Basic Standard Deduction Amounts

	Standard Deduction Amount	
Filing Status	**2005**	**2006**
Single	$ 5,000	$ 5,150
Married, filing jointly	10,000	10,300
Surviving spouse	10,000	10,300
Head of household	7,300	7,550
Married, filing separately	5,000	5,150

Amount of Each Additional Standard Deduction

Filing Status	2005	2006
Single	$1,250	$1,250
Married, filing jointly	1,000	1,000
Surviving spouse	1,000	1,000
Head of household	1,250	1,250
Married, filing separately	1,000	1,000

Personal and Dependency Exemption

2005	2006
$3,200	$3,300

Income Tax Rates—Corporations

Taxable Income	Tax Rate
Not over $50,000	15%
Over $50,000 but not over $75,000	25%
Over $75,000 but not over $100,000	34%
Over $100,000 but not over $335,000	39%*
Over $335,000 but not over $10,000,000	34%
Over $10,000,000 but not over $15,000,000	35%
Over $15,000,000 but not over $18,333,333	38%**
Over $18,333,333	35%

*Five percent of this rate represents a phaseout of the benefits of the lower tax rates on the first $75,000 of taxable income.

**Three percent of this rate represents a phaseout of the benefits of the lower tax rate (34% rather than 35%) on the first $10 million of taxable income.

West Federal Taxation

Taxation of Business Entities

EDITION 2007

General Editors

James E. Smith
Ph.D., CPA
College of William and Mary

William A. Raabe
Ph.D., CPA
Ohio State University

David M. Maloney
Ph.D., CPA
University of Virginia

THOMSON
SOUTH-WESTERN

Australia · Brazil · Canada · Mexico · Singapore · Spain · United Kingdom · United States

THOMSON
SOUTH-WESTERN

West Federal Taxation: Taxation of Business Entities, 2007 Edition

James E. Smith, William A. Raabe, David M. Maloney

Authors for the West Federal Taxation Series

James H. Boyd
Ph.D., CPA
Arizona State University

D. Larry Crumbley
Ph.D., CPA
Louisiana State University

Jon S. Davis
Ph.D., CPA
University of Wisconsin, Madison

Steven C. Dilley
J.D., Ph.D., CPA
Michigan State University

William H. Hoffman, Jr.
J.D., Ph.D., CPA
University of Houston

Gary A. McGill
Ph.D., CPA
University of Florida

Mark B. Persellin
Ph.D., CPA, CFP®
St. Mary's University

Boyd C. Randall
J.D., Ph.D.
Brigham Young University

Debra L. Sanders
Ph.D., CPA
Washington State University

W. Eugene Seago
J.D., Ph.D., CPA
Virginia Polytechnic Institute and State University

Eugene Willis
Ph.D., CPA
University of Illinois, Urbana-Champaign

VP/Editorial Director
Jack W. Calhoun

Publisher
Rob Dewey

Acquisitions Editor
Daniel Jones

Senior Developmental Editor
Craig Avery

Marketing Manager
Chris McNamee

Senior Production Project Manager
Tim Bailey

Manager of Technology, Editorial
Vicky True

Technology Project Editor
Kelly Reid

Web Coordinator
Scott Cook

Manufacturing Coordinator
Doug Wilke

Art Director
Michelle Kunkler

Internal Designer
Diane Gliebe/Design Matters

Cover Designer
Craig Ramsdell

Cover Images
© Getty Images, Inc.

Production
LEAP Publishing Services, Inc.

Composition
Cadmus Professional Communications

Printer
Quebecor World
Versailles, KY

Printed in the United States of America
1 2 3 4 5 08 07 06

For more information about our products, contact us at:

Thomson Learning Academic Resource Center

1-800-423-0563

Professional Edition ISBN: 0-324-31394-2
Student Edition with CD ISBN: 0-324-31395-0
Instructor's Edition ISBN: 0-324-31397-7

ISSN: 1544-3590
2007 Annual Edition

Thomson Higher Education
5191 Natorp Boulevard
Mason, OH 45040
USA

To the Student

The Leadership You Trust—The Innovation You Expect—The Service You Deserve

♦

West Federal Taxation (WFT) is the most trusted and largest selling brand in college taxation. We are focused exclusively on providing the most useful, comprehensive, and up-to-date tax texts, online study aids, tax preparation tools, and print study guides to help you succeed in your tax courses and beyond.

♦

More than just a textbook, the *WFT* series provides a dynamic learning experience in and out of the classroom. Built around the areas students have identified as the most important, our total integrated solution will offer you options in the way you learn.

Student Workflow

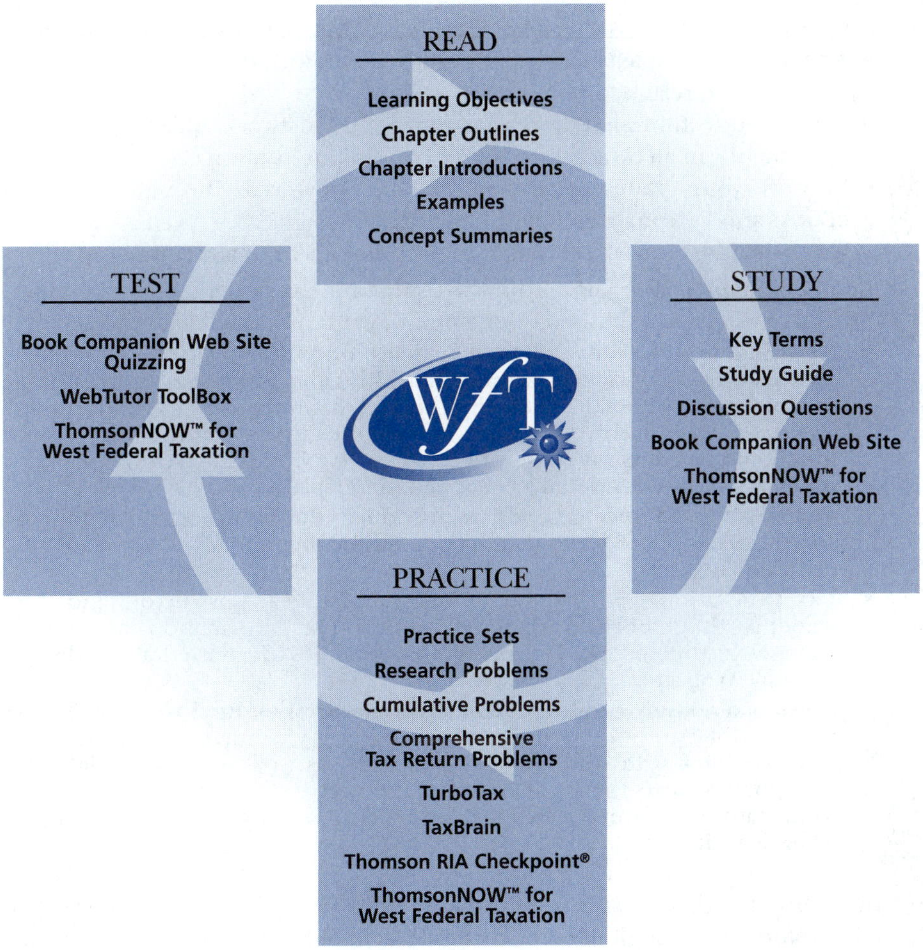

Today, the *WFT* series provides the most innovative solutions on the market. With integration of TurboTax, RIA Checkpoint®, TaxBrain®, and Deloitte Tax LLP, materials, *WFT* exposes you to the professional knowledge and tools you will use now and in your future career.

FREE RESOURCES AND STUDY TOOLS

- **Free TurboTax software** is included with every new copy of your text and provides access to tools for all your homework.
- **Free Online Access to TaxBrain® Tax Preparation Software,** which is used by more than 2,500 tax professionals every year. You can use TaxBrain® to work the income tax form problems in the text, developing your skills as you master course information. To access, log on to **http://www.taxbrain.com**. Take advantage of a 20% filing discount when filing your 2005 return with TaxBrain®—enter promotional code **SWL947**.
- **Exclusive Free Access to RIA's Checkpoint® Student Edition Online Tax Research Database.** Each *new* copy of the text contains an RIA Checkpoint® Student Edition access code, allowing you access to content from the research database most widely used by tax professionals. As you use Checkpoint® to complete problems within the text, you are building research skills and familiarity with the database—valuable preparation for your professional future.
- **Free Tutorial for RIA's Checkpoint®**. This self-paced tutorial from RIA orients you to Checkpoint® features and walks you through the application of RIA research strategies—giving you a running start on your class assignments that use Checkpoint®.
- **ThomsonNOW for *West Federal Taxation*.** This powerful, fully integrated online teaching and learning system provides you with the ultimate in flexibility, control, and results.
  - One place to find all of your assignments! Homework, quizzing, and self-assessment can all be accessed in one convenient location.
  - Improve your grades by accessing chapter materials through integrated eBooks and Personalized Learning Paths.
  - Save valuable time by accessing your assignments from any computer.
- **Book Companion Web Site – http://wft.swlearning.com**
  - **Tax newsletters** published twice a month written by the text authors.
  - **NewsEdge** pulls from full text articles from over 1,200 online news sources on a continuous basis and includes the following features: topic organization, personalization with the "Select My Topics/View My Topics" feature, 30-day archive, links to full online articles, and robust search functionality. NewsEdge also offers access to "Company News by Ticker," which includes stock detail, charts, and financials.
  - **Tax Tips for the Recent Graduate** introduces the college graduate to some common tax considerations that could be beneficial in reducing the dreaded "tax-bite."
  - **Tax Legislation Updates** is a resource available to instructors and their students that provides up-to-the-minute tax information and major changes to the tax law. Tax Legislation Updates are posted as needed on the *WFT* Web site.
  - **Download a Study Guide Chapter FREE before You Buy! Get one chapter of the print Study Guide free online**. The Study Guide contains **questions and problems with solutions for self-study**, as well as **chapter highlights** that point you to the right place in the text for further study. Order it from your bookstore (ISBN 0-324-31398-5) or buy it online at **http://wft.swlearning.com.**

For over 29 years, the *West Federal Taxation (WFT)* Series has guided more than 1.5 million students through the ever changing field of Federal taxation. With commitment to leadership, innovation, and service, we will continue to play a part in your success both now and in the future.

About the Editors

James E. Smith is the John S. Quinn Professor of Accounting at the College of William and Mary. He has been a member of the Accounting Faculty for over thirty years. He received his Ph.D. degree from the University of Arizona.

Professor Smith has served as a discussion leader for Continuing Professional Education programs for the AICPA, Federal Tax Workshops, and various state CPA societies. He has conducted programs in over 40 states for approximately 25,000 CPAs. He has been the recipient of the AICPAs' Outstanding Discussion Leader Award and the American Taxation Association/Arthur Andersen Teaching Innovation Award.

Other awards received by him include the Virginia Society of CPAs' Outstanding Accounting Educator Award and the James Madison University's Outstanding Accounting Educator Award. He was the President of the Administrators of Accounting Programs Group (AAPG) in 1991-1992. He was the faculty adviser for the William and Mary teams that received first place in the Andersen Tax Challenge in 1994, 1995, 1997, 2000, and 2001 and in the Deloitte & Touche Tax Case Study Competition in 2002, 2004, and 2005.

William A. Raabe teaches tax courses in the Fisher College of Business at the Ohio State University. A graduate of Carroll College (WI) and the University of Illinois, Dr. Raabe's teaching and research interests include international and multistate taxation, technology in tax education, personal financial planning, and the economic impact of sports teams and fine arts groups.

Professor Raabe also writes *Federal Tax Research* and *Fundamentals of California Income Taxation*. He coordinates the material on the West Federal Taxation Internet page, and he has written estate planning software used widely by tax professionals. Dr. Raabe has been a visiting tax faculty member for a number of public accounting firms, bar associations, and CPA societies. He has received numerous teaching awards, including the Accounting Educator of the Year award from the Wisconsin Institute of CPAs.

David M. Maloney, Ph.D., CPA, completed his undergraduate work at the University of Richmond and his graduate work at the University of Illinois at Urbana- Champaign. He teaches courses in Federal taxation in the graduate and undergraduate programs at the University of Virginia's McIntire School of Commerce. Since joining the Virginia faculty in January 1984, Professor Maloney has been a recipient of major research grants from the Ernst & Young and KPMG Foundation. In addition, his work has been published in numerous professional journals, including *The Journal of Taxation, The Tax Adviser, Tax Notes, The Journal of Corporate Taxation, Accounting Horizons,* and *The Journal of Accountancy.* He is a member of several professional organizations, including the American Accounting Association and the American Taxation Association.

http://wft.swlearning.com

CONTENTS IN BRIEF

PART 1: THE WORLD OF TAXATION

PART 2: STRUCTURE OF THE FEDERAL INCOME TAX

PART 3: PROPERTY TRANSACTIONS

PART 4: BUSINESS ENTITIES

http://wft.swlearning.com

CONTENTS

PART 1: THE WORLD OF TAXATION

PART 4: BUSINESS ENTITIES

CHAPTER 10 CORPORATIONS: EARNINGS & PROFITS AND DIVIDEND DISTRIBUTIONS 10–1

CHAPTER 11 PARTNERSHIPS AND LIMITED LIABILITY ENTITIES 11–1

PART 5: SPECIAL BUSINESS TOPICS

PART 6: TAXATION OF INDIVIDUALS

APPENDIXES

http://wft.swlearning.com

PART 1

The World of Taxation

Part I provides an introduction to taxation in the United States. Various taxes imposed by Federal, state, and local governments are discussed. A unique tax planning framework is developed that is applied throughout the book in developing tax planning strategies for business entities and for individual taxpayers. This tax planning framework serves as a unifying theme throughout the book. The role of the IRS and the courts in the evolution of the Federal tax system is presented. The tax research process, including the relevance of the legislative, administrative, and judicial sources of the tax law, is discussed. Part I concludes with a chapter on accounting for income taxes.

http://wft.swlearning.com

Introduction to Taxation

LEARNING OBJECTIVES

After completing Chapter 1, you should be able to:

LO.1

Understand the components of a tax.

LO.2

Identify the various taxes affecting business enterprises.

LO.3

Recall the basic tax formula for individuals and taxable business entities.

LO.4

Understand the relationship between business entities and their owners.

LO.5

Recognize tax planning opportunities and apply a general framework for tax planning.

LO.6

Recognize the economic, social, equity, and political considerations that underlie the tax law.

LO.7

Describe the role played by the IRS and the courts in the evolution of the Federal tax system.

OUTLINE

TAX *Talk*

How many people were taxed, who was taxed, and what was taxed tell more about a society than anything else.

—Charles Adams

Taxes have a pervasive impact on our lives. They affect every individual in the United States from birth to death, and even beyond death (through taxation of the individual's estate). Taxes likewise affect every business from formation of the business entity to its operations, distribution of profits to owners, and ultimate disposition or liquidation.

Despite the wide-ranging impact of taxes, most studies of the tax law overemphasize the provisions applying to individual taxpayers and ignore much of the tax law relevant to business. That approach fails to address the role of taxes in *business decisions*, and it fails to provide the broad knowledge base necessary to succeed in today's business environment. This text adopts a more balanced approach; it introduces the tax laws that apply to all business entities and surveys the tax rules specific to each type of entity. It also recognizes that both tax and nontax considerations are important in business planning and therefore presents the tax laws within the context of the business transactions to which they relate.

LO.1

Understand the components of a tax.

The Structure of Taxes

Most taxes have two components: a tax rate and a tax base (such as income, wages, value, or sales price). Tax liability is computed by multiplying these two components. Taxes vary by the structure of their rates and by the base subject to tax.

Tax Rates

Tax rates can be either progressive, proportional, or regressive. A tax rate is *progressive* if it increases as the tax base increases. The Federal income tax and the Federal estate and **gift taxes** are progressive. For example, the Federal income tax rates for

TAX *in the News* **CARRYING THE TAX BURDEN**

Data from the Congressional Budget Office indicate that the progressive nature of the Federal income tax, accelerated by laws passed under Presidents Bush I and Clinton, remains largely intact, even after the broad tax cuts issued under President Bush II. When considering the total Federal tax burden, though, such progressivity is not so apparent. Perhaps payroll, gasoline, and other Federal taxes tend to even out the total tax burden, if only slightly.

	Earners with Top 1% of AGI	Earners with Top 1–5% of AGI	Earners with Top 5–10% of AGI	Earners with Top 10–20% of AGI
Share of Federal income tax	32.3%	21.4%	13.0%	15.4%
Effective Federal income tax rate	19.7	17.6	16.0	14.2
Share of all Federal taxes	20.1	25.6	11.7	15.9
Effective overall Federal tax rate	26.7	25.6	24.9	23.8

corporations range from 15 to 39 percent. These rates increase with increases in taxable income.

EXAMPLE 1

Refer to the corporate Tax Rate Schedule inside the front cover of this text. If Abel Corporation has taxable income of $5,000, its income tax is $750 and its average tax rate is 15% ($750/$5,000, or the ratio of tax liability to the tax base). If, however, Abel's taxable income is $200,000, its income tax is $61,250 [$22,250 + 0.39($200,000 – $100,000)], and its average tax rate is 30.63% ($61,250/$200,000). The tax is progressive because the average tax rate increases with increases in the tax base (income). ■

A tax is *proportional* if the rate of tax is constant, regardless of the size of the tax base. State retail **sales taxes** are proportional, as is the Federal Medicare tax on salaries and wages. Proportional tax rates also underlie the various "flat tax" proposals recently in the news.[1]

EXAMPLE 2

Bob purchases an automobile for $6,000. If the sales tax on automobiles is 7% in Bob's state, he will pay a $420 tax. Alternatively, if Bob pays $20,000 for a car, his sales tax will be $1,400 (still 7% of the sales price). Because the average tax rate does not change with the tax base (sales price), the sales tax is proportional. ■

Finally, *regressive* tax rates decrease as the tax base increases. Federal **employment taxes**, such as FICA and FUTA, are regressive. When the tax base and the taxpayer's ability to pay generally are positively correlated (i.e., when they move in the same direction), many tax pundits view regressive tax rates as unfair. This is because the tax burden decreases as a *percentage* of the taxpayer's ability to pay.

EXAMPLE 3

In 2006, the combined Social Security and Medicare tax rate levied on the wages of employees is 7.65% up to a maximum of $94,200 and 1.45% on all wages over $94,200. Sarah earns a salary of $30,000. She will pay FICA taxes of $2,295, with an average tax rate of 7.65%. Alternatively, if Sarah earns $120,000, she will pay $7,580 [(0.0765 × $94,200) +

[1]Flat tax proposals call for a new tax with one low, proportional rate (usually between 15% and 20%). Such a tax would have a very broad base, taxing almost all forms of income with few deductions. To avoid taxing the poor, large personal exemptions would be provided (e.g., $30,000 for a family of four).

0.0145($120,000 – $94,200)], with an average tax rate of 6.32%. Once the FICA base exceeds the maximum amount subject to the Social Security part of FICA, the FICA tax is regressive, since the average tax rate decreases as the tax base increases. ■

Under all three tax rate structures, the *amount* of taxes due increases as the tax base increases. The structure of tax rates only affects the *rate* of increase (i.e., progressive taxes increase at an increasing rate, proportional taxes increase at a constant rate, and regressive taxes increase at a decreasing rate).

Tax Bases

Most taxes are levied on one of four kinds of tax bases.

- Transactions (including sales or purchases of goods and services and transfers of wealth).
- Property or wealth (including ownership of specific kinds of property).
- Privileges and rights (including the ability to do business as a corporation, the right to work in a certain profession, and the ability to move goods between countries).
- Income, on a gross or net-of-expenses basis.

Because the Federal income tax usually has the most significant influence on business decisions, it is the principal focus of this text. Other taxes can play an important role, however, so it is important to have at least some familiarity with them. The next section introduces many of the taxes imposed on individuals and businesses in the United States.

LO.2

Identify the various taxes affecting business enterprises.

Types of Taxes

After taxes on income, the various transaction taxes usually play the most important role in business (and personal) contexts. In many countries, transaction taxes are even more important than income taxes. There are three types of transaction taxes: sales and certain **excise taxes**, employment taxes, and taxes on the transfer of wealth.

Taxes on the Production and Sale of Goods

Sales tax and some excise taxes are imposed on the production, sale, or consumption of commodities or the use of services. Excise taxes and general sales taxes differ by the breadth of their bases. An excise tax base is limited to a specific kind of good or service while a general sales tax is broad based (e.g., it might be levied on all retail sales). All levels of government impose excise taxes while state and local governments make heavy use of the general sales tax.

Federal Excise Taxes. Together with customs duties, excise taxes served as the principal source of revenue for the United States during its first 150 years of existence. Since World War II, the role of excise taxes in the Federal government's fund-raising efforts has steadily declined, falling from about 30 to 40 percent of revenues just prior to the war to less than 4 percent now. During this time, the Federal government came to rely upon income and employment taxes as its principal sources of funds.

Despite the decreasing contribution of excise taxes to the Federal coffers, they continue to have a significant impact on specific industries. Currently, trucks, trailers, tires, liquor, tobacco, firearms, certain sporting equipment, air travel, and telephone service are all subject to Federal excise taxes. In the past, the sale and manufacture of a variety of other goods, including furs, jewelry, boats, luxury automobiles, and theater tickets, have been taxed. Excise taxes extend beyond sales transactions. They are also levied on privileges and rights, as discussed below.

The bases used for Federal excise taxes are as diverse as the goods that are taxed. Fuels are taxed by the gallon, vaccines by the dose, telephone service and air travel by the price paid for the service, water travel by the passenger, coal by the ton extracted or by the sales price, insurance by the premiums paid, and the gas guzzler tax by the mileage rating on the automobile produced. Some of these taxes are levied on producers, some on resellers, and some on consumers. In almost every circumstance, the tax rate structure is proportional.

With the exception of Federal excise taxes on alcohol, tobacco, and firearms, Federal excise taxes are due at least quarterly, when the Federal excise tax return (Form 720) is filed.

State Excise Taxes. Many states levy excise taxes on the same items taxed by the Federal government. For example, most states have excise taxes on gasoline, liquor, and tobacco. However, the tax on specific goods can vary dramatically among states. Compare New Jersey's $2.40 tax on each pack of cigarettes to Missouri's $0.17 tax. These differences at the state level provide ample incentive for smuggling between states and for state-line enterprises specializing in taxed goods.[2]

Other goods and services subject to state and local excise taxes include admission to amusement facilities, hotel occupancy, rental of other facilities, and sales of playing cards, oleomargarine products, and prepared foods. Most states impose a tax on transfers of property that require recording of documents (such as real estate sales and sales of stock and securities).

Local Excise Taxes. Over the last few years, two types of excise taxes imposed at the local level have become increasingly popular. These are the hotel occupancy tax and the rental car "surcharge." Since they tax the visitor who cannot vote, they are a political windfall and serve as a means of financing special projects that generate civic pride (e.g., convention centers, state-of-the-art sports arenas). That these levies can be significant is demonstrated by Houston's hotel tax of 17 percent and Boston's car rental tax of 28.7 percent.

General Sales Tax. The broad-based general sales tax is a major source of revenue for most state and local governments. It is used in all but five states (Alaska, Delaware, Montana, New Hampshire, and Oregon). While specific rules vary from state to state, the sales tax typically employs a proportional tax rate and includes retail sales of tangible personal property (and occasionally personal services) in the base. Some states exempt medicine and food from the base, and sometimes tax rates vary with the good being sold (e.g., the sales tax rate for automobiles may differ from the rate on other goods). The sales tax is collected by the retailer and then paid to the state government.

Local general sales taxes, over and above those levied by the state, are common. It is not unusual to find taxpayers living in the same state who pay different general rates of sales taxes due to the location of their residence.

EXAMPLE 4

Pete and Sam both live in a state that has a general sales tax of 3%. Sam, however, resides in a city that imposes an additional general sales tax of 2%. Even though Pete and Sam live in the same state, one is subject to a rate of 3%, while the other pays a tax of 5%. ■

For various reasons, some jurisdictions will suspend the application of a general sales tax. New York City does so to stimulate shopping. Illinois has permanently suspended the tax on construction materials used to build power-generating plants.

[2]Some excise taxes are referred to as "sin" taxes (because goods such as liquor and tobacco are subject to the tax). Although it is commonly believed that these taxes are imposed for the purpose of discouraging consumption, evidence frequently fails to show that sin taxes have a significant impact on consumption. Since demand for cigarettes and gasoline tends to be relatively inelastic (insensitive to price), the increase in price caused by excise taxes has little to do with rates of consumption.

GLOBAL *Tax Issues*

WHY IS GASOLINE EXPENSIVE? IT DEPENDS ON WHERE YOU LIVE

In recent years, increases in the cost of gasoline and fuel oil have sometimes aroused such a furor in the United States that supplies have been released from the national oil reserve. Whether such tactics reduce prices more than temporarily seems doubtful. But in the United States, unlike other countries, increases in the price of gasoline are largely attributable to the rising cost of crude oil. In 2004, the price of crude oil increased from approximately $30 to $50 per barrel. In January 2006, the average price per gallon of gasoline in the United States was over $2.00.

In other countries (and using selected European nations as examples), the real culprit is the amount of tax imposed. Consider the following situations.

Country	Price per Gallon*
United Kingdom	$4.16
France	3.31
Germany	3.49
Sweden	3.41

*Converted to U.S. dollars

While other factors may contribute to the higher European prices, the primary factor is the amount of tax charged in those countries. For example, in the United Kingdom, approximately 75 percent of the cost of gasoline is attributable to taxes.

Source: *European prices and taxes as of June 2002, compiled by the Energy Information Administration.*

Texas does so annually on clothing right before the beginning of the school year. Such suspensions are similar to the tax holidays granted for ad valorem tax purposes.

Use Taxes. One obvious approach to avoiding state and local sales taxes is to purchase goods in a state that has little or no sales tax and then transport the goods back to one's home state. **Use taxes** exist to prevent this tax reduction ploy. The use tax is a value-based tax, usually imposed at the same rate as the sales tax, on the use, consumption, or storage of tangible property. Every state that imposes a general sales tax levied on the consumer also has a use tax.

EXAMPLE 5

Orange, Inc., is located in a jurisdiction that imposes a 5% general sales tax, but is located near a state that has no sales or use tax. Orange purchases an automobile for $50,000 from a dealer located in the neighboring tax-free state. Though Orange will pay no sales tax to the dealer upon purchase of the car, it will be assessed a use tax when it brings the automobile back to its home state and licenses it. ■

The use tax is difficult to enforce for many other purchases and is therefore often avoided. In some cases, for example, it may be worthwhile to make purchases through an out-of-state mail-order business. In spite of shipping costs, the avoidance of the local sales tax that otherwise might be incurred often makes the price of such products as computer components cheaper. Some states are taking steps to curtail this loss of revenue.

Value Added Tax. The **value added tax (VAT)** is a sales tax levied at each stage of production on value added by the producer. VAT is in widespread use in many countries around the world (most notably in the European Union and in Canada). The tax typically serves as a major source of revenue for governments that use it. Some proposals to reduce the Federal government's reliance on income tax have focused on VAT as an alternative tax system.

EXAMPLE 6

Farmer Brown sells wheat to a flour mill for $100. If the wheat cost $65 for Brown to produce and if the VAT rate is 10%, then Brown will owe a VAT of $3.50 [0.10($100 – $65)]. If the mill sells the flour for $200 to a baker and if it cost the mill $120 to make the flour (including the cost of Brown's wheat), then it will pay a VAT of $8 [0.10($200 – $120)]. If the baker sells the bread he makes from the flour for $400 and if it cost the baker $280 to make the bread, then he will pay a VAT of $12 [0.10($400 – $280)]. The consumer who buys the bread will not pay any VAT directly. It is likely, however, that some or all of the total VAT paid of $23.50 ($3.50 + $8 + $12) will be paid by the consumer in the form of higher prices for the bread.[3] ■

Employment Taxes

Both Federal and state governments tax the salaries and wages paid to employees. On the Federal side, employment taxes represent a major source of funds. For example, the **FICA tax** accounts for about one-third of revenues in the Federal budget, second only to the income tax in its contribution.

The Federal government imposes two kinds of employment tax. The Federal Insurance Contributions Act (FICA) imposes a tax on self-employed individuals, employees, and employers. The proceeds of the tax are used to finance Social Security and Medicare payments. The Federal Unemployment Tax Act (FUTA) imposes a tax on employers. The **FUTA tax** provides funds to state unemployment benefit programs. Most state employment taxes are similar to the FUTA tax, with proceeds used to finance state unemployment benefit payments.

FICA Taxes. The FICA tax has two components: old age, survivors, and disability insurance payments (commonly referred to as Social Security) and Medicare health insurance payments. The Social Security tax rate is 6.2 percent, and the Medicare tax rate is 1.45 percent. The maximum base for the Social Security tax is $94,200 for 2006. There is no ceiling on the base amount for the Medicare tax. The employer must withhold the FICA tax from an employee's wages and must also pay a matching tax.

Payments are usually made through weekly or monthly deposits to a Federal depository. Employers must also file Form 941, Employer's Quarterly Federal Tax Return, by the end of the first month following each quarter of the calendar year (e.g., by July 31 for the quarter ending on June 30) and pay any remaining amount of employment taxes due for the previous quarter. Failure to pay can result in large and sometimes ruinous penalties.

EXAMPLE 7

Janet receives $115,000 in salary in 2006. She pays FICA taxes of $7,507.90 [(7.65% × $94,200) + 1.45%($115,000 – $94,200)]. Her employer is required to pay a matching FICA tax of $7,507.90. Janet's share of FICA taxes is withheld from her salary by her employer and deposited on a regular basis together with the employer's share of FICA. ■

Finally, FICA tax is not assessed on all wages paid. For example, wages paid to children under the age of 18 who are employed in a parent's trade or business are exempt from the tax.

[3]In the area of economics dealing with taxation (public finance), the issue of who ultimately pays a tax is known as *tax incidence*.

Self-Employment Tax. Self-employed individuals also pay FICA in the form of a self-employment (SE) tax (determined on Schedule SE, filed with Form 1040, U.S. Individual Income Tax Return). Self-employed individuals are required to pay both the employer and the employee portion of the FICA tax. Therefore, the 2006 SE tax rate is 15.3 percent (2 × 7.65%) on self-employment income up to $94,200 and 2.9 percent (2 × 1.45%) on all additional self-employment income. Self-employed individuals deduct half of the SE tax—the amount normally deductible by an employer as a business expense. The self-employment tax is discussed in more detail in Chapter 17.

Unemployment Taxes. In 2006, FUTA applies at a rate of 6.2 percent on the first $7,000 of covered wages paid during the year to each employee. As with FICA, this represents a regressive rate structure. The Federal government allows a credit for unemployment tax paid (or allowed under a merit rating system)[4] to the state. The credit cannot exceed 5.4 percent of the covered wages. Thus, the amount required to be paid to the IRS could be as low as 0.8 percent (6.2% – 5.4%).

FUTA and state unemployment taxes differ from FICA in that the tax is imposed only on the employer. A few states, however, levy a special tax on employees to provide either disability benefits or supplemental unemployment compensation, or both.

Employers must file Form 940, Employer's Annual Federal Employment Tax Return, to determine the amount of Federal unemployment taxes due in a given year. The return is due on or before January 31 of the following year.[5] Most states also require unemployment tax returns to be filed with quarterly estimated payments.

Death Taxes

A **death tax** is a tax on the transfer of property upon the death of the owner. If the death tax is imposed on the transferor at death, it is classified as an **estate tax**. If it taxes the recipient of the property, it is termed an **inheritance tax**. As is typical of other types of transaction taxes, the value of the property transferred provides the base for determining the amount of the death tax.

The Federal government imposes only an estate tax. State governments, however, levy inheritance taxes, estate taxes, or both.

EXAMPLE 8

At the time of her death, Wilma lived in a state that imposes an inheritance tax but not an estate tax. Mary, one of Wilma's heirs, lives in the same state. Wilma's estate is subject to the Federal estate tax, and Mary is subject to the state inheritance tax. ■

The Federal Estate Tax. Never designed to generate a large amount of revenue, the estate tax was originally intended to prevent large concentrations of wealth from being kept within a family for many generations. Whether this objective has been accomplished is debatable, because estate taxes can be substantially reduced (or deferred for decades) through careful planning.

Determination of the estate tax base begins with the gross estate, which includes property the decedent owned at the time of death. It also includes property interests, such as life insurance proceeds paid to the estate or to a beneficiary other than the estate if the deceased-insured had any ownership rights in the policy. Most property included in the gross estate is valued at fair market value as of the date of death.

[4]States follow a policy of reducing unemployment tax on employers with stable employment. Thus, an employer with no employee turnover might face state unemployment tax rates as low as 0.1% or, in some cases, zero. This *merit rating system* explicitly accounts for the savings generated by steady employment.

[5]Employers may be required to make more frequent payments of the tax (estimated payments) if their FUTA liability is sufficiently large.

Deductions from the gross estate in arriving at the taxable estate include funeral and administration expenses, certain taxes, debts of the decedent, transfers to charitable organizations, and, in some cases, an unlimited marital deduction. The marital deduction is available for amounts actually passing to a surviving spouse (a widow or widower).

Once the taxable estate has been determined and certain taxable gifts have been added to it, progressive estate tax rates ranging from 18 to 46 percent in 2006 are applied to determine a tentative tax liability. The tentative liability is reduced by a variety of credits to arrive at the amount due. Although many credits are available, probably the most significant is the *unified transfer tax credit.* This credit eliminates estate tax liability for most individuals. For 2006, the amount of the credit is $780,800. Based on the estate tax rates, the credit offsets a tax base of $2 million. The unified transfer tax credit is scheduled to increase until by 2009 it will be $3.5 million. By 2010, the Federal estate tax is scheduled to be eliminated.

EXAMPLE 9

Ildiko made no taxable gifts before her death in 2006. If Ildiko's taxable estate amounts to $2 million or less, no Federal estate tax is due because of the application of the unified transfer tax credit. Under the tax law, the tentative estate tax on a taxable estate of $2 million is $780,800, exactly equal to the maximum unified transfer tax credit allowed. ■

State Death Taxes. As noted earlier, states usually levy an inheritance tax, an estate tax, or both. The two forms of death taxes differ according to whether the tax is imposed on the heirs or on the estate.

Characteristically, an inheritance tax divides the heirs into classes based on their relationship to the decedent. The more closely related the heir, the lower the rates imposed and the greater the exemption allowed. Some states completely exempt amounts passing to a surviving spouse from taxation.

Gift Taxes

Like death taxes, the gift tax is an excise tax levied on the right to transfer property. In this case, however, the tax is imposed on transfers made during the owner's life rather than at death. A gift tax applies only to transfers that are not supported by full and adequate consideration (i.e., gifts).

EXAMPLE 10

Carl sells property worth $20,000 to his daughter for $1,000. Although property worth $20,000 has been transferred, only $19,000 represents a gift, since this is the portion not supported by full and adequate consideration. ■

The Federal Gift Tax. The Federal gift tax is intended to complement the estate tax. The gift tax base is the sum of all taxable gifts made *during one's lifetime.* Gifts are valued at the date of transfer. To compute the tax due in a year, the tax rate schedule is applied to the sum of all lifetime taxable gifts. The resulting tax is then reduced by gift taxes paid in prior years.

EXAMPLE 11

In 1995, Willie gave $700,000 of taxable gifts to his son. The gift tax paid in 1995 (before application of any credits) was $229,800. In 2006, Willie will give an additional $100,000 in taxable gifts to his son. The tax base in 2006 will be $800,000 of lifetime gifts, and the tax will be $267,800. However, the actual gift tax due in 2006 (before credits) will be $38,000 ($267,800 – $229,800 tax paid on prior-year gifts). ■

Under current law, the Federal gift tax and the Federal estate tax are *unified.*[6] The transfer of assets by a decedent at death is effectively treated as a final gift

[6]§§ 2010 and 2505.

under the tax law. Thus, the unified transfer tax credit available under the estate tax is also available to reduce the tax liability generated by lifetime gifts. If the credit is exhausted during one's lifetime, it will not be available to reduce the estate tax liability, except to the extent of the excess of the credit amount for estate tax purposes over that for gift tax purposes. In addition, the same tax rate schedule applies to both lifetime gifts and the estate tax.

EXAMPLE 12

Before his death, Ben gives $1 million of taxable gifts. Because the unified transfer tax credit was used during his life to offset the tax due on these gifts, only a partial credit is left to reduce Ben's estate tax liability. ■

Annual taxable gifts are determined by reducing the fair market value of gifts given by an *annual exclusion* of $12,000 per donee. A married couple can elect *gift splitting*, which enables them to transfer twice the annual exclusion ($24,000) per donee per year.

EXAMPLE 13

On December 31, 2006, Vera (a widow) gives $12,000 to each of her four married children, their spouses, and her eight grandchildren. On January 3, 2007, she repeats the same procedure. Due to the annual exclusion, Vera has *not* made a taxable gift, although she transferred $192,000 [$12,000 × 16 (the number of donees)] in 2006 and $192,000 [$12,000 × 16 (the number of donees)] in 2007 for a total of $384,000 ($192,000 + $192,000). If Vera were married, she could have given twice as much ($768,000) by electing gift splitting with her husband. ■

As noted previously, tax legislation has scheduled a phaseout of the Federal estate tax. The reason for the elimination of the estate tax does not apply to the gift tax. Unlike death, which is involuntary, the making of a gift is a voluntary parting of ownership. Thus, the ownership of a business can be transferred gradually without incurring drastic and immediate tax consequences. As a result, the Federal gift tax is to be retained with the unified transfer tax credit frozen at $345,800 (which covers a taxable gift of $1 million).

State Gift Taxes. The states currently imposing a gift tax are Connecticut, Louisiana, North Carolina, and Tennessee. Most of the laws provide for lifetime exemptions and annual exclusions. Unlike the Federal version, the amount of state gift tax often depends on the relationship between the donor and the donee. As with state inheritance taxes, larger exemptions and lower rates apply when the donor and donee are closely related to each other.

Property Taxes

A property tax can be a tax on the ownership of property or a tax on wealth, depending on the base used. Any measurable characteristic of the property being taxed can be used as a base (e.g., weight, size, number, or value). Most property taxes in the United States are taxes on wealth since they use value as a base. These value-based property taxes are known as **ad valorem taxes**. Property taxes are generally administered by state and local governments where they serve as a significant source of revenue.

Taxes on Realty. Property taxes on **realty** are used exclusively by states and their local political subdivisions such as cities, counties, and school districts. They represent a major source of revenue for local governments, but their importance at the state level has waned over the past few years. Some states, for example, have imposed freezes on the upward revaluations of residential housing.

How realty is defined can have an important bearing on which assets are subject to tax. This is especially true in jurisdictions that do not impose ad valorem taxes on **personalty**. Although the definition is primarily a question of state property law,

TAX *in the News* **A FEW PIGS AND CHICKENS MAY NOT BE ENOUGH**

Mel Gibson, the director of *The Passion of the Christ*, applied for an agricultural use exemption for 17 acres of his 75.7-acre estate in Greenwich, Connecticut. The $17.7 million estate features a 28-room mansion, pool, tennis court, and two guesthouses. In addition, it also includes a barn where Gibson has kept sheep, donkeys, and some chickens. The town officials, however, found that the property was not being held for a bona fide productive farming activity and turned down Gibson's request for an agricultural use exemption. Securing the exemption would have saved Gibson $10,000 per year in ad valorem property taxes.

Source: *Adapted from Associated Press, "Ol' Mel Gibson Didn't Have a Farm,"* Houston Chronicle, *January 17, 2005*, p. A2.

realty generally includes real estate and any capital improvements that are classified as fixtures. A fixture is something so permanently attached to the real estate that its removal will cause irreparable damage. A built-in bookcase might be a fixture, whereas a movable bookcase is not. Certain items such as electrical wiring and plumbing change from personalty to realty when installed in a building.

The following are some of the characteristics of ad valorem taxes on realty.

- Property owned by the Federal government is exempt from tax. Similar immunity usually is extended to property owned by state and local governments and by certain charitable organizations.
- Some states provide for lower valuations on property dedicated to agricultural use or other special uses (e.g., wildlife sanctuaries).
- Some states partially exempt the homestead, or personal residence, portion of property from taxation. Additionally, modern homestead laws normally protect some or all of a personal residence (including a farm or ranch) from the actions of creditors pursuing claims against the owner.
- Lower taxes may apply to a residence owned by a taxpayer age 65 or older.
- Some jurisdictions extend immunity from tax for a specified period of time (a tax holiday) to new or relocated businesses.

Taxes on Personalty. Personalty includes all assets that are not realty. It may be helpful to distinguish between the classification of an asset (realty or personalty) and the use to which it is put. Both realty and personalty can be either business-use or personal-use property. Examples include a residence (personal-use realty), an office building (business-use realty), surgical instruments (business-use personalty), and casual clothing (personal-use personalty).

Personalty can also be classified as tangible property or intangible property. For property tax purposes, intangible personalty includes stocks, bonds, and various other securities (e.g., bank shares).

The following generalizations may be made concerning the property taxes on personalty.

- Particularly with personalty devoted to personal use (e.g., jewelry, household furnishings), taxpayer compliance ranges from poor to zero. Some jurisdictions do not even attempt to enforce the tax on these items. For automobiles devoted to personal use, many jurisdictions have converted from value as the tax base to a tax based on the weight of the vehicle. Some jurisdictions also consider the vehicle's age (e.g., automobiles six years or older are not subject to the ad valorem tax because they are presumed to have little value).
- For personalty devoted to business use (e.g., inventories, trucks, machinery, equipment), taxpayer compliance and enforcement procedures are notably better.
- Some jurisdictions impose an ad valorem property tax on intangibles.

TAX FACT

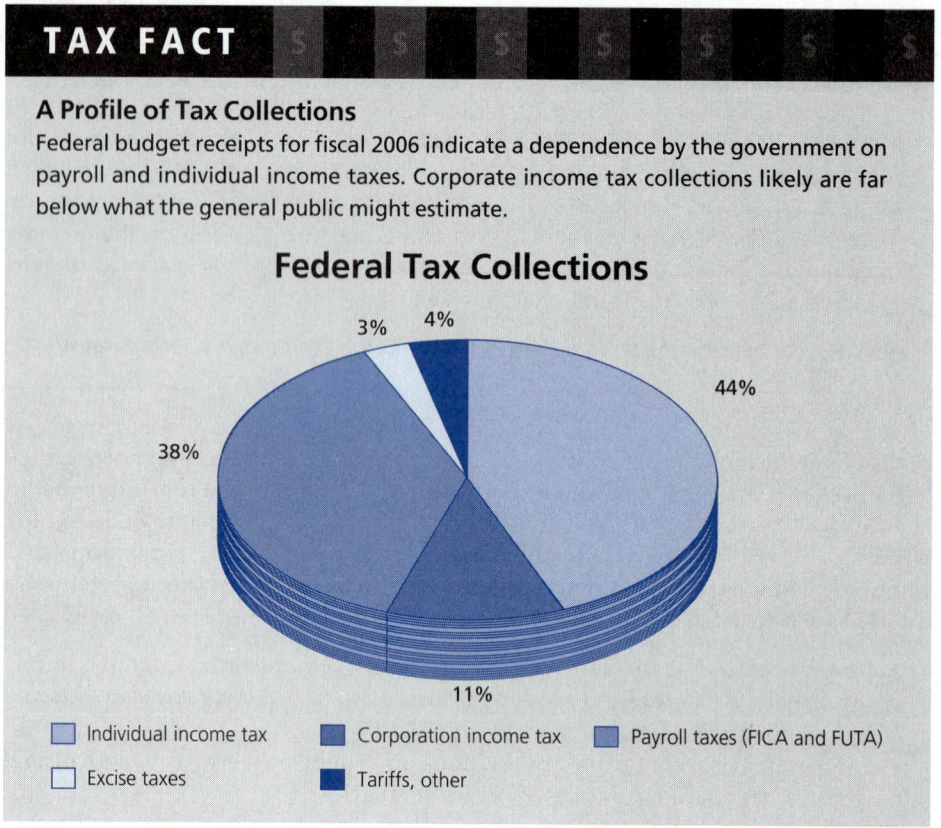

A Profile of Tax Collections

Federal budget receipts for fiscal 2006 indicate a dependence by the government on payroll and individual income taxes. Corporate income tax collections likely are far below what the general public might estimate.

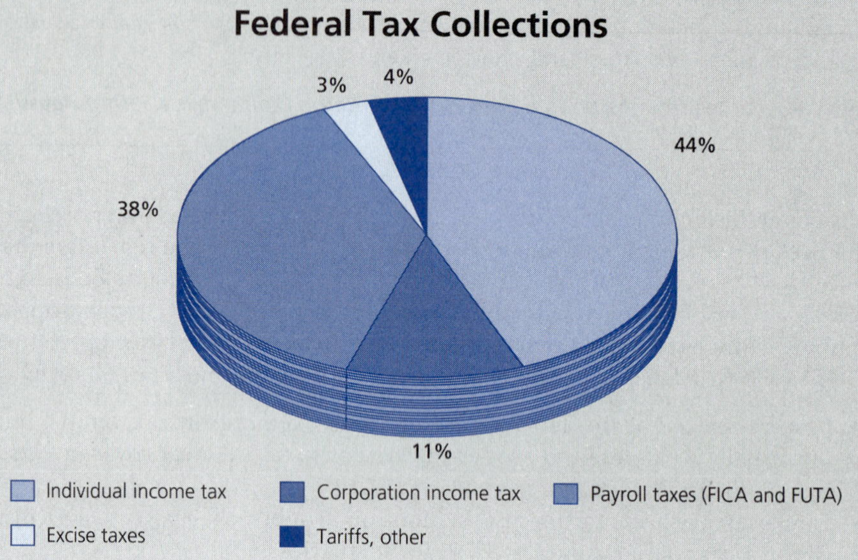

Taxes on Privileges and Rights

Taxes on privileges and rights are usually considered excise taxes. A few of the most important of these taxes are reviewed here.

Federal Customs Duties. Customs duties or tariffs can be characterized as a tax on the right to move goods across national borders. These taxes, together with selective excise taxes, provided most of the revenues needed by the Federal government during the nineteenth century. For example, tariffs and excise taxes alone paid off the national debt in 1835 and enabled the U.S. Treasury to pay a surplus of $28 million to the states. Today, however, customs duties account for only 1 percent of revenues in the Federal budget.

In recent years, tariffs have served the nation more as an instrument for carrying out protectionist policies than as a means of generating revenue. Thus, a particular U.S. industry might be saved from economic disaster, so the argument goes, by placing customs duties on the importation of foreign goods that can be sold at lower prices. Protectionists contend that the tariff therefore neutralizes the competitive edge held by the producer of the foreign goods.[7]

Protectionist policies seem more appropriate for less-developed countries whose industrial capacity has not yet matured. In a world where a developed country should have everything to gain by encouraging international free trade, such policies may be of dubious value since tariffs often lead to retaliatory action on the part of the nation or nations affected.

Franchise Taxes and Occupational Taxes. A **franchise tax** is a tax on the privilege of doing business in a state or local jurisdiction. Typically, the tax is imposed by

[7]The North American Free Trade Agreement (NAFTA) substantially reduced the tariffs on trade between Canada, Mexico, and the United States. General Agreement on Tariffs and Trade (GATT) legislation reduced tariffs on selected commodities among 124 countries.

TAX FACT

What Is the U.S. Tax Burden?

One popular measure of the burden of taxes in the U.S. economy is the Tax Foundation's "Tax Freedom Day." This statistic is a determination of the day upon which an individual has completed the entire year's obligation to governmental units (i.e., if all earnings were paid as taxes to this point, annual taxes would be paid up, and one would now begin to "work for your own account").

Being "free from taxes" may bring about a feeling of relief, but in reality tax burdens vary greatly from state to state. And as the U.S. economy has evolved and develops a more complex tax structure, adding emphasis on income and sales/use taxes, and reducing the relative reliance on tariffs and excise taxes, year-to-year comparisons become difficult. Nonetheless, as a rough measure of the presence of government in our lives, Tax Freedom Day carries some importance.

Year	Tax Freedom Day
1902	1/31
1930	2/12
1945	4/4
1960	4/15
1970	4/26
1990	5/1
1999	5/11
2000	5/3
2005	4/17

states on corporations, but the tax base varies from state to state. While some states use a measure of corporate net income as part of the base, most states base the tax on the capitalization of the corporation (with or without certain long-term debt).

Closely akin to the franchise tax are **occupational taxes** applicable to various trades or businesses, such as a liquor store license, a taxicab permit, or a fee to practice a profession such as law, medicine, or accounting. Most of these are not significant revenue producers and fall more into the category of licenses than taxes. The revenue derived is used to defray the cost incurred by the jurisdiction to regulate the business or profession for the public good.

Severance Taxes. Severance taxes are based on the extraction of natural resources (e.g., oil, gas, iron ore, and coal). They are an important source of revenue for many states (e.g., Alaska).

Income Taxes

Income taxes are levied by the Federal government, most states, and some local governments. In recent years, the trend in the United States has been to place greater reliance on this method of taxation while other countries are relying more heavily on transactions taxes such as the VAT.

Income taxes are generally imposed on individuals, corporations, and certain fiduciaries (estates and trusts). Most jurisdictions attempt to assure the collection of income taxes by requiring certain pay-as-you-go procedures, including withholding requirements for employees and estimated tax prepayments for all taxpayers.

FIGURE 1–1 **Basic Formula for Federal Income Tax**

Income (broadly conceived)	$xxx,xxx
Less: Exclusions (income that is not subject to tax)	(xx,xxx)
Gross income (income that is subject to tax)	$xxx,xxx
Less: Deductions	(xx,xxx)
Taxable income	$xxx,xxx
Federal income tax on taxable income (see Tax Rate Schedules inside front cover of text)	$ xx,xxx
Less: Tax credits (including Federal income tax withheld and other prepayments of Federal income taxes)	(x,xxx)
Tax owed (or refund)	$ xxx

LO.3

Recall the basic tax formula for individuals and taxable business entities.

The Structure of the Federal Income Tax. Although some variations exist, the basic Federal income tax formula is similar for all taxable entities. This formula is shown in Figure 1–1.

The income tax is based on the assumption that all income is subject to tax and that no deductions are allowed unless specifically provided for in the law. Some types of income are specifically excluded on the basis of various economic, social, equity, and political considerations. Examples include gifts, inheritance, life insurance proceeds received by reason of death, and interest income from state and local bonds. All entities are allowed to deduct business expenses from gross income, but a number of limitations and exceptions are applied. A variety of credits against the tax are also allowed, again on the basis of economic, social, equity, or political goals of Congress.

Income tax rates for all entities are progressive. The corporate rates range from 15 percent on the lowest level of taxable income to 35 percent on the highest level. Individual rates range from 10 percent to 35 percent. Estates and trusts are also subject to taxation, with rates ranging from 15 percent to 35 percent.

Partnerships, qualifying small business corporations, and some limited liability companies are not taxable entities, but must file information returns. Owners of these business entities then are taxed on the net taxable income of the enterprise, proportionate to their holdings.

In the case of individuals, deductions are separated into two categories—deductions *for* adjusted gross income (AGI) and deductions *from* AGI. Generally, deductions *for* AGI are related to business activities, while deductions *from* AGI are often personal in nature (e.g., medical expenses, mortgage interest and property taxes on a personal residence, charitable contributions, and personal casualty losses) or related to investment activities. Deductions *from* AGI take the form of *itemized deductions* and personal and dependency exemptions. Individuals may take a *standard deduction* (a specified amount based on filing status) rather than itemizing actual deductions. An overview of the individual income tax formula is provided in Figure 1–2.

State Income Taxes. Most states (except Alaska, Florida, Nevada, South Dakota, Texas, Washington, and Wyoming) impose a traditional income tax on individuals. Tennessee taxes only income from stocks and bonds, and New Hampshire taxes only dividend and interest income. Most states also impose either a corporate income tax or a franchise tax based in part on corporate income. The following additional points can be made about state income taxes.

- State income tax usually relies on Federal income tax laws to some degree—the states use Federal taxable income as a base, with a few adjustments (e.g., a

FIGURE 1–2 **Federal Income Tax Formula for Individuals**

Income (broadly conceived)	$xx,xxx
Less: Exclusions (income that is not subject to tax)	(x,xxx)
Gross income (income that is subject to tax)	$xx,xxx
Less: Certain business and investment deductions (usually referred to as deductions *for* adjusted gross income)	(x,xxx)
Adjusted gross income	$xx,xxx
Less: The greater of certain personal and employee deductions (usually referred to as *itemized deductions*) *or* The standard deduction (including any *additional* standard deduction)	(x,xxx)
Less: Personal and dependency exemptions	(x,xxx)
Taxable income	$xx,xxx
Federal income tax on taxable income (see Tax Rate Schedules inside front cover of text)	$ x,xxx
Less: Tax credits (including Federal income tax withheld and other prepayments of Federal income taxes)	(xxx)
Tax owed (or refund)	$ xxx

few allow a deduction for Federal income taxes paid and sometimes an exclusion on interest income earned on Federal securities).

- For individuals, a few states impose a flat rate on Federal AGI.
- Several states piggyback directly on the Federal income tax system by using the Federal income tax liability as a tax base.
- Most states also require withholding of state income tax from salaries and wages and estimated payments by corporations and self-employed individuals.
- Most states have their own set of rates, exemptions, and credits.
- Many states also allow a credit for taxes paid to other states.

Local Income Taxes. Cities imposing an income tax include Baltimore, Cincinnati, Cleveland, Detroit, Kansas City (Mo.), New York, Philadelphia, and St. Louis. City income taxes usually apply to anyone who earns income in a city. They are designed to collect contributions for government services from those who live in the suburbs but work in the city as well as from local residents.

Find more information on this topic at our Web site: ***http://wft-entities.swlearning.com.***

DIGGING DEEPER 1

Income Taxation of Business Entities

LO.4

Understand the relationship between business entities and their owners.

Proprietorships

The simplest form of business entity is a **proprietorship**, which is not a separate taxable entity. Instead, the proprietor reports the net profit of the business on his or her own individual tax return.

Individuals who own proprietorships often have specific tax goals with regard to their financial interactions with the business. Because a proprietorship is, by definition, owned by an individual, the individual has great flexibility in structuring the entity's transactions in a way that will minimize his or her income tax (or, in some cases, the income tax of the family unit).

BRIDGE *Discipline*

Bridge to Political Science and Sociology

The tax law and its effects on citizens and businesses of the United States are included in many other academic disciplines. Tax burdens are part of American fiction, family studies, and minority issues, as well as economics, finance, and management courses.

In the Bridge feature found in most chapters of this text, we relate the concerns of other disciplines to a more specific review of tax law, as presented here. With the topical knowledge obtained in this text, the reader can better understand the issues raised by other disciplines, sometimes to support beliefs held by others, and sometimes to refute them.

For instance, the structure of the U.S. tax system raises many issues of equity and fairness. Politicians and journalists discuss these issues freely, often without the requisite tax knowledge to draw proper conclusions.

- Should the property tax on real estate be used to finance the local public education system? Why should elderly taxpayers with grown children, or parents who send their children to private schools, continue to pay for public schools through these taxes?
- How will the repeal of the Federal estate tax affect legacy gifts made to charitable organizations? Would the lack of a charitable contribution deduction impair the ability of charities to raise operating and capital funds?
- Does a regressive sales/use tax fall harder on individuals of color?

EXAMPLE 14

Susan, a single individual, is the sole proprietor of Quality Fabrics, a retail store in which she works full-time. The business is her only source of income. Susan's taxable income in 2006 is $100,000, and her Federal income tax is $22,331.50 ($15,107.50 + 28% of the amount over $74,200). Thus, her *marginal tax rate*[8] is 28%. ■

EXAMPLE 15

Assume the same facts as in the previous example, except that Susan pays her nondependent 19-year-old son a $10,000 salary to work part-time at Quality Fabrics. This will reduce her 2006 taxable income by $10,000 and reduce her tax bill by $2,800 ($10,000 deduction × 28% marginal tax rate). Her son will have $1,550 in taxable income ($10,000 – $5,150 standard deduction – $3,300 personal exemption) and will be taxed at a 10% rate, which results in Federal income tax of $155. In summary, Susan (the individual taxpayer) is able to operate the business entity (Quality Fabrics) in a way that will save the family unit $2,645 in Federal income tax ($2,800 saved by Susan – $155 paid by her son). ■

Examples 14 and 15 reflect the fact that a proprietorship itself is not a taxpaying entity. The owner of the proprietorship must report the income and deductions of the business on a Schedule C (Profit or Loss from Business) and must report the net profit (or loss) of the proprietorship on his or her Form 1040 (U.S. Individual Income Tax Return). Specific issues related to the taxation of sole proprietorships are presented in detail in Chapter 17.

Corporations

Some corporations pay tax on corporate taxable income while others pay no tax at the corporate level. Corporations that are separate taxable entities are referred to as **C corporations**, because they are governed by Subchapter C of the Internal Revenue Code. Corporations that meet certain requirements and pay no tax at the corporate level are referred to as **S corporations**, because they are governed by

[8] A taxpayer's *marginal tax rate* (or *marginal tax bracket*) is the rate that would be paid on an additional dollar of taxable income.

Subchapter S of the Code. S corporations are discussed in detail in Chapter 12. C corporations are addressed in Chapters 9 and 10.

A C corporation is required to file a tax return (Form 1120) and is subject to the Federal income tax. The shareholders then pay income tax on the dividends they receive when the corporation distributes its profits. Thus, the profits of the corporation can be seen as subject to double taxation, first at the corporate level and then at the shareholder level.

EXAMPLE 16

Joseph is single, has no dependents, and does not itemize deductions. He is the president and sole shareholder of Falcon Corporation. Falcon's taxable income for 2006 is $100,000, and its tax liability is $22,250. If Joseph has the corporation pay all of its after-tax income to him as a dividend, he will receive $77,750, have taxable income of $69,300 (after the $5,150 standard deduction and $3,300 personal exemption), and will pay Federal income tax of $10,395 ($69,300 × 15% rate applicable to qualified dividends). The combined Federal income tax paid by Joseph and the corporation is $32,645 ($22,250 corporate tax + $10,395 individual tax). ■

Partnerships

A partnership is not a separate taxable entity. The partnership is required to file a tax return (Form 1065) on which it summarizes the financial results of the business. Each partner then reports his or her share of the net income or loss and other special items that were reported on the partnership return.

EXAMPLE 17

Cameron and Connor form a partnership in which they are equal partners. The partnership reports a $100,000 net profit on its tax return, but is not subject to the Federal income tax. Cameron and Connor each report $50,000 net income from the partnership on their separate individual income tax returns. ■

S Corporations

An S corporation is like a C corporation with regard to nontax factors. Shareholders have limited liability, shares are freely transferable, there is a centralized management (vested in the board of directors), and there is continuity of life (i.e., the corporation continues to exist after the withdrawal or death of a shareholder). With regard to tax factors, however, an S corporation is more like a partnership. The S corporation is not subject to the Federal *income tax.* Like a partnership, it does file a tax return (Form 1120S), but the shareholders report their share of net income or loss and other special items on their own tax returns.

EXAMPLE 18

Kay and Dawn form a corporation and elect to have it treated as an S corporation. Kay owns 60% of the stock of the corporation, and Dawn owns 40%. The S corporation reports a $100,000 net profit on its tax return, but is not subject to the income tax. Kay will report $60,000 net income from the S corporation on her individual income tax return, and Dawn will report $40,000 on her tax return. ■

The S corporation, limited liability company, and partnership forms of organization, which are referred to as *flow-through* entities, avoid the double taxation problem associated with the C corporation.

Limited Liability Companies and Limited Liability Partnerships

Limited liability companies (LLCs) and limited liability partnerships (LLPs) have grown rapidly in popularity over the last few years. These organizations exist under state laws, and the specific rules vary somewhat from state to state. Both forms offer limited liability and some (but not all) of the other nontax features of corporations. Additionally, both forms usually are treated as partnerships for tax purposes.

Dealings between Individuals and Entities

Many of the provisions in the tax law deal with the relationships between owners and the business entities they own. The following are some of the major interactions between owners and business entities.

- Owners put assets into a business when they establish a business entity (e.g., a proprietorship, partnership, or corporation).
- Owners take assets out of the business during its existence in the form of salary, dividends, withdrawals, redemptions of stock, etc.
- Through their entities, owner-employees set up retirement plans for themselves, including IRAs, Keogh plans, and qualified pension plans.
- Owners dispose of all or part of a business entity.

Every major transaction that occurs between an owner and a business entity has important tax ramifications. The following are a few of the many tax issues that arise.

- How to avoid taxation at both the owner level and the entity level (i.e., the multiple taxation problem).
- How to get assets into the business with the least adverse tax consequences.
- How to get assets out of the business with the least adverse tax consequences.
- How to dispose of the business entity with the least adverse tax consequences.

When addressing these (and other) tax issues, a common set of tax planning tools can be applied. These tax planning fundamentals are introduced in the next section.

LO.5

Recognize tax planning opportunities and apply a general framework for tax planning.

Tax Planning Fundamentals

Overview of Tax Planning

Taxpayers generally attempt to minimize their tax liabilities, and it is perfectly acceptable to do so by using legal means. It is a long-standing principle that taxpayers have no obligation to pay more than their fair share of taxes. The now-classic words of Judge Learned Hand in *Commissioner v. Newman,* reflect the true values a taxpayer should have.

> Over and over again courts have said that there is nothing sinister in so arranging one's affairs as to keep taxes as low as possible. Everybody does so, rich or poor; and all do right, for nobody owes any public duty to pay more than the law demands; taxes are enforced exactions, not voluntary contributions. To demand more in the name of morals is mere cant.[9]

Minimizing taxes legally is referred to as **tax avoidance**. On the other hand, some taxpayers attempt to *evade* income taxes through illegal actions. There is a major distinction between tax avoidance and **tax evasion**. Though eliminating or reducing taxes is also a goal of tax evasion, the term *evasion* implies the use of subterfuge and fraud as a means to this end. Tax avoidance is legal, while tax evasion subjects the taxpayer to numerous civil and criminal penalties, including prison sentences.

Clients expect tax practitioners to provide advice to help them minimize their tax costs. This part of the tax practitioner's practice is referred to as *tax planning.* To structure a sound tax minimization plan, a practitioner must have a thorough knowledge of the tax law. Tax planning skill is based on knowledge of tax saving

[9] 47–1 USTC ¶9175, 35 AFTR 857, 159 F.2d 848 (CA–2, 1947).

provisions in the tax law, as well as provisions that contain costly pitfalls for the unwary. Thorough study of the remainder of this text will provide a solid base of the knowledge required to recognize opportunities and avoid pitfalls. Tax planning requires the practitioner to have in mind both a framework for planning and an understanding of the tax planning implications of a client's situation.

A General Framework for Income Tax Planning

★ Tax Planning Framework

The primary goal of tax planning is to design a transaction so as to minimize its tax costs, while meeting the other nontax objectives of the client. Generally, this means that the client attempts to maximize the present value of its after-tax income and assets. Selecting a specific form of transaction solely for the sake of tax minimization often leads to a poor business decision. Effective tax planning requires careful consideration of the nontax issues involved in addition to the tax consequences.

Careful analysis of the tax formula (refer to Figure 1–1) reveals a series of tax minimization strategies. Through creative tax planning that also takes into consideration a client's nontax concerns, each component of the tax formula can be managed in a way that will help to minimize the client's tax liability. The General Framework for Income Tax Planning in Figure 1–3 lists each element in the income tax formula, develops tax planning strategies designed to minimize taxes, and provides brief summaries of specific examples of tax planning. The framework is followed by a discussion of the tax planning strategies, along with detailed examples of how the strategies can be applied. In Chapters 4–17 of this book, these strategies and their tax formula components provide the framework for Planning Strategies features.

Tax Minimization Strategies Related to Income

★ Framework Focus: Income

➤ *Tax Planning Strategy*

➤ ***Avoid Income Recognition.*** Section 61(a) defines gross income as "all income from whatever source derived." However, the Code contains provisions that allow various types of income to be excluded from the tax base. Numerous exclusions are available for individuals, but very few are available for corporations. However, a corporation can provide excludible income for its owners at no tax cost to the corporation.

EXAMPLE 19

The average employee of Penguin Corporation is a 25% bracket taxpayer. In negotiations with the employees' union, Penguin proposes that it will increase the amount it spends on nontaxable fringe benefits by an average of $3,000 per employee in lieu of granting a $3,000 average salary increase. The average employee will be better off by $750 if the union accepts Penguin's offer.

	Salary Increase	Fringe Benefit Increase
Value of compensation received	$3,000	$3,000
Tax on employee's compensation	750	–0–
After-tax increase in compensation	$2,250	$3,000

Although the average employee receives a $750 benefit, there is no tax cost to Penguin because both fringe benefits and salaries are deductible by the corporation. ■

➤ *Tax Planning Strategy*

➤ ***Postpone Recognition of Income to Achieve Tax Deferral.*** The IRS requires that both income and expenses be reported in the proper year. If not for this requirement, taxpayers could freely shift income and expenses from year to year to take advantage of tax rate differentials or could defer tax liabilities indefinitely.

FIGURE 1–3 **General Framework for Income Tax Planning**

Tax Formula	Tax Planning Strategy	Tax Planning Examples
Income and exclusions	➤ **Avoid income recognition.**	Compensate employees with nontaxable fringe benefits (see Example 19).
	➤ **Postpone recognition of income to achieve tax deferral.**	Postpone sale of assets (see Example 20).
− Deductions	➤ **Maximize deductible amounts.**	Invest in stock of another corporation (see Example 21).
	➤ **Accelerate recognition of deductions to achieve tax deferral.**	Elect to deduct charitable contribution in year of pledge rather than in year of payment (see Example 22).
= Taxable income		
× Tax rate	➤ **Shift net income from high-bracket years to low-bracket years.**	Postpone recognition of income to a low-bracket year (see Example 23).
		Postpone recognition of deductions to a high-bracket year (see Example 24).
	➤ **Shift net income from high-bracket taxpayers to low-bracket taxpayers.**	Pay children to work in the family business (see Example 25).
	➤ **Shift net income from high-tax jurisdictions to low-tax jurisdictions.**	Establish subsidiary operations in countries with low tax rates (see Examples 26 and 27).
	➤ **Control the character of income and deductions.**	Hold assets long enough to qualify for long-term capital gain rates before selling them (see Example 28).
		Invest in small business stock to obtain ordinary loss treatment under § 1244 (see Example 29).
	➤ **Avoid double taxation.**	Operate as a flow-through entity rather than a C corporation (see Example 30).
		Maximize deductible expenses paid by a C corporation to a shareholder/employee (see Example 31).
= Federal income tax		
− Tax credits	➤ **Maximize tax credits.**	Hire employees who qualify the business for the work opportunity tax credit (see Example 33).
= Tax owed (or refund)		

Although various rules limit the shifting of income and deductions across time periods, some opportunities still exist.

EXAMPLE 20

In 1996, Turquoise Corporation acquired land for investment purposes at a cost of $500,000. In November 2005, Turquoise is negotiating to sell the land to Aqua Corporation for $800,000. Aqua insists that the transaction be completed in 2005, but Turquoise wants to delay the sale until 2006, to defer the tax on the gain. In an effort to compromise, Turquoise agrees to sell the land in November of 2005 and asks Aqua to pay for the land in two installments, $400,000 in December 2005 and $400,000 in January 2006. This enables Turquoise to use the installment sale method, under which Turquoise will report $150,000 of the gain in 2005 and the remaining $150,000 in 2006. By electing the installment method, Turquoise defers the payment of tax on $150,000 of the gain for one year. Assuming that the marginal tax rate for Turquoise is 35%, this tax deferral strategy will provide $52,500 ($150,000 × 35%) to be invested or used in the business for a year. ■

Tax Minimization Strategies Related to Deductions

★ **Framework Focus: Deductions**

➤ *Tax Planning Strategy*

➤ ***Maximize Deductible Amounts.*** A corporation that owns stock in another corporation is eligible for a *dividends received deduction (DRD).* The DRD is equal to a specified percentage of the dividends received. The percentage is based on the amount of stock that the investor corporation owns in the investee corporation (70 percent deduction for ownership of less than 20 percent, 80 percent deduction for ownership of 20 percent or more but less than 80 percent, and 100 percent deduction for ownership of 80 percent or more).

EXAMPLE 21

Falcon Corporation invests in bonds of Sparrow Corporation and receives interest of $20,000. Red Hawk Corporation acquires 15% of the stock of Pheasant Corporation and receives a $20,000 dividend. Falcon's taxable income is increased by $20,000 of interest received. Red Hawk's income is increased by $20,000 in dividend income, but it is allowed a $14,000 dividends received deduction, thus increasing taxable income by only $6,000. ■

Example 21 clearly demonstrates the *tax* advantage of dividend income versus interest income. However, it is also important to consider *nontax* factors. Is the investment in bonds safer than the investment in stock? Does the potential growth in the value of stock outweigh the possible risk of investing in stock versus bonds?

➤ *Tax Planning Strategy*

➤ ***Accelerate Recognition of Deductions to Achieve Tax Deferral.*** Both corporate and noncorporate taxpayers may deduct charitable contributions if the recipient is a qualified charitable organization. Generally, a deduction is allowed only for the year in which the payment is made. However, an important exception is available for *accrual basis corporations.* They may claim the deduction in the year *preceding* payment if two requirements are met. First, the contribution must be authorized by the board of directors by the end of that year. Second, the contribution must be paid on or before the fifteenth day of the third month of the next year.

EXAMPLE 22

Blue, Inc., a calendar year, accrual basis corporation, wants to make a $10,000 donation to the Atlanta Symphony Association (a qualified charitable organization), but does not have adequate funds to make the contribution in 2006. On December 28, 2006, Blue's board of directors *authorizes* a $10,000 contribution to the Association. The donation is made on March 14, 2007. Because Blue is an accrual basis corporation, it may claim the $10,000 donation as a deduction for tax year 2006, even though payment is not made until 2007. ■

In the preceding example, Blue Corporation was able to take advantage of a tax provision and reduce 2006 taxable income by $10,000. Assuming that Blue is in the 35 percent marginal bracket, the corporation has been able to defer payment of $3,500 in Federal income tax. The $3,500 can be invested or used in the business for a year.

Tax Minimization Strategies Related to Tax Rates

★ **Framework Focus: Tax Rates**

➤ *Tax Planning Strategy*

➤ ***Shift Net Income from High-Bracket Years to Low-Bracket Years.*** One objective of shifting income is to defer the payment of income tax (refer to Example 20). A second time-shifting strategy is to shift *net* income from high-tax to low-tax years. This can be accomplished by shifting income from high-bracket years to low-bracket years or by shifting deductions from low-bracket years to high-bracket years.

EXAMPLE 23

Egret Corporation, a calendar year taxpayer, is in the 34% bracket in 2006, but expects to be in the 25% bracket in 2007. The corporation, which is negotiating a $10,000 service contract with a client, decides to wait until 2007 to sign the contract and perform the services. The client is indifferent as to when the contract is completed. Thus, Egret saves $900 in income tax by deferring the service contract income to 2007, when it will be taxed at the 25% rate instead of the current 34% rate. In this case, the income-shifting strategy is used to accomplish two tax planning objectives. First, shifting the income defers the payment of income tax from 2006 to 2007. Second, the shifting strategy results in the income being taxed at a rate of 25% rather than 34%. ■

EXAMPLE 24

Macaw Corporation has been sued for $125,000 damages by a customer, and the parties decided to settle out of court for $100,000. Macaw expects to be in the 25% bracket in 2006 and the 35% bracket in 2007. Macaw will save $10,000 in income tax if it finalizes the agreement in January 2007 rather than December 2006 [$100,000 × (35% − 25%)]. ■

➤ *Tax Planning Strategy*

➤ ***Shift Net Income from High-Bracket Taxpayers to Low-Bracket Taxpayers.*** Individual income tax rates range from 10 to 35 percent. Although several provisions in the tax law prevent shifting income from high-bracket taxpayers to low-bracket taxpayers, many opportunities to do so remain. Business entities can be effective vehicles for shifting income to low-bracket taxpayers.

EXAMPLE 25

Bill Gregory is the president and sole shareholder of Grayhawk, Inc., an S corporation. He projects that Grayhawk will earn $400,000 in 2006. Bill will be taxed on this income at a 35% marginal rate. Bill and his wife have four teenage children, all of whom are dependents. Bill decides to employ the children as part-time workers throughout 2006 and pay them $11,000 each. This will reduce Bill's income from Grayhawk by $44,000 and reduce his Federal income tax by $15,400 ($44,000 × 35%). Each child will report taxable income of $5,850 ($11,000 − $5,150 standard deduction) and will pay $585 of Federal income tax ($5,850 × 10% rate). As a result of this income-shifting strategy, the family unit will save $13,060 ($15,400 tax saved by Bill − $2,340 tax paid by children). ■

➤ *Tax Planning Strategy*

➤ ***Shift Net Income from High-Tax Jurisdictions to Low-Tax Jurisdictions.*** The state or country where income is earned (or where a deduction is incurred) can have a large impact on an entity's overall tax liability. Hence, shifting income from high-tax jurisdictions to low-tax jurisdictions or shifting deductions from low-tax jurisdictions to high-tax jurisdictions is an important tax planning strategy.

EXAMPLE 26

Gold International owns a sales subsidiary in Texas and a manufacturing subsidiary in Ireland (which imposes a 10% tax rate on certain types of business income). The Irish subsidiary makes drill presses and sells them for $4 million to the Texas subsidiary, which then modifies them and offers them for sale to businesses in the United States for $8.4 million. The cost of manufacturing and modifying each drill press is $3 million. Of the $5.4 million of profit earned, $1 million is attributable to the Irish corporation (which is subject to a 10% tax rate), and $4.4 million is attributable to the U.S. corporation (which is subject to a 34% tax rate). Gold's total tax liability is $1,596,000 [($1,000,000 × 10%) + ($4,400,000 × 34%)]. ■

EXAMPLE 27

Assume the same facts as in the previous example, except $5 million of the profit is attributable to the Irish corporation and $400,000 is attributable to the U.S. corporation. In this case, Gold's total tax liability is $636,000 [($5,000,000 × 10%) + ($400,000 × 34%)]. Thus, by altering the amount of work done in each of the two subsidiaries and the amount of income generated by each, Gold's tax liability is decreased by $960,000 ($1,596,000 − $636,000). ■

➤ *Tax Planning Strategy*

➤ ***Control the Character of Income and Deductions.*** For various policy reasons, Congress has chosen to treat certain categories of income and losses more favorably than others. For instance, the provisions that tax long-term capital gains at a maximum rate of 15 percent, compared to a 35 percent rate on ordinary income, were enacted to encourage individuals to make long-term investments of capital in the economy.

EXAMPLE 28

Lisa is the proprietor of Designer Enterprises. Because a proprietorship is a flow-through entity, Lisa must report all of Designer's transactions on her individual income tax return. On October 9, 2005, Lisa invested $25,000 of Designer's excess cash in Lavender Corporation stock. On October 1, 2006, the stock was worth $35,000.

Lisa, who is a 35% bracket taxpayer, has decided to sell the stock and use the cash to increase Designer's inventory. She must hold the stock until October 10, 2006, for the gain to qualify as long term (held more than a year). If she sells the stock before October 10, 2006, the gain will be taxed as short term, and she will pay 35% tax on the gain. If she sells the stock after October 9, 2006, the gain is long term, and she will pay 15% tax on the gain. ■

To encourage investment in small businesses, Congress enacted the § 1244 provisions, which provide favorable treatment of losses incurred on the sale of qualifying small business stock. Generally, losses on the sale of stock are treated as capital losses. Individuals with capital losses in excess of capital gains are permitted to deduct only $3,000 of such losses against ordinary income in a tax year. To make small business stock more attractive as an investment, § 1244 allows up to $50,000 ($100,000 if married filing jointly) of losses on such stock to be treated as ordinary losses, thus exempting the § 1244 losses from being offset against capital gains and then from the $3,000 limit that would otherwise apply to any excess capital losses.

EXAMPLE 29

Roberto invested $80,000 in Mauve Corporation stock and sold the stock in 2006 for $40,000. He has no other capital asset transactions and does not expect to have any in future years. If the Mauve stock qualifies as § 1244 stock, Roberto may deduct the entire $40,000 as an ordinary loss. If the stock does not qualify as § 1244 stock, Roberto may deduct only $3,000 as a capital loss in the current tax year. He carries the remaining loss of $37,000 forward. In future years, the loss will continue to be subject to the annual $3,000 limitation unless there are offsetting capital gains. ■

➤ Tax Planning Strategy

➤ Avoid Double Taxation. The owners of a corporation can choose between two entity forms. A C corporation, also referred to as a regular corporation, is a taxable entity that pays tax on corporate profits. Shareholders also pay tax on dividends received from a C corporation, resulting in what is commonly referred to as *double taxation* (refer to Example 16). Note, however, as discussed in Chapter 4, the dividends may be eligible for a beneficial tax rate.

Shareholders can avoid double taxation by electing to have a corporate entity become an S corporation. Unlike a C corporation, an S corporation is not a taxable entity. Instead, the profits and losses of the S corporation flow through to the shareholders and are reported on their tax returns (see Chapter 12).

EXAMPLE 30

Chickadee, Inc., a C corporation with net income of $100,000, pays Carl, its sole shareholder, a $77,750 dividend. Chickadee must pay corporate income tax of $22,250 on the net income of $100,000, and Carl must pay tax on the $77,750 dividend. Sparrow, Inc., an S corporation, also earns $100,000. Sparrow is not a taxable entity, so it pays no income tax on the $100,000 net income. Sam, who is the sole shareholder of Sparrow, includes $100,000 in computing his taxable income. ■

There are other entity choices that can be used to avoid double taxation, including partnerships and limited liability companies. Partnerships and limited liability companies, like S corporations, are flow-through entities rather than taxable entities (see Chapter 11).

Choosing to operate as a flow-through entity is not the only way to avoid double taxation. Double taxation can be avoided or minimized by having the corporation make payments, such as salaries, rent, and interest to the shareholders.

EXAMPLE 31

Walt is the president and sole shareholder of Meadowlark, Inc., a C corporation. Meadowlark's taxable income before any payment to Walt is $600,000. Walt, a skilled manager, is primarily responsible for the profitability of the corporation. If Meadowlark pays Walt a dividend of $400,000, the corporation must pay Federal income tax on $600,000, and Walt must include the $400,000 dividend in gross income. However, if Meadowlark pays Walt a salary of $400,000, the salary is deductible, and the corporation has only $200,000 of taxable income. Walt must include the $400,000 salary in gross income. In either case, Walt includes $400,000 in gross income (the dividends, however, may be eligible for a beneficial tax rate). Meadowlark, on the other hand, reports $400,000 less taxable income if the payment to Walt is a salary payment rather than a dividend payment. ■

★ **Framework Focus: Credits**

➤ *Tax Planning Strategy*

Tax Minimization Strategies Related to Credits

➤ ***Maximize Tax Credits.*** Congress uses the tax credit provisions of the Internal Revenue Code liberally in implementing tax policy. It is important to understand the difference between a credit and a deduction, both of which reduce a taxpayer's tax liability. A deduction reduces taxable income, which results in a reduction of the tax paid. The tax benefit of the deduction depends on the amount of the qualifying expenditure and the taxpayer's tax rate. A tax credit reduces the tax liability dollar for dollar and is not affected by the taxpayer's tax rate.

EXAMPLE 32

Oriole Corporation, which is in the 25% marginal bracket, has a $6,000 deduction for expenditures made to repair a machine. The deduction reduces taxable income by $6,000 and results in a tax liability reduction of $1,500 ($6,000 deduction × 25% marginal rate). Oriole also incurred expenditures of $6,000 to rehabilitate a building, which qualifies the corporation for a tax credit of $600 ($6,000 rehabilitation expenditures × 10% rate for the credit). The rehabilitation expenditures credit results in a $600 reduction of Oriole's tax liability. In addition, Oriole's depreciable basis for the building increases by $5,400 ($6,000 expenditures – $600 credit). ■

One example of the use of credits to influence taxpayer behavior is the work opportunity tax credit, which was enacted to encourage employers to hire employees from several targeted and economically disadvantaged groups, including high-risk youths, summer youth employees, and military veterans. The employee is certified to be a member of a qualifying targeted group. The work opportunity tax credit is 40 percent of the first $6,000 of wages paid during the first 12 months of employment.

EXAMPLE 33

Robin Corporation hired a high-risk youth for four months at a cost of $6,000. Robin qualifies for the work opportunity tax credit and is allowed a credit of $2,400 ($6,000 wages × 40% credit rate) and a wage deduction of $3,600 ($6,000 wages – $2,400 credit). Robin is a 34% bracket taxpayer. The $3,600 deduction reduces Robin's income tax by $1,224 ($3,600 × 34%). The total tax saving thus is $3,624 ($1,224 + $2,400 credit).

If the employee does not qualify Robin for the work opportunity tax credit, Robin is allowed a deduction of $6,000, which results in a tax saving of $2,040 ($6,000 × 34%). Thus, hiring an employee who qualifies Robin for the work opportunity tax credit will save an additional $1,584 in tax ($3,624 – $2,040). ■

Thinking Outside the Framework

Although the General Framework for Income Tax Planning in Figure 1–3 is broad and covers most tax planning strategies, some strategies fall outside the framework. In addition, other planning ideas can supplement the strategies in the framework. Some of these ideas are discussed below.

Determining the Tax Burden. To engage in effective tax planning, one must be able to identify the relevant tax rate that will be applied to a transaction. There are three kinds of tax rates. A taxpayer's *marginal* tax rate is paid on an additional dollar of taxable income. Referring to the corporate income tax rate schedule inside the front cover of this text, a C corporation's marginal tax rate on its first dollar of income is 15 percent. Similarly, the marginal tax rate faced by a corporation with $100,001 of income is 39 percent. The *average* tax rate is the ratio of taxes paid to the tax base. Thus, a corporation with $100,000 of taxable income is subject to an average tax rate of 22.25 percent ($22,250 in tax divided by $100,000 in taxable income). A third kind of tax rate, the *effective* tax rate, can be seen as either (1) the ratio of taxes paid to financial net income before tax or (2) the sum of currently payable and deferred tax expense divided by net income before tax. Of these approaches to determining a taxpayer's tax rate, the marginal tax rate is most appropriate for tax planning purposes.

EXAMPLE 34

Azure Corporation has taxable income of $80,000. Azure also has $10,000 of tax-free interest income from municipal bonds. Using the corporate tax rate schedule inside the front cover of this text, one can determine that the company's tax liability is $15,450. If Azure were to earn an additional dollar in taxable income, it would pay an extra $0.34 in tax. Thus, the company's marginal tax rate is 34%. Azure's average tax rate is the ratio of taxes paid to taxable income or 19.3% ($15,450/$80,000). Finally, the company has an effective rate of tax of 17.2% ($15,450/$90,000), the ratio of taxes paid to financial net income before tax (here, the sum of taxable income and tax-free income). ■

The actual tax paid may not always be apparent. For example, the amount of taxes paid should include both current taxes and the present value of future taxes generated by a transaction.

EXAMPLE 35

Magenta Corporation is a publishing company that specializes in electronic media. It is a new corporation that was formed on January 1, 2003. During that year, it generated a net operating loss (NOL) of $300,000. The NOL can be carried forward to offset future years' taxable income and thereby reduce Magenta's future tax liabilities. Magenta expects to earn $100,000 of income each year over the next four years. The NOL should completely offset the company's taxable income for the first three of these years.

At the beginning of 2004, Magenta must decide whether to invest in a project that will earn an additional $40,000 of taxable income during 2004 or a project that will generate $36,000 of tax-free income. The company's president reasons that, since the company has an NOL carryforward, the applicable tax rate is 0%, so the taxable project should be chosen.

The president's reasoning is incorrect, because an additional $40,000 of income now will result in $40,000 of taxable income in 2006 (since there will be $40,000 less NOL available in that year).

	2004	2005	2006	2007
Alternative 1 (tax-free investment)				
Pre-NOL taxable income	$ 100,000	$ 100,000	$ 100,000	$100,000
NOL carryforward (from 2003)	(300,000)	(200,000)	(100,000)	–0–
Taxable income	$ –0–	$ –0–	$ –0–	$100,000
Alternative 2 (taxable investment)				
Pre-NOL taxable income	$ 140,000	$ 100,000	$ 100,000	$100,000
NOL carryforward (from 2003)	(300,000)	(160,000)	(60,000)	–0–
Taxable income	$ –0–	$ –0–	$ 40,000	$100,000

The tax on the $40,000 project equals the discounted value of the tax due in 2006. Assuming a 10% discount rate and a 15% corporate tax rate, the present value of taxes paid in three years is $4,508, and the discounted tax rate is 11.27%. Thus, the after-tax proceeds on the taxable project will be $35,492, or $508 *less* than the $36,000 earnings on the tax-free project. ■

Finally, the amount of tax paid includes both *explicit* taxes (paid directly to the government) and **implicit taxes** (paid through higher prices or lower returns on tax-favored investments).

EXAMPLE 36

Sunflower, Inc., a C corporation with a 15% marginal tax rate, has accumulated excess cash of $100,000 that it wants to invest in bonds. Sunflower has the option of investing in taxable corporate bonds that yield 9% or tax-free municipal bonds that yield 6%. Assume that the bonds are identical, except for their tax status.

Sunflower's tax rate on the corporate bonds is explicit at 15%. The tax rate on the municipal bonds is implicit, evidenced by the lower return on the bonds. Since the bonds are identical, if the municipal bonds were taxable, they would yield a 9% pre-tax rate. Their after-tax rate is 6% because they are tax-free. Hence, the implicit tax rate on the municipal bonds equals 33%, or the tax rate that would generate a 6% after-tax return on a 9% bond [9% – (0.33 × 9%)].

Since Sunflower is in the 15%, tax bracket, it should invest in the taxable bonds because it would face a higher marginal tax rate (a 33% implicit rate) if it invested in the municipal bonds. Stated another way, Sunflower's after-tax return on the taxable bonds is greater than the 6% return available on the tax-free bonds. ■

LO.6

Recognize the economic, social, equity, and political considerations that underlie the tax law.

Understanding the Federal Tax Law

The Federal tax law is a mosaic of statutory laws, administrative pronouncements, and court decisions. Anyone who has attempted to work with these provisions would have to admit to their complexity. For the person who has to trudge through a mass of rules to find the solution to a tax problem, it may be of some consolation to know that the law's complexity can generally be explained. Whether sound or not, there are reasons for the formulation of every rule. Knowing these reasons, therefore, is an important step toward understanding the Federal tax law.

Revenue Needs

The foundation of the income tax system is the raising of revenue to cover the cost of government operations. Ideally, annual outlays should not exceed anticipated revenues, thereby leading to a balanced budget with no resulting deficit. Many states have achieved this objective by passing laws or constitutional amendments precluding deficit spending.

The U.S. Constitution allows deficit spending, and politicians often find it hard to resist the temptation to spend more than the tax system collects currently. Congress uses several approaches to reduce a tax bill's net revenue loss. When tax reductions are involved, the full impact of the legislation can be phased in over a period of years. Or, as an alternative, the tax reduction can be limited to a period of years. When the period expires, Congress can then renew or not renew the provision in light of budget considerations.

Economic Considerations

Using the tax system in an effort to accomplish economic objectives has become increasingly popular in recent years. Generally, proponents of this approach use tax legislation to promote measures designed to help control the economy or encourage certain economic activities and businesses.

Encouragement of Certain Activities. Without passing judgment on the wisdom of any such choices, it is quite clear that the tax law does encourage certain types of economic activity or segments of the economy. For example, the favorable treatment (immediate deduction) allowed research and development expenditures can be explained by the desire to foster technological progress.

Similarly, Congress has used depreciation deductions as a means of encouraging investment in business capital. Theoretically, shorter asset lives and accelerated methods should encourage additional investment in depreciable property acquired for business use. Conversely, longer asset lives and the required use of the straight-line method of depreciation dampen the tax incentive for capital outlays.

Is preserving the environment a desirable objective? Ecological considerations explain why the tax law permits favorable treatment for costs incurred in the installation of pollution control facilities.

Is it wise to stimulate U.S. exports of goods and services? Considering the pressing and continuing problem of a deficit in the U.S. balance of payments, the answer should be clear. In an international setting, Congress has deemed it advisable to establish incentives for U.S. citizens who accept employment overseas.

Is saving desirable for the economy? Saving leads to capital formation and thereby makes funds available to finance home construction and industrial expansion. The tax law encourages saving by according preferential treatment to private retirement plans. Not only are deductions allowed for contributions to certain retirement plans and Individual Retirement Accounts (IRAs), but income on the contributions is not taxed until withdrawn.

Encouragement of Certain Industries. No one can question the proposition that a sound agricultural base is necessary for a well-balanced national economy. Undoubtedly, this explains why farmers are accorded special treatment under the Federal income tax system. Among the benefits available to farmers are the election to expense rather than capitalize certain soil and water conservation expenditures and fertilizers and the election to defer the recognition of gain on the receipt of crop insurance proceeds.

Encouragement of Small Business. At least in the United States, a consensus exists that what is good for small business is good for the economy as a whole. Whether valid or not, this assumption has led to a definite bias in the tax law favoring small business. Several income tax provisions can be explained by the desire to benefit small business, including the low marginal tax rates applied to the first dollars of the entity's income.

Social Considerations

Some provisions of the Federal tax law, particularly those dealing with the income tax of individuals, can be explained by a desire to encourage certain social results.

- Certain benefits provided to employees through accident and health plans financed by employers are nontaxable to employees. Encouraging such plans is considered socially desirable since they provide medical benefits in the event of an employee's illness or injury.

- A contribution made by an employer to a qualified pension or profit sharing plan for an employee may receive special treatment. The contribution and any income it generates are not taxed to the employee until the funds are distributed. Such an arrangement also benefits the employer by allowing a tax deduction when the contribution is made to the qualified plan. Various types of retirement plans are encouraged to supplement the subsistence income level the employee would otherwise have under the Social Security system.
- A deduction is allowed for contributions to qualified charitable organizations. The deduction attempts to shift some of the financial and administrative burden of socially desirable programs from the public (government) to the private (citizens) sector.
- Various tax credits, deductions, and exclusions that are designed to encourage taxpayers to obtain or extend the level of education are allowed.
- A tax credit is allowed for amounts spent to furnish care for certain minor or disabled dependents to enable the taxpayer to seek or maintain gainful employment. Who could deny the social desirability of encouraging taxpayers to provide care for their children while they work?
- A tax deduction is denied for certain expenditures deemed to be contrary to public policy. This disallowance extends to such items as fines, penalties, illegal kickbacks, bribes to government officials, and gambling losses in excess of gains. Social considerations dictate that the tax law should not encourage these activities by permitting a deduction.

Equity Considerations

The concept of equity is relative. Reasonable persons can, and often do, disagree about what is fair or unfair. In the tax area, moreover, equity is most often tied to a particular taxpayer's personal situation. To illustrate, compare the tax positions of those who rent their personal residences with those who own their homes. Renters may not take a Federal income tax deduction for the rent they pay. For homeowners, however, a large portion of the house payments they make may qualify for the Federal mortgage interest and property tax deductions. Although renters may have difficulty understanding this difference in tax treatment, the encouragement of home ownership can be justified on both economic and social grounds.

In many other parts of the law, however, equity concerns are evident. The concept of equity appears in tax provisions that alleviate the effect of multiple taxation and postpone the recognition of gain when the taxpayer lacks the ability or **wherewithal to pay** the tax. Provisions that mitigate the effect of the application of the annual accounting period concept and help taxpayers cope with the eroding results of inflation also reflect equity considerations.

Alleviating the Effect of Multiple Taxation. The income earned by a taxpayer may be subject to taxes imposed by different taxing authorities. If, for example, the taxpayer is a resident of New York City, income might be subject to Federal, state of New York, and city of New York income taxes. To compensate for this apparent inequity, the Federal tax law allows a taxpayer to claim a deduction for state and local income taxes.

The deduction does not, however, neutralize the effect of multiple taxation, since the benefit derived depends on the taxpayer's Federal income tax rate. Only a tax credit, rather than a deduction, would completely eliminate the effects of multiple taxation on the same income. Equity considerations can also explain the Federal tax treatment of certain income from foreign sources.

The Wherewithal to Pay Concept. The wherewithal to pay concept recognizes the inequity of taxing a transaction when the taxpayer lacks the means to pay the tax. The wherewithal to pay concept underlies a provision in the tax law dealing with the treatment of gain resulting from an involuntary conversion. An involuntary conversion occurs when property is destroyed by casualty or taken by a public authority through condemnation. If gain results from the conversion, it need not be recognized if the taxpayer replaces the property within a specified time period. The replacement property must be similar or related in service or use to that involuntarily converted.

EXAMPLE 37

Ron, a rancher, has some pasture land that is condemned by the state for use as a game preserve. The condemned pasture land cost Ron $120,000, but the state pays him $150,000 (its fair market value). Shortly thereafter, Ron buys more pasture land for $150,000.

Ron has realized gain of $30,000 [$150,000 (condemnation award) – $120,000 (cost of land)]. It would be inequitable to require Ron to pay a tax on this gain for two reasons. First, without disposing of the property acquired (the new land), Ron would be hard-pressed to pay the tax. Second, his economic position has not changed. ■

EXAMPLE 38

Assume the same facts as in Example 37, except that Ron reinvests only $140,000 of the award in new pasture land. Now, Ron has a taxable gain of $10,000. Instead of ending up with only replacement property, Ron now has $10,000 in cash. ■

Mitigating the Effect of the Annual Accounting Period Concept. For purposes of effective administration of the tax law, all taxpayers must report to and settle with the Federal government at periodic intervals. Otherwise, taxpayers would remain uncertain as to their tax liabilities, and the government would have difficulty judging revenues and budgeting expenditures. The period selected for final settlement of most tax liabilities is one year.

The application of this annual accounting period concept can lead to dissimilar tax treatment for taxpayers who are, from a long-range standpoint, in the same economic position.

EXAMPLE 39

José and Alicia, both sole proprietors, experienced the following results during the indicated three tax years.

	Profit (or Loss)	
Year	**José**	**Alicia**
2005	$50,000	$150,000
2006	60,000	60,000
2007	60,000	(40,000)

Although José and Alicia have the same profit of $170,000 over the period from 2005 through 2007, the annual accounting period concept places Alicia at a disadvantage for tax purposes. However, the net operating loss deduction generated in 2007 offers Alicia some relief by allowing her to carry back some or all of her 2007 loss to the earlier profitable years (in this case, 2005). Thus, with an NOL carryback, Alicia can obtain an immediate refund for some of the taxes she paid on the $150,000 profit reported for 2005. ■

The installment method of recognizing gain on the sale of property allows a taxpayer to spread tax consequences over the payout period. The harsh effect of taxing all the gain in the year of sale is thereby avoided. The installment method can also be explained by the wherewithal to pay concept, since recognition of gain is tied to the collection of the installment notes received from the sale of the property.

Coping with Inflation. Because of the progressive nature of the income tax, a wage adjustment to compensate for inflation can push the recipient into a higher income tax bracket without increasing real income. Known as *bracket creep,* this phenomenon's overall impact is an erosion of purchasing power. Congress recognized this problem and began to adjust various income tax components, such as marginal tax brackets, standard deduction amounts, and personal and dependency exemptions. Indexation usually is based upon the rise in the consumer price index over the prior year.

Political Considerations

A large segment of the Federal tax law is made up of statutory provisions. Since these statutes are enacted by Congress, is it any surprise that political considerations influence tax law? For purposes of discussion, the effect of political considerations on the tax law is divided into the following topics: special interest legislation, political expediency, and state and local government influences.

Special Interest Legislation. There is no doubt that certain provisions of the tax law can largely be explained by the political influence some groups have had on Congress. For example, is there any other realistic reason that prepaid subscription and dues income is not taxed until earned, while prepaid rents are taxed to the landlord in the year received?

The American Jobs Creation Act of 2004 included several good examples of special interest legislation. One provision, sponsored by Senator Zell Miller (D–Ga.), suspended the import duties on ceiling fans. The nation's largest seller of ceiling fans is Home Depot, which is based in Atlanta, Georgia. Another provision, sponsored by House Speaker Dennis Hastert (R–Ill.), reduced the excise taxes on fishing tackle boxes. Representative Hastert's district includes Plano Molding, a major manufacturer of tackle boxes. The justification for this change was that it placed tackle boxes on a more level playing field with toolboxes (which are not subject to tax). Allegedly, fishermen had been buying and converting toolboxes to avoid the excise tax!

Special interest legislation is not necessarily to be condemned if it can be justified on economic, social, or some other utilitarian grounds. At any rate, it is an inevitable product of our political system.

Political Expediency. Various tax reform proposals rise and fall in favor with the shifting moods of the American public. That Congress is sensitive to popular feeling is an accepted fact. Therefore, certain provisions of the tax law can be explained by the political climate at the time they were enacted.

Measures that deter more affluent taxpayers from obtaining so-called preferential tax treatment have always had popular appeal and, consequently, the support of Congress. Provisions such as the limitation on the deductibility of interest on investment indebtedness can be explained on this basis.

State and Local Government Influences. State law has had an influence in shaping our present Federal tax law. One example of this effect is the evolution of Federal tax law in response to states with community property systems. The states with community property systems are Louisiana, Texas, New Mexico, Arizona, California, Washington, Idaho, Nevada, and Wisconsin. Spouses in Alaska can elect community property treatment. The rest of the states are common law jurisdictions. The difference between common law and community property systems centers around the property rights possessed by married persons. In a common law system, each spouse owns whatever he or she earns. Under a community property system, one-half of the earnings of each spouse is considered owned by the other spouse.

EXAMPLE 40

Al and Fran are husband and wife, and their only income is the $80,000 annual salary Al receives. If they live in New Jersey (a common law state), the $80,000 salary belongs to Al. If, however, they live in Arizona (a community property state), the $80,000 is divided equally, in terms of ownership, between Al and Fran. ■

BRIDGE *Discipline*

Bridge to Political Science and Sociology

Taxes and Marriage

The country's wrestling with the issue of gay marriage has important tax ramifications. One recent study noted that, if all committed gay couples were to be legally married under state laws (perhaps 400,000 now-single filers), the remnants of the marriage penalty would bring a small amount of extra income tax dollars into the Treasury. However, any income tax revenue increase would be offset many times over by the additional Social Security and Medicare claims from one member of the couple against the other's accounts.

But this issue is still working its way through the statehouses and courthouses. For instance, how should someone file a tax return given the current developments?

- Gay marriage is seemingly allowed in only a few cities and counties. On a Federal income tax return, what is the correct filing status for those with some form of a marriage certificate?
- How should someone in Oregon file a tax return? The state supreme court has held that localities there do not have the right to marry gay couples, but a few hundred marriages were performed in the state during 2004 before the court's ruling was made.
- Are we certain that the various forms of civil unions and other contractual arrangements allowed by dozens of localities do not qualify the parties for married status on a Federal income tax return? This is a court case waiting to happen. Federal law passed under President Clinton (the Defense of Marriage Act of 1996) makes it clear that a "marriage" consists of one male and one female. The IRS follows all Federal laws, but what about the couple's state and local income tax returns? Can an individual file as single on one tax return and married on another for the same tax year? And how would TurboTax handle this?

Gay advocates say that "Federal tax law requires us to perjure ourselves" in that a gay couple who sees itself as married must file as single on the Form 1040. They compare the situation to the "don't ask, don't tell" culture of the military (another Clinton rule). Will the Federal government require jail time for those who file knowingly inaccurate/fraudulent tax returns? Some have concluded that the proper filing status in this situation is Married – Separate, but that decision subjects the individual to the highest of the Form 1040 tax rate schedules.

IRS personnel assert that audits of filing status are low priority in the agency's workplans—the audit-effort to taxes-collected ratio likely is very low. Less-impassioned observers of the issue view the filing status matter as a minor bureaucratic decision, carrying only limited political or fiscal firepower.

State-Federal law conflicts have affected citizens at other times in U.S. history.

- A few states allowed voting by women before the U.S. constitution adopted the rule.
- "Nevada divorces" were not recognized by the home states of all couples. As recently as 1940, charges of bigamy were brought against those with Nevada divorces who remarried outside Nevada.
- A few states now recognize gay marriages performed outside of the United States.

Who would have thought that the important tax question "Are you married?" could become so difficult to answer?

At one time, the tax position of the residents of community property states was so advantageous that many common law states actually adopted community property systems. Needless to say, the political pressure placed on Congress to correct the disparity in tax treatment was considerable. To a large extent, this was accomplished in 1948 when the law extended many of the community property tax advantages to residents of common law jurisdictions.

The major advantage extended was the provision allowing married taxpayers to file joint returns and compute the tax liability as if the income had been earned one-half by each spouse. This result is automatic in a community property state, since half of the income earned by one spouse belongs to the other spouse. The income-splitting benefits of a joint return are now incorporated as part of the tax rates applicable to married taxpayers.

LO.7

Describe the role played by the IRS and the courts in the evolution of the Federal tax system.

Influence of the Internal Revenue Service

The influence of the IRS on tax law is apparent in many areas beyond its role in issuing the administrative pronouncements that make up a considerable portion of our tax law. The IRS has been instrumental in securing the passage of much legislation designed to curtail the most flagrant tax avoidance practices (to close tax loopholes). In addition, the IRS has sought and obtained legislation to make its own job easier (to attain administrative feasibility).

Closing Perceived Tax Loopholes. Certain tax provisions are intended to prevent a loophole from being used to avoid the tax consequences intended by Congress. Working within the letter of existing law, ingenious taxpayers and their advisers devise techniques that accomplish indirectly what cannot be accomplished directly. As a consequence, legislation is enacted to close the loopholes that taxpayers have located and exploited. Some tax law can be explained in this fashion and is discussed in the chapters to follow.

Administrative Feasibility. Some tax law is justified on the grounds that it simplifies the task of the IRS in collecting the revenue and administering the law. With regard to collecting the revenue, the IRS long ago realized the importance of placing taxpayers on a pay-as-you-go basis. Elaborate withholding procedures apply to wages, and accrual basis taxpayers often must pay taxes on prepaid income in the year received and not when earned. The approach may be contrary to generally accepted accounting principles, but it is consistent with the wherewithal to pay concept.

Of considerable aid to the IRS in collecting revenue are the numerous provisions that impose interest and penalties on taxpayers for noncompliance with the tax law. Provisions such as the penalties for failure to pay a tax or to file a return that is due, the negligence penalty for intentional disregard of rules and regulations, and various penalties for civil and criminal fraud serve as deterrents to taxpayer noncompliance.

One of the keys to an effective administration of our tax system is the audit process conducted by the IRS. To carry out this function, the IRS is aided by provisions that reduce the chance of taxpayer error or manipulation and therefore reduce the audit effort that is necessary. An increase in the amount of the standard deduction, for example, reduces the number of individual taxpayers who will choose the alternative of itemizing their personal deductions. With fewer deductions to check, the audit function is simplified.

DIGGING DEEPER 2

Find more information on this topic at our Web site: ***http://wft-entities.swlearning.com.***

Influence of the Courts

In addition to interpreting statutory provisions and the administrative pronouncements issued by the IRS, the Federal courts have influenced tax law in two other respects. First, the courts have formulated certain judicial concepts that serve as guides in the application of various tax provisions. Second, certain key decisions have led to changes in the Internal Revenue Code.

TAX FACT

The Costs of Complexity

A tax system that is designed to accomplish so many, sometimes contradictory, goals is bound to be a complex animal. According to the University of Michigan's Office of Tax Policy Research, the current system may actually be so complex as to be self-defeating. By one measure, the costs of complying with the individual income tax portions of the Internal Revenue Code—taxpayers' time, record-keeping systems and software, and costs for tax advisers and preparers—equal 14.5 cents for every dollar collected by the Treasury for the tax year.

Judicial Concepts Relating to Tax. Particularly in dealings between related parties, the courts test transactions by looking to whether the taxpayers acted in an arm's length manner. The question to be asked is: Would unrelated parties have handled the transaction in the same way?

EXAMPLE 41

Rex, the sole shareholder of Silver Corporation, leases property to the corporation for a yearly rent of $6,000. To test whether the corporation should be allowed a rent deduction for this amount, the IRS and the courts will apply the arm's length concept. Would Silver Corporation have paid $6,000 a year in rent if it had leased the same property from an unrelated party (rather than from Rex)? Suppose it is determined that an unrelated third party would have paid an annual rent for the property of only $5,000. Under these circumstances, Silver Corporation will be allowed a deduction of only $5,000. The other $1,000 it paid for the use of the property represents a nondeductible dividend. Accordingly, Rex will be treated as having received rent income of $5,000 and dividend income of $1,000. ■

Judicial Influence on Statutory Provisions. Some court decisions have been of such consequence that Congress has incorporated them into statutory tax law. For example, many years ago the courts found that stock dividends distributed to the shareholders of a corporation were not taxable as income. This result was largely accepted by Congress, and a provision in the tax statutes now addresses the issue.

On occasion, however, Congress has reacted negatively to judicial interpretations of the tax law.

EXAMPLE 42

Nora leases unimproved real estate to Wade for 40 years. At a cost of $200,000, Wade erects a building on the land. The building is worth $100,000 when the lease terminates and Nora takes possession of the property. Does Nora have any income either when the improvements are made or when the lease terminates? In a landmark decision, a court held that Nora must recognize income of $100,000 upon the termination of the lease. ■

Congress felt that the result reached in Example 42 was inequitable in that it was not consistent with the wherewithal to pay concept. Consequently, the tax law was amended to provide that a landlord does not recognize any income either when the improvements are made (unless made in lieu of rent) or when the lease terminates.

Summary

In addition to its necessary revenue-raising objective, the Federal tax law has developed in response to several other factors.

- *Economic considerations.* The emphasis here is on tax provisions that help regulate the economy and encourage certain activities and types of businesses.

- *Social considerations.* Some tax provisions are designed to encourage (or discourage) socially desirable (or undesirable) practices.
- *Equity considerations.* Of principal concern in this area are tax provisions that alleviate the effect of multiple taxation, recognize the wherewithal to pay concept, mitigate the effect of the annual accounting period concept, and recognize the eroding effect of inflation.
- *Political considerations.* Of significance in this regard are tax provisions that represent special interest legislation, reflect political expediency, and reflect the effect of state and local law.
- *Influence of the IRS.* Many tax provisions are intended to aid the IRS in the collection of revenue and the administration of the tax law.
- *Influence of the courts.* Court decisions have established a body of judicial concepts relating to tax law and have, on occasion, led Congress to enact statutory provisions to either clarify or negate their effect.

Suggested Further Readings

Ellen D. Cook, *et al.*, "Outsourcing Tax Returns," *Practical Tax Strategies*, August 2005, pp. 68–73.

John S. Irons and Michael Powers, "Tax Complexity: By the Numbers," October 2005, **www.americanprogress.org**.

Chaim V. Kofinas, "State & Local Taxation—Sales Tax Treatment of Internet Commerce," *The CPA Journal*, January 2004, pp. 36–40.

KEY TERMS

Ad valorem tax, 1–10
C corporation, 1–16
Death tax, 1–8
Employment tax, 1–3
Estate tax, 1–8
Excise tax, 1–4
FICA tax, 1–7
Franchise tax, 1–12
FUTA tax, 1–7
Gift tax, 1–2
Implicit tax, 1–26
Inheritance tax, 1–8
Occupational tax, 1–13
Personalty, 1–10
Proprietorship, 1–15
Realty, 1–10
S corporation, 1–16
Sales tax, 1–3
Tax avoidance, 1–18
Tax evasion, 1–18
Use tax, 1–6
Value added tax (VAT), 1–6
Wherewithal to pay, 1–28

PROBLEM MATERIALS

PROBLEMS

Issue ID

1. Aqua Corporation believes that it will have a better distribution location for its product if it relocates the corporation to another state. What considerations (both tax and nontax) should Aqua Corporation weigh before making a decision on whether to make the move?

2. Are the following taxes *proportional* or *progressive*?
   a. Federal estate tax.
   b. FUTA tax.
   c. Ad valorem tax on personalty.
   d. Hotel occupancy tax.

3. Is the Medicare component of FICA a proportional or a progressive tax? Explain.

4. Compare FICA and FUTA in connection with each of the following.
   a. Incidence of taxation.
   b. Justification for taxation.
   c. Rates and base involved.

5. Jim, a resident of Washington (which imposes a general sales tax), goes to Oregon (which does not impose a general sales tax) to purchase his automobile. Will Jim successfully avoid the Washington sales tax? Explain.

6. In 2005, Horace makes a taxable gift of $250,000 upon which he pays a Federal gift tax of $70,800. In 2006, Horace makes another taxable gift of $250,000. Will the 2006 taxable gift result in the same gift tax as the 2005 gift? Why or why not?

7. How much property can Herman, a widower, give to his four married children, their spouses, and eight grandchildren over a period of 10 years without making a taxable gift?

8. *Issue ID* Once its new facilities are finished, the Church of the Good Samaritan moves from downtown Madison City to the suburbs. Instead of disposing of the old location, the church leases it to a former mayor of Madison City who converts the church building and its parking lot into a high-end restaurant. Comment on any tax ramifications of this arrangement.

9. *Ethics* The Toth family lives in a residence that they have owned for several years. They purchased the residence from St. Matthew's Catholic Church, which had used the house as a rectory for its priest. To the Toths' surprise, since they purchased the residence, they have not received any ad valorem property tax bills from either the city or the county. Is there a plausible explanation for this? Explain. What, if anything, should the Toths do about the property tax matter?

10. *Issue ID* The Adams Independent School District desires to sell a parcel of unimproved land that it does not need. Its three best offers are as follows: from State Department of Public Safety (DPS), $2.3 million; from Second Baptist Church, $2.2 million; and from Baker Chevrolet Company, $2.1 million. DPS would use the property for a new state highway patrol barracks, Second Baptist would start a church school, and Baker would open a car dealership. As the financial adviser for the school district, which offer would you prefer? Why?

11. *Issue ID* Shaquille O'Neal, a perennial All-Star in the National Basketball Association, was traded by the Los Angeles Lakers to the Miami Heat. Discuss Shaq's state income tax situation both before and after the trade.

12. *Issue ID* Before she entered a nursing home, Doris signed a deed transferring title to her personal residence to her only son, Walt. Walt has never filed the deed with the county clerk's office and continues to pay the property taxes in his mother's name. Walt and his family are the only occupants of the property. Is there an explanation for Walt's actions?

13. The commissioners for Colby County are actively negotiating with Eagle Industries regarding the location of a new manufacturing facility in the county. As Eagle has several sites from which to pick, a "generous tax holiday" may be needed to influence its choice. The local school district is opposed to any "generous tax holiday."
    a. What might a proposal for a "generous tax holiday" entail?
    b. Why should the school district be opposed?

14. *Issue ID* The Mayo family is selected for ABC's *Extreme Makeover: Home Edition.* The program gives the Mayos' California home the royal treatment, increasing the living area from 1,200 square feet to about 4,300—more than doubling the value of the property. Do you envision any tax problems?

15. *Issue ID* During a social event, Muriel and Earl are discussing the home computer each recently purchased. Although the computers are identical makes and models, Muriel is surprised to learn that she paid a sales tax, while Earl did not. Comment as to why this could happen.

Issue ID

16. Jared wants to give his wife a $30,000 diamond necklace for her birthday. To avoid the state and local general sales tax of 8.5%, he asks his aunt (who lives in New Hampshire) to make the purchase. Has Jared saved $2,550 (8.5% × $30,000)?

17. Jill is a single individual. Jill has total income of $220,000, credits of $19,000, exclusions of $30,000, deductions *for* AGI of $38,000, itemized deductions of $20,000 (assume no AGI limitations are applicable), a standard deduction of $5,150, a personal exemption equal to $3,300, and estimated tax payments of $16,500.
    a. What is her 2006 tax due?
    b. If Jill were a corporation instead of an individual, and if all of her deductions were business related, what would be the tax due?

Decision Making

Communications

18. Cory and Cynthia have decided to go into business together. They will operate a sandwich delivery business. They expect to have a loss in the first and second years of the business and subsequently expect to make a substantial profit. Both are also concerned about potential liability if a customer ever gets sick. They have called your office and asked for advice about whether they should run their business as a partnership or as a corporation. Write a letter to Cynthia Clay, at 1206 Seventh Avenue, Fort Worth, TX 76101, describing the alternative forms of business that they can select. In your letter, explain what form or forms of business you recommend and why.

Decision Making

19. Ashley runs a small business in Boulder, Colorado, that makes snow skis. She expects the business to grow substantially over the next three years. Because she is concerned about product liability and is planning to take the company public in the year 2007, she is currently considering incorporating the business. Financial data are as follows.

	2006	2007	2008
Sales revenue	$150,000	$320,000	$600,000
Tax-free interest income	5,000	8,000	15,000
Deductible cash expenses	30,000	58,000	95,000
Tax depreciation	25,000	20,000	40,000

Ashley expects her marginal tax rate to be 35% over the next three years before any profits from the business are considered. Her cost of capital is 10%.
    a. Compute the present value of the future cash flows for 2006 to 2008, assuming Ashley incorporates the business and pays all after-tax income as dividends (that qualify for the 15% rate).
    b. Compute the present value of the future cash flows for 2006 to 2008, assuming Ashley continues to operate the business as a sole proprietorship.
    c. Should Ashley incorporate the business this year? Why or why not?

20. Sienna, Inc., faces a marginal tax rate of 25%, an average tax rate of 17.5%, and an effective marginal tax rate of 16.8%. Sienna is considering investing in Kiowa County bonds, which currently pay a 5% return (equivalent taxable bonds are paying an 8% return).
    a. What is the implicit tax rate on the Kiowa County bonds?
    b. Are the Kiowa County bonds a good investment for Sienna? Why or why not?

21. Chartreuse, Inc., has a net operating loss carryforward of $100,000. If Chartreuse continues its business with no changes, it will have $50,000 of taxable income (before the NOL) in both 2006 and 2007. If Chartreuse decides to invest in a new product line instead, it expects to have taxable income of $70,000 in 2006 and $50,000 in 2007. What marginal tax rate does the new product line face in 2006?

22. Mauve Supplies, Inc., reports total income of $120,000. The corporation's taxable income is $105,000. What are Mauve's marginal, average, and effective tax rates?

23. Franklin County is in dire financial straits and is considering a number of sources for additional revenue. Evaluate the following possibilities in terms of anticipated taxpayer compliance.
    a. A property tax on business inventories.
    b. A tax on intangibles (i.e., stocks and bonds) held as investments.
    c. A property tax on boats used for recreational purposes.

24. Some tax rules can be justified on multiple grounds (e.g., economic, social, etc.). In this connection, comment on the possible justification for the rules governing the following:
    a. Pension plans.
    b. Education.
    c. Home ownership.

25. What purpose is served by allowing individuals to deduct home mortgage interest and property taxes?

26. Go to **http://www.taxfoundation.org** and determine Tax Freedom Day for your state for 1950, 1960, 1970, 1980, 1990, 2000, and 2005. *Extender*

27. Contrast a value added tax (VAT) with a national sales tax in terms of anticipated taxpayer compliance. *Extender*

28. Send by e-mail to your instructor a graph that indicates IRS audit rates for individuals in each of the last 10 years. *Extender* *Communications*

BRIDGE *Discipline*

Communications

1. Prepare a two-page paper to submit to your sociology professor, titled "How I Would Apply Federal Tax Law to a Gay Married Couple."

http://wft.swlearning.com

CHAPTER 2

Working with the Tax Law

LEARNING OBJECTIVES

After completing Chapter 2, you should be able to:

LO.1

Understand the statutory, administrative, and judicial sources of the tax law and the purpose of each source.

LO.2

Locate and work with the tax law and understand the tax research process.

LO.3

Communicate the results of the tax research process in a client letter and a tax file memorandum.

LO.4

Have an awareness of how best to use a computer when performing tax research and in taking the CPA exam.

OUTLINE

TAX *Talk*

The less people know about how sausages and laws are made, the better they'll sleep at night.

—Otto von Bismarck

LO.1

Understand the statutory, administrative, and judicial sources of the tax law and the purpose of each source.

Tax Sources

Understanding taxation requires a mastery of the sources of the *rules of tax law.* These sources include not only legislative provisions in the form of the Internal Revenue Code, but also congressional Committee Reports, Treasury Department Regulations, other Treasury Department pronouncements, and court decisions. Thus, the *primary sources* of tax information include pronouncements from all three branches of government: legislative, executive, and judicial.

In addition to being able to locate and interpret the sources of the tax law, a tax professional must understand the relative weight of authority within these sources. The tax law is of little significance, however, until it is applied to a set of facts and circumstances. This chapter, therefore, both introduces the statutory, administrative, and judicial sources of the tax law *and* explains how the law is applied to individual and business transactions. It also explains how to apply research techniques effectively.

Tax research is necessary because the application of the law to a specific situation is often not clear. As complicated as the Internal Revenue Code is, it cannot clearly address every conceivable situation. Accordingly, the tax professional must search other sources (such as administrative rulings and judicial decisions) to determine the most likely tax treatment of a transaction.

Often, this research process will yield widely differing results for similar fact patterns. One of the goals of tax research is to discover which facts and which legal rules are most relevant in determining the ultimate tax consequences. Working with such knowledge, a tax professional can then advise the client about the tax consequences of several possible courses of action. Tax research, in other words, is of critical importance not only in properly characterizing completed events but also in planning proposed transactions.

Statutory Sources of the Tax Law

Origin of the Internal Revenue Code. Before 1939, the statutory provisions relating to taxation were contained in the individual revenue acts enacted by Congress. The inconvenience and confusion that resulted from dealing with many separate acts led Congress to codify all of the Federal tax laws. Known as the Internal Revenue Code of 1939, this codification arranged all Federal tax provisions in a logical sequence and placed them in a separate part of the Federal statutes. A further rearrangement took place in 1954 and resulted in the Internal Revenue Code of

TAX FACT

Scope of the U.S. Tax System

Although it started out in 1913 as a tax on only the uppermost-income individuals, the tax system today is pervasive in our lives.

- The annual tax expenditures by Congress for a number of popular items are estimated as follows ($B).

Home mortgage interest deduction	$72
Exclusion of the first $500,000 gain on sale of a personal residence	23
Exclusion for employer-provided health insurance fringe benefit	78
Child tax credit	46
State/local taxes deduction	46
Education tax credits	5

- Of the 130 million Forms 1040 filed for 2003, about one-third were filed by the end of February 2004. Presumably, these returns generated refunds for the taxpayers. The average refund received by a taxpayer filing a 2003 return was about $2,125. Refund payments for 2003 Forms 1040 came to over $200 billion.
- For 2003 returns, the IRS received about 18 million Forms 1040EZ and about 24 million Forms 1040A.
- Over the next 10 years, the alternative minimum tax on individuals will generate an increase of $500 billion in revenues. A tax this large is very hard to modify or repeal.
- The typical Form 1040 requires 7.25 hours to gather records and assemble the return, and 6.25 hours to prepare the form and attachments. The estimated cost of complying with tax rules is $225 billion per year.
- The Internal Revenue Code is now 3.5 million words long, and the Regulations require another 8 million words. Combined, these documents are 12 times the length of Shakespeare's combined works and 15 times the length of the King James Bible.
- In filing Federal income tax returns, almost 56 percent of all taxpayers employ a professional tax preparer. This is about a 10 percent increase in the last decade. The average taxpayer pays about $130 to have the Form 1040 prepared in this manner.
- The IRS goal is for 80 percent of all Forms 1040 to be filed electronically for the 2007 filing season.
- Every month, about 47 million people receive a benefits check from Social Security. Benefit payments under this program represent over 4 percent of the country's GDP.

1954, which continued in effect until it was replaced by the Internal Revenue Code of 1986.[1]

Now, statutory amendments to the tax law are integrated into the existing Code. Thus, subsequent tax legislation, such as the Working Families Tax Relief Act of 2004 and the American Jobs Creation Act of 2004, becomes part of the Internal Revenue Code of 1986.

The Legislative Process. Federal tax legislation generally originates in the House of Representatives, where it is first considered by the House Ways and Means

[1]Aside from changes due to a large tax act, the organization of the Internal Revenue Code of 1986 is not substantively different from the organization of the 1954 Code. In contrast, the numbering scheme of sections in the 1939 Code differs from that used in the 1954 Code.

Committee. Tax bills can originate in the Senate if they are attached as riders to other legislative proposals. If acceptable to the committee, the proposed bill is referred to the entire House of Representatives for approval or disapproval. Approved bills are sent to the Senate, where they initially are considered by the Senate Finance Committee.

The next step is referral from the Senate Finance Committee to the entire Senate. Assuming no disagreement between the House and Senate, passage by the Senate means referral to the President for approval or veto. If the bill is approved or if the President's veto is overridden, the bill becomes law and part of the Internal Revenue Code. The passage of JGTRRA of 2003 required the vote of the Vice President to break a 50–50 tie in the Senate.

When the Senate version of the bill differs from that passed by the House, the Conference Committee, which includes members of both the House Ways and Means Committee and the Senate Finance Committee, is called upon to resolve the differences. House and Senate versions of major tax bills frequently differ. One reason bills are often changed in the Senate is that each senator has considerable latitude to make amendments when the Senate as a whole is voting on a bill referred to it by the Senate Finance Committee. In contrast, the entire House of Representatives either accepts or rejects what is proposed by the House Ways and Means Committee, and changes from the floor are rare.

The deliberations of the Conference Committee usually produce a compromise between the two versions, which is then voted on by both the House and the Senate. If both bodies accept the revised bill, it is referred to the President for approval or veto. The typical legislative process dealing with tax bills is summarized in Figure 2–1.

The role of the Conference Committee indicates the importance of compromise in the legislative process. As an example of the practical effect of the compromise process, consider what happened to a provision allowing the amortization of certain intangible assets in the Revenue Reconciliation Act of 1993 (see Figure 2–2).

Referrals from the House Ways and Means Committee, the Senate Finance Committee, and the Conference Committee are usually accompanied by *Committee Reports.* These Committee Reports often explain the provisions of the proposed legislation and are therefore a valuable source for ascertaining the *intent of Congress.* What Congress had in mind when it considered and enacted tax legislation is the key to interpreting legislation. Since Regulations interpreting new legislation normally are not issued immediately after a statute is enacted, taxpayers and the courts look to Committee Reports to determine congressional intent.

Arrangement of the Code. The Internal Revenue Code is found in Title 26 of the U.S. Code. Here is a partial table of contents.

Subtitle A. Income Taxes
  Chapter 1. Normal Taxes and Surtaxes
    Subchapter A. Determination of Tax Liability
      Part I. Tax on Individuals
        Sections 1–5
      Part II. Tax on Corporations
        Sections 11–12

In referring to a provision of the Code, the tax professional usually cites the Section number. In referring to § 2(a) (dealing with the status of a surviving spouse), for example, it is unnecessary to include Subtitle A, Chapter 1, Subchapter A, Part I. Merely mentioning § 2(a) suffices, since the Section numbers run consecutively and do not begin again with each new Subtitle, Chapter, Subchapter, or Part. Not all

FIGURE 2–1 Legislative Process for Tax Bills

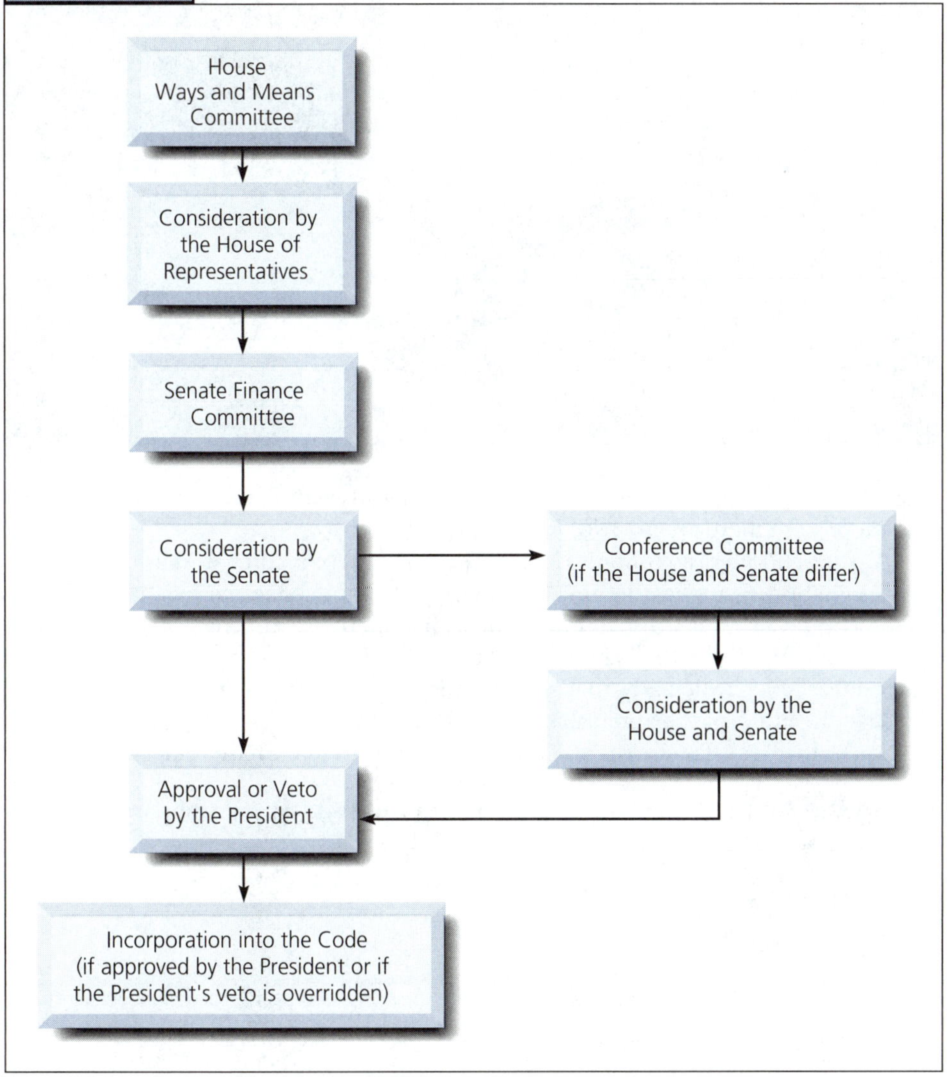

FIGURE 2–2 Example of Compromise in the Conference Committee

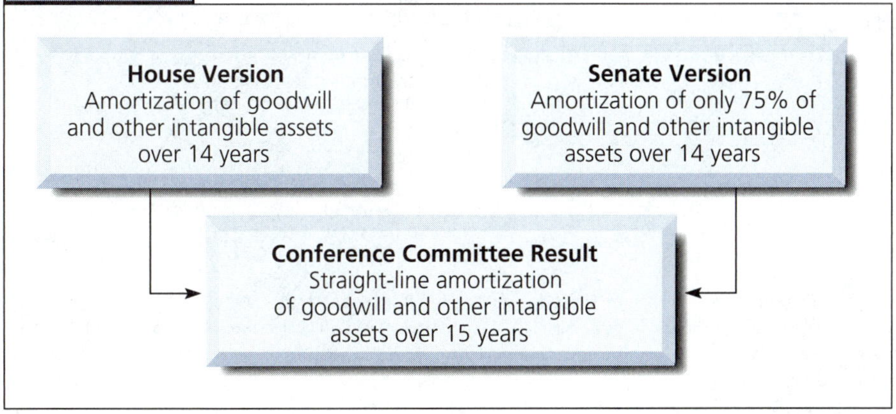

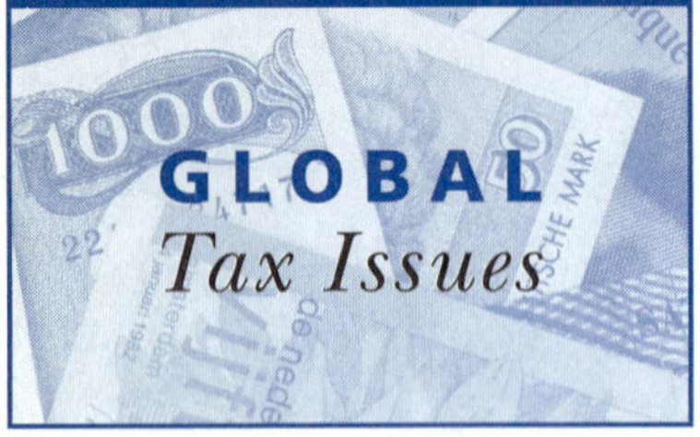

TAX TREATIES

The United States has entered into treaties with most of the major countries of the world, to eliminate possible double taxation. For example, nonresident alien students wishing to claim exemption from taxation are required to provide an information statement as set forth in several Revenue Procedures. The withholding agent must also certify the form.

Chinese students are required to prepare a four-part statement. Part 3 of the student's statement is as follows.

> I will receive compensation for personal services performed in the United States. This compensation qualifies for exemption from withholding of Federal income tax under the tax treaty between the United States and the People's Republic of China in an amount not in excess of $5,000 for any taxable year.

Code Section numbers are used, however. Part I ends with § 5 and Part II starts with § 11 (at present there are no §§ 6, 7, 8, 9, and 10).[2]

Tax practitioners commonly refer to certain areas of income tax law by Subchapter designation. Some of the more common Subchapter designations include Subchapter C ("Corporate Distributions and Adjustments"), Subchapter K ("Partners and Partnerships"), and Subchapter S ("Tax Treatment of S Corporations and Their Shareholders"). Particularly in the last situation, it is much more convenient to describe the effect of the applicable Code provisions (§§ 1361–1379) as "Subchapter S" than as the "Tax Treatment of S Corporations and Their Shareholders."

Citing the Code. Code Sections are often broken down into subparts.[3] Section 2(a)(1)(A) serves as an example.

Broken down by content, a citation for Code § 2(a)(1)(A) appears as follows.

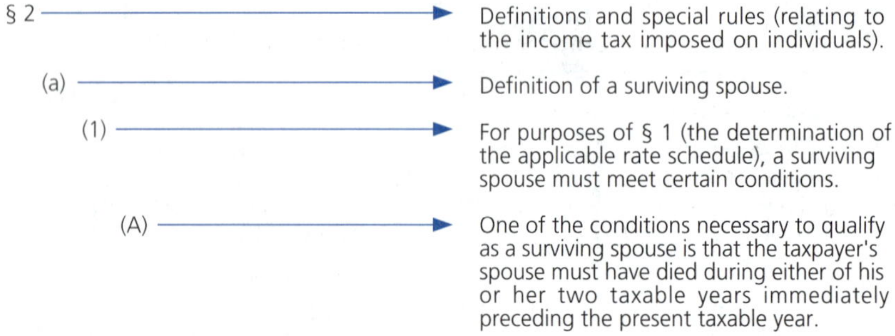

§ 2
Definitions and special rules (relating to the income tax imposed on individuals).
(a)
Definition of a surviving spouse.
(1)
For purposes of § 1 (the determination of the applicable rate schedule), a surviving spouse must meet certain conditions.
(A)
One of the conditions necessary to qualify as a surviving spouse is that the taxpayer's spouse must have died during either of his or her two taxable years immediately preceding the present taxable year.

[2]When the Code was drafted, Section numbers were intentionally omitted so that later changes could be incorporated into the Code without disrupting its organization. When Congress does not leave enough space, subsequent Code Sections are given A, B, C, etc., designations. A good example is the treatment of §§ 280A through 280H.

[3]Some Code Sections do not have subparts. See, for example, §§ 211 and 241.

[4]Some Code Sections omit the subsection designation and use, instead, the paragraph designation as the first subpart. See, for example, §§ 212(1) and 1222(1).

Throughout the text, references to the Code Sections are in the form given above. The symbols "§" and "§§" are used in place of "Section" and "Sections." The following table illustrates the format used in the text.

Complete Reference	Text Reference
Section 2(a)(1)(A) of the Internal Revenue Code of 1986	§ 2(a)(1)(A)
Sections 1 and 2 of the Internal Revenue Code of 1986	§§ 1 and 2
Section 2 of the Internal Revenue Code of 1954	§ 2 of the Internal Revenue Code of 1954
Section 12(d) of the Internal Revenue Code of 1939[5]	§ 12(d) of the Internal Revenue Code of 1939

Effect of Treaties. The United States signs certain tax treaties (sometimes called tax conventions) with foreign countries to render mutual assistance in tax enforcement and to avoid double taxation. These treaties affect transactions involving U.S. persons and entities operating or investing in a foreign country, as well as persons and entities of a foreign country operating or investing in the United States. Although these bilateral agreements are not codified in any one source, they are published in various Internal Revenue Service publications as well as in privately published tax services.

Neither a tax law nor a tax treaty automatically takes precedence. When there is a direct conflict, the most recent item will take precedence. With certain exceptions, a taxpayer must disclose on the tax return any position where a treaty overrides a tax law.[6] There is a $1,000 per *failure to disclose* penalty for individuals and a $10,000 per failure to disclose penalty for corporations.[7]

Administrative Sources of the Tax Law

The administrative sources of the Federal tax law can be grouped as follows: Treasury Department Regulations, Revenue Rulings and Revenue Procedures, and various other administrative pronouncements (see Exhibit 2–1). All are issued by either the U.S. Treasury Department or the IRS.

Treasury Department Regulations. Regulations are issued by the U.S. Treasury Department under authority granted by Congress.[8] Usually interpretive by nature, they provide taxpayers with considerable guidance on the meaning and application of the Code and often include examples. Regulations carry considerable authority as the official interpretation of tax statutes. They are an important factor to consider in complying with the tax law.

Treasury Regulations are arranged in the same sequence as the Code. A number is added at the beginning, however, to indicate the type of tax or other matter to which they relate. For example, the prefix 1 designates the Regulations under the income tax law. Thus, the Regulations under Code § 2 would be cited as Reg. § 1.2, with subparts added for further identification. The numbering pattern of these subparts often has no correlation with the Code subsections. The prefix 20 designates estate tax Regulations, 25 addresses gift tax Regulations, 31 relates to

[5]Section 12 (d) of the Internal Revenue Code of 1939 is the predecessor to § 2 of the Internal Revenue Codes of 1954 and 1986.

[6]§ 7852(d).

[7]§ 6712.

[8]§ 7805.

EXHIBIT 2–1 **Administrative Sources**

Source	Location	Authority***
Regulations	*Federal Register** *Internal Revenue Bulletin* *Cumulative Bulletin*	Force and effect of law. May be cited as precedent.
Temporary Regulations	*Federal Register** *Internal Revenue Bulletin* *Cumulative Bulletin*	May be cited as a precedent.
Proposed Regulations	*Federal Register** *Internal Revenue Bulletin* *Cumulative Bulletin*	Preview of final Regulations. Not precedent.
Revenue Rulings Revenue Procedures Treasury Decisions Actions on Decisions	*Internal Revenue Bulletin*** *Cumulative Bulletin*	Do not have the force and effect of law. Not precedent.
General Counsel Memoranda Technical Advice Memoranda	Tax Analysts' *Tax Notes* RIA's *Internal Memoranda of the IRS* CCH's *IRS Position Reporter*	May not be cited as precedent.
Letter Rulings	Research Institute of America and Commerce Clearing House tax services**	Applicable only to taxpayer addressed. Not precedent.

*Final, Temporary, and Proposed Regulations are published in soft-cover form and online by several publishers (including *RIA Checkpoint*).
**Revenue Rulings, Revenue Procedures, and letter rulings are also published online by several publishers (including *RIA Checkpoint*).
***Each of these sources may be substantial authority for purposes of the accuracy-related penalty in § 6662. Notice 90–20, 1990–1 C.B. 328.

employment taxes, and 301 refers to procedure and administration. This list is not all-inclusive. Reg. § 1.351–1(a)(2) is an example of a citation.

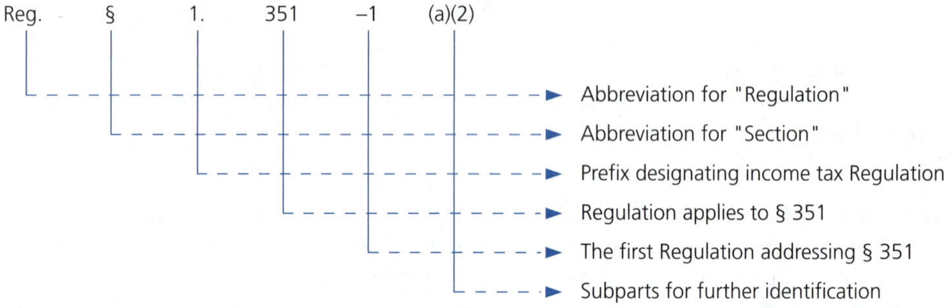

New Regulations and changes in existing Regulations usually are issued in proposed form before they are finalized. The interval between the proposal of a Regulation and its finalization permits taxpayers and other interested parties to comment on the propriety of the proposal. These comments are usually provided in writing, but oral comments can be offered at hearings held by the IRS on the Regulations in question pursuant to a public notice. This practice of notice-and-comment is a major distinction between Regulations and other forms of Treasury guidance such as Revenue Rulings, Revenue Procedures, and the like.

Proposed Regulations under Code § 2, for example, are cited as Prop.Reg. § 1.2. The Tax Court indicates that Proposed Regulations carry little weight—no more than a position advanced in a written brief prepared by a litigating party before the Tax Court.[9]

[9] *F. W. Woolworth Co.*, 54 T.C. 1233 (1970); *Harris M. Miller*, 70 T.C. 448 (1978); and *James O. Tomerlin Trust*, 87 T.C. 876 (1986).

TAX *in the News* **CHANGING THE FACE OF RUSSIA**

Peter the Great, the ruler of Russia from 1682 to 1725, imposed a tax on beards (except for clergy) because he felt that beards were "unnecessary, uncivilized, and ridiculous." If an individual did not pay the tax, a tax official would scrape off the beard. Without warning Peter himself would take a straight razor to the faces of bearded men appearing before him. When Peter attended a ceremony or banquet, anyone arriving with a beard would depart without it.

Source: *Adapted from Erik Jensen, "Taxation of Beards,"* Tax Notes, *January 5, 2004, pp. 153–157.*

The Treasury Department issues **Temporary Regulations** relating to matters where immediate guidance is important. These Regulations are issued without the comment period required for Proposed Regulations. Temporary Regulations have the same authoritative value as final Regulations and may be cited as precedents. Temporary Regulations also are issued as Proposed Regulations and automatically expire within three years after the date of their issuance.[10]

Proposed, Temporary, and **Final Regulations** are published in the *Federal Register*, the *Internal Revenue Bulletin*, and major tax services.

Regulations may also be classified as *legislative, interpretive,* or *procedural.* This classification scheme is discussed later in the chapter.

Revenue Rulings and Revenue Procedures. **Revenue Rulings** are official pronouncements of the National Office of the IRS.[11] Like Regulations, they are designed to provide interpretation of the tax law. However, they do not carry the same legal force and effect as Regulations and usually deal with more restricted problems. In addition, Regulations are approved by the Secretary of the Treasury, whereas Revenue Rulings generally are not.

Both Revenue Rulings and Revenue Procedures serve an important function in providing *guidance* to IRS personnel and taxpayers in handling routine tax matters. Revenue Rulings and Revenue Procedures generally apply retroactively and may be revoked or modified by subsequent rulings or procedures, Regulations, legislation, or court decisions.

Revenue Rulings typically provide one or more examples of how the IRS would apply a law to specific fact situations. Revenue Rulings may arise from technical advice memoranda of the IRS, court decisions, suggestions from tax practitioner groups, and various tax publications. A Revenue Ruling may also arise from a specific taxpayer's request for a letter ruling. If the IRS believes that a taxpayer's request for a letter ruling deserves official publication due to its widespread impact, the letter ruling will be converted into a Revenue Ruling and issued for the information and guidance of taxpayers, tax practitioners, and IRS personnel. Names, identifying descriptions, and money amounts are changed to conceal the identity of the requesting taxpayer.

Revenue Procedures are issued in the same manner as Revenue Rulings, but deal with the internal management practices and procedures of the IRS. Familiarity with these procedures increases taxpayer compliance and helps make the administration of the tax laws more efficient. The failure of a taxpayer to follow a Revenue Procedure can result in unnecessary delay or, in a discretionary situation, can cause the IRS to decline to act on behalf of the taxpayer.

Some recent Revenue Procedures dealt with the following matters.

- Deduction limits on luxury automobile depreciation.
- Revised procedures for the issuance of letter rulings.
- Automatic consent procedure for a change in accounting method.

[10] § 7805(e).

[11] § 7805(a).

Revenue Rulings and Revenue Procedures are published weekly by the U.S. Government in the *Internal Revenue Bulletin* (I.R.B.). Semiannually, the *Internal Revenue Bulletins* for a six-month period are gathered together and published in a bound volume called the *Cumulative Bulletin* (C.B.).[12]

The proper form for citing Rulings and Procedures depends on whether the item has been published in the *Cumulative Bulletin* or is available only in I.R.B. form. Consider, for example, the following sequence.

Temporary Citation	Rev.Rul. 2005–48, I.R.B. No. 32, 259. *Explanation:* Revenue Ruling Number 48, appearing on page 259 of the 32nd weekly issue of the *Internal Revenue Bulletin* for 2005.
Permanent Citation	Rev.Rul. 2005–48, 2005–1 C.B. 259. *Explanation:* Revenue Ruling Number 48, appearing on page 259 of Volume 1 of the *Cumulative Bulletin* for 2005.

Until the first volume of the 2005 *Cumulative Bulletin* is published, the I.R.B. citation is used. After the publication of the *Cumulative Bulletin*, the C.B. citation is preferred.

Note that the page reference of 259 is the same for both the I.R.B. (temporary) and C.B. (permanent) versions of the citation. The IRS numbers the pages of the I.R.B.s consecutively for each six-month period so as to facilitate their conversion to C.B. form. Revenue Procedures are cited in the same manner, except that "Rev.Proc." is substituted for "Rev.Rul."

Letter Rulings. **Letter rulings** are issued for a fee upon a taxpayer's request and describe how the IRS will treat a *proposed* transaction for tax purposes. Letter rulings can be useful to taxpayers who wish to be certain of how a transaction will be taxed before proceeding with it. Letter rulings allow taxpayers to avoid unexpected tax costs. The procedure for requesting a ruling can be quite cumbersome, although it sometimes is the most effective way to carry out tax planning. The IRS limits the issuance of individual rulings to restricted, pre-announced areas of taxation and generally will not rule on situations that are fact-intensive. Thus, a ruling may not be obtained on many of the problems that are particularly troublesome to taxpayers.[13]

Although letter rulings once were private and not available to the public, the law now requires the IRS to make such rulings available for public inspection after identifying details are deleted.[14] Published digests of private letter rulings can be found in RIA's *Private Letter Rulings*, BNA *Daily Tax Reports*, and Tax Analysts' *Tax Notes. IRS Letter Rulings Reports* (published by Commerce Clearing House) contain both digests and full texts of all letter rulings. *Letter Ruling Review* (published by Tax Analysts), a monthly publication, selects and discusses the most important of the approximately 40 letter rulings issued each week. In addition, computerized databases of letter rulings are also available through several private publishers.

Letter rulings are issued multidigit file numbers, which indicate the year and week of issuance as well as the number of the ruling during that week. Consider, for example, Ltr.Rul. 200530033, which waived the 60-day rollover requirement for distributions from an Individual Retirement Account for an investor.

2005	30	033
Year 2005	Issued during the 30th week of 2005	33rd ruling issued during the 30th week

[12]Usually, only two volumes of the *Cumulative Bulletin* are published in the typical year. However, when Congress has enacted major tax legislation, additional volumes may be published containing the congressional Committee Reports supporting the Revenue Act.

[13]The first *Internal Revenue Bulletin* issued each year contains a list of areas in which the IRS will not issue advance rulings. This list may be modified throughout the year. See, for example, Rev.Proc. 2005–68, I.R.B. No. 41, 694.

[14]§ 6110.

Other Administrative Pronouncements. *Treasury Decisions* (TDs) are issued by the Treasury Department to promulgate new Regulations, amend or otherwise change existing Regulations, or announce the position of the Government on selected court decisions. Like Revenue Rulings and Revenue Procedures, TDs are published initially in the *Internal Revenue Bulletin* and subsequently transferred to the *Cumulative Bulletin.*

The IRS publishes other administrative communications in the *Internal Revenue Bulletin,* such as Announcements, Notices, LRs (Proposed Regulations), Termination of Exempt Organization Status, Practitioner Disciplinary Actions, and Prohibited Transaction Exemptions.

Like letter rulings, **determination letters** are issued at the request of taxpayers and provide guidance on the application of the tax law. They differ from letter rulings in that the issuing source is an IRS Director rather than the National Office of the IRS. Further, determination letters usually involve *completed* (as opposed to proposed) transactions. Determination letters are not regularly published and are made known only to the party making the request.

EXAMPLE 1

The shareholders of Red Corporation and Green Corporation want assurance that the consolidation of their corporations into Blue Corporation will be a nontaxable reorganization. The proper approach is to ask the National Office of the IRS to issue a letter ruling concerning the income tax effect of the proposed transaction. ■

EXAMPLE 2

Chris operates a barber shop in which he employs eight barbers. To comply with the rules governing income tax and payroll tax withholdings, Chris wants to know whether the barbers working for him are employees or independent contractors. The proper procedure is to request a determination letter on their status from the appropriate IRS Director. ■

The National Office of the IRS releases **Technical Advice Memoranda (TAMs)** weekly. TAMs resemble letter rulings in that they give the IRS's determination of an issue. Letter rulings, however, are responses to requests by taxpayers, whereas TAMs are issued by the National Office of the IRS in response to questions raised by IRS field personnel during audits. TAMs deal with completed rather than proposed transactions and are often requested for questions relating to exempt organizations and employee plans.

The law requires that several internal memoranda that constitute the working law of the IRS be released. TAMs and General Counsel Memoranda (GCMs) are not officially published, and the IRS indicates that they may not be cited as precedents by taxpayers.[15] However, these working documents do explain the IRS's position on various issues.

Judicial Sources of the Tax Law

The Judicial Process in General. After a taxpayer has exhausted some or all of the remedies available within the IRS (no satisfactory settlement has been reached at the agent level or at the Appeals Division level), the dispute can be taken to the Federal courts. The dispute is first considered by a **court of original jurisdiction** (known as a trial court), with any appeal (either by the taxpayer or the IRS) taken to the appropriate appellate court. In most situations, the taxpayer has a choice of four trial courts: a **District Court**, the **Court of Federal Claims**, the **Tax Court**, or the **Small Cases Division** of the Tax Court. The court system for Federal tax litigation is illustrated in Figure 2–3.

[15]These are unofficially published by the sources listed in Exhibit 2–1. Internal memoranda may constitute substantial authority for purposes of the § 6662 accuracy-related penalty. Notice 90–20, 1990–1 C.B. 328.

FIGURE 2–3 **Federal Judicial System**

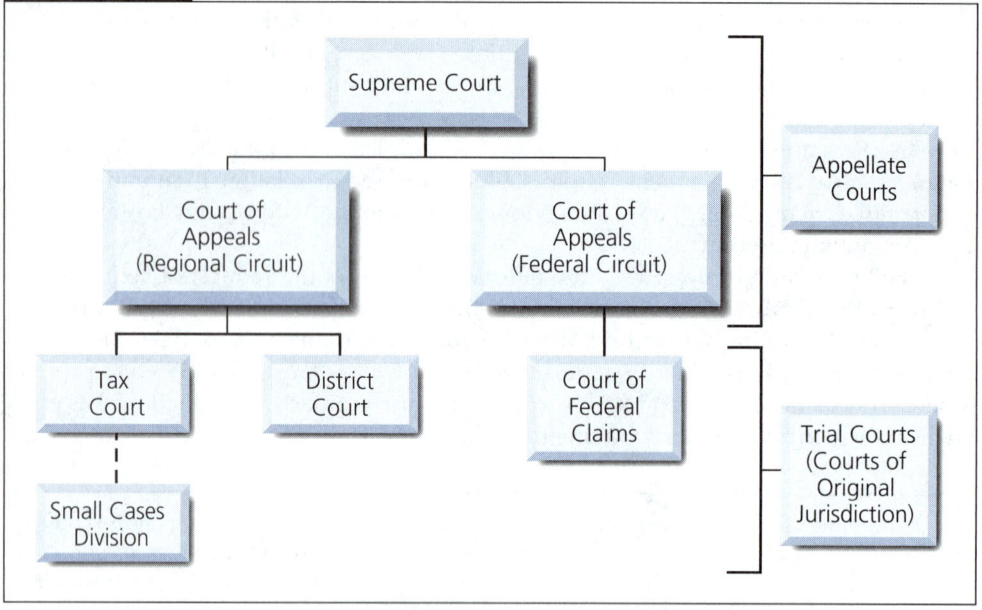

The broken line between the Tax Court and the Small Cases Division indicates that there is no appeal from the Small Cases Division. Decisions from the Small Cases Division have no precedential value. Some of these cases can now be found on the U.S. Tax Court Web site. They may not be relied upon by other taxpayers or even by the taxpayer in question in subsequent years. The jurisdiction of the Small Cases Division is limited to cases involving amounts of $50,000 or less.

DIGGING DEEPER 1

Find more information on this topic at our Web site: ***http://wft-entities.swlearning.com.***

Trial Courts. The differences among the various trial courts (courts of original jurisdiction) can be summarized as follows.

- *Number of courts.* There is only one Court of Federal Claims and only one Tax Court, but there are many District Courts. The taxpayer does not select the District Court that will hear the dispute but must sue in the one that has jurisdiction where the taxpayer resides.
- *Number of judges.* A case tried in a District Court is heard before only 1 judge. The Court of Federal Claims has 16 judges, and the Tax Court has 19 regular judges. The entire Tax Court, however, reviews a case (the case is sent to court conference) only when important or novel tax issues are involved. Most cases are heard and decided by 1 of the 19 judges.
- *Location.* The Court of Federal Claims meets most often in Washington, D.C., while a District Court meets at a prescribed seat for the particular district. Each state has at least one District Court, and many of the populous states have more than one. Choosing the District Court usually minimizes the inconvenience and expense of traveling for the taxpayer and his or her counsel. The Tax Court is based in Washington, D.C., but various judges travel to different parts of the country and hear cases at predetermined locations and dates. This procedure eases the distance problem for the taxpayer, but it can mean a delay before the case comes to trial.
- *Jurisdiction of the Court of Federal Claims.* The Court of Federal Claims has jurisdiction over any claim against the United States that is based upon the

TAX *in the News* **SO NOW WHO DO I TALK TO?**

Spending priorities in the IRS are changing, broadly from customer service to enforcement, reflecting the orientations of the last two commissioners. Some see this as an unraveling of the pro-taxpayer movements of the late 1990s, when the Taxpayer Bills of Rights were produced as a response to a series of congressional hearings that reflected badly on IRS operating procedures.

One manifestation of this trend is the permanent closing of about a third of the IRS walk-up assistance centers, where individuals could receive from the government answers to tax questions and help with filling in and filing their tax returns online. Those resources that continue to take live and telephone queries will reduce their operating hours. And the Tele-File system, which for about 20 years has allowed taxpayers to file a Form 1040 by punching buttons on their phones, was terminated as of the end of the 2005 filing season. These moves are projected to save about $20 million per year for the IRS's operating budget, about a 0.5 percent effect, but affecting over five million taxpayers. Most of this budget savings comes from the elimination of about 500 IRS jobs.

The IRS is pushing taxpayers to use **www.irs.gov** to find forms and publications, and to e-file their tax forms using various resources. One could see the current moves as reinforcing the "tax filing system of the future." But the low-income taxpayers who are likely to be most affected by this round of service cuts are perhaps not the most Internet-savvy of tax filers to begin with, so this rationale does not hold up well.

The commissioner-level sea change in approach was reflected in a recent quote by the past-commissioner, noting that because about 98 percent of tax revenues come in without any audit/enforcement effort, the better path would be to invest in helping those who are trying to comply with an ever-more-complex tax law. Contrary to that argument is the recent study measuring at $350 billion per year the tax revenues that the Treasury should be collecting but is not, due mostly to underreporting and nonfiling.

Constitution, any Act of Congress, or any Regulation of an executive department. Thus, the Court of Federal Claims hears nontax litigation as well as tax cases.

- *Jurisdiction of the Tax Court and District Courts.* The Tax Court hears only tax cases and is the most popular forum. The District Courts hear a wide variety of nontax cases, including drug crimes and other Federal violations, as well as tax cases. For this reason, some people suggest that the Tax Court has more expertise in tax matters.
- *Jury trial.* The only court in which a taxpayer can obtain a jury trial is a District Court. Juries can decide only questions of fact and not questions of law. Therefore, taxpayers who choose the District Court route often do not request a jury trial. If a jury trial is not elected, the judge will decide all issues. Note that a District Court decision is controlling only in the district in which the court has jurisdiction.
- *Payment of deficiency.* Before the Court of Federal Claims or a District Court can have jurisdiction, the taxpayer must pay the tax deficiency assessed by the IRS and then sue for a refund. If the taxpayer wins (assuming no successful appeal by the Government), the tax paid plus appropriate interest will be recovered. Jurisdiction in the Tax Court, however, is usually obtained without first paying the assessed tax deficiency.

DIGGING DEEPER 2

Find more information on this topic at our Web site: ***http://wft-entities.swlearning.com.***

- *Appeals.* Appeals from a District Court or a Tax Court decision go to the Court of Appeals for the circuit in which the taxpayer resides. Appeals from the Court of Federal Claims go to the Court of Appeals for the Federal Circuit. Few Tax Court cases are appealed, and when appeals are made, most are filed by the taxpayers rather than the IRS.
- *Bankruptcy.* When a taxpayer files a bankruptcy petition, the IRS, like other creditors, is prevented from taking action against the taxpayer. Sometimes a bankruptcy court may settle a tax claim.

For a summary of the Federal trial courts, see Concept Summary 2–1.

CONCEPT SUMMARY 2–1

Federal Judicial System: Trial Courts

Issue	Tax Court	District Court	Court of Federal Claims
Number of judges per court	19*	1 per case	16
Payment of deficiency before trial	No	Yes	Yes
Jury trial available	No	Yes	No
Types of disputes	Tax cases only	Mostly criminal and civil issues	Claims against the United States
Jurisdiction	Nationwide	Location of taxpayer	Nationwide
IRS acquiescence policy	Yes	Yes	Yes
Appeal route	U.S. Court of Appeals	U.S. Court of Appeals	Court of Appeals for the Federal Circuit

*There are also 14 special trial judges and 9 senior judges.

Appellate Courts. The losing party can appeal a trial court decision to a **Circuit Court of Appeals.** The 11 geographic circuits, the circuit for the District of Columbia, and the Federal Circuit[16] are shown in Figure 2–4.

If the Government loses at the trial court level (District Court, Tax Court, or Court of Federal Claims), it need not (and frequently does not) appeal. The fact that an appeal is not made, however, does not indicate that the IRS agrees with the result and will not litigate similar issues in the future. The IRS may decide not to appeal for a number of reasons. First, its current litigation load may be heavy. As a consequence, the IRS may decide that available personnel should be assigned to other, more important cases. Second, the IRS may not appeal for strategic reasons. For example, the taxpayer may be in a sympathetic position, or the facts may be particularly strong in his or her favor. In that event, the IRS may wait for a weaker case to test the legal issues involved. Third, if the appeal is from a District Court or the Tax Court, the Court of Appeals of jurisdiction could have some bearing on whether the IRS decides to pursue an appeal. Based on past experience and precedent, the IRS may conclude that the chance for success on a particular issue might be more promising in another Court of Appeals. If so, the IRS will wait for a similar case to arise in a different jurisdiction.

The Federal Circuit at the appellate level provides a taxpayer with an alternative forum to the Court of Appeals of his or her home circuit. When a particular circuit has issued an adverse decision, the taxpayer may prefer the Court of Federal Claims route since any appeal will be to the Court of Appeals for the Federal Circuit.

District Courts, the Tax Court, and the Court of Federal Claims must abide by the **precedents** set by the Court of Appeals of their jurisdiction. A particular Court of Appeals need not follow the decisions of another Court of Appeals. All courts, however, must follow decisions of the **Supreme Court**.

This pattern of appellate precedents raises an issue for the Tax Court. Because the Tax Court is a national court, it decides cases from all parts of the country. Appeals from its decisions, however, go to all of the Courts of Appeals except the Court of Appeals for the Federal Circuit. Accordingly, identical Tax Court cases might be appealed to different circuits with different results. As a result of the *Golsen*[17] case, the Tax Court will not follow its own precedents in a subsequent case

[16]The Court of Appeals for the Federal Circuit was created to hear decisions appealed from the Claims Court (now the Court of Federal Claims).

[17]*Jack E. Golsen*, 54 T.C. 742 (1970).

FIGURE 2–4 **The Circuit Courts of Appeals**

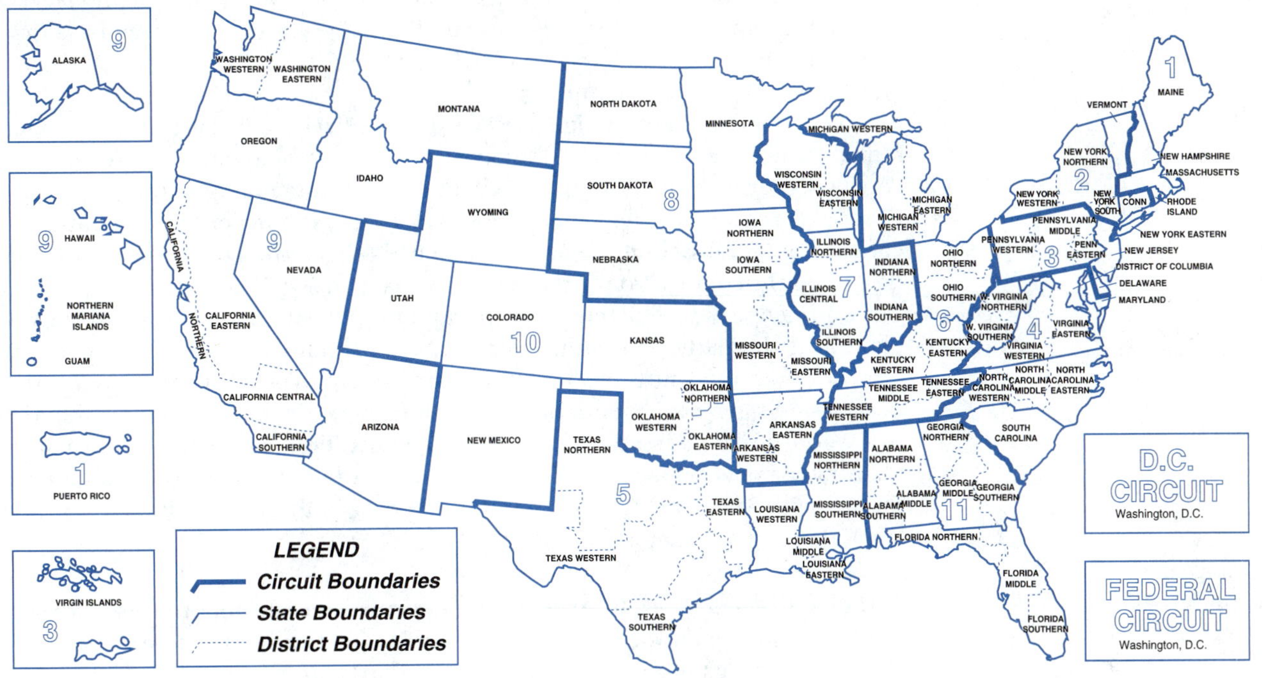

ADMINISTRATIVE OFFICE OF THE UNITED STATES SUPREME COURTS
APRIL 1988

if the Court of Appeals with jurisdiction over the taxpayer in question has previously reversed the Tax Court on the specific issue at hand.

EXAMPLE 3

Emily lives in Texas and sues in the Tax Court on Issue A. The Fifth Circuit Court of Appeals is the appellate court with jurisdiction. The Fifth Circuit has already decided, in a case involving similar facts but a different taxpayer, that Issue A should be resolved against the Government. Although the Tax Court feels that the Fifth Circuit is wrong, under its *Golsen* policy it will render judgment for Emily. Shortly thereafter, in a comparable case, Rashad, a resident of New York, sues in the Tax Court on Issue A. The Second Circuit Court of Appeals, the appellate court with jurisdiction in New York, has never expressed itself on Issue A. Presuming the Tax Court has not reconsidered its position on Issue A, it will decide against Rashad. Thus, it is entirely possible for two taxpayers suing in the same court to end up with opposite results merely because they live in different parts of the country. ■

Appeal to the Supreme Court is not automatic. It must be applied for via a **Writ of Certiorari**. If the Court agrees to hear the case, it will grant the Writ (*Cert. granted*). Most often, it will decline to hear the case (*Cert. denied*). In fact, the Supreme Court rarely hears tax cases. The Court usually grants certiorari to resolve a conflict among the Courts of Appeals (e.g., two or more appellate courts have opposing positions on a particular issue) or where the tax issue is extremely important. The granting of a *Writ of Certiorari* indicates that at least four members of the Supreme Court believe that the issue is of sufficient importance to be heard by the full Court.

The *role* of appellate courts is limited to a review of the record of trial compiled by the trial courts. Thus, the appellate process usually involves a determination of whether the trial court applied the proper law in arriving at its decision, rather than a consideration of the trial court's factual findings.

An appeal can have any of a number of possible outcomes. The appellate court may approve (affirm) or disapprove (reverse) the lower court's finding, or it may send the case back for further consideration (remand). When many issues are involved, a mixed result is not unusual. Thus, the lower court may be affirmed (*aff'd.*) on Issue A and reversed (*rev'd.*) on Issue B, while Issue C is remanded (*rem'd.*) for additional fact finding.

When more than one judge is involved in the decision-making process, disagreements are not uncommon. In addition to the majority view, one or more judges may concur (agree with the result reached but not with some or all of the reasoning) or dissent (disagree with the result). In any one case, the majority view controls. But concurring and dissenting views can influence other courts or, at some subsequent date when the composition of the court has changed, even the same court.

Knowledge of several terms is important in understanding court decisions. The plaintiff is the party requesting action in a court, and the defendant is the party against whom the suit is brought. Sometimes a court uses the terms *petitioner* and *respondent.* In general, "petitioner" is a synonym for "plaintiff," and "respondent" is a synonym for "defendant." At the trial court level, a taxpayer is normally the plaintiff (or petitioner), and the government is the defendant (or respondent). If the taxpayer wins and the Government appeals as the new petitioner (or appellant), the taxpayer now is the respondent.

Judicial Citations—General. Court decisions are an important source of tax law. The ability to locate a case and to cite it is therefore a must in working with the tax law. Judicial citations usually follow a standard pattern: case name, volume number, reporter series, page or paragraph number, court (where necessary), and the year of decision.

Judicial Citations—The Tax Court. The Tax Court issues two types of decisions: Regular and Memorandum. The Chief Judge decides whether the opinion is issued as a Regular or Memorandum decision. The distinction between the two involves both substance and form. In terms of substance, *Memorandum* decisions deal with situations necessitating only the application of already established principles of law. *Regular* decisions involve novel issues not previously resolved by the court. In actual practice, however, this distinction is not always so clear. Be that as it may, both Regular and Memorandum decisions represent the position of the Tax Court and, as such, can be relied on.

Regular and Memorandum decisions issued by the Tax Court also differ in form. Memorandum decisions are not officially published while Regular decisions are published by the U.S. Government in a series called *Tax Court of the United States Reports* (T.C.). Each volume of these *Reports* covers a six-month period (January 1 through June 30 and July 1 through December 31) and is given a succeeding volume number. But there is usually a time lag between the date a decision is rendered and the date it appears in official form. A temporary citation may be necessary to help the researcher locate a recent Regular decision. Consider, for example, the temporary and permanent citations for *Estate of Leona Engelman,* a decision filed on July 24, 2003.

Temporary Citation	*Estate of Leona Engelman,* 121 T.C. ___, No. 4 (2003). *Explanation:* Page number left blank because not yet known.
Permanent Citation	*Estate of Leona Engelman,* 121 T.C. 54 (2003). *Explanation:* Page number now available.

Both citations tell us that the case will ultimately appear in Volume 121 of the *Tax Court of the United States Reports.* Until this volume becomes available to the general public, however, the page number must be left blank. Instead, the temporary citation identifies the case as being the 4th Regular decision issued by the Tax Court since Volume 120 ended. With this information, the decision easily can be located in either of the special Tax Court services published by Commerce Clearing

House and Research Institute of America. Once Volume 121 is released, the permanent citation can be substituted and the number of the case dropped. Regular decisions and Memorandum decisions are published on the U.S. Tax Court Web site (**http://www.ustaxcourt.gov**).

Before 1943, the Tax Court was called the Board of Tax Appeals, and its decisions were published as the *United States Board of Tax Appeals Reports* (B.T.A.). These 47 volumes cover the period from 1924 to 1942. For example, the citation *Karl Pauli*, 11 B.T.A. 784 (1928) refers to the 11th volume of the *Board of Tax Appeals Reports*, page 784, issued in 1928.

If the IRS loses a decision, it may indicate whether it agrees or disagrees with the results reached by the court by publishing an **acquiescence** ("A" or "*Acq.*") or **nonacquiescence** ("NA" or "*Nonacq.*"), respectively. The acquiescence program is used where guidance is helpful, regardless of the court that issued the opinion. The acquiescence or nonacquiescence is published in the *Internal Revenue Bulletin* and the *Cumulative Bulletin* as an *Action on Decision.* The IRS can retroactively revoke an acquiescence.

Although Memorandum decisions were not published by the U.S. Government until recently, they were and continue to be published by Commerce Clearing House (CCH) and Research Institute of America (RIA). Consider, for example, the three different ways that *Jack D. Carr* can be cited.

Jack D. Carr, T.C.Memo. 1985–19.

The 19th Memorandum decision issued by the Tax Court in 1985.

Jack D. Carr, 49 TCM 507.

Page 507 of Volume 49 of the CCH *Tax Court Memorandum Decisions.*

Jack D. Carr, RIA T.C.Mem.Dec. ¶85,019.

Paragraph 85,019 of the RIA *T.C. Memorandum Decisions.*

The third citation contains the same information as the first. Thus, ¶85,019 indicates the following information about the case: year 1985, 19th T.C. Memo. decision. Although the RIA citation does not include a specific volume number, the paragraph citation (85,019) indicates that the decision can be found in the 1985 volume of the RIA Memorandum Decision service.

U.S. Tax Court Summary Opinions are published on the U.S. Tax Court Web site, with the warning that they may not be treated as precedent for any other case. For example, *James A. Wiese*, filed on July 19, 2005, is cited as follows.

James A. Wiese, T.C. Summary Opinion, 2005–91.

Judicial Citations—The District Courts, Court of Federal Claims, and Courts of Appeals. District Court, Court of Federal Claims, and Court of Appeals decisions dealing with Federal tax matters are reported in both the CCH *U.S. Tax Cases* (USTC) and the RIA *American Federal Tax Reports* (AFTR) series.

District Court decisions, dealing with *both* tax and nontax issues, are also published by West Publishing Company in its *Federal Supplement Series* (F.Supp.). Volume 999, published in 1998, was the last volume of the Federal Supplement Series. West now uses the *Federal Supplement Second Series* (F.Supp.2d). A District Court case can be cited in three different forms.

Simons-Eastern Co. v. U.S., 73–1 USTC ¶9279 (D.Ct.Ga., 1972).
Explanation: Reported in the first volume of the *U.S. Tax Cases* (USTC) published by Commerce Clearing House for calendar year 1973 (73–1) and located at paragraph 9279 (¶9279).

Simons-Eastern Co. v. U.S., 31 AFTR2d 73–640 (D.Ct.Ga., 1972).
Explanation: Reported in the 31st volume of the second series of the *American Federal Tax Reports* (AFTR2d) published by RIA, beginning on page 640. The "73" preceding the page number indicates the year the case was published but is a designation used only in recent decisions.

Simons-Eastern Co. v. U.S., 354 F.Supp. 1003 (D.Ct.Ga., 1972).
Explanation: Reported in the 354th volume of the *Federal Supplement Series* (F.Supp.) published by West Publishing Company, beginning on page 1003.

In all of the preceding citations, the name of the case is the same (Simons-Eastern Co. being the taxpayer), as are the references to the District Court of Georgia (D.Ct.Ga.) and the year the decision was rendered (1972).

Decisions of the Courts of Appeals are published in the USTCs, AFTRs, and the *Federal Second Series* (F.2d). Volume 999, published in 1993, was the last volume of the *Federal Second Series.* West now uses the *Federal Third Series* (F.3d). Decisions of the Court of Federal Claims are published in the USTCs, AFTRs, and the *Claims Court Reporter* (abbreviated as Cl.Ct.).

DIGGING DEEPER 3

Find more information on this topic at our Web site: ***http://wft-entities.swlearning.com.***

Finkbohner, Jr. v. U.S., (CA–11, 1986).

86–1 USTC ¶9393 (CCH citation)
57 AFTR2d 86–1400 (RIA citation)
788 F.2d 723 (West citation)

Apollo Computer, Inc. v. U.S., (Fed.Cl., 1994).

95–1 USTC ¶50,015 (CCH citation)
74 AFTR2d 94–7172 (RIA citation)
32 Fed.Cl. 334 (West citation)

Finkbohner, Jr. is a decision rendered by the Eleventh Circuit Court of Appeals in 1986 (CA–11, 1986), while *Apollo Computer, Inc.* was issued by the Court of Federal Claims in 1994 (Fed.Cl., 1994).

Judicial Citations—The Supreme Court. Like all other Federal tax decisions (except those rendered by the Tax Court), Supreme Court decisions dealing with Federal tax matters are published by Commerce Clearing House in the USTCs and by RIA in the AFTRs. The U.S. Government Printing Office publishes all Supreme Court decisions in the *United States Supreme Court Reports* (U.S.), as do West Publishing Company in its *Supreme Court Reporter* (S.Ct.) and the Lawyer's Co-operative Publishing Company in its *United States Reports, Lawyer's Edition* (L.Ed.).

U.S. v. The Donruss Co., (USSC, 1969).

69–1 USTC ¶9167 (CCH citation)
23 AFTR2d 69–418 (RIA citation)
89 S.Ct. 501 (West citation)
393 U.S. 297 (U.S. Government Printing Office citation)
21 L.Ed.2d 495 (Lawyer's Co-operative Publishing Co. citation)

The parenthetical reference (USSC, 1969) identifies the decision as having been rendered by the U.S. Supreme Court in 1969. In this text, the citations of Supreme Court decisions are limited to the CCH (USTC), RIA (AFTR), and West (S.Ct.) versions.

LO.2

Locate and work with the tax law and understand the tax research process.

Working with the Tax Law—Tax Research

Tax research is undertaken to determine the best available solution to a situation that has tax consequences. In the case of a completed transaction, the objective of the research is to determine the tax result of what has already taken place. For example, is the expenditure incurred by the taxpayer deductible or not deductible for tax purposes? When dealing with proposed transactions, tax research is concerned with the determination of possible alternative tax consequences to facilitate effective tax planning.

Tax research involves the following procedures.

- Identifying and refining the problem.
- Locating the appropriate tax law sources.
- Assessing the tax law sources.

FIGURE 2–5 **Tax Research Process**

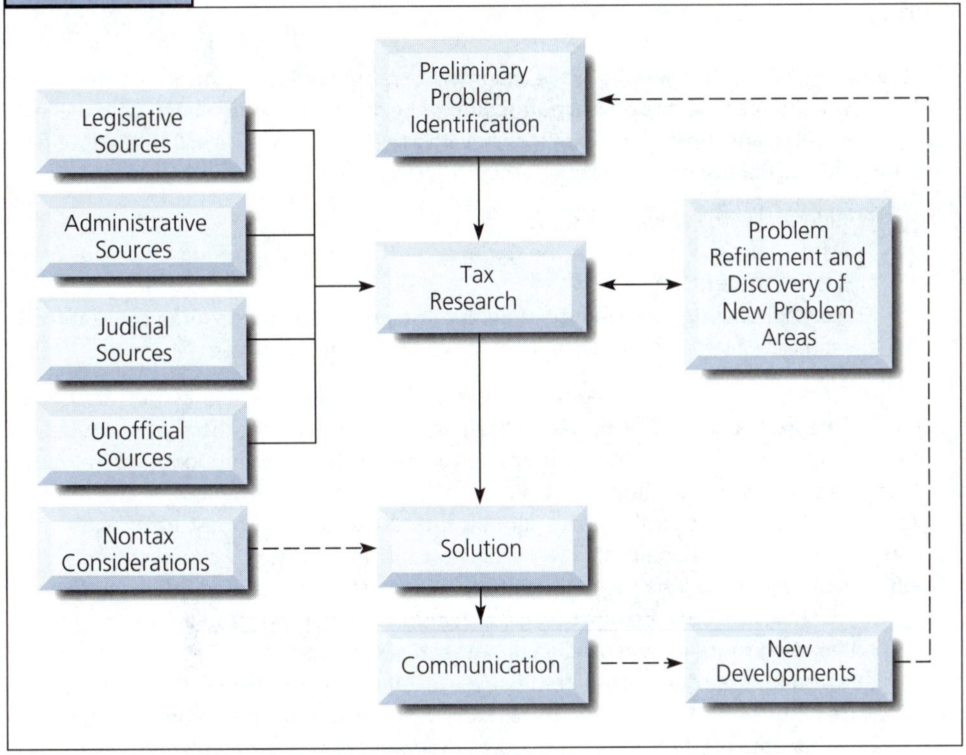

- Arriving at the solution or at alternative solutions while giving due consideration to nontax factors.
- Effectively communicating the solution to the taxpayer or the taxpayer's representative.
- Following up on the solution (where appropriate) in light of new developments.

This process is depicted schematically in Figure 2–5. The broken lines indicate steps of particular interest when tax research is directed toward proposed, rather than completed, transactions.

Identifying the Problem

Problem identification starts with a compilation of the relevant facts involved. In this regard, *all* of the facts that may have a bearing on the problem must be gathered, as any omission could modify the solution reached. To illustrate, consider what appears to be a very simple problem.

EXAMPLE 4

In reviewing their tax and financial situation, Fred and Megan, a married couple, notice that Fred's investment in Airways stock has declined from its purchase price of $8,000 to a current market value of $5,500. Megan wants to sell this stock now and claim the $2,500 loss ($5,500 value − $8,000 cost) as a deduction this year. Fred, however, believes that Airways Co. will yet prosper and does not want to part with its stock. Their daughter suggests that they sell the Airways Co. stock to Maple, Inc., a corporation owned equally by Fred and Megan. That way, they can claim the deduction this year while still holding the stock through their corporation. Will this suggestion work? ■

Refining the Problem

Fred and Megan in Example 4 face three choices: (1) sell the Airways stock through their regular investment broker and get a deduction in the current year

BRIDGE *Discipline*

Bridge to Business Law

U.S. income tax laws change daily by the action of Congress, tax administrators, and the courts. This process matches the three-branch structure of the rest of the government, with the legislative, executive, and judicial branches each having a say in making tax law. But this distinction among the functions of government is perhaps less clear when it involves the tax law.

- Presidential vetoes of tax legislation are rare.
- The Tax Court is a creation of the Congress in the Internal Revenue Code, not of the U.S. Constitution.
- The cost of tax litigation and the time that it takes for a case to work its way through the judicial system render the courts unavailable to most taxpayers.

Under the U.S. Constitution, legislation involving government revenues must start in the House of Representatives. This provision likely was included so that the public would have greater control over those who want greater access to their pocketbooks. Several recent pieces of tax legislation, though, have been initiated as bills in the Senate. And during the years of the deepest Federal deficits, all bills introduced in both houses of Congress are required to be "revenue neutral" (i.e., they must include provisions by which the legislation's new programs will be paid for). In both houses, this has resulted in amendments to the Internal Revenue Code being attached to legislation involving clean air and water standards, child care programs, and product import and export limitations.

In a few cases, the courts considered a taxpayer challenge to the way this tax legislation was crafted. But so far the courts have failed to overturn any tax provisions solely because they were initiated in the Senate. The courts' rationale for this seemingly unconstitutional position is that (1) the House and its committees heard a full discussion of the proposal, and (2) too much time has passed since adoption of the legislation to easily un-wind it and undertake a refund procedure.

(Megan's plan); (2) continue to hold the Airways stock (Fred's plan); and (3) sell the Airways stock to a corporation owned 50–50 by Fred and Megan (their daughter's suggestion). The tax consequences of plans (1) and (2) are clear, but the question that Fred and Megan want to resolve is whether plan (3) will work as anticipated. Refining the problem further, can shareholders deduct a loss from the sale of an asset to a corporation that they control? Section 267(a)(1) indicates that losses from the sale of property between persons specified in § 267(b) are not deductible. This subsection lists 12 different relationships, including, in § 267(b)(2): "an individual and a corporation more than 50 percent in value of the outstanding stock of which is owned, directly or indirectly, by or for such individual." Thus, if Fred and Megan each own 50 percent of Maple, neither owns *more than* 50 percent, as § 267(b) requires. Accordingly, the loss disallowance rule would not apply to Fred, and their daughter's suggestion would appear to be sound.

The language of the statute, however, indicates that any stock owned *directly or indirectly* by an individual is counted toward the 50 percent test. Might Megan's stock be considered owned "indirectly" by Fred? Further research is necessary. Section 267(c) contains rules for determining "constructive ownership of stock," or when stock owned by one person will be attributed to someone else. One of the rules in this subsection declares that an individual is considered to own any stock that is owned by that person's *family*, and family is defined in § 267(c)(4) as including a person's spouse, among others. Therefore, Megan's stock will be attributed to Fred, so that Fred is treated as owning all of the stock of Maple, Inc. As a result, § 267(a) would indeed apply, and no loss would be deductible if Fred sells his Airways stock to Maple. In short, the daughter's suggestion will not work.

Locating the Appropriate Tax Law Sources

Once the problem is clearly defined, what is the next step? While it is a matter of individual judgment, most tax research begins with the index volume of a paper-based tax service or a keyword search of an online or CD-ROM tax service. If the problem is not complex, the researcher may bypass the tax service and turn directly to the Internal Revenue Code and the Treasury Regulations. For the beginner, the latter procedure saves time and will solve many of the more basic problems. If the researcher does not have a personal copy of the Code or Regulations, use of the appropriate volume(s) of a tax service, an online service, or a CD-ROM is necessary.[18] The major tax services and their publishers are:

Standard Federal Tax Reporter, Commerce Clearing House.

United States Tax Reporter, Research Institute of America.

Federal Tax Coordinator 2d, Research Institute of America.

Tax Management Portfolios, Bureau of National Affairs.

Working with Tax Services. In this text, it is not feasible to explain the use of any particular tax service—this ability can be obtained with experience. However, several important observations about the use of tax services cannot be overemphasized. First, always check for current developments. The main text of any paper-based service is revised too infrequently to permit reliance on that portion as the *latest* word on any subject. Where current developments can be found depends on which service is being used. Commerce Clearing House's *Standard Federal Tax Reporter* contains a special volume devoted to current matters. Both RIA's *United States Tax Reporter* and *Federal Tax Coordinator 2d* integrate the new developments into the body of the service throughout the year. Second, there is no substitute for the original source. Do not base a conclusion solely on a tax service's commentary. If the Code Section, Regulation, or case is vital to the research, read it.

Tax Periodicals. Various tax periodicals are another source of information. The easiest way to locate a journal article on a particular tax problem is through CCH's *Federal Tax Articles.* This six-volume service includes a subject index, a Code Section number index, and an author's index. In addition, RIA's tax service has a topical "Index to Tax Articles" section that is organized using the RIA paragraph index system. *The Accounting & Tax Index* also is available in three quarterly issues plus a cumulative year-end volume covering all four quarters.

The following are some of the more useful tax periodicals.

The Journal of Taxation
Warren, Gorham and Lamont
395 Hudson Street
4th Floor
New York, NY 10014

Tax Law Review
Warren, Gorham and Lamont
395 Hudson Street
4th Floor
New York, NY 10014

Practical Tax Strategies
Warren, Gorham and Lamont
395 Hudson Street
4th Floor
New York, NY 10014

The Tax Executive
1200 G Street NW
Suite 300
Washington, D.C. 20005

[18]Several of the major tax services publish paperback editions of the Code and Treasury Regulations that can be purchased at modest prices. These editions are usually revised twice each year. For an annotated and abridged version of the Code and Regulations that is published annually, see James E. Smith, *West's Internal Revenue Code of 1986 and Treasury Regulations: Annotated and Selected* (West/South-Western College Publishing, 2007). The complete Code and Regulations are also available in *RIA Checkpoint.*

TAXES—The Tax Magazine
Commerce Clearing House, Inc.
2700 Lake Cook Road
Riverwood, IL 60015

National Tax Journal
725 15th Street NW
Suite 600
Washington, D.C. 20005

The Tax Adviser
AICPA
Harborside Financial Center
201 Plaza III
Jersey City, NJ 07311-3881

Estate Planning
Warren, Gorham and Lamont
395 Hudson Street
4th Floor
New York, NY 10014

Journal of Corporate Taxation
Warren, Gorham and Lamont
395 Hudson Street
4th Floor
New York, NY 10014

Tax Notes
6830 Fairfax Drive
Arlington, VA 22213

Assessing Tax Law Sources

Once a source has been located, the next step is to assess it in light of the problem at hand. Proper assessment involves careful interpretation of the tax law and consideration of its relevance and significance.

Interpreting the Internal Revenue Code. The language of the Code is often difficult to comprehend fully. Contrary to many people's suspicions, the Code is not written deliberately to confuse. Nevertheless, it often has that effect. The Code is intended to apply to more than 275 million citizens, most of whom are willing to exploit any linguistic imprecision to their benefit—to find a "loophole," in popular parlance. Moreover, many of the Code's provisions are limitations or restrictions involving two or more variables. Expressing such concepts algebraically would be more direct; using words to accomplish this task instead is often quite cumbersome. Among the worst such attempts was former § 341(e) relating to so-called collapsible corporations, which included one sentence with more than 450 words.

Nevertheless, the Code is the governing law, the only source of tax law (other than treaties) that has received the actual approval of Congress and the President. Accordingly, it is usually the first source to be consulted, and often it is the only source needed.

Assessing the Significance of a Treasury Regulation. Treasury Regulations are the official interpretation of the Code and are entitled to great deference. Occasionally, however, a court will invalidate a Regulation or a portion thereof on the grounds that the Regulation is contrary to the intent of Congress. Usually, courts do not question the validity of Regulations because of the belief that "the first administrative interpretation of a provision as it appears in a new act often expresses the general understanding of the times or the actual understanding of those who played an important part when the statute was drafted."[19]

Keep in mind the following observations when assessing the significance of a Regulation.

- IRS agents *must* give the Code and the Regulations issued thereunder equal weight when dealing with taxpayers and their representatives.
- Proposed Regulations provide a preview of future final Regulations, but they are not binding on the IRS or taxpayers.
- In a challenge, the burden of proof is on the taxpayer to show that a Regulation varies from the language of the statute and has no support in the Committee Reports.

[19] *Augustus v. Comm.*, 41–1 USTC ¶9255, 26 AFTR 612, 118 F.2d 38 (CA–6, 1941).

TAX *in the News* — **INTERNAL REVENUE CODE: INTERPRETATION PITFALLS**

One author has noted 10 common pitfalls in interpreting the Code.

1. Determine the limitations and exceptions to a provision. Do not permit the language of the Code Section to carry greater or lesser weight than was intended.
2. Just because a Section fails to mention an item does not necessarily mean that the item is excluded.
3. Read definitional clauses carefully.
4. Do not overlook small words such as *and* and *or*. There is a world of difference between these two words.
5. Read the Code Section completely; do not jump to conclusions.
6. Watch out for cross-referenced and related provisions, since many Sections of the Code are interrelated.
7. At times Congress is not careful when reconciling new Code provisions with existing Sections. Conflicts among Sections, therefore, do arise.
8. Be alert for hidden definitions; terms in a particular Code Section may be defined in the same Section or in a separate Section.
9. Some answers may not be found in the Code; therefore, a researcher may have to consult the Regulations and/or judicial decisions.
10. Take careful note of measuring words such as *less than 50 percent, more than 50 percent,* and *at least 80 percent.*

Source: *Adapted by permission from Henry G. Wong, "Ten Common Pitfalls in Reading the Internal Revenue Code,"* Journal of Business Strategy, *July–August 1972, pp. 30–33. Reprinted with permission by Faulkner & Gray, Inc., 11 Penn Plaza, New York, NY 10001.*

- Final Regulations can be classified as procedural, interpretive, or legislative. **Procedural Regulations** neither establish tax laws nor attempt to explain tax laws. Procedural Regulations often include procedural instructions, indicating information that taxpayers should provide the IRS, as well as information about the internal management and conduct of the IRS itself.
- **Interpretive Regulations** rephrase and elaborate what Congress stated in the Committee Reports that were issued when the tax legislation was enacted. Such Regulations are *hard and solid* and almost impossible to overturn unless they do not clearly reflect the intent of Congress.
- In some Code Sections, Congress has given the *Secretary or his delegate* the specific authority to prescribe Regulations to carry out the details of administration or to otherwise create rules not included in the Code. Under such circumstances, Congress is effectively delegating its legislative powers to the Treasury Department. Regulations issued pursuant to this type of authority possess the force and effect of law and are often called **Legislative Regulations** [e.g., see § 385(a)].

Assessing the Significance of Other Administrative Sources of the Tax Law. Revenue Rulings issued by the IRS carry much less weight than Treasury Department Regulations. Revenue Rulings are important, however, in that they reflect the position of the IRS on tax matters. In any dispute with the IRS on the interpretation of tax law, taxpayers should expect agents to follow the results reached in applicable Revenue Rulings. It is not unusual, however, for courts to overturn Revenue Rulings as incorrect applications of the law to the facts presented.

Actions on Decisions report the IRS's acquiescence or nonacquiescence to a published opinion. A nonacquiescence does not mean that a particular court decision is of no value, but it does indicate that the IRS may choose to litigate the issue involved.

Assessing the Significance of Judicial Sources of the Tax Law. The judicial process as it relates to the formulation of tax law has been described. How much reliance can be placed on a particular decision depends upon the following factors.

- *The level of the court.* A decision rendered by a trial court (e.g., a District Court) carries less weight than one issued by an appellate court (e.g., the Fifth Circuit Court of Appeals). Unless Congress changes the Code, decisions by the U.S. Supreme Court represent the last word on any tax issue.
- *The legal residence of the taxpayer.* If, for example, a taxpayer lives in Texas, a decision of the Fifth Circuit Court of Appeals means more than one rendered by the Second Circuit Court of Appeals. This is the case because any appeal from a District Court or the Tax Court would be to the Fifth Circuit Court of Appeals and not to the Second Circuit Court of Appeals.
- *The type of decision.* A Tax Court Regular decision carries more weight than a Memorandum decision because the Tax Court does not consider Memorandum decisions to have precedential value.[20]
- *The weight of the decision.* A decision that is supported by cases from other courts carries more weight than a decision that is not supported by other cases.
- *Subsequent events.* Was the decision affirmed or overruled on appeal?

In connection with the last two factors, a citator is helpful to tax research.[21] A citator provides the history of a case and lists subsequent published opinions that refer to the case being assessed. Reviewing these references enables the tax researcher to determine whether the decision in question has been reversed, affirmed, followed by other courts, or distinguished in some way. If one plans to rely on a judicial decision to any significant degree, "running" the case through a citator is imperative.

Understanding Judicial Opinions. Reading judicial opinions can be more productive if certain conventions of usage are understood. Some courts, including the Tax Court, apply the terms *petitioner* and *respondent* to the plaintiff and defendant, respectively, particularly when the case does not involve an appellate proceeding. Appellate courts often use the terms *appellant* and *appellee* instead.

It is also important to distinguish between a court's final determination, or *holding*, and passing comments made in the course of its opinion. These latter remarks, examples, and analogies, often collectively termed *dicta*, are not part of the court's conclusion and do not have precedential value. Nevertheless, they often facilitate one's understanding of the court's reasoning and can enable a tax adviser to better predict how the court might resolve some future tax case.

DIGGING DEEPER 4

Find more information on this topic at our Web site: ***http://wft-entities.swlearning.com.***

Assessing the Significance of Other Sources. *Primary sources* of tax law include the Constitution, legislative history materials (e.g., Committee Reports), statutes, treaties, Treasury Regulations, IRS pronouncements, and judicial decisions. In general, the IRS regards only primary sources as substantial authority. However, reference to *secondary materials* such as legal periodicals, treatises, legal opinions, General Counsel Memoranda, and written determinations may be useful. In general, secondary sources are not authority.

Although the statement that the IRS regards only primary sources as substantial authority is generally true, there is one exception. Substantial authority *for purposes of* the accuracy-related penalty in § 6662 includes a number of secondary materials (e.g., letter rulings and General Counsel Memoranda).[22] "Authority" does not include conclusions reached in treatises, legal periodicals, and opinions rendered by tax professionals.

[20] *Severino R. Nico, Jr.*, 67 T.C. 647 (1977).

[21] The major citators are published by Commerce Clearing House, RIA, and Shepard's Citations, Inc. These citators are available in print and electronic formats. WESTLAW's citator is available only in electronic format.

[22] Reg. § 1.6661–3(b)(2).

A letter ruling or determination letter can be relied upon *only* by the taxpayer to whom it is issued, except as noted above with respect to the accuracy-related penalty.

DIGGING DEEPER 5

Find more information on this topic at our Web site: ***http://wft-entities.swlearning.com.***

Arriving at the Solution or at Alternative Solutions

Example 4 raises the question of whether taxpayers would be denied a loss deduction from the sale of stock to a corporation that they own. The solution depends, in part, on the relationship of the corporation's shareholders to each other. Since Fred and Megan are married to each other, § 267(c)(2) attributes Megan's stock to Fred in applying the "more than 50 percent" test of § 267(b)(2). Accordingly, Fred and Maple, Inc., are considered related parties under § 267(a), and a sale between them does not provide a deductible loss. If Fred and Megan were not related to each other, the constructive stock ownership rules would not apply, and a loss could be deducted on a sale by Fred to Maple.

If Maple, Inc., were a *partnership* instead of a corporation, § 267 would not apply.[23] That Regulation, however, references a different Code Section, namely § 707, which produces the same result: no deduction of the loss from a sale between a "more than 50 percent" partner and the partnership. This additional research prevents Fred and Megan from erroneously selling their Airways stock to a partnership in hopes of obtaining a loss deduction from the sale. Accordingly, Fred must sell the Airways stock to an unrelated party in order to deduct the loss.

Since Fred still wants to own Airways stock, he might consider purchasing new Airways Co. stock to replace the stock he sells. Additional research reveals that for the loss on the sale to be deductible, the "wash sale" rule requires that 30 days elapse between the purchase of the new stock and the sale of the old stock.[24] This rule applies to purchases and sales of *substantially identical stock or securities.* As a result, to deduct the loss on the Airways stock, Fred must either wait at least 30 days after selling this stock to buy new Airways stock or acquire stock in a different company at any time. This new company can even be in the same general business as is Airways.[25]

Communicating Tax Research

LO.3

Communicate the results of the tax research process in a client letter and a tax file memorandum.

Once the problem has been researched adequately, a memorandum, letter, or speech setting forth the result may need to be prepared. The form the communication takes could depend on a number of considerations. For example, does an employer or instructor recommend a particular procedure or format for tax research memos? Is the memo to be given directly to the client or will it first go to the preparer's employer? If the communication is a speech, who is the audience? How long should one speak?[26] Whatever form it takes, a good research communication should contain the following elements.

- A clear statement of the issue.
- In more complex situations, a short review of the fact pattern that raises the issue.
- A review of the pertinent tax law sources (e.g., Code, Regulations, Revenue Rulings, judicial authority).
- Any assumptions made in arriving at the solution.
- The solution recommended and the logic or reasoning supporting it.
- The references consulted in the research process.

Illustrations of the memo for the tax file and the client letter associated with Example 4 appear in Figures 2–6 and 2–7.

[23] Reg. § 1.267(b)–1(b)(1).
[24] § 1091.
[25] Rev.Rul. 59–44, 1959–1 C.B. 205.
[26] See W. A. Raabe and G. E. Whittenburg, "Talking Tax: How to Make a Tax Presentation," *The Tax Adviser,* March 1997, pp.179–182.

FIGURE 2–6 **Tax File Memorandum**

August 26, 2006

TAX FILE MEMORANDUM

FROM: John J. Jones
SUBJECT: Fred and Megan Taxpayer Engagement

Today I talked to Fred Taxpayer with respect to his August 14, 2006 letter requesting tax assistance. He wishes to know if he can sell his stock in Airways Co. to Maple, Inc., and deduct the $2,500 loss on his Airways stock.

FACTS: Maple, Inc., is owned 50% by Fred and 50% by Megan. Fred wants to continue holding Airways stock in anticipation of a rebound in its value, and that is why he has asked about a proposed sale of this stock to Maple.

ISSUE: Can shareholders deduct a loss on the sale of an asset to a corporation all of whose stock they own?

ANALYSIS: Section 267(a) provides that no loss will be deductible on a sale or exchange between certain related parties. One of these relationships involves a corporation and a shareholder who owns "more than 50 percent" of that corporation's stock [see § 267(b)(2)]. Although Fred owns only 50% of Maple, Inc., his wife, Megan, owns the other 50%. The constructive ownership rule of § 267(c)(2) attributes stock held by family members, and a spouse is part of a taxpayer's family for this purpose, according to § 267(c)(4). Consequently, Megan's stock will be attributed to Fred, who is then treated as owning 100% of Maple, Inc. The related-party disallowance rule would then apply to the loss from Fred's selling his Airways stock to Maple. Accordingly, Fred must sell this stock to an unrelated party to make his loss deductible.

Since Fred really wants to retain an investment in Airways, he can purchase replacement stock either before or after he sells his original Airways stock. Section 1091(a), however, requires that at least 30 days elapse between the purchase and the sale, or the sale and the purchase, as the case may be. Moreover, for this purpose, an option to buy the stock is treated as equivalent to the stock itself. As a result, Fred must wait at least 30 days between transactions and cannot utilize stock options in the interim to minimize his stock market exposure.

A final alternative might be to replace the Airways stock with securities of a comparable company in the same industry. Although no two companies are exactly alike, there may be another company whose management philosophy, marketing strategy, and financial data are sufficiently similar to Airways to provide an equivalent return on investment. Under this alternative, Fred could acquire the new company's shares immediately without waiting the 30 days mandated by § 1091(a). Despite the two companies' investment similarity, they would not be treated as "substantially identical" for this purpose [see Rev.Rul. 59–44, 1959–1 C.B. 205].

CONCLUSION: Fred should *not* sell his Airways stock to Maple. Instead, he should sell this stock via his regular broker and either acquire new Airways stock at least 30 days before or after the date of sale, or acquire stock of a similar company whenever he chooses.

Follow-up Procedures

Because tax research may involve a proposed (as opposed to a completed) transaction, a change in the tax law (either legislative, administrative, or judicial) could alter the original conclusion. Additional research may be necessary to test the solution in light of current developments (refer to the broken lines at the right in Figure 2–5).

LO.4

Have an awareness of how best to use a computer when performing tax research and in taking the CPA exam.

Computers and Tax Research

Computer-based tax research tools hold a prominent position in tax practice. Electronic tax resources allow the tax library to better reflect the tax law's dynamic and daily changes. Nevertheless, using a computer to locate tax law sources cannot substitute for developing and maintaining a thorough knowledge of the tax law or for careful analysis when addressing tax research issues.

Accessing tax documents electronically offers several important advantages over a paper-based approach.

- Materials generally are available to the practitioner on a more timely basis through an electronic system.
- Commercial subscriptions to electronic tax services sometimes provide, at little or no cost, additional tax law sources to which the researcher would not have access through stand-alone purchases of traditional material. For example,

FIGURE 2–7 **Client Letter**

Smith, Raabe, and Maloney, CPAs
5191 Natorp Boulevard
Mason, OH 45040

August 30, 2006

Mr. and Ms. Fred Taxpayer
111 Boulevard
Williamsburg, Virginia 23185

Dear Mr. and Ms. Taxpayer:

This letter is in response to your request for us to review your family's financial and tax situation. Our conclusions are based upon the facts as outlined in your August 14th letter. Any change in the facts may affect our conclusions.

Mr. Taxpayer owns stock in Airways Co. that has declined in value, but he would like to retain this stock in anticipation of a rebound in its value. You have proposed a sale of this stock at its current market value to Maple, Inc., a corporation owned 50–50 by Mr. and Mrs. Taxpayer. Such a sale, however, would not permit the loss to be deducted.

A better approach would be to sell the Airways stock before year-end and repurchase this stock through your regular stockbroker. Please understand that the loss will not be deductible unless at least 30 days elapse between the sale and the repurchase of the stock. You can either sell the old stock first and then buy the new stock, or buy the new stock first and then sell the old stock. However, it is essential that at least 30 days elapse between the sale and purchase transactions. Using options during this 30-day period is ineffective and will prevent the loss from being deducted in the current taxable year.

If the 30-day requirement is unacceptable, you might consider replacing the Airways stock with securities of some other company, perhaps even a company in the same general business as is Airways. Your regular stockbroker should be able to suggest appropriate possibilities. In that situation, your loss on the Airways stock can be deducted without regard to when you buy the new stock.

Should you need more information or need to clarify our conclusions, do not hesitate to contact me.

Sincerely yours,

John J. Jones, CPA
Partner

the full text of private letter rulings is costly to acquire in a paper-based format, but electronic publishers may bundle the rulings with other materials for a reasonable cost.

- A user can create his or her own keywords and indexes. The software will electronically scan entire files and retrieve all of the documents that contain those words.
- A computerized tax service may retrieve documents that are no longer in print and may obtain regularly published documents to which a researcher does not otherwise have access.
- Most computerized services allow a user to retrieve documents in order of relevance, or in the order listed by database sources. Although this can be useful, just because a document is placed high on the relevance list does not mean it is valid law. Reading the primary sources, validating their authority, and checking the citator are essential in reaching a correct answer.

Strict cost comparisons of paper and electronic tax research materials are difficult to make, especially when the practitioner uses computers that are already in place and employed elsewhere in the practice. Over time, however, the convenience, cost, and reliability of electronic research tools clearly make them the dominant means of finding and analyzing tax law.

Using Electronic Tax Services. Usually, tax professionals use one of the following strategies when performing computer-based tax research.

- *Search* various databases using keywords that are likely to be found in the underlying documents, as written by Congress, the judiciary, or administrative sources.

TAX FACT

An Electronic IRS

The IRS is pushing for greater numbers of taxpayers to file their tax returns electronically. For tax year 2004 over 60 percent of all individuals filed their Forms 1040 using an electronic format. From the taxpayer's standpoint, electronic filing offers several advantages.

- Electronic filing better matches taxpayers' increasingly computer-oriented lifestyles. As many taxpayers use software to manage their bank and brokerage accounts, the transfer of tax data among programs becomes more effective.
- Refunds are processed and paid more quickly. Forty percent of returns receiving significant refunds and 60 percent of those using the earned income tax credit were e-filed. Nearly all of the e-filers chose to receive refunds by direct deposit.

The IRS benefits from electronic filing too.

- IRS computers capture all of the data submitted by an e-filing taxpayer, but only 40 percent from those filing returns on paper.
- The error rate for data entry into IRS computers is less than 2 percent for e-filed returns, but it is about 20 percent for paper-based returns.

- *Link* to tax documents for which all or part of the proper citation is known.
- *Browse* the tax databases, examining various tables of contents and indexes in a traditional manner or using cross-references in the documents to jump from one tax law source to another.

Virtually all of the major commercial tax publishers and most of the primary sources of the law itself, such as the Supreme Court and some of the Courts of Appeals, provide tax material in a variety of electronic formats, including CD-ROM services and online services. Exhibit 2–2 summarizes the most popular of the electronic tax services on the market today.

CD-ROM Services. CCH, RIA, WESTLAW, and others offer vast tax libraries to the practitioner on CDs, often in conjunction with a subscription to traditional paper-based resources and accompanied by newsletters, training seminars, and ongoing technical support.

At its best, a CD-ROM tax library provides the archival data that make up a permanent, core library of tax documents. For about $300 a year, a CD-ROM is updated quarterly, providing more comprehensive tax resources than the researcher is ever likely to need. The CD-ROM is comparable in scope to a paper-based library of a decade ago, which cost perhaps $20,000 to establish and $5,000 per year in perpetuity to maintain. If the library is contained on a small number of discs, it also can offer portability through use on notebook computers.

Online Services. Online research systems allow practitioners to obtain virtually instantaneous use of tax law sources by accessing databases via the Internet. Online services generally employ price-per-search cost structures, which can be as much as $200 per hour, significantly higher than the cost of CD materials. Thus, unless a practitioner can pass along related costs to clients or others, online searching generally is limited to the most important issues and to the researchers with the most experience and training in search techniques.

Perhaps the best combination of electronic tax resources is to conduct day-to-day work on a CD system, so that the budget for the related work is known in

EXHIBIT 2–2 **CD-Based Tax Services**

Tax Service	Description
CCH	Includes the CCH tax service, primary sources including treatises, and other subscription materials. Ten to 20 discs and online.
RIA	Includes primary sources, the *Federal Tax Coordinator 2d*, and the *United States Tax Reporter*. The citator has elaborate document-linking features. Major tax treatises and other subscription materials are provided. One to 10 discs and online.
WESTLAW	Code, Regulations, *Cumulative Bulletins*, cases, citators, and editorial material are included. Twelve discs and online.
Kleinrock's	A single disc with statutory, administrative, and judicial tax law. Another disc provides tax forms and instructions for Federal and state jurisdictions.

advance, and augment the CD search with online access where it is judged to be critical. Exhibit 2–3 provides details about the most commonly used commercial online tax services.

The Internet. The Internet provides a wealth of tax information in several popular forms, sometimes at no direct cost to the researcher. Using web browser software and an Internet connection, the tax professional can access information provided around the world that can aid the research process.

- *The World Wide Web* provides access to a number of sites maintained by accounting and consulting firms, publishers, tax academics and libraries, and governmental bodies. The best sites offer links to other sites and direct contact to the site providers. Exhibit 2–4 lists some of the Web sites that may be most useful to tax researchers and their Internet addresses as of press date.
- *Blogs and newsletters* provide a means by which information related to the tax law can be exchanged among taxpayers, tax professionals, and others who subscribe to the group's services. The tax professional can read the exchanges among other members and offer replies and suggestions to inquiries as desired. Discussions address the interpretation and application of existing law, analysis of proposals and new pronouncements, and reviews of tax software.

While tax information on the Internet is plentiful, freely accessed information should never be relied upon without referring to other, more reliable sources. Always remember that anyone can set up a Web site and quality control is often lacking.

In many situations, solutions to research problems benefit from, or require, the use of various electronic tax research tools. A competent tax professional must become familiar and proficient with these tools and be able to use them effectively, to meet the expectations of clients and the necessities of work in the modern world.[27]

[27]For a more detailed discussion of the use of electronic tax research in the modern tax practice, see W. A. Raabe, G. E. Whittenburg, and D. L. Sanders, *West's Federal Tax Research*, 7th ed. (Thomson/South-Western, 2006).

EXHIBIT 2–3 **Online Tax Services**

Online Service	Description
LEXIS/NEXIS	Includes Federal and state statutory, administrative, and judicial material. Extensive libraries of newspapers, magazines, patent records, and medical and economic databases, both U.S. and foreign-based.
RIA	Includes the RIA tax services, major tax treatises, Federal and state statutes, administrative documents, and court opinions. Extensive citator access, editorial material, and practitioner aids.
CCH	Includes the CCH tax service, primary sources including treatises, and other subscription materials. Tax and economic news sources, extensive editorial material, and practitioner support tools.
WESTLAW	Federal and state statutes, administrative documents, and court opinions. Extensive citator access, editorial material, and gateways to third-party publications. Extensive government document databases.

Tax Research on the CPA Examination

The CPA examination is computer-based, and it emphasizes information technology and general business knowledge. The 14-hour exam has four sections, and taxation is included in the 3-hour Regulation section, which covers these topics.

- Federal tax procedures and accounting issues.
- Federal taxation of property transactions.
- Federal taxation—individuals.
- Federal taxation—entities.

Each exam section includes both multiple-choice questions and case studies called simulations. The multiple-choice part consists of three sequential testlets, each containing 24 to 30 questions. These testlets are groups of questions prepared to appear together. In addition, each exam section includes a testlet, which consists of two simulations. A candidate may review and change answers within each testlet but cannot go back after exiting a testlet. Candidates take different, but equivalent exams.

Simulations are small case studies designed to test a candidate's tax knowledge and skills using real-life work-related situations. The simulations range from 30 to 50 minutes in length and complement the multiple-choice questions. Simulations include a four-function pop-up calculator, a blank spreadsheet with some elementary functionality, and authoritative literature for the candidate to research in completing the tax case study simulations (e.g., Internal Revenue Code and Federal tax forms). Examples of such simulations follow.

EXAMPLE 5

The tax *citation type* simulation requires the candidate to research the Internal Revenue Code and enter a Code Section and subsection citation. For example, Amber Company is considering using the simplified dollar-value method of pricing its inventory for purposes of the LIFO method that is available to certain small businesses. What Internal Revenue Code section is the relevant authority to which you should turn to determine whether the taxpayer is eligible to use this method? To be successful, the candidate needs to find § 474. ■

EXHIBIT 2–4 **Tax-Related Web Sites**

Web Site	WWW Address at Press Date	Description
Internal Revenue Service	**http://www.irs.gov/**	News releases, downloadable forms and instructions, tables, and e-mail.
Court opinions	**http://www.law.emory.edu/caselaw**	Allows the researcher to link to the site of the jurisdiction (other than the Tax Court) that is the subject of the query.
Tax Analysts	**http://www.taxanalysts.com**	Policy-oriented readings on tax laws and proposals to change it, moderated bulletins on various tax subjects.
Tax Sites Directory	**http://www.taxsites.com**	References and links to tax sites on the Internet, including state and Federal tax sites, academic and professional pages, tax forms, and software.
Tax laws online	**http://cfr.law.cornell.edu/cfr/**	Treasury Regulations.
	http://www4.law.cornell.edu/uscode/	Internal Revenue Code.
	http://uscode.house.gov/search/criteria.shtml	
Motley Fool Tax Page	**http://www.fool.com/taxes**	References and links to tax sites on the Internet.
Commercial tax publishers	For example, **http://cch.com**	Information about products and services available by subscription and newsletter excerpts.
Large accounting firms and professional organizations	For example, the AICPA's page is at **http://www.aicpa.org**, Ernst & Young is at **http://www.ey.com**, and KPMG is at **http://www.kpmg.com**	Tax planning newsletters, descriptions of services offered and career opportunities, and exchange of data with clients and subscribers.
Thomson South-Western	**http://wft.swlearning.com**	Informational updates, newsletters, support materials for students and adopters, and continuing education.
Tax Court decisions	**http://www.ustaxcourt.gov/**	Recent Tax Court decisions.

Caution: Addresses change frequently.

EXAMPLE 6

A *tax form completion* simulation requires the candidate to fill out a portion of a tax form. For example, Green Company is a limited liability company (LLC) for tax purposes. Complete the income section of the 2005 IRS Form 1065 for Green Company using the values found and calculated on previous tabs along with the following data.

Ordinary income from other partnerships	$ 5,200
Net gain (loss) from Form 4797	2,400
Management fee income	12,000

The candidate is provided with page 1 of Form 1065 on which to record the appropriate amounts. ■

Suggested Further Readings

Sheldon I. Banoff and Richard M. Lipton, editors Shop Talk, "Will Withdrawal of a Letter Ruling Request Lead to § 6662 Penalties?" *Journal of Taxation*, November 2003, pp. 316–317.

Ted Needleman, "What's New in Tax Research," *Practical Accountant*, June 2004, pp. 35–38.

Roger Russell, "Online Tax Research," *Accounting Today*, May 2003.

Michael G. Stevens, "What Are You Overlooking in Your Tax Tools?" *Practical Accountant*, June 2003, pp. 38–41.

KEY TERMS

Acquiescence, 2-17
Circuit Court of Appeals, 2-14
Court of Federal Claims, 2-11
Court of original jurisdiction, 2-11
Determination letters, 2-11
District Court, 2-11
Final Regulations, 2-9
Interpretive Regulations, 2-23
Legislative Regulations, 2-23
Letter rulings, 2-10
Nonacquiescence, 2-17
Precedents, 2-14
Procedural Regulations, 2-23
Proposed Regulations, 2-8
Revenue Procedures, 2-9
Revenue Rulings, 2-9
Small Cases Division, 2-11
Supreme Court, 2-14
Tax Court, 2-11
Technical Advice Memoranda (TAMs), 2-11
Temporary Regulations, 2-9
Writ of Certiorari, 2-15

PROBLEM MATERIALS

PROBLEMS

1. What is a primary source of tax information?

Communications

2. Barbara Brown operates a small international firm named Mallard, Inc. A new treaty between the United States and Ukraine conflicts with a Section of the Internal Revenue Code. Barbara asks you for advice. If she follows the treaty position, does she need to disclose this on her tax return? If she is required to disclose, are there any penalties for failure to disclose? Prepare a letter in which you respond to Barbara. Mallard's address is 100 International Drive, Tampa, FL 33620.

3. What is the function of the Joint Conference Committee of the House Ways and Means Committee and the Senate Finance Committee?

4. Distinguish between the following.
   a. Treasury Regulations and Revenue Rulings.
   b. Revenue Rulings and Revenue Procedures.
   c. Revenue Rulings and letter rulings.
   d. Letter rulings and determination letters.

5. Rank the following items from the highest authority to the lowest in the Federal tax law system.
   a. Interpretive Regulation.
   b. Legislative Regulation.
   c. Letter ruling.
   d. Revenue Ruling.
   e. Internal Revenue Code.
   f. Proposed Regulation.

6. Explain how Regulations are arranged. How would the following Regulations be cited?
   a. Finalized Regulations under § 442.
   b. Proposed Regulations under § 318.
   c. Temporary Regulations under § 446.

7. Interpret each of the following citations.
   a. Prop.Reg. § 1.280A–3(c)(4).
   b. Rev.Rul. 67–74, 1967–1 C.B. 194.
   c. Ltr.Rul. 200409001.

8. Which of the following would be considered advantages of the Small Cases Division of the Tax Court?
   a. Appeal to the Tax Court is possible.
   b. A hearing of a deficiency of $65,000 is considered on a timely basis.
   c. Taxpayer can handle the litigation without using a lawyer or certified public accountant.
   d. Taxpayer can use Small Cases Division decisions for precedential value.
   e. The actual hearing is conducted informally.
   f. Travel time will probably be reduced.

9. List an advantage and a disadvantage of using the U.S. District Court as the trial court for Federal tax litigation.

10. Carl Jensen is considering litigating a tax deficiency of approximately $274,000 in the court system. He asks you to provide him with a short description of his alternatives indicating the advantages and disadvantages of each. Prepare your response to Carl in the form of a letter. His address is 200 Mesa Drive, Tucson, AZ 85714.

Communications

11. A taxpayer lives in Michigan. In a controversy with the IRS, the taxpayer loses at the trial court level. Describe the appeal procedure for each of the following trial courts.
    a. Small Cases Division of the Tax Court.
    b. Tax Court.
    c. District Court.
    d. Court of Federal Claims.

12. Suppose the U.S. Government loses a tax case in the U.S. Tax Court and does not appeal the result. What does the failure to appeal signify?

13. For the Tax Court, District Court, and the Court of Federal Claims, indicate the following.
    a. Number of regular judges per court.
    b. Availability of a jury trial.
    c. Whether the deficiency must be paid before the trial.

14. In which of the following states could a taxpayer appeal the decision of a U.S. District Court to the Ninth Circuit Court of Appeals?
    a. Alaska.
    b. Arkansas.
    c. Florida.
    d. New York.
    e. South Carolina.

15. What is the Supreme Court's policy on hearing tax cases?

16. In assessing the validity of a prior court decision, discuss the significance of the following on the taxpayer's issue.
    a. The decision was rendered by the U.S. District Court of Wyoming. Taxpayer lives in Wyoming.
    b. The decision was rendered by the Court of Federal Claims. Taxpayer lives in Wyoming.
    c. The decision was rendered by the Second Circuit Court of Appeals. Taxpayer lives in California.
    d. The decision was rendered by the Supreme Court.
    e. The decision was rendered by the Tax Court. The IRS has acquiesced in the result.
    f. Same as (e), except that the IRS has nonacquiesced in the result.

17. What is the difference between a Regular decision, a Memorandum decision, and a Summary Opinion of the Tax Court?

18. Interpret each of the following citations.
 a. 54 T.C. 1514 (1970).
 b. 408 F.2d 117 (CA–2, 1969).
 c. 69–1 USTC ¶9319 (CA–2, 1969).
 d. 23 AFTR2d 69–1090 (CA–2, 1969).
 e. 293 F.Supp. 1129 (D.Ct.Miss., 1967).
 f. 67–1 USTC ¶9253 (D.Ct.Miss., 1967).
 g. 19 AFTR2d 647 (D.Ct.Miss., 1967).
 h. 56 S.Ct. 289 (USSC, 1935).
 i. 36–1 USTC ¶9020 (USSC, 1935).
 j. 16 AFTR 1274 (USSC, 1935).
 k. 422 F.2d 1336 (Ct.Cls., 1970).

19. Explain the following abbreviations.
 a. CA–2
 b. Fed.Cl.
 c. *aff'd.*
 d. *rev'd.*
 e. *rem'd.*
 f. *Cert. denied*
 g. *acq.*
 h. B.T.A.
 i. USTC
 j. AFTR
 k. F.3d
 l. F.Supp.
 m. USSC
 n. S.Ct.
 o. D.Ct.

20. Give the Commerce Clearing House citation for each of the following courts.
 a. Small Cases Division of the Tax Court.
 b. District Court.
 c. Supreme Court.
 d. Court of Federal Claims.
 e. Tax Court Memorandum decision.

21. Where can you locate a published decision of the U.S. Court of Federal Claims?

22. Which of the following items can probably be found in the *Cumulative Bulletin*?
 a. Action on Decision.
 b. Small Cases Division of the Tax Court decision.
 c. Letter ruling.
 d. Revenue Procedure.
 e. Final Regulation.
 f. Court of Appeals decision.
 g. Senate Finance Committee Report.
 h. Acquiescences to Tax Court decisions.
 i. U.S. Circuit Court of Appeals decision.

23. Answer the following questions based upon this citation: *United Draperies, Inc. v. Comm.*, 340 F.2d 936 (CA–7, 1964), *aff'g* 41 T.C. 457 (1963), *cert. denied* 382 U.S. 813 (1965).
 a. In which court did this decision first appear?
 b. Did the appellate court uphold the trial court?
 c. Who was the plaintiff?
 d. Did the Supreme Court uphold the appellate court decision?

Issue ID

24. Ashley is preparing a research paper discussing the credit for child and dependent care expenses for her tax class. Explain to Ashley how she can research this credit.

25. James has just been audited by the IRS and, as a result, has been assessed a substantial deficiency (which he has not yet paid) in additional income taxes. In preparing his defense, James advances the following possibilities.
 a. Although a resident of Texas, James plans to sue in a District Court in Oregon that appears to be more favorably inclined toward taxpayers.
 b. If (a) is not possible, James plans to take his case to a Texas state court where an uncle is the presiding judge.
 c. Since James has found a B.T.A. decision that seems to help his case, he plans to rely on it under alternative (a) or (b).

d. If he loses at the trial court level, James plans to appeal to either the Court of Federal Claims or the Eleventh Circuit Court of Appeals because he has relatives in both Washington, D.C., and Atlanta. Staying with these relatives could save James lodging expense while his appeal is being heard by the court selected.
e. Even if he does not win at the trial court or appeals court level, James feels certain of success on an appeal to the Supreme Court.

Evaluate James's notions concerning the judicial process as it applies to Federal income tax controversies.

26. Using the legend provided, classify each of the following statements (more than one answer per statement may be appropriate).

Legend

D = Applies to the District Court
T = Applies to the Tax Court
C = Applies to the Court of Federal Claims
A = Applies to the Circuit Court of Appeals
U = Applies to the Supreme Court
N = Applies to none of the above

a. Decides only Federal tax matters.
b. Decisions are reported in the F.3d Series.
c. Decisions are reported in the USTCs.
d. Decisions are reported in the AFTRs.
e. Appeal is by *Writ of Certiorari.*
f. Court meets most often in Washington, D.C.
g. Offers the choice of a jury trial.
h. Is a trial court.
i. Is an appellate court.
j. Allows appeal to the Court of Appeals for the Federal Circuit, and bypasses the taxpayer's particular Circuit Court of Appeals.
k. Has a Small Cases Division.
l. Is the only trial court where the taxpayer does not have to first pay the tax assessed by the IRS.

27. Using the legend provided, classify each of the following citations as to the type of court.

Legend

D = Applies to the District Court
T = Applies to the Tax Court
C = Applies to the Court of Federal Claims
A = Applies to the Circuit Court of Appeals
U = Applies to the Supreme Court
N = Applies to none of the above

a. Temp.Reg. § 1.79–4T.
b. *Whipple Chrysler Plymouth,* 31 TCM 230 (1972).
c. *Keller v. Comm.,* 723 F.2d 58 (CA–10, 1983).
d. *Borge v. Comm.,* 395 U.S. 933 (1969).
e. *Allen Leavell,* 104 T.C. 140 (1995).
f. *Shaffstall Corp. v. U.S.,* 639 F.Supp. 1041 (S.D. Ind., 1986).
g. *Mernard, Inc. v. Comm.,* T.C.Memo. 2004–207.
h. Rev.Rul. 84–68, 1984–1 C.B. 31.
i. 3 B.T.A. 1042 (1926).

28. Using the legend provided, classify each of the following tax sources.

Legend
P = Primary tax source
S = Secondary tax source
B = Both
N = Neither

a. Sixteenth Amendment to the Constitution.
b. Tax Treaty between the United States and France.
c. Revenue Procedure.
d. General Counsel Memoranda (1989).
e. Tax Court memorandum decision.
f. *Tax Notes* article.
g. Temporary Regulations (issued 2004).
h. Tax Court Memorandum decision.
i. Small Cases Division of the Tax Court decision.
j. Senate Finance Committee Report.

Ethics

29. An accountant friend of yours tells you that he "almost never" does any tax research, because he feels that "research usually reveals that some tax planning idea has already been thought up and shot down." Besides, he points out, most tax returns are never audited by the IRS. Can a tax adviser who is dedicated to reducing his client's tax liability justify the effort to engage in tax research? Do professional ethics *demand* such efforts? Which approach would a client probably prefer?

Ethics

30. Another friend of yours, who is a philosophy major, has overheard the conversation described in the previous problem and declares that all tax research is "immoral." She says that tax research enables people with substantial assets to shift the burden of financing public expenditures to those who "get up every morning, go to work, play by the rules, and pay their bills." How do you respond?

31. In general, most tax research can now be conducted and conclusions reached with the use of materials available on the Internet. Assess the validity of this statement.

Extender

32. Under what circumstances can court decisions lead to changes in the Code?

Extender
Communications

33. Locate the following Code provisions and give a brief description of each in an e-mail to your instructor.
a. § 61(a)(13).
b. § 643(a)(2).
c. § 2503(g)(2)(A).

Extender

34. Go to page 44,274 of the August 25, 1995 issue of the *Federal Register*. What action was taken by the IRS, and what was the subject matter?

BRIDGE *Discipline*

1. Comment on these statements.
a. The tax law is created and administered in the same way as other Federal provisions.
b. Most taxpayers find it too expensive and time-consuming to sue the government in a tax dispute.

RESEARCH PROBLEMS

Note: Solutions to Research Problems can be prepared by using the **RIA Checkpoint® Student Edition** online research product, which is available to accompany this text. It is also possible to prepare solutions to the Research Problems by using tax research materials found in a standard tax library.

THOMSON RIA

Research Problem 1. Locate the April 2005 issue of *The Tax Adviser* and find the article by Robert A. Briskin. What are the title and page numbers of the article he wrote? Define "incidental property."

Research Problem 2. Locate the following Code citations and give a brief topical description of each.

a. § 708(a).
b. § 1371(a)(1).
c. § 2503(a).

Research Problem 3. Locate the following Regulations and give a brief topical description of each.

a. Reg. § 1.170A–4A(b)(2)(ii)(C).
b. Reg. § 1.672(b)–1.
c. Reg. § 20.2031–7(f).

Research Problem 4. Locate the following items and give a brief summary of the results.

a. Prop.Reg. § 1.864(b)–1(b)(2)(ii)(E).
b. Rev.Proc. 2005–50, I.R.B. No. 32, 272.
c. FSA 200228005.
d. IRC § 32(c)(2)(A).
e. *Ramirez-Ota v. Comm.*, T.C. Summary Opinion, 2002–27.

Research Problem 5. Complete the following citations.

a. *Betty R. Carraway*, T.C.Memo. 1994–___.
b. *Robert E. Imel*, 61 T.C. ___ (1973).
c. *Higgins v. Comm.*, 312 U.S. 212 (___).
d. Rev.Rul. 68–378, 1968–___ C.B. ___.
e. *Dye v. U.S.*, 121 F.3d 1399 (___, 1997).
f. Rev.Proc. 2003–85, ___ C.B. 1184.
g. *Talen v. U.S.*, 355 F.Supp.2d 22 (D.D.C., ___).

Research Problem 6. Find *Kathryn Bernal*, 120 T.C. 102 (2003) and answer the following questions.

a. What was the docket number?
b. When was the dispute filed?
c. Who is the respondent?
d. Who was the attorney for the taxpayers?
e. Who was the judge who wrote the opinion?
f. What was the disposition of the dispute?

Communications

Research Problem 7. Determine how the term *person* is defined in the *Internal Revenue Code.* Specify the Code Section in which the term is defined. Describe your research path in a PowerPoint presentation for your classmates.

Internet *Activity*

Use the tax resources of the Internet to address the following questions. Do not restrict your search to the World Wide Web, but include a review of newsgroups and general reference materials, practitioner sites and resources, primary sources of the tax law, chat rooms and discussion groups, and other opportunities.

Research Problem 8. Find tax research documents for the following on the Internet.

a. The U.S. Supreme Court, a Circuit Court of Appeals, the Internal Revenue Service, and final Regulations.
b. Sources of proposed Federal tax legislation.
c. A collection of tax rules for your state.

Communications

Research Problem 9. Go to the U.S. Tax Court Internet site.

a. What types of cases can be found on the site?
b. What is a Summary Opinion? Find one.
c. What is a Memorandum Opinion? Find one.
d. Find the "Rules of Practice and Procedure."
e. Is the site user friendly? E-mail one suggested improvement to the webmaster.

Communications

Research Problem 10. In an e-mail to your professor, describe how to find the following tax law sources using only **http:// www.irs.gov**.

a. Internal Revenue Code.
b. Current Income Tax Regulations.
c. A recent Revenue Procedure.

Communications

Research Problem 11. Find three blogs on the Internet related to tax practice. On one PowerPoint slide, list the URLs for each blog, and the general topical areas addressed at each.

http://wft.swlearning.com

CHAPTER 3

Taxes on the Financial Statements

LEARNING OBJECTIVES

After completing Chapter 3, you should be able to:

LO.1

Recognize the difference between book and tax methods of computing income tax expense.

LO.2

Compute a corporation's book income tax expense under FAS 109.

LO.3

Describe the purpose of the valuation allowance.

LO.4

Recognize the effect of APB 23 on effective tax rates.

LO.5

Interpret the disclosure information contained in an income tax note.

LO.6

Use financial statement income tax information to benchmark a company's tax position.

OUTLINE

TAX *Talk*

Truth is, figuring out how much tax a company actually pays is impossible. . . . Tax disclosure is just inscrutable.

—Robert Willens

GlobalCo is a U.S. corporation with operations in 40 different states and 27 different countries. It pays income taxes in virtually all these jurisdictions. GlobalCo's investors and competitors are interested in understanding GlobalCo's effective tax rate. An examination of its financial statements indicates that GlobalCo has a 28 percent effective tax rate. How much of GlobalCo's tax expense is related to U.S. federal tax, state and local tax, or taxes in foreign countries? What portion of its tax cost is currently paid versus deferred to some future period? Has GlobalCo recorded any deferred tax assets, representing future tax savings, or deferred tax liabilities, representing future tax costs? How does GlobalCo's effective tax rate for the current year compare to prior years, or to other companies in the same industry? Why is GlobalCo's effective tax rate not simply 35 percent, the statutory corporate rate for large U.S. corporations?

The bottom line result of the many tax planning ideas, advice, and compliance efforts provided by tax professionals to their clients is captured in a simple summary number—income tax expense. A U.S. corporation's tax expense is reported in its annual Federal tax return, its financial statements, and other regulatory filings and is often the starting point for state and local tax returns. As it turns out, however, deriving a corporation's income tax expense is not so simple.

A corporation may report millions of dollars in tax expense in its financial statements and yet pay virtually nothing to the U.S., state, or foreign governments. Alternatively, a corporation may pay substantial amounts to the U.S., state, and foreign governments and report very little income tax expense in its financial statements. Why do such differences exist? Which income tax expense is the "correct" number? How can data regarding a corporation's income tax expense provide valuable information for the corporation, its competitors, and tax professionals assisting in the planning function? This chapter addresses these questions.

LO.1

Recognize the difference between book and tax methods of computing income tax expense.

Book-Tax Differences

A significant difference may exist between a corporation's Federal income tax liability as reported on its Form 1120 (tax) and the corporation's income tax expense as reported on its financial statements (book) prepared using **generally accepted accounting principles (GAAP)**. This book-tax difference is caused by any or all of the following.

- Differences in reporting entities included in the calculation.
- Different definition of taxes included in the income tax expense amount.
- Different accounting methods.

TAX *in the News* **HERE, THERE, AND EVERYWHERE—ENRON'S CORPORATE STRUCTURE**

The collapse of Enron Corporation gave the public a peek behind the scenes of a multinational corporation's financial and tax strategies. It turned out that Enron used many sophisticated techniques—some legal and some not—to increase its reported net income and decrease its taxes.

Enron used so-called special purpose entities structured so that the income or loss of the entities was not included in Enron's financial statements. Enron had over 900 subsidiaries located in a number of tax haven countries around the world. For example, Enron had 692 subsidiaries incorporated in the Cayman Islands, 119 subsidiaries in the Turks and Caicos Islands, and 43 subsidiaries in Mauritius.

Different Reporting Entities

A corporate group must consolidate all U.S. and foreign subsidiaries within a single financial statement for book purposes when the parent corporation controls more than 50 percent of the voting power of those subsidiaries.[1] In cases where the parent corporation owns between 20 and 50 percent of another corporation, the parent uses the **equity method** to account for the earnings of the subsidiary. Under the equity method, the parent currently records its share of the subsidiary's income or loss for the year.[2] Corporations that own less than 20 percent of other corporations typically use the *cost method* to account for income from these investments and include income only when actual dividends are received.

EXAMPLE 1

Fisher, Inc., a domestic corporation, owns 100% of Gator, Inc., a domestic corporation; 100% of Hurricane, Ltd., a foreign corporation; and 40% of Beach, Inc., a domestic corporation. Fisher's combined financial statement includes its own net income and the net income of both Gator and Hurricane. In addition, Fisher's financial statement includes its 40% share of Beach's net income. Fisher's financial statement includes the income of these subsidiaries regardless of whether Fisher receives any actual profit distributions from its subsidiaries. ■

For Federal tax purposes, a U.S. corporation may elect to include any *domestic* subsidiaries that are 80 percent or more owned in its consolidated U.S. tax return.[3] The income of foreign subsidiaries and less than 80 percent owned domestic subsidiaries is not included in the consolidated tax return.

EXAMPLE 2

If Fisher from Example 1 elects to include Gator as part of its consolidated Federal income tax return, Fisher's return includes its own taxable income and the taxable income generated by Gator. Hurricane's taxable income is not included in the consolidated return because it is a non-U.S. corporation. Beach, although a domestic corporation, cannot be consolidated with Fisher because Fisher owns only 40% of the stock. Income from Hurricane and Beach will be included in Fisher's U.S. taxable income only when Fisher receives actual or constructive dividends. ■

Different Taxes

The income tax expense reported on a corporation's financial statement is the combination of Federal, state, local, and foreign income taxes. Furthermore, this tax expense number includes both current and deferred tax expense amounts.

[1] *Statement of Financial Accounting Standards No. 94—Consolidation of All Majority-Owned Subsidiaries*, Financial Accounting Standards Board. Certain adjustments are made to reduce book income for the after-tax income related to minority shareholders.

[2] *Opinion No. 18—The Equity Method of Accounting for Investments in Common Stock*, Accounting Principles Board.

[3] §§ 1501–1504. The election to consolidate an 80% or more owned subsidiary can be changed only with the permission of the IRS.

TAX *in the News* **TO DEDUCT OR NOT TO DEDUCT—THE QUESTION IS ANSWERED**

In March 2004, the Financial Accounting Standards Board proposed that companies be required to report the value of options they provide to their employees as an expense on their financial statements beginning in 2005. The International Accounting Standards Board adopted a similar rule effective in 2004. Some companies fear the effect this rule might have on their share prices, with the lower net income that stock option expensing will produce. High-tech companies are particularly concerned with this proposal because they are heavy users of stock options to attract employees.

The opponents of stock option expensing lobbied Congress to intervene with the FASB and prevent the adoption of this rule. This is not the first time the option-expensing controversy has erupted. The FASB almost adopted a similar rule in 1994 but backed down after intervention by the U.S. Senate and the Securities and Exchange Commission. However, the recent history of corporate failure and fraud, combined with the push for more transparency in financial statements, made Congress hesitant to get involved this time around.

Ultimately, the FASB issued a revised *Statement of Financial Accounting Standards No. 123—Share-Based Payment*. The new standard requires that the compensation cost relating to share-based payments be recognized as an expense in the income statement. Most public companies may be required to apply the new statement to years beginning after June 15, 2005, unless the effective date is extended by Congress or the FASB. Nonpublic companies must apply the new statement to years beginning after December 15, 2005. The new standard applies to many types of stock-based compensation, including stock options, restricted share plans, performance-based awards, share appreciation rights, and employee share purchase plans. The FASB reports that approximately 750 companies voluntarily followed the new standard in 2004.

The distinction between current and deferred income taxes is discussed later in this chapter.

EXAMPLE 3

For book purposes, Fisher, Gator, and Hurricane from Example 1 combine their income and expenses into a single financial statement. The book tax expense for the year includes all Federal, state, local, and foreign income taxes paid or accrued by these three corporations. In addition, the tax expense amount includes any future Federal, state, local, or foreign income tax expenses (or tax savings) on income reported in the current income statement. ■

The income tax expense computed on the Federal income tax return is the U.S. *Federal* income tax expense. This amount is based on the U.S. corporation's taxable income. State income taxes are reported on the Federal tax return, but as deductions in arriving at taxable income.

EXAMPLE 4

Fisher and Gator, from Example 1, file a consolidated Federal tax return. The tax expense reported on the Form 1120 is only the U.S. Federal income tax expense for the consolidated taxable income of Fisher and Gator. This tax expense does not include the income taxes that Fisher and its subsidiaries paid to state, local, or foreign governments. ■

Different Methods

Many differences exist between book and tax accounting methods. Some are simply **temporary differences**, with income and expenses appearing in both the financial statement and tax return, but in different periods (i.e., a timing difference). Others are **permanent differences**, with items appearing in the financial statement or the tax return, but not both.

Examples of temporary differences include the following.

- *Depreciation on fixed assets.* Taxpayers may use an accelerated depreciation method under the modified accelerated cost recovery system (MACRS) rules but a straight-line method for book purposes. Even if identical methods are used, the period over which the asset is depreciated may differ between book and tax.

- *Compensation-related expenses.* Several differences exist in this category. For example, under GAAP, corporations must accrue the future expenses related to providing postretirement benefits other than pensions (e.g., health insurance coverage). However, these expenses are deductible for tax purposes only when paid.
- *Accrued income and expenses.* Although most income and expense items are recognized for tax and book purposes in the same period, a number of items potentially appear in different periods. For example, warranty expenses are accrued for book purposes but are not deductible for tax purposes until incurred. Inventory write-offs are accrued for book but are not deductible for tax until incurred. On the income side, different methods applicable to the timing of income recognition may create temporary differences.
- *Net operating losses.* Operating losses from one tax year may be used to offset taxable income in another tax year. Thus, the losses incurred in one year for book purposes may be used as a deduction for tax purposes in a different year.
- *Intangible assets.* Goodwill and some other intangibles are not amortizable for book purposes. However, GAAP requires an annual determination of whether the intangible has suffered a reduction in value (i.e., impairment).[4] If an intangible has suffered an impairment, a deduction is required to reduce the intangible's book value to the lower level. For tax purposes, post-1993 intangibles are amortized over 15 years.[5]

Examples of permanent differences include the following.[6]

- *Nontaxable income.* A common example is municipal bond interest, which is income for book purposes but is not taxable.
- *Nondeductible expenses.* For example, the disallowed portion of meals and entertainment expense and certain penalties are not deductible for tax purposes but are expensed in arriving at book income.
- *Tax credits.* Credits such as the research activities credit reduce Federal income tax liability but have no corresponding book treatment.

DIGGING DEEPER 1

Find more information on this topic at our Web site: ***http://wft-entities.swlearning.com.***

EXAMPLE 5

Wise, Inc., reported the following results for the current year.

Book income (before tax)	$ 685,000
Tax depreciation in excess of book	(125,000)
Nondeductible warranty expense	65,000
Municipal bond interest income	(35,000)
Taxable income (Form 1120)	$ 590,000

Wise reports net income before tax of $685,000 on its financial statement but must adjust this amount for differences between book and tax income. Tax depreciation in excess of book is a tax deduction not deducted for book purposes, and warranty expense is deductible for book purposes but not yet deductible for tax. Both these items are temporary differences

[4] *Statement of Financial Accounting Standards No. 142—Goodwill and Other Intangible Assets,* Financial Accounting Standards Board.

[5] § 197. Note that prior to 1994, goodwill and similar intangibles were not amortizable for tax purposes but were amortizable for book purposes over a maximum period of 40 years. Thus, goodwill acquired during this period triggered a permanent difference (amortizable for book but not for tax).

[6] Before the FASB changed the rules in 2004 for reporting stock options as an expense in financial statements, nonqualified stock option expenses also created a permanent difference because the corporation received a tax deduction on the date the employee exercised the option but was not required to deduct an expense for book purposes under prior GAAP. For an extended discussion of this issue, see M. Hanlon and T. Shevlin, "Accounting for Tax Benefits of Employee Stock Options and Implications for Research," *Accounting Horizons,* March 2002.

TAX *in the News* AUDIT ROADMAP EXPANDS

The IRS audit roadmap now includes country lanes and alleyways instead of only major highways. U.S. corporations will begin disclosing much more detailed information about the differences between their book and taxable income to the IRS in their tax returns for years beginning after 2004. The new book-tax reconciliation Schedule M–3 replaces the Schedule M–1 for consolidated tax groups with total year-end assets of $10 million or more. The new reconciliation schedule provides extensive detail on the differences between a corporation's book and taxable income, including information on entities included, income, and deductions.

The business community expressed concern over the compliance costs associated with providing this level of detail. These concerns did little to derail the new reporting requirements in an era of Sarbanes-Oxley, corporate fraud, and concern over whether corporations were paying their fair share of the tax burden.

because they will eventually reverse (with book depreciation eventually exceeding tax depreciation and the warranty expense ultimately deducted for tax when incurred). The municipal bond adjustment is a permanent difference because this income will never be subject to tax. ■

Figure 3–1 contains the **Schedule M–1** from Form 1120, the corporate income tax return. The purpose of Schedule M–1 is to reconcile book income to the taxable income reported on the tax return. Line 1 is the net income or loss per books, and line 2 adds back the book tax expense in order to get back to book income before tax.[7] The remainder of Schedule M–1 contains positive and negative adjustments for both temporary and permanent differences until arriving at taxable income on line 10. For tax years after 2004, **Schedule M–3** is required for a consolidated tax group with total year-end assets of $10 million or more. Other corporations may voluntarily file a Schedule M–3. Figure 3–2 contains the Schedule M–3. The income tax note of the financial statements also contains a tax reconciliation, but as discussed later, the purpose and content of this reconciliation are quite different.

FIGURE 3–1 **Schedule M–1**

Schedule M-1 **Reconciliation of Income (Loss) per Books With Income per Return** (see instructions)

1	Net income (loss) per books		7	Income recorded on books this year not included on this return (itemize):	
2	Federal income tax per books			Tax-exempt interest $	
3	Excess of capital losses over capital gains				
4	Income subject to tax not recorded on books this year (itemize):		8	Deductions on this return not charged against book income this year (itemize):	
5	Expenses recorded on books this year not deducted on this return (itemize):		a	Depreciation $	
a	Depreciation $		b	Charitable contributions $	
b	Charitable contributions $				
c	Travel and entertainment $		9	Add lines 7 and 8	
6	Add lines 1 through 5		10	Income (page 1, line 28)—line 6 less line 9	

[7]Line 1, "Net income (loss) per books" is not defined in the instructions to the form, and corporations seem to use various starting points in the Schedule M–1 (e.g., only the book income from U.S. members of the group). The new Schedule M–3 expands the M–1 and provides much more detail and consistency.

FIGURE 3–2 **Schedule M–3**

SCHEDULE M-3 (Form 1120)

Department of the Treasury
Internal Revenue Service

Net Income (Loss) Reconciliation for Corporations With Total Assets of $10 Million or More

▶ Attach to Form 1120.
▶ See separate instructions.

OMB No. 1545-0123

2005

Name of corporation (common parent, if consolidated return) | **Employer identification number**

Part I **Financial Information and Net Income (Loss) Reconciliation**

1a Did the corporation file SEC Form 10-K for its income statement period ending with or within this tax year?
☐ **Yes.** Skip lines 1b and 1c and complete lines 2a through 11 with respect to that SEC Form 10-K.
☐ **No.** Go to line 1b.

b Did the corporation prepare a certified audited income statement for that period?
☐ **Yes.** Skip line 1c and complete lines 2a through 11 with respect to that income statement.
☐ **No.** Go to line 1c.

c Did the corporation prepare an income statement for that period?
☐ **Yes.** Complete lines 2a through 11 with respect to that income statement.
☐ **No.** Skip lines 2a through 3c and enter the corporation's net income (loss) per its books and records on line 4.

2a Enter the income statement period: Beginning ___/___/___ Ending ___/___/___

b Has the corporation's income statement been restated for the income statement period on line 2a?
☐ **Yes.** (If "Yes," attach an explanation and the amount of each item restated.)
☐ **No.**

c Has the corporation's income statement been restated for any of the five income statement periods preceding the period on line 2a?
☐ **Yes.** (If "Yes," attach an explanation and the amount of each item restated.)
☐ **No.**

3a Is any of the corporation's voting common stock publicly traded?
☐ **Yes.**
☐ **No.** If "No," go to line 4.

b Enter the symbol of the corporation's primary U.S. publicly traded voting common stock . . . . ☐☐☐☐☐

c Enter the nine-digit CUSIP number of the corporation's primary publicly traded voting common stock . . . . ☐☐☐☐☐☐☐☐☐

4	Worldwide consolidated net income (loss) from income statement source identified in Part I, line 1	4	
5a	Net income from nonincludible foreign entities (attach schedule)	5a	( )
b	Net loss from nonincludible foreign entities (attach schedule and enter as a positive amount) .	5b	
6a	Net income from nonincludible U.S. entities (attach schedule)	6a	( )
b	Net loss from nonincludible U.S. entities (attach schedule and enter as a positive amount) . .	6b	
7a	Net income of other includible corporations (attach schedule)	7a	
b	Net loss of other includible corporations (attach schedule)	7b	( )
8	Adjustment to eliminations of transactions between includible corporations and nonincludible entities (attach schedule)	8	
9	Adjustment to reconcile income statement period to tax year (attach schedule)	9	
10	Other adjustments to reconcile to amount on line 11 (attach schedule)	10	
11	**Net income (loss) per income statement of includible corporations.** Combine lines 4 through 10	11	

For Privacy Act and Paperwork Reduction Act Notice, see the Instructions for Forms 1120 and 1120-A. Cat. No. 37961C **Schedule M-3 (Form 1120) 2005**

FIGURE 3-2 *(continued)*

Schedule M-3 (Form 1120) 2005 Page **2**

Name of corporation (common parent, if consolidated return)	**Employer identification number**

If consolidated return, check applicable box: **(1)** ☐ Consolidated group **(2)** ☐ Parent corporation **(3)** ☐ Consolidated eliminations **(4)** ☐ Subsidiary corporation

Name of subsidiary (if consolidated return)	**Employer identification number**

Part II **Reconciliation of Net Income (Loss) per Income Statement of Includible Corporations With Taxable Income per Return**

	Income (Loss) Items	(a) Income (Loss) per Income Statement	(b) Temporary Difference	(c) Permanent Difference	(d) Income (Loss) per Tax Return
1	Income (loss) from equity method foreign corporations				
2	Gross foreign dividends not previously taxed .				
3	Subpart F, QEF, and similar income inclusions .				
4	Section 78 gross-up				
5	Gross foreign distributions previously taxed . .				
6	Income (loss) from equity method U.S. corporations .				
7	U.S. dividends not eliminated in tax consolidation .				
8	Minority interest for includible corporations . .				
9	Income (loss) from U.S. partnerships (attach schedule) .				
10	Income (loss) from foreign partnerships (attach schedule)				
11	Income (loss) from other pass-through entities (attach schedule)				
12	Items relating to reportable transactions (attach details)				
13	Interest income				
14	Total accrual to cash adjustment				
15	Hedging transactions				
16	Mark-to-market income (loss)				
17	Cost of goods sold				
18	Sale versus lease (for sellers and/or lessors) . .				
19	Section 481(a) adjustments				
20	Unearned/deferred revenue				
21	Income recognition from long-term contracts .				
22	Original issue discount and other imputed interest				
23a	Income statement gain/loss on sale, exchange, abandonment, worthlessness, or other disposition of assets other than inventory and pass-through entities				
23b	Gross capital gains from Schedule D, excluding amounts from pass-through entities				
23c	Gross capital losses from Schedule D, excluding amounts from pass-through entities, abandonment losses, and worthless stock losses				
23d	Net gain/loss reported on Form 4797, line 17, excluding amounts from pass-through entities, abandonment losses, and worthless stock losses				
23e	Abandonment losses				
23f	Worthless stock losses (attach details) . . .				
23g	Other gain/loss on disposition of assets other than inventory				
24	Disallowed capital loss in excess of capital gains .				
25	Utilization of capital loss carryforward				
26	Other income (loss) items with differences (attach schedule)				
27	**Total income (loss) items.** Combine lines 1 through 26				
28	**Total expense/deduction items** (from Part III, line 36)				
29	Other income (loss) and expense/deduction items with no differences				
30	**Reconciliation totals.** Combine lines 27 through 29 .				

Note. Line 30, column (a), must equal the amount on Part I, line 11, and column (d) must equal Form 1120, page 1, line 28.

Schedule M-3 (Form 1120) 2005

FIGURE 3–2 *(continued)*

Schedule M-3 (Form 1120) 2005 Page **3**

Name of corporation (common parent, if consolidated return) | **Employer identification number**

If consolidated return, check applicable box: **(1)** ☐ Consolidated group **(2)** ☐ Parent corporation **(3)** ☐ Consolidated eliminations **(4)** ☐ Subsidiary corporation

Name of subsidiary (if consolidated return) | **Employer identification number**

Part III **Reconciliation of Net Income (Loss) per Income Statement of Includible Corporations With Taxable Income per Return—Expense/Deduction Items**

Expense/Deduction Items	**(a)** Expense per Income Statement	**(b)** Temporary Difference	**(c)** Permanent Difference	**(d)** Deduction per Tax Return
1 U.S. current income tax expense				
2 U.S. deferred income tax expense				
3 State and local current income tax expense				
4 State and local deferred income tax expense				
5 Foreign current income tax expense (other than foreign withholding taxes)				
6 Foreign deferred income tax expense				
7 Foreign withholding taxes				
8 Interest expense				
9 Stock option expense				
10 Other equity-based compensation				
11 Meals and entertainment				
12 Fines and penalties				
13 Judgments, damages, awards, and similar costs				
14 Parachute payments				
15 Compensation with section 162(m) limitation				
16 Pension and profit-sharing				
17 Other post-retirement benefits				
18 Deferred compensation				
19 Charitable contribution of cash and tangible property				
20 Charitable contribution of intangible property				
21 Charitable contribution limitation/carryforward				
22 Domestic production activities deduction				
23 Current year acquisition or reorganization investment banking fees				
24 Current year acquisition or reorganization legal and accounting fees				
25 Current year acquisition/reorganization other costs				
26 Amortization/impairment of goodwill				
27 Amortization of acquisition, reorganization, and start-up costs				
28 Other amortization or impairment write-offs				
29 Section 198 environmental remediation costs				
30 Depletion				
31 Depreciation				
32 Bad debt expense				
33 Corporate owned life insurance premiums				
34 Purchase versus lease (for purchasers and/or lessees)				
35 Other expense/deduction items with differences (attach schedule)				
36 **Total expense/deduction items.** Combine lines 1 through 35. Enter here and on Part II, line 28				

Printed on recycled paper **Schedule M-3 (Form 1120) 2005**

CONCEPT SUMMARY 3–1

Book versus Tax

Financial Statement	U.S. Federal Income Tax Return
Reporting entities	**Reporting entities**
• 50% or more owned domestic and foreign subsidiaries *must* be consolidated.	• 80% or more owned domestic subsidiaries *may* be consolidated.
• Share of income from 20 to 50% owned domestic and foreign corporations included in current income.	• Share of income from other corporations reported only when actual or constructive dividends are received.
Income tax expense	**Income tax expense**
• Federal income taxes.	• Federal income taxes.
• State income taxes.	• Current only.
• Local income taxes.	
• Foreign income taxes.	
• Current and deferred.	
Methods	**Methods**
• Temporary differences.	• Temporary differences.
• Permanent differences.	• Permanent differences.
• Income tax note reconciliation.	• Schedule M–1 or M–3 reconciliation.

Schedule M–1 or M–3 is typically the starting point for IRS audits of corporations. Identifying large differences between book and taxable income may offer the IRS auditor insights into tax saving strategies (some perhaps questionable) employed by the taxpayer. Concept Summary 3–1 summarizes the book-tax differences in arriving at income tax expense.

LO.2

Compute a corporation's book income tax expense under FAS 109.

Income Taxes in the Financial Statements

FAS 109 Principles

As pointed out earlier, a corporation's financial statements are prepared in accordance with GAAP. The purpose and objectives of these statements are quite different from the objective of the corporation's income tax return.

The **FAS 109** approach produces a total income tax expense (also called the **income tax provision**) for the income currently reported on a corporation's combined financial statement.[8] This approach follows the matching principle, where all the expenses related to earning income are reported in the same period as the income without regard to when the expenses are actually paid.

EXAMPLE 6

PanCo, Inc., earns $100,000 in book income before tax. PanCo has a single temporary difference. Tax depreciation exceeds book depreciation by $20,000. Accordingly, PanCo's taxable income is $80,000 ($100,000 – $20,000 additional tax deduction). On its income tax return, PanCo reports total Federal tax expense of $28,000 ($80,000 × 35%). On its financial

[8] *Statement of Financial Accounting Standards No. 109—Accounting for Income Taxes,* Financial Accounting Standards Board.

TAX *in the News* **THE BOOK-TAX INCOME GAP**

The corporate financial scandals of Enron, WorldCom, and others have heightened interest in whether corporations are making appropriate disclosures (i.e., transparency) and in whether they are shouldering their fair share of the tax burden. Adding fuel to the fire is the fact that the gap between book income and taxable income seems to be growing.

According to the Citizens for Tax Justice, 41 large companies reported over $28 billion in pretax book income but paid no U.S. taxes in at least one year between 1996 and 1998. An IRS study found that the aggregate difference between book and taxable income of active corporations increased by more than 70 percent between 1996 and 1998, with corporations reporting substantially more book income than taxable income during this period.

Congress and the U.S. Treasury are concerned about the increased use of tax shelters by corporations to reduce U.S. tax and have recently issued regulations that require disclosure of certain "tax shelter" transactions. Corporations counter that the large differences in book and tax income are a function of the different rules and objectives of GAAP for financial statements and the Internal Revenue Code for tax returns.

statement, PanCo reports a total tax expense of $35,000 ($100,000 × 35%). This $7,000 book-tax difference is the difference between book and taxable income times the current corporate tax rate ($7,000 = $20,000 × 35%). Although PanCo did not actually pay the $7,000 this year, in future years when the book-tax depreciation difference reverses, the $7,000 will eventually be paid. Hence, the *future* income tax expense related to the current book income is reported in the current year. ■

The total book tax expense under FAS 109 is made up of both current and deferred components.[9] The **current tax expense** theoretically represents the taxes actually payable to (or refund receivable from) the governmental authorities for the current period. Although an oversimplification, think of this amount as the actual check the taxpayer writes to the government (or refund received) for the current year. Keep in mind, though, that the current portion of the book income tax expense rarely matches the taxpayer's actual tax liability. Prior to 2005 a major cause of this disconnect was the tax deduction for employee stock options. The corporation received a tax deduction at the date of employee exercise but was not required to deduct an expense for book purposes. Although this was a book-tax difference, it is not treated as a temporary or permanent difference in the FAS 109 calculation.[10] Figure 3–3 summarizes the computation of a corporation's current tax expense.

The deferred component of the book tax expense is called the **deferred tax expense** or **deferred tax benefit**. This component represents the future tax cost (or savings) connected with income reported in the current-period financial statement. Deferred tax expense or benefit is created as a result of temporary differences. More technically, FAS 109 adopts a **balance sheet approach** to measuring deferred taxes. Under this approach, the deferred tax expense or benefit is the change from one year to the next in the net **deferred tax liability** or **deferred tax asset**.

A deferred tax liability is the expected future tax liability related to current income (measured using enacted tax rates and rules).[11] A deferred tax liability is created in the following situations.

[9]Corporations also may include a "cushion" in their provision for income tax expense in order to currently account for potential tax costs in the future (e.g., deficiencies related to losing a potential IRS audit). See *Statement of Financial Accounting Standards No. 5—Accounting for Contingencies*, Financial Accounting Standards Board.

[10]See G. A. McGill and E. Outslay, "Did Enron Pay Taxes? Using Accounting Information to Decipher Tax Status," *Tax Notes*, August 19, 2002, for a discussion of issues surrounding the interpretation of the current tax payable account.

[11]If the tax rate will be different in future years, the *enacted* future tax rate should be used in the computation.

FIGURE 3–3 **Current Tax Expense**

	Pretax book income
±	Schedule M–1 adjustments
	Taxable income before NOLs
–	NOL carryforwards
	Taxable income
×	Applicable tax rate
	Current tax expense (provision) before tax credits
–	Tax credits
	Current tax expense (tax provision)

- An expense is deductible for tax in the current period but is not deductible for book until some future period.
- Income is includible currently for book purposes but is not includible in taxable income until a future period.

EXAMPLE 7

PJ Enterprises earns net income before depreciation of $500,000 in 2005 and $600,000 in 2006. Assume that PJ has a single depreciable asset acquired in 2005 for $80,000 and that for tax purposes PJ may deduct $60,000 in depreciation expense for the first year and $20,000 in depreciation expense for the second year (i.e., an accelerated method). For book purposes, assume that PJ depreciates the asset on a straight-line basis over two years ($40,000 depreciation deduction per year).

2005

	Book	Tax
Income before depreciation	$500,000	$500,000
Depreciation	(40,000)	(60,000)
Income after depreciation	460,000	440,000
Corporate tax rate	× 35%	× 35%
Income tax expense	$161,000	$154,000
Current tax expense	$154,000	
Deferred tax expense	$ 7,000	
Starting adjusted basis in depreciable asset	$ 80,000	$ 80,000
Ending adjusted basis in depreciable asset	(40,000)	(20,000)
Change in adjusted basis	$ 40,000	$ 60,000

Book-tax balance sheet difference	$20,000
Corporate tax rate	× 35%
Deferred tax liability	$ 7,000

In this example, it is easy to "back into" the deferred tax expense amount of $7,000 by simply taking the difference between the tax expense per the tax return ($154,000) and the book tax expense ($161,000). However, the technical computation of the deferred tax expense is based on the difference between the book and tax asset basis numbers ($20,000) at the corporate tax rate (35%).

2006

	Book	Tax
Income before depreciation	$600,000	$600,000
Depreciation	(40,000)	(20,000)
Income after depreciation	560,000	580,000
Corporate tax rate	× 35%	× 35%
Income tax expense	$196,000	$203,000
Current tax expense	$203,000	
Deferred tax expense	($ 7,000)	
Starting adjusted basis in depreciable asset	$ 40,000	$ 20,000
Ending adjusted basis in depreciable asset	(–0–)	(–0–)
Change in adjusted basis	$ 40,000	$ 20,000
Book-tax balance sheet difference	($20,000)	
Corporate tax rate	× 35%	
Deferred tax liability	($ 7,000)	

In 2006, the book-tax difference in asset basis reverses, with a resulting reverse in the deferred tax liability account. ■

EXAMPLE 8

Continue with the facts in Example 7. The following journal entries record the book tax expense (provision) for each year. Notice that the book total tax expense combines the current amount (income tax payable) and the future amount (deferred tax liability).

2005 journal entry		
Income tax expense (provision)	$161,000	
Income tax payable		$154,000
Deferred tax liability		7,000
2006 journal entry		
Income tax expense (provision)	$196,000	
Deferred tax liability	7,000	
Income tax payable		$203,000

At the end of 2005, the balance sheet reflects a net deferred tax liability of $7,000. At the end of 2006, the balance sheet contains no deferred tax liability because the temporary difference that created the deferred tax liability has reversed itself. ■

A deferred tax asset is the expected future tax benefit related to current book income (measured using enacted tax rates and rules). A deferred tax asset is created in the following situations.

- An expense is deductible for book in the current period but is not deductible for tax until some future period.
- Income is includible in taxable income currently but is not includible in book income until a future period.

EXAMPLE 9

MollCo, Inc., earns net income before warranty expense of $400,000 in 2005 and $450,000 in 2006. In 2005, MollCo deducts $30,000 in warranty expense for book purposes related to expected warranty repairs. This warranty expense is not deductible for tax purposes until actually incurred. Assume the $30,000 warranty expense is actually incurred in 2006 and this is MollCo's only temporary difference.

2005

	Book	Tax
Income before warranty expense	$400,000	$400,000
Warranty expense	(30,000)	—
Income after warranty expense	$370,000	$400,000
Corporate tax rate	× 35%	× 35%
Income tax expense	$129,500	$140,000
Current tax expense	$140,000	
Deferred tax expense	($ 10,500)	
Basis in warranty expense payable	$ 30,000	$ -0-
Book-tax balance sheet difference	($30,000)	
Corporate tax rate	× 35%	
Deferred tax asset	($10,500)	

In this example, it is easy to "back into" the deferred tax expense amount of $10,500 by simply taking the difference between the tax expense per the tax return ($140,000) and the book tax expense ($129,500). However, the technical computation of the deferred tax expense is based on the difference between the book and tax basis in the warranty expense payable ($30,000) at the corporate tax rate (35%).

2006

	Book	Tax
Income before warranty expense	$450,000	$450,000
Warranty expense	—	(30,000)
Income after depreciation	$450,000	$420,000
Corporate tax rate	× 35%	× 35%
Income tax expense	$157,500	$147,000
Current tax expense	$147,000	
Deferred tax expense	$ 10,500	
Basis in warranty expense payable	$ -0-	$ 30,000
Book-tax balance sheet difference	$30,000	
Corporate tax rate	× 35%	
Deferred tax liability	$10,500	

In 2006, the book-tax difference in warranty expense payable reverses, with a resulting reverse in the deferred tax asset account. ■

EXAMPLE 10

Continue with the facts in Example 9. The following journal entries record the book tax expense (provision) for each year. Notice that the book total tax expense combines the current amount (income tax payable) and the future amount (deferred tax asset).

2005 journal entry

Income tax expense (provision)	$129,500	
Deferred tax asset	10,500	
Income tax payable		$140,000

2006 journal entry

Income tax expense (provision)	$157,500	
Deferred tax asset		$ 10,500
Income tax payable		147,000

At the end of 2005, the balance sheet reflects a net deferred tax asset of $10,500. At the end of 2006, the balance sheet contains no deferred tax asset because the temporary difference that created the deferred tax asset has reversed itself. ■

Deferred tax assets and liabilities are reported on the balance sheet just as any other asset or liability would be. However, the interpretation of these assets and liabilities is quite different. Typically, an asset is "good" because it represents a claim on something of value, and a liability is "bad" because it represents a future claim against the corporation's assets. In the case of deferred tax assets and liabilities, the interpretation is reversed. Deferred tax liabilities are "good" because they represent an amount that may be paid to the government in the future. In essence, deferred tax liabilities are like an interest-free loan from the government with a due date perhaps many years in the future. Deferred tax assets, on the other hand, are future tax benefits and thus are similar to a receivable from the government that may not received until many years in the future.

Valuation Allowance

LO.3

Describe the purpose of the valuation allowance.

Much of GAAP is based on the **conservatism principle**. That is, accounting rules are designed to provide assurance that assets are not overstated and liabilities are not understated. Current recognition of deferred tax liabilities does not require significant professional judgment because future tax liabilities are always expected to be settled. However, under FAS 109, deferred tax assets are recognized only when it is more likely than not that the future tax benefits will be realized.

EXAMPLE 11

Warren, Inc., reported book income before tax of $2 million in 2005. Warren's taxable income is also $2 million (no temporary or permanent differences). Warren has a current U.S. income tax liability for 2005 of $700,000 before tax credits ($2 million × 35%). During 2005, Warren paid $100,000 in foreign income taxes that it is not able to use as a credit on its 2005 tax return because of the foreign tax credit (FTC) limitation (see Chapter 13). Warren's auditors believe it is more likely than not that Warren will be able to use the $100,000 in FTCs within the next 10 years before they expire. Consequently, the future tax benefit of the FTCs is accounted for in the current year book tax expense as follows.

	Book	Tax
Income tax expense	$600,000	$700,000
Current tax expense	$700,000	
Deferred tax expense (benefit)	($100,000)	

Warren makes the following journal entry to record the book income tax expense and deferred tax asset related to the expected use of the FTCs.

Income tax expense (provision)	$600,000	
Deferred tax asset	100,000	
Income tax payable		$700,000

Because Warren is able to record the benefit of the future FTCs, its effective tax rate is 30% ($600,000 tax expense/$2 million book income before tax). ■

When a deferred tax asset does not meet the *more likely than not* threshold for recognition, FAS 109 requires that a **valuation allowance** be created. The valuation allowance is a contra-asset account that offsets all or a portion of the deferred tax asset.

EXAMPLE 12

Assume that the auditors in Example 11 believe that Warren will be able to use only $40,000 of the FTCs, with the remaining $60,000 expiring. In this case, the future tax benefit recognized currently should be only $40,000 rather than the full $100,000. To implement this reduction in the deferred tax asset, Warren must record a valuation allowance of $60,000, resulting in a book tax expense of $660,000 as follows.

	Book	Tax
Income tax expense	$660,000	$700,000
Current tax expense	$700,000	
Deferred tax expense (benefit)	($ 40,000)	

Warren makes the following journal entry to record the book income tax expense and deferred tax asset related to the expected use of the FTCs.

Income tax expense (provision)	$660,000	
Deferred tax asset	100,000	
Valuation allowance		$ 60,000
Income tax payable		700,000

Warren must reduce the deferred tax asset by $60,000, which increases its effective tax rate to 33% ($660,000 tax expense/$2 million book income before tax), compared with the 30% effective tax rate in Example 11. ■

To determine whether a valuation allowance is required, both positive and negative evidence must be evaluated. Examples of negative evidence (i.e., evidence suggesting that the deferred tax asset will not be realized) include the following.

- History of losses.
- Expected future losses.
- Short carryback/carryforward periods.
- History of tax credits expiring unused.

Positive evidence (i.e., support for realizing the current benefit of future tax savings) includes the following.

- Strong earnings history.
- Existing contracts.
- Unrealized appreciation in assets.
- Sales backlog of profitable orders.

The valuation allowance is examined for appropriateness each year. The allowance may be increased or decreased if facts and circumstances change in the future.

PLANNING *Strategies*

RELEASING VALUATION ALLOWANCES

★ **Framework Focus: Deductions**

Strategy ★ Maximize Deductible Amounts.

When a corporation records a valuation allowance, it loses the ability to recognize the benefit of future tax savings in the current period. However, all is not lost if the taxpayer can demonstrate that facts and circumstances have changed. For example, if a taxpayer generates a net operating loss (NOL), it records a deferred tax asset for the future tax savings related to using the NOL. However, if the evidence suggests that it is more likely than not that the NOL will expire unused, a valuation allowance must be recorded. To reduce this valuation allowance, the taxpayer must demonstrate that there will be future taxable income sufficient to absorb the NOL within the carryforward period. Sources of future taxable income include reversals of temporary differences that will produce future taxable income and other sources of future profits. Taxpayers also may demonstrate that the adoption of new tax planning strategies will allow the use of deferred tax assets.

For example, assume that Warren, Inc., from Example 12, adopts new planning strategies in 2006 that will allow it ultimately to use all $100,000 of its FTC carryforward. Warren earns $2.3 million in book income before tax and reports $2.3 million in taxable income in 2006 (i.e., no permanent or temporary differences). The current tax expense is $805,000 ($2.3 million × 35%). Based on new evidence (implementation of tax planning strategies), the auditors determine that the entire $100,000 in FTCs will be used in the future before expiration. Accordingly, the $60,000 valuation allowance from 2005 is "released," and the tax benefit of this release affects the 2006 financial results as follows.

	Book	Tax
Income tax expense	$745,000	$805,000
Current tax expense	$805,000	
Deferred tax expense	($ 60,000)	

Warren makes the following journal entry to record the book income tax expense and valuation allowance release related to the expected use of the FTCs.

Income tax expense (provision)	$745,000	
Valuation allowance	60,000	
Income tax payable		$805,000

Warren's effective tax rate for 2006 is 32.4 percent ($745,000/$2.3 million). Without the valuation allowance release, Warren's effective tax rate would have been 35 percent ($805,000/$2.3 million). Note that this tax rate benefit is realized even though the $100,000 in FTC carryforwards have yet to be actually used in Warren's tax return.

Find more information on this topic at our Web site: ***http://wft-entities.swlearning.com.***

DIGGING DEEPER 2

Earnings of Foreign Subsidiaries and APB 23

LO.4

Recognize the effect of APB 23 on effective tax rates.

As discussed earlier, a corporate group's financial statements include both domestic and foreign controlled subsidiaries. However, foreign corporations, even those controlled by U.S. shareholders, are not part of a U.S. consolidated tax return. Consequently, U.S. taxpayers can achieve deferral of current U.S. taxes on foreign income if they operate their foreign activities through foreign subsidiary corporations in jurisdictions with lower tax rates than the United States (see Chapter 13). Although the *actual* U.S. taxes on foreign corporations' profits are deferred, the reported effective tax rate for financial statement purposes may not reflect this deferral because FAS 109 requires that a corporate group report both current and deferred income tax expense.

EXAMPLE 13

USCo, a domestic corporation, operates a manufacturing facility in Singapore through a Singapore corporation. Assume that the U.S. tax rate is 35% and the Singapore tax rate is 6%. For the current year, USCo earns $600,000 in taxable income. The Singapore corporation earns $400,000 in taxable income from its operations, pays $24,000 in taxes to Singapore, and makes no distributions to its U.S. parent. The Singapore corporation is not taxed in the United States because it is not a U.S. person and has no activities in the United States. USCo is not taxed on the Singapore profits because it has not received any distributions of these profits. Accordingly, USCo has achieved deferral and reduced its worldwide cash tax costs.

However, for financial statement purposes, the USCo group must include the $400,000 in Singapore profits in its net income and report both the Singapore tax and any *potential* U.S. tax (after allowable FTCs) as its total tax expense.

TAX *in the News* **HOW SOFT IS THAT CUSHION?**

Companies take positions in their tax returns that may not ultimately survive the scrutiny of the IRS or other tax authorities. If a taxpayer loses the benefit of a favorable tax position after a future audit, the loss of this tax benefit may unfavorably affect the company's financial statement tax expense in that future year. The additional tax cost will become part of the current tax expense, yet the income this tax is related to would have been reported in the initial year. This result wreaks havoc with a company's effective tax rate.

To avoid this increase in effective tax rate, companies may book a reserve or "cushion" for the uncertain tax position in the initial year. That is, rather than book the entire tax benefit (and thus reduce tax expense in the current year), the company may book only a portion (or none) of the tax benefit. If company later loses the actual tax benefit upon audit, to the extent the additional tax imposed is charged against the reserve (or "cushion"), the additional tax does not affect the future-year tax expense. If the company's tax position is not challenged in the future (or the company successfully defends any challenge), the reserve can be released. This release reduces the current tax expense in the future (release) year and lowers the company's effective tax rate in that year.

FAS 5, Accounting for Contingencies, addresses the accounting for uncertain events in the financial statements and should be followed in determining any reserve required for an uncertain tax position. Even with *FAS 5*, the FASB is concerned that companies too freely use the tax reserve as a "cookie jar" to shift earnings from one period to another. To add more structure to the accounting for tax reserves, in July 2005 the FASB issued its *Exposure Draft on Accounting for Uncertain Tax Positions*. The approach suggested by this exposure draft will significantly change the rules for accounting for uncertain tax positions. The exposure draft is controversial (even among FASB members), and the FASB delayed the publication of any new guidance on this issue to the first quarter of 2006.

U.S. Tax Return		Potential U.S. Tax on Non-U.S. Income	
Income	$600,000	Income	$400,000
Tax rate	× 35%	Tax rate	× 35%
U.S. tax	$210,000	Total tax	$140,000
		Foreign tax credit	(24,000)
		Net U.S. tax	$116,000

Consequently, the total tax expense for financial statement purposes is $350,000.

Current U.S. tax	$210,000
Current foreign tax	24,000
Deferred U.S. tax	116,000
Total tax expense	$350,000

The financial statement effective tax rate on global income is 35% ($350,000 total tax expense/$1,000,000 net income). Thus, although USCo paid only $234,000 in taxes, its effective tax rate (and thus its after-tax book income) does not reflect the savings generated from operating in Singapore, a low-tax country. ■

APB 23 provides a special exception to FAS 109 for income from foreign subsidiaries.[12] If a corporation documents that it is **permanently reinvesting** the earnings of its foreign subsidiaries outside the United States, the corporation does not record as an expense any future U.S. income tax that the corporation may pay on such earnings.

[12] *Opinion No. 23—Accounting for Income Taxes—Special Areas*, Accounting Principles Board.

EXAMPLE 14

Assume that USCo, in Example 13, uses APB 23 to avoid reporting the $116,000 in deferred taxes. Because USCo plans to reinvest indefinitely its Singapore earnings outside the United States, it is not required to include the deferred U.S. taxes as part of its total tax expense. Thus, USCo's total financial statement income remains $1 million, but its total tax expense is only $234,000 (the taxes currently paid to the United States and Singapore). The resulting financial statement effective tax rate is 23.4% ($234,000/ $1,000,000), and the USCo group's after-tax book income reflects the Singapore tax savings. ■

Using APB 23 is not an "all or nothing" decision. It can be adopted in some years and not others. Even within a year it may be used for only a portion of foreign subsidiary earnings.

EXAMPLE 15

Larson, Inc., a domestic corporation, has two wholly owned foreign subsidiaries, Arendt, Ltd., and Carroll, Ltd. Larson can choose to apply APB 23 to both subsidiaries in 2005 and to only Arendt in 2006. In 2007, Larson can choose to use APB 23 for 40% of Arendt's earnings and 80% of Carroll's earnings. ■

PLANNING *Strategies*

REDUCING EFFECTIVE TAX RATES WITH APB 23 CAN BACKFIRE

★ Framework Focus: Deductions

Strategy ★ Maximize Deductible Amounts.

Because APB 23 allows for higher reported book earnings (no deferred U.S. tax expense is recorded), its use may be reflected in higher stock prices and increased shareholder wealth. Although academic studies find mixed evidence on this effect, many U.S. multinationals with foreign subsidiaries do in fact use APB 23 to avoid reporting U.S. deferred taxes on foreign earnings.

The "permanent reinvestment" exception should not be employed unless the corporation truly expects to keep its foreign earnings outside the United States. Using APB 23 and then repatriating foreign profits after all can cause extreme spikes in a corporation's effective tax rate.

For example, USCo, a domestic corporation, owns 100 percent of Shamrock, Ltd., an Irish corporation. Assume that the U.S. tax rate is 35 percent and the Irish tax rate is 10 percent. In 2005, USCo earns $100,000 in taxable income and pays $35,000 to the United States. Shamrock earns $400,000 in taxable income and pays $40,000 in taxes to Ireland. Shamrock makes no distributions to its U.S. parent and is not taxed in the United States because it is not a U.S. person and has no activities in the United States. USCo is not taxed on the Irish profits because it has not received any distributions of these profits. Furthermore, USCo uses APB 23 to avoid recording any deferred U.S. income tax expense on its financial statements. Accordingly, USCo has achieved deferral and reduced its worldwide cash tax costs and book income tax expense.

USCo's total tax expense for financial statement purposes is $75,000.

Current U.S. tax	$35,000
Current foreign tax	40,000
Total tax expense	$75,000

The financial statement effective tax rate on global income is 15 percent ($75,000 total tax expense/$500,000 net income). Thus, the USCo group has achieved higher after-tax book income and earnings per share.

In 2006, USCo earns $200,000 in taxable income and pays $70,000 to the United States. Shamrock breaks even for the year and pays no taxes to Ireland. In 2006, USCo decides to have Shamrock pay it a dividend of $360,000.

U.S. Tax Return	
U.S. income	$200,000
Foreign dividend*	400,000
Taxable income	$600,000
Tax rate	× 35%
	$210,000
FTC	(40,000)
Net U.S. tax	$170,000

*The foreign dividend is the $360,000 cash dividend grossed up by the $40,000 potential FTC (see Chapter 13).

For book purposes, USCo reports only $200,000 in net income (the $400,000 in Irish income was previously included in book income in 2005 and is not included again). The 2006 total tax expense for financial statement purposes is $170,000.

Current U.S. tax	$170,000
Current foreign tax	–0–
Total tax expense	$170,000

The financial statement effective tax rate on global income is 85 percent ($170,000 total tax expense/$200,000 net income). This extremely high effective rate is caused by the mismatching of the Irish income (reported in 2005) and the U.S. taxes on the Irish income (reported in 2006).

APB 23 is only a major issue when the foreign subsidiary is taxed at rates below the U.S. tax rate. Otherwise, there is no deferral potential. However, using APB 23 may limit the availability of creating deferred tax assets when foreign subsidiaries pay taxes at greater than the U.S. rate. Then the multinational group could use these excess foreign taxes as credits on the U.S. tax return. See Chapter 13.

EXAMPLE 16

AmeriCo, a domestic corporation, operates a manufacturing facility in the Netherlands through a Dutch corporation. Assume that the U.S. tax rate is 35% and the Netherlands tax rate is also 35%. For the current year, AmeriCo earns $400,000 in taxable income. The Netherlands corporation earns $300,000 in taxable income from its operations, pays $105,000 in taxes to the Netherlands, and makes no distributions to its U.S. parent. The Netherlands corporation is not taxed in the United States because it is not a U.S. person and has no activities in the United States. AmeriCo is not taxed on the Netherlands profits because it has not received any distributions of these profits.

For financial statement purposes, the AmeriCo group must include the $300,000 in Dutch profits in its net income and report both the Dutch tax and any *potential* U.S. tax (after allowable FTCs) as its total tax expense.

U.S. Tax Return		Potential U.S. Tax on Foreign Income	
Income	$400,000	Income	$ 300,000
Tax rate	× 35%	Tax rate	× 35%
U.S. tax	$140,000	Total tax	$ 105,000
		FTC	(105,000)
		Net U.S. tax	$ –0–

Consequently, the total tax expense for financial statement purposes is $245,000.

Current U.S. tax	$140,000
Current foreign tax	105,000
Total tax expense	$245,000

The financial statement effective tax rate on global income is 35% ($245,000 total tax expense/$700,000 book net income). Even without APB 23, there is no deferred U.S. tax on the Dutch income, because AmeriCo would pay no additional U.S. tax upon repatriation of the Netherlands earnings after its use of the available FTC. ■

LO.5

Interpret the disclosure information contained in an income tax note.

Tax Disclosures in the Financial Statements

As illustrated earlier, any temporary differences create deferred tax liabilities or deferred tax assets, and these amounts appear in the corporation's balance sheet. As with any asset or liability, these accounts must be classified as either current or noncurrent, based on the assets or liabilities that created the temporary difference. If the deferred tax liability or asset is not related to any asset, then the classification is based on the expected reversal period.

TAX *in the News* **PERMANENT REINVESTMENT, UNLESS I GET A BETTER OFFER**

The 2004 Jobs Act provided a temporary incentive for corporations to repatriate foreign profits back to the United States. Section 965 allows domestic corporations to elect to take a one-time 85 percent dividends received deduction for certain cash dividends received from controlled foreign corporations for either the taxpayer's last tax year that began before October 22, 2004, or the first tax year that began after October 22, 2004. Such dividends must be reinvested in the United States, and the eligible dividend amount is based on a calculation that considers prior-year average dividends and the amount of earnings considered "permanently reinvested" abroad under APB 23.

This rule was intended to provide a tax benefit only for earnings that would not have otherwise been repatriated to the United States. With an 85 percent dividends received deduction, the effective U.S. corporate tax rate on such dividends is 5.25 percent (35% corporate tax rate × 15% taxable amount). This low effective tax rate produces a relatively minor "hit" to a corporation's effective tax rate, because of the mismatch of income and tax expense (i.e., the income was included in prior-year financial statements without recording any residual U.S. tax).

Supporters of this measure argued that the inflow of cash back to the United States, along with the requirement for reinvestment here, would provide a boost to the domestic economy. The dividend income is lightly taxed but would otherwise have never been taxed in the United States. Critics argue that the tax break is simply a giveaway to U.S. multinational corporations and rewards outsourcing. They fear that with this precedent, U.S. multinationals may simply outsource more profits to low-tax countries and wait for future tax breaks before repatriating profits.

EXAMPLE 17

JenCo, Inc., has a deferred tax liability generated because tax depreciation exceeds book depreciation on manufacturing equipment. Because the equipment is classified as a noncurrent asset, the deferred tax liability is classified as noncurrent. JenCo also has a deferred tax asset related to bad debt expense deductible for book purposes but not yet deductible for tax purposes. Because the bad debt expense is related to accounts receivable, a current asset, the associated deferred tax asset is classified as current.

If JenCo incurs an NOL, a deferred tax asset is created, because of the future tax benefit provided by the NOL deduction. The NOL is not related to any specific asset or liability. Accordingly, the deferred tax asset is classified based on when the corporation expects to use the NOL. If the expected use is more than one year in the future, the deferred tax asset is classified as noncurrent. ■

A corporation may have both deferred tax assets and liabilities, current and noncurrent. The corporation reports the *net* current deferred tax assets or liabilities, and the *net* noncurrent deferred tax assets or liabilities.

EXAMPLE 18

Jordan, Inc., has the following deferred tax asset and liability accounts for the current year.

Current deferred tax assets	$50,000
Current deferred tax liabilities	72,000
Noncurrent deferred tax assets	93,000
Noncurrent deferred tax liabilities	28,000

On its balance sheet, Jordan reports a $22,000 current net deferred tax liability ($72,000 − $50,000) and a $65,000 noncurrent net deferred tax asset ($93,000 − $28,000). ■

In its income statement, a corporation reports a total income tax expense that consists of both the current tax expense (or benefit) and the deferred tax expense (or benefit). The tax expense must be allocated to income from continuing operations, discontinued operations, extraordinary items, prior-period adjustments, and the cumulative effect of accounting changes. Additional disclosures are required for tax expense allocated to income from continuing operations (e.g., current versus deferred, benefits of NOL deductions, changes in valuation allowances, etc.).

The income tax note contains a wealth of information, including the following.

- Breakdown of income between domestic and foreign.
- Detailed analysis of the provision for income tax expense.
- Detailed analysis of deferred tax assets and liabilities.
- Effective tax **rate reconciliation** (dollar amount or percentage).
- Information on use of APB 23 for the earnings of foreign subsidiaries.
- Discussion of significant tax matters.

Figure 3–4 contains selected information from Microsoft's 2005 financial statements. The balance sheet detail shows both deferred tax assets and liabilities. The

FIGURE 3–4 **Microsoft, Inc., Selected 2005 Financial Statement Information (in Millions)**

Balance Sheet	
Assets	
Current assets	
Cash and equivalents	$ 4,851
Short-term investments	32,900
Total cash and short-term investments	$ 37,751
Accounts receivable, net	7,180
Inventories	491
Deferred income taxes	1,701
Other	1,614
Total current assets	$ 48,737
Property and equipment, net	2,346
Equity and other investments	11,004
Goodwill	3,309
Intangible assets, net	499
Deferred income taxes	3,621
Other long-term assets	1,299
Total assets	$ 70,815
Liabilities and stockholders' equity	
Current liabilities	
Accounts payable	$ 2,086
Accrued compensation	1,662
Income taxes	2,020
Short-term unearned revenue	7,502
Other	3,607
Total current liabilities	$ 16,877
Long-term unearned revenue	1,665
Other long-term liabilities	4,158
Total liabilities	$ 22,700
Stockholders' equity	
Common stock and paid-in capital—shares authorized 24,000; Shares issued and outstanding 10,862 and 10,710	$ 60,413
Retained earnings (deficit), including accumulated other comprehensive income of $1,119 and $1,426	(12,298)
Total stockholders' equity	$ 48,115
Total liabilities and stockholders' equity	$ 70,815

(Continued on next page)

FIGURE 3–4 *(continued)*

Income Statement

Revenue	$ 39,788
Operating expenses	
Cost of revenue	$ (6,200)
Research and development	(6,184)
Sales and marketing	(8,677)
General and administrative	(4,166)
Total operating expenses	$(25,227)
Operating income	$ 14,561
Investment income and other	2,067
Income before income taxes	$ 16,628
Provision for income taxes	(4,374)
Net income	$ 12,254

Income Tax Note

U.S. and international components of income before income taxes were:

U.S.	$ 9,806
International	6,822
Income before income taxes	$ 16,628

The provision for income taxes consisted of:

Current taxes	
U.S. federal	$ 3,401
U.S. state and local	152
International	911
Current taxes	$ 4,464
Deferred taxes	(90)
Provision for income taxes	$ 4,374

Deferred income taxes were:

Deferred income tax assets	
Unearned revenue	$ 915
Impaired investments	861
Stock based compensation expense	3,994
Other revenue items	213
Other expense items	1,751
Other	173
Deferred income tax assets	$ 7,907
Deferred income tax liabilities	
Unrealized gain on investments	$ (1,169)
International earnings	(1,393)
Other	(23)
Deferred income tax liabilities	$ (2,585)

Effective Tax Rate Reconciliation

	$	%
Hypothetical income taxes at U.S. rate	$ 5,820	35.0
IRS examination settlement	(781)	(4.7)
Foreign earnings taxed at lower rates	(516)	(3.1)
Extraterritorial income exclusion benefit	(216)	(1.3)
Other reconciling items	67	0.4
Provision for income tax	$ 4,374	26.3

(Continued on next page)

FIGURE 3–4 *(concluded)*

We have not provided for U.S. deferred income taxes or foreign withholding taxes on $4.1 billion of our undistributed earnings for certain non-U.S. subsidiaries, all of which relate to fiscal 2002 through 2005 earnings, because these earnings are intended to be permanently reinvested in operations outside the United States.

The American Jobs Creation Act of 2004 (the "Act") was enacted in October 2004. The Act creates a temporary incentive for U.S. corporations to repatriate foreign subsidiary earnings by providing an elective 85% dividends received deduction for certain dividends from controlled foreign corporations. The deduction is subject to a number of limitations and requirements, including adoption of a specific domestic reinvestment plan for the repatriated funds. Based on our current understanding of the Act and subsequent guidance published by the U.S. Treasury, we have determined that we are eligible and intend to repatriate approximately $780 million in dividends subject to the elective 85% dividends received deduction. Accordingly, we recorded a corresponding tax provision benefit of $179 million from the reversal of previously provided U.S. deferred tax liabilities on these unremitted foreign subsidiary earnings. We intend to pay this dividend in fiscal year 2006.

Income taxes paid were $2.8 billion in fiscal year 2003, $2.5 billion in fiscal year 2004, and $4.3 billion in fiscal year 2005.

Tax Contingencies. We are subject to income taxes in the United States and numerous foreign jurisdictions. Significant judgment is required in determining our worldwide provision for income taxes and recording the related assets and liabilities. In the ordinary course of our business, there are many transactions and calculations where the ultimate tax determination is uncertain. We are regularly under audit by tax authorities. Accruals for tax contingencies are provided for in accordance with the requirements of SFAS No. 5, *Accounting for Contingencies*.

The Internal Revenue Service (IRS) has completed and closed its audits of our consolidated federal income tax returns through 1996. We recently entered into a closing agreement with the IRS for tax years 1997 through 1999 resulting in certain adjustments to our federal income tax liability for those years. Accordingly, our fiscal year 2005 tax provision has been reduced by $776 million as a result of reversing previously established reserves in excess of the additional tax liability assessed by the IRS for the 1997-1999 tax years. The IRS is currently conducting an audit of our consolidated federal income tax return for tax years 2000 through 2003.

Although we believe we have appropriate support for the positions taken on our tax returns, we have recorded a liability for our best estimate of the probable loss on certain of these positions, the non-current portion of which is included in other long-term liabilities. We believe that our accruals for tax liabilities are adequate for all open years, based on our assessment of many factors including past experience and interpretations of tax law applied to the facts of each matter, which matters result primarily from intercompany transfer pricing, tax benefits from the Foreign Sales Corporation and Extra Territorial Income tax rules and the amount of research and experimentation tax credits claimed. Although we believe our recorded assets and liabilities are reasonable, tax regulations are subject to interpretation and tax litigation is inherently uncertain; therefore our assessments can involve both a series of complex judgments about future events and rely heavily on estimates and assumptions. Although we believe that the estimates and assumptions supporting our assessments are reasonable, the final determination of tax audits and any related litigation could be materially different than that which is reflected in historical income tax provisions and recorded assets and liabilities. Based on the results of an audit or litigation a material effect on our income tax provision, net income, or cash flows in the period or periods for which that determination is made could result. Due to the complexity involved we are not able to estimate the range of reasonably possible losses in excess of amounts recorded.

income statement indicates that Microsoft's income before tax was $16,628 million, and its total income tax expense was $4,374 million. The income tax note indicates that $9,806 million of the book income was earned from domestic operations and $6,822 million from foreign operations. The $4,374 million total income tax expense reported in the income statement is further divided into $4,464 million of current tax expense ($911 million of which was paid to non-U.S. governments) and $90 million of deferred tax benefit (i.e., future tax savings related to current-year activities).

The note provides detail on the cumulative deferred tax assets and liabilities. Microsoft has a net deferred tax asset of $5,322 million ($7,907 deferred tax assets – $2,585 deferred tax liabilities). Microsoft's auditors must believe that these deferred tax assets will be fully realized because no valuation allowance is required. Because of the way the balance sheet accounts are summarized, the deferred tax asset and liability amounts in the balance sheet do not match the amounts reported in the income tax note. This is because the deferred tax assets and liabilities are separated into current and noncurrent components in the balance sheet and may be subsumed within other balance sheet accounts (e.g., other long-term assets).

Microsoft is using APB 23 to avoid currently recording a deferred tax expense for $4.1 billion of its foreign subsidiary earnings. Microsoft also reports on the status of audits and litigation matters with the IRS.

Microsoft's effective rate reconciliation starts with its book income before taxes at the U.S. corporate tax rate ($5,820 = $16,628 × 35%). Adjustments are made for permanent differences.

(1) the tax benefit from a tax settlement with the IRS [$781 or 4.7% ($781/$16,628)],
(2) the tax benefit of foreign earnings taxed at less than the U.S. rate [$516 or 3.1% ($516/$16,628)],
(3) the tax benefits related to excluding extraterritorial income [$216 or 1.3% ($216/$16,628)], and
(4) other tax increasing differences [$67 or 0.4% ($67/$16,628)]. The ending tax amount is $4,374, which ties to the total income tax expense reported in the income statement. This is an effective tax rate of 26.3 percent ($4,374/$16,628). Thus, Microsoft's overall effective tax rate (local, state, U.S., and foreign) on its worldwide income is less than the U.S. corporate tax rate.

The purpose of the rate reconciliation is to demonstrate how a corporation's actual book effective tax rate relates to its "hypothetical tax rate" as if the book income were taxed at the U.S. corporate rate of 35 percent. Although similar to Schedule M–1 or M–3, the tax note rate reconciliation only reports differences triggered by permanent differences. As discussed in the benchmarking section later in this chapter, an analysis of the rate reconciliation can provide substantial clues as to the tax planning strategies adopted (or not adopted) by a company.

Microsoft's income tax note states that the company "paid" $4.3 billion in income taxes for 2005. Notice that this amount does not match either the total income tax expense of $4,374 million or the current income tax expense of $4,464 million. This anomaly illustrates the difficulty in interpreting the true tax position of a corporation from its financial statements. The $4.3 billion in income taxes paid may relate to Federal, state, or foreign taxes and may be associated with income earned in years other than 2005 (i.e., estimated tax payments for 2006 or payments with prior-year tax returns filed in 2005).

The steps in determining a corporation's income tax expense for book purposes are summarized in Concept Summary 3–2.

EXAMPLE 19

BoxCo, Inc., a domestic corporation, owns 100% of PaperCo, Ltd., an Irish corporation. Assume that the U.S. corporate tax rate is 35% and the Irish rate is 10%. BoxCo is permanently reinvesting PaperCo's earnings outside the United States under APB 23. The corporations' book income, permanent and temporary differences, and current tax expense are as follows.

CONCEPT SUMMARY 3–2

Steps in Determining Book Tax Expense

Start with the corporation's book income after permanent differences.

↓

Determine the corporation's temporary differences.

↓

Compute the corporation's current tax provision.

↓

Compute the corporation's deferred tax provision.

↓

Determine if a valuation allowance is required.

↓

Prepare the income tax note disclosures.

	BoxCo	PaperCo
Book income before tax	$300,000	$200,000
Permanent differences		
Meals and entertainment expense	20,000	—
Municipal bond interest income	(50,000)	—
Book income after permanent differences	$270,000	$200,000
Temporary differences		
Tax > book depreciation	(50,000)	—
Book > tax bad debt expense	10,000	—
Taxable income	$230,000	$200,000
Tax rate	× 35%	× 10%
Current tax expense	$ 80,500	$ 20,000

Assume that the beginning-of-the-year difference between book and tax basis in the depreciable assets is $150,000 and the beginning-of-the-year difference between book and tax basis in the bad debt expense is $50,000. Thus, the beginning-of-the-year deferred tax liability is $35,000] ($150,000 – $50,000) × 35%]. To determine the deferred tax expense (benefit) for the current year, the change in these temporary differences from the beginning to the end of the year must be determined and then multiplied by the appropriate tax rate.

Temporary Differences	Beginning of Year	Change	End of Year
Depreciation	$150,000	$ 50,000	$200,000
Bad debts	(50,000)	(10,000)	(60,000)
Total temporary differences	$100,000	$ 40,000	$140,000
Tax rate	× 35%	× 35%	× 35%
	$ 35,000	$ 14,000	$ 49,000

The deferred tax liability increased by $14,000 for the year. Consequently, BoxCo's total tax expense for book purposes is $114,500.

Current tax expense:	
Domestic	$ 80,500
Foreign	20,000
Deferred tax expense:	
Domestic	14,000
Foreign	—
Total tax expense	$114,500

The journal entry to record the book income tax expense is as follows.

Income tax expense (provision)	$114,500	
Income tax payable		$100,500
Deferred tax liability		14,000

BoxCo's book income is $500,000 (the combined book income of both BoxCo and PaperCo). The effective tax rate reconciliation is based on this book income, with the dollar amounts in the table representing the tax expense (benefit) related to the item and the percentage representing the tax expense (benefit) as a percentage of book income. For example, the municipal bond interest of $50,000 reduces tax liability by $17,500 ($50,000 × 35%). This $17,500 as a percentage of the $500,000 book income is 3.5%.

	Effective Tax Rate Reconciliation	
	$	%
Hypothetical tax at U.S. rate	$175,000	35.0
Disallowed meals and entertainment expense	7,000	1.4
Municipal bond interest	(17,500)	(3.5)
Foreign income taxed at less than U.S. rate	(50,000)	(10.0)
Income tax expense (provision)	$114,500	22.9

Only permanent differences appear in the rate reconciliation. Temporary differences do not affect the *total* book income tax expense; they simply affect the amount of the tax expense that is current versus deferred. ■

EXAMPLE 20

Assume the same facts as Example 19, except that a new Federal income tax law is enacted before the end of the current year that will increase the corporate tax rate to 40% beginning next year. In this case, multiply the year-end total temporary differences of $140,000 by 40% rather than 35%. This results in an increase in the deferred tax liability of $21,000 as illustrated below.

Temporary Differences	Beginning of Year	End of Year	Effect
Depreciation	$150,000	$200,000	
Bad debts	(50,000)	(60,000)	
Total temporary differences	$100,000	$140,000	
Tax rate	× 35%	× 40%	
Deferred tax liability	$ 35,000	$ 56,000	$21,000

The current-year deferred tax liability amount is a function of both the change in temporary differences at the enacted rate ($40,000 × 40%) and the additional 5% tax on the beginning

TAX FACT

Effective Tax Rates for Selected Fortune 100 Companies

The following table shows the provisions for income taxes made by selected major corporations, as a percentage of their book income before taxes.

General Electric	17.9%
General Motors	(76.4)
Verizon	28.2
IBM	29.8
Citigroup	28.4
Ford	20.0
ExxonMobil	40.3
Wal-Mart	26.3
ChevronTexaco	36.6

Source: *2004 or 2005 10-K Filings with Securities and Exchange Commission.*

temporary differences [$100,000 × (40% − 35%)]. This example illustrates the "balance sheet" approach of FAS 109. ■

PLANNING *Strategies*

TAX SAVINGS ARE NOT ALWAYS CREATED EQUAL

★ **Framework Focus: Thinking Outside the Framework**

Many different types of tax planning strategies can produce tax savings. Yet, even when planning ideas produce identical current cash-flow effects, some ideas may have an edge. CEOs and CFOs of public companies are very focused on the bottom line—the company's net income after tax and related earnings per share. A CFO is likely just as interested in an idea's effect on the company's bottom line income as on the cash tax savings.

For example, consider two tax planning ideas that each produce $700,000 of current tax savings. The first idea generates its $700,000 in tax savings by increasing tax depreciation relative to book depreciation by $2 million ($700,000 = $2 million × 35%). The second idea produces research activities tax credits of $700,000, thus reducing current-year tax by $700,000.

Idea 1 produces its current tax savings via a temporary difference. Accordingly, the book tax expense will not reflect the $700,000 in tax savings. Instead, this $700,000 simply moves from the current tax category into the deferred tax category. Even if the book-tax difference is not expected to reverse in the next 30 years (effectively generating "permanent" savings), the book tax expense does not reflect this savings.

In contrast, idea 2 produces its current tax savings via a permanent difference. Thus, the book tax expense also declines by $700,000. This item is a reconciling item in the income tax note rate reconciliation.

LO.6

Use financial statement income tax information to benchmark a company's tax position.

Benchmarking

As the *outcome* of the taxpayer's activities combined with the tax professional's advice, the income tax expense amount may appear to be of little interest to anyone beyond the taxpayer that makes the payment and the government agencies that collect it. The tax year is over, the transactions completed, and the final costs tallied. Still, this historical tax information may prove very valuable. A company's income tax expense is one of the single largest expense items on its income statement, and

FIGURE 3–5 **Tax Rate Reconciliation for Tommy Hilfiger and Polo Ralph Lauren**

	Tommy Hilfiger		Polo Ralph Lauren	
	2004	2003	2004	2003
Hypothetical tax (benefit) at U.S. Federal rate	35.0%	(35.0)%	35.0%	35.0%
State and local income taxes, net of Federal benefits	(1.4)	(29.1)	0.8	1.1
Non-U.S. income taxed at different rates	(18.0)	(48.2)	1.8	0.2
Valuation allowance	3.5	53.3	—	—
Goodwill amortization	—	—	—	—
Goodwill impairment	—	75.9	—	—
U.S. tax on foreign dividends	2.9	—	—	—
Other	0.14	3.5	(1.3)	0.2
Provision for income tax expense (effective tax rate)	22.14%	20.4%	36.3%	36.5%
Book income before tax (in millions)	$170	($69)	$262	$274

Source: 2003 and 2004 10-K Filings with Securities and Exchange Commission.

understanding the components of this expense is a critical activity for the tax professional.

Consider a typical baseball game. Two teams meet, interact following a specific set of rules, and ultimately complete the game generating a final score. Of course, the final score is of immediate interest to the teams and the fans, but once the game is over, the score and associated statistics (runs, hits, errors) are relegated to the history books. Yet these statistics are still quite useful. A team coach may use the game statistics to evaluate the strengths and weaknesses of the players to assist in improving performance. Other teams in the league may use the statistics to develop strategies for upcoming games. Players can use the statistics to benchmark themselves against their own performance in prior games or against players in other teams. In short, there is a wealth of information in these historical data.

A taxpayer's reported income tax expense is likewise a valuable source of information for the company, its tax advisers, and its competitors. The reported information provides clues about a company's operational and tax planning strategies.

Companies may benchmark their tax situation to other years' results or to other companies within the same industry. The starting point for a **benchmarking** exercise is the data from the income tax note rate reconciliation.

Figure 3–5 contains the tax rate reconciliation information from the income tax notes of Tommy Hilfiger (Tommy) and Polo Ralph Lauren (Polo). Both companies have been listed on the New York Stock Exchange, are in the same industry (clothing and accessories), and operate around the world. Although the income and tax expense amounts of both companies are quite different, the tax amounts are converted to percentage of income numbers for comparability purposes. In 2003, Tommy has a very low effective tax rate at 20.4 percent, compared with Polo's 36.5 percent rate. Tommy's 2004 rate is also substantially lower than Polo's 2004 rate. What factors create this difference? Rate reconciliation information can provide clues.

BRIDGE *Discipline*

Financial Statement Analysis

Benchmarking a company's tax position with other companies in the same industry or against prior-year results is simply part of a more comprehensive benchmarking analysis of a company's financial results. For example, analysts often perform ratio analysis when benchmarking a company. The information gleaned from the debt-to-equity ratio, return on assets, return on equity, inventory turnover, and the like is useful in comparing the overall performance of two or more companies. Effective tax rates are simply one more bit of information for the analysts to compare and contrast.

Tax information, however, is often misunderstood by analysts, who may not understand the difference between current and deferred taxes (or that the reported current tax expense does not necessarily represent the taxes the company actually paid for the year). Add stock options, APB 23, and tax cushions under FAS 5 to the mix and the likelihood of the tax note producing a clear picture for the analyst is low. The subtle and sometimes confusing nature of accounting for income taxes creates a special demand for professionals who can demystify the income tax note.

The major difference between Tommy and Polo is in the foreign income taxed at less than the U.S. rate. In Tommy's case, this factor reduces the effective tax rate by 48.2 percentage points in 2003 and 18 percentage points in 2004. This factor increases the effective tax rate by 0.2 percentage points for Polo in 2003 and increases the rate by 1.8 percentage points in 2004. Closer examination of the financial statements provides an explanation for this difference. Tommy was incorporated in the British Virgin Islands, a tax haven (low or no tax) country, while Polo is incorporated in the United States. As discussed in Chapter 13, establishing a company offshore can generate substantial tax savings. Obviously, Tommy has used this strategy to its advantage in structuring its multinational operations.

Another difference between Tommy and Polo is the effect of state and local taxes. Tommy is actually receiving tax savings from state and local taxes (perhaps through local tax incentives and losses), while Polo is paying an effective state and local rate of 1.1 percent (2003) and 0.8 percent (2004).

If Polo could reduce its effective tax rate to 22.1 percent through tax planning or restructuring its operations, its after-tax net income in 2004 would have increased by $37.4 million [difference in tax rates (36.5% − 22.1%) × $262 million book income]. After examination of this simple benchmarking exercise, Polo might engage a tax adviser to investigate the potential of implementing state and local and international tax planning strategies. It appears that Polo has already reduced its state and local taxes (1.1 percent versus 0.8 percent).

When comparing effective tax rates, it is important to consider which components of the effective rate produce one-time effects. For example, the foreign tax rate differential for Tommy and Polo is likely a long-term structural difference in effective tax rates, as the two companies were incorporated in different jurisdictions. However, the large valuation allowance and goodwill impairment effects for Tommy may be a one-time reconciling item. Other typical one-time reconciling items are IRS tax settlements.

Note that Tommy delayed issuing its 2005 financial statements and the press reported potential concerns of tax authorities with some of Tommy's tax positions. Although the ultimate disposition of these tax matters is unknown at this time, this information is also useful in interpreting Tommy's effective tax rate.

In addition to comparing effective tax rates, companies can compare levels of deferred tax assets and liabilities.

EXAMPLE 21

Akiko Enterprises reports a net deferred tax liability of $280,000. Asare, Inc., a company in the same industry, reports a net deferred tax liability of $860,000. Seeing deferred tax liabilities on the balance sheet indicates that these companies are both benefiting from deferring actual tax payments (essentially, an interest-free loan from the government). At first glance it may appear that Asare is doing better in this regard. However, what if Akiko holds total assets of $2.6 million and Asare's assets total $19.2 million? This information indicates that Akiko has 10.8% ($280,000/$2.6 million) of its total assets "financed" with an interest-free loan from the government, while Asare has only 4.5% ($860,000/$19.2 million) of its assets "financed" with its deferred tax liabilities. ■

A company may do a more refined benchmarking analysis of its deferred tax assets and liabilities by examining each component of its deferred tax assets and liabilities as a percentage of total assets. For example, a company can examine how the deferred tax assets or liabilities related to property, plant, and equipment compare with its competitors. The nature of the components of deferred tax liabilities and deferred tax assets becomes quite important in a benchmarking analysis.

EXAMPLE 22

LinCo reports total book income before taxes of $10 million and a total tax expense of $3.2 million, producing a 32% effective tax rate. TuckCo also reports book income before taxes of $10 million. TuckCo's total tax expense is $3.1 million, producing an effective tax rate of 31%. At first glance it appears that both companies are similar with regard to effective tax rates. The total tax expense divided between current and deferred is as follows (in millions).

	LinCo	TuckCo
Current tax expense	$ 4.1	$ 4.2
Deferred tax benefit	(0.9)	(1.1)
Total tax expense	$ 3.2	$ 3.1

Again, it appears that both companies have created deferred tax assets in the current year that are expected to produce tax savings in the future. Knowing the nature of the underlying deferred tax assets will add greatly to the interpretation of the effective tax rates. The deferred tax asset generating LinCo's $900,000 expected future tax savings is the use of an NOL. The deferred tax asset generating TuckCo's expected future tax savings is generated by different book and tax methods in accounting for warranty expense. This additional information reveals that LinCo has previously incurred losses and it is critical that it earn future income in order to use the NOL.

This is quite different from TuckCo's situation, which reveals only that common differences in accounting methods exist. Although the tax positions of LinCo and TuckCo seem very similar on the surface, a closer look reveals a striking difference. ■

EXAMPLE 23

WageCo and SalaryCo are both in the same industry and both report a 38% effective tax rate. Their book income and current, deferred, and total tax expense were reported as:

	WageCo	SalaryCo
Book income before tax	$1,500,000	$2,300,000
Current tax expense	$ 980,000	$ 24,000
Deferred tax expense (benefit)	(410,000)	850,000
Total tax expense	$ 570,000	$ 874,000
Effective tax rate	38%	38%

WageCo's total tax expense is highly dependent on the current recognition of future tax savings of $410,000. SalaryCo appears to be deferring a substantial portion of its tax expense to future years. Although both companies report a 38% effective tax rate, the details indicate that the two companies face very different tax situations. ■

It is important in benchmarking exercises to remove the effect of one-time items in comparing sustainable effective tax rates across time or companies. Examples of one-time items include restructuring costs, legal settlements, and IRS settlements. A one-time item may seem beneficial or detrimental to a company's effective tax rate. But the very nature of such an item implies that it has little to do with the company's long-term sustainable tax costs.

EXAMPLE 24

MetalCo and IronCo are both in the same industry and report the following tax rate reconciliations in their tax footnotes.

	MetalCo	IronCo
Hypothetical tax at U.S. rate	35.0%	35.0%
State and local taxes	2.2	2.1
Foreign income taxed at less than U.S. rate	(6.2)	(6.1)
Tax court settlement on disputed tax issue	(18.6)	—
Effective tax rate	12.4%	31.0%

Although it appears that MetalCo has a significantly lower effective tax rate (12.4%) than IronCo's 31%, removing MetalCo's one-time item related to the court settlement indicates that both companies have a 31% effective tax rate (12.4% + 18.6% = 31%). ■

Benchmarking is part science and part art. A useful analysis requires both knowledge of how the underlying financial statements are constructed, including arriving at tax expense, and a detective's sense of where to look and what questions to ask.

Suggested Further Readings

S. Gupta and K. Newberry, "Corporate Effective Tax Rates after the Tax Reform Act of 1986," *Tax Notes*, May 4, 1992.

G. A. McGill and E. Outslay, "Lost in Translation: Detecting Tax Shelter Activity in Financial Statements," *National Tax Journal*, September 2004.

L. K. Mills K. Newberry and W. B. Trautman, "Trends in Book-Tax Income and Balance Sheet Differences, *Tax Notes*, August 19, 2002.

KEY TERMS

PROBLEM MATERIALS

DISCUSSION QUESTIONS

1. Evaluate the following statement: To avoid the appearance of tax evasion, a corporation's reported book and taxable income should be virtually identical in any given year. *Ethics*

2. USCo, a domestic corporation, owns 100% of ForCo, a foreign corporation, and SubCo, a domestic corporation. USCo also owns 35% of InvestCo, a domestic corporation. USCo receives no distributions from any of these corporations. Which of these entities' net income is included in USCo's income statement for current-year financial reporting purposes?

3. USCo, a domestic corporation, owns 100% of ForCo, a foreign corporation, and SubCo, a domestic corporation. USCo also owns 35% of InvestCo, a domestic corporation. USCo receives no distributions from any of these corporations. Which of these entities' taxable income is included in USCo's current-year Form 1120, U.S. income tax return? Assume USCo consolidates all eligible subsidiaries.

4. Sarah Carter, the CFO of Mac, Inc., notices that the tax expense reported on Mac's tax return differs from the tax expense reported on Mac's financial statement. Provide a letter to Sarah outlining why these two tax expense numbers differ. Mac's address is 482 Linden Road, Paris, KY 40362. *Communications*

5. Temporary and permanent differences both cause taxable income to differ from book income. Describe how these two book-tax differences affect the gap between book and taxable income. *Issue ID*

6. Identify two temporary differences and two permanent differences.

7. Indicate whether the following items create temporary or permanent differences.
   a. Tax depreciation in excess of book depreciation.
   b. Book depreciation in excess of tax depreciation.
   c. Municipal bond interest income.
   d. Increase in the allowance for doubtful accounts.
   e. Disallowed meals and entertainment expense for tax purposes.
   f. Deduction for legal expenses expected to be incurred to settle a lawsuit.

8. Indicate whether the following temporary differences produce deferred tax assets or deferred tax liabilities (considered independently).
   a. Tax depreciation in excess of book depreciation.
   b. Book depreciation in excess of tax depreciation.
   c. Increase in the allowance for doubtful accounts.
   d. Deduction for legal expenses expected to be incurred to settle a lawsuit.
   e. A current-year net operating loss.
   f. Foreign tax credits that are not allowed in the current year because of the foreign tax credit limitation.

9. Indicate whether the following temporary differences produce current or noncurrent deferred tax assets or deferred tax liabilities (considered independently).
   a. Tax depreciation in excess of book depreciation.
   b. Book depreciation in excess of tax depreciation.
   c. Increase in the allowance for doubtful accounts.
   d. Deduction for legal expenses expected to be incurred to settle a lawsuit.
   e. A current-year net operating loss.

10. Evaluate the following statement: The purpose of the Schedule M–1 is to report the book income tax expense to the IRS.

11. Idil, a stock analyst, wants to understand the income tax expense reported in financial statements. Briefly describe the objective of FAS 109 with regard to reporting income tax expense.

12. GlobalCo, Inc., earns book net income of $250,000 in 2006. GlobalCo acquires a depreciable asset in 2006, and first-year tax depreciation exceeds book depreciation by $25,000. GlobalCo has no other temporary or permanent differences. Assuming the U.S. tax rate is 35%, compute GlobalCo's total income tax expense, current income tax expense, and deferred income tax expense.

13. Using the facts of Problem 12, determine the 2006 end-of-year balance in GlobalCo's deferred tax asset and deferred tax liability balance sheet accounts.

14. GlobalCo, in Problem 12, reports $300,000 of book net income in 2007. GlobalCo's book depreciation exceeds tax depreciation in this year by $10,000. GlobalCo has no other temporary or permanent differences. Assuming the U.S. tax rate is 35%, compute GlobalCo's total income tax expense, current income tax expense, and deferred income tax expense.

15. Using the facts of Problem 14, determine the 2007 end-of-year balance in GlobalCo's deferred tax asset and deferred tax liability balance sheet accounts.

16. WorldCo, Inc., earns book net income of $500,000 in 2006. WorldCo deducted $60,000 in bad debt expense for book purposes. This expense is not yet deductible for tax purposes. WorldCo has no other temporary or permanent differences. Assuming the U.S. tax rate is 35%, compute WorldCo's total income tax expense, current income tax expense, and deferred income tax expense.

17. Using the facts of Problem 16, determine the 2006 end-of-year balance in WorldCo's deferred tax asset and deferred tax liability balance sheet accounts.

18. WorldCo, in Problem 16, reports $800,000 of book net income in 2007. WorldCo did not deduct any bad debt expense for book purposes but did deduct $40,000 in bad debt expense for tax purposes. WorldCo has no other temporary or permanent differences. Assuming the U.S. tax rate is 35%, compute WorldCo's total income tax expense, current income tax expense, and deferred income tax expense.

19. Using the facts of Problem 18, determine the 2007 end-of-year balance in WorldCo's deferred tax asset and deferred tax liability balance sheet accounts.

20. Zoom, Inc., hopes to report a total book tax expense of $50,000 in the current year. This $50,000 expense consists of $80,000 in current tax expense and a $30,000 tax benefit related to the expected future use of an NOL by Zoom. If the auditors determine that a valuation allowance of $20,000 must be placed against Zoom's deferred tax assets, what is Zoom's total book tax expense?

21. Describe the factors considered in evaluating the need for a valuation allowance.

22. How does the release of a valuation allowance in a future year affect the book effective tax rate for that year?

Decision Making

23. RadioCo, a domestic corporation, owns 100% of TVCo, a manufacturing facility in Ireland. TVCo has no operations or activities in the United States. The U.S. tax rate is 35%, and the Irish tax rate is 10%. For the current year, RadioCo earns $400,000 in taxable income. TVCo earns $800,000 in taxable income from its operations, pays $80,000 in taxes to Ireland, and makes no distributions to RadioCo. Determine RadioCo's effective tax rate for book purposes with and without the permanent reinvestment assumption of APB 23. Under what conditions should RadioCo adopt APB 23 for TVCo's earnings?

Issue ID

24. Shannon, the CFO of TechCo, Inc., has used APB 23 to avoid reporting any U.S. deferred tax expense on $30 million of the earnings of TechCo's foreign subsidiaries. All of these subsidiaries operate in countries with lower tax rates than the United States. Shannon wants to bring home $10 million in profits from these foreign subsidiaries in the form of dividends. How will this profit repatriation affect TechCo's book effective tax rate?

Issue ID

25. Brian, the CFO of AutoCo, Inc., has used APB 23 to avoid reporting any U.S. deferred tax expense on $60 million of the earnings of AutoCo's foreign subsidiaries. All of these subsidiaries operate in countries with higher tax rates than the ones that apply under U.S. law. Brian wants to bring home $20 million in profits from these foreign subsidiaries in the form of dividends. How will this profit repatriation affect AutoCo's book effective tax rate?

26. Rufus Enterprises acquires another corporation. This acquisition created $10 million of goodwill for both book and tax purposes. The $10 million in goodwill is amortized over 15 years for tax purposes but is not deductible for book purposes unless impaired. Will this book-tax difference create a permanent or temporary difference? *Extender*

27. Lydia is the CFO of FarmTime, Inc. FarmTime's tax advisers have recommended two tax planning ideas that will each provide $8 million of current-year cash tax savings. One idea is based on a timing difference and is expected to reverse 20 years in the future. The other idea creates a permanent difference that will never reverse. Determine whether these ideas will allow FarmTime to reduce its reported book income tax expense for the current year. Illustrate your preference for one planning strategy over the other in a spreadsheet. Which idea will you recommend to Lydia? *Decision Making*

28. Sam Taggart, the CEO of Skate, Inc., has reviewed Skate's tax return and its financial statement. He notices that both the Schedule M–3 and the rate reconciliation in the income tax note provide a reconciliation of tax information. However, he sees very little correspondence between the two schedules. Outline the differences between these two schedules in a letter to Sam. Skate's address is 499 Lucerne Avenue, Ocala, FL 34482. *Communications*

29. RoofCo reports total book income before taxes of $20 million and a total tax expense of $8 million. FloorCo reports book income before taxes of $30 million and a total tax expense of $12 million. The companies' breakdown between current and deferred tax expense (benefit) is as follows.

	RoofCo	FloorCo
Current tax expense	$ 8.2	$12.4
Deferred tax benefit	(0.2)	(0.4)
Total tax expense	$ 8.0	$12.0

RoofCo's deferred tax benefit is from a deferred tax asset created because of differences in depreciation methods for equipment. FloorCo's deferred tax benefit is created by the expected future use of a net operating loss. Compare and contrast these two companies' effective tax rates. How are they similar, and how are they different?

30. LawnCo and TreeCo are both in the same industry, and both report a 32% effective tax rate. Their book income and current, deferred, and total tax expense are reported below. *Communications*

	LawnCo	TreeCo
Book income before tax	$500,000	$650,000
Current tax expense	$310,000	$ 17,000
Deferred tax expense (benefit)	(150,000)	191,000
Total tax expense	$160,000	$208,000
Effective tax rate	32%	32%

ShrubCo is a competitor of both these companies. Prepare a memo to Laura Collins, VP-Taxation, outlining your analysis of the two companies' effective tax rates, using only the information above.

31. RedCo and BlueCo are both in the same industry and report the following tax rate reconciliations in their tax footnotes.

	RedCo	BlueCo
Hypothetical tax at U.S. rate	35.0%	35.0%
State and local taxes	3.2	3.9
Foreign income taxed at less than U.S. rate	(12.3)	(7.8)
Tax court settlement on disputed tax issue	5.3	—
Effective tax rate	31.2%	31.1%

Compare and contrast the effective tax rates of these two companies.

BRIDGE *Discipline*

1. Using publicly available Web resources, locate summary financial information for two companies in the same industry. Compare and contrast the following items across the two companies: debt-to-equity ratio, return on assets, return on equity, inventory turnover ratio, and effective tax rate.

RESEARCH PROBLEMS

Internet *Activity*

Use the tax resources of the Internet to address the following questions. Do not restrict your search to the World Wide Web, but include a review of newsgroups and general reference materials, practitioner sites and resources, primary sources of the tax law, chat rooms and discussion groups, and other opportunities.

Communications

Research Problem 1. Locate the Web page of Citizens for Tax Justice and find the report "Corporate Income Taxes in the 1990s." Using this report, identify the effective tax rates of three companies, as estimated in the report. Also locate the financial statements of these three companies (using the companies' Web sites or the SEC's Web site **http://www.sec.gov**). From the financial statement income tax note, identify the reported effective tax rate from the rate reconciliation for each company. Compare and contrast the financial statement effective tax rates with those estimated by the Citizens for Tax Justice report. Summarize this information in an e-mail to your instructor.

Communications

Research Problem 2. Locate the most recent financial statements of two companies in the same industry using the companies' Web sites or the SEC's Web site (**http://www.sec.gov**). Perform a benchmarking analysis of the two companies' effective tax rates, components of the effective tax rate reconciliation, levels of deferred tax assets and liabilities, and other relevant data. Summarize this information in an e-mail to your instructor.

Communications

Research Problem 3. Search the news archives available on the Web and locate four articles addressing the controversy over whether stock options should be included as a compensation expense on a company's income statement. Summarize these articles and write one or two paragraphs stating your own position on the FASB mandated reporting of stock options as an expense. Send your report as an e-mail to your instructor.

Communications

Research Problem 4. Both Schedule M–1 and Schedule M–3 of Form 1120 provide a reconciliation of book income to taxable income. Locate the instructions for both these schedules at the IRS Web site (**http://www.irs.gov**) and review the definition of book income for purposes of the two schedules. Identify three specific items included in the Schedule M–3 determination of book income and discuss why these items are useful in determining a corporation's appropriate book income to use in the reconciliation. Send your comments as an e-mail to your instructor.

http://wft.swlearning.com

PART 2

Structure of the Federal Income Tax

Part II introduces the components of the basic tax model. The gross income component, including the effect of exclusions, the accounting period, and the accounting method, are presented. This presentation is followed by an analysis of business deductions, including deductions that are allowed, deductions that are disallowed, and the effect of the accounting period and the accounting method on the timing of deductions. Included in the presentation are the deduction for charitable contributions, research and experimental expenditures, production activities, interest and taxes, cost recovery, amortization, and depletion. Part II concludes with a discussion of losses. Included are coverage on bad debts, casualty and theft losses, net operating losses, the tax shelter issue, the at-risk limitations, and the passive activity loss limitations.

http://wft.swlearning.com

Gross Income

LEARNING OBJECTIVES

After completing Chapter 4, you should be able to:

LO.1

Explain the concepts of gross income and realization and distinguish between the economic, accounting, and tax concepts of gross income.

LO.2

Understand when the cash, accrual, and hybrid methods of accounting are used and how they are applied.

LO.3

Identify who should pay the tax on an item of income.

LO.4

Understand that statutory authority is required to exclude an item from gross income.

LO.5

Apply the Internal Revenue Code provisions on loans made at below-market interest rates.

LO.6

Determine the extent to which receipts can be excluded under the tax benefit rule.

LO.7

Understand the Internal Revenue Code provision that excludes interest on state and local government obligations from gross income.

LO.8

Use the Internal Revenue Code's exclusion of leasehold improvements from gross income.

LO.9

Determine the extent to which life insurance proceeds are excluded from gross income.

LO.10

Describe the circumstances under which income must be reported from the discharge of indebtedness.

LO.11

Describe the tax consequences of property transactions.

OUTLINE

TAX *Talk*

The first nine pages of the Internal Revenue Code define income. The remaining 1,100 pages spin the web of exceptions and preferences.

—Warren G. Magnuson

Mary purchases a number of computer components from a supplier for $500. She hires an employee to assemble them into a computer that has a market value of $1,100. Keith, one of Mary's long-time customers, has been especially effective in sending new business to Mary's operation, so Mary sells the computer to Keith for $950. Direct labor costs for the computer totaled $150, and an allocable share of Mary's overhead for the current sale was determined to be $40.

Keith called in his order on December 15, 2006. Because he was going to be out of town, Keith told Mary to bring the computer to his office on January 6, 2007. The computer was fully assembled on December 22, 2006, but Mary delivered the machine on January 6, 2007.

Mary does business in a storefront in the local strip mall, using the name Home-Made Computers. Home-Made is a partnership, owned equally by Mary and her sister Sherry.

Some variation of this simple scenario is carried out millions of times every day in today's global economy. Several broad tax questions, such as the following, arise as a result of these transactions.

- What: What is income?
- When: In which tax period is the income recognized?
- Who: Who is taxed on the income?

The Tax Formula

The basic income tax formula was introduced in Chapter 1 and summarized in Figure 1-1. This chapter, together with Chapters 5 through 8, examines the elements of this formula in detail. However, before embarking on a detailed study of the income tax, a brief introduction of each component of the tax formula is provided below as an overview.

Components of the Tax Formula

Income (Broadly Conceived). This includes all of the taxpayer's income, both taxable and nontaxable. Although it is essentially equivalent to gross receipts, it does not include a return of capital or borrowed funds.

Exclusions. For various reasons, Congress has chosen to exclude certain types of income from the income tax base. The principal income exclusions that apply to all entities (e.g., life insurance proceeds received by reason of death of the insured and state and local bond interest) are discussed later in this chapter, while exclusions that are unique to individuals are addressed in Chapters 16 and 17.

Gross Income. Section 61 of the Internal Revenue Code provides the following definition of **gross income**.

> Except as otherwise provided in this subtitle, gross income means all income from whatever source derived.

This language is derived from the Sixteenth Amendment to the Constitution. The "except as otherwise provided" phrase refers to exclusions.

Supreme Court decisions have made it clear that *all* sources of income are subject to tax unless Congress specifically excludes the type of income received.

> The starting point in all cases dealing with the question of the scope of what is included in "gross income" begins with the basic premise that the purpose of Congress was to use the full measure of its taxing power.[1]

While it is clear that income is to be broadly construed, the statutory law fails to provide a satisfactory definition of the term and lists only a small set of items that are specifically included in income, including:

- Compensation for services.
- Business income.
- Gains from sales and other disposition of property.
- Interest.
- Dividends.
- Rents and royalties.
- Certain income arising from discharge of indebtedness.
- Income from partnerships.

Deductions. Generally, all ordinary and necessary trade or business expenses are deductible by taxpaying entities. Such expenses include the cost of goods sold, salaries, wages, operating expenses (such as rent and utilities), research and development expenditures, interest, taxes, depreciation, amortization, and depletion.

As noted in Chapter 1, individuals can use two categories of deductions—deductions *for* AGI and deductions *from* AGI. In addition, individuals are unique among taxpaying entities in that they are permitted to deduct a variety of personal expenses (i.e., expenses unrelated to business or investment), they are allowed a standard deduction if this amount exceeds the deductible personal expenses, and they are allowed a deduction for personal and dependency exemptions.

Determining the Tax. Taxable income is determined by subtracting deductions (after any applicable limitations) from gross income. The tax rates (located inside the front cover of this text) are then applied to determine the tax. Finally, tax prepayments (such as Federal income tax withholding on salaries and estimated tax

[1] *James v. U.S.*, 61–1 USTC ¶9449, 7 AFTR2d 1361, 81 S.Ct. 1052 (USSC, 1961).

FROM "ALL SOURCES" IS A BROAD DEFINITION

When § 61 refers to "income from whatever source derived," the taxing authorities are reaching far beyond the borders of the United States. Although one interpretation of "source" in this context is type of income (wages, interest, etc.), a broader interpretation revolves around the place where the income is generated. In this context, citizens and residents of the United States are subject to taxation on income earned from sources both inside and outside the country. This "worldwide income" tax base can cause potential double taxation problems, with other countries also taxing income earned within their borders, but mechanisms such as the foreign tax credit can alleviate these tax burdens.

Recently, some U.S. corporations have relocated to other countries to avoid the higher U.S. tax rates on income earned abroad.

payments) and a wide variety of credits are subtracted from the tax to determine the amount due to the Federal government or the refund due to the taxpayer.

LO.1

Explain the concepts of gross income and realization and distinguish between the economic, accounting, and tax concepts of gross income.

Gross Income—What Is It?

Economic and Accounting Concepts of Income

As noted above, Congress failed to provide in the Code a clear definition of income. Instead, it was left to the judicial and administrative branches of government to thrash out the meaning of income. As the income tax law developed, two competing models of income were considered by these agencies: economic income and accounting income.

The term **income** is used in the Code but is defined very broadly. Early in the history of our tax laws, the courts were required to interpret "the commonly understood meaning of the term which must have been in the minds of the people when they adopted the Sixteenth Amendment."[2]

Economists measure income (**economic income**) by determining the change (increase or decrease) in the fair market value of the entity's net assets from the beginning to the end of the year. This focus on change in *net worth* as a measure of income (or loss) requires no disposition of assets. For *individual* taxpayers, one adds the value of the year's personal consumption of goods and services (e.g., food, the rental value of owner-occupied housing, etc.).[3]

EXAMPLE 1

Helen's economic income is calculated by comparing her net worth at the end of the year (December 31) with her net worth at the beginning of the year (January 1) and adding her personal consumption.

Fair market value of Helen's assets on December 31	$220,000	
Less liabilities on December 31	(40,000)	
Net worth on December 31		$ 180,000
Fair market value of Helen's assets on January 1	$200,000	
Less liabilities on January 1	(80,000)	
Net worth on January 1		(120,000)
Increase in net worth		$ 60,000

[2] *Merchants Loan and Trust Co. v. Smietanka*, 1 USTC ¶42, 3 AFTR 3102, 41 S.Ct. 386 (USSC, 1921).

[3] See Henry C. Simons, *Personal Income Taxation* (Chicago: University of Chicago Press, 1933), Chapters 2–3.

Consumption			
Food, clothing, and other personal expenditures	$ 25,000		
Imputed rental value of the home Helen owns and occupies	12,000		
Total consumption		37,000	
Economic income		$ 97,000	■

The tax law relies to some extent on net worth as a measure of income.[6] Potentially, anything that increases net worth is income, and anything that decreases net worth is deductible (if permitted by statute). Thus, *windfall income* such as buried treasure found in one's backyard is taxable under the theory that net worth has been increased.[7] Likewise, a lender does *not* recognize gross income on receipt of loan principal repayments. The lender's investment simply changes from a loan receivable to cash, so net worth does not change.

Because the strict application of a tax based on economic income would require taxpayers to determine the value of their assets annually, compliance would be burdensome. Controversies between taxpayers and the IRS would inevitably arise under an economic approach to income determination because of the subjective nature of valuation in many circumstances. In addition, using market values to determine income for tax purposes could result in liquidity problems. That is, a taxpayer's assets could increase in value but not be easily converted into the cash needed to pay the resulting tax (e.g., increases in the value of commercial real estate).[8] Thus, the IRS, Congress, and the courts have rejected broad application of the economic income concept as impractical.

BRIDGE *Discipline*

Bridge to Financial Accounting

Accountants use a definition of income that relies on the realization principle.[4] **Accounting income** is not recognized until it is realized. For realization to occur:

- An exchange of goods or services must take place between the entity and some independent, external party, and
- The goods or services received by the entity must be capable of being objectively valued.[5]

Thus, an increase in the fair market value of an asset before its sale or other disposition is not sufficient to trigger the recognition of accounting income. Similarly, the imputed savings that arise when an entity creates assets for its own use (e.g., feed grown by a farmer for his or her livestock) do not constitute accounting income because no exchange has occurred.

Business taxpayers often reconcile their annual income computations for financial accounting and tax law purposes. Taxpayers required to prepare audited financial statements must explain in the footnotes to the statements (1) the most important accounting principles used in computing book income, and (2) the most important tax elections and other consequences of the tax law on earnings per share.

[4] See the American Accounting Association Committee Report on the "Realization Concept," *The Accounting Review* (April 1965): 312–322.

[5] Valuation is carried out in the local currency of the reporting entity.

[6] *Comm. v. Glenshaw Glass Co.*, 55–1 USTC ¶9308, 47 AFTR 162, 348 U.S. 426 (USSC, 1955).

[7] *Cesarini v. U.S.*, 69–1 USTC ¶9270, 23 AFTR2d 69–997, 296 F.Supp. 3 (D.Ct. Oh., 1969), *aff'd* 70–2 USTC ¶9509, 26 AFTR2d 70–5107, 428 F.2d 812 (CA–6, 1970); Rev.Rul. 61, 1953–1 C.B. 17.

[8] In Chapter 1, this was identified as a justification of the wherewithal to pay concept.

TAX *in the News* **IF FREE IS TAXED, IT'S NOT FREE**

Major League Baseball teams provide complimentary tickets to any of their players who ask for them. The tickets are given to family members, friends, or even the attendant in the stadium parking lot. The players have been happy to oblige because the tickets haven't cost them anything.

Now, however, the free tickets are disappearing. The reason is that "free is no longer free." The IRS now includes the value of the tickets in the player's gross income. Jimmy Banks, the traveling secretary for the Chicago Cubs, says he saw a tremendous decline in player requests for tickets this past season.

Now a computer system in the Chicago Cubs clubhouse keeps track of the tickets that players request on their laptops. The key to inclusion in gross income is the player's request for tickets rather than whether the tickets are picked up at the stadium ticket office.

As one Cubs player says, "We get paid well. But under this new system, I have to shake my head and tell lots of people . . . I just can't do anything for you."

Source: *Adapted from Joseph A. Reaves, "IRS Stems Flow of Free Tickets,"* USA Today, *September 20, 2005, p. 5C.*

Comparison of the Accounting and Tax Concepts of Income

Although income tax rules frequently parallel financial accounting measurement concepts, differences do exist. Of major significance, for example, is the fact that unearned (prepaid) income received by an accrual basis taxpayer often is taxed in the year of receipt. For financial accounting purposes, such prepayments are not treated as income until earned. Because of this and other differences, many corporations report financial accounting income that is substantially different from the amounts reported for tax purposes.

The Supreme Court provided an explanation for some of the variations between accounting and taxable income in a decision involving inventory and bad debt adjustments.

> The primary goal of financial accounting is to provide useful information to management, shareholders, creditors, and others properly interested; the major responsibility of the accountant is to protect these parties from being misled. The primary goal of the income tax system, in contrast, is the equitable collection of revenue. . . . Consistently with its goals and responsibilities, financial accounting has as its foundation the principle of conservatism, with its corollary that "possible errors in measurement [should] be in the direction of understatement rather than overstatement of net income and net assets." In view of the Treasury's markedly different goals and responsibilities, understatement of income is not destined to be its guiding light. . . .
>
> Financial accounting, in short, is hospitable to estimates, probabilities, and reasonable certainties; the tax law, with its mandate to preserve the revenue, can give no quarter to uncertainty.[9]

Form of Receipt

Gross income is not limited to cash received. "It includes income realized in any form, whether in money, property, or services. Income may be realized [and recognized], therefore, in the form of services, meals, accommodations, stock or other property, as well as in cash."[10]

[9] *Thor Power Tool Co. v. Comm.*, 79–1 USTC ¶9139, 43 AFTR2d 79–362, 99 S.Ct. 773 (USSC, 1979).

[10] Reg. § 1.61–1(a).

EXAMPLE 2

Ostrich Corporation allows Cameron, an employee, to use a company car for his vacation. Cameron realizes income equal to the rental value of the car for the time and mileage. ■

EXAMPLE 3

Plover, Inc., owes $10,000 on a mortgage. The creditor accepts $8,000 in full satisfaction of the debt. Plover realizes income of $2,000 from retiring the debt.[11] ■

EXAMPLE 4

Donna is a CPA specializing in individual tax return preparation. Her neighbor, Jill, is a dentist. Each year, Donna prepares Jill's tax return in exchange for two dental checkups. Jill and Donna both have gross income equal to the fair market value of the services they provide. ■

Year of Inclusion

Taxable Year

The annual accounting period or **taxable year** is a basic component of our tax system. Generally, an entity must use the *calendar year* to report its income. However, a *fiscal year* (a period of 12 months ending on the last day of any month other than December) can be elected if the taxpayer maintains adequate books and records. This fiscal year option generally is not available to partnerships, S corporations, and personal service corporations.

Determining the tax year in which the income is recognized is important for determining the tax consequences of the income.

- With a progressive tax rate system, a taxpayer's marginal tax rate can change from year to year.
- Congress may change the tax rates.
- The relevant rates may change because of a change in the entity's status (e.g., a proprietorship may incorporate).
- Several provisions in the Code depend on the taxpayer's income for the year (e.g., the charitable contribution deduction).

Accounting Methods

LO.2

Understand when the cash, accrual, and hybrid methods of accounting are used and how they are applied.

The year in which an item of income is subject to tax often depends upon the **accounting method** the taxpayer employs. The three primary methods of accounting are (1) the cash receipts and disbursements method, (2) the accrual method, and (3) the hybrid method. Most individuals use the cash receipts and disbursements method of accounting, whereas most corporations use the accrual method. Because the Regulations require the accrual method for determining purchases and sales when inventory is an income-producing factor,[12] some businesses employ a hybrid method that is a combination of the cash and accrual methods.

In addition to these overall accounting methods, a taxpayer may choose to spread the gain from an installment sale of property over the collection period by using the *installment method* of income recognition. Contractors may either spread profits from contracts over the period in which the work is done (the *percentage of completion method*) or defer all profit until the year in which the project is completed (the *completed contract method*) in limited circumstances.[13]

The IRS has the power to prescribe the accounting method to be used by the taxpayer. The IRS holds broad powers to determine if the accounting method used *clearly reflects income.*

[11] Reg. § 1.61–12. See *U.S. v. Kirby Lumber Co.*, 2 USTC ¶814, 10 AFTR 458, 52 S.Ct. 4 (USSC, 1931). Exceptions to this general rule exist.

[12] Reg. § 1.446–1(c)(2)(i).

[13] §§ 453 and 460.

> If no method of accounting has been regularly used by the taxpayer, or *if the method used does not clearly reflect income, the computation of taxable income shall be made under such method as, in the opinion of the Secretary . . . does clearly reflect income.*[14]

Cash Receipts Method. Under the **cash receipts method**, property or services received are included in the taxpayer's gross income in the year of actual or constructive receipt by the taxpayer or agent, regardless of whether the income was earned in that year.[15] The income received need not be reduced to cash in the same year. All that is necessary for income recognition is that property or services received have a fair market value—a cash equivalent.[16] Thus, a cash basis taxpayer that receives a note in payment for services has income in the year of receipt equal to the fair market value of the note. However, a creditor's mere promise to pay (e.g., an account receivable), with no supporting note, is not usually considered to have a fair market value.[17] Thus, the cash basis taxpayer defers income recognition until the account receivable is collected.

EXAMPLE 5

Finch & Thrush, a CPA firm, uses the cash receipts method of accounting. In 2006, the firm performs an audit for Orange Corporation and bills the client for $5,000, which is collected in 2007. In 2006, the firm also performs an audit for Blue Corporation. Because of Blue's precarious financial position, Finch & Thrush requires Blue to issue an $8,000 secured negotiable note in payment of the fee. The note has a fair market value of $6,000. The firm collects $8,000 on the note in 2007. Finch & Thrush has the following gross income for the two years.

	2006	2007
Fair market value of note received from Blue	$6,000	
Cash received		
From Orange on account receivable		$ 5,000
From Blue on note receivable		8,000
Less: Recovery of capital	-0-	(6,000)
Total gross income	$6,000	$ 7,000

■

Generally, a check received is considered a cash equivalent. Thus, a cash basis taxpayer must recognize the income when the check is received. This is true even if the taxpayer receives the check after banking hours.[18]

Certain taxpayers are not permitted to use the cash method of accounting regardless of whether inventories are material. Specifically, the accrual basis must be used to report the income earned by (1) corporations (other than S corporations), (2) partnerships with a corporate partner, and (3) tax shelters.[19] A number of other businesses still can use the cash method.

- A farming business.
- A qualified personal service corporation (e.g., a corporation performing services in health, law, engineering, architecture, accounting, actuarial science, performing arts, or consulting).
- Any entity that is not a tax shelter whose average annual gross receipts for the most recent three-year period are $5 million or less.[20]

[14]§ 446(b).

[15]*Julia A. Strauss*, 2 B.T.A. 598 (1925). The doctrine of *constructive receipt* holds that if income is unqualifiedly available although not physically in the taxpayer's possession, it is subject to the income tax. An example is accrued interest on a savings account. Under the doctrine of constructive receipt, the interest is taxed to a depositor in the year available, rather than the year actually withdrawn. The fact that the depositor uses the cash basis of accounting for tax purposes is irrelevant. Reg. § 1.451–2.

[16]Reg. §§ 1.446–1(a)(3) and (c)(1)(i).

[17]*Bedell v. Comm.*, 1 USTC ¶359, 7 AFTR 8469, 30 F.2d 622 (CA–2, 1929).

[18]*Charles F. Kahler*, 18 T.C. 31 (1952).

[19]§ 448(a).

[20]§ 448(b). Rev.Proc. 2002–28, 2002–1 C.B. 815.

PLANNING *Strategies*

CASH RECEIPTS METHOD

★ **Framework Focus: Income**

Strategy ★ Postpone Recognition of Income to Achieve Tax Deferral.

★ **Framework Focus: Tax Rate**

Strategy ★ Shift Net Income from High-Bracket Years to Low-Bracket Years.

The timing of income from services can often be controlled through the cash method of accounting. The usual lag between billings and collections (e.g., December's billings collected in January) will result in a deferral of some income until the last year of operations. For example, before rendering services, a corporate officer approaching retirement may contract with the corporation to defer a portion of his or her compensation to the lower tax bracket retirement years.

Accrual Method. Under the **accrual method**, an item generally is included in gross income for the year in which it is earned, regardless of when the income is collected. The income is earned when (1) all the events have occurred that fix the right to receive the income and (2) the amount to be received can be determined with reasonable accuracy.[21]

Generally, the taxpayer's rights to the income accrue when title to property passes to the buyer or the services are performed for the customer or client.[22] If the rights to the income have accrued but are subject to a potential refund claim (e.g., under a product warranty), the income is reported in the year of sale, and a deduction is allowed in subsequent years when actual claims accrue.[23]

Where the taxpayer's rights to the income are being contested (e.g., when a contractor fails to meet specifications), gross income is recognized only when payment has been received.[24] If the payment is received before the dispute is settled, however, the court-made **claim of right doctrine** requires the taxpayer to recognize the income in the year of receipt.[25]

EXAMPLE 6

Tangerine Construction, Inc., completes construction of a building in 2006 and presents a bill to the customer. The customer refuses to pay the bill and claims that Tangerine has not met specifications. A settlement with the customer is not reached until 2007. No income accrues to Tangerine until 2007. Alternatively, if the customer pays for the work and then files suit for damages, Tangerine cannot defer the income, and it is taxable in 2006. ■

EXAMPLE 7

Assume the same facts as in Example 5, except that Finch & Thrush uses the accrual basis of accounting. The firm must recognize $13,000 ($8,000 + $5,000) income in 2006, the year its rights to the income accrue. ■

Hybrid Method. The Regulations require that the accrual method be used for determining sales and cost of goods sold. To simplify record keeping, some taxpayers account for inventory using the accrual method and use the cash method for all other income and expense items. This approach, called the **hybrid method**, is used primarily by small businesses when inventory is an income-producing factor.

[21] Reg. § 1.451–1(a).

[22] *Lucas v. North Texas Lumber Co.*, 2 USTC ¶484, 8 AFTR 10276, 50 S.Ct. 184 (USSC, 1930).

[23] *Brown v. Helvering*, 4 USTC ¶1222, 13 AFTR 851, 54 S.Ct. 356 (USSC, 1933).

[24] *Burnet v. Sanford and Brooks*, 2 USTC ¶636, 9 AFTR 603, 51 S.Ct. 150 (USSC, 1931).

[25] *North American Oil Consolidated Co. v. Burnet*, 3 USTC ¶943, 11 AFTR 16, 52 S.Ct. 613 (USSC, 1932).

Special Rules for Cash Basis Taxpayers

Constructive Receipt. Income that has not actually been received by the taxpayer is taxed as though it had been received—the income is constructively received—under the following conditions.

- The amount is made readily available to the taxpayer.
- The taxpayer's actual receipt is not subject to substantial limitations or restrictions.[26]

The rationale for the **constructive receipt** doctrine is that if the income is available, the taxpayer should not be allowed to postpone income recognition. For instance, a taxpayer is not permitted to defer income for December services by refusing to accept payment until January.

EXAMPLE 8

Rob, a physician, conducts his medical practice as a sole proprietorship. Rob is also a member of a barter club. In 2006, Rob provided medical care for other club members and earned 3,000 points. Each point entitles him to $1 in goods and services sold by other members of the club; the points can be used at any time. In 2007, Rob exchanged his points for a new high definition TV. Rob recognizes $3,000 of gross income in 2006 when the 3,000 points were credited to his account.[27] ■

EXAMPLE 9

On December 31, an employer issued a bonus check to an employee but asked her to hold it for a few days until the company could make deposits to cover the check. The income was not constructively received on December 31 since the issuer did not have sufficient funds in its account to pay the debt.[28] ■

EXAMPLE 10

Mauve, Inc., an S corporation, owned interest coupons that matured on December 31. The coupons can be converted to cash at any bank at maturity. Thus, the income was constructively received on December 31, even though Mauve failed to cash in the coupons until the following year.[29] ■

EXAMPLE 11

Flamingo Company mails dividend checks on December 31, 2006. The checks will not be received by the shareholders until January. The shareholders do not realize gross income until 2007.[30] ■

The constructive receipt doctrine does not reach income that the taxpayer is not yet entitled to receive even though the taxpayer could have contracted to receive the income at an earlier date.

EXAMPLE 12

Murphy offers to pay Peach Corporation (a cash basis taxpayer) $100,000 for land in December 2006. Peach Corporation refuses but offers to sell the land to Murphy on January 1, 2007, when the corporation will be in a lower tax bracket. If Murphy accepts Peach's offer, the gain is taxed to Peach in 2007 when the sale is completed.[31] ■

Original Issue Discount. Lenders frequently make loans that require a payment at maturity of more than the amount of the original loan. The difference between the amount due at maturity and the amount of the original loan is actually interest but is referred to as **original issue discount**. Under the general rules of tax accounting, a cash basis lender would not report the original issue discount as

[26] Reg. § 1.451–2(a).
[27] Rev.Rul. 80–52, 1980–1 C.B. 100.
[28] *L. M. Fischer*, 14 T.C. 792 (1950).
[29] Reg. § 1.451–2(b).
[30] Reg. § 1.451–2(b).
[31] *Cowden v. Comm.*, 61–1 USTC ¶9382, 7 AFTR2d 1160, 289 F.2d 20 (CA–5, 1961).

TAX in the News **CONGRESS RESCUES LOTTERY WINNERS FROM CONSTRUCTIVE RECEIPT PROBLEMS**

Under the general rules of constructive receipt, a lottery winner who elected to receive the winnings in installments could face horrendous tax problems. If the winner had the right to receive the entire amount, but elected to be paid in installments, tax was due on all the amounts to be received in the future as well as the amount received currently. Frequently, the winner made the election without being aware of the tax consequences. To protect poorly advised, or unadvised, lottery winners, Congress changed § 451(h) so that the constructive receipt doctrine will not apply to "qualified prizes," a term crafted specifically to address the lottery and prize winner's situation. Thus, lottery winnings can be received in installments and included in gross income as the installments are actually received.

interest income until the year the amount is collected, although an accrual basis borrower would deduct the interest as it is earned. However, the Code puts the lender and borrower on parity by requiring that the original issue discount be reported when it is earned, regardless of the taxpayer's accounting method.[32] The *interest earned* is calculated by the effective interest rate method.

EXAMPLE 13

On January 1, 2006, Blue and White, a cash basis partnership, pays $82,645 for a 24-month certificate of deposit. The certificate is priced to yield 10% (the effective interest rate) with interest compounded annually. No interest is paid until maturity, when Blue and White receives $100,000. Thus, the partnership's gross income from the certificate is $17,355 ($100,000 – $82,645). Blue and White calculates income earned each year as follows.

2006: (0.10 × $82,645) =	$ 8,264
2007: [0.10($82,645 + $8,264)] =	9,091
	$17,355

■

The original issue discount rules do not apply to U.S. savings bonds or to obligations with a maturity date of one year or less from the date of issue.[33]

Amounts Received under an Obligation to Repay. The receipt of funds with an obligation to repay that amount in the future is the essence of borrowing. The taxpayer's assets and liabilities increase by the same amount, so no income is realized when the borrowed funds are received.

EXAMPLE 14

A landlord receives a damage deposit from a tenant. The landlord does not recognize income until the deposit is forfeited because the landlord has an obligation to repay the deposit if no damage occurs.[34] However, if the deposit is in fact a prepayment of rent, it is taxed in the year of receipt. ■

Special Rules for Accrual Basis Taxpayers

Prepaid Income. For financial reporting purposes, advance payments received from customers are reflected as prepaid income and as a liability of the seller. For tax purposes, however, the prepaid income often is taxed in the year of receipt.

EXAMPLE 15

In December 2006, a company pays its January 2007 rent of $1,000. The accrual basis landlord must include the $1,000 in 2006 gross income for tax purposes, although the unearned rent income is reported as a liability on the landlord's balance sheet for December 31, 2006. ■

[32] §§ 1272(a)(3) and 1273(a).

[33] § 1272(a)(2).

[34] *John Mantell*, 17 T.C. 1143 (1952).

Deferral of Advance Payments for Goods. Generally, an accrual basis taxpayer can elect to defer recognition of income from advance payments for goods if the method of accounting for the sale is the same for tax and financial reporting purposes.[35]

EXAMPLE 16

Brown Company ships goods only after payment for the goods has been received. In December 2006, Brown receives $10,000 for goods that are not shipped until January 2007. Brown can elect to report the income in 2007 for tax purposes, assuming the company reports the income in 2007 for financial reporting purposes. ■

Deferral of Advance Payments for Services. An accrual basis taxpayer can defer recognition of income for *advance payments for services* to be performed after the end of the tax year of receipt.[36] The portion of the advance payment that relates to services performed in the tax year of receipt is included in gross income in the tax year of receipt. The portion of the advance payment that relates to services to be performed after the tax year of receipt is included in gross income in the tax year following the tax year of receipt of the advance payment.

EXAMPLE 17

Yellow Corporation, an accrual basis calendar year taxpayer, sells its services under 12-month, 24-month, and 36-month contracts. The corporation provides services to each customer every month. On May 1, 2006, Yellow Corporation sold the following customer contracts.

Length of Contract	Total Proceeds
12 months	$3,000
24 months	4,800
36 months	7,200

Yellow may defer until 2007 all of the income that will be earned after 2006.

Length of Contract	Income Recorded in 2006	Income Recorded in 2007
12 months	$2,000 ($3,000 × 8/12)	$1,000 ($3,000 × 4/12)
24 months	1,600 ($4,800 × 8/24)	3,200 ($4,800 × 16/24)
36 months	1,600 ($7,200 × 8/36)	5,600 ($7,200 × 28/36)

■

Advance payments for prepaid rent or prepaid interest always are taxed in the year of receipt.

PLANNING *Strategies*

PREPAID INCOME

★ Framework Focus: Income

Strategy ★ Postpone Recognition of Income to Achieve Tax Deferral.

The accrual basis taxpayer who receives advance payments from customers should structure the transactions using the rules discussed above to avoid having to pay tax on income before the time the income is actually earned. In addition, both cash and accrual basis taxpayers can sometimes defer income by stipulating that the payments are deposits rather than prepaid income. For example, a landlord might consider requiring an equivalent damage deposit rather than prepayment of the last month's rent.

[35]Reg. § 1.451–5(b). See Reg. § 1.451–5(c) for exceptions to this deferral opportunity.

[36]Rev.Proc. 2004–34, 2004–1 C.B. 991.

Income Sources

LO.3

Identify who should pay the tax on an item of income.

Personal Services

It is a well-established principle of taxation that income from personal services must be included in the gross income of the person who performs the services. This principle was first established in a Supreme Court decision, *Lucas v. Earl.*[37] Mr. Earl entered into a binding agreement with his wife under which Mrs. Earl was to receive one-half of Mr. Earl's salary. Justice Holmes used the celebrated **fruit and tree metaphor** to explain that the fruit (income) must be attributed to the tree from which it came (Mr. Earl's services). A mere **assignment of income** does not shift the liability for the tax.

Services of an Employee. Services performed by an employee for the employer's customers are considered performed by the employer. Thus, the employer is taxed on the income from the services provided to the customer, and the employee is taxed on any compensation received from the employer.[38]

EXAMPLE 18

Dr. Carey incorporates her medical practice and enters into a contract to work for the corporation for a salary. All patients contract to receive their services from the corporation, and those services are provided through the corporation's employee, Dr. Carey. The corporation must include the patients' fees in its gross income. Dr. Carey must include her salary in her gross income. The corporation is allowed a deduction for a reasonable salary paid to Dr. Carey. ■

Income from Property

Income earned from property (interest, dividends, rent) must be included in the gross income of the owner of the property. If a shareholder clips interest coupons from bonds shortly before the interest payment date and transfers the coupons to his or her solely owned corporation, the interest still is taxed to the shareholder. Similarly, a parent who assigns rents from income-producing property to a subsidiary is taxed on the rent, since the parent retains ownership of the property.[39]

Often income-producing property is transferred after income from the property has accrued but before the income is recognized under the transferor's method of accounting. The IRS and the courts have developed rules to allocate the income between the transferor and the transferee. These allocation rules are addressed below. Other allocation rules address income in community property states.

DIGGING DEEPER 1

Find more information on this topic at our Web site: ***http://wft-entities.swlearning.com.***

Interest. According to the IRS, interest accrues daily. Therefore, the interest for the period that includes the date of the transfer is allocated between the transferor and the transferee based on the number of days during the period that each owned the property.

EXAMPLE 19

Floyd, a cash basis taxpayer, gives his son, Seth, bonds with a face amount of $10,000 and an 8% stated annual interest rate, payable December 31. The gift is made on January 31, 2006. Floyd recognizes $68 in interest income (8% × $10,000 × 31/365). Seth recognizes $732 in interest income ($800 – $68). ■

[37] 2 USTC ¶496, 8 AFTR 10287, 50 S.Ct. 241 (USSC, 1930).

[38] *Sargent v. Comm.*, 91–1 USTC ¶50,168, 67 AFTR2d 91–718, 929 F.2d 1252 (CA–8, 1991).

[39] *Galt v. Comm.*, 54–2 USTC ¶9457, 46 AFTR 633, 216 F.2d 41 (CA–7, 1954); *Helvering v. Horst*, 40–2 USTC ¶9787, 24 AFTR 1058, 61 S.Ct. 144 (USSC, 1940).

TAX FACT

How Much and What Type of Income?

Of the 130 million individual income tax returns filed for the 2002 tax year, 85 percent included wage or salary income, and about half included some amount of taxable interest income. But except for these two categories, no other type of income was found in even a quarter of the returns filed. Sales of business assets were found on fewer than 1 percent of the returns, and about 6 percent of the returns included flow-through income or loss from partnerships and S corporations. Capital gains showed up on about a quarter of the returns, but only when distributions from mutual fund investments were included.

When the transferor recognizes gross income from the property depends upon the method of accounting and the manner in which the property was transferred. In the case of a gift of income-producing property, the donor's share of the accrued income is recognized at the time it would have been recognized had the donor continued to own the property.[40] If the transfer is a sale, however, the transferor recognizes the accrued income at the time of the sale because the accrued interest is included in the sales proceeds.

EXAMPLE 20

Assume the same facts as in the preceding example, except that the interest payable on December 31 is not actually or constructively received by the bondholders until January 3, 2007. As a cash basis taxpayer, Floyd generally does not recognize interest income until it is received. If Floyd had continued to own the bonds, he would have included the interest in his gross income in 2007, the year he would have received it. Therefore, Floyd includes the $68 accrued income in his gross income as of January 3, 2007.

Further assume that Floyd sells identical bonds on the date of the gift. The bonds sell for $9,900, including accrued interest. On January 31, 2006, Floyd recognizes the accrued interest of $68 on the bonds sold. Thus, the selling price of the bonds is $9,832 ($9,900 – $68). ■

Dividends. A corporation is taxed on its earnings, and the shareholders are taxed on the dividends paid to them from the corporation's after-tax earnings. The dividend can take the form of an actual dividend or a constructive dividend (e.g., shareholder use of corporate assets).

Partial relief from the double taxation of dividends has been provided in that dividends generally are taxed at the same marginal rate that is applicable to a net capital gain.[41] Individuals subject to the 25, 28, 33, or 35 percent marginal tax rate pay a 15 percent tax on qualified dividends received. Individuals otherwise subject to the 10 or 15 percent marginal tax rate pay only a 5 percent tax on qualified dividends received. Thus, qualified dividends receive favorable treatment as compared to interest income.

Note that qualified dividends are not treated as capital gains in the gains and losses netting process; thus, they are *not* reduced by capital losses. Qualified dividend income merely is taxed at the rates that would apply to the taxpayer if he or she had an excess of net long-term capital gain over net short-term capital loss.

Because the beneficial tax rate is intended to mitigate double taxation, only certain dividends are eligible for the beneficial treatment. Excluded are certain dividends from foreign corporations, dividends from tax-exempt entities, and dividends that do not satisfy the holding period requirement.

To satisfy the holding period requirement, the stock on which the dividend is paid must have been held for more than 60 days during the 120-day period

[40] Rev.Rul. 72–312, 1972–1 C.B. 22.

[41] § 1(h)(11).

WHICH FOREIGN DIVIDENDS GET THE 15% RATE?

A dividend from a foreign corporation is eligible for qualified dividend status only if one of the following requirements is met: (1) the foreign corporation's stock is traded on an established U.S. securities market, or (2) the foreign corporation is eligible for the benefits of a comprehensive income tax treaty or information-sharing agreement between its country of incorporation and the United States.

beginning 60 days before the ex-dividend date.[42] The purpose of this requirement is to prevent the taxpayer from buying the stock shortly before the dividend is paid, receiving the dividend, and then selling the stock at a loss (a capital loss) after the stock goes ex-dividend. A stock's price often declines after the stock goes ex-dividend.

EXAMPLE 21

Green Corporation pays a dividend of $1.50 on each share of its common stock. Madison and Daniel, two unrelated shareholders, each own 1,000 shares of the stock. Consequently, each receives $1,500 (1,000 shares × $1.50). Assume Daniel satisfies the 60/120-day holding period rule, but Madison does not. The $1,500 Daniel receives is subject to preferential 15%/5% treatment. The $1,500 Madison receives, however, is not. Because Madison did not comply with the holding period rule, her dividend is not a *qualified dividend* and is taxed at ordinary income rates. ■

EXAMPLE 22

Assume that both Madison and Daniel in Example 21 are in the 35% tax bracket. Consequently, Madison pays a tax of $525 (35% × $1,500) on her dividend, while Daniel pays a tax of $225 (15% × $1,500) on his. The $300 saving that Daniel enjoys underscores the advantages of a qualified dividend. ■

Unlike interest, dividends do not accrue on a daily basis because the declaration of a dividend is at the discretion of the corporation's board of directors. Generally, dividends are taxed to the person who is entitled to receive them—the shareholder of record as of the corporation's record date.[43] Thus, if a taxpayer sells stock after a dividend has been declared but before the record date, the dividend generally will be taxed to the purchaser.

If a donor makes a gift of stock to someone (e.g., a family member) after the declaration date but before the record date, the Tax Court has held that the donor does not shift the dividend income to the donee. The *fruit* has sufficiently ripened as of the declaration date to tax the dividend income to the donor of the stock.[44] In a similar set of facts, the Fifth Circuit Court of Appeals concluded that the dividend income should be included in the gross income of the donee (the owner at the record date). In this case, the taxpayer gave stock to a qualified charity (a charitable contribution) after the declaration date and before the record date.[45]

Find more information on this topic at our Web site: ***http://wft-entities.swlearning.com.***

DIGGING DEEPER 2

EXAMPLE 23

On June 20, the board of directors of Black Corporation declares a $10 per share dividend. The dividend is payable on June 30, to shareholders of record on June 25. As of June 20, Kathleen owns 200 shares of Black Corporation's stock. On June 21, Kathleen sells 100 of the

[42] The ex-dividend date is the date following the record date on which the corporation finalizes the list of shareholders who will receive the dividends.

[43] Reg. § 1.61–9(c). The record date is the cutoff for determining the shareholders who are entitled to receive the dividend.

[44] *M. G. Anton*, 34 T.C. 842 (1960).

[45] *Caruth Corporation v. U.S.*, 89–1 USTC ¶9172, 63 AFTR2d 89–716, 865 F.2d 644 (CA–5, 1989).

TAX FACT

Business Income and Loss

Sole proprietors reporting net business income on Form 1040 constitute almost 15 percent of all returns filed. Flow-through income from partnerships and S corporations is found on only one-third as many returns, but the income reported is essentially the same in nominal dollars. Flow-through income has increased dramatically and consistently since the 1987 tax year, when changes in marginal tax rates shifted to favor individual rather than C corporation taxpayers. It will be interesting to see what effect, if any, the beneficial tax rates for qualified dividends will have on the choice of the form of business entity.

shares to Jon for their fair market value and gives 100 of the shares to Andrew (her son). Both Jon and Andrew are shareholders of record as of June 25. Jon (the purchaser) is taxed on $1,000 since he is entitled to receive the dividend. However, Kathleen (the donor) is taxed on the $1,000 received by Andrew (the donee) because the gift was made after the declaration date of the dividend. ■

Income Received by an Agent

Income received by the taxpayer's agent is considered to be received by the taxpayer. A cash basis principal must recognize the income at the time it is received by the agent.[46]

EXAMPLE 24

Longhorn, Inc., a cash basis corporation, delivers cattle to the auction barn in late December. The auctioneer, acting as the corporation's agent, sells the cattle and collects the proceeds in December. The auctioneer does not pay Longhorn until the following January. The corporation must include the sales proceeds in its gross income in the year the auctioneer received the funds. ■

PLANNING *Strategies*

TECHNIQUES FOR REDUCING GROSS INCOME

★ Framework Focus: Income

Strategy ★ Avoid Income Recognition.

★ Framework Focus: Tax Rate

Strategy ★ Shift Net Income from High-Bracket Years to Low-Bracket Years.

★ Framework Focus: Income

Strategy ★ Postpone Recognition of Income to Achieve Tax Deferral.

NONTAXABLE ECONOMIC BENEFITS

Home ownership is the prime example of economic income from capital that is not subject to tax. If the taxpayer uses his or her capital to purchase investments, but pays rent on a personal residence, the taxpayer would pay the rent from after-tax income. However, if the taxpayer purchases a personal residence instead of the investments, he or she would give up gross income from the forgone investments in exchange for the rent savings. The savings in rent enjoyed as a result of owning the home are not subject to tax. Thus, the homeowner will have substituted nontaxable for taxable income.

[46]Rev.Rul. 79–379, 1979–2 C.B. 204.

TAX DEFERRAL

General Since deferred taxes are tantamount to interest-free loans from the government, the deferral of taxes is a worthy goal of the tax planner. However, the tax planner must also consider the tax rates for the years the income is shifted from and to. For example, a one-year deferral of income from a year in which a corporate taxpayer's tax rate was 25 percent to a year in which the tax rate will be 35 percent would not be advisable if the taxpayer expects to earn less than a 10 percent after-tax return on the deferred tax dollars.

The taxpayer often can defer the recognition of income from appreciated property by postponing the event triggering realization (the final closing on a sale or an exchange of property). If the taxpayer needs cash, obtaining a loan by using the appreciated property as collateral may be the least costly alternative. When the taxpayer anticipates reinvesting the proceeds, a sale may be inadvisable.

EXAMPLE 25

Ira owns 100 shares of Pigeon Company common stock with a cost of $20,000 and a fair market value of $50,000. Although the stock's value has increased substantially in the past three years, Ira thinks the growth days are over. If he sells the Pigeon stock, Ira will invest the proceeds from the sale in other common stock. If Ira's marginal tax rate on the sale is 15%, he will have only $45,500 [$50,000 − .15($50,000 − $20,000)] to reinvest. The alternative investment must substantially outperform Pigeon in the future in order for the sale to be beneficial. ■

Selection of Investments Because no tax is due until a gain has been recognized, the law favors investments that yield appreciation rather than annual income.

EXAMPLE 26

Vera can buy a corporate bond or an acre of land for $10,000. The bond pays $1,000 of interest (10%) each year, and Vera expects the land to increase in value 10% each year for the next 10 years. She is in the 40% (combined Federal and state) tax bracket for ordinary income and 26% for qualifying capital gains. If the bond would mature or the land would be sold in 10 years and Vera would reinvest the interest at a 10% before-tax return, she would accumulate the following amount at the end of 10 years.

		Bond	Land
Original investment		$10,000	$10,000
Annual income	$1,000		
Less tax	(400)		
	$ 600		
Compound amount reinvested for 10 years at 6% after-tax	×13.18	7,908	
Future value		$17,908	
Compound amount, 10 years at 10%			× 2.59
			$25,900
Less tax on sale:			
26%($25,900 − $10,000)			(4,134)
Future value			$21,766

Therefore, the value of the deferral that results from investing in the land rather than in the bond is $3,858 ($21,766 − $17,908). ■

Specific Items of Gross Income

LO.4

Understand that statutory authority is required to exclude an item from gross income.

The all-inclusive principles of gross income determination as applied by the IRS and the courts have, on occasion, been expanded or modified by Congress through legislation. This legislation generally provides more specific rules for determining gross income from certain sources. Most of these special rules appear in §§ 71–90 of the Code.

In addition to provisions describing how specific sources of gross income are to be taxed, several specific rules *exclude* items from gross income. Authority for excluding specific items is provided in §§ 101–150 and in various other provisions in the Code.

Many statutory exclusions are unique to *individual taxpayers* (e.g., gifts and inheritances,[47] scholarships,[48] and a variety of fringe benefits paid to *employees*). These exclusions are discussed in Chapters 16 and 17. Other exclusions are broader and apply to all entities. These exclusions include interest on state and local bonds (§ 103), life insurance proceeds received by reason of death of the

[47] § 102.

[48] § 117.

insured (§ 101), the fair market value of leasehold improvements received by the lessor when a lease is terminated (§ 109),[49] and income from discharge of indebtedness (§ 108). Some of the broadly applied statutory rules describing inclusions and exclusions are discussed below.

LO.5

Apply the Internal Revenue Code provisions on loans made at below-market interest rates.

Imputed Interest on Below-Market Loans

As discussed earlier in the chapter, generally no income is recognized unless it is realized. Realization occurs when the taxpayer performs services or sells goods and thus becomes entitled to a payment from the other party. It follows that no income is realized if the goods or services are provided at no charge. Under this interpretation of the realization requirement, before 1984, interest-free loans were used to shift income between taxpayers.

EXAMPLE 27

Brown Corporation is in the 35% tax bracket and has $200,000 in a money market account earning 10% interest. Jack is the sole shareholder of Brown. He is in the 15% tax bracket and has no investment income. In view of the difference in tax rates, Jack believes that it would be better for him to receive and pay tax on the earnings from Brown's $200,000 investment. Jack does not wish to receive the $200,000 from Brown as a dividend because that would trigger a tax.

Before 1984, Jack could achieve his goals as follows. He could receive the money market account from Brown Corporation in exchange for a $200,000 non-interest-bearing note, payable on Brown's demand. As a result, Jack would receive the $20,000 earnings on the money market account, and the combined taxes of Brown Corporation and Jack would be decreased by $4,000.

Decrease in Brown's tax—(0.10 × $200,000) × 0.35	($7,000)
Increase in Jack's tax—(0.10 × $200,000) × 0.15	3,000
Overall decrease in tax liability	$4,000

■

Under 1984 amendments to the Code, Brown Corporation in the preceding example is deemed to have received an interest payment from Jack even though no interest was actually paid.[50] This payment of imputed interest is taxable to Brown. Jack may be able to deduct the imaginary interest payment on his return as investment interest if he itemizes deductions. To complete the fictitious series of transactions, Brown is deemed to return the interest to Jack in the form of a taxable dividend.

Imputed interest is calculated using rates the Federal government pays on new borrowings and is compounded semiannually. The Federal rates are adjusted monthly and are published by the IRS.[51] There are three Federal rates: short-term (not over three years and including demand loans), mid-term (over three years but not over nine years), and long-term (over nine years).

EXAMPLE 28

Assume the Federal rate applicable to the loan in the preceding example is 7% through June 30 and 8% from July 1 through December 31. Brown Corporation made the loan on January 1, and the loan is still outstanding on December 31. Brown must recognize interest income of $15,280, and Jack has interest expense of $15,280. Brown is deemed to have paid a $15,280 dividend to Jack.

Interest Calculations	
January 1 to June 30—(0.07 × $200,000)(½ year)	$ 7,000
July 1 to December 31—[0.08($200,000 + $7,000)] (½ year)	8,280
	$15,280

■

[49] If the tenant made the improvements in lieu of rent, the value of the improvements is not eligible for exclusion.

[50] § 7872(a)(1).

[51] §§ 7872(b)(2) and (f)(2).

CONCEPT SUMMARY 4–1

Effect of Certain Below-Market Loans on the Lender and Borrower

Type of Loan		Lender	Borrower
Gift	Step 1	Interest income	Interest expense
	Step 2	Gift made*	Gift received
Compensation related	Step 1	Interest income	Interest expense
	Step 2	Compensation expense	Compensation income
Corporation to shareholder	Step 1	Interest income	Interest expense
	Step 2	Dividend paid	Dividend income

*The gift may be subject to the gift tax (refer to Chapter 1).

If interest is charged on the loan but is less than the Federal rate, the imputed interest is the difference between the amount that would have been charged at the Federal rate and the amount actually charged.

EXAMPLE 29

Assume the same facts as in Example 28, except that Brown Corporation charged 6% interest, compounded annually.

Interest at the Federal rate	$ 15,280
Less interest charged (0.06 × $200,000)	(12,000)
Imputed interest	$ 3,280

■

The imputed interest rules apply to the following types of below-market loans.[52]

1. Gift loans (made out of love, respect, or generosity).
2. Compensation-related loans (employer loans to employees).
3. Corporation-shareholder loans (a corporation's loans to its shareholders, as in Example 27).
4. Tax avoidance loans and other loans that significantly affect the borrower's or lender's Federal tax liability (discussed in the following paragraphs).

The effects of the first three types of loans on the borrower and lender are summarized in Concept Summary 4–1.

Exceptions and Limitations. No interest is imputed on total outstanding *compensation-related loans* or *corporation-shareholder loans* of $10,000 or less unless the purpose of the loan is tax avoidance.[53] This vague tax avoidance standard exposes practically all compensation-related and corporation-shareholder loans to possible imputed interest problems. Nevertheless, the $10,000 exception should apply when an employee's borrowing was necessitated by personal needs (e.g., to meet unexpected expenses) rather than tax considerations.

Similarly, no interest is imputed on outstanding *gift loans* of $10,000 or less between individuals, unless the loan proceeds are used to purchase income-producing property.[54] This exemption eliminates from these complex provisions immaterial amounts that do not result in sizable shifts of income.

[52]§ 7872(c).

[53]§ 7872(c)(3).

[54]§ 7872(c)(2).

CONCEPT SUMMARY 4–2

Exceptions to the Imputed Interest Rules for Below-Market Loans

Exception	Eligible Loans	Ineligible Loans and Limitations
De minimis—aggregate loans of $10,000 or less	Gift loans	Proceeds used to purchase income-producing assets.
	Employer-employee	Principal purpose is tax avoidance.
	Corporation-shareholder	Principal purpose is tax avoidance.
Aggregate loans of $100,000 or less	Gift loans between individuals	Principal purpose is tax avoidance. For all other loans, interest is imputed to the extent of the borrower's net investment income, if it exceeds $1,000.

On loans of $100,000 or less between individuals, the imputed interest cannot exceed the borrower's net investment income for the year (gross income from all investments less the related expenses).[55] Through the gift loan provision, the imputed interest rules are designed to prevent high-income individuals from shifting income to relatives in a lower marginal bracket. This shifting of investment income is considered to occur only to the extent that the borrower has net investment income. Thus, the income imputed to the lender is limited to the borrower's net investment income.

As a further limitation or exemption, if the borrower's net investment income for the year does not exceed $1,000, no interest is imputed on loans of $100,000 or less. However, these limitations for loans of $100,000 or less do not apply if a principal purpose of a loan is tax avoidance. In such a case, interest is imputed, and the imputed interest is not limited to the borrower's net investment income.[56]

These exceptions to the imputed interest rules are summarized in Concept Summary 4–2.

LO.6

Determine the extent to which receipts can be excluded under the tax benefit rule.

Tax Benefit Rule

Generally, if a taxpayer obtains a deduction for an item in one year and in a later year recovers all or a portion of the prior deduction, the recovery is included in gross income in the year received.[57]

EXAMPLE 30

A business deducted as a loss a $1,000 receivable from a customer when it appeared the amount would never be collected. The following year, the customer paid $800 on the receivable. The business must report the $800 as gross income in the year it is received. ■

However, the § 111 **tax benefit rule** limits income recognition when a deduction does not yield a tax benefit in the year it is taken. If the taxpayer in Example 30 has no tax liability in the year of the deduction, the $800 receipt is excluded from gross income in the year of the recovery.

[55] § 7872(d). The $100,000 provision applies only to gift loans.

[56] *Deficit Reduction Tax Bill of 1984: Explanation of the Senate Finance Committee* (April 2, 1984), p. 484.

[57] § 111(a).

TAX in the News LOANS TO EXECUTIVES PROHIBITED

Interest-free loans have become a popular form of compensation for executives. Several examples of multimillion dollar loans have come to light as a result of recent bankruptcies by large corporations. The board of directors often justifies the loans as necessary to enable the executive to be able to purchase a residence or to buy stock in the company.

Loans by publicly held corporations to their executives are now generally prohibited by Federal law. The Sarbanes-Oxley provisions generally prohibit loans by corporations to their executives. However, an exception permits corporate loans to finance the acquisition of a personal residence for an executive.

EXAMPLE 31

Before deducting a $1,000 loss from an uncollectible business receivable, Tulip Company had taxable income of $200. The business bad debt deduction yields only a $200 tax benefit (assuming no loss carryback is made). That is, taxable income is reduced by only $200 (to zero) as a result of the bad debt deduction. Therefore, if the customer makes a payment on the previously deducted receivable in the following year, only the first $200 is a taxable recovery of a prior deduction. Any additional amount collected is nontaxable because only $200 of the loss yielded a reduction in taxable income (i.e., a tax benefit). ■

Interest on Certain State and Local Government Obligations

LO.7

Understand the Internal Revenue Code provision that excludes interest on state and local government obligations from gross income.

At the time the Sixteenth Amendment was ratified by the states, there was some question as to whether the Federal government possessed the constitutional authority to tax interest on state and local government obligations. Taxing such interest was thought to violate the doctrine of intergovernmental immunity because the tax would impair the ability of state and local governments to finance their operations.[58] Thus, interest on state and local government obligations was specifically exempted from Federal income taxation.[59] However, the Supreme Court has concluded that there is no constitutional prohibition against levying a nondiscriminatory Federal income tax on state and local government obligations.[60] Nevertheless, the statutory exclusion still exists.

The current exempt status applies solely to state and local government bonds. Thus, income received from the accrual of interest on a condemnation award or an overpayment of state tax is fully taxable.[61] Nor does the exemption apply to gains on the sale of tax-exempt securities.

Find more information on this topic at our Web site: ***http://wft-entities.swlearning.com.***

DIGGING DEEPER 3

EXAMPLE 32

Macaw Corporation purchases State of Virginia bonds for $10,000 on July 1, 2005. The bonds pay $400 interest each June 30 and December 31. On March 31, 2006, Macaw sells the bonds for $10,500 plus $200 of accrued interest. Macaw recognizes a $500 taxable gain ($10,500 – $10,000), but the $200 accrued interest is exempt from taxation. ■

Obviously, the interest exclusion reduces the cost of borrowing for state and local governments. A taxpayer with a 35 percent marginal tax rate requires only a 5.2 percent yield on a tax-exempt bond to obtain the same after-tax income as a taxable bond paying 8 percent interest [5.2% ÷ (1 – 0.35) = 8%].

[58] *Pollock v. Farmer's Loan & Trust Co.*, 3 AFTR 2602, 15 S.Ct. 912 (USSC, 1895).

[59] § 103(a).

[60] *South Carolina v. Baker III*, 88–1 USTC ¶9284, 61 AFTR2d 88–995, 108 S.Ct. 1355 (USSC, 1988).

[61] *Kieselbach v. Comm.*, 43–1 USTC ¶9220, 30 AFTR 370, 63 S.Ct. 303 (USSC, 1943); *U.S. Trust Co. of New York v. Anderson*, 3 USTC ¶1125, 12 AFTR 836, 65 F.2d 575 (CA–2, 1933).

State and local governments have developed sophisticated financial schemes to attract new industry. For example, local municipalities have issued bonds to finance construction of plants to be leased to private enterprise. By arranging the financing with low-interest municipal obligations, the plants could be leased at lower cost than other facilities the private business could obtain. However, Congress has placed limitations on the use of tax-exempt securities to finance private business.[62]

PLANNING *Strategies*

STATE AND MUNICIPAL BONDS

★ **Framework Focus: Income and Exclusion**

Strategy ★ Avoid Income Recognition.

Tax-exempt state and local bonds are almost irresistible investments for taxpayers with high marginal tax rates. To realize the maximum benefit from the exemption, the investor can purchase zero-coupon bonds, which pay interest only at maturity. The advantage of the zero-coupon feature is that the investor can earn tax-exempt interest on the accumulated principal and interest. If the investor purchases a tax-exempt bond that pays the interest each year, the interest received may be such a small amount that an additional tax-exempt investment cannot be made. In addition, reinvesting the interest may entail transaction costs (broker's fees). The zero-coupon feature avoids these problems. However, certain state and municipal bond interest may increase the base of the alternative minimum tax, as discussed in Chapter 14.

LO.8

Use the Internal Revenue Code's exclusion of leasehold improvements from gross income.

Improvements on Leased Property

When a real property lease expires, the landlord regains control of both the real property and any improvements to the property (e.g., buildings and landscaping) made by the tenant during the term of the lease. In 1940, the Supreme Court held that the fair market value of improvements made by a tenant to the landlord's property should be included in the landlord's gross income upon termination of the lease.[63] Congress effectively reversed this decision by enacting § 109, which defers tax on the value of the improvements until the property is sold. More specifically, any improvements made to the leased property are excluded from the landlord's gross income unless the improvement is made to the property in lieu of rent.

EXAMPLE 33

Mahogany Corporation leases office space to Zink and Silver, Attorneys-at-Law. When the law firm took possession of the office space, it added wall partitions, an in-wall computer network, and a variety of other improvements to the space. The improvements were not made in lieu of rent payments to Mahogany. When the lease expires and Mahogany regains possession of the space, the value of the improvements will be excluded from Mahogany's gross income. ■

LO.9

Determine the extent to which life insurance proceeds are excluded from gross income.

Life Insurance Proceeds

General Rule. **Life insurance proceeds** paid to the beneficiary because of the death of the insured are exempt from income tax.[64] Congress chose to exempt life insurance proceeds from gross income for the following reasons.

[62]See § 103(b). The alternative minimum tax may apply to some of this interest income.

[63]*Helvering v. Bruun*, 40–1 USTC ¶9337, 24 AFTR 652, 60 S.Ct. 631 (USSC, 1940).

[64]*Estate of D. R. Daly*, 3 B.T.A. 1042 (1926).

TAX in the News — **CORPORATE-OWNED LIFE INSURANCE MAY NOT YIELD CORPORATE BENEFITS**

Many corporations purchase insurance policies on the lives of key employees (employees who are extremely important to the company's success, such as the CEO and CFO). The corporation is the beneficiary, and the insurance proceeds are excluded from the corporation's gross income under § 101.

Before changes in the tax laws a decade ago, corporations could deduct the interest on loans to purchase the insurance policies. Many large corporations took advantage of these rules and purchased insurance policies not just on key employees but also on their rank-and-file employees (frequently referred to as "janitor's insurance"), with the corporation as the beneficiary.

In recent years, some heirs of deceased employees who were covered by such janitor's insurance have successfully sued the insurance companies and the employers to recover the insurance proceeds, on the theory that the employer did not have an "insurable interest." Such an interest is required under the laws of most states to prevent individuals from "gambling" on the lives of people in whom they otherwise have no financial interest. The next chapter in this judicial saga will determine whether the heirs who collect the insurance proceeds in this way are "beneficiaries" under § 101.

- For family members, life insurance proceeds serve much the same purpose as a nontaxable inheritance.
- In a business context (as well as in a family situation), life insurance proceeds replace an economic loss suffered by the beneficiary.

Thus, Congress concluded that, in general, making life insurance proceeds exempt from income tax was a good policy.

EXAMPLE 34

Sparrow Corporation purchased an insurance policy on the life of its CEO and named itself as the beneficiary. Sparrow paid $24,000 in premiums. When the company's CEO died, Sparrow collected the insurance proceeds of $60,000. The $60,000 is excluded from Sparrow's gross income. ■

Exceptions to Exclusion Treatment. The income tax exclusion applies only when the insurance proceeds are received because of the death of the insured. If the owner cancels the policy and receives the cash surrender value, he or she must recognize gain to the extent of the excess of the amount received over the cost of the policy.[65]

Another exception to exclusion treatment applies if the policy is transferred after the insurance company issues it. If the policy is transferred for valuable consideration, the insurance proceeds are includible in the gross income of the transferee to the extent the proceeds received exceed the amount paid for the policy by the transferee plus any subsequent premiums paid.

EXAMPLE 35

Platinum Corporation pays premiums of $5,000 for an insurance policy with a face amount of $12,000 on the life of Beth, an officer of the corporation. Subsequently, Platinum sells the policy to Beth's husband for $5,500. On Beth's death, her husband receives the proceeds of $12,000. Beth's husband can exclude from gross income $5,500 plus any premiums he paid subsequent to the transfer. ■

The Code, however, provides four exceptions to the rule illustrated in the preceding example.[66] These exceptions permit exclusion treatment for transfers to the following. The first three exceptions facilitate the use of insurance contracts to fund **buy-sell agreements**.

[65] *Landfield Finance Co. v. U.S.*, 69–2 USTC ¶9680, 24 AFTR2d 69–5744, 418 F.2d 172 (CA–7, 1969).

[66] § 101(a)(2).

1. A partner of the insured.
2. A partnership in which the insured is a partner.
3. A corporation in which the insured is an officer or shareholder.
4. A transferee whose basis in the policy is determined by reference to the transferor's basis, such as a gift or a transfer due to a divorce.

EXAMPLE 36

Rick and Sam are equal partners who have a buy-sell agreement that allows either partner to purchase the interest of a deceased partner for $500,000. Neither partner has sufficient cash to actually buy the other partner's interest, but each has a life insurance policy on his own life in the amount of $500,000. Rick and Sam could exchange their policies (usually at little or no taxable gain), and upon the death of either partner, the surviving partner could collect tax-free insurance proceeds. The proceeds could then be used to purchase the decedent's interest in the partnership. ■

Investment earnings arising from the reinvestment of life insurance proceeds are generally subject to income tax. For example, the beneficiary may elect to collect the insurance proceeds in installments that include taxable interest income. The interest portion of each installment is included in gross income.

PLANNING *Strategies*

LIFE INSURANCE

★ Framework Focus: Income and Exclusion

Strategy ★ Avoid Income Recognition.

Life insurance is a tax-favored investment. The annual increase in the cash surrender value of the policy is not taxable because it is subject to substantial restrictions (no income has been actually or constructively received). By borrowing on the policy's cash surrender value, the owner can receive the policy's increase in value in cash without recognizing income.

LO.10

Describe the circumstances under which income must be reported from the discharge of indebtedness.

Income from Discharge of Indebtedness

Income is generated when appreciated property is used to pay a debt or when the creditor cancels debt. If appreciated property is used to pay a debt, the transaction is treated as a sale of the appreciated property followed by payment of the debt.[67] Foreclosure by a creditor is also treated as a sale or exchange of the property.[68]

EXAMPLE 37

Juan owed the State Bank $100,000 on an unsecured note. Juan satisfied the note by transferring to the bank common stock with a basis of $60,000 and a fair market value of $100,000. Juan recognizes a $40,000 gain on the transfer. Juan also owed the bank $50,000 on a note secured by land. When Juan's basis in the land was $20,000 and the land's fair market value was $50,000, the bank foreclosed on the loan and took title to the land. Juan recognizes a $30,000 gain on the foreclosure. ■

A creditor may cancel debt to assure the vitality of the debtor. In such cases, the debtor's net worth is increased by the amount of debt forgiven.

[67] Reg. § 1.1001–2(a).

[68] *Estate of Delman v. Comm.*, 73 T.C. 15 (1979).

EXAMPLE 38

Brown Corporation is unable to meet the mortgage payments on its factory building. Both the corporation and the mortgage holder are aware of the depressed market for industrial property in the area. Foreclosure would only result in the creditor's obtaining unsellable property. To improve Brown's financial position and thus improve its chances of obtaining the additional credit necessary for survival from other lenders, the creditor agrees to forgive all amounts past due and to reduce the principal amount of the mortgage. Brown's net worth is increased by the amount of past due debt that was forgiven *plus* the reduction in the mortgage balance. ■

Generally, the debtor recognizes gross income equal to the amount of debt canceled.[69] The following two examples illustrate additional circumstances where gross income results from cancellation of indebtedness.

EXAMPLE 39

A corporation issues bonds with a face value of $500,000. Subsequently, the corporation repurchases the bonds in the market for $150,000. It has effectively canceled its $500,000 debt with a $150,000 payment, so it recognizes $350,000 in gross income.[70] ■

EXAMPLE 40

Turquoise Corporation borrowed $60,000 from National Bank to purchase a warehouse. Turquoise agreed to make monthly principal and interest payments for 15 years. The interest rate on the note was 4%. When the balance on the note had been reduced through monthly payments to $48,000, the bank offered to accept $45,000 in full settlement of the note. The bank made the offer because interest rates had increased to 7%. Turquoise accepted the bank's offer. As a result, Turquoise recognizes $3,000 ($48,000 – $45,000) of gross income.[71] ■

Though discharge of indebtedness generally increases the taxpayer's gross income, in the following cases, the reduction in debt is excluded from gross income.[72]

1. Creditors' gifts.
2. Discharges under Federal bankruptcy law.
3. Discharges that occur when the debtor is insolvent.
4. Discharge of the farm debt of a solvent taxpayer.
5. Discharge of **qualified real property business indebtedness**.
6. A seller's cancellation of a buyer's indebtedness.
7. A shareholder's cancellation of a corporation's indebtedness.
8. Forgiveness of certain loans to students.

Creditors' Gifts. If the creditor reduces the debt as an act of *love, respect, or generosity*, the debtor has simply received a nontaxable gift (situation 1). Such motivations generally arise only on loans between friends or family members. Rarely will a gift be found to have occurred in a business context. A businessperson may settle a debt for less than the amount due, but as a matter of business expediency (e.g., high collection costs or disputes as to contract terms) rather than generosity.[73]

Insolvency and Bankruptcy. Cancellation of indebtedness income is excluded when the debtor is insolvent (i.e., the debtor's liabilities exceed the fair market value of the assets) or when the cancellation of debt results from a bankruptcy proceeding (situations 2 and 3). The insolvency exclusion is limited to the amount of insolvency. The tax law permits this exclusion to avoid imposing undue hardship on the debtor (wherewithal to pay) and the debtor's limited resources.

[69] § 61(a)(12).

[70] See *U.S. v. Kirby Lumber Co.*, 2 USTC ¶814, 10 AFTR 458, 52 S.Ct. 4 (USSC, 1931).

[71] Rev.Rul. 82–202, 1982–1 C.B. 35.

[72] §§ 108 and 1017.

[73] *Comm. v. Jacobson*, 49–1 USTC ¶9133, 37 AFTR 516, 69 S.Ct. 358 (USSC, 1949).

The law imposes a cost for the insolvency and bankruptcy exclusion. More specifically, the debtor must decrease certain tax benefits (capital loss carryforwards, net operating loss carryforwards, some tax credits, and suspended passive losses)[74] by the amount of income excluded. In addition, if the amount of excluded income exceeds these tax benefits, the debtor must then reduce the basis in assets.[75] Thus, excluded cancellation of indebtedness income either accelerates recognition of future income (by reducing tax benefit carryforwards) or is deferred until the debtor's assets are sold (or depreciated).

EXAMPLE 41

Before any debt cancellation, Maroon Corporation has assets with a fair market value of $500,000 and liabilities of $600,000. A creditor agrees to cancel $125,000 of liabilities. Maroon excludes $100,000 of the debt cancellation income (the amount of insolvency) and is taxed on $25,000. Maroon also reduces any tax benefits and the basis of its assets by $100,000 (the excluded income). ■

Qualified Real Property Indebtedness. Taxpayers (other than C corporations) can elect to exclude income from cancellation of indebtedness if the canceled debt is secured by real property used in a trade or business (situation 5). In addition, the debt must have been used to acquire or improve real property in a trade or business to qualify for the exclusion.[76] The amount of the exclusion is limited to the *lesser of* (1) the excess of the debt over the fair market value of the real property or (2) the adjusted basis of all depreciable real property held. In addition, the basis of all depreciable real property held by the debtor must be reduced by the amount excluded.

EXAMPLE 42

Blue, Inc., owns a warehouse worth $5 million, with a $3 million basis. The warehouse is subject to a $7 million mortgage that was incurred in connection with the acquisition of the warehouse. In lieu of foreclosure, the lender decides that it will reduce the mortgage to $4.5 million. Blue may elect to exclude $2 million from gross income ($7 million – $5 million). If Blue makes the election, it must reduce the aggregate basis of its depreciable realty by $2 million. ■

EXAMPLE 43

Assume the same facts as in the preceding example, except that the basis of the warehouse is $1 million. If the warehouse is the only piece of depreciable realty that Blue owns, only $1 million of the debt cancellation income may be excluded. ■

Seller Cancellation. When a seller of property cancels debt previously incurred by a buyer in a purchase transaction, the cancellation generally is not treated as income to the buyer (situation 6). Instead, the reduction in debt is considered to be a reduction in the purchase price of the asset. Consequently, the basis of the asset is reduced in the hands of the buyer.[77]

EXAMPLE 44

Snipe, Inc., purchases a truck from Sparrow Autos for $10,000 in cash and a $25,000 note payable. Two days after the purchase, Sparrow announces a sale on the same model truck, with a sales price of $28,000. Snipe contacts Sparrow and asks to be given the sales price on the truck. Sparrow complies by canceling $7,000 of the note payable. The $7,000 is excluded from Snipe's gross income, and the basis of the truck to Snipe is $28,000. ■

Shareholder Cancellation. If a shareholder cancels the corporation's indebtedness to him or her (situation 7) and receives nothing in return, the cancellation usually is considered a contribution of capital to the corporation by the

[74]See Chapter 6 for a discussion of net operating loss carryforwards and suspended passive losses. Chapter 8 discusses capital loss carryforwards. Chapter 14 discusses tax credits.

[75]§ 108(b).

[76]§ 108(a)(1)(D).

[77]§ 108(e)(5).

shareholder. Thus, the corporation recognizes no income. Instead, its paid-in capital is increased, and its liabilities are decreased by the same amount.[78]

DIGGING DEEPER 4

Find more information on this topic at our Web site: ***http://wft-entities.swlearning.com.***

Student Loans. Many states make loans to students on the condition that the loan will be forgiven if the student practices a profession in the state upon completing his or her studies. The amount of the loan that is forgiven (situation 8) is excluded from gross income.[79]

Gains and Losses from Property Transactions

LO.11

Describe the tax consequences of property transactions.

In General. When property is sold or otherwise disposed of, gain or loss may result. Such gain or loss has an effect on the gross income of the party making the sale or other disposition when the gain or loss is *realized* and *recognized* for tax purposes. The concept of realized gain or loss is expressed as follows.

$$\text{Amount realized from the sale} - \text{Adjusted basis of the property} = \text{Realized gain (or loss)}$$

The amount realized is the selling price of the property less any costs of disposition (e.g., brokerage commissions) incurred by the seller. The adjusted basis of the property is determined as follows.

Cost (or other original basis) at date of acquisition[80]	
Add:	Capital additions
Subtract:	Depreciation (if appropriate) and other capital recoveries (see Chapter 5)
Equals:	Adjusted basis at date of sale or other disposition

Without realized gain or loss, generally, there can be no recognized (taxable) gain or loss. All realized gains are recognized unless some specific part of the tax law provides otherwise. Realized losses may or may not be recognized (deductible) for tax purposes, depending on the circumstances involved. For example, losses realized from the disposition of personal-use property (property held by individuals and not used for business or investment purposes) are not recognized.

EXAMPLE 45

During the current year, Ted sells his sailboat (adjusted basis of $4,000) for $5,500. Ted also sells one of his personal automobiles (adjusted basis of $8,000) for $5,000. Ted's realized gain of $1,500 from the sale of the sailboat is recognized. The $3,000 realized loss on the sale of the automobile, however, is not recognized. Thus, the gain is taxable, but the loss is not deductible. ■

Once it has been determined that the disposition of property results in a recognized gain or loss, the next step is to classify the gain or loss as capital or ordinary. Although ordinary gain is fully taxable and ordinary loss is fully deductible, the same is not true for capital gains and capital losses.

Capital Gains and Losses. Gains and losses from the disposition of capital assets receive special tax treatment. Capital assets are defined in the Code as any property held by the taxpayer *other than* property listed in § 1221. The list in § 1221

[78] § 108(e)(6).
[79] § 108(f).
[80] Cost usually means purchase price plus expenses related to the acquisition of the property and incurred by the purchaser (e.g., brokerage commissions). For the basis of property acquired by gift or inheritance and other basis rules, see Chapter 7.

includes, among other things, inventory, accounts receivable, and depreciable property or real estate used in a business. The sale or exchange of assets in these categories usually results in ordinary income or loss treatment (see Chapter 8). The sale of any other asset generally creates a capital gain or loss.

EXAMPLE 46

Cardinal, Inc., owns a pizza parlor. During the current year, Cardinal sells an automobile. The automobile, which had been used as a pizza delivery car for three years, was sold at a loss of $1,000. Because this automobile was a depreciable asset used in its business, Cardinal has an ordinary loss of $1,000, rather than a capital loss. Cardinal also sold securities held for investment during the current year. The securities were sold for a gain of $800. The securities are capital assets. Therefore, Cardinal has a capital gain of $800. ■

Individuals and corporations are taxed differently on capital gains and losses. An individual's *net capital gain* is subject to the following *maximum* tax rates.[81]

	Maximum Rate[82]
Short-term gains (assets held for one year or less)	35%
Long-term gains (assets held for more than one year)	15%

A corporation's net capital gain does not receive any beneficial tax treatment.

The net capital losses of individuals can be used to offset up to $3,000 of ordinary income each year. Any remaining capital loss is carried forward indefinitely until it is exhausted. Corporations may deduct capital losses only to the extent of capital gains. Capital losses of corporations in excess of capital gains may not be deducted against ordinary income. A corporation's unused capital losses can be carried back three years and then carried forward five years to offset capital gains in those years.[83]

EXAMPLE 47

Jones has a short-term capital loss of $5,000 during 2006 and no capital gains. If Jones is an individual, she can deduct $3,000 of this amount as an ordinary loss. The remaining $2,000 loss is carried over to 2007 and will continue to be carried forward until it is fully deducted.

If Jones is a C corporation, none of the capital loss is deductible in 2006. All of the $5,000 loss is carried back and offset against capital gains in 2003, 2004, and 2005 (generating an immediate tax refund). Any unused capital loss is carried forward and offset against capital gains in 2007 to 2011. ■

DIGGING DEEPER 5

Find more information on this topic at our Web site: ***http://wft-entities.swlearning.com.***

Suggested Further Readings

"Partnerships that Invest in Tax-Exempt Bonds," *Business Entities*, online, March/April 2003.

"Reduction in Employee's Debt is § 108 Compensation Income," *Practical Tax Strategies*, April 2004, p. 193.

Edward J. Roche, "Lease Cancellation Payments are Capital Gain? Yes! Section 1234A Overturns *Hort*," *Journal of Taxation*, June 2005, pp. 364–368.

Robert W. Wood and Dominic L. Daher, "Contingent Attorney's Fees in Class Action Cases—From Bad to Worse for Taxpayer-Plaintiffs," *Journal of Taxation*, October 2003, 228–233.

[81] § 1(h). Net capital gain is defined in § 1222(11) as the excess of the net long-term capital gain over the net short-term capital loss.

[82] Certain assets, such as collectibles (e.g., art, antiques, stamps, etc.) and some real estate, receive special treatment. Collectibles gain is taxed at a maximum rate of 28%, and certain real estate gain is taxed at a maximum rate of 25%. See Chapter 8.

[83] §§ 1211 and 1212.

KEY TERMS

PROBLEM MATERIALS

PROBLEMS

1. Cecil buys wrecked cars and stores them on his property. Recently, he purchased a 1990 Ford Taurus for $250. If he can sell all of the usable parts, his total proceeds from the Taurus will be over $2,000. As of the end of the year, he has sold only the radio for $50, and he does not know how many, if any, of the remaining parts will ever be sold. What are Cecil's income recognition issues? *Issue ID*

2. In each of the following, determine the taxpayer's "income" for the current year as computed by an economist and as computed for tax purposes. Explain any differences.
   a. A cash basis taxpayer overcharged a customer by billing her twice for the same item in 2005. The taxpayer notified the customer of the mistake in December 2005 and refunded the overcharge in January 2006.
   b. In the previous year, the taxpayer purchased stock for $4,000. By the end of the year, the stock had declined in value to $3,000. In the current year, the taxpayer sold the stock for $6,500.
   c. The taxpayer, a carpenter, purchased a house for investment for $100,000. He renovated the house. The taxpayer spent $14,000 on materials, and he estimates that the value of his time spent on the work (what he would have charged a customer for the same work) was $20,000. He sold the property the following year for $140,000.
   d. The sole shareholder in a corporation purchased property from the corporation for $10,000. The fair market value of the property was $15,000.

3. The roof of your corporation's office building recently suffered some damage as the result of a storm. You, the president of the corporation, are negotiating with a carpenter who has quoted two prices for the repair work: $600 if you pay in cash ("folding money") and $700 if you pay by check. The carpenter observes that the IRS can more readily discover his receipt of a check. Thus, he hints that he will report the receipt of the check (but not the cash). The carpenter has a full-time job and will do the work after hours and on the weekend. He comments that he should be allowed to keep all he earns after regular working hours. Evaluate what you should do. *Ethics*

4. Tom's job requires 40 hours of work each week, and he is never required to work overtime. He gets one month of vacation each year. Tom uses his weekends and two weeks of his vacation to make repairs and improvements to his personal residence. Ed's job requires considerable overtime, and he has only two weeks of vacation each year. Because his job demands so much of his time, Ed is required to pay others to make repairs and improvements to his personal residence. Under these circumstances, does the tax law favor Tom or Ed? *Decision Making*

5. Jared, a self-employed insect exterminator, uses the cash method of accounting to report his income. In December 2006, Jared received a check for $400 from a client. Jared deposited the check near the end of December. In early January 2007, the bank

notified him that the check did not clear because of insufficient funds in the customer's account. The bank sent the check through a second time, and it cleared in January 2007. Jared computes his income using his deposit records. Therefore, he included the $400 in his 2006 gross income.

a. In what year should Jared report the $400 of income?
b. Why does it matter to Jared whether he reports the income in 2006 or 2007, as long as he actually reports it?

Decision Making
Communications

6. Kevin, a cash basis taxpayer, received the following from his employer during 2006.

- Salary of $80,000.
- 2005 bonus of $12,000 received in 2006.

The 2005 bonus was not paid until 2006 because Kevin's employer suffered a computer crash and could not complete the bonus calculations in a timely manner. In addition, Kevin earned a 2006 bonus of $15,000 that was to be paid by the end of December 2006. However, in December, Kevin told his employer to delay the payment of the bonus until January 2007, when Kevin plans to retire.

a. Determine the effect of the above on Kevin's gross income in 2006.
b. Assume that Kevin is your client and he tells you that he now does not plan to retire until 2008. He is reasonably certain that he will be in a lower marginal tax bracket in that year. Write a memorandum to the tax file explaining what you plan to advise Kevin regarding his 2007 bonus.

Decision Making
Communications

7. Which of the following investments of $10,000 each will yield the greatest after-tax value, assuming the taxpayer is in the 35% tax bracket for ordinary income and 15% for qualifying capital gains in all years? The investments will be liquidated at the end of five years.

a. Land that will increase in value by 6% each year.
b. A taxable bond yielding 6% before tax. The interest can be reinvested at 6% before tax.
c. Common stock paying a 5% dividend each year that can be reinvested in common stock paying a 5% dividend each year. The value of the stock will not change.

Prepare a brief speech for your tax class in which you explain why the future value of the land will exceed the future value of the taxable bond. Explain why the after-tax return on the stock will exceed the after-tax return earned on the bond.

Compound amount of $1 and compound value of annuity payments at the end of five years are given as:

Interest Rate	$1 Compounded for Five Years	$1 Annuity Compounded for Five Years
6%	$1.34	$5.64
3.90%	1.20	5.39
4.25%	1.23	5.44

8. Determine the taxpayer's gross income for tax purposes in each of the following situations.

a. Olga, a cash basis taxpayer, sold a corporate bond with accrued interest of $200 for $10,500. Olga's cost of the bond was $10,000.
b. Olga needed $10,000 to make a down payment on her house. She instructed her broker to sell some stock to raise the $10,000. Olga's cost for the stock is $3,000. Based on her broker's advice, instead of selling the stock, she borrowed the $10,000 using the stock as collateral for the debt.
c. Olga owns a vacant lot that has been zoned for residential housing. She spends $900 in attorney fees to get the property rezoned as commercial. The property's value increases by $10,000 as a result of the rezoning.

Decision Making

9. Al is an attorney who conducts his practice as a sole proprietor. During 2006, he received cash of $150,000 for legal services. Of the amount collected, $25,000 was for services provided in 2005. At the end of 2006, Al had accounts receivable of $45,000, all for services rendered in 2006. During the year, Al billed a client $20,000, but the client

died and Al has no hope of collecting the balance due. At the end of the year, Al received $5,000 as a deposit on property a client was in the process of selling. Compute Al's gross income for 2006:

a. Using the cash basis of accounting.
b. Using the accrual basis of accounting.
c. Advise Al on which method of accounting he should use.

10. Autumn Company began operating a grocery store during the year. Autumn's only books and records are based on cash receipts and disbursements, but the company president has asked you to compute the company's gross profit from the business for tax purposes.

Sale of merchandise	$480,000
Purchases of merchandise	220,000

You determine that as of the end of the year Autumn has accounts payable for merchandise of $20,000 and accounts receivable from customers totaling $12,000. The cost of merchandise on hand at the end of the year was $9,000. Compute Autumn's accrual method gross profit for the year.

Communications

11. Color Paint Shop, Inc. (459 Ellis Avenue, Harrisburg, PA 17111), is an accrual basis taxpayer that paints automobiles. During 2006, the company painted Samuel's car and was to receive a $1,000 payment from his insurance company. Samuel was not satisfied with the work, however, and the insurance company refused to pay. In December 2006, Color and Samuel agreed that Color would receive $800 for the work, subject to final approval by the insurance company. In the past, Color had come to terms with customers only to have the insurance company negotiate an even smaller amount. In August 2007, the insurance company reviewed the claim and paid the $800 to Color. An IRS agent thinks that Color should report $1,000 of income in 2006 and deduct a $200 loss in 2007. Prepare a memo to Susan Apple, a tax partner for whom you are working, with the recommended treatment for the disputed income.

12. Dance, Inc., is a dance studio that sells dance lessons for cash, on open account, and for notes receivable. The company also collects interest on bonds held as an investment. The company's cash receipts for the year totaled $219,000.

Cash sales	$ 70,000
Collections on accounts receivable	120,000
Collections on notes receivable	20,000
Interest on bonds	9,000
	$219,000

The balances in accounts receivable, notes receivable, and accrued interest on bonds at the beginning and end of the year were as follows.

	1–1	12–31
Accounts receivable	$24,000	$24,000
Notes receivable	9,000	13,000
Accrued interest on bonds	2,500	4,000
	$35,500	$41,000

The fair market value of the notes is equal to 60% of their face amount. There were no bad debts for the year, and all notes were for services performed during the year. Compute the corporation's gross income:

a. Using the cash basis of accounting.
b. Using the accrual basis of accounting.
c. Using a hybrid method—accrual basis for lessons and cash basis for interest income.

13. Determine the effect of the following on a cash basis taxpayer's gross income for 2005 and 2006.

a. In December 2005, the taxpayer negotiated his employment contract for 2006. The employer offered to pay the taxpayer $10,000 in December 2005 as a signing bonus and a $100,000 salary to be paid in 2006. The taxpayer rejected that offer but agreed to receive the $100,000 salary in 2006, and $15,000 to be received in four years.

b. In addition to a signing bonus of $10,000 to be paid in December 2005, the taxpayer was to receive $10,000 on the last day of each month in 2006. On December 31, 2006, the taxpayer told his employer to pay the December salary on January 1, 2007.

c. The taxpayer charges $100 per hour for his services. On December 31, 2006, the taxpayer worked eight hours for a client. The client told the taxpayer that his wife had the checkbook, but if the taxpayer would wait until the wife returned, the client would pay the $800. The taxpayer had another appointment, however, and told the client to mail him a check instead. The taxpayer received the check on January 2, 2007.

14. Swan Appliance Company, an accrual basis taxpayer, sells home appliances and service contracts. Determine the effects of each of the following transactions on the company's 2006 gross income assuming that the company uses any available options to defer its taxes.

a. In December 2005, the company received a $1,200 advance payment from a customer for an appliance that Swan special ordered from the manufacturer. The appliance did not arrive from the manufacturer until January 2006, and Swan immediately delivered it to the customer. The sale was reported in 2006 for financial accounting purposes.

b. In June 2006, the company sold a 12-month service contract for $240. The company also sold a 24-month service contract for $480 in December 2006.

c. On December 31, 2006, the company sold an appliance for $1,200. The company received $500 cash and a note from the customer for $700 and $260 interest, to be paid at the rate of $40 a month for 24 months. Because of the customer's poor credit record, the fair market value of the note was only $600. The cost of the appliance was $750.

Ethics

15. Dr. Randolph, a cash basis taxpayer, knows that he will be in a lower marginal tax bracket next year. To take advantage of the expected decrease in his tax rate, Dr. Randolph instructs his office manager to delay filing the medical insurance claims for services performed in November and December until January of the following year. This will assure that the receipts will not be included in his current gross income. Is Dr. Randolph abusing the cash method of accounting rules?

Decision Making

Communications

16. Your client is a new partnership, Aspen Associates, which is an engineering consulting firm. Generally, Aspen bills clients for services at the end of each month. Client billings are about $50,000 each month. On average, it takes 45 days to collect the receivables. Aspen's expenses are primarily for salary and rent. Salaries are paid on the last day of each month, and rent is paid on the first day of each month. The partnership has a line of credit with a bank, which requires monthly financial statements. These must be prepared using the accrual method. Aspen's managing partner, Amanda Sims, has suggested that the firm should also use the accrual method for tax purposes and thus reduce accounting fees by $600.

The partners are in the 35% (combined Federal and state) marginal tax bracket. Write a letter to your client explaining why you believe it would be worthwhile for Aspen to file its tax return on the cash basis even though its financial statements are prepared on the accrual basis. Aspen's address is 100 James Tower, Denver, CO 80208.

17. Alva received dividends on her stocks as follows.

Amur Corporation (a French corporation whose stock is traded on an established U.S. securities market)	$55,000
Blaze, Inc., a Delaware corporation	25,000
Grape, Inc., a Virginia corporation	12,000

a. Alva purchased the Grape stock four years ago, and she purchased the Amur stock two years ago. She purchased the Blaze stock 15 days before it went ex-dividend and sold it 20 days later at a $22,000 loss. Alva had no other capital gains and losses for the year. She is in the 35% marginal tax bracket. Compute Alva's tax on her dividend income.

b. Alva's daughter, who is not Alva's dependent, had taxable income of $10,000, which included $1,000 of dividends on Grape, Inc. stock. The daughter had purchased the stock two years ago. Compute the daughter's tax liability on the dividends.

18. Bethany Investment Partners is a cash basis taxpayer. It purchased a 20-year zero-coupon bond (no annual interest is paid) for $4,291 on January 1. The maturity value of the bond in 20 years is $20,000, which is the principal plus 8% interest compounded annually.
    a. What is Bethany's interest income from the bond this year?
    b. What is its basis for the bond on December 31?
    c. Will the interest income from the bond be greater in 10 years? Explain.

19. Brad is the president of the Zinc Corporation. He and other members of his family control the corporation. Brad has a temporary need for $50,000, and the corporation has excess cash. He could borrow the money from a bank at 9%, and Zinc is earning 6% on its temporary investments. Zinc has made loans to other employees on several occasions. Therefore, Brad is considering borrowing $50,000 from the corporation. He will repay the loan principal in two years plus interest at 5%. Identify the relevant tax issues for Brad and Zinc Corporation.

Issue ID

20. On June 30, 2006, Ridge borrowed $62,000 from his employer. On July 1, 2006, Ridge used the money as follows.

Interest-free loan to Ridge's controlled corporation (operated by Ridge on a part-time basis)	$31,000
Interest-free loan to Tab (Ridge's son)	11,000
National Bank of Grundy 6% CD ($14,840 due at maturity, June 30, 2007)	14,000
National Bank of Grundy 6.25% CD ($6,773 due at maturity, June 30, 2008)	6,000
	$62,000

Ridge's employer did not charge him interest. The applicable Federal rate was 7% throughout the relevant period. Tab had investment income of $800 for the year, and he used the loan proceeds to pay medical school tuition. There were no other outstanding loans between Ridge and Tab. What are the effects of the preceding transactions on Ridge's 2006 taxable income?

21. Indicate whether the imputed interest rules apply in the following situations.
    a. Mike loaned his sister $80,000 to buy a new home. Mike did not charge interest on the loan. The Federal rate was 4.5%. Mike's sister had $900 of investment income for the year.
    b. Sam's employer maintains an emergency loan fund for its employees. During the year, Sam's wife was very ill, and he incurred unusually large medical expenses. He borrowed $9,000 from his employer's emergency loan fund for six months. The Federal rate was 5.5%. Sam and his wife had no investment income for the year.
    c. Jody borrowed $15,000 from her controlled corporation for six months. She used the funds to pay her daughter's college tuition. The corporation charged Jody 4% interest. The Federal rate was 4.5%. Jody had $3,500 of investment income for the year.

22. Vito is the sole shareholder of Vito, Inc. The corporation also employs him. On June 30, 2005, Vito borrowed $8,000 from Vito, Inc., and on July 1, 2006, he borrowed an additional $3,000. Both loans were due on demand. No interest was charged on the loans, and the Federal rate was 10% for all relevant dates. Vito used the money to purchase stock, and he had no investment income. Determine the tax consequences to Vito and Vito, Inc., if:
    a. The loans are considered employer-employee loans.
    b. The loans are considered corporation-shareholder loans.

23. White and Swan Modeling is a partnership. How does the tax benefit rule apply to White and Swan in the following transactions?
    a. In 2005, White and Swan paid Vera $5,000 for locating a potential client. The deal fell through, and in 2006, Vera refunded the $5,000 to the partnership.
    b. In 2005, White and Swan paid an attorney $300 for services in connection with a title search. Because the attorney was negligent, the partnership incurred some

additional costs in acquiring the land. In 2006, the attorney refunded his $300 fee to White and Swan.

24. Rita is a CPA. Her clients frequently ask her for advice about investing. The current rate quoted on tax-exempt state and local government bond funds is 4.4%, and the rate on taxable U.S. government obligations is 6.6%. Both types of accounts are considered "risk-free." What is the minimum marginal tax bracket in which Rita's clients can benefit from investing in the tax-exempt funds?

25. Determine Hazel's gross income from the following receipts for the year.

Gain on sale of Augusta County bonds	$600
Interest on U.S. government savings bonds	300
Interest on state income tax refund	150
Interest on Augusta County bonds	900

Decision Making

26. Tedra, a C corporation, is in the 35% marginal tax bracket, is very risk adverse, and is considering purchasing U.S. government bonds due in 10 years that yield 5.6% before tax. Triple A rated State of Virginia bonds due in 10 years yield 4%. Which is the better alternative, assuming the bonds are of equal risk?

27. Determine the taxable life insurance proceeds in the following cases.
   a. When Monty died, his wife collected $50,000 on a group term insurance policy purchased by Monty's employer. Monty had never included the premiums in gross income.
   b. The Cardinal Software Company purchased an insurance policy on the life of a key employee. The company paid $50,000 in premiums and collected $500,000 of insurance proceeds.
   c. When Barbara died, she and her husband owed $15,000 on a loan. Under the terms of the loan, Barbara was required to purchase life insurance to pay the creditor the amount due at the date of Barbara's death. The creditor collected from the life insurance company the amount due at the time of Barbara's death. Is the creditor required to recognize income from the collection of the life insurance proceeds?

Decision Making

28. The Egret Company, which has a 40% (combined Federal and state) marginal tax rate, estimated that if its current president should die, the company would incur $200,000 in costs to find a suitable replacement. In addition, profits on various projects the president is responsible for would likely decrease by $300,000. The president has recommended that Egret purchase a $500,000 life insurance policy. How much insurance should the company carry on the life of its president to compensate for the after-tax loss that would result from the president's death, assuming the $200,000 costs of finding a president are deductible and the lost profits would have been taxable?

29. Fay and Edward are partners in an accounting firm. The partners have entered into an arm's length agreement requiring Fay to purchase Edward's partnership interest from Edward's estate if he dies before Fay. The price is set at 150% of the book value of Edward's partnership interest at the time of his death. Fay purchased an insurance policy on Edward's life to fund this agreement. After Fay had paid $40,000 in premiums, Edward was killed in an automobile accident, and Fay collected $1.5 million of life insurance proceeds. Fay used the life insurance proceeds to purchase Edward's partnership interest.
   a. What amount should Fay include in her gross income from receiving the life insurance proceeds?
   b. The insurance company paid Fay $15,000 interest on the life insurance proceeds during the period Edward's estate was in administration. During this period, Fay had left the insurance proceeds with the insurance company. Is this interest taxable?
   c. When Fay purchased Edward's partnership interest for $1.5 million, as determined by specifications in the agreement, the fair market value of Edward's interest was $2 million. How much should Fay include in her gross income from this bargain purchase?

Issue ID

30. Hawk Industries, Inc., has experienced financial difficulties as a result of its struggling business. The corporation has been behind on its mortgage payments for the last six

months. The mortgage holder has offered to accept $80,000 in full payment of the $100,000 owed on the mortgage and payable over the next 10 years. The interest rate of the mortgage is 7%, and the market rate is now 8%. What tax issues are raised by the creditor's offer?

31. Wanda had the following transactions involving capital assets.

Extender

Short-term gain on the sale of a stock investment	$6,000
Long-term gain on the sale of a sailing boat owned for 4 years (used for pleasure)	3,000
Long-term loss on the sale of a power boat owned for 2 years (used for pleasure)	1,000
Long-term gain on the sale of real estate held for 3 years as an investment	7,000

a. If Wanda is in the 28% tax bracket, how much income tax do these transactions generate?
b. What if Wanda is in the 15% tax bracket?
c. What if Wanda is a C corporation in the 35% tax bracket? Assume that the power boat is used in the corporation's business.

32. Cole had the following gains and losses from the sale of capital assets.

Extender

Loss on Pigeon Corporation stock (held 9 months)	($4,000)
Gain on painting (held for 2 years as an investment)	5,000
Gain on unimproved land (held for 3 years as an investment)	3,000

a. If Cole is in the 35% tax bracket, how much income tax do these transactions generate?
b. What if Cole is in the 15% tax bracket?
c. What if Cole is a C corporation in the 35% tax bracket?

33. Selma opened a farm implements store in 2006. The only accounting records she maintains are her cash receipts and disbursements for the business. Cash receipts for 2006 total $500,000, and cash disbursements total $350,000. The cash receipts include the $50,000 Selma originally invested in the business and a $5,000 customer deposit on a new tractor that was to be delivered by the factory in January 2007. You determine that there were no accounts receivable at the beginning of the year. At the end of the year, receivables total $15,000. The inventory at the end of the year is $75,000, and the accounts payables are $40,000. Determine the 2006 gross income for the store.

Extender

34. In a two-page paper, evaluate the following alternative proposals for taxing the income from property.

Extender

Communications

a. All assets would be valued at the end of the year, any increase in value that occurred during the year would be included in gross income, and any decrease in value would be deductible from gross income.
b. No gain or loss would be recognized until the taxpayer sold or exchanged the property.
c. Increases or decreases in the value of property traded on a national exchange (e.g., the New York Stock Exchange) would be reflected in gross income for the years in which the changes in value occur. For all other assets, no gain or loss would be recognized until the owner disposes of the property.

35. The exclusion of state and local bond interest from Federal income tax is often criticized as creating a tax haven for the wealthy. Critics, however, often fail to take into account the effect of market forces. In recent months, the long-term tax-exempt interest rate has been 4.45% while the long-term taxable rate for bonds of comparable risk was approximately 6.4%. On the other hand, state and local governments do enjoy a savings in interest costs because of the tax-favored status of their bonds. To date, Congress has concluded that the benefits gained by the states and municipalities and their residents outweigh any damages to our progressive income tax system. Do you agree with the proponents of the exclusion? Why or why not?

Extender

BRIDGE *Discipline*

1. Using an online research service, find the audited financial statements of a major U.S. corporation.
   a. Summarize its most important financial accounting policies.
   b. Describe two elements of the Federal income tax law that significantly affected the corporation's earnings per share for the operating year.

RESEARCH PROBLEMS

THOMSON RIA

Note: Solutions to Research Problems can be prepared by using the **RIA Checkpoint® Student Edition** online research product, which is available to accompany this text. It is also possible to prepare solutions to the Research Problems by using tax research materials found in a standard tax library.

Communications

Research Problem 1. Tranquility Funeral Home, Inc., your client, is an accrual basis taxpayer that sells pre-need funeral contracts. Under these contracts, the customer pays in advance for goods and services to be provided at the contract beneficiary's death. These payments are refundable at the contract purchaser's request, pursuant to state law, at any time until the goods and services are furnished. Tranquility, consistent with its financial accounting reporting, includes the payments in income for the year the funeral service is provided. The IRS agent insists that the payments are prepaid income subject to tax in the year of receipt. Your client believes the amounts involved are customer deposits. Write a letter to Tranquility that contains your advice about how the issue should be resolved. The client's address is 400 Rock Street, Memphis, TN 38152.

Communications

Research Problem 2. Your client, the Cheyenne Golf and Tennis Club, requires its newly admitted members to purchase stock in the corporation and to make a deposit of $10,000. The deposit is to be repaid in 30 years, and no interest is charged. Is the deposit subject to the imputed interest rules for below-market loans? Outline the points you intend to make when you call the client back next week.

Partial list of research aids:
TAM 9735002.

Communications

Research Problem 3. Debra is a cash basis taxpayer. In December 2005, she purchased a used piano for $400. In 2006, she discovered $4,500 hidden inside the piano. Debra was unable to determine who placed the funds in the piano. She included the $4,500 in her 2006 gross income. When her 2006 return was examined, she explained the source of the $4,500 of other income she reported. Upon hearing the story, the IRS agent contended that Debra should have included the $4,500 on her 2005 return. Since she bought the piano in 2005, that is when her wealth actually increased. Debra was in the 35% marginal tax bracket in 2005, but was only in the 10% marginal tax bracket in 2006.

Debra has asked your advice about the correct year for reporting the $4,500. Summarize your analysis in a memo to the tax research file.

Partial list of research aids:
Cesarini v. U.S., 70–2 USTC ¶9509, 26 AFTR2d 70–5107, 428 F.2d 812 (CA–6, 1970).

Internet *Activity*

Use the tax resources of the Internet to address the following questions. Do not restrict your search to the World Wide Web, but include a review of newsgroups and general reference materials, practitioner sites and resources, primary sources of the tax law, chat rooms and discussion groups, and other opportunities.

Communications

Research Problem 4. Congress cut the individual's tax on dividend income a few years ago. As a result, did U.S. corporations increase their dividend payments? Find two studies addressing this point and summarize the authors' conclusions in an e-mail to your instructor.

Research Problem 5. Determine the applicable Federal rate as of today for purposes of below-market loans.

Research Problem 6. Go to the Web page for a securities broker or mutual fund. Use a "calculator" provided there to indicate the following.

Taxable Interest Rate	Your Marginal Tax Rate	Breakeven Exempt Interest Rate
6%	35%	?
6%	15%	?
8%	28%	?
8%	33%	?

Research Problem 7. Find an article about the tax and nontax advantages of a buy-sell agreement and summarize the major points for your classmates in no more than three Power Point slides.

Communications

http://wft.swlearning.com

CHAPTER 5

Business Deductions

LEARNING OBJECTIVES

After completing Chapter 5, you should be able to:

LO.1

Understand the meaning and application of the ordinary, necessary, and reasonableness requirements for the deduction of business expenses.

LO.2

Describe the cash and accrual methods of accounting for business deductions.

LO.3

Apply a variety of Internal Revenue Code deduction disallowance provisions.

LO.4

Understand the limitations applicable to the charitable contribution deduction for corporations.

LO.5

Recognize the alternative tax treatments for research and experimental expenditures and understand several other common business deductions.

LO.6

Determine the amount of cost recovery under MACRS, and apply the § 179 expensing election and the deduction limitations on listed property and automobiles when making the MACRS calculation.

LO.7

Identify intangible assets that are eligible for amortization and calculate the amount of the deduction.

LO.8

Determine the amount of depletion expense and recognize the alternative tax treatments for intangible drilling and development costs.

OUTLINE

TAX *Talk*

Last year I had difficulty with my income tax. I tried to take my analyst off as a business deduction. The Government said it was entertainment. We compromised finally and made it a religious contribution.

—Woody Allen

LO.1

Understand the meaning and application of the ordinary, necessary, and reasonableness requirements for the deduction of business expenses.

Overview of Business Deductions

Ordinary and Necessary Requirement

Section 162(a) permits a deduction for all **ordinary and necessary** expenses paid or incurred in carrying on a trade or business. To understand the scope of this provision, it is necessary to understand the meanings of the terms ordinary and necessary.

Neither ordinary nor necessary is defined in the Code or Regulations. However, the courts have had to deal with these terms on numerous occasions and have held that an expense is necessary if a prudent business person would incur the same expense and the expense is expected to be appropriate and helpful in the taxpayer's business.[1] Many expenses that are necessary are not ordinary.

EXAMPLE 1

Welch felt that it would be helpful for the development of his new business if he repaid the debts owed by a bankrupt corporation that he had worked for. Consequently, over a period of years, he took a portion of his income and repaid these debts, even though he was under no legal obligation to do so. Welch claimed these repayments as ordinary and necessary

[1] *Welch v. Helvering*, 3 USTC ¶1164, 12 AFTR 1456, 54 S.Ct. 8 (USSC, 1933).

business expenses. The Supreme Court indicated that the payments were *necessary* for the development of Welch's business because they contributed toward Welch's reputation and built goodwill. However, the Court also indicated that the expenses were *not ordinary*, since the act of repaying the debts of a bankrupt company was unusual and not a normal method of doing business. Instead, the repayments were more appropriately classified as capital expenditures for goodwill.[2] ■

An expense is ordinary if it is normal, usual, or customary in the type of business conducted by the taxpayer and is not capital in nature.[3] However, an expense need not be recurring to be deductible as ordinary.

EXAMPLE 2

Zebra Corporation engaged in a mail-order business. The post office judged that Zebra's advertisements were false and misleading. Under a fraud order, the post office stamped "fraudulent" on all letters addressed to Zebra's business and returned them to the senders. Zebra spent $30,000 on legal fees in an unsuccessful attempt to force the post office to stop. The legal fees (though not recurring) were ordinary business expenses because they were normal, usual, or customary in the circumstances.[4] ■

Reasonableness Requirement

Although § 162 is intended to allow taxpayers to deduct a broad range of trade or business expenses, certain expenses are mentioned specifically:

- *Reasonable* salaries paid for services.
- Expenses for the use of business property.

The Code applies the **reasonableness requirement** solely to salaries and other compensation for services.[5] However, the courts have held that for *any* business expense to be ordinary and necessary, it must also be reasonable in amount.[6]

What constitutes reasonableness is a question of fact.[7] If an expense is unreasonable, the excess amount is not allowed as a deduction. The question of reasonableness usually arises with respect to closely held corporations with no separation of ownership and management.

Transactions between shareholders and a closely held corporation may result in the disallowance of deductions for excessive salaries, rent, and other expenses paid by the corporation to the shareholders. The courts will view an unusually large salary in light of all relevant circumstances and may find that the salary is reasonable despite its size. If excessive payments for salaries, rent, and other expenses are closely related to the percentage of stock owned by the recipients, the payments are generally treated as dividends.[8] Since dividends are not deductible by the corporation, the disallowance results in an increase in corporate taxable income. Deductions for reasonable salaries will not be disallowed solely because the corporation has paid insubstantial portions of its earnings as dividends to its shareholders.

EXAMPLE 3

Sparrow Corporation, a closely held corporation, is owned equally by Lupe, Carlos, and Ramon. The company has been highly profitable for several years and has not paid dividends. Lupe, Carlos, and Ramon are key officers of the company, and each receives a salary of $200,000. Salaries for similar positions in comparable companies average only $100,000. Amounts paid the owners in excess of $100,000 may be deemed unreasonable, and, if so, a

[2] *Welch v. Helvering*, 3 USTC ¶1164, 12 AFTR 1456, 54 S.Ct. 8 (USSC, 1933). For a contrasting decision, see *Dunn and McCarthy, Inc. v. Comm.*, 43–2 USTC ¶9688, 31 AFTR 1043, 139 F.2d 242 (CA–2, 1943), involving an *existing* business, where repayments to employees of a bankrupt corporation were held to be both ordinary and necessary.

[3] *Deputy v. DuPont*, 40–1 USTC ¶9161, 23 AFTR 808, 60 S.Ct. 363 (USSC, 1940).

[4] *Comm. v. Heininger*, 44–1 USTC ¶9109, 31 AFTR 783, 64 S.Ct. 249 (USSC, 1943).

[5] § 162(a)(1).

[6] *Comm. v. Lincoln Electric Co.*, 49–2 USTC ¶9388, 38 AFTR 411, 176 F.2d 815 (CA–6, 1949).

[7] *Kennedy, Jr. v. Comm.*, 82–1 USTC ¶9186, 49 AFTR2d 82–628, 671 F.2d 167 (CA–6, 1982), *rev'g* 72 T.C. 793 (1979).

[8] Reg. § 1.162–8.

EXHIBIT 5–1 Partial List of Business Deductions

Advertising	Pension and profit sharing plans
Bad debts	Rent or lease payments
Commissions and fees	Repairs and maintenance
Depletion	Salaries and wages
Depreciation	Supplies
Employee benefit programs	Taxes and licenses
Insurance	Travel and transportation
Interest	Utilities

total of $300,000 in salary deductions by Sparrow is disallowed. The disallowed amounts are treated as dividends rather than salary income to Lupe, Carlos, and Ramon because the payments are proportional to stock ownership. Salaries are deductible by the corporation, but dividends are not. ■

PLANNING *Strategies*

UNREASONABLE COMPENSATION

★ Framework Focus: Tax Rate

Strategy ★ Avoid Double Taxation.

In substantiating the reasonableness of a shareholder-employee's compensation, an internal comparison test is sometimes useful. If it can be shown that nonshareholder-employees and shareholder-employees in comparable positions receive comparable compensation, it is indicative that compensation is not unreasonable.

Another possibility is to demonstrate that the shareholder-employee has been underpaid in prior years. For example, the shareholder-employee may have agreed to take a less-than-adequate salary during the unprofitable formative years of the business. He or she would expect the "postponed" compensation to be paid in later, more profitable years. The agreement should be documented, if possible, in the corporate minutes.

Keep in mind that in testing for reasonableness, the total pay package must be considered. Compensation includes all fringe benefits or perquisites, such as contributions by the corporation to a qualified pension plan, regardless of when the funds are available to the employee.

Common Business Deductions. The language of § 162 is broad enough to permit the deduction of many different types of ordinary and necessary business expenses. Some of the more common deductions are listed in Exhibit 5–1.

LO.2

Describe the cash and accrual methods of accounting for business deductions.

Timing of Expense Recognition

A taxpayer's accounting method is a major factor in determining taxable income. The method used determines *when* an item is includible in income and *when* an item is deductible on the tax return. Usually, the taxpayer's regular method of record keeping is used for income tax purposes.[9] The taxing authorities require that the method used clearly reflect income and that items be handled consistently.[10] The most common methods of accounting are the cash method and the accrual method.

[9] § 446(a).

[10] §§ 446(b) and (e); Reg. § 1.446–1(a)(2).

Throughout the portions of the Code dealing with deductions, the phrase "paid or incurred" is used. A cash basis taxpayer is allowed a deduction only in the year an expense is *paid.* An accrual basis taxpayer is allowed a deduction in the year in which the liability for the expense is *incurred* (becomes certain).

Cash Method Requirements

The expenses of cash basis taxpayers are deductible only when they are actually paid with cash or other property. Promising to pay or issuing a note does not satisfy the actually paid requirement.[11] However, the payment can be made with borrowed funds. Thus, taxpayers are allowed to claim the deduction at the time they charge expenses on credit cards. They are deemed to have simultaneously borrowed money from the credit card issuer and constructively paid the expenses.[12]

Although the cash basis taxpayer must have actually or constructively paid the expense, payment does not assure a current deduction. The Regulations require capitalization of any expenditure that creates an asset having a useful life that extends substantially beyond the end of the tax year.[13] Thus, cash basis and accrual basis taxpayers cannot take a current deduction for capital expenditures except through amortization, depletion, or depreciation over the tax life of the asset.

EXAMPLE 4

Redbird, Inc., a calendar year and cash basis taxpayer, rents property from Bluejay, Inc. On July 1, 2006, Redbird pays $24,000 rent for the 24 months ending June 30, 2008. The prepaid rent extends 18 months after the close of the tax year—substantially beyond the year of payment. Therefore, Redbird must capitalize the prepaid rent and amortize the expense on a monthly basis. Redbird's deduction for 2006 is $6,000. ■

DIGGING DEEPER 1

Find more information on this topic at our Web site: ***http://wft-entities.swlearning.com.***

PLANNING *Strategies*

TIME VALUE OF TAX DEDUCTIONS

★ **Framework Focus: Deductions**

Strategy ★ Accelerate Recognition of Deductions to Achieve Tax Deferral.

Cash basis taxpayers often have the ability to make early payments for their expenses at the end of the tax year. This may permit the payments to be deducted in the year of payment instead of in the following tax year. In view of the time value of money, a tax deduction this year may be worth more than the same deduction next year. Before employing this strategy, the taxpayer must consider next year's expected income and tax rates and whether a cash-flow problem may develop from early payments. Thus, a variety of considerations must be taken into account when planning the timing of tax deductions.

Accrual Method Requirements

The period in which an accrual basis taxpayer can deduct an expense is determined by applying the *all events test* and the *economic performance test.* A deduction cannot be claimed until (1) all the events have occurred to create the taxpayer's liability and (2) the amount of the liability can be determined with reasonable accuracy. Once

[11] *Page v. Rhode Island Trust Co., Exr.*, 37–1 USTC ¶9138, 19 AFTR 105, 88 F.2d 192 (CA–1, 1937).

[12] Rev.Rul. 78–39, 1978–1 C.B. 73. See also Rev.Rul. 80–335, 1980–2 C.B. 170, which applies to pay-by-phone arrangements.

[13] Reg. § 1.461–1(a).

these requirements are satisfied, the deduction is permitted only if economic performance has occurred. The economic performance test is met only when the service, property, or use of property giving rise to the liability is actually performed for, provided to, or used by the taxpayer.[14]

EXAMPLE 5

On December 22, 2006, Robin, Inc., an entertainment business, sponsored a jazz festival in a rented auditorium at City College. Robin is responsible for cleaning up the auditorium after the festival and for reinstalling seats that were removed so more people could attend the festival. Since the college is closed over the Christmas holidays, the company hired by Robin to perform the work did not begin these activities until January 2, 2007. The cost to Robin is $1,200. Robin cannot deduct the $1,200 until 2007, when the services are performed. ■

As illustrated in Examples 6 and 7, an exception to the economic performance requirement allows some *recurring* items to be deducted if certain conditions are met.[15]

DIGGING DEEPER 2

Find more information on this topic at our Web site: ***http://wft-entities.swlearning.com.***

EXAMPLE 6

Towhee Company, an accrual basis, calendar year taxpayer, entered into a monthly maintenance contract during the year. Towhee makes a monthly accrual at the end of every month for this service and pays the fee sometime between the first and fifteenth of the following month when services are performed. The December 2006 accrual is deductible in 2006 even though the service is performed on January 12, 2007. ■

EXAMPLE 7

Tanager, Inc., an accrual basis, calendar year taxpayer, shipped merchandise sold on December 30, 2006, via Greyhound Van Lines on January 2, 2007, and paid the freight charges at that time. Since Tanager reported the sale of the merchandise in 2006, the shipping charge should also be deductible in 2006. This procedure results in a better matching of income and expenses. ■

Reserves for estimated expenses (frequently employed for financial accounting purposes) generally are not allowed for tax purposes because the economic performance test cannot be satisfied.

EXAMPLE 8

Oriole Airlines is required by Federal law to test its engines after 3,000 flying hours. Aircraft cannot return to flight until the tests have been conducted. An unrelated aircraft maintenance company does all of the company's tests for $1,500 per engine. For financial reporting purposes, the company accrues an expense based upon $.50 per hour of flight and credits an allowance account. The actual amounts paid for maintenance are offset against the allowance account. For tax purposes, the economic performance test is not satisfied until the work has been done. Therefore, the reserve method cannot be used for tax purposes. ■

LO.3

Apply a variety of Internal Revenue Code deduction disallowance provisions.

Disallowance Possibilities

While most ordinary and necessary business expenses are deductible, the tax law contains provisions that disallow a deduction for certain expenditures. The most frequently encountered disallowance provisions are discussed below.

Public Policy Limitations

Justification for Denying Deductions. The courts developed the principle that a payment that is in violation of public policy is not a necessary expense and is

[14] § 461(h).

[15] § 461(h)(3)(A).

not deductible.[16] Although a bribe or fine may be appropriate, helpful, and even contribute to the profitability of an activity, allowing a deduction for such expenses would frustrate clearly defined public policy. A deduction would effectively represent an indirect governmental subsidy for taxpayer wrongdoing.

Under legislation enacted based on this principle, deductions are disallowed for specific types of expenditures that are considered contrary to public policy:

- Bribes and kickbacks illegal under either Federal or state law, including those associated with Medicare or Medicaid.
- Two-thirds of the treble damage payments made to claimants resulting from violation of antitrust law.[17]
- Fines and penalties paid to a government for violation of law.

EXAMPLE 9

Brown Corporation, a moving company, consistently loads its trucks with weights in excess of the limits allowed by state law. The additional revenue more than offsets the fines levied. The fines are for a violation of public policy and are not deductible. ■

DIGGING DEEPER 3

Find more information on this topic at our Web site: ***http://wft-entities.swlearning.com.***

Legal Expenses Incurred in Defense of Civil or Criminal Penalties. To deduct legal expenses as trade or business expenses, the taxpayer must be able to show that the origin and character of the claim are directly related to a trade or business. Personal legal expenses are not deductible. Thus, legal fees incurred in connection with a criminal defense are deductible only if the crime is associated with the taxpayer's trade or business.[18]

EXAMPLE 10

Debra, a majority shareholder and chief financial officer of Blue Corporation, incurs legal expenses in connection with her defense in a criminal indictment for evasion of Blue's income taxes. Debra may deduct her legal expenses because she is deemed to be in the trade or business of being an executive. The legal action impairs her ability to conduct this business activity.[19] ■

Expenses Related to an Illegal Business. The usual expenses of operating an illegal business (e.g., a numbers racket) are deductible.[20] However, § 162 disallows a deduction for fines, bribes to public officials, illegal kickbacks, and other illegal payments.

EXAMPLE 11

Grizzly, Inc., owns and operates a saloon. In addition, Grizzly operates an illegal gambling establishment out of the saloon's back room. In connection with the illegal gambling activity, Grizzly has the following expenses during the year:

Rent	$ 60,000
Payoffs to police	40,000
Depreciation on equipment	100,000
Wages	140,000
Interest	30,000
Criminal fines	50,000
Illegal kickbacks	10,000
Total	$430,000

[16]*Tank Truck Rentals, Inc. v. Comm.*, 58–1 USTC ¶9366, 1 AFTR2d 1154, 78 S.Ct. 507 (USSC, 1958).

[17]§§ 162(c), (f), and (g).

[18]*Comm. v. Tellier*, 66–1 USTC ¶9319, 17 AFTR2d 633, 86 S.Ct. 1118 (USSC, 1966).

[19]Rev.Rul. 68–662, 1968–2 C.B. 69.

[20]*Comm. v. Sullivan*, 58–1 USTC ¶9368, 1 AFTR2d 1158, 78 S.Ct. 512 (USSC, 1958).

All of the usual expenses (rent, depreciation, wages, and interest) are deductible; payoffs, fines, and kickbacks are not deductible. Of the $430,000 spent, $330,000 is deductible and $100,000 is not. ■

An exception applies to expenses incurred in illegal trafficking in drugs.[21] Drug dealers are not allowed a deduction for ordinary and necessary business expenses incurred in their business. In arriving at gross income from the business, however, dealers may reduce total sales by the cost of goods sold.[22]

Political Contributions and Lobbying Activities

Political Contributions. Generally, no business deduction is permitted for direct or indirect payments for political purposes.[23] Historically, the government has been reluctant to extend favorable tax treatment to political expenditures by businesses. Allowing deductions might encourage abuses and enable businesses to have undue influence upon the political process.

Lobbying Expenditures. The Code places severe restrictions on the deductibility of expenses incurred in connection with lobbying activities.[24] These provisions deny deductions for expenditures incurred in connection with:

- influencing state or Federal legislation;
- participating or intervening in any political campaign on behalf of, or in opposition to, any candidate for public office;
- attempting to influence voters with respect to elections, legislative matters, or referendums; and
- attempting to influence the actions of certain high-ranking public officials (including the President, Vice President, and cabinet-level officials).

There are three exceptions to the disallowance provisions. First, an exception is provided for influencing *local* legislation (e.g., city and county governments). Second, the disallowance provision does not apply to activities devoted solely to *monitoring* legislation. Third, a *de minimis* exception allows the deduction of up to $2,000 of annual *in-house expenditures,* if the expenditures are not otherwise disallowed under the provisions discussed above. In-house lobbying expenditures do not include expenses paid to professional lobbyists or any portion of dues used by associations for lobbying. If in-house expenditures exceed $2,000, none of the in-house expenditures can be deducted.

EXAMPLE 12

Egret Company pays a $10,000 annual membership fee to the Free Trade Group, a trade association for plumbing wholesalers. The trade association estimates that 70% of its dues are allocated to lobbying activities. Thus, Egret's deduction is limited to $3,000 ($10,000 × 30%), the amount that is not associated with lobbying activities. ■

Excessive Executive Compensation

The Code contains a *millionaires' provision* that applies to compensation paid by *publicly held* corporations.[25] The provision does not limit the amount of compensation that can be *paid* to an employee. Instead, it limits the amount the employer can *deduct* for the compensation of a covered executive to $1 million annually. Covered employees include the chief executive officer and the four other most

[21] § 280E.

[22] Reg. § 1.61–3(a). Gross income is defined as sales minus cost of goods sold. Thus, while § 280E prohibits any deductions for drug dealers, it does not modify the normal definition of gross income.

[23] § 276.

[24] § 162(e).

[25] § 162(m).

highly compensated officers. Employee compensation for this purpose *excludes* the following:

- Commissions based on individual performance.
- Certain performance-based compensation based on company performance according to a formula approved by a board of directors compensation committee (comprised solely of two or more outside directors) and by shareholder vote. The performance attainment must be certified by this compensation committee.
- Payments to tax-qualified retirement plans.
- Payments that are excludible from the employee's gross income (e.g., certain fringe benefits).

Disallowance of Deductions for Capital Expenditures

The Code specifically disallows a deduction for "any amount paid out for new buildings or for permanent improvements or betterments made to increase the value of any property or estate."[26] The Regulations further define capital expenditures to include expenditures that add to the value or prolong the life of property or adapt the property to a new or different use.[27] Incidental repairs and maintenance of the property are not capital expenditures and can be deducted as ordinary and necessary business expenses. Repairing a roof is a deductible expense, but replacing a roof is a capital expenditure subject to depreciation deductions over its useful life. The tune-up of a delivery truck is an expense; a complete overhaul probably is a capital expenditure.

Capitalization versus Expense. When an expenditure is capitalized rather than expensed, the deduction is at best deferred and at worst lost forever. Although an immediate tax benefit for a large cash expenditure is lost, the cost may be deductible in increments over a longer period of time.

If the expenditure is for a tangible asset that has an ascertainable life, it is capitalized and may be deducted as depreciation over the life of the asset or as a cost recovery allowance over a specified statutory period under MACRS.[28] Land is not subject to depreciation (or cost recovery) since it does not have an ascertainable life.

EXAMPLE 13

Buffalo Corporation purchases a prime piece of land and an old but usable apartment building located in an apartment-zoned area. Buffalo pays $500,000 for the property and immediately has the building demolished at a cost of $100,000. The $500,000 purchase price and the $100,000 demolition costs must be capitalized, and the tax basis of the land is $600,000. Since land is a nondepreciable asset, no deduction is allowed. More favorable tax treatment might result if Buffalo rents the apartments in the old building for a period of time to attempt to establish that there is no intent to demolish the building. If Buffalo's attempt is successful, it might be possible to allocate a substantial portion of the original purchase price of the property to the building (a depreciable asset). When the building is later demolished, any remaining adjusted basis can be deducted as an ordinary (§ 1231) loss. ■

Investigation of a Business

Investigation expenses are paid or incurred to determine the feasibility of entering a new business or expanding an existing business. They include such costs as travel, engineering and architectural surveys, marketing reports, and various legal and

[26]§ 263(a)(1).
[27]Reg. § 1.263(a)–1(b).
[28]Depreciation and cost recovery allowances are discussed later in this chapter.

accounting services. How such expenses are treated for tax purposes depends on a number of variables, including the following:

- The current business, if any, of the taxpayer.
- The nature of the business being investigated.
- Whether or not the acquisition actually takes place.

If the taxpayer is in a business the same as or similar to that being investigated, all investigation expenses are deductible in the year paid or incurred. The tax result is the same whether or not the taxpayer acquires the business being investigated.[29]

EXAMPLE 14

Terry, an accrual basis sole proprietor, owns and operates three motels in Georgia. In the current year, Terry incurs expenses of $8,500 in investigating the possibility of acquiring several additional motels located in South Carolina. The $8,500 is deductible in the current year whether or not Terry acquires the motels in South Carolina. ■

When the taxpayer is not in a business that is the same as or similar to the one being investigated, the tax result depends on whether the new business is acquired. If the business is not acquired, all investigation expenses generally are nondeductible.[30]

EXAMPLE 15

Lynn, president and sole shareholder of Marmot Corporation, incurs expenses when traveling from Rochester, New York, to California to investigate the feasibility of acquiring several auto care centers. Marmot is in the residential siding business. If no acquisition takes place, Marmot may not deduct any of the expenses. ■

If the taxpayer is not in a business that is the same as or similar to the one being investigated and actually acquires the new business, the expenses must be capitalized as startup expenses. At the election of the taxpayer, the first $5,000 of the expenses can be immediately deducted. Any excess expenses can be amortized over a period of 180 months (15 years). In arriving at the $5,000 immediate deduction allowed, a dollar-for-dollar reduction must be made for those expenses in excess of $50,000.[31]

EXAMPLE 16

Tina, a sole proprietor, owns and operates 10 restaurants located in various cities throughout the Southeast. She travels to Atlanta to discuss the acquisition of an auto dealership. In addition, she incurs legal and accounting costs associated with the potential acquisition. After incurring total investigation costs of $52,000, she acquires the auto dealership on October 1, 2006.

Tina may immediately deduct $3,000 [$5,000 – ($52,000 – $50,000)] and amortize the balance of $49,000 ($52,000 – $3,000) over a period of 180 months. For calendar year 2006, therefore, Tina can deduct $3,817 [$3,000 + ($49,000 × 3/180)]. ■

DIGGING DEEPER 4

Find more information on this topic at our Web site: ***http://wft-entities.swlearning.com.***

Transactions between Related Parties

The Code places restrictions on the recognition of gains and losses from **related-party transactions**. Without these restrictions, relationships created by birth, marriage, and business would provide endless possibilities for engaging in financial transactions that produce tax savings with no real economic substance or change.

[29] *York v. Comm.*, 58–2 USTC ¶9952, 2 AFTR2d 6178, 261 F.2d 421 (CA–4, 1958).

[30] Rev.Rul. 57–418, 1957–2 C.B. 143; *Morton Frank*, 20 T.C. 511 (1953); and *Dwight A. Ward*, 20 T.C. 332 (1953).

[31] § 195(b). Prior to October 22, 2004 (the effective date of the American Jobs Creation Act), no immediate deduction was available, but the amortization period was not less than 60 months.

For example, to create an artificial loss, a corporation could sell investment property to its sole shareholder at a loss and deduct the loss on the corporate return. The shareholder could then hold the asset indefinitely. Although title to the property has changed, there has been no real economic loss if the shareholder and corporation are considered as an economic unit. A complex set of laws has been designed to eliminate such possibilities.

Losses. The Code provides for the disallowance of any losses from sales or exchanges of property directly or indirectly between related parties.[32] In addition to specified family relationships (e.g., brothers and sisters), certain business relationships are subject to this disallowance rule. For instance, a corporation and a shareholder are considered related parties if the shareholder owns more than 50 percent of the corporation.

When the property is subsequently sold to an unrelated party, any gain recognized is reduced by the loss previously disallowed. Any disallowed loss not used by the related-party buyer to offset his or her recognized gain on a subsequent sale or exchange to an unrelated party is permanently lost.

EXAMPLE 17

Anna, sole shareholder of Leopard Corporation, sells common stock with a basis of $1,000 to the corporation for $800. Leopard sells the stock several years later for $1,100. Anna's $200 loss is disallowed upon the sale to Leopard, and only $100 of gain ($1,100 selling price − $800 basis − $200 disallowed loss) is taxable to Leopard upon the subsequent sale. ■

EXAMPLE 18

George sells common stock with a basis of $1,050 to his wholly owned corporation for $800. George's $250 loss is disallowed under the related-party rules. The corporation sells the stock eight months later to an unrelated party for $900. The corporation's gain of $100 ($900 selling price − $800 basis) is not recognized because of the offset from George's previously disallowed loss of $250. Note that the offset may result in only a partial tax benefit upon the subsequent sale (as in this case). If George had not sold the property to the corporation, he could have recognized a $150 loss upon the sale to the unrelated party ($900 selling price − $1,050 basis). ■

Unpaid Expenses and Interest. The law prevents related taxpayers from engaging in tax avoidance schemes where one related taxpayer uses the accrual method of accounting and the other uses the cash basis. The accrual basis allows the deduction of expenses when incurred, while the cash method requires that income be reported when received. In the absence of restrictions, an accrual basis, closely held corporation, for example, could borrow funds from a cash basis individual shareholder. At the end of the year, the corporation would accrue and deduct the interest expense, but the cash basis lender would not recognize interest income since no interest had been paid. Section 267 specifically defers the accrual of an interest deduction until the lender is required to include the interest in income; that is, when it is actually received by the cash basis taxpayer. This matching provision also applies to other expenses, such as salaries and bonuses.

The deduction deferral provision does not apply if both of the related taxpayers use the accrual method or both use the cash method. Likewise, it does not apply if the related party reporting income uses the accrual method and the related party taking the deduction uses the cash method.

Relationships and Constructive Ownership. Section 267 operates to disallow losses and defer deductions only between *related parties.* Losses or deductions

[32]§ 267(a)(1).

generated by similar transactions with an unrelated party are allowed. Related parties include the following:

- Brothers and sisters (whether whole, half, or adopted), spouse, ancestors (parents, grandparents), and lineal descendants (children, grandchildren) of the taxpayer.
- A corporation owned more than 50 percent (directly or indirectly) by the taxpayer.
- Two corporations that are members of a controlled group.
- A series of other complex relationships between trusts, corporations, and individual taxpayers.

Constructive ownership provisions are applied to determine whether the taxpayers are related. Under these provisions, stock owned by certain relatives or related entities is deemed to be owned by the taxpayer for purposes of applying the loss and expense deduction disallowance provisions. A taxpayer is deemed to own not only his or her stock but also the stock owned by his or her lineal descendants, ancestors, brothers and sisters or half-brothers and half-sisters, and spouse. The taxpayer is also deemed to own his or her proportionate share of stock owned by any partnership, corporation, estate, or trust of which he or she is a member. An individual is deemed to own any stock owned, directly or indirectly, by his or her partner. However, constructive ownership by an individual of the other partner's shares does not extend to the individual's spouse or other relatives (i.e., no double attribution).

EXAMPLE 19

The stock of Sparrow Corporation is owned 20% by Ted, 30% by Ted's father, 30% by Ted's mother, and 20% by Ted's sister. On July 1 of the current year, Ted loaned $10,000 to Sparrow Corporation at 8% annual interest, principal and interest payable on demand. For tax purposes, Sparrow uses the accrual basis, and Ted uses the cash basis. Both report on a calendar year basis. Since Ted is deemed to own the 80% owned by his parents and sister, he actually and constructively owns 100% of Sparrow. If the corporation accrues the interest within the taxable year, no deduction can be taken until payment is made to Ted. ■

Lack of Adequate Substantiation

The tax law is built on a voluntary system. Taxpayers file their tax returns, report income and take deductions to which they are entitled, and pay their taxes through withholding or estimated tax payments during the year. The taxpayer has the burden of proof for substantiating expenses deducted on the returns and must retain adequate records. Upon audit, the IRS will disallow any undocumented or unsubstantiated deductions. These requirements have resulted in numerous conflicts between taxpayers and the IRS.

Some events throughout the year should be documented as they occur. For example, it is generally advisable to receive a pledge payment statement from a charity, in addition to a canceled check (if available), for proper documentation of a charitable contribution.[33] In addition, for a charitable contribution of $250 or more, a donor must obtain a *receipt* from the donee. Other types of deductible expenditures (such as travel and entertainment expenses, and depreciation on property used for both business and personal purposes) may require receipts or some other type of support.

[33] Rev.Proc. 92–71, 1992–2 C.B. 437, addresses circumstances where checks are not returned by a financial institution or where electronic transfers are made.

Expenses and Interest Related to Tax-Exempt Income

Certain income, such as interest on municipal bonds, is tax-exempt.[34] The law also allows the taxpayer to deduct expenses incurred for the production of income.[35] Deduction disallowance provisions, however, make it impossible to make money at the expense of the government by excluding interest income and deducting interest expense.[36]

EXAMPLE 20

Oriole, Inc., a corporation in the 35% bracket, purchased $100,000 of 6% municipal bonds. At the same time, Oriole used the bonds as collateral on a bank loan of $100,000 at 8% interest. A positive cash flow would result from the tax benefit as follows:

Cash paid out on loan	($8,000)
Cash received from bonds	6,000
Tax savings from deducting interest expense ($8,000 × 35%)	2,800
Net positive cash flow	$ 800

■

To eliminate the possibility illustrated in the preceding example, the Code specifically disallows a deduction for the expenses of producing tax-exempt income. Interest on any indebtedness incurred or continued to purchase or carry tax-exempt obligations also is disallowed.

Judicial Interpretations. It is often difficult to show a direct relationship between borrowings and investment in tax-exempt securities. Suppose, for example, that a taxpayer borrows money, adds it to existing funds, buys inventory and stocks, then later sells the inventory and buys municipal bonds. A series of transactions such as these can completely obscure any connection between the loan and the tax-exempt investment. One solution would be to disallow interest on any debt to the extent that the taxpayer holds any tax-exempt securities. The law was not intended to go to such extremes. As a result, judicial interpretations have tried to be reasonable in disallowing interest deductions.[37]

DIGGING DEEPER 5

*Find more information on this topic at our Web site: **http://wft-entities.swlearning.com.***

EXAMPLE 21

In January of the current year, Crane Corporation borrowed $100,000 at 8% interest. Crane used the loan proceeds to purchase 5,000 shares of stock in White Corporation. In July, Crane sold the stock for $120,000 and reinvested the proceeds in City of Denver bonds, the income from which is tax-exempt. Assuming the $100,000 loan remained outstanding throughout the entire year, Crane cannot deduct the interest attributable to the period when it held the bonds. ■

Charitable Contributions

LO.4

Understand the limitations applicable to the charitable contribution deduction for corporations.

Corporations and individuals are allowed to deduct contributions made to qualified domestic charitable organizations.[38] Qualified organizations include:[39]

- A state or possession of the United States or any subdivisions thereof.
- A corporation, trust, or community chest, fund, or foundation that is situated in the United States and is organized and operated exclusively for religious,

[34]§ 103.
[35]§ 212.
[36]§ 265.
[37]See, for example, *The Wisconsin Cheeseman, Inc. v. U.S.*, 68–1 USTC ¶9145, 21 AFTR2d 383, 388 F.2d 420 (CA–7, 1968).
[38]§ 170.
[39]§ 170(c).

charitable, scientific, literary, or educational purposes or for the prevention of cruelty to children or animals.

DIGGING DEEPER 6

Find more information on this topic at our Web site: ***http://wft-entities.swlearning.com.***

Generally, a deduction for a **charitable contribution** will be allowed only for the year in which the payment is made. However, an important exception is made for *accrual basis* corporations. They may claim the deduction in the year preceding payment if two requirements are met. First, the contribution must be *authorized* by the board of directors by the end of that year. Second, it must be *paid* on or before the fifteenth day of the third month of the following year.

EXAMPLE 22

On December 28, 2006, Blue Company, a calendar year, accrual basis partnership, authorizes a $5,000 donation to the Atlanta Symphony Association (a qualified charitable organization). The donation is made on March 14, 2007. Because Blue Company is a partnership, the contribution can be deducted only in 2007.[40] However, if Blue Company is a corporation and the December 28, 2006 authorization was made by its board of directors, Blue may claim the $5,000 donation as a deduction for calendar year 2006. ■

Property Contributions

The amount that can be deducted for a noncash charitable contribution depends on the type of property contributed. Property must be identified as long-term **capital gain property** or ordinary income property. Long-term capital gain property is property that, if sold, would result in long-term capital gain for the taxpayer. Such property generally must be a capital asset and must be held for the long-term holding period (more than one year). **Ordinary income property** is property that, if sold, would result in ordinary income for the taxpayer. Examples of ordinary income property include inventory and capital assets held short term (one year or less). Refer to Chapter 4 for a brief introduction to the distinction between capital and ordinary assets.

The deduction for a charitable contribution of long-term capital gain property is generally measured by its *fair market value.*

EXAMPLE 23

During the current year, Mallard Corporation donates a parcel of land (a capital asset) to Oakland Community College. Mallard acquired the land in 1988 for $60,000, and the fair market value on the date of the contribution is $100,000. The corporation's charitable contribution deduction (subject to a percentage limitation discussed later) is measured by the asset's fair market value of $100,000, even though the $40,000 of appreciation on the land has never been included in Mallard's income. ■

In two situations, a charitable contribution of long-term capital gain property is measured by the basis of the property, rather than fair market value. If a corporation contributes tangible personal property and the charitable organization puts the property to an *unrelated use,* the appreciation on the property is not deductible. Unrelated use is defined as use that is not related to the purpose or function that qualifies the organization for exempt status.

EXAMPLE 24

White Corporation donates a painting worth $200,000 to Western States Art Museum (a qualified charity), which exhibits the painting. White had acquired the painting in 1980 for

[40]Each calendar year partner will report an allocable portion of the charitable contribution deduction as of December 31, 2007 (the end of the partnership's tax year). See Chapter 11.

$90,000. Because the museum put the painting to a related use, White is allowed to deduct $200,000, the fair market value of the painting. ■

EXAMPLE 25

Assume the same facts as in the previous example, except that White Corporation donates the painting to the American Cancer Society, which sells the painting and deposits the $200,000 proceeds in the organization's general fund. White's deduction is limited to the $90,000 basis because it contributed tangible personal property that was put to an unrelated use by the charitable organization. ■

The deduction for charitable contributions of long-term capital gain property to certain private nonoperating foundations (defined in §§ 4942 and 509) is also limited to the basis of the property.

As a general rule, the deduction for a contribution of ordinary income property is limited to the basis of the property. On certain contributions, however, corporations enjoy two special exceptions that allow a deduction for basis plus 50 percent of the appreciation on the property. The first exception concerns inventory if the property is used in a manner related to the exempt purpose of the donee. The charity must use the property solely for the care of the ill, the needy, or infants.

EXAMPLE 26

Lark Corporation, a grocery chain, donates canned goods to the Salvation Army to be used to feed the needy. Lark's basis in the canned goods is $2,000, and the fair market value (the sales price to customers) is $3,000. Lark's deduction is $2,500 [$2,000 basis + 50% ($3,000 – $2,000)]. ■

The second exception involves gifts of scientific property to colleges and certain scientific research organizations for use in research, provided certain conditions are met.[41]

Limitations Imposed on Charitable Contribution Deductions

Both corporations and individuals are subject to percentage limits on the charitable contribution deduction.[42] The complex limitations for individual taxpayers are covered in Chapter 16.

For any one year, a corporate taxpayer's contribution deduction is limited to 10 percent of taxable income. For this purpose, taxable income is computed without regard to the charitable contribution deduction, any net operating loss carryback or capital loss carryback, and the dividends received deduction. Any contributions in excess of the 10 percent limitation may be carried forward to the five succeeding tax years. Any carryforward must be added to subsequent contributions and will be subject to the 10 percent limitation. In applying this limitation, the current year's contributions must be deducted first, with excess deductions from previous years deducted in order of time.[43]

EXAMPLE 27

During 2006, Orange Corporation (a calendar year taxpayer) had the following income and expenses.

Income from operations	$140,000
Expenses from operations	110,000
Dividends received	10,000
Charitable contributions made in May 2006	5,000

[41]These conditions are set forth in § 170(e)(4). For the inventory exception, see § 170(e)(3).

[42]The percentage limitations applicable to individuals and corporations are set forth in § 170(b).

[43]The carryover rules relating to all taxpayers are in § 170(d).

TAX FACT

What Ten Percent Ceiling?

Just how generous is corporate America? Based on recent data, of the $601 billion of corporate income subject to tax, contributions and gifts totaled approximately $10.3 billion. In other words, approximately 1.7 percent of a corporation's income subject to tax, on average, goes to charity.

Source: *Corporation Income Tax Returns, 2002; Table 2—Selected Balance Sheet, Income Statement, and Tax Items by Asset Size; September 2005.*

For purposes of the 10% limitation only, Orange Corporation's taxable income is $40,000 ($140,000 − $110,000 + $10,000). Consequently, the allowable charitable contribution deduction for 2006 is $4,000 (10% × $40,000). The $1,000 unused portion of the contribution can be carried forward to 2007, 2008, 2009, 2010, and 2011 (in that order) until exhausted. ■

EXAMPLE 28

Assume the same facts as in the previous example. In 2007, Orange Corporation has taxable income (for purposes of the 10% limitation) of $50,000 and makes a charitable contribution of $4,500. The maximum deduction allowed for 2007 is $5,000 (10% × $50,000). The entire 2007 contribution of $4,500 and $500 of the 2006 charitable contribution carryforward are currently deductible. The remaining $500 of the 2006 carryforward may be carried over to 2008 (and later years, if necessary). ■

LO.5

Recognize the alternative tax treatments for research and experimental expenditures and understand several other common business deductions.

Research and Experimental Expenditures

Section 174 covers the treatment of **research and experimental expenditures**. The Regulations define research and experimental expenditures as follows:

> all such costs incident to the development of an experimental or pilot model, a plant process, a product, a formula, an invention, or similar property, and the improvement of already existing property of the type mentioned. The term does not include expenditures such as those for the ordinary testing or inspection of materials or products for quality control or those for efficiency surveys, management studies, consumer surveys, advertising, or promotions.[44]

The law permits three alternatives for the handling of research and experimental expenditures.

- Expense in the year paid or incurred.
- Defer and amortize.
- Capitalize.

If the costs are capitalized, a deduction is not available until the research project is abandoned or is deemed worthless. Since many products resulting from research projects do not have a definite and limited useful life, a taxpayer should ordinarily elect to write off the expenditures immediately or to defer and amortize them. It is generally preferable to elect an immediate write-off of the research expenditures because of the time value of the tax deduction.

The law also provides for a research activities credit. The credit amounts to 20 percent of certain research and experimental expenditures.[45]

[44]Reg. § 1.174–2(a)(1).

[45]§ 41. See Chapter 14 for a more detailed discussion of the research activities credit.

Expense Method

A taxpayer can elect to expense all of the research and experimental expenditures incurred in the current year and all subsequent years. The consent of the IRS is not required if the method is adopted for the first taxable year in which such expenditures were paid or incurred. Once the election is made, the taxpayer must continue to expense all qualifying expenditures unless a request for a change is made to, and approved by, the IRS. In certain instances, a taxpayer may incur research and experimental expenditures before actually engaging in any trade or business activity. In such instances, the Supreme Court has applied a liberal standard of deductibility and permitted a deduction in the year of incurrence.[46]

Deferral and Amortization Method

Alternatively, research and experimental expenditures may be deferred and amortized if the taxpayer makes an election.[47] Under the election, research and experimental expenditures are amortized ratably over a period of not less than 60 months. A deduction is allowed beginning with the month in which the taxpayer first realizes benefits from the research and experimental expenditures. The election is binding, and a change requires permission from the IRS.

EXAMPLE 29

Gold Corporation decides to develop a new line of adhesives. The project begins in 2006. Gold incurs the following expenses in 2006 and 2007 in connection with the project.

	2006	2007
Salaries	$25,000	$18,000
Materials	8,000	2,000
Depreciation on machinery	6,500	5,700

The benefits from the project will be realized starting in March 2008. If Gold Corporation elects a 60-month deferral and amortization period, there is no deduction prior to March 2008, the month benefits from the project begin to be realized. The deduction for 2008 is $10,867, computed as follows.

Salaries ($25,000 + $18,000)	$43,000
Materials ($8,000 + $2,000)	10,000
Depreciation ($6,500 + $5,700)	12,200
Total	$65,200
$65,200 × (10 months/60 months)	$10,867

■

The option to treat research and experimental expenditures as a deferred expense is usually employed when a company does not have sufficient income to offset the research and experimental expenses. Rather than create net operating loss carryovers that might not be utilized because of the 20-year limitation on such carryovers, the deferral and amortization method may be used. The deferral of research and experimental expenditures should also be considered if the taxpayer expects higher tax rates in the future.

Other Expense Rules

In addition to the provisions related to charitable contributions and research and experimental expenditures, a variety of other expenses are subject to special rules

46 *Snow v. Comm.*, 74–1 USTC ¶9432, 33 AFTR2d 74–1251, 94 S.Ct. 1876 (USSC, 1974).

47 § 174(b)(2).

and limitations. Some of these rules are noted briefly in the paragraphs that follow.

Interest Expense

Generally, corporations are not limited in the amount of interest expense they may deduct. However, the deductibility of expenses (including interest) from certain activities may be limited.[48] In contrast, individuals generally may not deduct interest expense on loans used for personal purposes, unless the loan is secured by a home. Furthermore, individuals may only deduct interest expense associated with investments to the extent of net investment income and interest on qualified education loans.[49]

Because the deductibility of interest expense associated with certain activities is limited, the IRS provides rules for allocating interest expense among activities. Under these rules, interest is allocated in the same manner as the debt with respect to which the interest is paid, and debt is allocated by tracing disbursements of the debt proceeds to specific expenditures. The interest tracing rules are complex and depend on whether loan proceeds are commingled with other cash and the length of time the loan proceeds are held before they are spent.

Taxes

As with interest expense, tax payments in a business or investment context are generally deductible. However, most Federal taxes are not deductible. Individuals may also deduct tax payments, subject to limitations (discussed in Chapter 16). One unique problem associated with determining the deductibility of taxes relates to real estate taxes paid during a year when the real estate is sold.

Real estate taxes for the entire year are apportioned between the buyer and seller based on the number of days the property was held by each during the real property tax year. This apportionment is required whether the tax is paid by the buyer or the seller or is prorated according to the purchase agreement. It is the apportionment that determines who is entitled to deduct the real estate taxes in the year of sale. The required apportionment prevents the shifting of the deduction for real estate taxes from buyer to seller, or vice versa.

In making the apportionment, the assessment date and the lien date are disregarded. The date of sale counts as a day the property is owned by the buyer. In leap years, the taxes are prorated over 366 days.

EXAMPLE 30

A county's real property tax year runs from April 1 to March 31. Nuthatch Corporation, the owner on April 1, 2006, of real property located in the county, sells the real property to Crane, Inc., on June 30, 2006. Crane owns the real property from June 30, 2006, through March 31, 2007. The tax for the real property tax year April 1, 2006, through March 31, 2007, is $3,650. The portion of the real property tax treated as imposed upon Nuthatch, the seller, is $900 [(90/365) × $3,650, April 1 through June 29, 2006], and $2,750 [(275/365) × $3,650, June 30, 2006, through March 31, 2007] of the tax is treated as imposed upon Crane, the purchaser. ■

If the actual real estate taxes are not prorated between the buyer and seller as part of the purchase agreement, adjustments are required. The adjustments are necessary to determine the amount realized by the seller and the adjusted basis of the property to the buyer. If the buyer pays the entire amount of the tax, it effectively has paid the seller's portion of the real estate tax and has therefore paid more for the property than the actual purchase price. Thus, the amount of real estate tax

[48]See, for example, the discussion of the passive activity limits in Chapter 6.

[49]See Chapter 16 for a more detailed discussion of the deductibility of interest by individuals.

that is apportioned to the seller (for Federal income tax purposes) and paid by the buyer is added to the buyer's adjusted basis. The seller must increase the amount realized on the sale by the same amount.

EXAMPLE 31

Seth sells real estate on October 3, 2007, for $100,000. The buyer, Winslow Company, pays the real estate taxes of $3,650 for the 2007 calendar year, which is the real estate property tax year. Of the real estate taxes, $2,750 (for 275 days) is apportioned to and is deductible by the seller, Seth, and $900 (for 90 days) of the taxes is deductible by Winslow. The buyer has paid Seth's real estate taxes of $2,750 and has therefore paid $102,750 for the property. Winslow's basis is increased to $102,750, and the amount realized by Seth from the sale is increased to $102,750. ■

The opposite result occurs if the seller (rather than the buyer) pays the real estate taxes. In this case, the seller reduces the amount realized from the sale by the amount that has been apportioned to the buyer. The buyer is required to reduce his or her adjusted basis by a corresponding amount.

EXAMPLE 32

Silver Corporation sells real estate to Butch for $50,000 on October 3, 2007. While Silver held the property, it paid the real estate taxes of $1,095 for the calendar year, which is the real estate property tax year. Although Silver paid the entire $1,095 of real estate taxes, $270 of that amount is apportioned to Butch, based on the number of days he owned the property, and is therefore deductible by him. The effect is that the buyer, Butch, has paid only $49,730 ($50,000 − $270) for the property. The amount realized by Silver, the seller, is reduced by $270, and Butch reduces his basis in the property to $49,730. ■

Domestic Production Activities Deduction

The American Jobs Creation Act of 2004 was enacted to replace certain tax provisions that our world trading partners regarded as allowing unfair advantage to U.S. exports. Among other changes, the Act created a new deduction based on the income from manufacturing activities (designated as *production activities*). The new **production activities deduction (PAD)** is contained in § 199.

Calculation of the Production Activities Deduction. For tax years beginning in 2005 or 2006, the PAD is based on the following formula:[50]

3% × Lesser of
- Qualified production activities income (QPAI)
- Taxable (or modified adjusted gross) income or alternative minimum taxable income

For tax years beginning in 2007 to 2009, the 3 percent factor is increased to 6 percent. For tax years beginning in 2010 and thereafter, the factor is increased to 9 percent.

Taxable income is determined without regard to the PAD. In the case of an individual (a sole proprietorship or an owner of a flow-through entity), **modified adjusted gross income** is substituted for taxable income.[51]

The taxable income limitation is determined after the application of any net operating loss (NOL) deduction for the tax year (NOLs are explained in Chapter 6). Thus, a company with an NOL carryforward for a tax year is ineligible for the PAD if the carryforward eliminates current taxable income. Further, a taxpayer that has an NOL carryback may lose part or all of the PAD benefit for that year. As taxable income is reduced by the NOL carryback, there is a corresponding reduction in the PAD. If qualified production activities income (QPAI) cannot be used in a particular

[50]§ 199(a). Generally, modified AGI is AGI prior to the effect of § 199.

[51]§ 199(d)(2).

year due to the taxable income limitation (see the above formula), it is lost forever. (The calculation of QPAI is explained in the next section.)

EXAMPLE 33

Opal, Inc., manufactures and sells costume jewelry. It also sells costume jewelry purchased from other manufacturers. During 2006, Opal had a *profit* of $200,000 (QPAI) from the sale of its own manufactured jewelry and a *loss* of $50,000 from the sale of the purchased jewelry. Based on this information, Opal's QPAI is $200,000, and its taxable income is $150,000 ($200,000 – $50,000). Opal's PAD becomes $4,500 [3% of the lesser of $200,000 (QPAI) or $150,000 (taxable income)]. ■

EXAMPLE 34

Assume the same facts as in Example 33, except that Opal also has an NOL carryover from 2005 of $300,000. As taxable income for 2006 is zero ($200,000 – $50,000 – $300,000), there is no PAD. ■

Another important limitation is that the amount of the PAD cannot exceed 50 percent of **W–2 wages** paid by the taxpayer during the tax year.[52] An employer's W–2 wages include the sum of the aggregate amount of wages and elective deferrals required to be included on the W–2 wage statements for employees during the employer's taxable year. Elective deferrals include those amounts deferred under § 457 plans and Roth IRA contributions. An employer includes wages paid to all workers during a tax year and not just the wages of the employees engaged in qualified production activities.

EXAMPLE 35

In 2006, Red, Inc., has QPAI of $2 million and taxable income of $2.1 million. Since Red outsources much of its work to independent contractors, its W–2 wage base, which for Red is related entirely to production activities, is $80,000. Although Red's PAD normally would be $60,000 [3% of the lesser of $2 million (QPAI) or $2.1 million (taxable income)], it is limited to $40,000 [50% of $80,000 (W–2 wages)]. ■

EXAMPLE 36

Assume the same facts as in Example 35, except that Red also pays salaries of $50,000 related to its *nonproduction* activities. As the wage limitation now becomes $65,000 [50% of $130,000 ($80,000 + $50,000)], the usual PAD amount of $60,000 can be claimed. ■

The purpose of this limitation is to preserve U.S. manufacturing jobs and to discourage their outsourcing.

Calculation of Qualified Production Activities Income. **Qualified production activities income (QPAI)** is the excess of **domestic production gross receipts (DPGR)** over the sum of:[53]

- The cost of goods sold allocated to such receipts.
- Other deductions, expenses, or losses directly allocated to such receipts.
- The ratable portion of deductions, expenses, and losses not directly allocable to such receipts or another class of income.

QPAI is determined on an item-by-item basis—not on a division-by-division or transaction-by-transaction basis. Because all items must be netted in the calculation, the final QPAI amount can be either positive or negative. The effect of the netting rule is to preclude taxpayers from selecting only profitable product lines or profitable transactions when calculating QPAI.

EXAMPLE 37

A taxpayer manufactures pants and shirts with the following QPAI results: $5 for one pair of pants and a negative $2 for one shirt. Because the two items are netted, the QPAI amount that controls is $3 ($5 – $2). ■

[52] § 199(b).

[53] § 199(c).

Five specific categories of DPGR qualify for the PAD.[54]

- The lease, license, sale, exchange, or other disposition of qualified production property (QPP) that was manufactured, produced, grown, or extracted (MPGE) in the United States.
- Qualified films largely created in the United States.
- The production of electricity, natural gas, or potable water.
- Construction (but not self-construction) performed in the United States.
- Engineering and architectural services for domestic construction.

The sale of food and beverages prepared by a taxpayer at a retail establishment and the transmission or distribution of electricity, natural gas, or potable water are specifically excluded from the definition of DPGR.

Eligible Taxpayers. The deduction is available to a variety of taxpayers including individuals, partnerships, S corporations, C corporations, cooperatives, estates, and trusts. For a pass-through entity (e.g., partnerships, S corporations), the deduction flows through to the individual owners. In the case of a sole proprietor, a deduction *for* AGI results and is claimed on Form 1040, line 35 on page 1. A Form 8903 must be attached to support the deduction.

Cost Recovery Allowances

LO.6

Determine the amount of cost recovery under MACRS, and apply the § 179 expensing election and the deduction limitations on listed property and automobiles when making the MACRS calculation.

Overview

Taxpayers may write off the cost of certain assets that are used in a trade or business or held for the production of income. A write-off may take the form of a *cost recovery allowance* (depreciation under prior law), depletion, or amortization. Tangible assets, other than natural resources, are written off through cost recovery allowances. Natural resources, such as oil, gas, coal, and timber, are *depleted.* Intangible assets, such as copyrights and patents, are *amortized.* Generally, no write-off is allowed for an asset that does not have a determinable useful life.

The tax rules for writing off the cost of business assets differ from the accounting rules. Several methods are available for determining depreciation for accounting purposes, including the straight-line, declining-balance, and sum-of-the-years' digits methods. Historically, *depreciation* for tax purposes was computed using variations of these accounting methods. Congress completely overhauled the **depreciation rules** in 1981 tax legislation by creating the **accelerated cost recovery system (ACRS)**. Substantial modifications were made to ACRS in 1986 tax legislation which resulted in the **modified accelerated cost recovery system (MACRS)** replacing ACRS.

The statutory changes that have taken place since 1980 have widened the gap that exists between the accounting and tax versions of depreciation. The tax rules that existed prior to 1981 were much more compatible with generally accepted accounting principles. This chapter focuses on the MACRS rules because they cover more recent property acquisitions (i.e., after 1986) and their use is more widespread.

Concepts Relating to Depreciation

Nature of Property. Property includes both realty (real property) and personalty (personal property). *Realty* generally includes land and buildings permanently affixed to the land. *Personalty* is defined as any asset that is not realty. Personalty includes furniture, machinery, equipment, and many other types of assets. Do not confuse personalty (or personal property) with personal-use property. Personal-use property is any property (realty or personalty) that is held for personal use rather than for use in a trade or business or an income-producing activity. Cost recovery is not allowed for personal-use assets.

[54] § 199(c)(4).

TAX FACT

Cost Recovery by Any Other Name

Not surprisingly, the most prevalent write-off of assets used in a trade or business or in the production of income comes in the form of the cost recovery or depreciation allowances. Of the approximately $835 billion of corporate deductions in a recent year, the relative use of the three broad types of write-offs is shown below.

	Percentage
Amortization	13.77
Cost recovery or depreciation	85.10
Depletion	1.13
	100.00

Source: *Corporation Income Tax Returns, 2002; Table 2—Selected Balance Sheet, Income Statement, and Tax Items by Asset Size; September 2005.*

In summary, both realty and personalty can be either business-use/income-producing property or personal-use property. Examples include a residence (realty that is personal use), an office building (realty that is business use), a dump truck (personalty that is business use), and regular wearing apparel (personalty that is personal use). It is imperative that this distinction between the classification of an asset (realty or personalty) and the use to which the asset is put (business or personal) be understood.

Assets used in a trade or business or for the production of income are eligible for cost recovery if they are subject to wear and tear, decay or decline from natural causes, or obsolescence. Assets that do not decline in value on a predictable basis or that do not have a determinable useful life (e.g., land, stock, antiques) are not eligible for cost recovery.

Placed in Service Requirement. The key date for the commencement of depreciation is the date an asset is placed in service. This date, and not the purchase date of an asset, is the relevant date. This distinction is particularly important for an asset that is purchased near the end of the tax year, but not placed in service until after the beginning of the following tax year.

Cost Recovery Allowed or Allowable. The basis of cost recovery property must be reduced by the cost recovery *allowed* and by not less than the *allowable* amount. The allowed cost recovery is the cost recovery actually taken, whereas the allowable cost recovery is the amount that could have been taken under the applicable cost recovery method. If the taxpayer does not claim any cost recovery on property during a particular year, the basis of the property must still be reduced by the amount of cost recovery that should have been deducted (the *allowable* cost recovery).

EXAMPLE 38

On March 15, Heron Corporation paid $10,000 for a copier to be used in its business. The copier is five-year property. Heron elected to use the straight-line method of cost recovery, but did not take any cost recovery allowance in year 3 or 4. Therefore, the allowed cost recovery (cost recovery actually deducted) and the allowable cost recovery are as follows:[55]

[55]The cost recovery allowances are based on the half-year convention, which allows a half-year's cost recovery in the first and last years of the recovery period.

BRIDGE *Discipline*

Bridge to Finance

For many business entities, success in producing goods for sale is dependent on the efficient use of fixed assets, such as machinery and equipment. An important question for such businesses to resolve is how they should gain access to the required complement of fixed assets: that is, whether the assets should be purchased or leased. To answer this question, the taxpayer must determine which alternative is more cost-effective. Critical to this assessment is quantifying the after-tax cost (including the associated tax benefits) of each option.

Purchasing productive assets for business use often necessitates an immediate cash outflow. However, the tax savings resulting from the available depreciation expense deductions mitigate the impact of that outflow, by reducing the taxpayer's taxable income and the income tax paid for the year. Consequently, the tax savings from the depreciation calculation associated with the purchase of an asset reduce the after-tax cost of employing the asset. The analysis can be refined further by evaluating the tax savings from the depreciation deductions in present value terms by quantifying the tax savings from the depreciation expense over the life of the asset. The asset's purchase also can be financed with debt.

Taxpayers who lease rather than buy an asset benefit by not giving up the use of funds that otherwise would have gone to purchase the asset. Lessees also forgo the opportunity to claim depreciation deductions; however, they reduce the cost of the leasing option by claiming the lease expense as a deduction against their tax base.

	Cost Recovery Allowed	Cost Recovery Allowable
Year 1	$1,000	$ 1,000
Year 2	2,000	2,000
Year 3	–0–	2,000
Year 4	–0–	2,000
Year 5	2,000	2,000
Year 6	1,000	1,000
Totals	$6,000	$10,000

The adjusted basis of the copier at the end of year 6 is $0 ($10,000 cost – $10,000 *allowable* cost recovery). If Heron sells the copier for $800 in year 7, it will recognize an $800 gain ($800 amount realized – $0 adjusted basis). ■

Cost Recovery Basis for Personal-Use Assets Converted to Business or Income-Producing Use. If personal-use assets are converted to business or income-producing use, the basis for cost recovery and for loss is the lower of the adjusted basis or the fair market value at the time the property was converted. As a result of this basis rule, losses that occurred while the property was personal-use property will not be recognized for tax purposes through the cost recovery of the property.

EXAMPLE 39

Hans acquires a personal residence for $120,000. Four years later, when the fair market value is only $100,000, he establishes a consulting company and uses the residence solely for office space. The basis for cost recovery is $100,000, since the fair market value is less than the adjusted basis. The $20,000 decline in value is deemed to be personal (since it occurred while Hans held the property for personal use). Therefore, depreciation deductions will be based on $100,000 rather than $120,000. ■

EXHIBIT 5–2 **Cost Recovery Periods: MACRS Personalty**

Class	Examples
3-year	Tractor units for use over-the-road
	Any horse that is not a racehorse and is more than 12 years old at the time it is placed in service
	Special tools used in the manufacturing of motor vehicles, such as dies, fixtures, molds, and patterns
5-year	Automobiles and taxis
	Light and heavy general-purpose trucks
	Typewriters, calculators, and copiers
	Computers and peripheral equipment
7-year	Office furniture, fixtures, and equipment
	Agricultural machinery and equipment
10-year	Vessels, barges, tugs, and similar water transportation equipment
	Assets used for petroleum refining or for the manufacture of grain and grain mill products, sugar and sugar products, or vegetable oils and vegetable oil products
	Single-purpose agricultural or horticultural structures
15-year	Land improvements
	Assets used for industrial steam and electric generation and/or distribution systems
	Assets used in the manufacture of cement
20-year	Farm buildings except single-purpose agricultural and horticultural structures
	Water utilities

Modified Accelerated Cost Recovery System (MACRS)

MACRS provides separate cost recovery tables for realty (real property) and personalty (personal property). Write-offs are not available for land because it does not have a determinable useful life. Cost recovery allowances for real property, other than land, are based on recovery lives specified in the law. The IRS provides tables that specify cost recovery allowances for personalty and for realty.

Cost Recovery for Personal Property

MACRS provides that the cost recovery basis of eligible personalty (and certain realty) is recovered over 3, 5, 7, 10, 15, or 20 years.[56] Examples of property in the different cost recovery categories are shown in Exhibit 5–2.[57]

Accelerated depreciation is allowed for these six MACRS classes of property. The appropriate computational methods and conventions are built into the tables, so, in general, it is not necessary to perform any calculations. To determine the amount of the cost recovery allowance, simply identify the asset by class and go to the appropriate table.[58] The MACRS percentages for personalty are shown in Table 5–1 (MACRS tables are located at the end of the chapter prior to the Problem Materials).

[56]Property is classified by recovery period under MACRS based on asset depreciation range (ADR) midpoint lives provided by the IRS. Rev.Proc. 87–56, 1987–2 C.B. 674 is the source for the ADR midpoint lives.

[57]§ 168(e).

[58]§ 168(b).

TAX INCENTIVES FOR THE TEXTILE INDUSTRY IN INDIA

The Indian Finance Ministry announced that it will retain the special depreciation benefits for textile machinery installed under the Technology Upgradation Fund Scheme (TUFS). The intent is to build the capacity of the textile industry. The incentive allows 50 percent depreciation in the first year the machinery is in service.

Source: *Adapted from "Depreciation Benefits under TUFS to Continue for Textile Sector,"* The Indian Express Online Media Ltd., *March 31, 2005.*

Taxpayers may *elect* the straight-line method to compute cost recovery allowances for each of these classes of property. Certain property is not eligible for accelerated cost recovery and must be depreciated under an alternative depreciation system (ADS). Both the straight-line election and ADS are discussed later in the chapter.

MACRS views property as placed in service in the middle of the first year and allows a half-year of cost recovery in the year of acquisition and in the final year of cost recovery (the **half-year convention**).[59] Thus, for example, the statutory recovery period for three-year property begins in the middle of the year the asset is placed in service and ends three years later. In practical terms, this means the actual write-off periods cover 4, 6, 8, 11, 16, and 21 tax years. MACRS also allows for a half-year of cost recovery in the year of disposition or retirement.

EXAMPLE 40

Robin Corporation acquires a five-year class asset on April 10, 2006, for $30,000. Robin's cost recovery deduction for 2006 is $6,000, computed as follows:

MACRS calculation based on Table 5–1 ($30,000 × .20)	$6,000

■

EXAMPLE 41

Assume the same facts as in Example 40 and that Robin disposes of the asset on March 5, 2008. Robin's cost recovery deduction for 2008 is $2,880 [$30,000 × ½ × .192 (Table 5–1)]. ■

Mid-Quarter Convention. If more than 40 percent of the value of property other than eligible real estate[60] is placed in service during the last quarter of the year, a **mid-quarter convention** applies.[61] Under the convention, property acquisitions are grouped by the quarter they were acquired for cost recovery purposes. Acquisitions during the first quarter are allowed 10.5 months of cost recovery; the second quarter, 7.5 months; the third quarter, 4.5 months; and the fourth quarter, 1.5 months. The percentages are shown in Table 5–2.

EXAMPLE 42

Silver Corporation acquires the following five-year class property in 2006.

Acquisition Dates	Cost
February 15	$ 200,000
July 10	400,000
December 5	600,000
Total	$1,200,000

[59] § 168(d)(4)(A).

[60] See Cost Recovery for Real Estate later in this chapter for a discussion of eligible real estate.

[61] § 168(d)(3).

TAX *in the News* **TAX HEADACHES FOR OWNERS OF SMALL BUSINESSES**

The President's Advisory Panel on Federal Tax Reform held meetings around the country with tax experts and others to learn about problems with the current tax system. This gave owners of small businesses hope that some relief from the complexities of the Code might become a reality. Currently, many small businesses find that tax compliance is both time-consuming and costly. The depreciation rules are an example of this complexity. To comply with the rules, businesses must keep records for a variety of assets that are depreciated over different time frames using different depreciation methods that start in different years. This means that owners must establish tracking systems for each asset year after year, for long periods of time.

Source: *Manuel Cosme, "Depressing Depreciation in Tax Code,"* The Business Press/California, *May 2, 2005, p. 31.*

If Silver Corporation uses the statutory percentage method, the cost recovery allowances for the first two years are computed as indicated below. Because more than 40% ($600,000/$1,200,000 = 50%) of the acquisitions are in the last quarter, the mid-quarter convention applies.

2006			
	Mid-Quarter Convention Depreciation		**Total Depreciation**
February 15	$200,000 × .35 (Table 5–2)	=	$ 70,000
July 10	$400,000 × .15	=	60,000
December 5	$600,000 × .05	=	30,000
Total			$160,000
2007			
February 15	$200,000 × .26 (Table 5–2)	=	$ 52,000
July 10	$400,000 × .34	=	136,000
December 5	$600,000 × .38	=	228,000
Total			$416,000

■

When property to which the mid-quarter convention applies is disposed of, the property is treated as though it were disposed of at the midpoint of the quarter. Hence, in the quarter of disposition, cost recovery is allowed for one-half of the quarter.

EXAMPLE 43

Assume the same facts as in Example 42, except that Silver Corporation sells the $400,000 asset on November 30, 2007. The cost recovery allowance for 2007 is computed as follows.

February 15	$200,000 × .26 (Table 5–2)	=	$ 52,000
July 10	$400,000 × .34 × (3.5/4)	=	119,000
December 5	$600,000 × .38	=	228,000
Total			$399,000

■

Cost Recovery for Real Estate

Under MACRS, the cost recovery period for residential rental real estate is 27.5 years, and the straight-line method is used for computing the cost recovery allowance. **Residential rental real estate** includes property where 80 percent or more of

CONCEPT SUMMARY 5–1

MACRS Computational Rules: Statutory Percentage and Straight-Line Methods

	Personal Property	Real Property
Convention	Half-year or mid-quarter	Mid-month
Cost recovery deduction in the year of disposition	Half-year for year of disposition or half-quarter for quarter of disposition	Half-month for month of disposition

the gross rental revenues are from nontransient dwelling units (e.g., an apartment building). Hotels, motels, and similar establishments are not residential rental property. Nonresidential real estate has a recovery period of 39 years (31.5 years for such property placed in service before May 13, 1993) and is also depreciated using the straight-line method.[62]

Some items of real property are not treated as real estate for purposes of MACRS. For example, single-purpose agricultural structures are in the 10-year MACRS class. Land improvements are in the 15-year MACRS class.

All eligible real estate placed in service after June 22, 1984 (under both ACRS and MACRS) is depreciated using the **mid-month convention**. Regardless of when during the month the property is placed in service, it is deemed to have been placed in service at the middle of the month. This allows for one-half month's cost recovery for the month the property is placed in service. If the property is disposed of before the end of the recovery period, one-half month's cost recovery is permitted for the month of disposition regardless of the specific date of disposition.

Cost recovery is computed by multiplying the applicable rate (taken from a table) by the cost recovery basis. The MACRS real property rates are provided in Table 5–3.

EXAMPLE 44

Badger Rentals, Inc., acquired a building on April 1, 1993, for $800,000. If the building is classified as residential rental real estate, the cost recovery allowance for 2006 is $29,088 (.03636 × $800,000). If the building is classified as nonresidential real estate, the 2006 cost recovery allowance is $25,400 (.03175 × $800,000). (See the first two sections of Table 5–3 for the percentages.) ■

EXAMPLE 45

Assume the same facts as in Example 44, except that Badger acquired the nonresidential building on November 19, 2006. The 2006 cost recovery allowance is $2,568 [$800,000 × .00321 (Table 5–3)]. (See the last section of Table 5–3 for the percentage.) ■

An overview of MACRS rules is provided in Concept Summary 5–1.

Straight-Line Election

Although MACRS requires straight-line depreciation for all eligible real estate as previously discussed, the taxpayer may *elect* to use the straight-line method for personal property.[63] The property is depreciated using the class life (recovery period) of the asset with a half-year convention or a mid-quarter convention, whichever is applicable. The election is available on a class-by-class and year-by-year basis. The percentages for the straight-line election with a half-year convention appear in Table 5–4.

[62]§§ 168(b), (c), and (e).

[63]§ 168(b)(5).

EXAMPLE 46

Terry acquires a 10-year class asset on August 4, 2006, for $100,000. He elects the straight-line method of cost recovery. Terry's cost recovery deduction for 2006 is $5,000 ($100,000 × .05). His cost recovery deduction for 2007 is $10,000 ($100,000 × .10). (See Table 5–4 for the percentages.) ■

Election to Expense Assets under § 179

Section 179 (Election to Expense Certain Depreciable Business Assets) permits a taxpayer to elect to deduct up to $108,000 in 2006[64] of the acquisition cost of *tangible personal property* used in a trade or business. Amounts that are expensed under § 179 may not be capitalized and depreciated. The **§ 179 expensing election** is an annual election and applies to the acquisition cost of property placed in service that year. The immediate expense election is not available for real property or for property used for the production of income.[65] The base for calculating the standard MACRS deduction is net of the § 179 expense.

EXAMPLE 47

Kodiak Corporation acquires machinery (five-year class asset) on February 1, 2006, at a cost of $152,000 and elects to expense $108,000 under § 179. Kodiak also takes the statutory percentage cost recovery (see Table 5–1 for the percentage) for 2006. As a result, the total deduction for the year is calculated as follows.

§ 179 expense	$108,000
Standard MACRS calculation	
[($152,000 – $108,000) × .20]	8,800
Total	$116,800

■

Annual Limitations. Two additional limitations apply to the amount deductible under § 179. First, the ceiling amount on the deduction is reduced dollar-for-dollar when property (other than ineligible real estate) placed in service during the taxable year exceeds $430,000 in 2006 ($420,000 in 2005). Second, the amount expensed under § 179 cannot exceed the aggregate amount of taxable income derived from the conduct of any trade or business by the taxpayer. Taxable income of a trade or business is computed without regard to the amount expensed under § 179. Any § 179 deduction in excess of taxable income is carried forward to future taxable years and added to other amounts eligible for expensing. The § 179 amount eligible for expensing in a carryforward year is limited to the *lesser* of (1) the appropriate statutory dollar amount ($108,000 in 2006) reduced by the cost of § 179 property placed in service in excess of $430,000 in the carryforward year or (2) the business income limitation in the carryforward year.

EXAMPLE 48

Jill owns a computer service and operates it as a sole proprietorship. In 2006, she will net $11,000 before considering any § 179 deduction. If Jill spends $491,000 on new equipment, her § 179 expense deduction is computed as follows.

§ 179 deduction before adjustment	$108,000
Less: Dollar limitation reduction ($491,000 – $430,000)	(61,000)
Remaining § 179 deduction	$ 47,000
Business income limitation	$ 11,000
§ 179 deduction allowed	$ 11,000
§ 179 deduction carryforward ($47,000 – $11,000)	$ 36,000

■

[64]The expense amount was $102,000 for assets placed in service in 2004 and $105,000 for assets placed in service in 2005.

[65]§§ 179(b) and (d).

TAX in the News — **TAX INCENTIVES FOR WIND ENERGY**

Even though wind energy costs are dropping, most projects are feasible only because of tax incentives. MidAmerica Energy Company, a utility based in Des Moines, Iowa, is erecting a large wind farm in that state. The company has indicated that it would not have undertaken the $386 million project if it had not received tax incentives. One of the incentives that helped MidAmerica was the extension of the § 179 expensing provision.

Source: *Adapted from Nancy Gaarder, "The Power Behind the Wind,"* Omaha World-Herald, *March 27, 2005, Business, p. 1D.*

Effect on Basis. The basis of the property for cost recovery purposes is reduced by the § 179 amount after it is adjusted for property placed in service in excess of $430,000. This adjusted amount does not reflect any business income limitation.

EXAMPLE 49

Assume the same facts as in Example 48 and that the new equipment is five-year class property. After considering the § 179 deduction, Jill's cost recovery deduction for 2006 is calculated as follows. (See Table 5–1 for the percentage.)

Standard MACRS calculation	
[($491,000 – $47,000) × .20]	$88,800

■

Business and Personal Use of Automobiles and Other Listed Property

Limits exist on MACRS deductions for automobiles and other **listed property** used for both personal and business purposes.[66] These limits would apply, for example, to an automobile used by a sole proprietor partly for business purposes and partly for personal use.

If the listed property is *predominantly* used for business, the taxpayer is allowed to use the *statutory percentage method* to recover the cost. In cases where the property is *not predominantly* used for business, the cost is recovered using the *straight-line method.* The statutory percentage method results in a faster recovery of cost than the straight-line method. Listed property includes the following:

- Any passenger automobile.
- Any other property used as a means of transportation.
- Any property of a type generally used for purposes of entertainment, recreation, or amusement.
- Any computer or peripheral equipment, with the exception of equipment used exclusively at a regular business establishment, including a qualifying home office.
- Any cellular telephone or other similar telecommunications equipment.
- Any other property specified in the Regulations.

Automobiles and Other Listed Property Used Predominantly in Business. For listed property to be considered as predominantly used in business, its *business usage* must exceed 50 percent.[67] The use of listed property for production of income does not qualify as business use for purposes of the more-than-50 percent test. However, both production-of-income and business-use percentages are used to compute the cost recovery deduction.

[66] § 280F.

[67] § 280F(b)(3).

EXAMPLE 50

On September 1, 2006, Emma places in service listed five-year recovery property. The property cost $10,000. If Emma uses the property 40% for business and 25% for the production of income, the property is not considered as predominantly used for business. The cost is recovered using straight-line cost recovery. Emma's cost recovery allowance for the year is $650 ($10,000 × .10 × .65). If, however, Emma uses the property 60% for business and 25% for the production of income, the property is considered as used predominantly for business. Therefore, she may use the statutory percentage method. Emma's cost recovery allowance for the year is $1,700 ($10,000 × .20 × .85). ■

The method for determining the percentage of business usage for listed property is specified in the Regulations. The Regulations provide that for automobiles a mileage-based percentage is to be used. Other listed property is to use the most appropriate unit of time (e.g., hours) the property is actually used (rather than available for use).[68]

Limits on Cost Recovery for Automobiles. The law places special limitations on the cost recovery deduction for *passenger automobiles.*[69] These statutory dollar limits were imposed on passenger automobiles because of the belief that the tax system was being used to underwrite automobiles whose cost and luxury far exceeded what was needed for their business use.

The following limits apply to the cost recovery deductions for passenger automobiles for 2005.[70]

Year of Use	Recovery Limitation*
1	$2,960
2	4,700
3	2,850
Succeeding years until all cost is recovered	1,675

* The indexed amounts for 2006 were not available at the time of this writing.

For an automobile placed in service in 2005, the limitation for subsequent years' cost recovery will be based on the limits for the year the automobile was placed in service. Hence, the limit for the third year's cost recovery for an automobile placed in service in 2005 is $2,850 and not a limit published in 2007.[71]

There are also separate cost recovery limitations for trucks and vans and for electric automobiles. Because these limitations are applied in the same manner as those imposed on passenger automobiles, these additional limitations are not discussed further in this chapter.

The limits are imposed before any percentage reduction for personal use. In addition, the limitation in the first year includes any amount the taxpayer elects to expense under § 179.[72] If the passenger automobile is used partly for personal use, the personal-use percentage is ignored for the purpose of determining the unrecovered cost available for deduction in later years.

EXAMPLE 51

On July 1, 2006, Dan places in service a new automobile that cost $40,000. He does not elect § 179 expensing. The car is always used 80% for business and 20% for personal purposes. Dan chooses the MACRS 200% declining-balance method of cost recovery (see the 5-year column in Table 5–1). The depreciation computation for 2006–2011 is summarized below:

[68] Reg. § 1.280F–6T(e).

[69] § 280F(d)(5).

[70] § 280F(a)(1). Because the 2006 indexed amounts were not available at the time of this writing, the 2005 amounts are used in the Examples and Problem Materials.

[71] Cost recovery limitations for prior years can be found in IRS Publication 463.

[72] § 280F(d)(1).

Year	MACRS Amount	Recovery Limitation	Depreciation Allowed
2006	$6,400	$2,368	$2,368
	($40,000 × 20% × 80%)	($2,960 × 80%)	
2007	$10,240	$3,760	$3,760
	($40,000 × 32% × 80%)	($4,700 × 80%)	
2008	$6,144	$2,280	$2,280
	($40,000 × 19.2% × 80%)	($2,850 × 80%)	
2009	$3,686	$1,340	$1,340
	($40,000 × 11.52% × 80%)	($1,675 × 80%)	
2010	$3,686	$1,340	$1,340
	($40,000 × 11.52% × 80%)	($1,675 × 80%)	
2011	$1,843	$1,340	$1,340
	($40,000 × 5.76% × 80%)	($1,675 × 80%)	

The cost recovery allowed is the lesser of the MACRS amount or the recovery limitation. If Dan continues to use the car after 2011, his cost recovery is limited to the lesser of the recoverable basis or the recovery limitation (i.e., $1,675 × business use percentage). For this purpose, the recoverable basis is computed as if the full recovery limitation was allowed even if it was not. Thus, the recoverable basis as of January 1, 2012, is $24,465 ($40,000 – $2,960 – $4,700 – $2,850 – $1,675 – $1,675 – $1,675). ■

The cost recovery limitations are maximum amounts. If the regular calculation produces a lesser amount of cost recovery, the lesser amount is used.

EXAMPLE 52

On April 2, 2006, Gail places in service a pre-owned automobile that cost $10,000. The car is always used 70% for business and 30% for personal use. Therefore, the cost recovery allowance for 2006 is $1,400 ($10,000 × .20 × .70), which is less than $2,072 ($2,960 × .70). ■

The cost recovery limitations apply *only* to passenger automobiles and not to other listed property.

Special Limitation. The American Jobs Creation Act of 2004 (AJCA) placed a limit on the § 179 deduction for certain vehicles not subject to the statutory dollar limits on cost recovery deductions that are imposed on passenger automobiles. This new limit is $25,000. The limit applies to sport utility vehicles with an unloaded GVW rating of more than 6,000 pounds and not more than 14,000 pounds.[73]

EXAMPLE 53

During 2006, Jay acquires and places in service a sport utility vehicle that cost $70,000 and has a GVW of 8,000 pounds. Jay uses the vehicle 100% of the time for business purposes. The total deduction for 2006 with respect to the SUV is $34,000, computed as follows:

§ 179 expense	$25,000
Standard MACRS calculation	
[($70,000 – $25,000) × .20 (Table 5–1)]	9,000
Total	$34,000

■

Automobiles and Other Listed Property Not Used Predominantly in Business. The cost of listed property that does not pass the more-than-50 percent business usage test in the year the property is placed in service must be recovered

[73]§ 179(b)(6).

using the straight-line method.[74] The straight-line method to be used is that required under the alternative depreciation system (introduced later in the chapter). This system requires a straight-line recovery period of five years for automobiles. However, even though the straight-line method is used, the cost recovery allowance for passenger automobiles cannot exceed the dollar limitations noted above.

If the listed property fails the more-than-50 percent business usage test, the straight-line method must be used for the remainder of the property's life. This applies even if at some later date the business usage of the property increases to more than 50 percent. Even though the straight-line method must continue to be used, however, the amount of cost recovery will reflect the increase in business usage.

Change from Predominantly Business Use. If the business-use percentage of listed property falls to 50 percent or lower after the year the property is placed in service, the property is subject to *cost recovery recapture.* The amount required to be recaptured and included in the taxpayer's return as ordinary income is the excess cost recovery. *Excess cost recovery* is the excess of the cost recovery deduction taken in prior years using the statutory percentage method over the amount that would have been allowed if the straight-line method had been used since the property was placed in service.[75]

After the business usage of the listed property drops below the more-than-50 percent level, the straight-line method must be used for the remaining life of the property.

Leased Automobiles. A taxpayer who leases a passenger automobile for business purposes must report an *inclusion amount* in gross income. The inclusion amount is computed from an IRS table for each taxable year for which the taxpayer leases the automobile. The purpose of this provision is to prevent taxpayers from circumventing the cost recovery dollar limitations by leasing, instead of purchasing, an automobile.

The dollar amount of the inclusion is based on the fair market value of the automobile and is prorated for the number of days the auto is used during the taxable year. The prorated dollar amount is then multiplied by the business and income-producing usage percentage to determine the amount to be included in gross income.[76] The taxpayer deducts the lease payments, multiplied by the business and income-producing usage percentage. The net effect is that the annual deduction for the lease payment is reduced by the inclusion amount.

EXAMPLE 54

On April 1, 2006, Jim leases and places in service a passenger automobile worth $40,000. The lease is to be for a period of five years. During the taxable years 2006 and 2007, Jim uses the automobile 70% for business and 30% for personal use. Assuming the dollar amounts from the IRS table for 2006 and 2007 are $83 and $184, Jim must include $44 in gross income for 2006 and $129 for 2007, computed as follows.

2006	$\$83 \times (275/365) \times .70 = \$44$
2007	$\$184 \times (365/365) \times .70 = \$129$

In addition, Jim can deduct 70% of the lease payments each year because this is the business-use percentage. ■

Substantiation Requirements. Listed property is subject to the substantiation requirements of § 274. This means that the taxpayer must prove the business usage as to the amount of expense or use, the time and place of use, the business purpose

[74] § 280F(b)(1).
[75] § 280F(b)(2).
[76] Reg. § 1.280F–7(a).

TAX *in the News* **LEASING VERSUS BUYING AN AUTOMOBILE**

The decision to lease or buy an automobile often will depend on how long a person plans to use the car. Although leasing may be more advantageous over the short term, buying is probably better for those planning on using their vehicle over a long period.

From a tax standpoint, the lessee may be able to deduct most of the lease payment. For the purchaser, depreciation is deductible, but is subject to IRS limitations. Note that the depreciation amount included in the lease payment is not so limited. The lease payment consists of the expected depreciation during the term of the lease plus an interest factor. As a result of this limit, however, the lessee may be required to include an amount in gross income (i.e., the lease inclusion amount).

Source: *Adapted from Ken Levy, "Leasing versus Buying—Time Is Key to Choosing,"* Idaho Business Review, *July 25, 2005, News.*

for the use, and the business relationship to the taxpayer of persons using the property. Substantiation requires adequate records or sufficient evidence corroborating the taxpayer's statement. However, these substantiation requirements do not apply to vehicles that, by reason of their nature, are not likely to be used more than a *de minimis* amount for personal purposes.[77]

Alternative Depreciation System (ADS)

The **alternative depreciation system (ADS)** must be used in lieu of MACRS for the following.[78]

- To calculate the portion of depreciation treated as an alternative minimum tax (AMT) adjustment for purposes of the corporate and individual AMT (see Chapter 14).[79]
- To compute depreciation allowances for property for which any of the following is true:
  - Used predominantly outside the United States.
  - Leased or otherwise used by a tax-exempt entity.
  - Financed with the proceeds of tax-exempt bonds.
  - Imported from foreign countries that maintain discriminatory trade practices or otherwise engage in discriminatory acts.
- To compute depreciation allowances for earnings and profits purposes (see Chapter 10).

Tables 5–5, 5–6, and 5–7 provide cost recovery rates under the ADS method. Additional details of the ADS method are beyond the scope of this chapter.

Amortization

LO.7

Identify intangible assets that are eligible for amortization and calculate the amount of the deduction.

Taxpayers can claim an **amortization** deduction on certain intangible assets. The amount of the deduction is determined by amortizing the adjusted basis of such intangibles ratably over a 15-year period beginning in the month in which the intangible is acquired.[80]

An amortizable § 197 intangible is any § 197 intangible acquired after August 10, 1993, and held in connection with the conduct of a trade or business or for the production of income. Section 197 intangibles include goodwill and going-concern value, franchises, trademarks, and trade names. Covenants not to compete, copyrights, and

[77] §§ 274(d) and (i).

[78] § 168(g).

[79] This AMT adjustment applies for real and personal property placed in service before 1999. However, it will continue to apply for personal property placed in service after 1998, if the taxpayer uses the 200% declining-balance method for regular income tax purposes. See Chapter 14.

[80] § 197(a).

patents are also included if they are acquired in connection with the acquisition of a business. Generally, self-created intangibles are not § 197 intangibles. The 15-year amortization period applies regardless of the actual useful life of an amortizable § 197 intangible. No other depreciation or amortization deduction is permitted with respect to any amortizable § 197 intangible except those permitted under the 15-year amortization rules.

EXAMPLE 55

On June 1, 2006, Sally purchased and began operating the Falcon Café. Of the purchase price, $90,000 is correctly allocated to goodwill. The amortization deduction for 2006 is $3,500 [($90,000/15) × (7/12)]. ■

PLANNING *Strategies*

STRUCTURING THE SALE OF A BUSINESS

★ **Framework Focus: Tax Rate**

Strategy ★ Control the Character of Income and Deductions.

On the sale of a sole proprietorship where the sales price exceeds the fair market value of the tangible assets and stated intangible assets, a planning opportunity may exist for both the seller and the buyer.

The seller's preference is for the excess amount to be allocated to *goodwill* because goodwill is a capital asset whose sale may result in favorably taxed long-term capital gain. Amounts received for a *covenant not to compete,* however, produce ordinary income, which is not subject to favorable long-term capital gain rates.

Because a covenant and goodwill both are amortized over a statutory 15-year period, the tax results of a covenant not to compete versus goodwill are the same for the *buyer*. However, the buyer should recognize that an allocation to goodwill rather than a covenant may provide a tax benefit to the seller. Therefore, the buyer, in negotiating the purchase price, should factor in the tax benefit to the seller of having the excess amount labeled goodwill rather than a covenant not to compete. Of course, if the noncompetition aspects of a covenant are important to the buyer, a portion of the excess amount can be assigned to a covenant.

LO.8

Determine the amount of depletion expense and recognize the alternative tax treatments for intangible drilling and development costs.

Depletion

Natural resources (e.g., oil, gas, coal, gravel, timber) are subject to **depletion**, which is simply a form of depreciation applicable to natural resources. Land generally cannot be depleted.

The owner of an interest in the natural resource is entitled to deduct depletion. An owner is one who has an economic interest in the property.[81] An economic interest requires the acquisition of an interest in the resource in place and the receipt of income from the extraction or severance of that resource. Although all natural resources are subject to depletion, oil and gas wells are used as an example in the following paragraphs to illustrate the related costs and issues.

In developing an oil or gas well, the producer must make four types of expenditures.

- Natural resource costs.
- Intangible drilling and development costs.
- Tangible asset costs.
- Operating costs.

[81] Reg. § 1.611–1(b).

Natural resources are physically limited, and the costs to acquire them (e.g., oil under the ground) are, therefore, recovered through depletion. Costs incurred in making the property ready for drilling such as the cost of labor in clearing the property, erecting derricks, and drilling the hole are **intangible drilling and development costs (IDC)**. These costs generally have no salvage value and are a lost cost if the well is not productive (dry). Costs for tangible assets such as tools, pipes, and engines are capital in nature. These costs must be capitalized and recovered through depreciation (cost recovery). Costs incurred after the well is producing are operating costs. These costs would include expenditures for such items as labor, fuel, and supplies. Operating costs are deductible when incurred (on the accrual basis) or when paid (on the cash basis).

The expenditures for depreciable assets and operating costs pose no unusual problems for producers of natural resources. The tax treatment of depletable costs and intangible drilling and development costs is quite a different matter.

Intangible Drilling and Development Costs (IDC)

Intangible drilling and development costs can be handled in one of two ways at the option of the taxpayer. They can be either charged off as an expense in the year in which they are incurred or capitalized and written off through depletion. The taxpayer makes the election in the first year such expenditures are incurred either by taking a deduction on the return or by adding them to the depletable basis. No formal statement of intent is required. Once made, the election is binding on both the taxpayer and the IRS for all such expenditures in the future. If the taxpayer fails to make the election to expense IDC on the original timely filed return the first year such expenditures are incurred, an automatic election to capitalize them has been made and is irrevocable.

As a general rule, it is more advantageous to expense IDC. The obvious benefit of an immediate write-off (as opposed to a deferred write-off through depletion) is not the only advantage. Since a taxpayer can use percentage depletion, which is calculated without reference to basis, the IDC may be completely lost as a deduction if they are capitalized.

Depletion Methods

There are two methods of calculating depletion: cost and percentage. **Cost depletion** can be used on any wasting asset (and is the only method allowed for timber). **Percentage depletion** is subject to a number of limitations, particularly for oil and gas deposits. Depletion should be calculated both ways, and generally the method that results in the larger deduction is used. The choice between cost and percentage depletion is an annual election.

Cost Depletion. Cost depletion is determined by using the adjusted basis of the asset.[82] The basis is divided by the estimated recoverable units of the asset (e.g., barrels, tons) to arrive at the depletion per unit. The depletion per unit then is multiplied by the number of units sold (not the units produced) during the year to arrive at the cost depletion allowed. Cost depletion, therefore, resembles the units-of-production method of calculating depreciation.

[82] § 612.

EXHIBIT 5–3 **Sample of Percentage Depletion Rates**

22% Depletion	
Cobalt	Sulfur
Lead	Tin
15% Depletion	
Copper	Oil and gas
Gold	Silver
10% Depletion	
Coal	Perlite
5% Depletion	
Gravel	Sand

EXAMPLE 56

On January 1, 2006, Pablo purchases the rights to a mineral interest for $1 million. At that time, the remaining recoverable units in the mineral interest are estimated to be 200,000. The depletion per unit is $5 [$1,000,000 (adjusted basis)/200,000 (estimated recoverable units)]. If during the year 60,000 units are mined and 25,000 are sold, the cost depletion is $125,000 [$5 (depletion per unit) × 25,000 (units sold)]. ■

If the taxpayer later discovers that the original estimate was incorrect, the depletion per unit for future calculations must be redetermined based on the revised estimate.[83]

EXAMPLE 57

Assume the same facts as in Example 56. In 2007, Pablo realizes that an incorrect estimate was made. The remaining recoverable units now are determined to be 400,000. Based on this new information, the revised depletion per unit is $2.1875 [$875,000 (adjusted basis)/ 400,000 (estimated recoverable units)]. The adjusted basis is the original cost ($1,000,000) reduced by the depletion claimed in 2006 ($125,000). If 30,000 units are sold in 2007, the depletion for the year is $65,625 [$2.1875 (depletion per unit) × 30,000 (units sold)]. ■

Percentage Depletion. Percentage depletion (also referred to as statutory depletion) is based on a specified percentage provided for in the Code. The percentage varies according to the type of mineral interest involved. A sample of these percentages is shown in Exhibit 5–3. The rate is applied to the gross income from the property, but in no event may percentage depletion exceed 50 percent of the taxable income from the property before the allowance for depletion.[84]

[83] § 611(a).

[84] § 613(a). Special rules apply for certain oil and gas wells under § 613A (e.g., the 50% ceiling is replaced with a 100% ceiling, and the percentage depletion may not exceed 65% of the taxpayer's taxable income from all sources before the allowance for depletion).

EXAMPLE 58

Assuming gross income of $100,000, a depletion rate of 22%, and other expenses relating to the property of $60,000, the depletion allowance is determined as follows:

Gross income	$100,000
Less: Other expenses	(60,000)
Taxable income before depletion	$ 40,000
Depreciation allowance [the lesser of $22,000 (22% × $100,000) or $20,000 (50% × $40,000)]	(20,000)
Taxable income after depletion	$ 20,000

The adjusted basis of the property is reduced by $20,000, the depletion allowed. If the other expenses had been only $55,000, the full $22,000 could have been deducted, and the adjusted basis would have been reduced by $22,000. ■

Note that percentage depletion is based on a percentage of the gross income from the property and makes no reference to cost. Thus, when percentage depletion is used, it is possible to deduct more than the original cost of the property. If percentage depletion is used, however, the adjusted basis of the property (for computing cost depletion) must be reduced by the amount of percentage depletion taken until the adjusted basis reaches zero.

PLANNING *Strategies* SWITCHING DEPLETION METHODS

★ **Framework Focus: Deductions**

Strategy ★ Maximize Deductible Amounts.

Since the election to use the cost or percentage depletion method is an annual election, a taxpayer can use cost depletion (if higher) until the basis is exhausted and then switch to percentage depletion in the following years.

EXAMPLE 59

Assume the following facts for Warbler Company.

Remaining depletable basis	$ 11,000
Gross income (10,000 units)	100,000
Expenses (other than depletion)	$30,000
Percentage depletion rate	22%

Since cost depletion is limited to the basis of $11,000 and the percentage depletion is $22,000, Warbler would choose the latter. The company's basis is then reduced to zero. In future years, however, Warbler can continue to take percentage depletion since percentage depletion is taken without reference to the remaining basis. ■

Cost Recovery Tables

Summary of Cost Recovery Tables

Table 5–1	MACRS statutory percentage table for personalty.
	Applicable depreciation methods: 200 or 150 percent declining-balance switching to straight-line.
	Applicable recovery periods: 3, 5, 7, 10, 15, 20 years.
	Applicable convention: half-year.
Table 5–2	MACRS statutory percentage table for personalty.
	Applicable depreciation method: 200 percent declining-balance switching to straight-line.
	Applicable recovery periods: 3, 5, 7 years.
	Applicable convention: mid-quarter.
Table 5–3	MACRS straight-line table for realty.
	Applicable depreciation method: straight-line.
	Applicable recovery periods: 27.5, 31.5, 39 years.
	Applicable convention: mid-month.
Table 5–4	MACRS optional straight-line table for personalty.
	Applicable depreciation method: straight-line.
	Applicable recovery periods: 3, 5, 7, 10, 15, 20 years.
	Applicable convention: half-year.
Table 5–5	Alternative minimum tax declining-balance table for personalty.
	Applicable depreciation method: 150 percent declining-balance switching to straight-line.
	Applicable recovery periods: 3, 5, 7, 9.5, 10, 12 years.
	Applicable convention: half-year.
Table 5–6	ADS straight-line table for personalty.
	Applicable depreciation method: straight-line.
	Applicable recovery periods: 5, 9.5, 12 years.
	Applicable convention: half-year.
Table 5–7	ADS straight-line table for realty.
	Applicable depreciation method: straight-line.
	Applicable recovery period: 40 years.
	Applicable convention: mid-month.

TABLE 5–1 **MACRS Accelerated Depreciation for Personal Property Assuming Half-Year Convention**

For Property Placed in Service after December 31, 1986

Recovery Year	3-Year (200% DB)	5-Year (200% DB)	7-Year (200% DB)	10-Year (200% DB)	15-Year (150% DB)	20-Year (150% DB)
1	33.33	20.00	14.29	10.00	5.00	3.750
2	44.45	32.00	24.49	18.00	9.50	7.219
3	14.81*	19.20	17.49	14.40	8.55	6.677
4	7.41	11.52*	12.49	11.52	7.70	6.177
5		11.52	8.93*	9.22	6.93	5.713
6		5.76	8.92	7.37	6.23	5.285
7			8.93	6.55*	5.90*	4.888
8			4.46	6.55	5.90	4.522
9				6.56	5.91	4.462*
10				6.55	5.90	4.461
11				3.28	5.91	4.462
12					5.90	4.461
13					5.91	4.462
14					5.90	4.461
15					5.91	4.462
16					2.95	4.461
17						4.462
18						4.461
19						4.462
20						4.461
21						2.231

*Switchover to straight-line depreciation.

TABLE 5–2 **MACRS Accelerated Depreciation for Personal Property Assuming Mid-Quarter Convention**

For Property Placed in Service after December 31, 1986 (Partial Table*)

		3-Year		
Recovery Year	First Quarter	Second Quarter	Third Quarter	Fourth Quarter
1	58.33	41.67	25.00	8.33
2	27.78	38.89	50.00	61.11
		5-Year		
Recovery Year	First Quarter	Second Quarter	Third Quarter	Fourth Quarter
1	35.00	25.00	15.00	5.00
2	26.00	30.00	34.00	38.00
		7-Year		
Recovery Year	First Quarter	Second Quarter	Third Quarter	Fourth Quarter
1	25.00	17.85	10.71	3.57
2	21.43	23.47	25.51	27.55

*The figures in this table are taken from the official tables that appear in Rev.Proc. 87–57, 1987–2 C.B. 687. Because of their length, the complete tables are not presented.

TABLE 5-3 **MACRS Straight-Line Depreciation for Real Property Assuming Mid-Month Convention***

For Property Placed in Service after December 31, 1986: 27.5-Year Residential Real Property

Recovery Year(s)	The Applicable Percentage Is (Use the Column for the Month in the First Year the Property Is Placed in Service): 1	2	3	4	5	6	7	8	9	10	11	12
1	3.485	3.182	2.879	2.576	2.273	1.970	1.667	1.364	1.061	0.758	0.455	0.152
2–18	3.636	3.636	3.636	3.636	3.636	3.636	3.636	3.636	3.636	3.636	3.636	3.636
19–27	3.637	3.637	3.637	3.637	3.637	3.637	3.637	3.637	3.637	3.637	3.637	3.637
28	1.970	2.273	2.576	2.879	3.182	3.485	3.636	3.636	3.636	3.636	3.636	3.636
29	0.000	0.000	0.000	0.000	0.000	0.000	0.152	0.455	0.758	1.061	1.364	1.667

For Property Placed in Service after December 31, 1986, and before May 13, 1993: 31.5-Year Nonresidential Real Property

Recovery Year(s)	The Applicable Percentage Is (Use the Column for the Month in the First Year the Property Is Placed in Service): 1	2	3	4	5	6	7	8	9	10	11	12
1	3.042	2.778	2.513	2.249	1.984	1.720	1.455	1.190	0.926	0.661	0.397	0.132
2–19	3.175	3.175	3.175	3.175	3.175	3.175	3.175	3.175	3.175	3.175	3.175	3.175
20–31	3.174	3.174	3.174	3.174	3.174	3.174	3.174	3.174	3.174	3.174	3.174	3.174
32	1.720	1.984	2.249	2.513	2.778	3.042	3.175	3.175	3.175	3.175	3.175	3.175
33	0.000	0.000	0.000	0.000	0.000	0.000	0.132	0.397	0.661	0.926	1.190	1.455

For Property Placed in Service after May 12, 1993: 39-Year Nonresidential Real Property

Recovery Year(s)	The Applicable Percentage Is (Use the Column for the Month in the First Year the Property Is Placed in Service): 1	2	3	4	5	6	7	8	9	10	11	12
1	2.461	2.247	2.033	1.819	1.605	1.391	1.177	0.963	0.749	0.535	0.321	0.107
2–39	2.564	2.564	2.564	2.564	2.564	2.564	2.564	2.564	2.564	2.564	2.564	2.564
40	0.107	0.321	0.535	0.749	0.963	1.177	1.391	1.605	1.819	2.033	2.247	2.461

*The official tables contain a separate row for each year. For ease of presentation, certain years are grouped in these tables. In some instances, this will produce a difference of .001 for the last digit when compared with the official tables.

TABLE 5-4 **MACRS Straight-Line Depreciation for Personal Property Assuming Half-Year Convention***

For Property Placed in Service after December 31, 1986

MACRS Class	% First Recovery Year	Other Recovery Years: Years	Other Recovery Years: %	Last Recovery Year: Year	Last Recovery Year: %
3-year	16.67	2–3	33.33	4	16.67
5-year	10.00	2–5	20.00	6	10.00
7-year	7.14	2–7	14.29	8	7.14
10-year	5.00	2–10	10.00	11	5.00
15-year	3.33	2–15	6.67	16	3.33
20-year	2.50	2–20	5.00	21	2.50

*The official table contains a separate row for each year. For ease of presentation, certain years are grouped in this table. In some instances, this will produce a difference of .01 for the last digit when compared with the official table.

TABLE 5–5 **Alternative Minimum Tax: 150% Declining-Balance Assuming Half-Year Convention**

For Property Placed in Service after December 31, 1986 (Partial Table*)

Recovery Year	3-Year 150%	5-Year 150%	7-Year 150%	9.5-Year 150%	10-Year 150%	12-Year 150%
1	25.00	15.00	10.71	7.89	7.50	6.25
2	37.50	25.50	19.13	14.54	13.88	11.72
3	25.00**	17.85	15.03	12.25	11.79	10.25
4	12.50	16.66**	12.25**	10.31	10.02	8.97
5		16.66	12.25	9.17**	8.74**	7.85
6		8.33	12.25	9.17	8.74	7.33**
7			12.25	9.17	8.74	7.33
8			6.13	9.17	8.74	7.33
9				9.17	8.74	7.33
10				9.16	8.74	7.33
11					4.37	7.32
12						7.33
13						3.66

*The figures in this table are taken from the official table that appears in Rev.Proc. 87–57, 1987–2 C.B. 687. Because of its length, the complete table is not presented.

**Switchover to straight-line depreciation.

TABLE 5–6 **ADS Straight-Line for Personal Property Assuming Half-Year Convention**

For Property Placed in Service after December 31, 1986 (Partial Table*)

Recovery Year	5-Year Class	9.5-Year Class	12-Year Class
1	10.00	5.26	4.17
2	20.00	10.53	8.33
3	20.00	10.53	8.33
4	20.00	10.53	8.33
5	20.00	10.52	8.33
6	10.00	10.53	8.33
7		10.52	8.34
8		10.53	8.33
9		10.52	8.34
10		10.53	8.33
11			8.34
12			8.33
13			4.17

*The figures in this table are taken from the official table that appears in Rev.Proc. 87–57, 1987–2 C.B. 687. Because of its length, the complete table is not presented. The tables for the mid-quarter convention also appear in Rev.Proc. 87–57.

TABLE 5-7 **ADS Straight-Line for Real Property Assuming Mid-Month Convention**

For Property Placed in Service after December 31, 1986

Recovery Year(s)	Month Placed in Service 1	2	3	4	5	6	7	8	9	10	11	12
1	2.396	2.188	1.979	1.771	1.563	1.354	1.146	0.938	0.729	0.521	0.313	0.104
2–40	2.500	2.500	2.500	2.500	2.500	2.500	2.500	2.500	2.500	2.500	2.500	2.500
41	0.104	0.312	0.521	0.729	0.937	1.146	1.354	1.562	1.771	1.979	2.187	2.396

Suggested Further Readings

"Final Regs. Offer Guidance on Changes to Section 179," *Practical Tax Strategies*, September 2005, p. 176.

Claudia L. Kelley and Susan E. Anderson, "Tax Planning for Land Preparation Costs," *The Tax Adviser*, May 2005, pp. 276–279.

Gary L. Maydew, "Section 199 Offers New Deduction Opportunities and Complexity," *Practical Tax Strategies*, July 2005, pp. 4–10.

"Sec. 179 Recapture and SUVs," *The Tax Adviser*, July 2005, p. 438.

KEY TERMS

Accelerated cost recovery system (ACRS), 5–21

Alternative depreciation system (ADS), 5–33

Amortization, 5–33

Capital gain property, 5–14

Charitable contribution, 5–14

Cost depletion, 5–35

Depletion, 5–34

Depreciation rules, 5–21

Domestic production gross receipts (DPGR), 5–20

Half-year convention, 5–25

Intangible drilling and development costs (IDC), 5–35

Listed property, 5–29

Mid-month convention, 5–27

Mid-quarter convention, 5–25

Modified accelerated cost recovery system (MACRS), 5–21

Modified adjusted gross income, 5–19

Ordinary and necessary, 5–2

Ordinary income property, 5–14

Percentage depletion, 5–35

Production activities deduction (PAD), 5–19

Qualified production activities income (QPAI), 5–20

Reasonableness requirement, 5–3

Related-party transactions, 5–10

Research and experimental expenditures, 5–16

Residential rental real estate, 5–26

Section 179 expensing election, 5–28

W–2 wages, 5–20

PROBLEM MATERIALS

PROBLEMS

Issue ID

1. Ted is an agent for Waxwing Corporation, an airline manufacturer, and is negotiating a sale with a representative of the U.S. government and with a representative of a developing country. Waxwing has sufficient capacity to handle only one of the orders. Both orders will have the same contract price. Ted believes that if Waxwing will authorize a $500,000 payment to the representative of the foreign country, he can

guarantee the sale. He is not sure that he can obtain the same result with the U.S. government. Identify the relevant tax issues for Waxwing.

2. Linda operates a drug-running operation. Which of the following expenses she incurs can reduce taxable income?
   a. Bribes paid to border guards.
   b. Salaries to employees.
   c. Price paid for drugs purchased for resale.
   d. Kickbacks to police.
   e. Rent on an office.
   f. Depreciation on office furniture and equipment.
   g. Tenant's casualty insurance.

3. *Ethics* Cardinal Corporation is a trucking firm that operates in the Mid-Atlantic states. One of Cardinal's major customers frequently ships goods between Charlotte and Baltimore. Occasionally, the customer sends last-minute shipments that are outbound for Europe on a freighter sailing from Baltimore. To satisfy the delivery schedule in these cases, Cardinal's drivers must substantially exceed the speed limit. Cardinal pays for any related speeding tickets. During the past year, two drivers had their licenses suspended for 30 days each for driving at such excessive speeds. Cardinal continues to pay each driver's salary during the suspension periods.

   Cardinal believes that it is necessary to conduct its business in this manner if it is to be profitable, maintain the support of the drivers, and maintain the goodwill of customers. Evaluate Cardinal's business practices.

4. Quail Corporation anticipates that being positively perceived by the individual who is elected mayor will be beneficial for business. Therefore, Quail contributes to the campaigns of both the Democratic and the Republican candidates. The Republican candidate is elected mayor. Can Quail deduct any of the political contributions it made?

5. Melissa, the owner of a sole proprietorship, does not provide health insurance for her 20 employees. She plans to spend $1,500 lobbying in opposition to legislation that would require her to provide health insurance for her employees. Discuss the tax advantages and disadvantages of paying the $1,500 to a professional lobbyist rather than spending the $1,500 on in-house lobbying expenditures.

6. *Issue ID* a. Which of the following is a related party under § 267?
      - Mother
      - Sister
      - Nephew
      - Aunt
      - Cousin
      - Granddaughter
      - Corporation and a shareholder who owns 45% of the stock
   b. What negative tax consequences can result from being classified as a related party?

7. Jake owns City of Charleston bonds with an adjusted basis of $100,000. During the year, he receives interest payments of $4,000. Jake partially financed the purchase of the bonds by borrowing $70,000 at 6% interest. Jake's interest payments on the loan this year are $4,100, and his principal payments are $1,000.
   a. Should Jake report any interest income this year?
   b. Can Jake deduct any interest expense this year?

8. Drew and his wife Cassie own all of the stock of Thrush, Inc. Cassie is the president and Drew is the vice president. Cassie and Drew are paid salaries of $400,000 and $300,000, respectively, each year. They consider the salaries to be reasonable based on a comparison with salaries paid for comparable positions in comparable companies. They project Thrush's taxable income for next year, before their salaries, to be $800,000. They decide to place their four teenage children on the payroll and to pay them total salaries of $100,000. The children will each work about five hours per week for Thrush.
   a. What are Drew and Cassie trying to achieve by hiring the children?
   b. Calculate the tax consequences of hiring the children on Thrush, Inc., and on Drew and Cassie's family.

9. Polly made the following political contributions:

To national Republican Party	$1,000
To national Democratic Party	1,000
To local candidate for mayor	700
To candidate for state Senate	200
To candidate for school board	250

How much can Polly deduct?

10. Jenny, the owner of a very successful restaurant chain, is exploring the possibility of expanding the chain into a city in the neighboring state. She incurs $25,000 of expenses associated with this investigation. Based on the regulatory environment for restaurants in the city, she decides not to do so. During the year, she also investigates opening a hotel that will be part of a national hotel chain. Her expenses for this are $51,000. The hotel begins operations on November 1. Determine the amount that Jenny can deduct in the current year for investigating these two businesses.

Decision Making

Communications

11. Eleanor Saxon sold stock (basis of $68,000) to her brother, Ridge, for $55,000, the fair market value.
   a. What are the tax consequences to Eleanor?
   b. What are the tax consequences to Ridge if he later sells the stock for $90,000? For $49,000? For $66,000?
   c. Write a letter to Eleanor in which you inform her of the tax consequences if she sells the stock to Ridge for $55,000 and explain how a sales transaction could be structured that would produce better tax consequences for her. Eleanor's address is 32 Country Lane, Lawrence, KS 66045.

12. Giraffe, Inc., a calendar year C corporation, reported the following income and expenses in 2007.

Income from operations	$300,000
Expenses from operations	120,000
Dividends received (less than 20% ownership)	13,500
Capital loss carryback	10,500
Charitable contribution	24,000

   a. How much is Giraffe, Inc.'s charitable contribution deduction for 2007?
   b. What happens to the portion of the contribution that is not deductible in 2007?

Decision Making

Communications

13. Dan Simms is the president and sole shareholder of Simms Corporation, 1121 Madison Street, Seattle, WA 98121. Dan plans for the corporation to make a charitable contribution to the University of Washington, a qualified public charity. He will have the corporation donate Jaybird Corporation stock, held for five years, with a basis of $8,000 and a fair market value of $20,000. Dan projects a $200,000 net profit for Simms Corporation in 2006 and a $100,000 net profit in 2007. Dan calls you on December 3, 2006, and asks whether he should make the contribution in 2006 or 2007. Write a letter advising Dan about the timing of the contribution.

14. Blue Corporation, a manufacturing company, decided to develop a new line of merchandise. The project began in 2006. Blue had the following expenses in connection with the project.

	2006	2007
Salaries	$300,000	$400,000
Materials	80,000	70,000
Insurance	10,000	15,000
Utilities	7,000	8,000
Cost of inspection of materials for quality control	4,000	4,000
Promotion expenses	10,000	7,000
Advertising	-0-	30,000
Equipment depreciation	10,000	12,000
Cost of market survey	8,000	-0-

The new product will be introduced for sale beginning in July 2008. Determine the amount of the deduction for research and experimental expenditures for 2006, 2007, and 2008 if:

a. Blue Corporation elects to expense the research and experimental expenditures.
b. Blue Corporation elects to amortize the research and experimental expenditures over 60 months.

15. In 2006, Purple, Inc., a C corporation, has QPAI of $100,000 and a marginal tax rate of 35%. Calculate the tax savings resulting from the PAD.

16. In 2006, Rose, Inc., has QPAI of $2 million and taxable income of $1 million. Since Rose outsources much of its work to independent contractors, its W–2 wage base is only $600,000. Calculate any PAD for this company. What suggestions might you make to enable Rose to increase its PAD?

Decision Making

17. On November 4, 2004, Blue Company acquired an asset (27.5-year residential real property) for $100,000 for use in its business. In 2004 and 2005, respectively, Blue took $321 and $2,564 of cost recovery. These amounts were incorrect because Blue applied the wrong percentages (i.e., those for 39-year rather than 27.5-year property). Blue should have taken $455 and $3,636 of cost recovery in 2004 and 2005. On January 1, 2006, the asset was sold for $98,000. Calculate the gain or loss on the sale of the asset in 2006.

18. Juan, a sole proprietor, acquires a new five-year class asset on March 14, 2006, for $200,000. This is the only asset acquired by Juan during the year. He does not elect immediate expensing under § 179. On July 15, 2007, Juan sells the asset.

a. Determine Juan's cost recovery for 2006.
b. Determine Juan's cost recovery for 2007.

19. On November 5, 2006, Chris, a sole proprietor, acquires land with a warehouse on it for $3 million. The land was valued at $1 million. On January 10, 2017, Chris sells the land and warehouse for $4.5 million. Calculate Chris's cost recovery for 2006. For 2017.

20. Janice acquired an apartment building on June 4, 2006, for $1.4 million. The value of the land is $200,000. Janice sold the apartment building on November 29, 2012.

a. Determine Janice's cost recovery for 2006.
b. Determine Janice's cost recovery for 2012.

21. On July 10, 1997, Wade purchased and placed in service a warehouse. The warehouse cost $850,000. On May 7, 2006, Wade sold the warehouse.

Extender

a. Determine Wade's cost recovery for 1997.
b. Determine Wade's cost recovery for 2006.

22. Lori, who is single, purchased a new copier (five-year class property) for $30,000 and new furniture (seven-year class property) for $112,000 on May 20, 2006. Lori expects the taxable income derived from her business (without regard to the amount expensed under § 179) to be about $200,000. Lori wants to elect immediate § 179 expensing, but she doesn't know which asset she should expense under § 179.

Decision Making

a. Determine Lori's total deduction if the § 179 expense is first taken with respect to the copier.
b. Determine Lori's total deduction if the § 179 expense is first taken with respect to the furniture.
c. What is your advice to Lori?

23. Jack owns a small business that he operates as a sole proprietor. In 2006, Jack will net $80,000 of business income before consideration of any § 179 deduction. Jack spends $432,000 on new equipment in 2006. If Jack also has $4,000 of § 179 deduction carryforwards from 2005, determine his § 179 expense deduction for 2006 and the amount of any carryforward.

24. Olga is the proprietor of a small business. In 2006, the business income, before consideration of any cost recovery or § 179 deduction, is $180,000. Olga spends $132,000 for new furniture and elects to take the § 179 deduction on the furniture. Olga's cost recovery deduction for 2006, except for the cost recovery deduction with respect to the furniture, is $86,000. Determine Olga's total cost recovery for 2006 with respect to the furniture and the amount of any § 179 carryforward.

Decision Making

25. On March 10, 2006, Yoon purchased three-year class property for $20,000. On December 15, 2006, he purchased five-year class property for $127,000. Yoon has net business income of $140,000 before consideration of any § 179 deduction.
    a. Calculate Yoon's cost recovery for 2006, assuming he does not make the § 179 election or use straight-line cost recovery.
    b. Calculate Yoon's cost recovery for 2006, assuming he does elect to use § 179 and does not elect to use straight-line cost recovery.
    c. Assuming Yoon's marginal tax rate is 33%, determine his tax benefit from electing § 179.

Communications

26. John Johnson is considering acquiring an automobile at the beginning of 2006 that he will use 100% of the time as a taxi. The purchase price of the automobile is $35,000. John has heard of cost recovery limits on automobiles and wants to know the maximum amount of the $35,000 he can deduct in the first year. Write a letter to John in which you present your calculations. Also, prepare a memo for the tax files. John's address is 100 Morningside, Clinton, MS 39058.

27. On October 15, 2006, Jon purchased and placed in service a new car. The purchase price was $30,000. This was the only business-use asset Jon acquired in 2006. He used the car 80% of the time for business and 20% for personal use. Jon used the statutory percentage method of cost recovery. Calculate the total deduction Jon may take for 2006 with respect to the car.

28. On June 5, 2006, Leo purchased and placed in service a new car that cost $18,000. The business-use percentage for the car is always 100%. Compute Leo's cost recovery deduction in 2006 and 2007.

Extender

29. On May 28, 2006, Mary purchased and placed in service a new $20,000 car. The car was used 60% for business, 20% for production of income, and 20% for personal use. In 2007, the usage changed to 40% for business, 30% for production of income, and 30% for personal use. Mary did not elect immediate expensing under § 179. Compute the cost recovery and any cost recovery recapture in 2007.

30. At the beginning of the current year, Abdel purchased a new computer (five-year class property) for $8,000. During the year, Abdel used the computer 80% of the time for his personal investments and 20% of the time for personal use. Calculate the maximum total deduction Abdel can take with respect to the computer for the current tax year.

31. Midway through 2006, Abdel leases and places in service a passenger automobile. The lease will run for five years, and the payments are $700 per month. During 2006, Abdel uses the car 65% for business use and 35% for personal use. Assuming the inclusion dollar amount from the IRS table is $85, determine the tax consequences to Abdel from the lease for the year 2006.

Decision Making
Communications

32. Mike Saxon is negotiating the purchase of a business. The final purchase price has been agreed upon, but the allocation of the purchase price to the assets is still being discussed. Appraisals on a warehouse range from $1,200,000 to $1,500,000. If a value of $1,200,000 is used for the warehouse, the remainder of the purchase price, $800,000, will be allocated to goodwill. If $1,500,000 is allocated to the warehouse, goodwill will be $500,000. Mike wants to know what effect each alternative will have on cost recovery and amortization during the first year. Under the agreement, Mike will take over the business on January 1 of next year. Write a letter to Mike in which you present your calculations and recommendation. Also, prepare a memo for the tax files. Mike's address is 200 Rolling Hills Drive, Shavertown, PA 18708.

Ethics

33. Sam Jones owns a granite stone quarry. When he acquired the land, Sam allocated $800,000 of the purchase price to the quarry's recoverable mineral reserves, which were estimated at 10 million tons of granite stone. Based on these estimates, the cost depletion was $.08 per ton. In April of the current year, Sam received a letter from the State Department of Highways notifying him that part of his property was being condemned so the state could build a new road. At that time, the recoverable mineral reserves had an adjusted basis of $600,000 and 7.5 million tons of granite rock. Sam estimates that the land being condemned contains about 2 million tons of granite. Therefore, for the current year, Sam has computed his cost depletion at $.11 [$600,000/(7,500,000 – 2,000,000)] per ton. Evaluate the appropriateness of what Sam is doing.

34. Wes acquired a mineral interest during the year for $10 million. A geological survey estimated that 250,000 tons of the mineral remained in the deposit. During the year, 80,000 tons were mined, and 45,000 tons were sold for $12 million. Other expenses amounted to $5 million. Assuming the mineral depletion rate is 22%, calculate Wes's lowest taxable income.

BRIDGE *Discipline*

1. Sparrow Corporation is considering the acquisition of an asset for use in its business over the next five years. However, Sparrow must decide whether it would be better served by leasing the asset or buying it. An appropriate asset could be purchased for $15,000, and it would qualify as a three-year asset under the MACRS classification. Assume that the election to expense assets under § 179 is not available and that the asset is not expected to have a salvage value at the end of its use by Sparrow. Alternatively, Sparrow could lease the asset for a $3,625 annual cost over the five-year period. If Sparrow is in the 34% tax bracket, would you recommend that Sparrow buy or lease the asset? In your calculations, assume that 10% is an appropriate discount factor. *Decision Making*

2. Lark Corporation is considering the acquisition of an asset for use in its business over the next five years. However, Lark must decide whether it would be better served by leasing the asset or buying it. An appropriate asset could be purchased for $15,000, and it would qualify as a three-year asset under the MACRS classification. Assume that the election to expense assets under § 179 is made and that the asset is not expected to have a salvage value at the end of its use by Lark. Alternatively, Lark could lease the asset for a $3,625 annual cost over the five-year period. If Lark is in the 34% tax bracket, would you recommend that Lark buy or lease the asset? In your calculations, assume that 10% is an appropriate discount factor. *Decision Making*

3. Wayside Fruit Company is a sole proprietorship owned by Neil Stephenson. The company's records reflect the following.

Sales revenue	$185,000
Operating expenses	125,000
Depreciation expense for book	13,000
Cost recovery allowance for tax	17,500
Loss on the sale of delivery truck to Neil's brother	5,000
Amount paid to fruit inspector to overlook below-standard fruit shipped to various vendors	3,000

Compute the net income before tax for book purposes and the amount of taxable income for Wayside Fruit Company.

RESEARCH PROBLEMS

Note: Solutions to Research Problems can be prepared by using the **RIA Checkpoint® Student Edition** online research product, which is available to accompany this text. It is also possible to prepare solutions to the Research Problems by using tax research materials found in a standard tax library.

THOMSON RIA™

Research Problem 1. Green Motor Transportation Corporation is a nationwide long-haul freight concern that owns and operates approximately 15,000 trucks. For tax purposes, Green uses a calendar year and the accrual method of accounting.

Every year, Green is required to pay for a large number of fees, licenses, insurance, and permits (designated as FLIP expenses) in order to legally operate its fleet of vehicles in the large number of states in which it does business. Although the FLIP expenses are accrued for financial accounting purposes, they are expensed for tax purposes. None of the FLIP expenses covers a period of more than one year in duration. This practice has been followed consistently by Green for many years and, until recently, has never been questioned by the IRS.

Upon audit of Green's tax return, the IRS disallowed approximately 55% of the FLIP expenses that had been claimed as a deduction. Although the disallowed expenses were paid in 2003, the IRS held that they were applicable to year 2004. Because Green used the accrual method both for accounting and for tax purposes, the IRS found that a prorating of these expenses was necessary. Green disputed the proration based on the notion that the expenses did not provide a "substantial" benefit to future years. Under an informal policy followed by the IRS, prepaid expenses of less than a year can be expensed in the year paid if certain conditions are met. Green contended that these conditions were met as the FLIP expenses were routine in nature, did not distort income, and were not designed to be manipulative.

The IRS disputed the existence of any such "one-year rule" being available to preclude deducting prepaid expenses. But regardless of whether the rule existed, it would, in any event, not apply to *accrual basis* taxpayers.

Who is right? Can Green Motor Transportation Corporation deduct all of the FLIP expenses paid in 2003, or must 55% of this amount be deferred to 2004?

Research Problem 2. Bud purchased farmland from Enos. Bud paid Enos $400,000 for the land. Bud also paid Enos $100,000 for the peanut base acres and payment yield assigned to the land. Bud would like to know whether he can take cost recovery or amortization on the $100,000 payment.

Communications

Research Problem 3. Keith Larson has just finished building a new golf course. He would like to know whether he can take a cost recovery deduction with respect to the golf course greens. Write him a letter summarizing the pertinent tax law. Keith's address is: Whitehall Golf Course, 1 Chipping Avenue, Nashville TN, 37213.

Research Problem 4. Juan owns a business that acquires exotic automobiles that are high-tech, state-of-the-art vehicles with unique design features or equipment. The exotic automobiles are not licensed nor are they set up to be used on the road. Rather, the cars are used exclusively for car shows or related promotional photography. Juan would like to know whether he can take a cost recovery deduction with respect to the exotic automobiles on his Federal income tax return.

Partial list of research aids:
Bruce Selig, 70 TCM 1125, T.C.Memo. 1995–519.

Communications

Research Problem 5. United Bank is a federally chartered banking institution engaged in the business of issuing credit cards to customers. United also regularly purchases credit card receivables and/or cardholders' accounts from other financial institutions. Thereafter, United may extend additional credit to the customers on these accounts. In connection with its credit card business, United derives interest income, fees, and other income. United wants to know whether costs incurred in connection with the acquisition of credit card receivables must be capitalized under § 263 or whether they can be amortized under § 195. Summarize your findings in a memo to the tax research file.

Internet *Activity*

Use the tax resources of the Internet to address the following questions. Do not restrict your search to the World Wide Web, but include a review of newsgroups and general reference materials, practitioner sites and resources, primary sources of the tax law, chat rooms and discussion groups, and other opportunities.

Research Problem 6. The $1 million maximum compensation deduction does not seem to have deterred large corporations from remunerating their executives at very high levels. What techniques are being used to work around the millionaires' provision? Are executives taking pay cuts, or are their salaries being deferred or changed in nature due to § 162(m)?

Research Problem 7. Changes to depreciation systems often are discussed by policy makers and observers of the tax system. Outline the terms and policy objectives of one of the changes currently proposed by the Treasury, a member of Congress, or a tax policy think tank.

http://wft.swlearning.com

CHAPTER 6

Losses and Loss Limitations

LEARNING OBJECTIVES

After completing Chapter 6, you should be able to:

LO.1

Determine the amount, classification, and timing of the bad debt deduction.

LO.2

Understand the tax treatment of worthless securities including § 1244 stock.

LO.3

Identify a casualty and determine the amount, classification, and timing of casualty and theft losses.

LO.4

Recognize the impact of the net operating loss carryback and carryover provisions.

LO.5

Discuss tax shelters and the reasons for at-risk and passive loss limitations.

LO.6

Describe how the at-risk limitation and the passive loss rules limit deductions for losses and identify taxpayers subject to these restrictions.

LO.7

Discuss and be able to apply the definitions of activity, material participation, and rental activity under the passive loss rules.

LO.8

Recognize the relationship between the at-risk and passive activity limitations.

LO.9

Discuss the special treatment available to real estate activities.

OUTLINE

TAX *Talk*

The income tax has made more liars out of the American people than golf has. Even when you make a tax form out on the level, you don't know when it's through if you are a crook or a martyr.

—Will Rogers

Chapter 5 introduced rules governing the deductibility of trade and business expenses. This chapter extends the notion of deductibility to losses occurring in the course of business operations. In particular, special rules concerning the tax treatment of bad debts, casualty losses, and operating losses are reviewed. In addition, tax shelters and the rules that limit their usefulness as tax avoidance devices are discussed.

LO.1

Determine the amount, classification, and timing of the bad debt deduction.

Bad Debts

If a taxpayer lends money or purchases a debt instrument and the debt is not repaid, a **bad debt** deduction is allowed. Similarly, if an accrual basis taxpayer sells goods or provides services on credit and the account receivable subsequently becomes worthless, a bad debt deduction is permitted.[1] No deduction is allowed, however, for a bad debt arising from the sale of a product or service when the taxpayer is on the cash basis because no income is reported until the cash has been collected. Permitting a bad debt deduction for a cash basis taxpayer would amount to a double deduction because the expenses of the product or service rendered are deducted when payments are made to suppliers and to employees or at the time of the sale.

EXAMPLE 1

Ella, a sole proprietor engaged in the practice of accounting, performed services for Pat for which she charged $8,000. Pat never paid the bill, and his whereabouts are unknown.

If Ella is an accrual basis taxpayer, she includes the $8,000 in income when the services are performed. When she determines that Pat's account will not be collected, she deducts the $8,000 as a bad debt.

If Ella is a cash basis taxpayer, she does not include the $8,000 in income until payment is received. When she determines that Pat's account will not be collected, she cannot deduct the $8,000 as a bad debt expense because it was never recognized as income. ■

[1]Reg. § 1.166–1(e).

TAX FACT

Just How Good Is Your Credit?

To be successful, a business must generate sales among customers who are willing and able to pay their obligations. Nonetheless, if a sale is made and it is determined that the related account receivable is uncollectible, an accrual method business is allowed to claim a bad debt deduction. Recently, corporations claimed bad debt deductions of approximately $168 billion against business receipts of nearly $17.3 trillion.

Source: *Corporation Income Tax Returns, 2002; Table 2—Selected Balance Sheet, Income Statement, and Tax Items, by Asset Size; Summer 2005.*

Specific Charge-Off Method

Most taxpayers are required to use the **specific charge-off method** when accounting for bad debts. Some financial institutions are permitted to use an alternative **reserve method** for computing bad debt deductions.

A taxpayer using the specific charge-off method may claim a deduction when a specific *business* debt becomes either partially or wholly worthless or when a specific *nonbusiness* debt becomes wholly worthless.[2] For a business debt, the taxpayer must satisfy the IRS that the debt is partially worthless and must demonstrate the amount of worthlessness. If a business debt previously deducted as partially worthless becomes totally worthless in a future year, only the remainder not previously deducted can be deducted in the future year.

In the case of total worthlessness, a deduction is allowed for the entire amount in the year that the debt becomes worthless. The amount of the deduction depends on the taxpayer's basis in the bad debt. If the debt arose from the sale of services or products and the face amount was previously included in income, that amount is deductible. If the taxpayer purchased the debt, the deduction equals the amount the taxpayer paid for the debt instrument.

Determining when a bad debt becomes worthless can be a difficult task. Legal proceedings need not be initiated against the debtor when the surrounding facts indicate that such action will not result in collection.

EXAMPLE 2

In 2004, Partridge Company lent $1,000 to Kay, who agreed to repay the loan in two years. In 2006, Kay disappeared after the note became delinquent. If a reasonable investigation by Partridge indicates that Kay cannot be found or that a suit against Kay would not result in collection, Partridge can deduct the $1,000 in 2006. ■

Bankruptcy is generally an indication of at least partial worthlessness of a debt. Bankruptcy may create worthlessness before the settlement date. If this is the case, the deduction may be taken in the year of worthlessness.

EXAMPLE 3

In Example 2, assume that Kay filed for personal bankruptcy in 2005 and that the debt is a business debt. At that time, Partridge learned that unsecured creditors (including Partridge) were ultimately expected to receive 20 cents on the dollar. In 2006, settlement is made and Partridge receives only $150. Partridge should deduct $800 ($1,000 loan – $200 expected settlement) in 2005 and $50 in 2006 ($200 balance – $150 proceeds). ■

If a receivable is written off as uncollectible and is subsequently collected during the same tax year, the write-off entry is reversed. If a receivable has been written off as uncollectible, collection in a later tax year may result in income being

[2]§ 166(a) and Reg. § 1.166.

GLOBAL *Tax Issues*

WRITING OFF BAD DEBTS IN AUSTRALIA

In Australia, a small business must identify bad debts and physically write them off by June 30, or the business will not be allowed a deduction. Even if the debts have been referred to a collection agency, they must be physically written off the books. To claim a bad debt under Australian law, the business must be on the accrual basis, there must be little possibility of the debt being paid, and the debt must be written off before June 30.

recognized. Income will result if the deduction yielded a tax benefit in the year it was taken (the tax benefit rule).

Business versus Nonbusiness Bad Debts

The nature of a debt depends upon whether the lender is engaged in the business of lending money or whether there is a proximate relationship between the creation of the debt and the *lender's* trade or business. Where either of these conditions is true, a bad debt is classified as a **business bad debt**. If these conditions are not met, a bad debt is classified as a **nonbusiness bad debt**. The use to which the borrowed funds are put is of no consequence when making this classification decision.

EXAMPLE 4

Jamil lent his friend, Esther, $1,500. Esther used the money to start a business, which subsequently failed. Even though the proceeds of the loan were used in a business, the loan is a nonbusiness bad debt, because the business was Esther's, and not Jamil's. ■

EXAMPLE 5

Horace operates a sole proprietorship that sells premium stereo equipment. Horace uses the accrual basis to account for sales of the stereo equipment. During the year, he sold a $4,000 stereo system to Herbie on credit. Later that year, the account receivable becomes worthless. The loan is a business bad debt, because the debt was related to Horace's business. ■

Generally, nonbusiness bad debts are incurred only by individuals. It is assumed that any loans made by a corporation are related to its trade or business. Therefore, any bad debts resulting from loans made by a corporation are automatically business bad debts.

The distinction between a business bad debt and a nonbusiness bad debt is important. A business bad debt is deductible as an ordinary loss in the year incurred, whereas a nonbusiness bad debt is always treated as a short-term capital loss. Thus, regardless of the age of a nonbusiness bad debt, the deduction may be of limited benefit due to the $3,000 capital loss limitation for individuals (refer to the discussion in Chapter 4).

Loans between Related Parties

Loans between related parties raise the issue of whether the transaction was a *bona fide* loan or some other transfer, such as a gift, a disguised dividend payment, or a contribution to capital. The Regulations state that a bona fide debt arises from a debtor-creditor relationship based on a valid and enforceable obligation to pay a fixed or determinable sum of money. Thus, individual circumstances must be examined to determine whether advances between related parties are loans. Some considerations are these:

- Was a note properly executed?
- Was there a reasonable rate of interest?
- Was collateral provided?
- What collection efforts were made?
- What was the intent of the parties?

CONCEPT SUMMARY 6–1

The Tax Treatment of Bad Debts Using the Specific Charge-Off Method

	Business Bad Debts	Nonbusiness Bad Debts
Timing of deduction	A deduction is allowed when the debt becomes either partially or wholly worthless.	A deduction is allowed *only* when the debt becomes wholly worthless.
Character of deduction	The bad debt may be deducted as an ordinary loss.	The bad debt is classified as a short-term capital loss, subject to the $3,000 capital loss limitation for individuals.
Recovery of amounts previously deducted	If the account recovered was written off during the current tax year, the write-off entry is reversed. If the account was written off in a previous tax year, income is created subject to the tax benefit rule.	If the account recovered was written off during the current tax year, the write-off entry is reversed. If the account was written off in a previous tax year, income is created subject to the tax benefit rule.

EXAMPLE 6

Ted, who is the sole shareholder of Penguin Corporation, lends the corporation $10,000 so that it can continue business operations. The note specifies a 2% interest rate and is payable on demand. Penguin has shown losses in each year of its five-year existence. The corporation also has liabilities greatly in excess of its assets. It is likely that Ted's transfer to the corporation would be treated as a contribution to capital rather than a liability. Consequently, no bad debt deduction would be allowed upon default by Penguin. ■

Worthless Securities

LO.2

Understand the tax treatment of worthless securities including § 1244 stock.

A loss is allowed for securities that become *completely* worthless during the year (**worthless securities**).[3] Such securities are shares of stock, bonds, notes, or other evidence of indebtedness issued by a corporation or government. The losses generated are treated as capital losses (refer to Chapter 4) deemed to have occurred on the *last day* of the tax year. By treating losses as having occurred on the last day of the tax year, a loss that would otherwise have been classified as short term (if the date of worthlessness were used) may be classified as long term.

EXAMPLE 7

Falcon Company, a calendar year taxpayer, owns stock in Owl Corporation (a publicly held company). The stock was acquired as an investment on May 31, 2005, at a cost of $5,000. On April 1, 2006, the stock became worthless. Because the stock is deemed to have become worthless as of December 31, 2006, Falcon has a capital loss from an asset held for 19 months (a long-term capital loss). ■

Small Business Stock

The general rule is that shareholders receive capital loss treatment for losses from the sale or exchange of corporate stock. As noted in Chapter 4, the deductibility of capital losses is limited. However, it is possible to avoid capital loss limitations if the loss is sustained on **small business stock (§ 1244 stock)**. Such a loss could arise from a sale of the stock or from the stock becoming worthless. Only *individuals*[4] who

[3] § 165(g).

[4] The term *individuals* for this purpose includes a partnership but not a trust or an estate.

acquired the stock *from* the issuing corporation are eligible to receive ordinary loss treatment under § 1244. The ordinary loss treatment is limited to $50,000 ($100,000 for married individuals filing jointly) per year. Losses on § 1244 stock in excess of the statutory limits are treated as capital losses.

The issuing corporation must meet certain requirements for the loss on § 1244 stock to be treated as an *ordinary*—rather than a capital—loss. The principal requirement is that the total capitalization of the corporation is limited to a maximum of $1 million. This capital limit includes all money and other property received by the corporation for stock and all capital contributions made to the corporation. The $1 million test is made at the time the stock is issued. There are no requirements regarding the kind of stock issued. Section 1244 stock can be either common or preferred.

Section 1244 applies only to losses. If § 1244 stock is sold at a gain, the provision does not apply and the gain is capital gain (which, for individuals, may be subject to preferential tax treatment, as discussed in Chapter 4).

EXAMPLE 8

On July 1, 2004, Iris, a single individual, purchased 100 shares of Eagle Corporation common stock for $100,000. The Eagle stock qualifies as § 1244 stock. On June 20, 2006, Iris sells all of the Eagle stock for $20,000, which results in a loss of $80,000. Because the Eagle stock is § 1244 stock, Iris has $50,000 of ordinary loss and $30,000 of long-term capital loss. ■

PLANNING *Strategies*

MAXIMIZING THE BENEFITS OF § 1244

★ Framework Focus: Tax Rate

Strategy ★ Control the Character of Income and Deductions.

Because § 1244 limits the amount of loss classified as ordinary loss on a yearly basis, a taxpayer might maximize the benefits of § 1244 by selling the stock in more than one taxable year.

EXAMPLE 9

Mitch, a single individual, purchased small business stock in 2004 for $150,000 (150 shares at $1,000 per share). On December 20, 2006, the stock is worth $60,000 (150 shares at $400 per share). Mitch wants to sell the stock at this time. He earns a salary of $80,000 a year, has no other capital transactions, and does not expect any in the future. If Mitch sells all of the small business stock in 2006, his recognized loss will be $90,000 ($60,000 selling price − $150,000 cost). The loss will be characterized as a $50,000 ordinary loss and a $40,000 long-term capital loss. In computing taxable income for 2006, Mitch could deduct the $50,000 ordinary loss but could deduct only $3,000 of the capital loss (assuming he has no capital gains). The remainder of the capital loss could be carried over and used in future years subject to the capital loss limitations.

Alternatively, if Mitch sells 82 shares in 2006, he will recognize an ordinary loss of $49,200 [82 × ($400 − $1,000)]. If Mitch then sells the remainder of the shares in 2007, he will recognize an ordinary loss of $40,800 [68 × ($400 − $1,000)], successfully avoiding the capital loss limitation. Mitch could deduct the $49,200 ordinary loss in computing 2006 taxable income and the $40,800 ordinary loss in computing 2007 taxable income. ■

LO.3

Identify a casualty and determine the amount, classification, and timing of casualty and theft losses.

Casualty and Theft Losses

Losses on business property are deductible, whether attributable to casualty, theft, or some other cause (e.g., rust, termite damage). While all *business* property losses are generally deductible, the amount and timing of casualty and theft losses are determined using special rules. Furthermore, for individual taxpayers, who may deduct casualty losses on personal-use (nonbusiness) property as well as on business and investment property (held in partnerships and S corporations or in an individual capacity), a set of special limitations applies. Casualty gains are also afforded special consideration in the tax law.

TAX *in the News* **A CASUALTY LOSS DEDUCTION?**

The Alabama Department of Revenue is pushing a bill that will allow the department to stop unscrupulous tax preparers. One of the schemes used by the preparers is to claim casualty losses on property not even owned by the taxpayer.

Source: *Adapted from "Bill to Put Fraudulent Tax Preparers Out of Business Passes Committee,"* The Associated Press State & Local Wire, *May 4, 2005.*

Definition of Casualty

The term *casualty* generally includes *fire, storm, shipwreck,* and *theft.* In addition, losses from *other casualties* are deductible. Such losses generally include any loss resulting from an event that is (1) identifiable; (2) damaging to property; and (3) sudden, unexpected, and unusual in nature. The term also includes accidental loss of property provided the loss qualifies under the same rules as any other casualty.

A *sudden event* is one that is swift and precipitous and not gradual or progressive. An *unexpected event* is one that is ordinarily unanticipated and occurs without the intent of the taxpayer who suffers the loss. An *unusual event* is one that is extraordinary and nonrecurring and does not commonly occur during the activity in which the taxpayer was engaged when the destruction occurred.[5] Examples include hurricanes, tornadoes, floods, storms, shipwrecks, fires, sonic booms, vandalism, and mine cave-ins. A taxpayer also can take a deduction for a casualty loss from an automobile accident if the accident is not attributable to the taxpayer's willful act or willful negligence. Weather that causes damage (drought, for example) must be unusual and severe for the particular region to qualify as a casualty. Furthermore, damage must be to the *taxpayer's* property to be deductible.

Events That Are Not Casualties. Not all acts of God are treated as **casualty losses** for income tax purposes. Because a casualty must be sudden, unexpected, and unusual, progressive deterioration (such as erosion due to wind or rain) is not a casualty because it does not meet the suddenness test.

An example of an event that generally does not qualify as a casualty is insect damage. When termites caused damage over a period of several years, some courts have disallowed a casualty loss deduction.[6] On the other hand, some courts have held that termite damage over periods of up to 15 months after infestation constituted a sudden event and was, therefore, deductible as a casualty loss.[7] Despite the existence of some judicial support for the deductibility of termite damage as a casualty loss, the current position of the IRS is that termite damage is not deductible.[8]

Other examples of events that are not casualties are losses resulting from a decline in value rather than an actual loss of the property. For example, a taxpayer was allowed a loss for the actual flood damage to his property but not for the decline in market value due to the property's being flood-prone.[9] Similarly, a decline in value of an office building due to fire damage to nearby buildings is not deductible as a casualty.

Definition of Theft

Theft includes, but is not necessarily limited to, larceny, embezzlement, and robbery.[10] Theft does not include misplaced items.[11]

[5] Rev.Rul. 72–592, 1972–2 C.B. 101.

[6] *Fay v. Helvering,* 41–2 USTC ¶9494, 27 AFTR 432, 120 F.2d 253 (CA–2, 1941); *U.S. v. Rogers,* 41–1 USTC ¶9442, 27 AFTR 423, 120 F.2d 244 (CA–9, 1941).

[7] *Rosenberg v. Comm.,* 52–2 USTC ¶9377, 42 AFTR 303, 198 F.2d 46 (CA–8, 1952); *Shopmaker v. U.S.,* 54–1 USTC ¶9195, 45 AFTR 758, 119 F.Supp. 705 (D.Ct. Mo., 1953).

[8] Rev.Rul. 63–232, 1963–2 C.B. 97.

[9] *S. L. Solomon,* 39 TCM 1282, T.C.Memo. 1980–87.

[10] Reg. § 1.165–8(d).

[11] *Mary Francis Allen,* 16 T.C. 163 (1951).

Theft losses are treated like other casualty losses, but the *timing* of recognition of the loss differs. A theft loss is deducted in the *year of discovery*, not the year of the theft (unless, of course, the discovery occurs in the same year as the theft). If, in the year of the discovery, a claim exists (e.g., against an insurance company) and there is a reasonable expectation of recovering the adjusted basis of the asset from the insurance company, no deduction is permitted.[12] If, in the year of settlement, the recovery is less than the asset's adjusted basis, a deduction may be available. If the recovery is greater than the asset's adjusted basis, *casualty gain* may be recognized.

EXAMPLE 10

Sakura, Inc., owned a computer that was stolen from its offices in December 2005. The theft was discovered on June 3, 2006, and the corporation filed a claim with its insurance company that was settled on January 30, 2007. Assuming there is a reasonable expectation of full recovery, no deduction is allowed in 2006. A deduction may be available in 2007 if the actual insurance proceeds are less than the adjusted basis of the asset. (Loss measurement rules are discussed later in this chapter.) ■

PLANNING *Strategies*

DOCUMENTATION OF RELATED-TAXPAYER LOANS, CASUALTY LOSSES, AND THEFT LOSSES

★ **Framework Focus: Deductions**

Strategy ★ Maximize Deductible Amounts.

Since the validity of loans between related taxpayers might be questioned, adequate documentation is needed to substantiate a bad debt deduction if the loan subsequently becomes worthless. Documentation should include proper execution of the note (legal form) and the establishment of a bona fide purpose for the loan. In addition, it is desirable to stipulate a reasonable rate of interest and a fixed maturity date.

Because a theft loss deduction is not permitted for misplaced items, a police report and evidence of the value of the property (e.g., appraisals, pictures of the property, purchase receipts) are necessary to document a theft.

Similar documentation of the value of property should be provided to support a casualty loss deduction because the amount of loss is measured, in part, by the decline in fair market value of the property.

When to Deduct Casualty Losses

General Rule. Generally, a casualty loss is deducted in the year the loss occurs. However, no casualty loss is permitted if a reimbursement claim with a reasonable *prospect of full recovery* exists.[13] If the taxpayer has a partial claim, only part of the loss can be claimed in the year of the casualty, and the remainder is deducted in the year the claim is settled.

EXAMPLE 11

Fuchsia Corporation's new warehouse was completely destroyed by fire in 2006. Its cost and fair market value were $250,000. Fuchsia's only claim against the insurance company was on a $70,000 policy and was not settled by year-end. The following year, 2007, Fuchsia settled with the insurance company for $60,000. Fuchsia is entitled to a $180,000 deduction in 2006 and a $10,000 deduction in 2007. ■

If a taxpayer receives reimbursement for a casualty loss sustained and deducted in a previous year, an amended return is not filed for that year. Instead, the taxpayer must include the reimbursement in gross income on the return for the year

[12] Reg. §§ 1.165–1(d)(2) and 1.165–8(a)(2).

[13] Reg. § 1.165–1(d)(2)(i).

in which it is received to the extent that the previous deduction resulted in a tax benefit (refer to Chapter 4).

EXAMPLE 12

Golden Hawk, Inc., had a deductible casualty loss of $15,000 on its 2005 tax return. Golden Hawk's taxable income for 2005 was $60,000 after deducting the $15,000 loss. In June 2006, the corporation is reimbursed $13,000 for the prior year's casualty loss. Golden Hawk includes the entire $13,000 in gross income for 2006 because the deduction in 2005 produced a tax benefit. ■

Disaster Area Losses. An exception to the general rule for the time of deduction is allowed for **disaster area losses**, which are casualties or disaster-related business losses sustained in an area designated as a disaster area by the President of the United States.[14] In such cases, the taxpayer may *elect* to treat the loss as having occurred in the taxable year immediately *preceding* the taxable year in which the disaster actually occurred. The rationale for this exception is to provide immediate relief to disaster victims in the form of accelerated tax benefits.

If the due date, plus extensions, for the prior year's return has not passed, a taxpayer makes the election to claim the disaster area loss on the prior year's tax return. If a disaster area is designated after the prior year's return has been filed, it is necessary to file either an amended return or a refund claim. In any case, the taxpayer must show clearly that such an election is being made.

Measuring the Amount of Loss

Amount of Loss. The rules for determining the amount of a loss depend in part on whether business, investment, or personal-use (nonbusiness) property was involved. Another factor that must be considered is whether the property was partially or completely destroyed.

If business property or investment property (e.g., rental property) is *completely destroyed,* the loss is equal to the adjusted basis[15] (typically cost less depreciation) of the property at the time of destruction.

EXAMPLE 13

Monty's Movers owned a truck, which was used only for business purposes. The truck was destroyed by fire. Monty, the proprietor, had unintentionally allowed his insurance coverage to expire. The fair market value of the truck was $39,000 at the time of the fire, and its adjusted basis was $40,000. Monty is allowed a loss deduction of $40,000 (the adjusted basis of the truck). ■

A different measurement rule applies for *partial destruction* of business and investment property and for *partial* or *complete destruction* of personal-use property held by individuals. In these situations, the loss is the *lesser* of:

- the adjusted basis of the property, or
- the difference between the fair market value of the property before the event and the fair market value immediately after the event.

EXAMPLE 14

Wynd and Rain, a law firm, owned an airplane that was used only for business purposes. The airplane was damaged in an accident. At the date of the accident, the fair market value of the plane was $52,000, and its adjusted basis was $32,000. After the accident, the plane was appraised at $24,000. The law firm's loss deduction is $28,000 (the lesser of the adjusted basis or the decrease in fair market value). ■

Any insurance recovery reduces the loss for business, investment, and personal-use losses. In fact, a taxpayer may realize a gain if the insurance proceeds exceed

[14] § 165(h).

[15] See Chapter 7 for a detailed discussion of basis rules.

the adjusted basis of the property. Chapter 8 discusses the treatment of net gains and losses on business property and income-producing property.

A special rule on insurance recovery applies to *personal-use property*. In particular, individuals are not permitted to deduct a casualty loss for damage to insured personal-use property unless an insurance claim is filed. This rule applies, whether the insurance provides partial or full reimbursement for the loss.[16]

Generally, an appraisal before and after the casualty is needed to measure the amount of loss. However, the *cost of repairs* to the damaged property generally is acceptable as a method of establishing the loss in value.[17]

DIGGING DEEPER 1

Find more information on this topic at our Web site: ***http://wft-entities.swlearning.com.***

Multiple Losses. When multiple casualty losses occur during the year, the amount of each loss is computed separately. The rules for computing loss deductions where multiple losses have occurred are illustrated in Example 15.

EXAMPLE 15

During the year, Swan Enterprises had the following business casualty losses:

		Fair Market Value of the Asset		
Asset	Adjusted Basis	Before the Casualty	After the Casualty	Insurance Recovery
A	$900	$600	$-0-	$400
B	300	800	250	150

The following losses are allowed:

- Asset A: $500. The complete destruction of a business asset results in a deduction of the adjusted basis of the property (reduced by any insurance recovery) regardless of the asset's fair market value.
- Asset B: $150. The partial destruction of a business asset results in a deduction equal to the lesser of the adjusted basis ($300) or the decline in value ($550), reduced by any insurance recovery ($150). ■

Casualty and Theft Losses of Individuals

Recall from Chapter 4 that the individual income tax formula distinguishes between deductions *for* AGI and deductions *from* AGI. Casualty and theft losses incurred by an individual in connection with a business or with rental and royalty activities are deductible *for* AGI and are limited only by the rules previously discussed.[18] Losses from most other investment activities and personal-use losses are generally deducted *from* AGI. Investment casualty and theft losses (e.g., the theft of a security) are classified as other miscellaneous itemized deductions (not subject to a 2 percent-of-AGI floor as explained in Chapter 16). Casualty and theft losses of personal-use property are subject to special limitations discussed below.

Personal-Use Property. In addition to the valuation rules discussed above, casualty and theft loss deductions from personal-use property must be reduced by a $100 *per event* floor and a 10 percent-of-AGI *aggregate* floor.[19] The $100 floor applies separately to each casualty or theft and applies to the entire loss from each casualty (e.g., if a storm damages both a taxpayer's residence and automobile, only $100 is subtracted from the total amount of the loss) or theft. All personal-use losses incurred during the year are then added together, and the total is reduced by

[16] § 165(h)(4)(E).

[17] Reg. § 1.165–7(a)(2)(ii).

[18] § 62(a)(1).

[19] §§ 165(c)(3) and (h).

CONCEPT SUMMARY 6–2

Casualty Gains and Losses

	Business-Use or Income-Producing Property	Personal-Use Property
Event creating the loss	Any event.	Casualty or theft.
Amount	The lesser of the decline in fair market value or the adjusted basis, but always the adjusted basis if the property is totally destroyed.	The lesser of the decline in fair market value or the adjusted basis.
Insurance	Insurance proceeds received reduce the amount of the loss.	Insurance proceeds received (or for which there is an unfiled claim) reduce the amount of the loss.
$100 floor	Not applicable.	Applicable per event.
Gains and losses	Gains and losses are netted (see detailed discussion in Chapter 8).	Personal casualty and theft gains and losses are netted.
Gains exceeding losses		The gains and losses are treated as gains and losses from the sale of capital assets.
Losses exceeding gains		The gains—and the losses to the extent of gains—are treated as ordinary items in computing AGI. The losses in excess of gains, to the extent that they exceed 10% of AGI, are itemized deductions (*from* AGI).

10 percent of the taxpayer's AGI. The resulting amount is the taxpayer's itemized deduction for personal-use casualty and theft losses.

EXAMPLE 16

Rocky, who had AGI of $30,000, was involved in a motorcycle accident. His motorcycle, which was used only for personal use and had a fair market value of $12,000 and an adjusted basis of $9,000, was completely destroyed. He received $5,000 from his insurance company. Rocky's casualty loss deduction is $900 [$9,000 basis − $5,000 insurance − $100 floor − $3,000 (.10 × $30,000 AGI)]. The $900 casualty loss is an itemized deduction (*from* AGI). ■

Where there are both casualty and theft gains and losses from personal-use property, special netting rules apply. Generally, if casualty and theft gains exceed losses during the year, the gains and losses are treated as capital gains and losses. Alternatively, if losses exceed gains, the casualty and theft gains (and losses to the extent of gains) are treated as ordinary gains and losses. Any excess losses are deductible as personal-use casualty and theft losses.

DIGGING DEEPER 2

Find more information on this topic at our Web site: ***http://wft-entities.swlearning.com.***

Net Operating Losses

LO.4

Recognize the impact of the net operating loss carryback and carryover provisions.

Introduction

The requirement that every taxpayer file an annual income tax return (whether on a calendar year or a fiscal year) can lead to inequities for taxpayers who experience

TAX FACT

The Utility of the NOL Deduction

Recently, corporations claimed net operating loss deductions of approximately $62.4 billion against business receipts of nearly $17.3 trillion.

Source: *Corporation Income Tax Returns, 2002; Table 2—Selected Balance Sheet, Income Statement, and Tax Items, by Asset Size; Summer 2005.*

uneven income over a series of years. These inequities result from the application of progressive tax rates to taxable income determined on an annual basis.

EXAMPLE 17

Orange, Inc., realizes the following taxable income or loss over a five-year period: Year 1, $50,000; Year 2, ($30,000); Year 3, $100,000; Year 4, ($200,000); and Year 5, $380,000. Blue Corporation has taxable income of $60,000 every year. Note that both corporations have total taxable income of $300,000 over the five-year period. Assume there is no provision for carryback or carryover of net operating losses. Orange and Blue would have the following five-year tax liabilities:

Year	Orange's Tax	Blue's Tax
1	$ 7,500	$10,000
2	–0–	10,000
3	22,250	10,000
4	–0–	10,000
5	129,200	10,000
	$158,950	$50,000

The computation of tax is made without regard to any NOL benefit. Rates applicable to 2006 are used to compute the tax.

Even though Orange and Blue realized the same total taxable income ($300,000) over the five-year period, Orange would have to pay taxes of $158,950, while Blue would pay taxes of only $50,000. ■

To provide partial relief from this inequitable tax treatment, a deduction is allowed for **net operating losses (NOLs)**.[20] This provision permits an NOL for any one year to offset taxable income in other years. The NOL provision provides relief only for losses from the operation of a trade or business or from casualty and theft.

Only C corporations and individuals are permitted an NOL deduction, since losses of partnerships and S corporations pass through to their owners. For C corporations, the NOL equals any negative taxable income for the year, with an adjustment for the dividends received deduction (see Chapter 9). In addition, deductions for prior-year NOLs are not allowed when determining a current-year NOL.

NOLs of individuals are computed by adding back to negative taxable income the excess of nonbusiness deductions (e.g., the standard deduction, charitable contributions, alimony payments) over nonbusiness income, personal and dependency exemptions, and any net capital loss deducted in calculating taxable income. Business deductions that are allowed for determining the NOL include moving expenses, losses on rental property, loss on the sale of small business stock, one-half of the self-employment tax (refer to Chapter 1), and losses from a sole proprietorship, partnership, or S corporation.

[20] § 172.

TAX *in the News* **WINDFALL FROM A NET OPERATING LOSS**

Under a tentative agreement reached with the IRS, Lucent Technologies will receive a $816 million tax refund. In the year 2001, Lucent lost $16.2 billion. Under the Job Creation and Worker Assistance Act of 2002, companies were allowed to carry NOLs from years 2001 and 2002 back five years instead of the usual two years. Under this provision, Lucent carried its 2001 loss back to the year 1996.

Source: *Adapted from "Back to the Present,"* CFO: The Magazine for Senior Financial Executives, *November 2004, p. 18.*

Carryback and Carryover Periods

General Rules. A current-year NOL is usually carried back and deducted against income over the two preceding tax years.[21] It is carried back first to the second year before the loss year and then to the year immediately preceding the loss year (until it fully offsets income). If the loss is not completely used against income in the carryback period, it is carried forward for 20 years following the loss year. NOLs that are not used within the 20-year carryforward period are lost. Thus, an NOL sustained in 2006 is used first in 2004 and then 2005. Then, the loss is carried forward and offsets income in 2007 through 2026.

When an NOL is carried back, the taxpayer requests an immediate refund of prior years' taxes by filing an amended return for the previous two years. When an NOL is carried forward, the current return shows an NOL deduction for the prior year's loss. Thus, a struggling business with an NOL can receive rapid cash-flow assistance.

NOLs from Multiple Tax Years. When the taxpayer has NOLs in two or more years, the earliest year's loss is used first. Later years' losses can then be used until they are offset against income or lost. Thus, one year's return could show NOL carryovers from two or more years. Each loss is computed and applied separately.

Election to Forgo Carryback. A taxpayer can *irrevocably elect* not to carry back an NOL. The election is made on a corporate tax return (Form 1120) by checking the appropriate box. Individuals can make the election by attaching a statement to their tax return. If the election is made, the loss can *only* be carried forward for 20 years. This election may be desirable in circumstances where marginal tax rates in future years are expected to exceed rates in prior years.

The Tax Shelter Problem

LO.5

Discuss tax shelters and the reasons for at-risk and passive loss limitations.

Before Congress enacted legislation to reduce or eliminate their effectiveness, **tax shelters** were popular investments for tax avoidance purposes because they could generate losses and other benefits that could be used to offset income from other sources. Because of the tax avoidance potential of many tax shelters, they were attractive to wealthy taxpayers with high marginal tax rates. Many tax shelters merely provided an opportunity for "investors" to buy deductions and credits in ventures that were not expected to generate a profit, even in the long run.

[21]A three-year carryback period is available for any portion of an individual's NOL resulting from a casualty or theft loss. The three-year carryback rule also applies to NOLs that are attributable to presidentially declared disaster areas that are incurred by a small business or a taxpayer engaged in farming. For purposes of this provision, a small business is one whose average annual gross receipts for a three-year period are $5 million or less.

TAX *in the News* — **WITH TAX SHELTERS IN THE SPOTLIGHT, TAXPAYERS SHOULD BE CAUTIOUS!**

Over the years, the at-risk and passive loss rules have gone a long way toward curbing abusive tax shelters. To the IRS's chagrin, however, some tax shelters are not restricted by these rules and continue to be a problem, as many reports in the media have shown. In response, the IRS has launched a major assault on tax shelters marketed to wealthy individuals. Already, the IRS has collected over $3.2 billion from taxpayers involved in the "Son of Boss" tax shelter. With other tax shelters also under attack, taxpayers who entered transactions that sounded too good to be true should be concerned.

Meanwhile, the publicity surrounding the IRS's efforts has driven a wedge between shelter marketers and their clients. As a consequence, many clients have sought damages from the accounting and law firms that developed the questionable shelters. Those firms and executives whose shelters are under scrutiny by the IRS are at risk of losing enormous amounts of money as well as their reputations.

Although it may seem odd that a taxpayer would intentionally invest in an activity that was designed to produce losses, there is a logical explanation. The typical tax shelter operated as a partnership and relied heavily on nonrecourse financing.[22] Accelerated depreciation and interest expense deductions generated large losses in the early years of the activity. At the very least, the tax shelter deductions deferred the recognition of any net income from the venture until the activity was sold. In the best of situations, the investor could realize additional tax savings by offsetting other income (e.g., salary, interest, and dividends) with losses flowing from the tax shelter. Ultimately, the sale of the investment would result in *tax-favored* capital gain. The following examples illustrate what was possible *before* Congress enacted legislation to curb tax shelter abuses.

EXAMPLE 18

Bob, who earned a salary of $400,000 as a business executive and dividend income of $15,000, invested $20,000 for a 10% interest in a cattle-breeding tax shelter. He did not participate in the operation of the business. Through the use of $800,000 of nonrecourse financing and available cash of $200,000, the partnership acquired a herd of an exotic breed of cattle costing $1 million. Depreciation, interest, and other deductions related to the activity resulted in a loss of $400,000, of which Bob's share was $40,000. Bob was allowed to deduct the $40,000 loss, even though he had invested and stood to lose only $20,000 if the investment became worthless. The net effect of the $40,000 deduction from the partnership was that a portion of Bob's salary and dividend income was "sheltered," and as a result, he was required to calculate his tax liability on only $375,000 of income [$415,000 (salary and dividends) – $40,000 (deduction)] rather than $415,000. If this deduction were available under current law and if Bob was in a combined Federal and state income tax bracket of 40%, a tax savings of $16,000 ($40,000 × 40%) would be generated in the first year alone! ■

A review of Example 18 shows that the taxpayer took a two-for-one write-off ($40,000 deduction, $20,000 investment). In the heyday of tax shelters, promoters often promised even larger write-offs for the investor.

The first major provision aimed at tax shelters is the **at-risk limitation**. Its objective is to limit a taxpayer's deductions to the amount that the taxpayer could actually lose from the investment (the amount "at risk") if it turns out to be a financial disaster.

EXAMPLE 19

Returning to the facts of the preceding example, under the current at-risk rules Bob would be allowed to deduct $20,000 (i.e., the amount that he could lose if the business failed). This deduction would reduce his other income, and as a result, Bob would report $395,000 of

[22]Nonrecourse debt is an obligation for which the borrower is not personally liable. An example of nonrecourse debt is a liability on real estate acquired by a partnership without the partnership or any of the partners assuming any liability for the mortgage. The acquired property generally is pledged as collateral for the loan.

BRIDGE *Discipline*

Bridge to Finance

An overarching requirement to maximizing wealth is to reduce the present value cost of taxation. One way to reduce the cost of taxation in present value terms is to defer the payment of a tax into the future for as long as possible. This can be accomplished by reducing the taxpayer's tax base (i.e., taxable income) either by deferring the recognition of income or by accelerating the timing of deductions. As a result, to the extent that the tax cost associated with an investment alternative is reduced, the after-tax benefit from that investment and the investor's wealth position are enhanced.

For example, a common attribute of many tax-advantaged investments is the availability of tax losses that investors may claim on their own income tax returns. Many times, these tax losses are the result of investment-level deductions, such as interest and depreciation expenses, that are bunched in the early years of the life of the investment rather than being due to economic woes of the investment itself.

Through the at-risk limitations and the passive loss rules, the tax law works to scale back the ability of taxpayers to claim tax losses flowing from certain investments. These limitations have a direct impact on *when* investors can claim loss deductions flowing from affected investments. The typical result of these provisions is that the loss deductions are deferred. As a result, when evaluating competing investment alternatives, taxpayers must address the impact of these tax limitations in projecting the after-tax benefits that can be expected to follow.

income ($415,000 – $20,000). The remaining nondeductible $20,000 loss and any future losses flowing from the partnership would be suspended under the at-risk rules and would be deductible in the future only as Bob's at-risk amount increased. ■

The second major attack on tax shelters came with the passage of the **passive loss** rules. These rules are intended to halt an investor's ability to benefit from the mismatching of an entity's expenses and income that often occurs in the early years of the business. Congress observed that despite the at-risk limitations, investors could still deduct losses flowing from an entity and thereby defer their tax liability on other income. These passive loss rules have, to a great degree, made the term *tax shelter* obsolete by suspending the deductibility of losses.

The passive loss rules require the taxpayer to segregate all income and losses into three categories: active, passive, and portfolio. In general, the passive loss limits *disallow* the deduction of passive losses *against active or portfolio income*, even when the taxpayer is at risk to the extent of the loss. In general, passive losses can only offset passive income.

EXAMPLE 20

Returning to the facts of Example 18, the passive activity loss rules further restrict Bob's ability to claim the $20,000 tax deduction shown in Example 19. Because Bob is a passive investor and does not materially participate in any meaningful way in the activities of the cattle-breeding operation, the $20,000 loss allowed under the at-risk rules is disallowed under the passive loss rules. The passive loss is disallowed because Bob does not generate any passive income that could absorb his passive loss. His salary (active income) and dividends (portfolio income) cannot be sheltered by any of the passive loss. Consequently, Bob's current-year taxable income is $415,000, and he receives no current benefit for his share of the partnership loss. However, all is not lost because Bob's share of the entity's loss is *suspended*. That is, it is carried forward and can be deducted in the future when he has passive income or sells his interest in the activity. ■

The following two sections explore the nature of the at-risk limits and passive activity loss rules and their impact on investors. Congress intentionally structured these rules so that investors evaluating potential investments must consider mainly the *economics* of the venture instead of the *tax benefits* or tax avoidance possibilities that an investment may generate.

LO.6

Describe how the at-risk limitation and the passive loss rules limit deductions for losses and identify taxpayers subject to these restrictions.

At-Risk Limitations

The at-risk provisions limit the deductibility of losses from business and income-producing activities. These provisions, which apply to individuals and closely held corporations, are designed to prevent taxpayers from deducting losses in excess of their actual economic investment in an activity. In the case of an S corporation or a partnership, the at-risk limits apply at the owner level. Under the at-risk rules, a taxpayer's deductible loss from an activity for any taxable year is limited to the amount the taxpayer has at risk at the end of the taxable year (i.e., the amount the taxpayer could actually lose in the activity).

While the amount at risk generally vacillates over time, the initial amount considered at risk consists of the following:[23]

- The amount of cash and the adjusted basis of property contributed to the activity by the taxpayer.
- Amounts borrowed for use in the activity for which the taxpayer is personally liable.
- The adjusted basis of property pledged as security that is not used in the activity.

This amount generally is increased each year by the taxpayer's share of income and is decreased by the taxpayer's share of losses and withdrawals from the activity. In addition, because *general partners* are jointly and severally liable for recourse debts of the partnership, their at-risk amounts are increased when the partnership increases its debt and are decreased when the partnership reduces its debt. However, a taxpayer generally is not considered at risk with respect to borrowed amounts if either of the following is true:

- The taxpayer is not personally liable for repayment of the debt (e.g., nonrecourse debt).
- The lender has an interest (other than as a creditor) in the activity.

An important exception provides that, in the case of an activity involving the holding of real property, a taxpayer is considered at risk for his or her share of any *qualified nonrecourse financing* that is secured by real property used in the activity.[24]

Subject to the passive activity rules discussed later in the chapter, a taxpayer may deduct a loss as long as the at-risk amount is positive. However, once the at-risk amount is exhausted, any remaining loss cannot be deducted until a later year. Any losses disallowed for any given taxable year by the at-risk rules may be deducted in the first succeeding year in which the rules do not prevent the deduction—that is, when there is, and to the extent of, a positive at-risk amount.

EXAMPLE 21

In 2006, Sue invests $40,000 in an oil partnership. The partnership, through the use of nonrecourse loans, spends $60,000 on deductible intangible drilling costs applicable to Sue's interest. Assume Sue's interest in the partnership is subject to the at-risk limits but is not subject to the passive loss limits. Since Sue has only $40,000 of capital at risk, she cannot deduct more than $40,000 against her other income and must reduce her at-risk amount to zero ($40,000 at-risk amount – $40,000 loss deducted). The nondeductible loss of $20,000 ($60,000 loss generated – $40,000 loss allowed) can be carried over to 2007.

In 2007, Sue has taxable income of $15,000 from the oil partnership and invests an additional $10,000 in the venture. Her at-risk amount is now $25,000 ($0 beginning balance + $15,000 taxable income + $10,000 additional investment). This enables Sue to deduct the $20,000 carryover loss and requires her to reduce her at-risk amount to $5,000 ($25,000 at-risk amount – $20,000 carryover loss allowed). ■

[23]§ 465(b)(1).

[24]Section 465(b)(6) defines qualified nonrecourse financing.

CONCEPT SUMMARY 6–3

Calculation of At-Risk Amount

Increases to a taxpayer's at-risk amount:

- Cash and the adjusted basis of property contributed to the activity.
- Amounts borrowed for use in the activity for which the taxpayer is personally liable.
- The adjusted basis of property pledged as security that is not used in the activity.
- Taxpayer's share of amounts borrowed for use in the activity that are qualified nonrecourse financing.
- Taxpayer's share of the activity's income.

Decreases to a taxpayer's at-risk amount:

- Withdrawals from the activity.
- Taxpayer's share of the activity's loss.
- Taxpayer's share of any reductions of debt for which recourse against the taxpayer exists or reductions of qualified nonrecourse debt.

An additional complicating factor is that previously allowed losses must be recaptured as income to the extent the at-risk amount is reduced below zero.[25] This rule applies in situations such as when the amount at risk is reduced below zero by distributions to the taxpayer or when the status of indebtedness changes from recourse to nonrecourse.

Passive Loss Limits

Classification and Impact of Passive Income and Loss

Classification. The passive loss rules require income and loss to be classified into one of three categories: *active, passive,* or *portfolio.* **Active income** includes the following:

- Wages, salary, commissions, bonuses, and other payments for services rendered by the taxpayer.
- Profit from a trade or business in which the taxpayer is a material participant.

Portfolio income includes the following:

- Interest, dividends, annuities, and royalties not derived in the ordinary course of a trade or business.
- Gain or loss from the disposition of property that produces portfolio income or is held for investment purposes.

Section 469 provides that income or loss from the following activities is treated as *passive:*

- Any trade or business or income-producing activity in which the taxpayer does not materially participate.
- Subject to certain exceptions, all rental activities, whether the taxpayer materially participates or not.

Although the Code defines rental activities as passive activities, several exceptions allow losses from certain real estate rental activities to offset nonpassive (active or portfolio) income. The exceptions are discussed under Special Rules for Real Estate later in the chapter.

[25] § 465(e).

TAX FACT

The Declining Interest in Limited Partnerships

Based on the most recently available data compiled by the IRS, the number of taxpayers investing in limited partnerships appears to have peaked at about the time the passive activity loss rules were enacted by Congress. Since that time, the number of limited partnership interests has declined. It may well be no accident that with the constraints placed on a taxpayer's ability to claim losses by the passive activity provisions, fewer taxpayers are interested in investment opportunities that promote tax losses.

Year	Number of Partners in Limited Partnerships
1985	13,244,824
1990	11,986,542
1995	10,223,901
1998	9,325,111
2000	6,468,292
2003	6,262,103

Sources: *Partnership Returns: Selected Balance Sheet and Income Statement Items for Specified Income Years, 1985–2001, Table 11,* SOI Bulletin, *Summer 2003; Partnership Returns: Selected Balance Sheet and Income Statement Items for Specified Income Years, 1995–2003, Table 11,* SOI Bulletin, *Summer 2005.*

General Impact. Losses or expenses generated by passive activities can only be deducted to the extent of income from passive activities. Any excess may not be used to offset income from active or portfolio income. Instead, any unused passive losses are suspended and carried forward to future years to offset passive income generated in those years. Otherwise, suspended losses may be used only when a taxpayer disposes of his or her entire interest in an activity. In that event, all current and suspended losses related to the activity may offset active and portfolio income.

EXAMPLE 22

Kim, a physician, earns $150,000 from her full-time practice. She also receives $10,000 in dividends and interest from various portfolio investments, and her share of a passive loss from a tax shelter not limited by the at-risk rules is $60,000. Because the loss is a passive loss, it is not deductible against her other income. The loss is suspended and is carried over to the future. If Kim has passive income from this investment or from other passive investments in the future, she can offset the suspended loss against that passive income. If she does not have passive income to offset this suspended loss in the future, she will be allowed to offset the loss against other types of income when she eventually disposes of the passive activity. ■

Impact of Suspended Losses. The actual economic gain or loss from a passive investment (including any suspended losses) can be determined when a taxpayer disposes of his or her entire interest in the investment. As a result, under the passive loss rules, upon a fully taxable disposition, any overall loss realized from the activity by the taxpayer is recognized and can be offset against passive, active, and portfolio income.

A fully taxable disposition generally involves a sale of the property to a third party at arm's length and thus, presumably, for a price equal to the property's fair market value. Gain recognized upon a transfer of an interest in a passive activity generally is treated as passive and is first offset by the suspended losses from that activity.

EXAMPLE 23

Rex sells an apartment building, a passive activity, with an adjusted basis of $100,000 for $180,000. In addition, he has suspended passive losses of $60,000 associated with the building. His total gain, $80,000, and his taxable gain, $20,000, are calculated as follows:

Net sales price	$ 180,000
Less: Adjusted basis	(100,000)
Total gain	$ 80,000
Less: Suspended losses	(60,000)
Taxable gain (passive)	$ 20,000

■

If current and suspended losses of the passive activity exceed the gain realized from the sale or if the sale results in a realized loss, the amount of

- any loss from the activity for the tax year (including losses suspended in the activity disposed of)

in excess of

- net income or gain for the tax year from all passive activities (without regard to the activity disposed of)

is treated as a loss that is not from a passive activity. In computing the loss from the activity for the year of disposition, any gain or loss recognized is included in the calculation.

EXAMPLE 24

Dean sells an apartment building, a passive activity, with an adjusted basis of $100,000 for $150,000. In addition, he has current and suspended passive losses of $60,000 associated with the building and has no other passive activities. His total gain of $50,000 and his deductible loss of $10,000 are calculated as follows:

Net sales price	$ 150,000
Less: Adjusted basis	(100,000)
Total gain	$ 50,000
Less: Suspended losses	(60,000)
Deductible loss (not passive)	($ 10,000)

The $10,000 loss can be deducted against Dean's active and portfolio income. ■

Carryovers of Suspended Losses. In the above examples, it was assumed that the taxpayer had an interest in only one passive activity, and as a result, the suspended loss was related exclusively to the activity that was disposed of. When a taxpayer owns more than one passive activity, however, any suspended losses must be allocated among the activities. The allocation to an activity is made by multiplying the disallowed passive activity loss from all activities by the following fraction:

$$\frac{\text{Loss from activity}}{\text{Sum of losses for taxable year from all activities having losses}}$$

EXAMPLE 25

Diego has investments in three passive activities with the following income and losses for 2005:

Activity A	($ 30,000)
Activity B	(20,000)
Activity C	25,000
Net passive loss	($ 25,000)
Net passive loss allocated to:	
Activity A [$25,000 × ($30,000/$50,000)]	($ 15,000)
Activity B [$25,000 × ($20,000/$50,000)]	(10,000)
Total suspended losses	($ 25,000)

■

Suspended losses are carried over indefinitely and are offset in the future against any passive income from the activities to which they relate.[26]

EXAMPLE 26

Assume the same facts as in the preceding example and that Activity A produces $10,000 of income in 2006. Of the suspended loss of $15,000 from 2005 for Activity A, $10,000 is offset against the income from this activity. If Diego sells Activity A in early 2007, then the remaining $5,000 suspended loss is used in determining his final gain or loss. ■

Passive Credits. Credits arising from passive activities are limited in much the same way as passive losses. Passive credits can be utilized only against regular tax attributable to passive income,[27] which is calculated by comparing the tax on all income (including passive income) with the tax on income excluding passive income.

EXAMPLE 27

Sam owes $50,000 of tax, disregarding net passive income, and $80,000 of tax, considering both net passive and other taxable income (disregarding the credits in both cases). The amount of tax attributable to the passive income is $30,000. ■

Sam in the preceding example can claim a maximum of $30,000 of passive activity credits; the excess credits are carried over. These passive activity credits (such as the rehabilitation credit—discussed in Chapter 14) can be used only against the *regular* tax attributable to passive income. If a taxpayer has a net loss from passive activities during a given year, no credits can be used.

Carryovers of Passive Credits. Tax credits attributable to passive activities can be carried forward indefinitely, much like suspended passive losses. Unlike passive losses, however, passive credits are lost forever when the activity is disposed of in a taxable transaction where loss is recognized. Credits are allowed on dispositions only when there is sufficient tax on passive income to absorb them.

EXAMPLE 28

Alicia sells a passive activity for a gain of $10,000. The activity had suspended losses of $40,000 and suspended credits of $15,000. The $10,000 gain is offset by $10,000 of the suspended losses, and the remaining $30,000 of suspended losses is deductible against Alicia's active and portfolio income. The suspended credits are lost forever because the sale of the activity did not generate any tax after considering the effect of the suspended losses. This is true even if Alicia has positive taxable income or is subject to the alternative minimum tax (discussed in Chapter 14). ■

[26] § 469(b).

[27] § 469(d)(2).

EXAMPLE 29

If Alicia in the preceding example had realized a $100,000 gain on the sale of the passive activity, the suspended credits could have been used to the extent of regular tax attributable to the net passive income.

Gain on sale	$100,000
Less: Suspended losses	(40,000)
Net gain	$ 60,000

If the tax attributable to the net gain of $60,000 is $15,000 or more, the entire $15,000 of suspended credits can be used. If the tax attributable to the gain is less than $15,000, the excess of the suspended credits over the tax attributable to the gain is lost forever. ■

When a taxpayer has an adequate regular tax liability from passive activities to trigger the use of suspended credits, the credits lose their character as passive credits. They are reclassified as regular tax credits and made subject to the same limits as other credits (see Chapter 14).

Passive Activity Changes to Active. If a formerly passive activity becomes active, suspended losses are allowed to the extent of income from the now active business.[28] If any of the suspended loss remains, it continues to be treated as a loss from a passive activity. The excess suspended loss can be deducted against passive income or carried over to the next tax year and deducted to the extent of income from the now active business in the succeeding year(s).

Taxpayers Subject to the Passive Loss Rules

The passive loss rules apply to individuals, estates, trusts, personal service corporations, and closely held C corporations.[29] Passive income or loss from investments in partnerships or S corporations (see Chapters 11 and 12) flows through to the owners, and the passive loss rules are applied at the owner level. Consequently, it is necessary to understand how the passive activity rules apply to both entities *and* their owners (including individual taxpayers).

Personal Service Corporations. Application of the passive loss limitations to **personal service corporations** is intended to prevent taxpayers from sheltering personal service income by creating personal service corporations and acquiring passive activities at the corporate level.

EXAMPLE 30

Five tax accountants, who earn a total of $1 million a year in their individual practices, agree to work together in a newly formed personal service corporation. Shortly after its formation, the corporation invests in a passive activity that produces a $200,000 loss during the year. Because the passive loss rules apply to personal service corporations, the corporation may not deduct the $200,000 loss against the $1 million of active income. ■

Determination of whether a corporation is a *personal service corporation* is based on rather broad definitions. A personal service corporation is a corporation that meets both of the following conditions:

- The principal activity is the performance of personal services.
- Such services are substantially performed by owner-employees.

Generally, personal service corporations include those in the fields of health, law, engineering, architecture, accounting, actuarial science, performing arts, and consulting.[30]

DIGGING DEEPER 3

Find more information on this topic at our Web site: ***http://wft-entities.swlearning.com.***

[28] § 469(f).
[29] § 469(a).
[30] § 448(d)(2)(A).

Closely Held C Corporations. Application of the passive loss rules to closely held (non-personal service) C corporations is also intended to prevent individuals from incorporating to avoid the passive loss limitations. A corporation is classified as a **closely held C corporation** if at any time during the taxable year, more than 50 percent of the value of its outstanding stock is owned, directly or indirectly, by or for five or fewer individuals. Closely held C corporations (other than personal service corporations) may use passive losses to offset *active* income, but *not portfolio* income.

EXAMPLE 31

Silver Corporation, a closely held (non-personal service) C corporation, has a $500,000 passive loss from a rental activity, $400,000 of active income, and $100,000 of portfolio income. The corporation may offset $400,000 of the $500,000 passive loss against the $400,000 of active business income, but may not offset the remainder against the $100,000 of portfolio income. Thus, $100,000 of the passive loss is suspended ($500,000 passive loss – $400,000 offset against active income). ■

Application of the passive loss limitations to closely held C corporations prevents shareholders from transferring their portfolio investments to such corporations in order to offset passive losses against portfolio income.

LO.7

Discuss and be able to apply the definitions of activity, material participation, and rental activity under the passive loss rules.

Activity Defined

Identifying what constitutes an activity is a necessary first step in applying the passive loss limitation. The current rules used to delineate an activity state that, in general, a taxpayer can treat one or more trade or business activities or rental activities as a single activity if those activities form an *appropriate economic unit* for measuring gain or loss. The Regulations provide guidelines for identifying appropriate economic units.[31] These guidelines are designed to prevent taxpayers from arbitrarily combining different businesses in an attempt to circumvent the passive loss limitation. For example, combining a profitable active business and a passive business generating losses into one activity would allow the taxpayer to offset passive losses against active income.

DIGGING DEEPER 4

Find more information on this topic at our Web site: ***http://wft-entities.swlearning.com.***

To determine which ventures form an appropriate economic unit, all of the relevant facts and circumstances must be considered. However, special rules restrict the grouping of rental and nonrental activities.[32] The example below, adapted from the Regulations, illustrates the application of the activity grouping rules.[33]

EXAMPLE 32

George owns a men's clothing store and a video game parlor in Chicago. He also owns a men's clothing store and a video game parlor in Milwaukee. Reasonable methods of applying the facts and circumstances test may result in any of the following groupings:

- All four businesses may be grouped into a single activity because of common ownership and control.
- The clothing stores may be grouped into an activity, and the video game parlors may be grouped into an activity.
- The Chicago businesses may be grouped into an activity, and the Milwaukee businesses may be grouped into an activity.
- Each of the four businesses may be treated as a separate activity. ■

[31]Reg. § 1.469–4.
[32]Reg. § 1.469–4(d).
[33]Reg. § 1.469–4(c)(3).

Once a set of activities has been grouped by the taxpayer using the above rules, the grouping cannot be changed unless a material change in the facts and circumstances occurs or the original grouping was clearly inappropriate. In addition, the Regulations also grant the IRS the right to regroup activities when one of the primary purposes of the taxpayer's grouping is to avoid the passive loss limitation and the grouping fails to reflect an appropriate economic unit.[34]

Material Participation

If a taxpayer materially participates in a nonrental trade or business activity, any loss from that activity is treated as an active loss that can offset active or portfolio income. If a taxpayer does not materially participate, however, the loss is treated as a passive loss, which can only offset passive income. Therefore, controlling whether a particular activity is treated as active or passive is an important part of the tax strategy of a taxpayer who owns an interest in one or more businesses. Consider the following examples.

EXAMPLE 33

Cameron, a corporate executive, earns a salary of $600,000 per year. In addition, he owns a separate business in which he participates. The business produces a loss of $100,000 during the year. If Cameron materially participates in the business, the $100,000 loss is an active loss that may offset his active income from his corporate employer. If he does not materially participate, the loss is passive and is suspended. Cameron may use the suspended loss in the future only when he has passive income or disposes of the activity. ■

EXAMPLE 34

Connor, an attorney, earns $350,000 a year in his law practice. He owns interests in two activities, A and B, in which he participates. Activity A, in which he does not *materially* participate, produces a loss of $50,000. Connor has not yet met the material participation standard for Activity B, which produces income of $80,000. However, he can meet the material participation standard if he spends an additional 50 hours in Activity B during the year. Should Connor attempt to meet the material participation standard for Activity B? If he continues working in Activity B and becomes a material participant, the $80,000 of income from the activity is active, and the $50,000 passive loss from Activity A must be suspended. A more favorable tax strategy is for Connor to *not meet* the material participation standard for Activity B, thus making the income from that activity passive. This enables him to offset the $50,000 passive loss from Activity A against the passive income from Activity B. ■

It is possible to devise numerous scenarios in which the taxpayer could control the tax outcome by increasing or decreasing participation in different activities. Examples 33 and 34 demonstrate two of the possibilities. The conclusion reached in most analyses of this type is that taxpayers will benefit by having profitable activities classified as passive so that any passive losses can be used to offset that passive income. If the activity produces a loss, however, the taxpayer will benefit if it is classified as active so that the loss is not subject to the passive loss limitations.

Temporary Regulations[35] provide seven tests that are intended to help taxpayers determine when **material participation** is achieved.

Tests Based on Current Participation. The first four tests are quantitative tests that require measurement, in hours, of the individual's participation in the activity during the year.

1. *Does the individual participate in the activity for more than 500 hours during the year?*

The purpose of the 500-hour requirement is to restrict deductions from the types of trade or business activities that Congress intended to treat as passive

[34]Reg. § 1.469–4(f).

[35]Temp.Reg. § 1.469–5T(a).

activities. The 500-hour standard for material participation was adopted for the following reasons:[36]

- Few investors in traditional tax shelters devote more than 500 hours a year to such an investment.
- The IRS believes that income from an activity in which the taxpayer participates for more than 500 hours a year should not be treated as passive.

2. *Does the individual's participation in the activity for the taxable year constitute substantially all of the participation in the activity of all individuals (including nonowner employees) for the year?*

EXAMPLE 35

Ned, a physician, operates a separate business in which he participates for 80 hours during the year. He is the only participant and has no employees in the separate business. Ned meets the material participation standard of Test 2. If he had employees, it could be difficult to apply Test 2, because the Temporary Regulations do not define the term "substantially all." ■

3. *Does the individual participate in the activity for more than 100 hours during the year, and is the individual's participation in the activity for the year not less than the participation of any other individual (including nonowner employees) for the year?*

EXAMPLE 36

Adam, a college professor, owns a separate business in which he participates 110 hours during the year. He has an employee who works 90 hours during the year. Adam meets the material participation standard under Test 3, but probably does not meet it under Test 2 because his participation is only 55% of the total participation. It is unlikely that 55% would meet the substantially all requirement of Test 2. ■

Tests 2 and 3 are included because the IRS recognizes that the operation of some activities does not require more than 500 hours of participation during the year.

4. *Is the activity a significant participation activity for the taxable year, and does the individual's aggregate participation in all significant participation activities during the year exceed 500 hours?*

A **significant participation activity** is a trade or business in which the individual's participation exceeds 100 hours during the year. This test treats taxpayers as material participants if their aggregate participation in several significant participation activities exceeds 500 hours. Test 4 thus accords the same treatment to an individual who devotes an aggregate of more than 500 hours to several significant participation activities as to an individual who devotes more than 500 hours to a single activity.

EXAMPLE 37

Mike owns five different businesses. He participates in each activity during the year as follows:

Activity	Hours of Participation
A	110
B	140
C	120
D	150
E	100

[36]T.D. 8175, 1988–1 C.B. 191.

Activities A, B, C, and D are significant participation activities, and Mike's aggregate participation in those activities is 520 hours. Therefore, Activities A, B, C, and D are *not* treated as passive activities. Activity E is not a significant participation activity (not more than 100 hours), so it is not included in applying the 500-hour test. Activity E is treated as a passive activity, unless Mike meets one of the other material participation tests for that activity. ■

EXAMPLE 38

Assume the same facts as in the preceding example, except that Activity A does not exist. All of the activities are now treated as passive. Activity E is not counted in applying the more-than-500-hour test, so Mike's aggregate participation in significant participation activities is 410 hours (140 in Activity B + 120 in Activity C + 150 in Activity D). He could meet the significant participation test for Activity E by participating for one more hour in the activity. This would cause Activities B, C, D, and E to be treated as nonpassive activities. However, before deciding whether to participate for at least one more hour in Activity E, Mike should assess how the participation would affect his overall tax liability. ■

Tests Based on Prior Participation. Tests 5 and 6 are based on material participation in prior years. Under these tests, a taxpayer no longer participating in an activity can continue to be *classified* as a material participant. The IRS takes the position that material participation in a trade or business for a long period of time is likely to indicate that the activity represents the individual's principal livelihood, rather than a passive investment. Consequently, withdrawal from the activity or reduction of participation to the point where it is not material does not change the classification of the activity from active to passive.

5. *Did the individual materially participate in the activity for any five taxable years (whether consecutive or not) during the 10 taxable years that immediately precede the taxable year?*

EXAMPLE 39

Dawn, who owns a 50% interest in a restaurant, was a material participant in the operations of the restaurant from 2000 through 2004. She retired at the end of 2004 and is no longer involved in the restaurant except as an investor. Dawn will be treated as a material participant in the restaurant in 2005. Even if she does not become involved in the restaurant as a material participant again, she will continue to be treated as a material participant in 2006, 2007, 2008, and 2009. In 2010 and later years, Dawn's share of income or loss from the restaurant will be classified as passive unless she materially participates in those years. ■

6. *Is the activity a personal service activity, and did the individual materially participate in the activity for any three preceding taxable years (whether consecutive or not)?*

As indicated above, the material participation standards for personal service activities differ from other businesses. An individual who was a material participant in a personal service activity for *any three years* prior to the taxable year continues to be treated as a material participant after withdrawal from the activity.

EXAMPLE 40

Evan, a CPA, retires from the EFG Partnership after working full-time in the partnership for 30 years. As a retired partner, he will continue to receive a share of the profits of the firm for the next 10 years, even though he will not participate in the firm's operations. Evan also owns an interest in a passive activity that produces a loss for the year. Because he continues to be treated as a material participant in the EFG Partnership, his income from the partnership is active income. Therefore, he is not allowed to offset the loss from his passive investment against the income from the EFG Partnership. ■

Test Based on Facts and Circumstances. Test 7 assesses the facts and circumstances to determine whether the taxpayer has materially participated.

7. *Based on all the facts and circumstances, did the individual participate in the activity on a regular, continuous, and substantial basis during the year?*

DIGGING DEEPER 5

Find more information on this topic at our Web site: ***http://wft-entities.swlearning.com.***

Unfortunately, the Temporary Regulations do not define what constitutes regular, continuous, and substantial participation.[37]

Participation Defined. Participation generally includes any work done by an individual in an activity that he or she owns. Participation does not include work if it is of a type not customarily done by owners *and* if one of its principal purposes is to avoid the disallowance of passive losses or credits. Also, work done in an individual's capacity as an investor (e.g., reviewing financial reports in a nonmanagerial capacity) is not counted in applying the material participation tests. However, participation by an owner's spouse counts as participation by the owner.[38]

EXAMPLE 41

Tom, who is a partner in a CPA firm, owns a computer store that has operated at a loss during the year. In order to offset this loss against the income from his CPA practice, Tom would like to avoid having the computer business classified as a passive activity. Through December 15, he has worked 400 hours in the business in management and selling activities. During the last two weeks of December, he works 80 hours in management and selling activities and 30 hours doing janitorial chores. Also during the last two weeks in December, Tom's wife participates 40 hours as a salesperson. She has worked as a salesperson in the computer store in prior years, but has not done so during the current year. If any of Tom's work is of a type not customarily done by owners and if one of its principal purposes is to avoid the disallowance of passive losses or credits, it is not counted in applying the material participation tests. It is likely that Tom's 480 hours of participation in management and selling activities will count as participation, but the 30 hours spent doing janitorial chores will not. However, the 40 hours of participation by his wife will count, and as a result, Tom will qualify as a material participant under the more-than-500-hour rule (480 + 40 = 520). ■

Limited Partners. A *limited* partner is one whose liability to third-party creditors of the partnership is limited to the amount the partner has invested in the partnership. Such a partnership must have at least one *general* partner, who is fully liable in an individual capacity for the debts of the partnership to third parties. Generally, a *limited partner* is not considered a material participant unless he or she qualifies under Test 1, 5, or 6 in the above list. However, a *general partner* may qualify as a material participant by meeting any of the seven tests. If a general partner also owns a limited interest in the same limited partnership, all interests are treated as a general interest.[39]

Corporations. Personal service corporations and closely held C corporations cannot directly participate in an activity. However, a corporation is deemed to materially participate if its owners materially participate in an activity of the corporation. Together, the participating owners must own directly or indirectly more than 50 percent of the value of the outstanding stock of the corporation.[40] Alternatively, a closely held C corporation may be deemed to materially participate in an activity if, during the entire year, it has at least one full-time employee actively managing the business and at least three full-time nonowner employees working for the business. In addition, the corporation's trade or business expenses must exceed the gross income from that business by 15 percent for the year.[41]

[37] Temp.Reg. § 1.469–5T(b)(2).
[38] Temp.Reg. § 1.469–5T(f)(3).
[39] Temp.Reg. § 1.469–5T(e)(3)(ii).
[40] Temp.Reg. § 1.469–1T(g)(3)(i)(A).
[41] Temp.Reg. § 1.469–1T(g)(3)(i)(B).

CONCEPT SUMMARY 6–4

Passive Activity Loss Rules: General Concepts

What is the fundamental passive activity rule?	Passive activity losses may be deducted only against passive activity income and gains. Losses not allowed are suspended and used in future years.
Who is subject to the passive activity rules?	Individuals. Estates. Trusts. Personal service corporations. Closely held C corporations.
What is a passive activity?	Trade or business or income-producing activity in which the taxpayer does not materially participate during the year, or rental activities, subject to certain exceptions, regardless of the taxpayer's level of participation.
What is an activity?	One or more trades or businesses or rental activities that comprise an appropriate economic unit.
How is an appropriate economic unit determined?	Based on a reasonable application of the relevant facts and circumstances.
What is material participation?	In general, the taxpayer participates on a regular, continuous, and substantial basis. More specifically, when the taxpayer meets the conditions of one of the seven tests provided in the Regulations.
What is a rental activity?	In general, an activity where payments are received for the use of tangible property. More specifically, a rental activity that does *not* meet one of the six exceptions provided in the Regulations. Special rules apply to rental real estate.

Rental Activities

The Code specifies that, subject to certain exceptions, all rental activities are to be treated as passive activities.[42] A **rental activity** is defined as any activity where payments are received principally for the use of tangible (real or personal) property.[43] Importantly, an activity that is classified as a rental activity is subject to the passive activity loss rules, even if the taxpayer involved is a material participant.

EXAMPLE 42

Sarah owns an apartment building and spends an average of 60 hours a week in its operation. Assuming that the apartment building operation is classified as a rental activity, it is automatically subject to the passive activity rules, even though Sarah spends more than 500 hours a year in its operation. ■

Temporary Regulations, however, provide exceptions for certain situations where activities involving rentals of real and personal property are *not* to be treated as rental activities.[44] Activities covered by any of the exceptions provided by the Temporary Regulations are not *automatically* treated as passive activities because

[42] § 469(c)(2).

[43] § 469(j)(8).

[44] Temp.Reg. § 1.469–1T(e)(3)(ii).

they would not be classified as rental activities. Instead, the activities are subject to the material participation tests.

DIGGING DEEPER 6

Find more information on this topic at our Web site: ***http://wft-entities.swlearning.com.***

EXAMPLE 43

Dan owns a DVD rental business. Because the average period of customer use is seven days or less, Dan's business is not treated as a rental activity. ■

The fact that Dan's DVD business in the previous example is not treated as a rental activity does not necessarily mean that it is classified as a nonpassive activity. Instead, the DVD business is treated as a trade or business activity subject to the material participation standards. If Dan is a material participant, the business is treated as active. If he is not a material participant, it is treated as a passive activity.

LO.8

Recognize the relationship between the at-risk and passive activity limitations.

Interaction of At-Risk and Passive Activity Limits

The determination of whether a loss is suspended under the passive loss rules is made *after* application of the at-risk rules, as well as other provisions relating to the measurement of taxable income. A loss that is not allowed for the year because the taxpayer is not at risk with respect to it is suspended under the at-risk provision and not under the passive loss rules. Further, a taxpayer's basis is reduced by deductions (e.g., depreciation) even if the deductions are not currently usable because of the passive loss rules.

EXAMPLE 44

Jack's adjusted basis in a passive activity is $10,000 at the beginning of 2005. His loss from the activity in 2005 is $4,000. Since Jack has no passive activity income, the $4,000 cannot be deducted. At year-end, Jack has an adjusted basis and an at-risk amount of $6,000 in the activity and a suspended passive loss of $4,000. ■

EXAMPLE 45

Jack in the preceding example has a loss of $9,000 in the activity in 2006. Since the $9,000 exceeds his at-risk amount ($6,000) by $3,000, that $3,000 loss is disallowed by the at-risk rules. If Jack has no passive activity income, the remaining $6,000 is suspended under the passive activity rules. At year-end, he has:

- A $3,000 loss suspended under the at-risk rules.
- $10,000 of suspended passive losses.
- An adjusted basis and at-risk amount in the activity of zero. ■

EXAMPLE 46

Jack in Example 45 realizes $1,000 of passive income from the activity in 2007. Because the $1,000 increases his at-risk amount, $1,000 of the $3,000 unused loss is reclassified as a passive loss. If he has no other passive income, the $1,000 income is offset by $1,000 of suspended passive losses. At the end of 2007, Jack has:

- No taxable passive income.
- $2,000 ($3,000 – $1,000) of unused losses under the at-risk rules.
- $10,000 of (reclassified) suspended passive losses ($10,000 + $1,000 of reclassified unused at-risk losses – $1,000 of passive losses offset against passive income).
- An adjusted basis and an at-risk amount in the activity of zero. ■

EXAMPLE 47

In 2008, Jack has no gain or loss from the activity in Example 46. He contributes $5,000 more to the passive activity. Because the $5,000 contribution increases his at-risk amount, the $2,000 of losses suspended under the at-risk rules is reclassified as passive. Jack gets no passive loss deduction in 2008. At year-end, he has:

TAX *in the News* **NEWLY DEVELOPED TAX SHELTER STRATEGIES NOW PROTECTED BY PATENTS**

A patent is generally thought of as an intangible asset that protects the intellectual property underlying a new drug, manufacturing process, or consumer item. In such cases, the U.S. Patent and Trademark Office grants a patent that legally protects the holder's exclusive right to the invention. Now, tax and financial planners are patenting their newest tax shelters and strategies to prevent competitors from using them. Some of the patented strategies involve making mixed gifts of art to charities and family or transferring appreciated assets to heirs with minimal tax consequences.

The applicant for a patent should be aware of the potential costs associated with acquiring such legal protection, however. Even if the Patent and Trademark Office grants a so-called business method patent, there is no assurance that the IRS will approve of the technique. In addition, obtaining a patent can be an expensive and complicated process that can take years. Nonetheless, in a recent year, over 6,000 patent applications involving business methods were submitted for approval.

Source: *Adapted from Rachel Emma Silverman, "The Patented Tax Shelter,"* Wall Street Journal, *June 24, 2004, pp. D1–D2.*

- No suspended losses under the at-risk rules.
- $12,000 of suspended passive losses ($10,000 + $2,000 of reclassified suspended at-risk losses).
- An adjusted basis and an at-risk amount of $3,000 ($5,000 additional investment − $2,000 of reclassified losses). ■

Special Rules for Real Estate

LO.9

Discuss the special treatment available to real estate activities.

The passive loss rules contain two exceptions related to real estate activities. These exceptions allow all or part of real estate rental losses to offset active or portfolio income, even though the activity otherwise is defined as a passive activity.

Real Estate Professionals. The first exception allows certain real estate professionals to avoid passive loss treatment for losses from real estate rental activities.[45] To qualify for nonpassive treatment, a taxpayer must satisfy both of the following requirements:

- More than half of the personal services that the taxpayer performs in trades or businesses are performed in real property trades or businesses in which the taxpayer materially participates.
- The taxpayer performs more than 750 hours of services in these real property trades or businesses as a material participant.

Taxpayers who do not satisfy the above requirements must continue to treat losses from real estate rental activities as passive losses.

EXAMPLE 48

During the current year, Della performs personal service activities as follows: 900 hours as a personal financial planner, 550 hours in a real estate development business, and 600 hours in a real estate rental activity. Any loss Della incurs in the real estate rental activity will not be subject to the passive loss rules, since more than 50% of her personal services are devoted to real property trades or businesses and her material participation in those real estate activities exceeds 750 hours. Thus, any loss from the real estate rental activity can offset active and portfolio income. ■

As discussed earlier, a spouse's work is taken into consideration in satisfying the material participation requirement. However, the hours worked by a spouse are not taken into account when ascertaining whether a taxpayer has worked for more than

[45] § 469(c)(7).

750 hours in real property trades or businesses during a year. Services performed by an employee are not treated as being related to a real estate trade or business unless the employee performing the services owns more than a 5 percent interest in the employer. Additionally, a closely held C corporation may also qualify for the passive loss relief if more than 50 percent of its gross receipts for the year are derived from real property trades or businesses in which it materially participates.[46]

Rental Real Estate Deduction. The second exception is more significant in that it is not restricted to real estate professionals. This exception allows individuals to deduct up to $25,000 of losses from real estate rental activities against active and portfolio income.[47] The potential annual $25,000 deduction is reduced by 50 percent of the taxpayer's adjusted gross income (AGI) in excess of $100,000. Thus, the entire deduction is phased out at $150,000. If married individuals file separately, the $25,000 deduction is reduced to zero unless they lived apart for the entire year. If they lived apart for the entire year, the loss amount is $12,500 each, and the phaseout begins at $50,000.

To qualify for the $25,000 exception, a taxpayer must:[48]

- *Actively participate* in the real estate rental activity.
- Own 10 percent or more (in value) of all interests in the activity during the entire taxable year (or shorter period during which the taxpayer held an interest in the activity).

The difference between *active participation* and *material participation* is that the former can be satisfied without regular, continuous, and substantial involvement in operations as long as the taxpayer participates in making management decisions in a significant and bona fide sense. In this context, relevant management decisions include such decisions as approving new tenants, deciding on rental terms, and approving capital or repair expenditures.

The $25,000 allowance is available after all active participation rental losses and gains are netted and applied to other passive income. If a taxpayer has a real estate rental loss in excess of the amount that can be deducted under the real estate rental exception, that excess is treated as a passive loss.

EXAMPLE 49

Brad, who has $90,000 of AGI before considering rental activities, has $85,000 of losses from a real estate rental activity in which he actively participates. He also actively participates in another real estate rental activity from which he has $25,000 of income. He has other passive income of $36,000. Of the net rental loss of $60,000, $36,000 is absorbed by the $36,000 of passive income, leaving $24,000 that can be deducted against active or portfolio income because of the availability of the $25,000 allowance. ■

The $25,000 offset allowance is an aggregate of both deductions and credits in deduction equivalents. The deduction equivalent of a passive activity credit is the amount of deductions that reduces the tax liability for the taxable year by an amount equal to the credit.[49] A taxpayer with $5,000 of credits and a marginal tax rate of 25 percent would have a deduction equivalent of $20,000 ($5,000/25%).

If total deductions and deduction equivalents exceed $25,000, the taxpayer must allocate the benefit on a pro rata basis. First, the allowance must be allocated among the losses (including real estate rental activity losses suspended in prior years) and then to credits.

EXAMPLE 50

Kevin is an active participant in a real estate rental activity that produces $8,000 of income, $26,000 of deductions, and $1,500 of credits. Kevin, whose marginal tax rate is 25%, may

[46] § 469(c)(7)(B) and Reg. § 1.469–9.
[47] § 469(i).
[48] § 469(i)(6).
[49] § 469(j)(5).

deduct the net passive loss of $18,000 ($8,000 – $26,000). After deducting the loss, he has an available deduction equivalent of $7,000 ($25,000 – $18,000 passive loss). Therefore, the maximum amount of credits that he may claim is $1,750 ($7,000 × 25%). Since the actual credits are less than this amount, Kevin may claim the entire $1,500 credit. ■

EXAMPLE 51

Kelly, whose marginal tax rate is 25%, actively participates in three separate real estate rental activities. The relevant tax results for each activity are as follows:

- Activity A: $20,000 of losses.
- Activity B: $10,000 of losses.
- Activity C: $4,200 of credits.

Kelly's deduction equivalent from the credits is $16,800 ($4,200/25%). Therefore, the total passive deductions and deduction equivalents are $46,800 ($20,000 + $10,000 + $16,800), which exceeds the maximum allowable amount of $25,000. Consequently, Kelly must allocate pro rata first from among losses and then from among credits. Deductions from losses are limited as follows:

- Activity A: $25,000 × [$20,000/($20,000 + $10,000)] = $16,667.
- Activity B: $25,000 × [$10,000/($20,000 + $10,000)] = $8,333.

Since the amount of passive deductions exceeds the $25,000 maximum, the deduction balance of $5,000 and passive credits of $4,200 must be carried forward. Kelly's suspended losses and credits by activity are as follows:

		Activity		
	Total	A	B	C
Allocated losses	$ 30,000	$ 20,000	$10,000	$ -0-
Allocated credits	4,200	-0-	-0-	4,200
Utilized losses	(25,000)	(16,667)	(8,333)	-0-
Suspended losses	5,000	3,333	1,667	-0-
Suspended credits	4,200	-0-	-0-	4,200 ■

Disposition of Passive Activities

Recall from an earlier discussion that if a taxpayer disposes of an entire interest in a passive activity, any suspended losses (and in certain cases, suspended credits) may be utilized when calculating the final economic gain or loss on the investment. In addition, if a loss ultimately results, that loss can offset other types of income. However, the consequences may differ if the activity is disposed of in a transaction that is not fully taxable. The following discusses the treatment of suspended passive losses in two such dispositions.

Disposition of a Passive Activity at Death. A transfer of a taxpayer's interest in an activity by reason of the taxpayer's death results in suspended losses being allowed (to the decedent) to the extent they exceed the amount, if any, of the step-up in basis allowed.[50] Suspended losses are lost to the extent of the amount of the basis increase. The losses allowed generally are reported on the final return of the deceased taxpayer.

EXAMPLE 52

A taxpayer dies with passive activity property having an adjusted basis of $40,000, suspended losses of $10,000, and a fair market value at the date of the decedent's death of $75,000. The

[50] § 469(g)(2).

increase (i.e., step-up) in basis (see Chapter 7) is $35,000 (fair market value at date of death in excess of adjusted basis). None of the $10,000 suspended loss is deductible by either the decedent or the beneficiary. The suspended losses ($10,000) are lost because they do not exceed the step-up in basis ($35,000). ■

EXAMPLE 53

A taxpayer dies with passive activity property having an adjusted basis of $40,000, suspended losses of $10,000, and a fair market value at the date of the decedent's death of $47,000. Since the step-up in basis is only $7,000 ($47,000 − $40,000), the suspended losses allowed are limited to $3,000 ($10,000 suspended loss at time of death − $7,000 increase in basis). The $3,000 loss available to the decedent is reported on the decedent's final income tax return. ■

Disposition of a Passive Activity by Gift. In a disposition of a taxpayer's interest in a passive activity by gift, the suspended losses are added to the basis of the property.[51]

EXAMPLE 54

A taxpayer makes a gift of passive activity property having an adjusted basis of $40,000, suspended losses of $10,000, and a fair market value at the date of the gift of $100,000. The taxpayer cannot deduct the suspended losses in the year of the disposition. However, the suspended losses of $10,000 transfer with the property and are added to the adjusted basis of the property in the hands of the donee. ■

PLANNING *Strategies*

UTILIZING PASSIVE LOSSES

★ **Framework Focus: Tax Rate**

Strategy ★ Control the Character of Income and Deductions.

Perhaps the biggest challenge individuals face with the passive loss rules is to recognize the potential impact of the rules and then to structure their affairs to minimize this impact. Taxpayers who have passive activity losses (PALs) should adopt a strategy of generating passive activity income that can be sheltered by existing passive losses. One approach is to buy an interest in a passive activity that is generating income (referred to as a passive income generator, or PIG). Then the PAL can offset income from the PIG. From a tax perspective, it would be foolish to buy a loss-generating passive activity unless one has passive income to shelter or the activity is rental real estate that can qualify for the $25,000 exception or the exception available to real estate professionals.

If a taxpayer does invest in an activity that produces losses subject to the passive loss rules, the following strategies may help to minimize the loss of current deductions:

- If money is borrowed to finance the purchase of a passive activity, the associated interest expense is generally treated as part of any passive loss. Consequently, by increasing the amount of cash used to purchase the passive investment, the investor will need less debt and will incur less interest expense. By incurring less interest expense, a possible suspended passive loss deduction is reduced.
- If the investor does not have sufficient cash readily available for the larger down payment, it can be obtained by borrowing against the equity in his or her personal residence. The interest expense on such debt will be deductible under the qualified residence interest provisions (see Chapter 16) and will not be subject to the passive loss limitations. Thus, the taxpayer avoids the passive loss limitation and secures a currently deductible interest expense.

Often unusable passive losses accumulate and provide no current tax benefit because the taxpayer has no passive income. When the taxpayer disposes of the entire interest in a passive activity, however, any suspended losses from that activity are used to reduce the taxable gain. If any taxable gain still remains, it can be offset by losses from other passive activities. As a result, the taxpayer should carefully select the year in which a passive activity is disposed of. It is to the taxpayer's advantage to wait until sufficient passive losses have accumulated to offset any gain recognized on the asset's disposition.

[51] § 469(j)(6).

EXAMPLE 55

Bill, a calendar year taxpayer, owns interests in two passive activities: Activity A, which he plans to sell in December of this year at a gain of $100,000; and Activity B, which he plans to keep indefinitely. Current and suspended losses associated with Activity B total $60,000, and Bill expects losses from the activity to be $40,000 next year. If Bill sells Activity A this year, the $100,000 gain can be offset by the current and suspended losses of $60,000 from Activity B, producing a net taxable gain of $40,000. However, if Bill delays the sale of Activity A until January of next year, the $100,000 gain will be fully offset by the $100,000 of losses generated by Activity B ($60,000 current and prior losses + $40,000 next year's loss). Consequently, by postponing the sale by one month, he could avoid recognizing $40,000 of gain that would otherwise result. ■

Taxpayers with passive losses should consider the level of their involvement in all other trades or businesses in which they have an interest. If they show that they do not materially participate in a profitable activity, the activity becomes a passive activity. Current and suspended passive losses then could shelter any income generated by the profitable business. Family partnerships in which certain members do not materially participate would qualify. The silent partner in any general partnership engaged in a trade or business would also qualify.

EXAMPLE 56

Gail has an investment in a limited partnership that produces annual passive losses of approximately $25,000. She also owns a newly acquired interest in a convenience store where she works. Her share of the store's income is $35,000. If she works enough to be classified as a material participant, her $35,000 share of income is treated as active income. This results in $35,000 being subject to tax every year, while her $25,000 loss is suspended. However, if Gail reduces her involvement at the store so that she is not a material participant, the $35,000 of income receives passive treatment. Consequently, the $35,000 of income can be offset by the $25,000 passive loss, resulting in only $10,000 being subject to tax. Thus, by reducing her involvement, Gail ensures that the income from the profitable trade or business receives passive treatment and can then be used to absorb passive losses from other passive activities. ■

The passive loss rules can have a dramatic effect on a taxpayer's ability to claim passive losses currently. As a result, it is important to keep accurate records of all sources of income and losses, particularly any suspended passive losses and credits and the activities to which they relate, so that their potential tax benefit will not be lost.

Suggested Further Readings

"At-Risk Rules—Sec. 465 Prop. Regs., " *The Tax Adviser*, August 2005, pp. 466–468.

"Equipment Leasing Losses Were Not Passive, " *The Tax Adviser*, October 2005, p. 594.

Claudia L. Kelley and John M. Norman, "Repayments of Business Debt after Business Ceases," *The Tax Adviser*, September 2004, pp. 566–570.

Susan Megaard, "Recent Corporate Scandals Focus Attention on Tax Treatment of Stock Losses," *Journal of Taxation*, August 2004, pp. 101–109.

KEY TERMS

PROBLEM MATERIALS

PROBLEMS

Communications

1. Several years ago, Loon Finance Company, which is in the lending business, loaned Sara $30,000 to purchase an automobile to be used for personal purposes. In August of the current year, Sara filed for bankruptcy, and Loon was notified that it could not expect to receive more than $4,000. As of the end of the current year, Loon has received $1,000. Loon has contacted you about the possibility of taking a bad debt deduction for the current year.

   Write a letter to Loon Finance Company that contains your advice as to whether it can claim a bad debt deduction for the current year. Also, prepare a memo for the tax files. Loon's address is 100 Tyler Lane, Erie, PA 16563.

2. Sue loaned her sister Janice $10,000 three years ago. Janice has never made any payments to Sue, and Sue has never tried to collect from Janice. This year, Janice filed for bankruptcy and told Sue that she would not be able to repay any of the $10,000 loan. Determine Sue's tax treatment for the loan for the current year.

Issue ID

3. John was the sole shareholder of Blonde, Inc. The corporation had 26 salaried employees, which included John. Several years ago, Blonde began experiencing financial difficulties. As a result, John made several loans to the corporation in an attempt to continue business operations and pay employee salaries. The corporation eventually filed for bankruptcy under Chapter 7 of the bankruptcy code. Upon the final discharge of the corporation's debts, John's loans remained unpaid and were worthless. Identify the relevant tax issues for John with respect to his loans to Blonde, Inc.

4. Mable and Jack file a joint return. For the current year, they had the following items:

Salaries	$180,000
Loss on sale of § 1244 stock acquired two years ago	95,000
Gain on sale of § 1244 stock acquired six months ago	12,000
Nonbusiness bad debt	16,000

   Determine the impact of the above items on Mable and Jack's income for the current year.

Decision Making

5. Mary, a single taxpayer, purchased 10,000 shares of § 1244 stock several years ago at a cost of $20 per share. In November of the current year, Mary receives an offer to sell the stock for $12 per share. She has the option of either selling all of the stock now or selling half of the stock now and half of the stock in January of next year. Mary's salary is $80,000 for the current year, and it will be $90,000 next year. Mary has long-term capital gains of $8,000 for the current year and will have $10,000 next year. If Mary's goal is to minimize her AGI for the two years, determine whether she should sell all of her stock this year or half of her stock this year and half next year.

Extender

Communications

6. Paul Sanders, a married taxpayer who files a joint return with his wife, acquired stock in a corporation that qualified as a small business corporation under § 1244. The stock cost $30,000 and was acquired three years ago. A few months after he acquired the stock he gave it to his brother, Mike Sanders. The stock was worth $30,000 on the date of the gift. Mike, who is married and files a joint return with his wife, sells the stock for $10,000 in the current tax year. You represent Mike who asks you whether he can take a loss deduction on the sale of the stock. If so, how will the loss be treated for tax purposes? Prepare a letter to your client and a memo to the files. Mike's address is 2600 Riverview Drive, Plank, MO 63701.

Ethics

7. In the case of a casualty loss, if property used in a trade or business is damaged, the amount of the loss is the lesser of the decline in fair market value or the adjusted basis of the property.

Many years ago, Joe purchased a parcel of land for $300,000. The land was to be used in Joe's business. On the land was an existing road that was in poor condition. Joe made improvements to the road that cost $40,000. He computed his basis for the road to be $50,000—$40,000 from the improvements and $10,000 allocated from the original purchase price of the land. Joe has taken depreciation on the road, and consequently, at the beginning of the current year, the road has an adjusted basis of $20,000. During the current year, severe rainstorms washed out the road, and Joe paid $80,000 to have it repaired. Joe is considering claiming a loss deduction of $80,000 for the damage to the road. Evaluate Joe's plan.

8. Grackle Farming, Inc., owns a 500-acre farm in Minnesota. A tornado hit the area and destroyed a farm building and some farm equipment and damaged a barn. Fortunately for Grackle, the tornado occurred after the company had harvested its corn crop. Applicable information is as follows:

Decision Making

Asset	Basis	FMV Before	FMV After	Insurance Recovery
Building	$90,000	$ 70,000	$ –0–	$70,000
Equipment	40,000	50,000	–0–	25,000
Barn	90,000	120,000	70,000	25,000

Because of the extensive damage caused by the tornado, the President of the United States designated the area as a disaster area.

Grackle had $95,000 of taxable income last year. The company's taxable income for the current year, excluding the loss from the tornado, is $250,000. Determine the amount of the corporation's loss and the year in which it should take the loss.

9. Marydale Farms, Inc., owned 1,000 acres of unimproved farmland. During the spring of the current year, shortly after the company had tilled the ground, a storm blew away four inches of topsoil from 60% of the acreage. Identify the relevant tax issues for Marydale Farms.

Issue ID

10. On November 1 of the current year, Sam dropped off to sleep while driving home from a business trip. Luckily, he was only slightly injured in the resulting accident, but the company car that he was driving was completely destroyed.

Decision Making

Communications

Sam is an employee of Snipe Industries. The corporation purchased the car new two years ago for $40,000. The automobile had a fair market value of $30,000 before the accident and $12,000 after the accident. The car was covered by an insurance policy that had a $3,000 deductible clause. The corporation is afraid that the policy will be canceled if it makes a claim for the damages. Therefore, Snipe is considering not filing a claim. The company believes that the casualty loss deduction will help mitigate the loss of the insurance reimbursement. The corporation's taxable income for the current year is $25,000.

Write a letter to Snipe Industries that contains your advice regarding the filing of an insurance claim for reimbursement for the damages to the company's car. Snipe Industries' address is 450 Colonel's Way, Warrensburg, MO 64093.

11. Mary, a single taxpayer with two dependent children, has the following items of income and expense during 2006:

Extender

Gross receipts from business	$144,000
Business expenses	180,000
Alimony received	22,000
Interest income	40,000
Itemized deductions (no casualty or theft)	28,000

a. Determine Mary's taxable income for 2006.
b. Determine Mary's NOL for 2006.

12. In the current year, Lionel invests $20,000 for an interest in a partnership engaged in the wholesale distribution of plumbing supplies. Lionel is a material participant, and his

share of the partnership loss is $25,000. Discuss the tax treatment of Lionel's share of the loss, and compute his at-risk amount.

Communications

13. In the current year, Bill Parker (54 Oak Drive, St. Paul, MN 55162) is considering making an investment of $60,000 in Best Choice Partnership. The prospectus provided by Bill's broker indicates that the partnership investment is not a passive activity and that Bill's share of the entity's loss in the current year will likely be $40,000, while his share of the partnership loss next year will probably be $25,000. Write a letter to Bill in which you indicate how the losses would be treated for tax purposes in the current and next years.

Issue ID

14. Since his college days, Charles has developed an entrepreneurial streak. After working in his family's grocery business, he has decided to start several ventures on his own. Even though Charles is independently wealthy, he is looking forward to working in each of the ventures. He plans to "drop in" on the businesses from time to time between personal trips to Europe, the Caribbean, and the South Pacific. As of the end of the year, he has established computer software stores in Dayton, Austin, and Seattle; bagel bakeries in Albany, Athens (Georgia), and Tallahassee; and mountain bike and ski rental shops in small towns in Vermont, West Virginia, Colorado, and California. Identify the tax issues facing Charles.

15. Hazel has investments in two nonrental passive activities: Activity A, acquired seven years ago and profitable until the current year, and Activity B, acquired this year. Currently, Hazel's shares of the activities' losses are $10,000 from Activity A and $6,000 from Activity B. What is the total of Hazel's suspended losses from these activities?

16. Ray acquired an activity several years ago, and in the current year, it generated a loss of $50,000. Ray has AGI of $140,000 before considering the loss from the activity. If the activity is a bakery and Ray is not a material participant, what is his AGI?

17. Saundra has investments in four passive activity partnerships purchased several years ago. Last year, the income and losses were as follows:

Activity	Income (Loss)
A	$ 10,000
B	(5,000)
C	(25,000)
D	(20,000)

In the current year, she sold her interest in Activity D for a $19,000 gain. Activity D, which had been profitable until last year, had a current loss of $1,000. How will the sale of Activity D affect Saundra's taxable income in the current year?

18. Leon sells his interest in a passive activity for $100,000. Determine the tax effect of the sale based on each of the following independent facts:
    a. Adjusted basis in this investment is $35,000. Losses from prior years that were not deductible due to the passive loss restrictions total $40,000.
    b. Adjusted basis in this investment is $75,000. Losses from prior years that were not deductible due to the passive loss restrictions total $40,000.
    c. Adjusted basis in this investment is $75,000. Losses from prior years that were not deductible due to the passive loss restrictions total $40,000. In addition, suspended credits total $10,000.

19. Orange, Inc., a closely held personal service corporation, has $100,000 of passive losses. In addition, Orange has $80,000 of active business income and $20,000 of portfolio income. How much of the passive loss may Orange use to offset the other types of income?

20. White, Inc., earns $400,000 from operations in the current year. White also receives $36,000 in interest on various investments. During the year, White pays $150,000 to acquire a 20% interest in a passive activity that produces a $200,000 loss. How will these facts affect White's taxable income, assuming the corporation is:

a. A personal service corporation?
b. A closely held (non-personal service) C corporation?

21. Kristin Graf (123 Baskerville Mill Road, Jamison, PA 18929) is trying to decide how to invest a $10,000 inheritance. One option is to make an additional investment in Rocky Road Adventures in which she has an at-risk basis of $0, suspended losses under the at-risk rules of $7,000, and suspended passive losses of $1,000. If Kristin makes this investment, her share of the expected profits this year would be $8,000. If her investment stays the same, her share of profits from Rocky Road Adventures would be $1,000. Another option is to invest $10,000 as a limited partner in the Ragged Mountain Winery; this investment would produce passive income of $9,000. Write a letter to Kristin to review the tax consequences of each alternative. Kristin is in the 28% tax bracket.

Decision Making
Communications

22. Suzanne owns interests in a bagel shop, a lawn and garden store, and a convenience store. Several full-time employees work at each of the enterprises. As of the end of November of the current year, Suzanne has worked 150 hours in the bagel shop, 250 hours at the lawn and garden store, and 70 hours at the convenience store. In reviewing her financial records, you learn that she has no passive investments that are generating income and that she expects these three ventures collectively to produce a loss. What recommendation would you offer Suzanne as she plans her activities for the remainder of the year?

Decision Making

23. Rene retired from public accounting after a long and successful career of 45 years. As part of her retirement package, she continues to share in the profits and losses of the firm, albeit at a lower rate than when she was working full-time. Because Rene wants to stay busy during her retirement years, she has invested and works in a local hardware business, operated as a partnership. Unfortunately, the business has recently gone through a slump and has not been generating profits. Identify relevant tax issues for Rene.

Issue ID

24. Last year, Juan, a real estate developer, purchased 25 acres of farmland on the outskirts of town for $100,000. He expects that the land's value will appreciate rapidly as the town expands in that direction. Since the property was recently reappraised at $115,000, some of the appreciation has already taken place. To enhance his return from the investment, Juan decides he will begin renting the land to a local farmer. He has determined that a fair rent would be at least $1,500 but no more than $3,500 per year. Juan also has an interest in a passive activity that generates a $2,800 loss annually. How do the passive loss rules affect Juan's decision on how much rent to charge for the farmland?

Extender
Decision Making

25. The end of the year is approaching, and Maxine has begun to focus on ways of minimizing her income tax liability. Several years ago, she purchased an investment in Teal Limited Partnership, which is subject to both the at-risk and the passive activity loss rules. (Last year, Maxine sold a different investment that was subject to these rules but produced passive income.) She believes that her investment in Teal has good long-term economic prospects. However, it has been generating tax losses for several years in a row. In fact, when she was discussing last year's income tax return with her tax accountant, he said that unless "things change" with respect to her investments, she would not be able to deduct losses this year.
   a. What was the accountant referring to in his comment?
   b. You learn that Maxine's current at-risk basis in her investment is $1,000 and her share of the current loss is expected to be $13,000. Based on these facts, how will her loss be treated?
   c. After reviewing her situation, Maxine's financial adviser suggests that she invest at least an additional $12,000 in Teal in order to ensure a full loss deduction in the current year. How do you react to his suggestion?
   d. What would you suggest Maxine consider as she attempts to maximize her current-year deductible loss?

Decision Making

26. A number of years ago, Lee acquired a 20% interest in the BlueSky Partnership for $60,000. The partnership was profitable through 2005, and Lee's amount at risk in the partnership interest was $120,000 at the beginning of 2006. BlueSky incurred a loss of $400,000 in 2006 and reported income of $200,000 in 2007. Assuming Lee is not a

material participant, how much of his loss from BlueSky Partnership is deductible in 2006 and 2007?

27. Last year, Fran invested $40,000 for an interest in a partnership in which she is a material participant. Her share of the partnership's loss for the year was $50,000. In the current year, Fran's share of the partnership's income is $30,000. What is the effect on her taxable income for the current year?

28. Jonathan, a physician, earns $200,000 from his practice. He also receives $18,000 in dividends and interest on various portfolio investments. During the year, he pays $45,000 to acquire a 20% interest in a partnership that produces a $300,000 loss.
    a. Compute Jonathan's AGI, assuming he does not participate in the operations of the partnership.
    b. Compute Jonathan's AGI, assuming he is a material participant in the operations of the partnership.

29. Five years ago, Gerald invested $150,000 in a passive activity, his sole investment venture. On January 1, 2005, his amount at risk in the activity was $30,000. His shares of the income and losses were as follows:

Year	Income (Loss)
2005	($ 40,000)
2006	(30,000)
2007	50,000

How much can Gerald deduct in 2005 and 2006? What is his taxable income from the activity in 2007? Consider the at-risk rules as well as the passive loss rules.

30. During the current year, Maria Gonzales works 1,200 hours as a computer consultant, 320 hours in a real estate development business, and 400 hours in real estate rental activities. Jorge, her husband, works 250 hours in the real estate development business and 180 hours in the real estate rental business. Maria earns $60,000 as a computer consultant, while she and Jorge lost $18,000 in the real estate development business and $26,000 in the real estate rental business. How should they treat the losses?

Ethics

Communications

31. You have just met with Scott Myers (603 Pittsfield Dr., Champaign, IL 61821), a successful full-time real estate developer and investor. During your meeting you discussed his tax situation, because you are starting to prepare his 2005 Federal income tax return. During your meeting, Scott mentioned that he and his wife, Susan, went to great lengths to maximize their participation in an apartment complex that they own and manage. In particular, Scott included the following activities in the 540 hours of participation for the current year:

    - Time spent thinking about the rentals.
    - Time spent by Susan on weekdays visiting the apartment complex to oversee operations of the buildings (i.e., in a management role).
    - Time spent by both Scott and Susan on weekends visiting the apartment complex to assess operations. Scott and Susan always visited the complex together on weekends and both counted their hours (i.e., one hour at the complex was two hours of participation).
    - Time spent on weekends driving around the community looking for other potential rental properties to purchase. Again, both Scott's hours and Susan's hours were counted, even when they drove together.

    After reviewing Scott's records, you note that the apartment complex generated a significant loss this year. Prepare a letter to Scott describing your position on the deductibility of the loss.

Decision Making

32. Bonnie and Adam are married with no dependents and live in New Hampshire (not a community property state). Since Adam has large medical expenses, they seek your advice about filing separately to save taxes. Their income and expenses for 2006 are as follows:

Bonnie's salary	$ 40,000
Adam's salary	25,000
Interest income (joint)	1,800
Rental loss from actively managed rental property	22,000
Adam's unreimbursed medical expenses	8,000
All other itemized deductions:*	
Bonnie	9,000
Adam	3,000

*None subject to limitations.

Determine whether Bonnie and Adam should file jointly or separately for 2006.

33. During the current year, Gene performs services as follows: 1,800 hours as a CPA in his tax practice and 50 hours in an apartment leasing operation in which he has a 15% interest. Because of his oversight duties, Gene is considered to be an active participant in the leasing operation. He expects that his share of the loss realized from the apartment leasing operation will be $30,000 while his tax practice will show a profit of approximately $80,000. Gene is single and has no other income besides that stated above. Discuss the character of income and losses generated by these activities.

34. Ida, who has AGI of $80,000 before considering rental activities, is active in three separate real estate rental activities. Ida has a marginal tax rate of 28%. She has $12,000 of losses from Activity A, $18,000 of losses from Activity B, and income of $10,000 from Activity C. She also has $2,100 of tax credits from Activity A. Calculate her deductions and credits allowed and the suspended losses and credits.

35. Ella has $105,000 of losses from a real estate rental activity in which she actively participates. She has other rent income of $25,000 and other passive income of $32,000. How much rental loss can Ella deduct against active and portfolio income (ignoring the at-risk rules)? Does she have any suspended losses to carry over?

36. Lucien dies in the current year owning a limited partnership interest in a partnership that owns and operates an apartment complex. Associated with Lucien's interest is a $10,000 suspended passive activity loss that he had not been able to claim. Ron, the executor of Lucien's estate, learns from the partnership's general partner that she is not aware of any recent qualified appraisals or sales that would help determine the fair market value of the limited partnership interest. Ron feels that the cost of hiring a qualified appraiser to determine the value of the interest is not necessary because Lucien's estate is not large enough to be subject to the Federal estate tax. Lucien's records reflect a basis of $65,000 for the partnership interest immediately before his death. *Ethics*

The partnership's bookkeeper has a "gut feeling" that the partnership interest is worth anywhere between $65,000 and $80,000. This is good news to Ron. Based on her "guesstimate," Ron sets the value of the interest at $65,000.

What is Ron trying to accomplish in setting this valuation? What ethical issues arise?

37. In 2005, Nina gave her son a passive activity (adjusted basis of $100,000, fair market value of $180,000, and $25,000 of suspended losses). In 2006, the son realizes income of $12,000 from the passive activity. What are the tax effects to Nina and her son in 2005 and 2006?

BRIDGE *Discipline*

1. Marketplace, Inc., has recognized over time that a certain percentage of its customer accounts receivable will not be collected. To ensure the appropriate matching of revenues and expenditures in its financial reports, Marketplace uses the reserve method for bad debts. Records show the following pertaining to its treatment of bad debts.

Beginning allowance for bad debts	$120,000
Ending allowance for bad debts	123,000
Bad debts written off during the year	33,000

a. What was the bad debt expense for financial accounting purposes during the year?
b. What was the bad debt expense for income tax purposes during the year?
c. Assuming the before-tax net income for financial accounting purposes was $545,000, what is the taxable income for the year if the treatment of bad debts is the only book/tax difference?

2. Amanda wishes to invest $40,000 in a relatively safe venture and has discovered two alternatives that would produce the following ordinary income and loss over the next three years:

Year	Alternative 1 Income (Loss)	Alternative 2 Income (Loss)
1	($ 24,000)	($48,000)
2	(24,000)	32,000
3	72,000	40,000

She is interested in the after-tax effects of these alternatives over a three-year horizon. Assume that:

- Amanda's investment portfolio produces sufficient passive income to offset any potential passive loss that may arise from these alternatives.
- Amanda's marginal tax rate is 25%, and her cost of capital is 8% (the present value factors are 0.92593, 0.85734, and 0.79383).
- Each investment alternative possesses equal growth potential and comparable financial risk.
- In the loss years for each alternative, there is no cash flow from or to the investment (i.e., the loss is due to depreciation), while in those years when the income is positive, cash flows to Amanda equal the amount of the income.

Based on these facts, compute the present value of these two investment alternatives and determine which option Amanda should choose.

Decision Making

3. Emily has $100,000 that she wishes to invest and is considering the following two options:

- Option A: Investment in Redbird Mutual Fund, which is expected to produce interest income of $8,000 per year.
- Option B: Investment in Cardinal Limited Partnership (buys, sells, and operates wine vineyards). Emily's share of the partnership's ordinary income and loss over the next three years would be:

Year	Income (Loss)
1	($ 8,000)
2	(2,000)
3	34,000

Emily is interested in the after-tax effects of these alternatives over a three-year horizon. Assume that Emily's investment portfolio produces ample passive income to offset any passive losses that may be generated. Her cost of capital is 8% (the present value factors are 0.92593, 0.85734, and 0.79383), and she is in the 28% tax bracket. The two investment alternatives possess equal growth potential and comparable financial risk. Based on these facts, compute the present value of these two investment alternatives and determine which option Emily should choose.

RESEARCH PROBLEMS

THOMSON RIA™

Note: Solutions to Research Problems can be prepared by using the **RIA Checkpoint®** **Student Edition** online research product, which is available to accompany this text. It is also possible to prepare solutions to the Research Problems by using tax research materials found in a standard tax library.

Research Problem 1. Jeb Simmons operated an illegal gambling business out of his home. While executing a search warrant, the local sheriff seized gambling paraphernalia and $200,000 in cash. Subsequently, Jeb voluntarily consented to forfeit to the state the cash that had been seized in connection with the execution of the search warrant. Write a letter to Jeb advising him as to whether he can claim a loss under § 165 for the seized cash. Also, prepare a memo for the tax files. Jeb's address is 100 Honey Lane, Macon, GA 62108.

Communications

Research Problem 2. George and Judy Cash own a 30-foot yacht that is moored at Oregon Inlet on the Outer Banks of North Carolina. The yacht is offered for rent to tourists during March through November every year. George and Judy live too far away to be involved in the yacht's routine operation and maintenance. They are, however, able to perform certain periodic tasks, such as cleaning and winterizing it. Routine daily management, operating, and chartering responsibilities have been contracted to "Captain Mac." George and Judy are able to document spending 120 hours on the yacht chartering activities during the year. Determine how any losses resulting from the activity are treated under the passive activity loss rules.

Research Problem 3. David Drayer (2632 Holkham Drive, Lewisburg, PA 17837) is the lead partner in a local accounting firm whose practice consists of tax consulting and compliance. The firm also serves clients by providing write-up and payroll processing services. As his firm has grown, David has developed various ways to build its business prospects.

Communications

David and his wife, Judy, created DJ Partnership to purchase an office building where David moved his practice. Because the building is larger than the practice currently needs, space is rented to other tax practitioners. In addition to providing office space, the partnership offers professional and administrative services on an exclusive basis to the tenants. These services include secretarial support, telephone answering service, tax professionals available for special projects, access to a tax research library, computer hardware technology, and miscellaneous administrative support. DJ Partnership considers its primary activity to be providing professional and administrative services to its tenants rather than being a lessor.

Because of the attractiveness of the services offered to its tenants, the building is fully leased. In the first year, Judy works full-time at the partnership, and David commits about 550 hours to its affairs. For the first year, the partnership incurs a tax loss of $60,000. Without considering the impact of the loss, David and Judy's AGI is $175,000. Write a letter to David in which you provide advice on the deductibility of the $60,000 loss for Federal income tax purposes. Because David is a professional, feel free to make use of technical language in your letter.

Partial list of research aids:
Reg. § 1.469–1T(e)(3)(ii).

Use the tax resources of the Internet to address the following questions. Do not restrict your search to the World Wide Web, but include a review of newsgroups and general reference materials, practitioner sites and resources, primary sources of the tax law, chat rooms and discussion groups, and other opportunities.

Internet *Activity*

Research Problem 4. Scan several publications that are read by owners of small businesses. Some of the articles in these publications address tax-related issues such as how to structure a new business. Do these articles do an adequate job of conveying the benefits of issuing § 1244 small business stock? Prepare a short memo explaining the use of § 1244 stock and post it to a newsgroup that is frequented by inventors, engineers, and others involved in start-up corporations.

Communications

Research Problem 5. Scan the materials offered in several newsgroups frequented by tax advisers and consultants. Summarize the government's current strategies for identifying and sanctioning taxpayers and entities benefiting from and promoting abusive tax shelters.

http://wft.swlearning.com

PART 3

Property Transactions

Part III presents the tax treatment of sales, exchanges, and other dispositions of property. Included are the determination of the realized gain or loss, recognized gain or loss, and the classification of the recognized gain or loss as capital or ordinary. The topic of basis is evaluated both in terms of its effect on the calculation of the gain or loss and in terms of the determination of the basis of any contemporaneous or related subsequent acquisitions of property.

http://wft.swlearning.com

CHAPTER 7

Property Transactions: Basis, Gain and Loss, and Nontaxable Exchanges

LEARNING OBJECTIVES

After completing Chapter 7, you should be able to:

LO.1
Understand the computation of realized gain or loss on property dispositions.

LO.2
Distinguish between realized and recognized gain or loss.

LO.3
Explain how basis is determined for various methods of asset acquisition.

LO.4
Describe various loss disallowance provisions.

LO.5
Apply the nonrecognition provisions and basis determination rules for like-kind exchanges.

LO.6
Explain the nonrecognition provisions available on the involuntary conversion of property.

LO.7
Identify other nonrecognition provisions contained in the Code.

OUTLINE

TAX *Talk*

To base all of your decisions on tax consequences is not necessarily to maintain the proper balance and perspective on what you are doing.

—Barber Conable

This chapter and the following chapter are concerned with the income tax consequences of property transactions, including the sale or other disposition of property. The following questions are considered with respect to the sale or other disposition of property:

- Is there a realized gain or loss?
- If so, is that gain or loss recognized for tax purposes?
- If that gain or loss is recognized, is it ordinary or capital?
- What is the basis of any replacement property that is acquired?

This chapter discusses the determination of realized and recognized gain or loss and the basis of property. The following chapter covers the classification of recognized gain or loss as ordinary or capital.

For the most part, the rules discussed in Chapters 7 and 8 apply to all types of taxpayers. Individuals, partnerships, closely held corporations, limited liability companies, and publicly held corporations all own assets for use in business activities or as investments in entities that themselves conduct business activities. Individuals, however, are unique among taxpayers because they also own assets that are used in daily life and have no significant business or investment component. Because of that possibility, some property transaction concepts apply somewhat differently to individual taxpayers depending upon how a person uses the specific asset in question. Nevertheless, the material that follows pertains to taxpayers generally except where otherwise noted.

Determination of Gain or Loss

LO.1

Understand the computation of realized gain or loss on property dispositions.

Realized Gain or Loss

For tax purposes, gain or loss is the difference between the *amount realized* from the sale or other disposition of property and the property's *adjusted basis* on the date of disposition. If the amount realized exceeds the property's adjusted basis, the result is a **realized gain**. Conversely, if the property's adjusted basis exceeds the amount realized, the result is a **realized loss**.[1]

EXAMPLE 1

Lavender, Inc., sells Swan Corporation stock with an adjusted basis of $3,000 for $5,000. Lavender's realized gain is $2,000. If Lavender had sold the stock for $2,000, it would have had a realized loss of $1,000. ■

Sale or Other Disposition. The term *sale or other disposition* is defined broadly to include virtually any disposition of property. Thus, trade-ins, casualties, condemnations, thefts, and bond retirements are all treated as dispositions of property. The most common disposition of property is a sale or exchange. Usually, the key factor in determining whether a disposition has taken place is whether an identifiable event has occurred[2] as opposed to a mere fluctuation in the value of the property.[3]

EXAMPLE 2

Heron & Associates owns Tan Corporation stock that cost $3,000. The stock has appreciated in value by $2,000 since Heron purchased it. Heron has no realized gain since mere fluctuation in value is not a disposition or identifiable event for tax purposes. Nor would Heron have a realized loss had the stock declined in value. ■

Amount Realized. The **amount realized** from a sale or other disposition of property is the sum of any money received plus the fair market value of other property received. The amount realized also includes any real property taxes treated as imposed on the seller that are actually paid by the buyer.[4] The reason for including these taxes in the amount realized is that by paying the taxes, the purchaser is, in effect, paying an additional amount to the seller of the property.

The amount realized also includes any liability on the property disposed of, such as a mortgage debt, if the buyer assumes the mortgage or the property is sold subject to the mortgage.[5] The amount of the liability is included in the amount realized, even if the debt is nonrecourse and even if the amount of the debt is greater than the fair market value of the mortgaged property.[6]

EXAMPLE 3

Bunting & Co. sells property to Orange, Inc., for $50,000 cash. There is a $20,000 mortgage on the property. Bunting's amount realized from the sale is $70,000 if Orange assumes the mortgage or takes the property subject to the mortgage. ■

The **fair market value** of property received in a sale or other disposition has been defined by the courts as the price at which the property will change hands between a willing seller and a willing buyer when neither is compelled to sell or buy.[7] Fair market value is determined by considering the relevant factors in each case.[8] An expert appraiser is often required to evaluate these factors in arriving at

[1] § 1001(a) and Reg. § 1.1001–1(a).

[2] Reg. § 1.1001–1(c)(1).

[3] *Lynch v. Turrish*, 1 USTC ¶18, 3 AFTR 2986, 38 S.Ct. 537 (USSC, 1918).

[4] § 1001(b) and Reg. § 1.1001–1(b).

[5] *Crane v. Comm.*, 47–1 USTC ¶9217, 35 AFTR 776, 67 S.Ct. 1047 (USSC, 1947). Although a legal distinction exists between the direct assumption of a mortgage and taking property subject to a mortgage, the tax consequences in calculating the amount realized are the same.

[6] *Comm. v. Tufts*, 83–1 USTC ¶9328, 51 AFTR2d 83–1132, 103 S.Ct. 1826 (USSC, 1983).

[7] *Comm. v. Marshman*, 60–2 USTC ¶9484, 5 AFTR2d 1528, 279 F.2d 27 (CA–6, 1960).

[8] *O'Malley v. Ames*, 52–1 USTC ¶9361, 42 AFTR 19, 197 F.2d 256 (CA–8, 1952).

TAX *in the News* **PUTTING THE HOUSE AT RISK**

Investing for the future, and especially for retirement, is a good thing. An indirect investment that can produce a sizable return is the equity buildup in the taxpayer's principal residence. An additional benefit is that much (if not all) of the gain from the sale of a principal residence can be excluded from the taxpayer's gross income (see the discussion at the end of this chapter).

A technique for increasing the value of an investment is to leverage the investment (i.e., use borrowed funds to produce a greater rate of return). A potential source for leveraging is to borrow against the equity in a home in order to invest in stock.

The National Association of Securities Dealers, the main self-regulatory arm of the securities industry, is investigating whether certain brokers are pushing homeowners to use the equity in their homes to invest in the stock market. One concern is that brokers are not adequately disclosing the related risks and the potential conflicts of interest. Among the potential negative consequences of using home equity loans to buy stock is that investors could lose their homes if they default on the loans. Furthermore, such investments may cause the investor's asset-diversification mix to become unbalanced (i.e., too much stock and too little home equity).

Unfortunately, an increasing number of homeowners view their personal residence as not merely a place to live, but as a cash machine they can use to rapidly build wealth.

Source: *Adapted from Ann Davis, "Betting the House on the Stock Market,"* Wall Street Journal, *December 9, 2004, p. D1.*

fair market value. When the fair market value of the property received cannot be determined, the value of the property given up by the taxpayer may be used.[9]

In calculating the amount realized, selling expenses such as advertising, commissions, and legal fees relating to the disposition are deducted. The amount realized is the net amount that the taxpayer received directly or indirectly, in the form of cash or anything else of value, from the disposition of the property.

Adjusted Basis. The **adjusted basis** of property disposed of is the property's original basis adjusted to the date of disposition.[10] Original basis is the cost or other basis of the property on the date the property is acquired by the taxpayer. Considerations involving original basis are discussed later in this chapter. *Capital additions* increase and *recoveries of capital* decrease the original basis so that on the date of disposition the adjusted basis reflects the unrecovered cost or other basis of the property.[11] Adjusted basis is determined as follows:

Cost (or other adjusted basis) on date of acquisition
\+ Capital additions
− Capital recoveries
= Adjusted basis on date of disposition

Capital Additions. Capital additions include the cost of capital improvements and betterments made to the property by the taxpayer. These expenditures are distinguishable from expenditures for the ordinary repair and maintenance of the property, which are neither capitalized nor added to the original basis (refer to Chapter 5). The latter expenditures are deductible in the current taxable year if they are related to business or income-producing property. Amounts representing real property taxes treated as imposed on the seller but paid or assumed by the buyer are part of the cost of the property.[12] Any liability on property that is assumed by the buyer is also included in the buyer's original basis of the property. The same

[9] *U.S. v. Davis*, 62–2 USTC ¶9509, 9 AFTR2d 1625, 82 S.Ct. 1190 (USSC, 1962).

[10] § 1011(a) and Reg. § 1.1011–1.

[11] § 1016(a) and Reg. § 1.1016–1.

[12] Reg. §§ 1.1001–1(b)(2) and 1.1012–1(b). Refer to Chapter 5 for a discussion of this subject.

rule applies if property is acquired subject to a liability. In a similar fashion, amortization of the discount on bonds increases the adjusted basis of the bonds.[13]

EXAMPLE 4

Bluebird Corporation purchased some manufacturing equipment for $25,000. Whether Bluebird uses $25,000 from the business's cash account to pay for this equipment or uses $5,000 from that account and borrows the remaining $20,000, the basis of this equipment will be the same—namely, $25,000. Moreover, it does not matter whether Bluebird borrowed the $20,000 from the equipment's manufacturer, from a local bank, or from any other lender. ■

Capital Recoveries. Capital recoveries decrease the adjusted basis of property. The following are examples of capital recoveries:

1. *Depreciation and cost recovery allowances.* The original basis of depreciable property is reduced by the annual depreciation charges (or cost recovery allowances) while the property is held by the taxpayer. The amount of depreciation that is subtracted from the original basis is the greater of the *allowed* or *allowable* depreciation calculated on an annual basis.[14] In most circumstances, the allowed and allowable depreciation amounts are the same (refer to Chapter 5).
2. *Casualties and thefts.* A casualty or theft may result in the reduction of the adjusted basis of property.[15] The adjusted basis is reduced by the amount of the deductible loss. In addition, the adjusted basis is reduced by the amount of insurance proceeds received. However, the receipt of insurance proceeds may result in a recognized gain rather than a deductible loss. The gain increases the adjusted basis of the property.[16]

EXAMPLE 5

An insured truck owned by the Falcon Corporation is destroyed in an accident. The adjusted basis is $8,000, and the fair market value is $6,500. Falcon received insurance proceeds of $6,500. The amount of the casualty loss is $1,500 ($6,500 insurance proceeds – $8,000 adjusted basis). The adjusted basis becomes $0 ($8,000 pre-accident adjusted basis, reduced by the $1,500 casualty loss and the $6,500 of insurance proceeds received). ■

EXAMPLE 6

Osprey, Inc., owned an insured truck that was destroyed in an accident. The adjusted basis and fair market value of the truck were $6,500 and $8,000, respectively. Osprey received insurance proceeds of $8,000. The amount of the casualty *gain* is $1,500 ($8,000 insurance proceeds – $6,500 adjusted basis). The adjusted basis is increased by the $1,500 casualty gain and is reduced by the $8,000 of insurance proceeds received ($6,500 basis before casualty + $1,500 casualty gain – $8,000 insurance proceeds = $0 basis). ■

3. *Certain corporate distributions.* A corporate distribution to a shareholder that is not taxable is treated as a return of capital, and it reduces the basis of the shareholder's stock in the corporation.[17] Once the basis of the stock is reduced to zero, the amount of any subsequent distributions is a capital gain if the stock is a capital asset. See Chapter 10.
4. *Amortizable bond premium.* The basis in a bond purchased at a premium is reduced by the amortizable portion of the bond premium.[18] Investors in taxable bonds may *elect* to amortize the bond premium.[19] The amount of the amortized premium on taxable bonds is permitted as an interest deduction. Therefore, the election enables the taxpayer to take an annual interest deduction to offset

[13]See Chapter 4 for a discussion of bond discount and the related amortization.

[14]§ 1016(a)(2) and Reg. § 1.1016–3(a)(1)(i).

[15]Refer to Chapter 6 for the discussion of casualties and thefts.

[16]Reg. § 1.1016–6(a).

[17]§ 1016(a)(4) and Reg. § 1.1016–5(a).

[18]§ 1016(a)(5) and Reg. § 1.1016–5(b). The accounting treatment of bond premium amortization is the same as for tax purposes. The amortization results in a decrease in the bond investment account.

[19]§ 171(c).

BRIDGE *Discipline*

Bridge to Financial Accounting

Certain property transactions discussed later in this chapter are treated differently for tax purposes than for financial accounting purposes. For example, the category of transactions generally referred to as "nontaxable exchanges," such as like-kind exchanges and involuntary conversions, gives taxpayers the opportunity to defer the recognition of income on the disposition of property in qualifying transactions. The gains or losses deferred under tax law, however, are not deferred for financial reporting purposes. Instead, the actual gain or loss realized is reflected in the entity's financial reports.

Identifying and calculating the book-tax differences that arise from *taxable* dispositions of certain other property may not be so easy. For example, as discussed in Chapter 5, cost recovery (i.e., depreciation) rules provided by the tax law specify various ways in which an asset's cost may be recovered over time. These methods often differ from the methods used to depreciate an asset for book purposes. Consequently, the annual book-tax differences in these depreciation expense calculations are noted in the financial reports. But, in addition, these cumulative differences, as reflected in the accumulated depreciation account, will also produce a book-tax difference on the asset's disposition. That is, because an asset's accumulated depreciation may differ for book and tax purposes, its adjusted basis will also differ. Consequently, when the asset is sold, the amount of gain or loss for book purposes will differ from that recognized for tax purposes.

ordinary income in exchange for a larger capital gain or smaller capital loss on the disposition of the bond (due to the basis reduction).

DIGGING DEEPER 1

Find more information on this topic at our Web site: ***http://wft-entities.swlearning.com.***

In contrast to the treatment of taxable bonds, the premium on tax-exempt bonds *must* be amortized, and no interest deduction is permitted. Furthermore, the basis of tax-exempt bonds is reduced even though the amortization is not allowed as a deduction. No amortization deduction is permitted on tax-exempt bonds because the interest income is exempt from tax, and the amortization of the bond premium merely represents an adjustment of the effective amount of such income.

EXAMPLE 7

Navy, Inc., purchases Eagle Corporation taxable bonds with a face value of $100,000 for $110,000, thus paying a premium of $10,000. The annual interest rate is 7%, and the bonds mature 10 years from the date of purchase. The annual interest income is $7,000 (7% × $100,000). If Navy elects to amortize the bond premium, the $10,000 premium is deducted over the 10-year period. Navy's basis for the bonds is reduced each year by the amount of the amortization deduction. If the bonds were tax-exempt, amortization of the bond premium and the basis adjustment would be mandatory, and no deduction would be allowed for the amortization. ■

5. *Easements.* An easement is the legal right to use another's land for a special purpose. Historically, easements were commonly used to obtain rights-of-way for utility lines and roads. In recent years, grants of conservation easements have become a popular means of obtaining charitable contribution deductions and reducing the value of real estate for transfer tax (i.e., estate and gift) purposes. Likewise, scenic easements are used to reduce the value of land as assessed for ad valorem property tax purposes.

   If the taxpayer does not retain any right to the use of the land, all of the basis is assigned to the easement. However, if the use of the land is only partially restricted, an allocation of some of the basis to the easement is appropriate.

CONCEPT SUMMARY 7–1

Recognized Gain or Loss

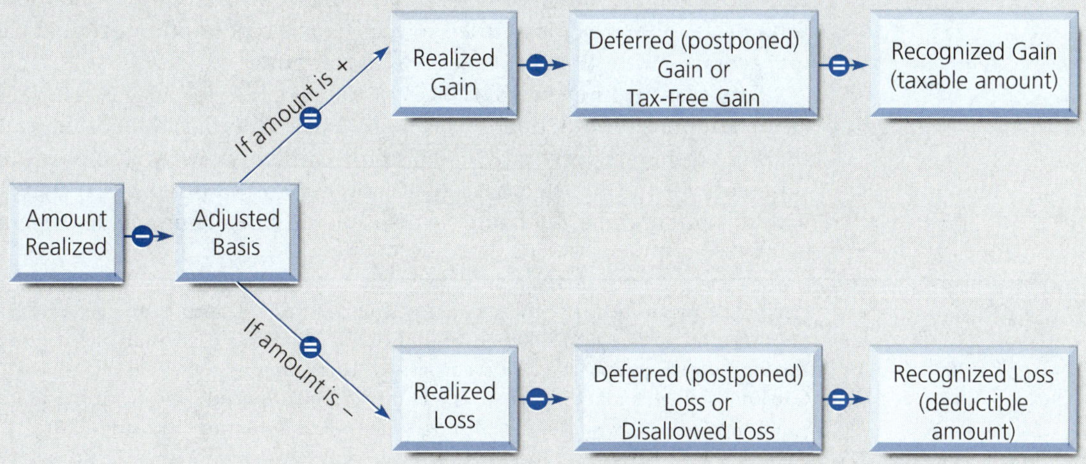

Recognized Gain or Loss

LO.2

Distinguish between realized and recognized gain or loss.

Recognized gain is the amount of the realized gain that is included in the taxpayer's gross income.[20] A **recognized loss**, on the other hand, is the amount of a realized loss that is deductible for tax purposes.[21] As a general rule, the entire amount of a realized gain or loss is recognized when it is realized.[22]

Concept Summary 7–1 summarizes the realized gain or loss and recognized gain or loss concepts.

Nonrecognition of Gain or Loss

In certain cases, a realized gain or loss is not recognized upon the sale or other disposition of property. One such case involves nontaxable exchanges, which are covered later in this chapter. In addition, realized losses from the sale or exchange of property between certain related parties are not recognized.[23]

Dispositions of Personal-Use Assets. For individual taxpayers, special rules apply to *personal-use* assets, that is, assets such as a residence or automobile that are not used in any business or investment activity. A loss from the sale, exchange, or condemnation of such assets is not recognized for tax purposes. An exception exists for casualty or theft losses from personal-use assets (refer to Chapter 6). In contrast, any gain realized from the disposition of personal-use assets is generally taxable.

EXAMPLE 8

Freda sells an automobile, which she has held exclusively for personal use, for $6,000. The adjusted basis of the automobile is $5,000. Freda has a realized and recognized gain of $1,000. If she sold this automobile for $4,500, she would have a realized loss of $500, but the loss would not be recognized for tax purposes. ■

[20] § 61(a)(3) and Reg. § 1.61–6(a).
[21] § 165(a) and Reg. § 1.165–1(a).
[22] § 1001(c) and Reg. § 1.1002–1(a).
[23] § 267(a)(1).

Recovery of Capital Doctrine

Doctrine Defined. The **recovery of capital doctrine** pervades all the tax rules relating to property transactions. The doctrine derives its roots from the very essence of the income tax—a tax on income or profit. Because the focus of the tax is on profit, a taxpayer is entitled to recover the cost or other original basis of property acquired without being taxed on that amount.

The cost or other original basis of depreciable property is recovered through annual depreciation deductions. The basis is reduced as the cost is recovered over the period the property is held. Therefore, when property is sold or otherwise disposed of, it is the adjusted basis (unrecovered cost or other basis) that is compared with the amount realized from the disposition to determine realized gain or loss.

EXAMPLE 9

Cardinal Corporation purchased a machine for $20,000 four years ago and has deducted depreciation totaling $13,000 during those years. Since Cardinal has recovered $13,000 through depreciation, the adjusted basis of this machine is $7,000 ($20,000 – $13,000). If Cardinal sells this machine, it subtracts the $7,000 adjusted basis from the amount realized when determining whether it realized a gain or loss upon the disposition. ■

DIGGING DEEPER 2

Find more information on this topic at our Web site: ***http://wft-entities.swlearning.com.***

LO.3

Explain how basis is determined for various methods of asset acquisition.

Basis Considerations

Determination of Cost Basis

As noted earlier, the basis of property is generally the property's cost. Cost is the amount paid for the property in cash or other property.[24] This general rule follows logically from the recovery of capital doctrine; that is, the cost or other basis of property is to be recovered tax-free by the taxpayer.

A *bargain purchase* of property is an exception to the general rule for determining basis. A bargain purchase may result when an employer transfers property to an employee at less than the property's fair market value (as compensation for services) or when a corporation transfers property to a shareholder at less than the property's fair market value (a dividend). These transfers create taxable income for the purchaser equal to the difference between fair market value and purchase price. The basis of property acquired in a bargain purchase is the property's fair market value.[25] If the basis of the property were not increased by the bargain amount, the taxpayer would be taxed on this amount again at disposition.

EXAMPLE 10

Wade buys land from his employer for $10,000. The fair market value of the land is $15,000. Wade must include the $5,000 difference between the cost and the fair market value of the land in his gross income. The bargain element represents additional compensation to Wade. His basis for the land is $15,000, the land's fair market value. ■

Identification Problems. Sometimes, it can be difficult to determine the cost of an asset being sold. This problem is frequently encountered in sales of corporate stock, because a taxpayer may purchase separate lots of a company's stock on different dates and at different prices. When the stock is sold, if the taxpayer cannot

[24] § 1012 and Reg. § 1.1012–1(a).

[25] Reg. §§ 1.61–2(d)(2)(i) and 1.301–1(j). See the discussion in Chapter 17 of the circumstances under which what appears to be a taxable bargain purchase is an excludible qualified employee discount.

TAX *in the News* **WHAT'S YOUR STOCK BASIS?**

AT&T has 2.7 million shareholders. Some of these are other corporations and wealthy investors, but many are widows and orphans. Each of these shareholders may encounter the same problem: What is the basis of their AT&T stock?

Under SBC Communications' proposal to buy AT&T (approved by the shareholders to be completed in 2006), the shareholders will need to know their stock basis in order to calculate their realized gain or loss. This is likely to be a complicated process. A shareholder who bought AT&T stock before the government broke up the Ma Bell monopoly in 1984 could face substantial difficulties in making this calculation. Such a shareholder who held onto those shares could have owned, at one time or another, shares of 20 different companies. Even with subsequent mergers and acquisitions, that same shareholder today would own stock in nearly a dozen corporations. The key issue then will be to allocate the shareholder's original basis for the AT&T stock among the shares of the various corporations. This assumes, however, that the shareholder knows the amount of the original stock basis.

Chuck Carlson, who runs a Web site that sells software to aid in such basis allocations, refers to the AT&T shareholder basis situation as a "train wreck." There is some good news, though: the train wreck can be postponed to the future. Since SBC's acquisition of AT&T will be a tax-free reorganization, the shareholder will not need to make the basis determinations until the SBC stock is sold later.

Source: *Adapted from Jane J. Kim, "AT&T Investors Face Tax Headache,"* Wall Street Journal, *February 3, 2005, p. D1.*

identify the specific shares being sold, the stock sold is determined on a first-in, first-out (FIFO) basis. Thus, the holding period and cost of the stock sold are determined by referring to the purchase date and cost of the first lot of stock acquired.[26] But if the stock being sold can be adequately identified, then the basis and holding period of the specific stock sold are used in determining the nature and amount of gain or loss.[27] Thus, to avoid FIFO treatment when the sold securities are held by a broker, it is often necessary to provide specific instructions and receive written confirmation of the securities being sold.

EXAMPLE 11

Pelican, Inc., purchases 100 shares of Olive Corporation stock on July 1, 2004, for $5,000 ($50 a share) and another 100 shares of Olive stock on July 1, 2005, for $6,000 ($60 a share). Pelican sells 50 shares of the stock on January 2, 2006. The cost of the stock sold, assuming Pelican cannot adequately identify the shares, is $50 a share (from shares purchased on July 1, 2004), or $2,500. This is the cost Pelican will compare with the amount realized in determining the gain or loss from the sale. ■

Allocation Problems. When a taxpayer acquires *several assets in a lump-sum purchase,* the total cost must be allocated among the individual assets.[28] Allocation is necessary for several reasons:

- Some of the assets acquired may be depreciable (e.g., buildings), while others may not be (e.g., land).
- Only a portion of the assets acquired may be sold.
- Some of the assets may be capital or depreciable assets that receive special tax treatment upon subsequent sale or other disposition.

The lump-sum cost is allocated on the basis of the fair market values of the individual assets acquired.

EXAMPLE 12

Magenta Corporation purchases a building and land for $800,000. Because of the depressed nature of the industry in which the seller was operating, Magenta was able to negotiate a very

[26] *Kluger Associates, Inc.,* 69 T.C. 925 (1978).

[27] Reg. § 1.1012–1(c)(1).

[28] Reg. § 1.61–6(a).

favorable purchase price. Appraisals of the individual assets indicate that the fair market value of the building is $600,000 and that of the land is $400,000. Magenta's basis for the building is $480,000 [($600,000/$1,000,000) × $800,000], and its basis for the land is $320,000 [($400,000/$1,000,000) × $800,000]. ■

If a business is purchased and **goodwill** (or any other § 197 intangible asset) is involved, a special *residual allocation* rule applies. Initially, the purchase price of the business is allocated to four classes of assets in the following order:

- Class 1—cash, demand deposits, etc.
- Class 2—marketable securities, certificates of deposit, and foreign currency.
- Class 3—all other assets, except for § 197 intangible assets.
- Class 4—goodwill and other § 197 intangible assets.

Within each class of assets, the purchase price is allocated among the assets on the basis of their respective fair market values, and the amount allocated to any specific asset cannot exceed its fair market value. Therefore, any amount paid in excess of fair market value for tangible assets (classes 1 through 3) is allocated to goodwill and other intangible assets of the acquired business (class 4). This allocation of purchase price is applicable to both the buyer and the seller.[29]

EXAMPLE 13

Roadrunner, Inc., sells its business to Coyote Corporation. The two companies agree that the values of the specific assets are as follows:

Cash	$ 10,000
Marketable securities	5,000
Inventory	35,000
Building	500,000
Land	200,000

After negotiations, Roadrunner and Coyote agree on a sales price of $1 million. Applying the residual method, the purchase price is allocated first to cash, then to marketable securities up to their fair market value. Next, the purchase price is allocated to inventory, building, and land, all on the basis of their fair market values. The residual purchase price is allocated to goodwill, resulting in the following basis of assets to Coyote Corporation:

Cash	$ 10,000
Marketable securities	5,000
Inventory	35,000
Building	500,000
Land	200,000
Goodwill	250,000

■

In the case of *nontaxable stock dividends*, the allocation depends on whether the dividend is a common stock dividend on common stock or a preferred stock dividend on common stock. If the dividend is common on common, the cost of the original common shares is allocated to the total shares owned after the dividend.[30]

EXAMPLE 14

Yellow, Inc., owns 100 shares of Sparrow Corporation common stock for which it paid $1,100. Yellow receives a 10% common stock dividend, giving it a new total of 110 shares. Before the stock dividend, Yellow's basis was $11 per share ($1,100 ÷ 100 shares). The basis of each share after the stock dividend is $10 ($1,100 ÷ 110 shares). ■

[29] § 1060 and Temp.Reg. § 1.338(b)–1T.

[30] §§ 305(a) and 307(a). The holding period of the new shares includes the holding period of the old shares. § 1223(5) and Reg. § 1.1223–1(e). See Chapter 8 for a discussion of the importance of the holding period.

If the nontaxable stock dividend is preferred stock on common, the cost of the original common shares is allocated between the common and preferred shares on the basis of their relative fair market values on the date of distribution.[31]

EXAMPLE 15

Brown Company owns 100 shares of Cardinal Corporation common stock for which it paid $1,000. Brown receives a nontaxable stock dividend of 50 shares of preferred stock on the Cardinal common stock. The fair market values on the date of distribution of the preferred stock dividend are $30 a share for common stock and $40 a share for preferred stock.

Fair market value of common ($30 × 100 shares)	$3,000
Fair market value of preferred ($40 × 50 shares)	2,000
	$5,000
Basis of common: 3/5 × $1,000	$ 600
Basis of preferred: 2/5 × $1,000	$ 400

The basis per share for the common stock is $6 ($600/100 shares). The basis per share for the preferred stock is $8 ($400/50 shares). ■

Gift Basis

Although business entities can neither make nor receive gratuitous transfers, ownership interests in such entities are frequently the subject of lifetime and testamentary gifts. Partnership interests, stock in closely or publicly held corporations, and other assets are regularly passed from one generation of owners to another for a variety of family and business reasons. Special basis rules apply to such transfers.

When a taxpayer receives property as a gift, there is no cost to the donee (recipient). Thus, under the cost basis provision, the donee's basis would be zero. With a zero basis, if the donee sold the property, the entire amount realized would be treated as taxable gain. Instead, the Code[32] assigns a basis to the property received that depends upon the following:

- The date of the gift.
- The basis of the property to the donor.
- The fair market value of the property.
- The amount of the gift tax paid, if any.

Gift Basis Rules if No Gift Tax Is Paid. If a property's fair market value on the date of gift exceeds the donor's basis in the property, the donor's basis carries over to the new owner.[33] This basis is called a *carryover basis* and is used in determining the donee's gain or loss.

EXAMPLE 16

Melissa purchased stock two years ago for $10,000. She gave the stock to her son, Joe, this year, when the fair market value was $15,000. No gift tax was paid on the transfer. Joe subsequently sells the property for $15,000. Joe's basis is $10,000, and he has a realized gain of $5,000. ■

If the property's fair market value on the date of gift is *lower* than the donor's basis in the property, the donee's basis cannot be determined until the donee disposes of the property. For the purpose of determining *gain*, the donor's basis will

[31]Reg. § 1.307–1(a).

[32]§ 1015(a).

[33]§ 1015(a) and Reg. § 1.1015–1(a)(1). See Reg. § 1.1015–1(a)(3) for cases in which the facts necessary to determine the donor's adjusted basis are unknown. See Example 22 for the effect of depreciation deductions by the donee.

carry over, as in the preceding example. But for determining *loss*, the property's basis will be its fair market value when the gift was made.

EXAMPLE 17

Burt purchased stock three years ago for $10,000. He gave the stock to his son, Cliff, this year, when the fair market value was $7,000. No gift tax was paid on the transfer. Cliff later sells the stock for $6,000. For determining loss, Cliff's basis is $7,000, and the realized loss from the sale is $1,000 ($6,000 amount realized – $7,000 basis). ■

Note that this loss basis rule prevents the donee from receiving a tax benefit from a decline in value that occurred while the donor held the property. Therefore, in the preceding example, Cliff has a loss of only $1,000 rather than a loss of $4,000. The $3,000 difference represents the decline in value that occurred while Burt held the property. Ironically, however, a donee might be subject to income tax on the appreciation that occurred while the donor held the property, as illustrated in Example 16.

In any case, the operation of this dual basis rule produces a curious anomaly: if the sales proceeds fall *between* the donor's adjusted basis and the property's fair market value at the date of gift, no gain or loss is recognized.

EXAMPLE 18

Assume the same facts as in the preceding example, except that Cliff sells the stock for $8,000. To calculate gain, he would use a basis of $10,000, the donor's adjusted basis. But when a $10,000 basis is compared to $8,000 of sales proceeds, a *loss* is produced. Yet in determining loss, Cliff must use the property's fair market value at the date of gift—namely, $7,000. When a $7,000 basis is compared to sales proceeds of $8,000, a *gain* is produced. Accordingly, no gain or loss is recognized on this transaction. ■

PLANNING *Strategies*

GIFT PLANNING

★ Framework Focus: Tax Rate

Strategy ★ Shift Net Income from High-Bracket Taxpayers to Low-Bracket Taxpayers.

★ Framework Focus: Deductions

Strategy ★ Maximize Deductible Amounts.

Gifts of *appreciated property* can produce tax savings if the donee is in a lower tax bracket than the donor. The carryover basis rule effectively shifts the tax on the property's appreciation to the new owner, even if all of the appreciation arose while the property was owned by the donor.

On the other hand, donors should generally avoid making gifts of property that is worth less than the donor's adjusted basis (loss property). The operation of the basis rule for losses may result in either (1) a realized loss that is not deductible by either the donor or the donee or (2) reduced tax benefits when the loss is recognized by a donee facing lower marginal tax rates. Unless the property is expected to rebound in value before it is sold, a donor would be better advised to sell the property that has declined in value, deduct the resulting loss, and then transfer the proceeds to the prospective donee.

Adjustment for Gift Tax. If gift taxes are paid by the donor, the donee's basis may exceed the donor's basis. This occurs only if the fair market value of the property at the date of the gift exceeds the donor's adjusted basis (i.e., the property has appreciated in value). The portion of the gift tax paid that is related to the appreciation is added to the donor's basis in calculating the donee's basis for the property. In this circumstance, the following formula is used for calculating the donee's basis:[34]

$$\text{Donee's basis} = \text{Donor's adjusted basis} + \left(\frac{\text{Unrealized appreciation}}{\text{Taxable gift*}} \times \text{Gift tax paid}\right)$$

*The taxable gift is the fair market value of the gift less the per donee annual exclusion.

EXAMPLE 19

Bonnie made a gift of stock (adjusted basis of $15,000) to Peggy earlier this year. The stock had a fair market value of $50,000, and the transfer resulted in a gift tax of $4,000. The unrealized appreciation of the stock is $35,000 ($50,000 fair market value – $15,000 adjusted basis), and the taxable gift is $38,000 ($50,000 fair market value of gift – $12,000 per donee annual exclusion). Peggy's basis in the stock is $18,680, determined as follows:

Donor's adjusted basis	$15,000
Gift tax attributable to appreciation—	
$35,000/$38,000 = 92% (rounded) × $4,000	3,680
Donee's gain basis	$18,680

■

EXAMPLE 20

Don made a gift of stock to Matt earlier this year, when the fair market value of the stock was $50,000. Don paid gift tax of $4,000. Don had purchased the stock in 1987 for $65,000. Because there is no unrealized appreciation at the date of the gift, none of the gift tax paid is added to Don's basis in calculating Matt's basis. Thus, Matt's gain basis is $65,000. ■

For *gifts made before 1977,* the full amount of the gift tax paid is added to the donor's basis. However, the ceiling on this total is the fair market value of the property at the date of the gift. Thus, in Example 19, if the gift had been made before 1977, the basis of the property would be $19,000 ($15,000 + $4,000). In Example 20, the donee's basis would still be $65,000 ($65,000 + $0) for gain and $50,000 for loss.

Holding Period. The **holding period** for property acquired by gift begins on the date the donor acquired the property,[35] unless the special circumstance requiring use of the property's fair market value at the date of gift applies. If so, the holding period starts on the date of the gift.[36] The significance of the holding period for capital assets is discussed in Chapter 8.

The following example summarizes the basis and holding period rules for gift property.

EXAMPLE 21

Jill acquired 100 shares of Wren Corporation stock on December 30, 1998, for $40,000. On January 3 of this year, when the stock has a fair market value of $38,000, Jill gives it to Dennis and pays gift tax of $4,000. The basis is not increased by a portion of the gift tax paid because the property has not appreciated in value at the time of the gift. Therefore, Dennis's basis for determining gain is $40,000. Dennis's basis for determining loss is $38,000 (fair market value), because the fair market value on the date of the gift is less than the donor's adjusted basis.

[34] § 1015(d)(6) and Reg. § 1.1015–5(c)(2).

[35] § 1223(2) and Reg. § 1.1223–1(b).

[36] Rev.Rul. 59–86, 1959–1 C.B. 209.

- If Dennis sells the stock for $45,000, he has a recognized gain of $5,000. The holding period for determining whether the capital gain is short term or long term begins on December 30, 1998, the date Jill acquired the property.
- If Dennis sells the stock for $36,000, he has a recognized loss of $2,000. The holding period for determining whether the capital loss is short term or long term begins on January 3 of this year, the date of the gift.
- If Dennis sells the property for $39,000, no gain or loss is recognized because the amount realized is between the property's fair market value when given ($38,000) and the donor's adjusted basis of $40,000. ■

Basis for Depreciation. The basis for depreciation on depreciable gift property is the donee's basis for determining gain.[37] This rule is applicable even if the donee later sells the property at a loss and uses the property's fair market value at the date of gift in calculating the amount of the realized loss.

EXAMPLE 22

Vito gave a machine to Tina earlier this year. At that time, the adjusted basis was $32,000 (cost of $40,000 – accumulated depreciation of $8,000), and the fair market value was $26,000. No gift tax was due. Tina's basis for determining gain is $32,000, and her loss basis is $26,000. During this year, Tina deducts depreciation (cost recovery) of $6,400 ($32,000 × 20%). (Refer to Chapter 5 for the cost recovery tables.) At the end of this year, Tina's basis determinations are calculated as follows:

	Gain Basis	Loss Basis
Donor's basis or fair market value	$32,000	$26,000
Depreciation	(6,400)	(6,400)
	$25,600	$19,600

■

Property Acquired from a Decedent

General Rules. The basis of property acquired from a decedent is generally the property's fair market value at the date of death (referred to as the *primary valuation amount*).[38] The property's basis is the fair market value six months after the date of death if the executor or administrator of the estate *elects* the alternate valuation date for estate tax purposes. This amount is referred to as the *alternate valuation amount.*

DIGGING DEEPER 3

Find more information on this topic at our Web site: ***http://wft-entities.swlearning.com.***

EXAMPLE 23

Linda and various other family members inherited stock in a closely held corporation from Linda's father, who died earlier this year. At the date of death, her father's adjusted basis for the stock Linda inherited was $35,000. The stock's fair market value at the date of death was $50,000. The alternate valuation date was not elected. Linda's basis for income tax purposes is $50,000. This is commonly referred to as a *stepped-up basis.* ■

EXAMPLE 24

Assume the same facts as in the preceding example, except that the stock's fair market value at the date of death was $20,000. Linda's basis for income tax purposes is $20,000. This is commonly referred to as a *stepped-down basis.* ■

[37] § 1011 and Reg. §§ 1.1011–1 and 1.167(g)–1.

[38] § 1014(a).

TAX *in the News* **EFFECT OF 2001 TAX LEGISLATION ON THE BASIS OF INHERITED PROPERTY: BAD NEWS/GOOD NEWS!**

The *bad news* is that the Tax Relief Reconciliation Act of 2001 repeals the current step-up or step-down (i.e., fair market value) rules for the beneficiary's basis in inherited property and replaces them with a modified carryover basis. By itself, this change significantly increases the complexity of the tax law. A potential decedent will need to maintain detailed records on the cost of his or her assets and have such data readily available for the executor. Otherwise, the executor will be unable to determine the cost of many assets included in the estate.

So what is the *good news*? First, the effective date for this new carryover basis provision is deferred to deaths occurring after December 31, 2009. Second, the carryover basis approach for inherited property has been tried before. The results were so unsuccessful that the legislation was repealed retroactively by Congress. Hopefully, if the new carryover basis ever becomes effective, history will repeat itself, and another retroactive repeal by Congress will occur.

No estate tax return must be filed for estates below a threshold amount (refer to Chapter 1). In such cases, the alternate valuation date and amount are not available. Even if an estate tax return is filed and the executor elects the alternate valuation date, the six-months-after-death date is available only for property that the executor has not distributed before this date. For any property distributed or otherwise disposed of by the executor during the six-month period preceding the alternate valuation date, the adjusted basis to the beneficiary will equal the fair market value on the date of distribution or other disposition.[39]

The alternate valuation date can be elected *only if*, as a result of the election, *both* the value of the gross estate and the estate tax liability are lower than they would have been if the primary valuation date had been used. This provision prevents the alternate valuation election from being used to increase the basis of the property to the beneficiary for income tax purposes without simultaneously increasing the estate tax liability (because of estate tax deductions or credits).[40]

EXAMPLE 25

Nancy inherited investment real estate from her father, who died earlier this year. Her father's adjusted basis for the property at the date of death was $650,000. The property's fair market value was $2,750,000 at the date of death and $2,760,000 six months after death. The alternate valuation date cannot be elected because the value of the gross estate has increased during the six-month period. Nancy's basis for income tax purposes is $2,750,000. ■

EXAMPLE 26

Assume the same facts as in Example 25, except that the property's fair market value six months after death was $2,745,000. If the executor elects the alternate valuation date, Nancy's basis for income tax purposes is $2,745,000. ■

EXAMPLE 27

Assume the same facts as in Example 26, except that the property is distributed four months after the date of the decedent's death. At the distribution date, the property's fair market value is $2,747,500. Since the executor elected the alternate valuation date, Nancy's basis for income tax purposes is $2,747,500. ■

DIGGING DEEPER 4

Find more information on this topic at our Web site: ***http://wft-entities.swlearning.com.***

[39] § 2032(a)(1) and Rev.Rul. 56–60, 1956–1 C.B. 443.

[40] § 2032(c).

PLANNING *Strategies*

PROPERTY FROM A DECEDENT

★ **Framework Focus: Income**

Strategy ★ Avoid Income Recognition.

★ **Framework Focus: Deductions**

Strategy ★ Maximize Deductible Amounts.

If a taxpayer *retains appreciated property* until death, the property's basis will be "stepped up" to its fair market value at that time. Thus, no income tax will be paid on the property's appreciation by either the former owner (the decedent) or the new owner (the heir).

On the other hand, *depreciated property should be sold* prior to death. Otherwise, the property's basis in the heir's hands will be its declined fair market value, and neither the decedent nor the heir will be able to deduct the loss that occurred while the property was owned by the decedent.

Deathbed Gifts. The Code contains a provision designed to eliminate a tax avoidance technique occasionally described as *deathbed gifts.* With this technique, a donor makes a gift of appreciated property to a dying person with the understanding that the donor (or the donor's spouse) will inherit the property on the donee's death. If a person (or that person's spouse) receives from a decedent property that this person gave to the decedent during the year before the decedent's death, the property does *not* get a stepped-up basis. Instead, the basis of that property is the donor's adjusted basis.[41]

EXAMPLE 28

Ned gives stock to his uncle, Vern, this year. Ned's basis for the stock is $1,000, and the fair market value is $9,000. No gift tax is due. Eight months later, Ned inherits the stock from Vern. At the date of Vern's death, the fair market value of the stock is $12,000. Ned's adjusted basis for the stock is $1,000. ■

Holding Period of Property Acquired from a Decedent. The holding period of property acquired from a decedent is *deemed to be long term* (held for the required long-term holding period). This provision applies regardless of whether the property is disposed of at a gain or at a loss.[42]

LO.4

Describe various loss disallowance provisions.

Disallowed Losses

Related Taxpayers. Section 267 provides that realized losses from sales or exchanges of property between certain related parties are not recognized. This loss disallowance provision applies to several types of related-party transactions. The most common involve (1) members of a family and (2) an individual and a corporation in which the individual owns, directly or indirectly, more than 50 percent in value of the corporation's outstanding stock. Section 707 provides a similar loss disallowance provision where the related parties are a partner and a partnership in which the partner owns, directly or indirectly, more than 50 percent of the capital interests or profits interests in the partnership. Neither provision, however, prevents the recognition of *gains* between related parties. The rules governing the relationships covered by § 267 were discussed in Chapter 5.

[41] § 1014(e).

[42] § 1223(11).

If income-producing or business property is transferred to a related party and a loss is disallowed, the basis of the property to the recipient is the property's cost to the transferee. However, if a subsequent sale or other disposition of the property by the original transferee results in a realized gain, the amount of gain is reduced by the loss that was previously disallowed. This *right of offset* is not applicable if the original sale involved the sale of a personal-use asset (e.g., a personal residence). Furthermore, the right of offset is available only to the original transferee (the related-party buyer). See Example 17 and Example 18 in Chapter 5.

DIGGING DEEPER 5

Find more information on this topic at our Web site: ***http://wft-entities.swlearning.com.***

Wash Sales. Section 1091 stipulates that in certain cases, a realized loss on the sale or exchange of stock or securities is not recognized. Specifically, if a taxpayer sells or exchanges stock or securities and within 30 days before *or* after the date of the sale or exchange acquires *substantially identical* stock or securities, any loss realized from the sale or exchange is not recognized because the transaction is a **wash sale**.[43] The term *acquire* means acquire by purchase or in a taxable exchange and includes an option to purchase substantially identical securities. *Substantially identical* means the same in all important particulars. Corporate bonds and preferred stock are normally not considered substantially identical to a corporation's common stock. However, if the bonds and preferred stock are convertible into common stock, they may be considered substantially identical under certain circumstances.[44] Attempts to avoid the application of the wash sale rules by having a related taxpayer repurchase the securities have been unsuccessful.[45] The wash sale provisions do *not* apply to gains.

Recognition of the loss is disallowed because the taxpayer is considered to be in substantially the same economic position after the sale and repurchase as before. This disallowance rule does not apply to taxpayers engaged in the business of buying and selling securities.[46] Investors, however, are not allowed to create losses through wash sales to offset income for tax purposes.

A realized loss that is not recognized is added to the *basis* of the substantially identical stock or securities whose acquisition resulted in the nonrecognition of loss.[47] In other words, the basis of the replacement stock or securities is increased by the amount of the unrecognized loss. If the loss were not added to the basis of the newly acquired stock or securities, the taxpayer would never recover the entire basis of the old stock or securities. As a result, the wash sale rule operates to *defer* the recognition of the taxpayer's loss.

EXAMPLE 29

Oriole Manufacturing Company sold 50 shares of Green Corporation stock (adjusted basis of $10,000) for $8,000. Ten days later, Oriole purchased 50 shares of the same stock for $7,000. Oriole's realized loss of $2,000 ($8,000 amount realized – $10,000 adjusted basis) is not recognized because it resulted from a wash sale. Oriole's basis in the newly acquired stock is $9,000 ($7,000 purchase price + $2,000 unrecognized loss from the wash sale). ■

The basis of the new stock or securities includes the unrecovered portion of the basis of the formerly held stock or securities. Therefore, the *holding period* of the new stock or securities begins on the date of acquisition of the old stock or securities.[48]

A taxpayer may acquire fewer shares than the number sold in a wash sale. In this case, the loss from the sale is prorated between recognized and unrecognized loss on the basis of the ratio of the number of shares acquired to the number of shares sold.[49]

[43] § 1091(a) and Reg. §§ 1.1091–1(a) and (f).

[44] Rev.Rul. 56–406, 1956–2 C.B. 523.

[45] *McWilliams v. Comm.*, 47–1 USTC ¶9289, 35 AFTR 1184, 67 S.Ct. 1477 (USSC, 1947).

[46] Reg. § 1.1091–1(a).

[47] § 1091(d) and Reg. § 1.1091–2(a).

[48] § 1223(4) and Reg. § 1.1223–1(d).

[49] § 1091(b) and Reg. § 1.1091–1(c).

PLANNING *Strategies*

AVOIDING WASH SALES

★ **Framework Focus: Deductions**

Strategy ★ Maximize Deductible Amounts.

The wash sale restriction can be avoided by replacing the sold security with a *similar* but not "substantially identical" security. For example, if IBM common stock is sold to claim an unrealized loss, the taxpayer could immediately acquire Intel common stock without triggering the wash sale rule.

Nontax considerations must also come into play, however, because IBM and Intel are two different companies with different investment prospects. Though both securities will be affected by many of the same factors, they will also be subject to different factors that may be even more significant than the ones they share.

Conversion of Property from Personal Use to Business or Income-Producing Use

As discussed previously, losses from the sale of personal-use assets are not recognized for tax purposes, but losses from the sale of business and income-producing assets are deductible. Can a taxpayer convert a personal-use asset that has declined in value to business or income-producing use and then sell the asset to recognize a business or income-producing loss? The tax law prevents this practice by specifying that the *basis for determining loss* on personal-use assets converted to business or income-producing use is the *lower* of the property's adjusted basis or its fair market value on the date of conversion.[50] The *gain basis* for converted property is the property's adjusted basis on the date of conversion, regardless of whether the property's use is business, income-producing, or personal in nature.

EXAMPLE 30

Diane's personal residence has an adjusted basis of $175,000 and a fair market value of $160,000. When she converts the personal residence to residential rental property on January 1, her basis for determining loss is $160,000 (lower of $175,000 adjusted basis and fair market value of $160,000). The $15,000 decline in value is a personal loss and can never be recognized for tax purposes. Diane's basis for determining gain is $175,000. ■

The basis for determining loss is also the *basis for depreciating* the converted property.[51] This is an exception to the general rule that the basis for depreciation is the basis for determining gain (e.g., property received by gift). This exception prevents the taxpayer from recovering a personal loss indirectly through depreciation of the higher original basis. Once property is converted, both its basis for loss and its basis for gain are adjusted for depreciation deductions from the date of conversion to the date of disposition.

EXAMPLE 31

Assume the same facts as in Example 30. The MACRS cost recovery deduction for the current year is $5,576 ($160,000 × 3.485%). Thus, at the end of the current year, Diane's adjusted basis for gain for the rental property is $169,424 ($175,000 – $5,576), and her adjusted basis for loss is $154,424 ($160,000 – $5,576). ■

DIGGING DEEPER 6 7

Find more information on this topic at our Web site: ***http://wft-entities.swlearning.com.***

[50] Reg. § 1.165–9(b)(2).

[51] Reg. § 1.167(g)–1.

CONCEPT SUMMARY 7–2

Adjustments to Basis

Item	Effect	Refer to Chapter	Explanation
Amortization of bond discount.	Increase	7	Amortization is mandatory for certain taxable bonds and elective for tax-exempt bonds.
Amortization of bond premium.	Decrease	7	Amortization is mandatory for tax-exempt bonds and elective for taxable bonds.
Amortization of covenant not to compete.	Decrease	5	Covenant must be for a definite and limited time period. The amortization period is a statutory period of 15 years.
Amortization of intangibles.	Decrease	5	Intangibles are amortized over a 15-year period.
Bad debts.	Decrease	6	Most taxpayers must use the specific charge-off method.
Capital additions.	Increase	7	Certain items, at the taxpayer's election, can be capitalized or deducted.
Casualty.	Decrease	7	For a casualty loss, the amount of the adjustment is the sum of the deductible loss and the insurance proceeds received. For a casualty gain, the amount of the adjustment is the insurance proceeds received reduced by the recognized gain.
Condemnation.	Decrease	7	See casualty explanation.
Cost recovery.	Decrease	5	§ 168 is applicable to tangible assets placed in service after 1980 whose useful life is expressed in terms of years.
Depletion.	Decrease	5	Use the greater of cost or percentage depletion. Percentage depletion can be deducted even when the basis is zero.
Depreciation.	Decrease	5	§ 167 is applicable to tangible assets placed in service before 1981 and to tangible assets not depreciated in terms of years.
Easement.	Decrease	7	If the taxpayer does not retain any use of the land, all of the basis is allocable to the easement transaction. However, if only part of the land is affected by the easement, only part of the basis is allocable to the easement transaction.
Improvements by lessee to lessor's property.	Increase	4	Adjustment occurs only if the lessor is required to include the fair market value of the improvements in gross income under § 109.
Imputed interest.	Decrease		Amount deducted is not part of the cost of the asset.
Inventory: lower of cost or market.	Decrease		Not available if the LIFO method is used.
Limited expensing under § 179.	Decrease	5	Occurs only if the taxpayer elects § 179 treatment.

Summary of Basis Adjustments

Some of the more common items that either increase or decrease the basis of an asset appear in Concept Summary 7–2.

In discussing the topic of basis, a number of specific techniques for determining basis have been presented. Although the various techniques are responsive to

Item	Effect	Refer to Chapter	Explanation
Medical capital expenditure deducted as a medical expense.	Decrease	16	Adjustment is the amount of the deduction (the effect on basis is to increase it by the amount of the capital expenditure net of the deduction).
Real estate taxes: apportionment between the buyer and seller.	Increase or decrease	5	To the extent the buyer pays the seller's pro rata share, the buyer's basis is increased. To the extent the seller pays the buyer's pro rata share, the buyer's basis is decreased.
Rebate from manufacturer.	Decrease		Since the rebate is treated as an adjustment to the purchase price, it is not included in the buyer's gross income.
Stock dividend.	Decrease	7	Adjustment occurs only if the stock dividend is nontaxable. While the basis per share decreases, the total stock basis does not change.
Stock rights.	Decrease	10	Adjustment to stock basis occurs only for nontaxable stock rights and only if the fair market value of the rights is at least 15% of the fair market value of the stock or, if less than 15%, the taxpayer elects to allocate the basis between the stock and the rights.
Theft.	Decrease	6	See casualty explanation.

and mandated by transactions occurring in the marketplace, they possess enough common characteristics to be categorized as follows:

- The basis of the asset may be determined by its cost.
- The basis of the asset may be determined by the basis of another asset.
- The basis of the asset may be determined by its fair market value.
- The basis of the asset may be determined by the basis of the asset in the hands of another taxpayer.

General Concept of a Nontaxable Exchange

A taxpayer who is going to replace a productive asset (e.g., machinery) used in a trade or business may structure the transaction as a sale of the old asset and the purchase of a new asset. When this approach is used, any realized gain or loss on the sale of the old asset is recognized. The basis of the new asset is its cost. Alternatively, the taxpayer may be able to trade the old asset for the new asset. This exchange of assets may produce beneficial tax consequences as a nontaxable exchange.

The tax law recognizes that nontaxable exchanges result in a change in the *form* but not the *substance* of a taxpayer's relative economic position. The replacement property received in the exchange is viewed as essentially a continuation of the old investment.[52] Additional justification for nontaxable treatment is that this type of transaction does not provide the taxpayer with the wherewithal to pay the tax on any realized gain.

The nonrecognition provisions for nontaxable exchanges do not apply to realized losses from the sale or exchange of personal-use assets. Such losses are never recognized (i.e., they are disallowed) because they are personal in nature.

[52]Reg. § 1.1002–1(c).

In contrast, in a **nontaxable exchange**, recognition of gains or losses is *postponed* (i.e., deferred) until the new property received in the nontaxable exchange is subsequently disposed of in a taxable transaction. This is accomplished by assigning a carryover basis to the replacement property.

EXAMPLE 32

Starling Management Company exchanges property with an adjusted basis of $10,000 and a fair market value of $12,000 for property with a fair market value of $12,000. The transaction qualifies for nontaxable exchange treatment. Starling has a realized gain of $2,000 ($12,000 amount realized − $10,000 adjusted basis). Its recognized gain is $0. Starling's basis in the replacement property is a carryover basis of $10,000. Assume the replacement property is nondepreciable and Starling subsequently sells it for $12,000. The realized and recognized gain will be the $2,000 gain that was postponed (deferred) in the nontaxable transaction. If the replacement property is depreciable, the carryover basis of $10,000 is used in calculating depreciation. ■

In some nontaxable exchanges, only some of the property involved in the transaction qualifies for nonrecognition treatment. If the taxpayer receives cash or other nonqualifying property, part or all of the realized gain from the exchange is recognized. In these situations, gain is recognized because the taxpayer has changed or improved its relative economic position and has the wherewithal to pay income tax to the extent of cash or other property received.

It is important to distinguish between a nontaxable disposition (or nonrecognition transaction, as the term is used in the statute) and a tax-free transaction. As previously mentioned, the term *nontaxable* refers to postponement of recognition via some version of carryover basis. In a *tax-free* transaction, the nonrecognition is permanent (e.g., see the discussion later in this chapter of the exclusion of gain from the sale of a principal residence).

Either way, nontaxable and tax-free transactions must be understood as exceptions to the Code's general rule that gains and losses are recognized when they are realized. These exceptions have their own sets of requirements, limitations, and restrictions, all of which must be satisfied for a transaction to be characterized as nontaxable or tax-free. Otherwise, the general rule of recognition applies to the gain or loss at hand.

Like-Kind Exchanges—§ 1031

LO.5

Apply the nonrecognition provisions and basis determination rules for like-kind exchanges.

Section 1031 provides for nontaxable exchange treatment if the following requirements are satisfied:[53]

- The form of the transaction is an exchange.
- Both the property transferred and the property received are held either for productive use in a trade or business or for investment.
- The property is like-kind property.

Qualifying **like-kind exchanges** include exchanges of business for business, business for investment, investment for business, or investment for investment property. Property held for personal use does not qualify under the like-kind exchange provisions. Thus, the purpose for which the property is held by the taxpayer in question is critical. For example, if Janet uses a small truck in her trade or business, it may qualify for like-kind treatment, but if she uses this truck as her personal-use vehicle, it is ineligible for nonrecognition treatment under § 1031.

Some assets are excluded from like-kind treatment by statute. These excluded assets include a taxpayer's inventory or "stock in trade," as well as most forms of investment other than real estate. Thus, stocks, bonds, partnership interests

[53] § 1031(a) and Reg. § 1.1031(a)–1(a).

(whether general or limited), and other securities, even though held for investment, do not qualify for like-kind exchange treatment.

The nonrecognition provision for like-kind exchanges is *mandatory* rather than elective. A taxpayer who wants to recognize a realized gain or loss will have to structure the transaction in a form that does not satisfy the statutory requirements for a like-kind exchange.

PLANNING *Strategies*

LIKE-KIND EXCHANGES

★ **Framework Focus: Deductions**

Strategy ★ Maximize Deductible Amounts.

Because nonrecognition of gain or loss is mandatory in like-kind exchanges, a taxpayer must affirmatively *avoid such exchanges* if nonrecognition treatment is not desired. If an asset is worth less than its adjusted basis, a *loss would result* from its disposition. Accordingly, the taxpayer should sell this property outright to ensure the deductibility of the loss, assuming it would otherwise be deductible.

Even if *disposition would result in a gain*, a taxpayer might want to recognize this gain in the current taxable year. If so, a like-kind exchange should be avoided. Circumstances suggesting this strategy include:

- Unused capital loss carryovers, especially if the taxpayer is a corporation for which such carryovers are limited in duration (see Chapters 4 and 8).
- Unused net operating loss carryovers (see Chapter 6).
- Unused general business credit carryovers (see Chapter 14).
- Suspended or current passive activity losses (see Chapter 6).
- Expectations of higher tax rates in future years.

Like-Kind Property

The term *like-kind* is explained in the Regulations as follows: "The words 'like-kind' refer to the nature or character of the property and not to its grade or quality. One kind or class of property may not . . . be exchanged for property of a different kind or class."[54] The Regulations go on to explain that although real estate can be exchanged only for other real estate, the definition of real estate is quite broad. *Real estate* (or realty) includes principally rental buildings, office and store buildings, manufacturing plants, warehouses, and land. It is immaterial whether real estate is improved or unimproved. Thus, unimproved land can be exchanged for an apartment house. On the other hand, real property located in the United States exchanged for foreign real property (and vice versa) does not qualify as like-kind property. A similar provision applies to exchanges of foreign and domestic personalty.

In any case, real estate cannot be exchanged in a like-kind transaction for personalty. *Personalty* includes tangible assets other than real estate, such as machinery, equipment, trucks, automobiles, furniture, and fixtures. Thus, an exchange of a machine (personalty) for a small office building (realty) is not a like-kind exchange. Finally, the Code mandates that livestock of different sexes are not like-kind property.

EXAMPLE 33

Pheasant, Inc., made the following exchanges during the taxable year:

a. Inventory for a machine used in business.
b. Land held for investment for a building used in business.

[54]Reg. § 1.1031(a)–1(b).

c. Stock held for investment for equipment used in business.
d. A business truck for a business truck.
e. Livestock for livestock of a different sex.
f. Land held for investment in New York for land held for investment in London.

Exchanges (b), investment real property for business real property, and (d), business personalty for business personalty, qualify as exchanges of like-kind property. Exchanges (a), inventory; (c), stock; (e), livestock of different sexes; and (f), U.S. and foreign real estate do not qualify. ■

DIGGING DEEPER 8

Find more information on this topic at our Web site: ***http://wft-entities.swlearning.com.***

The Regulations dealing with § 1031 like-kind exchanges provide greater specificity when determining whether depreciable tangible personalty is of a like kind. Such property held for productive use in a business is of like kind only if the exchanged property is within the same *general business asset class* (as specified by the IRS in Rev.Proc. 87–56 or as subsequently modified) or the same *product class* (as specified by the Department of Commerce). Property included in a general business asset class is evaluated exclusively under the Revenue Procedure, rather than under the product class system.

The following are examples of general business asset classes:

- Office furniture, fixtures, and equipment.
- Information systems (computers and peripheral equipment).
- Airplanes.
- Automobiles and taxis.
- Buses.
- Light general-purpose trucks.
- Heavy general-purpose trucks.

These Regulations narrow the range of depreciable tangible personalty subject to § 1031 like-kind exchange treatment. For example, the exchange of office equipment for a computer does not qualify as an exchange of like-kind property. Even though both assets are depreciable tangible personalty, they are not like-kind property because they are in different general business asset classes. Accordingly, any realized *gain or loss* on the office equipment would be recognized currently.

DIGGING DEEPER 9

Find more information on this topic at our Web site: ***http://wft-entities.swlearning.com.***

Finally, a special provision applies if the taxpayers involved in the exchange are *related parties* under § 267(b). To qualify for like-kind exchange treatment, the taxpayer and the related party must not dispose of the like-kind property received in the exchange for two years after the date of the exchange. If such a disposition does occur, the postponed gain is recognized as of the date of that disposition. Dispositions due to death, involuntary conversions, and certain non-tax avoidance transactions are excepted from this rule.

Exchange Requirement

The transaction must generally involve a direct exchange of property to qualify as a like-kind exchange. The sale of old property and the purchase of new property, even though like kind, is not an exchange. However, the Code does provide a limited procedure for real estate to be exchanged for qualifying property that is acquired subsequent to the exchange.[55]

[55] § 1031(a)(3).

Of course, the taxpayer may want to avoid nontaxable exchange treatment. Recognition of gain gives the taxpayer a higher basis for depreciation. To the extent that such gains would, if recognized, either receive favorable capital gain treatment or be passive activity income that could be offset by passive activity losses, it might be preferable to avoid the nonrecognition provisions through an indirect exchange transaction. For example, a taxpayer may sell property to one company, recognize the gain, and subsequently purchase similar property from another company. The taxpayer may also want to avoid nontaxable exchange treatment so that a realized loss can be recognized.

DIGGING DEEPER 10

Find more information on this topic at our Web site: ***http://wft-entities.swlearning.com.***

Boot

If the taxpayer in a like-kind exchange gives or receives some property that is not like-kind property, recognition may occur. Property that is not like-kind property, including cash, is often referred to as **boot**. Although the term *boot* does not appear in the Code, tax practitioners commonly use it rather than saying "property that does not qualify as like-kind property."

The *receipt* of boot will trigger recognition of gain if there is realized gain. The amount of the recognized gain is the *lesser* of the boot received or the realized gain (realized gain serves as the ceiling on recognition).

EXAMPLE 34

Blue, Inc., and White Corporation exchange machinery, and the exchange qualifies as like kind under § 1031. Since Blue's machinery (adjusted basis of $20,000) is worth $24,000 and White's machine has a fair market value of $19,000, White also gives Blue cash of $5,000. Blue's recognized gain is $4,000, the lesser of the realized gain of $4,000 ($24,000 amount realized – $20,000 adjusted basis) or the fair market value of the boot received of $5,000. ■

EXAMPLE 35

Assume the same facts as in the preceding example, except that White's machine is worth $21,000 (not $19,000). Under these circumstances, White gives Blue cash of $3,000 to make up the difference. Blue's recognized gain is $3,000, the lesser of the realized gain of $4,000 ($24,000 amount realized – $20,000 adjusted basis) or the fair market value of the boot received of $3,000. ■

The receipt of boot does not result in recognition if there is realized loss.

EXAMPLE 36

Assume the same facts as in Example 34, except that the adjusted basis of Blue's machine is $30,000. Blue's realized loss is $6,000 ($24,000 amount realized – $30,000 adjusted basis). The receipt of the boot of $5,000 does not trigger recognition of Blue's loss. ■

The *giving* of boot does not trigger recognition if the boot consists solely of cash.

EXAMPLE 37

Flicker, Inc., and Gadwall Corporation exchange equipment in a like-kind exchange. Flicker receives equipment with a fair market value of $25,000 and transfers equipment worth $21,000 (adjusted basis of $15,000) and cash of $4,000. Flicker's realized gain is $6,000 ($25,000 amount realized – $15,000 adjusted basis – $4,000 cash), none of which is recognized. ■

If, however, the boot given is appreciated or depreciated property, gain or loss is recognized to the extent of the difference between the adjusted basis and the fair market value of the boot. For this purpose, *appreciated or depreciated property* is property with an adjusted basis that differs from fair market value.

EXAMPLE 38

Assume the same facts as in the preceding example, except that Flicker transfers equipment worth $10,000 (adjusted basis of $12,000) and boot worth $15,000 (adjusted basis of $9,000). Flicker's realized gain appears to be $4,000 ($25,000 amount realized − $21,000 adjusted basis). Since realization previously has served as a ceiling on recognition, it appears that the recognized gain is $4,000 (lower of realized gain of $4,000 or amount of appreciation on boot of $6,000). However, the recognized gain actually is $6,000 (full amount of the appreciation on the boot). In effect, Flicker must calculate the like-kind and boot parts of the transaction separately. That is, the realized loss of $2,000 on the like-kind property *is not* recognized ($10,000 fair market value − $12,000 adjusted basis), but the $6,000 realized gain on the boot *is* recognized ($15,000 fair market value − $9,000 adjusted basis). ■

Basis and Holding Period of Property Received

If an exchange does not qualify as nontaxable under § 1031, gain or loss is recognized, and the basis of property received in the exchange is the property's fair market value. If the exchange qualifies for nonrecognition, the basis of property received must be adjusted to reflect any postponed (deferred) gain or loss. The *basis of like-kind property* received in the exchange is the property's fair market value less postponed gain or plus postponed loss. The *basis* of any *boot* received is the boot's fair market value.

EXAMPLE 39

Vireo Property Management Company exchanges a building (used in its business) with an adjusted basis of $300,000 and a fair market value of $380,000 for land with a fair market value of $380,000. The land is to be held as an investment. The exchange qualifies as like kind (an exchange of business real property for investment real property). Thus, the basis of the land is $300,000 (the land's fair market value of $380,000 less the $80,000 postponed gain on the building). If the land is later sold for its fair market value of $380,000, the $80,000 postponed gain is recognized. ■

EXAMPLE 40

Assume the same facts as in the preceding example, except that the building has an adjusted basis of $480,000 and a fair market value of only $380,000. The basis in the newly acquired land is $480,000 (fair market value of $380,000 plus the $100,000 postponed loss on the building). If the land is later sold for its fair market value of $380,000, the $100,000 postponed loss is recognized. ■

The Code provides an alternative approach for determining the basis of like-kind property received:

Adjusted basis of like-kind property surrendered
\+ Adjusted basis of boot given
\+ Gain recognized
− Fair market value of boot received
− Loss recognized
= *Basis of like-kind property received*

This approach accords with the recovery of capital doctrine. That is, the unrecovered cost or other basis is increased by additional cost (boot given) or decreased by cost recovered (boot received). Any gain recognized is included in the basis of the new property. The taxpayer has been taxed on this amount and is now entitled to recover it tax-free. Any loss recognized is deducted from the basis of the new property since the taxpayer has already received a tax benefit on that amount.

The holding period of the property surrendered in the exchange carries over and *tacks on* to the holding period of the like-kind property received.[56] This rule derives from the basic concept that the new property is a continuation of the old

[56] § 1223(1) and Reg. § 1.1223–1(a). For like-kind exchanges after March 1, 1954, the tacked-on holding period applies only if the like-kind property surrendered was either a capital asset or § 1231 property. See Chapter 8 for the discussion of capital assets and § 1231 property.

investment. The boot received has a new holding period (from the date of exchange) rather than a carryover holding period.

Depreciation recapture potential carries over to the property received in a like-kind exchange.[57] See Chapter 8 for a discussion of this topic.

DIGGING DEEPER 11

Find more information on this topic at our Web site: ***http://wft-entities.swlearning.com.***

If the taxpayer either assumes a liability or takes property subject to a liability, the amount of the liability is treated as boot given. For the taxpayer whose liability is assumed or whose property is taken subject to the liability, the amount of the liability is treated as boot received. The following example illustrates the effect of such a liability. In addition, the example illustrates the tax consequences for both parties involved in the like-kind exchange.

EXAMPLE 41

Jaeger & Company and Lark Enterprises, Inc., exchange real estate investments. Jaeger gives up property with an adjusted basis of $250,000 (fair market value of $400,000) that is subject to a mortgage of $75,000 (assumed by Lark). In return for this property, Jaeger receives property with a fair market value of $300,000 (adjusted basis of $200,000) and cash of $25,000.[58]

	Jaeger	Lark
Amount realized:		
Like-kind property received	$ 300,000	$ 400,000
Boot received:		
Cash	25,000	
Mortgage assumed	75,000	
	$ 400,000	$ 400,000
Adjusted basis:		
Like-kind property given	(250,000)	(200,000)
Boot given:		
Cash		(25,000)
Mortgage assumed		(75,000)
Realized gain	$ 150,000	$ 100,000
Recognized gain	100,000*	–0–**
Deferred gain	$ 50,000	$ 100,000
Basis of property transferred:		
Like-kind property	$ 250,000	$ 200,000
Cash		25,000
Mortgage assumed		75,000
	$ 250,000	$ 300,000
Plus: Gain recognized	100,000	
Less: Boot received	(100,000)	
Basis of new property	$ 250,000	$ 300,000

*Lesser of boot received ($25,000 cash + $75,000 mortgage assumed = $100,000) or gain realized ($150,000).

**No boot received.

■

[57]Reg. §§ 1.1245–2(a)(4) and 1.1250–2(d)(1).

[58]Example (2) of Reg. § 1.1031(d)–2 illustrates a special situation in which both the buyer and the seller transfer liabilities that are assumed by the other party or both parties acquire property that is subject to a liability.

BRIDGE *Discipline*

Bridge to Economics

One can assert that the "tax variable" is neutralized in nontaxable exchanges when taxable gains or losses do not arise. Neutralizing potential tax consequences can have a positive result given that tax costs tend to dampen economic activity. For example, in a like-kind exchange, a taxpayer can exchange one asset for another asset of like kind without having to recognize a gain or pay a tax. The justification for the tax deferral is that the taxpayer is viewed as having an equivalent economic investment after the transaction as before the transaction. But the tax-neutral result changes when the taxpayer receives property that is not "like kind" because the taxpayer's economic standing has changed.

If, for example, the taxpayer receives investment land *and* cash in exchange for investment land, her ownership in the land given up has, at least in part, been converted to cash, and to that degree, her investment has substantively changed. That is, the taxpayer's economic investment has changed from an ownership exclusively in land to ownership in land *and* cash. Alternatively, if the taxpayer gives up her investment land for corporate stock in a high-tech venture, the nature of her investment also would substantively change as a result of the transaction. These differences in the taxpayer's economic position after the transaction lead to the transactions being taxed.

Involuntary Conversions—§ 1033

LO.6

Explain the nonrecognition provisions available on the involuntary conversion of property.

Section 1033 provides that a taxpayer who suffers an involuntary conversion of property may postpone recognition of *gain* realized from the conversion, if that taxpayer *reinvests* the amount realized from the conversion in replacement property. Thus, if the amount reinvested in replacement property is *less than* the amount realized, realized gain *is recognized*, but only to the extent of the amount not reinvested. Any realized gain not recognized reduces the taxpayer's basis in the replacement property.[59] Thus, recognition of the gain is deferred until the replacement property is disposed of.

EXAMPLE 42

Sandpiper, Inc., receives insurance proceeds of $29,000 when some of its manufacturing equipment (adjusted basis of $25,000) is destroyed by fire. Sandpiper purchases new equipment costing $30,000, so none of its $4,000 realized gain ($29,000 amount realized – $25,000 adjusted basis) is recognized. Sandpiper's basis in the new equipment is $26,000 ($30,000 cost – $4,000 deferred gain). ■

EXAMPLE 43

If Sandpiper, Inc., in the preceding example purchases new equipment that costs $28,000, it would recognize gain of $1,000, the difference between the $29,000 of insurance proceeds realized on the conversion and the $28,000 cost of the new equipment. The remaining $3,000 of realized gain would not be recognized; instead, it would reduce the company's basis in the new equipment to $25,000 ($28,000 cost – $3,000 deferred gain). ■

By its terms, § 1033 is *elective.* A taxpayer need not postpone recognition of gain, even if replacement property is acquired. In essence, a taxpayer has three options:

- Reinvest the proceeds and elect § 1033's nonrecognition of gain.
- Reinvest the proceeds and not elect § 1033, thereby triggering recognition of realized gain under the customary rules applicable to property transactions.
- Not reinvest the proceeds and recognize the realized gain accordingly.

[59] § 1033(b)(2).

If a *loss* occurs on an involuntary conversion, § 1033 does not apply, and the general rules for loss recognition are effective. See Chapter 6 for the discussion of the deduction of losses.

PLANNING *Strategies*

RECOGNIZING INVOLUNTARY CONVERSION GAINS

★ **Framework Focus: Tax Rate**

Strategy ★ Shift Net Income from High-Bracket Years to Low-Bracket Years.

★ **Framework Focus: Deductions**

Strategy ★ Maximize Deductible Amounts.

Sometimes, a taxpayer may prefer to *recognize a gain from an involuntary conversion* and will choose not to elect § 1033, even though replacement property is acquired. Circumstances suggesting this strategy would include:

- The taxpayer realized the gain in a low-bracket tax year, quite possibly because of the events that caused the involuntary conversion, such as a flood and its aftermath that seriously disrupted the business.
- The taxpayer has an expiring net operating loss carryover that can offset most, if not all, of the gain from the involuntary conversion.
- The replacement property is depreciable, and the taxpayer would prefer an unreduced basis for this asset to maximize depreciation deductions in future years.

Nontax considerations might also come into play, perhaps suggesting that the property not be replaced at all. Even before the event that produced the involuntary conversion, the taxpayer might have been wanting to downsize the business or terminate it outright. In any case, the taxpayer might prefer to recognize the gain, pay the tax involved, and thereby free up the remaining proceeds for other uses—business, investment, or even personal—especially if the gain is small compared to the amount of proceeds received.

Involuntary Conversion Defined

An **involuntary conversion** results from the destruction (complete or partial), theft, seizure, requisition or condemnation, or sale or exchange under threat or imminence of requisition or condemnation of the taxpayer's property.[60] This description includes fires (other than arson),[61] tornadoes, hurricanes, earthquakes, floods, and other natural disasters. In these circumstances, *gain* can result from insurance proceeds received in an amount that exceeds the taxpayer's historical cost of the property, especially if depreciation deductions have lowered the property's adjusted basis.

For requisitions and condemnations, the amount realized includes the compensation paid by the public authority acquiring the taxpayer's property. To prove the existence of a threat or imminence of condemnation, the taxpayer must obtain confirmation that there has been a decision to acquire the property for public use. In addition, the taxpayer must have reasonable grounds to believe the property will be taken.[62] The property does not have to be sold to the authority threatening to condemn it to qualify for § 1033 postponement. If the taxpayer satisfies the confirmation and reasonable grounds requirements, he or she can sell the property to another party.[63] Likewise, the sale of property to a condemning authority by a

[60] § 1033(a) and Reg. §§ 1.1033(a)–1(a) and –2(a).

[61] Rev.Rul. 82–74, 1982–1 C.B. 110.

[62] Rev.Rul. 63–221, 1963–2 C.B. 332, and *Joseph P. Balistrieri*, 38 TCM 526, T.C.Memo. 1979–115.

[63] Rev.Rul. 81–180, 1981–2 C.B. 161.

TAX *in the News*

THE SUPREME COURT UPHOLDS THE GOVERNMENT'S TAKING OF PROPERTY

Under eminent domain, governmental units have the right to take private property for public use. As fair compensation must be paid, disagreement often arises over the fair market value of condemned property.

In recent years, there has also been controversy over what constitutes "public use." Courts have expanded the definition of public use beyond the traditional public projects (such as roads, bridges, schools, hospitals, and slum clearance) to allow the taking of unblighted property for commercial development purposes. The objective in taking such property is to create jobs and increase tax revenues by means of new office parks, big box stores, racetracks, and other businesses.

The U.S. Supreme Court addressed this issue of what constitutes "public use" in its 2005 decision in *Kelo v. City of New London* (125 S.Ct. 2655 [USSC, 2005]). The Court, in a 5-to-4 decision, ruled that the "takings clause" in the Fifth Amendment to the U.S. Constitution permits the condemnation of private property for uses that are primarily commercial, as long as such use serves a demonstrated "public use." Here, the City of New London condemned 15 properties to enable the construction of a resort hotel and facilities for a major pharmaceutical company. "Public use" in this case was deemed to occur because benefits would accrue to the city in the form of new jobs and increased tax revenues.

Some have criticized the decision because it leaves few limits on the ability of local governments to take private property. In addition, for those property owners whose property is either condemned or threatened with condemnation, the decision may impair their ability to receive fair compensation. It appears that the only way now available to limit this government condemnation power is for the states to enact laws restricting its use.

taxpayer who acquired the property from its former owner with the knowledge that the property was under threat of condemnation also qualifies as an involuntary conversion under § 1033.[64]

Find more information on this topic at our Web site: ***http://wft-entities.swlearning.com.***

DIGGING DEEPER 12

Replacement Property

The requirements for replacement property under the involuntary conversion rules generally are more restrictive than those for like-kind property under § 1031. The basic requirement is that the replacement property be similar or related in service or use to the involuntarily converted property.[65]

Different interpretations of the phrase *similar or related in service or use* apply depending on whether the involuntarily converted property is held by an *owner-user* or by an *owner-investor* (e.g., lessor). For an owner-user, the *functional use test* applies, and for an owner-investor, the *taxpayer use test* applies.

Functional Use Test. Under this test, a taxpayer's use of the replacement property and of the involuntarily converted property must be the same. Replacing a manufacturing plant with a wholesale grocery warehouse does not meet this test. Instead, the plant must be replaced with another facility of similar functional use.

Taxpayer Use Test. The taxpayer use test for owner-investors provides the taxpayer with more flexibility in terms of what qualifies as replacement property than does the functional use test for owner-users. Essentially, the properties must be used by the taxpayer (the owner-investor) in similar endeavors. For example, rental property held by an owner-investor qualifies if replaced by other rental property, regardless of the type of rental property involved. The test is met when an investor

[64]Rev.Rul. 81–181, 1981–2 C.B. 162.

[65]§ 1033(a) and Reg. § 1.1033(a)–1.

CONCEPT SUMMARY 7–3

Replacement Property Tests

Type of Property and User	Like-Kind Test	Taxpayer Use Test	Functional Use Test
Land used by a manufacturing company is condemned by a local government authority.	X		
Apartment and land held by an investor are sold due to the threat or imminence of condemnation.	X		
An investor's rented shopping mall is destroyed by fire; the mall may be replaced by other rental properties (e.g., an apartment building).		X	
A manufacturing plant is destroyed by fire; replacement property must consist of another manufacturing plant that is functionally the same as the property converted.			X
Personal residence of taxpayer is condemned by a local government authority; replacement property must consist of another personal residence.			X

replaces a manufacturing plant with a wholesale grocery warehouse if both properties are held for the production of rental income.[66] The replacement of a rental residence with a personal residence does not meet the test.[67]

Special Real Property Test. In addition to the functional and taxpayer use tests, the Code provides a special rule for business or investment real property *that is condemned.* This rule applies the broad like-kind classification for real estate to such circumstances. Accordingly, improved real property can be replaced with unimproved real property.

The rules concerning the nature of replacement property are illustrated in Concept Summary 7–3.

Time Limitation on Replacement

The taxpayer normally has a two-year period after the close of the taxable year in which gain is realized from an involuntary conversion to replace the property (*the latest date*).[68] This rule affords as much as three years from the date of realization of gain to replace the property if the realization of gain took place on the first day of the taxable year.[69] If the involuntary conversion involved the condemnation of real property used in a trade or business or held for investment, the Code substitutes a three-year period for the normal two-year period. In this case, a taxpayer might have as much as four years from the date of realization of gain to replace the property.

EXAMPLE 44

Magpie, Inc.'s warehouse is destroyed by fire on December 16, 2005. The adjusted basis is $325,000. Magpie receives $400,000 from the insurance company on January 10, 2006. The company is a calendar year taxpayer. The latest date for replacement is December 31, 2008

[66] *Loco Realty Co. v. Comm.*, 62–2 USTC ¶9657, 10 AFTR2d 5359, 306 F.2d 207 (CA–8, 1962).

[67] Rev.Rul. 70–466, 1970–2 C.B. 165.

[68] §§ 1033(a)(2)(B) and (g)(4) and Reg. § 1.1033(a)–2(c)(3).

[69] A taxpayer can apply for an extension of this time period anytime before its expiration [Reg. § 1.1033(a)–2(c)(3)]. Also, the period for filing the application for extension can be extended if a taxpayer shows reasonable cause.

(the end of the taxable year in which realized gain occurred plus two years). The critical date is not the date the involuntary conversion occurred, but rather the date of gain realization (when the insurance proceeds are received). ■

EXAMPLE 45

Assume the same facts as in the preceding example, except that Magpie's warehouse is condemned. The latest date for replacement is December 31, 2009 (the end of the taxable year in which realized gain occurred plus three years). ■

The *earliest date* for replacement typically is the date the involuntary conversion occurs. However, if the property is condemned, it is possible to replace the condemned property before this date. In this case, the earliest date is the date of the threat or imminence of requisition or condemnation of the property. The purpose of this provision is to enable the taxpayer to make an orderly replacement of the condemned property.

Other Nonrecognition Provisions

LO.7

Identify other nonrecognition provisions contained in the Code.

Several additional nonrecognition provisions are treated briefly in the remainder of this chapter.

Transfer of Assets to Business Entity—§§ 351 and 721

Taxpayers can transfer assets to corporations in exchange for stock without recognizing gain or loss on the transfer according to § 351. See Chapter 9 for the applicable restrictions and corresponding basis adjustments for the stock acquired. A similar provision (§ 721) allows the nontaxable transfer of assets to a partnership in exchange for an interest in that partnership. See Chapter 11 for a description of § 721.

Exchange of Stock for Property—§ 1032

Under § 1032, a corporation does not recognize gain or loss on the receipt of money or other property in exchange for its stock (including treasury stock). In other words, a corporation does not recognize gain or loss when it deals in its own stock. This provision accords with the accounting treatment of such transactions.

Certain Exchanges of Insurance Policies—§ 1035

Under § 1035, no gain or loss is recognized from the exchange of certain insurance contracts or policies. The rules relating to exchanges not solely in kind (i.e., with boot) and the basis of the property acquired are the same as under § 1031. Exchanges qualifying for nonrecognition include the following:

- The exchange of life insurance contracts.
- The exchange of a life insurance contract for an endowment or annuity contract.
- The exchange of an endowment contract for another endowment contract that provides for regular payments beginning at a date not later than the date payments would have begun under the contract exchanged.
- The exchange of an endowment contract for an annuity contract.
- The exchange of annuity contracts.

Exchange of Stock for Stock of the Same Corporation—§ 1036

Section 1036 provides that a shareholder does not recognize gain or loss on the exchange of common stock solely for common stock in the same corporation or from the exchange of preferred stock for preferred stock in the same corporation. Exchanges between individual shareholders as well as between a shareholder and the corporation are included under this nonrecognition provision. The rules relating to exchanges not solely in kind and the basis of the property acquired are the same as under § 1031. For example, a nonrecognition exchange occurs when common stock with different rights, such as voting for nonvoting, is exchanged. A shareholder usually recognizes gain or loss from the exchange of common for preferred or preferred for common even though the stock exchanged is in the same corporation.

Rollovers into Specialized Small Business Investment Companies—§ 1044

Section 1044 provides a postponement opportunity associated with the sale of publicly traded securities. If the amount realized is reinvested in the common stock or partnership interest of a specialized small business investment company (SSBIC), the realized gain is not recognized. Gain will be recognized, however, to the extent of any amount not reinvested. To qualify, the taxpayer must reinvest the proceeds within 60 days of the date of sale. In calculating the basis of the SSBIC stock, the amount of the purchase price is reduced by the amount of the postponed gain.

Statutory ceilings are imposed on the amount of realized gain that can be postponed for any taxable year as follows:

- For an individual taxpayer, the lesser of:
  - $50,000 ($25,000 for married filing separately).
  - $500,000 ($250,000 for married filing separately) reduced by the amount of such nonrecognized gain in all preceding taxable years.
- For a corporate taxpayer, the lesser of:
  - $250,000.
  - $1 million reduced by the amount of such nonrecognized gain in all preceding taxable years.

Investors ineligible for this postponement treatment include partnerships, S corporations, estates, and trusts.

DIGGING DEEPER 13

Find more information on this topic at our Web site: ***http://wft-entities.swlearning.com.***

Sale of a Principal Residence—§ 121

Section 121 allows individual taxpayers to exclude gain from the sale of a *principal residence.* This provision applies to the first $250,000 of realized gain, or $500,000 on a joint return. For this purpose, the residence must have been owned and used by the taxpayer as the primary residence for at least two of the five years preceding the date of sale. In addition, the exclusion is not available for sales occurring within two years of its last use. This exclusion can be prorated, however, if a taxpayer failed to meet one or more of these time period requirements due to a change in his or her place of employment or health. Moreover, a surviving spouse counts the ownership and usage periods of the decedent spouse in meeting the two-year test. This provision applies only to gains; losses on residences, like those of other personal-use assets, are not recognized for tax purposes.

DIGGING DEEPER 14 15 16

Find more information on this topic at our Web site: ***http://wft-entities.swlearning.com.***

Transfers of Property between Spouses or Incident to Divorce—§ 1041

Section 1041 provides for nontaxable exchange treatment on property transfers *between spouses during marriage.* The basis to the recipient spouse is a carryover basis.

Section 1041 also provides that transfers of property *between spouses or former spouses incident to divorce* are nontaxable transactions. Therefore, the basis to the recipient is a carryover basis. To be treated as incident to the divorce, the transfer must be related to the cessation of marriage or must occur within one year after the date on which the marriage ceases.

Suggested Further Readings

Robert A. Briskin, "Like-Kind Exchanges—Common Problems and Solutions," *The Tax Adviser*, April 2005, pp. 204–213.

Steven Dilley, "Tax Planning for the Sale of a Principal Residence (Part I)," *The Tax Adviser*, January 2004, pp. 30–34.

Steven Dilley, "Tax Planning for the Sale of a Principal Residence (Part II)," *The Tax Adviser*, February 2004, pp. 90–94.

"IRS Approves 1031 Exchange of Water Rights for Farmland," *Journal of Taxation*, June 2004, pp. 370–371.

KEY TERMS

Adjusted basis, 7–4
Amount realized, 7–3
Boot, 7–24
Fair market value, 7–3
Goodwill, 7–10
Holding period, 7–13
Involuntary conversion, 7–28
Like-kind exchanges, 7–21
Nontaxable exchange, 7–21
Realized gain, 7–3
Realized loss, 7–3
Recognized gain, 7–7
Recognized loss, 7–7
Recovery of capital doctrine, 7–8
Wash sale, 7–17

PROBLEM MATERIALS

PROBLEMS

1. If a taxpayer sells property for cash, the amount realized consists of the net proceeds from the sale. For each of the following, indicate the effect on the amount realized:
   a. The property is sold on credit.
   b. A mortgage on the property is assumed by the buyer.
   c. The buyer acquires the property subject to a mortgage of the seller.
   d. The seller pays real property taxes that are treated as imposed on the purchaser.
   e. Stock that has a basis to the purchaser of $6,000 and a fair market value of $10,000 is received by the seller as part of the consideration.

2. Black, Inc., owns a building (adjusted basis of $375,000 on January 1) that it rents to Lapwing & Longspur, which operates a restaurant in the building. The municipal health department closed the restaurant for two months this year because of health code violations. Under MACRS, the cost recovery deduction for this year would be $24,000. However, Black deducted cost recovery only for the 10 months the restaurant was open since it waived the rent income during the two-month period the restaurant was closed.
   a. What is the amount of the cost recovery deduction that Black should report on this year's income tax return?
   b. Calculate the adjusted basis of the building at the end of this year.

3. Nina owns a personal-use boat that has a fair market value of $12,500 and an adjusted basis of $17,000. Nina's AGI is $60,000. Calculate the realized and recognized loss if:
   a. Nina sells the boat for $12,500.

b. Nina exchanges the boat for another boat worth $12,500.
c. The boat is stolen and Nina receives insurance proceeds of $12,500.

4. Hubert's personal residence is condemned as part of an urban renewal project. His adjusted basis for the residence is $325,000. He receives condemnation proceeds of $300,000 and invests the proceeds in stock.
   a. Calculate Hubert's realized and recognized gain or loss.
   b. If the condemnation proceeds are $355,000, what are Hubert's realized and recognized gain or loss?
   c. What are Hubert's realized and recognized gain or loss in (a) if the house was rental property?

Issue ID

5. A warehouse owned by Marmot & Squirrel (a partnership) and used in its business (i.e., to store inventory) is being condemned by the city to provide a right of way for a highway. The warehouse has appreciated by $100,000 based on an estimate of fair market value. In the negotiations, the city is offering $40,000 less than what Marmot & Squirrel believes the property is worth. Alan, a real estate broker, has offered to purchase the property for $25,000 more than the city's offer. The partnership plans to invest the proceeds it will receive in an office building that it will lease to various tenants. Identify the relevant tax issues for Marmot & Squirrel.

6. Finch, Inc., purchases 1,000 shares of Bluebird Corporation stock on October 3, 2006, for $200,000. On December 12, 2006, Finch purchases an additional 500 shares of Bluebird stock for $112,500. According to market quotations, Bluebird stock is selling for $240 per share on December 31, 2006. Finch sells 400 shares of Bluebird stock on March 1, 2007, for $100,000.
   a. What is the adjusted basis of Finch's Bluebird stock on December 31, 2006?
   b. What is Finch's recognized gain or loss from the sale of Bluebird stock on March 1, 2007, assuming the shares sold are from the shares purchased on December 12, 2006?
   c. What is Finch's recognized gain or loss from the sale of Bluebird stock on March 1, 2007, assuming Finch cannot adequately identify the shares sold?

Communications

7. Rod Mitchell purchases Agnes's sole proprietorship for $975,000 on August 15, 2006. The assets of the business are as follows:

Asset	Agnes's Adjusted Basis	FMV
Accounts receivable	$ 70,000	$ 70,000
Inventory	90,000	100,000
Equipment	150,000	160,000
Furniture and fixtures	95,000	130,000
Building	190,000	250,000
Land	25,000	75,000

Rod and Agnes agree that $50,000 of the purchase price is for Agnes's five-year covenant not to compete.
   a. Calculate Agnes's realized and recognized gain.
   b. Determine Rod's basis for each of the assets.
   c. Write a letter to Rod informing him of the tax consequences of the purchase. His address is 300 Riverview Drive, Delaware, OH 43015.

8. Juanita has decided to dispose of the following assets that she received as gifts:
   a. In 1990, she received land worth $62,000. The donor's adjusted basis was $75,000. Juanita sells the land for $58,000 this year.
   b. In 1996, she received stock worth $50,000. The donor's adjusted basis was $65,000. Juanita sells the stock this year for $59,000.

What is the recognized gain or loss from each of the preceding transactions? Assume in each transaction that no gift tax was paid.

9. Holly owns stock with an adjusted basis of $2,500 and fair market value of $9,500. Holly expects the stock to continue to appreciate. Alice, Holly's best friend, has recently been operated on for cancer. Alice's physicians have told her that her life expectancy is between six months and one and a half years. One day at lunch, the two friends were discussing their tax situations (both feel they pay too much), when Alice mentioned that she had read a newspaper article about a tax planning opportunity that might be suitable for Holly. Holly would make a gift of the appreciated stock to Alice. In her will, Alice would bequeath the stock back to Holly. Since Alice is confident that she will live longer than a year, the basis of the stock to Holly would be the fair market value on the date of Alice's death. Alice would "feel good" because she had helped Holly "beat the tax system." You are Holly's tax adviser. How will you respond to Alice's proposal? Would your response change if the stock were a painting that Alice could enjoy for her remaining days? *Ethics*

10. Beth receives a car from Sam as a gift. Sam paid $18,000 for the car. He had used it for business purposes and had deducted $8,000 for depreciation up to the time he gave the car to Beth. The fair market value of the car is $6,000.
    a. Assuming Beth uses the car for business purposes, what is her basis for depreciation?
    b. If the estimated useful life is two years (from the date of the gift), what is her depreciation deduction for each year? Use the straight-line method.
    c. If Beth sells the car for $900 one year after receiving it, what is her gain or loss?
    d. If Beth sells the car for $6,000 one year after receiving it, what is her gain or loss?

11. In 2006, Felix receives a gift of property with a fair market value of $111,000 (adjusted basis to the donor of $40,000). Assume the donor paid gift tax of $30,000 on the transfer.
    a. What is Felix's basis for gain and loss and for depreciation?
    b. If the gift occurred in 1975, what is Felix's basis for gain and loss and for depreciation?

12. Simon, who is retired, owns Teal, Inc. stock that has declined in value since he purchased it. He has decided either to give the stock to his nephew, Fred, who is a high school teacher, or to sell the stock and give the proceeds to Fred. Because nearly all of his wealth is invested in tax-exempt bonds, Simon faces a 15% marginal tax rate. Fred will use the cash or the proceeds from his sale of the stock to make the down payment on the purchase of a house. Based on a recent conversation, Simon is aware that Fred is in the 25% marginal tax bracket. Identify the tax issues relevant to Simon in deciding whether to give the stock or the sale proceeds to Fred. *Issue ID*

13. On September 18, 2006, Gerald received land and a building from his Uncle Frank as a gift. Uncle Frank's adjusted basis and the fair market value at the date of the gift were as follows:

Asset	Adjusted Basis	FMV
Land	$100,000	$212,000
Building	80,000	100,000

    Uncle Frank paid gift tax of $45,000.
    a. Determine Gerald's adjusted basis for the land and building.
    b. Assume instead that the fair market value of the land was $87,000 and that of the building was $65,000. Determine Gerald's adjusted basis for the land and building.

14. Catherine died in March 2006 leaving real estate (adjusted basis of $500,000) to her niece, Amanda. The fair market value of the real estate at the date of Catherine's death is $1,825,000. The executor of the estate does not distribute the real estate to Amanda until November 2006, when its fair market value is $1,813,000. The fair market value of the real estate six months after Catherine's death is $1,815,000.
    a. What are the possibilities as to Amanda's adjusted basis in the real estate?
    b. What purpose does the alternate valuation date serve?
    c. Assume instead that the fair market value six months after Catherine's death is $1,860,000. What is Amanda's basis in the real estate?

15. Dan bought a hotel for $2,600,000 in January 2003. In May 2006, he died and left the hotel to Ed. Dan had deducted $289,000 of cost recovery on the hotel before his death. The fair market value in May 2006 was $2,800,000. The fair market value six months later was $2,850,000.
    a. What is the basis of the property to Ed?
    b. What is the basis of the property to Ed if the fair market value six months later was $2,500,000 and the objective of the executor was to minimize the estate tax liability?

16. Sheila sells land to Elane, her sister, for the fair market value of $40,000. Six months later when the land is worth $42,000, Elane gives it to Jacob, her son. No gift taxes are paid. Shortly thereafter, Jacob sells the land for $43,000.
    a. Assuming Sheila's adjusted basis for the land is $25,000, what are Sheila's and Jacob's recognized gain or loss on their respective sales?
    b. Assuming Sheila's adjusted basis for the land is $50,000, what are Sheila's and Jacob's recognized gain or loss on their respective sales?

Decision Making

17. Justin owns 1,000 shares of Oriole Corporation common stock (adjusted basis of $9,800). On April 27, 2006, he sells 300 of these shares for $2,800. On May 5, 2006, Justin purchases 200 shares of Oriole Corporation common stock for $2,500.
    a. What is Justin's recognized gain or loss resulting from these transactions?
    b. What is Justin's basis for the stock acquired on May 5?
    c. Could Justin have obtained different tax consequences in (a) and (b) if he had sold the 300 shares on December 27, 2006, and purchased the 200 shares on January 5, 2007?

18. Jeffrey leaves a public accounting firm to enter private practice. He had bought a home two years earlier for $300,000 (ignore land). When starting his business, he converts one-fourth of the home into an office. The fair market value of the home on the date of the conversion (January 1, 2001) is $350,000, while the adjusted basis remains at $300,000. Jeffery lives and works in the home for six years and sells it at the end of the sixth year. He deducted $11,400 of cost recovery (using the statutory percentage method). How much gain or loss is recognized if Jeffrey sells the home for:
    a. $280,000?
    b. $400,000?

Extender

19. Surendra's personal residence originally cost $180,000 (ignore land). After living in the house for five years, he converts it to rental property. At the date of conversion, the fair market value of the house is $150,000. As to the rental property, calculate Surendra's basis for:
    a. Loss.
    b. Depreciation.
    c. Gain.

20. Heron Industries, Inc., owns undeveloped land with an adjusted basis of $212,000. Heron exchanges this land for other undeveloped land worth $290,000.
    a. What are Heron's realized and recognized gain or loss?
    b. What is Heron's basis in the undeveloped land it receives?

Decision Making
Communications

21. Tex Watson owns undeveloped land (basis of $350,000) held as an investment. On October 7, 2006, he exchanges the land with his 27-year-old daughter, Porchia, for other undeveloped land also to be held as an investment. The appraised value of Porchia's land is $500,000.
    a. On February 15, 2007, Tex sells the land to Baxter, a real estate broker, for $600,000. Calculate Tex's realized and recognized gain or loss from the exchange with Porchia and on the subsequent sale of the land to Baxter.
    b. Calculate Tex's realized and recognized gain or loss on the exchange with Porchia if Tex does not sell the land. Instead, on February 15, 2007, Porchia sells the land received from Tex. Calculate Tex's basis for the land on October 7, 2006, and on February 15, 2007.
    c. Write a letter to Tex advising him on how he could avoid any recognition of gain associated with the October 7, 2006 exchange. His address is The Corral, El Paso, TX 79968.

22. Starling Corporation owns a computer with an adjusted basis of $3,000. Starling exchanges the computer and cash of $5,000 for a laser printer worth $14,000.
    a. Calculate Starling's recognized gain or loss on the exchange.
    b. Calculate its basis for the printer.

23. Ivyway, Inc., owns a machine (adjusted basis of $60,000; fair market value of $95,000) that it uses in its business. The company exchanges it for another machine (worth $70,000) and stock (worth $25,000). Determine Ivyway's:
    a. Realized and recognized gain or loss on the exchange.
    b. Basis in the new machine.
    c. Basis in the stock it received.

24. Tulip, Inc., would like to dispose of some land that it acquired four years ago because the land will not continue to appreciate. Its value has increased by $50,000 over the four-year period. The company also intends to sell stock that has declined in value by $50,000 during the six months since its purchase. Tulip has four offers to acquire the stock and land:

Issue ID

Buyer number 1: Exchange land.
Buyer number 2: Purchase land for cash.
Buyer number 3: Exchange stock.
Buyer number 4: Purchase stock for cash.

Identify the tax issues relevant to Tulip in disposing of this land and stock.

25. What is the basis of the new property in each of the following exchanges?
    a. Apartment building held for investment (adjusted basis, $145,000) for office building to be held for investment (fair market value, $225,000).
    b. Land and building used as a barber shop (adjusted basis, $190,000) for land and building used as a grocery store (fair market value, $350,000).
    c. Office building (adjusted basis, $45,000) for bulldozer (fair market value, $42,000), both held for business use.
    d. IBM common stock (adjusted basis, $20,000) for ExxonMobil common stock (fair market value, $28,000).
    e. Rental house (adjusted basis, $90,000) for mountain cabin to be held for personal use (fair market value, $225,000).

26. Hyacinth Realty Company owns land in Iowa that was originally purchased for $130,000. Hyacinth has received an all-cash offer in the amount of $400,000 from a well-known shopping center developer. An international real estate broker has now offered some land located outside Florence, Italy, that is worth $400,000 in exchange for the Iowa property. Please write the company a letter analyzing these options from a tax standpoint. Hyacinth's address is 2501 Longview Lane, Des Moines, IA 50311.

Decision Making

Communications

27. Normandy Company owns Machine A (adjusted basis of $12,000; fair market value of $18,000), which it uses in its business. Normandy is considering two options for the disposal of Machine A. Under the first option, it will transfer Machine A and $3,000 cash to Joan, a dealer, in exchange for Machine B (fair market value of $21,000). Under the second option, Normandy will sell Machine A for $18,000 to Tim, another dealer, and then purchase Machine B from Joan for $21,000. Machines A and B qualify as like-kind property.
    a. Calculate Normandy's recognized gain or loss and the basis of Machine B under the first option.
    b. Calculate Normandy's recognized gain or loss and the basis of Machine B under the second option.
    c. Advise Normandy on which option is preferable.

Decision Making

28. Cardinal Properties, Inc., exchanges real estate held for investment plus stock for real estate to be held for investment. The stock transferred has an adjusted basis of $30,000 and a fair market value of $20,000. The real estate transferred has an adjusted basis of $30,000 and a fair market value of $90,000. The real estate acquired has a fair market value of $110,000.
    a. What is Cardinal's realized gain or loss?
    b. Its recognized gain or loss?
    c. The basis of the newly acquired real estate?

Decision Making

29. Avocet Management Company exchanges a warehouse and the related land with Indigo, Inc., for an office building and the related land. Avocet's adjusted basis for the warehouse and land is $420,000. The fair market value of Indigo's office building and land is $410,000. Avocet's property has a $90,000 mortgage that Indigo assumes.
    a. Calculate Avocet's realized and recognized gain or loss.
    b. Calculate Avocet's adjusted basis for the office building and land received.
    c. As an alternative, Indigo has proposed that rather than assuming the mortgage, it will transfer cash of $90,000 to Avocet, which would use the cash to pay off the mortgage. Advise Avocet on whether this alternative would be beneficial to it from a tax perspective.

30. Determine the realized, recognized, and postponed gain or loss and the new basis for each of the following like-kind exchanges:

	Adjusted Basis of Old Asset	Boot Given	Fair Market Value of New Asset	Boot Received
a.	$ 7,000	$ –0–	$12,000	$4,000
b.	14,000	2,000	15,000	–0–
c.	3,000	7,000	8,000	500
d.	22,000	–0–	32,000	–0–
e.	10,000	–0–	11,000	1,000
f.	10,000	–0–	8,000	–0–

31. Turquoise Realty Company owns an apartment house that has an adjusted basis of $950,000 but is subject to a mortgage of $240,000. Turquoise transfers the apartment house to Dove, Inc., and receives from Dove $150,000 in cash and an office building with a fair market value of $975,000 at the time of the exchange. Dove assumes the $240,000 mortgage on the apartment house.
    a. What is Turquoise's realized gain or loss?
    b. What is its recognized gain or loss?
    c. What is the basis of the newly acquired office building?

32. For each of the following involuntary conversions, indicate whether the property acquired qualifies as replacement property, the recognized gain, and the basis for the property acquired:
    a. A warehouse is destroyed by a tornado. The space in the warehouse was rented to various tenants. The adjusted basis was $470,000. The owner of the warehouse uses all of the insurance proceeds of $700,000 to build a shopping mall in a neighboring community where no property has been damaged by tornadoes. The shopping mall is rented to various tenants.
    b. A warehouse is destroyed by fire. The adjusted basis is $300,000. Because of economic conditions in the area, the owner decides not to rebuild the warehouse. Instead, it uses all of the insurance proceeds of $400,000 to build a warehouse in another state.
    c. Swallow Fashions, Inc., owns a building that is destroyed by a hurricane. The adjusted basis is $250,000. Because of an economic downturn in the area caused by the closing of a military base, Swallow decides to rent space for its retail outlet rather than to replace the building. It uses all of the insurance proceeds of $300,000 to buy a four-unit apartment building in another city. A realtor in that city will handle the rental of the apartments.
    d. Susan and Rick's personal residence is destroyed by a tornado. The adjusted basis was $170,000. Since they would like to travel, they decide not to acquire a replacement residence. Instead, they invest all of the insurance proceeds of $200,000 in a duplex, which they rent to tenants.

Ethics

33. The City of Richmond is going to condemn some buildings to build a park. Steve's principal residence is among those to be condemned. His adjusted basis for the house and land is $120,000. The appraised value of the house and land is $104,000. Steve is unaware of the future condemnation proceedings, but would like his family to move to a better neighborhood. Therefore, when Ross, a realtor, mentions that he may have a corporate client who would like to purchase the property for $130,000, Steve is ecstatic and indicates a willingness to sell.

    Ross is having some "second thoughts" about his conversation with Steve. The potential corporate purchaser is a company owned by Ross and his wife. Ross is aware of the future condemnation proceedings. He considers himself a skilled negotiator and thinks he can negotiate a $260,000 price for the house. Ross is considering telling Steve that the corporate client has changed its mind. Ross would then indicate that he has learned the city will be condemning several buildings in order to create a park, but has not yet established the prices it will pay for the condemned property. He would also tell Steve that because he believes he can get more from the city than Steve would obtain, he is willing to gamble and purchase the property now from Steve for $130,000.

Ross will point out several benefits available to Steve. These include (1) not having to deal with the city, (2) receiving an amount that exceeds both the appraised value and the original purchase cost of the home, and (3) receiving the money now. While admitting that he could reap a substantial profit, Ross would emphasize that he would also be taking on substantial risks. In addition, Ross would explain that when he sells the property to the city, he will defer the taxes by reinvesting the sales proceeds (due to involuntary conversion).

Should Ross make a new proposal to Steve based on his "second thoughts"? How do you think Steve will respond?

34. Lark Corporation's office building is destroyed by a hurricane in September. The adjusted basis is $210,000. Lark receives insurance proceeds of $390,000 in October.
   a. Calculate Lark's realized gain or loss, recognized gain or loss, and basis for the replacement property if it acquires an office building for $390,000 in October.
   b. Calculate Lark's realized gain or loss, recognized gain or loss, and basis for the replacement property if it acquires a warehouse for $350,000 in October.
   c. Calculate Lark's realized gain or loss and recognized gain or loss if it does not acquire replacement property.

35. Magenta, Inc.'s warehouse, which has an adjusted basis of $300,000 and a fair market value of $420,000, is condemned by an agency of the Federal government to make way for a highway interchange. The initial condemnation offer is $400,000. After substantial negotiations, the agency agrees to transfer to Magenta a surplus warehouse that it believes is worth $420,000. *Decision Making*
   a. What are the recognized gain or loss and the basis of the replacement warehouse if Magenta's objective is to recognize as much gain as possible?
   b. Advise Magenta regarding what it needs to do by what date in order to achieve its objective.

36. What are the *maximum* postponed gain or loss and the basis for the replacement property for the following involuntary conversions?

	Property	Type of Conversion	Amount Realized	Adjusted Basis	Amount Reinvested
a.	Drugstore (business)	Condemned	$160,000	$120,000	$100,000
b.	Apartments (investment)	Casualty	100,000	120,000	200,000
c.	Grocery store (business)	Casualty	400,000	300,000	350,000
d.	Residence (personal)	Casualty	16,000	18,000	17,000
e.	Vacant lot (investment)	Condemned	240,000	160,000	240,000
f.	Residence (personal)	Casualty	20,000	18,000	19,000
g.	Residence (personal)	Condemned	18,000	20,000	26,000
h.	Apartments (investment)	Condemned	150,000	100,000	200,000

37. Milton, who is single, listed his personal residence with a realtor on March 3, 2006, at a price of $250,000. He rejected several offers in the $200,000 range during the summer. Finally, on August 16, 2006, he and the purchaser signed a contract to sell for $245,000. The sale (i.e., closing) took place on September 7, 2006. The closing statement showed the following disbursements: *Extender*

Realtor's commission	$ 14,000
Appraisal fee	500
Exterminator's certificate	300
Recording fees	400
Mortgage to First Bank	180,000
Cash to seller	49,800

Milton's adjusted basis for the house is $150,000. He owned and occupied the house for eight years. On October 1, 2006, Milton purchases another residence for $210,000.

a. Calculate Milton's recognized gain on the sale.
b. What is Milton's adjusted basis for the new residence?
c. Assume instead that the selling price is $735,000. What is Milton's recognized gain? His adjusted basis for the new residence?

Extender

Decision Making

38. Jeff and Jill are divorced on August 1, 2006. According to the terms of the divorce decree, Jeff's ownership interest in the house is to be transferred to Jill in exchange for the release of marital rights. The house was separately owned by Jeff and on the date of the transfer has an adjusted basis of $175,000 and a fair market value of $200,000.
    a. Does the transfer cause recognized gain to either Jeff or Jill?
    b. What is the basis of the house to Jill?
    c. If instead Jeff sold the house to Jill for $200,000 two months prior to the divorce, would either Jeff or Jill have recognized gain?
    d. Which transaction, (a) or (c), would be preferable for Jeff?

BRIDGE *Discipline*

1. In April of the current year, Blue Corporation purchased an asset to be used in its manufacturing operations for $100,000. Blue's management expects the asset to ratably provide valuable services in the production process for eight years and have a salvage value of $12,000. The asset is a five-year asset for tax purposes. Blue has adopted the half-year convention for book purposes in the year of acquisition and disposition; Blue uses MACRS for tax purposes.
    a. Compute the depreciation expense in the year of acquisition for book and tax purposes.
    b. Identify the book-tax difference related to the depreciation expense in the year of acquisition.

2. Refer to the facts in the preceding problem. Assume Blue Corporation disposes of the manufacturing asset at the beginning of year seven for $40,000. Compute the amount of gain or loss recognized for book and tax purposes. What is the book-tax difference in the year of disposition?

3. Identify whether the taxpayer's economic position has changed in the following exchanges such that they are subject to current taxation. That is, identify whether the following qualify as like-kind exchanges under § 1031.
    a. Improved for unimproved real estate.
    b. Vending machine (used in business) for inventory.
    c. Rental house for personal residence.
    d. Business equipment for securities.
    e. Warehouse for office building (both used for business).
    f. Truck for computer (both used in business).
    g. Rental house for land (both held for investment).
    h. Ten shares of stock in Blue Corporation for 10 shares of stock in Red Corporation.
    i. Office furniture for office equipment (both used in business).
    j. Unimproved land in Jackson, Mississippi, for unimproved land in Toledo, Spain.

RESEARCH PROBLEMS

Note: Solutions to Research Problems can be prepared by using the **RIA Checkpoint®** **Student Edition** online research product, which is available to accompany this text. It is also possible to prepare solutions to the Research Problems by using tax research materials found in a standard tax library.

Research Problem 1. Abner gives stock worth $400,000 to Hattie. Abner's adjusted basis in the stock is $95,000, and the gift taxes generated as a result of the transfer are $122,400.

As a condition for receiving the stock, Hattie agrees to pay the gift tax. The stock is transferred to Hattie on February 5, 2006.

a. What are the income tax consequences to Abner?
b. What are the income tax consequences to Abner if the gift was made on February 5, 1981?

Research Problem 2. Asa operated his business in a building on Mason Drive. Due to changing residential housing patterns in the city, he decided to move the business to a new location on Leigh Lane. His adjusted basis for the Mason Drive property is $120,000, and the fair market value is $500,000. He purchased the Leigh Lane property for $500,000 on September 1, 2006. Asa quitclaimed title to the Leigh Lane property to Ivory Enterprises on September 1, 2006, in exchange for a nonrecourse and non-interest-bearing single payment note for $500,000 (to be paid at the second closing). Ivory was to have a building constructed on the Leigh Lane property in accordance with specifications provided by Asa. The construction of the building was financed by a $700,000 note that was guaranteed by Asa and was nonrecourse to Ivory.

Another agreement provided that Asa would convey the Mason Drive property to Ivory on completion of the building in exchange for the Leigh Lane property and the new building. At that time, Asa would assume the $700,000 note.

On December 1, the Leigh Lane property was conveyed to Asa, the Mason Drive property was conveyed to Ivory, and Ivory paid the $500,000 note to Asa (the second closing). Asa assumed the $700,000 note associated with the construction and reported his recognized gain as follows:

	Exchange of Mason Drive	Sale of Leigh Lane
Amount realized	$ 500,000	$ 1,210,000
Basis	(120,000)	(1,200,000)
Realized gain	$ 380,000	$ 10,000
Recognized gain	$ -0-*	$ 10,000

*§ 1031 like-kind exchange.

An IRS agent treated the transactions as the sale of the Mason Drive property and a § 1031 exchange of the Leigh Lane property, producing a recognized gain of $380,000 rather than $10,000.

Evaluate the position of the IRS and of Asa.

Research Problem 3. Brown Construction, Inc., is in the road construction business. Brown exchanges a grader used in its business and $45,000 in cash for a scraper to be used in its business. The adjusted basis of the grader is $50,000, and the fair market value of the scraper is $102,000. What are the tax consequences to Brown of the exchange?

Use the tax resources of the Internet to address the following questions. Do not restrict your search to the World Wide Web, but include a review of newsgroups and general reference materials, practitioner sites and resources, primary sources of the tax law, chat rooms and discussion groups, and other opportunities.

Internet *Activity*

Research Problem 4. A number of public policy think tanks, taxpayer unions, and other private interest groups have proposed changes to the tax rules that apply to like-kind exchanges of realty. Summarize several of these proposals, including your assessment of the motivations underlying the suggested changes.

Research Problem 5. When taxpayers sell some of their mutual fund shares, they may compute their basis in the shares sold by utilizing the specific identification method. Go to the site of an investment adviser or mutual fund to find instructions on how to apply the specific identification method. What other options are described in the information you find? Illustrate each of the alternatives.

http://wft.swlearning.com

CHAPTER 8

Property Transactions: Capital Gains and Losses, Section 1231, and Recapture Provisions

LEARNING OBJECTIVES

After completing Chapter 8, you should be able to:

LO.1
Distinguish capital assets from ordinary assets.

LO.2
Understand the relevance of a sale or exchange to classification as a capital gain or loss.

LO.3
Determine the applicable holding period for a capital asset.

LO.4
Describe the tax treatment of capital gains and losses for noncorporate taxpayers.

LO.5
Describe the tax treatment of capital gains and losses for corporate taxpayers.

LO.6
Distinguish § 1231 assets from ordinary and capital assets, and calculate § 1231 gain or loss.

LO.7
Determine when recapture provisions apply and derive their effects.

OUTLINE

TAX *Talk*

Governments likely to confiscate wealth are unlikely to find much wealth to confiscate in the long run.

—Thomas Sowell

General Considerations

Rationale for Separate Reporting of Capital Gains and Losses

Since the earliest days of the Federal income tax, **capital assets** have received special treatment upon their disposition. Gains from these assets have historically received *preferential treatment* in the form of either partial exclusion of gain, lower rates, or a maximum tax rate. Losses from capital assets, however, have historically received less desirable treatment than losses from other assets. Further, because a taxpayer has complete control over the timing of dispositions, the Code imposes limitations on when capital losses can be deducted to prevent taxpayers from manipulating their tax liability excessively.

During World War II, capital asset treatment was extended to other assets. These assets are now called "§ 1231 assets" after the Code Section that prescribes their special treatment. Several years after World War II ended, Congress believed that this special treatment was no longer entirely warranted. Instead of repealing § 1231, however, Congress left that section in place but eroded many—but not all—of its benefits through *recapture provisions* in § 1245 and § 1250. Together, these Code Sections constitute one of the most complicated areas of tax law affecting both individual taxpayers and business entities.

TAX *in the News* **AVOIDING A RECOGNIZED GAIN**

Until recently the New York Stock Exchange (NYSE) was not a corporation. Instead, it was a partnership owned by its members. A membership in the NYSE was sold for $3 million during 2005. In early 2006, the NYSE merged with Archipelago Holdings, Inc. The members of the NYSE exchanged their membership interests in the NYSE for shares in the new corporation resulting from the merger of these two entities. If proper tax planning was done, the NYSE members did not have a *recognized* gain or loss from this transaction.

As already intimated, one concern is that taxpayers can time the realization of gains and losses by choosing when or even whether to sell the asset in question. If Lark Enterprises, Inc., owns stock with a basis of $20 per share and a current value of $80 per share, it does not pay tax on the $60 gain until it chooses to dispose of this stock in a taxable transaction. And for the most part, Lark has complete control over that decision. When it does dispose of the stock, however, its $60 gain is taxable in full, even though this gain may have accrued over many years. To mitigate the impact of this *bunching* of income in a single year and to offset the effect of inflation over the period of Lark's ownership of the stock, preferential treatment is prescribed for this **capital gain**.

The nature of this preferential treatment is discussed later in this chapter, but the essential point for now is that preferential treatment is confined to the excess of net long-term capital gains over net short-term **capital losses**. This cumbersome description requires taxpayers to separate their capital asset transactions from their transactions involving noncapital assets. It further requires taxpayers to separate their long-term (i.e., more than one year) transactions from their short-term (i.e., one year or less) transactions. Moreover, certain types of capital assets (principally real estate and "collectibles") receive specific treatment apart from the rates generally applicable to capital assets.

General Scheme of Taxation

Recognized gains and losses must be properly classified. Proper classification depends upon three characteristics.

- The tax status of the property, including the specific type of asset.
- The manner of the property's disposition.
- The holding period of the property.

The three possible tax statuses are capital asset, § 1231 asset, and ordinary asset. Property disposition may be by sale, exchange, casualty, theft, or condemnation. The two relevant holding periods are one year or less (short term) and more than one year (long term).

Capital Assets

LO.1

Distinguish capital assets from ordinary assets.

Definition of a Capital Asset

Investments comprise the most typical category of capital assets and include corporate stocks and bonds, mutual funds, partnership interests, government securities, and vacant land. These assets can be held by any type of taxpayer—individuals, partnerships, limited liability companies, and corporations, whether closely held or publicly held. In addition, individuals own certain capital assets that are part of their daily life, such as residences, automobiles, furniture, and artwork. The classification of these *personal-use* assets as capital assets is relevant only when their disposition produces a recognized gain. Losses from the disposition of personal-use assets are not recognized for tax purposes, as explained in the preceding chapter. For businesses, goodwill is often the only capital asset.

Capital assets are not directly defined in the Code. Instead, § 1221(a) defines what is *not* a capital asset. A capital asset is property held by the taxpayer that is *not* any of the following.

- Inventory or property held primarily for sale to customers in the ordinary course of a business. The Supreme Court, in *Malat v. Riddell,*[1] defined *primarily* as meaning *of first importance* or *principally.*
- Accounts and notes receivable acquired from the sale of inventory or acquired for services rendered in the ordinary course of business.
- Depreciable property or real estate used in a business.
- Certain copyrights; literary, musical, or artistic compositions; or letters, memoranda, or similar property held by (1) a taxpayer whose efforts created the property; (2) in the case of a letter, memorandum, or similar property, a taxpayer for whom it was produced; or (3) a taxpayer who received the property as a lifetime gift from someone described in (1) or (2).
- U.S. government publications that are (1) received by a taxpayer from the U.S. government other than by purchase at the price at which they are offered for sale to the public or (2) held by a taxpayer who received the publication as a lifetime gift from someone described in (1).
- Supplies of a type regularly used or consumed in the ordinary course of a business.

Inventory. What constitutes inventory is determined by reference to the taxpayer's business.

EXAMPLE 1

Green Company buys and sells used cars. Its cars are inventory. Its gains from the sale of the cars are ordinary income. ■

EXAMPLE 2

Soong sells her personal-use automobile at a $500 gain. The automobile is a personal-use asset and, therefore, a capital asset. The gain is a capital gain. ■

No asset is inherently capital or ordinary. If Soong in Example 2 sells her capital asset automobile to Green Company in Example 1, that very same automobile loses its capital asset status, because it is inventory to Green Company. Similar transformations can occur if, for example, an art dealer sells a painting (inventory; *not* a capital asset) to a private collector (now a capital asset). Whether an asset is capital or ordinary, therefore, depends entirely on the relationship of *that asset* to the taxpayer who sold it. This classification dilemma is but one feature of capital asset treatment that makes this area so confusing and perennially complicated.

Accounts and Notes Receivable. Collection of an accrual basis account receivable usually does not result in a gain or loss because the amount collected equals the receivable's basis. The *sale* of an account or note receivable may generate a gain or loss, however, because it will probably be sold for more or less than its basis. That gain or loss will be ordinary because the receivable is not a capital asset. A cash basis account receivable has no basis, so sale of such a receivable generates a gain, and that gain is ordinary income. Collection of a cash basis receivable also generates ordinary income.

EXAMPLE 3

Oriole Company, an accrual basis taxpayer, has accounts receivable of $100,000. Revenue of $100,000 was recorded and a $100,000 basis was established when the receivable was created. Because Oriole needs working capital, it sells the receivables for $83,000 to a financial institu-

[1] 66–1 USTC ¶9317, 17 AFTR2d 604, 86 S.Ct. 1030 (USSC, 1966).

tion. Accordingly, it has a $17,000 ordinary loss. If Oriole is a cash basis taxpayer, it has $83,000 of ordinary income because it would not have recorded any revenue earlier and the receivable would have no tax basis. ■

Business Fixed Assets. Depreciable personal property and real estate (both depreciable and nondepreciable) used by a business are not capital assets. Thus, *business fixed assets* are not capital assets. Business fixed assets can sometimes be treated as capital assets pursuant to § 1231, however, as discussed later in this chapter.

Copyrights and Creative Works. Generally, the person whose efforts led to the copyright or creative work has an ordinary asset, not a capital asset. This rule makes the creator comparable to a taxpayer whose customary activity (salary, business profits) is taxed as ordinary income. *Creative works* include the works of authors, composers, and artists. Also, the person for whom a letter, memorandum, or other similar property was created has an ordinary asset. Finally, a person receiving a copyright, creative work, letter, memorandum, or similar property by lifetime gift from the creator or the person for whom the work was created also has an ordinary asset.

EXAMPLE 4

Wanda is a part-time music composer. A music publisher purchases one of her songs for $5,000. Wanda has a $5,000 ordinary gain from the sale of an ordinary asset. ■

EXAMPLE 5

Ed received a letter from the President of the United States in 1994. In the current year, Ed sells the letter to a collector for $300. Ed has a $300 ordinary gain from the sale of an ordinary asset (because the letter was created for Ed). ■

EXAMPLE 6

Isabella gives a song she composed to her son. Her son sells the song to a music publisher for $5,000. Her son has a $5,000 ordinary gain from the sale of an ordinary asset. If he inherits the song from Isabella, his basis for the song is its fair market value at Isabella's death. The song is a capital asset because the son's basis is not related to Isabella's basis for the song (i.e., the song was not a *lifetime* gift). ■

U.S. Government Publications. U.S. government publications received from the U.S. government (or its agencies) for a reduced price are not capital assets. This prevents a taxpayer from later donating the publications to charity and claiming a charitable contribution equal to the fair market value of the publications. A charitable contribution of a capital asset generally yields a deduction equal to the asset's fair market value. If such property is received by gift from the original purchaser, the property is not a capital asset to the donee. (For a more comprehensive explanation of charitable contributions of property, refer to Chapter 5.)

Statutory Expansions

Because of the uncertainty often associated with capital asset status, Congress has occasionally enacted Code Sections to clarify the definition in particular circumstances. These statutory expansions of the capital asset definition are discussed in this section.

DIGGING DEEPER 1

Find more information on this topic at our Web site: ***http://wft-entities.swlearning.com.***

Dealers in Securities. As a general rule, securities (stocks, bonds, and other financial instruments) held by a dealer are considered to be inventory and are, therefore, not subject to capital gain or loss treatment. A *dealer in securities* is a merchant (e.g., a brokerage firm) that regularly engages in the purchase and resale of securities to customers. However, under the following circumstances, a dealer will have capital gain or capital loss. If a dealer clearly identifies certain securities as held for investment purposes by the close of business on the acquisition date, gain from the securities' sale will be capital gain. The gain will be ordinary if the dealer ceases to hold the securities for investment prior to the sale. Losses are capital losses if at any time the securities have been clearly identified by the dealer as held for investment.[2]

DIGGING DEEPER 2

Find more information on this topic at our Web site: ***http://wft-entities.swlearning.com.***

Real Property Subdivided for Sale. Substantial real property development activities may result in the owner being considered a dealer for tax purposes. If so, income from the sale of real estate property lots will be treated as the sale of inventory and therefore will be taxed as ordinary income. However, § 1237 allows real estate investors to claim capital gain treatment if they engage *only* in *limited* development activities. To be eligible for § 1237 treatment, the following requirements must be met.

- The taxpayer is not a corporation.
- The taxpayer is not a real estate dealer.
- No substantial improvements have been made to the lots sold. *Substantial* generally means more than a 10 percent increase in the value of a lot. Shopping centers and other commercial or residential buildings are considered substantial, while filling, draining, leveling, and clearing operations are not.
- The taxpayer has held the lots sold for at least 5 years, except for inherited property. The substantial improvements test is less stringent if the property is held at least 10 years.

If the preceding requirements are met, all gain is capital gain until the taxable year in which the *sixth* lot is sold. Sales of contiguous lots to a single buyer in the same transaction count as the sale of one lot. Beginning with the taxable year in which the *sixth* lot is sold, 5 percent of the revenue from lot sales is potential ordinary income. That potential ordinary income is offset by any selling expenses from the lot sales. Practically, sales commissions often are at least 5 percent of the sales price, so usually none of the gain is treated as ordinary income.

Section 1237 does not apply to losses. A loss from the sale of subdivided real property is ordinary loss unless the property qualifies as a capital asset under § 1221. The following example illustrates the application of § 1237.

EXAMPLE 7

Ahmed owns a large tract of land and subdivides it for sale. Assume Ahmed meets all the requirements of § 1237 and during the tax year sells the first 10 lots to 10 different buyers for $10,000 each. Ahmed's basis in each lot sold is $3,000, and he incurs total selling expenses of $4,000 on the sales. Ahmed's gain is computed as follows.

Selling price (10 × $10,000)	$100,000	
Less: Selling expenses (10 × $400)	(4,000)	
Amount realized		$ 96,000
Basis (10 × $3,000)		(30,000)
Realized and recognized gain		$ 66,000
Classification of recognized gain:		
Ordinary income		
Five percent of selling price (5% × $100,000)	$ 5,000	
Less: Selling expenses	(4,000)	
Ordinary gain		1,000
Capital gain		$ 65,000

■

[2]§§ 1236(a) and (b) and Reg. § 1.1236–1(a).

TAX *in the News* **KNOW YOUR LOSSES**

A local wealthy investor (single) recently lost her entire investment in a golf course development corporation. She had invested $250,000 in the corporation's stock several years ago. The golf course never opened because of environmental damage caused by its construction, and her stock became worthless. The local paper quoted the investor's comments on her bad luck: "My investment loss is only usable against capital gains and, since I do not have any such gains, I cannot deduct any of this loss." In reality, she may have qualified for the $50,000 ordinary loss deduction on § 1244 stock and the $3,000 per year capital loss deduction. Also, any unused capital losses carry forward and may be offset against future capital gains.

Sale or Exchange

LO.2

Understand the relevance of a sale or exchange to classification as a capital gain or loss.

Recognition of capital gain or loss usually requires a **sale or exchange** of a capital asset. The Code uses the term *sale or exchange*, but does not define it. Generally, a property sale involves the receipt of money by the seller and/or the assumption by the purchaser of the seller's liabilities. An exchange involves the transfer of property for other property. Thus, an involuntary conversion (casualty, theft, or condemnation) is not a sale or exchange. In several situations, the determination of whether or when a sale or exchange has taken place has been clarified by the enactment of Code Sections that specifically provide for sale or exchange treatment. These situations are discussed below.

Recognized gains or losses from the cancellation, lapse, expiration, or any other termination of a right or obligation with respect to personal property (other than stock) that is or would be a capital asset in the hands of the taxpayer are capital gains or losses.[3] See the discussion under Options later in the chapter for more details.

Worthless Securities and § 1244 Stock

Occasionally, securities such as stock and bonds may become worthless due to the insolvency of their issuer. If the security is a capital asset, the loss is deemed to have occurred as the result of a sale or exchange on the *last day* of the tax year.[4] This last-day rule may have the effect of converting a short-term capital loss into a long-term capital loss. See Capital Losses later in this chapter.

Section 1244 allows an *ordinary* deduction on disposition of stock at a loss. The stock must be that of a small business corporation, and the ordinary deduction is limited to $50,000 ($100,000 for married individuals filing jointly) per year.

Retirement of Corporate Obligations

A debt obligation (e.g., a bond or note payable) may have a tax basis different from its redemption value because it may have been acquired at a premium or discount. Consequently, the collection of the redemption value may result in a loss or a gain. Generally, the collection of a debt obligation is *treated* as a sale or exchange.[5] Therefore, any loss or gain is capital because a sale or exchange has taken place.

Find more information on this topic at our Web site: ***http://wft-entities.swlearning.com.***

DIGGING DEEPER 3

[3] § 1234A.
[4] § 165(g)(1).
[5] § 1271.

EXAMPLE 8

Osprey, Inc., purchases $1,000 of General Motors Corporation bonds for $1,020 in the open market. If the bonds are held to maturity, the $20 difference between Osprey's collection of the $1,000 redemption value and its cost of $1,020 is treated as capital loss. ■

Options

Frequently, a potential buyer of property wants to defer a final purchase decision, but wants to control the sale and/or the sale price in the meantime. **Options** are used to achieve such control. The potential purchaser (grantee) pays the property owner (grantor) for an option on the property. The grantee then becomes the option holder. An option usually sets the price at which a grantee can buy the property and expires after a specified period of time.

Sale of an Option. In addition to exercising an option or letting it expire, a grantee can often arrange for its sale or exchange. Such a sale or exchange generally results in capital gain or loss if the option property is (or would be) a capital asset to the grantee.[6]

EXAMPLE 9

Robin & Associates wants to buy some vacant land for investment purposes, but cannot afford the full purchase price. Instead, the firm convinces the landowner (grantor) to sell it the right to purchase the land for $100,000 anytime in the next two years. Robin & Associates (grantee) pays $3,000 for this option to buy the land. The option is a capital asset to Robin because if the firm actually purchased the land (the option property), the land would be a capital asset. Three months after purchasing the option, Robin sells it for $7,000. The firm has a $4,000 ($7,000 – $3,000) capital gain on this sale. ■

Failure to Exercise Options. If an option holder (grantee) fails to exercise the option, the lapse of the option is considered a sale or exchange on the option expiration date. Thus, the resulting loss is a capital loss if the property subject to the option is (or would be) a capital asset in the hands of the grantee.

The grantor of an option on *stocks, securities, commodities, or commodity futures* receives short-term capital gain treatment upon the expiration of the option.[7] For example, an individual investor who owns stock (a capital asset) may sell a call option, entitling the buyer of the option to acquire the stock at a specified price higher than the stock's value at the date the option is granted. The writer of the call (the grantor) receives a premium for writing the option. If the price of the stock does not increase during the option period, the option will expire unexercised. Upon the expiration of the option, the grantor must recognize a short-term capital gain equal to the premium received. These provisions do not apply to options held for sale to customers (the inventory of a securities dealer).

Options on property *other than* stocks, securities, commodities, or commodity futures result in ordinary income to the grantor when the option expires. For instance, the landowner in the preceding example would have ordinary income of $3,000 if Robin (the grantee) had allowed the option to expire.

Exercise of Options by Grantee. If an option is exercised, the amount paid for the option is added to the optioned property's selling price. This increases the gain (or reduces the loss) to the grantor resulting from the sale of the property. The grantor's gain or loss is capital or ordinary depending on the tax status of the property. The grantee adds the cost of the option to the basis of the property purchased.

[6] § 1234(a) and Reg. § 1.1234–1(a)(1).

[7] § 1234(b)(1).

CONCEPT SUMMARY 8–1

Options

	Effect on	
Event	**Grantor**	**Grantee**
Option is granted.	Receives value and has a contract obligation (a liability).	Pays value and has a contract right (an asset).
Option expires.	Has a short-term capital gain if the option property is stocks, securities, commodities, or commodity futures. Otherwise, gain is ordinary income.	Has a loss (capital loss if option property would have been a capital asset for the grantee). Otherwise, loss is ordinary.
Option is exercised.	Amount received for option increases proceeds from sale of the option property.	Amount paid for option becomes part of the basis of the option property purchased.
Option is sold or exchanged by grantee.	Result depends upon whether option later expires or is exercised (see above).	Could have gain or loss (capital gain or loss if option property would have been a capital asset for the grantee).

EXAMPLE 10

Several years ago, Indigo, Inc., purchased 100 shares of Eagle Company stock for $5,000. On April 1 of this year, Indigo writes a call option on the stock, giving the grantee the right to buy the stock for $6,000 during the following six-month period. Indigo (the grantor) receives a call premium of $500 for writing the call.

- If the call is exercised by the grantee on August 1, Indigo has $1,500 ($6,000 + $500 – $5,000) of long-term capital gain from the sale of the stock. The grantee has a $6,500 ($500 option premium + $6,000 purchase price) basis for the stock.
- Assume that the option expired unexercised. Indigo has a $500 short-term capital gain equal to the call premium received for writing the option. This gain is not recognized until the option expires. The grantee has a loss from expiration of the option. The nature of that loss will depend upon whether the option was a capital asset or an ordinary asset in the hands of the grantee. ■

Patents

Transfer of a **patent** is treated as the sale or exchange of a long-term capital asset when *all substantial rights* to the patent (or an undivided interest that includes all such rights) are transferred by a *holder*.[8] The transferor/holder may receive payment in virtually any form. Lump-sum or periodic payments are most common. The amount of the payments may also be contingent on the transferee/purchaser's productivity, use, or disposition of the patent. If the transfer meets these requirements, any gain or loss is *automatically a long-term* capital gain or loss. Whether the asset was a capital asset for the transferor, whether a sale or exchange occurred, and how long the transferor held the patent are all irrelevant.

EXAMPLE 11

Mei-Yen, a druggist, invents a pill-counting machine, which she patents. In consideration of a lump-sum payment of $200,000 plus $10 per machine sold, Mei-Yen assigns the patent to Drug Products, Inc. Assuming Mei-Yen has transferred all substantial rights, she automatically

[8] § 1235.

has a long-term capital gain from both the lump-sum payment and the $10 per machine royalty to the extent these proceeds exceed her basis for the patent. ■

This special long-term capital gain or loss treatment for patents is intended to encourage technological development and scientific progress. In contrast, books, songs, and artists' works may be copyrighted, but copyrights and the assets they represent are not capital assets. Thus, the disposition of these assets by their creators usually results in ordinary gain or loss.

Substantial Rights. To receive favorable capital gain treatment, all *substantial rights* to the patent (or an undivided interest in it) must be transferred. All substantial rights to a patent means all rights that are valuable at the time the patent rights (or an undivided interest in the patent) are transferred. All substantial rights have not been transferred when the transfer is limited geographically within the issuing country or when the transfer is for a period less than the remaining legal life of the patent. The circumstances of the entire transaction, rather than merely the language used in the transfer instrument, are to be considered in deciding whether all substantial rights have been transferred.[9]

EXAMPLE 12

Assume Mei-Yen, the druggist in the preceding example, only licensed Drug Products, Inc., to manufacture and sell the invention in Michigan. She retained the right to license the machine elsewhere in the United States. Mei-Yen has retained a substantial right and is not eligible for automatic long-term capital gain treatment. ■

Holder Defined. The *holder* of a patent must be an *individual* and is usually the invention's creator. A holder may also be an individual who purchases the patent rights from the creator before the patented invention has been reduced to practice. However, the creator's employer and certain parties related to the creator do not qualify as holders. Thus, in the common situation where an employer has all rights to an employee's inventions, the employer is not eligible for long-term capital gain treatment. More than likely, the employer will have an ordinary asset because the patent was developed as part of its business.

Franchises, Trademarks, and Trade Names

A mode of operation, a widely recognized brand name (trade name), and a widely known business symbol (trademark) are all valuable assets. These assets may be licensed (commonly known as *franchising*) by their owner for use by other businesses. Many fast-food restaurants (such as McDonald's and Taco Bell) are franchises. The franchisee usually pays the owner (franchisor) an initial fee plus a contingent fee. The contingent fee is often based upon the franchisee's sales volume.

For Federal income tax purposes, a **franchise** is an agreement that gives the franchisee the right to distribute, sell, or provide goods, services, or facilities within a specified area.[10] A franchise transfer includes the grant of a franchise, a transfer by one franchisee to another person, or the renewal of a franchise.

Section 1253 provides that a transfer of a franchise, trademark, or trade name is *not* a sale or exchange of a capital asset when the transferor retains any significant power, right, or continuing interest in the property transferred.

DIGGING DEEPER 4

Find more information on this topic at our Web site: ***http://wft-entities.swlearning.com.***

Significant Power, Right, or Continuing Interest. *Significant powers, rights, or continuing interests* include control over assignment of the franchise, trademark,

[9]Reg. § 1.1235–2(b)(1).

[10]§ 1253(b)(1).

CONCEPT SUMMARY 8–2

Franchises

Event	Effect on: Franchisor	Effect on: Franchisee
Franchisor Retains Significant Powers and Rights		
Noncontingent payment	Ordinary income.	Capitalized and amortized over 15 years as an ordinary deduction; if franchise is sold, amortization is subject to recapture under § 1245.
Contingent payment	Ordinary income.	Ordinary deduction.
Franchisor Does *Not* Retain Significant Powers and Rights		
Noncontingent payment	Ordinary income if franchise rights are an ordinary asset; capital gain if franchise rights are a capital asset (unlikely).	Capitalized and amortized over 15 years as an ordinary deduction; if the franchise is sold, amortization is subject to recapture under § 1245.
Contingent payment	Ordinary income.	Ordinary deduction.

or trade name, as well as the quality of the transferee's products or services. The following rights also are included.

- Right to require the transferee to sell or advertise *only* the transferor's products or services.
- Right to require the transferee to purchase substantially all supplies and equipment from the transferor.
- Right to receive substantial contingent payments.
- Right to terminate the franchise, trademark, or trade name at will.

In the unusual case where no significant power, right, or continuing interest is retained by the transferor, a sale or exchange may occur, and capital gain or loss treatment may be available. For capital gain or loss treatment to be available, the asset transferred must still qualify as a capital asset.

EXAMPLE 13

Orange, Inc., a franchisee, sells the franchise to a third party. Payments to Orange are not contingent, and all significant powers, rights, and continuing interests are transferred. The gain (payments – adjusted basis) on the sale is a capital gain to Orange. ■

Noncontingent Payments. When the transferor retains a significant power, right, or continuing interest, the transferee's noncontingent payments to the transferor are ordinary income to the transferor. The franchisee capitalizes the payments and amortizes them over 15 years. The amortization is subject to recapture under § 1245, discussed later in this chapter.

EXAMPLE 14

Grey Company signs a 10-year franchise agreement with DOH Donuts. Grey (the franchisee) makes payments of $3,000 per year for the first 8 years of the franchise agreement—a total of $24,000. Grey cannot deduct $3,000 per year as the payments are made. Instead, Grey must amortize the $24,000 total over 15 years. Thus, Grey may deduct $1,600 per year for each of the 15 years of the amortization period. The same result would occur if Grey had made a $24,000 lump-sum payment at the beginning of the franchise period. Assuming DOH

Donuts (the franchisor) retains significant powers, rights, or a continuing interest, it will have ordinary income when it receives the payments from Grey. ■

Contingent Payments. Whether or not the transferor retains a significant power, right, or continuing interest, contingent franchise payments are ordinary income for the franchisor and an ordinary deduction for the franchisee.

EXAMPLE 15

TAK, a spicy chicken franchisor, transfers an eight-year franchise to Egret Corporation. TAK retains a significant power, right, or continuing interest. Egret, the franchisee, agrees to pay TAK 15% of sales. This contingent payment is ordinary income to TAK and a business deduction for Egret as the payments are made. ■

Lease Cancellation Payments

The tax treatment of payments received for canceling a lease depends on whether the recipient of the payments is the **lessor** or the **lessee** and whether the lease is a capital asset or not.

Lessee Treatment. Lease cancellation payments received by a lessee (the tenant) are treated as an exchange.[11] Thus, these payments are capital gains if the lease is a capital asset. Generally, a lessee's lease is a capital asset if the property (either personalty or realty) is used for the lessee's personal use (e.g., his or her residence). A lease held one year or less is an ordinary income asset if the property is used in the lessee's trade or business.[12]

EXAMPLE 16

Merganser, Inc., owns an apartment building that it is going to convert into an office building. Vicki is one of the apartment tenants and receives $1,000 from Merganser to cancel the lease. Vicki has a capital gain of $1,000 (which is long term or short term depending upon how long she has held the lease). Merganser has an ordinary deduction of $1,000. ■

Lessor Treatment. Payments received by a lessor (the landlord) for a lease cancellation are always ordinary income because they are considered to be in lieu of rental payments.[13]

EXAMPLE 17

Finch & Company owns an apartment building near a university campus. Hui-Fen is one of the tenants. Hui-Fen is graduating early and offers Finch $800 to cancel the apartment lease. Finch accepts the offer. Finch has ordinary income of $800. Hui-Fen has a nondeductible payment since the apartment was personal-use property. ■

LO.3

Determine the applicable holding period for a capital asset.

Holding Period

Property must be held more than one year to qualify for long-term capital gain or loss treatment.[14] Property not held for the required long-term period results in short-term capital gain or loss. To compute the **holding period**, start counting on the day after the property was acquired and include the day of disposition.

EXAMPLE 18

Mallard & Co. purchases a capital asset on January 15, 2005, and sells it on January 16, 2006. Mallard's holding period is more than one year. If Mallard had sold the asset on January 15,

[11] § 1241 and Reg. § 1.1241–1(a).

[12] Reg. § 1.1221–1(b), PLR 200045019. If the lease was held for more than one year before cancellation, it is a § 1231 asset.

[13] *Hort v. Comm.*, 41–1 USTC ¶9354, 25 AFTR 1207, 61 S.Ct. 757 (USSC, 1941).

[14] § 1222.

2006, the holding period would have been exactly one year, and the gain or loss would have been short term. ■

To be held for more than one year, a capital asset acquired on the last day of any month must not be disposed of until on or after the first day of the thirteenth succeeding month.[15]

EXAMPLE 19

Purple, Inc., purchases a capital asset on March 31, 2005. If Purple sells the asset on March 31, 2006, the holding period is one year, and Purple will have a short-term capital gain or loss. If Purple sells the asset on April 1, 2006, the holding period is more than one year, and it will have a long-term capital gain or loss. ■

Special Holding Period Rules

There are several special holding period rules.[16] The application of these rules depends on the type of asset and how it was acquired.

Nontaxable Exchanges. The holding period of property received in a like-kind exchange (and certain other qualified nontaxable exchanges) includes the holding period of the former asset if the property that was exchanged was either a capital asset or a § 1231 asset.

EXAMPLE 20

Red Manufacturing Corporation exchanges some vacant real estate it owns (a capital asset) for land closer to its factory. The transaction is a like-kind exchange, so the holding period of the new land includes the holding period of the old land. ■

EXAMPLE 21

A lightning strike destroyed Vireo Company's generator (a § 1231 asset) in March. Vireo uses the entire insurance proceeds it received to acquire a comparable generator. The holding period of the new generator includes the holding period of the old generator. ■

Nontaxable Transactions Involving Carryover of Another Taxpayer's Basis. If a transaction is nontaxable and the former owner's basis carries over to the present owner, the former owner's holding period is included in (tacked on to) the present owner's holding period.

EXAMPLE 22

Kareem acquired 100 shares of Robin Corporation stock for $1,000 on December 31, 2002. He transferred the shares by gift to Megan on December 31, 2005, when the stock was worth $2,000. Kareem's basis of $1,000 becomes the basis for determining gain or loss on a subsequent sale by Megan. Megan's holding period begins with the date the stock was acquired by Kareem. ■

EXAMPLE 23

Assume the same facts as in the preceding example, except that the fair market value of the shares was only $800 on the date of the gift. If Megan sells the stock for a loss, its value at the date of the gift is her basis. Accordingly, the tacked-on holding period rule does not apply, and Megan's holding period begins with the date of the gift. So, if she sells the shares for $500 on April 1, 2006, Megan has a $300 recognized capital loss, and the holding period is from December 31, 2005, to April 1, 2006. The loss is short term. ■

Disallowed Loss Transactions. Under several Code provisions, realized losses are disallowed. When a loss is disallowed, there is no carryover of holding period. Losses can be disallowed under § 267 (sale or exchange between related taxpayers) and § 262 (sale or exchange of personal-use assets) as well as other Code Sections.

[15]Rev.Rul. 66–7, 1966–1 C.B. 188.

[16]§ 1223.

TRADING ADRs ON U.S. STOCK EXCHANGES

Many non-U.S. companies now have subsidiaries that were formerly U.S. companies. For instance, Chrysler Corporation is now a subsidiary of DaimlerChrysler (formed when the German company Daimler-Benz acquired Chrysler). Shares in such non-U.S. companies generally cannot be traded directly on U.S. stock exchanges. Instead, the offshore companies issue instruments called American Depository Receipts (ADRs) that can be traded on U.S. stock exchanges. Purchases and sales of ADRs are treated for tax purposes as though the ADRs were shares in the corporation that issued them.

Taxpayers who acquire property in a disallowed loss transaction begin a new holding period and have a basis equal to the purchase price.

EXAMPLE 24

Janet sells her personal automobile at a loss. She may not deduct the loss because it arises from the sale of personal-use property. Janet purchases a replacement automobile for more than the selling price of her former automobile. Janet has a basis equal to the cost of the replacement automobile, and her holding period begins when she acquires the replacement automobile. ■

Inherited Property. The holding period for inherited property is treated as long term no matter how long the property is actually held by the heir. The holding period of the decedent or the decedent's estate is not relevant to the heir's holding period.

EXAMPLE 25

Shonda inherits Blue Company stock from her father. She receives the stock on April 1, 2006, and sells it on November 1, 2006. Even though Shonda did not hold the stock more than one year, she receives long-term capital gain or loss treatment on the sale. ■

Short Sales

A **short sale** occurs when a taxpayer sells borrowed property and repays the lender with substantially identical property either held on the date of the sale or purchased after the sale. Short sales typically involve corporate stock. The seller's objective is to make a profit in anticipation of a decline in the stock's price. If the price declines, the seller in a short sale recognizes a profit equal to the difference between the sales price of the borrowed stock and the price paid for its replacement.

Section 1233 provides that a short sale gain or loss is a capital gain or loss to the extent that the short sale property constitutes a capital asset of the taxpayer. This gain or loss is not recognized until the short sale is closed. Generally, the holding period of the short sale property is determined by how long the property used to close the short sale was held.

EXAMPLE 26

On January 4, Green & Associates sold short 100 shares of Osprey Corporation for $1,500. Green closed the transaction on July 28 of the same year by purchasing 100 shares of Osprey for $1,000 and delivering them to the broker from whom the securities were borrowed. Because this stock was held less than one year (actually less than a day), Green's gain ($1,500 sale price – $1,000 cost) is short term. ■

EXAMPLE 27

Assume the same facts as in the preceding example, except that the January 4 short sale was not closed until January 28 of the *following* year. The result is the same, because the stock was acquired and used to close the transaction on the same day; that is, it was not held more than a year. ■

If a taxpayer owns securities that are "substantially identical" to those sold short, § 1259 subjects the short sale to potential *constructive sale treatment,* and the taxpayer recognizes gain (but not loss) as of that date. If the taxpayer has not closed the short sale by delivering the short sale securities to the broker from whom the securities were borrowed before January 31 of the year following the short sale, the short sale is deemed to have closed on the short sale date. The holding period in such circumstances is determined by how long the securities in question were held.

EXAMPLE 28

Assume the same facts as in Example 26, except that Green & Associates owned 100 shares of Osprey Corporation when it sold short 100 shares on January 4. Green does not close the short sale before January 31 of the following year. Green must recognize any gain on its 100 shares of Osprey as of January 4 of the current year. If Green owned those shares more than one year as of that date, the gain is long term. ■

DIGGING DEEPER 5

Find more information on this topic at our Web site: ***http://wft-entities.swlearning.com.***

Tax Treatment of Capital Gains and Losses of Noncorporate Taxpayers

LO.4

Describe the tax treatment of capital gains and losses for noncorporate taxpayers.

This section discusses how capital gains and losses are taxed to noncorporate taxpayers, that is, individuals, noncorporate partners, trusts, and estates. The rules applicable to corporations are considered in the following section of this chapter.

Capital Gains

Gains from the sale or exchange of capital assets are taxed at various rates, depending upon the holding period, the taxpayer's regular tax rate, and the type of asset involved.

Short-Term Gains. Gains on capital assets held one year or less are taxed as *ordinary income.* Accordingly, the applicable tax rates vary from 10 percent to 35 percent. Although short-term capital gains receive no preferential tax treatment compared to ordinary income, they do have one advantage: they can absorb capital losses without limit. As discussed later in this section, *capital losses* are deducted first against capital gains (without limit) and then against ordinary income, but only up to $3,000 per year.[17] Thus, someone with a large capital loss will find short-term capital gains attractive, even though such gains do not qualify for lower tax rates.

PLANNING *Strategies* **TIMING CAPITAL GAINS**

★ **Framework Focus: Income and Exclusions**

Strategy ★ Postpone Recognition of Income to Achieve Tax Deferral.

★ **Framework Focus: Deductions**

Strategy ★ Maximize Deductible Amounts.

Taxpayers have considerable control over the timing of their capital gains through the mechanism of realization. Accordingly, a taxpayer might want to defer recognizing a large capital gain in a year with *substantial itemized deductions,* such as large personal casualty losses or the purchase of a new residence with large up-front interest expenses. In so

[17] § 1211(b).

doing, the taxpayer minimizes the loss of such deductions due to AGI limitations and deduction phaseouts applicable to some high-income individuals.

Nontax considerations, of course, often dictate when assets are sold. If a particular stock is peaking in popularity, selling it might be a wise investment strategy, even if the taxpayer's current tax situation is not optimal. Similarly, if a taxpayer needs cash to start a business, purchase a home, or pay for a child's education or medical costs, the capital asset might need to be sold at a time when investment *and* tax considerations counsel otherwise. In these circumstances, however, a taxpayer might choose to *borrow* the money required and use the capital asset as collateral for the loan, rather than sell the asset. A loan does not trigger tax consequences, and the taxpayer can continue to hold the asset until a more opportune time—albeit at the cost of paying interest, which may be nondeductible.

Long-Term Gains. Gains on capital assets held more than one year are classified as *long-term* gains and are eligible for a special 15 percent tax rate, or 5 percent rate for taxpayers in the 10 or 15 percent tax bracket. The benefit of these long-term capital gain tax rates, therefore, is as follows.

Tax Rates		Differential
Ordinary Income	Capital Gain	(Percentage Points)
10%	5%	5
15	5	10
25	15	10
28	15	13
33	15	18
35	15	20

In point of fact, relatively few capital gains are realized by persons in the 10 or 15 percent tax bracket. Thus, the tax rate that generally applies to long-term capital gains is 15 percent.

There are two major exceptions, however, to this general treatment. The first exception is so-called *28% property*, which consists of the following items.

- **Collectibles** (works of art, rugs, antiques, gems, coins, stamps, and alcoholic beverages) held more than one year.[18]
- The taxable half of the gain on sales of *qualified small business stock* (see the end of this section).

These assets are labeled *28% property*, because the gains that they produce are taxed at 28 percent. But this 28 percent rate is a *maximum* rate, so a taxpayer in a lower tax bracket would pay at that rate. As a result, the benefit of the applicable tax rates for gains on 28% property is as follows.

Ordinary Income Tax Rates	Applicable Tax Rates	Differential (Percentage Points)
10%	10%	None
15	15	None
25	25	None
28	28	None
33	28	5
35	28	7

[18] § 408(m) and Reg. § 1.408–10(b).

TAX FACT

Individual Returns Reporting Capital Gains

The number of individual income tax returns including net capital gain in AGI is shown in the table below. About 130 million individual returns are filed annually, so based on the most current data about 18.6 percent of all returns report capital gain income. During the stock market boom of the late 1990s, though, this number was higher. After the turn of the century, reduced capital gain tax rates have contributed to this increasing percentage.

Year	Number of Returns (in Millions)
1975	5.8
1980	7.0
1985	10.0
1990	9.2
1995	14.8
2000	22.7
2002	24.2

Source: *Individual Income Tax Returns, 2002,* SOI Bulletin, *Fall 2004, Figure B.*

Gains on 28% property receive preferential tax treatment only when realized by taxpayers in the top two tax brackets.

PLANNING *Strategies*

GIFTS OF APPRECIATED SECURITIES

★ **Framework Focus: Tax Rate**

Strategy ★ Shift Net Income from High-Bracket Taxpayers to Low-Bracket Taxpayers.

Persons with appreciated securities that have been held over one year may reduce the tax due on their sale by giving the securities to someone (often a child) who is in the *lowest tax bracket*. The donor's holding period carries over, along with his or her basis, and the donee's lower tax rate applies when the securities are sold. As a result, the gain could be taxed at the donee's 5 percent, rather than the donor's 15 percent. The donee should be over age 13 by year-end, however, or a *kiddie tax* will nullify most of the tax advantage being sought. The kiddie tax subjects the gain to the parents' tax rate. See Chapter 16.

Such gifts usually bear no gift tax due to the annual $12,000 exclusion. But the property received after payment of the tax belongs to the donee. It is not available to the donor, nor may it be used to pay a parent's essential support obligations. Moreover, these assets may affect a child's eligibility for need-based financial aid when applying to college.

The second major exception involves depreciable real estate that has been held more than one year. Some—but not all—of the gain attributable to depreciation deductions on apartments, office buildings, shopping centers, and warehouses is taxable at 25 percent rather than 5 or 15 percent. The amount that is taxed in this manner depends upon how much depreciation is "recaptured" as ordinary income under § 1250, as explained later in this chapter. Accordingly, these gains are called *unrecaptured § 1250 gain* [§ 1(h)(7)]. In any case, the 25 percent rate is a *maximum*

GLOBAL *Tax Issues*

CAPITAL GAIN TREATMENT IN THE UNITED STATES AND OTHER COUNTRIES

Few other countries apply an alternative tax rate or other incentive to long-term capital gains. Instead, those gains are taxed in the same manner as other income. Consequently, even though the U.S. system of identifying and taxing capital assets is complex, it may be preferable because of the lower tax rates, and because the lower rates are available to taxpayers in all tax brackets.

rate, so the benefit of the applicable tax rates for gains from the sale of depreciable real estate is as follows.

Ordinary Income Tax Rates	Applicable Tax Rates	Differential (Percentage Points)
10%	10%	None
15	15	None
25	25	None
28	25	3
33	25	8
35	25	10

Capital Losses

As explained above, capital gains can be classified into four general categories.

- Short term—taxed as ordinary income.
- 28% property—taxed at no more than 28 percent.
- Unrecaptured § 1250 gain—taxed at no more than 25 percent.
- Regular long term—taxed at 5 percent or 15 percent.

A taxpayer can also have losses from capital assets in *three* of these four categories. The *unrecaptured § 1250 gain* category contains only gain. When both gains and losses occur in the year, they must be netted against each other in the order specified below.

Step 1. Group all gains and losses into short-term, 28% property, unrecaptured § 1250, and regular long-term categories.

Step 2. Net the gains and losses within each category to obtain net short-term, 28% property, unrecaptured § 1250, and regular long-term gain or loss.

Step 3. Offset the net 28% property and unrecaptured § 1250 amounts if they are of opposite sign. Add them if they have the same sign. Then, offset the resulting amount against the regular net long-term amount if they are of opposite sign, or add the amounts if they have the same sign.

Step 4. Offset the result of step 3 with the net short-term gain *or loss* from step 2 if they are of opposite sign.

These netting rules offset net short-term capital loss against the *highest taxed gain first.* Consequently, if there is a net short-term capital loss, it first offsets any net 28% property gain, any remaining loss offsets unrecaptured § 1250 gain, and then any remaining loss offsets regular long-term gain.

If the result of step 4 is *only* a short-term capital gain, the taxpayer is not eligible for a reduced tax rate. If the result of step 4 is a loss, a **net capital loss** exists, and the taxpayer may be eligible for a *capital loss deduction* (discussed later in this chapter).

CONCEPT SUMMARY 8–3

Capital Gains of Noncorporate Taxpayers

Type of Asset	Applicable Rate
Held not more than one year.	10%–35%, same as ordinary income.
Collectibles held more than one year.	10/15/25% for lowest bracket taxpayers, 28% for all others.
Taxable portion (50%) of gain on qualified small business stock held more than five years.	10/15/25% for lowest bracket taxpayers, 28% for all others.
Unrecaptured § 1250 gain on depreciable real estate held more than one year.	10/15% for lowest bracket taxpayers, 25% for all others.
Other capital assets held more than one year.	5% for lowest bracket taxpayers, 15% for all others.

If there was no offsetting in step 4 because the short-term and step 3 results were both gains *or* if the result of the offsetting is either a 28% property, an unrecaptured § 1250 property, and/or a regular long-term gain, a **net capital gain** exists, and the taxpayer may be eligible for a reduced tax rate. The net capital gain may consist of regular *long-term gain, unrecaptured § 1250 gain,* and/or *28% property gain.* Each of these gains may be taxed at a different rate.

EXAMPLE 29

Joe is in the 35% Federal income tax bracket. He is taxed as follows.

Ordinary income	35%
Unrecaptured § 1250 gain	25%
28% gain	28%
Short-term capital gain	35%
Other long-term capital gain	15%

■

EXAMPLE 30

This example shows how a net long-term capital loss is applied.

Step	Short Term	28% Gain	Unrecaptured § 1250 Gain	Regular Long Term	Comment
1	$ 3,000	$ 1,000		$ 3,000	
				(8,000)	
2	$ 3,000	$ 1,000		($ 5,000)	
3		(1,000)	→	1,000	Netted because of opposite sign.
		$ -0-		($ 4,000)	
4	(3,000)	→	→	3,000	The net short-term gain is netted against the net regular long-term loss, and the remaining loss is eligible for the capital loss deduction.
	$ -0-			($1,000)	

■

EXAMPLE 31

This example shows how net short-term and regular long-term capital losses are applied.

Step	Short Term	28% Gain	Unrecaptured § 1250 Gain	Regular Long Term	Comment
1	$ 3,000	$15,000	$4,000	$ 3,000	
	(5,000)	(7,000)		(8,000)	
2	($ 2,000)	$ 8,000	$4,000	($ 5,000)	
3		(5,000)	←	5,000	Net regular long-term loss is netted against 28% gain first.
		$ 3,000		$ -0-	
4	$ 2,000 →	(2,000)			Short-term loss is netted against 28% gain first.
	$ -0-	$ 1,000	$4,000		
		Net 28% gain	Net 25% gain		

■

If a net loss remains after applying these rules for offsetting losses, a noncorporate taxpayer may deduct up to $3,000 of that loss against ordinary income.[19] Losses in excess of $3,000 are carried over to future years where they are applied first against capital gains and then deducted up to $3,000 per year. Capital loss carryovers expire, however, when the taxpayer dies.

EXAMPLE 32

James incurred a $10,000 loss on his only capital asset transaction in 2006. If he has no other capital asset transactions from that point on, his $10,000 loss is deducted as follows.

Year	Deduction
2006	$3,000
2007	3,000
2008	3,000
2009	1,000

■

EXAMPLE 33

Assume the same facts as in the preceding example, except that James realizes a capital gain of $4,500 in 2008. At that time, his remaining capital loss carryover is $4,000 ($10,000 – $6,000 deducted previously). Since his capital gain in 2008 (i.e., $4,500) exceeds this loss carryforward, James can deduct the entire $4,000 against that year's capital gain. ■

EXAMPLE 34

Assume the same facts as in Example 32, except that James died in late 2007. His remaining capital loss carryforward of $4,000 ($10,000 – $6,000 deducted in 2006 and 2007) expires unused. ■

When a taxpayer's capital loss exceeds $3,000 and derives from more than one category, it is used in the following order: first, short term; then, 28% property; then, unrecaptured § 1250 property; and finally, regular long term. Unused losses are carried forward as follows: short-term losses carry forward as short-term losses, and long-term losses carry forward as long-term losses.

[19] § 1211(b)(1). Married persons filing separate returns are limited to a $1,500 deduction per tax year.

TAX FACT

Detrimental Tax Treatment for Capital Losses

A corporate taxpayer cannot deduct a net capital loss against ordinary income. It can carry the loss back three years and forward five years in search of capital gains. An individual taxpayer can deduct a maximum of $3,000 of net capital loss against ordinary income in the current tax year. Any excess can be carried forward indefinitely in search of capital gains. After capital gains are exhausted in each carryforward year, a maximum of $3,000 of the remaining net capital loss can be deducted against ordinary income.

The number of individual income tax returns with a net capital loss in AGI is as follows. These numbers are much higher lately, due to drops in stock prices.

Year	Number of Returns (in Millions)
1975	2.5
1980	2.0
1985	2.7
1990	5.0
1995	5.1
2000	6.9
2002	13.3

Source: *Individual Income Tax Returns, 2002,* SOI Bulletin, *Fall 2004, Figure C.*

EXAMPLE 35

Nancy incurs a long-term capital loss of $8,500 this year, of which $3,000 is deducted against her ordinary income. The remaining $5,500 ($8,500 loss − $3,000 deducted) carries forward as a long-term capital loss. ■

Find more information on this topic at our Web site: ***http://wft-entities.swlearning.com.***

DIGGING DEEPER 6

PLANNING *Strategies* MATCHING GAINS WITH LOSSES

★ **Framework Focus: Income and Exclusions**

Strategy ★ Avoid Income Recognition.

A taxpayer who has already realized a large capital gain may want to *match this gain* with an *offsetting capital loss.* Doing so will shelter the capital gain from taxation and will also free up an asset that has declined in value. Without the capital gain, after all, the taxpayer might hesitate to sell a loss asset, because the resulting capital loss may be deductible only in $3,000 annual increments.

Similarly, a taxpayer with a large realized capital loss might use the occasion to sell some appreciated assets. Doing so would enable the taxpayer to use the capital loss immediately and at the same time realize the benefit of the asset appreciation at little or no tax cost.

On the other hand, matching capital losses and long-term capital gains means that the taxpayer utilizes the capital loss against income that would otherwise qualify for a preferential tax rate of 5 or 15 percent. If the taxpayer's ordinary income is taxed at a higher rate, he or she might prefer to deduct the loss against that higher taxed income, even on a schedule of $3,000 per year. The *time value of money* must be considered; a current-year deduction at 5 or 15 percent might be worth more than a series of annual deductions at higher rates spread over several years.

Nontax considerations, such as investment prospects for the assets in question, are also important. Future investment prospects are often unknowable or at least highly speculative, while tax effects can be determined with relative certainty—which explains some of the late December selling activity in publicly traded securities and mutual funds.

Small Business Stock

A special 50 percent *exclusion* is available to noncorporate taxpayers who derive capital gains from the sale or exchange of **qualified small business stock.**[20] Half of the gain is excluded from the taxpayer's gross income, and the other half is subjected to a maximum tax rate of 28 percent, as noted earlier.

EXAMPLE 36

Yolanda realized a $100,000 gain on the sale of qualified small business stock. Yolanda has a 35% marginal tax rate without considering this gain. So $50,000 of this gain is excluded from her gross income, and the other $50,000 is taxed at a maximum tax rate of 28%. Thus, Yolanda owes tax of $14,000 ($50,000 × 28%), an effective tax rate of 14% on the entire $100,000 capital gain. ■

This treatment is more favorable than the capital gain tax treatment explained previously. Accordingly, Congress imposed additional restrictions to ensure that the gains receiving this treatment were derived in the circumstances that Congress intended to promote. These restrictions include the following.

- The stock must have been newly issued *after* August 10, 1993.
- The taxpayer must have held the stock *more than five years.*
- The issuing corporation must use at least 80 percent of its assets, determined by their value, in the *active conduct* of a trade or business.
- When the stock was issued, the issuing corporation's assets must not have exceeded $50 million, at adjusted basis, including the proceeds of the stock issuance.
- The corporation does not engage in banking, financing, insurance, investing, leasing, farming, mineral extraction, hotel or motel operation, restaurant operation, or any business whose principal asset is the *reputation or skill* of its employees (such as accounting, architecture, health, law, engineering, or financial services).

Even if each of these requirements is met, the amount of gain eligible for the exclusion is limited to the *greater* of 10 times the taxpayer's basis in the stock or $10 million per taxpayer per company,[21] computed on an aggregate basis.

EXAMPLE 37

Vanita purchased $100,000 of qualified small business stock when it was first issued in October 1996. This year, she sells the stock for $4 million. Her gain is $3.9 million ($4,000,000 – $100,000). Although this amount exceeds 10 times her basis ($100,000 × 10 = $1,000,000), it is *less* than $10 million, so the entire $3.9 million gain is eligible for the 50% exclusion. ■

Transactions that fail to satisfy *any one* of the applicable requirements are taxed as capital gains (and losses) realized by noncorporate taxpayers generally.

Gains are also eligible for *nonrecognition* treatment if the sale proceeds are invested in other qualified small business stock within 60 days.[22] To the extent that the sale proceeds are not so invested, gain is recognized, but the 50 percent exclusion still applies. To be eligible for this treatment, the stock sold must have been held more than six months.

EXAMPLE 38

Assume the same facts as in the preceding example, except that Vanita sold her stock in January 2007 and used $3.5 million of the sale proceeds to purchase other qualified small business stock one month later. Vanita's gain is recognized to the extent that the sale proceeds were not reinvested—namely, $500,000 ($4,000,000 sale proceeds – $3,500,000 reinvested). The 50% exclusion will apply, however, to this amount. ■

[20] § 1202(a).

[21] For married persons filing separately, the limitation is $5 million.

[22] § 1045(a).

CAPITAL GAIN TREATMENT AND NON-U.S. STOCK

GLOBAL Tax Issues

U.S. shareholders of certain non-U.S. corporations may find that they are denied capital gain treatment upon sale or other disposal of their stock. If the entity that issued the stock is considered a controlled foreign corporation (CFC) because certain U.S. shareholders as a group own more than 50 percent by vote or value, any gain recognized upon disposition of the stock is recharacterized as dividend income to the extent of the entity's earnings and profits yet to be taxed in the United States.

U.S. persons investing in non-U.S. corporations ultimately receive income taxable in the United States through dividends or capital gains upon disposition of the stock. If an offshore corporation pays no dividends, the U.S. shareholder's entire return from the stock investment is in the form of a gain on disposition of the stock, with the accumulated earnings of the non-U.S. corporation reflected in that gain. This provision protects the ability of the United States to tax these accumulated earnings as ordinary dividend income when they ultimately are realized by U.S. persons.

DIGGING DEEPER 7

Find more information on this topic at our Web site: ***http://wft-entities.swlearning.com.***

Tax Treatment of Capital Gains and Losses of Corporate Taxpayers

LO.5

Describe the tax treatment of capital gains and losses for corporate taxpayers.

The treatment of a corporation's net capital gain or loss differs dramatically from the rules for noncorporate taxpayers discussed in the preceding section. Briefly, the differences are as follows.

- Capital gains are taxed at the ordinary income tax rates.[23]
- Capital losses offset only capital gains. No deduction of capital losses is permitted against ordinary taxable income.
- There is a three-year carryback and a five-year carryforward period for net capital losses.[24] Capital loss carrybacks and carryforwards are always treated as short term, regardless of their original nature.

EXAMPLE 39

Sparrow Corporation has a $15,000 long-term capital loss for the current year and $57,000 of ordinary taxable income. Sparrow may not offset the $15,000 long-term capital loss against its ordinary income by taking a capital loss deduction. The $15,000 long-term capital loss becomes a $15,000 short-term capital loss for carryback and carryforward purposes. This amount may offset capital gains in the three-year carryback period or, if not absorbed there, offset capital gains in the five-year carryforward period. Any amount remaining after this carryforward period expires is permanently lost. ■

Section 1231 Assets

LO.6

Distinguish § 1231 assets from ordinary and capital assets, and calculate § 1231 gain or loss.

Businesses own many assets that are used in the business rather than held for resale. In financial accounting, such assets are known as "fixed assets." For example, a foundry's 30,000-pound stamping machine is a fixed asset. It is also a depreciable asset. The building housing the foundry is another fixed asset. The remainder of this chapter largely deals with how to *classify* the gains and losses from the disposition of fixed assets. Chapter 5 discussed how to depreciate such assets. Chapter 7 discussed how to determine the adjusted basis and the amount of gain or loss from their disposition.

[23]§ 1201. The alternative tax rate of 35% produces no beneficial results.

[24]§ 1212(a)(1).

TAX FACT

Capital Gains for the Wealthy?

Economists and other observers of society often accuse the Code of favoring those with higher levels of income and wealth, despite a fairly substantial progressivity in the Federal income tax rate structure. The claim is that the wealthy are the sole possessors of capital assets, and that capital gains are subject to highly favorable tax treatment. Current tax return data may confirm those assertions.

Net Capital Gain Income as a Percentage of AGI, 2002 Returns

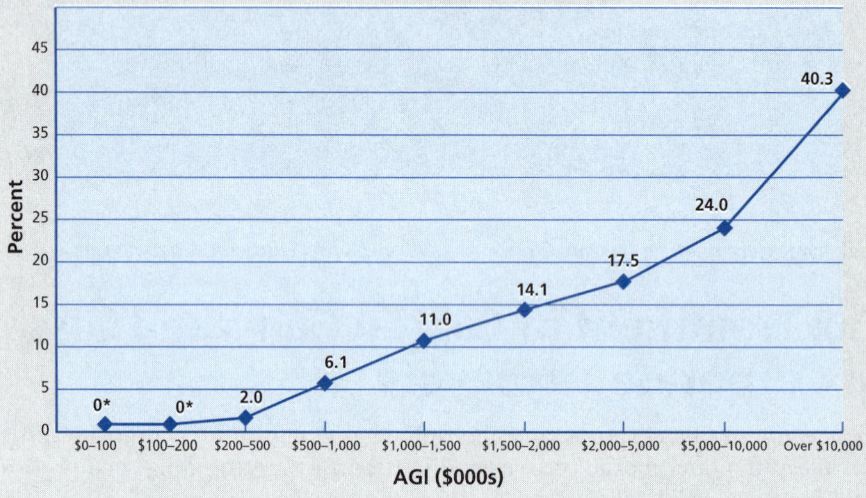

*Capital losses exceeded long-term capital gains.

Source: *Individual Income Tax Returns, 2002,* SOI Bulletin, *Fall 2004, Figure F.*

Relationship to Capital Assets

At first glance, the *classification of fixed assets* ought to be straightforward. Section 1221(a)(2) specifically excludes from the capital asset definition any property that is depreciable or that is real estate "used in a trade or business." Accordingly, the foundry's stamping machine and the building housing the foundry described above are not capital assets. Therefore, one would expect gains to be taxed as ordinary income and losses to be deductible as ordinary losses. Since World War II, however, certain business assets have received more favorable treatment.

Section 1231 provides that business assets held for more than one year can receive the best of both worlds: capital gain treatment on gains and ordinary loss treatment on losses. More specifically, this provision requires that gains and losses from **§ 1231 property** be compiled at the end of the taxable year; the *net result* is then classified as capital gain if a net gain is produced, or as ordinary loss if a net loss is produced. As a result, a particular disposition's character as capital or ordinary is not determined until the taxable year has concluded and all of the taxpayer's **§ 1231 gains and losses** are tabulated.

EXAMPLE 40

Brown & Co. sells business land and building at a $5,000 gain and equipment at a $3,000 loss. Both properties were held for more than one year. Brown's net gain is $2,000, and that net gain may be treated as a long-term capital gain under § 1231. ■

EXAMPLE 41

Chickadee, Inc., sells equipment at a $10,000 loss and business land at a $2,000 gain. Both properties were held for more than one year. Chickadee's net loss is $8,000, and that net loss is an ordinary loss. ■

Find more information on this topic at our Web site: ***http://wft-entities.swlearning.com.***

DIGGING DEEPER 8

Property Included

Section 1231 property includes the following.

- Depreciable or real property used in business (principally machinery and equipment, buildings, and land).
- Property held for the production of income if it has been involuntarily converted.
- Timber, coal, or domestic iron ore to which § 631 applies.
- Livestock held for draft, breeding, dairy, or sporting purposes.
- Unharvested crops on land used in business.
- Certain *purchased* intangible assets (such as patents and goodwill) that are eligible for amortization.

Find more information on this topic at our Web site: ***http://wft-entities.swlearning.com.***

DIGGING DEEPER 9 10

Property Excluded

Section 1231 property generally does *not* include the following.

- Property not held more than one year. Livestock must be held at least 12 months (24 months in some cases). Unharvested crops do not have to be held more than one year, but the land must be so held.
- Property not put to a personal use, where casualty losses exceed casualty gains for the taxable year. If a taxpayer has a net casualty loss, the casualty gains and losses are treated as ordinary gains and losses.
- Inventory and property held primarily for sale to customers.
- Copyrights; literary, musical, or artistic compositions, etc.; and certain U.S. government publications.
- Accounts receivable and notes receivable arising in the ordinary course of the trade or business.

Casualty or Theft and Nonpersonal-Use Capital Assets

When § 1231 assets are disposed of by casualty or theft, a special netting rule is applied. For simplicity, the term *casualty* is used to mean both casualty and theft dispositions. First, the casualty gains and losses from § 1231 assets *and* the casualty gains and losses from **long-term nonpersonal-use capital assets** are determined. For business entities, virtually any capital asset is a nonpersonal-use capital asset, because partnerships, limited liability companies, and corporations are incapable of using assets *personally*. This classification, therefore, is most significant to individual taxpayers who might use certain capital assets as part of their daily life.

Once the casualty gains and losses from § 1231 assets and nonpersonal-use capital assets are determined, they are netted together. If the result is a *net gain*, the net gain is treated as § 1231 gain, but if the result is a *net loss*, the net loss is deducted outside § 1231. Thus, whether these casualties get § 1231 treatment depends on the results of the casualty netting process.

Casualties and thefts are *involuntary conversions*, it should be recalled, and gains from such conversions need not be recognized if the proceeds are timely reinvested in similar property. Thus, the netting process described above would not consider any casualty and theft gains that are being deferred because insurance proceeds were reinvested according to the requirements of § 1033 (see Chapter 7). Section 1231, in other words, has no effect on whether a *realized* gain or loss is recognized. Instead, § 1231 merely dictates how a *recognized* gain will be classified.

This special netting process for casualties and thefts does not apply to *condemnation* gains and losses. As a result, if a § 1231 asset is disposed of by condemnation, any resulting gain or loss will get § 1231 treatment.

General Procedure for § 1231 Computation

The tax treatment of § 1231 gains and losses depends on the results of a rather complex *netting* procedure. The steps in this netting procedure are as follows.

Step 1: Casualty Netting. Net all recognized long-term gains and losses from casualties of § 1231 assets and nonpersonal-use capital assets. This casualty netting is beneficial because if there is a net gain, the gain may receive long-term capital gain treatment. If there is a net loss, it receives ordinary loss treatment.

a. If the casualty gains exceed the casualty losses, add the net gain to the other § 1231 gains for the taxable year.
b. If the casualty losses exceed the casualty gains, exclude all casualty losses and gains from further § 1231 computation. The casualty gains are ordinary income and the casualty losses are deductible. For individual taxpayers, the casualty losses must be classified further. For individual taxpayers, § 1231 asset casualty losses are deductible *for* AGI, while other casualty losses are deductible *from* AGI (see Chapter 16).

Step 2: § 1231 Netting. After adding any net casualty gain from step 1a above to the other § 1231 gains and losses (including *recognized* § 1231 asset condemnation gains and losses), net all § 1231 gains and losses.

a. If the gains exceed the losses, the net gain is offset by the "lookback" nonrecaptured § 1231 losses (see step 3 below) from the prior five tax years. To the extent of this offset, the net § 1231 gain is classified as ordinary income. Any remaining gain is long-term capital gain.
b. If the losses exceed the gains, the net loss is deducted against ordinary income. For individual taxpayers only, the gains are ordinary income, the § 1231 asset losses are deductible *for* AGI, and the other casualty losses are deductible *from* AGI.

EXAMPLE 42

Falcon Management, Inc., recognized the following gains and losses this year.

Capital Gains and Losses	
Long-term capital gain	$ 3,000
Long-term capital loss	(400)
Short-term capital gain	1,000
Short-term capital loss	(200)
Casualties	
Gain from insurance recovery on fire loss to building, owned five years	$ 1,200
Loss from theft of computer (uninsured), owned two years	(1,000)

§ 1231 Gains and Losses from Depreciable Business Assets Held Long Term	
Asset A	$ 300
Asset B	1,100
Asset C	(500)

Gains and Losses from Sale of Depreciable Business Assets Held Short Term	
Asset D	$ 200
Asset E	(300)

Falcon had no net § 1231 losses in prior tax years.

Disregarding the recapture of depreciation (discussed later in this chapter), Falcon's gains and losses receive the following tax treatment.

- The casualty netting of the § 1231 and nonpersonal-use capital assets contains two items—the $1,200 gain from the business building and the $1,000 loss from the computer. Consequently, there is a $200 net gain and that gain is treated as a § 1231 gain (added to the § 1231 gains).
- The gains from § 1231 transactions (Assets A, B, and C and the § 1231 asset casualty gain) exceed the losses by $1,100 ($1,600 – $500). This excess is a long-term capital gain and is added to Falcon's other long-term capital gains.
- Falcon's net long-term capital gain is $3,700 ($3,000 + $1,100 from § 1231 transactions – $400 long-term capital loss). Its net short-term capital gain is $800 ($1,000 – $200). The result is capital gain income of $4,500, which will be taxed at ordinary rates. If Falcon were an individual rather than a corporation, the $3,700 net long-term capital gain portion would be eligible for preferential capital gain treatment, and the $800 net short-term capital gain would be taxed as ordinary income.
- Falcon treats the gain and loss from Assets D and E as ordinary gain and loss, because § 1231 does not apply unless the assets have been held more than one year.[25]

Results of the Gains and Losses on Falcon's Tax Computation	
Net long-term capital gain	$3,700
Net short-term capital gain	800
Ordinary gain from sale of Asset D	200
Ordinary loss from sale of Asset E	(300)
Gross income	$4,400

■

EXAMPLE 43

Assume the same facts as in the preceding example, except that the loss from Asset C was $1,700 instead of $500.

- The treatment of the casualty gains and losses is the same.
- The losses from § 1231 transactions now exceed the gains by $100 ($1,700 – $1,600). As a result, the net loss is deducted in full as an ordinary loss.
- Capital gain income is $3,400 ($2,600 long term + $800 short term).

Results of the Gains and Losses on Falcon's Tax Computation	
Net long-term capital gain	$2,600
Net short-term capital gain	800
Net ordinary loss on Assets A, B, and C and § 1231 casualty gain	(100)
Ordinary gain from sale of Asset D	200
Ordinary loss from sale of Asset E	(300)
Gross income	$3,200

■

[25] § 1231(b)(1).

Step 3: § 1231 Lookback Provision. The net § 1231 gain from step 2a above is offset by the nonrecaptured net § 1231 losses for the five preceding taxable years.[26] For 2006, the lookback years are 2001, 2002, 2003, 2004, and 2005. To the extent of the nonrecaptured net § 1231 loss, the current-year net § 1231 gain is ordinary income. The *nonrecaptured* net § 1231 losses are those that have not already been used to offset net § 1231 gains. Only the net § 1231 gain exceeding this net § 1231 loss carryforward is given long-term capital gain treatment. The **§ 1231 lookback** provision reduces the taxpayer's ability to gain a tax advantage by "timing" sales artificially.

EXAMPLE 44

Komodo Manufacturing Corporation sold various used machines and some business real estate during 2006 for a net § 1231 gain of $25,000. During 2005, Komodo had no § 1231 transactions, but in 2004, it had a net § 1231 loss of $17,000. This loss causes $17,000 of the 2006 gain to be classified as ordinary income. The remaining 2006 gain of $8,000 ($25,000 of § 1231 gain – $17,000 nonrecaptured loss) is § 1231 gain. ■

EXAMPLE 45

Assume the same facts as in the preceding example, except that Komodo had a net § 1231 loss of $37,000 in 2004 and a net § 1231 gain of $10,000 in 2005.

- The 2004 net § 1231 loss of $37,000 would cause the net § 1231 gain of $10,000 in 2005 to be classified as ordinary income, and $27,000 ($37,000 loss – $10,000 recaptured) would carry over to 2006.
- The remaining nonrecaptured § 1231 loss of $27,000 from 2004 completely offsets the § 1231 gain of $25,000 from 2006, making that entire gain ordinary income.
- The remaining nonrecaptured § 1231 loss from 2004 is $2,000 ($27,000 carried to 2006 – $25,000 recaptured). This recapture potential carries over to 2007. ■

LO.7

Determine when recapture provisions apply and derive their effects.

Section 1245 Recapture

As explained earlier, when Congress determined that § 1231 was unduly generous, it chose to *recapture* some of § 1231's benefits rather than repeal that section altogether. This recapture phenomenon applies exclusively to the gain side of § 1231; the ordinary loss feature applicable to § 1231 property is not affected by the Code's recapture provisions. In essence, recapture takes part—often all—of the gain from the sale or exchange of a § 1231 asset and classifies it as *ordinary income* before the netting process of § 1231 begins. Accordingly, recaptured gain is computed *first,* without considering the other § 1231 transactions that occurred during the taxable year. This section discusses the § 1245 recapture rules, and the next section discusses the § 1250 recapture rules.

Section 1245 requires taxpayers to treat all gain as ordinary gain unless the property is sold for more than its original cost. This result is accomplished by requiring that all gain be treated as ordinary gain to the extent of the depreciation taken on the property disposed of. Section 1231 gain results only if the property is disposed of for more than its original cost. The excess of the sales price over the original cost is § 1231 gain. Section 1245 applies primarily to personalty such as machinery, trucks, and office furniture.

EXAMPLE 46

Avocet, Inc., purchased a $100,000 machine and deducted $70,000 depreciation before selling it for $80,000. Avocet's gain is $50,000 [$80,000 amount realized – $30,000 adjusted basis

[26] § 1231(c).

CONCEPT SUMMARY 8–4

Section 1231 Netting Procedure

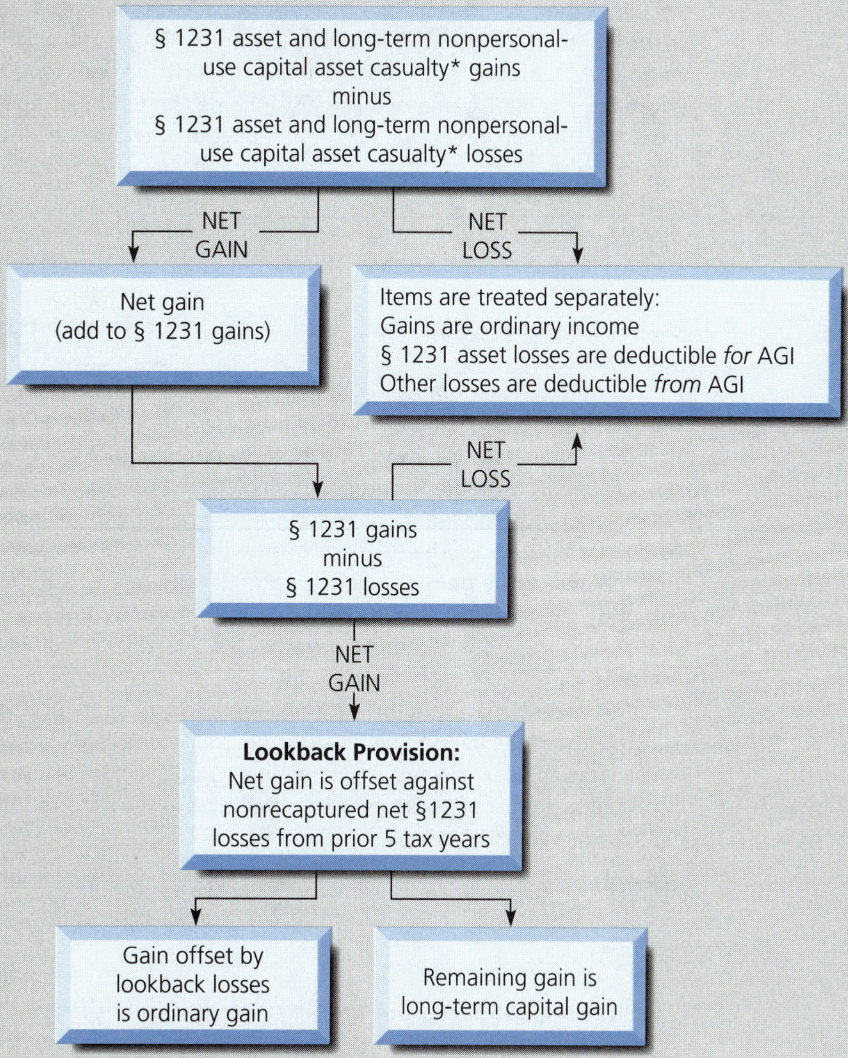
§ 1231 asset and long-term nonpersonal-use capital asset casualty* gains
minus
§ 1231 asset and long-term nonpersonal-use capital asset casualty* losses
NET GAIN
NET LOSS
Net gain (add to § 1231 gains)
Items are treated separately:
Gains are ordinary income
§ 1231 asset losses are deductible *for* AGI
Other losses are deductible *from* AGI
NET LOSS
§ 1231 gains
minus
§ 1231 losses
NET GAIN
Lookback Provision:
Net gain is offset against nonrecaptured net §1231 losses from prior 5 tax years
Gain offset by lookback losses is ordinary gain
Remaining gain is long-term capital gain

*Includes casualties and thefts.

($100,000 cost – $70,000 depreciation taken)]. Section 1245 treats as ordinary income (not as § 1231 gain) any gain to the extent of depreciation taken. In this example, the entire $50,000 gain would be ordinary income. ■

EXAMPLE 47

If Avocet, Inc., in the preceding example sold the machine for $120,000, it would have a gain of $90,000 ($120,000 amount realized – $30,000 adjusted basis). The § 1245 gain would be $70,000 (equal to the depreciation taken), and the remaining gain of $20,000 (equal to the excess of the sales price over the original cost) would be § 1231 gain. ■

EXAMPLE 48

Assume the same facts as in Example 46, except that the asset is sold for $25,000 instead of $80,000. Avocet's loss is $5,000 ($25,000 amount realized – $30,000 adjusted basis). Since there is a loss, there is no depreciation recapture. All of the loss is § 1231 loss. ■

BRIDGE *Discipline*

Bridge to Financial Accounting

The essence of much of the tax code is to create definitions that discriminate among certain types of income or expenditures, so that special tax treatment can be afforded to one of the definitional groups. For instance, municipal bond interest might be favored over corporate bond interest income, long-term capital gains over short-term capital gains or ordinary income, and processing fees to bribes. In each case, the former generally allows a reduction of taxable income or the tax liability and helps the taxpayer to meet its goal of maximizing the available after-tax income that it generates.

Maximizing net income also is a goal of financial accounting, at least from the viewpoint of current and potential shareholders. In the long run, stock prices may advance solely because of the positive earnings that the corporation generates relative to the rest of the capital markets. The greater the net earnings, the greater the increase in stock price and private wealth.

But financial accounting makes far fewer distinctions when classifying the reporting entity's revenues and expenses. Most of the tax code's definitions and distinctions are politically or economically motivated means by which to reduce the effective tax rate of the taxpayer, perhaps without affecting its nominal rate.

The preferential treatment of long-term capital gains is one of the most long-lived of these tax fictions. The "best of both worlds" § 1231 treatment is over 60 years old itself. Whereas the gain or loss generated by the sale of a business or investment asset is merely included in the body of the income statement of the reporting entity, § 1221 and § 1231 can reduce the taxpayer's effective tax rate, and § 1245 and § 1250 can increase it.

Differences in classification of income and deductions created solely by the tax code constitute most of the items to be reconciled in the Schedule M–1 or M–3 of the C corporation, S corporation, partnership, and limited liability entity. Many of these items must be reported as permanent or temporary differences in the Deferred Tax Liability account regulated by APB 23 and SFAS 109.

Section 1245 recapture applies to the portion of *recognized* gain from the sale or other disposition of § 1245 property that represents depreciation, including § 167 depreciation, § 168 cost recovery, § 179 immediate expensing, and § 197 amortization. Section 1245 merely *classifies* gain as ordinary income; it does not cause gain to be recognized. Thus, in Example 46, Avocet, Inc., recaptures as ordinary income only the $50,000 of actual gain, not the entire $70,000 of depreciation taken. In other words, § 1245 recaptures the *lower* of the depreciation taken or the gain recognized.

The method of depreciation (e.g., accelerated or straight-line) does not matter. All depreciation taken is potentially subject to recapture. Thus, § 1245 recapture is often referred to as *full recapture.* Any remaining gain after subtracting the amount recaptured as ordinary income will usually be § 1231 gain. The remaining gain is casualty gain, however, if the asset is disposed of in a casualty event. For example, if the machine in Example 47 had been disposed of by casualty and the $120,000 received had been an insurance recovery, Avocet would still have a gain of $90,000, and $70,000 of that gain would still be recaptured by § 1245 as ordinary gain. The other $20,000 of gain, however, would be casualty gain.

If § 1245 property is disposed of in a transaction other than a sale, exchange, or involuntary conversion, the maximum amount recaptured is the excess of the

TAX in the News — **ASK THE CPA ABOUT RECAPTURE**

A local newspaper includes a column called "Ask the CPA." A subscriber asked whether there were any differences between § 1245 recapture related to depreciable tangible personal property and that related to amortizable intangible personal property. The CPA wrote back that accelerated depreciation is usually used for tangible personal property, whereas straight-line amortization is used for intangible personal property. Consequently, the adjusted basis for the tangible personal property tends to be lower than that of the intangible personal property. If the properties had the same original cost and the same fair market value when they were sold, the tangible personal property would result in the larger gain and, therefore, the larger amount subject to recapture as ordinary income under § 1245.

property's fair market value over its adjusted basis. See the discussion under Exceptions to §§ 1245 and 1250 later in this chapter.

Section 1245 Property

Generally, **§ 1245 property** includes all depreciable personal property (e.g., machinery and equipment), including livestock. Buildings and their structural components usually are not § 1245 property. The following property is *also* subject to § 1245 treatment.

- Amortizable personal property such as goodwill, patents, copyrights, and leaseholds of § 1245 property.
- Professional baseball and football player contracts.
- Expensing of costs to remove architectural and transportation barriers that restrict the handicapped and/or elderly.
- Section 179 immediate expensing of depreciable tangible personal property.
- Certain depreciable tangible real property (other than buildings and their structural components) employed as an integral part of certain activities such as manufacturing and production. For example, a natural gas storage tank where the gas is used in the manufacturing process is § 1245 property.
- Pollution control facilities, railroad grading and tunnel bores, on-the-job training facilities, and child care facilities on which amortization is taken.
- Single-purpose agricultural and horticultural structures and petroleum storage facilities (e.g., a greenhouse or silo).

Observations on § 1245

- In most instances, the total depreciation taken will exceed the recognized gain. Therefore, the disposition of § 1245 property usually results in ordinary income rather than § 1231 gain. Refer to Example 46.
- Recapture applies to the total amount of depreciation allowed or allowable regardless of the depreciation method used (i.e., full recapture).
- Recapture applies regardless of the holding period of the property. Of course, the entire recognized gain would be ordinary income if the property was not held more than one year, because then § 1231 would not apply.
- Section 1245 does not apply to losses, which receive § 1231 treatment.
- Gains from the disposition of § 1245 assets may also be treated as passive activity gains (refer to Chapter 6).

EXAMPLE 49

Upon sale of some business equipment held for five years, Pink Corporation recognized a $7,500 loss. All of the $20,000 § 1245 depreciation recapture potential for the asset disappears as a result of the disposition. The transaction receives § 1231 loss treatment, and none of Pink's cost recovery deductions are recaptured into ordinary income for this asset. ■

PLANNING *Strategies*

DEPRECIATION RECAPTURE AND § 179

★ **Framework Focus: Deductions**

Strategy ★ Accelerate Recognition of Deductions to Achieve Tax Deferral.

Section 1245 recapture applies to all types of depreciation, including § 179 *immediate expensing*. Expensing under § 179, however, is elective and entirely within the discretion of the taxpayer. Choosing this option accelerates depreciation on the affected property but increases the potential recapture as well. Therefore, if a taxpayer anticipates that an asset will generate a gain when it is sold and that such sale will occur in the early years of the asset's life, the taxpayer might decide to forgo electing the additional depreciation under § 179.

On the other hand, electing § 179 remains attractive if little or no gain is anticipated upon an asset's disposition. After all, § 1245 recapture applies only to the extent that gain is actually realized. Moreover, even if a substantial gain is anticipated upon an asset's disposition, the *time value of money* might suggest that § 179 be elected if the disposition is expected to be many years away. In any case, the taxpayer can usually control when an asset is sold or exchanged and can thereby extend the time before the taxes saved by electing § 179 must be returned as § 1245 recapture.

Section 1250 Recapture

Some depreciable property that is not subject to § 1245 recapture faces a separate recapture computation mechanism in § 1250. For the most part, § 1250 applies to *depreciable real property* (principally buildings and their structural components), such as apartments, office buildings, factories, stores, and warehouses. Intangible real property, such as leaseholds of **§ 1250 property**, also is included.

Section 1250 recapture is much less onerous than § 1245 recapture, but it is also much more complex. Section 1250 recaptures only a property's **additional depreciation**, which is the excess of the depreciation actually deducted over the amount that would have been allowed under the straight-line method of depreciation. For this reason, § 1250 recapture is often referred to as *partial recapture*, in contrast to § 1245's full recapture.

Since § 1250 recaptures only the excess over straight-line depreciation, the concept does not apply to properties that were depreciated using the straight-line method (unless they were held for one year or less). Real property placed in service *after 1986* can only be depreciated using the straight-line method, so there is *no § 1250 recapture* upon the disposition of such properties that are held for longer than one year.

But real estate is particularly long-lived, and many dispositions of such assets involve properties placed in service *before 1987*, when accelerated depreciation was often available for real estate. Finally, § 1250 does not affect the § 1231 treatment of realized losses.

When straight-line depreciation is used, there is no § 1250 recapture potential unless the property is disposed of in the first year of use. For real property placed in service after 1986, only straight-line depreciation is allowed. Therefore, the application of § 1250 is limited to first-year dispositions.

EXAMPLE 50

Sanjay Enterprises, Ltd., acquires a residential rental building on January 1, 2005, for $300,000. It receives an offer of $450,000 for the building and sells it on December 23, 2006.

CONCEPT SUMMARY 8–5

Comparison of § 1245 and § 1250 Depreciation Recapture

	§ 1245	§ 1250
Property affected	All depreciable personal property, including items such as § 179 expense and § 197 amortization of intangibles such as goodwill, patents, and copyrights.	Nonresidential real property acquired after 1969 and before 1981, on which accelerated depreciation was taken. Residential rental real property acquired after 1975 and before 1987, on which accelerated depreciation was taken.
Depreciation recaptured	Potentially all depreciation taken. If the selling price is greater than or equal to the original cost, all depreciation is recaptured. If the selling price is between the adjusted basis and the original cost, only some depreciation is recaptured.	Additional depreciation (the excess of accelerated depreciation over straight-line depreciation). All depreciation taken if property disposed of in first year.
Limit on recapture	Lower of depreciation taken or gain recognized.	Lower of additional depreciation or gain recognized.
Treatment of gain exceeding recapture gain	Usually § 1231 gain.	Usually § 1231 gain.
Treatment of loss	No depreciation recapture; loss is usually § 1231 loss.	No depreciation recapture; loss is usually § 1231 loss.

- Sanjay takes $20,909 [($300,000 × .03485) + ($300,000 × .03636 × $^{11.5}/_{12}$) = $20,909] of total depreciation for 2005 and 2006. The adjusted basis of the property is $279,091 ($300,000 − $20,909).
- Sanjay's recognized gain is $170,909 ($450,000 − $279,091).
- All of the gain is § 1231 gain. ■

Concept Summary 8–5 compares and contrasts the § 1245 and § 1250 depreciation recapture rules.

Unrecaptured § 1250 Gain (Real Estate 25% Gain)

As noted previously, *noncorporate taxpayers* pay tax at a maximum rate of 25 percent on their **unrecaptured § 1250 gain**. This gain represents that part of the gain on § 1250 property that is attributable to depreciation that was not recaptured by § 1250.

The procedure for computing this amount involves three distinct steps.

Step 1. Determine the part of the recognized gain that is attributable to *depreciation deductions* claimed in prior years.

Step 2. Apply § 1250 to determine the portion of the gain calculated in step 1 that is recaptured as ordinary income.

Step 3. Subtract the gain recaptured under § 1250 (step 2) from the gain derived in step 1. This amount is the *unrecaptured § 1250 gain.*

EXAMPLE 51

Linda placed two apartment buildings in service at a cost of $100,000 each. On each building, she claimed accelerated depreciation deductions of $78,000, and straight-line depreciation would have been $64,000. Thus, her adjusted basis for each building is $22,000

($100,000 cost − $78,000 depreciation deducted), and her potential § 1250 recapture on each building is $14,000 ($78,000 accelerated depreciation − $64,000 straight-line). She now sells these buildings for $96,000 and $110,000, respectively, and computes her gain as follows.

	Building A	Building B
Amount realized	$ 96,000	$110,000
Adjusted basis	(22,000)	(22,000)
Recognized gain	$ 74,000	$ 88,000
Depreciation recaptured by § 1250	(14,000)	(14,000)
Remaining gain	$ 60,000	$ 74,000
Unrecaptured § 1250 gain	(60,000)	(64,000)
§ 1231 gain	None	$ 10,000

■

For property placed in service after 1986, § 1250 generally does not apply, because such property may use only straight-line depreciation under MACRS. As a result, *all* of the gain attributable to depreciation on such assets is unrecaptured § 1250 gain.

PLANNING *Strategies*

SELLING DEPRECIABLE REAL ESTATE

★ **Framework Focus: Deductions**

Strategy ★ Maximize Deductible Amounts.

★ **Framework Focus: Tax Rate**

Strategy ★ Control the Character of Income and Deductions.

A building depreciated on an accelerated method eventually generates annual allowances that are smaller than the amount that the straight-line method would have produced. Beyond that "cross-over" point, the *cumulative* amount of "additional depreciation" is reduced every year the asset is operated. Doing so effectively converts gain that would otherwise be subject to § 1250 recapture into "unrecaptured § 1250 gain," enabling the taxpayer to save the difference between the applicable tax rate on ordinary income and 25 percent.

Continuing to operate the building, however, brings forth an array of important *nontax considerations*. Each year a building is used subjects it to additional maintenance expenses to keep it in operating condition. Moreover, a building's appeal to current and prospective tenants tends to decline over time as newer structures appear offering more modern amenities, such as wireless high-speed Internet access, and other conveniences. Finally, local real estate developments might produce lower resale prices that offset much, if not all, of the tax advantage obtained by holding the property for the additional time.

Additional Recapture for Corporations

Although depreciation recapture is generally the same for all taxpayers, corporations that sell depreciable real estate face an additional amount of depreciation recapture. Section 291(a)(1) requires recapture of 20 percent of the excess of the amount that would be recaptured under § 1245 over the amount actually recaptured under § 1250.

EXAMPLE 52

Franklin Corporation purchased an apartment building for $300,000. Accelerated depreciation was taken in the amount of $260,000 before the building was sold for $250,000. Straight-line depreciation would have been $245,000. The corporation's depreciation recapture and § 1231 gain are computed as follows.

Sales price	$250,000
Less: Adjusted basis [$300,000 (cost of building) – $260,000 (MACRS depreciation)]	(40,000)
Recognized gain	$210,000
Ordinary income if property were § 1245 property	$210,000
Less: Gain recaptured under § 1250 ($260,000 – $245,000)	(15,000)
Excess § 1245 gain	$195,000
Apply § 291 percentage	× 20%
Additional § 291 gain recaptured	$ 39,000
Ordinary income from depreciation recapture ($15,000 + $39,000)	$ 54,000
Section 1231 gain ($210,000 – $54,000)	156,000
Total recognized gain	$210,000 ■

EXAMPLE 53

If the building in the preceding example were commercial property and straight-line depreciation was used, no § 1250 recapture results. A corporate taxpayer still must recapture as ordinary income 20% of the depreciation that would be ordinary income if the property were § 1245 property.

Sales price	$250,000
Less: Adjusted basis [$300,000 (cost of building) – $245,000 (straight-line depreciation)]	(55,000)
Recognized gain	$195,000
Ordinary income if property were § 1245 property	$195,000
Less: Ordinary income under § 1250	(–0–)
Excess ordinary income under § 1245	$195,000
Apply § 291 percentage	× 20%
Ordinary income under § 291	$ 39,000

Thus, $39,000 of the $195,000 gain would be ordinary income, and $156,000 would be § 1231 gain. ■

Exceptions to §§ 1245 and 1250

Recapture under §§ 1245 and 1250 does not apply to the following transactions.

Gifts

Depreciation recapture potential carries over to the donee.[27]

EXAMPLE 54

Wade gives his daughter, Helen, § 1245 property with an adjusted basis of $1,000. The amount of recapture potential is $700. Helen uses the property in her business and claims further depreciation of $100 before selling it for $1,900. Helen's recognized gain is $1,000 [$1,900 amount realized – $900 adjusted basis ($1,000 carryover basis – $100 depreciation taken by Helen)], of which $800 is recaptured as ordinary income ($100 depreciation taken

[27] §§ 1245(b)(1) and 1250(d)(1) and Reg. §§ 1.1245–4(a)(1) and 1.1250–3(a)(1).

GLOBAL *Tax Issues*

EXCHANGE FOR FOREIGN PROPERTY YIELDS RECOGNIZED RECAPTURE GAIN

Tangible personal property used in a trade or business may be the subject of a like-kind exchange, and the postponed gain is most likely postponed § 1245 gain. However, tangible personal property used predominantly within the United States cannot be exchanged for tangible personal property used predominantly outside the United States. Thus, such an exchange would cause recognized gain, and, as long as the fair market value of the property given up does not exceed its original cost, all of the gain is § 1245 depreciation recapture gain.

by Helen + $700 recapture potential carried over from Wade). The remaining gain of $200 is § 1231 gain. Even if Helen had used the property for personal purposes, the $700 recapture potential would have carried over. ■

Death

Although not an attractive tax planning approach, death eliminates all recapture potential.[28] Depreciation recapture potential does not carry over from a decedent to an estate or an heir.

EXAMPLE 55

Assume the same facts as in the preceding example, except that Helen receives the property as a result of Wade's death. The $700 recapture potential from Wade is extinguished at his death. Helen has a basis in the property equal to its fair market value (assume $1,700) at Wade's death. She will have a $300 gain when the property is sold because the selling price ($1,900) exceeds the property's adjusted basis of $1,600 ($1,700 basis to Helen – $100 depreciation) by $300. Because of § 1245, Helen has ordinary income of $100. The remaining gain of $200 is § 1231 gain. ■

Charitable Transfers

Depreciation recapture potential reduces the amount of any charitable contribution deduction.[29]

EXAMPLE 56

Bullfinch Corporation donates to a museum § 1245 property with a fair market value of $10,000 and an adjusted basis of $7,000. Depreciation recapture potential is $2,000 (the amount of recapture that would occur if the property were sold). The company's charitable contribution deduction (subject to the limitations discussed in Chapter 5) is $8,000 ($10,000 fair market value – $2,000 recapture potential). ■

Certain Nontaxable Transactions

In certain transactions, the transferor's adjusted basis for the property carries over to the transferee. Then, depreciation recapture potential also carries over to the transferee.[30] Included in this category are transfers of property pursuant to the following.

- Nontaxable incorporations under § 351.
- Certain liquidations of subsidiary corporations under § 332.
- Nontaxable contributions to a partnership under § 721.
- Nontaxable corporate reorganizations.

[28] §§ 1245(b)(2) and 1250(d)(2).

[29] § 170(e)(1)(A) and Reg. § 1.170A–4(b)(1). In certain circumstances, § 1231 gain also reduces the amount of the charitable contribution. See § 170(e)(1)(B).

[30] §§ 1245(b)(3) and 1250(d)(3). Reg. §§ 1.1245–2(a)(4) and (c)(2), 1.1245–4(c), 1.1250–2(d)(1) and (3).

Gain may be recognized in these transactions if boot is received. If gain is recognized, it is treated as ordinary income to the extent of the recapture potential or the recognized gain, whichever is lower.[31]

Like-Kind Exchanges and Involuntary Conversions

As explained in Chapter 7, realized gain is recognized to the extent of boot received in a like-kind exchange. Realized gain is also recognized to the extent the proceeds from an involuntary conversion are not reinvested in similar property. Such recognized gain is subject to recapture as ordinary income under §§ 1245 and 1250. Any remaining recapture potential carries over to the property received in the exchange.

EXAMPLE 57

Crane Corporation exchanges § 1245 property with an adjusted basis of $300 for § 1245 property with a fair market value of $6,000 plus $1,000 cash (boot). The exchange qualifies as a like-kind exchange under § 1031. Crane's realized gain is $6,700 ($7,000 amount realized – $300 adjusted basis of property).

Since Crane received boot of $1,000, it recognizes gain to this extent. Assuming the recapture potential is $7,500, Crane recognizes § 1245 gain of $1,000. The remaining recapture potential of $6,500 carries over to the like-kind property received. ■

DIGGING DEEPER 11

Find more information on this topic at our Web site: ***http://wft-entities.swlearning.com.***

Reporting Procedures

Noncapital gains and losses are reported on Form 4797, Sales of Business Property. Before filling out Form 4797, however, Form 4684, Casualties and Thefts, Part B, must be completed to determine whether any casualties will enter into the § 1231 computation procedure. Recall that gains from § 1231 asset casualties may be recaptured by § 1245 or § 1250. These gains do not appear on Form 4684. The § 1231 gains and nonpersonal-use long-term capital gains are netted against § 1231 and nonpersonal-use long-term capital losses on Form 4684 to determine if there is a net gain to transfer to Form 4797, Part I.

DIGGING DEEPER 12

Find more information on this topic at our Web site: ***http://wft-entities.swlearning.com.***

PLANNING *Strategies*

TIMING OF RECAPTURE

★ **Framework Focus: Tax Rate**

Strategy ★ Shift Net Income from High-Bracket Years to Low-Bracket Years.
★ Shift Net Income from High-Bracket Taxpayers to Low-Bracket Taxpayers.

Since recapture is usually not triggered until the property is sold or disposed of, it may be possible to plan for recapture in low-bracket or loss years. If a taxpayer has net operating loss carryovers that are about to expire, the recognition of ordinary income from recapture may be advisable to absorb the loss carryovers.

EXAMPLE 58

Angel Corporation has a $15,000 net operating loss carryover that will expire this year. It owns a machine that it plans to sell in the early part of next year. The expected gain of $17,000 from the sale of the machine will be recaptured as

[31] §§ 1245(b)(3) and 1250(d)(3), and Reg. §§ 1.1245–4(c) and 1.1250–3(c).

ordinary income under § 1245. Angel sells the machine before the end of this year and offsets $15,000 of the ordinary income against the net operating loss carryover. ■

It is also possible to postpone recapture or to shift the burden of recapture to others. For example, recapture is avoided upon the disposition of a § 1231 asset if the taxpayer replaces the property by entering into a like-kind exchange. In this instance, recapture potential is merely carried over to the newly acquired property (refer to Example 57).

Recapture can be shifted to others through the gratuitous transfer of § 1245 or § 1250 property to family members. A subsequent sale of such property by the donee will trigger recapture to the donee rather than the donor (refer to Example 54). This technique is advisable when the donee is in a lower income tax bracket than the donor.

Summary

The lower tax rates afforded long-term capital gains present numerous definitional and computational challenges. Most of these rules are found in court decisions and Regulations rather than in the Code. The tax professional needs to use good software to analyze all of the possibilities that are available.

Suggested Further Readings

John O. Everett and Debra M. Grace, "The Ins and Outs of Recapture (Part I)," *The Tax Adviser*, July 2005, pp. 418–423.

John O. Everett and Debra M. Grace, "The Ins and Outs of Recapture (Part II)," *The Tax Adviser*, August 2005, pp. 480–483.

"Loss on Classic Car Sales Was Not Capital Loss," *Practical Tax Strategies*, July 2005, pp. 58–59.

"Securing Capital Gains on Development Property," *The Tax Adviser*, October 2005, pp. 606–608.

KEY TERMS

Additional depreciation, 8–32
Capital asset, 8–2
Capital gain, 8–3
Capital loss, 8–3
Collectibles, 8–16
Franchise, 8–10
Holding period, 8–12
Lessee, 8–12
Lessor, 8–12
Long-term nonpersonal-use capital assets, 8–25
Net capital gain, 8–19
Net capital loss, 8–18
Options, 8–8
Patent, 8–9
Qualified small business stock, 8–22
Sale or exchange, 8–7
Section 1231 gains and losses, 8–24
Section 1231 lookback, 8–28
Section 1231 property, 8–24
Section 1245 property, 8–31
Section 1245 recapture, 8–30
Section 1250 property, 8–32
Section 1250 recapture, 8–32
Short sale, 8–14
Unrecaptured § 1250 gain, 8–33

PROBLEM MATERIALS

PROBLEMS

1. Mariah had three property transactions during the year. She sold a vacation home used only for personal purposes at a $35,000 loss. The home had been held for five years and

had never been rented. Mariah also sold an antique clock for $13,500 that she had inherited from her grandmother. The clock was valued in Mariah's grandmother's estate at $12,000. Mariah owned the clock for only four months. She sold these assets to finance her full-time occupation as a song writer. Near the end of the year, Mariah sold one of the songs she had written two years earlier. She received cash of $50,000 and a royalty interest in revenues derived from the merchandising of the song. Mariah had no tax basis for the song. What is Mariah's gross income?

2. All of the following assets are held by Chuck, not in his trade or business. Which are capital assets?
   a. Ten shares of Green Motors common stock.
   b. A note Chuck received when he loaned $3,000 to a friend.
   c. Chuck's personal use automobile.
   d. A letter written by Abraham Lincoln that Chuck purchased at an auction. Chuck is a collector of Lincoln memorabilia.

3. Hyacinth, Inc., is a dealer in securities. The firm has spotted a fast-rising company and would like to buy and hold its stock for investment. The stock is currently selling for $15 per share, and Hyacinth thinks it will climb to $63 a share within two years. How can Hyacinth ensure that any gain it realizes will be taxed as long-term capital gain? Draft a letter responding to Hyacinth's inquiry. The firm's address is 200 Morningside Drive, Hattisburg, MS 39406.

Communications

4. Eagle Partners meets all the requirements of § 1237 (subdivided realty). In 2006, Eagle Partners begins selling lots and sells four separate lots to four different purchasers. Eagle Partners also sells two contiguous lots to another purchaser. The sale price of each lot is $20,000. The partnership's basis for each lot is $15,000. Selling expenses are $500 per lot.
   a. What are the realized and recognized gain?
   b. Explain the nature of the gain (i.e., ordinary income or capital gain).
   c. Would your answers change if, instead, the lots sold to the fifth purchaser were not contiguous? If so, how?

5. Swan Songs, Inc., is in the business of buying song copyrights from struggling songwriters, holding those copyrights, and then reselling the songs to major record companies and singers. Swan has a four-month option to purchase a song copyright. The firm paid $2,000 for this option. A famous singer has heard the song and is willing to buy the option for $10,000. Swan thinks the song may be worth $35,000 in six months. If Swan exercises the option, it will have to pay $20,000 for the song. Assuming Swan is in the 34% tax bracket, which of these alternatives will give it a better after-tax cash flow?

Decision Making

6. Daffodil Enterprises Company purchased a one-year option on 20 acres of farmland for $245,000. Daffodil's plans for the property did not work out, so it let the option expire unexercised. What tax issues does the company face in determining how to treat the $245,000?

Issue ID

7. An investment partnership is looking for vacant land to buy. For $20,000, it is granted an 11-month option to buy 20 acres of vacant land for $400,000. The owner (who is holding the land for investment) paid $62,000 for the land several years ago.
   a. Does the landowner have gross income when $20,000 is received for granting the option?
   b. Does the partnership have an asset when the option is granted?
   c. If the option lapses, does the landowner have a recognized gain? If so, what type of gain? Does the partnership have a recognized loss? If so, what type of loss?
   d. If the option is exercised and an additional $400,000 is paid for the land, how much recognized gain does the seller have? What type of gain? What is the partnership's tax basis for the property?

8. Freys, Inc., sells a 12-year franchise to Red Company. The franchise contains many restrictions on how Red may operate its store. For instance, Red cannot use less than Grade 10 Idaho potatoes, must fry the potatoes at a constant 410 degrees, dress store personnel in Freys-approved uniforms, and have a Freys sign that meets detailed specifications on size, color, and construction. When the franchise contract is signed,

Red makes a noncontingent $160,000 payment to Freys. During the same year, Red pays Freys $300,000—14% of Red's sales. How does Freys treat each of these payments? How does Red treat each of the payments?

Issue ID

9. Jeremy is a sole proprietor running a video store. A large national chain has made an offer to purchase all of his store's assets. What issues does Jeremy face in determining what the results of this sale would be?

10. Tricia sells an automobile used in her business to her daughter, Felicia. Tricia has a realized loss of $9,000 on the sale even though the sale was for the full fair market value of the automobile. Tricia is unable to deduct this loss because of the loss disallowance rules for sales between related taxpayers. When does Felicia's holding period begin?

11. Magenta is an accrual basis corporation that is having cash-flow problems. It sells its account receivable to a financing company for 85% of the receivable's $236,000 face value. What is the nature of the loss from the disposition of the receivable?

Communications

12. Elaine Case (single with no dependents) has the following transactions in 2006:

AGI (exclusive of capital gains and losses)	$240,000
Long-term capital gain	22,000
Long-term capital loss	(5,000)
Short-term capital gain	19,000
Short-term capital loss	(23,000)

What is Elaine's net capital gain or loss? Draft a letter to Elaine describing how the net capital gain or loss will be treated on her tax return. Assume Elaine's income from other sources puts her in the 35% bracket. Elaine's address is 300 Ireland Avenue, Shepherdstown, WV 25443.

Decision Making

13. Sally has taxable income of $160,000 as of November 30 of this year. She wants to sell a Rodin sculpture that has appreciated $90,000 since she purchased it six years ago, but she does not want to pay more than $15,000 of additional tax on the transaction. Sally also owns various stocks, some of which are currently worth less than their basis. How can she achieve her desired result?

14. Platinum, Inc., has determined its taxable income as $215,000 before considering the results of its capital gain or loss transactions. Platinum has a short-term capital loss of $24,000, a long-term capital loss of $38,000, and a short-term capital gain of $39,000. What is Platinum's taxable income, and what (if any) are the amount and nature of its capital loss carryover?

Ethics

15. The taxpayer is an antiques collector and is going to sell an antique purchased many years ago for a large gain. The facts and circumstances indicate that the taxpayer might be classified as a dealer rather than an investor in antiques. The taxpayer will save $40,000 in taxes if the gain is treated as long-term capital gain rather than as ordinary income. The taxpayer is considering the following options as ways to assure the $40,000 tax savings.

- Give the antique to his daughter, who is an investment banker, to sell.
- Merely assume that he has held the antique as an investment.
- Exchange the antique in a like-kind exchange for another antique he wants.

One of the tax preparers the taxpayer has contacted has said he would be willing to prepare the return under the second option. Would you? Why? Evaluate the other options.

Issue ID

16. Bridgette is known as the "doll lady." She started collecting dolls as a child, always received one or more dolls as gifts on her birthday, never sold any dolls, and eventually owned 600 dolls. She is retiring and moving to a small apartment and has decided to sell her collection. She lists the dolls on an Internet auction site and, to her great surprise, receives an offer from another doll collector of $45,000 for the entire collection. Bridgette sells the entire collection, except for five dolls that she purchased during the last year. She had owned all the dolls sold for more than a year. What tax factors should Bridgette consider in deciding how to report the sale?

17. During the year, Eric had the four property transactions summarized below. Eric is a collector of antique automobiles and occasionally sells one to get funds to buy another. What are the amount and nature of the gain or loss from each of these transactions?

Property	Date Acquired	Date Sold	Adjusted Basis	Sale Price
Antique truck	06/18/98	05/23/06	$47,000	$35,000
Blue Growth Fund (100 shares)	12/23/00	11/22/06	12,000	23,000
Orange bonds	02/12/01	04/11/06	34,000	42,000*
Green stock (100 shares)	02/14/06	11/23/06	13,000	11,000

* The sale price included $750 of accrued interest income.

18. Mateen, an inventor, obtained a patent on a chemical process to clean old aluminum siding so that it can be easily repainted. Mateen has a zero tax basis in the patent. Mateen does not have the capital to begin manufacturing and selling this product, so he has done nothing with the patent since obtaining it two years ago.

Decision Making

Now a group of individuals has approached him and offered two alternatives. Under one alternative, they will pay Mateen $400,000 (payable evenly over the next 10 years) for the exclusive right to manufacture and sell the product. Under the other, they will form a business and contribute capital to it to begin manufacturing and selling the product; Mateen will receive 20% of the company's shares of stock in exchange for all of his patent rights. Discuss which alternative is better for Mateen.

19. A painting that Tulip & Co. held for investment was destroyed in a flood. The painting was insured, and Tulip had a $30,000 gain from this casualty. It also had a $17,000 loss from an uninsured antique vase that was destroyed by the flood. The vase was also held for investment. Tulip had no other property transactions during the year and has no nonrecaptured § 1231 losses from prior years. Compute Tulip's net gain or loss and identify how it would be treated. Write a letter to Tulip explaining the nature of the gain or loss. Tulip's address is 2367 Meridian Road, Hannibal Point, MO 34901.

Communications

20. Sylvia owns two items of business equipment. They were both purchased in 2002 for $100,000, both have a seven-year recovery period, and both have an adjusted basis of $37,490. Sylvia is considering selling these assets in 2006. One of them is worth $40,000, and the other is worth $23,000. Since both items were used in her business, Sylvia simply assumes that the loss on one will be offset against the gain from the other and the net gain or loss will increase or reduce her business income. Is she correct?

Issue ID

21. Harold, a CPA, has a new client who recently moved to town. Harold prepares the client's current-year tax return, which shows a net § 1231 gain. Harold calls the client to request copies of the returns for the preceding five years to determine if there are any § 1231 lookback losses. The client says that the returns are "still buried in the moving mess somewhere" and cannot be found. The client also says that he does not remember any § 1231 net losses on the prior-year returns. What should Harold do? Justify your answer.

Ethics

22. Geranium, Inc., has the following net § 1231 results for each of the years shown. What is the nature of the net gain in 2005 and 2006?

Tax Year	Net § 1231 Loss	Net § 1231 Gain
2001	$16,000	
2002	33,000	
2003	32,000	
2004		$42,000
2005		30,000
2006		39,000

Decision Making

23. Delphinium Company owns two parcels of land (§ 1231 assets). One parcel can be sold at a loss of $30,000, and the other parcel can be sold at a gain of $40,000. The company has no nonrecaptured § 1231 losses from prior years. The parcels could be sold at any time because potential purchasers are abundant. The company has a $25,000 short-term capital loss carryover from a prior tax year and no capital assets that could be sold to generate long-term capital gains. What should Delphinium do based upon these facts?

24. Green Industries (a sole proprietorship) sold three § 1231 assets on October 10, 2006. Data on these property dispositions are as follows.

Asset	Cost	Acquired	Depreciation	Sold for
Rack	$100,000	10/10/02	$60,000	$75,000
Forklift	35,000	10/16/03	23,000	5,000
Bin	87,000	3/12/05	34,000	60,000

a. Determine the amount and the character of the recognized gain or loss from the disposition of each asset in 2006.
b. Assuming Green has no nonrecaptured net § 1231 losses from prior years, how much of the recognized gains are treated as long-term capital gains?

Communications

25. On December 1, 2004, Gray Manufacturing Company (a corporation) purchased another company's assets, including a patent. The patent was used in Gray's manufacturing operations; $40,500 was allocated to the patent, and it was amortized at the rate of $225 per month. On June 30, 2006, Gray sold the patent for $70,000. Twenty months of amortization had been taken on the patent. What are the amount and nature of the gain Gray recognizes on the disposition of the patent? Write a letter to Gray discussing the treatment of the gain. Gray's address is 6734 Grover Street, Back Bay Harbor, ME 23890. The letter should be addressed to Siddim Sadatha, Controller.

26. Dave is the sole proprietor of a trampoline shop. During 2006, the following transactions occurred.

- Unimproved land adjacent to the store was condemned by the city on February 1. The condemnation proceeds were $25,000. The land, acquired in 1983, had an allocable basis of $40,000. Dave has additional parking across the street and plans to use the condemnation proceeds to build his inventory.
- A truck used to deliver trampolines was sold on January 2 for $3,500. The truck was purchased on January 2, 2002, for $6,000. On the date of sale, the adjusted basis was $2,509.
- Dave sold an antique rowing machine at an auction. Net proceeds were $3,900. The rowing machine was purchased as used equipment 17 years ago for $5,200 and is fully depreciated.
- Dave sold an apartment building for $200,000 on September 1. The rental property was purchased on September 1, 2003, for $150,000 and was being depreciated over a 27.5-year life using the straight-line method. At the date of sale, the adjusted basis was $124,783.
- Dave's personal yacht was stolen on September 5. The yacht had been purchased in August at a cost of $25,000. The fair market value immediately preceding the theft was $20,000. Dave was insured for 50% of the original cost, and he received $12,500 on December 1.
- Dave sold a Buick on May 1 for $9,600. The vehicle had been used exclusively for personal purposes. It was purchased on September 1, 2002, for $20,800.
- Dave's trampoline stretching machine (owned two years) was stolen on May 5, but the business's insurance company will not pay any of the machine's value because Dave failed to pay the insurance premium. The machine had a fair market value of $8,000 and an adjusted basis of $6,000 at the time of theft.
- Dave had AGI of $402,000 from sources other than those described above.
- Dave has no nonrecaptured § 1231 lookback losses.

a. For each transaction, what are the amount and nature of recognized gain or loss?
b. What is Dave's 2006 AGI?

27. Vermilion Corporation sold a machine used in its business for $453,000 on the installment basis. It received a $53,000 down payment in 2006 and will receive payments of $100,000 (plus fair market value interest) for each of the next four years. The machine was originally purchased for $1 million in 1994 and had a zero adjusted basis at the time of its sale. How much gain must be recognized, when must it be recognized, and what is the nature of the gain from this sale?

Extender

28. Nicholas owns business equipment with a $155,000 adjusted basis; he paid $200,000 for the equipment, and it is currently worth $173,000. Nicholas dies suddenly, and his son Alvin inherits the property. What is Alvin's basis for the property, and what happens to the § 1245 depreciation recapture potential?

29. Two years ago, Hsui Company (an unincorporated entity) developed a process for preserving fresh fruit that gives the fruit a much longer shelf life. The process is not patented or copyrighted, and only Hsui knows how it works. A conglomerate has approached Hsui with an offer to purchase the formula for the process. Specifically, the offer allows Hsui to choose between the following. Which option should Hsui accept?

Extender

- $850,000 cash for the formula and a 10-year covenant not to compete, paying Hsui $45,000 per year for 10 years.
- $850,000 cash for a 10-year covenant not to compete, and an annual $45,000 royalty for the formula, payable for 10 years.

30. In March 2004, the Sue-Jen Partnership contracted for $100,000 to cut timber on a 100-acre tract of undeveloped South Dakota land. On January 1, 2005, the timber was worth $110,000. The value in November 2005 when the timber was cut was $115,000. On January 30, 2006, the wood was sold for $78,000.

Extender

   a. If Sue-Jen elects to treat the timber cutting as a sale, what is its recognized gain or loss for 2004, 2005, and 2006?
   b. In each case, what is the character of this gain or loss?
   c. How does the result change if the wood is sold in December 2005? Why?
   d. If the timber was worth only $48,000 on January 1, 2005, was cut in November when worth $21,000, and was sold in December for $49,000, how would the answers in (a) and (b) change?

31. Thrasher Corporation sells short 100 shares of ARC stock at $20 per share on January 15, 2006. It buys 200 shares of ARC stock on April 1, 2006, at $25 per share. On May 2, 2006, Thrasher closes the short sale by delivering 100 of the shares purchased on April 1.

Extender

   a. What are the amount and nature of Thrasher's loss upon closing the short sale?
   b. When does the holding period for the remaining 100 shares begin?
   c. If Thrasher sells (at $27 per share) the remaining 100 shares on January 20, 2007, what will be the nature of its gain or loss?

BRIDGE *Discipline*

1. Using an online research service, find the audited financial statements of a major U.S. corporation.
   a. List some of the items that the corporation reports as having different treatment for tax and financial accounting purposes. These items often are mentioned in the footnotes to the statements.
   b. List two or more such items that seem to increase the taxpayer's after-tax income and two or more that seem to decrease it.

RESEARCH PROBLEMS

Note: Solutions to Research Problems can be prepared by using the **RIA Checkpoint® Student Edition** online research product, which is available to accompany this text. It is also possible to prepare solutions to the Research Problems by using tax research materials found in a standard tax library.

THOMSON RIA™

Research Problem 1. Siva Nathaniel owns various plots of land in Fulton County, Georgia. He acquired the land at various times during the last 20 years. About every fourth year, Siva subdivides one of the properties he owns into lots. He then has water, sewer, natural gas, and electricity hookups put in on each lot and paves the new streets. Siva has always treated his sales of such lots as sales of capital assets. His previous tax returns were prepared by an accountant whose practice you recently purchased. Has the proper tax treatment been used on the prior tax returns?

Partial list of research aids:
§§ 1221 and 1237.
Jesse W. and Betty J. English, 65 TCM 2160, T.C.Memo. 1993–111.

Decision Making

Research Problem 2. Ali owns 100 shares of Brown Corporation stock. He purchased the stock at five different times and at five different prices per share as indicated.

Share Block	Number of Shares	Per Share Price	Purchase Date
A	10	$60	10/10/94
B	20	20	8/11/95
C	15	15	10/24/95
D	35	30	4/23/97
E	20	25	7/28/97

On April 28, 2006, Ali will sell 40 shares of Brown stock for $40 per share. All of Ali's shares are held by his stockbroker. The broker's records track when the shares were purchased. May Ali designate the shares he sells, and, if so, which shares should he sell? Assume Ali wants to maximize his gain because he has a capital loss carryforward.

Research Problem 3. Mobley is a retired high school teacher. He has $65,000 of AGI from his retirement income. He is an avid player of the stock market. During 2006, he made 3,000 transactions buying and selling stocks. All the sales involved stocks held short term. His net loss for the year was $17,000. He incurred $7,000 of expenses for subscriptions to various publications dealing with how to buy and sell stocks. He has two questions. (1) Is the loss a short-term capital loss or an ordinary loss? (2) Is the $7,000 of expenses deductible *for* or *from* AGI?

Partial list of research aids:
Marlowe King, 89 T.C. 445 (1987), *acq.* 1988–2 C.B. 1.
Frederick Mayer, T.C.Memo. 1994–209 (1994), 67 TCM 2949.

Communications

Research Problem 4. Clean Corporation runs a chain of dry cleaners. Borax is used heavily in Clean's dry cleaning process and has been in short supply several times in the past. Several years ago, Clean Corporation bought a controlling interest in Dig Corporation—a borax mining concern—to assure Clean of a continuous supply of borax if another shortage developed. Clean has just sold the stock at a loss because Dig is in difficult financial straits and because Clean has obtained an alternative source of borax. What is the nature of Clean's loss on the disposition of the Dig Corporation stock? Write a letter to the controller, Salvio Guitterez, that contains your advice and prepare a memo for the tax files. The mailing address of Clean Corporation is 4455 Whitman Way, San Mateo, CA 44589.

Research Problem 5. Walter is both a real estate developer and the owner and manager of residential rental real estate. Walter is retiring and is going to sell both the land he is holding for future development and the rental properties he owns. Straight-line depreciation was used to depreciate the rental real estate. The rental properties will be sold at a substantial loss, and the development property will be sold at a substantial gain. What is the nature of these gains and losses?

Partial list of research aids:
§§ 1221 and 1231.
Zane R. Tollis, 65 TCM 1951, T.C.Memo. 1993–63.

Research Problem 6. Brown Corporation, a software development company, was formed in 1996 and has always been a C corporation. In 2003, it acquired all the assets of another software company, including $400,000 worth of copyrights developed by the acquired company. Brown treated these copyrights as § 197 intangible assets and amortized 30 months' worth of the 180-month life of the assets before selling the copyrights for $1.2 million on June 28, 2005. What was the tax status of these copyrights, and what is the nature of the gain or loss from their disposition?

Use the tax resources of the Internet to address the following questions. Do not restrict your search to the World Wide Web, but include a review of newsgroups and general reference materials, practitioner sites and resources, primary sources of the tax law, chat rooms and discussion groups, and other opportunities.

Internet *Activity*

Research Problem 7. Summarize tax planning strategies related to each of the following topics that are presented on the Internet by tax advisers looking for clients. Send your findings in an e-mail to your instructor.

Communications

a. A strategy for maximizing gains that are eligible for the 5%/15% alternative tax rate rather than the 25% rate.
b. A strategy for maximizing gains that are eligible for the 5%/15% alternative tax rate rather than the 28% rate.

Research Problem 8. Find a Web site that discusses the income tax in Australia. Determine whether Australia has an alternative tax on net long-term capital gains similar to that in the United States. Summarize your findings in an e-mail to your instructor.

Communications

Research Problem 9. Investors are flooded with performance data and rankings of mutual funds. The "tax efficiency" of these funds is much more difficult to determine, even though this information often has an enormous impact on taxable accounts (i.e., non-retirement-oriented accounts). Examine various Web sites to determine recent distribution history of mutual funds and compare their pre-tax and after-tax performance data to assess the impact of this information on investment planning.

Research Problem 10. Go to the the IRS Web site and download a Form 4797 and its instructions. Use the form to complete Problem 24.

Research Problem 11. How does your state tax the sale of a plot of investment land, owned by a resident of your state, but located in Arizona?

http://wft.swlearning.com

PART 4

Business Entities

The materials in Parts I through III have dealt with tax concepts that generally are taxpayer neutral with respect to the different types of business entities. Some of these tax concepts are equally applicable to individual taxpayers. Part IV focuses on the different types of business entities and includes a life cycle coverage of formation, operations, and termination. The specific business entities covered are the C corporation, the S corporation, the partnership, and the LLC.

http://wft.swlearning.com

CHAPTER 9

Corporations: Organization, Capital Structure, and Operating Rules

LEARNING OBJECTIVES

After completing Chapter 9, you should be able to:

LO.1

Identify the tax consequences of incorporating and transferring assets to controlled corporations.

LO.2

Understand the special rules that apply when a corporation assumes a shareholder's liability.

LO.3

Recognize the basis issues relevant to the shareholder and the corporation.

LO.4

Understand the tax aspects of the capital structure of a corporation.

LO.5

Recognize the tax differences between debt and equity investments.

LO.6

Understand the tax rules unique to corporations.

LO.7

Compute the corporate income tax.

LO.8

Explain the rules unique to computing the tax of multiple corporations.

LO.9

Describe the reporting process for corporations.

OUTLINE

TAX *Talk*

Taxes owing to the Government ... are the price that business has to pay for protection and security.

—Benjamin N. Cardozo

Business operations may be conducted in a number of different forms. As with many business decisions, consideration must be given to the tax consequences of choosing a particular business entity. This chapter deals with the unique tax consequences of operating an entity as a regular corporation, including:

- Classification of the entity as a corporation.
- The tax consequences to the shareholders and the corporation upon the formation of the corporation.
- The capital structure of the corporation.
- Determination of the corporate income tax liability.
- Corporate tax filing requirements.

An Introduction to Corporate Tax

Corporations are governed by Subchapter C or Subchapter S of the Internal Revenue Code. Those governed by Subchapter C are referred to as **C corporations** or **regular corporations**. Corporations governed by Subchapter S are referred to as **S corporations**.

S corporations, which generally do not pay Federal income tax, are similar to partnerships in that net profit or loss flows through to the shareholders to be reported on their separate returns. Also like partnerships, S corporations do not aggregate all income and expense items in computing net profit or loss. Certain items flow through to the shareholders and retain their separate character when reported on the shareholders' returns. See Chapter 12 for detailed coverage of S corporations.

Double Taxation of Corporate Income

Unlike proprietorships, partnerships, and S corporations, C corporations are taxpaying entities. This results in what is known as a *double tax* effect. A C corporation reports its income and expenses on Form 1120 (or Form 1120–A, the corporate

GLOBAL *Tax Issues*

CHOICE OF ORGANIZATIONAL FORM WHEN OPERATING OVERSEAS

When the management of a corporation decides to expand its business by establishing a presence in a foreign market, the new business venture may take one of several organizational forms. As each form comes with its respective advantages and disadvantages, making the best choice can be difficult.

One common approach is to conduct the foreign activity as a *branch* operation of the U.S. corporation. The foreign branch is not a separate legal entity, but a division of the U.S. corporation established overseas. As a result, any gains and losses produced by the foreign unit are included in the corporation's overall financial results.

Another possibility is to organize the foreign operations as a *subsidiary* of the U.S. parent corporation. If this route is chosen, the subsidiary may be either a *domestic* subsidiary (i.e., organized in the United States) or a *foreign* subsidiary (organized under the laws of a foreign country).

One fundamental tax difference between these two approaches is that the gains and losses of a domestic subsidiary may be consolidated with the operations of the U.S. parent, while the operations of a foreign subsidiary may not. Thus, the use of a domestic subsidiary to conduct foreign operations will yield generally the same final result as the use of a branch. With both approaches, the financial statements of the U.S. parent reflect the results of its worldwide operations.

short form). The corporation computes tax on the taxable income reported on the corporate tax return using the rate schedule applicable to corporations (refer to the rate schedule inside the front cover of this text). When a corporation distributes its income, the corporation's shareholders report dividend income on their own tax returns. Thus, income that has already been taxed at the corporate level is also taxed at the shareholder level. The effects of double taxation (disregarding the effect of payroll and self-employment taxes) are illustrated in Examples 1 and 2.

EXAMPLE 1

Lavender Corporation earned net profit of $100,000 in 2006. It paid corporate tax of $22,250 (refer to the corporate rate schedule on the inside front cover of this text). This left $77,750, all of which was distributed as a dividend to Mike, the corporation's sole shareholder. Mike had taxable income of $69,300 ($77,750 – $5,150 standard deduction – $3,300 personal exemption). He paid tax at the 15% rate applicable to dividends received by individuals. His tax was $10,395 ($69,300 × 15%). The combined tax on the corporation's net profit was $32,645 ($22,250 paid by the corporation + $10,395 paid by the shareholder). ■

EXAMPLE 2

Assume the same facts as in Example 1, except that the business is organized as a sole proprietorship. Mike reports the $100,000 net profit from the business on his tax return. He has taxable income of $91,550 ($100,000 – $5,150 standard deduction – $3,300 personal exemption) and pays tax of $19,966. Therefore, operating the business as a sole proprietorship resulted in tax *savings* of $12,679 in 2006 ($32,645 tax from Example 1 – $19,966). ■

Examples 1 and 2 deal with a specific set of facts. The conclusions reached in this situation cannot be extended to all decisions about a form of business organization. Each specific set of facts and circumstances requires a thorough analysis of the tax factors. In many cases, the tax burden will be greater if the business is operated as a corporation (as in Example 1), but sometimes operating as a corporation can result in tax savings, as illustrated in Examples 3 and 4.

EXAMPLE 3

In 2006, Tan Corporation filed Form 1120 reporting net profit of $100,000. The corporation paid tax of $22,250 and distributed the remaining $77,750 as a dividend to Carla, the sole

TAX FACT

Corporations' Reporting Responsibilities

Like individuals, corporations are required to report their taxable income and other financial information to the IRS on an annual basis. The forms used depend on the type and size of the corporation. Based on projections, the IRS expects to receive over 6 million corporate income tax returns during the 2006 filing season.

Type of Corporation	Form	Percentage
C Corporation	1120 and 1120–A	35.9%
C Corporation	Others	3.6
S Corporation	1120S	60.5
		100.0%

Interestingly, only about 6.9 percent of C and S corporations are expected to submit their returns electronically.

Source: *Fiscal Year Return Projections for the United States: 2005–2012, IRS, Document 6292, Fall 2005 Update, Table 1.*

shareholder of the corporation. Carla had income from other sources and was in the top individual tax bracket of 35% in 2006. As a result, she paid tax of $11,663 ($77,750 × 15% rate on dividends) on the distribution. The combined tax on the corporation's net profit was $33,913 ($22,250 paid by the corporation + $11,663 paid by the shareholder). ■

EXAMPLE 4

Assume the same facts as in Example 3, except that the business is a sole proprietorship. Carla reports the $100,000 net profit from the business on her tax return and pays tax of $35,000 ($100,000 net profit × 35% marginal rate). Therefore, operating the business as a sole proprietorship resulted in a tax *cost* of $1,087 in 2006 ($35,000 – $33,913 tax from Example 3). ■

Shareholders in closely held corporations frequently attempt to avoid double taxation by paying out all the profit of the corporation as salary to themselves.

EXAMPLE 5

Orange Corporation has net income of $180,000 during the year ($300,000 revenue – $120,000 operating expenses). Emilio is the sole shareholder of Orange Corporation. In an effort to avoid tax at the corporate level, Emilio has Orange pay him a salary of $180,000, which results in zero taxable income for the corporation. ■

Will the strategy described in Example 5 effectively avoid double taxation? The answer depends on whether the compensation paid to the shareholder is *reasonable.* Section 162 provides that compensation is deductible only to the extent that it is reasonable in amount. The IRS is aware that many taxpayers use this strategy to bail out corporate profits and, in an audit, looks closely at compensation expense.

If the IRS believes that compensation is too high based on the amount and quality of services performed by the shareholder, the compensation deduction of the corporation is reduced to a reasonable amount. Compensation that is determined to be unreasonable is usually treated as a constructive dividend to the shareholder and is not deductible by the corporation.

EXAMPLE 6

Assume the same facts as in Example 5, and that the IRS determines that $80,000 of the amount paid to Emilio is unreasonable compensation. As a result, $80,000 of the corporation's compen-

TAX *in the News* **CORPORATE TAX BREAKS**

Although rates in the corporate tax schedule range from 15 percent to 39 percent, a recent Government Accountability Office study found that fewer than 40 percent of U.S. corporations paid *any* Federal income taxes from 1996 to 2000. The Commerce Department provides additional evidence of the low tax burden borne by U.S. corporations. Throughout the 1990s, the average rate paid by U.S. corporations was approximately 30 percent. Since 2001, the rate has been approximately 20 percent. A Duke University study found that the rate in 2002 was 12 percent, compared to 15 percent in 1999 and 18 percent in 1995. All of these studies show that the actual rate of Federal income tax paid by corporations is low and that it has declined steadily from the early 1990s through 2002.

Source: *"Corporate Tax Burden Shows Sharp Decline,"* Wall Street Journal, *April 13, 2004, pp. C1–C3.*

sation deduction is disallowed and treated as a constructive dividend to Emilio. Orange has taxable income of $80,000. Emilio would report salary of $100,000 and a taxable dividend of $80,000. The net effect is that $80,000 would be subject to double taxation. ■

Taxation of Dividends. The Jobs and Growth Tax Relief Reconciliation Act (JGTRRA) of 2003 reduced the impact of double taxation. Before 2003, dividends received by individuals were subject to the same rates as ordinary income. JGTRRA changed the top individual rate from 38.6 percent to 35 percent and the rate on dividend income to 15 percent (5 percent for low-income taxpayers).

This tax-favored treatment of dividends is having a marked impact on many closely held corporations. Prior to JGTRRA, the motivation was to avoid paying dividends, as they were nondeductible to the corporation and fully taxed to the shareholders (as illustrated in Examples 1 and 3 above). To counter this problem of double taxation, corporate profits were bailed out in a manner that provided tax benefits to the corporation (refer to Example 5). Hence, liberal use was made of compensation, loan, and lease arrangements, as salaries, interest, and rent are deductible items. Now, another variable has been interjected. Who should benefit? Shareholders prefer dividends because salaries, interest, and rent are fully taxed, while dividends are taxed at the 15 percent rate (5 percent for low-income taxpayers). Corporations, however, continue to favor distributions that are deductible (e.g., salaries, interest, and rent). The ideal is a good mix of the two approaches. Besides being attractive to shareholders, the payment of dividends helps the corporation ease the problems of unreasonable compensation, thin capitalization, and meeting the arm's length test as to rents. Chapter 10 presents a detailed discussion of the taxation of dividends.

Comparison of Corporations and Other Forms of Doing Business

Chapter 15 presents a detailed comparison of sole proprietorships, partnerships, S corporations, and C corporations as forms of doing business. However, it is appropriate at this point to consider some of the tax and nontax factors that favor corporations over other business entities.

Consideration of tax factors requires an examination of the corporate rate structure. The income tax rate schedule applicable to corporations is reproduced on the inside front cover of the text. As this schedule shows, corporate rates on taxable income up to $75,000 are lower than individual rates for persons in the 28 percent and higher brackets. Therefore, corporate tax will be lower than individual tax. Furthermore, only the corporate marginal rates of 38 and 39 percent are higher than the 35 percent top bracket for individuals. When dividends are paid, however, the double taxation problem occurs.

BRIDGE *Discipline*

Bridge to Finance

Investment brokers and promoters often try to entice individuals to invest their disposable income in ventures designed to produce handsome returns. In most situations, the type of business entity in which the funds are invested takes the form of a "flow-through" entity, such as a limited partnership. Such investment ventures rarely operate as regular corporations.

A limited partnership is the favored investment vehicle for several reasons. One of the most significant reasons is that the investors who become limited partners are protected from exposure to unlimited liability. In addition, any operating losses of the entity (which may be expected in the venture's early years) flow through to the partners and, as a result, may provide an immediate tax benefit on the partners' returns. Another major advantage of the partnership form, in contrast to the corporate form, is that the business earnings are subject to only one level of tax—at the partner or investor level. If the investments were housed in a corporation, a tax would be levied first on the corporate earnings and then at the investor level when the corporation makes distributions to the shareholders.

Another tax consideration involves the nature of dividend income. All income and expense items of a proprietorship retain their character when reported on the proprietor's tax return. In the case of a partnership, several separately reported items (e.g., charitable contributions and long-term capital gains) retain their character when passed through to the partners. However, the tax attributes of income and expense items of a corporation do not pass through the corporate entity to the shareholders.

Losses of a C corporation are treated differently than losses of a proprietorship, partnership, or S corporation. A loss incurred by a proprietorship may be deductible by the owner, because all income and expense items are reported by the proprietor. Partnership and S corporation losses are passed through the entity and may be deductible by the partners or shareholders. C corporation losses, however, have no effect on the taxable income of the shareholders.

EXAMPLE 7

Franco plans to start a business this year. He expects the business will incur operating losses for the first three years and then become highly profitable. Franco decides to operate as an S corporation during the loss period because the losses will flow through and be deductible on his personal return. When the business becomes profitable, he intends to switch to C corporation status. ■

Nontax Considerations

Nontax considerations will sometimes override tax considerations and lead to the conclusion that a business should be operated as a corporation. The following are some of the more important nontax considerations:

- Sole proprietors and *general* partners in partnerships face the danger of *unlimited liability*. That is, creditors of the business may file claims not only against the assets of the business but also against the *personal* assets of proprietors or general partners. Shareholders are protected from claims against their personal assets by state corporate law.
- The corporate form of business organization can provide a vehicle for raising large amounts of capital through widespread stock ownership. Most major businesses in the United States are operated as corporations.

- Shares of stock in a corporation are freely transferable, whereas a partner's sale of his or her partnership interest is subject to approval by the other partners.
- Shareholders may come and go, but a corporation can continue to exist. Death or withdrawal of a partner, on the other hand, may terminate the existing partnership and cause financial difficulties that result in dissolution of the entity. Thus, *continuity of life* is a distinct advantage of the corporate form of doing business.
- Corporations have *centralized management.* All management responsibility is assigned to a board of directors, which appoints officers to carry out the corporation's business. Partnerships, by contrast, may have decentralized management, in which every owner has a right to participate in the organization's business decisions; **limited partnerships**, though, may have centralized management. Centralized management is essential for the smooth operation of a widely held business.

Limited Liability Companies

The **limited liability company (LLC)** has proliferated greatly in recent years, particularly since 1988 when the IRS first ruled that it would treat qualifying LLCs as partnerships for tax purposes. All 50 states and the District of Columbia have passed laws that allow LLCs, and thousands of companies have chosen LLC status. As with a corporation, operating as an LLC allows its owners to avoid unlimited liability, which is a primary *nontax* consideration in choosing this form of business organization. The tax advantage of LLCs is that qualifying businesses may be treated as partnerships for tax purposes, thereby avoiding the problem of double taxation associated with regular corporations.

Some states allow an LLC to have centralized management, but not continuity of life or free transferability of interests. Other states allow LLCs to adopt any or all of the corporate characteristics of centralized management, continuity of life, and free transferability of interests. The comparison of business entities in Chapter 15 includes a discussion of LLCs.

Entity Classification

In late 1996, the IRS issued its so-called **check-the-box Regulations**.[1] Effective beginning in 1997, the Regulations enable taxpayers to choose the tax status of a business entity without regard to its corporate (or noncorporate) characteristics. These rules have simplified tax administration considerably and eliminated the type of litigation that arose under prior law.

Under these rules, entities with more than one owner can elect to be classified as either a partnership or a corporation. An entity with only one owner can elect to be classified as a sole proprietorship or as a corporation. In the event of default (i.e., no election is made), multi-owner entities are classified as partnerships and single-person businesses as sole proprietorships.

The election is not available to entities that are actually incorporated under state law or to entities that are required to be corporations under Federal law (e.g., certain publicly traded partnerships). Otherwise, LLCs are not treated as being incorporated under state law. Consequently, they can elect either corporation or partnership status.

DIGGING DEEPER 1

Find more information on this topic at our Web site: ***http://wft-entities.swlearning.com.***

[1]Reg. §§ 301.7701–1 through –4, and –7.

PLANNING *Strategies*

CONSOLIDATED GROUPS MAY UTILIZE CHECK-THE-BOX REGULATIONS

★ **Framework Focus: Thinking outside the Framework**

The check-the-box Regulations allow a single-owner eligible entity to be treated as a corporation or a division. Since LLCs are eligible entities, a C corporation that owns 100 percent of an LLC can treat the LLC as a division. At the same time, the parent corporation can enjoy the benefit of limited liability in the LLC operations. By electing division treatment, the income of the LLC flows directly to the parent corporation for tax purposes. Consequently, the parent corporation is able to avoid detailed and complex consolidated return Regulations and filing requirements.

LO.1

Identify the tax consequences of incorporating and transferring assets to controlled corporations.

Organization of and Transfers to Controlled Corporations

In General

Property transactions normally produce tax consequences if a gain or loss is realized. As a result, unless special provisions in the Code apply, a transfer of property to a corporation in exchange for stock is a taxable transaction. The amount of gain or loss is measured by the difference between the fair market value of the stock received and the tax basis of the property transferred.

The Code, however, permits nonrecognition of gain or loss in limited circumstances. For example, when a taxpayer exchanges some of his or her property for other property of a like kind, § 1031 provides that gain (or loss) on the exchange is deferred because there has not been a substantive change in the taxpayer's investment. The deferral of gain or loss is accomplished by calculating a substituted basis for the like-kind property received. With this substituted basis, the potential gain or loss on the property given up is recognized when the property received in the exchange is sold.

In a similar fashion, § 351 provides that gain or loss is not recognized upon the transfer of property to a corporation in exchange for stock. The nonrecognition of gain or loss under § 351 reflects the principle that gain should not be recognized when a taxpayer's investment has not substantively changed. For example, when a business is incorporated, the owner's economic status remains the same; only the *form* of the investment has changed. The investment in the business assets carries over to an investment in corporate stock. When only stock in the corporation is received, the shareholder is hardly in a position to pay a tax on any realized gain. As noted later, however, when the taxpayer receives property other than stock (i.e., *boot*) from the corporation, realized gain may be recognized.

The same principles govern the nonrecognition of gain or loss under § 1031 and § 351. The concept of nonrecognition of gain or loss, present in both provisions, causes gain or loss to be deferred until a substantive change in the taxpayer's investment occurs (such as a sale to or a taxable exchange with third parties). This approach is justified under the wherewithal to pay concept discussed in Chapter 1. A further justification for the nonrecognition of gain or loss provisions under § 351 is that tax rules should not impede the exercise of sound business judgment (e.g., choice of the corporate form of doing business).

EXAMPLE 8

Ron is considering incorporating his sole proprietorship. He is concerned about his personal liability for the obligations of the business. Ron realizes that if he incorporates, he will be liable only for the debts of the business that he has personally guaranteed. If Ron incorporates his business, the following assets will be transferred to the corporation:

	Tax Basis	Fair Market Value
Cash	$10,000	$ 10,000
Furniture and fixtures	20,000	60,000
Land and building	40,000	100,000
	$70,000	$170,000

In exchange, Ron will receive stock in the newly formed corporation worth $170,000. Without the nonrecognition provisions of § 351, Ron would recognize a taxable gain of $100,000 ($170,000 – $70,000) on the transfer. Under § 351, however, Ron does not recognize any gain because his economic status has not changed. Ron's investment in the assets of his sole proprietorship ($70,000) carries over to his investment in the incorporated business, which is now represented by his ownership of stock in the corporation. Thus, § 351 provides for tax neutrality on the initial incorporation of Ron's sole proprietorship. ■

When a taxpayer participates in a like-kind exchange, gain is deferred to the extent that the taxpayer receives like-kind property. The taxpayer must recognize any realized gain when receiving "boot" (i.e., property of an unlike kind). For example, if a taxpayer exchanges a truck used in a business for another truck to be used in the business and also receives cash, the taxpayer has the wherewithal to pay an income tax on the cash involved. Further, the taxpayer's economic status has changed to the extent of the cash (not like-kind property) received. Thus, any "realized" gain on the exchange is recognized to the extent of the cash received. In like manner, if a taxpayer transfers property to a corporation and receives money or property other than stock, § 351(b) provides that gain is recognized to the extent of the lesser of the gain realized or the boot received (the amount of money and the fair market value of other property received). Gain is characterized according to the type of asset transferred.[2] Loss on a § 351 transaction is never recognized. The nonrecognition of gain or loss is accompanied by a substituted basis in the shareholder's stock.[3]

EXAMPLE 9

Abby and Bill form White Corporation. Abby transfers property with an adjusted basis of $30,000 and a fair market value of $60,000 for 50% of White's stock. Bill transfers property with an adjusted basis of $70,000 and a fair market value of $60,000 for the remaining 50% of the stock. The transfers qualify under § 351. Abby has a deferred gain of $30,000, and Bill has a deferred loss of $10,000. Both have a substituted basis in the stock of White Corporation. Abby has a basis of $30,000 in her stock, and Bill has a basis of $70,000 in his stock. Assume instead that Abby receives stock and cash of $10,000. Abby would recognize a gain of $10,000. ■

Section 351 is mandatory if a transaction satisfies the provision's requirements. There are three requirements for nonrecognition of gain or loss: (1) *property* is transferred (2) in exchange for *stock* and (3) the transferors must be in *control* of the transferee corporation immediately after the transfer. These three requirements are discussed below.

Transfer of Property

Questions have arisen concerning what constitutes **property** for purposes of § 351. The Code specifically excludes services rendered from the definition of property. With this exception, the definition of property is comprehensive. For example,

[2]Rev.Rul. 68–55, 1968–1 C.B. 140.

[3]§ 358(a). See the discussion preceding Example 28.

along with plant and equipment, unrealized receivables for a cash basis taxpayer and installment obligations are considered property.[4] The transfer of an installment obligation in a transaction qualifying under § 351 is not a disposition of the installment obligation. Thus, gain is not recognized to the transferor. Secret processes and formulas, as well as secret information in the general nature of a patentable invention, also qualify as property under § 351.[5]

Services are not considered to be property under § 351 for a critical reason. A taxpayer must report as income the fair market value of any consideration received as compensation for services rendered.[6] Thus, if a taxpayer receives stock in a corporation as consideration for rendering services to the corporation, the taxpayer has taxable income. In this case, the amount of income recognized by the taxpayer is equal to the fair market value of the stock received. The taxpayer's basis in the stock received is its fair market value.

EXAMPLE 10

Ann and Bob form Brown Corporation and transfer the following consideration:

	Consideration Transferred		
	Basis to Transferor	Fair Market Value	Number of Shares Issued
From Ann:			
Personal services rendered to Brown Corporation	$ –0–	$20,000	200
From Bob:			
Installment obligation	5,000	40,000	
Inventory	10,000	30,000	800
Secret process	–0–	10,000	

The value of each share in Brown Corporation is $100.[7] Ann has taxable income of $20,000 on the transfer because services do not qualify as "property." She has a basis of $20,000 in her 200 shares of stock in Brown. Bob recognizes no gain on the transfer because all of the consideration he transferred to Brown qualifies as "property" and he has "control" of Brown after the transfer. (See the discussion concerning control below.) Bob has a substituted basis of $15,000 in the Brown stock. ■

If property is transferred to a corporation in exchange for any property other than stock, the property received constitutes boot. The boot is taxable to the transferor-shareholder to the extent of any realized gain.[8]

Stock

Generally, the term "stock" needs no clarification. It includes both common stock and most preferred stock. However, the Regulations state that the term "stock" does not include stock rights and stock warrants.[9] In addition, it does not include "nonqualified preferred stock," which possesses many of the attributes of debt.[10]

[4]*Hempt Brothers, Inc. v. U.S.*, 74–1 USTC ¶9188, 33 AFTR2d 74–570, 490 F.2d 1172 (CA–3, 1974), and Reg. § 1.453–9(c)(2).

[5]Rev.Rul. 64–56, 1964–1 C.B. 133; Rev.Rul. 71–564, 1971–2 C.B. 179.

[6]§§ 61 and 83.

[7]The value of closely held stock normally is presumed to be equal to the value of the property transferred.

[8]§ 351(b).

[9]Reg. § 1.351–1(a)(1)(ii).

[10]§ 351(g). Examples of nonqualified preferred stock include preferred stock that is redeemable within 20 years of issuance and whose dividend rate is based on factors other than corporate performance. Therefore, gain is recognized up to the fair market value of the nonqualified preferred stock received. Loss may be recognized when the transferor receives *only* nonqualified preferred stock (or nonqualified preferred stock and other boot) in exchange for property. See also Reg. § 1.351–1(a)(1)(ii).

Thus, any corporate debt or **securities** (i.e., long-term debt, such as bonds) are treated as boot because they do not qualify as stock. Therefore, the receipt of debt in exchange for the transfer of appreciated property to a controlled corporation causes recognition of gain.

Control of the Corporation

For a transaction to qualify as nontaxable under § 351, the transferor(s) of the property must be in **control** of the corporation immediately after the exchange. Control means that the person or persons transferring *property* must have at least an 80 percent stock ownership in the corporation. The property transferors must own stock possessing at least 80 percent of the total combined voting power of all classes of stock entitled to vote *and* at least 80 percent of the total *number* of shares of all other classes of stock.[11]

Control Immediately after the Transfer. Immediately after the exchange, the property transferors must control the corporation. Control can apply to a single person or to several taxpayers if they are all parties to an integrated transaction. The Regulations provide that when more than one person is involved, the exchange does not necessarily require simultaneous exchanges by two or more persons. The Regulations do, however, require that the rights of the parties (i.e., those transferring property to the corporation) be previously set out and determined. Also, the agreement to transfer property should be executed "with an expedition consistent with orderly procedure."[12]

If two or more persons transfer property to a corporation for stock, the transfers should occur close together in time and should be made in accordance with an agreement among the parties.

EXAMPLE 11

Jack exchanges property with a basis of $60,000 and a fair market value of $100,000 for 70% of the stock of Gray Corporation. The other 30% is owned by Jane, who acquired it several years ago. The fair market value of Jack's stock is $100,000. Jack recognizes a taxable gain of $40,000 on the transfer because he does not have control immediately after the exchange and his transaction cannot be integrated with Jane's for purposes of the control requirement. ■

EXAMPLE 12

Lana, Leo, and Lori incorporate their respective businesses by forming Green Corporation. Lana exchanges her property for 300 shares in Green on January 6, 2006. Leo exchanges his property for 400 shares in Green on January 12, 2006, and Lori exchanges her property for 300 shares in Green on March 6, 2006. The three exchanges are part of a prearranged plan, so the control requirement is met. The nonrecognition provisions of § 351 apply to all of the exchanges. ■

Stock need not be issued to the property transferors in the same proportion as the relative value of the property transferred by each. However, when stock received is not proportionate to the value of the property transferred, the actual effect of the transaction must be properly characterized. For example, in such situations one transferor may actually be making a gift of valuable consideration to another transferor.

EXAMPLE 13

Ron and Shelia, father and daughter, form Oak Corporation. Ron transfers property worth $50,000 in exchange for 100 shares of stock, while Shelia transfers property worth $50,000 for 400 shares of stock. The transfers qualify under § 351 because Ron and Shelia have control of the Oak stock immediately after the transfers of property. However, the implicit gift by Ron to Shelia must be recognized and appropriately characterized. As such, the value of the gift might be subject to the gift tax. ■

[11] § 368(c). Nonqualified preferred stock is treated as stock, and not boot, for purposes of this control test.

[12] Reg. § 1.351–1(a)(1).

Once control has been achieved, it is not necessarily lost if stock received by shareholders in a § 351 exchange is sold or given to persons who are not parties to the exchange shortly after the transaction. However, failure to meet the control requirement might result if a *plan* for the ultimate disposition of the stock existed *before* the exchange.[13]

EXAMPLE 14

Mark and Carl form Black Corporation. They transfer appreciated property to the corporation with each receiving 50 shares of the stock. Shortly after the formation, Mark gives 25 shares to his son. Because Mark was not committed to make the gift, he is considered to own his original shares of Black Corporation stock and, along with Carl, to control Black Corporation "immediately after the exchange." The requirements of § 351 are met, and neither Mark nor Carl is taxed on the exchange. Alternatively, had Mark immediately given 25 shares to a business associate pursuant to a plan to satisfy an outstanding obligation, the formation of Black would be taxable to Mark and Carl because of their lack of control (i.e., Mark and Carl, the property transferors, would own only 75% of the stock). ■

PLANNING *Strategies*

UTILIZING § 351

★ **Framework Focus: Income and Exclusions**

Strategy ★ Avoid Income Recognition.

When using § 351, ensure that all parties transferring property (including cash) receive control of the corporation. Simultaneous transfers are not necessary, but a long period of time between transfers makes the transaction vulnerable to taxation if the transfers are not properly documented as part of a single plan. To do this, the parties should document and preserve evidence of their intentions. Also, it is helpful to have some reasonable explanation for any delay in the transfers.

To meet the requirements of § 351, mere momentary control on the part of the transferor may not suffice if loss of control is compelled by a prearranged agreement.[14]

EXAMPLE 15

For many years, Todd operated a business as a sole proprietor employing Linda as manager. To dissuade Linda from quitting and going out on her own, Todd promised her a 30% interest in the business. To fulfill this promise, Todd transferred the business to newly formed Green Corporation in return for all its stock. Immediately thereafter, Todd transfers 30% of the stock to Linda. As a consequence, he no longer meets the 80% control requirement. Section 351 probably does not apply to Todd's transfer to Green Corporation. It appears that Todd was under an obligation to relinquish control. If this is not the case and the loss of control was voluntary on Todd's part, momentary control would suffice.[15] ■

Be sure that later transfers of property to an existing corporation satisfy the 80 percent control requirement if recognition of gain is to be avoided. Also with respect to later transfers, a transferor's interest cannot be counted if the value of stock received is relatively small compared with the value of stock already owned. Further, the primary purpose of the transfer may not be to qualify other transferors for § 351 treatment.[16]

Transfers for Property and Services. Section 351 treatment is lost if stock is transferred to persons who did not contribute property, causing those who did to lack control immediately after the exchange.

[13] *Wilgard Realty Co. v. Comm.*, 42–1 USTC ¶9452, 29 AFTR 325, 127 F.2d 514 (CA–2, 1942).

[14] Rev.Rul. 54–96, 1954–1 C.B. 111.

[15] Compare *Fahs v. Florida Machine and Foundry Co.*, 48–2 USTC ¶9329, 36 AFTR 1161, 168 F.2d 957 (CA–5, 1948), with *John C. O'Connor*, 16 TCM 213, T.C.Memo. 1957–50, *aff'd* in 58–2 USTC ¶9913, 2 AFTR2d 6011, 260 F.2d 358 (CA–6, 1958).

[16] Reg. § 1.351–1(a)(1)(ii).

EXAMPLE 16

Kate transfers property with a value of $60,000 and a basis of $5,000 for 600 shares of stock in newly formed Wren Corporation. Brian receives 400 shares in Wren for services rendered to the corporation. Each share of stock is worth $100. Both Kate and Brian have taxable gain on the transaction. Brian is not part of the control group because he does not transfer property for stock. He has taxable income of $40,000 (400 shares × $100). Kate has a taxable gain of $55,000 [$60,000 (fair market value of the stock in Wren Corporation) – $5,000 (basis in the transferred property)]. Kate is taxed on the exchange because she receives only 60% of the stock in Wren Corporation. ■

A person who performs services for the corporation in exchange for stock and also transfers some property is treated as a member of the transferring group. That person is taxed on the value of the stock issued for services but not on the stock issued for property. In such a case, all the stock received by the person transferring both property and services is counted in determining whether the transferors acquired control of the corporation.[17]

EXAMPLE 17

Assume the same facts as in Example 16, except that Brian transfers property worth $30,000 (basis of $3,000) in addition to services rendered to the corporation (valued at $10,000). Now Brian becomes a part of the control group. Kate and Brian together receive 100% of the stock in Wren Corporation. Consequently, § 351 is applicable to the exchanges. Kate has no recognized gain. Brian does not recognize gain on the transfer of the property, but he has taxable income to the extent of the value of the shares issued for services rendered. Thus, Brian recognizes income of $10,000. ■

Transfers for Services and Nominal Property. To be a member of the group and aid in qualifying all transferors under the 80 percent control test, the person contributing services must transfer property having more than a "relatively small value" compared to the value of services performed. Section 351 will not apply when a small amount of property is transferred and the primary purpose of the transfer is to qualify the transaction under § 351 for concurrent transferors.[18]

EXAMPLE 18

Kim and Eric transfer property to Redbird Corporation, each in exchange for one-third of the stock. Howie receives the other one-third of the stock for services rendered. The transaction will not qualify under § 351 because Howie is not a member of the group transferring property and Kim and Eric together received only 66⅔% of the stock. Thus, the post-transfer control requirement is not met.

Assume instead that Howie also transfers property. Then he is a member of the group, and the transaction qualifies under § 351. Howie is taxed on the value of the stock issued for services, but the remainder of the transaction is tax-free. However, if the property transferred by Howie is of a relatively small value in comparison to the stock he receives for his services, and the primary purpose for transferring the property is to cause the transaction to be tax-free for Kim and Eric, the exchange does not qualify under § 351. Gain or loss is recognized by all parties. ■

The IRS generally requires that before a transferor who receives stock for both property and services can be included in the control group, the value of the property transferred must be at least 10 percent of the value of the services provided.[19] If the value of the property transferred is less than this amount, the IRS will not issue an advance ruling that the exchange meets the requirements of § 351.

EXAMPLE 19

Sara and Rick form White Corporation. Sara transfers land (worth $100,000, basis of $20,000) for 50% of the stock in White. Rick transfers equipment (worth $5,000, adjusted

[17]Reg. § 1.351–1(a)(2), Ex. 3.

[18]Reg. § 1.351–1(a)(1)(ii).

[19]Rev.Proc. 77–37, 1977–2 C.B. 568.

GLOBAL *Tax Issues*

DOES § 351 COVER THE INCORPORATION OF A FOREIGN BUSINESS?

When a taxpayer wishes to incorporate a business overseas by moving assets across U.S. borders, the deferral mechanism of § 351 applies in certain situations, but not in others. In general, § 351 is available to defer gain recognition when starting up a new corporation outside the United States unless so-called tainted assets are involved. Under § 367, tainted assets, which include assets such as inventory and accounts receivable, are treated as having been sold by the taxpayer prior to the corporate formation; therefore, their transfer results in the current recognition of gain. The presence of tainted assets triggers gain because Congress does not want taxpayers to be able to shift the gain outside of U.S. jurisdiction. The gain recognized is ordinary or capital, depending on the nature of the asset involved.

basis of $1,000) and provides services worth $95,000 for 50% of the stock. Rick's stock in White Corporation is unlikely to be counted in determining control for purposes of § 351; thus, the control requirement is not met. None of Rick's stock is counted in determining control because the property he transfers has a nominal value in comparison to the value of the services he renders. Sara recognizes $80,000 of gain on the transfer of the land. She has a basis of $100,000 in her White stock. Rick must recognize income of $95,000 on the transfer for services rendered and a gain of $4,000 for the property transferred. Rick also has a $100,000 basis in his White stock. ■

Transfers to Existing Corporations. Once a corporation is in operation, § 351 also applies to any later transfers of property for stock by either new or existing shareholders.

EXAMPLE 20

Sam and Beth formed Blue Corporation three years ago. Both Sam and Beth transferred appreciated property to Blue in exchange for 500 shares each in the corporation. The original transfers qualified under § 351, and neither Sam nor Beth was taxed on the exchange. In the current year, Sam transfers property (worth $100,000, adjusted basis of $5,000) for 500 additional Blue shares. Sam has a taxable gain of $95,000 on the transfer. The exchange does not qualify under § 351 because Sam does not have 80% control of Blue Corporation immediately after the transfer; he owns 1,000 shares of the 1,500 shares outstanding, or a $66\frac{2}{3}$% interest. ■

If current shareholders transfer property with a small value relative to the value of stock already owned, a special rule applies (similar to the nominal property rule noted previously). In particular, if the purpose of the transfer is to qualify a transaction under § 351, the ownership of the current shareholders is not counted when determining control. Thus, in the preceding example, if Beth had contributed $200 for one share of stock at the time of Sam's contribution, Beth's ownership would not count toward the 80 percent control requirement and Sam would still have a taxable exchange.

LO.2

Understand the special rules that apply when a corporation assumes a shareholder's liability.

Assumption of Liabilities—§ 357

Without a provision to the contrary, the transfer of mortgaged property to a controlled corporation could require recognition of gain by the transferor if the corporation took over the mortgage. This would be consistent with the treatment given in like-kind exchanges under § 1031. Liabilities assumed by the other party are considered the equivalent of cash and treated as boot received. Section 357(a) provides, however, that when the acquiring corporation **assumes a liability** in a § 351 transaction, the transfer does *not* result in boot to the transferor-shareholder. Nevertheless, liabilities assumed by the transferee corporation are treated as boot in determining the basis of the stock received. As a result, the basis of the stock received is reduced by the amount of the liabilities assumed by the corporation.

EXAMPLE 21

Vera transfers property with an adjusted basis of $60,000, fair market value of $100,000, to Gray Corporation for 100% of the stock in Gray. The property is subject to a liability of $25,000 that Gray Corporation assumes. The exchange is tax-free under §§ 351 and 357. However, the basis to Vera of the Gray stock is $35,000 [$60,000 (basis of property transferred) – $25,000 (amount of the liability assumed by Gray)]. ■

The general rule of § 357(a) has two exceptions: (1) § 357(b) provides that if the principal purpose of the assumption of the liabilities is to avoid tax *or* if there is no bona fide business purpose behind the exchange, the liabilities are treated as boot; and (2) § 357(c) provides that if the sum of the liabilities exceeds the adjusted basis of the properties transferred, the excess is taxable gain.

Exception (1): Tax Avoidance or No Bona Fide Business Purpose. Unless liabilities are incurred shortly before incorporation, § 357(b) generally poses few problems. A tax avoidance purpose for transferring liabilities to a controlled corporation normally is not a concern in view of the basis adjustment as noted above. Since the liabilities transferred reduce the basis of the stock received, any realized gain merely is deferred and not completely eliminated. Any postponed gain is recognized when and if the stock is disposed of in a taxable sale or exchange.

Satisfying the bona fide business purpose is not difficult if the liabilities were incurred in connection with the transferor's normal course of conducting a trade or business. But the bona fide business purpose requirement can cause difficulty if the liability is taken out shortly before the property is transferred and the proceeds are utilized for personal purposes.[20] This type of situation is analogous to a cash distribution by the corporation, which is taxed as boot.

EXAMPLE 22

Dan transfers real estate (basis of $40,000 and fair market value of $90,000) to a controlled corporation in return for stock in the corporation. Shortly before the transfer, Dan mortgages the real estate and uses the $20,000 of proceeds to meet personal obligations. Thus, along with the real estate, the mortgage is transferred to the corporation. In this case, the assumption of the mortgage lacks a bona fide business purpose. Consequently, the release of the liability is treated as boot received, and Dan has a taxable gain on the transfer of $20,000, computed as follows:[21]

Stock	$ 70,000
Release of liability—treated as boot	20,000
Total amount realized	$ 90,000
Less: Basis of real estate	(40,000)
Realized gain	$ 50,000
Recognized gain	$ 20,000

■

The effect of the application of § 357(b) is to taint *all* liabilities transferred, even if some are supported by a bona fide business purpose.

EXAMPLE 23

Tim, an accrual basis taxpayer, incorporates his sole proprietorship. Among the liabilities transferred to the new corporation are trade accounts payable of $100,000 and a credit card bill of $5,000. Tim had used the credit card to purchase a wedding anniversary gift for his

[20]See, for example, *Campbell, Jr. v. Wheeler*, 65–1 USTC ¶9294, 15 AFTR2d 578, 342 F.2d 837 (CA–5, 1965).

[21]§ 351(b).

wife. Under these circumstances, the *entire* $105,000 of liabilities is boot and triggers the recognition of gain to the extent gain is realized. ■

Exception (2): Liabilities in Excess of Basis. Section 357(c) states that, if the amount of the liabilities assumed *exceeds* the total of the adjusted bases of the properties transferred, the excess is taxable gain. Without this provision, if liabilities exceed basis in property exchanged, a taxpayer would have a negative basis in the stock received in the controlled corporation.[22] Section 357(c) precludes the negative basis possibility by treating the excess over basis as gain to the transferor.

EXAMPLE 24

Andre transfers land and equipment with adjusted bases of $35,000 and $5,000, respectively, to a newly formed corporation in exchange for 100% of the stock. The corporation assumes $50,000 of liabilities on the transferred land. Without § 357(c), Andre's basis in the stock of the new corporation would be a negative $10,000 [$40,000 (bases of properties transferred) + $0 (gain recognized) – $0 (boot received) – $50,000 (liabilities assumed)]. Section 357(c), however, causes Andre to recognize a gain of $10,000 ($50,000 liabilities assumed – $40,000 bases of assets transferred). As a result, the stock has a zero basis in Andre's hands, determined as follows:

Bases in the properties transferred ($35,000 + $5,000)	$ 40,000
Plus: Gain recognized	10,000
Less: Boot received	(–0–)
Less: Liabilities assumed	(50,000)
Basis in the stock received	$ –0–

Thus, Andre recognizes $10,000 of gain, and a negative stock basis is avoided. ■

The definition of liabilities under § 357(c) excludes obligations that would have been deductible to the transferor had those obligations been paid before the transfer. Thus, accounts payable of a cash basis taxpayer that give rise to a deduction are not considered to be liabilities for purposes of § 357(c). In addition, they are not considered in the computation of stock basis.

EXAMPLE 25

Tina, a cash basis taxpayer, incorporates her sole proprietorship. In return for all of the stock of the new corporation, she transfers the following items:

	Adjusted Basis	Fair Market Value
Cash	$10,000	$10,000
Unrealized accounts receivable (amounts due to Tina but not yet received by her)	–0–	40,000
Trade accounts payable	–0–	30,000
Note payable	5,000	5,000

Unrealized accounts receivable and trade accounts payable have a zero basis. Under the cash method of accounting, no income is recognized until the receivables are collected, and no deduction materializes until the payables are satisfied. The note payable has a basis because it was issued for consideration received.

In this situation, the trade accounts payable are disregarded for gain recognition purposes and in determining Tina's stock basis. Thus, because the balance of the note payable

[22] *Jack L. Easson*, 33 T.C. 963 (1960), *rev'd* in 61–2 USTC ¶9654, 8 AFTR2d 5448, 294 F.2d 653 (CA–9, 1961).

does not exceed the basis of the assets transferred, Tina does not have a problem of liabilities in excess of basis (i.e., the note payable of $5,000 does not exceed the aggregate basis in the cash and accounts receivable of $10,000). ■

If §§ 357(b) and (c) both apply to the same transfer, § 357(b) dominates.[23] This could be significant because § 357(b) does not create gain on the transfer, as does § 357(c), but merely converts the liability to boot. Thus, the realized gain limitation continues to apply to § 357(b) transactions.

EXAMPLE 26

Chris owns land with a basis of $100,000 and a fair market value of $1 million. The land is subject to a mortgage of $300,000. One month prior to transferring the land to Robin Corporation, Chris borrows an additional $200,000 for personal purposes and gives the lender a second mortgage on the land. Therefore, upon the incorporation, Robin Corporation issues stock worth $500,000 to Chris and assumes the mortgages on the land.

Both § 357(c) and § 357(b) apply to the transfer. The mortgages on the property ($500,000) exceed the basis of the property ($100,000). Thus, Chris has a gain of $400,000 under § 357(c). Chris borrowed $200,000 just prior to the transfer and used the loan proceeds for personal purposes. Under § 357(b), Chris has boot of $500,000 in the amount of the liabilities. Note that *all* of the liabilities are treated as boot, not just the "tainted" $200,000 liability. He has realized gain of $900,000 [$1,000,000 (stock of $500,000 and assumption of liabilities of $500,000) – $100,000 (basis in the land)]. Gain is recognized to the extent of the boot of $500,000. Section 357(b) dominates over § 357(c). ■

PLANNING *Strategies*

AVOIDING § 351

★ **Framework Focus: Tax Rate**

Strategy ★ Shift Net Income from High-Bracket Years to Low-Bracket Years.
★ Control the Character of Income and Deductions.

Section 351(a) provides for the nonrecognition of gain on transfers to controlled corporations. As such, it is often regarded as a relief provision favoring taxpayers. In some situations, however, avoiding § 351(a) may produce a more advantageous tax result. The transferors might prefer to recognize gain on the transfer of property if the tax cost is low. For example, they may be in low tax brackets, or the gain may be a capital gain from which substantial capital losses can be offset. Also, recognition of gain will lead to a stepped-up basis in the transferred property in the corporation.

Another reason a particular transferor might wish to avoid § 351 concerns possible loss recognition. Recall that § 351 refers to the nonrecognition of both gains and losses. Section 351(b)(2) specifically states: "No loss to such recipient shall be recognized." A transferor who wishes to recognize loss has several alternatives:

- Sell the property to the corporation for its stock. The IRS could attempt to collapse the "sale," however, by taking the approach that the transfer really falls under § 351(a).[24]
- Sell the property to the corporation for other property or boot. Because the transferor receives no stock, § 351 is inapplicable.
- Transfer the property to the corporation in return for securities or nonqualified preferred stock. Recall that § 351 does not apply to a transferor who receives securities or nonqualified preferred stock. In both this and the previous alternatives, watch for the possible disallowance of the loss under the related-party rules.

Suppose loss property is to be transferred to the corporation and no loss is recognized by the transferor due to § 351(a). This could present an interesting problem in terms of assessing the economic realities involved.

EXAMPLE 27

Iris and Ivan form Wren Corporation with the following investments: property by Iris (basis of $40,000 and fair market value of $50,000) and property by Ivan (basis of $60,000 and fair market value of $50,000). Each receives 50% of the Wren

[23] § 357(c)(2)(A).

[24] *U.S. v. Hertwig*, 68–2 USTC ¶9495, 22 AFTR2d 5249, 398 F.2d 452 (CA–5, 1968).

stock. Has Ivan acted wisely in settling for only 50% of the stock? At first, it would appear so, since Iris and Ivan each invested property of the same value ($50,000). But what about tax considerations? By applying the general carryover basis rules, the corporation now has a basis of $40,000 in Iris's property and $60,000 in Ivan's property. In essence, Iris has shifted a possible $10,000 gain to the corporation while Ivan has transferred a $10,000 potential loss. With this in mind, an equitable allocation of the Wren stock would call for Ivan to receive a greater percentage interest than Iris.

This issue is further complicated by the special basis adjustment required when a shareholder, such as Ivan, contributes property with a built-in loss to a corporation. (See the discussion of this basis adjustment for loss property below.) In this situation, if Wren is to take a carryover basis in Ivan's property, Ivan must reduce his stock basis by the $10,000 built-in loss. This reduced stock basis, of course, could lead to a greater tax burden on Ivan when he sells the Wren stock. This may suggest additional support for Ivan having a greater percentage interest than Iris. ■

LO.3

Recognize the basis issues relevant to the shareholder and the corporation.

Basis Determination and Other Issues

Recall that § 351(a) postpones gain or loss recognition until the taxpayer's investment changes substantively. By virtue of the basis rules described below, the postponed gain or loss is recognized when the stock is disposed of in a taxable transaction.

Basis of Stock to Shareholder. For a taxpayer transferring property to a corporation in a § 351 transaction, the basis of *stock* received in the transaction is the same as the basis the taxpayer had in the property transferred, increased by any gain recognized on the exchange and decreased by boot received. For basis purposes, boot received includes any liabilities transferred by the shareholder to the corporation. Also note that if the shareholder receives any *other property* (i.e., boot) along with the stock, it takes a basis equal to its fair market value.[25] See Figure 9–1 and the discussion that follows relating to an elective stock basis reduction that may be taken when a shareholder contributes property with a net built-in loss.

Basis of Property to Corporation. The basis of property received by the corporation generally is the basis of the exchanged property in the hands of the transferor increased by the amount of any gain recognized by the transferor-shareholder.[26]

These basis rules are illustrated in Examples 28 and 29.

EXAMPLE 28

Maria and Ned form Brown Corporation. Maria transfers land (basis of $30,000 and fair market value of $70,000); Ned invests cash ($60,000). They each receive 50 shares in Brown Corporation, worth $1,200 per share, but Maria also receives $10,000 cash from Brown. The transfers of property, the realized and recognized gain on the transfers, and the basis of the stock in Brown Corporation to Maria and Ned are as follows:

	A	B	C	D	E	F
	Basis of Property Transferred	FMV of Stock Received	Boot Received	Realized Gain (B + C – A)	Recognized Gain (Lesser of C or D)	Basis of Stock in Brown (A – C + E)
From Maria:						
Land	$30,000	$60,000	$10,000	$40,000	$10,000	$30,000
From Ned:						
Cash	60,000	60,000	–0–	–0–	–0–	60,000

[25] § 358(a).

[26] § 362(a).

FIGURE 9–1 **Shareholder's Basis in Stock Received**

Adjusted basis of property transferred	$xx,xxx
Plus: Gain recognized	xxx
Minus: Boot received (including any liabilities transferred)	(xxx)
Minus: Adjustment for loss property (if elected)	(xxx)
Equals: Basis of stock received	$xx,xxx

Brown Corporation has a basis of $40,000 in the land: Maria's basis of $30,000 plus her recognized gain of $10,000. ■

EXAMPLE 29

Assume the same facts as in Example 28 except that Maria's basis in the land is $68,000 (instead of $30,000). Because recognized gain cannot exceed realized gain, the transfer generates only $2,000 of gain to Maria. The realized and recognized gain and the basis of the stock in Brown Corporation to Maria are as follows:

	A	B	C	D	E	F
	Basis of Property Transferred	FMV of Stock Received	Boot Received	Realized Gain (B + C – A)	Recognized Gain (Lesser of C or D)	Basis of Stock in Brown (A – C + E)
Land	$68,000	$60,000	$10,000	$2,000	$2,000	$60,000

Brown's basis in the land is $70,000 ($68,000 basis to Maria + $2,000 gain recognized by Maria). ■

Figure 9–2 summarizes the basis calculation for property received by a corporation.

Basis Adjustment for Loss Property. As noted above, when a corporation receives property in a § 351 transaction, the basis for that property is carried over from the shareholder. As a result, the corporation's basis for the property has no correlation to its fair market value. However, in certain situations when built-in loss property is contributed to a corporation, its aggregate basis in the property may have to be stepped down so that the basis does not exceed the fair market value of the property transferred. This basis adjustment is necessary to prevent the parties from obtaining a double benefit from the losses involved.

The anti-loss duplication rule applies when the aggregate basis of the assets transferred by a shareholder exceeds their fair market value. When this built-in loss situation exists, the basis in the loss properties is stepped down. The step-down in basis is allocated proportionately among the assets with the built-in loss.[27]

FIGURE 9–2 **Corporation's Basis in Property Received**

Adjusted basis of property transferred	$xx,xxx
Plus: Gain recognized by transferor-shareholder	xxx
Minus: Adjustment for loss property (if required)	(xxx)
Equals: Basis of property to corporation	$xx,xxx

[27]§ 362(e)(2). This adjustment is determined separately with respect to each property transferor. In addition, this adjustment also is required in the case of a contribution to capital by a shareholder.

EXAMPLE 30

In a transaction qualifying under § 351, Charles transfers the following assets to Blue Corporation in exchange for all of its stock

	Tax Basis	Fair Market Value	Built-In Gain/ (Loss)
Equipment	$100,000	$ 90,000	($10,000)
Land	200,000	230,000	30,000
Building	150,000	100,000	(50,000)
	$450,000	$420,000	($30,000)

Charles's stock basis is $450,000 [$450,000 (basis of the property transferred) + $0 (gain recognized) − $0 (boot received)]. However, Blue's basis for the loss assets transferred must be reduced by the amount of the net built-in loss ($30,000) in proportion to each asset's share of the loss.

	Unadjusted Tax Basis	Adjustment	Adjusted Tax Basis
Equipment	$100,000	($ 5,000)*	$ 95,000
Land	200,000		200,000
Building	150,000	(25,000)**	125,000
	$450,000	($30,000)	$420,000

*$\frac{\$10{,}000 \text{ (loss attributable to equipment)}}{\$60{,}000 \text{ (\textit{total} built-in loss)}} \times \$30{,}000 \text{ (\textit{net} built-in loss)}$

= $5,000 (adjustment to basis in equipment).

**$\frac{\$50{,}000 \text{ (loss attributable to building)}}{\$60{,}000 \text{ (\textit{total} built-in loss)}} \times \$30{,}000 \text{ (\textit{net} built-in loss)}$

= $25,000 (adjustment to basis in building). ■

Note the end result of Example 30:

- Charles still has a built-in loss in his stock basis. Thus, if he sells the Blue Corporation stock, he will recognize a loss of $30,000 [$420,000 (selling price based on presumed value of the stock) − $450,000 (basis in the stock)].
- Blue Corporation can no longer recognize any loss on the sale of *all* of its assets [$420,000 (selling price based on value of assets) − $420,000 (adjusted basis in assets) = $0 (gain or loss)].

In the event a corporation is subject to the built-in loss adjustment, an alternative approach is available. If the shareholder and the corporation both elect, the basis reduction can be made to the shareholder's stock.

EXAMPLE 31

Assume the same facts as in the previous example. If Charles and Blue elect, Charles can reduce his stock basis to $420,000 ($450,000 − $30,000). As a result, Blue's aggregate basis in the assets it receives is $450,000. If Charles has no intention of selling his stock, this election could be desirable as it benefits Blue by giving the corporation a higher depreciable basis in the equipment and building. ■

Note the end result of Example 31:

- Charles has no built-in loss. Thus, if he sells the Blue Corporation stock, he will recognize no gain or loss [$420,000 (presumed value of the stock) − $420,000 (basis in the stock)].
- Blue Corporation has a built-in loss. Thus, if it sells *all* of its assets [$420,000 (selling price based on value of assets) − $450,000 (basis in assets)], it recognizes a loss of $30,000.

Consequently, the built-in loss adjustment places the loss with either the shareholder or the corporation but not both (compare Examples 30 and 31).

Stock Issued for Services Rendered. A corporation's transfer of stock for property is not a taxable exchange.[28] A transfer of shares for services is also not a taxable transaction to a corporation.[29] Can a corporation deduct the fair market value of the stock it issues in consideration of services as a business expense? Yes, unless the services are such that the payment is characterized as a capital expenditure.[30]

EXAMPLE 32

Carol and Carl form White Corporation. Carol transfers cash of $500,000 for 100 shares of White Corporation stock. Carl transfers property worth $400,000 (basis of $90,000) and agrees to serve as manager of the corporation for one year; in return, Carl receives 100 shares of stock in White. The value of Carl's services to White Corporation is $100,000. Carol's and Carl's transfers qualify under § 351. Neither Carol nor Carl is taxed on the transfer of their property. However, Carl has income of $100,000, the value of the services he will render to White Corporation. White has a basis of $90,000 in the property it acquired from Carl, and it may claim a compensation expense deduction under § 162 for $100,000. Carl's stock basis is $190,000 ($90,000 + $100,000). ■

EXAMPLE 33

Assume, in the preceding example, that Carl receives the 100 shares of White Corporation stock as consideration for the appreciated property and for providing legal services in organizing the corporation. The value of Carl's legal services is $100,000. Carl has no gain on the transfer of the property but has income of $100,000 for the value of the services rendered. White Corporation has a basis of $90,000 in the property it acquired from Carl and must capitalize the $100,000 as an organizational expenditure. Carl's stock basis is $190,000 ($90,000 + $100,000). ■

Holding Period for Shareholder and Transferee Corporation. The shareholder's holding period for stock received for a capital asset or for § 1231 property includes the holding period of the property transferred to the corporation. The holding period of the property is *tacked on* to the holding period of the stock. The holding period for stock received for any other property (e.g., inventory) begins on the day after the exchange. The transferee corporation's holding period for property acquired in a § 351 transfer is the holding period of the transferor-shareholder regardless of the character of the property to the transferor.[31]

Recapture Considerations

In a pure § 351(a) nontaxable transfer (no boot involved) to a controlled corporation, the depreciation recapture rules do not apply.[32] Instead, any recapture potential of the property carries over to the corporation as it steps into the shoes of the transferor-shareholder for purposes of basis determination. However, to the extent that gain is recognized, the recapture rules are applied.

EXAMPLE 34

Paul transfers equipment (adjusted basis of $30,000, original cost of $120,000, and fair market value of $100,000) to a controlled corporation in return for additional stock. If Paul had sold the equipment, it would have yielded a gain of $70,000, all of which would be recaptured as ordinary income under § 1245. If the transfer comes within § 351(a), Paul has no recognized gain and no depreciation to recapture. If the corporation later disposes of the equipment in a taxable transaction, it must take into account the § 1245 recapture potential originating with Paul.

[28] § 1032.

[29] Reg. § 1.1032–1(a).

[30] Rev.Rul. 62–217, 1962–2 C.B. 59, modified by Rev.Rul. 74–503, 1974–2 C.B. 117.

[31] §§ 1223(1) and (2).

[32] §§ 1245(b)(3) and 1250(d)(3).

If Paul had received boot of $60,000 on the transfer, all of the recognized gain would be recaptured as ordinary income. The remaining $10,000 of recapture potential would carry over to the corporation. ■

PLANNING *Strategies*

OTHER CONSIDERATIONS WHEN INCORPORATING A BUSINESS

★ **Framework Focus: Tax Rate**

Strategy ★ Control the Character of Income and Deductions.
★ Shift Net Income from High-Bracket Taxpayers to Low-Bracket Taxpayers.

★ **Framework Focus: Deductions**

Strategy ★ Maximize Deductible Amounts.

★ **Framework Focus: Income and Exclusions**

Strategy ★ Avoid Income Recognition.

When a business is incorporated, the organizers must determine which assets and liabilities should be transferred to the corporation. A transfer of assets that produce passive income (rents, royalties, dividends, and interest) can cause the corporation to be a personal holding company in a tax year when operating income is low. Thus, the corporation could be subject to the personal holding company penalty tax (see the discussion in Chapter 10).

A transfer of the accounts payable of a cash basis taxpayer may prevent the taxpayer from taking a tax deduction when the accounts are paid. These payables should generally be retained.

Leasing property to the corporation may be a more attractive alternative than transferring ownership. Leasing provides the taxpayer with the opportunity of withdrawing money from the corporation in a deductible form without the payment being characterized as a nondeductible dividend. If the property is donated to a family member in a lower tax bracket, the lease income can be shifted as well. If the depreciation and other deductions available in connection with the property are larger than the lease income, a high tax rate taxpayer could retain the property until the income exceeds the deductions.

Another way to shift income to other taxpayers is by the use of corporate debt. Shareholder debt in a corporation can be given to family members with low marginal tax rates. This technique also shifts income without a loss of control of the corporation.

LO.4

Understand the tax aspects of the capital structure of a corporation.

Capital Structure of a Corporation

Capital Contributions

When a corporation receives money or property in exchange for capital stock (including treasury stock), neither gain nor loss is recognized by the recipient corporation.[33] The corporation's gross income also does not include shareholders' contributions of money or property to the capital of the corporation. Additional funds received from shareholders through voluntary pro-rata payments are not income to the corporation. This is the case even though there is no increase in the number of outstanding shares of stock of the corporation. The payments represent an additional price paid for the shares held by the shareholders (increasing their basis) and are treated as additions to the operating capital of the corporation.[34]

Contributions by nonshareholders, such as land contributed to a corporation by a civic group or a governmental group to induce the corporation to locate in a

[33] § 1032.

[34] § 118 and Reg. § 1.118–1.

TAX *in the News* **TAX BREAKS MAKE A DIFFERENCE IN EXPANSION PLANS**

As a business grows, management must be on the lookout for locations for expansion. Proximity to markets, access to an educated workforce, the general business climate, and appropriate infrastructure are factors to consider when making the choice. Another factor that can make a critical difference in the expansion decision is the availability of tax incentives that are offered as inducements by often competing state and local governments.

Dell, Inc., the world's largest maker of personal computers, apparently knows how to play the expansion game. Recently, it chose three expansion sites—Oklahoma City, Oklahoma; West Chester, Ohio; and Winston-Salem, North Carolina—largely because of the tax inducements offered by these communities.

particular community, are also excluded from the gross income of a corporation.[35] However, property that is transferred to a corporation by a nonshareholder in exchange for goods or services rendered is taxable income to the corporation.[36]

EXAMPLE 35

A cable company charges its customers an initial fee to hook up to a new cable system installed in the area. These payments are used to finance the total cost of constructing the cable facilities. The customers will make monthly payments for the cable service. The initial payments are used for capital expenditures, but they represent payments for services to be rendered by the cable company. As such, they are taxable income and not contributions to capital by nonshareholders. ■

The basis of property received by a corporation from a shareholder as a **capital contribution** is equal to the basis of the property in the hands of the shareholder, although the basis may be subject to a downward adjustment when loss property is contributed. The basis of property transferred to a corporation by a nonshareholder as a contribution to capital is zero.

If a corporation receives *money* as a contribution to capital from a nonshareholder, a special rule applies. The basis of any property acquired with the money during a 12-month period beginning on the day the contribution was received is reduced by the amount of the contribution. The excess of money received over the cost of new property is used to reduce the basis of other property held by the corporation and is applied in the following order:

- Depreciable property.
- Property subject to amortization.
- Property subject to depletion.
- All other remaining properties.

The basis of property within each category is reduced in proportion to the relative bases of the properties.[37]

EXAMPLE 36

A city donates land to Brown Corporation as an inducement for Brown to locate in the city. The receipt of the land produces no taxable income to Brown, and the land's basis to the corporation is zero. If, in addition, the city gives the corporation $100,000 in cash, the money is not taxable income to the corporation. However, if the corporation purchases property with the $100,000 within the next 12 months, the basis of the property is reduced by $100,000. Any excess cash not used is handled according to the ordering rules noted above. ■

[35]See *Edwards v. Cuba Railroad Co.*, 1 USTC ¶139, 5 AFTR 5398, 45 S.Ct. 614 (USSC, 1925).

[36]Reg. § 1.118–1. See also *Teleservice Co. of Wyoming Valley*, 27 T.C. 722 (1957), *aff'd* in 58–1 USTC ¶9383, 1 AFTR2d 1249, 254 F.2d 105 (CA–3, 1958), *cert. den.* 78 S.Ct. 1360 (USSC, 1958).

[37]§ 362(c); Reg. §§ 1.362–2(b) and 1.118–1.

TAX in the News — **CONFLICT ARISES BETWEEN CORPORATIONS AND THEIR SHAREHOLDERS**

Throughout the history of income taxation in the United States, applicable law has favored financing regular corporations with debt rather than equity. This corporate preference for debt exists because interest is deductible by the corporation, while dividends are not. Thus, if a corporation raises capital by issuing debt, the deductibility of the interest reduces the after-tax cost of obtaining financing. From the shareholders' perspective, the difference between debt and equity was not important because both interest and dividend income were taxed at ordinary income tax rates.

Now, with most dividend income being taxed at lower rates than interest income, investors will have a bias toward dividends. In contrast, corporations will still prefer debt financing because interest payments remain deductible while dividend payments are not. The chart in Example 37 illustrates this divergence between corporate and shareholder preferences. It will be interesting to see how corporations and their shareholders will work through their differences!

LO.5

Recognize the tax differences between debt and equity investments.

Debt in the Capital Structure

Advantages of Debt. Significant tax differences exist between debt and equity in the capital structure, and shareholders must be aware of these differences. The advantages of issuing long-term debt are numerous. Interest on debt is deductible by the corporation, while dividend payments are not. Further, the shareholders are not taxed on debt repayments unless the repayments exceed basis. An investment in stock usually cannot be withdrawn tax-free as long as a corporation has earnings and profits. Withdrawals will be deemed to be taxable dividends to the extent of earnings and profits of the distributing corporation. (The concept of earnings and profits is discussed in Chapter 10.)

Currently, another distinction between debt and equity relates to the taxation of dividend and interest income. Dividend income on equity holdings now is taxed to individual investors at the low capital gains rates, while interest income on debt continues to be taxed at the higher ordinary income rates.

EXAMPLE 37

Wade transfers cash of $100,000 to a newly formed corporation for 100% of the stock. In the first year of operations, the corporation has net income of $40,000. If the corporation distributes $9,500 to Wade, the distribution is a taxable dividend with no corresponding deduction to the corporation. Assume, instead, that Wade transfers to the corporation cash of $50,000 for stock. In addition, he lends the corporation $50,000. The note is payable in equal annual installments of $5,000 and bears interest at the rate of 9%. At the end of the year, the corporation pays Wade interest of $4,500 ($50,000 × 9%), and a note repayment of $5,000. The interest payment is taxable to Wade and deductible to the corporation. The $5,000 principal repayment on the loan is neither taxed to Wade nor deductible by the corporation. The after-tax impact to Wade and the corporation under each alternative is illustrated below.

	If the Distribution Is	
	$9,500 Dividend	**$5,000 Note Repayment and $4,500 Interest**
*After-tax benefit to Wade**		
[$9,500 × (1 – 15%)]	$8,075	
{$5,000 + [$4,500 × (1 – 35%)]}		$7,925
*After-tax cost to corporation***		
No deduction to corporation	9,500	
{$5,000 + [$4,500 × (1 – 35%)]}		7,925

*Assumes Wade's dividend income is taxed at the 15% capital gains rate and his interest income is taxed at the 35% ordinary income rate.

**Assumes the corporation is in the 35% marginal tax bracket. ■

Reclassification of Debt as Equity (Thin Capitalization Problem). In situations where the corporation is said to be thinly capitalized, the IRS contends that debt is really an equity interest and denies the corporation the tax advantages of debt financing. If a debt instrument has too many features of stock, it may be treated as a form of stock by the IRS. As a result, the principal and interest payments are considered dividends. Under § 385, the IRS has the authority to characterize corporate debt wholly as equity or as part debt and part equity. In the current environment, however, the IRS may be less inclined to raise the thin capitalization issue because the conversion of interest income to dividend income would produce a tax benefit to individual investors.

For the most part, the principles used to classify debt as equity developed in connection with closely held corporations where the holders of the debt are often shareholders. The rules have often proved inadequate for dealing with large, publicly traded corporations.

Section 385 lists several factors that *may* be used to determine whether a debtor-creditor relationship or a shareholder-corporation relationship exists. The thrust of § 385 is to authorize the Treasury to prescribe Regulations that provide more definite guidelines for determining when debt should be reclassified as equity. To date, the Treasury Department has not drafted final Regulations. Consequently, taxpayers must rely on judicial decisions to determine whether a true debtor-creditor relationship exists.

The courts have identified the following factors to be considered when classifying a security as debt or equity:

- Whether the debt instrument is in proper form. An open account advance is more easily characterized as a contribution to capital than a loan evidenced by a properly written note executed by the shareholder.[38]
- Whether the debt instrument bears a reasonable rate of interest and has a definite maturity date. When a shareholder advance does not provide for interest, the return expected is that inherent in an equity interest (e.g., a share of the profits or an increase in the value of the shares).[39] Likewise, a lender unrelated to the corporation will usually be unwilling to commit funds to the corporation for an indefinite period of time (i.e., no definite due date).
- Whether the debt is paid on a timely basis. A lender's failure to insist upon timely repayment (or satisfactory renegotiation) indicates that the return sought does not depend upon interest income and the repayment of principal.
- Whether payment is contingent upon earnings. A lender ordinarily will not advance funds that are likely to be repaid only if the venture is successful.
- Whether the debt is subordinated to other liabilities. Subordination tends to eliminate a significant characteristic of the creditor-debtor relationship. Creditors should have the right to share with other general creditors in the event of the corporation's dissolution or liquidation. Subordination also destroys another basic attribute of creditor status—the power to demand payment at a fixed maturity date.[40]
- Whether holdings of debt and stock are proportionate (e.g., each shareholder owns the same percentages of debt and stock). When debt and equity obligations are held in the same proportion, shareholders are, apart from tax considerations, indifferent as to whether corporate distributions are in the form of interest or dividends.
- Whether funds loaned to the corporation are used to finance initial operations or capital asset acquisitions. Funds used to finance initial operations or

[38] *Estate of Mixon, Jr. v. U.S.*, 72–2 USTC ¶9537, 30 AFTR2d 72–5094, 464 F.2d 394 (CA–5, 1972).

[39] *Slappey Drive Industrial Park v. U.S.*, 77–2 USTC ¶9696, 40 AFTR2d 77–5940, 561 F.2d 572 (CA–5, 1977).

[40] *Fin Hay Realty Co. v. U.S.*, 68–2 USTC ¶9438, 22 AFTR2d 5004, 398 F.2d 694 (CA–3, 1968).

to acquire capital assets the corporation needs to operate are generally obtained through equity investments.

- Whether the corporation has a high ratio of shareholder debt to shareholder equity. **Thin capitalization** occurs when shareholder debt is high relative to shareholder equity. This indicates the corporation lacks reserves to pay interest and principal on debt when corporate income is insufficient to meet current needs.[41] In determining a corporation's debt-equity ratio, courts look at the relation of the debt both to the book value of the corporation's assets and to their actual fair market value.[42]

Section 385 also authorizes the Treasury to issue Regulations classifying an instrument either as *wholly* debt or equity or as *part* debt and *part* equity. This flexible approach is important because some instruments cannot readily be classified either wholly as stock or wholly as debt. It may also provide an avenue for the IRS to address problems in publicly traded corporations.

Corporate Operations

The rules related to gross income, deductions, and losses discussed in previous chapters of this text generally apply to corporations. In a few instances, it was noted that corporations face unique limitations such as the 10 percent of taxable income limitation for charitable contributions and the limitation allowing corporate capital losses to be deductible only against capital gains. Corporations also are permitted some deductions not generally available to other entities. These special deductions and other special rules regarding the determination of corporate income tax liability are discussed in the following pages.

LO.6

Understand the tax rules unique to corporations.

Deductions Available Only to Corporations

Dividends Received Deduction. The purpose of the **dividends received deduction** is to mitigate multiple levels of taxation. Without the deduction, dividends paid between corporations could be subject to several levels of tax. For example, if Corporation A pays Corporation B a dividend, and B passes the dividend on to its shareholders, the dividend is taxed at three levels: Corporation A, Corporation B, and Corporation B's shareholders. The dividends received deduction alleviates this inequity by limiting or eliminating the amount of dividend income taxable to corporations.

As the following table illustrates, the amount of the dividends received deduction depends on the percentage of ownership the recipient corporate shareholder holds in a domestic corporation making the dividend distribution.[43]

Percentage of Ownership by Corporate Shareholder	Deduction Percentage
Less than 20%	70%
20% or more (but less than 80%)	80%
80% or more*	100%

* The payor corporation must be a member of an affiliated group with the recipient corporation.

[41] A court held that a debt-equity ratio of approximately 14.6:1 was not excessive. See *Tomlinson v. 1661 Corp.*, 67–1 USTC ¶9438, 19 AFTR2d 1413, 377 F.2d 291 (CA–5, 1967). A 26:1 ratio was found acceptable in *Delta Plastics, Inc.*, 85 TCM 940, T.C.Memo. 2003–54.

[42] In *Bauer v. Comm.*, 84–2 USTC ¶9996, 55 AFTR2d 85–433, 748 F.2d 1365 (CA–9, 1984), a debt-equity ratio of 92:1 resulted when book value was used. But the ratio ranged from 2:1 to 8:1 when equity included both paid-in capital and accumulated earnings.

[43] § 243(a).

The dividends received deduction is limited to a percentage of the taxable income of the shareholder-corporation. For this purpose, taxable income is computed without regard to the net operating loss (NOL), the dividends received deduction, and any capital loss carryback to the current tax year. The percentage of taxable income limitation corresponds to the deduction percentage. Thus, if a corporate shareholder owns less than 20 percent of the stock in the distributing corporation, the dividends received deduction is limited to 70 percent of taxable income. However, the taxable income limitation does not apply if the corporation has an NOL for the current taxable year.[44]

The following steps summarize the computation of the deduction:

1. Multiply the dividends received by the deduction percentage.
2. Multiply the taxable income by the deduction percentage.
3. The deduction is limited to the lesser of Step 1 or Step 2, unless subtracting the amount derived in Step 1 from taxable income *generates* an NOL. If so, the amount derived in Step 1 should be used. This is referred to as the *NOL rule*.

EXAMPLE 38

Red, White, and Blue Corporations, three unrelated calendar year corporations, have the following transactions for the year:

	Red Corporation	White Corporation	Blue Corporation
Gross income from operations	$ 400,000	$ 320,000	$ 260,000
Expenses from operations	(340,000)	(340,000)	(340,000)
Dividends received from domestic corporations (less than 20% ownership)	200,000	200,000	200,000
Taxable income before the dividends received deduction	$ 260,000	$ 180,000	$ 120,000

In determining the dividends received deduction, use the three-step procedure described above:

Step 1 (70% × $200,000)	$140,000	$140,000	$140,000
Step 2			
70% × $260,000 (taxable income)	$182,000		
70% × $180,000 (taxable income)		$126,000	
70% × $120,000 (taxable income)			$ 84,000
Step 3			
Lesser of Step 1 or Step 2	$140,000	$126,000	
Step 1 amount generates an NOL			$140,000

White Corporation is subject to the 70% of taxable income limitation. It does not qualify for NOL rule treatment since subtracting $140,000 (Step 1) from $180,000 (100% of taxable income before the dividends received deduction) does not yield a negative figure. Blue Corporation qualifies under the NOL rule because subtracting $140,000 (Step 1) from $120,000 (100% of taxable income before the dividends received deduction) yields a negative figure. In summary, each corporation has a dividends received deduction for the year as follows: $140,000 for Red Corporation, $126,000 for White Corporation, and $140,000 for Blue Corporation. ■

[44]§ 246(b)(2).

Deduction of Organizational Expenditures. Expenses incurred in connection with the organization of a corporation normally are chargeable to a capital account. That they benefit the corporation during its existence seems clear. But over what period should organizational expenses be amortized? The lack of a determinable and limited estimated useful life makes such a determination difficult. Section 248 was enacted to solve this problem.

Under § 248, a corporation may elect to amortize **organizational expenditures** over a period of 180 months or more. The period begins with the month in which the corporation begins business.[45] Organizational expenditures *subject to the election* include:

- Legal services incident to organization (e.g., drafting the corporate charter, bylaws, minutes of organizational meetings, terms of original stock certificates).
- Necessary accounting services.
- Expenses of temporary directors and of organizational meetings of directors or shareholders.
- Fees paid to the state of incorporation.

Expenditures that *do not qualify* include those connected with issuing or selling shares of stock or other securities (e.g., commissions, professional fees, and printing costs) or with the transfer of assets to a corporation. Such expenditures reduce the amount of capital raised and are not deductible.

A special exception allows the corporation to immediately expense the first $5,000 of organizational costs. The exception, however, is phased out on a dollar-for-dollar basis when these expenses exceed $50,000. A corporation, for example, with $52,000 of organizational expenditures could elect to expense $3,000 [$5,000 – ($52,000 – $50,000)] of this amount and amortize the $49,000 balance ($52,000 – $3,000) over 180 months.[46]

To qualify for the election, the expenditure must be *incurred* before the end of the tax year in which the corporation begins business. In this regard, the corporation's method of accounting is of no consequence. Thus, an expense incurred by a cash basis corporation in its first tax year qualifies even though the expense is not paid until a subsequent year.

The election is made in a statement attached to the corporation's tax return for its first tax year. The return and statement must be filed no later than the due date of the return (including any extensions).

If the election is *not* made on a timely basis, organizational expenditures cannot be deducted until the corporation ceases to do business and liquidates. These expenditures will be deductible if the corporate charter limits the life of the corporation.

EXAMPLE 39

Black Corporation, an accrual basis, calendar year taxpayer, was formed and began operations on May 1, 2006. The following expenses were incurred during its first year of operations (May 1–December 31, 2006):

Expenses of temporary directors and of organizational meetings	$15,000
Fee paid to the state of incorporation	2,000
Accounting services incident to organization	18,000
Legal services for drafting the corporate charter and bylaws	32,000
Expenses incident to the printing and sale of stock certificates	48,000

[45]The month in which a corporation begins business may not be immediately apparent. See Reg. § 1.248–1(a)(3). For a similar problem in the Subchapter S area, see Chapter 12.

[46]Organizational expenditures incurred before October 23, 2004, could not be immediately expensed but could be amortized over a period of 60 months or more. The change to § 248 was made by the American Jobs Creation Act of 2004.

Because of the dollar cap (i.e., dollar-for-dollar reduction for amounts in excess of $50,000), no immediate expensing under the $5,000 rule is available. Assume, however, that Black Corporation elects to amortize the qualifying organizational expenses over a period of 180 months. The monthly amortization is $372 [($15,000 + $2,000 + $18,000 + $32,000) ÷ 180 months], and $2,976 ($372 × 8 months) is deductible for tax year 2006. Note that the $48,000 of expenses incident to the printing and sale of stock certificates does not qualify for the election. These expenses cannot be deducted. Instead, they reduce the amount of the capital realized from the sale of stock. ■

Organizational expenditures are distinguished from startup expenditures covered by § 195. Startup expenditures include various investigation expenses involved in entering a new business, whether incurred by a corporate or a noncorporate taxpayer. Startup expenses also include operating expenses, such as rent and payroll, that are incurred by a corporation before it actually begins to produce any gross income. At the election of the taxpayer, such expenditures (e.g., travel, market surveys, financial audits, legal fees) can be treated in the same manner as organizational expenditures. Thus, up to $5,000 can be immediately expensed (subject to the dollar cap and excess-of-$50,000 phaseout) and any remaining amounts amortized over a period of 180 months or longer.

PLANNING *Strategies*

ORGANIZATIONAL EXPENDITURES

★ **Framework Focus: Deductions**

Strategy ★ Maximize Deductible Amounts.

To qualify for the 180-month amortization procedure of § 248, only organizational expenditures incurred in the first taxable year of the corporation can be considered. This rule could prove to be an unfortunate trap for corporations formed late in the year.

EXAMPLE 40

Thrush Corporation is formed in December 2006. Qualified organizational expenditures are incurred as follows: $62,000 in December 2006 and $30,000 in January 2007. If Thrush uses the calendar year for tax purposes, only $62,000 of the organizational expenditures qualify for amortization. ■

A solution to the problem posed by Example 40 may be for Thrush Corporation to adopt a fiscal year that ends on or beyond January 31. All organizational expenditures will then have been incurred before the close of the first tax year.

Determining the Corporate Income Tax Liability

LO.7

Compute the corporate income tax.

Corporate Income Tax Rates. Corporate income tax rates have fluctuated widely over past years. Refer to the inside front cover of the text for a schedule of current corporate income tax rates.

EXAMPLE 41

Gold Corporation, a calendar year taxpayer, has taxable income of $90,000 for 2006. Its income tax liability is $18,850, determined as follows:

Tax on $75,000	$13,750
Tax on $15,000 × 34%	5,100
Tax liability	$18,850

■

For a corporation that has taxable income in excess of $100,000 for any tax year, the amount of the tax is increased by the lesser of (1) 5 percent of the excess or (2) $11,750. In effect, the additional tax means a 39 percent rate for every dollar of taxable income from $100,000 to $335,000.

EXAMPLE 42

Silver Corporation, a calendar year taxpayer, has taxable income of $335,000 for 2006. Its income tax liability is $113,900, determined as follows:

Tax on $100,000	$ 22,250
Tax on $235,000 × 39%	91,650
Tax liability	$113,900

Note that the tax liability of $113,900 is 34% of $335,000. Thus, due to the 39% rate (34% normal rate + 5% additional tax on taxable income between $100,000 and $335,000), the benefit of the lower rates on the first $75,000 of taxable income completely phases out at $335,000. The normal rate drops back to 34% on taxable income between $335,000 and $10 million. ■

Section 11(b) provides that qualified **personal service corporations (PSCs)** are taxed at a flat 35 percent rate on all taxable income. Thus, PSCs do not enjoy the tax savings of being in the 15 percent to 34 percent brackets applicable to other corporations. For this purpose, a PSC is a corporation that is substantially employee owned. Also, it must engage in one of the following activities: health, law, engineering, architecture, accounting, actuarial science, performing arts, or consulting.

LO.8

Explain the rules unique to computing the tax of multiple corporations.

Tax Liability of Related Corporations

Related corporations are subject to special rules for computing the income tax, the AMT exemption, and the § 179 election to expense certain depreciable assets.[47] If these restrictions did not exist, the shareholders of a corporation could gain significant tax advantages by splitting a single corporation into *multiple* corporations. The next two examples illustrate the potential *income tax* advantage of multiple corporations.

EXAMPLE 43

Gray Corporation annually yields taxable income of $300,000. The corporate tax on $300,000 is $100,250, computed as follows:

Tax on $100,000	$ 22,250
Tax on $200,000 × 39%	78,000
Tax liability	$100,250

■

EXAMPLE 44

Assume that Gray Corporation in the previous example is divided equally into four corporations. Each corporation would have taxable income of $75,000, and the tax for each (absent the special provisions for related corporations) would be computed as follows:

Tax on $50,000	$ 7,500
Tax on $25,000 × 25%	6,250
Tax liability	$13,750

The total liability for the four corporations would be $55,000 ($13,750 × 4). Consequently, the savings would be $45,250 ($100,250 – $55,000). ■

[47] § 1561(a).

To preclude the advantages that could be gained by using multiple corporations, the tax law requires special treatment for *controlled groups* of corporations. A comparison of Examples 43 and 44 reveals that the income tax savings that could be achieved by using multiple corporations result from having more of the total income taxed at lower rates. To close this potential loophole, the law limits a controlled group's taxable income in the tax brackets below 35 percent to the amount the corporations in the group would have if they were one corporation. Thus, in Example 44, under the controlled corporation rules, only $12,500 (one-fourth of the first $50,000 of taxable income) for each of the four related corporations would be taxed at the 15 percent rate. The 25 percent rate would apply to the next $6,250 (one-fourth of the next $25,000) of taxable income of each corporation. This equal allocation of the $50,000 and $25,000 amounts is required unless all members of the controlled group consent to an apportionment plan providing for an unequal allocation.

Similar limitations apply to the § 179 expense election (see Chapter 5) and to the $40,000 exemption amount for purposes of computing the AMT (see Chapter 14).

Controlled Groups

A **controlled group** of corporations includes parent-subsidiary groups, brother-sister groups, combined groups, and certain insurance companies. Parent-subsidiary controlled groups are discussed in the following section.

Parent-Subsidiary Controlled Group. A **parent-subsidiary controlled group** consists of one or more *chains* of corporations connected through stock ownership with a common parent corporation. The ownership connection can be established through either a *voting power test* or a *value test.* The voting power test requires ownership of stock possessing at least 80 percent of the total voting power of all classes of stock entitled to vote. The value test requires ownership of at least 80 percent of the total value of all shares of all classes of stock of each of the corporations, except the parent corporation, by one or more of the other corporations.[48]

EXAMPLE 45

Aqua Corporation owns 80% of White Corporation. Aqua and White Corporations are members of a parent-subsidiary controlled group. Aqua is the parent corporation and White is the subsidiary. ■

The parent-subsidiary relationship described in Example 45 is easy to recognize because Aqua Corporation is the direct owner of White Corporation. Real-world business organizations are often much more complex, sometimes including numerous corporations with chains of ownership connecting them. In these complex corporate structures, determining whether the controlled group classification is appropriate becomes more difficult. The ownership requirements can be met through direct ownership (refer to Example 45) or through indirect ownership, as illustrated in the following example.

EXAMPLE 46

Red Corporation owns 80% of the voting stock of White Corporation, and White Corporation owns 80% of the voting stock of Blue Corporation. Red, White, and Blue Corporations constitute a controlled group in which Red is the common parent and White and Blue are subsidiaries. This parent-subsidiary relationship is diagrammed in Figure 9–3. The same result would occur if Red Corporation, rather than White Corporation, owned the Blue Corporation stock. ■

Find more information on this topic at our Web site: ***http://wft-entities.swlearning.com.***

DIGGING DEEPER 7

[48]§ 1563(a)(1).

FIGURE 9–3 **Controlled Groups—Parent-Subsidiary Corporations**

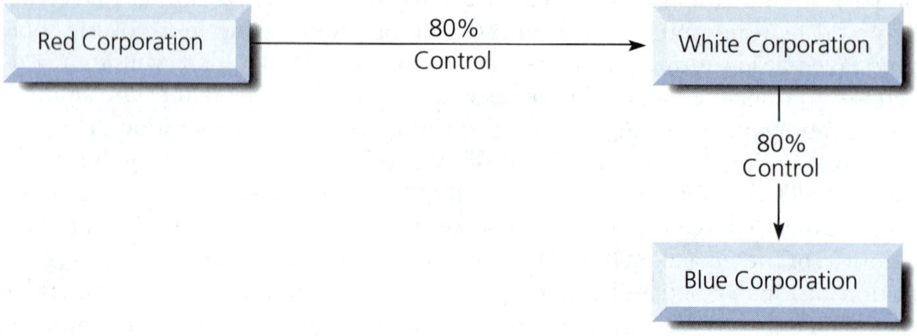

Red is the common parent of a parent-subsidiary controlled group consisting of Red, White, and Blue Corporations.

Application of § 482. Congress has recognized that a parent corporation has the power to shift income among its subsidiaries. Likewise, shareholders who control other related groups of corporations can shift income and deductions among the related corporations.

When the true taxable income of a subsidiary or other related corporation has been understated or overstated, the IRS can reallocate the income and deductions of the related corporations under § 482. Section 482 permits the IRS to allocate gross income, deductions, and credits between any two or more organizations, trades, or businesses that are owned or controlled by the same interests. This is appropriate when the allocation is necessary to prevent avoidance of taxes or to reflect income correctly. Controlled groups of corporations, especially multinational corporations, are particularly vulnerable to § 482.

LO.9

Describe the reporting process for corporations.

Procedural Matters

Filing Requirements for Corporations

A corporation must file a Federal income tax return whether or not it has taxable income.[49] A corporation that was not in existence throughout an entire annual accounting period is required to file a return for the fraction of the year during which it was in existence. In addition, a corporation must file a return even though it has ceased to do business if it has valuable claims for which it will bring suit. A corporation is relieved of filing income tax returns only when it ceases to do business and retains no assets.

DIGGING DEEPER 3

Find more information on this topic at our Web site: ***http://wft-entities.swlearning.com.***

The return must be filed on or before the fifteenth day of the third month following the close of a corporation's tax year. A regular corporation, other than a PSC, can use either a calendar or a fiscal year to report its taxable income. The tax year of the shareholders has no effect on the corporation's tax year.

[49] § 6012(a)(2).

TAX FACT

Sources of Federal Government Revenues

This pie chart shows the relative sizes of the major categories of Federal income for fiscal year 2004.

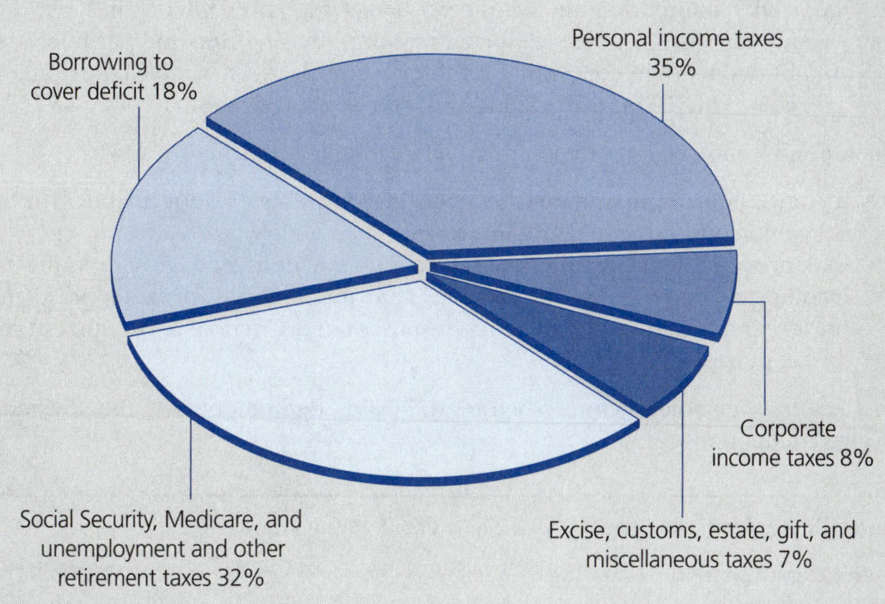

Source: *Form 1040 Instructions.*

Estimated Tax Payments

A corporation must make payments of estimated tax unless its tax liability can reasonably be expected to be less than $500. The required annual payment (which includes any estimated AMT liability) is the lesser of (1) 100 percent of the corporation's final tax or (2) 100 percent of the tax for the preceding year (if that was a 12-month tax year and the return filed showed a tax liability).[50] Estimated payments can be made in four installments due on or before the fifteenth day of the fourth month, the sixth month, the ninth month, and the twelfth month of the corporate taxable year. The full amount of the unpaid tax is due on the due date of the return without regard to extensions. A corporation failing to pay its required estimated tax payments will be subjected to a nondeductible penalty on the amount by which the installments are less than the tax due.

Schedule M–1—Reconciliation of Taxable Income and Financial Net Income

Schedule M–1 of Form 1120 is used to *reconcile* net income as computed for financial accounting purposes with taxable income reported on the corporation's income tax return (commonly referred to as book/tax differences). Schedule M–1 is required of corporations with less than $10 million of total assets.

The starting point on Schedule M–1 is net income per books (financial accounting net income). Additions and subtractions are entered for items that

[50]§§ 6655(d) and (e).

affect net income per books and taxable income differently. The following items are entered as additions (see lines 2 through 5 of Schedule M–1 below):

- Federal income tax expense (deducted in computing net income per books but not deductible in computing taxable income).
- The excess of capital losses over capital gains (deducted for financial accounting purposes but not deductible by corporations for income tax purposes).
- Income that is reported in the current year for tax purposes that is not reported in computing net income per books (e.g., prepaid income).
- Various expenses that are deducted in computing net income per books but are not deducted in computing taxable income (e.g., charitable contributions in excess of the 10 percent ceiling applicable to corporations).

The following subtractions are entered on lines 7 and 8 of Schedule M–1:

- Income reported for financial accounting purposes but not included in taxable income (e.g., tax-exempt interest).
- Expenses deducted on the tax return but not deducted in computing net income per books (e.g., a charitable contributions carryover deducted in a prior year for financial accounting purposes but deductible in the current year for tax purposes).

The result is taxable income (before the NOL deduction and the dividends received deduction).

EXAMPLE 47

During the current year, Tern Corporation had the following transactions:

Net income per books (after tax)	$92,400
Taxable income	50,000
Federal income tax expense per books	7,500
Interest income from tax-exempt bonds	5,000
Interest paid on loan, the proceeds of which were used to purchase the tax-exempt bonds	500
Life insurance proceeds received as a result of the death of a key employee	50,000
Premiums paid on key employee life insurance policy	2,600
Excess of capital losses over capital gains	2,000

For book and tax purposes, Tern Corporation determines depreciation under the straight-line method. Tern's Schedule M–1 for the current year is as follows:

Schedule M-1 **Reconciliation of Income (Loss) per Books With Income per Return**

1 Net income (loss) per books	92,400	7 Income recorded on books this year not included on this return (itemize): Tax-exempt interest $ 5,000 *Life insurance proceeds on key employee $50,000*	55,000
2 Federal income tax per books	7,500	8 Deductions on this return not charged against book income this year (itemize):	
3 Excess of capital losses over capital gains	2,000	a Depreciation $	
4 Income subject to tax not recorded on books this year (itemize):		b Charitable contributions $	
5 Expenses recorded on books this year not deducted on this return (itemize): a Depreciation $ b Charitable contributions $ c Travel and entertainment $ *Prem.–life ins. $2,600; Int.–exempt bonds $500*	3,100	9 Add lines 7 and 8	55,000
6 Add lines 1 through 5	105,000	10 Income (page 1, line 28)—line 6 less line 9	50,000

■

Schedule M–2 reconciles unappropriated retained earnings at the beginning of the year with unappropriated retained earnings at year-end. Beginning balance plus net income per books, as entered on line 1 of Schedule M–1, less dividend distributions during the year equals ending retained earnings. Other sources of increases or decreases in retained earnings are also listed on Schedule M–2.

BRIDGE *Discipline*

Bridge to Financial Accounting

Measures of corporate income for financial reporting and income tax purposes differ because the objectives of these measures differ. Income measures for financial reporting purposes are intended to help various stakeholders have a clear view of the corporation's financial position and operational results. Income measures for Federal income tax purposes, on the other hand, must comply with the relevant provisions of the Internal Revenue Code. The tax law is intended not only to raise revenues to fund government operations, but to reflect the objectives of government fiscal policy as well.

As a consequence of these differing objectives, revenue and expense measurements used to determine taxable income may differ from those used in financial reporting. In most cases, differences between book and tax measurements are temporary in nature. Two such temporary differences relate to the different methods of calculating depreciation expense and the limits placed on the deductibility of net capital losses for tax purposes. Permanent differences between book and tax income, such as the dividends received deduction and the production activities deduction, also may exist.

Accounting standards for reporting income tax expenses and liabilities require that the tax impact of *temporary* differences be recognized currently in the financial statements. Because many temporary differences allow a firm to postpone its tax payments to later years, the financial statements must show the amount of the expense that is paid currently and that portion that is to be paid in a later period. The portion of the taxes to be paid in a later period is shown as a liability for such future income taxes. The liability for future income taxes is referred to as a deferred income tax liability.

EXAMPLE 48

Assume the same facts as in the preceding example. Tern Corporation's beginning balance in unappropriated retained earnings is $125,000. During the year, Tern distributed a cash dividend of $30,000 to its shareholders. Based on these further assumptions, Tern's Schedule M–2 for the current year is as follows:

Schedule M-2 **Analysis of Unappropriated Retained Earnings per Books**

1	Balance at beginning of year	*125,000*	5	Distributions: a Cash	*30,000*
2	Net income (loss) per books	*92,400*		b Stock	
3	Other increases (itemize):			c Property	
			6	Other decreases (itemize):	
			7	Add lines 5 and 6	*30,000*
4	Add lines 1, 2, and 3	*217,400*	8	Balance at end of year (line 4 less line 7)	*187,400*

■

DIGGING DEEPER 4

Find more information on this topic at our Web site: ***http://wft-entities.swlearning.com.***

Schedule M–3—Net Income (Loss) Reconciliation for Corporations with Total Assets of $10 Million or More

Corporate taxpayers with total assets of $10 million or more are required to report much greater detail relative to differences between income (loss) reported for financial accounting purposes and income (loss) reported for tax purposes. This expanded reconciliation of book and tax income (loss) is reported on **Schedule M–3**. Corporations that are not required to file Schedule M–3 may do so voluntarily. Any corporation that files Schedule M–3 is not allowed to file Schedule M–1. Comparison of Schedule M–3 (see **http://www.irs.gov**) with Schedule M–1 (illustrated in Example 47) reveals the significantly greater disclosure requirements that apply to corporations that are required to file Schedule M–3.

Schedule M–3 is a response, at least in part, to recent financial reporting scandals, including Enron, WorldCom, and others. One objective of Schedule M–3 is to create greater transparency between corporate financial statements and tax returns. Another objective is to identify corporations that engage in aggressive tax practices by requiring that transactions that create book/tax differences be disclosed on corporate tax returns.

Total assets for purposes of the $10 million test are determined from the taxpayer's financial reports. If the taxpayer files Form 10–K with the Securities and Exchange Commission (SEC), that statement is used. If no 10–K is filed, information from another financial source is used, in the following order: certified financial statements, prepared financial statements, or the taxpayer's books and records.

The Paperwork Reduction Notice Act reports the following estimates related to the filing of Schedule M–3: 76 hours 3 minutes for record keeping, 3 hours 40 minutes for learning about the schedule, and 5 hours 4 minutes to prepare the schedule. High-level tax executives generally believe these estimates are much too low and that Schedule M–3 compliance will be expensive and time consuming. Software producers will also incur considerable costs to modify their software to include Schedule M–3. Examination of the IRS instructions for Schedule M–3 reinforces the impression of its complexity. The instructions grew from 16 pages for 2004 to more than 40 pages for 2005.

DIGGING DEEPER 5 6

Find more information on this topic at our Web site: ***http://wft-entities.swlearning.com.***

Summary

The evolution of the check-the-box Regulations has provided taxpayers with a simplified method for determining an entity's tax classification. Nevertheless, taxpayers should not discount the importance of choosing the appropriate form of entity. As demonstrated in this chapter and Chapter 10, a variety of tax provisions applicable to corporations do not extend to other entities. Of particular importance are the different deductions available to corporations and the corporate income tax rate structure. Corporations must also be aware of their levels of debt to avoid equity reclassification. Such reclassification causes deductible interest paid on debt to become nondeductible dividend payments. Equally important are the timing and completeness requirements of the corporate filing provisions. Failure to comply with the appropriate filing provisions may result in heavy penalties and interest.

Suggested Further Readings

"Common Schedule M-1 Adjustments," *The Tax Adviser*, October 2005, pp. 586–588.

Brian E. Keller, "Sec. 351 Transfers Involving Boot and Encumbered Assets," *The Tax Adviser*, September 2004, pp. 536–539.

Phillip J. Korb, John N. Sigler, and Thomas E. Vermeer, "Dividend Tax Rate Cuts Benefit Closely Held Corporations," *The CPA Journal*, October 2004, pp. 40–41.

John R. McGowan and David Killion, "Schedule M-3: Closing the Corporate Book-Tax Gap," *The Tax Adviser*, July 2005, pp. 408–416.

KEY TERMS

Assumption of liabilities, 9–14
C corporations, 9–2
Capital contribution, 9–23
Check-the-box Regulations, 9–7
Control, 9–11
Controlled group, 9–31
Dividends received deduction, 9–26
Limited liability company (LLC), 9–7
Limited partnership, 9–7
Organizational expenditures, 9–28
Parent-subsidiary controlled group, 9–31
Personal service corporation (PSC), 9–30
Property, 9–9
Regular corporation, 9–2
Related corporations, 9–30
S corporation, 9–2
Schedule M–1, 9–33
Schedule M–3, 9–35
Securities, 9–11
Thin capitalization, 9–26

PROBLEM MATERIALS

PROBLEMS

1. Conner is the sole owner of Service Enterprises (SE). SE earned net operating income of $90,000 during the year and had a long-term capital loss of $12,000. Conner withdrew $45,000 of the profit from SE. How should Conner report this information on his individual tax return for 2006 if SE is:
   a. A proprietorship?
   b. A C corporation?
   c. An S corporation?

2. On June 17, 2006, Susan and Valerie started an investment firm called B & W Investments. During 2006, both Susan and Valerie lived and conducted their business in Illinois. B & W Investments is an unincorporated entity under Illinois state law. Neither Susan nor Valerie filed an election regarding the Federal tax classification of B & W Investments. Susan's husband, Bill, told Valerie and Susan that they must file a Form 1120 for the 2006 taxable year and will be taxed twice on B & W's earnings. Is Bill correct in his assessment?

3. Emu Company, which was formed in 2006, had operating income of $100,000 and operating expenses of $80,000 in 2006. In addition, Emu had a long-term capital loss of $5,000. How does Andrew, the owner of Emu Company, report this information on his individual tax return under the following assumptions?
   a. Emu Company is a proprietorship, and Andrew does not withdraw any funds from Emu during the year.
   b. Emu Company is a corporation and pays no dividends during the year.

4. Charlotte and Catherine are equal owners in Woodchuck Enterprises, a calendar year business. During the year, Woodchuck Enterprises had $1 million of gross income and $600,000 of operating expenses. In addition, Woodchuck sold land that had been held for investment purposes for a long-term capital gain of $120,000. During the year, Charlotte and Catherine each received a distribution of $80,000 from Woodchuck. Discuss the impact of this information on the taxable income of Woodchuck, Charlotte, and Catherine if Woodchuck is:
   a. A partnership.
   b. An S corporation.
   c. A C corporation.

5. Mesquite Company had a $200,000 net profit from operations in 2006 and paid Sheryl, its sole shareholder, a dividend of $138,750 ($200,000 net profit – $61,250 corporate tax). Sheryl has a large amount of income from other sources and is in the 35% marginal tax bracket. Would Sheryl's tax situation be better or worse if Mesquite

Company were a proprietorship and Sheryl withdrew $138,750 from the business during the year?

Issue ID

6. Emily incorporates her sole proprietorship, but does not transfer a building used by the business to the corporation. Instead, the building is leased to the corporation for an annual rent. What tax reasons might Emily have for not transferring the building to the corporation when the business was incorporated?

7. Sam, Carl, Lucy, and Sylvia form Pine Corporation with the following consideration:

	Consideration Transferred		
	Basis to Transferor	Fair Market Value	Number of Shares Issued
From Sam—			
Inventory	$30,000	$96,000	30*
From Carl—			
Equipment ($30,000 of depreciation taken by Carl in prior years)	45,000	99,000	30 **
From Lucy—			
Secret process	15,000	90,000	30
From Sylvia—			
Cash	30,000	30,000	10

*Sam receives $6,000 in cash in addition to the 30 shares.

**Carl receives $9,000 in cash in addition to the 30 shares.

Assume the value of each share of Pine Corporation stock is $3,000. As to these transactions, provide the following information:

a. Sam's recognized gain or loss. Identify the treatment given to any such gain or loss.
b. Sam's basis in the Pine Corporation stock.
c. Pine Corporation's basis in the inventory.
d. Carl's recognized gain or loss. Identify the treatment given to any such gain or loss.
e. Carl's basis in the Pine Corporation stock.
f. Pine Corporation's basis in the equipment.
g. Lucy's recognized gain or loss.
h. Lucy's basis in the Pine Corporation stock.
i. Pine Corporation's basis in the secret process.
j. Sylvia's recognized gain or loss.
k. Sylvia's basis in the Pine Corporation stock.

8. Mark and Gail form Maple Corporation with the following consideration:

	Consideration Transferred		
	Basis to Transferor	Fair Market Value	Number of Shares Issued
From Mark—			
Cash	$ 50,000	$ 50,000	
Installment obligation	140,000	250,000	30
From Gail—			
Cash	150,000	150,000	
Equipment	125,000	250,000	
Patent	10,000	300,000	70

The installment obligation has a face amount of $250,000 and was acquired last year from the sale of land held for investment purposes (adjusted basis of $140,000). As to these transactions, provide the following information:

a. Mark's recognized gain or loss.
b. Mark's basis in the Maple Corporation stock.

c. Maple Corporation's basis in the installment obligation.
d. Gail's recognized gain or loss.
e. Gail's basis in the Maple Corporation stock.
f. Maple Corporation's basis in the equipment and the patent.
g. How would your answers to the preceding questions change if Mark received common stock and Gail received preferred stock?
h. How would your answers change if Gail was a partnership?

Decision Making

9. Jane, Jon, and Clyde incorporate their respective businesses and form Starling Corporation. On March 1 of the current year, Jane exchanges her property (basis of $100,000 and value of $400,000) for 200 shares in Starling Corporation. On April 15, Jon exchanges his property (basis of $140,000 and value of $600,000) for 300 shares in Starling. On May 10, Clyde transfers his property (basis of $1,180,000 and value of $1 million) for 500 shares in Starling.
   a. If the three exchanges are part of a prearranged plan, what gain or loss will each of the parties recognize on the exchanges?
   b. Assume Jane and Jon exchanged their property for stock four years ago while Clyde transfers his property for 500 shares in the current year. Clyde's transfer is not part of a prearranged plan with Jane and Jon to incorporate their businesses. What gain or loss will Clyde recognize on the transfer?
   c. What arrangement—part (a) or part (b)—would the parties prefer?

Communications

10. Jim Yancey (1635 Maple Street, Syracuse, NY 13201) exchanges property, basis of $200,000 and fair market value of $850,000, for 75% of the stock of Red Corporation. The other 25% is owned by Joy Perry, who acquired her stock several years ago. You represent Jim, who asks whether he must report gain on the transfer. Prepare a letter to Jim and a memorandum for the tax files documenting your response.

Issue ID

11. Barbara exchanges property, basis of $20,000 and fair market value of $500,000, for 65% of the stock of Pelican Corporation. Alice, Barbara's daughter, who acquired her stock last year, owns the other 35% of Pelican. What are the tax issues?

12. Dan and Vera form Crane Corporation. Dan transfers land (worth $200,000, basis of $60,000) for 50% of the stock in Crane. Vera transfers machinery (worth $150,000, adjusted basis of $30,000) and provides services worth $50,000 for 50% of the stock.
   a. Will the transfers qualify under § 351?
   b. What are the tax consequences to Dan and Vera?
   c. What is Crane Corporation's basis in the land and the machinery?

13. Juan organized Red Corporation 10 years ago. He contributed property worth $1 million (basis of $200,000) for 2,000 shares of stock in Red (representing 100% ownership). Juan later gave each of his children, Julie and Rachel, 500 shares of the stock. In the current year, Juan transfers property worth $400,000 (basis of $150,000) to Red for 500 more of its shares. What gain, if any, will Juan recognize on the transfer?

14. Ann and Bob form Robin Corporation. Ann transfers property worth $420,000 (basis of $150,000) for 70 shares in Robin Corporation. Bob receives 30 shares for property worth $165,000 (basis of $30,000) and for legal services in organizing the corporation; the services are worth $15,000.
   a. What gain, if any, will the parties recognize on the transfer?
   b. What basis do Ann and Bob have in the stock in Robin Corporation?
   c. What is Robin Corporation's basis in the property and services it received from Ann and Bob?

15. Assume in Problem 14 that the property Bob transfers to Robin Corporation is worth $15,000 (basis of $3,000) and his services in organizing the corporation are worth $165,000. What are the tax consequences to Ann, Bob, and Robin Corporation?

Decision Making

16. Rhonda Johnson owns 50% of the stock of Peach Corporation. She and the other 50% shareholder, Rachel Powell, have decided that additional contributions of capital are needed if Peach is to remain successful in its competitive industry. The two shareholders have agreed that Rhonda will contribute assets having a value of $200,000 (adjusted basis of $15,000) in exchange for additional shares of stock. After the transaction, Rhonda will hold 75% of Peach Corporation and Rachel's interest will fall to 25%.

a. What gain is realized on the transaction? How much of the gain will be recognized?
b. Rhonda is not satisfied with the transaction as proposed. How would the consequences change if Rachel agrees to transfer $1,000 of cash in exchange for additional stock? In this case, Rhonda will own slightly less than 75% of Peach and Rachel's interest will be slightly more than 25%.
c. If Rhonda still is not satisfied with the result, what should be done to avoid any gain recognition?

17. Paul transfers property with an adjusted basis of $50,000, fair market value of $400,000, to Swift Corporation for 90% of the stock. The property is subject to a liability of $60,000, which Swift assumes. What is the basis of the Swift stock to Paul? What is the basis of the property to Swift Corporation?

18. Lori, a sole proprietor, was engaged in a service business and reported her income on the cash basis. On February 1, 2006, she incorporates the business and transfers the assets to the corporation in return for all the stock plus the corporation's assumption of her proprietorship's liabilities. All the receivables and the unpaid trade payables are transferred to the newly formed Green Corporation. The balance sheet of Green immediately following its formation is as follows:

GREEN CORPORATION
BALANCE SHEET
FEBRUARY 1, 2006

Assets

	Basis to Green	Fair Market Value
Cash	$ 80,000	$ 80,000
Accounts receivable	–0–	240,000
Equipment (cost $180,000; depreciation claimed $60,000)	120,000	320,000
Building (straight-line depreciation)	160,000	400,000
Land	40,000	160,000
Total	400,000	$1,200,000

Liabilities and Stockholder's Equity

Liabilities:	
Accounts payable—trade	$ 120,000
Notes payable—bank	360,000
Stockholder's equity:	
Common stock	720,000
Total	$1,200,000

Discuss the tax consequences of the incorporation to Lori and to Green Corporation.

19. Allie forms Blue Corporation by transferring land with a basis of $125,000 (fair market value of $775,000). The land is subject to a mortgage of $375,000. One month prior to incorporating Blue, Allie borrows $100,000 for personal purposes and gives the lender a second mortgage on the land. Blue Corporation issues stock worth $300,000 to Allie and assumes the mortgages on the land.
a. What are the tax consequences to Allie and to Blue Corporation?
b. How would the tax consequences to Allie differ if she had not borrowed the $100,000?

20. Fay, a sole proprietor, is engaged in a cash basis, service business. In the current year, she incorporates the business to form Robin Corporation. She transfers assets with a basis of $400,000 (fair market value of $1.2 million), a bank loan of $360,000 (which Robin assumes), and $80,000 in trade payables in return for all of Robin's stock. What are the tax consequences of the incorporation of the business?

Issue ID

21. Nancy and her daughter, Margaret, have been working together in a cattery called "The Perfect Cat." Nancy formed the business in 1990 as a sole proprietorship. Because of the

high quality and exotic lineage of the cats that Nancy breeds, the business has been very successful. It currently has assets with a fair market value of $250,000 and a basis of $180,000. On the advice of her tax accountant, Nancy decides to incorporate "The Perfect Cat." Because of Margaret's loyalty, Nancy would like her to have shares in the corporation. What are the relevant tax issues?

22. Early in the year, Charles, Lane, and Tami form the Harrier Corporation for the express purpose of developing a shopping center. All parties are experienced contractors, and they transfer various business assets (e.g., building materials, land) to Harrier in exchange for all of its stock. Three months after it is formed, Harrier purchases two cranes from Lane for their fair market value of $400,000 by issuing four annual installment notes of $100,000 each. Since the adjusted basis of the cranes is $550,000, Lane plans to recognize a § 1231 loss of $150,000 in the year of the sale. Does Lane have any potential income tax problem with this plan? *Ethics*

23. Sara and Jane form Wren Corporation. Sara transfers property, basis of $25,000 and fair market value of $200,000, for 50 shares in Wren Corporation. Jane transfers property, basis of $10,000 and fair market value of $185,000, and agrees to serve as manager of Wren for one year; in return Jane receives 50 shares in Wren. The value of Jane's services to Wren is $15,000.
   a. What gain will Sara and Jane recognize on the exchange?
   b. What basis will Wren Corporation have in the property transferred by Sara and Jane? How should Wren treat the value of the services Jane renders?

24. Assume in Problem 23, that Jane receives the 50 shares of Wren Corporation stock in consideration for the appreciated property and for providing legal services in organizing the corporation. The value of Jane's services is $15,000.
   a. What gain does Jane recognize?
   b. What is Wren Corporation's basis in the property transferred by Jane? How should Wren treat the value of the services Jane renders?

25. On January 10, 2006, Carol transferred machinery worth $100,000 (adjusted basis of $20,000) to a controlled corporation, Lark. The transfer qualified under § 351. Carol had deducted $85,000 of depreciation on the machinery while it was used in her proprietorship. On November 15, 2006, Lark Corporation sells the machinery for $95,000. What are the tax consequences to Carol and to Lark Corporation on the sale of the machinery?

26. Blue Corporation desires to set up a manufacturing facility in a southern state. After considerable negotiations with a small town in Arkansas, Blue accepts the following offer: land (fair market value of $3 million) and cash of $1 million.
   a. How much gain, if any, must Blue Corporation recognize?
   b. What basis will Blue Corporation have in the land?
   c. Within one year of the contribution, Blue constructs a building for $800,000 and purchases inventory for $300,000. What basis will Blue Corporation have in each of these assets?

27. Emily Patrick (36 Paradise Road, Northampton, MA 01060) formed Teal Corporation a number of years ago with an investment of $200,000 of cash, for which she received $20,000 in stock and $180,000 in bonds bearing interest of 8% and maturing in nine years. Several years later, Emily lent the corporation an additional $50,000 on open account. In the current year, Teal Corporation becomes insolvent and is declared bankrupt. During the corporation's existence, Emily was paid an annual salary of $60,000. Write a letter to Emily in which you explain how she should treat her losses for tax purposes. *Extender* *Communications*

28. In each of the following independent situations, determine the dividends received deduction. Assume that none of the corporate shareholders owns 20% or more of the stock in the corporations paying the dividends.

	Green Corporation	Orange Corporation	Yellow Corporation
Income from operations	$ 350,000	$ 1,200,000	$ 1,500,000
Expenses from operations	(300,000)	(1,350,000)	(1,580,000)
Qualifying dividends	50,000	300,000	400,000

29. Owl Corporation was formed on December 1, 2006. Qualifying organizational expenses were incurred and paid as follows:

Incurred and paid in December 2006	$12,000
Incurred in December 2006 but paid in January 2007	6,000
Incurred and paid in February 2007	3,600

Assuming that Owl Corporation makes a timely election under § 248 to expense and amortize its organizational expenditures, what amount may be deducted in the corporation's first tax year under each of the following assumptions?

a. Owl Corporation adopts a calendar year and the cash basis of accounting for tax purposes.
b. Same as (a), except that Owl Corporation chooses a fiscal year of December 1–November 30.
c. Owl Corporation adopts a calendar year and the accrual basis of accounting for tax purposes.
d. Same as (c), except that Owl Corporation chooses a fiscal year of December 1–November 30.

30. Hummingbird Corporation, an accrual basis taxpayer, was formed and began operations on July 1, 2006. The following expenses were incurred during the first tax year (July 1 to December 31, 2006) of operations:

Expenses of temporary directors and of organizational meetings	$12,000
Fee paid to the state of incorporation	3,000
Accounting services incident to organization	15,000
Legal services for drafting the corporate charter and bylaws	21,000
Expenses incident to the printing and sale of stock certificates	18,000
	$69,000

Assume Hummingbird Corporation makes an appropriate and timely election under § 248 and the related Regulations. What is the maximum organizational expense Hummingbird may write off for tax year 2006?

31. In each of the following *independent* situations, determine the corporation's income tax liability. Assume that all corporations use a calendar year for tax purposes and that the tax year involved is 2006.

	Taxable Income
Violet Corporation	$ 32,000
Indigo Corporation	280,000
Orange Corporation	335,000
Blue Corporation	4,335,000
Green Corporation	20,000,000

Extender

32. The outstanding stock in Red, Blue, and Green Corporations, each of which has only one class of stock, is owned by the following unrelated individuals:

	Corporations		
Shareholders	Red	Blue	Green
Marrin	20%	10%	30%
Murray	10%	50%	20%
Moses	50%	30%	35%

a. Determine whether Red, Blue, and Green Corporations constitute a brother-sister controlled group.
b. Assume that Murray does not own stock in any of the corporations. Would a brother-sister controlled group exist?

33. Indicate in each of the following *independent* situations whether the corporation may file Form 1120–A:

Extender

	Jay Corporation	Shrike Corporation	Martin Corporation
Sales of merchandise	$600,000	$400,000	$300,000
Total assets	200,000	360,000	400,000
Total income (gross profit plus other income, including gains)	480,000	490,000	380,000
Member of controlled group	no	yes	no
Ownership in foreign corporation	no	no	no

34. The following information for 2006 relates to Oak Corporation, a calendar year, accrual basis taxpayer. You are to determine the amount of Oak's taxable income for the year using this information. You may use Schedule M–1, which is available on the IRS Web site.

Net income per books (after tax)	$209,710
Federal income tax expense per books	30,050
Interest income from tax-exempt bonds	22,000
Interest paid on loan incurred to purchase tax-exempt bonds	2,800
Life insurance proceeds received as a result of the death of the president of the corporation	110,000
Premiums paid on policy on the life of the president of the corporation	5,240
Excess of capital losses over capital gains	4,200

35. For 2006, Cedar Corporation, an accrual basis, calendar year taxpayer, had net income per books of $172,750 and the following special transactions:

Life insurance proceeds received as a result of the death of the corporation's president	$100,000
Premiums paid on the life insurance policy on the president	10,000
Prepaid rent received and properly taxed in 2005 but credited as rent income in 2006	15,000
Rent income received in 2006 ($10,000 is prepaid and relates to 2007)	25,000
Interest income on tax-exempt bonds	5,000
Interest on loan to carry tax-exempt bonds	3,000
MACRS depreciation in excess of straight-line (straight-line was used for book purposes)	4,000
Capital loss in excess of capital gains	6,000
Federal income tax liability and accrued tax provision for 2006	22,250

Using Schedule M–1 of Form 1120 (the most current version available), determine Cedar Corporation's taxable income for 2006.

36. For years ending after December 31, 2004, corporate taxpayers with total assets of $10 million or more are required to report much greater detail relative to differences between book and tax income (loss). What were the government's objectives in creating this reporting requirement?

37. Pro Golf Warehouse, Inc. (PGW), sells golf equipment throughout the United States. PGW also sells golf equipment in Canada through its subsidiary, Canadian Golf Warehouse (CGW), which is organized as a Canadian corporation. In addition, PGW has an American subsidiary, Tennis Supplies, Inc. (TSI). PGW includes income (loss) from both subsidiaries on its audited financial statements, which show net income of $120 million in 2006. CGW, which is not consolidated by PGW for U.S. tax purposes, had net income of $22 million. TSI, which is consolidated for U.S. tax purposes, had a loss of $11 million. How is this information reported on Schedule M–3?

Extender

Extender

38. PGW acquired intellectual property in 2006 and deducted amortization of $50,000 on its financial statements, which were prepared according to GAAP. For Federal income tax purposes, PGW deducted $75,000. How is this information reported on Schedule M–3?

Extender

39. In January 2006, PGW established an allowance for uncollectible accounts (bad debt reserve) of $105,000 on its books and increased the allowance by $195,000 during the year. As a result of a client's bankruptcy, PGW decreased the allowance by $75,000 in November 2006. PGW deducted the $300,000 of increases to the allowance on its 2006 income statement, but was not allowed to deduct that amount on its tax return. On its 2006 tax return, the corporation was allowed to deduct the $75,000 actual loss sustained because of its client's bankruptcy. On its financial statements, PGW treated the $300,000 increase in the bad debt reserve as an expense that gave rise to a temporary difference. On its 2006 tax return, PGW took a $75,000 deduction for bad debt expense. How is this information reported on Schedule M–3?

COMPREHENSIVE TAX RETURN PROBLEM

Tax Return Problem

40. Dwayne Gordon and Craig Murray each own 50% of the common stock of Educational Software, Inc. (ESI). No other class of stock is authorized. On January 4, 1996, they formed ESI to market educational software acquired from independent developers. Pertinent information regarding ESI is summarized as follows:

- ESI's business address is 4010 Hansen Street, Ithaca, NY 14850, and its telephone number is (607) 555–1217. The corporation's e-mail address is esihq@esi.com.
- The employer identification number is 54–3044456; the principal business activity code is 611000.
- Dwayne is president of the company, and Craig is vice president.
- Both Dwayne and Craig are full-time employees of the corporation, and each receives a salary of $95,000. Dwayne's Social Security number is 842–48–1181; Craig's Social Security number is 384–28–3121.
- ESI is an accrual method, calendar year taxpayer. Inventories are determined using FIFO and the lower of cost or market method. ESI uses the straight-line method of depreciation for both book and tax purposes.
- During 2005, the corporation distributed a cash dividend of $30,000.

ESI's financial statements for 2005 are shown below.

Income Statement

Operating Income		
Gross sales		$1,893,536
Sales returns and allowances		(60,465)
Net sales		$1,833,071
Cost of goods sold:		
Beginning inventory	$ 254,345	
Purchases	905,866	
Cost of goods available for sale	$1,160,211	
Ending inventory	(354,099)	
Cost of goods sold		(806,112)
Gross profit from operations		$1,026,959

Operating Expenses			
Salaries—officers:			
Dwayne Gordon	$95,000		
Craig Murray	95,000	$190,000	
Salaries—clerical and sales		361,247	
Taxes:			
Property	$22,869		
Payroll	37,239		
State income	13,796		
Other miscellaneous	11,642	85,546	
Repairs and maintenance		34,816	
Meals and entertainment		4,284	
Travel		8,264	
Charitable contributions		14,300	
Fine paid to City of Ithaca for building code violation		2,683	
Interest expense on business loans		13,068	
Advertising		45,851	
Rental expense		84,233	
Depreciation*		29,948	
Contributions to pension plans		38,587	
Employee benefit programs		11,025	
Accounting services		25,000	
Dues and subscriptions		867	
Insurance		24,321	
Legal and professional services		8,199	
Miscellaneous expenses		3,874	
Telephone		2,248	
Premiums on term life insurance policies on the lives of Dwayne and Craig; ESI is the designated beneficiary		11,000	
Total expenses			$ 999,361
Net operating income			$ 27,598
Other Income			
Dividends received from stock investments in less-than-20%-owned U.S. corporations			$ 50,000
Interest income:			
State of Nevada bonds		$ 3,037	
Federal bonds		864	
Certificates of deposit		4,462	8,363
Other Expense			
Interest expense to purchase state bonds			2,266
Net income before Federal income taxes			$ 83,695

*You are not provided enough detailed data to complete a Form 4562 (depreciation). If you solve this problem using TurboTax, enter the amount of depreciation on line 20c of Form 1120 using the override feature (right click on line 20c, select *override* from the pop-up menu, and enter the amount of depreciation).

Balance Sheet

Assets	January 1, 2005	December 31, 2005
Cash	$ 58,856	$ 55,889
Trade notes and accounts receivable	70,385	56,264
Inventories	254,345	354,099
Federal bonds	23,500	18,500
State bonds	121,500	121,500
Certificates of deposit	154,075	164,880
Stock investment	346,198	346,198
Buildings and other depreciable assets	316,077	315,908
Accumulated depreciation	(79,925)	(109,873)
Land	125,550	128,580
Other assets	7,117	2,628
Total assets	$1,397,678	$1,454,573
Liabilities and Equity	**January 1, 2005**	**December 31, 2005**
Accounts payable	$ 153,518	$ 209,304
Other current liabilities	53,436	22,136
Mortgages	220,114	209,765
Capital stock	125,000	125,000
Retained earnings	845,610	888,368
Total liabilities and equity	$1,397,678	$1,454,573

During 2005, ESI made estimated tax payments of $3,000 each quarter to the IRS. Prepare a Form 1120 for ESI for tax year 2005. Suggested software. TurboTax.

BRIDGE *Discipline*

1. Charles is planning to invest $10,000 in a venture whose management is undecided as to whether it should be structured as a regular corporation or as a partnership. Charles will hold a 10% interest in the entity. Determine the treatment to Charles if the entity is a corporation and if it is a partnership. In the analysis, assume Charles is in the 35% marginal tax bracket, and the entity, if operating as a corporation, is in the 34% marginal tax bracket. Also, assume that the passive activity rules do not apply to Charles.
   a. If the entity incurs an $80,000 operating loss in year 1, what is Charles's cash outflow if the entity is a corporation? A partnership?
   b. In year 2, the entity earns operating income of $200,000 and makes no distribution to any of the owners. What is the tax burden on Charles if the investment is a corporation? A partnership?
   c. In year 3, the entity earns operating income of $200,000 and distributes all of that year's after-tax proceeds to the owners. What amount of cash is available to Charles if the entity operates as a corporation (assume any distribution is a qualified dividend)? A partnership?

2. On your review of the books and records of Ridge Corporation, you note the following information pertaining to its tax provision.

Net income per books	$525,400
Book income tax expense	234,600
Dividends received deduction	70,000
Capital gains	50,000
Capital losses	(60,000)
MACRS depreciation	80,000
Book depreciation	65,000

   a. Calculate Ridge's taxable income and Federal income tax liability for the year.
   b. Calculate Ridge's deferred income tax liability.

RESEARCH PROBLEMS

Note: Solutions to Research Problems can be prepared by using the **RIA Checkpoint® Student Edition** online research product, which is available to accompany this text. It is also possible to prepare solutions to the Research Problems by using tax research materials found in a standard tax library.

THOMSON RIA™

Decision Making

Communications

Research Problem 1. Lynn Jones, Shawn, Walt, and Donna are trying to decide whether they should organize a corporation and transfer their shares of stock in several corporations to this new corporation. All their shares are listed on the New York Stock Exchange and are readily marketable. Lynn would transfer shares in Brown Corporation; Shawn would transfer stock in Rust Corporation; Walt would transfer stock in White Corporation; and Donna would transfer stock in several corporations. The stock would be held by the newly formed corporation for investment purposes. Lynn asks you, her tax adviser, if she would have gain on the transfer of her substantially appreciated shares in Brown Corporation if she transfers the shares to a newly formed corporation. She also asks whether there will be tax consequences if she, Shawn, Walt, and Donna form a partnership, rather than a corporation, to which they would transfer their readily marketable stock. Your input will be critical as they make their decision. Prepare a letter to the client, Lynn Jones, and a memo for the firm's files. Lynn's address is 1540 Maxwell Avenue, Highland, KY 41099.

Communications

Research Problem 2. Joe and Tom Moore are brothers and equal shareholders in Black Corporation, a calendar year taxpayer. In 2003, they incurred certain travel and entertainment expenditures, as employees, on behalf of Black Corporation. Because Black was in a precarious financial condition, Joe and Tom decided not to seek reimbursement for these expenditures. Instead, each brother deducted what he spent on his own individual return (Form 1040). Upon audit of the returns filed by Joe and Tom for 2003, the IRS disallowed these expenditures. Write a letter to Joe at 568 Inwood Avenue, Waynesburg, PA 15370, and indicate whether he should challenge the IRS action. Explain your conclusion using nontechnical language.

Research Problem 3. Tim is a real estate broker who specializes in commercial real estate. Although he usually buys and sells on behalf of others, he does maintain a portfolio of property of his own. He holds this property, mainly unimproved land, either as an investment or for sale to others.

In early 2005, Irene and Al contact Tim regarding a tract of land located just outside the city limits. Tim bought the property, which is known as the Moore farm, several years ago for $600,000. At that time, no one knew that it was located on a geological fault line. Irene, a well-known architect, and Al, a building contractor, want Tim to join them in developing the property for residential use. They are aware of the fault line but believe they can circumvent the problem by using newly developed design and construction technology. Because of the geological flaw, however, they regard the Moore farm as being worth only $450,000. Their intent is to organize a corporation to build the housing project, and each party will receive stock commensurate to the property or services contributed.

After consulting his tax adviser, Tim agrees to join the venture if certain modifications to the proposed arrangement are made. The transfer of the land would be structured as a sale to the corporation. Instead of receiving stock, Tim would receive a note from the corporation. The note would be interest bearing and become due in five years. The maturity value of the note would be $450,000—the amount that even Tim concedes is the fair market value of the Moore farm.

What income tax consequences ensue from Tim's suggested approach? Compare this result with what would happen if Tim merely transferred the Moore farm in return for stock in the new corporation.

Internet *Activity*

Use the tax resources of the Internet to address the following questions. Do not restrict your search to the World Wide Web, but include a review of newsgroups and general reference materials, practitioner sites and resources, primary sources of the tax law, chat rooms and discussion groups, and other opportunities.

Research Problem 4. Find the IRS Web site and print a copy of Schedule M–3. Compare it with the Schedule M–1 used in Example 47 and discuss the differences.

Research Problem 5. Identify two publicly traded corporations that have issued more than one class of stock to their shareholders. Was the issuance of the additional classes of stock part of the original incorporation, or did it occur later? Determine the rationale for the corporations' actions.

http://wft.swlearning.com

CHAPTER 10

Corporations: Earnings & Profits and Dividend Distributions

LEARNING OBJECTIVES

After completing Chapter 10, you should be able to:

LO.1

Understand the role that earnings and profits play in determining the tax treatment of distributions.

LO.2

Compute a corporation's earnings and profits.

LO.3

Apply the rules for allocating earnings and profits to distributions.

LO.4

Understand the tax impact of property dividends on the recipient shareholder and the corporation making the distribution.

LO.5

Understand the nature and treatment of constructive dividends.

LO.6

Distinguish between taxable and nontaxable stock dividends.

LO.7

Discuss the tax treatment of stock redemptions.

OUTLINE

TAX *Talk*

The relative stability of profits after taxes is evidence that the corporation profits tax is, in effect, almost entirely shifted; the government simply uses the corporation as a tax collector.

—K. E. Boulding

Generally, a corporation cannot deduct distributions made to its shareholders. In contrast, shareholders may be required to treat distributions as fully subject to tax, a nontaxable recovery of capital, or capital gain.

Since distributions provide no deduction to the paying corporation and often require income recognition by the shareholders, a double tax seemingly results (i.e., at both the corporate and the shareholder levels). Because of the possibility of a double tax when dealing with corporations, the tax treatment of distributions often raises issues such as the following.

- The availability of earnings to be distributed.
- The basis of the stock in the hands of the shareholder.
- The character of the property being distributed.
- Whether the shareholder gives up ownership in return for the distribution.
- Whether the distribution is liquidating or nonliquidating.

LO.1

Understand the role that earnings and profits play in determining the tax treatment of distributions.

Corporate Distributions—In General

To the extent that a distribution is made from corporate earnings and profits (E & P), the shareholder is deemed to receive a **dividend**, usually taxed in a preferential manner.[1] Generally, corporate distributions are presumed to be paid out of E & P (defined later in this chapter) and are treated as dividends, *unless* the parties to the transaction can show otherwise.

The portion of a corporate distribution that is not taxed as a dividend (because of insufficient E & P) is nontaxable to the extent of the shareholder's basis in the stock. The stock basis is reduced accordingly. The excess of the distribution over the shareholder's basis is treated as a gain from the sale or exchange of the stock.[2]

EXAMPLE 1

At the beginning of the year, Amber Corporation (a calendar year taxpayer) has accumulated E & P of $30,000. The corporation has no current E & P. During the year, the corporation distributes $40,000 to its *equal* shareholders, Bob and Bonnie. Only $30,000 of the $40,000 distribution is a taxable dividend. Suppose Bob's basis in his stock is $8,000, while Bonnie's basis is $4,000. Under these conditions, Bob recognizes a taxable dividend of

[1]§§ 301(c)(1) and 316(a). Corporate shareholders claim a dividends received deduction. Others typically pay a tax on dividends at a maximum 15% rate.

[2]§ 301(c).

TAX *in the News* — **WAS THE DIVIDEND TAX CUT A SUCCESS OR A FAILURE?**

In 2004, 374 companies in the Standard & Poor's 500 stock index paid dividends, up from 351 in 2002 and 370 in 2003. This was the highest rate since 1999. Furthermore, the amount of dividends paid in 2004 was a record $183 billion.

According to equity market analysts, the growth in dividend payments was fueled both by larger dividends from companies with an established dividend-paying history (e.g., Wal-Mart Stores, Coca-Cola, and Harley-Davidson) and by first-time dividends from growth companies that hadn't paid dividends in the past (e.g., Staples, Cendant Corporation, and Costco Wholesale Corporation). The biggest dividend standout in 2004, however, was Microsoft, which paid a record onetime $32 billion dividend and doubled its usual quarterly dividend to boot.

Recent research into the impact of the tax cut on corporate dividend policies provides a clearer picture of its effectiveness. Economists have offered convincing evidence that dividend payments increased following the reduction in tax rates on dividends, even when onetime dividends are not considered. Other research, however, suggests that corporations did not increase total payments to shareholders but substituted dividend payments for stock buybacks. Thus, the change in the tax law may not have led to the effect that was originally intended.

$15,000 and reduces the basis of his stock from $8,000 to $3,000. The $20,000 Bonnie receives from Amber Corporation is accounted for as follows.

- Taxable dividend of $15,000.
- Reduction in stock basis from $4,000 to zero.
- Taxable gain of $1,000. ■

Earnings and Profits (E & P)

LO.2

Compute a corporation's earnings and profits.

The notion of **earnings and profits** is similar in many respects to the accounting concept of retained earnings. Both are measures of the firm's accumulated capital. However, these two concepts differ in a fundamental way. The computation of retained earnings is based on financial accounting rules, while E & P is determined using rules specified in the tax law.

E & P fixes the upper limit on the amount of dividend income that shareholders must recognize as a result of a distribution by the corporation. In this sense, E & P represents the corporation's economic ability to pay a dividend without impairing its capital. Thus, the effect of a specific transaction on the E & P account often can be determined by considering whether the transaction increases or decreases the corporation's capacity to pay a dividend.

Computation of E & P

The Code does not explicitly define the term *earnings and profits.* Instead, a series of adjustments to taxable income are identified to provide a measure of the corporation's economic income.[3] In general, E & P determinations are applied in the same manner for cash and accrual basis taxpayers.

Accumulated E & P is fixed as of the beginning of the tax year, which is the sum of the undistributed earnings of the entity since February 28, 1913. **Current E & P** is that portion of E & P attributable to the current tax year's operations. It is computed by using the corporation's Federal taxable income and then applying a series of adjustments to more closely approximate the cash flow of the entity.[4]

[3] Reg. § 1.312–6(a).

[4] Section 312 describes many of the adjustments to taxable income necessary to determine E & P. Regulation § 1.312–6 addresses the effect of accounting methods on E & P.

Additions to Taxable Income. It is necessary to add certain previously excluded income items back to taxable income to determine current E & P. Included among these positive adjustments are interest income on municipal bonds, excluded life insurance proceeds (in excess of cash surrender value), and Federal income tax refunds from taxes paid in prior years.

In addition to excluded income items, the dividends received deduction and the production activities deduction are added back to taxable income to determine E & P. Neither of these deductions decreases the corporation's assets. Instead, they are partial exclusions for specific types of income (dividend income and income from production activities). Since they do not impair the corporation's ability to pay dividends, they do not reduce E & P.

EXAMPLE 2

A corporation collects $100,000 on a key employee life insurance policy (the corporation is the owner and beneficiary of the policy). At the time the policy matured on the death of the insured employee, it possessed a cash surrender value of $30,000. None of the $100,000 is included in the corporation's taxable income, but $70,000 is added to taxable income when computing current E & P. ■

Subtractions from Taxable Income. Some of the corporation's nondeductible expenditures are subtracted from taxable income to arrive at E & P. These negative adjustments include the nondeductible portion of meals and entertainment expenses, related-party losses, expenses incurred to produce tax-exempt income, Federal income taxes paid, nondeductible key employee life insurance premiums (net of increases in cash surrender value), and nondeductible fines, penalties, and lobbying costs.

EXAMPLE 3

A corporation sells property (basis of $10,000) to its sole shareholder for $8,000. Because of § 267 (disallowance of losses on sales between related parties), the $2,000 loss cannot be deducted in arriving at the corporation's taxable income. But since the overall economic effect of the transaction is a decrease in the corporation's assets by $2,000, the loss reduces the current E & P for the year of the sale. ■

EXAMPLE 4

A corporation pays a $10,000 premium on a key employee life insurance policy covering the life of its president. As a result of the payment, the cash surrender value of the policy is increased by $7,000. Although none of the $10,000 premium is deductible for tax purposes, current E & P is reduced by $3,000. ■

Timing Adjustments. Some E & P adjustments shift the effect of a transaction from the year of its inclusion in or deduction from taxable income to the year in which it has an economic effect on the corporation. Charitable contribution carryovers, net operating loss carryovers, and capital loss carryovers all give rise to this kind of adjustment.

EXAMPLE 5

During 2006, Raven Corporation makes charitable contributions, $12,000 of which cannot be deducted in arriving at the taxable income for the year because of the 10% taxable income limitation. Consequently, the $12,000 is carried forward to 2007 and fully deducted in that year. The excess charitable contribution reduces the corporation's current E & P for 2006 by $12,000 and increases its current E & P for 2007, when the deduction is allowed, by a like amount. The increase in E & P in 2007 is necessary because the charitable contribution carryover reduces the taxable income for that year (the starting point for computing E & P) and already has been taken into account in determining the E & P for 2006. ■

Gains and losses from property transactions generally affect the determination of E & P only to the extent that they are recognized for tax purposes. Thus, gains and losses deferred under the like-kind exchange provision and deferred involuntary conversion gains do not affect E & P until recognized. Accordingly, no timing adjustment is required for these items.

Accounting Method Adjustments. In addition to the above adjustments, accounting methods used for determining E & P are generally more conservative than those allowed under the income tax rules. For example, the installment method is not permitted for E & P purposes even though, in some cases, it is allowed when computing taxable income. Thus, an adjustment is required for the deferred gain attributable to sales of property made during the year under the installment method. Specifically, all principal payments are treated as having been received in the year of sale.[5]

EXAMPLE 6

In 2006, Cardinal Corporation, a calendar year taxpayer, sells unimproved real estate (basis of $20,000) for $100,000. Under the terms of the sale, beginning in 2007, Cardinal will receive two annual payments of $50,000 each with interest of 9%. Cardinal Corporation does not elect out of the installment method. Since Cardinal's taxable income for 2006 will not reflect any of the gain from the sale, the corporation must make an $80,000 positive adjustment for 2006 (the deferred gain from the sale) in computing E & P. Similarly, $40,000 negative adjustments will be required in 2007 and 2008 when the deferred gain is recognized under the installment method. ■

The alternative depreciation system (ADS) must be used for purposes of computing E & P.[6] This method requires straight-line depreciation over a recovery period equal to the Asset Depreciation Range (ADR) midpoint life.[7] If MACRS cost recovery is used for income tax purposes, a positive or negative adjustment equal to the difference between MACRS and ADS must be made each year. Finally, none of the 30 or 50 percent additional first-year depreciation is allowed under the ADS.[8]

Likewise, when assets are disposed of, an additional adjustment to taxable income is required to allow for the difference in gain or loss resulting from the difference in income tax basis and E & P basis.[9] The adjustments arising from depreciation are illustrated in the following example.

EXAMPLE 7

On January 2, 2005, White Corporation purchased equipment with an ADR midpoint life of 10 years for $30,000. The equipment was then depreciated over its 7-year MACRS class life. The asset was sold on July 2, 2007, for $27,000. For purposes of determining taxable income and E & P, cost recovery claimed on the equipment is summarized below.

Year	Cost Recovery Computation	MACRS	ADS	Adjustment Amount
2005	$30,000 × 14.29%	$ 4,287		
	$30,000 ÷ 10-year ADR recovery period × ½ (half-year for first year of service)		$1,500	$2,787
2006	$30,000 × 24.49%	7,347		
	$30,000 ÷ 10-year ADR recovery period		3,000	4,347
2007	$30,000 × 17.49% × ½ (half-year for year of disposal)	2,624		
	$30,000 ÷ 10-year ADR recovery period × ½ (half-year for year of disposal)		1,500	1,124
	Total cost recovery	$14,258	$6,000	$8,258

[5] § 312(n)(5).

[6] § 312(k)(3)(A).

[7] See § 168(g)(2). The ADR midpoint life for most assets is set out in Rev.Proc. 87–56, 1987–2 C.B. 674. The recovery period is 5 years for automobiles and light-duty trucks and 40 years for real property. For assets with no class life, the recovery period is 12 years.

[8] § 168(k)(2)(C). This provision applied only for certain assets placed in service after September 10, 2001 and before January 1, 2005.

[9] § 312(f)(1).

Each year White Corporation increases its taxable income by the adjustment amount indicated above to determine E & P. In addition, when computing E & P for 2007, White reduces taxable income by $8,258 to account for the excess gain recognized for income tax purposes.

	Income Tax	E & P
Amount realized	$ 27,000	$ 27,000
Adjusted basis for income tax ($30,000 cost – $14,258 MACRS)	(15,742)	
Adjusted basis for E & P ($30,000 cost – $6,000 ADS)		(24,000)
Gain on sale	$ 11,258	$ 3,000
Adjustment amount ($3,000 – $11,258)	($ 8,258)	

■

In addition to more conservative depreciation methods, the E & P rules impose limitations on the deductibility of § 179 expense.[10] In particular, this expense is deducted over a period of five years for E & P purposes. Thus, in any year that § 179 is elected, 80 percent of the resulting expense is added back to taxable income to determine current E & P. In each of the following four years, a negative adjustment equal to 20 percent of the § 179 expense is made.

The E & P rules also require specific accounting methods in various situations, making adjustments necessary when different methods are used for income tax purposes. For example, E & P requires cost depletion rather than percentage depletion. When accounting for long-term contracts, E & P rules specify the percentage of completion method rather than the completed contract method. As the E & P determination does not allow for the amortization of organizational expenses, any such expense deducted when computing taxable income must be added back. To account for income deferral under the LIFO inventory method, the E & P computation requires an adjustment for changes in the LIFO recapture amount (the excess of FIFO over LIFO inventory value) during the year. Increases in LIFO recapture are added to taxable income and decreases are subtracted, to the extent of prior-year increases. E & P rules also specify that intangible drilling costs and mine exploration and development costs be amortized over a period of 60 months and 120 months, respectively. For income tax purposes, however, these costs can be deducted currently.[11]

Summary of E & P Adjustments

E & P serves as a measure of the earnings of the corporation that are available for distribution as taxable dividends to the shareholders. Current E & P is determined by making a series of adjustments to the corporation's taxable income. These adjustments are reviewed in Concept Summary 10–1.

LO.3

Apply the rules for allocating earnings and profits to distributions.

Allocating E & P to Distributions

When a positive balance exists in both the current and the accumulated E & P accounts, corporate distributions are deemed to be made first from current E & P and then from accumulated E & P. When distributions exceed the amount of current E & P, it becomes necessary to allocate current and accumulated E & P to each distribution made during the year. Current E & P is allocated on a pro rata basis to each distribution. Accumulated E & P is applied in chronological order, beginning with the earliest distribution. This allocation is important if any shareholder sells stock during the year.

[10] § 312(k)(3)(B).

[11] § 312(n).

CONCEPT SUMMARY 10–1

Computing E & P

Transaction	Adjustment to Taxable Income to Determine Current E & P: Addition	Subtraction
Tax-exempt income	X	
Dividends received deduction	X	
Collection of proceeds from insurance policy on life of corporate officer (in excess of cash surrender value)	X	
Deferred gain on installment sale (all gain is added to E & P in year of sale)	X	
Future recognition of installment sale gross profit		X
Excess capital loss and excess charitable contribution (over 10% limitation) in year incurred		X
Deduction of charitable contribution, NOL, or capital loss carryovers in succeeding taxable years (increase E & P because deduction reduces taxable income while E & P was reduced in a prior year)	X	
Federal income taxes paid		X
Federal income tax refund	X	
Loss on sale between related parties		X
Nondeductible fines, penalties, lobbying costs, meals, and entertainment		X
Payment of premiums on insurance policy on life of corporate officer (in excess of increase in cash surrender value of policy)		X
Realized gain (not recognized) on an involuntary conversion	No effect	
Realized gain or loss (not recognized) on a like-kind exchange	No effect	
Percentage depletion (only cost depletion can reduce E & P)	X	
Accelerated depreciation (E & P is reduced only by straight-line, units-of-production, or machine hours depreciation)	X	X
Production activities deduction	X	
§ 179 expense in year elected (80%)	X	
§ 179 expense in four years following election (20% each year)		X
Increase (decrease) in LIFO recapture amount	X	X
Intangible drilling costs deducted currently (reduce E & P in future years by amortizing costs over 60 months)	X	
Mine exploration and development costs (reduce E & P in future years by amortizing costs over 120 months)	X	

EXAMPLE 8

As of January 1 of the current year, Black Corporation has accumulated E & P of $10,000. Current E & P for the year amounts to $30,000. Megan and Matt are sole *equal* shareholders of Black from January 1 to July 31. On August 1, Megan sells all of her stock to Helen. Black makes two distributions to shareholders during the year: $40,000 to Megan and Matt ($20,000 to each) on July 1, and $40,000 to Matt and Helen ($20,000 to each) on December 1. Current and accumulated E & P are allocated to the two distributions as follows.

CONCEPT SUMMARY 10–2

Allocating E & P to Distributions

1. Current E & P is allocated first to distributions on a pro rata basis; then, accumulated E & P is applied (to the extent necessary) in chronological order beginning with the earliest distribution. See Example 8.
2. Unless and until the parties can show otherwise, it is presumed that current E & P covers all distributions. See Example 9.
3. When a deficit exists in accumulated E & P and a positive balance exists in current E & P, distributions are regarded as dividends to the extent of current E & P. See Example 10.
4. When a deficit exists in current E & P and a positive balance exists in accumulated E & P, the two accounts are netted at the date of distribution. If the resulting balance is zero or a deficit, the distribution is treated as a return of capital, first reducing the basis of the stock to zero, then generating taxable gain. If a positive balance results, the distribution is a dividend to the extent of the balance. Any loss in current E & P is allocated ratably during the year unless the parties can show otherwise. See Example 11.

	Source of Distribution		
	Current E & P	Accumulated E & P	Return of Capital
July 1 distribution ($40,000)	$15,000	$10,000	$15,000
December 1 distribution ($40,000)	15,000	–0–	25,000

Since 50% of the total distributions are made on July 1 and December 1, respectively, one-half of current E & P is allocated to each of the two distributions. Accumulated E & P is applied in chronological order, so the entire amount is applied to the July 1 distribution. The tax consequences to the shareholders are presented below.

	Shareholder		
	Megan	Matt	Helen
July distribution ($40,000)			
Dividend income—			
From current E & P ($15,000)	$ 7,500	$ 7,500	$ –0–
From accumulated E & P ($10,000)	5,000	5,000	–0–
Return of capital ($15,000)	7,500	7,500	–0–
December distribution ($40,000)			
Dividend income—			
From current E & P ($15,000)	–0–	7,500	7,500
From accumulated E & P ($0)	–0–	–0–	–0–
Return of capital ($25,000)	–0–	12,500	12,500
Total dividend income	$12,500	$20,000	$ 7,500
Nontaxable return of capital (assuming sufficient basis in the stock investment)	$ 7,500	$20,000	$12,500

Because the balance in the accumulated E & P account is exhausted when it is applied to the July 1 distribution, Megan has more dividend income than Helen, even though both receive equal distributions during the year. In addition, each shareholder's basis is reduced by the nontaxable return of capital; any excess over basis results in taxable gain. ■

GLOBAL *Tax Issues*

A WORLDWIDE VIEW OF DIVIDENDS

From an international perspective, the double taxation of dividends is unusual. Most developed countries have adopted a policy of corporate integration, which imposes a single tax on corporate profits. Corporate integration takes several forms. One popular approach is to impose a tax at the corporate level, but allow shareholders to claim a credit for corporate-level taxes paid when dividends are received. A second alternative is to allow a corporate-level deduction for dividends paid to shareholders. A third approach is to allow shareholders to exclude corporate dividends from income. A fourth alternative suggested in the past by the U.S. Treasury is the "comprehensive business income tax," which excludes both dividend and interest income while disallowing deductions for interest expense.

Facing trade-offs between equity and the economic distortions introduced by the double tax and the prevalence of corporate integration throughout the world, the United States continues to struggle with the issue of how corporate distributions should be taxed. Corporate integration has been a recurring suggestion since the Treasury advanced the idea in 1992. The current reduced tax rate on dividends began as a proposal by President Bush in 2003 to exempt qualified dividends from tax. However, because estimates indicated that the proposed dividend exclusion would result in a loss of revenue in excess of $600 billion, the process of political compromise eventually led to a reduced tax rate instead of a complete exemption from tax.

When the tax years of the corporation and its shareholders are not the same, it may be impossible to determine the amount of current E & P on a timely basis. For example, if shareholders use a calendar year and the corporation uses a fiscal year, then current E & P may not be ascertainable until after the shareholders' tax returns have been filed. To address this timing problem, the allocation rules presume that current E & P is sufficient to cover every distribution made during the year unless or until the parties can show otherwise.

EXAMPLE 9

Green Corporation uses the fiscal year of July 1 through June 30 for tax purposes. Carol, Green's only shareholder, uses a calendar year. As of July 1, 2006, Green Corporation has a zero balance in its accumulated E & P account. For fiscal year 2006–2007, the corporation incurs a $5,000 deficit in current E & P. On August 1, 2006, Green distributed $10,000 to Carol. The distribution is dividend income to Carol and is reported when she files her income tax return for the 2006 calendar year, on or before April 15, 2007.

Because Carol cannot prove until June 30, 2007, that the corporation has a deficit for the 2006–2007 fiscal year, she must assume the $10,000 distribution is fully covered by current E & P. When Carol learns of the deficit, she can file an amended return for 2006 showing the $10,000 as a return of capital. Alternatively, Carol can file for an extension for her returns, while she awaits Green Corporation's fiscal year-end. ■

Additional difficulties arise when either the current or the accumulated E & P account has a deficit balance. In particular, when current E & P is positive and accumulated E & P has a deficit balance, accumulated E & P is *not* netted against current E & P. Instead, the distribution is deemed to be a taxable dividend to the extent of the positive current E & P balance.

EXAMPLE 10

At the beginning of the current year, Brown Corporation has a deficit of $30,000 in accumulated E & P. For the year, it has current E & P of $10,000 and distributes $5,000 to its shareholders. The $5,000 distribution is treated as a taxable dividend since it is deemed to have been made from current E & P. This is the case even though Brown Corporation still has a deficit in accumulated E & P at the end of the year. ■

BRIDGE *Discipline*

Bridge to Finance

Investors often have tried to read the dividend policies of a corporation as indicators of the strength of the entity: Constant dividend payments indicated a stable financial structure for the corporation, while dividend increases were a predictor of good times and triggered stock price increases. Reductions in historic dividend payment patterns foreshadowed financial difficulties and often caused a quick and sizable drop in share price.

Nobel Prize winners Merton Miller, University of Chicago, and Franco Modigliani, MIT, saw things differently. They viewed dividends as a remnant of various financing sources available to the corporation: If it was cheaper to finance future growth by retaining profits and decreasing or eliminating dividend payments, so be it. The entity must reduce its cost of capital wherever possible, and, under this interpretation, a dividend decrease might indicate the internal financial strength of the corporation. Conversely, the payment of a dividend reduces the capital available to the entity, thereby forcing the entity to finance its operations and growth from some third-party source and risking future weakness if the cost of that capital increases.

Miller and Modigliani held that stock price and dividend policy were unrelated, and that changes in dividend patterns should not affect the capitalized value of the business. Their original studies are more than 40 years old, but the market seems to have adopted them. Even with lower tax rates on dividends, few shareholders complain that the typical growth stock never pays dividends.

Nevertheless, shares of companies that pay dividends outperform those that don't pay dividends. In the first half of 2004, this trend continued. Stock prices of dividend payers in the S&P 500 fell by only about half a percent, while the stock prices of non-dividend-paying companies declined almost 5 percent.

In contrast to the above rule, when a deficit exists in current E & P and a positive balance exists in accumulated E & P, the accounts are netted at the date of distribution. If the resulting balance is zero or negative, the distribution is a return of capital. If a positive balance results, the distribution is a dividend to the extent of the balance. Any current E & P deficit is allocated ratably during the year unless the parties can show otherwise.

EXAMPLE 11

At the beginning of the current year, Gray Corporation (a calendar year taxpayer) has accumulated E & P of $10,000. During the year, the corporation incurs a $15,000 deficit in current E & P that accrues ratably. On July 1, Gray Corporation distributes $6,000 in cash to Hal, its sole shareholder. To determine how much of the $6,000 cash distribution represents dividend income to Hal, the balances of both accumulated and current E & P as of July 1 are determined and netted. This is necessary because of the deficit in current E & P.

	Source of Distribution	
	Current E & P	Accumulated E & P
January 1		$10,000
July 1 (½ of $15,000 deficit in current E & P)	($7,500)	2,500
July 1 distribution—$6,000		
Dividend income: $2,500		
Return of capital: $3,500		

The balance in E & P on July 1 is $2,500. Thus, of the $6,000 distribution, $2,500 is taxed as a dividend, and $3,500 represents a return of capital. ■

PLANNING *Strategies*

CORPORATE DISTRIBUTIONS

★ **Framework Focus: Income and Exclusions**

Strategy ★ Avoid Income Recognition.

In connection with the discussion of corporate distributions, the following points need reinforcement.

- Because E & P is the measure of dividend income, its periodic determination is essential to corporate planning. Thus, an E & P account should be established and maintained, particularly if the possibility exists that a corporate distribution might be a return of capital.
- Accumulated E & P is the sum of all past years' current E & P. Because there is no statute of limitations on the computation of E & P, the IRS can redetermine a corporation's current E & P for a tax year long since passed. Such a change affects accumulated E & P and has a direct impact on the taxability of current distributions to shareholders.
- Distributions can be planned to avoid or minimize dividend exposure.

EXAMPLE 12

Flicker Corporation has accumulated E & P of $100,000 as of January 1 of the current year. During the year, it expects to generate earnings from operations of $80,000 and to sell an asset for a loss of $100,000. Thus, it anticipates a current E & P deficit of $20,000. Flicker also expects to make a cash distribution of $60,000. The best approach is to recognize the loss as soon as possible and immediately thereafter make the cash distribution to the shareholders. Suppose these two steps take place on January 1. Because the current E & P has a deficit, the accumulated E & P account must be brought up to date (refer to Example 11). Thus, at the time of the distribution, the combined E & P balance is zero [$100,000 (beginning balance in accumulated E & P) – $100,000 (existing deficit in current E & P)], and the $60,000 distribution to the shareholders constitutes a return of capital. Current deficits are allocated pro rata throughout the year unless the parties can prove otherwise. Here they can. ■

EXAMPLE 13

After several unprofitable years, Darter Corporation has a deficit in accumulated E & P of $100,000 as of January 1, 2006. Starting in 2006, Darter expects to generate annual E & P of $50,000 for the next four years and would like to distribute this amount to its shareholders. The corporation's cash position (for dividend purposes) will correspond to the current E & P generated. Compare the following possibilities.

1. On December 31 of 2006, 2007, 2008, and 2009, Darter Corporation distributes a cash dividend of $50,000.
2. On December 31 of 2007 and 2009, Darter Corporation distributes a cash dividend of $100,000.

The two alternatives are illustrated as follows.

Year	Accumulated E & P (First of Year)	Current E & P	Distribution	Amount of Dividend
		Alternative 1		
2006	($100,000)	$50,000	$50,000	$50,000
2007	(100,000)	50,000	50,000	50,000
2008	(100,000)	50,000	50,000	50,000
2009	(100,000)	50,000	50,000	50,000
		Alternative 2		
2006	($100,000)	$50,000	$ –0–	$ –0–
2007	(50,000)	50,000	100,000	50,000
2008	(50,000)	50,000	–0–	–0–
2009	–0–	50,000	100,000	50,000

Alternative 1 produces $200,000 of dividend income because each $50,000 distribution is fully covered by current E & P. Alternative 2, however, produces only $100,000 of dividend income to the shareholders. The remaining $100,000 is a return of capital. Why? At the time Darter Corporation made its first distribution of $100,000 on December 31, 2007, it had a deficit of $50,000 in accumulated E & P (the original deficit of $100,000 is reduced by the $50,000 of current E & P from 2006). Consequently, the $100,000 distribution yields a $50,000 dividend (the current E & P for 2007), and $50,000 is treated as a return of capital. As of January 1, 2008, Darter's accumulated E & P now has a deficit balance of $50,000, since a distribution cannot increase a deficit in E & P. Adding the remaining $50,000 of current E & P from 2008, the balance as of January 1, 2009, is zero. Thus, the second distribution of $100,000 made on December 31, 2009, also yields $50,000 of dividends (the current E & P for 2009) and a $50,000 return of capital. ■

BRIDGE *Discipline*

Bridge to Investments

Most investors look to the stocks of utilities, real estate investment trusts, and tobacco companies as the source of steady dividend payments. This is a prudent decision on the investor's part, as the typical S&P 500 stock offers a dividend yield of just over 1 percent. But an investor could put together a fairly diversified portfolio using only stocks that regularly produce dividend yields of at least 2 percent. Using recent data, these companies include the following.

- Bank of America
- Dow Chemical
- Hong Kong Telecommunications
- Emerson Electric
- Telefonos de Mexico
- Weyerhauser
- General Electric
- ChevronTexaco
- Citigroup
- BellSouth
- Honeywell
- Kimberly–Clark
- Sara Lee

Dividends can be important to the investor because:

- They can be used in a tax-sheltered account, like a § 401(k) plan, such that the tax inefficiency of the dividends is not recognized immediately by the investor.
- Even today, about 40 percent of the total return from an investment can be traced to holding stocks that make regular distributions.
- Generally, a dividend-paying company is a profitable company, and corporate profits often are hard to come by.
- Earning and reinvesting dividends is an easy way to put into place an investment policy of dollar-cost averaging, a technique that forces the investor to buy more shares when prices are low and fewer shares when prices are high. Dollar-cost averaging often implements a contrarian investment strategy.

LO.4

Understand the tax impact of property dividends on the recipient shareholder and the corporation making the distribution.

Property Dividends

The previous discussion assumed that all distributions by a corporation to its shareholders are in the form of cash. Although most corporate distributions are paid in cash, a corporation may distribute a **property dividend** for various reasons. The shareholders may want a particular property that is held by the corporation. Or a corporation that is strapped for cash may want to distribute a dividend to its shareholders.

Property distributions have the same tax impact as distributions of cash except for effects attributable to any difference between the basis and the fair market value of the distributed property. In most situations, distributed property is appreciated, so its sale would result in a gain to the corporation. Distributions of property with a basis that differs from fair market value raise several tax questions.

- For the shareholder:
  - What is the amount of the distribution?
  - What is the basis of the property in the shareholder's hands?
- For the corporation:
  - Is a gain or loss recognized as a result of the distribution?
  - What is the effect of the distribution on E & P?

TAX FACT

So Who Is Paying Dividends?

Tax return data for 2002 indicate that over $400 billion were paid out by C corporations as dividends, including about $6 billion from entities with zero or negative assets. (Zero-asset corporations likely are in startup or liquidation mode or, during the tax year, were merged into another corporation.) Most of the distributions were made by the largest corporations by asset size, those likely to be publicly traded.

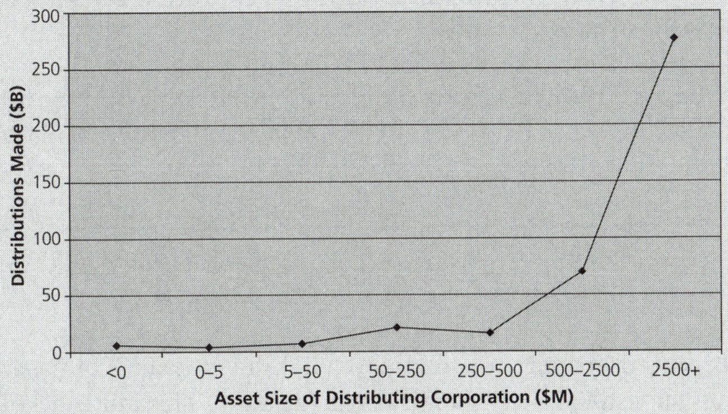

Property Dividends—Effect on the Shareholder

When a corporation distributes property rather than cash to a shareholder, the amount distributed is measured by the fair market value of the property on the date of distribution.[12] As with a cash distribution, the portion of a property distribution covered by existing E & P is a dividend, and any excess is treated as a return of capital. If the fair market value of the property distributed exceeds the corporation's E & P and the shareholder's basis in the stock investment, a capital gain usually results.

The amount distributed is reduced by any liabilities to which the distributed property is subject immediately before and immediately after the distribution and by any liabilities of the corporation assumed by the shareholder. The basis in the distributed property to the shareholder is the fair market value of the property on the date of the distribution.

EXAMPLE 14

Robin Corporation has E & P of $60,000. It distributes land with a fair market value of $50,000 (adjusted basis of $30,000) to its sole shareholder, Charles. The land is subject to a liability of $10,000, which Charles assumes. Charles has a taxable dividend of $40,000 [$50,000 (fair market value) – $10,000 (liability)]. The basis of the land to Charles is $50,000. ■

EXAMPLE 15

Red Corporation owns 10% of Tan Corporation. Tan has ample E & P to cover any distributions made during the year. One distribution made to Red consists of a vacant lot with a basis of $50,000 and a fair market value of $30,000. Red recognizes a taxable dividend of $30,000, and its basis in the lot becomes $30,000. ■

Distributing property that has depreciated in value as a property dividend may reflect poor planning. Note what happens in Example 15. Basis of $20,000 disappears due to the loss (basis $50,000, fair market value $30,000). As an alternative, if Tan Corporation sells the lot, it could use the loss to reduce its taxes. Then Tan could distribute the $30,000 of proceeds to its shareholders.

[12] § 301.

Property Dividends—Effect on the Corporation

As noted earlier, the distribution of a property dividend raises two questions related to the corporation's tax position: Is a gain or loss recognized? What is the effect on E & P?

Recognition of Gain or Loss. All distributions of appreciated property generate gain to the distributing corporation.[13] In effect, a corporation that distributes appreciated property is treated as if it had sold the property to the shareholder for its fair market value. However, the distributing corporation does *not* recognize loss on distributions of property.

EXAMPLE 16

A corporation distributes land (basis of $10,000 and fair market value of $30,000) to a shareholder. The corporation recognizes a gain of $20,000. ■

EXAMPLE 17

Assume the property in Example 16 has a basis of $30,000 and a fair market value of $10,000. The corporation does not recognize a loss on the distribution. ■

If the distributed property is subject to a liability in excess of basis or the shareholder assumes such a liability, a special rule applies. The fair market value of the property for purposes of determining gain on the distribution is treated as not being less than the amount of the liability.[14]

EXAMPLE 18

Assume the land in Example 16 is subject to a liability of $35,000. The corporation recognizes gain of $25,000 on the distribution ($35,000 – $10,000). ■

Effect of Corporate Distributions on E & P. Corporate distributions reduce E & P by the amount of money distributed or by the greater of the fair market value or the adjusted basis of property distributed, less the amount of any liability on the property.[15] E & P is increased by gain recognized on appreciated property distributed as a property dividend.

EXAMPLE 19

Crimson Corporation distributes property (basis of $10,000 and fair market value of $20,000) to Brenda, its shareholder. Crimson Corporation recognizes a gain of $10,000, which is added to its E & P. E & P is then reduced by $20,000, the fair market value of the property. Brenda has dividend income of $20,000 (presuming sufficient E & P). ■

EXAMPLE 20

Assume the same facts as in Example 19, except that the property's adjusted basis in the hands of Crimson Corporation is $25,000. Because loss is not recognized and the property's adjusted basis is greater than its fair market value, E & P is reduced by $25,000. Brenda reports dividend income of $20,000 (the fair market value of the property received). ■

EXAMPLE 21

Assume the same facts as in Example 20, except that the property is subject to a liability of $6,000. E & P is now reduced by $19,000 [$25,000 (adjusted basis) – $6,000 (liability)]. Brenda has a dividend of $14,000 [$20,000 (amount of the distribution) – $6,000 (liability)], and her basis in the property is $20,000. ■

Under no circumstances can a distribution, whether cash or property, either generate a deficit in E & P or add to a deficit in E & P. Deficits can arise only through recognized corporate losses.

[13] § 311.

[14] § 311(b)(2).

[15] §§ 312(a), (b), and (c).

BRIDGE *Discipline*

Bridge to Public Finance

The double tax on corporate income has always been controversial. Reformers have argued that taxing corporate profits twice creates several distortions in the economy, including:

- An incentive to invest in noncorporate rather than corporate businesses.
- An incentive for corporations to finance operations with debt rather than new equity because interest payments are deductible.
- An incentive for corporations to retain earnings and to structure distributions of profits to avoid the double tax.

Taken together, these distortions raise the cost of capital for corporate investments and increase the vulnerability of corporations in economic downturns due to excessive debt financing. Reformers argue that eliminating the double tax would remove these distortions, stimulate the economy (with estimated gains of up to $25 billion annually), and increase capital stock in the corporate sector by as much as $500 billion. They also argue that elimination of the double tax would make the United States more competitive internationally, because the majority of our trading partners assess only one tax on corporate income.

In contrast, supporters of the double tax argue that in view of the economic power held by publicly traded corporations, the tax is appropriate, especially since the income tax is based on notions of ability to pay and fairness. They also argue that many of the distortions can already be avoided through the use of deductible payments by closely held C corporations and through partnerships, limited liability companies, and S corporations.

EXAMPLE 22

Teal Corporation has accumulated E & P of $10,000 at the beginning of the current tax year. During the year, it has current E & P of $15,000. At the end of the year, it distributes cash of $30,000 to its sole shareholder, Walter. Teal's E & P at the end of the year is zero. The accumulated E & P of $10,000 is increased by current E & P of $15,000 and reduced $25,000 by the dividend distribution. The remaining $5,000 of the distribution to Walter does not reduce E & P because a distribution cannot generate a deficit in E & P. ■

Constructive Dividends

LO.5

Understand the nature and treatment of constructive dividends.

Any measurable economic benefit conveyed by a corporation to its shareholders can be treated as a dividend for Federal income tax purposes even though it is not formally declared or designated as a dividend. A distribution need not be issued pro rata to all shareholders.[16] Nor must the distribution satisfy the legal requirements of a dividend as set forth by applicable state law. This benefit, often described as a **constructive dividend**, is distinguishable from actual corporate distributions of cash and property in form only.

Constructive dividend situations usually arise in closely held corporations. Here, the dealings between the parties are less structured, and frequently, formalities are not preserved. The constructive dividend serves as a substitute for actual distributions. Usually, it is intended to accomplish some tax objective not available through the use of direct dividends. The shareholders may be attempting to distribute corporate profits in a form deductible to the corporation, like compensation.[17] Alternatively, the shareholders may be seeking benefits for themselves while avoiding the recognition of income. Some constructive dividends are, in reality, disguised dividends. But not all constructive dividends are deliberate attempts to

[16]See *Lengsfield v. Comm.*, 57–1 USTC ¶9437, 50 AFTR 1683, 241 F.2d 508 (CA–5, 1957).

[17]Recall that dividend distributions do not provide the distributing corporation with an income tax deduction, although they do reduce E & P.

avoid actual and formal dividends; many are inadvertent. Thus, an awareness of the various constructive dividend situations is essential to protect the parties from unanticipated, undesirable tax consequences.

Types of Constructive Dividends

The most frequently encountered types of constructive dividends are summarized on the following pages.

Shareholder Use of Corporate-Owned Property. A constructive dividend can occur when a shareholder uses the corporation's property for personal purposes at no cost. Personal use of corporate-owned automobiles, airplanes, yachts, fishing camps, hunting lodges, and other entertainment facilities is commonplace in some closely held corporations. The shareholder has dividend income to the extent of the fair rental value of the property for the period of its personal use.

Bargain Sale of Corporate Property to a Shareholder. Shareholders often purchase property from a corporation at a cost below the fair market value of the property. These bargain sales produce dividend income to the extent that the property's fair market value on the date of sale differs from the amount the shareholder paid for the property.[18] These situations might be avoided by appraising the property on or about the date of the sale. The appraised value should become the price to be paid by the shareholder.

Bargain Rental of Corporate Property. A bargain rental of corporate property by a shareholder also produces dividend income. Here the measure of the constructive dividend is the excess of the property's fair rental value over the rent actually paid. Again, appraisal data should be used to avoid any questionable situations.

Payments for the Benefit of a Shareholder. If a corporation pays an obligation of a shareholder, the payment is treated as a constructive dividend. The obligation involved need not be legally binding on the shareholder; it may, in fact, be a moral obligation.[19] Forgiveness of shareholder indebtedness by the corporation creates an identical problem.[20] Excessive rentals paid by a corporation for the use of shareholder property also are treated as constructive dividends.

Unreasonable Compensation. A salary payment to a shareholder-employee that is deemed to be **unreasonable compensation** is frequently treated as a constructive dividend. As a consequence, it is not deductible by the corporation. In determining the reasonableness of salary payments, the following factors are considered.

- The employee's qualifications.
- A comparison of salaries with dividend distributions.
- The prevailing rates of compensation for comparable positions in comparable business concerns.
- The nature and scope of the employee's work.
- The size and complexity of the business.
- A comparison of salaries paid with both gross and net income.
- The taxpayer's salary policy toward all employees.
- For small corporations with a limited number of officers, the amount of compensation paid to the employee in question in previous years.

[18] Reg. § 1.301–1(j).

[19] *Montgomery Engineering Co. v. U.S.*, 64–2 USTC ¶9618, 13 AFTR2d 1747, 230 F.Supp. 838 (D.Ct. N.J., 1964), *aff'd* in 65–1 USTC ¶9368, 15 AFTR2d 746, 344 F.2d 996 (CA–3, 1965).

[20] Reg. § 1.301–1(m).

TAX *in the News* **THE $6,000 SHOWER CURTAIN: COMPENSATION OR CONSTRUCTIVE DIVIDEND?**

Recently, there have been several well-publicized accounts of compensation abuse (to some) and illegal looting of corporate coffers (to others) by corporate executives. At the forefront of these scandals are the payments to L. Dennis Kozlowski by Tyco International (a large multinational conglomerate).

Kozlowski, during a four-year stint as CEO of Tyco, received about $400 million from the company in salary and stock-related compensation. In addition, Kozlowski received fringe benefits valued at $135 million. The benefits purportedly included:

- A new 15,000-square-foot home in Boca Raton, Florida, complete with pool, tennis court, and fountain. Tyco initially loaned the money interest-free to Kozlowski and then later forgave the entire loan. It paid him an extra $13 million to help him handle the income taxes on the income that resulted from forgiveness of the debt.
- More than $11 million in corporate funds used to decorate an $18 million Fifth Avenue apartment that Kozlowski stayed in when visiting New York. The funds were used to purchase antiques, art, a $17,000 umbrella stand, and a $6,000 gold-and-burgundy floral-patterned shower curtain.
- Half the cost of a $2.1 million birthday party for Kozlowski's wife, on the island of Sardinia. The week-long party included a performance by singer Jimmy Buffett.
- Flowers costing $96,943 for Kozlowski's homes.

Kozlowski and other officers of Tyco are facing criminal indictments alleging that the compensation represents theft of the corporation's assets. Tyco is suing Kozlowski, seeking repayment of $244 million in back pay and benefits.

How should the compensation payments be treated? Kozlowski owned stock in his employer. Should Tyco treat the payments as compensation, a constructive dividend, or a theft loss? Avoidance of the double tax does not seem to have been a motive for the payments (recall that compensation in excess of $1 million is not deductible unless it is contingent on performance), and the corporation is publicly traded. Consequently, it would be difficult for the IRS to argue for constructive dividend treatment. The payments to Kozlowski were apparently not authorized, so they may be treated as a theft of Tyco's assets.

- For large corporations, whether a reasonable shareholder would have agreed to the level of compensation paid.[21]

Loans to Shareholders. Advances to shareholders that are not bona fide loans are constructive dividends. Whether an advance qualifies as a bona fide loan is a question of fact to be determined in light of the particular circumstances. Factors considered in determining whether the advance is a bona fide loan include the following.[22]

- Whether the advance is on open account or is evidenced by a written instrument.
- Whether the shareholder furnished collateral or other security for the advance.
- How long the advance has been outstanding.
- Whether any repayments have been made.
- The shareholder's ability to repay the advance.
- The shareholder's use of the funds (e.g., payment of routine bills versus nonrecurring, extraordinary expenses).
- The regularity of the advances.
- The dividend-paying history of the corporation.

Even when a corporation makes a bona fide loan to a shareholder, a constructive dividend may be triggered, equal to the amount of any imputed (forgone)

[21] *Mayson Manufacturing Co. v. Comm.*, 49–2 USTC ¶9467, 38 AFTR 1028, 178 F.2d 115 (CA–6, 1949) and *Alpha Medical v. Comm.*, 99–1 USTC ¶50,461, 83 AFTR2d 99–697, 172 F.3d 942 (CA–6, 1999).

[22] *Fin Hay Realty Co. v. U.S.*, 68–2 USTC ¶9438, 22 AFTR2d 5004, 398 F.2d 694 (CA–3, 1968).

TAX *in the News* **HARD WORK PAYS OFF!**

By 1985, William Rogers, a pharmacist with 25 years of experience in health care, had successfully developed and sold two businesses—a pharmacy chain and a medical supply company. In 1986, after turning down a $1 million offer to manage the home health care division of a large corporation, Rogers founded Alpha Medical, Inc., with a $1,000 contribution. Over the next four years, Rogers built Alpha Medical into a business with 60 employees, a taxable income of almost $7 million, and a 1990 return on equity of almost 100 percent. The business provided both financial management and medical consulting services to hospitals and home health care companies. Rogers was the company's sole shareholder and president. He regularly worked 12 hours a day and was on call 24 hours a day. Rogers made all major decisions for Alpha Medical, acquired all of the company's clients, and personally negotiated all of the company's contracts. In addition, he personally developed many of the company's products and collaborated with programmers to develop proprietary software used by the company.

In 1986, Rogers received only $67,000 in compensation. The amount increased to $431,000 in 1988 and $928,000 in 1989. In 1990, Rogers was paid over $4.4 million, 64 percent of the company's taxable income, while the company paid only a $1,500 dividend.

During an audit of Alpha Medical, the IRS argued that only $400,000 of Rogers' compensation in 1990 was reasonable and that the remaining $4 million was not deductible. As a result, the IRS assessed a $1.3 million tax deficiency and an accuracy-related penalty.

The Tax Court split the difference between the IRS and the taxpayer, holding that $2.3 million of Rogers' pay was reasonable. On appeal, however, the Sixth Circuit Court of Appeals ruled that all $4.4 million of the compensation paid to Rogers was reasonable. In its decision, the Court of Appeals said that "in light of Rogers' record of accomplishment, risks he assumed, and amazing growth, reasonable shareholders would have gladly agreed to Rogers' level of compensation." The Court of Appeals also explicitly noted that Rogers had been undercompensated in prior years and that he had incurred a substantial opportunity cost when he refused the $1 million job offer so that he could start Alpha Medical.

Source: *Alpha Medical, Inc. v. Comm.*, 99–1 USTC ¶50,461, 83 AFTR2d 99–697, 172 F.3d 942 (CA–6, 1999).

interest on the loan.[23] Imputed interest equals the amount of interest (using the rate the Federal government pays on new borrowings, compounded semiannually) that exceeds the interest charged on the loan. When the imputed interest provision applies, the shareholder is deemed to have made an interest payment to the corporation equal to the amount of imputed interest, and the corporation is deemed to have repaid the imputed interest to the shareholder through a constructive dividend. As a result, the corporation receives interest income and makes a nondeductible dividend payment, and the shareholder has taxable dividend income that may be offset with an interest deduction.

EXAMPLE 23

Mallard Corporation lends its principal shareholder, Henry, $100,000 on January 2 of the current year. The loan is interest-free and payable on demand. On December 31, the imputed interest rules are applied. Assuming the Federal rate is 6%, compounded semiannually, the amount of imputed interest is $6,090. This amount is deemed paid by Henry to Mallard in the form of interest. Mallard is then deemed to return the amount to Henry as a constructive dividend. Thus, Henry has dividend income of $6,090, which may be offset with a deduction for the interest deemed paid to Mallard. Mallard has interest income of $6,090 for the interest received, with no offsetting deduction for the dividend payment. ■

Loans to a Corporation by Shareholders. Shareholder loans to a corporation may be reclassified as equity if the debt has too many features of stock. Any interest and principal payments made by the corporation to the shareholder are then treated as constructive dividends. This topic was covered more thoroughly in the discussion of "thin capitalization" in Chapter 9.

[23]See § 7872. A more detailed discussion of imputed interest is found in Chapter 4.

TAX FACT

Executive Compensation: Amount and Composition

Median executive compensation exceeds $2 million in the following five industries: insurance, communications, telecommunications, energy, and financial services. While stock options accounted for less than 20 percent of a CEO's direct pay in 1980, long-term compensation—mostly from exercised stock options—now makes up 80 percent of the average CEO's pay package.

Tax Treatment of Constructive Dividends

For tax purposes, constructive distributions are treated the same as actual distributions.[24] Thus, a corporate shareholder is entitled to the dividends received deduction (refer to Chapter 9). The constructive distribution is taxable as a dividend only to the extent of the corporation's current and accumulated E & P. The burden of proving that the distribution constitutes a return of capital because of inadequate E & P rests with the taxpayer.[25]

PLANNING *Strategies*

CONSTRUCTIVE DIVIDENDS

★ **Framework Focus: Income and Exclusions**

Strategy ★ Avoid Income Recognition.

Tax planning can be particularly effective in avoiding constructive dividend situations. Shareholders should try to structure their dealings with the corporation on an arm's length basis. For example, reasonable rent should be paid for the use of corporate property, and a fair price should be paid for its purchase. The parties should make every effort to support the amount involved with appraisal data or market information obtained from reliable sources at or near the time of the transaction. Dealings between shareholders and a closely held corporation should be as formal as possible. In the case of loans to shareholders, for example, the parties should provide for an adequate rate of interest and written evidence of the debt. Shareholders also should establish and follow a realistic repayment schedule.

If shareholders wish to distribute corporate profits in a form deductible to the corporation, a balanced mix of the possible alternatives lessens the risk of constructive dividend treatment. Rent for the use of shareholder property, interest on amounts borrowed from shareholders, or salaries for services rendered by shareholders are all feasible substitutes for dividend distributions. But overdoing any one approach may attract the attention of the IRS. Too much interest, for example, may mean the corporation is thinly capitalized, and some of the debt may be reclassified as equity.

Much can be done to protect against the disallowance of unreasonable compensation. Example 24 is an illustration, all too common in a family corporation, of what *not* to do.

EXAMPLE 24

Bob Cole wholly owns Eagle Corporation. Corporate employees and annual salaries include Mrs. Cole ($30,000), Cole, Jr. ($20,000), Bob Cole ($160,000), and Ed ($80,000). The operation of Eagle Corporation is shared about equally between Bob Cole and Ed, who is an unrelated party. Mrs. Cole performed significant services for Eagle during its formative years but now merely attends the annual meeting of the board of directors. Cole, Jr., Bob Cole's son, is a full-time student and occasionally signs papers for the corporation in his capacity as treasurer. Eagle Corporation has not distributed a dividend for 10 years, although it has accumulated substantial E & P. Mrs. Cole, Cole, Jr., and Bob Cole run the risk of a finding of unreasonable compensation, based on the following factors.

[24] *Simon v. Comm.*, 57–2 USTC ¶9989, 52 AFTR 698, 248 F.2d 869 (CA–8, 1957).

[25] *DiZenzo v. Comm.*, 65–2 USTC ¶9518, 16 AFTR2d 5107, 348 F.2d 122 (CA–2, 1965).

- Mrs. Cole's salary is vulnerable unless proof is available that some or all of her $30,000 annual salary is payment for services rendered to the corporation in prior years and that she was underpaid for those years.[26]
- Cole, Jr.'s salary is also vulnerable; he does not appear to earn the $20,000 paid to him by the corporation. Although neither Cole, Jr., nor Mrs. Cole is a shareholder, each one's relationship to Bob Cole is enough of a tie-in to raise the unreasonable compensation issue.
- Bob Cole's salary appears susceptible to challenge. Why is he receiving $80,000 more than Ed when it appears that they share equally in the operation of the corporation?
- The fact that Eagle Corporation has not distributed dividends over the past 10 years, even though it is capable of doing so, increases the likelihood of a constructive dividend. ■

What could have been done to improve the tax position of the parties in Example 24? Mrs. Cole and Cole, Jr., are not entitled to a salary as neither seems to be performing any services for the corporation. Paying them a salary simply aggravates the problem. The IRS is more apt to consider *all* the salaries to members of the family as being excessive under the circumstances. Bob Cole should probably reduce his compensation to correspond to that paid Ed. He can then attempt to distribute corporate earnings to himself in some other form.

Paying some dividends to Bob Cole would also help alleviate the problems raised in Example 24. The IRS has been successful in denying a deduction for salary paid to a shareholder-employee, even when the payment was reasonable, in a situation where the corporation had not distributed any dividends.[27] Most courts, however, have not denied deductions for compensation solely because a dividend was not paid. A better approach is to compare an employee's compensation with the level of compensation prevalent in the particular industry.

The corporation can substitute *indirect* compensation for Bob Cole by paying expenses that benefit him personally but are nevertheless deductible to the corporation. For example, premiums paid by the corporation for sickness, accident, and hospitalization insurance for Bob Cole are deductible to the corporation and generally nontaxable to him.[28] Any payments under the policy are not taxable to Bob Cole unless they exceed his medical expenses.[29] The corporation can also pay for travel and entertainment expenses incurred by Cole on behalf of the corporation. If these expenditures are primarily for the benefit of the corporation, Bob Cole will not recognize any taxable income and the corporation will receive a deduction.[30] The tax treatment of these benefits is discussed in more detail in Chapter 17.

When testing for reasonableness, the IRS looks at the total compensation package, including indirect compensation payments to a shareholder-employee. Thus, indirect payments must not be overlooked.

EXAMPLE 25

Cora, the president and sole shareholder of Willet Corporation, is paid an annual salary of $100,000 by the corporation. Cora would like to draw funds from the corporation but is concerned that additional salary payments might cause the IRS to contend her salary is unreasonable. Cora does not want Willet to pay any dividends. She also wishes to donate $50,000 to her alma mater to establish scholarships for needy students. Willet Corporation could make the contribution on Cora's behalf. The payment clearly benefits Cora, but the amount of the contribution will not be taxed to her.[31] Willet can take a charitable contribution deduction for the payment. ■

EXAMPLE 26

Assume in Example 25 that Cora has made an individual pledge to the university to provide $50,000 for scholarships for needy students. Willet Corporation satisfies Cora's pledge by paying the $50,000 to the university. The $50,000 will be taxed to Cora.[32] In this context, the $50,000 payment to the university may be treated as *indirect* compensation to Cora. In determining whether Cora's salary is unreasonable, both the *direct* payment of $100,000 and the *indirect* $50,000 payment will be considered. Cora's total compensation package is $150,000. Cora may be eligible for a charitable contribution deduction, up to 50% of her adjusted gross income. However, the phaseout of itemized deductions for high-income individuals may limit the deduction. (see Chapter 16). ■

[26]See, for example, *R. J. Nicoll Co.*, 59 T.C. 37 (1972).

[27]*McCandless Tile Service v. U.S.*, 70–1 USTC ¶9284, 25 AFTR2d 70–870, 422 F.2d 1336 (Ct.Cls., 1970). The court in *McCandless* concluded that a return on equity of 15% of net profits was reasonable.

[28]Reg. § 1.162–10.

[29]The medical reimbursement plan must meet certain nondiscrimination requirements. § 105(h)(2).

[30]Reg. § 1.62–2(c)(4).

[31]*Henry J. Knott*, 67 T.C. 681 (1977).

[32]*Schalk Chemical Co. v. Comm.*, 62–1 USTC ¶9496, 9 AFTR2d 1579, 304 F.2d 48 (CA–9, 1962).

Find more information on this topic at our Web site: ***http://wft-entities.swlearning.com.***

DIGGING DEEPER 1

Stock Dividends

LO.6

Distinguish between taxable and nontaxable stock dividends.

As a general rule, **stock dividends** are excluded from income if they are pro rata distributions of stock or stock rights, paid on common stock.[33] However, there are five exceptions to this general rule. These exceptions to nontaxability of stock dividends deal with various disproportionate distribution situations.

Find more information on this topic at our Web site: ***http://wft-entities.swlearning.com.***

DIGGING DEEPER 2

If a stock dividend is not taxable, the corporation's E & P is not reduced.[34] If a stock dividend is taxable, the distributing corporation treats the distribution in the same manner as any other taxable property dividend.

If a stock dividend is taxable, the shareholder's basis of the newly received shares is fair market value, and the holding period starts on the date of receipt. If a stock dividend is not taxable, the basis of the stock on which the dividend is distributed is reallocated.[35] If the dividend shares are identical to these formerly held shares, basis in the old stock is reallocated by dividing the taxpayer's cost in the old stock by the total number of shares. If the dividend stock is not identical to the underlying shares (e.g., a stock dividend of preferred on common), basis is determined by allocating the basis of the formerly held shares between the old and new stock according to the fair market value of each. The holding period includes the holding period of the previously held stock.[36]

EXAMPLE 27

Gail bought 1,000 shares of common stock two years ago for $10,000. In the current tax year, Gail receives 10 shares of common stock as a nontaxable stock dividend. Gail's basis of $10,000 is divided by 1,010. Consequently, each share of stock has a basis of $9.90 instead of the pre-dividend $10 basis. ■

EXAMPLE 28

Assume instead that Gail received a nontaxable preferred stock dividend of 100 shares. The preferred stock has a fair market value of $1,000, and the common stock, on which the preferred is distributed, has a fair market value of $19,000. After the receipt of the stock dividend, the basis of the common stock is $9,500, and the basis of the preferred is $500, computed as follows.

Fair market value of common	$19,000
Fair market value of preferred	1,000
	$20,000
Basis of common: $^{19}/_{20} \times$ $10,000	$ 9,500
Basis of preferred: $^{1}/_{20} \times$ $10,000	$ 500

■

Find more information on this topic at our Web site: ***http://wft-entities.swlearning.com.***

DIGGING DEEPER 3

[33] Companies often issue stock dividends or authorize stock splits to keep the stock price in an affordable range. Stock splits do not change the total value of an investment. For example, 100 shares at $100 will become 200 shares at $50 after the split. However, some studies show that a stock split often leads to an upward price trend over the year following the split.

[34] § 312(d)(1).

[35] § 307(a).

[36] § 1223(5).

TAX *in the News* — **CORPORATE CASH RESERVES AFFECT THE FREQUENCY OF STOCK REDEMPTIONS**

The economic and financial market slumps of 2001 and 2002, along with the uneven economic recovery that followed, prompted many executives to build up corporate cash reserves to record levels. However, finding productive uses for this cash in the current economic environment can be challenging. One consequence of the higher cash reserves has been an increase in stock buybacks (i.e., redemptions) over the last few years. Many corporations have also increased their dividend payouts in response to the reduction in tax rates applicable to dividends. Debt reduction also appears to have been a favorite use for the excess cash reserves.

LO.7

Discuss the tax treatment of stock redemptions.

Stock Redemptions

Many investors are tempted to use a "no dividends" strategy in working with a healthy corporation whose accumulated profits and market value continue to rise over time.

EXAMPLE 29

Sally invests $100,000 in the new Cream Corporation. Cream is successful in generating operating profits, and it reinvests its accumulated profits in the business rather than paying dividends. Fifteen years later, Sally's shares are worth $300,000, and her share of Cream's E & P exceeds $1 million. Sally sells the shares for a $200,000 long-term capital gain, taxed at a rate of only 15%. By selling her stock to a third party, Sally can reduce the sales proceeds by her stock basis, resulting in a significant tax savings to her, at no detriment to Cream. ■

A similar strategy would seem to work where several shareholders can act in concert. Using a **stock redemption** to carry out this strategy, the corporation buys back shares from its shareholders in a market transaction.

EXAMPLE 30

Mike and Cheryl are husband and wife, and each owns 100 shares in Mauve Corporation, the total of all of Mauve's outstanding stock. Mauve's operations have produced a sizable aggregated operating profit over the years, such that its E & P exceeds $5 million. Mike and Cheryl both have realized appreciation of $600,000 on their original investment of $100,000 each, and they would like to enjoy some of the cash that Mauve has accumulated during their holding period. At Mike's request, instead of paying a dividend, Mauve buys back one-half of Mike's shares for $350,000. This seems to produce a $300,000 long-term capital gain [$350,000 (sales proceeds) – $50,000 (basis in 50 shares of Mauve stock)], rather than a $350,000 dividend for Mike. ■

Stock redemptions, however, generally result in dividend income for the shareholder whose stock is redeemed, rather than a sale or exchange, unless the shareholder surrenders significant control in the entity as a result of the redemption. Section 302 allows sale or exchange treatment where either:

- All of the shareholder's stock is redeemed.[37]
- After the redemption, the investor is a minority shareholder and owns less than 80 percent of the interest owned in the corporation before the redemption.[38]

DIGGING DEEPER 4

Find more information on this topic at our Web site: ***http://wft-entities.swlearning.com.***

[37] § 302(b)(3).

[38] § 302(b)(2).

GLOBAL Tax Issues

FOREIGN SHAREHOLDERS PREFER SALE OR EXCHANGE TREATMENT IN STOCK REDEMPTIONS

As a general rule, foreign shareholders of U.S. corporations are subject to U.S. tax on dividend income but not on capital gains. In some situations, a nonresident alien is taxed on a capital gain from the disposition of stock in a U.S. corporation, but only if the stock was effectively connected with the conduct of a U.S. trade or business of the individual. Foreign corporations are similarly taxed on gains from the sale of U.S. stock investments. Whether a stock redemption qualifies for sale or exchange treatment therefore takes on added significance for foreign shareholders. If one of the qualifying stock redemption rules can be satisfied, the foreign shareholder typically will avoid U.S. tax on the transaction. If, instead, dividend income is the result, a 30 percent withholding tax typically applies.

When the transaction is treated as a dividend, the investor's basis in the redeemed shares *does not disappear* but attaches to any remaining shares that he or she owns. Corporate E & P is reduced by the amount of the dividend.

Some redemptions can be structured so that shareholders recognize a capital gain, not a dividend.[39] In measuring the investor's stock holdings before and after the redemption, shares owned by related taxpayers also are counted.[40]

DIGGING DEEPER 5

Find more information on this topic at our Web site: ***http://wft-entities.swlearning.com.***

Stock redemptions occur for numerous reasons, including the following.

- To acquire the holdings of a retiring or deceased shareholder.
- To carry out a property settlement related to a divorce.
- To increase the per-share price of the stock as it trades in a market.

The tax consequences for the redeeming corporation are summarized as follows.

- If noncash property is used to acquire the redeemed shares, the corporation recognizes any realized gain (but not loss) on the distributed assets.[41]
- When the shareholder is taxed as having received a capital gain, E & P of the redeeming corporation *disappears* to the extent of the number of shares redeemed as a percentage of the shares outstanding before the buyback.[42]

Thus, a dividend likely results in Example 30. The strategy illustrated in Example 29, though, can be effective in avoiding dividend income and converting it instead into a long-term capital gain.

Restrictions on Corporate Accumulations

Two provisions of the Code are designed to prevent corporations and their shareholders from avoiding the double tax on dividend distributions. Both provisions impose a penalty tax on undistributed income retained by the corporation. The rules underlying these provisions are complex and beyond the scope of this text. However, a brief description is provided as an introduction.

The *accumulated earnings tax* (in §§ 531–537) imposes a 15 percent tax on the current year's corporate earnings that have been accumulated without a reasonable business need. The burden of proving what constitutes a reasonable need is borne by the taxpayer. In determining accumulated income, most businesses are

[39]For example, see §§ 302(b)(1), 302(b)(4), and 303.

[40]Section 318 is used for this purpose.

[41]§ 311.

[42]The E & P reduction cannot exceed the amount of the redemption proceeds. § 312(n)(7).

allowed a $250,000 minimum credit. Thus, most corporations can accumulate $250,000 in earnings over a series of years without fear of an accumulated earnings tax. Beyond the minimum credit, earnings can be accumulated for:

- Working capital needs (to purchase inventory),
- Retirement of debt incurred in connection with the business,
- Investment or loans to suppliers or customers (if necessary to maintain the corporation's business), or
- Realistic business contingencies, including lawsuits or self-insurance.

The *personal holding company (PHC) tax* (described in §§ 541–547) was enacted to discourage the sheltering of certain kinds of passive income in corporations owned by individuals with high marginal tax rates. Historically, the tax was aimed at "incorporated pocketbooks" that were frequently found in the entertainment and construction industries. For example, a taxpayer could shelter income from securities in a corporation, which would pay no dividends, and allow the corporation's stock to increase in value. Like the accumulated earnings tax, the PHC tax employs a 15 percent rate and is designed to force a corporation to distribute earnings to shareholders. However, in any single year, the IRS cannot impose both the PHC tax and the accumulated earnings tax. Generally, a company is considered a PHC and may be subject to the tax if:

- More than 50 percent of the value of the outstanding stock was owned by five or fewer individuals at any time during the last half of the year, and
- A substantial portion (60 percent or more) of the corporation's income is comprised of passive types of income, including dividends, interest, rents, royalties, or certain personal service income.

Suggested Further Readings

Richard W. Bailine, "When Is a Dividend Not a Dividend?" *Journal of Corporate Taxation*, March/April 2004, pp. 30–33.

"Exclusive Discounts Treated as Constructive Distributions," *Business Entities*, July/August 2002, p. 51.

Andrew R. Lee, "Dividend Planning Strategies for Shareholders and Corporations," *Practical Tax Strategies*, October 2003, pp. 204–211.

Robert Willens, "When Is a Distribution a Dividend?" *Journal of Taxation*, June 2005, pp. 345–350.

KEY TERMS

Accumulated earnings and profits, 10–3

Constructive dividend, 10–15

Current earnings and profits, 10–3

Dividend, 10–2

Earnings and profits, 10–3

Property dividend, 10–12

Stock dividends, 10–21

Stock redemption, 10–22

Unreasonable compensation, 10–16

PROBLEM MATERIALS

PROBLEMS

1. At the start of the current year, Swan Corporation (a calendar year taxpayer) has accumulated E & P of $200,000. Its current E & P is $60,000. During the year, Swan distributes $280,000 ($140,000 each) to its equal shareholders, George and Albert.

George has a basis of $48,000 in his stock, and Albert has a basis of $8,000 in his stock. How is the distribution treated for tax purposes?

2. During the year, Vireo Corporation received dividend income of $300,000 from a corporation in which it holds a 10% interest. Vireo also received interest income of $50,000 from municipal bonds. The municipality used the proceeds from the sale of the bonds to construct a needed facility to house county documents and to provide office space for several county officials. Vireo borrowed funds to purchase the municipal bonds and paid $25,000 in interest on the loan this year. Vireo's taxable income exclusive of the items noted above was $225,000.
   a. What is Vireo Corporation's taxable income after considering the dividend income, the interest from the municipal bonds, and the interest paid on the indebtedness to purchase the municipals?
   b. What is Vireo Corporation's E & P as of December 31 if its E & P account balance was $80,000 as of January 1?

3. Tern Corporation (a calendar year, accrual basis taxpayer) had the following transactions during 2006, its second year of operation.

Taxable income	$320,000
Federal income tax liability	108,050
Interest income from tax-exempt payors	4,000
Meals and entertainment expenses	2,000
Premiums paid on key employee life insurance	2,500
Increase in cash surrender value attributable to life insurance premiums	600
Proceeds from key employee life insurance policy	120,000
Cash surrender value of life insurance policy at distribution	15,000
Excess of capital losses over capital gains	11,000
MACRS deductions	24,000
Straight-line depreciation using ADS lives	14,000
Section 179 expense elected during 2005	90,000
Organizational expenses incurred in 2005	12,000
Dividends received from domestic corporations (less than 20% owned)	20,000

Tern uses the LIFO inventory method, and its LIFO recapture amount increased by $9,000 during 2006. In addition, Tern sold property on installment during 2005. The property was sold for $30,000 and had an adjusted basis at sale of $22,000. During 2006, Tern received a $10,000 payment on the installment sale. Tern elected to amortize its qualified organizational expenses in 2005. Compute Tern Corporation's current E & P.

4. On November 15, 2006, Red Corporation sold a parcel of land. The land had a basis of $350,000, and Red received a $900,000 note as consideration in the sale. The note is to be paid in five installments, the first of which is due on December 15, 2007. Because Red did not elect out of the installment method, none of the $550,000 gain is included in taxable income for 2006.

   Red Corporation had a deficit in accumulated E & P of $280,000 on January 1, 2006. For 2006, before considering the effect of the land sale, Red had a deficit in current E & P of $120,000.

   Buck, the sole shareholder in Red, has a basis of $100,000 in his stock. If Red distributes $300,000 to Buck on December 31, 2006, how much gross income must Buck report from the distribution?

5. In determining Greene Corporation's current E & P for 2006, how should taxable income be adjusted by the following transactions?
   a. Sale of inventory on installment in 2006, with the first payment due in 2007.
   b. A net operating loss carryover from 2005, fully used in 2006.
   c. Excess capital losses incurred in 2006 that are carried forward to 2007.

d. Gain deferred in a qualifying like-kind exchange that occurred in 2006.
e. A Federal income tax refund received in 2006.
f. Section 179 expenses elected and deducted in 2004.

6. Gadwall Corporation is a calendar year taxpayer. At the beginning of the current year, Gadwall has accumulated E & P of $350,000. The corporation incurs a current E & P deficit of $400,000 that accrues ratably throughout the year. On September 30, Gadwall distributes $200,000 to its sole individual shareholder, Richard. If Richard has a basis in his stock of $15,000, how is the distribution taxed to him?

7. Complete the following schedule. For each case, assume the shareholder has ample basis in the stock investment.

	Accumulated E & P Beginning of Year	Current E & P	Cash Distributions (All on Last Day of Year)	Dividend Income	Return of Capital
a.	($150,000)	$ 70,000	$130,000	$ ______	$ ______
b.	200,000	(60,000)	210,000	______	______
c.	130,000	50,000	150,000	______	______
d.	120,000	(40,000)	130,000	______	______
e.	Same as (d), except the distribution of $130,000 is made on June 30 and the corporation uses the calendar year for tax purposes.			______	______

8. Carrie Lynn, the sole shareholder of Junco Corporation, had a basis of $50,000 in Junco stock that she sold to Rajib on July 30 for $200,000. Junco had accumulated E & P of $95,000 on January 1 and current E & P of $80,000. During the year, Junco made the following distributions: $150,000 of cash to Carrie Lynn on July 1, and $150,000 of cash to Rajib on December 30. How will the distributions be taxed to Carrie Lynn and Rajib? What gain will Carrie Lynn recognize on the sale of her stock to Rajib?

9. In each of the following *independent* situations, indicate the effect on taxable income and E & P, stating the amount of any increase (or decrease) as a result of the transaction. Assume E & P has already been increased by taxable income.

	Transaction	Taxable Income Increase (Decrease)	E & P Increase (Decrease)
a.	Realized gain of $80,000 on involuntary conversion of building ($10,000 of gain is recognized).	______	______
b.	Mining exploration costs incurred on May 1 of the current year; $24,000 is deductible from current-year taxable income.	______	______
c.	Sale of equipment to unrelated third party for $240,000; basis is $120,000 (no election out of installment method; no payments are received in the current year).	______	______
d.	Dividends of $20,000 received from 5%-owned corporation, together with dividends received deduction (assume taxable income limit does not apply).	______	______
e.	Production activities deduction of $45,000 claimed in current year.	______	______
f.	Section 179 expense deduction of $100,000 in current year.	______	______

Transaction	Taxable Income Increase (Decrease)	E & P Increase (Decrease)
g. Impact of current-year § 179 expense deduction in succeeding year.	__________	__________
h. MACRS depreciation of $80,000. ADS depreciation would have been $90,000.	__________	__________
i. Federal income taxes paid in the current year of $80,000.	__________	__________

10. Penguin Corporation (a cash basis, calendar year taxpayer) had the following income and expenses in the current year.

Income from services	$400,000
Salaries paid to employees	70,000
Tax-exempt interest income	24,000
Dividends from a corporation in which Penguin holds a 12% interest	40,000
Short-term capital loss the sale of stock	17,000
Estimated Federal income taxes paid	110,000

Penguin Corporation purchased seven-year MACRS property in the current year for $80,000. No § 179 election was made. The property has a 10-year ADR midpoint life. Determine taxable income and E & P for Penguin Corporation.

11. At the beginning of its taxable year, Teal Corporation had E & P of $225,000. Teal Corporation sold an asset at a loss of $225,000 on March 30. For the calendar year, Teal incurred a deficit in current E & P of $305,000, which includes the $225,000 loss on the sale of the asset. If Teal made a distribution of $50,000 to its sole shareholder on April 1, how will the shareholder be taxed?

12. Bunting Corporation (a calendar year taxpayer) had a deficit in accumulated E & P of $250,000 at the beginning of the current year. Its net profit for the period January 1 through September 30 was $300,000, but its E & P for the entire taxable year was only $40,000. If Bunting made a distribution of $60,000 to its sole shareholder on October 1, how will the shareholder be taxed?

13. Woodpecker Corporation and Tim each own 50% of Cormorant Corporation's common stock. On January 1, Cormorant has a deficit in accumulated E & P of $200,000. Its current E & P is $90,000. During the year, Cormorant makes cash distributions of $40,000 each to Woodpecker and Tim.
    a. How are the two shareholders taxed on the distribution?
    b. What is Cormorant Corporation's accumulated E & P at the end of the year?

14. Taylor, an individual, owns all of the outstanding stock in Violet Corporation. Taylor purchased his stock in Violet 11 years ago, and his basis is $15,000. At the beginning of this year, the corporation has $35,000 of accumulated E & P and no current E & P (before considering the effect of distributions). What are the tax consequences to Taylor (amount of dividend income and basis in property received) and Violet Corporation (gain or loss and effect on E & P) in each of the following situations?
    a. Violet distributes land to Taylor. The land was held as an investment and has a fair market value of $25,000 and an adjusted basis of $18,000.
    b. Violet Corporation has no current or accumulated E & P prior to the distribution. How would your answer to (a) change?
    c. The land distributed in (a) is subject to a $22,000 mortgage (which Taylor assumes). How would your answer change?
    d. The land has a fair market value of $25,000 and an adjusted basis of $28,000 on the date of distribution. How would your answer to (a) change?
    e. Instead of distributing land, Violet decides to distribute furniture used in its business. The furniture has a $6,000 fair market value and $500 adjusted basis for income tax purposes and a $2,500 adjusted basis for E & P purposes. The original fair market value of the furniture when it was purchased four years ago was $8,000.

15. Pearl Corporation, with E & P of $600,000, distributes land worth $175,000, adjusted basis of $220,000, to Azure, a corporate shareholder. The land is subject to a liability of $50,000, which Azure assumes.
    a. What is the amount of dividend income to Azure?
    b. What is Azure's basis in the land it received?
    c. How does the distribution affect Pearl Corporation's E & P account?

Decision Making

16. Crimson Corporation owns three automobiles that it uses in its business. It no longer needs two of these cars and is considering the possibility of distributing them to its two shareholders as a property dividend. All three automobiles have a fair market value of $15,000. Automobile A has a basis of $8,000; automobile B has a basis of $15,000; and automobile C has a basis of $20,000. The corporation has asked you for advice. What actions do you recommend?

17. Petrel Corporation has accumulated E & P of $63,000 at the beginning of the year. Its current-year taxable income is $300,000. On December 31, Petrel distributed business property (worth $120,000, adjusted basis of $270,000) to Juan, its sole shareholder. Juan assumes a $78,000 liability on the property. Included in the determination of Petrel's current taxable income is $14,000 of income recognized from an installment sale in a previous year. In addition, the corporation incurred a Federal income tax liability of $108,050, paid life insurance premiums of $3,000, and received term life insurance proceeds of $54,300 on the death of an officer.
    a. What is the amount of taxable income to Juan?
    b. What is the E & P of Petrel Corporation after the property distribution?
    c. What is Juan's tax basis in the property received?
    d. How would your answers to (a) and (b) change if Petrel had sold the property at its fair market value, used $78,000 of the proceeds to pay off the liability, and then distributed the remaining cash and any tax savings to Juan?

Issue ID

18. Copper Corporation has two equal shareholders, Cybil and Sally. Cybil acquired her Copper stock three years ago by transferring property worth $600,000, basis of $200,000, for 60 shares of the stock. Sally acquired 60 shares in Copper Corporation two years ago by transferring property worth $620,000, basis of $70,000. Copper Corporation's accumulated E & P as of January 1 of the current year is $300,000. On March 1 of the current year, the corporation distributed to Cybil property worth $100,000, basis to Copper of $30,000. It distributed cash of $200,000 to Sally. On July 1 of the current year, Sally sold her stock to Dana for $800,000. On December 1 of the current year, Copper distributed cash of $80,000 each to Dana and to Cybil. What are the tax issues?

19. Blackbird Corporation is a closely held company with accumulated E & P of $200,000 and current E & P of $250,000. Dan and Patrick are brothers, and each owns a 50% share in Blackbird. On a day-to-day basis, Dan and Patrick share management responsibilities equally. What are the tax consequences of the following independent transactions involving Blackbird, Dan, and Patrick? How does each transaction affect Blackbird's E & P?
    a. Blackbird sells an office building (adjusted basis of $250,000, fair market value of $200,000) to Dan for $175,000.
    b. Blackbird lends Patrick $150,000 on July 1 of this year. The loan is evidenced by a note and is payable on demand. No interest is charged on the loan (the current applicable Federal interest rate is 8%).
    c. Blackbird owns an airplane that it rents to others for a specified rental rate. Dan and Patrick also use the airplane for personal use and pay no rent. During the year, Dan used the airplane for 80 hours, while Patrick used it for 120 hours. The rental value of the airplane is $200 per hour, and its maintenance costs average $40 per hour.
    d. Dan leases equipment to Blackbird for $15,000 per year. The same equipment can be leased from another company for $11,000.

Decision Making

20. Sparrow Corporation would like to transfer excess cash to its sole shareholder, Adam, who is also an employee. Adam is in the 28% tax bracket, and Sparrow is in the 34% bracket. Because Adam's contribution to the business is substantial, Sparrow believes that a $25,000 bonus in the current year would be viewed as reasonable compensation and would be deductible by the corporation. However, Sparrow is leaning toward paying Adam a $25,000 dividend because the tax rate on dividends is lower than the tax rate on

compensation. Is Sparrow correct in believing that a dividend is the better choice? Why or why not?

21. Diver Corporation has a deficit in accumulated E & P of $200,000 as of January 1. Diver Corporation expects to generate annual E & P of $100,000 for the next four years, starting this year, and would like to distribute this amount to its shareholders. How should Diver Corporation distribute the $400,000 over the four-year period to provide the least amount of dividend income to its shareholders (all individuals)? Prepare a letter to your client, Diver Corporation, and a memo for the file. Diver Corporation's address is 1010 Oak Street, Oldtown, MD 20742. *Decision Making* *Communications*

22. Stan purchased 6,000 shares of Robin Corporation common stock five years ago for $30,000. In the current year, Stan receives a nontaxable preferred stock dividend of 300 shares. The preferred stock has a fair market value of $10,000. Stan's common stock in Robin has a fair market value of $50,000. What is Stan's basis in the preferred stock and common stock after the dividend is received?

23. Your client, Cormorant Corporation, declares a dividend permitting its common stockholders to elect to receive 8 shares of cumulative preferred stock or 2 additional shares of common stock for every 10 shares of common stock currently held. Cormorant currently has only common stock outstanding, with a fair market value of $50 per share. Two shareholders elect to receive preferred stock, and all the remaining shareholders elect to receive common stock. Cormorant asks you whether the shareholders must recognize any taxable income on the receipt of the stock. Prepare a letter to Cormorant and a memo to the file. Cormorant's address is 6730 Pima Drive, Madison, WI 53708. *Extender* *Communications*

24. Sarah Beckert bought 3,000 shares of Grebe Corporation stock two years ago for $10,000. Last year, Sarah received a nontaxable stock dividend of 1,000 shares in Grebe. In the current tax year, Sarah sold all of the stock received as a dividend for $8,000. Prepare a letter to Sarah and a memo to the file describing the tax consequences of the stock sale. Sarah's address is 1822 N. Sarnoff Road, Tucson, AZ 85710. *Communications*

25. Stork Corporation declares a nontaxable dividend payable in rights to subscribe to common stock. One right and $50 entitle the holder to subscribe to one share of stock. One right is issued for every two shares of stock owned. At the date of distribution of the rights, the market value of the stock was $100 per share, and the market value of the rights was $45 per right. Cindy, a shareholder, owns 200 shares of stock that she purchased two years ago for $6,000. Cindy received 100 rights, of which she exercises 70 to purchase 70 additional shares. She sells the remaining 30 rights for $1,650. What are the tax consequences of these transactions to Cindy? *Extender*

26. Becca is a shareholder in Blue Corporation. This year, she receives a $4,000 qualified dividend from Blue. Becca is in the 35% tax bracket, has investment interest expense of $8,000, and net investment income of $4,500 (not including the qualified dividend). Assume that Becca expects to have more than enough net investment income next year to permit the deduction of any investment interest expense that is carried forward. Should Becca subject the qualified dividend to a 15% tax rate or treat it as net investment income? *Extender* *Decision Making*

27. Ivana, the president and a shareholder of Robin Corporation, has earned a salary bonus of $15,000 for the current year. Because of the recent reduction in tax rates on qualified dividends, Robin is considering substituting a dividend for the bonus. Pertinent tax rates are 28% for Ivana and 34% for Robin Corporation. *Decision Making*
    a. How much better off would Ivana be if she were paid a dividend rather than salary?
    b. How much better off would Robin Corporation be if it paid Ivana salary rather than a dividend?
    c. If Robin Corporation pays Ivana a salary bonus of $20,000 instead of a $15,000 dividend, how would your answers to (a) and (b) change?
    d. What should Robin do?

28. Corporate shareholders typically prefer dividend income treatment for a stock redemption. Assess the validity of this statement.

29. The stock in Brown Corporation is owned equally by Petra and Salvador, a couple in the process of divorce. Pursuant to a settlement agreement being negotiated between the *Issue ID*

two taxpayers, Salvador would be required to sell his Brown stock either to Petra or to the corporation. What issues should be considered in determining whether a redemption of Salvador's stock by Brown Corporation is the preferable alternative?

30. Julio is in the 33% tax bracket. He acquired 600 shares of stock in Gray Corporation seven years ago at a cost of $75 per share. In the current year, Julio received a payment of $100,000 from Gray Corporation in exchange for 200 of his shares in Gray. Gray has E & P of $1 million. What tax liability would Julio incur on the $100,000 payment in each of the following situations? Assume that Julio has no capital losses.
    a. The payment qualifies for stock redemption (i.e., sale or exchange) treatment.
    b. The payment does not qualify for stock redemption (i.e., sale or exchange treatment is not applicable) treatment.

31. How would your answer to Problem 30 differ if Julio were a corporate shareholder (in the 34% tax bracket) rather than an individual shareholder and the stock ownership in Gray Corporation represented a 25% interest?

Decision Making

32. Assume in Problem 30 that Julio has a capital loss carryover of $40,000 in the current tax year. Julio has no other capital gain transactions during the year. What amount of the capital loss may Julio deduct in the current year in the following situations?
    a. The $100,000 payment from Gray Corporation is a qualifying stock redemption for tax purposes (i.e., receives sale or exchange treatment).
    b. The $100,000 payment from Gray Corporation does not qualify as a stock redemption for tax purposes (i.e., does not receive sale or exchange treatment).
    c. If Julio had the flexibility to structure the transaction as described in either (a) or (b), which form would he choose?

33. How would your answer to parts (a) and (b) of Problem 32 differ if Julio were a corporate shareholder (in the 34% tax bracket) rather than an individual shareholder and the stock ownership in Gray Corporation represented a 25% interest?

34. Shonda owns 110 shares of the 200 outstanding shares of Hawk Corporation. Shonda paid $1,000 per share for the stock five years ago. The remaining Hawk stock is owned by several unrelated individuals. In the current year, Hawk redeems 20 of Shonda's shares for $60,000 ($3,000 per share). Hawk's E & P at the time of the redemption was $200,000.
    a. How does Shonda report the $60,000?
    b. What is Shonda's basis in her remaining shares?
    c. What is Hawk's E & P after the redemption?

35. Teal Corporation's 100 shares of outstanding common stock are held equally by Ann and Bonnie. The shareholders are not related to each other. Each paid $1,000 per share for the Teal stock 10 years ago. Teal shows $20,000 of current E & P and $100,000 of accumulated E & P. Teal distributes $80,000 of cash to Ann in exchange for 25 of her shares.
    a. What are the tax consequences of the exchange for Ann?
    b. What is Teal's E & P balance after the exchange?

Extender

36. Blue Jay Corporation was organized eight years ago to construct family dwellings. Six years ago, it began selling furniture. Because of a glut in the real estate market, Blue Jay discontinues its construction business in the current year. Blue Jay sells all the assets used in the construction business for $4 million and distributes the proceeds to its two equal shareholders, Walt (an individual) and Redbird Corporation, in the redemption of half of their stock. Walt has a basis of $110,000 in his redeemed stock, and Redbird has a basis of $200,000 in its redeemed stock. Blue Jay's E & P was $7 million on the date of the distribution. What are the tax consequences of the redemption to Walt, Redbird, and Blue Jay?

Extender

Communications

37. Stork Corporation has 1,000 shares of common stock outstanding. The shares are owned as follows.
    - Leo Jones, 700 shares
    - Lori Johnson, 100 shares
    - Lana Pierce, 200 shares

Lori is Lana's mother. Leo is not related to the two other shareholders. Stork redeems 100 of Lana's shares for $45,000. Lana paid $100 per share for her stock two years ago. On the date of the redemption, Stork's E & P was $400,000.

Prepare a memo to the tax research file and a letter to Lana (1000 Main Street, Oldtown, MN 55166) outlining the tax effects of the redemption to her.

Extender

38. Cardinal Corporation has 200 shares of common stock outstanding. Hubert owns 80 of the shares, Hubert's mother owns 50 shares, Hubert's brother owns 20 shares, and Redbird Corporation owns 20 shares. Hubert owns 80% of the stock in Redbird.
    a. Applying the § 318 stock attribution rules, how many shares does Hubert own in Cardinal?
    b. Assume Hubert owns only 25% of Redbird. How many shares does Hubert own directly and indirectly in Cardinal?
    c. Assume the same facts as in (a) above, but in addition, Hubert owns 40% of Yellow Partnership. The partnership owns 30 shares in Cardinal. How many shares does Hubert own directly and indirectly in Cardinal?

BRIDGE *Discipline*

1. Find the audited financial statements of five major U.S. corporations, each in a different operating industry (e.g., manufacturing, energy, financial services, health care).
    a. Compute the total return on each corporation's stock for the past two years.
    b. Compute the dividend yield of the stock for the past two years.

RESEARCH PROBLEMS

Note: Solutions to Research Problems can be prepared by using the **RIA Checkpoint® Student Edition** online research product, which is available to accompany this text. It is also possible to prepare solutions to the Research Problems by using tax research materials found in a standard tax library.

THOMSON RIA™

Communications

Research Problem 1. Spifficar, Inc., owns and operates several car washes in Tucson, Arizona. A married couple, Joe and Simone Simpson, are the sole shareholders of Spifficar, and they have been your clients for the last decade. Over the course of several years, Joe and Simone made weekly deposits of their receipts from the car washes to corporate and personal bank accounts. In a recent phone conversation with Joe, he told you some very disturbing news. It turns out that the Simpsons regularly took a portion of the weekly collections home rather than depositing them at the bank. These amounts were hidden in shoe boxes under the Simpsons' bed and were not reported as taxable income by them. The total hidden under their bed amounts to approximately $250,000. Joe says that the IRS notified them that criminal tax evasion charges under § 7201 are being brought against them. The IRS believes that the Simpsons' actions provide prima facie evidence that they intended to defraud the government.

As Joe and Simone's accountant, you recognize that Spifficar has a deficit in its current and accumulated E & P accounts and that a deficit has existed over the period at issue with the IRS. In addition, your records indicate that the Simpsons' basis in the Spifficar stock is $300,000 (before taking into consideration the money hidden under their bed). You believe that these facts may have some bearing on the evasion charges being made against them. Investigate the tax law related to this situation and prepare a letter to the Simpsons' attorney reporting the results of your research. Their attorney is Monty Davis, 1212 S. Camino Seco, Tucson, AZ 85710.

Communications

Research Problem 2. Patrick Zimbrick and his son, Dan, own all of the outstanding stock of Osprey Corporation. Both Dan and Patrick are officers in the corporation and, together with their uncle, John, comprise the entire board of directors. Osprey uses the cash method of accounting and a calendar year-end. In late 2002, the board of directors adopted the following legally enforceable resolution (agreed to in writing by each of the officers).

Salary payments made to an officer of the corporation that are disallowed in whole or in part as a deductible expense for Federal income tax purposes shall be reimbursed by such officer to the corporation to the full extent of any disallowance. It is the duty of the board of directors to enforce repayment of each such amount.

In 2003, Osprey paid Patrick $560,000 in compensation. Dan received $400,000. On audit in late 2006, the IRS found the compensation of both officers to be excessive. It disallowed deductions for $200,000 of the payment to Patrick and $150,000 of the payment to Dan. The IRS recharacterized the disallowed payments as constructive dividends. Complying with the resolution by the board of directors, both Patrick and Dan repaid the disallowed compensation to Osprey Corporation in early 2007. Dan and Patrick have asked you to determine how their repayments should be treated for tax purposes. Prepare a memo to your files describing the results of your research.

Communications

Research Problem 3. Aqua Corporation wholly owns Egret Corporation. Aqua formed Egret four years ago with the transfer of several assets to the corporation, together with a substantial amount of cash. Aqua's basis in Egret stock is $5.5 million. Since it was formed, Egret has been a very profitable software company and currently has accumulated E & P of $4 million. The company's principal assets are software patents currently worth $5 million and cash and marketable securities of approximately $4.5 million (a total fair market value of $9.5 million).

Aqua and Egret are members of an affiliated group and have made the election under § 243(b) so that Aqua is entitled to a 100% dividends received deduction. From a strategic perspective, Aqua is no longer interested in the software industry and so is considering a sale of Egret. In anticipation of a sale in the next year or two, the management of Aqua has contacted you for advice. If Egret is sold outright, then Aqua Corporation will have a capital gain of $4 million ($9.5 million fair market value less a basis of $5.5 million). As an alternative, it has been suggested that taxes on a future sale would be minimized if Egret pays Aqua a dividend (using existing cash and securities) equal to its E & P. With the 100% dividends received deduction, this payment would be a tax-free transfer from Egret to Aqua. Subsequent to the dividend payment, Egret could be sold for its remaining value of $5.5 million ($5 million in software patents plus $500,000 in cash), generating no additional loss or gain to Aqua.

a. Prepare a letter to the president of Aqua Corporation describing the results of your research on the proposed plan. The president's name and address is Bill Gateson, 601 Pittsfield Dr., Champaign, IL 61821.
b. Prepare a memo for your firm's client files.

Partial list of research aids:

Waterman Steamship Corp. v. Comm., 70–2 USTC ¶9514, 26 AFTR2d 70–5185, 430 F.2d 1185 (CA–5, 1970).

Research Problem 4. In the summer of this year, Tangerine Corporation announced that it would pay a special one-time dividend of about $32 billion ($3 per share) on December 2 (with an ex-dividend date of November 15). It also announced that it would double its regular quarterly per-share dividend from $0.04 to $0.08, for the dividends payable on September 14 (with an ex-dividend date of August 23) and December 2 (with an ex-dividend date of November 15).

Motivated by these announcements, Samantha (a high-income taxpayer) purchased 50,000 shares of Tangerine stock on August 20 at $27 per share and sold the stock in late December (after receiving the dividends) for $26 per share. The highest trading price reached by Tangerine stock during the year was $29.98 per share on the day before the special dividend ex-dividend date. Before considering the Tangerine sale, Samantha has $50,000 of short-term capital gains and $50,000 of 15% long-term capital gains. The dividend paid by Tangerine qualifies for the 15% dividend tax rate. What are the tax consequences of the dividends and stock sale to Samantha?

Internet *Activity*

Use the tax resources of the Internet to address the following questions. Do not restrict your search to the World Wide Web, but include a review of newsgroups and general reference materials, practitioner sites and resources, primary sources of the tax law, chat rooms and discussion groups, and other opportunities.

Research Problem 5. Just how common are dividend distributions? Are dividends concentrated in the companies traded on the New York Stock Exchange, or do closely held corporations pay dividends with the same frequency and at the same rates? Financial institutions and observers are acutely interested in these issues. Search for comments on such questions at various commercial Web sites as well as one or two academic journals or newsgroups.

Communications

Research Problem 6. Investigate Web sites of for-profit investment managers and summarize the information you find in a two-page discussion, entitled "The Market in Stock Splits: How You Can Profit." Submit the summary to your professor.

Communications

Research Problem 7. Write an e-mail query to two tax consultants who practice in your state. Ask each for an example or two of a constructive dividend that a client recently has paid. Give your instructor copies of your query and the responses you receive.

http://wft.swlearning.com

CHAPTER 11

Partnerships and Limited Liability Entities

LEARNING OBJECTIVES

After completing Chapter 11, you should be able to:

LO.1

Discuss governing principles and theories of partnership taxation.

LO.2

Describe the tax effects of forming a partnership with cash and property contributions.

LO.3

Examine the tax treatment of expenditures of a newly formed partnership and identify elections available to the partnership.

LO.4

Calculate partnership taxable income and describe how partnership items affect a partner's income tax return.

LO.5

Determine a partner's basis in the partnership interest.

LO.6

Describe the limitations on deducting partnership losses.

LO.7

Review the treatment of transactions between a partner and the partnership.

LO.8

Describe the application of partnership tax law provisions to limited liability companies (LLCs) and limited liability partnerships (LLPs).

OUTLINE

TAX *Talk*

Today is the first day of the rest of your taxable year.

—Jeffrey L. Yablon

Overview of Partnership Taxation

Much of the new business in today's world of commerce is conducted in what the Internal Revenue Code would classify as *partnerships.* As evidence of their popularity, more than 2 million partnership tax returns are filed with the IRS annually.

Whether termed a *joint venture, working agreement, shared operating arrangement,* or some other designation, a partnership is formed when individuals or separate business entities get together for the specific purpose of earning profits by jointly operating a trade or business. For example, a partnership likely exists when a U.S. business enters into a joint venture with a foreign distributor to gain access to an overseas consumer market. Or a number of businesses located in a blighted downtown area might work together to boost sales and customer traffic by forming a group that unifies and improves the appearance of the storefronts in the area, conducts joint advertising, and coordinates sales and coupon activities.

Partnerships allow a great degree of flexibility in the conduct of business: for example, a group can limit its goals to a specific list of agreed-to projects or to a given time period, or businesses can work together without altering any of their underlying capital structures. In many service professions, such as law, medicine, and accounting, state laws prohibit the owners from using a corporation to limit their liability to clients or patients, so the partnership form prevails.

The tax law addressing the transactions of partners and partnerships is found in Subchapter K of the Code. These provisions comprise only a few short pages in the Code, however. Most of the details of partnership tax law have evolved through extensive Regulations and a healthy number of court cases.

Forms of Doing Business—Federal Tax Consequences

This chapter and the next chapter analyze business forms that offer certain advantages over C corporations. These entities are partnerships and S corporations, which are called *flow-through* or *pass-through* entities because the owners of the trade

TAX FACT

Partnership Power

Partnerships represent a sizable number of business entities, and they generate a significant part of the net income of the economy, especially in the investment sectors.

Partnership Activities, Tax Year 2003	
Number of partnerships	2,375,000
Number of partners	14,110,000
Reported partnership net income—total	$303 billion
Reported partnership business income	$155 billion
Reported partnership portfolio income	$189 billion
Reported partnership rental real estate income	$31 billion

or business elect to avoid treating the enterprise as a separate taxable entity. Instead, the owners are taxed on a proportionate share of the firm's taxable income at the end of each of its taxable years, regardless of the amount of cash or property distributions the owners receive during the year. The entity serves as an information provider to the IRS and its owners with respect to the proportionate income shares, and the tax falls directly upon the owners of those shares.

A partnership may be especially advantageous in many cases. A partnership's income is subject to only a single level of taxation, whereas C corporation income is subject to *double taxation.* Corporate income is taxed at the entity level at rates up to 35 percent. Any after-tax income that is distributed to corporate owners is taxed again as a dividend at the owner level. Though partnership income may be subject to high individual rates, the resulting tax will likely be lower than a combined corporate-level tax and a second tax on dividends.

In addition, administrative and filing requirements are relatively simple for a partnership, and the entity offers certain planning opportunities not available to other entities. Both C and S corporations are subject to rigorous allocation and distribution requirements (generally, each allocation or distribution is proportionate to the ownership interest of the shareholder). A partnership, though, may adjust its allocations of income and cash flow among the partners each year according to their needs, as long as certain standards are met. Any previously unrealized income (such as appreciation of corporate assets) of a C corporation is taxed at the entity level when the corporation liquidates, but a partnership generally may liquidate tax-free. Finally, many states impose reporting and licensing requirements on corporate entities, including S corporations. These include franchise or capital stock tax returns that may require annual assessments and costly professional preparation assistance. Partnerships, on the other hand, often have no reporting requirements beyond Federal and state informational tax returns.

Although partnerships may avoid many of the income tax and reporting burdens faced by other entities, they are subject to all other taxes in the same manner as any other business. Thus, the partnership files returns and pays the outstanding amount of pertinent sales taxes, property taxes, and payroll taxes.

In summary, partnerships offer advantages to both large and small businesses. For smaller business operations, a partnership enables several owners to combine their resources at low cost. It also offers simple filing requirements, the taxation of income only once, and the ability to discontinue operations relatively inexpensively. For larger business operations, a partnership offers a unique ability to raise capital with low filing and reporting costs (compared to corporate bond issuances, for example).

BRIDGE *Discipline*

Bridge to Finance

As movies have become more expensive to produce, many production studios have turned to limited partnerships as a lucrative source of investment capital. For example, the Walt Disney Company has sold limited partnership or LLC interests in entities formed to produce specific movies.

The sponsoring studio usually injects capital for a small (1–5 percent) general partnership interest, and the limited partners contribute the remaining capital—millions of dollars in most cases. The partnership agreement spells out the number and types of films the partnership intends to produce and provides a formula for allocating cash flows to the partners. The agreement includes various benefits for the general partner (studio), such as a preferred allocation of cash flows (the first $1 million per year, for example), distribution fees for marketing the movies, and/or reimbursement of specified amounts of corporate overhead. Any cash remaining after these expenses is allocated under a fixed formula between the general and limited partners (for example, the limited partners may receive 90 percent of remaining cash flows).

These film-financing partnerships are not necessarily private operations. A layperson with a well-connected tax or investment adviser can become a partner in the next Julia Roberts project, perhaps financed by Silver Screen Partners XXII. Partnership shares sell for multiples of $100,000 or more, and in return the investor can become part-owner in an entity that is certain to throw off operating losses for many years to come.

Especially interested in movie financing of this type can be non-U.S. investors. The use of partnerships and limited liability entities is a common way to attract cross-border investment, as many developed countries treat such joint ventures favorably under their tax laws, allowing deferral of income recognition and lower tax withholding on the income of these entities. U.S. investors are attracted to joint venture financing of film projects in several countries, including Canada, that offer generous tax credits for projects that are filmed and processed chiefly within their borders. The partnership tax regime can offer an immediate flow-through of these tax benefits.

Think about traditional bank financing of manufacturing or distribution activities in comparison, and you will see why the movie studio finds partnerships so appealing: How many banks would allow the general partner to receive reimbursements and allocations before debt principal and interest are paid?

This capital-raising technique has proved so advantageous to the studios that some related industries, such as movie lighting contractors and special effects companies, have also used limited partnerships to raise capital. The next time you go to a movie, watch the credits at the end and think about the large number of people who invested cash in the movie hoping for a blockbuster!

What Is a Partnership?

A partnership is an association of two or more persons formed to carry on a trade or business, with each contributing money, property, labor, or skill, and with all expecting to share in profits and losses. A "person" can be an individual, a corporation, or another partnership. For Federal income tax purposes, a partnership includes a syndicate, group, pool, joint venture, or other unincorporated organization, through which any business, financial operation, or venture is carried on. The entity must not be otherwise classified as a corporation, trust, or estate.[1]

An eligible entity can "check the box" on the partnership tax return indicating that the entity wants to be taxed as a partnership.[2] A partnership must have at least

[1] § 7701(a)(2).

[2] Reg. §§ 301.7701–1 to 301.7701–3, as discussed in Chapter 9 of this text.

two owners, so a sole proprietor or one-shareholder corporation cannot "check the box" and be taxed as a partnership.[3]

Businesses operating in several forms are taxed as partnerships. Provisions controlling these legal forms of doing business typically are dictated by the laws of the states in which the businesses operate.

- In a **general partnership**, the partners share profits and losses in some specified manner, as dictated by the partnership agreement. Creditors can reach the assets of the business and the personal assets of the general partners to satisfy any outstanding debts. A general partner can be bankrupted by a judgment against the entity, even though the partner did not cause the violation triggering the damages.
- In a **limited partnership**, profits and losses are shared as the partners agree, but ownership interests are either general (creditors can reach the personal assets of the partner) or limited (a partner's exposure to entity liabilities is limited to the partner's own capital contributions). Usually, the general partners conduct most of the partnership business, and they have a greater say in making decisions that affect the entity operations.
- The **limited liability partnership (LLP)** is used chiefly in the service professions, such as accounting and consulting. The primary difference between an LLP and a general partnership is that an LLP partner is not personally liable for acts of negligence, fraud, or malpractice committed by other partners.
- The **limited liability company (LLC)** is discussed in more detail later in this chapter. This entity is taxed as a partnership, but its capital structure resembles that of a corporation, with shares for sale and an owner's liability limited almost strictly to the extent of capital contributions. Some states allow LLCs to be owned solely by one person.

Partnership Taxation and Reporting

LO.1

Discuss governing principles and theories of partnership taxation.

A partnership is not a taxable entity.[4] Rather, the taxable income or loss of the partnership flows through to the partners at the end of the entity's tax year.[5] Partners report their allocable share of the partnership's income or loss for the year on their tax returns. As a result, the partnership itself pays no Federal income tax on its income; instead, the partners' individual tax liabilities are affected by the activities of the entity.

EXAMPLE 1

Adam is a 40% partner in the ABC Partnership. Both Adam's and the partnership's tax years end on December 31. This year, the partnership generates $200,000 of ordinary taxable income. However, because the partnership needs capital for expansion and debt reduction, Adam makes no cash withdrawals during the year. He meets his living expenses by reducing his investment portfolio. Adam is taxed on his $80,000 allocable share of the partnership's income ($200,000 × 40%), even though he received no distributions from the entity during the year. This allocated income is included in Adam's gross income. ■

EXAMPLE 2

Assume the same facts as in Example 1, except that the partnership realizes a taxable loss of $100,000. Adam's $40,000 proportionate share of the loss flows through to him from the partnership, and he can deduct the loss. (Note: Loss limitation rules discussed later in the chapter may result in some or all of this loss being deducted by Adam in a later year.) ■

Many items of partnership income, expense, gain, or loss retain their tax identity as they flow through to the partners. These **separately stated items** include

[3] § 761(a).

[4] § 701.

[5] § 702.

TAX FACT

Look at All the LLCs

LLCs and LLPs have become so popular in the last decade that there are more of them than there are reporting general partnerships.

Number of U.S. Entities Reporting (000s), Tax Year 2003

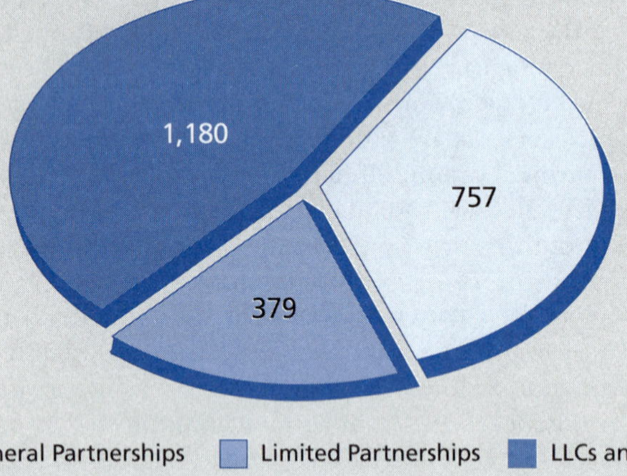

those items that may affect any two partners' tax liability computations differently.[6] For example, the § 179 expense of a partnership is separately stated because one partner might be able to deduct his or her share of the expense completely, while another's deduction might be limited. Separately stated items include recognized gains and losses from property transactions, dividend income, preferences and adjustments for the alternative minimum tax (see Chapter 14), foreign tax payments, and expenditures that individual partners would treat as itemized deductions (e.g., charitable contributions).

Items that are not separately stated, because all partners will treat them the same on their income tax returns, are aggregated and form the *ordinary income* of the partnership. Thus, profits from product sales, advertising expenses, and depreciation recapture amounts are combined to form the entity's ordinary income. This amount is then allocated among the partners and flows through to their tax returns. The ordinary income that flows through to a general partner, as well as any salary-like guaranteed payments (discussed in a later section) received, usually is subject to self-employment tax, as well as Federal income tax.[7]

EXAMPLE 3

Beth is a 25% partner in the BR Partnership. The cash basis entity collected sales income of $60,000 and incurred $15,000 in business expenses. In addition, it sold a corporate bond for a $9,000 long-term capital gain. Finally, the partnership made a $1,000 contribution to the local Performing Arts Fund drive. The fund is a qualifying charity. BR and all of its partners use a calendar tax year.

Beth is allocated ordinary taxable income of $11,250 [($60,000 − $15,000) × 25%] from the partnership. She also is allocated a flow-through of a $2,250 long-term capital gain and a $250 charitable contribution deduction. The ordinary income increases Beth's gross income, and the capital gain and charitable contribution are combined with her other similar activities for the year as though she had incurred them herself. These items could be treated

[6] § 703(a)(1). Certain large partnerships can elect to limit the number of separately stated items.

[7] § 1402(a).

differently on the tax returns of the various partners (e.g., because a partner may be subject to a percentage limitation on charitable contribution deductions), so they are not included in the computation of ordinary partnership income. Instead, the items flow through to the partners separately. ■

DIGGING DEEPER 1

Find more information on this topic at our Web site: ***http://wft-entities.swlearning.com.***

Even though it is not a taxpaying entity, the partnership files an information tax return, Form 1065. Look at Form 1065 in Appendix B, and refer to it during the following discussion. The ordinary income and expense items generated by the partnership's trade or business activities are netted to produce a single income or loss amount. The partnership reports this ordinary income or loss from its trade or business activities on Form 1065, page 1. Schedule K (page 3 of Form 1065) accumulates all items that must be separately reported to the partners, including net trade or business income or loss (from page 1). The amounts on Schedule K are allocated to all the partners. Each partner receives a Schedule K–1, which shows that partner's share of partnership items.

EXAMPLE 4

The BR Partnership in Example 3 reports its $60,000 of sales income on Form 1065, page 1, line 1. The $15,000 of business expenses are reported in the appropriate amounts on page 1, line 2 or lines 9–20. Partnership ordinary income of $45,000 is shown on page 1, line 22, and on Schedule K, line 1. The $9,000 capital gain and the $1,000 charitable contribution are reported only on Schedule K, on lines 9a and 13, respectively.

Beth receives a Schedule K–1 from the partnership that shows her shares of partnership ordinary income of $11,250, long-term capital gain of $2,250, and charitable contributions of $250 on lines 1, 9a, and 13, respectively.

She combines these amounts with similar items from other sources on her personal tax return. For example, if she has a $5,000 long-term capital loss from a stock transaction during the year, her overall net capital loss is $2,750. She then evaluates this net amount to determine the amount she may deduct on her Form 1040. ■

Thus, one must look at both page 1 and Schedule K to get complete information regarding a partnership's operations for the year.

Certain items reported on Schedule K are netted and entered on line 1 of the Analysis of Net Income (Loss) on page 4. This total agrees with the total amount on line 9 of Schedule M–1, Reconciliation of Income (Loss) per Books with Income (Loss) per Return. Schedule L generally shows an accounting-basis balance sheet, and Schedule M–2 reconciles beginning and ending partners' capital accounts.

Partner's Ownership Interest in a Partnership

Each partner typically owns both a **capital interest** and a **profits (loss) interest** in the partnership. A capital interest is measured by a partner's **capital sharing ratio**, which is the partner's percentage ownership of the capital of the partnership. A partner's capital interest can be determined in several ways. The most widely accepted method measures the capital interest as the percentage of net asset value (asset value remaining after payment of all partnership liabilities) a partner would receive on immediate liquidation of the partnership.

A profits (loss) interest is simply the partner's percentage allocation of current partnership operating results. **Profit and loss sharing ratios** usually are specified in the partnership agreement. They are used to determine each partner's allocation of partnership ordinary taxable income and separately stated items.[8] The partnership can change its profit and loss allocations at any time by amending the partnership agreement.

[8] § 704(a).

BRIDGE *Discipline*

Bridge to Financial Accounting

The equivalent in financial accounting to the partner's basis in his or her partnership interest is the capital account. A partner's ending balance in the capital account rarely is the same as his or her basis in the partnership interest. Just as the tax and accounting bases of a specific asset may differ, a partner's capital account and basis in the partnership interest usually are not equal.

Whereas contributions and most distributions from the partnership do not create financial accounting income, the capital account is "written up" or down to aggregate fair market value when the entity is formed. For most partnerships with simple financial transactions, *changes* to the capital account parallel closely the annual changes to the partner's basis in the partnership. Basis in one's partnership interest cannot be a negative number, but the capital account can become negative.

Oddly, the Schedules K-1 for the partners require an accounting for their capital accounts, but there is no required reconciliation for the partner's tax basis on the Schedule K-1. As a result, the tax adviser may find that a new partnership client has poor records with respect to the basis amounts of the partners, and a reconstruction must take place so that future computations will be correct. Sometimes, lacking adequate information with which to make this computation, the capital account is used because it is "close enough" and forms a good surrogate for the partner's basis in the partnership.

The partnership agreement may, in some cases, provide for a **special allocation** of certain items to specified partners, or it may allocate items in a different proportion from the general profit and loss sharing ratios. These items are separately reported to the partner receiving the allocation. For a special allocation to be recognized for tax purposes, it must produce nontax economic consequences to the partners receiving the allocation.[9]

EXAMPLE 5

When the George-Helen Partnership was formed, George contributed cash and Helen contributed some City of Iuka bonds that she had held for investment purposes. The partnership agreement allocates all of the tax-exempt interest income from the bonds to Helen as an inducement for her to remain a partner. This is an acceptable special allocation for income tax purposes; it reflects the differing economic circumstances that underlie the partners' contributions to the capital of the entity. Since Helen would have received the tax-exempt income if she had not joined the partnership, she can retain the tax-favored treatment via the special allocation. ■

EXAMPLE 6

Assume the same facts as in Example 5. Three years after it was formed, the George-Helen Partnership purchased some City of Butte bonds. The municipal bond interest income of $15,000 flows through to the partners as a separately stated item, so it retains its tax-exempt status. The partnership agreement allocates all of this income to George because he is subject to a higher marginal income tax rate than is Helen. The partnership then allocates $15,000 more of the partnership's ordinary income to Helen than to George. These allocations are not effective for income tax purposes because they have no purpose other than a reduction of the partners' combined income tax liability. ■

A partner has a **basis in the partnership interest**, just as he or she would have a tax basis in any asset owned. When income flows through to a partner from the partnership, the partner's basis in the partnership interest increases accordingly. When a loss flows through to a partner, basis is reduced.[10] A partner's basis is important when determining the treatment of distributions from the partnership to

[9] § 704(b).

[10] §§ 705, 722, and 723.

the partner, establishing the deductibility of partnership losses, and calculating gain or loss on the disposition of the partnership interest.

EXAMPLE 7

The Philly Clinic contributes $20,000 cash to acquire a 30% capital and profits interest in the Red Robin Partnership. In its first year of operations, the partnership earns ordinary income of $40,000 and makes no distributions to the partners. The Clinic's initial basis is the $20,000 that it paid for the interest. Philly recognizes ordinary income of $12,000 (30% × $40,000 partnership income) and increases its basis in Red Robin by the same amount, to $32,000. ■

The Code provides for increases and decreases in a partner's basis so that the income or loss from partnership operations is taxed only once. In Example 7, if the Philly Clinic sold its interest at the end of the first year for $32,000, it would have no gain or loss. If the Code did not provide for an adjustment of a partner's basis, Philly's basis would still be $20,000, and it would be taxed on the gain of $12,000 in addition to being taxed on its $12,000 share of income.

DIGGING DEEPER 2

Find more information on this topic at our Web site: ***http://wft-entities.swlearning.com.***

Formation of a Partnership: Tax Effects

LO.2

Describe the tax effects of forming a partnership with cash and property contributions.

Gain or Loss on Contributions to the Partnership

When a taxpayer transfers property to an entity in exchange for valuable consideration, a taxable exchange usually results. Typically, both the taxpayer and the entity realize and recognize gain or loss on the exchange.[11] The gain or loss recognized by the transferor is the difference between the fair market value of the consideration received and the adjusted basis of the property transferred.[12]

In most situations, however, neither the partner nor the partnership recognizes the gain or loss that is realized when a partner contributes property to a partnership in exchange for a partnership interest. Instead, recognition of any realized gain or loss is deferred.[13]

There are two reasons for this nonrecognition treatment. First, forming a partnership allows investors to combine their assets toward greater economic goals than could be achieved separately. Only the form of ownership, rather than the amount owned by each investor, has changed. Requiring that gain be recognized on such transfers would make the formation of some partnerships economically unfeasible. Second, because the partnership interest received is typically not a liquid asset, the partner may not be able to generate the cash to pay the tax. Thus, deferral of the gain recognizes the economic realities of the business world and follows the wherewithal to pay principle.

EXAMPLE 8

Alicia transfers two assets to the Wren Partnership on the day the entity is created, in exchange for a 60% profits and loss interest worth $60,000. She contributes cash of $40,000 and retail display equipment (basis to her as a sole proprietor, $8,000; fair market value, $20,000). Since an exchange has occurred between two parties, Alicia *realizes* a $12,000 gain on this transaction. The gain realized is the fair market value of the partnership interest of $60,000 less the basis of the assets that Alicia surrendered to the partnership [$40,000 (cash) + $8,000 (equipment)].

Under § 721, Alicia *does not recognize* the $12,000 realized gain in the year of contribution. Alicia might not have had sufficient cash if she had been required to pay tax on the $12,000 gain. All that she received from the partnership was an illiquid partnership interest; she received no cash with which to pay any resulting tax liability. ■

[11] § 1001(c).
[12] § 1001(a).
[13] § 721.

EXAMPLE 9

Assume the same facts as in Example 8, except that the equipment Alicia contributes to the partnership has an adjusted basis of $25,000. She has a $5,000 *realized* loss [$60,000 – ($40,000 + $25,000)], but she cannot deduct the loss. Realized losses, as well as realized gains, are deferred by § 721.

Unless it was essential that the partnership receive Alicia's display equipment rather than similar equipment purchased from an outside supplier, Alicia should have considered selling the equipment to a third party. This would have allowed her to deduct a $5,000 loss in the year of the sale. Alicia then could have contributed $60,000 of cash (including the proceeds from the sale) for her interest in the partnership, and the partnership would have funds to purchase similar equipment. ■

EXAMPLE 10

Five years after the Wren Partnership (Examples 8 and 9) was created, Alicia contributes another piece of equipment to the entity. This property has a basis of $35,000 and a fair market value of $50,000. Alicia will defer the recognition of the $15,000 realized gain. Section 721 is effective *whenever* a partner makes a contribution to the capital of the partnership, not just when the partnership is formed. ■

Exceptions to Nonrecognition

The nonrecognition provisions of § 721 do *not* apply where:

- the transaction is essentially a taxable exchange of properties;
- the transaction is a disguised sale of properties; or
- the partnership interest is received in exchange for services rendered to the partnership by the partner.[14]

Exchange. If a transaction is essentially a taxable exchange of properties, tax on the gain is not deferred under the nonrecognition provisions of § 721.[15]

EXAMPLE 11

Sara owns land, and Bob owns stock. Sara would like to have Bob's stock, and Bob wants Sara's land. If Sara and Bob both contribute their property to newly formed SB Partnership in exchange for interests in the partnership, the tax on the transaction appears to be deferred under § 721. The tax on a subsequent distribution by the partnership of the land to Bob and the stock to Sara also appears to be deferred under § 731. According to a literal interpretation of the statutes, no taxable exchange has occurred. Sara and Bob will find, however, that this type of tax subterfuge is not permitted. The IRS will disregard the passage of the properties through the partnership and will hold, instead, that Sara and Bob exchanged the land and stock directly. Thus, the transactions will be treated as any other taxable exchange. ■

Disguised Sale. A similar result (i.e., recognition) occurs in a **disguised sale** of property or of a partnership interest. A disguised sale is deemed to occur when a partner contributes property to a partnership and soon thereafter receives a distribution from the partnership. This distribution could be viewed as a payment by the partnership for purchase of the property.[16]

EXAMPLE 12

Kim transfers property to the KLM Partnership. The property has an adjusted basis of $10,000 and a fair market value of $30,000. Two weeks later, the partnership makes a distribution of $30,000 of cash to Kim. Under the rules of § 731, the distribution would not be taxable to Kim if the basis for her partnership interest prior to the distribution was greater than the $30,000 of cash distributed. However, the transaction appears to be a disguised purchase-sale transaction, rather than a contribution and distribution. Therefore, Kim must recognize gain of $20,000 on transfer of the property, and the partnership is deemed to have purchased the property for $30,000. ■

[14] § 721(b). A few other exceptions to § 721 treatment also exist.

[15] Reg. § 1.731–1(c)(3).

[16] § 707(a)(2)(B).

A disguised sale is presumed to exist when a contribution by one partner is followed within two years by a specified distribution to him or her from the partnership.

Services. Another exception to the nonrecognition provision of § 721 occurs when a partner receives an interest in the partnership as compensation for services rendered to the partnership. This is not a tax-deferred transaction because services are not treated as "property" that can be transferred to a partnership on a tax-free basis. Instead, the partner performing the services recognizes ordinary compensation income equal to the fair market value of the partnership interest received.[17]

The partnership may deduct the amount included in the *service partner's* income if the services are of a deductible nature. If the services are not deductible by the partnership, they are capitalized. For example, architectural plans created by a partner are capitalized to the structure built with those plans. Alternatively, day-to-day management services performed by a partner for the partnership usually are deductible by the partnership.

EXAMPLE 13

Bill, Carol, and Dave form the BCD Partnership, with each receiving a one-third interest in the entity. Dave receives his one-third interest as compensation for the accounting and tax planning services he will render after the formation of the partnership. The value of a one-third interest in the partnership (for each of the parties) is $20,000. The partnership deducts $20,000 for Dave's services in computing ordinary income. Dave recognizes $20,000 of compensation income, and he has a $20,000 basis in his partnership interest. The same result would occur if the partnership had paid Dave $20,000 for his services and he immediately contributed that amount to the entity for a one-third ownership interest. ■

Tax Issues Related to Contributed Property

When a partner makes a tax-deferred contribution of an asset to the capital of a partnership, the entity assigns a *carryover basis* to the property.[18] The partnership's basis in the asset is equal to the basis the partner held in the property prior to its transfer to the partnership. The partner's basis in the new partnership interest equals the prior basis in the contributed asset. The tax term for this basis concept is *substituted basis.* Thus, two assets are created out of one when a partnership is formed, namely, the property in the hands of the new entity and the new asset (the partnership interest) in the hands of the partner. Both assets are assigned a basis that is derived from the partner's basis in the contributed property.

The holding period of a partner's interest includes that of the contributed property when the property was a § 1231 asset or capital asset in the partner's hands. Otherwise, the holding period starts on the day the interest is acquired. The holding period of an interest acquired by a cash contribution starts at acquisition.

To understand the logic of these rules, consider what Congress was attempting to accomplish in this deferral transaction. For both parties, realized gain is deferred, under the wherewithal to pay concept, until the asset or ownership interest is subsequently disposed of in a taxable transaction. The deferral is accomplished through the use of a substituted basis by the partner and a carryover basis by the partnership. This treatment is similar to the treatment of assets transferred to a controlled corporation and the treatment of like-kind exchanges.[19]

EXAMPLE 14

On June 1, José transfers property to the JKL Partnership in exchange for a one-third interest in the partnership. The property has an adjusted basis to José of $10,000 and a fair market value of $30,000. José has a $20,000 realized gain on the exchange ($30,000 – $10,000), but he does not recognize any of the gain. José's basis for his partnership interest is the amount necessary to recognize the $20,000 deferred gain if his partnership interest is subsequently

[17] § 83(a).

[18] § 723.

[19] §§ 351 and 1031.

sold for its $30,000 fair market value. This amount, $10,000, is the substituted basis. The basis of the property contributed to the partnership is the amount necessary to allow for the recognition of the $20,000 deferred gain if the property is subsequently sold for its $30,000 fair market value. This amount, also $10,000, is the carryover basis. ■

The holding period for the contributed asset also carries over to the partnership. Thus, the partnership's holding period for the asset includes the period during which the partner owned the asset individually.

Depreciation Method and Period. If depreciable property is contributed to the partnership, the partnership usually is required to use the same cost recovery method and life used by the partner. The partnership merely "steps into the shoes" of the partner and continues the same cost recovery calculations. Thus, the partnership may not expense any part of the basis of depreciable property it receives from the transferor partner under § 179.

Intangible Assets. If a partner contributes an existing "§ 197" intangible asset to the partnership, the partnership generally will "step into the shoes" of the partner in determining future amortization deductions. Section 197 intangible assets include goodwill, going-concern value, information systems, customer- or supplier-related intangible assets, patents, licenses obtained from a governmental unit, franchises, trademarks, covenants not to compete, and other items.

Receivables, Inventory, and Losses. To prevent ordinary income from being converted into capital gain, gain or loss is treated as ordinary when the partnership disposes of either of the following.[20]

- Contributed receivables that were unrealized in the contributing partner's hands at the contribution date. Such receivables include the right to receive payment for goods or services.
- Contributed property that was inventory in the contributor's hands on the contribution date, if the partnership disposes of the property within *five years of the contribution.* For this purpose, inventory includes all tangible property except capital and real or depreciable business assets.

EXAMPLE 15

Tyrone operates a cash basis retail electronics and television store as a sole proprietor. Ramon is an enterprising individual who likes to invest in small businesses. On January 2 of the current year, Tyrone and Ramon form the TR Partnership. Their partnership contributions are listed below.

	Adjusted Basis	Fair Market Value
From Tyrone:		
Receivables	$ -0-	$ 2,000
Inventory	2,500	5,000
Land used as parking lot*	1,200	5,000
From Ramon:		
Cash	12,000	12,000

*The parking lot had been held for nine months at the contribution date.

[20] § 724. For this purpose, § 724(d)(2) waives the holding period requirement in defining § 1231 property.

CONCEPT SUMMARY 11–1

Partnership Formation and Basis Computation

1. Generally, partners or partnerships do not recognize gain or loss when property is contributed for capital interests.
2. Partners contributing property for partnership interests take the contributed property's adjusted basis for their *outside basis* in their partnership interest. The partners are said to take a substituted basis in their partnership interest.
3. The partnership will continue to use the contributing partner's basis for the *inside basis* in property it receives. The contributed property is said to take a carryover basis.
4. The partnership's holding period for contributed property may include the contributing partner's holding period.
5. Gain is recognized by a contributing partner when services are contributed or when the capital contribution is a disguised sale or exchange.
6. Special rules may apply when the partnership disposes of contributed receivables, inventory, or loss assets.

Within 30 days of formation, TR collects the receivables and sells the inventory for $5,000. It uses the land for the next 10 months as a parking lot, then sells it for $3,500. TR realized the following income in the current year from these transactions.

- Ordinary income of $2,000 from collecting the receivables.
- Ordinary income of $2,500 from the sale of inventory.
- § 1231 gain of $2,300 from the sale of land.

Since the land takes a carryover holding period, it is treated as having been held 19 months at the sale date. ■

A similar rule is designed to prevent a capital loss from being converted into an ordinary loss. Under the rule, if contributed property is disposed of at a loss and the property had a "built-in" capital loss on the contribution date, the loss is treated as a capital loss if the partnership disposes of the property *within five years of the contribution.* The capital loss is limited to the "built-in" loss on the date of contribution.[21]

Inside and Outside Bases

In this chapter, reference is made to the partnership's inside basis and the partners' outside basis. **Inside basis** refers to the adjusted basis of each partnership asset, as determined from the partnership's tax accounts. **Outside basis** represents each partner's basis in the partnership interest. Each partner "owns" a share of the partnership's inside basis for all its assets, and all partners should maintain a record of their respective outside bases.

In many cases—especially on formation of the partnership—the total of all the partners' outside bases equals the partnership's inside bases for all its assets. Differences between inside and outside basis arise when a partner's interest is sold to another person for more or less than the selling partner's share of the inside basis of partnership assets. The buying partner's outside basis equals the price paid for the interest, but the buyer's share of the partnership's inside basis is the same amount as the seller's share of the inside basis.

Concept Summary 11–1 reviews the rules that apply to partnership asset contributions and basis adjustments.

Tax Accounting Elections

LO.3

Examine the tax treatment of expenditures of a newly formed partnership and identify elections available to the partnership.

A newly formed partnership must make numerous tax accounting elections. These elections are formal decisions on how a particular transaction or tax attribute should be handled. Most of these elections must be made by the partnership rather

[21] § 724(c).

than by the partners individually.[22] The *partnership* makes the elections involving the following items.

- Inventory method.
- Cost or percentage depletion method, excluding oil and gas wells.
- Accounting method (cash, accrual, or hybrid).
- Cost recovery methods and assumptions.
- Tax year.
- Amortization of organization costs and amortization period.
- Amortization of startup expenditures and amortization period.
- First-year cost recovery deductions for certain tangible personal property.
- Nonrecognition treatment for gains from involuntary conversions.

Each partner is bound by the decisions made by the partnership relative to the elections. If the partnership fails to make an election, a partner cannot compensate for the error by making the election individually.

Though most elections are made by the partnership, each *partner* individually makes a specific election on the following relatively narrow tax issues.

- Whether to take a deduction or a credit for taxes paid to foreign countries.
- Whether to claim the cost or percentage depletion method for oil and gas wells.
- Whether to reduce the basis of depreciable property first when excluding income from discharge of indebtedness.

Initial Costs of a Partnership

In its initial stages, a partnership incurs expenses relating to some or all of the following: forming the partnership (organization costs), admitting partners to the partnership, marketing and selling partnership units to prospective partners (**syndication costs**), acquiring assets, starting business operations (startup costs), negotiating contracts, and other items. Many of these expenditures are not currently deductible. However, the Code permits a deduction or ratable amortization (straight-line) of "organization" and "startup" costs; acquisition costs incurred to acquire depreciable assets are included in the initial basis of the acquired assets; and costs related to some intangible assets may be amortized. "Syndication costs" may be neither amortized nor deducted.[23]

Organization Costs. Organization costs are incurred incident to the creation of the partnership and are capital in nature. Such costs include accounting and legal fees associated with the partnership formation.[24] Costs incurred for the following purposes are *not* organization costs.

- Acquiring assets for the partnership.
- Transferring assets to the partnership.
- Admitting partners, other than at formation.
- Removing partners, other than at formation.
- Negotiating operating contracts.

A partnership may elect to deduct up to $5,000 of the costs in the year in which it begins business. This amount is reduced, however, by the organization costs that exceed $50,000. Any organization costs that cannot be deducted under this provision are amortizable over 180 months beginning with the month in which the partnership begins business.

[22] § 703(b).
[23] § 709(a).
[24] § 709(b)(2).

The election to deduct or amortize these amounts must be made by the due date (including extensions) of the partnership return for the year in which it begins business. Failure to make a proper election results in no deduction or amortization of the organization costs until the partnership is liquidated.

EXAMPLE 16

The Bluejay Partnership, which was formed on March 1, 2006, incurs $52,000 in organization costs. On its first tax return for the period March–December 2006, Bluejay can deduct $5,722 for these items. This deduction is the sum of:

- $5,000 reduced by the $2,000 ($52,000 – $50,000) amount by which the organization costs exceed $50,000.
- $2,722 ($49,000 × 10/180) amortization of the remaining $49,000 ($52,000 – $3,000) of organization costs for 10 months.

If Bluejay had failed to make a proper election to deduct or amortize the organization costs, none of these costs would be deductible until the partnership liquidated. ■

Startup Costs. Operating costs that are incurred after the entity is formed but before it begins business are known as startup costs. Like organization costs, startup costs are capitalized and may be immediately expensed and/or amortized.[25] Such costs include marketing surveys prior to conducting business, pre-operating advertising expenses, costs of establishing an accounting system, and salaries paid to executives and employees before the start of business.

A partnership may elect to deduct up to $5,000 of startup costs in the year in which it begins business. This amount is reduced, however, by the startup costs that exceed $50,000. Costs that are not deductible under this provision are amortizable over 180 months beginning with the month in which the partnership begins business. Failure to make a proper election results in no deduction or amortization of the startup costs until the partnership is liquidated.

Find more information on this topic at our Web site: ***http://wft-entities.swlearning.com.***

DIGGING DEEPER 3

Operations of the Partnership

LO.4

Calculate partnership taxable income and describe how partnership items affect a partner's income tax return.

A key consideration in the taxation of partnerships is that a variety of entities can be partners and each may be affected differently by the partnership's operations. In particular, any combination of individuals, corporations, trusts, estates, or other partnerships may be partners. Furthermore, at the end of each year, every partner receives a share of the partnership's income, deductions, credits, and alternative minimum tax (AMT) preferences and adjustments.[26] These flow-through items ultimately may be reported and taxed on a wide variety of income tax returns [e.g., Forms 1040 (Individuals), 1041 (Fiduciaries), 1120 (C corporations), and 1120S (S corporations)], each facing different limitations and rules. Thus, the ultimate tax treatment of partnership operations is directly affected by how the partnership reports its operating results.

Reporting Operating Results

Form 1065 is due on the fifteenth day of the fourth month following the close of the partnership's tax year; for a calendar year partnership, this is April 15.

Classifying Income and Deductions. The measurement and reporting of partnership income require a two-step approach. Some items are not reported separately. These are netted at the partnership level and flow through to the partners as an aggregate number. Other items must be segregated and reported separately

[25]§ 195.

[26]§ 702(a).

GLOBAL *Tax Issues*

VARIOUS WITHHOLDING PROCEDURES APPLY TO FOREIGN PARTNERS

A U.S. partnership may have foreign partners, and these partners are taxed on their U.S. income. Because it might be difficult for the IRS to collect the tax owed by such foreign partners, several Code sections provide for various withholding procedures. The procedures differ depending on whether the income is "effectively connected with a U.S. trade or business," derived from investment property, or related to real estate transactions.

If the partnership purchases real property from a foreign seller, for example, the partnership is required to withhold 10 percent of the purchase price. Further, if the partnership receives "fixed and determinable annual or periodic payments" (FDAP), such as dividends, interest, or rents, it is required to withhold 30 percent of the amounts paid to any foreign person. (The 30 percent withholding rate can be reduced to a lower rate by a tax treaty between the United States and the foreign country.)

Finally, if the partnership reports U.S. business income, it must withhold and pay an amount equal to the highest U.S. tax rate applicable to the foreign taxpayer. For a foreign individual or corporate partner, the partnership would withhold 35 percent of any amounts related to a U.S. business.

on the partnership return and each partner's Schedule K–1. Items passed through separately include the following.[27]

- Net short-term and net long-term capital gains or losses.
- Section 1231 gains and losses.
- Charitable contributions.
- Portfolio income items (qualified and ordinary dividends, interest, and royalties).
- Expenses related to portfolio income.
- Immediately expensed tangible personal property (§ 179).
- Deduction for domestic production activities.[28]
- Items allocated differently from the general profit and loss ratio.
- Recovery of items previously deducted (tax benefit items).
- AMT preference and adjustment items.
- Self-employment income.
- Passive activity items (e.g., rental real estate income or loss).
- Intangible drilling and development costs.
- Taxes paid to foreign countries and U.S. possessions.

A partnership is not allowed the following deductions.

- Net operating loss.
- Dividends received deduction.

In addition, items that are allowed only to individuals, such as standard deductions or personal exemptions, are not allowed to the partnership.

EXAMPLE 17

Tiwanda is a one-third partner in the TUV Partnership. The partnership experienced a $20,000 net loss from operations last year, its first year of business. The partnership's transactions for this year are summarized below.

Fees received	$100,000
Salaries paid	30,000
Cost recovery deductions	10,000

[27] § 702(b).

[28] § 199.

Supplies, repairs	$ 3,000
Payroll taxes paid	9,000
Contribution to art museum	6,000
Short-term capital gain	12,000
Passive income (rental operations)	7,500
Qualified dividends received	1,500
Tax-exempt income (bond interest)	2,100
AMT adjustment (private activity bond interest)	3,600
Payment of partner Vern's alimony obligations	4,000

The two-step computational process that is used to determine partnership income is applied in the following manner.

Nonseparately Stated Items (Ordinary Income)	
Fees received	$100,000
Salaries paid	(30,000)
Cost recovery deductions	(10,000)
Supplies, repairs	(3,000)
Payroll taxes paid	(9,000)
Ordinary income	$ 48,000
Separately Stated Items	
Contribution to art museum	$ 6,000
Short-term capital gain	12,000
Passive income (rental operations)	7,500
Qualified dividends received	1,500
Tax-exempt income (bond interest)	2,100
AMT adjustment (private activity bond interest)	3,600

Each of the separately stated items passes through proportionately to each partner and is included on the appropriate schedule or netted with similar items that the partner generated for the year. Thus, in determining her tax liability, Tiwanda includes a $2,000 charitable contribution, a $4,000 short-term capital gain, $2,500 of passive rent income, $500 of qualified dividend income, and a $1,200 positive adjustment in computing alternative minimum taxable income. Tiwanda treats these items as if she had generated them herself. She must disclose her $700 share of tax-exempt interest on the first page of her Form 1040. In addition, Tiwanda reports $16,000 as her share of the partnership's ordinary income, the net amount of the nonseparately stated items.

The partnership is not allowed a deduction for last year's $20,000 net operating loss—this item was passed through to the partners in the previous year. Moreover, the partnership is not allowed a deduction for personal expenditures (payment of Vern's alimony). ■

Find more information on this topic at our Web site: ***http://wft-entities.swlearning.com.***

DIGGING DEEPER 4

Withdrawals. Capital withdrawals by partners during the year do not affect the partnership's income classification and reporting process.[29] These items usually are treated as distributions made on the last day of the partnership's tax year. In Example 17, the payment of Vern's alimony by the partnership is probably treated as a distribution from the partnership to Vern. Such distributions reduce the

[29]§ 731(a).

CONCEPT SUMMARY 11–2

Tax Reporting of Partnership Activities

Event	Partnership Level	Partner Level
1. Compute partnership ordinary income.	Form 1065, line 22, page 1. Schedule K, Form 1065, line 1, page 3.	Schedule K–1 (Form 1065), line 1. Each partner's share is passed through for separate reporting. Each partner's basis is increased.
2. Compute partnership ordinary loss.	Form 1065, line 22, page 1. Schedule K, Form 1065, line 1, page 3.	Schedule K–1 (Form 1065), line 1. Each partner's share is passed through for separate reporting. Each partner's basis is decreased. The amount of a partner's loss deduction may be limited. Losses that may not be deducted are carried forward for use in future years.
3. Separately reported items like portfolio income, capital gain and loss, and § 179 deductions.	Schedule K, Form 1065, various lines, page 3.	Schedule K–1 (Form 1065), various lines. Each partner's share of each item is passed through for separate reporting.
4. Net earnings from self-employment.	Schedule K, Form 1065, line 14, page 3.	Schedule K–1 (Form 1065), line 14.

partner's outside basis by the amount of the cash received. The partnership's inside basis in assets is similarly reduced.

EXAMPLE 18

Bill is a partner in the BB Partnership. The basis in his partnership interest is $10,000. The partnership distributes $3,000 cash to Bill at the end of the year. Bill does not recognize any gain on the distribution and reduces his basis by $3,000 (the amount of the distribution) to $7,000. Bill's basis in the cash he received is $3,000, and the partnership's inside basis for its assets is reduced by the $3,000 cash distributed. ■

The result in Example 18 arises whether or not a similar distribution is made to other partners. In a partnership, it is not critical that all partners receive a distribution at the same time as long as capital account balances are maintained appropriately.

DIGGING DEEPER 5

Find more information on this topic at our Web site: ***http://wft-entities.swlearning.com.***

Partnership Allocations

Two key special allocation rules also can affect a partner's Schedule K–1 results.[30]

Economic Effect. The partnership agreement can provide that any partner may share capital, profits, and losses in different ratios.[31] For example, a partner could have a 25 percent capital sharing ratio, yet be allocated 30 percent of the profits and 20 percent of the losses of the partnership, or, as in Examples 5 and 6, a partner

[30] The Code requires certain other allocations not discussed here.

[31] § 704(a).

BRIDGE *Discipline*

Bridge to Business Law

Although a written partnership agreement is not required, many rules governing the tax consequences to partners and their partnerships refer to such an agreement. Remember that a partner's distributive share of income, gain, loss, deduction, or credit is determined in accordance with the partnership agreement. Consequently, if taxpayers operating a business in partnership form want a measure of certainty as to the tax consequences of their activities, a carefully drafted partnership agreement is crucial. An agreement that sets forth the obligations, rights, and powers of the partners should prove invaluable in settling controversies among them and provide some degree of certainty as to the tax consequences of the partners' actions.

could be allocated a specific amount or items of income, deduction, gain, or loss. Such special allocations are permissible if they meet the **economic effect test**.[32] The rules prevent partners from shifting income and loss items merely to reduce current taxes.

DIGGING DEEPER 6

Find more information on this topic at our Web site: ***http://wft-entities.swlearning.com.***

Precontribution Gain or Loss. Certain income, gain, loss, and deductions relative to contributed property may not be allocated under the economic effect rules.[33] Instead, **precontribution gain or loss** is allocated among the partners to take into account the variation between the basis of the property and its fair market value on the date of contribution.[34] For nondepreciable property, this means that *built-in* gain or loss on the date of contribution is allocated to the contributing partner when the property is eventually disposed of by the partnership in a taxable transaction.

EXAMPLE 19

Seth and Tim form the equal profit and loss sharing ST Partnership. Seth contributes cash of $10,000, and Tim contributes land purchased two years ago and held for investment. The land has an adjusted basis of $6,000 and fair market value of $10,000 at the contribution date. For accounting purposes, the partnership records the land at its fair market value of $10,000. For tax purposes, the partnership takes a carryover basis of $6,000 in the land. After using the land as a parking lot for five months, ST sells it for $10,600. No other transactions have taken place.

The accounting and tax gain from the land sale are computed as follows.

	Accounting	Tax
Amount realized	$ 10,600	$10,600
Less: Adjusted basis	(10,000)	(6,000)
Gain realized	$ 600	$ 4,600
Built-in gain to Tim	(–0–)	(4,000)
Remaining gain (split equally)	$ 600	$ 600

Seth recognizes $300 of the gain ($600 remaining gain ÷ 2), and Tim recognizes $4,300 [$4,000 built-in gain + ($600 remaining gain ÷ 2)]. ■

[32] Reg. § 1.704–1(b).

[33] § 704(b).

[34] § 704(c)(1)(A).

TAX FACT

What Do Partnerships Do?

The partnership form seems to be especially popular for businesses operating in financial services, real estate, information, and other service industries.

Assets of Partnerships, Tax Year 2003

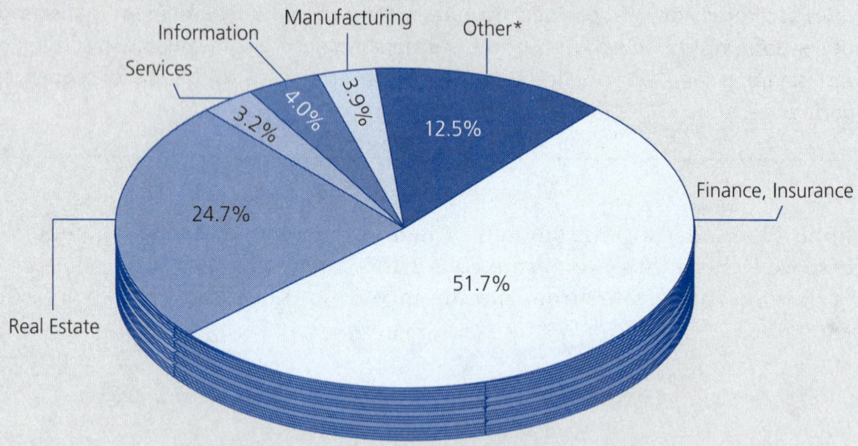

*"Other" includes agriculture, health care, construction, wholesale and retail, education, and arts and entertainment.

LO.5

Determine a partner's basis in the partnership interest.

Basis of a Partnership Interest

A partner's adjusted basis in a newly formed partnership usually equals (1) the adjusted basis in any property contributed to the partnership plus (2) the fair market value of any services the partner performed for the partnership (i.e., the amount of ordinary income reported by the partner for services rendered to the partnership).

A partnership interest also can be acquired after the partnership has been formed. The method of acquisition controls how the partner's initial basis is computed. If the partnership interest is purchased from another partner, the purchasing partner's basis is the amount paid (cost basis) for the partnership interest. The basis of a partnership interest acquired by gift is the donor's basis for the interest plus, in certain cases, some or all of the transfer (gift) tax paid by the donor. The basis of a partnership interest acquired through inheritance generally is the fair market value of the interest on the date the partner dies.

After the partnership begins its activities, or after a new partner is admitted to the partnership, the partner's basis is adjusted for numerous items. The following operating results *increase* a partner's adjusted basis.

- The partner's proportionate share of partnership income (including capital gains and tax-exempt income).
- The partner's proportionate share of any increase in partnership liabilities.

The following operating results *decrease* the partner's adjusted basis in the partnership. A partner's adjusted basis for the partnership interest cannot be reduced below zero.

- The partner's proportionate share of partnership deductions and losses (including capital losses).

- The partner's proportionate share of nondeductible expenses.
- The partner's proportionate share of any reduction in partnership liabilities.[35]

Increasing the adjusted basis for the partner's share of partnership taxable income is logical since the partner has already been taxed on the income. By increasing the partner's basis, the Code ensures that the partner is not taxed again on the income when he or she sells the interest or receives a distribution from the partnership.

It is also logical that tax-exempt income should increase the partner's basis. If the income is exempt in the current period, it should not contribute to the recognition of gain when the partner either sells the interest or receives a distribution from the partnership.

Decreasing the adjusted basis for the partner's share of deductible losses, deductions, and noncapitalizable, nondeductible expenditures is logical for the same reasons.

EXAMPLE 20

Yuri is a one-third partner in the XYZ Partnership. His proportionate share of the partnership income during the current year consists of $20,000 of ordinary taxable income and $10,000 of tax-exempt income. None of the income is distributed to Yuri. The adjusted basis of Yuri's partnership interest before adjusting for his share of income is $35,000, and the fair market value of the interest before considering the income items is $50,000.

The unrealized gain inherent in Yuri's investment in the partnership is $15,000 ($50,000 − $35,000). Yuri's proportionate share of the income items should increase the fair market value of the interest to $80,000 ($50,000 + $20,000 + $10,000). By increasing the adjusted basis of Yuri's partnership interest to $65,000 ($35,000 + $20,000 + $10,000), the Code ensures that the unrealized gain inherent in Yuri's partnership investment remains at $15,000. This makes sense because the $20,000 of ordinary taxable income is taxed to Yuri this year and should not be taxed again when Yuri either sells his interest or receives a distribution. Similarly, the tax-exempt income is exempt this year and should not increase Yuri's gain when he either sells his interest or receives a distribution from the partnership. ■

Partnership Liabilities. A partner's adjusted basis is affected by the partner's share of partnership debt.[36] Partnership debt includes most debt that is considered a liability under financial accounting rules except for accounts payable of a cash basis partnership and certain contingent liabilities.

Two major types of partnership debt exist.[37] **Recourse debt** is partnership debt for which the partnership or at least one of the partners is personally liable. This liability can exist, for example, through the operation of state law or through personal guarantees that a partner makes to the creditor. Personal liability of a party related to a partner (under attribution rules) is treated as the personal liability of the partner. **Nonrecourse debt** is debt for which no partner (or party related to a partner) is personally liable. Lenders of nonrecourse debt generally require that collateral be pledged against the loan. Upon default, the lender can claim only the collateral, not the partners' personal assets.

EXAMPLE 21

The Bay Partnership financed its asset acquisitions with debt. If the partnership defaults on the debt, the lender can place a lien on the partners' salaries and personal assets. This constitutes recourse debt. ■

[35] §§ 705 and 752.

[36] § 752.

[37] Reg. § 1.752–1(a).

EXAMPLE 22

The Tray Partnership financed its asset acquisitions with debt. If the partnership defaults on the debt, the lender can repossess the equipment purchased with the loan proceeds. This constitutes nonrecourse debt. ■

EXAMPLE 23

When Ray bought into the Sleigh Partnership, the entity was in the midst of settling litigation as to its liability to those who had purchased its products and were making warranty claims against the entity. Ray's basis in his partnership interest does not include his share of these contingent liabilities. ■

A partner's share of entity-level debt usually increases as a result of increases in outstanding partnership debt.

EXAMPLE 24

Jim and Becky contribute property to form the JB Partnership. Jim contributes cash of $30,000. Becky contributes land with an adjusted basis and fair market value of $45,000, subject to a liability of $15,000. The partnership borrows $50,000 to finance construction of a building on the contributed land. At the end of the first year, the accrual basis partnership owes $3,500 in trade accounts payable to various vendors. No other operating activities occurred. If Jim and Becky share equally in liabilities, the partners' bases in their partnership interests are determined as follows.

Jim's Basis		**Becky's Basis**	
Contributed cash	$30,000	Basis in contributed land	$ 45,000
Share of debt on land (assumed by partnership)	7,500	Less: Debt assumed by partnership	(15,000)
Share of construction loan	25,000	Share of debt on land (assumed by partnership)	7,500
Share of trade accounts payable	1,750	Share of construction loan	25,000
		Share of trade accounts payable	1,750
Basis, end of Year 1	$64,250	Basis, end of Year 1	$ 64,250

In this case, it is reasonable that the parties have an equal basis after contributing their respective properties, because each is a 50% owner and they contributed property with identical net bases and identical *net* fair market values. ■

A decrease in a partner's share of partnership debt decreases the partner's basis. A partner's share of partnership debt decreases as a result of (1) decreases in total partnership debt and (2) assumption of a partner's debt by the entity. This limits the partner's ability to deduct current-year flow-through losses.

DIGGING DEEPER 7

Find more information on this topic at our Web site: ***http://wft-entities.swlearning.com.***

Partner's Basis, Gain, and Loss

The partner's basis is also affected by (1) postacquisition contributions of cash or property to the partnership and (2) postacquisition distributions of cash or property from the partnership.

EXAMPLE 25

Ed is a one-third partner in the ERM Partnership. On January 1, 2006, Ed's basis in his partnership interest was $50,000. During 2006, the calendar year, accrual basis partnership generated ordinary taxable income of $210,000. It also received $60,000 of tax-exempt interest income from City of Buffalo bonds. It paid $3,000 in nondeductible bribes to local law enforcement officials, so that the police would not notify the Federal government about the products that the entity had imported without paying the proper tariffs. On July 1, 2006, Ed contributed $20,000 cash and a computer (zero basis to him) to the partnership. Ed's monthly draw from the partnership is $3,000; this is not a guaranteed payment. The only liabilities that the partnership has incurred are trade accounts payable. On January 1, 2006, the trade accounts payable totaled $45,000; this account balance was $21,000 on December 31, 2006. Ed shares in one-third of the partnership liabilities for basis purposes.

Ed's basis in the partnership on December 31, 2006, is $115,000, computed as follows.

Beginning balance	$ 50,000
Share of ordinary partnership income	70,000
Share of tax-exempt income	20,000
Share of nondeductible expenditures	(1,000)
Ed's basis in noncash capital contribution (computer)	–0–
Additional cash contributions	20,000
Capital withdrawal ($3,000 per month)	(36,000)
Share of net decrease in partnership liabilities [$^1/_3$ × ($45,000 – $21,000)]	(8,000)
	$115,000

■

EXAMPLE 26

Assume the same facts as in Example 25. If Ed withdraws cash of $115,000 from the partnership on January 1, 2007, the withdrawal is tax-free to him and reduces his basis to zero. The distribution is tax-free because Ed has recognized his share of the partnership's net income throughout his association with the entity via the annual flow-through of his share of the partnership's income and expense items to his personal tax return. Note that the $20,000 cash withdrawal of his share of the municipal bond interest retains its nontaxable character in this distribution. Ed receives the $20,000 tax-free because his basis was increased in 2006 when the partnership received the interest income. ■

Distributions. When a distribution involves something other than cash, the recipient partner (1) reduces the basis in the partnership interest and (2) assigns a basis to the asset received, both by the amount of the inside basis of the distributed asset. When cash and another asset are distributed at the same time, the partner first accounts for the cash received. Loss is never recognized when a partnership makes a distribution other than in its own liquidation. A partner recognizes gain only when receiving cash in an amount in excess of the partner's basis.

EXAMPLE 27

Pert Corporation has a $100,000 basis in the PQR Partnership. Pert receives a distribution from PQR in the form of a plot of land (basis to PQR of $40,000, fair market value of $50,000). Pert recognizes no income from the distribution. Pert's basis in the land is $40,000 (i.e., a carryover basis), and its basis in PQR now is $60,000 ($100,000 – $40,000). ■

EXAMPLE 28

Pert Corporation has a $100,000 basis in the PQR Partnership. Pert receives a distribution from PQR in the form of a plot of land (basis to PQR of $40,000, fair market value of $50,000), and $75,000 of cash. Pert recognizes no income from the distribution because the cash received ($75,000) does not exceed Pert's partnership basis ($100,000). Pert's basis in the land is $25,000, the basis in PQR remaining after accounting for the cash ($100,000 partnership basis – $75,000 cash = $25,000 basis assigned to land). Pert's basis in the partnership now is zero ($25,000 basis after accounting for the cash – $25,000 assigned to the land). ■

FIGURE 11–1 **Partner's Basis in Partnership Interest**

Basis generally is adjusted in the following order.

Initial basis. Amount paid for partnership interest, or gift or inherited basis (including share of partnership debt).

+ Partner's subsequent asset contributions.
+ Since interest acquired, partner's share of the partnership's

- Debt increase.
- Income items.
- Tax-exempt income items.
- Excess of depletion deductions over adjusted basis of property subject to depletion.

– Partner's distributions and withdrawals.
– Since interest acquired, partner's share of the partnership's

- Debt decrease.
- Nondeductible items not chargeable to a capital account.
- Special depletion deduction for oil and gas wells.
- Loss items.

The basis of a partner's interest can never be negative.

EXAMPLE 29

Pert Corporation has a $100,000 basis in the PQR Partnership. Pert receives a distribution from PQR in the form of a plot of land (basis to PQR of $40,000, fair market value of $50,000), and $125,000 of cash. Pert recognizes $25,000 of income from the distribution ($125,000 cash received – $100,000 basis in PQR). Pert's basis in the land is $0, as there is no basis in PQR remaining after accounting for the cash. Pert's basis in the partnership also is zero. ■

Entity-level liabilities, and thus a partner's interest basis, change from day to day, but the partner's interest basis generally needs to be computed only once or twice a year. Figure 11–1 summarizes the rules for computing a partner's basis in a partnership interest.

Capital Changes. When a partnership interest is sold, exchanged, or retired, the partner must compute the adjusted basis as of the date the transaction occurs. The partner recognizes gain or loss on the disposition of the partnership interest, and this usually is a capital gain or loss. Income "bunching" may occur if the partner recognizes the pass-through of operating income in the same tax year during which the sale of the interest occurs. To the extent that the partner is allocated a share of ordinary income items that have yet to be recognized by the partnership (i.e., "hot assets"), some of the capital gain is converted to ordinary income.[38]

EXAMPLE 30

When its basis in the TUV Partnership is $100,000, taking into account all earnings to date and the sale-date liabilities of the partnership, Kurt Corporation sells its interest in the entity to Gloria for $120,000. Kurt recognizes a $20,000 capital gain [$120,000 (amount realized) – $100,000 (basis in partnership interest)]. ■

[38]Partnership items that hold unrecognized ordinary income are known as *hot assets.* Hot assets include the unrealized receivables of a cash basis partnership, and a broadly defined concept of appreciated inventory. §§ 751(a) and (d).

EXAMPLE 31

When its basis in the TUV Partnership is $100,000, taking into account all earnings to date and the sale-date liabilities of the partnership, Kurt Corporation sells its interest in the entity to Gloria for $120,000. At the time of the sale, Kurt's share of the TUV hot assets is $8,000. Kurt recognizes $8,000 of ordinary income and $12,000 of capital gain (i.e., the total gain of $20,000 is comprised of $8,000 of ordinary income and $12,000 of capital gain). ■

EXAMPLE 32

When its basis in the TUV Partnership is $100,000, taking into account all earnings to date and the sale-date liabilities of the partnership, Kurt Corporation sells its interest in the entity to Gloria for $120,000. At the time of the sale, Kurt's share of the TUV hot assets is $28,000. Kurt recognizes $28,000 of ordinary income and $8,000 of capital loss (i.e., the total gain of $20,000 is comprised of $28,000 of ordinary income and $8,000 of capital loss). ■

Loss Limitations

LO.6

Describe the limitations on deducting partnership losses.

Partnership losses flow through to the partners for use on their tax returns. However, the amount and nature of the losses that may be used in a partner's tax computations may be limited. When limitations apply, all or a portion of the losses are suspended and carried forward until the rules allow them to be used. Only then can the losses decrease the partner's tax liability.

Three different limitations may apply to partnership losses that are passed through to a partner. The first allows the deduction of *losses* only to the extent the partner has adjusted basis for the partnership interest. Losses that are deductible under this basis limitation may then be subject to the *at-risk* limitations. Losses are deductible under this provision only to the extent the partner is at risk for the partnership interest. Any losses that survive this second limitation may be subject to a third limitation, the *passive* loss rules. Only losses that make it through all of these applicable limitations are eligible to be deducted on the partner's tax return.

EXAMPLE 33

Meg is a partner in a partnership that does not invest in real estate. On January 1, Meg's adjusted basis for her partnership interest is $50,000, and her at-risk amount is $35,000. Her share of losses from the partnership for the year is $60,000, all of which is passive. She has one other passive income-producing investment that produced $25,000 of passive income during the year. Meg can deduct $25,000 of partnership losses on her Form 1040.

Applicable Provision	Deductible Loss	Suspended Loss
Basis limitation	$50,000	$10,000
At-risk limitation	35,000	15,000
Passive loss limitation	25,000	10,000

Meg can deduct only $50,000 under the basis limitation. Of this $50,000, only $35,000 is deductible under the at-risk limitation. Under the passive loss limitation, passive losses can only be deducted against passive income. Thus, Meg can deduct only $25,000 on her return. The remaining $35,000 of losses is suspended. ■

Basis Limitation. A partner may only deduct losses flowing through from the partnership to the extent of the partner's adjusted basis in the partnership.[39] A partner's adjusted basis in the partnership is determined at the end of the partnership's taxable year. It is adjusted for distributions and any partnership gains during the year, but it is determined *before considering any losses for the year.*

Losses that cannot be deducted because of this rule are suspended and carried forward (never back) for use against future increases in the partner's adjusted basis.

[39] § 704(d).

Such increases might result from additional capital contributions, from sharing in additional partnership debts, or from future partnership income.

EXAMPLE 34

Carol and Dan do business as the CD Partnership, sharing profits and losses equally. All parties use the calendar year. At the start of the current year, the basis of Carol's partnership interest is $25,000. The partnership sustains an operating loss of $80,000 in the current year. Only $25,000 of Carol's $40,000 allocable share of the partnership loss can be deducted under the basis limitation. As a result, the basis of Carol's partnership interest is zero as of January 1 of the following year, and Carol must carry forward the remaining $15,000 of partnership losses. ■

EXAMPLE 35

Assume the same facts as in Example 34, and that the partnership earns a profit of $70,000 for the next calendar year. Carol reports net partnership income of $20,000 ($35,000 distributive share of income – $15,000 carryforward loss). The basis of Carol's partnership interest becomes $20,000. ■

PLANNING *Strategies*

MAKE YOUR OWN TAX SHELTER

★ **Framework Focus: Deductions**

Strategy ★ Maximize Deductible Amounts.

In Example 34, Carol's entire $40,000 share of the current-year partnership loss could have been deducted under the basis limitation in the current year if she had contributed an additional $15,000 or more in capital by December 31. Alternatively, if the partnership had incurred additional debt by the end of the current year, Carol's basis might have been increased to permit some or all of the loss to be deducted in that year. Thus, if partnership losses are projected for a given year, careful tax planning can ensure their deductibility under the basis limitation. Note in the discussion below, however, that the effects of the at-risk and passive activity limitations also must be considered.

Figure 11–1 shows that contributions to capital, partnership income items, and distributions from the partnership are taken into account before loss items. This *losses last* rule can produce some unusual results in taxation of partnership distributions and deductibility of losses.

EXAMPLE 36

The Ellen-Glenn Partnership is owned equally by partners Ellen and the Glenn Hospital. At the beginning of the year, Ellen's basis in her partnership interest is exactly $0. Her share of partnership income is $10,000 for the year, and she receives a $10,000 distribution from the partnership.

Under the basis adjustment ordering rules of Figure 11–1, Ellen's basis is first increased by the $10,000 of partnership income; then it is decreased by her $10,000 distribution. She reports her $10,000 share of partnership taxable income on her personal tax return. Her basis at the end of the year is exactly $0 ($0 + $10,000 income – $10,000 distribution). ■

EXAMPLE 37

Assume the same facts as in Example 36, except that Ellen's share of partnership operating results is a $10,000 loss instead of $10,000 income. She again receives a $10,000 distribution.

A distribution of cash in excess of basis in the partnership interest results in a gain to the distributee partner to the extent of the excess. Ellen's distribution is considered before the deductibility of the loss is evaluated under the basis limitation.

Therefore, Ellen recognizes gain on the $10,000 distribution because she has no basis in her partnership interest. The gain effectively ensures that she still has a $0 basis after the

TAX FACT

Whose Money Are We Losing?

Net operating losses are more likely to be found in the limited partnership and LLC/LLP than in the general partnership.

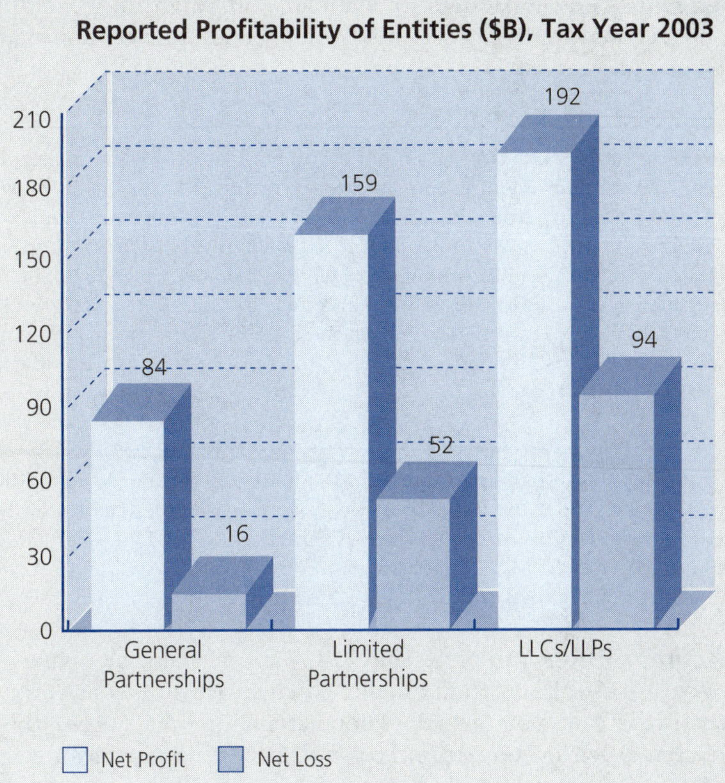

distribution. The loss cannot be deducted under the basis limitation rule because Ellen has no basis in her partnership interest. ■

Given this $20,000 difference in partnership earnings in the two examples ($10,000 income versus $10,000 loss), does income taxed to Ellen differ in the same way? Actually, she reports $10,000 of income (gain) in each case: ordinary income in Example 36, and (probably) a capital gain from the distribution in Example 37. In Example 37, she also has a $10,000 suspended loss carryforward. These results are due solely to the basis adjustment ordering rules.

At-Risk Limitation. Under the at-risk rules, the partnership losses from business and income-producing activities that noncorporate partners and closely held C corporation partners can deduct are limited to amounts that are economically invested in the partnership. Invested amounts include the cash and the adjusted basis of property contributed by the partner and the partner's share of partnership earnings that has not been withdrawn.[40] A closely held C corporation exists when five or fewer individuals own more than 50 percent of the entity's stock under appropriate attribution and ownership rules.

When some or all of the partners are personally liable for partnership recourse debt, that debt is included in the adjusted basis of those partners. Usually, those partners also include the debt in their amount at risk.

[40] § 465(a).

No partner, however, carries any financial risk on nonrecourse debt. Therefore, as a general rule, partners cannot include nonrecourse debt in their amount at risk even though that debt is included in the adjusted basis of their partnership interest. This rule has an exception, however, that applies in many cases. Real estate nonrecourse financing provided by a bank, retirement plan, or similar party or by a Federal, state, or local government generally is deemed to be at risk.[41] Such debt is termed **qualified nonrecourse debt**. In summary, although the general rule provides that nonrecourse debt is not at risk, the overriding exception may provide that it is deemed to be at risk.

EXAMPLE 38

Kelly invests $5,000 in the Kelly Green Limited Partnership as a 5% general partner. Shortly thereafter, the partnership acquires the master recording of a well-known vocalist for $250,000 ($50,000 from the partnership and $200,000 secured from a local bank via a *recourse* mortgage). Kelly's share of the recourse debt is $10,000, and her basis in her partnership interest is $15,000 ($5,000 cash investment + $10,000 debt share). Since the debt is recourse, Kelly's at-risk amount also is $15,000. Kelly's share of partnership losses in the first year of operations is $11,000. Kelly is entitled to deduct the full $11,000 of partnership losses under both the basis and the at-risk limitations because this amount is less than both her outside basis and at-risk amount. ■

EXAMPLE 39

Assume the same facts as in Example 38, except the bank loan is nonrecourse (the partners have no direct liability under the terms of the loan in the case of a default). Kelly's basis in her partnership interest still is $15,000, but she can deduct only $5,000 of the flow-through loss. The amount she has at risk in the partnership does not include the nonrecourse debt. (The debt does not relate to real estate so it is not qualified nonrecourse debt.) ■

Passive Activity Rules. A partnership loss share may also be disallowed under the passive activity rules. Recall from Chapter 6 that an activity is considered passive if the taxpayer (in this case, a partner) does not materially participate or if the activity is considered a rental activity. Losses from passive partnership activities are aggregated by each partner with his or her other passive income and losses. Any net loss is suspended and carried forward to future years. Thus, the passive activity limitation applies at the partner level and is computed after the basis and at-risk limitations.

PLANNING *Strategies*

FORMATION AND OPERATION OF A PARTNERSHIP

★ Framework Focus: Income and Exclusions

Strategy ★ Postpone Recognition of Income to Achieve Tax Deferral.

In transferring assets to a partnership, potential partners should be cautious to ensure that they are not required to recognize any gain upon the creation of the entity. The nonrecognition provisions of § 721 are relatively straightforward and resemble the provisions under § 351. However, any partner can make a tax-deferred contribution of assets to the entity either at the inception of the partnership or later. This possibility is not available to less-than-controlling shareholders in a corporation.

The partners should anticipate the tax benefits and pitfalls that are presented in Subchapter K and should take appropriate actions to resolve any resulting problems. Typically, all that is needed is an appropriate provision in the partnership agreement (e.g., with respect to differing allocation percentages for gains and losses). Recall, however, that a special allocation of income, expense, or credit items in the partnership agreement must satisfy certain requirements before it is effective.

[41] § 465(b)(6).

Transactions between Partner and Partnership

LO.7

Review the treatment of transactions between a partner and the partnership.

Many types of transactions occur between a partnership and its partners. A partner may contribute property to the partnership, perform services for the partnership, or receive distributions from the partnership. A partner may borrow money from or lend money to the partnership. Property may be bought and sold between a partner and the partnership. Several of these transactions were discussed earlier in the chapter. The remaining types of partner-partnership transactions are the focus of this section.

Guaranteed Payments

If a partnership makes a payment to a partner in his or her capacity as a partner, the payment may be a draw against the partner's share of partnership income; a return of some or all of the partner's original capital contribution; or a guaranteed payment, among other treatments. A **guaranteed payment** is a payment for services performed by the partner or for the use of the partner's capital. The payment may not be determined by reference to partnership income. Guaranteed payments are usually expressed as a fixed-dollar amount or as a percentage of capital that the partner has invested in the partnership. Whether the partnership deducts or capitalizes the guaranteed payment depends on the nature of the payment.

EXAMPLE 40

David, Donald, and Dale formed the accrual basis DDD Partnership. The partnership and each of the partners are calendar year taxpayers. According to the partnership agreement, David is to manage the partnership and receive a $21,000 distribution from the entity every year, payable in 12 monthly installments. Donald is to receive an amount that is equal to 18% of his capital account, as it is computed by the firm's accountant at the beginning of the year, payable in 12 monthly installments. Dale is the partnership's advertising specialist. He withdraws about 3% of the partnership's net income every month for his personal use. David and Donald receive guaranteed payments from the partnership, but Dale does not. ■

Guaranteed payments resemble the salary or interest payments of other businesses and receive somewhat similar income tax treatment.[42] In contrast to the provision that usually applies to withdrawals of assets by partners from their partnerships, guaranteed payments are deductible (or capitalized) by the entity. Deductible guaranteed payments, like any other deductible expenses of a partnership, can create an ordinary loss for the entity. Partners receiving a guaranteed payment report ordinary income, treated as paid on the last day of the entity's tax year.

EXAMPLE 41

Continue with the situation introduced in Example 40. For calendar year 2006, David receives the $21,000 as provided by the partnership agreement, Donald's guaranteed payment for 2006 is $17,000, and Dale withdraws $20,000 under his personal expenditures clause. Before considering these amounts, the partnership's ordinary income for 2006 is $650,000.

The partnership can deduct its payments to David and Donald, so the final amount of its 2006 ordinary income is $612,000 ($650,000 – $21,000 – $17,000). Thus, each of the equal partners is allocated $204,000 of ordinary partnership income for their 2006 individual income tax returns ($612,000 ÷ 3). In addition, David reports the $21,000 guaranteed payment as income, and Donald includes the $17,000 guaranteed payment in his 2006 income. Dale's partnership draw is deemed to have come from his allocated $204,000 (or from the accumulated partnership income that was taxed to him in prior years) and is not taxed separately to him. ■

EXAMPLE 42

Assume the same facts as in Example 41, except that the partnership's tax year ends on March 31, 2007. The total amount of the guaranteed payments is taxable to the partners on

[42] § 707(c).

CONCEPT SUMMARY 11–3

Partner-Partnership Transactions

1. Partners can transact business with their partnerships in a nonpartner capacity. These transactions include the sale and exchange of property, rentals, loans of funds, etc.
2. A payment to a partner may be classified as a guaranteed payment if it is for services or use of the partner's capital and is not based on partnership income. A guaranteed payment usually is deductible by the partnership and is included in the partner's income on the last day of the partnership's tax year.
3. A payment to a partner may be treated as being to an outside (though related) party. Such a payment is deductible or capitalizable by the partnership at the time it must be included in income under the partner's method of accounting.
4. Guaranteed payments and payments to a partner that are treated as being to an outside party are deductible if the payment constitutes an ordinary and necessary (rather than capitalizable) business expense.
5. Losses are disallowed between a partner or related party and a partnership when the partner or related party owns more than a 50% interest in the partnership's capital or profits.
6. Income from a related-party sale is treated as ordinary income if the property is not a capital asset to both the transferor and the transferee.
7. Partners are not employees of their partnership, so the entity cannot deduct payments for partner fringe benefits, nor need it withhold or pay any payroll tax for payments to partners.

that date. Thus, even though David received 9 of his 12 payments for fiscal 2007 in the 2006 calendar year, all of his guaranteed payments are taxable to him in 2007. Similarly, all of Donald's guaranteed payments are taxable to him in 2007, rather than when they are received. The deduction for, and the gross income from, guaranteed payments is allowed on the same date that all of the other income and expense items relative to the partnership are allocated to the partners (i.e., on the last day of the entity's tax year). ■

Other Transactions between a Partner and a Partnership

Certain transactions between a partner and the partnership are treated as if the partner were an outsider, dealing with the partnership at arm's length.[43] Loan transactions, rental payments, and sales of property between the partner and the partnership are generally treated in this manner.

EXAMPLE 43

The Eastside Co-op, a one-third partner in the ABC Partnership, owns a tract of land that the partnership wishes to purchase. The land has a fair market value of $30,000 and an adjusted basis to Eastside of $17,000. If Eastside sells the land to the partnership, it recognizes a $13,000 gain on the sale, and the partnership takes a $30,000 cost basis in the land. If the land has a fair market value of $10,000 on the sale date, the Co-op recognizes a $7,000 loss. ■

DIGGING DEEPER 8

Find more information on this topic at our Web site: ***http://wft-entities.swlearning.com.***

Sales of Property. No loss is recognized on a sale of property between a person and a partnership when the person owns, directly or indirectly, more than 50 percent of partnership capital or profits.[44] The disallowed loss may not vanish entirely, however. If the person eventually sells the property at a gain, the disallowed loss reduces the gain that would otherwise be recognized.[45]

[43] § 707(a).
[44] § 707(b).
[45] This is similar to treatment under § 267.

EXAMPLE 44

Barry sells land (adjusted basis, $30,000; fair market value, $45,000) to a partnership in which he controls a 60% capital interest. The partnership pays him only $20,000 for the land. Barry cannot deduct his $10,000 realized loss. The sale apparently was not at arm's length, but the taxpayer's intentions are irrelevant. Barry and the partnership are related parties, and the loss is disallowed.

When the partnership sells the land to an outsider at a later date, it receives a sales price of $44,000. The partnership can offset the recognition of its $24,000 realized gain on the subsequent sale ($44,000 sales proceeds − $20,000 adjusted basis) by the amount of the $10,000 prior disallowed loss ($20,000 − $30,000). Thus, the partnership recognizes a $14,000 gain on its sale of the land. ■

Using a similar rationale, any gain that is realized on a sale or exchange between a partner and a partnership in which the partner controls a capital or profits interest of more than 50 percent is recognized as ordinary income, unless the asset is a capital asset to both the seller and the purchaser.[46]

EXAMPLE 45

The Kent School purchases some land (adjusted basis, $30,000; fair market value, $45,000) for $45,000 from a partnership in which it controls a 90% profits interest. The land was a capital asset to the partnership. If Kent holds the land as a capital asset, the partnership recognizes a $15,000 capital gain. However, if the school also is a land developer and the property is not a capital asset to it, the partnership must recognize $15,000 of ordinary income from the sale, even though the property was a capital asset to the partnership. ■

Partners as Employees

A partner usually does not qualify as an employee for tax purposes. For example, a partner receiving guaranteed payments is not regarded as an employee of the partnership for purposes of payroll taxes (e.g., FICA or FUTA). Moreover, since a partner is not an employee, the partnership cannot deduct its payments for the partner's fringe benefits. Nonetheless, a general partner's distributive share of ordinary partnership income and guaranteed payments for services are generally subject to the Federal self-employment tax.[47]

Find more information on this topic at our Web site: ***http://wft-entities.swlearning.com.***

DIGGING DEEPER 9

PLANNING *Strategies*

TRANSACTIONS BETWEEN PARTNERS AND PARTNERSHIPS

★ **Framework Focus: Deductions**

Strategy ★ Maximize Deductible Amounts.

Partners should be careful when engaging in transactions with the partnership to ensure that no negative tax results occur. A partner who owns a majority of the partnership generally should not sell property at a loss to the partnership because the loss is disallowed. Similarly, a majority partner should not sell a capital asset to the partnership at a gain, if the asset is to be used by the partnership as other than a capital asset. The gain on this transaction is taxed as ordinary income to the selling partner rather than as capital gain.

As an alternative to selling property to a partnership, the partner may lease it to the partnership. The partner recognizes rent income, and the partnership has a rent expense. A partner who needs more cash immediately can sell the property to an outside third party; then the third party can lease the property to the partnership for a fair rental.

The timing of the deduction for payments by accrual basis partnerships to cash basis partners varies depending on whether the payment is a guaranteed payment or is treated as a payment to an outsider. If the payment is a guaranteed payment, the deduction occurs when the partnership properly accrues the payment. If the payment is treated as a payment to an outsider, the actual date the payment is made controls the timing of the deduction.

[46] § 707(b)(2).

[47] § 1402(a).

LO.8

Describe the application of partnership tax law provisions to limited liability companies (LLCs) and limited liability partnerships (LLPs).

Limited Liability Entities

Limited Liability Companies

The *limited liability company (LLC)* combines partnership taxation with limited personal liability for all owners of the entity. All states and the District of Columbia have passed legislation permitting the establishment of LLCs.

Taxation of LLCs. A properly structured LLC may be taxed as a partnership under the "check-the-box" rules. Because LLC members are not personally liable for the debts of the entity, the LLC is effectively treated as a limited partnership with no general partners. This may result in an unusual application of partnership taxation rules. The IRS has not specifically ruled on most aspects of LLC taxation, so several of the following comments are based on speculation about how a partnership with no general partners would be taxed.

- Formation of a new LLC is treated in the same manner as formation of a partnership. Generally, no gain or loss is recognized by the LLC member or the LLC, the member takes a substituted basis in the LLC interest, and the LLC takes a carryover basis in the assets it receives.
- An LLC's income and losses are allocated proportionately. Special allocations are permitted, as long as they demonstrate economic effect.
- An LLC member contributing property with built-in gains can be subject to tax on certain distributions within seven years of the contribution.
- A loss must meet the basis, at-risk, and passive loss limitations to be currently deductible. Because debt of an LLC is considered nonrecourse to each of the members, it may not be included in the at-risk limitation unless it is "qualified nonrecourse financing." The IRS has not issued rulings as to whether a member is treated as a material or active participant of an LLC for passive loss purposes. Presumably, passive or active status will be based on the time the member spends in LLC activities.
- The initial accounting period and accounting method elections are available to an LLC.
- Property takes a carryover or substituted basis when distributed from an LLC.

Advantages of an LLC. An LLC offers certain advantages over a limited partnership.

- Generally, none of the members of an LLC is personally liable for the entity's debts. In contrast, general partners in a limited partnership have personal liability for partnership recourse debts.
- Limited partners cannot participate in the management of a partnership. All owners of an LLC have the legal right to participate in the entity's management.

An LLC also offers certain advantages over an S corporation (see Chapter 12), including the following.

- An LLC can have an unlimited number of owners, while an S corporation is limited to 100 shareholders.
- Any taxpayers, including corporations, nonresident aliens, other partnerships, and trusts, can be owners of an LLC. S corporation shares can be held only by specified parties.
- The transfer of property to an LLC in exchange for an ownership interest in the entity is governed by partnership tax provisions rather than corporate tax provisions. Thus, the transfers need not satisfy the 80 percent control requirement needed for tax-free treatment under the corporate tax statutes.
- The S corporation taxes on built-in gains and passive income do not apply to LLCs.

CONCEPT SUMMARY 11–4

Advantages and Disadvantages of the Partnership Form

The partnership form may be attractive when one or more of the following factors is present:

- The entity is generating net taxable losses and/or valuable tax credits, which will be of use to the owners.
- The owners want to avoid complex corporate administrative and filing requirements.
- Other means of reducing the effects of the double taxation of corporate business income (e.g., compensation to owners, interest, and rental payments) have been exhausted.
- The entity does not generate material amounts of tax preference and adjustment items, which increase the alternative minimum tax liabilities of its owners.
- The entity is generating net passive income, which its owners can use to claim immediate deductions for net passive losses that they have generated from other sources.
- The owners wish to make special allocations of certain income or deduction items that are not possible under the C or S corporation forms.
- The owners have adequate bases in their ownership interests to facilitate the deduction of flow-through losses and the assignment of an adequate basis to assets distributed in-kind to the owners.

The partnership form may be less attractive when one or more of the following factors is present:

- The tax paid by the owners on the entity's income is greater than that payable by the entity as a C corporation, and the income is not expected to be distributed soon. (If distributed by a C corporation, double taxation would likely occur.)
- The entity is generating net taxable income without distributing any cash to the owners. The owners may not have sufficient cash with which to pay the tax on the entity's earnings.
- The type of income that the entity is generating (e.g., business and portfolio income) is not as attractive to its owners as net passive income would be because the owners could use net passive income to offset the net passive losses that they have generated on their own.
- The entity is in a high-exposure business, and the owners desire protection from personal liability. An LLC or LLP structure may be available, however, to limit personal liability.
- The owners want to avoid Federal self-employment tax.
- Partnership operations are complex (indicating that Form 1065 might not be filed until near the due date for the return), but partners with the same tax year need to file their returns as early as possible for personal reasons (e.g., to meet debt requirements or to receive a tax refund).

- An owner's basis in an LLC includes the owner's share of almost all LLC liabilities under § 752. Only certain entity liabilities are included in the S corporation shareholder's basis.
- An LLC may make special allocations, whereas S corporations must allocate income, loss, etc., only on a per share/per day basis.

Disadvantages of an LLC. The disadvantages of an LLC stem primarily from the entity's relative newness. There is no established body of case law interpreting the various state statutes, so the application of specific provisions is uncertain. An additional uncertainty for LLCs that operate in more than one jurisdiction is which state's law will prevail and how it will be applied.

Among other factors, statutes differ from state to state as to the type of business an LLC can conduct—primarily the extent to which a service-providing firm can operate as an LLC. A service entity may find it cannot operate as an LLC in several jurisdictions where it conducts business. Despite these uncertainties and limitations, LLCs are being formed at increasing rates, and the ranks of multistate LLCs are rising quickly.

GLOBAL *Tax Issues*

PARTNERSHIPS AROUND THE WORLD—AND BEYOND

Technology continues to act as a catalyst—and incentive—for the creation of joint ventures. From Web kiosks at gas stations to global satellite networks, high-tech companies are forging alliances to bring technology to consumers.

Microsoft has teamed up with BP to provide news, weather, and other content for customers to watch while they fill up at the gas station. TimeWarner and Radiant Systems, Inc., formed their own venture to offer programming at other gas stations, pizza parlors, and numerous other retail outlets. These ventures appear to be spurred by a desire to capture larger shares of the ever-expanding global market.

Meanwhile, various domestic telephone companies are continuing to align themselves with partners in foreign telecommunications markets: each wants to have the widest possible service coverage area so it can offer efficient communications and computer networking to business clients with a global presence.

Primestar is a partnership formed by several media and cable companies to offer digital satellite television services on numerous channels to customers for a monthly rental fee. And several partnerships have been formed to establish satellite-based Web communications around the world.

Limited Liability Partnerships

The difference between a general partnership and a limited liability partnership (LLP) is small, but very significant. Recall that general partners are jointly and severally liable for all partnership debts. Partners in a registered LLP are jointly and severally liable for contractual liability (i.e., they are treated as general partners for commercial debt). They are also personally liable for their own malpractice or other torts. They are not, however, personally liable for the malpractice and torts of their partners. As a result, the exposure of their personal assets to lawsuits filed against other partners and the partnership is considerably reduced.

An LLP must have formal documents of organization and register with the state. LLPs are taxed as partnerships under Federal tax rules.

Summary

Partnerships are popular among business owners because formation of the entity is relatively simple and tax-free. The Code places very few restrictions on who can be a partner. Partnerships are especially attractive when operating losses are anticipated, or when marginal rates that would apply to partnership income are less than those that would be paid by a C corporation. Partnerships do not offer the limited liability of a corporate entity, but the use of limited partnerships, LLCs, and LLPs can offer some protection to the owners.

Partnerships are tax-reporting, not taxpaying, entities. Distributive shares of ordinary income and separately stated items are taxed to the partners on the last day of the tax year. Special allocations and guaranteed payments are allowed and offer partners the ability to tailor the cash-flow and taxable amounts that are distributed by the entity to its owners. Deductions for flow-through losses may be limited by the passive activity, related-party, and at-risk rules, as well as by the partner's interest basis. The flexibility of the partnership rules makes this form continually attractive to new businesses, especially in a global setting.

Suggested Further Readings

"Are LLC Members GPs or LPs for Federal or State Tax Purposes?" *Journal of Taxation*, January 2003, p. 62.

C. Curry, S. Harrington, and K. Milani, "Tax Choice When Receiving Partnership Interest for Services," *Practical Tax Strategies*, February 2004, pp. 112–118.

Catherine E. Livingston, "Accepting Charitable Contributions Through a Single-Member LLC," *Taxation of Exempts*, November/December 2001, pp. 107–111.

Peter C. Mahoney and Elizabeth Williams, "Opportunities, Pitfalls, and Developments in the Disguised Sale Rules," *Real Estate Taxation*, WG&L Online, 2005.

KEY TERMS

Basis in partnership interest, 11–8
Capital account, 11–8
Capital interest, 11–7
Capital sharing ratio, 11–7
Disguised sale, 11–10
Economic effect test, 11–19
General partnership, 11–5
Guaranteed payment, 11–29
Inside basis, 11–13
Limited liability company (LLC), 11–5
Limited liability partnership (LLP), 11–5
Limited partnership, 11–5
Nonrecourse debt, 11–21
Outside basis, 11–13
Precontribution gain or loss, 11–19
Profit and loss sharing ratios, 11–7
Profits (loss) interest, 11–7
Qualified nonrecourse debt, 11–28
Recourse debt, 11–21
Separately stated items, 11–5
Special allocation, 11–8
Syndication costs, 11–14

PROBLEM MATERIALS

PROBLEMS

1. Justin and Tiffany will contribute property to form the equal TJ Partnership. Justin will contribute cash of $20,000 plus land with a fair market value of $80,000 and an adjusted basis of $65,000. Tiffany currently operates a sole proprietorship with assets valued at $100,000 and an adjusted basis of $125,000. Tiffany will contribute these assets in-kind to the partnership. Describe the tax consequences of the formation to Tiffany, Justin, and the partnership. *Issue ID*

2. Larry and Ken form an equal partnership with a cash contribution of $50,000 from Larry and a property contribution (adjusted basis of $30,000 and a fair market value of $50,000) from Ken.
   a. How much gain, if any, must Larry recognize on the transfer? Must Ken recognize any gain?
   b. What is Larry's basis in his partnership interest?
   c. What is Ken's basis in his partnership interest?
   d. What basis does the partnership take in the property transferred by Ken?

3. Tom and Katie form an equal partnership with an $80,000 cash contribution from Tom and a contribution of property (basis of $100,000, fair market value of $80,000) from Katie. *Decision Making*
   a. Compute Katie's realized and recognized gain or loss from the contribution.
   b. Compute Tom's basis in his partnership interest.
   c. Compute Katie's basis in her partnership interest.
   d. What basis does the partnership take in Katie's contributed asset?
   e. Are there more tax-effective ways to structure the transaction?

4. Three years after the S&P Partnership is formed, Sylvia, a 25% partner, contributes an additional $50,000 of cash and land she has held for investment. Sylvia's basis in the land is $60,000, and its fair market value is $100,000. Her basis in the partnership interest was $50,000 before this contribution. The partnership uses the land as a parking lot for four years and then sells it for $120,000.
   a. How much gain or loss does Sylvia recognize on the contribution?
   b. What is Sylvia's basis in her partnership interest immediately following this contribution?
   c. How much gain or loss does S&P recognize on this contribution?
   d. What is S&P's basis in the property it receives from Sylvia?
   e. How much gain or loss does the partnership recognize on the later sale of the land, and what is the character of the gain or loss? How much is allocated to Sylvia?

Issue ID

5. Block, Inc., a calendar year general contractor, and Strauss, Inc., a development corporation with a July 31 year-end, formed the equal SB Partnership on January 1 of the current year. Both partners are C corporations. The partnership was formed to construct and lease shopping centers in Wilmington, Delaware. Block contributed equipment (basis of $650,000, fair market value of $650,000), building permits, and architectural designs created by Block's employees (basis $0, fair market value $100,000). Strauss contributed land (basis $50,000, fair market value $250,000) and cash of $500,000. The cash was used as follows.

Legal fees for drafting partnership agreement	$ 10,000
Materials and labor costs for construction in progress on shopping center	400,000
Office expense (utilities, rent, overhead, etc.)	90,000

What issues must the partnership address in preparing its initial tax return?

Decision Making

6. Craig and Beth are equal members of the CB Partnership, formed on June 1 of the current year. Craig contributed land that he inherited from his father three years ago. Craig's father purchased the land in 1946 for $6,000. The land was worth $50,000 when the father died. The fair market value of the land was $75,000 at the date it was contributed to the partnership.

   Beth has significant experience developing real estate. After the partnership is formed, she will prepare a plan for developing the property and secure zoning approvals for the partnership. She would normally bill a third party $25,000 for these efforts. Beth will also contribute $50,000 of cash in exchange for her 50% interest in the partnership. The value of her 50% interest is $75,000.
   a. How much gain or income will Craig recognize on his contribution of the land to the partnership? What is the character of any gain or income recognized?
   b. What basis will Craig take in his partnership interest?
   c. How much gain or income will Beth recognize on the formation of the partnership? What is the character of any gain or income recognized?
   d. What basis will Beth take in her partnership interest?
   e. Construct an opening balance sheet for the partnership reflecting the partnership's basis in the assets and the fair market value of these assets.
   f. Outline any planning opportunities that may minimize current taxation to any of the parties.

7. Continue with the facts presented in Problem 6. At the end of the first year, the partnership distributes the $50,000 of cash to Craig. No distribution is made to Beth.
   a. How does Craig treat the payment?
   b. How much income or gain would Craig recognize as a result of the payment?
   c. Under general tax rules, what basis would the partnership take in the land Craig contributed?

8. Describe the tax treatment of a proportionate nonliquidating distribution of cash, land, and inventory. How are the partner's basis in the property received and the partner's gain or loss on the distribution determined? What are the tax effects to the partnership?

Issue ID

9. The SueBart Partnership distributes the following assets to partner Bart:

   - $10,000 cash.
   - An account receivable with a $10,000 value and a $0 basis to the partnership.
   - A parcel of land with a $10,000 value and a $2,000 basis to the partnership.

   What issues must be considered in determining the tax treatment of the distribution?

10. On July 1 of the current year, the R&R Partnership was formed to operate a bed and breakfast inn. The partnership paid $3,000 in legal fees for drafting the partnership agreement, and $5,000 for accounting fees related to organizing the entity. It also paid $10,000 in syndication costs to locate and secure investments from limited partners. In addition, before opening the inn for business, the entity paid $15,500 for advertising and $36,000 in costs related to an open house just before the grand opening of the property. The partnership opened the inn for business on October 1.
    a. How are these expenses classified?
    b. How much may the partnership deduct in its initial year of operations?
    c. How are costs treated that are not deducted currently?
    d. What elections must the partnership make in its initial tax return?

11. Lisa and Lori are equal members of the Redbird Partnership. They are real estate investors who formed the partnership several years ago with equal cash contributions. Redbird then purchased a piece of land.

    On January 1 of the current year, to acquire a one-third interest in the entity, Lana contributed some land she had held for investment to the partnership. Lana purchased the land three years ago for $30,000; its fair market value at the contribution date was $40,000. No special allocation agreements were in effect before or after Lana was admitted to the partnership. The Redbird Partnership holds all land for investment.

    Immediately before Lana's property contribution, the balance sheet of the Redbird Partnership was as follows.

	Basis	FMV		Basis	FMV
Land	$5,000	$80,000	Lisa, capital	$2,500	$40,000
			Lori, capital	2,500	40,000
	$5,000	$80,000		$5,000	$80,000

    a. At the contribution date, what is Lana's basis in her interest in the Redbird Partnership?
    b. When does the partnership's holding period begin for the contributed land?
    c. On June 30 of the current year, the partnership sold the land contributed by Lana for $40,000. How much is the recognized gain or loss, and how is it allocated among the partners?
    d. Prepare a balance sheet reflecting basis and fair market value for the partnership immediately after the land sale.

12. Assume the same facts as in Problem 11, with the following exceptions.

    - Lana purchased the land three years ago for $50,000. Its fair market value was $40,000 when it was contributed to the partnership.
    - Redbird sold the land contributed by Lana for $34,000.

    a. How much is the recognized gain or loss, and how is it allocated among the partners?
    b. Prepare a balance sheet reflecting basis and fair market value for the partnership immediately after the land sale. Complete schedules that support the amount in each partner's capital account.

13. Carrie and Matt are equal partners in the accrual basis CM Partnership. At the beginning of the current year, Carrie's capital account has a balance of $60,000, and the partnership has recourse debts of $80,000 payable to unrelated parties. All partnership recourse debt is shared equally between the partners. The following information about CM's operations for the current year is obtained from the partnership's records.

Taxable income	$80,000
Interest income from City of Huntsville bond	5,000
§ 1231 gain	6,000
Long-term capital gain	500
Short-term capital loss	4,000

IRS penalty	$ 3,000
Charitable contribution to Red Cross	1,000
Cash distribution to Carrie	14,000
Payment of Carrie's medical expenses	2,000

Assume that year-end partnership debt payable to unrelated parties is $100,000.

a. If all transactions are reflected in her beginning capital and basis in the same manner, what is Carrie's basis in the partnership interest at the beginning of the year?
b. What is Carrie's basis in the partnership interest at the end of the current year?

14. Martin and Morgan formed the equal M&M Partnership on January 1. Martin contributed $25,000 cash, and land with a fair market value of $10,000 and an adjusted basis of $2,000. Morgan contributed equipment with a fair market value of $35,000 and an adjusted basis of $20,000. Morgan previously had used the equipment in his sole proprietorship. As to the partnership formation:
a. How much gain or loss will Martin, Morgan, and the partnership realize?
b. How much gain or loss will Martin, Morgan, and the partnership recognize?
c. What bases will Martin and Morgan take in their partnership interests?
d. What bases will M&M take in the assets it receives?
e. Are there any differences between inside and outside basis?
f. How will the partnership depreciate any assets it receives from the partners?

Decision Making
Communications

15. Your client, the Williams Institute of Technology (WIT), is a 60% partner in the Research Industries Partnership (RIP). WIT is located at 76 Bradford Lane, St. Paul, MN 55164. The controller, Jeanine West, has sent you the following note and a copy of WIT's 2005 Schedule K–1 from the partnership.

Excerpt from client's note
"RIP" expects its 2006 operations to include the following.

Net loss from operations	$200,000
Capital gain from sale of land	100,000

The land was contributed by DASH, the other partner, when its value was $260,000. The partnership sold the land for $300,000. The partnership used this cash to repay all the partnership debt and pay for research and development expenditures, which a tax partner in your firm has said RIP can deduct this year.

We want to be sure we can deduct our full share of this loss, but we do not believe we will have enough basis. We are a material participant in this partnership's activities.

Items Reported on the 2005 Schedule K–1	
WIT's share of partnership recourse liabilities	$90,000
WIT's ending capital account balance	30,000

Draft a letter to the controller that describes the following.

- WIT's allocation of partnership items.
- WIT's basis in the partnership interest following the allocation.
- Any limitations on loss deductions.
- Any recommendations you have that would allow WIT to claim the full amount of losses in 2006.

WIT's 2005 Schedule K–1 accurately reflects the information needed to compute its basis in the partnership interest. The research expenditures are fully deductible this year, as the partner said.

Your client has experience researching issues in the Internal Revenue Code, so you may use some citations. However, be sure that the letter is written in layperson's terms and that legal citations are minimized.

16. Lee, Brad, and Rick form the LBR Partnership on January 1 of the current year. In return for a 25% interest, Lee transfers property (basis of $15,000, fair market value of $17,500) subject to a nonrecourse liability of $10,000. The liability is assumed by the

partnership. Brad transfers property (basis of $16,000, fair market value of $7,500) for a 25% interest, and Rick transfers cash of $15,000 for the remaining 50% interest.

a. How much gain must Lee recognize on the transfer?
b. What is Lee's basis in his interest in the partnership?
c. How much loss may Brad recognize on the transfer?
d. What is Brad's basis in his interest in the partnership?
e. What is Rick's basis in his interest in the partnership?
f. What basis does the LBR Partnership take in the property transferred by Lee?
g. What is the partnership's basis in the property transferred by Brad?

17. Assume the same facts as in Problem 16, except that the property contributed by Lee has a fair market value of $27,500 and is subject to a nonrecourse mortgage of $20,000. *Extender*
a. What is Lee's basis in his partnership interest?
b. How much gain must Lee recognize on the transfer?
c. What is Brad's basis in his partnership interest?
d. What is Rick's basis in his partnership interest?
e. What basis does the LBR Partnership take in the property transferred by Lee?

18. Sam has operated a microbrewery (sole proprietorship) in southern Oregon for the past 15 years. The business has been highly profitable lately, and demand for the product will soon exceed the amount Sam can produce with his present facilities. Marcie, a long-time fan of the brewery, has offered to invest $1,500,000 for equipment to expand production. The assets and goodwill of the brewery are currently worth $1,000,000 (tax basis is only $200,000). Sam will continue to manage the business. He is not willing to own less than 50% of whatever arrangement they arrive at. What issues should Sam and Marcie address and document before finalizing their venture? *Issue ID*

19. The BCD Partnership plans to distribute cash of $20,000 to partner Brad at the end of the tax year. The partnership reported a loss for the year, and Brad's share of the loss is $10,000. Brad has a basis of $15,000 in the partnership interest, including his share of partnership liabilities. The partnership expects to report substantial income in future years. *Issue ID* *Decision Making*
a. What rules are used to calculate Brad's ending basis in his partnership interest?
b. How much income or loss will Brad report for the tax year?
c. Will any of the $10,000 be suspended?
d. Could any planning opportunities be used to minimize the tax ramifications of the distribution?

20. The Warbler Partnership was formed on July 1 of the current year and admitted Ross and Rachel as equal partners on that date. The partners contributed $100,000 of cash each to establish an apparel shop in the local mall. The partners spent July and August buying inventory, equipment, supplies, and advertising for their "Grand Opening" on September 1. The partnership will use the accrual method of accounting. The partnership incurred the following costs during its first year of operations.

- Purchased all assets of Jenny B. Apparel of New York, which was going out of business, including:

Trade name and logo	$30,000
Inventory	95,000
Shop fixtures, racks, shelves, etc.	25,000

- Other costs:

Additional inventory	$40,000
Legal fees to form partnership	3,000
Advertising for "Grand Opening"	10,000
Advertising after opening	6,000
Consulting fees for establishing accounting system	3,000
Rent, at $3,000 per month	18,000
Utilities, at $400 per month	2,400
Salaries to sales clerks	15,000
Payments to Ross and Rachel for services ($3,500 per month each for four months)	28,000
Tax return preparation expense	3,000

- Revenues during the year included the following.

Sales revenues	$200,000
Interest income on bank balances	1,500

- Inventory remaining at the end of the year was valued at $35,000 on a FIFO basis.

a. Determine how each of the above costs and revenues is treated by the partnership, and identify the period over which the costs can be deducted, if any.
b. Calculate the deduction for startup and organization costs.
c. Identify any elections the partnership should make on its initial tax return.

21. Four Lakes Partnership is owned by four sisters. Anne holds a 70% interest; each of the others owns 10%. Anne sells investment property to the partnership for its fair market value of $100,000. Her tax basis was $150,000.
    a. How much loss, if any, may Anne recognize?
    b. If the partnership later sells the property for $160,000, how much gain must it recognize?
    c. If Anne's basis in the investment property was $20,000 instead of $150,000, how much, if any, gain would she recognize on the sale, and how would it be characterized?

22. Comment on the validity of each of the following statements.
    a. Since a partnership is not a taxable entity, it is not required to file any type of tax return.
    b. Each partner can choose a different method of accounting and depreciation computation in determining the gross income from the entity.
    c. Generally, a transfer of appreciated property to a partnership results in recognized gain to the contributing partner at the time of the transfer.
    d. A partner can carry forward, for an unlimited period of time, the partner's share of any partnership operating losses that exceed the partner's basis in the entity, provided the partner retains an ownership interest in the partnership.
    e. When a partner renders services to the entity in exchange for an unrestricted interest, that partner does not recognize any gross income.
    f. Losses on sales between a partner and the partnership always are nondeductible.
    g. A partnership may choose a year that results in the least aggregate deferral of tax to the partners, unless the IRS requires the use of a natural business year.
    h. A partner's basis in a partnership interest includes that partner's share of partnership recourse and nonrecourse liabilities.
    i. Built-in loss related to nondepreciable property contributed to a partnership must be allocated to the contributing partner to the extent the loss is eventually recognized by the partnership.
    j. Property that was held as inventory by a contributing partner, but is a capital asset in the hands of the partnership, results in a capital gain if the partnership immediately sells the property.

23. Sonya is a 20% owner of Philadelphia Cheese Treats, Inc., a C corporation that was formed on February 1, 2006. She receives a $5,000 monthly salary from the corporation, and Cheese Treats generates $200,000 of taxable income (after the salary payment) for its tax year ending January 31, 2007.
    a. How do these activities affect Sonya's 2006 adjusted gross income?
    b. Assume, instead, that Cheese Treats is a partnership with a January 31 year-end and consider Sonya's salary to be a guaranteed payment. How do these activities affect Sonya's 2006 and 2007 adjusted gross income?

24. Ned, a 50% partner in the MN Partnership, is to receive a payment of $35,000 for services. He will also be allocated 50% of the partnership's profits or losses. After deducting the payment to Ned, the partnership has a loss of $25,000. Ned's basis in his partnership interest was $10,000 before these items.
    a. How much, if any, of the $25,000 partnership loss is allocated to Ned?
    b. What is the net income from the partnership that Ned must report on his Federal income tax return?
    c. What is Ned's basis in his partnership interest following the guaranteed payment and loss allocation?

25. As of January 1 of last year, the outside basis and at-risk limitation of Rashad's 25% interest in the RST Partnership were $24,000. Rashad and the partnership use the calendar year for tax purposes. The partnership incurred an operating loss of $100,000 for last year and a profit of $8,000 for the current year. Rashad is a material participant in the partnership.
   a. How much loss, if any, may Rashad recognize for last year?
   b. How much net reportable income must Rashad recognize for the current year?
   c. What is Rashad's basis in the partnership interest as of January 1 of the current year?
   d. What is Rashad's basis in the partnership interest as of January 1 of the next year?
   e. What year-end tax planning would you suggest to ensure that Rashad can deduct his share of the partnership losses?

26. Peggy and Cindy, parent and child, operate a local apparel shop as a partnership. The PC Partnership earned a profit of $80,000 in the current year. Cindy's equal partnership interest was acquired by gift from Peggy. Assume that capital is a material income-producing factor and that Peggy manages the day-to-day operations of the shop without any help from Cindy. Reasonable compensation for Peggy's services is $30,000. *Extender*
   a. How much of the partnership income is allocated to Peggy?
   b. What is the maximum amount of partnership income that can be allocated to Cindy?
   c. Assuming that Cindy is five years old, has no other income, and is claimed as a dependent by Peggy, how is Cindy's income from the partnership taxed?

27. Melinda, Gabe, and Pat each contributed $10,000 cash to start up the MGP General Partnership on January 1 this year. Each partner shares equally in partnership income, losses, deductions, gains, and credits. At the end of the year, the partnership balance sheet reads as follows. *Extender*

	Basis	FMV		Basis	FMV
Assets	$60,000	$75,000	Recourse debt	$30,000	$30,000
			Melinda, capital	14,000	19,000
			Gabe, capital	14,000	19,000
			Pat, capital	2,000	7,000
				$60,000	$75,000

How will the basis computations of the partners' interests be affected by the partnership debt?

28. The Cardinal Partnership leases apartments to individuals. Chris is a 15% partner in Cardinal, and her share of this year's operating losses totals $70,000. Before accounting for this loss, Chris reported the following amounts. *Extender* *Communications*

Share of partnership recourse liabilities	$10,000
Share of partnership nonrecourse liabilities	6,000
Capital account in Cardinal	40,000

Chris also is a partner in the Bluebird Partnership, which earns income from equipment rentals of more than 30 days. Chris's share of Bluebird's income this year is $23,000.

Chris performs substantial services for Bluebird and spends several hundred hours a year working for Cardinal. Chris's AGI before accounting for the partnership investments totals $100,000.

Your manager has asked you to determine how much of the Cardinal loss that Chris can deduct this year. Draft a memo to the tax research file describing the various loss limitations that apply to Chris.

COMPREHENSIVE TAX RETURN PROBLEM

Tax Return Problem

TurboTax

29. Craig Howard (623–98–0123), Josh Edwards (410–63–4297), and Dana Prosky (896–49–1235) are equal partners in TDP—the "Tile Doctors Partnership"—a general partnership engaged in residential tile installation in Baton Rouge, Louisiana. TDP's Federal ID number is 42–1234598. The partnership uses the accrual method of accounting and the calendar year for reporting purposes. It began business operations on October 15, 2003. Its current address is 5917 La Rue, Baton Rouge, LA 70825. The 2005 income statement for the partnership reflected net income of $161,520. The following information was taken from the partnership's financial statements for the current year.

Receipts	
Sales revenues	$740,925
Qualified dividend income	2,700
Long-term capital gain	1,275
Long-term capital loss	(300)
Total revenues	$744,600
Cash payments related to cost of goods sold	
Materials purchases	$162,250
Direct job costs	26,450
Additional § 263A costs	2,950
Contract labor	278,300
Total cash payments—work-in-progress	$469,950
Other cash disbursements (net of additional § 263A costs)	
Rent	$ 18,400
Utilities	11,580
Administrative services	10,680
Contribution to Red Cross	1,500
Meals and entertainment, subject to 50% disallowance	1,200
Guaranteed payment, Dana Prosky, managing partner	30,000
Office expense	2,820
Legal fees	3,500
Janitorial services	2,400
Business interest on operating line of credit	9,500
Repairs	1,420
Payment of beginning accounts payable	8,200
Tile cutting equipment	9,000
Total other cash disbursements	$110,200
Noncash expenses	
Amortization	$ 600
Accrual of ending accounts payable	–0–
Depreciation on equipment owned previously (reported on Schedule A)	16,620

The beginning and ending balance sheets for the partnership were as follows for 2005.

	Beginning	Ending
Cash	$ 28,730	$ 38,180
Inventory (jobs in progress)	36,850	42,940
Long-term investments	46,000	42,000
Equipment	95,000	104,000
Accumulated depreciation	(26,660)	(52,280)
Organization fees	3,000	3,000
Accumulated amortization	(750)	(1,350)
Total assets	$182,170	$176,490

	Beginning	Ending
Accounts payable	$ 8,200	$ -0-
Recourse operating line of credit (note payable in less than one year)	75,000	60,000
Capital, Howard	32,990	38,830
Capital, Edwards	32,990	38,830
Capital, Prosky	32,990	38,830
Total liabilities and capital	$182,170	$176,490

The partnership uses the lower of cost or market method for valuing inventory. TDP is subject to § 263A; for simplicity, assume § 263A costs are reflected in the same manner for book and tax purposes. TDP did not change its inventory accounting method during the year. There were no write-downs of inventory items, and TDP does not use the LIFO method.

The partnership claimed $16,620 of depreciation expense for both tax and financial accounting purposes; all $16,620 should be reported on Schedule A. None of the depreciation creates a tax preference. The partnership will claim a § 179 deduction for the tile cutting equipment purchased during the year.

None of the long-term capital gain or loss is taxable at a 28% rate. All line-of-credit borrowings were used exclusively for business operations; consequently, none of the interest expense is considered investment interest expense.

In order to avoid the cost and compliance burden of being an employer, the partnership uses contract labor. All of its artisans are properly classified as independent contractors, and the partnership retains several support organizations to provide accounting and janitorial services.

No guaranteed payments were paid to partners other than Dana Prosky. Instead, each partner (including Prosky) withdrew $4,000 per month as a distribution (draw) of operating profits. There were no distributions of noncash property.

All debts are recourse debt. The partners share equally in all partnership liabilities, since all initial contributions and all ongoing allocations and distributions are pro rata. All partners are considered "active" for purposes of the passive loss rules.

None of the partners sold any portion of their interests in the partnership during 2005. The partnership's operations are entirely restricted to southern Louisiana. All partners are U.S. citizens. The partnership had no foreign operations, no foreign bank accounts, and no ownership of any foreign trusts or other partnerships. The partnership is not publicly traded and is not a statutory tax shelter. No Forms 8865 are required to be attached to the return.

The IRS's business code for "tile contractors" is 238340. The partnership is not subject to the consolidated audit procedures and does not have a tax matters partner. The partnership files its tax return in Ogden, Utah. Partner Dana Prosky lives at 1423 N. Louisiana Boulevard, Baton Rouge, LA 70823. The capital account reconciliation on Schedule K–1 is prepared according to GAAP, which, in this case, corresponds to the tax basis.

a. Prepare pages 1–4 of Form 1065 for TDP. Do not prepare Form 4562. Leave any items blank where insufficient information has been provided. Prepare supporting schedules as necessary if adequate information is provided. (You will not be able to prepare a schedule for additional § 263A costs.) *Hint:* Prepare Schedule A first to determine cost of goods sold.
b. Prepare Schedule K–1 for partner Dana Prosky.

BRIDGE *Discipline*

1. Jim Dunn, Amy Lauersen, and Tony Packard have agreed to form a partnership. In return for a 30% capital interest, Dunn transferred machinery (basis $268,000, fair market value $400,000) subject to a liability of $100,000. The liability was assumed by the partnership. Lauersen transferred land (basis $450,000, fair market value $300,000) for a 30% capital interest. Packard transferred cash of $400,000 for the remaining 40% interest. Compute the initial values of Dunn's basis and capital account.

RESEARCH PROBLEMS

THOMSON RIA

Note: Solutions to Research Problems can be prepared by using the **RIA Checkpoint® Student Edition** online research product, which is available to accompany this text. It is also possible to prepare solutions to the Research Problems by using tax research materials found in a standard tax library.

Decision Making

Communications

Research Problem 1. Your clients, Mark Henderson and John Burton, each contributed $10,000 cash to form the Realty Management Partnership, a limited partnership. Mark is the general partner, and John is the limited partner. The partnership used the $20,000 cash to make a down payment on a building. The rest of the building's $200,000 purchase price was financed with an interest-only nonrecourse loan of $180,000, which was obtained from an independent third-party bank. The partnership allocates all partnership items equally between the partners except for the MACRS deductions and building maintenance, which are allocated 70% to John and 30% to Mark. The partnership definitely wishes to satisfy the "economic effect" requirements of Reg. §§ 1.704–1 and 1.704–2 and will reallocate MACRS, if necessary, to satisfy the requirements of the Regulations.

Under the partnership agreement, liquidation distributions will be paid in proportion to the partners' positive capital account balances. Capital accounts are maintained as required in the Regulations. Mark has an unlimited obligation to restore his capital account while John is subject to a qualified income offset provision.

All partnership items, except for MACRS, net to zero throughout the first three years of the partnership operations. Each year's MACRS deduction is $10,000 (to simplify the calculations).

Draft a letter to the partnership evaluating the allocation of MACRS in each of the three years. The partnership's address is 53 East Marsh Ave., Smyrna, GA 30082. Do not address the "substantial" test.

Decision Making

Communications

Research Problem 2. Harrison has considerable experience as a leasing agent for residential rental properties. He is disappointed, though, that his salary with his present employer does not reflect the effort he puts forth.

Alameda Properties has offered Harrison a position handling leasing activities for a new limited partnership that is being formed to construct and manage three apartment complexes in southern California. Alameda is willing to hire Harrison for two years to lease the properties, but is unable to pay the $100,000 salary Harrison requires without impairing its ability to pay necessary cash distributions to the limited partners.

Alameda is willing to pay a $60,000 salary for two years, increasing to a market salary thereafter. Alameda is also willing to allow Harrison to purchase a 10% interest in the partnership, but Harrison cannot afford the required $20,000 capital contribution.

The partnership expects to distribute cash flows from operations of approximately $200,000 per year, for an estimated seven-year holding period (taxable income will be much lower because depreciation and interest deductions will be greater than mortgage payments).

Harrison and Alameda Properties have approached you for assistance in structuring a mutually satisfactory arrangement. You are aware that a partner can be awarded an interest in the future profits of a partnership. You have learned from a colleague that in 2005, the IRS issued a Notice and Proposed Regulations that outline procedures for structuring an interest to avoid current taxation of the expected future profits. You are also aware of a 2001 Notice and a 1993 Revenue Procedure that provide additional guidance in this area.

You have suggested that Alameda could grant Harrison a 10% interest in Alameda's future profits. In a memo to the tax research file, address the following points.

a. Until the Regulations are finalized, the IRS indicates that Rev.Proc. 93–27 remains the authority for determining taxation of a profits interest received in exchange for services. What requirements must the profits interest meet to be nontaxable under this rule?

b. Under Notice 2005–43, what actions must the partnership take to ensure that the profits interest is nontaxable? What is the tax result for receipt of a nonforfeitable future profits interest?

c. Alameda has an interest in making sure that Harrison remains with the company and wants to attach a three-year forfeiture clause to the profits interest. In other words, if Harrison leaves the company within three years, his profits interest is terminated. What additional considerations arise under Notice 2005–43 if the profits interest is not fully vested?

d. What are the advantages and disadvantages of this structure to each party?

Research Problem 3. Cameron, an individual, and Totco, Inc., a domestic C corporation, form CT, a California LLC. The new LLC will produce a product that Cameron has recently developed and patented. Cameron and Totco, Inc., each take a 50% capital and profits interest in the LLC. Cameron is a calendar year taxpayer, while Totco uses a fiscal year ending June 30. The LLC does not have a "natural business year" and elects to be taxed as a partnership.

a. Determine the taxable year of the LLC under existing Code and Regulations.

b. Two years after formation of the LLC, Cameron sells half of his interest (25%) to Totco, Inc. Can the LLC retain the taxable year determined in (a)?

Research Problem 4. Fred and Grady have formed the FG Partnership as a retail establishment to sell antique household furnishings. Fred is the general partner, and Grady is the limited partner. Both partners contribute $15,000 to form the partnership. The partnership uses the $30,000 contributed by the partners and a recourse loan of $100,000 (obtained from an unrelated third-party lender) to acquire $130,000 of initial inventory.

The partners believe they will have extensive losses in the first year due to advertising and initial cash-flow requirements. Fred and Grady have agreed to share losses equally. To make sure the losses can be allocated to both partners, they have included a provision in the partnership agreement requiring each partner to restore any deficit balance in his partnership capital account upon liquidation of the partnership.

Fred was also willing to include a provision that requires him to make up any deficit balance within 90 days of liquidation of the partnership. As a limited partner, Grady argued that he should not be subject to such a time requirement. The partners compromised and included a provision that requires Grady to restore a deficit balance in his capital account within two years of liquidation of the partnership. No interest will be owed on the deferred restoration payment.

Determine whether FG can allocate the $100,000 recourse debt equally to the two partners, to ensure they will be able to deduct their respective shares of partnership losses.

Use the tax resources of the Internet to address the following questions. Do not restrict your search to the World Wide Web, but include a review of newsgroups and general reference materials, practitioner sites and resources, primary sources of the tax law, chat rooms and discussion groups, and other opportunities.

Internet *Activity*

Research Problem 5. Find a solicitation for funds posted by investors in an Internet start-up company. Summarize the partner's rights to profits and any tax implications discussed in the prospectus, in a PowerPoint presentation to your class.

Communications

Research Problem 6. Find a discussion group that concentrates on the taxation of partners and partnerships. Post to the group a message defining the terms "inside and outside basis" and illustrating why the distinction between them is important. Respond to any replies you receive. Print your message and one or two of the replies.

Research Problem 7. Determine the statutory tax treatment in your state of a one-member LLC. Write an e-mail message to your professor, comparing this rule with Federal tax law.

Communications

Research Problem 8. Graph the increases in the numbers of LLCs and LLPs filing Federal tax returns, for five-year periods beginning with 1970. Explain any trends in the data that you identify. Send your report as an e-mail to your instructor.

Communications

http://wft.swlearning.com

CHAPTER 12

S Corporations

LEARNING OBJECTIVES

After completing Chapter 12, you should be able to:

LO.1

Explain the tax effects associated with S corporation status.

LO.2

Identify corporations that qualify for the S election.

LO.3

Understand how to make and terminate an S election.

LO.4

Compute nonseparately stated income and allocate income, deductions, and credits to shareholders.

LO.5

Understand how distributions to S corporation shareholders are taxed.

LO.6

Calculate a shareholder's basis in S corporation stock.

LO.7

Explain the tax effects of losses on S shareholders.

LO.8

Compute the entity-level taxes on S corporations.

OUTLINE

TAX *Talk*

In levying taxes and in shearing sheep it is well to stop when you get down to the skin.

—Austin O'Malley

LO.1

Explain the tax effects associated with S corporation status.

An individual establishing a business has a number of choices as to the form of business entity under which to operate. Chapters 9 and 10 outline many of the rules, advantages, and disadvantages of operating as a regular C corporation. Chapter 11 discusses the partnership entity, as well as the limited liability company (LLC) and limited liability partnership (LLP) forms.

Another alternative, the **S corporation**, provides many of the benefits of partnership taxation and at the same time gives the owners limited liability protection from creditors. The S corporation rules, which are contained in **Subchapter S** of the Internal Revenue Code (§§ 1361–1379), were enacted to minimize the role of tax considerations in the entity choice that businesspeople face. Thus, S status combines the legal environment of C corporations with taxation similar to that applying to partnerships. S corporation status is obtained through an election by a *qualifying* corporation with the consent of its shareholders.

S corporations are treated as corporations under state law. They are recognized as separate legal entities and generally provide shareholders with the same liability protection afforded by C corporations. Some states (such as Michigan) treat S corporations as C corporations for tax purposes, resulting in a state corporate income or franchise tax liability. For Federal income tax purposes, however, taxation of S corporations resembles that of partnerships. As with partnerships, the income, deductions, and tax credits of an S corporation flow through to shareholders annually, regardless of whether distributions are made. Thus, income generally is taxed at the shareholder level and not at the corporate level. Distributions made to S shareholders by the corporation are tax-free to the extent that the distributed earnings were previously taxed.

Although the tax treatment of S corporations and partnerships is similar, it is not identical. For example, liabilities affect an owner's basis differently, and S corporations may incur a tax liability at the corporate level. In addition, a variety of C corporation provisions apply to S corporations. For example, the liquidation of C and S corporations is taxed in the same way. As a rule, where the S corporation provisions are silent, C corporation rules apply.

An Overview of S Corporations

Since the inception of S corporations in 1958, their popularity has waxed and waned with changes in the tax law. Before the Tax Reform Act of 1986, their ranks

TAX FACT

The Business of S Corporations

S corporations file over 3 million tax returns every year, concentrated in the service and merchandising industries.

S Corporation Returns Filed (000s), 2002 Tax Year

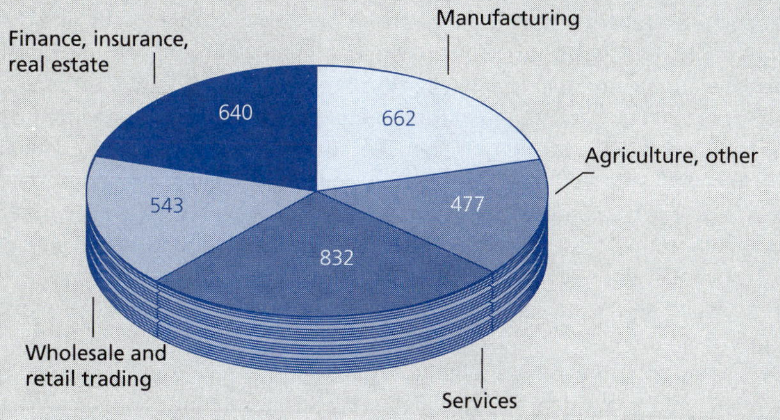

grew slowly. In contrast, in the two years following the 1986 law change, the number of S corporations increased by 52 percent. Now, over 3 million of the country's 5.5 million corporations have elected S status. The IRS projects that S corporations and limited liability companies (LLCs) will be the most-chosen forms of business entity for the next decade.

EXAMPLE 1

An S corporation earns $300,000, and all after-tax income is distributed currently. The marginal individual tax rate applicable to its shareholders is 35% for ordinary income and 15% for dividend income. The marginal corporate tax rate is 34%. The entity's available after-tax earnings, compared with those of a similar C corporation, are computed below.

	C Corporation	S Corporation
Earnings	$ 300,000	$ 300,000
Less: Corporate income tax	(102,000)	(–0–)
Amount available for distribution	$ 198,000	$ 300,000
Less: Income tax at owner level	(29,700)*	(105,000)**
Available after-tax earnings	$ 168,300	$ 195,000

*$198,000 × 15% dividend income tax rate.

**$300,000 × 35% ordinary income tax rate.

The S corporation generates an extra $26,700 of after-tax earnings ($195,000 − $168,300), when compared with a similar C corporation. The C corporation might be able to reduce this disadvantage, however, by paying out its earnings as compensation, rents, or interest to its owners. In addition, tax at the owner level can also be deferred or avoided by not distributing after-tax earnings. ■

EXAMPLE 2

A new corporation elects S status and incurs a net operating loss (NOL) of $300,000. The shareholders may use their proportionate shares of the NOL to offset other taxable income in the current year, providing an immediate tax savings. In contrast, a newly formed C corporation is required to carry the NOL forward for up to 20 years and receives no tax benefit in

BRIDGE *Discipline*

Bridge to Business Law

An S corporation is a corporation for all purposes other than its Federal and state income tax law treatment. The entity registers as a corporation with the secretary of state of the state of its incorporation. It issues shares and may hold some treasury stock. Dealings in its own stock are not taxable to the S corporation.

The corporation itself is attractive as a form of business ownership because it offers limited liability to all shareholders from the claims of customers, employees, and others. This is not the case for any type of partnership, where there always is at least one general partner bearing the ultimate personal liability for the operations of the entity. Forming an entity as an S corporation facilitates the raising of capital for the business, as an infinite number of shares can be divided in any way imaginable, so as to pass income and deductions, gains, losses, and credits through to the owners, assuming that the fairly generous "type of shareholder" requirements continue to be met.

An S corporation must comply with all licensing and registration requirements of its home state under the rules applicable to corporate entities. Some states levy privilege taxes on the right to do business in the corporate form, and the S corporation typically is not exempted from this tax.

Because an S corporation is a separate legal entity from its owners, shareholders can be treated as employees and receive qualified retirement and fringe benefits under the Code, as well as unemployment and worker's compensation protection through the corporation. Some limitations apply to the deductibility of fringe benefits, though.

The tax fiction of the S corporation is attractive to investors, as over one-half of all U.S. corporations have an S election in effect.

the current year. Hence, an S corporation can accelerate the use of NOL deductions and thereby provide a greater present value for the tax savings generated by the loss. ■

Limited liability companies can provide tax results similar to those of an S corporation, while avoiding some of the key restrictions that are imposed on S corporations and their shareholders. However, recent changes to a number of S corporation election and operating rules provide greater flexibility in using S corporations as a viable alternative to LLCs.

PLANNING *Strategies*

WHEN TO ELECT S CORPORATION STATUS

★ **Framework Focus: Deductions**

Strategy ★ Maximize Deductible Amounts.

★ **Framework Focus: Tax Rate**

Strategy ★ Shift Net Income from High-Bracket Taxpayers to Low-Bracket Taxpayers.
★ Shift Net Income from High-Tax Jurisdictions to Low-Tax Jurisdictions.

The planner begins by determining whether an S election is appropriate for the entity. The following factors should be considered.

- If shareholders are subject to high marginal rates relative to C corporation rates, it may be desirable to avoid S corporation status. Although a C corporation may be subject to double taxation, this result can be mitigated by paying compensation to employee-shareholders. Likewise, profits of the corporation may be taken out by the shareholders through other compensation arrangements, as interest, or as rent income. Corporate profits can be transferred to shareholders as capital gain income through capital structure changes, such as stock redemptions, liquidations, or sales of stock to others. Alternatively, profits may be paid out as dividends at a 15 percent tax rate. Any distribution of profits or sale of stock can be deferred to a later year, thereby reducing the present value of shareholder taxes. Finally, potential shareholder-level tax on corporate profits can be eliminated by a step-up in the basis of the stock upon the shareholder's death.

- S corporations status allows shareholders to realize tax benefits from corporate losses immediately—an important consideration in new business enterprises where operating losses are common. Thus, if corporate NOLs are anticipated and there is unlikely to be corporate income over the near term to offset with the NOLs, S corporation status is advisable. However, the deductibility of the losses to shareholders must also be considered. The at-risk and passive loss limitations (refer to Chapter 6) apply to losses generated by an S corporation. In addition, as discussed later in this chapter, shareholders may not deduct losses in excess of the tax basis in their S corporation stock. Together with the time value of money considerations of deferring any loss deduction, these limits may significantly reduce the benefits of an S corporation election in a loss setting.
- If the entity electing S status is currently a C corporation, NOL carryovers from prior years (refer to Chapter 6) generally cannot be used in an S corporation year. Even worse, S corporation years use up the 20-year carryover period.
- Distributions of earnings from C corporations are usually taxed using the preferential 15 percent tax rate. In contrast, because S corporations are flow-through entities, all deduction and income items retain any special tax characteristics when they are reported on shareholders' returns. Whether this consideration favors S status depends upon the character of income and deductions of the S corporation.
- Because S corporations are flow-through entities, separately-stated items retain their tax characteristics on the shareholders' returns. For instance, it may be an advantage to receive the flow-through of passive income, or the qualified production activities deduction, on the shareholder's tax return, making the S election more attractive.
- State and local tax laws also should be considered when making the S corporation election. Although an S corporation usually escapes Federal income tax, it may not be immune from all state and local income taxes.

Qualifying for S Corporation Status

LO.2

Identify corporations that qualify for the S election.

Definition of a Small Business Corporation

To achieve S corporation status, a corporation must *first* qualify as a **small business corporation**. A small business corporation:

- Is a domestic corporation (incorporated and organized in the United States).
- Is eligible to elect S corporation status.
- Issues only one class of stock.
- Is limited to a maximum of 100 shareholders.
- Has only individuals, estates, and certain trusts and exempt organizations as shareholders.
- Has no nonresident alien shareholders.

Unlike other small business provisions in the tax law (e.g., § 1244), no maximum or minimum dollar sales or capitalization restrictions apply to S corporations.

Ineligible Corporations. S status is not permitted for foreign corporations, certain banks, or insurance companies. S corporations are permitted to have wholly owned C and S corporation subsidiaries.[1]

[1]Other eligibility rules exist. § 1361(b).

One Class of Stock. A small business corporation may have only one class of stock issued and outstanding.[2] This restriction permits differences in voting rights, but not differences in distribution or liquidation rights.[3] Thus, two classes of common stock that are identical except that one class is voting and the other is nonvoting would be treated as a single class of stock for small business corporation purposes. In contrast, voting common stock and voting preferred stock (with a preference on dividends) would be treated as two classes of stock. Authorized and unissued stock or treasury stock of another class does not disqualify the corporation. Likewise, unexercised stock options, phantom stock, stock appreciation rights, warrants, and convertible debentures usually do not constitute a second class of stock.[4]

DIGGING DEEPER 1

Find more information on this topic at our Web site: ***http://wft-entities.swlearning.com.***

Although the one-class-of-stock requirement seems straightforward, it is possible for debt to be reclassified as stock, resulting in an unexpected loss of S corporation status.[5] To mitigate concern over possible reclassification of debt as a second class of stock, the law provides a set of *safe harbor* provisions. Neither straight debt[6] nor short-term advances[7] constitute a second class of stock.

DIGGING DEEPER 2

Find more information on this topic at our Web site: ***http://wft-entities.swlearning.com.***

Number of Shareholders. A small business corporation is limited to 100 shareholders. If shares of stock are owned jointly by two individuals, they will generally be treated as separate shareholders. However, family members (ancestors, descendants, spouses, and former spouses) of the investor can elect to be counted as one shareholder for purposes of determining the number of shareholders.[8]

EXAMPLE 3

Fred and Wilma (husband and wife) jointly own 10 shares in Oriole, Inc., an S corporation, with the remaining 90 shares outstanding owned by 99 other shareholders. Fred and Wilma are divorced. Both before and after the divorce, the 100-shareholder limit is met, and Oriole can qualify as a small business corporation. ■

Type of Shareholder Limitation. Small business corporation shareholders may be individuals, estates, or certain trusts and exempt organizations.[9] This limitation prevents partnerships, corporations, LLCs, LLPs, and IRAs from owning S corporation stock. Without this rule, partnerships and corporate shareholders could easily circumvent the 100-shareholder limitation.

EXAMPLE 4

Paul and 200 other individuals wish to form an S corporation. Paul reasons that if the group forms a partnership, the partnership can then form an S corporation and act as a single shareholder, thereby avoiding the 100-shareholder rule. Paul's plan will not work, because partnerships cannot own stock in an S corporation. ■

[2] § 1361(b)(1)(D).
[3] § 1361(c)(4).
[4] Reg. § 1.1361–1(l)(2).
[5] Refer to the discussion of debt-versus-equity classification in Chapter 9.
[6] § 1361(c)(5)(A).
[7] Reg. § 1.1361–1(l)(4).
[8] § 1361(c)(1). Narrower rules applied for tax years prior to 2005.
[9] § 1361(b)(1)(B).

PLANNING *Strategies*

BEATING THE 100-SHAREHOLDER LIMIT

★ **Framework Focus: Tax Rate**

Strategy ★ Avoid Double Taxation.

Although partnerships and corporations cannot own small business corporation stock, S corporations themselves can be partners in a partnership or shareholders in a corporation. In this way, the 100-shareholder requirement can be bypassed in a limited sense. For example, if two S corporations, each with 80 shareholders, form a partnership, then the shareholders of both corporations can enjoy the limited liability conferred by S corporation status and a single level of tax on the resulting profits.

Nonresident Aliens. Nonresident aliens cannot own stock in a small business corporation.[10] Thus, individuals who are not U.S. citizens *must live in the United States* to own S corporation stock. Shareholders with nonresident alien spouses in community property states[11] cannot own S corporation stock because the nonresident alien spouse is treated as owning half of the stock.[12] Similarly, if a resident alien shareholder moves outside the United States, the S election is terminated.

Making the Election

LO.3

Understand how to make and terminate an S election.

To become an S corporation, the entity must file a valid election with the IRS. The election is made on Form 2553. For the election to be valid, it must be filed on a timely basis and all shareholders must consent. For S corporation status to apply in the current tax year, the election must be filed either in the previous year or on or before the fifteenth day of the third month of the current year.[13]

EXAMPLE 5

In 2006, a calendar year C corporation decides to become an S corporation beginning January 1, 2007. The S corporation election can be made at any time in 2006 or by March 15, 2007. An election after March 15, 2007, will not be effective until the 2008 tax year. ■

Even if the 2½-month deadline is met, a current election is not valid unless the corporation qualifies as a small business corporation for the *entire* tax year. Otherwise, the election will be effective for the following tax year. Late current-year elections, after the 2½-month deadline, may be considered timely if there is reasonable cause for the late filing.

A corporation that does not yet exist cannot make an S corporation election.[14] Thus, for new corporations, a premature election may not be effective. A new corporation's 2½-month election period begins at the earliest occurrence of any of the following events.

- When the corporation has shareholders.
- When it acquires assets.
- When it begins doing business.[15]

[10] § 1362(b)(1)(C).

[11] Assets acquired by a married couple are generally considered community property in these states: Alaska (by election), Arizona, California, Idaho, Louisiana, Nevada, New Mexico, Texas, Washington, and Wisconsin.

[12] See *Ward v. U.S.*, 81–2 USTC ¶9674, 48 AFTR2d 81–5942, 661 F.2d 226 (Ct.Cls., 1981), where the court found that the stock was owned as community property. Since the taxpayer-shareholder (a U.S. citizen) was married to a citizen and resident of Mexico, the nonresident alien prohibition was violated. If the taxpayer-shareholder had held the stock as separate property, the S election would have been valid.

[13] § 1362(b).

[14] See, for example, *T.H. Campbell & Bros., Inc.*, 34 TCM 695, T.C.Memo. 1975–149; Ltr.Rul. 8807070.

[15] Reg. § 1.1372–2(b)(1). Also see, for example, *Nick A. Artukovich*, 61 T.C. 100 (1973).

Shareholder Consent

A qualifying election requires the consent of all of the corporation's shareholders.[16] Consent must be in writing, and it must generally be filed by the election deadline. However, although no statutory authority exists for obtaining an extension of time for filing an S election (Form 2553), a shareholder may receive an extension of time to file a consent. Both husband and wife must consent if they own their stock jointly (as joint tenants, tenants in common, tenants by the entirety, or community property).[17]

EXAMPLE 6

Vern and Yvonne decide to convert their C corporation into a calendar year S corporation for 2006. At the end of February 2006 (before the election is filed), Yvonne travels to Ukraine and forgets to sign a consent to the election. Yvonne will not return to the United States until June and cannot be reached by fax or e-mail. Vern files the S election on Form 2553 and also requests an extension of time to file Yvonne's consent to the election. Vern indicates that there is a reasonable cause for the extension: a shareholder is out of the country. Since the government's interest is not jeopardized, the IRS probably will grant Yvonne an extension of time to file the consent. Vern must file the election on Form 2553 on or before March 15, 2006, for the election to be effective for the 2006 calendar year. ■

PLANNING *Strategies*

MAKING A PROPER ELECTION

★ **Framework Focus: Tax Rate**

Strategy ★ Avoid Double Taxation.

- Because S corporation status is *elected*, strict compliance with the requirements is demanded by both the IRS and the courts. Any failure to meet a condition in the law may lead to loss of the S election and raise the specter of double tax.
- Make sure all shareholders consent. If any doubt exists concerning the shareholder status of an individual, it would be wise to request that he or she sign a consent anyway.[18] Missing consents are fatal to the election; the same cannot be said for too many consents.
- Be sure that the election is timely and properly filed. Either deliver the election to an IRS office in person, or send it by certified or registered mail or via a major overnight delivery service. The date used to determine timeliness is the postmark date, not the date the IRS receives the election.

Loss of the Election

An S election remains in force until it is revoked or lost. Election or consent forms are not required for future years. However, an S election can terminate if any of the following occurs.[19]

- Shareholders owning a majority of shares (voting and nonvoting) voluntarily revoke the election.
- A new shareholder owning more than one-half of the stock affirmatively refuses to consent to the election.
- The corporation no longer qualifies as a small business corporation.
- The corporation does not meet the passive investment income limitation.

[16] § 1362(a)(2).

[17] Rev.Rul. 60–183, 1960–1 C.B. 625; *William Pestcoe*, 40 T.C. 195 (1963); Reg. § 1.1362–6(b)(3)(iii). This rule likely applies to all family members electing to be treated as one shareholder.

[18] See *William B. Wilson*, 34 TCM 463, T.C.Memo. 1975–92.

[19] § 1362(d).

TAX *in the News* **THE IRS LAUNCHES AN S CORPORATION RESEARCH PROGRAM**

In August 2005, the IRS announced a plan to study S corporations' reporting compliance. The National Research Program will audit 5,000 randomly selected S corporation tax returns for 2003 and 2004 (an insignificant number considering that more than 3 million Forms 1120S are filed each year). The IRS last examined S corporation compliance in 1984.

Benson Goldstein, technical manager for the AICPA Tax Division, says that "recent research points to S corporations as a significant source of noncompliance, particularly among high-income individuals." But Tom Ochsenschlager, vice president of taxation for the AICPA, points out that "a lot of the errors made are errors, not malfeasance."

Voluntary Revocation. A **voluntary revocation** of the S election requires the consent of shareholders owning a majority of shares on the day that the revocation is to be made.[20] A revocation filed up to and including the fifteenth day of the third month of the tax year is effective for the entire tax year, unless a later date is specified. Similarly, unless an effective date is specified, revocation made after the first 2½ months of the current tax year is effective for the following tax year.

EXAMPLE 7

The shareholders of Petunia Corporation, a calendar year S corporation, voluntarily revoke the S election on January 5, 2006. They do not specify a future effective date in the revocation. Assuming the revocation is properly executed and timely filed, Petunia will be a C corporation for the entire 2006 tax year. If the revocation is not made until June 2006, Petunia remains an S corporation in 2006 and becomes a C corporation at the beginning of 2007. ■

A corporation can revoke its S status *prospectively* by specifying a future date when the revocation is to be effective. A revocation that designates a future effective date splits the corporation's tax year into a short S corporation year and a short C corporation year. The day on which the revocation occurs is treated as the first day of the C corporation year. The corporation allocates income or loss for the entire year on a pro rata basis, based on the number of days in each short year.

EXAMPLE 8

Assume the same facts as in the preceding example, except that Petunia designates July 1, 2006, as the revocation date. Accordingly, June 30, 2006, is the last day of the S corporation's tax year. The C corporation's tax year runs from July 1, 2006, to December 31, 2006. Income or loss for the 12-month period is allocated between the two short years (i.e., 184/365 to the C corporation year). ■

Rather than using pro rata allocation, the corporation can elect to compute the actual income or loss attributable to the two short years. This election requires the consent of everyone who was a shareholder at any time during the S corporation's short year and everyone who owns stock on the first day of the C corporation's year.[21]

Loss of Small Business Corporation Status. If an S corporation fails to qualify as a small business corporation at any time after the election has become effective, its status as an S corporation ends. The termination occurs on the day that the corporation ceases to be a small business corporation.[22] Thus, if the corporation ever has more than 100 shareholders, a second class of stock, or a nonqualifying shareholder, or otherwise fails to meet the definition of a small business corporation, the S election is terminated immediately.

[20] § 1362(d)(1)(B).

[21] § 1362(e)(3).

[22] § 1362(d)(2)(B).

EXAMPLE 9

Peony Corporation has been a calendar year S corporation for three years. On August 13, 2006, one of its 100 shareholders sells *some* of her stock to an outsider. Peony now has 101 shareholders, and it ceases to be a small business corporation. Peony is an S corporation through August 12, 2006, and a C corporation from August 13 to December 31, 2006. ■

Passive Investment Income Limitation. The Code provides a **passive investment income (PII)** limitation for some S corporations that were previously C corporations or for S corporations that have merged with C corporations. If an S corporation has C corporation E & P and passive income in excess of 25 percent of its gross receipts for three consecutive taxable years, the S election is terminated as of the beginning of the fourth year.[23]

EXAMPLE 10

For 2003, 2004, and 2005, Chrysanthemum Corporation, a calendar year S corporation, derived passive income in excess of 25% of its gross receipts. If Chrysanthemum holds accumulated E & P from years in which it was a C corporation, its S election is terminated as of January 1, 2006. ■

PII includes dividends, interest, rents, gains and losses from sales of securities, and royalties net of investment deductions. Rents are not considered PII if the corporation renders significant personal services to the occupant.

EXAMPLE 11

Violet Corporation owns and operates an apartment building. The corporation provides utilities for the building, maintains the lobby, and furnishes trash collection for tenants. These activities are not considered significant personal services, so any rent income earned by the corporation will be considered PII.

Alternatively, if Violet also furnishes maid services to its tenants (personal services beyond what normally would be expected from a landlord in an apartment building), the rent income would no longer be PII. ■

Reelection after Termination. After an S election has been terminated, the corporation must wait five years before reelecting S corporation status. The five-year waiting period is waived if:

- there is a more-than-50-percent change in ownership of the corporation after the first year for which the termination is applicable, or
- the event causing the termination was not reasonably within the control of the S corporation or its majority shareholders.

PLANNING *Strategies*

PRESERVING THE S ELECTION

★ **Framework Focus: Tax Rate**

Strategy ★ Avoid Double Taxation.

Unexpected loss of S corporation status can be costly to a corporation and its shareholders. Given the complexity of the rules facing these entities, constant vigilance is necessary to preserve the S election.

- As a starting point, the corporation's management and shareholders should be made aware of the various transactions that can lead to the loss of an election.
- Prevent violations of the small business corporation limitations. Since most such violations result from transfers

[23] § 1362(d)(3)(A)(ii).

of stock, the corporation and its shareholders should consider adopting a set of stock transfer restrictions. A carefully designed set of restrictions could prevent sale of stock to nonqualifying entities or violation of the 100-shareholder rule. Similarly, stock could be repurchased by the corporation under a buy-sell agreement upon the death of a shareholder, thereby preventing nonqualifying trusts from becoming shareholders.[24]

Operational Rules

LO.4

Compute nonseparately stated income and allocate income, deductions, and credits to shareholders.

S corporations are treated much like partnerships for tax purposes. With a few exceptions, S corporations generally make tax accounting and other elections at the corporate level.[25] Each year, the S corporation determines nonseparately stated income or loss and separately stated income, deductions, and credits. These items are taxed only once, as they pass through to shareholders. All items are allocated to each shareholder based on average ownership of stock throughout the year.[26] The flow-through of each item of income, deduction, and credit from the corporation to the shareholder is illustrated in Figure 12–1.

Computation of Taxable Income

Subchapter S taxable income or loss is determined in a manner similar to the tax rules that apply to partnerships, except that S corporations recognize gains (but not losses) on distributions of appreciated property to shareholders.[27] Other special provisions affecting only the computation of C corporation income, such as the dividends received deduction, do not extend to S corporations.[28] Finally, as with partnerships, certain deductions of individuals are not permitted, including alimony payments, personal moving expenses, certain dependent care expenses, the personal exemption, and the standard deduction.

FIGURE 12–1 **Flow-Through of Items of Income and Loss to S Corporation Shareholders**

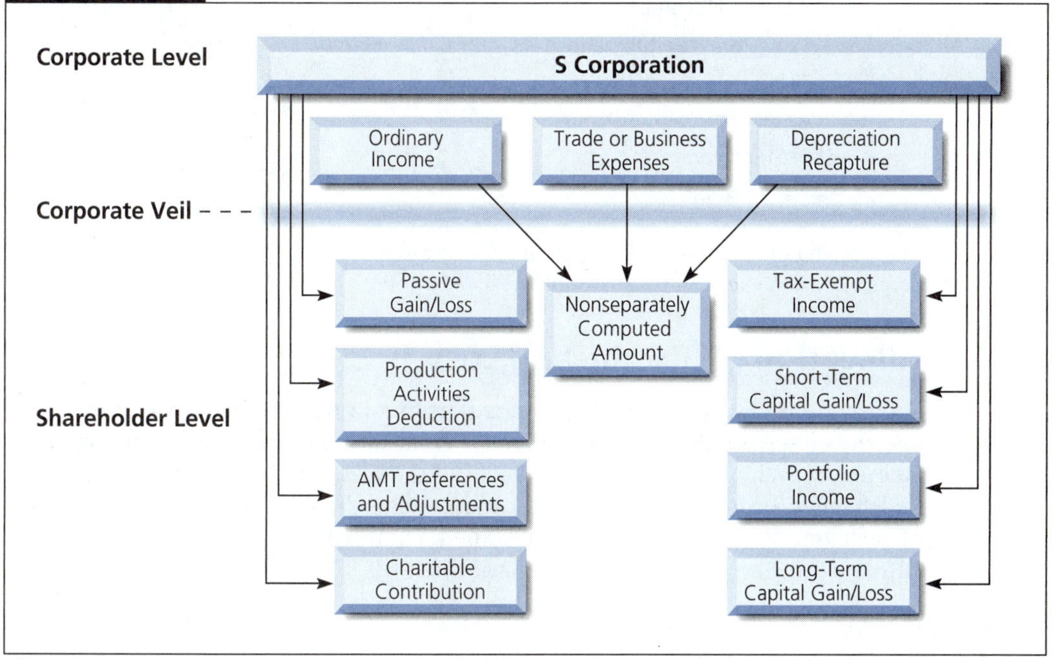

[24]Most such agreements do not create a second class of stock. Rev.Rul. 85–161, 1985–2 C.B. 191; *Portage Plastics Co. v. U.S.*, 72–2 USTC ¶9567, 30 AFTR2d 72–5229, 470 F.2d 308 (CA–7, 1973).

[25]Certain elections are made at the shareholder level (e.g., the choice between a foreign tax deduction or credit).

[26]§§ 1366(a), (b), and (c).

[27]§ 1363(d).

[28]§ 703(a)(2).

In general, S corporation items are divided into (1) nonseparately stated income or loss and (2) separately stated income, losses, deductions, and credits that could uniquely affect the tax liability of any shareholder. In essence, nonseparate items are aggregated into an undifferentiated amount that constitutes Subchapter S taxable income or loss.

EXAMPLE 12

The following is the income statement for Larkspur, Inc., an S corporation.

Sales		$ 40,000
Less: Cost of goods sold		(23,000)
Gross profit on sales		$ 17,000
Less: Interest expense	$1,200	
Charitable contributions	400	
Advertising expenses	1,500	
Other operating expenses	2,000	(5,100)
		$ 11,900
Add: Tax-exempt interest	$ 300	
Dividend income	200	
Long-term capital gain	500	1,000
Less: Short-term capital loss		(150)
Net income per books		$ 12,750

Subchapter S taxable income (i.e., nonseparately stated income) for Larkspur is calculated as follows, using net income for book purposes as the starting point.

Net income per books		$12,750
Separately stated items		
Deduct: Tax-exempt interest	$300	
Dividend income	200	
Long-term capital gain	500	(1,000)
		$11,750
Add: Charitable contributions	$400	
Short-term capital loss	150	550
Subchapter S taxable income		$12,300

The $12,300 of Subchapter S taxable income, as well as each of the five separately stated items, are divided among the shareholders based upon their stock ownership. ■

Allocation of Income and Loss

Each shareholder is allocated a pro rata portion of nonseparately stated income or loss and all separately stated items. The pro rata allocation method assigns an equal amount of each of the S items to each day of the year. If a shareholder's stock holding changes during the year, this allocation assigns the shareholder a pro rata share of each item for each day the stock is owned. On the date of transfer, the transferor (not the transferee) is considered to own the stock.[29]

S corporation item × Percentage of shares owned × Percentage of year shares were owned = Amount of item to be reported

[29] Reg. § 1.1377–1(a)(2)(ii).

TAX FACT

A "Small" Business Corporation

The majority of S corporations have only one shareholder.

Returns Filed by Number of S Corporation Shareholders, 2002 Tax Year

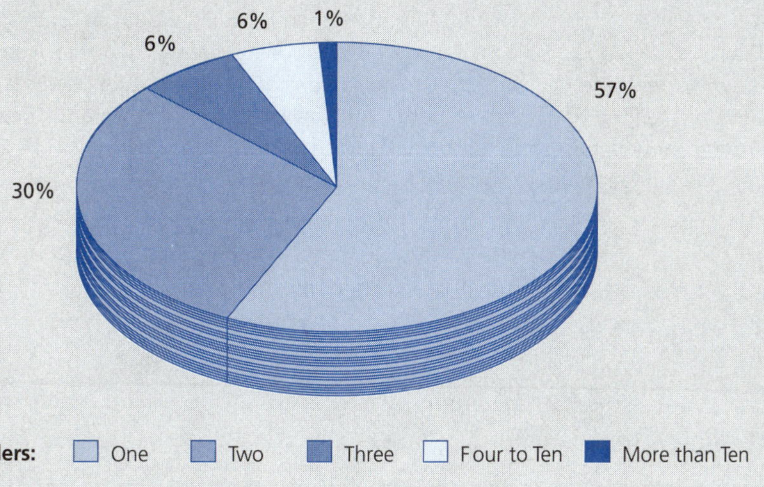

The per-day allocation must be used, unless the shareholder disposes of his or her entire interest in the entity.[30] In case of a complete termination, a short year may result, as discussed below. If a shareholder dies during the year, his or her share of the pro rata items up to the date of death is reported on the final individual income tax return.

EXAMPLE 13

Pat, a shareholder, owned 10% of Larkspur's stock (from Example 12) for 100 days and 12% for the remaining 265 days. Using the required per-day allocation method, Pat's share of the Subchapter S taxable income is the total of $12,300 × [10% × (100/365)] plus $12,300 × [12% × (265/365)], or $1,409. All of Pat's Schedule K–1 totals flow through to the corresponding lines on his individual income tax return (Form 1040). ■

The Short-Year Election. If a shareholder's interest is completely terminated during the tax year by disposition or death, all shareholders owning stock during the year and the corporation may elect to treat the S taxable year as two taxable years. The first year ends on the date of the termination. Under this election, an interim closing of the books is undertaken, and the shareholders report their shares of the S corporation items as they occurred during the short tax year.[31]

The short-year election provides an opportunity to shift income, losses, and credits among shareholders. The election is desirable in circumstances where more loss can be allocated to taxpayers with higher marginal tax rates.

Find more information on this topic at our Web site: ***http://wft-entities.swlearning.com.***

DIGGING DEEPER 3

EXAMPLE 14

Alicia, the owner of all of the shares of an S corporation, transfers her stock to Cindy halfway through the tax year. There is a $100,000 NOL for the entire tax year, but $30,000 of the loss occurs during the first half of the year. Without a short-year election, $50,000 of the loss is allocated to Alicia and $50,000 is allocated to Cindy. If the corporation makes the short-year

[30] §§ 1366(a)(1) and 1377(a)(1).

[31] § 1377(a)(2).

TAX *in the News* AN ABUSIVE TAX SHELTER?

During the 2004 presidential campaign, some tax practitioners pointed out that Democratic vice presidential candidate John Edwards had approximately $20 million of legal fees inside his S corporation in 1995. By paying himself a salary of only $360,000, he avoided paying almost $600,000 for the Medicare portion of FICA taxes (imposed at a rate of 2.9 percent).

There was considerable discussion of Edwards's tax situation in the media, and Vice President Dick Cheney mentioned the issue in the vice presidential debate. Reactions tended to follow the party affiliation of the commentator. In general, the $360,000 was probably less than reasonable compensation for Edwards (less than 2 percent of his legal fees), and the IRS could deem any distributions (i.e., recharacterize them) to be wages subject to the FICA and FUTA taxes.

Even one of Edwards's defenders said that if these funds were distributed to the senator, he "was making use of an alleged 'tax shelter' and the IRS would be quite justified in treating the distributions as salary." Another commentator said that it was somewhat hypocritical for Edwards to express concern about the solvency of Medicare and Social Security when he had engaged in what seemed to be an attempt to evade the Medicare tax.

election, Cindy is allocated $70,000 of the loss. The sales price of the stock probably would be increased to recognize the tax benefits being transferred from Alicia to Cindy. ■

PLANNING *Strategies* SALARY STRUCTURE

★ **Framework Focus: Tax Rate**

Strategy ★ Shift Net Income from High-Bracket Taxpayers to Low-Bracket Taxpayers.
★ Avoid Double Taxation.

The amount of salary paid to a shareholder-employee of an S corporation can have varying tax consequences and should be considered carefully. Larger amounts might be advantageous if the maximum contribution allowed under the retirement plan has not been reached. Smaller amounts may be beneficial if the parties are trying to shift taxable income to lower-bracket shareholders, reduce payroll taxes, curtail a reduction of Social Security benefits, or restrict losses that do not pass through because of the basis limitation.

A strategy of decreasing compensation and correspondingly increasing distributions to shareholder-employees often results in substantial savings in employment taxes. However, a shareholder of an S corporation cannot always perform substantial services and arrange to receive distributions rather than compensation so that the corporation may avoid paying employment taxes. The shareholder may be deemed an employee, and any distributions will be recharacterized as wages subject to FICA and FUTA taxes.[32] For planning purposes, some level of compensation should be paid to all shareholder-employees to avoid any recharacterization of distributions as deductible salaries—especially in personal service corporations.

Use of S corporations as an income-shifting device within a family (e.g., through a gift of stock from a high-marginal-rate taxpayer to a low-marginal-rate taxpayer) may be ineffective. The IRS can ignore such transfers unless the stock is purchased at fair market value.[33] Effectively, the IRS can require that reasonable compensation be paid to family members who render services or provide capital to the S corporation.

LO.5

Understand how distributions to S corporation shareholders are taxed.

Tax Treatment of Distributions to Shareholders

S corporations do not generate earnings and profits (E & P) while the S election is in effect. Indeed, all profits are taxed in the year earned, as though they were distributed on a pro rata basis to the shareholders. Thus, distributions from S corporations do not constitute dividends in the traditional sense—there is no corporate E & P to distribute.

[32] Rev.Rul. 74–44, 1974–1 C.B. 287; *Spicer Accounting, Inc. v. U.S.*, 91–1 USTC ¶50,103, 66 AFTR2d 90–5806, 918 F.2d 90 (CA–9, 1990); *Radtke v. U.S.*, 90–1 USTC ¶50,113, 65 AFTR2d 90–1155, 895 F.2d 1196 (CA–7, 1990).

[33] § 1366(e) and Reg. § 1.1373–1(a).

CONCEPT SUMMARY 12–1

Distributions from an S Corporation

Where Earnings and Profits Exist	Where No Earnings and Profits Exist
1. Distributions are tax-free to the extent of the AAA.*	
2. Any PTI from pre-1983 tax years can be distributed tax-free.	
3. The remaining distribution constitutes dividend income from AEP.†	
4. Distributions are tax-free to the extent of the other adjustments account (OAA).	
5. Any residual amount is applied as a tax-free reduction in basis of stock.	1. Distributions are nontaxable to the extent of adjusted basis in stock.
6. Excess is treated as gain from a sale or exchange of stock (capital gain in most cases).	2. Excess is treated as gain from a sale or exchange of stock (capital gain in most cases).

*A shareholder's stock basis serves as a limit on the amount that may be received tax-free.

†The AAA bypass election is available to pay out AEP before reducing the AAA [§ 1368(e)(3)].

It is possible, however, for S corporations to have an accumulated E & P (AEP) account. This can occur when:

- the S corporation was previously a C corporation, or
- a C corporation with its own AEP merged into the S corporation.

Distributions from S corporations are measured as the cash received plus the fair market value of any other distributed property. The tax treatment of distributions differs, depending upon whether the S corporation has AEP.

S Corporation with No AEP. If the S corporation has no AEP, the distribution is a tax-free recovery of capital to the extent that it does not exceed the adjusted basis of the shareholder's stock. When the amount of the distribution exceeds the adjusted basis of the stock, the excess is treated as a gain from the sale or exchange of property (capital gain in most cases).

EXAMPLE 15

Hyacinth, Inc., a calendar year S corporation, has no AEP. During the year, Juan, an individual shareholder of the corporation, receives a cash distribution of $12,200 from Hyacinth. Juan's basis in his stock is $9,700. Juan recognizes a capital gain of $2,500, the excess of the distribution over the stock basis ($12,200 – $9,700). The remaining $9,700 is tax-free, but it reduces Juan's basis in his stock to zero. ■

S Corporation with AEP. For S corporations with AEP, a more complex set of rules applies. These rules blend the entity and conduit approaches to taxation, treating distributions of pre-election (C corporation) and postelection (S corporation) earnings differently. Distributions of C corporation AEP are taxed as dividends (5/15 percent rate), while distributions of previously taxed S corporation earnings are tax-free to the extent of the shareholder's adjusted basis in the stock.

The treatment of distributions is determined by their order. Specifically, distributions are deemed to be first from previously taxed, undistributed earnings of the S corporation. Such distributions are tax-free and are determined by reference to a special account, the **accumulated adjustments account (AAA)**.[34] Next, AEP is distributed

[34]For S corporations in existence prior to 1983, an account similar to the AAA was used. This account, called *previously taxed income* (PTI), can be distributed in cash tax-free to shareholders after AAA has been distributed. See §§ 1368(c)(1) and (e)(1).

as taxable dividends (i.e., as payments from AEP). After AEP is depleted, distributions are made from the **other adjustments account (OAA)**. These amounts are received tax-free by the shareholder. Remaining amounts of the distribution are received tax-free to the extent of the shareholder's remaining stock basis,[35] with any excess being treated typically as capital gain.

EXAMPLE 16

Salvia, a calendar year S corporation, distributes $1,300 of cash to its only shareholder, Otis, on December 31. Otis's basis in his stock is $1,400, AAA is $500, and the corporation has AEP of $750 before the distribution.

The first $500 of the distribution is a tax-free recovery of basis from the AAA. The next $750 is a taxable dividend distribution from AEP. Finally, the remaining $50 of cash is a tax-free recovery of basis. Immediately after the distribution, Salvia has no AAA or AEP. Otis's stock basis now is $850.

	Corporate AAA	Corporate AEP	Otis's Stock Basis
Beginning balance	$ 500	$ 750	$1,400
Distribution from AAA	(500)		(500)
Distribution from AEP		(750)	
Distribution of capital			(50)
Ending balance	$ -0-	$ -0-	$ 850

■

EXAMPLE 17

Assume the same facts as in the preceding example. The next year, Salvia has no earnings and distributes $1,000 to Otis. Of the distribution, $850 is a tax-free recovery of the stock basis, and then $150 is taxed to Otis as a capital gain. ■

With the consent of all of its shareholders, an S corporation can elect to have a distribution treated as if it were made from AEP rather than from the AAA. This mechanism is known as an **AAA bypass election**. This election may be desirable when making distributions to move the entity to the no-AEP system of accounting for distributions, at a tax cost of 15 percent of the AEP.

EXAMPLE 18

Rotor is a valid S corporation. It has $50 of AEP. An AAA bypass election for Rotor's next shareholder distribution would eliminate the need to track the AAA and would greatly simplify the accounting for future distributions. The cost for this simplification is the tax on $50 of dividend income. ■

Accumulated Adjustments Account. The AAA is the cumulative total of undistributed nonseparately and separately stated income and deduction items for S corporation years beginning after 1982. As noted above, it provides a mechanism to ensure that earnings of an S corporation are taxed only once. Changes to the AAA are reported annually in Schedule M–2 on page 4 of the Form 1120S.

AAA is computed at the end of each tax year rather than at the time of a distribution. First, add to the year's beginning balance any current nonseparately computed income and positive separately stated items (except tax-exempt income). Next, account for distributions *prior* to subtracting the negative items.

AAA is applied to the distributions made during the year on a pro rata basis (in a fashion similar to the application of current E & P, discussed in Chapter 10). The determination of AAA is summarized in Exhibit 12–1.

[35] § 1368(c).

EXHIBIT 12–1 **Adjustments to the Corporate AAA**

Increase by:

1. Positive separately stated items other than tax-exempt income.
2. Nonseparately computed income.

Decrease by:

3. Distribution(s) from AAA (but not below zero).
4. Adjustments other than distributions (e.g., losses, deductions).

Although adjustments to AAA and stock basis adjustments are similar, there are some important differences between the two amounts. In particular,

- The AAA is not affected by tax-exempt income and related expenses.
- Unlike stock basis, the AAA can have a negative balance. All losses decrease the AAA balance, even those in excess of the shareholder's basis. However, distributions may not make the AAA negative or increase a negative balance in the account.
- Every shareholder has a proportionate interest in the AAA, regardless of the amount of his or her stock basis.[36] In fact, AAA is a corporate account, so there is no connection between the amount and any specific shareholder.[37] Thus, the benefits of AAA can be shifted from one shareholder to another. For example, when an S corporation shareholder sells stock to another party, any AAA balance on the purchase date can be distributed tax-free to the purchaser.

Other Adjustments Account. The OAA tracks the entity's net items that affect basis but not the AAA, such as tax-exempt income and any related nondeductible expenses. Distributions are made from the OAA after AEP and the AAA are reduced to zero. Distributions from this account are tax-free.

Schedule M–2. Page 4 of the Form 1120S includes Schedule M–2, a reconciliation of beginning and ending balances in the AAA, PTI, and OAA accounts. Most tax professionals recommend that the Schedule M–2 be kept current even if the entity has retained no AEP, so that if future events require the use of these amounts, they need not be reconstructed after the fact.

EXAMPLE 19

Poinsettia, an S corporation, records the following items.

AAA, beginning of year	$ 8,500
OAA, beginning of year	–0–
Ordinary income	25,000
Tax-exempt interest	4,000
Key employee life insurance proceeds received	5,000
Payroll penalty expense	2,000
Charitable contributions	3,000
Unreasonable compensation	5,000
Premiums on key employee life insurance	2,100
Distributions to shareholders	16,000

[36] § 1368(c).

[37] § 1368(e)(1)(A).

Poinsettia's Schedule M–2 appears as follows.

Schedule M-2 **Analysis of Accumulated Adjustments Account, Other Adjustments Account, and Shareholders' Undistributed Taxable Income Previously Taxed**

		(a) Accumulated adjustments account	(b) Other adjustments account
1	Balance at beginning of tax year	8,500	0
2	Ordinary income from page 1, line 21	25,000	
3	Other additions		9,000**
4	Loss from page 1, line 21	( )	
5	Other reductions	(10,000*)	(2,100)
6	Combine lines 1 through 5	23,500	6,900
7	Distributions other than dividend distributions	16,000	
8	Balance at end of tax year. Subtract line 7 from line 6	7,500	6,900

**$2,000 (payroll penalty) + $3,000 (charitable contributions) + $5,000 (unreasonable compensation).*
***$4,000 (tax-exempt interest) + $5,000 (life insurance proceeds).* ■

Effect of Terminating the S Election. Normally, distributions to shareholders from a C corporation are taxed as dividends to the extent of E & P. However, any distribution of *cash* by a C corporation to shareholders during a one-year period[38] following an S election termination receives special treatment. Such a distribution is treated as a tax-free recovery of stock basis to the extent that it does not exceed the AAA.[39] Since *only* cash distributions reduce the AAA during this *postelection termination period*, a corporation should not make property distributions during this time. Instead, the entity should sell property and distribute the proceeds to shareholders.

EXAMPLE 20

Quinn, the sole shareholder of Azalea, Inc., a calendar year S corporation, decides during 2006 to terminate the S election, effective January 1, 2007. As of the end of 2006, Azalea has an AAA of $1,300. Quinn can receive a nontaxable distribution of cash during the post-termination period to the extent of Azalea's AAA. Cash distributions of $1,300 during 2007 are nontaxable to Quinn, but they reduce the adjusted basis of his stock. ■

PLANNING *Strategies*

THE ACCUMULATED ADJUSTMENTS ACCOUNT

★ **Framework Focus: Tax Rate**

Strategy ★ Avoid Double Taxation.

The AAA is needed to determine the tax treatment of distributions from S corporations with AEP *and* distributions made during the post-termination election period. Therefore, it is important for all S corporations (even those with no AEP) to maintain a current AAA (and OAA) balance. Without an accurate AAA balance, distributions could needlessly be classified as taxable dividends. Alternatively, it will be costly to reconstruct the AAA after the S election terminates.

Distributions should be made when AAA is positive. If future years bring operating losses, AAA is reduced, and shareholder exposure to AEP and taxable dividends increases.

Tax Treatment of Property Distributions by the Corporation

An S corporation recognizes a gain on any distribution of appreciated property (other than in a reorganization) in the same manner as if the asset had been sold

[38] § 1377(b).

[39] § 1371(e). Termination-period distributions from the OAA are taxed as capital gains.

CONCEPT SUMMARY 12–2

Distribution of Property In-Kind

	Appreciated Property	Depreciated Property
S corporation	Realized gain is recognized by the corporation, which passes it through to the shareholders. Such gain increases a shareholder's stock basis, generating a basis in the property equal to FMV. On the distribution, the shareholder's stock basis is reduced by the FMV of the property (but not below zero).	Realized loss is not recognized. The shareholder assumes an FMV basis in the property.
C corporation	Realized gain is recognized under § 311(b) and increases E & P (net of tax). The shareholder has a taxable dividend to the extent of E & P.	Realized loss is not recognized. The shareholder assumes an FMV basis in the property.
Partnership	No gain to the partnership or partner. The partner takes a carryover basis in the asset, but the asset basis is limited to the partner's basis in the partnership.	Realized loss is not recognized. The partner takes a carryover basis in the asset, but the asset basis is limited to the partner's basis in the partnership.

to the shareholder at its fair market value.[40] The corporate gain is passed through to the shareholders. There is an important reason for this rule. Without it, property might be distributed tax-free (other than for certain recapture items) and later sold without income recognition to the shareholder because the shareholder's basis equals the asset's fair market value. The character of the gain—capital gain or ordinary income—depends upon the type of asset being distributed.

The S corporation does not recognize a loss when distributing assets that are worth less than their basis. As with gain property, the shareholder's basis is equal to the asset's fair market value. Thus, the potential loss is postponed until the shareholder sells the stock of the S corporation. Since loss property receives a step-down in basis without any loss recognition by the S corporation, distributions of loss property should be avoided. See Concept Summary 12–2.

EXAMPLE 21

Yarrow, Inc., an S corporation for 10 years, distributes a tract of land held as an investment to one of its shareholders. The land was purchased for $22,000 many years ago and is currently worth $82,000. Yarrow recognizes a capital gain of $60,000, which increases the AAA by $60,000. The gain flows through proportionately to Yarrow's shareholders and is taxed to them.

Then a tax-free property distribution reduces AAA and shareholder stock basis by $82,000 (fair market value). The tax consequences are the same for appreciated property, whether it is distributed to the shareholders and they dispose of it, or the corporation sells the property and distributes the proceeds to the shareholders. ■

EXAMPLE 22

Continue with the facts of Example 21. If the land had been purchased for $82,000 and was currently worth $22,000, the shareholder would take a $22,000 basis in the land. The $60,000 realized loss is not recognized at the corporate level. The loss does not reduce Yarrow's AAA. Only when the S corporation sells the asset does it recognize the loss and reduce AAA. ■

[40] § 311(b).

EXAMPLE 23

Assume the same facts as in Examples 21 and 22, except that Yarrow is a C corporation (E & P balance of $1 million) or a partnership. Assume the partner's basis in the partnership interest is $100,000 and ignore any corporate-level taxes. Compare the results.

	Appreciated Property		
	S Corporation	C Corporation	Partnership
Entity gain/loss	$60,000	$60,000	$ –0–
Owner's gain/loss/dividend	60,000	82,000	–0–
Owner's basis in land	82,000	82,000	22,000
	Property That Has Declined in Value		
	S Corporation	C Corporation	Partnership
Entity gain/loss	$ –0–	$ –0–	$ –0–
Owner's gain/loss/dividend	–0–	22,000	–0–
Owner's basis in land	22,000	22,000	82,000

■

LO.6

Calculate a shareholder's basis in S corporation stock.

Shareholder's Basis

The calculation of the initial tax basis of stock in an S corporation is similar to that for the basis of stock in a C corporation and depends upon the manner in which the shares are acquired (e.g., gift, inheritance, purchase, exchange under § 351). Once the initial tax basis is determined, various transactions during the life of the corporation affect the shareholder's basis in the stock. Although each shareholder is required to compute his or her own basis in the S shares, neither Form 1120S nor Schedule K–1 provides a place for tracking this amount.

A shareholder's basis is increased by stock purchases and capital contributions. Operations during the year cause the following additional upward adjustments to basis.[41]

- Nonseparately computed income.
- Separately stated income items (e.g., nontaxable income).

Basis then is reduced by distributions not reported as income by the shareholder (e.g., an AAA or PTI distribution). Next, the following items reduce basis (but not below zero).

- Nondeductible expenses of the corporation (e.g., fines, penalties, illegal kickbacks).
- Nonseparately computed loss.
- Separately stated loss and deduction items.

As under the partnership rules, basis first is increased by income items; then it is decreased by distributions and finally by losses.[42] In most cases, this *losses last* rule is advantageous.

EXAMPLE 24

In its first year of operations, Iris, Inc., a calendar year S corporation, earns income of $2,000. On February 2 in its second year of operations, Iris distributes $2,000 to Marty, its sole shareholder. During the remainder of the second year, the corporation incurs a $2,000 loss.

Under the S corporation ordering rules, the $2,000 distribution is tax-free AAA to Marty. The distribution is accounted for before the loss. The $2,000 loss is *not* passed through, though, because stock basis cannot be reduced below zero. ■

[41]§ 1367(a).

[42]Reg. § 1.1367–1(f).

A shareholder's basis in S corporation stock can never be reduced below zero. Once stock basis is zero, any additional basis reductions (losses or deductions, but *not* distributions) decrease (but not below zero) the shareholder's basis in loans made to the S corporation. Any excess of losses or deductions over both stock and loan bases is not deductible in the current year. Losses can be deducted only to the extent that they offset stock or loan basis. Thus, until additional basis is created due to capital contributions or flow-through income, the loss deductions are suspended.

When there is a capital contribution or an item of flow-through income, basis is first restored to the shareholder loans, up to the original principal amount.[43] Then, basis in the stock is restored.

EXAMPLE 25

Stacey, a sole shareholder, has a $7,000 stock basis and a $2,000 basis in a loan that she made to a calendar year S corporation. At the beginning of the year, the corporation's AAA and OAA balances are $0. Subchapter S ordinary income for the year is $8,200. During the year, the corporation also received $2,000 of tax-exempt interest income.

Cash of $17,300 is distributed to Stacey on November 15. As a result, Stacey recognizes only a $100 capital gain.

	Corporate AAA	Corporate OAA	Stacey's Stock Basis	Stacey's Loan Basis
Beginning balance	$ -0-	$ -0-	$ 7,000	$2,000
Ordinary income	8,200		8,200	
Tax-exempt income		2,000	2,000	
Subtotal	$ 8,200	$ 2,000	$17,200	$2,000
Distribution ($17,300)				
From AAA	(8,200)		(8,200)	
From OAA		(2,000)	(2,000)	
From stock basis			(7,000)	
Ending balance	$ -0-	$ -0-	$ -0-	$2,000
Distribution in excess of stock basis (capital gain)			$ 100	

Pass-through losses can reduce loan basis, but distributions do not. Stock basis cannot be reduced below zero, and the $100 excess distribution does not reduce Stacey's loan basis. ■

The basis rules for S corporation stock are similar to the rules for determining a partner's basis in a partnership interest. However, a partner's basis in the partnership interest includes the partner's direct investment plus a *ratable share* of partnership liabilities.[44] If a partnership borrows from a partner, the partner receives a basis increase as if the partnership had borrowed from an unrelated third party.[45] In contrast, except for loans from the shareholder to the corporation, corporate borrowing has no effect on S corporation shareholder basis. Loans from a shareholder to the S corporation have a tax basis only for the shareholder making the loan.

If a loan's basis has been reduced and is not restored, income is recognized when the corporation repays the loan. If the corporation issued a note as evidence of the debt, repayment constitutes an amount received in exchange for a capital

[43] § 1367(b)(2).

[44] § 752(a).

[45] Reg. § 1.752–1(e).

asset, and the amount that exceeds the shareholder's basis is capital gain.[46] However, if the loan is made on open account, the repayment constitutes ordinary income to the extent that it exceeds the shareholder's basis in the loan. Thus, a note should be given to ensure capital gain treatment for the income that results from a loan's repayment.

EXAMPLE 26

Phil is the sole shareholder of Falcon, a valid S corporation. At the beginning of 2006, Phil's basis in his stock was $10,000. During 2006, he made a $4,000 loan to the corporation, using a written debt instrument and market interest rates. Falcon has no other outstanding debt.

Falcon generated a $13,000 taxable loss for 2006. Thus, at the beginning of 2007, Phil's stock basis was zero, and the basis in his loan to Falcon was $1,000.

Falcon repaid the loan in full on March 1, 2007. Phil recognized a $3,000 capital gain on the repayment. ■

DIGGING DEEPER 4

Find more information on this topic at our Web site: ***http://wft-entities.swlearning.com.***

PLANNING *Strategies*

WORKING WITH SUSPENDED LOSSES

★ **Framework Focus: Income and Exclusion**

Strategy ★ Avoid Income Recognition.

Distributions made to shareholders with suspended losses usually create capital gain income because there is no stock basis to offset. Usually, distributions should be deferred until the shareholder creates stock basis in some form. In this way, no gross income is recognized until the suspended losses are fully used.

EXAMPLE 27

Continue with the facts of Example 26 except that Falcon's loss cannot be deducted by Phil because of the lack of basis. Phil purchases $5,000 of additional stock in Falcon. Phil gets an immediate deduction for his investment, due to his $13,000 in suspended losses. Alternatively, if Falcon shows a $5,000 profit for the year, Phil pays no tax on the flow-through income, due to his $13,000 in suspended losses.

However, if Falcon distributes $5,000 to Phil in 2007 without earning any profit for the year, and prior to any capital contribution by him, Phil recognizes a $5,000 capital gain, because his stock basis is zero. ■

LO.7

Explain the tax effects of losses on S shareholders.

Treatment of Losses

Net Operating Loss. One major advantage of an S election is the ability to pass through any net operating loss (NOL) of the corporation directly to the shareholders. A shareholder can deduct an NOL for the year in which the S corporation's tax year ends. The corporation is not entitled to any deduction for the NOL. A shareholder's basis in the stock is reduced to the extent of any pass-through of the NOL, and the shareholder's AAA is reduced by the same deductible amount.[47]

Deductions for an S corporation's NOL pass-through cannot exceed a shareholder's adjusted basis in the stock *plus* the basis of any loans made by the shareholder to the corporation.[48] A shareholder is entitled to carry forward a loss to the extent that the loss for the year exceeds basis. Any loss carried forward may be deducted *only* by

[46] *Joe M. Smith,* 48 T.C. 872 (1967), *aff'd* and *rev'd* in 70–1 USTC ¶9327, 25 AFTR2d 70–936, 424 F.2d 219 (CA–9, 1970); Rev.Rul. 64–162, 1964–1 C.B. 304.

[47] §§ 1368(a)(1)(A) and (e)(1)(A).

[48] See *Donald J. Sauvigne,* 30 TCM 123, T.C.Memo. 1971–30.

the *same* shareholder if and when the basis in the stock of or loans to the corporation is restored.[49]

Find more information on this topic at our Web site: ***http://wft-entities.swlearning.com.***

DIGGING DEEPER 5

EXAMPLE 28

Ginny owns 10% of the stock of Pilot, a calendar year S corporation. Her basis in the shares is $10,000 at the beginning of 2004. The indicated events are accounted for under the S corporation rules as follows.

Tax Year	Event	Tax Consequences
2004	Ginny's share of Pilot's operating loss is $15,000.	Ginny deducts $10,000. Her stock basis is reduced to zero. She holds a $5,000 suspended loss.
2005	Ginny's share of Pilot's operating loss is $4,000.	No deduction for the loss, as Ginny has no stock basis to offset. Her suspended loss is now $9,000.
2006	Ginny's share of Pilot's operating loss is $7,000. She purchases an additional $10,000 of stock from Pilot.	The purchase creates $10,000 of stock basis. Ginny deducts $10,000—the current $7,000 loss and $3,000 of the suspended loss. Stock basis again is zero, and the new suspended loss is $6,000.
2007	Ginny sells all of her Pilot shares to Christina on January 1.	The $6,000 suspended loss disappears—it cannot be transferred to Christina.

■

PLANNING *Strategies* LOSS CONSIDERATIONS

★ **Framework Focus: Deductions**

Strategy ★ Maximize Deductible Amounts.

A loss in excess of tax basis may be carried forward and deducted only by the same shareholder in succeeding years. Thus, before disposing of the stock, a shareholder should increase stock/loan basis to flow through the loss. The next shareholder cannot acquire the loss carryover.

The NOL provisions create a need for sound tax planning during the last election year and the post-termination transition period. If it appears that the S corporation is going to sustain an NOL or use up any loss carryover, each shareholder's basis should be analyzed to determine if it can absorb the owner's share of the loss. If basis is insufficient to absorb the loss, further investments should be considered before the end of the post-termination period. Such investments can be accomplished through additional stock purchases from the corporation, or from other shareholders, to increase basis.

EXAMPLE 29

A calendar year C corporation has an NOL of $20,000 in 2005. The corporation makes a valid S election in 2006 and has another $20,000 NOL in that year. At all times during 2006, the stock of the corporation was owned by the same 10 shareholders, each of whom owned 10% of the stock. Tim, one of the shareholders, has an adjusted basis in his stock of $1,800 at the beginning of 2006. None of the 2005 NOL may be carried forward into the S year. Although Tim's share of the 2006 NOL is $2,000, his deduction for the loss is limited to $1,800 in 2006 with a $200 carryover to 2007. ■

[49] § 1366(d).

At-Risk Rules. S corporation shareholders, like partners, are limited in the amount of loss that they may deduct by their "at-risk" amounts. The rules for determining at-risk amounts are similar, but not identical, to the partnership at-risk rules.

An amount at risk is determined separately for each shareholder. The amount of the corporate losses that are passed through and deductible by the shareholders is not affected by the amount the corporation has at risk. A shareholder usually is considered at risk with respect to an activity to the extent of cash and the adjusted basis of other property contributed to the electing corporation, any amount borrowed for use in the activity for which the taxpayer has personal liability for payment from personal assets, and the net fair market value of personal assets that secure nonrecourse borrowing. Any losses that are suspended under the at-risk rules are carried forward and are available during the post-termination period. The S stock basis limitations and at-risk limitations are applied before the passive activity limitations (see below).

EXAMPLE 30

Carl has a basis of $35,000 in his S corporation stock. He takes a $15,000 nonrecourse loan from a relative and lends the proceeds to the S corporation. Carl now has a stock basis of $35,000 and a loan basis of $15,000. However, due to the at-risk limitation, he can deduct only $35,000 of losses from the S corporation. ■

Passive Losses and Credits. Net passive losses and credits are not deductible when incurred and must be carried over to a year when there is passive income. Thus, one must be aware of three major classes of income, losses, and credits—active, portfolio, and passive. S corporations are not directly subject to the passive activity limits, but corporate rental activities are inherently passive, and other activities of an S corporation may be passive unless the shareholder(s) materially participate(s) in operating the business. An S corporation may engage in more than one such activity.

If the corporate activity is rental or the shareholders do not materially participate, any passive losses or credits flow through. The shareholders are able to apply the losses or credits only against their income from other passive activities. An S shareholder's stock basis is reduced by passive losses that flow through to the shareholder, even though the shareholder may not be entitled to a current deduction due to the passive loss limitations.

Other Operational Rules

Several other points may be made about the possible effects of various Code provisions on S corporations.

- An S corporation must make estimated tax payments with respect to any recognized built-in gain and excess passive investment income tax (discussed next).
- An S corporation may own stock in another corporation, but an S corporation may not have a C corporation shareholder. An S corporation is *not* eligible for the dividends received deduction.
- An S corporation is *not* subject to the 10 percent of taxable income limitation applicable to charitable contributions made by a C corporation.
- Any family member who renders services or furnishes capital to an S corporation must be paid reasonable compensation. Otherwise, the IRS can make adjustments to reflect the value of the services or capital. This rule may make it more difficult for related parties to shift Subchapter S taxable income to children or other family members.
- Although § 1366(a)(1) provides for a flow-through of S items to a shareholder, this amount is not self-employment income and is not subject to the self-employment tax.[50] Compensation for services rendered to an S corporation is, however, subject to FICA taxes.

[50]Rev.Rul. 59–221, 1959–1 C.B. 225. Recall from Chapter 11 that flow-through ordinary income is self-employment income to a partner or LLC member.

CONCEPT SUMMARY 12–3

Treatment of S Corporation Losses

Step 1. Allocate total loss to the shareholder on a daily basis, based upon stock ownership.

Step 2. If the shareholder's loss exceeds his or her stock basis, apply any excess to the adjusted basis of indebtedness to the shareholder. Loss allocations do not reduce stock or loan basis below zero.

Step 3. Where a flow-through loss exceeds the stock and loan basis, any excess is suspended and carried over to succeeding tax years.

Step 4. In succeeding tax years, any net increase in basis restores the debt basis first, up to its original amount.

Step 5. Once debt basis is restored, any remaining net increase restores stock basis.

Step 6. Any suspended loss from a previous year now reduces stock basis first and debt basis second.

Step 7. If the S election terminates, any suspended loss carryover may be deducted during the post-termination period to the extent of the stock basis at the end of this period. Any loss remaining at the end of this period is lost forever.

- An S corporation is placed on the cash method of accounting for purposes of deducting business expenses and interest owed to a cash basis related party.[51] Thus, the timing of the shareholder's income and the corporate deduction must match.
- The S election is not recognized by the District of Columbia and several states, including Louisiana, New Hampshire, and Tennessee. Thus, some or all of the entity's income may be subject to a state-level income tax.
- An S corporation may issue § 1244 stock to its shareholders to obtain ordinary loss treatment.
- Losses may be disallowed due to a lack of a profit motive. If the activities at the corporate level are not profit motivated, the losses may be disallowed under the hobby loss rules of § 183 (see Chapter 17).[52]

Entity-Level Taxes

LO.8

Compute the entity-level taxes on S corporations.

Tax on Pre-Election Built-in Gain

Normally, an S corporation does *not* pay an income tax, since all items flow through to the shareholders. But an S corporation that was previously a C corporation may be required to pay a built-in gains tax, a LIFO recapture tax, or a passive investment income tax.

Without the **built-in gains tax**, it would be possible to avoid the corporate double tax on a disposition of appreciated property, by electing S corporation status.

EXAMPLE 31

Zinnia, Inc., a C corporation, owns a single asset with a basis of $100,000 and a fair market value of $500,000. If Zinnia sells this asset and distributes the cash to its shareholders, there are two levels of tax, one at the corporate level and one at the shareholder level. Alternatively, if Zinnia distributes the asset to its shareholders as a dividend, a double tax still results. In an attempt to avoid the double tax, Zinnia elects S corporation status. It then sells the asset and distributes the proceeds to shareholders. Without the built-in gains tax, the gain would be taxed only once, at the shareholder level. The distribution of the sales proceeds would be a tax-free reduction of the AAA. ■

The built-in gains tax generally applies to C corporations converting to S status after 1986. It is a *corporate-level* tax on any built-in gain recognized when the

[51] § 267(b).

[52] *Michael J. Houston*, 69 TCM 2360, T.C.Memo. 1995–159; *Mario G. De Mendoza, III*, 68 TCM 42, T.C.Memo. 1994–314.

CONCEPT SUMMARY 12–4

Calculation of the Built-in Gains Tax Liability

Step 1. Select the smaller of built-in gain or taxable income.*

Step 2. Deduct unexpired NOLs and capital losses from C corporation tax years.

Step 3. Multiply the tax base obtained in step 2 by the top corporate income tax rate.

Step 4. Deduct any business credit carryforwards and AMT credit carryforwards arising in a C corporation tax year from the amount obtained in step 3.

Step 5. The corporation pays any tax resulting in step 4.

*Any net recognized built-in gain in excess of taxable income is carried forward to the next year within the 10-year recognition period.

S corporation disposes of an asset in a taxable disposition within 10 calendar years after the date on which the S election took effect. The steps in computing the tax are summarized in Concept Summary 12–4.

General Rules. The base for the built-in gains tax includes any unrealized gain on appreciated assets (e.g., real estate, cash basis receivables, goodwill) held by a corporation on the day it elects S status. The highest corporate tax rate (currently 35 percent) is applied to the unrealized gain when any of the assets are sold. Any gain from the sale (net of the built-in gains tax)[53] also passes through as a taxable gain to shareholders.

EXAMPLE 32

Assume the same facts as in the preceding example. Section 1374 imposes a corporate-level built-in gains tax that must be paid by Zinnia if it sells the asset after electing S status. Upon sale of the asset, the corporation owes a tax of $140,000 ($400,000 × 35%). In addition, the shareholders report a $260,000 taxable gain ($400,000 − $140,000). Hence, the built-in gains tax effectively imposes a double tax on Zinnia and its shareholders. ■

DIGGING DEEPER 6

Find more information on this topic at our Web site: ***http://wft-entities.swlearning.com.***

The amount of built-in gain recognized in any year is limited to an *as if* taxable income for the year, computed as if the corporation were a C corporation. Any built-in gain that escapes taxation due to the taxable income limitation is carried forward and recognized in future tax years. Thus, a corporation can defer a built-in gain tax liability whenever it has a low or negative taxable income.

EXAMPLE 33

Vinca's recognized built-in gain for 2006 is $400,000. If Vinca were a C corporation, its 2006 taxable income would be $300,000. The amount of built-in gain subject to tax in 2006 is $300,000. The excess built-in gain of $100,000 is carried forward and taxed in 2007 (assuming adequate C corporation taxable income in that year). There is no statutory limit on the carryforward period, but the gain would effectively expire at the end of the 10-year recognition period applicable to all built-in gains.[54] ■

Normally, tax attributes of a C corporation do not carry over to a converted S corporation. For purposes of the built-in gains tax, however, certain carryovers are allowed. In particular, an S corporation can offset built-in gains with unexpired NOLs or capital losses from C corporation years.

[53] § 1366(f)(2).

[54] § 1374(d)(7); Notice 90–27, 1990–1 C.B. 336.

EXAMPLE 34

An S corporation has a built-in gain of $100,000 and taxable income of $90,000. The built-in gains tax liability is calculated as follows, applying the indicated loss carryforwards.

Lesser of taxable income or built-in gain	$ 90,000
Less: NOL carryforward from C year	(12,000)
Capital loss carryforward from C year	(8,000)
Tax base	$ 70,000
Highest corporate income tax rate	× 0.35
Tentative tax	$ 24,500
Less: Business credit carryforward from C year	(4,000)
Built-in gains tax liability	$ 20,500

The $10,000 realized (but not taxed) built-in gain in excess of taxable income is carried forward to the next year, as long as the next year is within the 10-year recognition period. ■

PLANNING *Strategies* MANAGING THE BUILT-IN GAINS TAX

★ **Framework Focus: Income and Exclusion**

Strategy ★ Avoid Income Recognition.
★ Postpone Recognition of Income to Achieve Tax Deferral.

Although limitations exist on contributions of loss property to the corporation before electing S status, it still is possible for a corporation to minimize built-in gains and maximize built-in losses prior to the S election. A cash basis S corporation can accomplish this by reducing receivables, accelerating payables, and accruing compensation costs.

To further reduce or defer the tax, the corporation may take advantage of the taxable income limitation by shifting income and deductions to minimize taxable income in years when built-in gain is recognized. Although the postponed built-in gain is carried forward to future years, the time value of money makes the postponement beneficial. For example, paying compensation to shareholder-employees in place of a distribution creates a deduction that reduces taxable income and postpones the built-in gains tax.

EXAMPLE 35

Tulip, Inc., an S corporation, has built-in gain of $110,000 and taxable income of $120,000 before payment of salaries to its shareholders. If Tulip pays at least $120,000 in salaries to the shareholders (rather than making a distribution), its taxable income drops to zero, and the built-in gains tax is postponed. Thus, Tulip needs to keep the salaries as high as possible to postpone the built-in gains tax in future years and reap a benefit from the time value of money. Of course, paying the salaries may increase the payroll tax burden if the salaries are initially below FICA and FUTA limits. ■

Giving built-in gain property to a charitable organization does not trigger the built-in gains tax. Built-in *loss* property may be sold in the same year that built-in gain property is sold to reduce or eliminate the built-in gains tax. Generally, the taxpayer should sell built-in loss property in a year when an equivalent amount of built-in gain property is sold. Otherwise, the built-in loss could be wasted.

LIFO Recapture Tax. When a corporation uses the FIFO method for its last year before making the S election, any built-in gain is recognized and taxed as the inventory is sold. A LIFO-basis corporation does not recognize this gain unless the corporation invades the LIFO layer during the 10-year built-in gains tax period. To preclude deferral of gain recognition under LIFO, any LIFO recapture amount at the time of the S election is subject to a corporate-level tax.

TAX FACT

No Double Taxation?

S corporations paid almost $400 million in Federal corporate-level taxes for tax year 2002, a significant level of collections from "tax-exempt" entities.

Federal Income Taxes Paid by S Corporations ($M)

	2001	2002
Built-in gains, LIFO recapture taxes	$303	$277
Passive investment income penalty tax	9	12
Audit adjustments, other	57	76
Totals	$369	$365

For 2002, corporate-level Federal income taxes were reported by about 9,230 S corporations, about 0.30 percent of all S returns filed.

The taxable LIFO recapture amount equals the excess of the inventory's value under FIFO over the LIFO value. The resulting tax is payable in four equal installments, with the first payment due on or before the due date for the corporate return for the last C corporation year (without regard to any extensions). The remaining three installments must be paid on or before the due dates of the succeeding corporate returns. No interest is due if payments are made by the due dates, and no estimated taxes are due on the four tax installments. No refund is allowed if the LIFO value is higher than the FIFO value.

EXAMPLE 36

Daffodil Corporation converts from a C corporation to an S corporation at the beginning of 2006. Daffodil used the LIFO inventory method in 2005 and had an ending LIFO inventory of $110,000 (FIFO value of $190,000). Daffodil must add $80,000 of LIFO recapture amount to its 2005 taxable income, resulting in an increased tax liability of $28,000 ($80,000 × 35%). Daffodil must pay one-fourth of the tax (or $7,000) with its 2005 corporate tax return. The three succeeding installments of $7,000 each are paid with Daffodil's 2006–2008 tax returns. ■

Passive Investment Income Penalty Tax

A tax is imposed on the excess passive income of S corporations that possess AEP from C corporation years. The tax rate is the highest corporate income tax rate for the year. The rate is applied to excess net passive income (ENPI), which is determined using the following formula.

$$\text{Excess net passive income} = \frac{\text{Passive investment income in excess of 25\% of gross receipts for the year}}{\text{Passive investment income for the year}} \times \text{Net passive investment income for the year}$$

Passive investment income (PII) includes gross receipts derived from royalties, rents, dividends, interest, annuities, and sales and exchanges of stocks and securities.[55] Only the net gain from the disposition of capital assets (other than stocks

[55] § 1362(d)(3)(C)(i).

and securities) is taken into account in computing gross receipts. Net passive income is passive income reduced by any deductions directly connected with the production of that income. Any passive income tax reduces the amount the shareholders must take into income.

The excess net passive income cannot exceed a hypothetical C corporate taxable income for the year, before considering special C corporation deductions (like the dividends received deduction) or an NOL carryover.[56]

EXAMPLE 37

Lilac Corporation, an electing S corporation, has gross receipts totaling $264,000 (of which $110,000 is PII). Expenditures directly connected to the production of the PII total $30,000. Therefore, Lilac has net PII of $80,000 ($110,000 – $30,000), and its PII exceeds 25% of its gross receipts by $44,000 [$110,000 PII – (25% × $264,000)]. Excess net passive income (ENPI) is $32,000, calculated as follows.

$$\text{ENPI} = \frac{\$44{,}000}{\$110{,}000} \times \$80{,}000 = \$32{,}000$$

Lilac's PII tax is $11,200 ($32,000 × 35%). ■

PLANNING *Strategies*

AVOID PII PITFALLS

★ **Framework Focus: Tax Rate**

Strategy ★ Avoid Double Taxation.

Watch for a possible violation of the PII limitation. Avoid a consecutive third year with excess passive income when the corporation has accumulated E & P from C corporation years. In this connection, assets that produce passive income (e.g., stocks and bonds, certain rental assets) might be retained by the shareholders in their individual capacities and kept out of the corporation.

DIGGING DEEPER 7

Find more information on this topic at our Web site: ***http://wft-entities.swlearning.com.***

Summary

The S corporation rules are elective and can be used to benefit a number of owners of small businesses.

- When the business is profitable, the S corporation election removes the threat of double taxation on corporate profits.
- When the business is generating losses, deductions for allocable losses are immediately available to the shareholders.

Over one-half of all U.S. corporations operate under the S rules. Flow-through income is taxed to the shareholders, who increase basis in their corporate stock accordingly. In this manner, subsequent distributions to shareholders can be made tax-free. Flow-through losses reduce stock and debt basis, but loss deductions are suspended when basis reaches zero. Flow-through items that could be treated differently by various shareholders are separately stated on Schedule K–1 of the Form 1120S.

Corporate-level taxes are seldom assessed on S corporations, but they guard against abuses of the S rules, such as shifting appreciated assets from higher

[56]§§ 1374(d)(4), and 1375(a) and (b).

TAX FACT

The S Corporation Economy

Total assets controlled by even the smallest S corporations make up a significant part of the economy. The 3.2 million S corporations filing returns, representing over 5.5 million shareholders, employ $2.02 trillion in assets in their investments and operations.

Assets Controlled ($B) by S Corporations, by Number of Shareholders, 2002 Tax Year

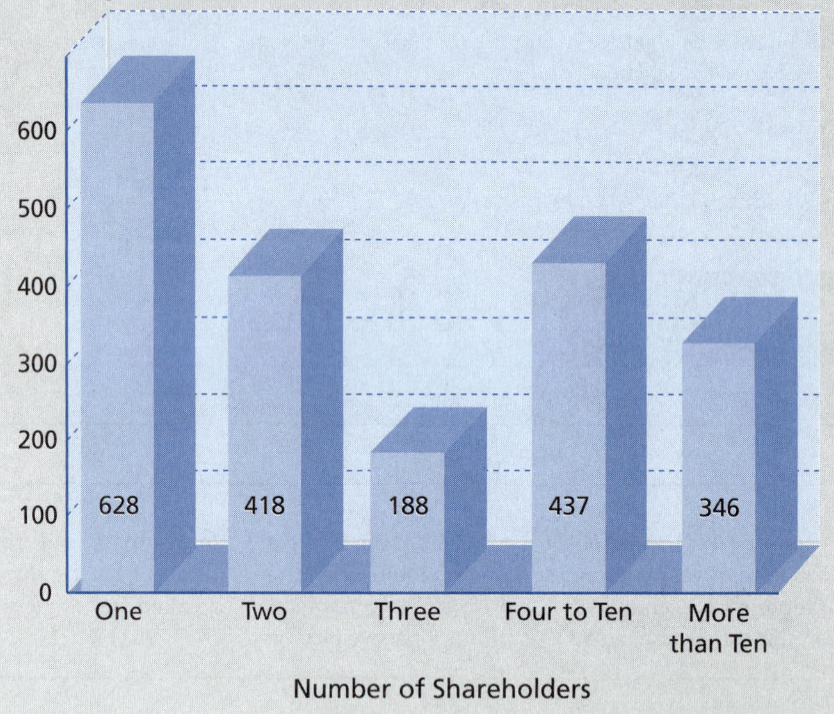

C corporation rates to lower individual rates (the built-in gains tax) or doing the same with investment assets (the tax on excessive PII).

The S rules are designed for closely held businesses with simple capital structures. Eligibility rules are not oppressive, and they do not include any limitations on the corporation's capitalization value, sales, number or distribution of employees, or other operating measures. The S election process can be complex, though, and maintenance of S status must be monitored on an ongoing basis.

Suggested Further Readings

Donald Cunningham and Paul Erickson, "Employment Taxes and the Entity Choice Decision," *Business Entities Online*, July/August 2004.

James P. Dawson and David W. LaRue, "Eluding the LIFO Recapture Provisions of Subchapter S," *Business Entities*, September/October 2003, pp. 22–30.

Charles M. Steines, "S Corporation Distribution Subject to City Earnings Tax," *Journal of Multistate Taxation and Incentives*, October 2002, pp. 38–40.

James L. Wittenbach and Ken Milani, "FICA Factors for S Corporation Payments to Owner/Employees," *Practical Tax Strategies*, December 2005, pp. 338–345.

KEY TERMS

AAA bypass election, 12–16
Accumulated adjustments account (AAA), 12–15
Built-in gains tax, 12–25
Other adjustments account (OAA), 12–16
Passive investment income (PII), 12–10
S corporation, 12–2
Small business corporation, 12–5
Subchapter S, 12–2
Voluntary revocation, 12–9

PROBLEM MATERIALS

PROBLEMS

1. What are some tax differences between a partnership and an S corporation?

2. On March 2, the two 50% shareholders of a calendar year corporation decide to elect S status. One of the shareholders, Terry, purchased her stock from a previous shareholder (a nonresident alien) on January 18 of the same year. Identify any potential problems for Terry or the corporation. *Issue ID*

3. Burt is the custodian at Quaker Inn, an S corporation that has paid him bonuses over the years in the form of shares in the corporation. Burt now holds 276 shares in Quaker Inn. *Ethics*

   While listening to a television debate about a national health care plan, Burt decides that the company's health coverage is unfair. He is concerned about this because his wife, Dora, is seriously ill.

   During the second week in December, Burt informs Quaker's president that he would like a Christmas bonus of $75,000 cash, or else he will sell 10 shares of his stock to one of his relatives, a nonresident alien. The resulting loss of the S election would trigger about $135,000 in Federal corporate income taxes for the current year alone. Can you defend Burt's position?

4. Ninety-nine individuals own all of the shares of Woodpecker Corporation. Hal and Mary Jones want to buy into the corporation, and then to direct the entity to make an S election. Can Woodpecker so elect? How many signatures must appear on the consent form making the S election?

5. Which of the following entities may be S corporation shareholders?
   a. An estate.
   b. A partnership.
   c. A corporation.
   d. A resident individual.
   e. A limited liability partnership.
   f. An LLC.
   g. An IRA.
   h. A minor child.
   i. A nonresident alien.

6. Which of the following items are *not* considered passive investment income?
   a. Dividends.
   b. Interest.
   c. Rent income (no significant services).
   d. Gain from sale of inventory.
   e. Royalties.
   f. Gain from sale of stock.
   g. Gain from sale of equipment.

Issue ID

7. Lynch's share of her S corporation's net operating loss is $41,000, but her stock basis is only $29,000. Point out any tax consequences to Lynch.

8. Zebra, Inc., a calendar year S corporation, incurred the following items. Sammy is a 40% shareholder in Zebra throughout the year.

Sales	$100,000
Cost of goods sold	40,000
Depreciation expense	10,000
Administrative expenses	5,000
§ 1231 gain	21,000
§ 1250 gain	20,000
Short-term capital loss from stock sale	6,000
Long-term capital loss from stock sale	4,000
Long-term capital gain from stock sale	15,000
Charitable contributions	4,500

a. Calculate Sammy's share of nonseparately computed income.
b. Calculate Sammy's share of any net long-term capital gain.

9. An S corporation's profit and loss statement shows net profits of $90,000 (book income). The corporation has three equal shareholders. From supplemental data, you obtain the following information about the corporation. All of the indicated items are included in book income.

Selling expenses	$21,200
Municipal bond interest income	2,000
Dividends received on IBM stock	9,000
§ 1231 gain	6,000
§ 1250 gain	12,000
Recovery of bad debts	4,000
Long-term capital losses	6,000
Salary paid to owners (each)	10,000
Cost of goods sold	95,000

a. Determine nonseparately computed income or loss.
b. What would be the portion of taxable income or loss for Chang, one of the shareholders?

10. Polly has been the sole shareholder of a calendar year S corporation since its inception. Polly's stock basis is $15,500, and she receives a distribution of $19,000. Corporate-level accounts are as follows.

AAA	$6,000	AEP	$500

How is Polly taxed on the distribution?

11. Suresh, Inc., an S corporation, has a beginning AAA balance of $782,000. During the year, the following items occur.

Operating income	$472,000
Interest income	6,500
Dividend income	14,050
Municipal bond interest income	6,000
Long-term capital loss from sale of land	7,400
§ 179 expense	6,000
Charitable contributions	19,000
Cash distributions	57,000

Calculate Suresh's ending AAA balance.

Issue ID

12. Berger, Inc., a calendar year S corporation, is owned equally by three individuals: Adam, Bonnie, and Charlene. The company owns a plot of land, purchased for $110,000 three years ago. When the land is worth $170,000, it is distributed to Charlene. Assuming

Charlene's stock basis is $300,000 on the distribution date, what are the potential tax ramifications?

Decision Making

13. Goblins, Inc., a calendar year S corporation, has $90,000 of AEP. Tobias, the sole shareholder, has an adjusted basis of $80,000 in his stock with a zero balance in the AAA.
   a. Determine the tax aspects if a $90,000 salary is paid to Tobias.
   b. Same as (a), except that Tobias receives a cash distribution of $90,000.

14. At the beginning of the year, Malcolm, a 50% shareholder of a calendar year S corporation, has a stock basis of $22,000. During the year, the corporation has taxable income of $32,000. The following data are obtained from supplemental sources.

Dividends received from IBM	$12,000
Municipal bond interest income	18,000
Short-term capital gain	6,000
§ 1245 gain	10,000
§ 1231 gain	7,000
Charitable contributions	5,000
Political contributions	8,000
Short-term capital loss	12,000
Distribution to Malcolm	6,000
Selling expense	14,000
Beginning AAA	40,000

   a. Compute Malcolm's ending stock basis.
   b. Compute ending AAA.

Issue ID

15. Red Dragon, Inc., is an S corporation with a sizable amount of AEP from a C corporation year. The S corporation has $300,000 of investment income and $300,000 of investment expenses. The company makes cash distributions to enable its sole shareholder to pay her taxes. What are the tax aspects to consider?

16. On January 1, Bobby and Alicia own equally all of the stock of an electing S corporation called Prairie Dirt Delight. The company has a $60,000 loss for the year (not a leap year). On the 219th day of the year, Bobby sells his half of the stock to his son, Bubba. How much of the $60,000 loss, if any, is allocated to Bubba?

Communications

17. A calendar year S corporation has a taxable loss of $80,000 and a capital loss of $20,000. Ms. Muhammad owns 30% of the corporate stock and has a $24,000 basis in her stock. Determine the amounts of the taxable loss and capital loss, if any, that flow through to Ms. Muhammad. Prepare a tax memo for the files.

18. Money, Inc., a calendar year S corporation, has two unrelated shareholders, each owning 50% of the stock. Both shareholders have a $400,000 stock basis as of January 1, and Money has AAA of $300,000 and AEP of $600,000. During the year, Money has operating income of $100,000. At the end of the year, Money distributes securities worth $1 million, with an adjusted basis of $800,000. Determine the tax effects of these transactions.

Decision Making

19. Assume the same facts as in Problem 18, except that the two shareholders consent to an AAA bypass election (i.e., to distribute AEP first).

20. An S corporation's Form 1120S shows taxable income of $88,000 for the year. Daniel owns 40% of the stock throughout the year. The following information is obtained from the corporate records.

Salary paid to Daniel	$52,000
Tax-exempt interest income	3,000
Charitable contributions	6,000
Dividends received from a non-U.S. corporation	5,000
Long-term capital loss	6,000
§ 1245 gain	11,000
Refund of prior state income taxes	5,000
Cost of goods sold	72,000
Short-term capital loss	7,000

Administrative expenses	$18,000
Short-term capital gain	14,000
Selling expenses	11,000
Daniel's beginning stock basis	32,000
Daniel's additional stock purchases	9,000
Beginning AAA	31,000
Daniel's loan to corporation	20,000

a. Compute book income or loss.
b. Compute Daniel's ending stock basis.
c. Calculate ending corporate AAA.

21. Cloris owns 35% of the stock of an S corporation and lends the corporation $7,000 during the year. Her stock basis in the corporation at the end of the year is $25,000. If the corporation sustains a $110,000 operating loss during the year, what amount, if any, can Cloris deduct with respect to the operating loss?

Communications

22. Candy owns 40% of the stock of Park, a valid S corporation. Her stock basis is $25,000, and she loaned $8,000 to the corporation during the year. How much of Park's $110,000 operating loss can Candy deduct for this year? Show your computation of the tax consequences in spreadsheet form and include them in a memo to your manager.

23. Crew Corporation elected S status effective for tax year 2006. As of January 1, 2006, Crew's assets were appraised as follows.

	Adjusted Basis	Fair Market Value
Cash	$ 16,010	$ 16,010
Accounts receivable	–0–	55,400
Investment in land	110,000	215,000
Building	220,000	275,000
Goodwill	–0–	93,000

In each of the following situations, calculate any built-in gains tax, assuming that the highest corporate tax rate is 35%. C corporation taxable income would have been $100,000.

a. During 2006, Crew collects $40,000 of the accounts receivable.
b. In 2007, Crew sells the land held for investment for $203,000.
c. In 2008, the building is sold for $270,000.

24. Chris Valletta, the sole shareholder of Taylor, Inc., elects to terminate the S election, effective at the end of the year. As of the end of the year, Taylor, Inc., has AAA of $120,000 and OAA of $13,000. This amount reflects the fact that Chris received a cash dividend of $130,000 on January 15. If his stock basis was $220,000 before the distribution, calculate his taxable amount and his ending stock basis.

25. Opal, the owner of *all* of the shares of an S corporation in Richmond, Virginia, transfers all of the stock to Will at the middle of the tax year. There is a $200,000 NOL for the entire year, but $130,000 of the loss occurs during the first half of the year. With a short-year election, how much of the loss is allocated to Will?

26. Jeff, a 52% owner of an S corporation, has a stock basis of zero at the beginning of the year. Jeff's basis in a $10,000 loan made to the corporation and evidenced by a corporate note has been reduced to zero by pass-through losses. During the year, his net share of the corporate taxable income is $11,000. At the end of the year, Jeff receives a $15,000 distribution. Discuss the tax effects of the distribution.

27. Assume the same facts as in Problem 26, except that there is no $15,000 distribution, but the corporation repays the loan principal to Jeff. Discuss the tax effects.

28. Assume the same facts as in Problem 26, except that Jeff's share of corporate taxable income is only $8,000, and there is no distribution. However, the corporation repays the

$10,000 loan principal to Jeff. Discuss the tax effects. Assume there was no corporate note (i.e., only an account payable). Does this change your answer?

29. An S corporation in Polly Beach, South Carolina, has a recognized built-in gain of $95,000 and taxable income of $80,000. It holds a $7,000 NOL carryforward and a $9,000 business credit carryforward from a C corporation year. There are no earnings and profits from C corporation years. Calculate the built-in gains tax liability.

30. Ruff Ltd., an S corporation in Flint, Michigan, recognizes an $80,000 built-in gain and a $10,000 built-in loss. Ruff also holds an $8,000 unexpired NOL from a C corporation year. Currently, Ruff generates ordinary income of $65,000. Calculate any built-in gains tax.

31. Lejeune, Inc., an S corporation in Boone, North Carolina, has operating revenues of $400,000, taxable interest of $380,000, operating expenses of $250,000, and deductions attributable to the interest income of $140,000. Lejeune's accumulated E & P amounts to $2 million. Calculate any penalty tax payable by this S corporation or its shareholders.

Issue ID

Communications

32. Friedman, Inc., an S corporation, holds some highly appreciated land and inventory, and some marketable securities that have declined in value. It anticipates a sale of these assets and a complete liquidation of the company over the next two years. Arnold Schwartz, the CFO, calls you, asking how to treat these transactions. Prepare a tax memo indicating what you told Arnold over the phone.

Extender

33. Claude Bergeron sold 1,000 shares of Ditta, Inc., an S corporation located in Concord, North Carolina, for $9,000. He has a stock basis of $107,000 in the shares. Assuming that Claude is single and that he is the original owner of these § 1244 stock shares, calculate the appropriate tax treatment of any gain or loss. If he sold the stock for $201,000, could he obtain a 50% exclusion under § 1202 for one-half of the gain?

Extender

Decision Making

34. Gert is the owner of all of the shares of an S corporation. Gert is considering receiving a salary of $80,000 from the business. She will pay 7.65% FICA taxes on the salary, and the S corporation will pay the same amount of FICA tax. If Gert reduces her salary to $60,000 and takes an additional $20,000 as a distribution, how much total tax could be saved?

Extender

Decision Making

35. One of your clients, Sweet Tea Corporation, is considering electing S status. Both of Sweet Tea's equal shareholders paid $30,000 for their stock. As of the beginning of 2004, Sweet Tea's Subchapter C NOL carryforward is $110,000. Its taxable income projections for the next few years are as follows.

2004	$40,000
2005	25,000
2006	25,000
2007	25,000

Will you counsel Sweet Tea to make the S election?

Extender

36. C&C Properties is an S corporation and owns two rental real estate undertakings: Carrot Plaza and Cantaloupe Place. Both properties produce an annual $10,000 operating loss. C&C's Schedule K aggregates the results of the two locations into one number.

Dan and Marta, C&C's two equal shareholders, both hold a $7,000 stock basis in C&C as of the beginning of the year. Marta actively participates in the Cantaloupe location, but not at Carrot. Dan actively participates at neither location. Determine the amount of the available loss pass-throughs for both shareholders.

COMPREHENSIVE TAX RETURN PROBLEM

Tax Return Problem

37. Donald Jacobs (654–12–8756) and Ryan Pearson (324–21–4211) are 30% and 70% owners of JR, Inc. (74–7654321), a building contractor, located at 86135 Marble Canyon Drive, Ft. Worth, TX 76137. The company's S corporation election was effective on May 28, 1995. The following information was taken from the income statement for 2005.

Gross receipts	$1,769,965	
Other income	7,030	
Interest income (taxable)	1,630	
Tax-exempt interest	8,031	
Dividend income (not qualified)	1,280	$1,787,936
Salaries and wages	$ 420,580	
Repairs	24,961	
Rents (operating expenses)	135,207	
Taxes (payroll)	45,311	
Interest expense	21,774	
Depreciation	144,898	
Advertising	15,544	
Employee benefits programs	7,908	
Other deductions—miscellaneous	216,594	
§ 179 depreciation	23,967	1,056,744
Book income		$ 731,192

A partially completed comparative balance sheet appears as follows.

	Beginning of the Year	End of the Year
Cash	$ 19,243	$ 166,437
Other investments	152,789	684,550
Buildings and other depreciable assets	899,505	993,352
Accumulated depreciation	(564,744)	(733,609)
Total	$ 506,793	$1,110,730
Mortgages, notes, bonds (payable in one year or more)	$ 410,742	$ 378,538
Capital stock	1,000	1,000
Retained earnings	95,051	?
Total	$ 506,793	$?

The corporation distributed a total of $95,051 to the two shareholders during the year. The distributions were made from the entity's:

Accumulated adjustments account	$95,051
Other adjustments account	–0–
Previously taxed income	–0–

Prepare Form 1120S and Schedule K–1 for Ryan Pearson. If any information is missing, make realistic assumptions and list them.

BRIDGE *Discipline*

1. Using an online research service, determine whether your state:
   a. Allows flow-through treatment for Federal S corporations.
   b. Requires any state-specific form to elect or elect out of S treatment at the state level.
   c. Places any additional withholding tax burdens on out-of-state U.S. shareholders or on non-U.S. shareholders of an S corporation.
   d. Requires any additional information disclosures or compliance deadlines for S corporations operating in the state *other than* to the revenue department (e.g., a report that must be filed with the secretary of state).

RESEARCH PROBLEMS

Note: Solutions to Research Problems can be prepared by using the **RIA Checkpoint® Student Edition** online research product, which is available to accompany this text. It is also possible to prepare solutions to the Research Problems by using tax research materials found in a standard tax library.

THOMSON RIA

Decision Making

Research Problem 1. Eel Corporation, in Spivey Corners, North Carolina, has filed a Form 1120S for six years, and the local office of the IRS has sent the company a letter requesting an audit next month. Carrie, who is in charge of tax matters at Eel, cannot find a copy of the original S election, Form 2553.

The original shareholders and officers all agree that a local accountant filed the form, but he passed away last year. Several of the shareholders instruct Carrie to prepare a backdated Form 2553, which they will sign. Carrie could then copy the form and tell the agent that this was a copy of the original Form 2553. What should Carrie do? She estimates that any proposed deficiency would be in the range of $625,000.

Partial list of research aids:
§§ 1362(b)(5) and (f).
Rev.Proc. 97–48, 1997–2 C.B. 521.
Ltr.Rul. 9748033.

Research Problem 2. Ewing Ballman owned a major league baseball team (the Rattlers), an S corporation. In 1995, Ballman sold 49% of his stock to Avon Fogel. Fogel also bought an option to purchase more of the stock. In 1999, Fogel purchased 2% more of the shares of the team, but later he encountered financial problems. In 2006, Ballman loaned $34 million to the team; then the Rattlers lent the money to Fogel, secured by his stock shares. Fogel's stock was auctioned off, but no acceptable bids were obtained.

Fogel defaulted on the $34 million loan and signed a waiver allowing the Rattlers to take his stock and options. The Rattlers claimed that the collateral had no value and deducted the full amount of the loan. Ballman deducted the losses on his 2007 tax return. Do you agree with Ballman's action?

Research Problem 3. Charles, Inc., was a closely held C corporation engaged in the real estate rental business in 2005. The company had $6 million in passive activity losses. In 2006, Charles elected to be taxed as an S corporation, and the company sold a number of rental properties. May these suspended passive activity losses (PAL) be claimed as deductions under § 469(g)(1)(A)?

Recall that § 1371(b)(1) prohibits an S corporation from using any carryforwards from a year in which it was a C corporation. If the PAL deductions are disallowed, may Charles increase its cost basis in the sold property?

Research Problem 4. Peter Sleiman entered into a lease agreement with Blockbuster Video, Inc., to purchase land, build a video rental store, and lease the property to Blockbuster. Sleiman formed an S corporation and assigned his rights under the lease to the corporation, REE, Inc. REE then obtained bank loans of approximately $1 million, pledging the property that the S corporation had purchased as collateral under the contract. Sleiman personally guaranteed the corporation's loans, but the banks never asked him for repayment. Does Sleiman get a $1 million step-up in basis for the guaranteed loans?

Partial list of research aids:
Selfe v. U.S., 86–1 USTC ¶9115, 75 AFTR2d 86–464, 778 F.2d 769 (CA–11, 1985).
Plantation Patterns, Inc. v. Comm., 72–2 USTC ¶9494, 29 AFTR2d 72–1408, 462 F.2d 712 (CA–5, 1972).

Internet *Activity*

Use the tax resources of the Internet to address the following questions. Do not restrict your search to the World Wide Web, but include a review of newsgroups and general reference materials, practitioner sites and resources, primary sources of the tax law, chat rooms and discussion groups, and other opportunities.

Communications

Research Problem 5. Go to the Internet site of a newspaper or business magazine and find a case study of how to start a small business and choose the best tax entity (e.g., C corporation, S corporation, etc.). Summarize your findings in an e-mail to your instructor.

Communications

Research Problem 6. Use a spreadsheet program to graph the growth in the number of S corporation returns filed. Obtain data for these years: 1975, 1980, 1985, 1990, 1995, 2000, and 2005. In a note to your instructor, explain the trends that you found in S returns filed.

Communications

Research Problem 7. Which types of trusts can own S corporation stock? Summarize your findings in a PowerPoint presentation (maximum 3 slides) for your classmates.

http://wft.swlearning.com

PART 5

Special Business Topics

Part V covers several topics that are relevant to all types of business entities. Business entities operate in both the international arena and state arenas. Therefore, multijurisdictional taxation is addressed from both a multinational business perspective and a multistate business perspective. A very important component of the basic tax model, tax credits, is presented next. This is followed by a discussion of the alternative tax system applicable to certain C corporations, that is, the AMT. Part V concludes with a comparative analysis of the different types of business entities previously discussed. This analysis recognizes the relevance of each of the three life cycle components in selecting a business entity form.

http://wft.swlearning.com

CHAPTER 13

Multijurisdictional Taxation

LEARNING OBJECTIVES

After completing Chapter 13, you should be able to:

LO.1

Recognize the computational and compliance issues that arise when a taxpayer operates in more than one taxing jurisdiction.

LO.2

Identify the sources of tax law applicable to a taxpayer operating in more than one country.

LO.3

Outline the U.S. tax effects related to the offshore operations of a U.S. taxpayer.

LO.4

Describe the tax effects related to the U.S. operations of a non-U.S. taxpayer.

LO.5

Identify the sources of tax law applicable to a taxpayer operating in more than one U.S. state.

LO.6

Apply computational principles designed for a taxpayer operating in more than one U.S. state.

LO.7

Synthesize the international and multistate tax systems and recognize common issues faced by both systems.

OUTLINE

TAX *Talk*

Don't tax you, don't tax me; tax the fellow behind the tree.

—Russell B. Long

Don't tax you, don't tax me; tax the companies across the sea.

—Dan Rostenkowski

One of the tax planning principles that has been discussed throughout this text relates to the use of favorable tax jurisdictions—moving income into lower-taxed districts and deductions into higher-taxed ones. Many individuals dream of moving all of their income and wealth to a tax-friendly state or a proverbial island in the tropics, never to be taxed again. This chapter examines the temptations that attract taxpayers to this idea and various ways in which this goal can and cannot be accomplished.

LO.1

Recognize the computational and compliance issues that arise when a taxpayer operates in more than one taxing jurisdiction.

The Multijurisdictional Taxpayer

Companies large and small must deal with the consequences of earning income through activities in different jurisdictions. A small business may have its center of operations in a single city but have customers in many states and countries. Consider the typical U.S. multinational corporation. Its assets, employees, customers, suppliers, lenders, and owners are located in numerous locations, crossing city, county, state, national, and even "virtual" borders.

EXAMPLE 1

RobotCo, a corporation created and organized in Delaware, produces and sells robotic manufacturing equipment. It holds its valuable patents and intangible property in Delaware and Bermuda. The company has manufacturing operations in Ireland, Singapore, Germany, Texas, and New Jersey. It has distribution centers in Canada, the United Kingdom, Germany, Hong Kong, Texas, New Jersey, Georgia, California, Illinois, and Arizona. RobotCo's sales force spends time in Europe, Asia, Mexico, Canada, and almost every state in the union. RobotCo's engineers likewise provide technical service to customers wherever they may be located. And in recent years, RobotCo has developed a substantial Web presence.

RobotCo must determine its potential exposure to tax in each of these jurisdictions. Such exposure usually is based on RobotCo's nexus (or economic connection) to the various locations. Unfortunately for all concerned, each of these taxing jurisdictions uses a different taxing system and methods, imposes taxes under differing structures, and even defines the tax base differently. How does RobotCo divide its income among the various jurisdictions that want a piece of the tax pie, determine its tax costs, mitigate any potential double taxation, and file the appropriate information returns with this diverse set of taxing authorities? Such questions and more must be addressed by modern-day businesses. ■

BRIDGE *Discipline*

Bridge to International Law

Many of the provisions of the U.S. tax law relating to international transactions are thinly disguised extensions of a principle of international law—the ability of sovereign countries to protect the safety and privacy of their citizens abroad.

For instance, U.S. tax auditors often have difficulty obtaining or reviewing the documentation supporting deductions claimed by U.S. taxpayers operating overseas. Banking, credit card, and other records that are available (in the course of business or forcibly by summons) for strictly U.S. transactions are not available once those same transactions cross national borders.

How could the U.S. tax base include rental and royalty income of a U.S. investor operating through a corporation in another country when property ownership and taxation records are not available for substantiation or audit outside the country of the investment? Perhaps this explains why the U.S. tax base typically excludes such items.

Conversely, when the taxing agencies of multiple countries are allowed by law to trade among themselves information about business operations and taxpayers, the fairness and completeness of the taxing process may improve. But such lengthening of the reach of the taxing authorities results from diplomatic negotiations among the countries, not from the passage of legislation.

Thousands of state and local jurisdictions are involved in the taxation of interstate transactions through income, property, sales, or other taxes. State and local taxes make up over one-third of all taxes collected in the United States. Global trade also represents a major portion of the U.S. economy. In recent years, U.S. exports of goods and services have averaged over $1 trillion a year, with imports reaching $1.8 trillion. As of the beginning of 2005, U.S. companies had direct investments abroad exceeding $2 trillion, and foreign companies had invested $1.8 trillion in U.S. businesses. Hundreds of countries and many more political subdivisions participated in the taxation of these transactions. These interstate and international trade flows, along with cross-state and cross-country investments, create significant Federal, state, and local tax consequences for both U.S. and foreign entities.

U.S. Taxation of Multinational Transactions

Cross-country transactions create the need for special tax considerations for both the United States and its trading partners. From a U.S. perspective, international tax laws should promote the global competitiveness of U.S. enterprises and at the same time protect the tax revenue base of the United States. These two objectives sometimes conflict, however. The need to deal with both objectives contributes to the complexity of the rules governing the U.S. taxation of cross-border transactions.

EXAMPLE 2

U.S. persons engage in activities outside the United States for many different reasons. Consider two U.S. corporations that have established sales subsidiaries in foreign countries. Dedalus, Inc., operates in Germany, a high-tax country, because customers demand local attention from sales agents. Mulligan, Inc., operates in the Cayman Islands, a tax haven country, simply to shift income outside the United States. U.S. tax law must fairly address both situations with the same law. ■

FIGURE 13–1 **U.S. Taxation of International Transactions**

	U.S. Person	Foreign Person
U.S.-Source Income	Domestic taxation only	"Inbound" taxation
Foreign-Source Income	"Outbound" taxation	Limited U.S. authority to tax

U.S. international tax provisions are concerned primarily with two types of potential taxpayers: U.S. persons earning income from outside the United States and non-U.S. persons earning income from inside the United States.[1] U.S. persons earning income only from inside the United States do not create any international tax issues and are taxed under the purely domestic provisions of the Internal Revenue Code. Foreign persons earning income from outside the United States are not within the taxing jurisdiction of the United States (unless this income is somehow directly connected to U.S. operations).

The U.S. taxation of international transactions can be organized in terms of "outbound" and "inbound" taxation. **Outbound taxation** refers to the U.S. taxation of foreign-source income earned by U.S. taxpayers. **Inbound taxation** refers to the U.S. taxation of U.S.-source income earned by foreign taxpayers. Figure 13–1 summarizes these concepts.

LO.2

Identify the sources of tax law applicable to a taxpayer operating in more than one country.

Sources of Law

U.S. individuals and companies operating across national borders are subject to both U.S. law and the laws of the other jurisdictions in which they operate or invest. Accordingly, the source of law depends on the nature of a taxpayer's connection with a particular country. For U.S. persons, the Internal Revenue Code addresses the tax consequences of earning income anywhere in the world. However, U.S. persons must also comply with the local tax law of the other nations in which they operate. For non-U.S. persons, U.S. statutory law is relevant to income they earn that is connected to U.S. income-producing activities, whether those activities involve a passive investment or an active trade or business. Whether non-U.S. persons are also subject to potential tax in their home countries on their U.S. income depends on their own local tax law.

It is difficult for the United States (or any country) to craft local tax laws that equitably address all of the potential issues that arise when two countries attempt to tax the same income. Furthermore, any uncertainty as to tax consequences can be an impediment to global business investment. Consequently, countries enter into **income tax treaties** with each other to provide more certainty to taxpayers.

Tax treaties are the result of specific negotiations with each treaty partner, so each treaty is unique. Nevertheless, all tax treaties are organized in the same way and address similar issues. For example, all treaties include provisions regarding the taxation of investment income, business profits from a **permanent establishment (PE)**, personal service income, and exceptions for certain persons (e.g., athletes, entertainers, students, and teachers). Treaty provisions generally override the treatment otherwise called for under the Internal Revenue Code or foreign tax statutes.

Permanent establishment (PE) is an important concept that is defined in all income tax treaties. A person has a PE within a country when its activities within that country rise beyond a minimal level. Tax treaties outline the activities that create a PE, including an office, plant, or other fixed place of business. Treaties also specify specific activities that do not create a PE (e.g., maintaining goods in a

[1]The term "person" includes an individual, corporation, partnership, trust, estate, or association. § 7701(a)(1). The terms "domestic" and "foreign" are defined in §§ 7701(a)(4) and (5).

TAX FACT

U.S. Income Tax Treaties in Force

The United States has entered into income tax treaties with the following nations:

Australia	Finland	Korea	Russia
Austria	France	Latvia	Slovak Republic
Barbados	Germany	Lithuania	Slovenia
Belgium	Greece	Luxembourg	South Africa
Canada	Hungary	Mexico	Spain
China	Iceland	Morocco	Sweden
Commonwealth of Independent States*	India	Netherlands	Switzerland
	Indonesia	New Zealand	Thailand
	Ireland	Norway	Trinidad and Tobago
Cyprus	Israel	Pakistan	Tunisia
Czech Republic	Italy	Philippines	Turkey
Denmark	Jamaica	Poland	United Kingdom
Egypt	Japan	Portugal	Venezuela
Estonia	Kazakhstan	Romania	

*The income tax treaty between the United States and the former Soviet Union applies to the countries of Armenia, Azerbaijan, Belarus, Georgia, Kyrgyzstan, Moldova, Tajikistan, Turkmenistan, Ukraine, and Uzbekistan. The Commonwealth of Independent States is an association of many of the former constituent republics of the Soviet Union.

warehouse or a temporary construction project). Once a person has a PE within a country, the business profits associated with the PE become subject to tax in that country.

EXAMPLE 3

Amelia, Inc., a U.S. corporation, sells boating supplies to customers in the United States and Canada. Amelia has no assets in Canada. All Canadian sales transactions are conducted via the Internet or telephone from Amelia's Florida office. Because Amelia does not have any assets in Canada or conduct any activities within Canada, it does not have a Canadian PE. Consequently, Canada does not impose an income tax on the profit associated with Amelia's Canadian sales. However, if Amelia opens a sales office in Canada, a PE will exist, and Canada will tax the profits associated with the PE. ■

Although the United States has entered into more than 50 income tax treaties, many jurisdictions where U.S. taxpayers operate are not covered by a treaty. Where there is no tax treaty, the more subjective test of whether a person is "engaged in a trade or business" within a country replaces the PE determination. Both the PE concept and the engaged in a trade or business concept are closely related to the determination of whether a person has nexus within a jurisdiction for state and local tax purposes.

PLANNING *Strategies*

TREATY SHOPPING

★ **Framework Focus: Tax Rate**

Strategy ★ Avoid Double Taxation.

U.S. taxpayers with operations in countries that do not have a treaty with the United States may attempt to arrange their activities to take advantage of other countries' tax treaties. In some cases, structuring a company's global operations in this way is simply good tax planning. In other cases, attempts to benefit from tax treaties constitute unwarranted treaty shopping.

USCo, a domestic corporation, owns subsidiaries in Country A and Country B. The U.S. parent wants to obtain a loan from its A subsidiary. The United States does not have a tax treaty with A, but it does have a tax treaty with B. Countries A and B have a tax treaty with each other. The home tax laws of all three countries impose a withholding tax on payments of interest to persons outside the country. However, the existing tax treaties exempt interest payments from withholding.

If the U.S. parent borrows money directly from its A subsidiary, any interest paid to the subsidiary is subject to a 30 percent withholding tax under the Internal Revenue Code (loan option 1). If the U.S. parent instead borrows money from its B subsidiary, any interest paid to the subsidiary is not subject to withholding under the treaty (loan option 2). Thus, USCo's choice of obtaining the loan from its A subsidiary or its B subsidiary possesses major tax consequences. Making such decisions is part of an appropriate global tax plan.

Alternatively, the U.S. parent could use the B subsidiary as a mere conduit by funneling A funds to B via a loan and then having the B subsidiary lend these funds to the U.S. parent (loan option 3). In this case, however, the ability of the U.S. parent to benefit from the tax treaty with B may be restricted by the provisions of the treaty itself or by U.S. tax law. The United States is likely to take an anti-treaty-shopping position. In such case, it would ignore the intermediate payment to the B subsidiary and treat the interest as being paid directly to the A subsidiary, resulting in a 30 percent withholding tax.

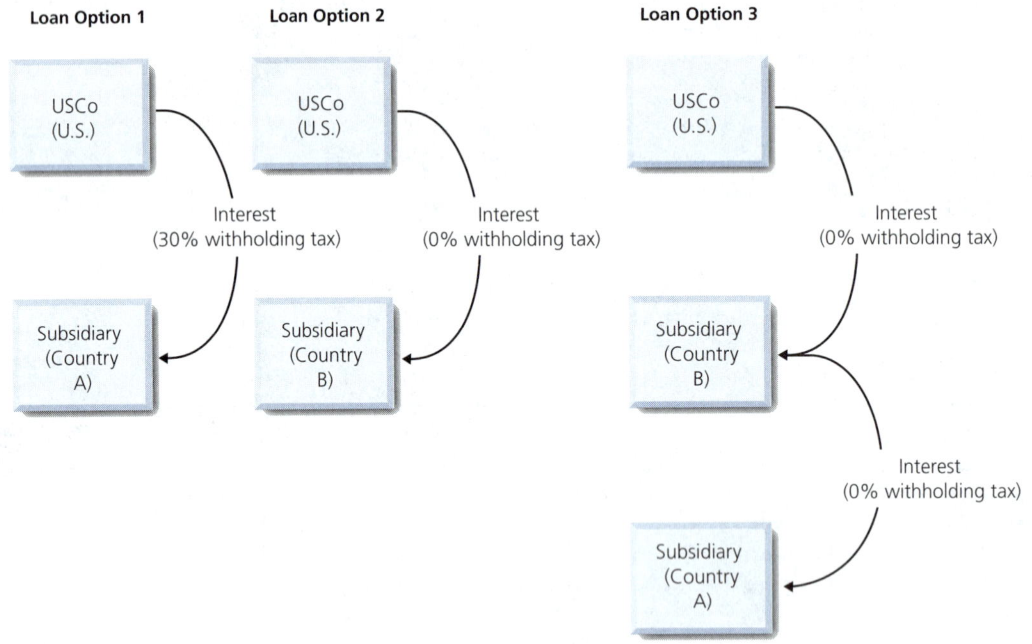

LO.3

Outline the U.S. tax effects related to the offshore operations of a U.S. taxpayer.

Tax Issues

Authority to Tax. The United States taxes the worldwide income of U.S. taxpayers.[2] The United States claims the right to tax all of a U.S. person's income because of the protection of U.S. law provided to a person connected to the United States through citizenship, residency, or place of organization.

Because non-U.S. governments may also tax some of the U.S. person's income when it is earned within their borders, U.S. taxpayers may be subjected to double taxation. There are two broad methods of mitigating this double taxation problem. Under the territorial approach, a country simply exempts from tax the income derived from sources outside its borders. Some European and Asian countries have adopted this approach.[3] The second approach, and the one adopted by the United

[2]Gross income for a U.S. person includes all income from whatever source derived. "Source" in this context means not only type of income (e.g., wages or interest) but geographic source as well (e.g., the United States or Belgium). § 61.

[3]In some cases, countries allow the territorial exemption from home country taxation only if the income has been subject to tax in another country. Other countries, however, exempt such income even if no source country tax is imposed.

TAX *in the News* EXPORT INCENTIVES FADE AWAY

To improve the U.S. balance of trade, Congress has used various export tax incentives to encourage exports of U.S.-produced property. In the late 1970s, Congress created the domestic international sales corporation (DISC) provisions, allowing a DISC to defer the tax on a portion of its export income until actual repatriation of the earnings. After the General Agreement on Tariffs and Trade (GATT) charged that the DISC provisions were a prohibited *export subsidy*, the provisions were curtailed. As an alternative, in 1984 the foreign sales corporation (FSC) provisions (§§ 921–927) were enacted to provide similar tax incentives to U.S. exporters while appeasing the GATT members. FSCs were not allowed to defer the tax on export income. Instead, a certain percentage of export income was permanently exempt from U.S. taxation. In 2000, the United States was forced to repeal the FSC provisions after the World Trade Organization (WTO) found that the FSC benefits constituted an illegal export subsidy. Congress replaced the FSC with a benefit that excluded extraterritorial income from U.S. taxation.

The new extraterritorial income (ETI) regime preserved the basic incentives provided by the FSC rules. Consequently, it is not surprising that the WTO found that the ETI provisions also violated its rules. After losing its appeal to the WTO, the United States repealed the ETI rules in October 2004, but provided a transition rule that allows partial ETI benefits for 2005 and 2006. Congress did not replace the ETI benefit with a new tax benefit for U.S. exporters. Instead, it created a new broad-based "domestic production activities deduction" for U.S. manufacturers and certain other domestic producers equal to 9 percent of the taxpayer's *qualified production activities income* subject to several limitations. The deduction is phased in, beginning with a 3 percent deduction for tax years beginning in 2005 or 2006, a 6 percent deduction for tax years beginning in 2007, 2008, or 2009, and a 9 percent deduction for tax years thereafter. This production activities deduction replacement for ETI is no longer an "international tax" issue, as the deduction does not require exporting or any other activity outside the United States.

States, is to provide a **foreign tax credit** against home country taxes for taxes paid to other countries on the same income. The United States allows its taxpayers to reduce their U.S. tax liability by some or all of the foreign income taxes paid on income earned outside the United States.

EXAMPLE 4

Gator Enterprises, Inc., a U.S. corporation, operates a manufacturing branch in Italy because of customer demand in Italy, local availability of raw materials, and the high cost of shipping finished goods. This branch income is taxed in the United States as part of Gator's worldwide income, but it is also taxed in Italy. Without the availability of a foreign tax credit to mitigate this double taxation, Gator Enterprises would suffer an excessive tax burden and could not compete with local Italian companies. ■

The United States does adopt the territorial approach in taxing foreign persons. Such "inbound" taxpayers generally are subject to tax only on income earned within U.S. borders.

EXAMPLE 5

Purdie, Ltd., a corporation based in the United Kingdom, operates in the United States. Although not a U.S. person, Purdie is taxed in the United States on its U.S.-source business income. If Purdie, Ltd., could operate free of U.S. tax, its U.S.-based competitors would face a serious disadvantage. ■

Income Sourcing. Determining the source of net income is a critical component in calculating the U.S. tax consequences to both U.S. and foreign persons. A number of specific provisions contained in §§ 861 through 865 address the income-sourcing rules for all types of income, including interest, dividends, rents, royalties, services, and sales of assets. Although sometimes complex and subject to various special exceptions, these sourcing rules generally assign income to a geographic source based on the location where the economic activity producing the income took place. In some cases, this relationship is clear, and in others the connection is more obscure.

TAX *in the News* **SOURCING INCOME IN CYBERSPACE**

The use of the Internet in more consumer and business transactions is posing problems for the taxing authorities. Consumers purchase books, music, clothing, and food from Internet retailers. Businesses negotiate with suppliers via online auctions of products and services. Consultants provide services to their clients over the Web. Very few transactions do not have a counterpart that takes place in cyberspace. The existing income-sourcing rules were developed long before the existence of the Internet, and taxing authorities are finding it challenging to apply these rules to Internet transactions.

Where does a sale take place when the Web server is in the Cayman Islands, the seller is in Singapore, and the customer is in Texas? Where is a service performed when all activities take place over the Web? These questions and more must be answered by the United States and its trading partners as the Internet economy grows in size and importance.

EXAMPLE 6

Wickless, Inc., a U.S. corporation, provides scuba diving lessons to customers in Florida and in the Bahamas. These services are sourced based on the place where the activity is performed. The services performed in Florida are U.S.-source income, and those performed in the Bahamas are foreign-source income. Because Wickless, Inc., is a U.S. person, all the income, U.S. and foreign, is subject to U.S. taxation. But the foreign-source portion is important in determining any available foreign tax credits for Wickless. ■

EXAMPLE 7

Brown, Inc., a U.S. corporation, receives dividend income from Takeda Corporation, a Japanese corporation, based on its ownership of Takeda common stock. Brown purchased the stock in the United States and receives all payments in the United States. At first glance, it appears that all of the activities related to earning the dividend income take place in the United States. Nevertheless, the dividend income is treated as foreign source because it is paid by a foreign corporation.[4] ■

In addition to sourcing income, the U.S. rules require taxpayers to assign deductions to U.S.- or foreign-source categories. Deductions that are directly related to an activity or property are first allocated to classes of income to which they directly relate. This is followed by an apportionment between the U.S. and foreign groupings using some reasonable basis (e.g., revenue, gross profit, assets, units sold, time spent). If a deduction is not definitely related to any class of gross income, the deduction is first assigned to all classes of gross income and then apportioned between U.S.- and foreign-source income.

EXAMPLE 8

Ace, Inc., a domestic corporation, has $2 million of gross income and a $50,000 expense, all related to real estate sales and rental activities. The expense is allocated and apportioned using gross income as a basis.

	Gross Income			Apportionment	
	Foreign	U.S.	Allocation	Foreign	U.S.
Sales	$1,000,000	$500,000	$37,500*	$25,000	$12,500**
Rentals	400,000	100,000	12,500	10,000	2,500***
			$50,000	$35,000	$15,000

*$50,000 × ($1,500,000/$2,000,000).
**$37,500 × ($500,000/$1,500,000).
***$12,500 × ($100,000/$500,000).

[4]Section 861(a)(2) establishes that only dividends from domestic corporations are U.S.-source income. Prior to 2005, certain dividends from foreign corporations could be treated as U.S.-source income.

If Ace could show that $45,000 of the expense was directly related to sales income, the $45,000 would be allocated directly to that class of gross income, with the remainder allocated and apportioned between U.S. and foreign source ratably based on gross income. ■

Many deductions may be allocated and apportioned based on any reasonable method the taxpayer chooses.[5] However, the U.S. tax rules impose a specific method for certain types of deductions, including interest and research and experimentation expenses. Interest expense is allocated and apportioned based on the theory that money is fungible. For example, if a taxpayer borrows to support its manufacturing activity, this frees up other funds for use to support its investment activities. Accordingly, the tax rules require that interest expense be allocated and apportioned to all the activities and property of the taxpayer, regardless of the specific purpose for incurring the debt on which interest is paid. Taxpayers must allocate and apportion interest expense on the basis of asset location, using either the fair market value or the tax book value of the assets.

EXAMPLE 9

Fisher, Inc., a domestic corporation, generates both U.S.-source and foreign-source gross income for the current year. Fisher's assets (tax book value) are as follows.

Assets generating U.S.-source income	$18,000,000
Assets generating foreign-source income	5,000,000
	$23,000,000

Fisher incurs interest expense of $800,000 for the current year. Using the tax book value method, interest expense is apportioned to foreign-source income as follows.

$$\frac{\$5{,}000{,}000 \text{ (foreign assets)}}{\$23{,}000{,}000 \text{ (total assets)}} \times \$800{,}000 \text{ (interest expense)} = \$173{,}913.$$ ■

PLANNING *Strategies*

SOURCING INCOME FROM SALES OF INVENTORY

★ **Framework Focus: Tax Rate**

Strategy ★ Control the Character of Income and Deductions.

Generally, income from the sale of personal property is sourced according to the residence of the seller under § 865. Several important exceptions exist for inventory. Income from the sale of purchased inventory is sourced in the country in which the sale takes place under the "title passage" rule. This rule provides the taxpayer with flexibility with regard to sourcing and allows for the creation of zero-taxed foreign-source income.

USCo, a domestic corporation, purchases inventory for resale from unrelated parties and sells the inventory to customers in the United States and Brazil. If title on the Brazilian sales passes in the United States (i.e., risks of loss shift to the Brazilian customers at the shipping point), the inventory income is U.S. source. If title passes outside the United States (e.g., at the customer's warehouse in Brazil), the inventory income is foreign source. Although the Code identifies the income item as foreign source, this income likely is not subject to any Brazilian tax because USCo has no employees, assets, or activities in Brazil. Although the income is subject to U.S. tax in either case (as it represents taxable income to USCo), in the latter case USCo has generated foreign-source income with no corresponding foreign income tax. This will prove very useful in managing USCo's ability to use foreign tax credits, as discussed later in this chapter.

When a taxpayer both produces and sells inventory, the income is apportioned between the country of production and the country of sale. Taxpayers often use a 50–50 allocation method as allowed by § 863(b), where 50 percent of the profits from the sale are automatically assigned to the location of the production assets, and 50 percent of the profits are assigned to the location where title passes.

[5] Reg. § 1.861–8.

Assume that USCo manufactures inventory in its Texas plant and sells the inventory to customers in Mexico. Regardless of the actual economic profit relationship between the manufacturing and selling activities, 50 percent of the profit on the Mexican sales can be assigned to foreign-source income by simply passing title outside the United States.

The Foreign Tax Credit. As discussed earlier, the United States retains the right to tax its citizens and residents on their worldwide taxable income. This approach can result in double taxation, presenting a potential problem to U.S. persons who operate abroad. To reduce the possibility of double taxation, Congress created the foreign tax credit (FTC). A qualified taxpayer is allowed a tax credit for foreign income taxes paid or accrued. The credit is a dollar-for-dollar reduction of U.S. income tax liability. For the most recent years data are available, corporations filing U.S. tax returns claimed $41 billion in FTCs, and individuals claimed $6.3 billion in FTCs. Income receipts on U.S. direct investment abroad were $164.7 billion. Without the benefit of the FTC, much of this income would have been subject to double taxation.

EXAMPLE 10

Caulkin Tools, Inc., a U.S. corporation, has a branch operation in Mexico from which it earns taxable income of $750,000 for the current year. Caulkin pays income tax of $150,000 on these earnings to the Mexican tax authorities. Caulkin must also include the $750,000 in gross income for U.S. tax purposes. Before considering the FTC, Caulkin owes $255,000 in U.S. income taxes on this foreign-source income. Thus, total taxes on the $750,000 could equal $405,000 ($150,000 + $255,000), a 54% effective rate. But Caulkin takes an FTC of $150,000 against its U.S. tax liability on the foreign-source income. Caulkin's total taxes on the $750,000 now are $255,000 ($150,000 + $105,000), a 34% effective rate. ■

The FTC is elective for any particular tax year. If the taxpayer does not "choose" to take the FTC, § 164 allows a deduction for foreign taxes paid or incurred. A taxpayer cannot take a credit and a deduction for the same foreign income taxes, and in most situations the FTC is more valuable to the taxpayer.

U.S. taxpayers may claim FTCs for foreign taxes they pay directly or through withholding as so-called direct credits. In addition, U.S. corporate taxpayers may claim FTCs for foreign taxes paid indirectly. If a U.S. corporation operates in a foreign country through a branch, the direct credit is available for foreign taxes paid. If, however, a U.S. corporation operates in a country through a foreign subsidiary, the direct credit is not available for foreign taxes paid by the foreign corporation. An indirect or **deemed-paid credit** is available to U.S. corporate taxpayers that receive actual or constructive dividends from foreign corporations that have paid foreign income taxes.[6] These foreign taxes are deemed paid by the corporate shareholders in the same proportion as the dividends actually or constructively received bear to the foreign corporation's post-1986 undistributed E & P.

$$\text{Deemed-paid credit} = \frac{\text{Actual or constructive dividend}}{\text{Post-1986 undistributed E \& P}} \times \begin{array}{c}\text{Post-1986}\\ \text{foreign taxes}\end{array}$$

If a U.S. taxpayer claims a deemed-paid credit, § 78 requires the corporation to *gross up* (add to income) the dividend income by the amount of the deemed-paid credit.

EXAMPLE 11

Wren, Inc., a domestic corporation, owns 50% of Finch, Inc., a foreign corporation. Wren receives a dividend of $120,000 from Finch. Finch paid foreign taxes of $500,000 on post-

[6]U.S. corporations must meet certain minimum ownership requirements under § 902 to claim a deemed-paid credit.

TAX FACT

Income Subject to U.S. Tax, Foreign-Source Taxable Income, Current-Year Foreign Taxes, and Foreign Tax Credit: Tax Years 1994–1999

The following table shows some of the most recent data available on the foreign tax credit. Amounts are in millions of dollars.

			U.S. Income Tax before Credits		Foreign-Source Taxable Income (Less Loss)		Current-Year Foreign Taxes		Foreign Tax Credit Claimed	
Tax Year	Number of U.S. Corporation Returns	Income Subject to U.S. Tax	Amount	As a Percentage of Income Subject to U.S. Tax	Amount	As a Percentage of Income Subject to U.S. Tax	Amount	As a Percentage of Foreign-Source Taxable Income	Amount	As a Percentage of U.S. Income Tax before Credits
1994	7,199	$255,439	$ 90,786	35.5%	$101,521	39.7%	$26,470	26.1%	$25,419	28.0%
1995	6,710	303,308	107,996	35.6	120,518	39.7	30,930	25.7	30,416	28.2
1996	6,100	370,049	130,748	35.3	150,826	40.8	41,177	27.3	40,255	30.8
1997	6,569	410,126	144,779	35.3	157,989	38.5	45,080	28.5	42,223	29.2
1998	5,927	377,129	132,740	35.2	147,129	35.9	47,576	32.3	37,338	28.1
1999	5,789	385,832	135,855	35.2	165,713	42.9	41,309	24.9	38,271	28.2

Source: *IRS,* Statistics of Income Bulletin, *Fall 2003. Publication 1136 (Rev. 12–2003), Figure F.*

1986 E & P, which totals $1.2 million. Wren's deemed-paid foreign taxes for FTC purposes are $50,000.

Cash dividend from Finch	$120,000
Deemed-paid foreign taxes	
[($120,000/$1,200,000) × $500,000]	50,000
Gross income to Wren	$170,000

Wren includes $170,000 in gross income for the year. As a result of the dividend received, Wren can claim a credit for the $50,000 in deemed-paid foreign taxes. ■

The United States does not automatically grant an FTC for all foreign taxes paid, and there are limits on the amount of foreign taxes that can be taken as a credit. First, only foreign *income* taxes are potentially creditable. Second, the FTC allowed in any tax year is limited to the U.S. tax imposed on the foreign-source income included on the U.S. tax return.[7] Thus, taxpayers are allowed a credit for the lesser of the foreign income taxes paid or accrued, or the following limitation.

$$\text{FTC limit} = \frac{\text{Foreign-source taxable income}}{\text{Worldwide taxable income}} \times \text{U.S tax liability before FTC}$$

Worldwide taxable income is the total taxable income reported on the taxpayer's U.S. tax return, not the total worldwide income of a group of related domestic and foreign entities. Any potential FTCs disallowed because of the FTC limitation may be carried back one year or forward 10 years, subject to the FTC limits in those tax years.

EXAMPLE 12

Lassaline, Inc., a domestic corporation, invests in the bonds of non-U.S. corporations. Lassaline's worldwide taxable income for the tax year is $1.2 million, consisting of $1 million of profits from U.S. sales and $200,000 of interest income from foreign sources. Foreign taxes of $90,000 were withheld on these interest payments. Lassaline's U.S. tax before the FTC is

[7] Sections 901, 902, and 903 provide definitions of creditable foreign taxes. Section 904 contains the FTC limitation rules.

$420,000. Its FTC is limited to $70,000 [($200,000/$1,200,000) × $420,000]. Thus, Lassaline's net U.S. tax liability is $350,000 after allowing the $70,000 FTC. The remaining $20,000 of FTCs may be carried back or forward. ■

PLANNING *Strategies*

UTILIZING THE FOREIGN TAX CREDIT

★ **Framework Focus: Tax Credits**

Strategy ★ Maximize Tax Credits.

The FTC limitation can prevent the total amount of foreign taxes paid in high-tax jurisdictions from being credited. Taxpayers can overcome this problem by generating additional foreign-source income that is subject to no, or low, foreign taxation. A U.S. taxpayer's ability to use FTCs is directly related to its level of foreign-source income relative to its total taxable income. To the extent that a U.S. taxpayer can keep the average tax rate on its foreign-source income at or below the U.S. tax rate on such income, the foreign taxes will be fully creditable. Consequently, combining high- and low-tax foreign-source income is an important planning objective.

Compare the two situations at the right where a U.S. corporation's FTC situations differ depending on its ability to mix high- and low-taxed income. In the first scenario, the corporation has only $500,000 of highly taxed foreign-source income. In the second scenario, the corporation also has $100,000 of low-taxed foreign-source interest income.

	Only Highly Taxed Income	With Low-Taxed Interest Income
Foreign-source income	$500,000	$600,000
Foreign taxes	275,000	280,000
U.S.-source income	700,000	700,000
U.S. taxes (34%)	408,000	442,000
FTC limitation	170,000*	204,000**

*($500,000/$1,200,000) × $408,000.

**($600,000/$1,300,000) × $442,000.

The corporation's actual foreign taxes increase by only $5,000 ($280,000 versus $275,000), but its FTC limitation increases by $34,000 (from $170,000 to $204,000). The ability to "cross-credit" high- and low-taxed foreign income is available only when the foreign-source income is all classified within the same category.

To limit the ability of U.S. taxpayers to cross-credit foreign taxes, the FTC rules provide for several **separate foreign tax credit limitation categories** (or baskets). In any tax year, taxpayers are allowed to credit the lesser of foreign income taxes paid or accrued or the FTC limit *within each separate basket.* The separate FTC limitation categories for different types of income each use this same basic FTC limitation formula. The separate limitation categories affect the amount of FTC that can be taken by generally segregating income subject to a high level of foreign tax from lower-taxed foreign income.

Figure 13–2 summarizes the current separate income categories. Any income that does not fit into one of the specific categories falls into the general (or residual) category. The general limitation basket is where most active income is classified and provides the best opportunity for combining high- and low-taxed foreign-source income. For tax years beginning after 2006, only two baskets exist: passive income and all other (general). Any FTC carryforwards into post-2006 years will be assigned to one of these two categories.

EXAMPLE 13

BenCo, Inc., a U.S. corporation, has a foreign branch in Germany that earns taxable income of $1.5 million from manufacturing operations and $600,000 from passive activities. BenCo also earns German-source high withholding tax interest of $100,000. BenCo pays foreign taxes of $600,000 (40%), $300,000 (50%), and $15,000 (15%), respectively, on this foreign-source income. The corporation also earns $4 million of U.S.-source taxable income, resulting

FIGURE 13-2 **Foreign Tax Credit: Separate Income Limitations for Tax Years Beginning before 2007**

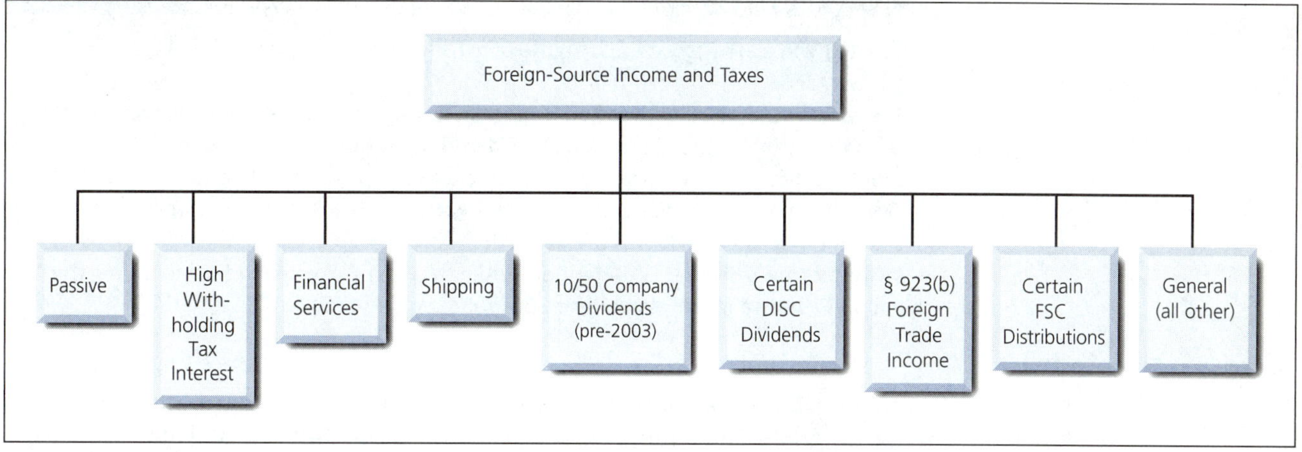

Note: DISCs are domestic international sales corporations; FSCs are foreign sales corporations.

in worldwide taxable income of $6.2 million. BenCo's U.S. taxes before the FTC are $2,108,000 (at 34%). The following table illustrates the effect of the separate limitation baskets on cross-crediting in pre-2007 years.

Separate Foreign Income Category	Net Taxable Amount	Foreign Taxes	U.S. Tax before FTC at 34%	FTC Allowed with Separate Limits
Manufacturing	$1,500,000	$600,000	$510,000	$510,000
Passive	600,000	300,000	204,000	204,000
High withholding tax interest	100,000	15,000	34,000	15,000
Total	$2,200,000	$915,000	$748,000	$729,000

Without the separate limitation provisions, the FTC would be the lesser of (1) $915,000 foreign taxes or (2) $748,000 share of U.S. tax [($2,200,000/$6,200,000) × $2,108,000]. The separate limitation provisions reduce the FTC by $19,000 ($748,000 versus $729,000). The effect of the separate limitation rules is that the foreign-source income taxed at the foreign tax rates of 40% and 50% cannot be aggregated with foreign-source income taxed at only 15%. The reduction in the number of baskets in post-2006 years will be helpful to BenCo. ■

Find more information on this topic at our Web site: ***http://wft-entities.swlearning.com.***

DIGGING DEEPER 1

Controlled Foreign Corporations. Foreign corporations—even those controlled by U.S. shareholders—generally are not included in a U.S. consolidated income tax return. Consequently, in the absence of some other provision, the income of a foreign corporation is included on the U.S. shareholder's U.S. income tax return only when dividend income is received. To minimize current U.S. tax liability, taxpayers often attempt to defer the recognition of taxable income. One way to do this is to shift the income-generating activity to a foreign entity where the income earned will not be subject to U.S. tax until repatriated.

For example, a U.S. person can create a foreign holding company to own the stock of foreign operating affiliates or intangible assets, such as patents and trademarks. Thus, the income generated by these foreign holdings would escape current U.S. taxation. A non-U.S. corporation can also be used to accumulate income from sales or service activities by acting as an intermediary between the U.S. corporation

TAX FACT

Taxing the Earnings of Controlled Foreign Corporations: A Tale of Two JFKs

The current Subpart F regime had its genesis as the centerpiece of a major reform of U.S. international tax rules in 1962. President John F. Kennedy and his administration sought to limit the ability of U.S. companies to easily shift income out of the United States into lower tax countries with the creation of the Subpart F regime. Over 40 years later, another JFK wanted to further limit the ability of U.S. corporations to move income offshore. Presidential candidate John F. Kerry made tightening the Subpart F rules a major plank in his 2004 campaign.

and an offshore customer. The foreign subsidiary corporation would be used to purchase goods from the U.S. parent or domestic affiliates and then resell the goods to foreign customers or provide services on behalf of the U.S. parent or affiliates.

In some cases, the use of intermediate foreign subsidiaries is based on a substantive business purpose. In other cases, they are employed only to reduce tax costs. Because of this potential for abuse, Congress has enacted various provisions to limit the availability of deferral.

The most important of these antideferral provisions are those affecting **controlled foreign corporations (CFCs)**. Subpart F, §§ 951–964 of the Code, provides that certain types of "tainted" income generated by CFCs are currently included in gross income by the U.S. shareholders without regard to actual distributions. U.S. shareholders must include in gross income their pro rata share of **Subpart F income**. This rule applies to U.S. shareholders who own stock in the corporation on the last day of the tax year or on the last day the foreign corporation is a CFC.

EXAMPLE 14

Jordan, Ltd., a calendar year foreign corporation, is a CFC for the entire tax year. Taylor, Inc., a U.S. corporation, owns 60% of Jordan's one class of stock for the entire year. Jordan earned $100,000 of Subpart F income for the year and makes no actual distributions during the year. Taylor, a calendar year taxpayer, includes $60,000 in gross income as a constructive dividend for the tax year. To the extent Jordan has paid any foreign income taxes, Taylor may claim a deemed-paid foreign tax credit for the portion of the foreign taxes related to the $60,000 constructive dividend. ■

A CFC is any foreign corporation in which more than 50 percent of the total combined voting power of all classes of stock entitled to vote or the total value of the stock of the corporation is owned by U.S. shareholders on any day during the taxable year of the foreign corporation. The foreign subsidiaries of most multinational U.S. parent corporations are CFCs.

For purposes of determining if a foreign corporation is a CFC, a **U.S. shareholder** is defined as a U.S. person who owns, or is considered to own, 10 percent or more of the total combined voting power of all classes of voting stock of the foreign corporation. Stock owned directly, indirectly, and constructively is counted. Indirect ownership involves stock held through a foreign entity, such as a foreign corporation, foreign partnership, or foreign trust. This stock is considered to be actually owned proportionately by the shareholders, partners, or beneficiaries. Constructive ownership rules, with certain modifications, apply in determining if a U.S. person is a U.S. shareholder, in determining whether a foreign corporation is a CFC, and for certain related-party provisions of Subpart F.

A U.S. shareholder of a CFC does not necessarily lose the ability to defer U.S. taxation of income earned by the CFC. Only certain income earned by the CFC triggers immediate U.S. taxation as a constructive dividend. This tainted income, referred to as Subpart F income, can be characterized as income that is easily shifted or has little or no economic connection with the CFC's country of incorporation. Examples include:

- Passive income such as interest, dividends, rents, and royalties.
- Sales income where neither the manufacturing activity nor the customer base is in the CFC's country and either the property supplier or the customer is related to the CFC.
- Service income where the CFC is providing services on behalf of its U.S. owners outside the CFC's country.

EXAMPLE 15

Collins, Inc., a domestic corporation, sells $1 million of its products to customers in Europe. All manufacturing and sales activities take place in the United States. Collins has no employees, assets, or operations in Europe and thus is not subject to income tax in any European jurisdiction.

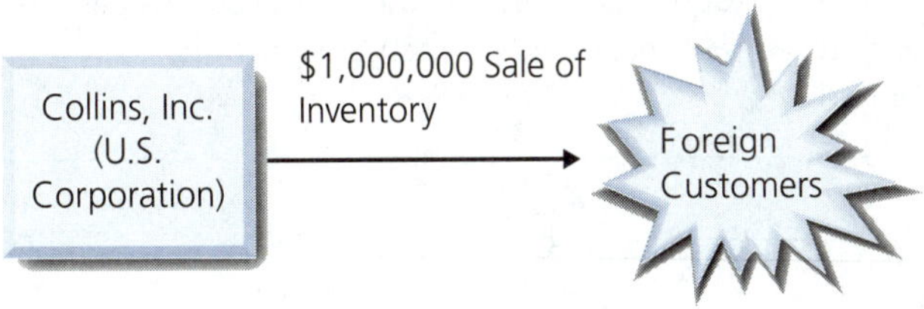

Collins reported the following tax consequences from these inventory sales.

Sales revenue	$1,000,000
Cost of goods sold	(600,000)
Net income	$ 400,000
U.S. tax at 35%	$ 140,000

Assume that Collins instead creates a wholly owned foreign subsidiary in the Cayman Islands, where no income taxes are imposed on corporate income. Collins then sells the inventory to the subsidiary at an intercompany transfer price of $700,000, and the subsidiary sells the inventory to the ultimate European customers for $1 million. The subsidiary does not further process the inventory and is only minimally involved in the sales function, as Collins' employees arrange the transactions with the ultimate customers. In essence, the sale to the subsidiary is simply a "paper" transaction.

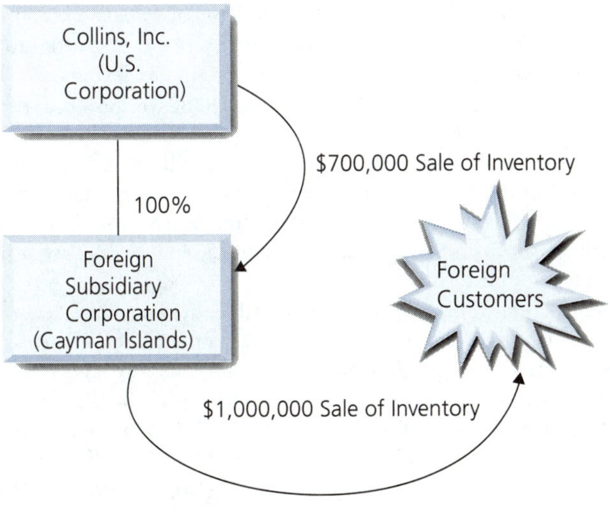

TAX *in the News*

A BOOST TO DOMESTIC INVESTMENT OR A TAX AMNESTY FOR OUTSOURCERS?

The American Jobs Creation Act of 2004 provided a temporary incentive to repatriate foreign profits back to the United States. Section 965 allows domestic corporations to elect to take a onetime 85 percent dividends received deduction for certain cash dividends received from controlled foreign corporations for either the taxpayer's last tax year that began before October 22, 2004, or the first tax year that began after October 22, 2004. Such dividends must be reinvested in the United States, and the eligible dividend amount is based on a calculation that considers prior-year average dividends and the amount of earnings considered "permanently reinvested" abroad under financial accounting principles. The intent was to provide a tax benefit only for earnings that would not otherwise have been repatriated to the United States. With an 85 percent dividends received deduction, the effective U.S. corporate tax rate on such dividends is 5.25 percent (35% corporate tax rate × 15% taxable amount).

Supporters of this measure argued that the inflow of cash back to the United States, along with the requirement for reinvestment here, will provide a boost to the domestic economy. The dividend income is lightly taxed but would otherwise never have been taxed in the United States. Critics argue that the tax break is simply a giveaway to U.S. multinational corporations and rewards outsourcing. They fear that with this precedent, U.S. multinationals may simply outsource more profits to low-tax countries and wait for future tax breaks before repatriating profits.

If there were no tax law restrictions, this structure would create the following tax consequences.

	Collins, Inc.	Foreign Subsidiary
Sales revenue	$ 700,000	$1,000,000
Cost of goods sold	(600,000)	(700,000)
Net income	$ 100,000	$ 300,000
U.S. tax at 35%	$ 35,000	
Foreign tax at 0%		$ -0-

Because the Cayman Island subsidiary is not engaged in a U.S. trade or business, it is not subject to any U.S. tax on its income. So long as the subsidiary's profits are kept outside the United States, Collins believes it can avoid any U.S. income tax on these profits (i.e., the deferral privilege). Thus, at first glance it appears that using the foreign subsidiary significantly reduces Collins' current tax cost from $140,000 to $35,000.

However, Collins will find this strategy attacked by the U.S. taxing authorities on two fronts, either of which results in the loss of all or most of the tax savings.

First, the IRS may use the transfer pricing rules of § 482 to claim that the $700,000 intercompany transfer price between Collins and its subsidiary is not a correct **arm's length price**. The IRS may claim that the transfer price should be $1 million because the subsidiary does not add any value to the inventory through further processing or sales activities and all the risks of the transaction are borne by Collins. With this transfer pricing adjustment, Collins will have a $400,000 profit from the sales and the same $140,000 tax cost as if it had not used the foreign subsidiary as an intermediary.

Determining a correct transfer price is a very subjective exercise. Accordingly, Congress enacted the Subpart F provisions to create more certainty in the effort to prevent unwarranted tax benefits from accruing to U.S. taxpayers using offshore subsidiaries to shield profits from the reach of the U.S. tax authorities. Under the Subpart F rules, the subsidiary's $300,000 income creates a constructive dividend for Collins, thus producing a $105,000 tax cost ($300,000 × 35%). Combined with its original $35,000 tax, Collins' total tax cost for the sales is $140,000 ($35,000 + $105,000), and the use of the foreign subsidiary does not achieve any tax savings. ■

TAX FACT

Who Are These CFCs?

The 7,500 largest CFCs accounted for $4.4 trillion of the assets and more than $2.2 trillion of the gross receipts of all CFCs during the latest year for which complete data are available. These CFCs were engaged primarily in manufacturing (29 percent), services (26 percent), or finance, insurance, or real estate (23 percent). Although these 7,500 CFCs were incorporated in over 100 different countries, CFCs in Europe, Canada, and Japan accounted for over 80 percent of the gross receipts. In 2000, CFCs distributed $95 billion of profits to their U.S. parents and other shareholders. A "large" CFC is one having $500 million or more in assets.

Source: Statistics of Income Bulletin, *Summer 2004, Publication 1136 (Rev. 09–2004).*

EXAMPLE 16

Assume that in Example 15 Collins' foreign subsidiary instead was incorporated in Ireland, where the tax rate on such sales income is 12.5%. The subsidiary purchases raw materials from Collins and performs substantial manufacturing activity in Ireland before selling the inventory to customers in Hong Kong. In this case, the sales income is not Subpart F income. Even without the manufacturing activity, sales to customers within Ireland would not produce Subpart F income. In both instances, there is economic substance to the non-U.S. subsidiary earning the income. The fact that the Irish subsidiary pays a substantially lower tax rate than the U.S. parent does not by itself trigger a constructive dividend. However, Collins must still document the appropriateness of its intercompany transfer price on raw material sales to its Irish subsidiary. ■

The Subpart F provisions are quite complex and subject to numerous exceptions. But, in general, any time a CFC earns income that has little economic connection to its local country, the income is potentially tainted income under Subpart F and will generate a constructive dividend to the CFC's U.S. shareholders. Alternatively, if the CFC is actively generating the income, it is likely not Subpart F income. Unfortunately, the mechanistic application required by the Subpart F provisions sometimes catches active foreign corporations within the Subpart F web.

EXAMPLE 17

Murphy, Inc., a U.S. corporation owns all of GreenCo, Ltd., an Irish manufacturing corporation, and SwissCo, a Swiss distribution corporation. Both GreenCo and SwissCo are CFCs. GreenCo sells its inventory production to SwissCo. SwissCo sells the inventory to unrelated customers located in Switzerland, Italy, and Germany. Because SwissCo does not manufacture the inventory and acquires it from a related supplier, any sales to customers outside Switzerland will produce Subpart F income and a constructive dividend to Murphy, Inc. This is true even though SwissCo is engaged in an active business and is not merely a "paper" corporation. To avoid Subpart F treatment, Murphy, Inc., should create a distribution company within each country where it operates to sell to customers only within that country. ■

PLANNING *Strategies*

AVOIDING CONSTRUCTIVE DIVIDENDS

★ Framework Focus: Deductions

Strategy ★ Maximize Deductible Amounts.

To defer U.S. taxes on foreign income, U.S. taxpayers often create separate foreign subsidiaries to hold their foreign operations. This approach is successful so long as the foreign subsidiaries do not pay dividends to the U.S. owners and do not earn Subpart F income that creates constructive dividends. U.S. companies often set up foreign holding companies in tax-favorable jurisdictions to hold the foreign operating subsidiaries.

For example, a U.S. parent might create a CFC holding company to hold its two operating subsidiaries. The subsidiaries both pay interest to the holding company on intercompany loans. The interest is deductible by the operating subsidiaries at a high tax rate (providing tax savings in those countries) and is taxed to the holding company at a relatively low tax rate. This approach provides a net tax savings to the foreign group. However, the interest payments to the holding company may constitute Subpart F income and trigger a constructive dividend back to the U.S. parent. If so, the tax savings related to the intercompany loans are offset by the U.S. taxes on the Subpart F income.

Fortunately, a mechanism exists that allows the holding company to avoid Subpart F treatment for the interest income. The **check-the-box** Regulations under § 7701 provide a great deal of flexibility for U.S.-based multinational corporations. For example, corporations are allowed to elect (i.e., check the box on a form) to treat certain foreign subsidiaries as unincorporated branches for U.S. purposes rather than separate legal entities. This election does not change the treatment of the entities under local tax law.

Using the check-the-box rules, the U.S. parent can elect to treat the foreign subsidiaries as branches for U.S. purposes. In this case, the two foreign subsidiaries are treated as mere divisions of the holding company. Accordingly, the intercompany loans do not exist from a U.S. perspective, and there is no interest income because the interest payments are treated as simply fund transfers within a single corporation. Without the interest income, there is no Subpart F income and thus no constructive dividends. However, the foreign tax savings still exist because the interest payments do exist from a foreign tax perspective and continue to provide interest deductions at the subsidiary level.

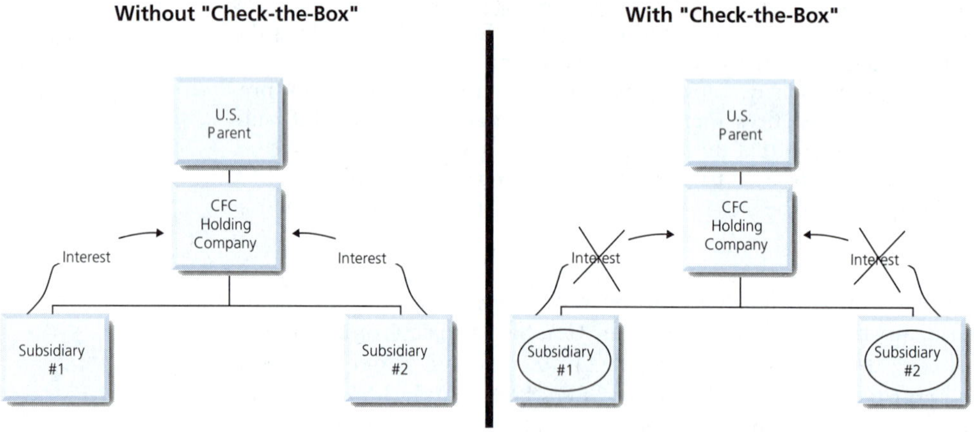

LO.4

Describe the tax effects related to the U.S. operations of a non-U.S. taxpayer.

Inbound Issues. Generally, only the U.S.-source income of nonresident alien individuals and foreign corporations is subject to U.S. taxation. This reflects the reach of the U.S. tax jurisdiction. This constraint, however, does not prevent the United States from also taxing the foreign-source income of nonresident alien individuals and foreign corporations when that income is effectively connected with the conduct of a U.S. trade or business.

A **nonresident alien (NRA)** is an individual who is not a citizen or resident of the United States. Citizenship is determined under the immigration and naturalization laws of the United States. Residency is determined under § 7701(b). A person is treated as a resident of the United States for income tax purposes if he or she meets either the green card test or the substantial presence test. If either of these tests is met for the calendar year, the individual is deemed a U.S. resident for the year. Section 7701(a)(5) defines a foreign corporation as one that is not domestic.

Two important definitions determine the U.S. tax consequences to foreign persons with U.S.-source income: "the conduct of a U.S. trade or business" and "**effectively connected income**." Specifically, for a foreign person's noninvestment income to be subject to U.S. taxation, the foreign person must be considered engaged in a U.S. trade or business and must earn income effectively connected with that business. General criteria for determining if a U.S. trade or business exists include the location of production activities, management, distribution activities, and other business functions. The Code does not explicitly define a U.S. trade or business, but case law has described the concept as activities carried on in the

CONCEPT SUMMARY 13–1

U.S. Tax Treatment of Foreign Person's Income

Type of Income	Tax Rate
U.S.-source fixed, determinable, annual, or periodic (FDAP) income (not effectively connected to a U.S. business)	Generally 30% withholding on gross amount (or lower treaty rate) with certain limited exceptions.
U.S.-source income effectively connected with a U.S. business	Regular individual or corporate rates applied against net income (after deductions).
Gain on U.S. real property (direct or indirect interest)	Taxed as if effectively connected to a U.S. trade or business.
Capital gains (other than on U.S. real property) not effectively connected to a U.S. business	• Foreign corporation: Not subject to U.S. tax. • Individual: Generally not taxed but may be subject to a 30% U.S. tax if taxpayer is physically present in the United States for 183 days or more in a taxable year.
Foreign-source business income	Generally not subject to U.S. taxation unless attributable to a U.S. office or fixed place of business.

United States that are regular, substantial, and continuous. Once a foreign person is considered engaged in a U.S. trade or business, all U.S.-source income other than investment and capital gain income is considered effectively connected to that trade or business and is therefore subject to U.S. taxation. Effectively connected income is taxed at the same rates that apply to U.S. persons, and deductions for expenses attributable to that income are allowed.

Certain U.S.-source income that is *not* effectively connected with the conduct of a U.S. trade or business is subject to a flat 30 percent tax. This income includes dividends, interest, rents, royalties, certain compensation, premiums, annuities, and other fixed, determinable, annual or periodic **(FDAP)** income. This tax generally is levied by a withholding mechanism that requires the payors of the income to withhold 30 percent of gross amounts (or a lower rate as established by a treaty). This method eliminates the problems of assuring payment by nonresidents and foreign corporations.

EXAMPLE 18

Robert, a citizen and resident of New Zealand, produces wine for export. During the current year, Robert earns $500,000 from exporting wine to unrelated wholesalers in the United States. The title to the wine passes to the U.S. wholesalers in New York. Robert has no offices or employees in the United States. The income from the wine sales is U.S.-source income, but because Robert is not engaged in a U.S. trade or business, the income is not subject to taxation in the United States.

Robert begins operating a hot dog cart in New York City. This activity constitutes a U.S. trade or business. Consequently, all U.S.-source income other than FDAP or capital gain income is taxed in the United States as income effectively connected with a U.S. trade or business. Thus, both the hot dog cart profits and the $500,000 in wine income are taxed in the United States. ■

Several exceptions exempt foreign persons from U.S. taxation on their U.S. investment income that is not connected with a U.S. business. For example, certain U.S.-sourced portfolio debt investments and capital gains (other than gains on U.S. real property investments) are exempt from U.S. tax for most foreign investors. Gains from investments in U.S. real property (held directly or indirectly through other entities) are subject to U.S. taxation. Concept Summary 13–1 summarizes the U.S. taxation of foreign persons.

DIGGING DEEPER 2

Find more information on this topic at our Web site: ***http://wft-entities.swlearning.com.***

Crossing State Lines: State and Local Income Taxation in the United States

Very few taxpayers sell goods and services solely in the state in which they are based. Sales in other states are attractive for a variety of business reasons, including the expansion of market share and the achievement of economies of scale. By extending its operations into other states, a firm may be able to lower its labor and distribution costs, obtain additional sources of long-term debt and equity, and perhaps find a more favorable tax climate.

Many of the same issues discussed earlier in the chapter concerning international operations are encountered when a multistate operation is in place. Both international and multistate operations raise basic questions such as where did the transaction occur and who is liable for the collection of the tax.

However, as state and local income taxation has evolved within the United States, differences in terminology, definitions, and scope of the tax have arisen. Although prior knowledge of the U.S. international tax regime can be helpful in studying the state and local income tax structure, there still is much to learn. In addition, the sheer number of income taxing districts at the state and local level make an encounter with the state and local income tax laws of the United States a challenging experience.

LO.5

Identify the sources of tax law applicable to a taxpayer operating in more than one U.S. state.

Sources of Law

Think of how complicated a tax professional's work would be if there were several hundred different Internal Revenue Codes, each with its own Regulations, rulings, and court decisions. That description is hardly an exaggeration of the state and local income tax law faced by a taxpayer operating in more than one jurisdiction. Unless a firm's salable goods or services are designed, made, and sold strictly within one taxing jurisdiction, the multistate regime comes into effect.

Almost every U.S. state taxes the business income of proprietors, corporations, and other entities that have a presence in the state.[8] Those states all have constitutional provisions allowing an income tax and aggregated legislation defining the tax base, specifying when the tax is due and from whom, and otherwise administering the tax. A separate revenue department interprets the law and administers the annual taxing process.

Every one of these systems is distinct and different in multiple ways—the name and location of the chief tax official, the definitions of what is taxable and deductible and what is not, the due dates and filing requirements applicable to the tax, and the taxpayer-friendliness of the audit and appeals system.

Despite the no-new-taxes pledge of many politicians on election day, income taxes are still popular in the United States. Income taxes are levied by states, cities, counties, villages, commuter districts, stadium boards, and numerous other bodies that have been granted taxing authority by their states. And politicians think that they can gain economic development advantages over their neighbors by granting special tax breaks—"Locate your assembly plant here and we'll exempt one-half of your employees' wages from the state income tax"—so the laws are constantly changing. By one estimate, a business taxpayer might be exposed to almost 500 different income taxing jurisdictions in the United States.

The Federal government has stayed out of the fray and has not attempted to force states and localities to use a single common tax formula and administrative organization. Only in **Public Law 86–272** has Congress attempted to bring order to the multistate income tax process. This 1957 pro-interstate commerce provision exempts from state and local taxation a sale of tangible personal property where the only contact with the state was the **solicitation** activity of the taxpayer.

[8]Some states tax the investment income of individuals, but those taxes are not addressed in this chapter. Nevada, South Dakota, Washington, and Wyoming do not have a corporate income tax. Washington uses a business and occupation tax, Michigan uses a form of value added tax, and several states impose a tax on the gross receipts of a business.

TAX FACT

State Tax Revenue Sources

The corporate income tax accounts for only a small portion of total tax revenues of the states. For 2004, almost $600 billion in taxes were collected by the states (i.e., over $2,000 per person).

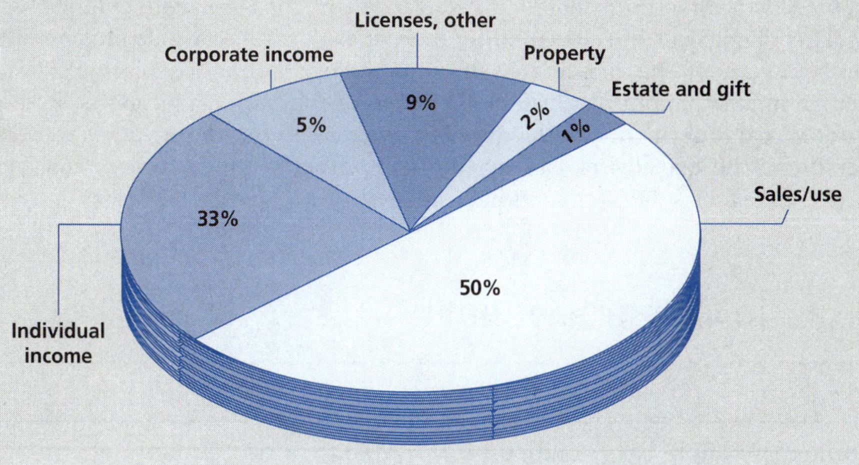

In the past 20 or 30 years, the states have taken some steps to coordinate their activities. Several groups of states exchange information as to the seller and purchase price for cross-border sales, so that income and sales/use tax obligations can be computed and collected properly. A few states have reciprocity arrangements with their neighbors so as to straighten out the complications that can arise when an employee lives in one jurisdiction but works in another.

EXAMPLE 19

Harry works at the Illinois plant of Big Corporation, but he lives in Iowa. His wages are subject to Iowa tax. If Illinois and Iowa had a reciprocity agreement in place, either (1) Big would collect and remit income tax at Iowa's rates and remit the tax to the Iowa revenue department, or (2) Big would collect Illinois tax, and that state would keep the withholdings paid, in full satisfaction of Harry's Iowa tax obligations for the year. ■

About half of the states are members of the **Multistate Tax Commission (MTC)**, a body that proposes legislation to the states and localities and issues its own regulations and informational materials. A majority of the non-MTC members follow the agency's rules virtually without exception. The Uniform Division of Income for Tax Purposes Act (UDITPA) is made available to states and localities interested in a coherent set of income assignment rules, and it forms the basis for the income tax statutes in most of the MTC member states.

The MTC, which provides very specific formulas and definitions to be used in computing state taxable income, is as close as the states have come so far to a multilateral tax treaty process. If all states and localities followed all of the MTC rules, taxpayers would be unable to gain any "border advantages" or disadvantages. But political concerns will keep this coordinated result from ever happening.

Tax Issues

The key issues facing a state or locality in drafting and implementing an income tax model are the same as those facing the international tax community. The results of the deliberative process, though, have produced somewhat different sets of rules and terminology.

Authority to Tax. A business is taxable in the state in which it is resident, organized, or incorporated. Tax liabilities also arise in other jurisdictions where **nexus** exists; that is, a sufficient presence in the other state has been established on an ongoing basis. Such presence might come about because the corporation was organized there, the proprietor lives there, an in-state customer made a purchase, or the business employed people or equipment within the borders of the state. The precise activities that create nexus vary from jurisdiction to jurisdiction, although most of the taxing states follow the broad rules of Public Law 86–272 and the regulations of the MTC.[9]

When a taxpayer operates in more than one state, total taxable income for the year is split among the jurisdictions in which the operations take place. Portions of the total income amount are assigned to each of the business locations, so several tax returns and payments will be due. For a taxpayer considering an expansion of operations, the tax adviser can make an important contribution in helping to decide with which state(s) nexus will be created.

PLANNING *Strategies*

NEXUS: TO HAVE OR HAVE NOT

★ Framework Focus: Tax Rate

Strategy ★ Shift Net Income from High-Tax Jurisdictions to Low-Tax Jurisdictions.

Most taxpayers try to avoid establishing nexus in a new state, for example, by providing a sales representative with a cash auto allowance rather than a company car, by restricting the situs of inventory to only a few states, or by limiting a sales person's activities to those that are protected by the solicitation standard of Public Law 86–272. This effort to avoid nexus stems in part from the additional compliance burden that falls upon the taxpayer when a new set of income tax returns, information forms, and deadlines must be dealt with in the new state.

Another concern is that the marginal tax rate that applies to the net taxable income generated by the taxpayer may increase. Such a tax increase occurs, of course, only when the applicable tax rate in the new state is higher than the rate that would apply in the home state. If a business is already based in a tax-friendly state such as Alabama or Illinois or in a no-tax state such as Nevada, its aggregate tax liability is sure to increase.

Still, nexus is not necessarily a bad thing. Consider what happens if a business based in Minnesota, Massachusetts, Wisconsin, or another high-tax jurisdiction purposely creates nexus in a low- or no-tax state. If the new state applies a lower marginal rate than is available in the home state, or offers special exemptions or exclusions that match the taxpayer's operations, the aggregate tax bill can decrease. Then the planning efforts include determining which activities will *create* nexus in the new jurisdiction and meeting or maintaining that standard.

For instance, an entertainer based in Manhattan is subject to the relatively high income taxes of New York City and New York State. By establishing a permanent office in Tennessee, nexus will be created, and some portion of the taxpayer's income will subject to taxation there, instead of in New York. These are permanent savings, accruing immediately to after-tax income and the share price of the stock of the taxpayer.

Notice that the nexus rules of state/local taxation serve much the same function as do the permanent establishment provisions of international taxation. The PE standards are based in the language of the applicable tax treaty and interpretive court decisions. They look for real estate holdings and manufacturing equipment. Permanent establishment is found when an office in the host country participates significantly in the making of a sales or service contract.

DIGGING DEEPER 3

Find more information on this topic at our Web site: ***http://wft-entities.swlearning.com.***

[9]Income and sales/use tax regimes use different nexus standards. Generally, it has been "easier" to establish nexus for sales/use tax purposes; most states have a separate set of rules to determine the taxability of income or a transaction. But recent U.S. Supreme Court cases seem to apply a "physical presence" test for the sales/use tax, a somewhat stricter and smokestack-industry test than the income tax nexus rules of the MTC. This chapter concentrates on income tax nexus provisions for the most part.

TAX *in the News* **SO WHERE DID YOU WORK TODAY?**

It is the dream of many intellectual-property employees to work at home with the latest in computer and telecommunications equipment. Not only is the dress code there targeted to the worker's comfort, but the employee can avoid the time and cost of commuting. The employer saves by not having to provide office space.

But what are the tax effects when the employee or independent contractor submits work to an employer located in a different state? The general rule in the past has been that state income taxes fall in full in the state where the work is done. Is this still the rule, or must the employee use the ultimate destination concept and apportion the hours of the day among the various states that receive the work product? If so, on what basis should such apportionment be made? Furthermore, how will the worker avoid double taxation of the same income by more than one state?

A few states and cities, most notably in New York, are aggressively trying to impose income taxes on the work of telecommuters that enters the state. In these situations, enough nexus purportedly exists to permit the levying of income taxes on telecommuters based in other states. The finding of nexus with New York (both the city and the state) can be an expensive proposition for the worker and employer. Not only do additional taxes result but compliance costs are incurred.

The first round of court cases challenging this extension of nexus has resulted in rulings in favor of the state. Such success may encourage other states (and cities) to impose similar taxes.

Several bills have been introduced in Congress to attempt to coordinate the definitions of nexus for telecommuters, but no legislation has been enacted. For now, it will be up to the states considering this form of taxation to decide if the additional revenue is worth the risk of angering the desirable high-tech, information workers who play a large role in our economy.

LO.6

Apply computational principles designed for a taxpayer operating in more than one U.S. state.

Income Sourcing. The multistate business, like its international counterpart, must divide up the taxable income generated for the year among the states in which it operates. Then tax liability is computed for the states in which nexus has been established. The computational template illustrated in Figure 13–3 indicates how most states derive their shares of the entity's aggregate taxable income. Usually, the starting point for this computation is Federal taxable income.

State modification items come about because each state creates its own tax base in the legislative process, and some of the rules adopted may differ from those used in the Internal Revenue Code. The modification items reflect such differences in the tax base. For example, modifications might be created to reflect the following differences between state and Federal taxable income.

- The state might allow a different cost recovery schedule.
- The state might tax interest income from its own bonds or from those of other states.
- The state might allow a deduction for Federal income taxes paid.
- The state might disallow a deduction for payment of its own income taxes.
- The state might allow a net operating loss (NOL) deduction only for losses generated in the state.
- The state's NOL deduction might reflect different carryover periods than Federal law allows.

State tax modifications are made even if the taxpayer operates only in its home state.

The next step in computing state taxable income is to **allocate** items of nonbusiness income and loss to the states in which such items are derived. For instance, a Kansas entity might recognize some net income from the rental of a Missouri office building to a tenant. The net rental amount is in Federal taxable income, but it must appear only and fully in Missouri taxable income. So, by means of the modification process, the rents are removed from the taxable income for both states and then added back into Missouri taxable income. The allocation process is very much like the income-sourcing procedures employed in international taxation.

FIGURE 13–3 **Computing State Income Tax Liability**

	Federal taxable income
±	State modification items
	State tax base
±	Nonbusiness income/loss (for allocation)
	Business income (for apportionment)
×	Apportionment percentage for the state
	Taxable income apportioned to the state
±	Taxable income/loss allocated to the state
	State taxable income/loss
	State tax, per tax table or rate schedule
–	State's tax credits
	Net state tax liability

EXAMPLE 20

HammerCo reports $400,000 in taxable income for the year from its sales operations, based exclusively in Mississippi and Arkansas. HammerCo recognized net rent income of $60,000 from a building it owns in Mississippi. It earned $20,000 in interest income from Arkansas bonds. This amount is excluded from Federal taxable income, and it is taxed by Mississippi but not Arkansas. HammerCo also claimed a Federal NOL carryforward of $75,000 from a prior period. Mississippi follows Federal law for NOLs, but Arkansas does not allow such carryovers at all. The modifications to the state tax base are as follows.

Mississippi		Arkansas	
Amount	**Modification**	**Amount**	**Modification**
–$60,000	Total nonbusiness income	–$60,000	Total nonbusiness income
+$20,000	Municipal bond interest income	+$75,000	Remove Federal NOL deduction
+$60,000	Net rent income from Mississippi rentals		

■

The business income of the taxpayer is **apportioned** among the states in which it operates. The apportionment percentage for the state is multiplied times the business income of the taxpayer to measure the extent of the taxpayer's exposure to the state's income tax. The application of the apportionment percentage is illustrated in Figure 13–3.

Most states apply an apportionment procedure involving three factors, each meant to estimate the taxpayer's relative activities in the state.

- The **sales factor** = In-state sales/total sales.
- The **payroll factor** = In-state payroll/total payroll.
- The **property factor** = In-state property/total property.

The state's apportionment percentage is the average of these three factors. This three-factor apportionment can be traced to the earliest days of state income taxation. Today, most states add additional weight to the sales factor, believing it to be the most accurate and measurable reflection of the taxpayer's in-state activities. It is common to "double-weight" the sales factor. A few states use only the sales factor in the apportionment procedure.

EXAMPLE 21

LinkCo, Inc., operates in two states. It reports the following results for the year. LinkCo's apportionment percentages for both states are computed as shown. Amounts are stated in millions of dollars.

	State A	State B	Totals
Sales	\$30	\$20	\$50
Payroll	40	20	60
Property	45	5	50
Sales factor	\$30/\$50 = .6	\$20/\$50 = .4	
Payroll factor	\$40/\$60 = .67	\$20/\$60 = .33	
Property factor	\$45/\$50 = .9	\$5/\$50 = .1	
Apportionment percentage	(.6 + .67 + .9)/3 = .72	(.4 + .33 + .1)/3 = .28	

Note that 100% of the business income is apportioned between the two states: 72% to State A and 28% to State B. ■

EXAMPLE 22

Continue with the facts of Example 21, but now assume that State A double-weights the sales factor. LinkCo's apportionment percentages are computed as follows.

	State A´	State B	Totals
Sales	\$30	\$20	\$50
Payroll	40	20	60
Property	45	5	50
Sales factor	\$30/\$50 = .6	\$20/\$50 = .4	
Payroll factor	\$40/\$60 = .67	\$20/\$60 = .33	
Property factor	\$45/\$50 = .9	\$5/\$50 = .1	
Apportionment percentage	(.6 + .6 + .67 + .9)/4 = .69	(.4 + .33 + .1)/3 = .28	

State B's apportionment computations are not affected by A's double-weighting of the sales factor. The percentages now do not total to 100%. The effect of the special weighting is to reduce LinkCo's tax liability in A. This is likely LinkCo's "home state" given the location of its personnel and plant and equipment. ■

EXAMPLE 23

Continue with the facts of Example 22, but now assume that State B uses a "sales-factor-only" weighting. The A apportionment percentage is .69, and the B percentage is .4. Now the apportionment percentages *exceed* 100%. ■

Most states follow the regulations of the MTC and the outline of the UDITPA in defining and applying the apportionment factors. But because the states do not follow identical rules in the makeup of the factors, the apportionment percentages seldom total precisely to 100 percent. Some other aspects of the three-factor approach include the following.

- Sales are assigned using the tax accounting methods of the taxpayer. Sales are assigned using the "ultimate destination" concept; that is, a sale is usually assigned to the state of the purchaser.
- If a sale is made into a state with no income tax or a state with which the taxpayer has not established nexus, tax is likely escaped. But over a third of the states apply a **throwback rule** that causes the sale to be sourced to the state of the seller (i.e., by overriding the "ultimate destination" rule).

TAX *in the News* — STATE DEFICITS CHANGE HOW REVENUE DEPARTMENTS WORK

The current crunch in state budget making has lasted for several years, and with a U.S. president who is inclined to hold Federal taxes steady and push down to lower-level governments the fiscal obligations for large programs such as Medicare and welfare entitlements, new sources of revenue and new attitudes toward enforcement are prime goals of state and local operations.

Much of this budget squeeze has been felt in the increased attention toward sales and use taxes, with many states now dedicating more resources toward those taxes than toward the individual and corporate income taxes. Collecting unpaid use taxes on Internet and mail-order sales and finding new taxpayers to add to the income and sales/use tax rolls are prime enforcement targets for many states.

But a sustained revenue shortfall tends to make some revenue departments either more desperate or more creative. In either event, we can observe the use of new or recycled approaches to tax enforcement that can surprise the taxpayer who has not been paying attention. Some of the techniques observed lately include the following.

- Applying local business and occupation taxes, payroll taxes, and license fees to telecommuters and work-at-home entrepreneurs and creative workers.
- Increasing audit staff and travel resources, resulting in increased and better-targeted auditing of returns.
- Temporary increases in underpayment and nonfiling fines and penalties, and reductions in grace periods for late filing or payment.
- Denial of other licenses and permits (like hunting and boating permissions, driver's licenses, and professional certifications) where income and sales/use taxes are underpaid.
- Adding "unpaid use tax" lines to the income tax return. This does result in some revenue collected from taxpayers who have guilty consciences or high levels of integrity, but mainly it sets up the taxpayer for penalties on a later audit, when the sworn-to-be-complete income tax return shows a zero balance on the use tax line.
- Refusing legislatively to adopt certain Federal tax breaks, such as special cost recovery elections or the increases in deductible or tax-deferred retirement and education allowances.
- Increased use of private collection agencies to find delinquent taxpayers and produce dollars for the state treasury.

- Payroll is assigned to the state in which the employee's services primarily are performed. Payroll includes wages, bonuses, commissions, and taxable fringe benefits. Some states exclude officer compensation because it can distort the computations. Some states exclude contributions to a § 401(k) plan.
- The property factor uses an average historical cost basis, net of accumulated depreciation. Idle property is ignored, but construction in progress is included. Property in transit is assigned to the state of its presumed destination.
- Property leased but not owned by the taxpayer is included in the property factor at eight times the annual rentals paid.

Many states use specialized apportionment percentages for industries whose sales and asset profile is not properly reflected in the traditional three-factor formula. For instance, the airline industry might divide its income based on passenger-miles beginning and ending in the state. Truckers might be able to divide taxable income among the states based on in-state vehicle-trips or tons-per-day. Communications companies might use the in-state miles of cable or number of wireless devices to make up an apportionment formula.

About a dozen states use a **unitary approach** to computing the apportionment factors. Conglomerates are required, or can elect, to base their computations on the data for all of their affiliated corporations, not just the legal entities that do business with the state. Affiliates included under the unitary theory share a majority ownership with a parent or group of shareholders. They also often share data processing, sales force, and marketing resources.

The *combined return* that the unitary business files includes much more data than might be expected on a separate-entity basis, but the taxing jurisdictions often believe that the unitary figures offer a more accurate reflection of the taxpayer's activity within the state and that, therefore, a more accurate tax liability can be derived.

CONCEPT SUMMARY 13–2

Corporate Multistate Income Taxation

1. A taxpayer is subject to income tax in the state in which it resides or is organized.
2. A taxpayer is subject to income tax in states where it has a business presence and enjoys the resources of the host state in conducting its operations.
3. A multistate taxpayer must divide its aggregate taxable income for the year among the states in which it conducts business.
4. Nonbusiness income is allocated to the state in which it is generated.
5. Business income is apportioned among the states in which the taxpayer has nexus.
6. Apportionment usually is conducted using a formula based on the relative sales, employment, and asset holdings in the various states.
7. The sales factor uses a destination test, while the payroll and property factors use a source test.
8. Most states weight the sales factor higher than the other apportionment factors.
9. Some states apply a special apportionment formula for certain industries, when the traditional three-factor formula could distort the income division procedure in some way.
10. About a dozen states employ the unitary theory in deriving the apportionment factors, using the data from a group of corporations to compute the apportionment formula. Other states allow or require a consolidated return from a conglomerate.

EXAMPLE 24

Kipp Industries is a holding company for three subsidiaries: GrapeCo operating in California, PotatoCo operating in Idaho, and BratCo operating in Germany. Only GrapeCo has nexus with California. But because California is a unitary state, the California apportionment percentage is computed also using PotatoCo and BratCo data. ■

PLANNING *Strategies* WHERE SHOULD MY INCOME GO?

★ **Framework Focus: Tax Rate**

Strategy ★ Shift Net Income from High-Tax Jurisdictions to Low-Tax Jurisdictions.

Every state defines its apportionment factors in a slightly different manner. The multistate taxpayer needs to keep track of these differences and place activities in the state that will serve them best.

Planning with the sales factor includes a detailed analysis of the destination point of the product shipments for the year, especially when the firm has customers in low- and no-tax states. The property factor should include only assets that are used in the taxpayer's trade or business, not the investment, leasing, or research functions. Permanently idle property is excluded from the property factor as well. The payroll factor can be manipulated by hiring independent contractors to carry out certain sales and distribution work, or by relocating highly paid managers to low-tax states.

By setting up an investment holding company in a no- or low-tax state, such as Delaware or Nevada, and transferring income-producing securities and intangible assets to that entity, significant tax reductions can be obtained. When the net investment income is paid back to the parent corporation, the dividends received deduction eliminates the tax liability there.

The unitary system does not always result in a tax increase, although the additional record-keeping burden of operating in a unitary state cannot be understated. If the affiliates make available less profitable operations or a presence in low- or no-tax states or countries, the current tax liability may be reduced. The record-keeping burden can be reduced if the taxpayer makes a **waters'-edge election**, which allows it to include only affiliate data from within the boundaries of the United States.

EXAMPLE 25

Return to the facts of Example 24. If Kipp Industries files a waters'-edge election, the unitary group that files a California income tax return can be limited to GrapeCo and PotatoCo. ■

DIGGING DEEPER 4

Find more information on this topic at our Web site: ***http://wft-entities.swlearning.com.***

Common Challenges

Practical and policy issues facing the U.S. states, developed countries, and the taxpayers operating in all of them show a great degree of similarity between the multistate and international tax regimes. Terminology may differ, and the evolution of tax solutions may take radically different paths, but the key issues that face the multijurisdictional community are at once challenging and rewarding.

LO.7

Synthesize the international and multistate tax systems and recognize common issues faced by both systems.

Authority to Tax

The old-economy orientation of the nexus and permanent establishment rules presents great difficulty in today's economy, as jurisdictions attempt to describe the income and sales/use tax base fairly. An electronic presence also exploits the resources of the host country and should trigger a tax in the visited jurisdiction. Mathematically, the apportionment and sourcing rules should result in only a modest tax liability in the host jurisdiction, but to maintain that no presence exists and no tax should be paid in the context of an 800 telephone number or Internet sale is improper.

But perhaps the notion of *presence* is becoming less important over time, and the level of resource usage in the host jurisdiction also is declining. For example, just-in-time manufacturing and purchasing strategies reduce the need for warehousing by some taxpayers. Human capital can be dispersed through telecommuting, video conferencing, and project rotation using work-group software that provides acceptable levels of data security. If the future is to a great degree wireless, perhaps the standard of presence will diminish, as the buyer and the seller are both "everywhere."

Division of Income

The multistate apportionment procedure could use an overhaul. The fact that a majority of states change the weighting of the sales factor indicates that some other income division method might better serve taxpayers and governments. Three-factor apportionment was designed for an age of traveling sales representatives and sales of built, grown, and manufactured goods. Sales reps were assigned territories that they could drive through on short notice, so they usually lived close to their customer base. In that case, the sales and payroll factors could be highly redundant. Today, with communication and distribution systems more highly developed, the sales factor appears incrementally to be the preferred income-sourcing device. Sales of goods and services should be assigned based on a destination test so that the transaction is assigned to the state of the purchaser.

The three-factor formula further breaks down for income derived from specialized industries, as evidenced by the special computational methods allowed by many states. Perhaps the economy is so specialized today that income simply cannot be assigned by the use of one simple formula. Nonetheless, more uniformity among the states as to definitions and computational rules for the factors would be welcome.

The U.S. Treasury has held hearings in the last decade concerning the adoption of an apportionment approach to the sourcing of international taxable income. Although a formulary apportionment would represent a more reliable and predictable method of dividing multinational income and deduction amounts, the

TAX in the News STATES IN A BIND ON SALES/USE TAX ON INTERNET SALES

In the mid-1960s, the Supreme Court held in *National Bellas Hess* that the seller had no sales/use tax nexus with a state into which a sale was made using catalogs and other general advertising materials. In the early 1990s, the Court's decision in *Quill* extended this no-nexus holding to 800 telephone numbers and Internet sales. As a result, states find it difficult to collect taxes on remote sales of personal property, electronic goods and software downloads, and services that clearly are taxable under existing law.

This issue addresses who should collect the tax, not whether a tax is due, or the amount of the liability. Existing law allows the states to collect a tax, but they have found it impossible to chase down all the Internet sellers around the world who deal with local residents, get them to register for the sales/use tax, and remit the tax liability due. Aware of this difficulty, most sellers today still charge no use tax on out-of-state transactions, with little to fear from understaffed state and local tax audit staffs. Correcting this problem does not constitute a tax increase, but it does require a new approach to enforcement and collection.

The stakes are extremely high. Internet sales are estimated at $60 billion for 2005, and are projected to reach $105 billion by 2007. This situation is not just a battle between the "bricks" and "clicks" economies—it is a problem in which we all share as taxpayers and recipients of government goods and services.

The court battles that will follow any state that forces sellers to start collecting use tax on its cross-border Internet sales are "worth it" in terms of the future revenues that any victory would bring. The counterargument that appearing to increase taxes on e-commerce will hurt business and economic development forces a political dispute. Should a politician come down on the side of $200 million per year in new Internet sales tax collections or a $200 million cut in public health care for lower-income citizens?

data collection burden that such a system would create may be too much to expect from most of the trading partners in the short term. Moreover, the model treaties developed by the United States and the Organization for Economic Cooperation and Development (OECD) include language relating to the income-sourcing rules and transfer pricing at arm's length, not an apportionment approach.

Transfer Pricing

The transfer pricing system used in international trade requires the taxpayer to keep a database of comparable prices and transactions, even though often no such comparability exists. Especially when dealing with proprietary goods and design, it may be impossible to find comparable goods and, therefore, an acceptable transfer price for them. One solution to this situation would be to allow additional definitions of comparable goods, or of ranges of acceptable transfer prices, perhaps subjected to audit on a rotating five-year basis. The use of advance pricing agreements further allows a greater degree of control by the governments in data collection and analysis, ideally prior to the undertaking of the sales or manufacturing transactions.

Tax Havens

When taxpayers perceive effective tax rates as too high, planning usually includes seeking out a tax haven. If income-producing securities or profitable service operations can be moved to another jurisdiction, ideally one with significantly lower marginal tax rates on that type of income, permanent tax savings can be achieved.

When a government witnesses a loss of its tax base due to the transfer of assets and income out of the jurisdiction, anti-tax-haven legislation becomes attractive. The U.S. international tax regime shows several distinct attempts to find and tax income moved offshore, but those taxes collect few dollars in the typical tax year. The investment holding company structure currently used by multistate taxpayers has been met with little effective restrictive legislation from the states, probably out of fear of being branded "anti-business."

TAX FACT

The OECD's Tax Haven Blacklist

In 2000, the OECD identified these jurisdictions as tax havens that had not cooperated with its campaign to stop harmful global tax practices. As of 2005, only the countries marked with an asterisk remained on the list.

Andorra*	Guernsey	Samoa
Anguilla	Isle of Man	Seychelles
Antigua and Barbuda	Jersey	St. Christopher and Nevis
Aruba	Liberia*	St. Lucia
Bahamas	Liechtenstein*	St. Vincent and the Grenadines
Bahrain	Maldives	Tonga
Barbados	Marshall Islands*	Turks and Caicos Islands
Belize	Monaco*	U.S. Virgin Islands
British Virgin Islands	Montserrat	Vanuatu
Cook Island	Nauru	
Dominica	Netherlands Antilles	
Gibraltar	Niue	
Grenada	Panama	

Sources: *Organization for Economic Cooperation and Development (OECD),* Towards Global Tax Cooperation: Progress in Identifying and Eliminating Harmful Tax Practices, *2000; OECD News Release, April 18, 2002; and the OECD's* Project on Harmful Tax Practices: The 2004 Progress Report, *February 4, 2004.*

Perhaps a separate set of nexus rules could be created to address the most portable types of income, such as that from interest and dividends. But this difficult problem likely needs a multilateral solution, which is unlikely to be found in the short term among states and countries, each with unique revenue shortfalls and political profiles.

PLANNING *Strategies*

HOLDING COMPANIES MAKE OTHER STATES ANGRY

★ **Framework Focus: Tax Rate**

Strategy ★ Shift Net Income from High-Tax Jurisdictions to Low-Tax Jurisdictions.

A tax dollar saved in one state is a tax dollar lost in another. That's how some state tax administrators and observers view the use of the **passive investment holding company**. A spokesman for the Multistate Tax Commission asserts that the average state income tax rate paid by larger conglomerates has fallen from about 9.6 percent in 1980 to about 5.2 percent today. And the Secretary of Revenue in North Carolina says it's not fair that corporate tax savings must be recovered from income and sales/use taxes on individuals.

The Delaware version of the investment holding company is the great offender being blamed here. By isolating intangible assets like trademarks, and investment assets generating income, in tax-friendly states like Delaware, corporate giants can achieve major tax reductions.

These savings may not be easily obtained for long, however. State tax authorities have worked hard to target the holding companies operated by such familiar names as Home Depot, Circuit City, Staples, The Gap and The Limited, and Burger King. Tax advisers tell their clients to comply with the tax laws, but they also devise strategies to use holding companies and other "nowhere income" devices. Passive investment companies seem to be here to stay until Congress or the courts force a change.

TAX *in the News* **A MOVE TO THE BEACH FOR U.S. CORPORATIONS SEEKING A VACATION FROM U.S. TAX RULES**

A number of U.S.-based companies have decided to cast their lot on the golden shores of Bermuda, reincorporating as Bermuda companies and enjoying Bermuda's low-tax environment. Recent examples include such well-known companies as Fruit of the Loom, Cooper Industries, Foster Wheeler, and Ingersoll Rand. Even Accenture, formerly Andersen Consulting, established itself in Bermuda. Many of these companies argue that U.S. international tax policy compromises their ability to compete in the global marketplace. The stock market often rewarded these so-called inversion transactions (i.e., conversion from U.S. to foreign based) with increased stock prices.

Although an inversion transaction often entailed a current tax cost, the long-term tax benefits were considered more important. For example, with a Bermuda parent company rather than a U.S. parent company, many of the lower-tier foreign subsidiaries would not constitute CFCs. Many other companies were preparing to invert when Congress began developing anti-inversion legislation and the public began reacting negatively to these corporate expatriates. Toolmaker Stanley Works called off its previously announced, and very controversial, inversion plans, and subsequent years saw very few inversions of U.S. companies. The 2004 Jobs Act contained provisions that further curtailed the benefits of moving offshore.

Interjurisdictional Agreements

Treaties are documents that address many issues other than the taxable income computation. They involve several players within the governmental structure, and they take several years to draft and adopt. Treaties involving the United States tend to be only bilateral, meaning that it is difficult to anticipate and coordinate the interaction of several treaties as they apply to a single taxpayer.

At the multistate level, the Federal government has been slow to take up issues involving a synchronization of the income tax systems used by the states. Although this reluctance may be partly for strictly constitutional reasons, it is largely because of the difficulties presented by the lack of uniformity among the states' tax laws and enforcement efforts.

But the future must hold a greater degree of cooperation among various taxing jurisdictions, at least in the trading of information and the coordination of enforcement efforts. The United States must create additional treaties or information-sharing agreements with countries in South America and Africa. And the future of the European Union probably holds a series of highly developed agreements addressing tax issues with the United States.

Procedural developments may accomplish the same result. For instance, block filing by S corporations and their shareholders with various states accomplishes a number of income division and information-sharing goals. Applying the same approach to partnerships and limited liability entities, and perhaps C corporations with a small number of shareholders, would be an important step forward. Including the multinational activities of such flow-through and closely held entities would also allow for a more coordinated result. Sharing data, while still respecting the confidentiality needs of the taxpayer and requirements of the governments, represents a technologically sound method of collecting taxes in today's multijurisdictional economy.

DIGGING DEEPER 5

Find more information on this topic at our Web site: ***http://wft-entities.swlearning.com.***

Suggested Further Readings

Timothy H. Gillis, "Sixth Circuit Casts a Pall on Incentives," *Journal of Taxation*, December 2004.

Walter Hellerstein, "Federal Statutory Restraints on State Tax Nexus Generate Continuing Controversy," *Journal of Taxation*, November 2002, pp. 290–296.

John Mongan and Amrit Johal, "Tax Planning with European Holding Companies," *Journal of International Taxation*, January 2005.

Michael S. Schadewald and William A. Raabe, "Present and Future Directions in Federal and State Taxation of Income from Cross Border Trade," *TAXES*, April 1997, pp. 218–229.

David E. Spencer, "OECD Model Agreement Is a Major Advance in Information Exchange," *Journal of International Taxation*, November 2002, pp. 10–46.

William Zink, "Shrinking World Expands Relevance of International Tax Concepts," *Taxation for Accountants*, September 1998.

KEY TERMS

Allocate, 13–23
Apportion, 13–24
Arm's length price, 13–16
Check-the-box, 13–18
Controlled foreign corporation (CFC), 13–14
Deemed-paid credit, 13–10
Effectively connected income, 13–18
FDAP, 13–19
Foreign tax credit, 13–7
Inbound taxation, 13–4
Income tax treaties, 13–4
Multistate Tax Commission (MTC), 13–21
Nexus, 13–22
Nonresident alien (NRA), 13–18
Outbound taxation, 13–4
Passive investment holding company, 13–30
Payroll factor, 13–24
Permanent establishment (PE), 13–4
Property factor, 13–24
Public Law 86–272, 13–20
Sales factor, 13–24
Separate foreign tax credit limitation category, 13–12
Solicitation, 13–20
Subpart F income, 13–14
Throwback rule, 13–25
Unitary approach, 13–26
U.S. shareholder, 13–14
Waters'-edge election, 13–27

PROBLEM MATERIALS

PROBLEMS

1. Evaluate this statement: It is unfair that the United States taxes its citizens and residents on their worldwide income.

2. Explain why an income tax treaty between the United States and Germany can be very favorable to a U.S. person who earns investment or business income from Germany.

3. Describe the different approaches used by countries to tax the earnings of their citizens and residents generated outside the borders of the country.

4. Determine the source (U.S. or foreign) of the following items of income.
   a. Interest income paid by a U.S. corporation.
   b. Dividend income paid by a foreign corporation that has no U.S. operations.
   c. Dividend income paid by a foreign corporation that has U.S. operations that historically produce 76% of the corporation's income.
   d. Income from providing consulting services to clients with 12% of the services provided to clients on-site in Canada.

Decision Making

5. ERP, Inc., produces inventory in its foreign manufacturing plants for sale in the United States. Its foreign manufacturing assets have a tax book value of \$3 million and a fair market value of \$8 million. Its assets related to the sales activity have a tax book value of \$400,000 and a fair market value of \$100,000. ERP's interest expense totaled \$50,000 for the current year.
   a. What amount of interest expense is allocated and apportioned to foreign-source income using the tax book value method? What amount of interest expense is

allocated and apportioned to foreign-source income using the fair market value method?

b. If ERP wishes to maximize its FTC, which method should it use?

6. Lynn, Inc., a domestic corporation, operates in both Mexico and the United States. This year, the business generated taxable income of $600,000 from foreign sources and $200,000 from U.S. sources. All of Lynn's foreign-source income is in the general limitation basket. Lynn's total worldwide taxable income is $800,000. Lynn pays Mexican taxes of $300,000. What is Lynn's allowed FTC for the tax year? Assume a 35% U.S. income tax rate.

7. Drake, Inc., a U.S. corporation, operates a branch sales office in Turkey. During the current year, Drake earned $500,000 in taxable income from U.S. sources and $100,000 in taxable income from sources within Turkey. Drake paid $40,000 in income taxes to Turkey. All the income is characterized as general limitation income. Compute Drake's U.S. income tax liability after consideration of any foreign tax credit. Drake's U.S. tax rate is 35%.

8. Crank, Inc., a U.S. corporation, operates a branch sales office in Ghana. During the current year, Crank earned $200,000 in taxable income from U.S. sources and $50,000 in taxable income from sources within Ghana. Crank paid $5,000 in income taxes to Ghana. All the income is characterized as general limitation income. Compute Crank's U.S. income tax liability after consideration of any foreign tax credit. Crank's U.S. tax rate is 35%.

9. Harold, Inc., a domestic corporation, earned $500,000 from foreign manufacturing activities on which it paid $150,000 of foreign income taxes. Harold's foreign sales income is taxed at a 45% foreign tax rate. Both sales and manufacturing income are assigned to the general limitation basket. What amount of foreign sales income can Harold earn without generating any excess FTCs for the current year? Assume a 35% U.S. rate.

10. Food, Inc., a domestic corporation, owns 70% of the stock of Drink, Inc., a foreign corporation. For the current year, Food receives a dividend of $20,000 from Drink. Drink's post-1986 E & P (after taxes) and foreign taxes are $6 million and $800,000, respectively. What is Food's total gross income from receipt of this dividend if it elects to claim the FTC for deemed-paid foreign taxes?

11. Hightower, Inc., a U.S. corporation, has foreign-source income and pays foreign taxes as follows.

	Income	Taxes
Shipping category	$ 50,000	$ 10,000
Passive category	100,000	3,000
General category	300,000	150,000

Hightower's worldwide taxable income is $600,000, and U.S. taxes before the FTC are $210,000 (assume a 35% rate). What is Hightower's U.S. tax liability after the FTC?

12. Discuss the policy reasons for the existence of the Subpart F rules. Give two examples of Subpart F income. *Issue ID*

13. Snowball Enterprises, a domestic corporation, owns 100% of Aussie, Ltd., an Australian corporation. Determine whether any of the following transactions produce Subpart F gross income for the current year.

- Aussie earned $300,000 from sales of products purchased from Snowball and sold to customers outside Australia.
- Aussie earned $500,000 from sales of products purchased from Snowball and sold to customers in Australia.
- Aussie earned $200,000 from sales of products purchased from unrelated suppliers and sold to customers in Ireland.

- Aussie purchased raw materials from Snowball, used these materials to manufacture finished goods, and sold these goods to customers in New Zealand. Aussie earned $100,000 from these sales.
- Aussie earned $60,000 for the performance of warranty services on behalf of Snowball. These services were performed in Japan for customers located in Japan.
- Aussie earned $30,000 in dividend income from passive investments.

14. Ames, Inc., a U.S. corporation, owns 100% of Boone, Ltd., a United Kingdom corporation. Boone purchases finished inventory from Ames and sells the inventory to customers in the U.K. and Germany. During the current year, Ames earned $600,000 in profits from sales to U.K. customers and $400,000 in profits from sales to German customers. Boone operates a sales office in London with 12 full-time employees. How much of Boone's $1 million in profits will be characterized as Subpart F income?

15. Explain the purpose of determining whether a foreign person is engaged in a U.S. trade or business.

16. Evaluate the following statement: Foreign persons are never subject to U.S. taxation on U.S.-source investment income so long as they are not engaged in a U.S. trade or business.

Extender

17. Lili, Inc., a domestic corporation, operates a branch in France. The earnings record of the branch is as follows.

Year	Taxable Income (Loss)	Foreign Taxes Paid
2004	($ 25,000)	$ -0-
2005	(40,000)	-0-
2006	(10,000)	-0-
2007	120,000	40,000

For 2004–2007, Lili, Inc., has U.S.-source taxable income of $500,000 each year. What is the allowed FTC for 2007? Assume a 35% U.S. tax rate.

18. Evaluate this statement: A state can tax only its resident individuals and the corporations and partnerships that are organized in-state.

19. What is the function of the Multistate Tax Commission? Why have some U.S. states not joined the MTC?

Decision Making

20. Considering only the aggregate state income tax liability, how should a taxpayer, resident in State A and selling widgets, deploy its sales force? Assume the following flat income tax rates for the indicated states, which entail the entire customer base of the taxpayer.

State A	5%
State B	3
State C	6
State D	0

Ethics

21. Continue to consider the case of the taxpayer in Problem 20. Is it acceptable to you if the taxpayer purposely shifts its sales force among the states so as to reduce its tax liabilities?

22. Compute state taxable income for HippCo, Inc. Its Federal taxable income for the year is $1 million. Its operations are confined to Oregon and Montana. HippCo generates only business and interest income for the year.

- Federal cost recovery deductions totaled $200,000. Montana used this amount, but Oregon allowed only $140,000.

- Interest income of $45,000 from Oregon bonds was excluded from Federal taxable income. Oregon taxes all municipal bond income, while Montana taxes all such interest except that from its own bonds.
- Interest income from Treasury bonds that was recognized on the Federal return came to $46,000. Neither state taxes such income.

23. Continue with the facts of Problem 22. Using the format of Figure 13–3, compute state taxable income for HippCo, assuming also that the taxpayer recognized $225,000 of net rent income during the year from a warehouse building in Montana. Federal taxable income still is $1 million.

24. PinkCo, Inc., operates in two states. It reports the following results for the year. Compute the apportionment percentage for both states. Amounts are stated in millions of dollars.

	State A	State B	Totals
Sales	$25	$ 75	$100
Payroll	5	45	50
Property	0	100	100

25. Repeat the computations of Problem 24, but now assume that State B uses a double-weighted sales factor in its apportionment formula.

26. Repeat the computations of Problem 24, but now assume that State A is a sales-factor-only state and that State B uses the following weights: sales .70, payroll .15, and property .15.

27. Diagram the creation of an investment subsidiary in Delaware, by Parent, a Massachusetts corporation conducting all of its current sales activities through a single subsidiary, Junior, Inc.

Extender

28. Determine for your state and two of its neighbors:
    a. Whether a Federal affiliated group is allowed to file a consolidated return with the state.
    b. What the return is called (i.e., a "combined," "consolidated," or other type of return).
    c. Whether any special rules apply to the use of consolidated returns in the state (e.g., a special election is required, a limitation on deductible losses applies, a specified term exists during which the election to consolidate is binding).

Extender

29. The administrators of many of the U.S. states have developed model legislation for determining sales/use tax nexus for Internet sales. Look for a discussion of the Streamlined Sales Tax in various newspapers and Web sites and state whether:
    a. Your state is a participant in the Streamlined Sales Tax movement.
    b. You believe that the legislation needed to implement a Streamlined Sales Tax will be in place by the scheduled date. What issues might slow down the adoption date?

Communications

30. As the director of the multistate tax planning department of a consulting firm, you are developing a brochure to highlight the services it can provide. Part of the brochure is a list of five or so key techniques that clients can use to reduce state income tax liabilities. Develop this list for the brochure and send it to your instructor as two PowerPoint slides.

BRIDGE *Discipline*

1. What type of information-sharing agreements does the IRS have with the revenue agency of the Bahamas? Canada? Germany?

RESEARCH PROBLEMS

Internet *Activity*

Use the tax resources of the Internet to address the following questions. Do not restrict your search to the World Wide Web, but include a review of newsgroups and general reference materials, practitioner sites and resources, primary sources of the tax law, chat rooms and discussion groups, and other opportunities.

Communications

Research Problem 1. Review the last six months' archive of articles in one of the newspapers that you read. Use search terms such as "expatriate" and "tax haven" to look for articles that examine the ability of a taxpayer to move U.S. income offshore. Summarize two of the articles in an e-mail sent to your instructor.

Research Problem 2. Make a list of the countries with which the United States currently has an income tax treaty. Then make a list of the countries with which the United States currently is negotiating an income tax treaty. For the second list, include the date on which negotiations started and the current status of the negotiations.

Communications

Research Problem 3. Locate the most recent financial statements of four different publicly traded U.S. companies. Examine their tax footnotes and determine (1) the percentage of total income before taxes earned from foreign sources, (2) the overall effective tax rate, and (3) the effect, if any, on the effective tax rate of earning income outside the United States. Summarize this information in an e-mail to your instructor.

Research Problem 4. Shane, plc. is a corporation created and organized in France. All of Shane's owners are French citizens and residents. Most of Shane's income is derived from active business operations within France. During the current year, Shane invested excess cash into bonds issued by a U.S. corporation. Under Article 11 of the U.S.-French tax treaty, the interest income from the bonds is exempt from withholding. The U.S. corporation has requested that Shane complete a Form W-8BEN to document this treatment. Shane's address is 25 Rue Blomet, Paris, France, 75015. Visit the IRS Web site, locate a Form W-8BEN, complete Shane's form online using the "fill in" function of the IRS form, and print the completed form.

Communications

Research Problem 5. Locate data on the size of the international economy, including data on international trade, foreign direct investment of U.S. firms, investments in the United States by foreign firms, etc. Useful Web locations include **http://www.census.gov** and **http://www.bea.gov**. Prepare an analysis of these data for a three-year period using spreadsheet and graphing software, and e-mail your findings to your instructor.

Research Problem 6. Determine which, if any, of the multistate information-sharing groups your state has joined, as to either income or sales/use tax transactions.

Communications

Research Problem 7. For your state and one of its neighbors, determine the following. (Place your data in a chart and e-mail it to your professor.)

a. To what extent does it follow the rulings of the Multistate Tax Commission?
b. When are income tax estimated payments due?
c. What are the factors and weightings of the income tax apportionment formula?
d. What apportionment factors and weightings apply to an airline operator, like Delta?

Communications

Research Problem 8. Read the "tax footnote" of five publicly traded U.S. corporations. Find the effective state/local income tax rates of each. Create a PowerPoint presentation for your instructor, summarizing the search and reporting the findings.

Communications

Research Problem 9. Use **http://taxsites.com** or some other index to find a state/local tax organization (e.g., the Council on State Taxation). Read its current newsletter. In an e-mail to your instructor, summarize a major article at the site.

http://wft.swlearning.com

CHAPTER 14

Business Tax Credits and Corporate Alternative Minimum Tax

LEARNING OBJECTIVES

After completing Chapter 14, you should be able to:

LO.1
Explain how tax credits are used as a tool of Federal tax policy.

LO.2
Work with various business-related tax credits.

LO.3
Explain the reason for the alternative minimum tax.

LO.4
Identify and calculate the tax preferences that are included in determining the AMT.

LO.5
Identify and calculate AMT adjustments.

LO.6
Understand the function of adjusted current earnings (ACE).

LO.7
Compute the AMT liability for corporations.

OUTLINE

TAX *Talk*

A government which robs Peter to pay Paul can always count on the support of Paul.

—George Bernard Shaw

LO.1

Explain how tax credits are used as a tool of Federal tax policy.

Tax Policy and Tax Credits

Federal tax law often serves other purposes besides merely raising revenue for the government. Evidence of equity, social, and economic considerations, among others, is found throughout the tax law. These considerations also have considerable import in the area of **tax credits**. Congress has generally used tax credits to promote social or economic objectives or to work toward greater tax equity among different types of taxpayers. For example, the disabled access credit was enacted to accomplish a social objective: to encourage taxpayers to renovate older buildings so they would be in compliance with the Americans with Disabilities Act. This Act requires businesses and institutions to make their facilities more accessible to persons with various types of disabilities. As another example, the foreign tax credit, which has been a part of the law for decades, has as its chief purpose the economic and equity objectives of mitigating the burden of multiple taxation on a single stream of income.

A tax credit should not be confused with an income tax deduction. Certain expenditures (e.g., business expenses) are permitted as deductions from gross income in arriving at taxable income. While the tax benefit received from a tax deduction depends on the tax rate, a tax credit is not affected by the tax rate of the taxpayer. All taxpayers can benefit equally when a tax credit is used.

EXAMPLE 1

Assume Congress wishes to encourage a certain type of expenditure. One way to accomplish this objective is to allow a tax credit of 25% for such expenditures. Another way is to allow a deduction for the expenditures. Assume Red Corporation's tax rate is 15%, while Blue Corporation's tax rate is 34%. The following tax benefits are available to each corporation for a $1,000 expenditure.

	Red	Blue
Tax benefit if a 25% credit is allowed	$250	$250
Tax benefit if a deduction is allowed	150	340

As these results indicate, tax credits can provide benefits on a more equitable basis than tax deductions often do. ■

TAX FACT

Where Have All the Credits Gone?

The number of individual income tax returns claiming tax credits has fluctuated substantially over the years as indicated below.

Year	Returns Claiming Credits (in Millions)
1975	65.9
1980	19.7
1985	21.0
1990	12.5
1995	15.2
2000	17.1

The probable cause of the decline between 1975 and 1980 was tax reform legislation enacted in 1976. Likewise the probable cause of the decline between 1985 and 1990 was tax reform legislation enacted in 1986.

Source: *IRS Tax Statistics.*

Specific Business-Related Tax Credit Provisions

LO.2

Work with various business-related tax credits.

General Business Credit

As shown in Exhibit 14–1, the **general business credit** is comprised of a number of other credits, each of which is computed separately under its own set of rules. The general business credit combines these credits into one amount to limit the annual credit that can be used to offset a taxpayer's income tax liability. The idea behind combining the credits is to prevent a taxpayer from completely avoiding an income tax liability in any one year by offsetting it with several business credits that would otherwise be available.

Two special rules apply to the general business credit. First, any unused credit must be carried back 1 year, then forward 20 years. Second, for any tax year, the general business credit is limited to the taxpayer's *net income tax* reduced by the greater of:[1]

- The *tentative minimum tax* (see the discussion of AMT later in this chapter).
- 25 percent of *net regular tax liability* that exceeds $25,000.[2]

To understand these general business credit limitations, several terms need defining.

- *Net income tax* is the sum of the regular tax liability and the alternative minimum tax reduced by certain nonrefundable tax credits.
- *Tentative minimum tax* (discussed later in this chapter) is reduced by any foreign tax credit allowed, as specified in Exhibit 14–2.
- *Regular tax liability* is determined from the appropriate tax table or tax rate schedule, based on taxable income. However, the regular tax liability does not include certain taxes (e.g., alternative minimum tax).
- *Net regular tax liability* is the regular tax liability reduced by certain nonrefundable credits (e.g., foreign tax credit).

[1] § 38(c). This rule works to keep the general business credit from completely eliminating the tax liability for many taxpayers.

[2] § 38(c)(3)(B). The $25,000 amount is apportioned among the members of a controlled group.

TAX *in the News* **FEDERAL TAX LAW IS A KEY COMPONENT OF U.S. ENERGY POLICY**

To help stem the increasing dependence of the United States on foreign sources of energy, Congress enacted the Energy Tax Incentives Act of 2005. The legislation provides numerous tax breaks for power producers as well as for consumers, many of which take the form of tax credits. The primary goals of the tax provisions are to improve energy-related infrastructure, provide more incentives for traditional fossil fuel production, and encourage higher levels of energy conservation.

Some of the more widely applicable provisions include credits for:

- Builders who construct energy-efficient homes.
- Individuals who make energy-saving improvements to their residences.
- Manufacturers that make energy-efficient appliances.
- Businesses that buy fuel cell and microturbine power plants.
- Taxpayers who purchase alternative power motor vehicles and refueling property.

Like many other tax credits, the new energy credits have been designed to modify taxpayer behavior. More specifically, in this case, Congress's intention is that these credits will lead to greater conservation and more efficient use of energy. At the bill-signing ceremony, President Bush remarked that the legislation is "not a bill for today or necessarily a bill for tomorrow, but it's a bill for the future." Only time will tell whether Congress's intentions and President Bush's prediction of greater energy independence for the United States will prove to be true.

EXHIBIT 14-1 **Principal Components of the General Business Credit**

The general business credit combines (but is not limited to) the following.

- Tax credit for rehabilitation expenditures
- Work opportunity tax credit
- Welfare-to-work credit
- Research activities credit
- Low-income housing credit
- Disabled access credit
- Credit for small employer pension plan startup costs
- Credit for employer-provided child care

EXAMPLE 2

Tanager Corporation's general business credit for the current year is $70,000. Tanager's net income tax is $150,000, tentative minimum tax is $130,000, and net regular tax liability is $150,000. Tanager has no other tax credits. The general business credit allowed for the tax year is computed as follows.

Net income tax	$ 150,000
Less: The greater of—	
• $130,000 (tentative minimum tax)	
• $31,250 [25% × ($150,000 – $25,000)]	(130,000)
Amount of general business credit allowed for tax year	$ 20,000

Tanager then has $50,000 ($70,000 – $20,000) of unused general business credits that may be carried back or forward. ■

Treatment of Unused General Business Credits. Unused general business credits are initially carried back one year and reduce the tax liability of that year. Thus, the taxpayer may receive a tax refund as a result of the carryback. Any remaining unused credits are then carried forward 20 years.[3]

[3]§ 39(a)(1).

BRIDGE *Discipline*

Bridge to Finance

When calculating the cash-flow benefit of particular tax attributes and making a decision based on this analysis, an inappropriate decision can be made unless present value analysis is incorporated into the calculation.

The general business credit and the related carryback and carryover provisions can be used to illustrate the cash-flow impact.

Blonde, Inc.'s general business credit for 2006 is $400,000. However, the amount that may be used to reduce the current-year tax liability is only $280,000. None can be used in 2005 (the carryback year), so the $120,000 is carried forward. The $120,000 of unused general business credit is expected to offset Blonde's future tax liability as follows.

2007	$20,000
2008	40,000
2009	60,000

It appears that the cash-flow benefit to Blonde is $400,000. In nominal dollars, this result is correct. However, when the present value concept is applied, the cash-flow benefit is only $376,280 (assuming Blonde's discount rate is 10 percent).

2006	$280,000 × 1.0	=	$280,000
2007	20,000 × .909	=	18,180
2008	40,000 × .826	=	33,040
2009	60,000 × .751	=	45,060
			$376,280

The carryforward period for the general business credit is 20 years. Using a 10 percent discount rate, one dollar in 20 years is worth $0.149 ($1 × .149) today. So it behooves the taxpayer to use the general business credit to offset tax liability as rapidly as possible.

A FIFO method is applied to the carryback, carryovers, and utilization of credits earned during a particular year. The oldest credits are used first in determining the amount of the general business credit. The FIFO method minimizes the potential for loss of a general business credit benefit due to the expiration of credit carryovers and generally works to the taxpayer's benefit.

EXAMPLE 3

This example illustrates the use of general business credit carryovers for the taxpayer's 2006 tax year.

General business credit carryovers (unused in prior tax years)		
2003	$ 4,000	
2004	6,000	
2005	2,000	
Total carryovers	$12,000	
2006 general business credit		$ 40,000
Total credit allowed in 2006 (based on tax liability)	$50,000	
Less: Carryovers used		
2003	(4,000)	
2004	(6,000)	
2005	(2,000)	
Remaining credit allowed in 2006	$38,000	
2006 general business credit used		(38,000)
2006 unused amount carried forward to 2007		$ 2,000 ■

Most of the various credits that make up the general business credit are discussed in the paragraphs below.

Tax Credit for Rehabilitation Expenditures

Taxpayers are allowed a tax credit for expenditures incurred to rehabilitate older industrial and commercial buildings and certified historic structures. The **rehabilitation expenditures credit** is intended to discourage businesses from moving from economically distressed areas (e.g., an inner city) to outlying locations and to encourage the preservation of historic structures. The current operating features of this credit follow.[4]

Rate of the Credit for Rehabilitation Expenses	Nature of the Property
10%	Nonresidential buildings and residential rental property, other than certified historic structures, originally placed in service before 1936
20%	Nonresidential and residential certified historic structures

Taxpayers who claim the rehabilitation credit must reduce the basis of the rehabilitated building by the credit allowed.[5]

EXAMPLE 4

Grosbeak, Inc., spent $60,000 to rehabilitate a building (adjusted basis of $40,000) that originally had been placed in service in 1932. Grosbeak is allowed a credit of $6,000 (10% × $60,000) for rehabilitation expenditures. The corporation then increases the basis of the building by $54,000 [$60,000 (rehabilitation expenditures) – $6,000 (credit allowed)]. If the building were a historic structure, the credit allowed would be $12,000 (20% × $60,000), and the building's depreciable basis would increase by $48,000 [$60,000 (rehabilitation expenditures) – $12,000 (credit allowed)]. ■

To qualify for the credit, buildings must be substantially rehabilitated. A building has been *substantially rehabilitated* if qualified rehabilitation expenditures exceed the *greater of*:

- the adjusted basis of the property before the rehabilitation expenditures, or
- $5,000.

Qualified rehabilitation expenditures do not include the cost of acquiring a building, the cost of facilities related to a building (such as a parking lot), and the cost of enlarging an existing building. Stringent rules apply concerning the retention of the building's original internal and external walls.

Recapture of Tax Credit for Rehabilitation Expenditures. The rehabilitation credit taken is recaptured if the rehabilitated property is disposed of prematurely or if it ceases to be qualifying property. The **rehabilitation expenditures credit recapture** is added to the taxpayer's regular tax liability in the recapture year. The recapture amount also is *added* to the adjusted basis of the building.

The portion of the credit recaptured is a specified percentage of the credit that was taken by the taxpayer. This percentage is based on the period the property was held by the taxpayer, as shown in Table 14–1. If the property is held at least five years, no recapture can result.

[4] § 47.

[5] § 50(c).

TABLE 14–1 **Recapture Calculation for Rehabilitation Expenditures Credit**

If the Property Is Held for	The Recapture Percentage Is
Less than 1 year	100
One year or more but less than 2 years	80
Two years or more but less than 3 years	60
Three years or more but less than 4 years	40
Four years or more but less than 5 years	20
Five years or more	0

EXAMPLE 5

On March 15, 2003, Chickadee Corporation rehabilitated a building qualifying for the 10% credit. The company spent $30,000 in qualifying rehabilitation expenditures and claimed a $3,000 credit ($30,000 × 10%). The basis of the building was increased by $27,000 ($30,000 – $3,000).

Chickadee sold the building on December 15, 2006. Chickadee recaptures a portion of the rehabilitation credit based on the schedule in Table 14–1. Because Chickadee held the rehabilitated property for more than three years but less than four, 40% of the credit, or $1,200, is added to the company's 2006 income tax liability. In addition, the adjusted basis of the building is increased by the $1,200 recapture amount. ■

Work Opportunity Tax Credit

The **work opportunity tax credit**[6] was enacted to encourage employers to hire individuals from a variety of targeted and economically disadvantaged groups. Examples of such targeted persons include qualified ex-felons, high-risk youths, food stamp recipients, veterans, summer youth employees, and persons receiving certain welfare benefits.

Computation of the Work Opportunity Tax Credit: General. The credit generally is equal to 40 percent of the first $6,000 of wages (per eligible employee) for the first 12 months of employment. The credit is not available for wages paid to an employee after the *first year* of employment. If the employee's first year overlaps two of the employer's tax years, however, the employer may take the credit over two tax years. If the credit is claimed, the employer's tax deduction for wages is reduced by the amount of the credit.

To qualify an employer for the 40 percent credit, the employee must (1) be certified by a designated local agency as being a member of one of the targeted groups and (2) have completed at least 400 hours of service to the employer. If an employee meets the first condition but not the second, the credit is reduced to 25 percent, provided the employee has completed a minimum of 120 hours of service to the employer.

Find more information on this topic at our Web site: ***http://wft-entities.swlearning.com.***

DIGGING DEEPER 1

[6]§ 51. At the time of this writing, the credit is available only if qualifying employees start work by December 31, 2005. However, the general consensus is that Congress will extend this provision for 2006. Therefore, Chapter 14 examples and problems assume its continuing availability for qualifying employees who start work by December 31, 2006.

EXAMPLE 6

In January 2006, Green hires four individuals who are certified to be members of a qualifying targeted group. Each employee works 1,000 hours and is paid wages of $8,000 during the year. Green's work opportunity credit is $9,600 [($6,000 × 40%) × 4 employees]. If the tax credit is taken, Green reduces its deduction for wages paid by $9,600. No credit is available for wages paid to these employees after their first year of employment. ■

EXAMPLE 7

On June 1, 2006, Maria, a calendar year taxpayer, hires Joe, a member of a targeted group, and obtains the required certification to qualify Maria for the work opportunity credit. During his seven months of work in 2006, Joe is paid $3,500 for 500 hours of work. Maria is allowed a credit of $1,400 ($3,500 × 40%) for 2006.

Joe continues to work for Maria in 2007 and is paid $7,000 through May 31, 2007. Because up to $6,000 of first-year wages are eligible for the credit, Maria is also allowed a 40% credit on $2,500 [$6,000 – $3,500 (wages paid in 2006)] of 2007 wages paid, or $1,000 ($2,500 × 40%). None of Joe's wages paid after May 31, 2007, the end of the first year of employment, is eligible for the credit. ■

Welfare-to-Work Credit

The **welfare-to-work credit**[7] is available to employers hiring individuals who have been long-term recipients of family assistance welfare benefits. In general, *long-term recipients* are those individuals who are certified by a designated local agency as being members of a family receiving assistance under a public aid program for the 18-month period ending on the hiring date. Unlike the work opportunity credit, which applies only to first-year wages paid to qualified individuals, the welfare-to-work credit is available for qualified wages paid in the first *two years* of employment. If an employee's first and second work years overlap two or more of the employer's tax years, the employer may take the credit during the applicable tax years. If the welfare-to-work credit is taken, the employer's tax deduction for wages is reduced by the amount of the credit.

An employer is prohibited from taking both the work opportunity credit and the welfare-to-work credit for wages paid to a qualified employee in a given tax year.

Maximum Credit. The credit is equal to 35 percent of the first $10,000 of qualified wages paid to an employee in the first year of employment, plus 50 percent of the first $10,000 of qualified wages in the second year of employment, resulting in a maximum credit per qualified employee of $8,500 [$3,500 (year 1) + $5,000 (year 2)]. The credit rate is higher for second-year wages to encourage employers to retain qualified individuals, thereby promoting the overall welfare-to-work goal.

EXAMPLE 8

In April 2006, Blue hired three individuals who are certified as long-term family assistance recipients. Each employee is paid $12,000 during 2006. Two of the three individuals continue to work for Blue in 2007, earning $9,000 each during the year. Blue's welfare-to-work credit is $10,500 [(35% × $10,000) × 3 employees] for 2006 and $9,000 [(50% × $9,000) × 2 employees] for 2007. ■

Research Activities Credit

To encourage research and development (R & D) in the U.S. business community, a credit is allowed for certain qualifying expenditures paid or incurred by a taxpayer. The **research activities credit** is the *sum* of two components: (1) an incremental research activities credit and (2) a basic research credit.[8]

[7]§ 51A. At the time of this writing, the credit is available only if qualifying employees start work by December 31, 2005. However, the general consensus is that Congress will extend this provision for 2006. Therefore, Chapter 14 examples and problems assume its continuing availability for qualifying employees who start work by December 31, 2006.

[8]§ 41. At the time of this writing, both components of the research credit are available only if qualifying expenditures are paid or incurred by December 31, 2005. However, the general consensus is that Congress will extend this provision for 2006. Therefore, Chapter 14 examples and problems assume its continuing availability in 2006.

Incremental Research Activities Credit. The incremental research activities credit applies at a 20 percent rate to the *excess* of qualified research expenses for the taxable year (the credit year) over a base amount.

In general, *research expenditures* qualify if the research relates to discovering technological information that is intended for use in the development of a new or improved business component of the taxpayer. Such expenses qualify fully if the research is performed in-house (by the taxpayer or its employees). If the research is conducted by persons outside the taxpayer's business (under contract), only 65 percent of the amount paid qualifies for the credit.[9]

EXAMPLE 9

Bobwhite Company incurs the following research expenditures:

In-house wages, supplies, computer time	$50,000
Payment to Cutting Edge Scientific Foundation for research	30,000

Bobwhite's qualified research expenditures are $69,500 [$50,000 + ($30,000 × 65%)]. ■

Beyond the general guidelines described above, the Code does not give specific examples of qualifying research. However, the credit is *not* allowed for research that falls into certain categories, including the following.[10]

- Research conducted after the beginning of commercial production of the business component.
- Surveys and studies such as market research, testing, and routine data collection.
- Research conducted *outside* the United States (other than research undertaken in Puerto Rico and possessions of the United States).
- Research in the social sciences, arts, or humanities.

Determining the *base amount* involves a relatively complex series of computations, meant to approximate recent historical levels of research activity by the taxpayer. Thus, the credit is allowed only for increases in research expenses.

EXAMPLE 10

Hawk, Inc., a calendar year taxpayer, incurs qualifying research expenditures of $200,000 during the year. If the base amount is $100,000, the incremental research activities credit is $20,000 [($200,000 – $100,000) × 20%]. ■

Qualified research and experimentation expenditures are not only eligible for the 20 percent credit, but can also be *expensed* in the year incurred. In this regard, a taxpayer has two choices.[11]

- Use the full credit and reduce the expense deduction for research expenses by 100 percent of the credit.
- Retain the full expense deduction and reduce the credit by the product of 100 percent of the credit times the maximum corporate tax rate (35 percent).

As an alternative to the expense deduction, the taxpayer may *capitalize* the research expenses and *amortize* them over 60 months or more. In this case, the amount capitalized and subject to amortization is reduced by the full amount of the credit *only* if the credit exceeds the amount allowable as a deduction.

[9] § 41(b)(3)(A). In the case of payments to a qualified research consortium, § 41(b)(3)(A) provides that 75% of the amount paid qualifies for the credit. For amounts paid to an energy research consortium, § 41(b)(3)(D) allows the full amount to qualify for the credit.

[10] § 41(d).

[11] §§ 174 and 280C(c). Recall the discussion of rules for deducting research and experimental expenditures in Chapter 5.

EXAMPLE 11

This year, Thin Corporation's potential incremental research activities credit is $20,000. The amounts that Thin can deduct and the credit amount are computed as follows.

	Credit Amount	Deduction Amount
• Full credit and reduced deduction		
$20,000 – $0	$20,000	
$200,000 – $20,000		$180,000
• Reduced credit and full deduction		
$20,000 – [(1.00 × $20,000) × .35]	13,000	
$200,000 – $0		200,000
• Full credit and capitalize and elect to amortize costs over 60 months		
$20,000 – $0	20,000	
($200,000/60) × 12		40,000

The value of the deduction depends on Thin's marginal tax rates. ■

Basic Research Credit. Corporations (other than S corporations or personal service corporations) are allowed an additional 20 percent credit for basic research expenditures incurred, in *excess* of a base amount.[12] This credit is not available to individual taxpayers. *Basic research expenditures* are defined as amounts paid in cash to a qualified basic research organization, such as a college or university or a tax-exempt organization operated primarily to conduct scientific research.

Basic research is defined generally as any original investigation for the advancement of scientific knowledge not having a specific commercial objective. The definition excludes basic research conducted outside the United States and basic research in the social sciences, arts, or humanities.

Disabled Access Credit

The **disabled access credit** is designed to encourage small businesses to make their facilities more accessible to disabled individuals. The credit is available for any eligible access expenditures paid or incurred by an eligible small business. The credit is calculated at the rate of 50 percent of the eligible expenditures that exceed $250 but do not exceed $10,250. Thus, the maximum amount for the credit is $5,000 ($10,000 × 50%).[13]

An *eligible small business* is one that during the previous year either had gross receipts of $1 million or less or had no more than 30 full-time employees. A sole proprietorship, partnership, regular corporation, or S corporation can qualify as such an entity.

Eligible access expenditures generally include any reasonable and necessary amounts that are paid or incurred to make certain changes to facilities. These changes must involve the removal of architectural, communication, physical, or transportation barriers that would otherwise make a business inaccessible to disabled and handicapped individuals. Examples of qualifying projects include installing ramps, widening doorways, and adding raised markings on elevator control buttons. However, the improved facility must have been placed into service prior to the enactment of the credit (i.e., November 5, 1990).

[12] § 41(e).

[13] § 44.

To the extent a disabled access credit is available, no deduction or credit is allowed under any other provision of the tax law. The asset's adjusted basis is reduced by the amount of the credit.

EXAMPLE 12

This year Red, Inc., an eligible business, makes $11,000 of capital improvements to business realty that had been placed in service in June 1990. The expenditures are intended to make Red's business more accessible to the disabled and are considered eligible expenditures for purposes of the disabled access credit. The amount of the credit is $5,000 [($10,250 maximum − $250 floor) × 50%]. The depreciable basis of the capital improvement is $6,000 [$11,000 (cost) − $5,000 (amount of the credit)]. ■

Credit for Small Employer Pension Plan Startup Costs

Small businesses are entitled to a nonrefundable credit for administrative costs associated with establishing and maintaining certain qualified retirement plans.[14] While such costs (e.g., payroll system changes, consulting fees) generally are deductible as ordinary and necessary business expenses, the credit is intended to lower the after-tax cost of establishing a qualified retirement program and thereby to encourage qualifying businesses to offer retirement plans for their employees.

The **credit for small employer pension plan startup costs** is available for eligible employers at the rate of 50 percent of qualified startup costs. An eligible employer is one with fewer than 100 employees who have earned at least $5,000 of compensation. Qualified startup costs include ordinary and necessary expenses incurred in connection with establishing or maintaining an employer pension plan and retirement-related education costs.[15] The maximum credit is $500 (based on a maximum $1,000 of qualifying expenses), and the deduction for the startup costs incurred is reduced by the amount of the credit. The credit can be claimed for qualifying costs incurred in each of the three years beginning with the tax year in which the retirement plan becomes effective (maximum total credit of $1,500).

EXAMPLE 13

Maple Company decides to establish a qualified retirement plan for its employees. In the process, it pays consulting fees of $1,200 to a firm that will provide educational seminars to Maple's employees and will assist the payroll department in making necessary changes to the payroll system. Maple may claim a credit for the pension plan startup costs of $500 ($1,200 of qualifying costs, limited to $1,000 × 50%), and its deduction for these expenses is reduced to $700 ($1,200 − $500). ■

Credit for Employer-Provided Child Care

The scope of § 162 trade or business expenses includes an employer's expenditures incurred to provide for the care of children of employees as ordinary and necessary business expenses. Another option now available permits employers to claim a credit for qualifying expenditures incurred while providing child care facilities to their employees during normal working hours.[16]

The **credit for employer-provided child care**, limited annually to $150,000, is composed of the aggregate of two components: 25 percent of qualified child care expenses and 10 percent of qualified child care resource and referral services. *Qualified child care expenses* include the costs of acquiring, constructing, rehabilitating, expanding, and operating a child care facility. *Child care resource and referral services* include amounts paid or incurred under a contract to provide child care resource and referral services to an employee.

[14] § 45E. Currently this credit is scheduled to expire for years after December 31, 2010.

[15] §§ 45E(c) and (d)(1).

[16] § 45F. Currently, this credit is scheduled to expire for years after December 31, 2010.

GLOBAL Tax Issues

SOURCING INCOME IN CYBERSPACE—GETTING IT RIGHT WHEN CALCULATING THE FOREIGN TAX CREDIT

The overall limitation on the foreign tax credit plays a critical role in restricting the amount of the credit available to a taxpayer. In the overall limitation formula, the taxpayer must characterize the year's taxable income as either earned (or sourced) inside the United States or earned from sources outside the United States. As a general rule, a relatively greater percentage of foreign-source income in the formula will lead to a larger foreign tax credit. Therefore, determining the source of various types of income is critical in the proper calculation of the credit. However, classifying income as either foreign or U.S. source is not always a simple matter.

For example, consumers and business are using the Internet to conduct more and more commerce involving both products and services. The problem is that the existing income-sourcing rules were developed long before the existence of the Internet, and taxing authorities are finding it challenging to apply these rules to Internet transactions. Where does a sale take place when the Web server is in Scotland, the seller is in India, and the customer is in Illinois? Where is a service performed when all activities take place over the Net? These questions and more will have to be answered by the United States and its trading partners as the Internet economy grows in size and importance.

To prevent an employer from obtaining a double benefit by claiming a credit and the associated deductions on the same expenditures, any qualifying expenses otherwise deductible by the taxpayer must be reduced by the amount of the credit. In addition, the taxpayer's basis for any property acquired or constructed and used for qualifying purposes is reduced by the amount of the credit. If within 10 years of being placed in service, a child care facility ceases to be used for a qualified use, the taxpayer will be required to recapture a portion of the credit previously claimed.[17]

EXAMPLE 14

During the year, Tan Company constructed a child care facility for $400,000 to be used by its employees who have preschool-aged children in need of child care services while their parents are at work. In addition, Tan incurred salaries for child care workers and other administrative costs associated with the facility of $100,000 during the year. As a result, Tan's credit for employer-provided child care is $125,000 [($400,000 + $100,000) × 25%]. Correspondingly, the basis of the facility is reduced to $300,000 ($400,000 − $100,000), and the deduction for salaries and administrative costs is reduced to $75,000 ($100,000 − $25,000). ■

DIGGING DEEPER 2

Find more information on this topic at our Web site: ***http://wft-entities.swlearning.com.***

Foreign Tax Credit

Both individual taxpayers and corporations may claim a credit for foreign income tax paid on income earned and subject to tax in another country or a U.S. possession.[18] The purpose of the **foreign tax credit (FTC)** is to reduce the possibility of double taxation of foreign income.

EXAMPLE 15

Ace Tools, Inc., a U.S. corporation, has a branch operation in Mexico, from which it earns taxable income of $750,000 for the current year. Ace pays income tax of $150,000 on these

[17] § 45F(d).

[18] § 27 provides for the credit, but the qualifications and calculation procedure for the credit are contained in §§ 901–908. Alternatively, the taxpayer can *deduct* the foreign taxes paid.

earnings to the Mexican tax authorities. Ace must also include the $750,000 in gross income for U.S. tax purposes. Assume that, before considering the FTC, Ace would owe $255,000 in U.S. income taxes on this foreign-source income. Thus, total taxes on the $750,000 could equal $405,000 ($150,000 + $255,000), a 54% effective rate. But Ace takes the FTC of $150,000 against its U.S. tax liability on the foreign-source income. Ace Tools' total taxes on the $750,000 now are $255,000 ($150,000 + $105,000), a 34% effective rate. ■

The tax year's FTC equals the *lesser* of the foreign taxes imposed or the *overall limitation* determined according to the following formula. Thus, where applicable foreign tax rates exceed those of the United States, the credit offsets no more than the marginal U.S. tax on the double-taxed income.

$$\frac{\text{Foreign-source taxable income}}{\text{Worldwide taxable income}} \times \text{U.S. tax before FTC}$$

Foreign taxes paid but not allowed as a credit due to the overall limitation are carried back 1 tax year and then forward 10 years.[19]

EXAMPLE 16

Oriole, Inc., a U.S. corporation, conducts business in a foreign country. Oriole's worldwide taxable income for the tax year is $120,000, consisting of $100,000 in income from U.S. operations and $20,000 of income from the foreign source. Foreign tax of $6,000 was paid to foreign tax authorities on the $20,000. Before the FTC, Oriole's U.S. tax on the $120,000 is $30,050. The corporation's FTC is $5,008 {lesser of $6,000 paid or $5,008 limitation [$30,050 × ($20,000/$120,000)]}. Oriole's net U.S. tax liability is $25,042 ($30,050 – $5,008). Thus, Oriole carries over (back 1 year and forward 10 years) $992 FTC ($6,000 – $5,008) because of the overall limitation. ■

Corporate Alternative Minimum Tax

LO.3

Explain the reason for the alternative minimum tax.

A perception that many large corporations were not paying their fair share of Federal income tax was especially widespread in the early 1980s. A study released in 1986 reported that 130 of the 250 largest corporations in the United States (e.g., Reynolds Metals, General Dynamics, Georgia Pacific, and Texas Commerce Bankshares) paid no Federal tax, or received refunds, in at least one year between 1981 and 1985. Political pressure subsequently led to the adoption of an **alternative minimum tax (AMT)** to ensure that corporations with substantial economic income pay at least a minimum amount of Federal taxes.

The AMT limits the tax savings for some taxpayers who are seen as gaining "too much" from exclusions, deductions, and credits available under the law. A separate tax system with a proportional tax rate is applied each year to a corporation's economic income. If the tentative AMT is greater than the regular corporate income tax, then the corporation must pay the regular tax plus this excess, the AMT.

Since its inception, the AMT has been vulnerable to criticisms that it is too complex. Smaller corporations especially find that the imposition of a second tax structure unduly increases their compliance burdens. Thus, proposals to cut back or even repeal the AMT were considered by Congress throughout the 1990s. A special exemption from the AMT finally was adopted in 1997. For tax years beginning after 1997, most smaller corporations are not subject to the AMT at all. A corporation is exempted from the AMT if it meets the following tests.

- *Initial test.* The corporation must report average annual gross receipts of no more than $5 million for the three-year period beginning after December 1993.

[19]This treatment of unused FTCs applies to tax years ending after October 22, 2004. Prior law provided a two-year carryback and a five-year carryforward.

CONCEPT SUMMARY 14–1

Tax Credits

Credit	Computation	Comments
General business (§ 38)	May not exceed net income tax minus the greater of tentative minimum tax or 25% of net regular tax liability that exceeds $25,000.	Components include tax credit for rehabilitation expenditures, work opportunity tax credit, welfare-to-work credit, research activities credit, low-income housing credit, disabled access credit, credit for small employer pension plan startup costs, and credit for employer-provided child care. Unused credit may be carried back 1 year and forward 20 years. FIFO method applies to carrybacks, carryovers, and credits earned during current year.
Rehabilitation expenditures (§ 47)	Qualifying investment times rehabilitation percentage, depending on type of property. Regular rehabilitation rate is 10%; rate for certified historic structures is 20%.	Part of general business credit and therefore subject to same carryback, carryover, and FIFO rules. Purpose is to discourage businesses from moving from economically distressed areas to new locations.
Work opportunity (§ 51)	Credit is limited to 40% of the first $6,000 of wages paid to each eligible employee.	Part of the general business credit and therefore subject to the same carryback, carryover, and FIFO rules. Purpose is to encourage employment of members of economically disadvantaged groups.
Welfare-to-work (§ 51A)	Credit is limited to 35% of first $10,000 of wages paid to each eligible employee in first year of employment, plus 50% of first $10,000 of wages paid to same employee in second year of employment.	Part of general business credit and therefore subject to same carryback, carryover, and FIFO rules. Purpose is to encourage employment of long-term recipients of family assistance welfare benefits.
Research activities (§ 41)	Incremental credit is 20% of excess of computation-year expenditures over a base amount. Basic research credit is allowed to certain corporations for 20% of cash payments to qualified organizations that exceed a specially calculated base amount.	Part of general business credit and therefore subject to same carryback, carryover, and FIFO rules. Purpose is to encourage high-tech research in the United States.
Low-income housing (§ 42)	Appropriate rate times eligible basis (portion of project attributable to low-income units).	Part of general business credit and therefore subject to same carryback, carryover, and FIFO rules. Recapture may apply. Purpose is to encourage construction of housing for low-income individuals. Credit is available each year for 10 years.
Disabled access (§ 44)	Credit is 50% of eligible access expenditures that exceed $250, but do not exceed $10,250. Maximum credit is $5,000.	Part of general business credit and therefore subject to same carryback, carryover, and FIFO rules. Purpose is to encourage small businesses to become more accessible to disabled individuals. Available only to eligible small businesses.

Credit	Computation	Comments
Credit for small employer pension plan startup costs (§ 45E)	The credit equals 50% of qualified startup costs incurred by eligible employers. Maximum annual credit is $500. Deduction for related expenses is reduced by the amount of the credit.	Part of general business credit and therefore subject to same carryback, carryover, and FIFO rules. Purpose is to encourage small employers to establish qualified retirement plans for their employees.
Credit for employer-provided child care (§ 45F)	Credit is equal to 25% of qualified child care expenses plus 10% of qualified expenses for child care resource and referral services. Maximum credit is $150,000. Deduction for related expenses or basis must be reduced by the amount of the credit.	Part of general business credit and therefore subject to same carryback, carryover, and FIFO rules. Purpose is to encourage employers to provide child care for their employees' children during normal working hours.
Foreign tax (§ 27)	Foreign taxable income/total worldwide taxable income × U.S. tax = overall limitation. Lesser of foreign taxes imposed or overall limitation.	Unused credits may be carried back 1 year and forward 10 years. Purpose is to reduce double taxation of foreign income.

- *Ongoing test.* If the initial test is passed, the corporation is exempt from the AMT as long as its average annual gross receipts for the three-year period preceding the current tax year and any intervening three-year periods do not exceed $7.5 million.

A corporation that fails the initial test *never* (other than the first year exception below) can be exempt from the AMT. Furthermore, if the ongoing test is failed, the taxpayer is subject to the AMT provisions for that year and all subsequent tax years. Congress estimates that this provision will exempt up to 95 percent of all C corporations from the AMT. A corporation *automatically* is classified as a small corporation in the first tax year of existence.

The AMT Formula

The AMT is imposed in addition to the regular corporate income tax, but is computed in a manner wholly separate and independent from it.[20] The AMT is a parallel income tax system that generally uses more conservative accounting methods than the regular income tax. Typically, more items are subject to tax under AMT rules, some gross income items are accelerated, and some deductions are deferred.

The formula for determining the AMT liability of corporate taxpayers appears in Exhibit 14–2 and follows the format of Form 4626 (Alternative Minimum Tax—Corporations).

The base for the AMT, **alternative minimum taxable income (AMTI),** begins with regular taxable income before any deductions for net operating losses (NOLs). A series of adjustments are then made. Most AMT adjustments relate to *timing differences* that arise because of separate regular income tax and AMT treatments. Adjustments that are caused by timing differences eventually reverse; that is, positive adjustments are offset by negative adjustments in the future, and vice versa.

The adjustments related to *circulation expenditures* illustrate this concept. Circulation expenditures include expenses incurred to establish, maintain, or increase the circulation of a newspaper, magazine, or other periodical.

[20]The AMT provisions are contained in §§ 55 through 59.

EXHIBIT 14–2 **AMT Formula for Corporations**

Regular taxable income before NOL deduction
Plus/minus: AMT adjustments (except ACE adjustment)
Plus: Tax preferences
Equals: AMTI before AMT NOL deduction and ACE adjustment
Plus/minus: ACE adjustment
Equals: AMTI before AMT NOL deduction
Minus: AMT NOL deduction (limited to 90%)
Equals: Alternative minimum taxable income (AMTI)
Minus: Exemption
Equals: AMT base
Times: 20% rate
Equals: Tentative AMT before AMT foreign tax credit
Minus: AMT foreign tax credit
Equals: Tentative minimum tax
Minus: Regular income tax liability before credits minus regular foreign tax credit
Equals: Alternative minimum tax (AMT) if positive

In computing *taxable income*, corporations that are personal holding companies are allowed to deduct circulation expenditures in the year incurred. In computing AMTI, however, these expenditures must be capitalized and amortized ratably over the three-year period beginning with the year in which the expenditures were made.

EXAMPLE 17

Bobwhite, Inc., a personal holding company, incurred circulation expenditures of $30,000 in 2006. For regular income tax purposes, Bobwhite deducts $30,000 in 2006. For AMT purposes, the corporation is required to capitalize the expenditures and amortize them over a three-year period. Therefore, the deduction for AMT purposes is only $10,000. The AMT adjustment for 2006 is computed as follows.

Circulation expenditures deducted for regular income tax purposes	$ 30,000
Circulation expenditures deducted for AMT purposes	(10,000)
AMT adjustment (positive)	$ 20,000

■

EXAMPLE 18

Assume the same facts as in Example 17. The timing difference that gave rise to the positive adjustment in 2006 will reverse in the future. For AMT purposes, Bobwhite will deduct $10,000 in 2007 and $10,000 in 2008. The regular income tax deduction for circulation expenditures in each of those years will be $0, because the entire $30,000 expenditure was deducted in 2006. This results in a negative AMT adjustment of $10,000 each in 2007 and 2008. The AMT adjustments over the three-year period are summarized below.

Year	Regular Income Tax Deduction	AMT Deduction	AMT Adjustment
2006	$30,000	$10,000	$ 20,000
2007	–0–	10,000	(10,000)
2008	–0–	10,000	(10,000)
Totals	$30,000	$30,000	$ –0–

Timing differences eventually reverse. Thus, positive AMT adjustments can be offset later by negative adjustments. ■

TAX FACT

The Reach of the AMT

The total number of returns subject to the AMT is projected to increase as follows.

Year	Number of Returns
2000	1,300,000
2005	3,100,000
2011	35,500,000

Tax year 2000 is representative of the increases that are likely to occur because of the AMT unless the Code is modified.

Number of returns with AMT	1,300,000
Percentage increase in number of returns with AMT over prior year	28.1%
Percentage increase in AMT liability over prior year	48.2%
Revenue generated by AMT	$9 billion

The revenue generated by the corporate AMT as a percentage of corporate tax liabilities, however, is declining. The probable cause for this decline is the exemption from the AMT for small corporations.

Year	AMT as Percentage of Corporate Tax Liabilities
1990	8.0%
2000	1.8%

Source: *IRS Tax Statistics.*

Tax Preferences

LO.4

Identify and calculate the tax preferences that are included in determining the AMT.

AMTI includes designated **tax preference items**. In many cases, this part of the AMT formula has the effect of subjecting otherwise nontaxable income to the AMT. Tax preferences always increase AMTI. Some of the principal tax preferences are discussed below.

Percentage Depletion. Congress originally enacted the percentage depletion rules to provide taxpayers with incentives to invest in the development of specified natural resources. Percentage depletion is computed by multiplying a rate specified in the Code times the gross income from the property (refer to Chapter 5). The percentage rate is based on the type of mineral involved. The basis of the property is reduced by the amount of depletion taken until the basis reaches zero. However, once the basis of the property reaches zero, taxpayers are allowed to continue taking percentage depletion deductions. Thus, over the life of the property, depletion deductions may greatly exceed the cost of the property.

The percentage depletion preference is equal to the excess of the regular income tax deduction for percentage depletion over the adjusted basis of the property at the end of the taxable year.[21] Basis is determined without regard to the

[21] § 57(a)(1). Percentage depletion on oil and gas wells taken by independent producers and royalty owners does not create an AMT preference. See § 613A(c).

TAX *in the News* **THE AMT: FROM 155 TO 35.5 MILLION**

Often the tax law is changed to prevent or reduce certain perceived abuses. Such was the case when the AMT was enacted in 1969. The identifiable perceived abuse was that 155 individual taxpayers had zero Federal income tax liability despite having incomes in excess of $200,000.

Thus, the original idea behind the AMT was one of fairness, based on the premise that taxpayers with significant economic income should pay at least a minimum amount of tax. Although this idea has not changed, the tax is fast becoming anything but fair, according to most observers. That same concept of fairness later led Nina Olsen, the IRS's Taxpayer Advocate, to identify the expanding scope of the AMT as the number one problem facing taxpayers that needs to be legislatively addressed. A key problem is that Congress has not significantly updated the provisions of the AMT to account for inflation.

What has caused this shift in what is deemed fair? The idea that taxpayers with significant economic income should pay at least a minimum amount of tax has not changed. What is new is the number of taxpayers that are becoming subject to the AMT—an estimated 35.5 million taxpayers in 2011 if the law is not changed. Thus, a tax that was perceived as fair when it affected only a "few" now is perceived as unfair because it affects "many."

depletion deduction for the taxable year. This preference item is figured separately for each piece of property for which the taxpayer is claiming depletion.

EXAMPLE 19

Finch, Inc., owns a mineral property that qualifies for a 22% depletion rate. The basis of the property at the beginning of the year is $10,000. Gross income from the property for the year is $100,000. For regular income tax purposes, Finch's percentage depletion deduction (assume it is not limited by taxable income from the property) is $22,000. For AMT purposes, Finch has a tax preference of $12,000 ($22,000 – $10,000). ■

Interest on Private Activity Bonds. Income from private activity bonds is not included in taxable income, and expenses related to carrying such bonds are not deductible for regular income tax purposes. However, interest on private activity bonds is included as a preference in computing AMTI. Expenses incurred in carrying the bonds are offset against the interest income in computing the tax preference.[22]

The Code contains a lengthy, complex definition of **private activity bonds.**[23] In general, such debt is issued by states or municipalities, but more than 10 percent of the proceeds are used to benefit private business. For example, a bond issued by a city whose proceeds are used to construct a factory that is leased to a private business at a favorable rate is a private activity bond.

DIGGING DEEPER 3

*Find more information on this topic at our Web site: **http://wft-entities.swlearning.com.***

LO.5

Identify and calculate AMT adjustments.

AMT Adjustments

As Exhibit 14–2 indicates, the starting point for computing AMTI is the taxable income of the corporation before any NOL deduction. Certain *adjustments* must be made to this amount. Unlike tax preference items, which always increase AMTI, the adjustments may be either increases or decreases to taxable income.

Although NOLs are separately stated in Exhibit 14–2, they are actually negative adjustments. They are separately stated in Exhibit 14–2 and on Form 4626 because they may not exceed more than 90 percent of AMTI. Thus, such adjustments cannot be determined until all other adjustments and tax preference items are considered.

[22] § 57(a)(5).

[23] § 141.

TAX *in the News*

DISTINGUISHING BETWEEN TAXABLE AND EXEMPT BONDS FOR AMT PURPOSES

Interest on state and local bonds generally is exempt from the regular income tax, but it may be subject to the AMT.

If the state or local bond is a private activity bond, then the interest is a tax preference for AMT purposes. According to the Bond Market Association, interest from almost 8.7 percent of the $1.9 trillion municipal bond market is subject to the AMT. The association's Web site (**http://www.investinginbonds.com**) provides a primer on the AMT's effect on municipal bonds and explains how to determine if the related interest is subject to the AMT.

The IRS has developed a free online calculator to help taxpayers determine if they will be subject to the AMT in 2005 (**http://apps.irs.gov/app/amt**).

Computing Adjustments. It is necessary to determine not only the amount of an adjustment, but also whether the adjustment is positive or negative. Careful study of Examples 17 and 18 reveals the following pattern with regard to *deductions.*

- If the deduction allowed for regular income tax purposes exceeds the deduction allowed for AMT purposes, the difference is a positive adjustment.
- If the deduction allowed for AMT purposes exceeds the deduction allowed for regular income tax purposes, the difference is a negative adjustment.

Conversely, the direction of an adjustment attributable to an *income* item can be determined as follows.

- If the income reported for regular income tax purposes exceeds the income reported for AMT purposes, the difference is a negative adjustment.
- If the income reported for AMT purposes exceeds the income reported for regular income tax purposes, the difference is a positive adjustment.

The principal AMT adjustments are discussed below. The adjustment for circulation expenditures was discussed previously.

Depreciation of Post-1986 Real Property. Tax legislation enacted in 1997 eliminated the AMT depreciation adjustment for real property by providing that the MACRS recovery periods (see Table 5–3) used in calculating the regular income tax apply in calculating the AMT. Note, however, that this AMT recovery period conformity provision applies only to property placed in service after December 31, 1998.[24] Thus, the AMT depreciation adjustment discussed below does apply for real property placed in service before January 1, 1999.

For real property placed in service after 1986 (MACRS property) and before January 1, 1999, AMT depreciation is computed under the alternative depreciation system (ADS), which uses the straight-line method over a 40-year life. The depreciation lives for regular income tax purposes are 27.5 years for residential rental property and 39 years for all other real property.[25] The difference between AMT depreciation and regular income tax depreciation is treated as an adjustment in computing the AMT. The differences will be positive during the regular income tax life of the asset because the cost is written off over a shorter period for regular income tax purposes. For example, during the 27.5-year income tax life of residential real property, the regular income tax depreciation will exceed the AMT depreciation because AMT depreciation is computed over a 40-year period.

Table 5–3 is used to compute regular income tax depreciation on real property placed in service after 1986. For AMT purposes, depreciation on real property placed in service after 1986 and before January 1, 1999, is computed under the ADS (refer to Table 5–7).

[24]§ 56(a)(1)(A)(i).

[25]The 39-year life generally applies to nonresidential real property placed in service on or after May 13, 1993.

EXAMPLE 20

In January 1998, Robin Rentals placed in service a residential building that cost $100,000. Regular income tax depreciation, AMT depreciation, and the AMT adjustment are as follows:

	Depreciation		
Year	Regular Income Tax	AMT	AMT Adjustment
1998	$3,485[1]	$2,396[2]	$1,089
1999	3,636[3]	2,500[4]	1,136
2000	3,636	2,500	1,136
2001	3,636	2,500	1,136
2002	3,636	2,500	1,136
2003	3,636	2,500	1,136
2004	3,636	2,500	1,136
2005	3,636	2,500	1,136
2006	3,636	2,500	1,136

[1]$100,000 cost × 3.485% (Table 5–3) = $3,485
[2]$100,000 cost × 2.396% (Table 5–7) = $2,396
[3]$100,000 cost × 3.636% (Table 5–3) = $3,636
[4]$100,000 cost × 2.500% (Table 5–7) = $2,500

If the building had been placed in service after 1998, there would have been no AMT depreciation adjustment for the tax year it is placed in service or for subsequent years. The depreciation for the tax year the building was placed in service for both regular income tax purposes and AMT purposes would have been $3,485 ($100,000 × 3.485%). ■

After real property placed in service before 1999 has been held for the entire depreciation period for regular income tax purposes, the asset will be fully depreciated. However, the depreciation period under the ADS is 41 years due to application of the mid-month convention, so depreciation will continue for AMT purposes. This causes negative adjustments after the property has been fully depreciated for regular income tax purposes.

EXAMPLE 21

Assume the same facts as in the previous example for the building placed in service in 1998. Regular income tax depreciation in the year 2026 (the twenty-ninth year of the asset's life) is zero (refer to Table 5–3). AMT depreciation is $2,500 ($100,000 cost × 2.500% from Table 5–7). Therefore, Robin has a negative AMT adjustment of $2,500 ($0 regular income tax depreciation – $2,500 AMT depreciation). ■

After real property is fully depreciated for both regular income tax and AMT purposes, the positive and negative adjustments that have been made for AMT purposes will net to zero.

Depreciation of Post-1986 Personal Property. For most personal property placed in service after 1986 (MACRS property), the MACRS deduction for regular income tax purposes is based on the 200 percent declining-balance method with a switch to straight-line when that method produces a larger depreciation deduction for the asset. Refer to Table 5–1 for computing regular income tax depreciation.

For AMT purposes, the taxpayer must use the ADS for such property placed in service before 1999. This method is based on the 150 percent declining-balance method with a similar switch to straight-line for all personal property.[26] Refer to Table 5–5 for percentages to be used in computing AMT depreciation.

[26]§ 56(a)(1).

The MACRS deduction for personal property is larger than the ADS deduction in the early years of an asset's life. However, the ADS deduction is larger in the later years. This is so because ADS lives are sometimes longer than MACRS lives and use less accelerated depreciation methods.[27] Over the ADS life of the asset, the same aggregate amount of depreciation is deducted for both regular income tax and AMT purposes. In the same manner as other timing adjustments, the AMT adjustments for depreciation will net to zero over the ADS life of the asset.

The taxpayer may elect to use the ADS for regular income tax purposes. If this election is made, no AMT adjustment is required because the depreciation deduction is the same for regular income tax and for the AMT. The election eliminates the burden of maintaining two sets of tax depreciation records at the cost of a higher regular tax liability.

Tax legislation enacted in 1997 either reduces or eliminates the AMT adjustment for the depreciation of personal property. Prior to the effective date of this provision, the difference between regular income tax depreciation and AMT depreciation was caused by longer recovery periods for the AMT (class life versus MACRS recovery periods) and more accelerated depreciation methods for the regular income tax (200 percent declining balance rather than 150 percent declining balance).

Now, MACRS recovery periods are used in calculating AMT depreciation. Thus, if the taxpayer elects to use the 150 percent declining-balance method for regular income tax purposes, there are no AMT adjustments. Conversely, if the taxpayer uses the 200 percent declining-balance method for regular income tax purposes, there is an AMT adjustment for depreciation. This AMT recovery period conformity provision applies only to property placed in service after 1998. Thus, the adjustment continues to apply for personal property placed in service before 1999.

Pollution Control Facilities. For regular income tax purposes, the cost of certified pollution control facilities may be amortized over a period of 60 months. For AMT purposes, the cost of these facilities placed in service after 1986 and before 1999 is depreciated under the ADS over the appropriate class life, determined as explained above for depreciation of post-1986 property.[28] The required adjustment for AMTI is the difference between the amortization deduction allowed for regular income tax purposes and the depreciation deduction computed under the ADS. The adjustment may be positive or negative.

The AMT adjustment for pollution control facilities is reduced for property placed in service after 1998. This reduction is achieved by providing conformity in the recovery periods used for regular income tax purposes and AMT purposes (MACRS recovery periods).

DIGGING DEEPER 4

Find more information on this topic at our Web site: ***http://wft-entities.swlearning.com.***

Use of Completed Contract Method of Accounting. For a long-term contract, taxpayers are required to use the percentage of completion method for AMT purposes.[29] However, in limited circumstances, taxpayers can use the completed contract method for regular income tax purposes.[30] The resulting AMT adjustment is equal to the difference between income reported under the percentage of completion method and the amount reported using the completed contract method.[31] The adjustment can be either positive or negative, depending on the amount of income recognized under the different methods.

[27] Class lives and recovery periods are established for all assets in Rev.Proc. 87–56, 1987–2 C.B. 674.

[28] § 56(a)(5).

[29] § 56(a)(3).

[30] See Chapter 12 of *Advanced Business Entity Taxation* for a detailed discussion of the completed contract and percentage of completion methods of accounting.

[31] § 56(a)(3).

A taxpayer can avoid an AMT adjustment on long-term contracts by using the percentage of completion method for regular income tax purposes rather than the completed contract method.

Adjusted Gain or Loss. When property is sold during the year or a casualty occurs to business or income-producing property, gain or loss reported for regular income tax may be different than gain or loss determined for the AMT. This difference occurs because the adjusted basis of the property for AMT purposes must reflect any current and prior AMT adjustments for the following.[32]

- Depreciation.
- Circulation expenditures.
- Amortization of certified pollution control facilities.

A negative gain or loss adjustment is required if:

- the gain for AMT purposes is less than the gain for regular income tax purposes;
- the loss for AMT purposes is more than the loss for regular income tax purposes; or
- a loss is computed for AMT purposes and a gain is computed for regular income tax purposes.

Otherwise, the AMT gain or loss adjustment is positive.

EXAMPLE 22

In January 1998, Cardinal Corporation paid $100,000 for a duplex acquired for rental purposes. Regular income tax depreciation, AMT depreciation, and the AMT adjustment are as follows:

	Depreciation		
Year	**Regular Income Tax**	**AMT**	**AMT Adjustment**
1998	$3,485[1]	$2,396[2]	$1,089
1999	3,636[3]	2,500[4]	1,136
2000	3,636	2,500	1,136
2001	3,636	2,500	1,136
2002	3,636	2,500	1,136
2003	3,636	2,500	1,136
2004	3,636	2,500	1,136
2005	3,636	2,500	1,136

[1]$100,000 cost × 3.485% (Table 5–3) = $3,485
[2]$100,000 cost × 2.396% (Table 5–7) = $2,396
[3]$100,000 cost × 3.636% (Table 5–3) = $3,636
[4]$100,000 cost × 2.500% (Table 5–7) = $2,500

Cardinal then sold the duplex on December 20, 2006, for $105,000. Regular income tax depreciation for 2006 is $3,485 [($100,000 cost × 3.636% from Table 5–3) × (11.5/12)]. AMT depreciation for 2006 is $2,396 [($100,000 cost × 2.500% from Table 5–7) × (11.5/12)]. Cardinal's positive AMT adjustment for 2006 is $1,089 ($3,485 regular income tax depreciation − $2,396 AMT depreciation).

Because depreciation on the duplex differs for regular income tax and AMT purposes, Cardinal's adjusted basis for the property is different for regular income tax and AMT purposes. Consequently, the gain or loss on disposition of the duplex is different for regular income tax and AMT purposes.

[32]§ 56(a)(6).

The adjusted basis for Cardinal's duplex for regular income tax purposes is $67,578 and for AMT purposes is $77,708.

	Regular Income Tax	AMT
Cost	$100,000	$100,000
Depreciation:		
1998	(3,485)	(2,396)
1999	(3,636)	(2,500)
2000	(3,636)	(2,500)
2001	(3,636)	(2,500)
2002	(3,636)	(2,500)
2003	(3,636)	(2,500)
2004	(3,636)	(2,500)
2005	(3,636)	(2,500)
2006	(3,485)	(2,396)
Adjusted basis	$ 67,578	$ 77,708

The regular income tax gain is $37,422 and the AMT gain is $27,292.

	Regular Income Tax	AMT
Amount realized	$105,000	$105,000
Adjusted basis	(67,578)	(77,708)
Recognized gain	$ 37,422	$ 27,292

Because the regular income tax and AMT gain on the sale of the duplex differ, Cardinal makes a negative AMT adjustment of $10,130 ($37,422 regular income tax gain − $27,292 AMT gain). The negative adjustment matches the $10,130 total of the nine positive adjustments for depreciation ($1,089 in 1998 + $1,136 in 1999 + $1,136 in 2000 + $1,136 in 2001 + $1,136 in 2002 + $1,136 in 2003 + $1,136 in 2004 + $1,136 in 2005 + $1,089 in 2006). ■

Passive Activity Losses. Net losses on passive activities are not deductible in computing either the regular income tax or the AMT for closely held C corporations (cannot offset portfolio income) and personal service corporations (cannot offset either active income or portfolio income).[33] This does not, however, eliminate the possibility of adjustments attributable to passive activities.

The rules for computing taxable income differ from the rules for computing AMTI. It follows, then, that the rules for computing a loss for regular income tax purposes differ from the AMT rules for computing a loss. Therefore, any *passive loss* computed for regular income tax purposes may differ from the passive loss computed for AMT purposes.

EXAMPLE 23

Robin, Inc., a personal service corporation, acquired two passive activities in 2006. Robin received net passive income of $10,000 from Activity A and had no AMT adjustments or preferences in connection with the activity. Activity B had gross income of $27,000 and operating expenses (not affected by AMT adjustments or preferences) of $19,000. Robin claimed MACRS depreciation of $20,000 for Activity B; depreciation under the ADS would have been $15,000. In addition, Robin deducted $10,000 of percentage depletion in excess of basis.

[33] § 469(a).

The following comparison illustrates the differences in the computation of the passive loss for regular income tax and AMT purposes for Activity B.

	Regular Income Tax	AMT
Gross income	$ 27,000	$27,000
Deductions:		
Operating expenses	($ 19,000)	($ 19,000)
Depreciation	(20,000)	(15,000)
Depletion	(10,000)	–0–
Total deductions	($ 49,000)	($ 34,000)
Passive loss	($ 22,000)	($ 7,000)

Because the adjustment for depreciation ($5,000) applies and the preference for depletion ($10,000) is not taken into account in computing AMTI, the regular income tax passive activity loss of $22,000 for Activity B is reduced by these amounts, resulting in a passive activity loss of $7,000 for AMT purposes.

For regular income tax purposes, Robin would offset the $10,000 of net passive income from Activity A with $10,000 of the passive loss from Activity B. For AMT purposes, the corporation would offset the $10,000 of net passive income from Activity A with the $7,000 passive activity loss allowed from Activity B, resulting in passive activity income of $3,000. Thus, in computing AMTI, Robin makes a positive passive loss adjustment of $3,000 [$10,000 (passive activity loss allowed for regular income tax) – $7,000 (passive activity loss allowed for the AMT)].[34]

For regular income tax purposes, Robin, Inc., has a suspended passive loss of $12,000 [$22,000 (amount of loss) – $10,000 (used in 2006)]. This suspended passive loss can offset passive income in the future or can offset active or portfolio income when the corporation disposes of the loss activity (refer to Chapter 6). For AMT purposes, Robin's suspended passive loss is $0 [$7,000 (amount of loss) – $7,000 (amount used in 2006)]. ■

PLANNING *Strategies*

AVOIDING PREFERENCES AND ADJUSTMENTS

★ **Framework Focus: Tax Rate**

Strategy ★ Control the Character of Income and Deductions.

Investments in state and local bonds are attractive for income tax purposes because the interest is not included in gross income. Some of these bonds (private activity bonds) are issued to generate funds that are not used for an essential function of the government (e.g., to provide infrastructure for shopping malls or industrial parks or to build sports facilities). The interest on such bonds is a tax preference item and could lead to the imposition of the AMT. When the AMT applies, investors should take this factor into account. Perhaps an investment in regular tax-exempt bonds or even fully taxed private-sector bonds might yield a higher after-tax rate of return.

For a corporation anticipating AMT problems, capitalizing rather than expensing certain costs can avoid generating preferences and adjustments. The decision should be based on the present discounted value of after-tax cash flows under the available alternatives. Costs that may be capitalized and amortized, rather than expensed, include circulation expenditures, mining exploration and development costs, and research and experimentation expenditures.

[34]The depreciation adjustment and depletion preference are combined as part of the passive loss adjustment and are *not* reported separately.

FIGURE 14–1 **Determining the ACE Adjustment***

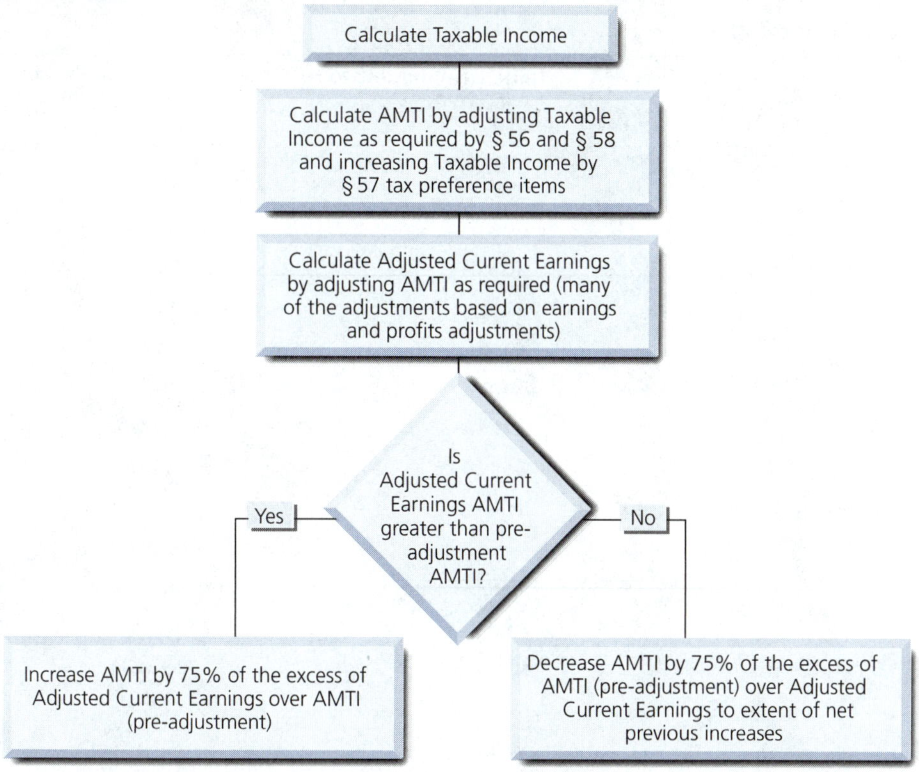
Calculate Taxable Income
Calculate AMTI by adjusting Taxable Income as required by § 56 and § 58 and increasing Taxable Income by § 57 tax preference items
Calculate Adjusted Current Earnings by adjusting AMTI as required (many of the adjustments based on earnings and profits adjustments)
Is Adjusted Current Earnings AMTI greater than pre-adjustment AMTI?
Yes
No
Increase AMTI by 75% of the excess of Adjusted Current Earnings over AMTI (pre-adjustment)
Decrease AMTI by 75% of the excess of AMTI (pre-adjustment) over Adjusted Current Earnings to extent of net previous increases

*Reprinted with permission *Oil and Gas Tax Quarterly*. Copyright 1989 Matthew Bender & Company, Inc., a member of the LexisNexis Group. All Rights Reserved.

Adjusted Current Earnings (ACE)

LO.6

Understand the function of adjusted current earnings (ACE).

The **adjusted current earnings (ACE)** rules make up a third, separate tax system, parallel to both AMT and taxable income. S corporations, real estate investment trusts, regulated investment companies, and real estate mortgage investment conduits are not subject to the ACE provisions.

The purpose of the ACE adjustment is to ensure that the mismatching of financial statement income and taxable income will not produce inequitable results. ACE represents another attempt by Congress to assure that large corporations with significant financial accounting income pay a fair share of Federal corporate income tax.

The ACE adjustment is tax-based and can be negative or positive. AMTI is increased by 75 percent of the excess of ACE over unadjusted AMTI, or AMTI is reduced by 75 percent of the excess of unadjusted AMTI over ACE. Any negative ACE adjustment is limited to the aggregate of the positive adjustments under ACE for prior years reduced by the previously claimed negative adjustments (see Figure 14–1).[35] Any unused negative adjustment is lost forever.

[35]§§ 56(g)(1) and (2). *Unadjusted AMTI* is AMTI before the ACE adjustment and the AMT NOL deduction.

CONCEPT SUMMARY 14–2

Impact of Various Transactions on ACE and E & P

	Effect on Unadjusted AMTI in Arriving at ACE	Effect on Taxable Income in Arriving at E & P
Tax-exempt income (net of expenses)	Add	Add
Federal income tax	No effect	Subtract
Dividends received deduction (80% and 100% rules)	No effect	Add
Dividends received deduction (70% rule)	Add	Add
Exemption amount of $40,000	No effect	No effect
Key employee insurance proceeds	Add	Add
Excess charitable contribution	No effect	Subtract
Excess capital losses	No effect	Subtract
Disallowed meals and entertainment expenses	No effect	Subtract
Penalties and fines	No effect	Subtract
Intangible drilling costs deducted currently	Add	Add
Deferred gain on installment sales	Add	Add
Realized (not recognized) gain on an involuntary conversion	No effect	No effect
Loss on sale between related parties	No effect	Subtract
Gift received	No effect	No effect
Net buildup on life insurance policy	Add	Add
Organization expense amortization	Add	Add

EXAMPLE 24

A calendar year corporation reports the following.

	2005	2006	2007
Unadjusted AMTI	$3,000,000	$3,000,000	$3,100,000
Adjusted current earnings	4,000,000	3,000,000	2,000,000

In 2005, since ACE exceeds unadjusted AMTI by $1 million, $750,000 (75% × $1,000,000) is the positive ACE adjustment. No adjustment is necessary for 2006. Unadjusted AMTI exceeds ACE by $1,100,000 in 2007, so there is a potential negative ACE adjustment of $825,000. Since the total increases to AMTI for prior years equal $750,000 (and there are no negative adjustments), only $750,000 of the potential negative ACE adjustment reduces AMTI for 2007. Further, $75,000 of negative ACE is lost forever. ■

The starting point for computing ACE is AMTI, which is regular taxable income after AMT adjustments (other than the NOL and ACE adjustments) and tax preferences.[36] Pre-NOL AMTI is adjusted for certain items to determine ACE. See Concept Summary 14–2.

DIGGING DEEPER 5

Find more information on this topic at our Web site: ***http://wft-entities.swlearning.com.***

[36]§ 56(g)(3).

EXAMPLE 25

Crimson Corporation makes the ACE adjustment calculation as follows.

AMTI		$ 5,780,000
Plus:		
Municipal bond interest	$210,000	
Installment gain	140,000	
70% dividends received deduction	300,000	
Income element in cash surrender life insurance	60,000	
Organization expense amortization	70,000	780,000
Subtotal		$ 6,560,000
Less:		
Related-party loss disallowance	$240,000	(240,000)
Adjusted current earnings		$ 6,320,000
AMTI		(5,780,000)
Base amount		$ 540,000
Times		.75
ACE adjustment (positive)		$ 405,000

■

ACE should not be confused with current E & P. Many items are treated in the same manner, but certain items that are deductible in computing E & P (but are not deductible in calculating taxable income) generally are not deductible in computing ACE (e.g., Federal income taxes). Concept Summary 14–2 compares the impact various transactions will have on the determination of ACE and E & P.

Computing Alternative Minimum Taxable Income

LO.7

Compute the AMT liability for corporations.

The following example illustrates the effect of tax preferences and adjustments in arriving at AMTI.

EXAMPLE 26

For 2006, Tan Corporation (a calendar year company) had the following transactions.

Taxable income	$4,250,000
Income deferred by using completed contract method (versus percentage of completion method)	450,000
Percentage depletion claimed (the property has a zero adjusted basis)	1,575,000
Interest on City of Elmira (Michigan) private activity bonds	1,175,000

Tan Corporation's AMTI for 2006 is determined as follows.

Taxable income		$4,250,000
Adjustments		
Income deferred by using completed contract method (versus percentage of completion method)		450,000
Tax preferences		
Excess depletion deduction	$1,575,000	
Interest on private activity municipal bonds	1,175,000	2,750,000
AMTI		$7,450,000

■

PLANNING *Strategies*

OPTIMUM USE OF THE AMT AND REGULAR CORPORATE INCOME TAX RATE DIFFERENCE

★ **Framework Focus: Tax Rate**

Strategy ★ Shift Net Income from High-Bracket Years to Low-Bracket Years.

A corporation that cannot avoid the AMT in a particular year often can save taxes by taking advantage of the difference between the AMT and the regular income tax rates. In general, a corporation that expects to be subject to the AMT should consider accelerating income and deferring deductions for the remainder of the year. Since the difference between the regular income tax rate and the AMT rate may be as much as 14 or 15 percentage points, this strategy may result in the income being taxed at less than it would be if reported in the next year (a non-AMT year). If the same corporation expects to be subject to the AMT for the next year (or years) and is not subject to AMT this year, this technique should be reversed.

EXAMPLE 27

Falcon Corporation expects to be in the 34% regular income tax bracket in 2007, but is subject to the AMT in 2006. In late 2006, Falcon is contemplating selling a tract of unimproved land (basis of $200,000 and fair market value of $1 million), which is classified as inventory. Under these circumstances, it may be preferable to sell the land in 2006. The gain of $800,000 ($1,000,000 – $200,000) generates a tax of $160,000 [$800,000 (recognized gain) × 20% (AMT rate)]. However, if the land is sold in 2007, the resulting tax is $272,000 [$800,000 (recognized gain) × 34% (regular corporate income tax rate)]. A nominal savings of $112,000 ($272,000 – $160,000) materializes by making the sale in 2006. ■

Whenever one accelerates income or defers deductions, a present value analysis should be conducted. This technique to accelerate gross income is attractive only if it reduces the present value of tax liabilities.

AMT Rate and Exemption

The AMT rate is 20 percent. The rate is applied to the *AMT base*, which is AMTI reduced by the *AMT exemption*. The exemption amount for a corporation is $40,000 reduced by 25 percent of the amount by which AMTI exceeds $150,000. The exemption phases out entirely when AMTI reaches $310,000.

EXAMPLE 28

Beige Corporation has AMTI of $180,000. Since the exemption amount is reduced by $7,500 [25% × ($180,000 – $150,000)], the amount remaining is $32,500 ($40,000 – $7,500). Thus, Beige Corporation's alternative minimum tax base (refer to Exhibit 14–2) is $147,500 ($180,000 – $32,500). ■

PLANNING *Strategies*

CONTROLLING THE TIMING OF PREFERENCES AND ADJUSTMENTS

★ **Framework Focus: Tax Rate**

Strategy ★ Control the Character of Income and Deductions.

In many situations, corporations with modest levels of income may be able to avoid the AMT by making use of the exemption. To maximize the exemption, taxpayers should attempt to avoid bunching positive adjustments and tax preferences in any one year. Rather, net these items against negative adjustments to keep AMTI low. When the expenditure is largely within the control of the taxpayer, timing to avoid bunching is more easily accomplished.

BRIDGE *Discipline*

Bridge to Finance

For entities other than C corporations, each year more taxpayers are subject to the AMT. In addition, for taxpayers who are paying the AMT, the amount of AMT increases annually, even when both the total Federal taxable income and the tentative AMT are constant. This increase is even more noticeable in light of the statutory tax rate decreases for individual taxpayers provided for in the Tax Relief Reconciliation Act of 2001 commencing in 2002. The next scheduled decrease in the individual income tax rates under the 2001 Act was to be effective for 2004. However, the reduced tax rates for 2004 and thereafter were accelerated into 2003 by the Jobs Growth and Tax Relief Reconciliation Act of 2003 (JGTRRA of 2003).

Rose, Inc., an S corporation, has one shareholder, Jack, who is single. In 2002 and 2003, Rose has taxable income of $100,000, which is reported to Jack each year on a Schedule K–1. Jack's taxable income, excluding the $100,000 from Rose, is $300,000 each year. Jack's tentative AMT each year is $150,000.

Jack's regular income tax liability, AMT, and total Federal income tax liability for 2002 and 2003 are as follows.

2002		
Regular income tax liability		
Tax on $307,050	=	$ 94,720
92,950 × 38.6%	=	35,879
$400,000		$130,599
AMT ($150,000 – $130,599)		$ 19,401
Regular income tax		$130,599
AMT		19,401
Total tax liability		$150,000

2003		
Regular income tax liability		
Tax on $311,950	=	$ 90,514
88,050 × 35%	=	30,818
$400,000		$121,332
AMT ($150,000 – $121,332)		$ 28,668
Regular income tax		$121,332
AMT		28,668
Total tax liability		$150,000

When Jack's taxable income remains the same each year, why does the AMT increase by $9,267 ($28,668 – $19,401)? The reasons are as follows: (1) the tax rates used in calculating the regular income tax (§ 1) are indexed for the effect of inflation each year, while the AMT tax rates (§ 55) are not subject to indexing, and (2) the statutory tax rates for the regular income tax for 2002 versus 2003 have been reduced by the JGTRRA of 2003 while the AMT rates have not changed. Note that if the tax years being compared were 2004, 2005, and 2006, only the indexing effect would be present. That is, the 2004, 2005, and 2006 statutory tax rates are the same.

The inflation effect could easily be fixed by indexing the AMT tax rates. Corporations are not subject to inflation-caused effects because neither the regular income tax rates (§ 11) nor the AMT rates (§ 55) are indexed. In addition, the Tax Relief Reconciliation Act of 2001 did not modify either the regular income tax rates or the AMT rates for C corporations.

Minimum Tax Credit

The **minimum tax credit** acts to make the AMT merely a *prepayment of tax* for corporations. Essentially, the AMT paid in one tax year may be carried forward indefinitely and used as a credit against the corporation's future *regular* tax liability that exceeds its tentative minimum tax. The minimum tax credit may not be carried back and may not be offset against any future AMT liability.

EXAMPLE 29

Return to the facts of Example 26. AMTI exceeds $310,000, so there is no exemption amount. The tentative minimum tax is $1,490,000 (20% of $7,450,000). Since Tan's regular income tax liability for 2006 is $1,445,000, the AMT liability is $45,000 ($1,490,000 – $1,445,000). The minimum tax credit carried forward is $45,000, the current year's AMT. The credit can be used to reduce regular income tax liability in future years (but not below the tentative alternative minimum tax). ■

Other Aspects of the AMT

In addition to paying their regular income tax liability, corporations must make estimated tax payments of the AMT liability. Even corporations that prepare quarterly financial statements may find this requirement adds to compliance costs.

The only credit that can be used to offset the AMT is the foreign tax credit (FTC). The general business credit and other credits discussed earlier in the chapter are unavailable in AMT years.

The corporate AMT is computed and reported by completing Form 4626.

PLANNING *Strategies*

THE SUBCHAPTER S OPTION

★ **Framework Focus: Tax Rate**

Strategy ★ Avoid Double Taxation.

Corporations that make the S election are not subject to the corporate AMT. As noted in Chapter 12, however, various AMT adjustments and preferences pass through to the individual shareholders. But one troublesome adjustment, the one involving the ACE adjustment, is avoided since it does not apply to individual taxpayers.

Individual Alternative Minimum Tax

The AMT applicable to individuals is similar to the corporate AMT. Most of the adjustments and preferences discussed above apply equally to individuals and corporations. However, there are several important differences.

- The individual AMT rate is slightly progressive, with rates at 26 percent on the first $175,000 of AMTI and at 28 percent on any additional AMTI.
- The alternative rate on net capital gain of 5 or 15 percent applies.
- The AMT exemption and phaseout amounts are tied to the individual's filing status for the year. The exemption phases out at a rate of $1 for every $4 of AMTI.[37]

Filing Status	Initial Exemption Amount in 2006	Phaseout Range	
		Begins at	Ends at
Married, joint	$58,000	$150,000	$382,000
Married, separate	29,000	75,000	191,000
Single, head of household	40,250	112,500	273,500

[37] §§ 55(d)(1) and (3). For tax years beginning in 2006 and thereafter, the exemption amount is scheduled to be reduced to the following amounts: married taxpayers filing jointly—$45,000, single taxpayers—$33,750, married taxpayers filing separately—$22,500. However, the general consensus is that Congress is highly likely to extend the increased exemption amounts for 2006. Thus, these increased amounts are used in all AMT calculations in this chapter.

- Individuals make no AMT adjustment for ACE.
- Some additional adjustments apply to individual taxpayers. Taxes and miscellaneous itemized deductions subject to the 2 percent-of-AGI floor are not allowed as deductions for AMTI. Medical expenses are allowed only to the extent that they exceed 10 percent of AGI (instead of a 7.5 percent limitation for regular income tax purposes). Interest expense deductions are limited to qualified residence interest, interest on certain student loans, and investment interest (subject to limitations). Finally, the standard deduction and personal and dependency exemptions are not allowed as deductions when computing AMTI. Other individual-specific adjustments also exist, including an adjustment accelerating the taxation of incentive stock options.
- Determination of the minimum tax credit is more complex for individual taxpayers. The credit applies only to AMT generated as a result of *timing* differences.

Although there are several computational differences, the individual AMT and the corporate AMT have the same objective: to force taxpayers who have more economic income than that reflected in taxable income to pay a fair share of Federal income tax.

Suggested Further Readings

Steven D. Arkin and James M. Eberle, "The New Research Credit Final Regs.—What's Gone, What's New, and What's Missing," *Journal of Taxation,* March 2004, pp. 144–151.

Albert B. Ellentuck, "Case Study: Avoiding the AMT Depreciation Adjustment," *The Tax Adviser,* January 2003, pp. 54–55.

Matt Given, "Aim to Take Advantage of Various Targeted Tax Credits," *Practical Tax Strategies,* April 2004, pp. 220–235.

Alan L. Kennard, "The Historic Credit: An Opportunity for Corporate Taxpayers," *Corporate Taxation,* July/August 2005, pp. 24–44.

Michael I. Sanders, "The New Markets Tax Credit: Stimulating Investment While Facilitating Economic Development," *Journal of Taxation,* November 2002, pp. 94–101.

James P. Trebby and George W. Kutner, "Seek Ways to Minimize the Mushrooming Alternative Minimum Tax," *Practical Tax Strategies,* June 2005, pp. 351–355.

KEY TERMS

Adjusted current earnings (ACE), 14–25

Alternative minimum tax (AMT), 14–13

Alternative minimum taxable income (AMTI), 14–15

Credit for employer-provided child care, 14–11

Credit for small employer pension plan startup costs, 14–11

Disabled access credit, 14–10

Foreign tax credit (FTC), 14–12

General business credit, 14–3

Minimum tax credit, 14–29

Private activity bonds, 14–18

Rehabilitation expenditures credit, 14–6

Rehabilitation expenditures credit recapture, 14–6

Research activities credit, 14–8

Tax credits, 14–2

Tax preference items, 14–17

Welfare-to-work credit, 14–8

Work opportunity tax credit, 14–7

PROBLEM MATERIALS

PROBLEMS

1. Canary, Inc., has a tentative general business credit of $85,000 for 2006. Canary's net regular tax liability before the general business credit is $95,000, and its tentative minimum tax is $90,000. Compute Canary's allowable general business credit for the year.

2. Oak Corporation holds the following general business credit carryovers.

2002	$ 20,000
2003	60,000
2004	20,000
2005	80,000
Total carryovers	$180,000

If the general business credit generated by activities during 2006 equals $170,000 and the total credit allowed during the current year is $320,000 (based on tax liability), what amounts of the current general business credit and carryovers are utilized against the 2006 income tax liability? What is the amount of the unused credit carried forward to 2007?

Issue ID

3. Clint, a self-employed engineering consultant, is contemplating purchasing an old building for renovation. After the work is completed, Clint plans to rent out two-thirds of the floor space to businesses and to live and work in the remaining portion. Identify the relevant tax issues for Clint.

4. In January 2004, Iris Corporation purchased and placed into service a 1933 building that houses retail businesses. The cost was $240,000, of which $25,000 applied to the land. In modernizing the facility, Iris Corporation incurred $280,000 of renovation costs of the type that qualify for the rehabilitation credit. These improvements were placed into service in October 2006.
   a. Compute Iris Corporation's rehabilitation tax credit for 2006.
   b. Calculate the cost recovery deductions for the building and the renovation costs for 2006.

Decision Making
Communications

5. In the current year, Diane Lawson (127 Peachtree Drive, Savannah, GA 31419) acquires a qualifying historic structure for $250,000 (excluding the cost of land) with full intentions of substantially rehabilitating the building. Write a letter to Diane and a memo to the tax files explaining the computation that determines the rehabilitation tax credit available to her and the impact on the depreciable basis, assuming she incurs either $200,000 or $400,000 for the rehabilitation project.

Ethics

6. The tax credit for rehabilitation expenditures is available to help offset the costs related to substantially rehabilitating certain buildings. The credit is calculated on the rehabilitation expenditures incurred and not on the acquisition cost of the building itself.

   You are a developer who buys, sells, and does construction work on real estate in the inner city of your metropolitan area. A potential customer approaches you about acquiring one of your buildings that easily could qualify for the 20% rehabilitation credit on historic structures. The stated sales price of the structure is $100,000 (based on appraisals ranging from $80,000 to $120,000), and the rehabilitation expenditures, if the job is done correctly, would be about $150,000.

   Your business has been slow recently due to the sluggish real estate market in your area, and the potential customer makes the following proposal: if you reduce the sales price of the building to $75,000, he will pay you $175,000 to perform the rehabilitation work. Although the buyer's total expenditures would be the same, he would benefit from this approach by obtaining a larger tax credit ($25,000 increased rehabilitation costs × 20% = $5,000).

It has been a long time since you have sold any of your real estate. How will you respond?

7. Red Company hires six individuals on January 15, 2006, qualifying Red for the work opportunity tax credit. Three of these individuals receive wages of $9,000 each during 2006, for working 900 hours each. The other three receive wages of $2,500 each, for working 325 hours each.
   a. Calculate the amount of Red's work opportunity tax credit for 2006.
   b. Assume Red pays total wages of $175,000 to its employees during the year. How much of this amount is deductible in 2006 if the work opportunity tax credit is taken?

8. In March 2006, Wren Corporation hired three individuals, Trent, Bernice, and Benita, all of whom are certified as long-term family assistance recipients. Each employee is paid $11,000 during 2006. Only Bernice continued to work for Wren in 2007, earning $13,500. Wren does not claim the work opportunity credit with respect to any employees hired in 2006.
   a. Compute Wren's welfare-to-work credit for 2006 and 2007.
   b. Wren pays total wages of $325,000 to its employees during 2006 and $342,000 during 2007. How much may Wren claim as a wage deduction for 2006 and 2007 if the welfare-to-work credit is claimed in both years?

Decision Making

9. Martin, Inc., a calendar year taxpayer, informs you that during the year it incurs expenditures of $50,000 that qualify for the incremental research activities credit. In addition, it is determined that the corporation's base amount for the year is $35,000.
   a. Determine Martin's incremental research activities credit for the year.
   b. Martin is in the 25% tax bracket. Determine which approach to the research expenditures and the research activities credit would provide the greatest tax benefit to Martin.

Communications

10. Ahmed Zinna (16 Southside Drive, Charlotte, NC 28204), one of your clients, owns two restaurants in downtown Charlotte and has come to you seeking advice concerning the tax consequences of complying with the Americans with Disabilities Act. He understands that he needs to install various features at his businesses (e.g., ramps, doorways, and restrooms that are handicapped accessible) to make them more accessible to disabled individuals. He inquires whether any tax credits are available to help offset the cost of the necessary changes. He estimates the cost of the planned changes to his facilities as follows.

Location	Projected Cost
Calvin Street	$22,000
Stowe Avenue	8,500

He reminds you that the Calvin Street restaurant was constructed in 2001 while the Stowe Avenue restaurant is in a building that was constructed in 1986. Ahmed operates his business as a sole proprietorship and has approximately eight employees at each location. Write a letter to Ahmed in which you summarize your conclusions concerning the tax consequences of his proposed capital improvements.

11. Zinnia Corporation is an international wholesaler headquartered in the United States. Of its worldwide taxable income of $3 billion, $1.25 billion is foreign sourced. Before any credits, Zinnia's U.S. income tax liability is $1.05 billion. If income taxes paid to foreign countries total $600 million, what is Zinnia's U.S. income tax liability after benefiting from the foreign tax credit?

12. Aqua, Inc., a calendar year corporation, has the following gross receipts and taxable income for 1993–2006.

Year	Gross Receipts	Taxable Income
1993	$11,000,000	$3,000,000
1994	4,800,000	900,000
1995	5,300,000	1,500,000
1996	4,600,000	700,000
1997	8,200,000	1,200,000
1998	8,500,000	1,900,000
1999	5,200,000	1,300,000
2000	8,000,000	1,500,000
2001	6,000,000	1,450,000
2002	6,200,000	1,375,000
2003	6,100,000	1,425,000
2004	8,000,000	1,400,000
2005	7,000,000	1,312,000
2006	7,500,000	985,000

a. When is Aqua first exempt from the AMT as a small corporation?
b. Is Aqua subject to the AMT for 2006?

13. Falcon, Inc., owns a silver mine that it purchased several years ago for $925,000. The adjusted basis at the beginning of the year is $400,000. For the year, Falcon deducts depletion of $700,000 (greater of cost depletion of $290,000 or percentage depletion of $700,000) for regular income tax purposes.
    a. Calculate Falcon's AMT adjustment.
    b. Calculate Falcon's adjusted basis for regular income tax purposes.
    c. Calculate Falcon's adjusted basis for AMT purposes.

Decision Making
Communications

14. In March 2006, Grackle, Inc., acquired used equipment for its business at a cost of $300,000. The equipment is five-year class property for regular income tax purposes and for AMT purposes.
    a. If Grackle depreciates the equipment using the method that will produce the greatest deduction for 2006 for regular income tax purposes, what is the amount of the AMT adjustment? Grackle does not elect §179 limited expensing.
    b. How can Grackle reduce the AMT adjustment to $0? What circumstances would motivate Grackle to do so?
    c. Draft a letter to Helen Carlon, Grackle's controller, regarding the choice of depreciation methods. Helen's address is 500 Monticello Avenue, Glendale, AZ 85306.

15. Rust Company is a real estate construction company with average annual gross receipts of $3 million. Rust uses the completed contract method on a contract that requires 16 months to complete. The contract is for $500,000 with estimated costs of $300,000. At the end of 2006, $180,000 of costs had been incurred. The contract is completed in 2007 with the total cost being $295,000. Determine the amount of adjustments for AMT purposes for 2006 and 2007.

Ethics

16. Allie, who was an accounting major in college, is the controller of a medium-size construction corporation. She prepares the corporate tax return each year. Due to reporting a home construction contract using the completed contract method, the corporation is subject to the AMT in 2006. Allie files the 2006 corporate tax return in early February 2007. The total tax liability is $58,000 ($53,000 regular income tax liability + $5,000 AMT).

    In early March, Allie reads an article on minimizing income taxes. Based on this article, she decides that it would be beneficial for the corporation to report the home construction contract using the percentage of completion method on its 2006 return. Although this will increase the corporation's 2006 income tax liability, it will minimize the total income tax liability over the two-year construction period. Therefore, Allie files an amended return on March 14, 2007. Evaluate Allie's actions from both a tax avoidance and an ethical perspective.

17. Buford sells an apartment building for $720,000. His adjusted basis is $406,000 for regular income tax purposes and $450,000 for AMT purposes. Calculate Buford's:
    a. Gain for regular income tax purposes.
    b. Gain for AMT purposes.
    c. AMT adjustment, if any.

18. Pheasant, Inc., is going to be subject to the AMT in 2006. The corporation owns an investment building and is considering disposing of it and investing in other realty. Based on an appraisal of the building's value, the realized gain would be $85,000. Ed has offered to purchase the building from Pheasant with the closing date being December 29, 2006. Ed wants to close the transaction in 2006 because certain beneficial tax consequences will result only if the transaction is closed prior to the beginning of 2007. Abby has offered to purchase the building with the closing date being January 2, 2007. The building has a $95,000 greater AMT adjusted basis. For regular income tax purposes, Pheasant expects to be in the 34% tax bracket. What are the relevant tax issues that Pheasant faces in making its decision? *Issue ID*

19. Flicker, Inc., a closely held corporation, acquired a passive activity in 2006. Gross income from operations of the activity was $160,000. Operating expenses, not including depreciation, were $122,000. Regular income tax depreciation of $49,750 was computed under MACRS. AMT depreciation, computed under ADS, was $41,000. Compute Flicker's passive loss deduction and passive loss suspended for regular income tax purposes and for AMT purposes.

20. Maize Corporation (a calendar year corporation) reports the following information for the years listed:

	2004	2005	2006
Adjusted current earnings	$5,000,000	$5,000,000	$7,000,000
Unadjusted AMTI	8,000,000	5,000,000	3,000,000

Compute the ACE adjustment for each year.

21. Based upon the following facts, calculate adjusted current earnings (ACE).

Alternative minimum taxable income (AMTI)	$5,120,000
Municipal bond interest	630,000
Expenses related to municipal bonds	50,000
Key employee life insurance proceeds in excess of cash surrender value	2,000,000
Organization expense amortization	100,000
Cost of goods sold	6,220,000
Advertising expenses	760,000
Loss between related parties	260,000
Life insurance expense	300,000

22. Purple Corporation, a calendar year taxpayer, reported the following amounts. Calculate Purple's positive and negative ACE adjustments.

	Preadjusted AMTI	ACE
2005	$80,000,000	$70,000,000
2006	60,000,000	90,000,000
2007	50,000,000	40,000,000
2008	60,000,000	20,000,000

23. Determine whether each of the following transactions is a preference (P), an adjustment (A), or not applicable (NA) for purposes of the corporate AMT.
   a. Depletion in excess of basis taken by Giant Oil Company.
   b. Accelerated depreciation on property.
   c. Charitable contributions of cash.
   d. Adjusted current earnings.
   e. Tax-exempt interest on private activity bonds.
   f. Untaxed appreciation on property donated to charity.
   g. Dividends received deduction.

24. In each of the following *independent* situations, determine the tentative minimum tax. Assume the company is not in small corporation status.

	AMTI (Before the Exemption Amount)
Quincy Corporation	$150,000
Redland Corporation	160,000
Tanzen Corporation	320,000

25. For 2006, Peach Corporation (a calendar year company) had the following transactions.

Taxable income	$5,000,000
Regular tax depreciation on realty in excess of ADS (placed in service in 1990)	1,700,000
Amortization of certified pollution control facilities (in excess of ADS amortization)	200,000
Tax-exempt interest on private activity bonds	300,000
Percentage depletion in excess of the property's adjusted basis	700,000

a. Determine Peach Corporation's AMTI.
b. Determine the tentative minimum tax base (refer to Exhibit 14–2).
c. Determine the tentative AMT.
d. What is the amount of the AMT?

26. Included in Alice's regular taxable income and in her AMT base is a $200,000 capital gain on the sale of stocks that she owned for three years. Alice is in the 35% tax bracket for regular income tax purposes. In calculating her regular income tax liability, she uses the appropriate alternative tax rate on net capital gain of 15%.
a. What rate should Alice use in calculating her tentative AMT?
b. What is Alice's AMT adjustment?
c. How would your answers in (a) and (b) change if the taxpayer were a C corporation in the 34% tax bracket for regular income tax purposes?

Extender

27. Calculate the AMT for the following cases in 2006. The taxpayer reports regular taxable income of $525,000 and no tax credits.

	Tentative AMT	
Filing Status	Case 1	Case 2
Single	$194,000	$175,000
Married, filing jointly	194,000	175,000

Extender

28. Grayson, who is single with no dependents and does not itemize, provides you with the following information for 2006.

Short-term capital loss	$ 4,000
Long-term capital gain	19,000
Municipal bond interest received on private activity bonds acquired in 1995	17,000
Dividends from General Motors	6,500
Excess of FMV over cost for incentive stock options (the rights became freely transferable and not subject to a substantial risk of forfeiture in 2006)	40,000
Charitable contributions	10,000
Qualified residence interest	9,000

What are Grayson's tax preference items and AMT adjustments for 2006?

BRIDGE *Discipline*

1. Balm, Inc., has a general business credit for 2006 of $90,000. Balm's regular income tax liability before credits is $140,000, and its tentative AMT is $132,000.
   a. Calculate the amount of general business credit that Balm can use in 2006 and calculate its general business credit carryback and carryforward, if any.
   b. Balm projects a $140,000 regular 2007 income tax liability. Its tentative AMT will be $132,000. Balm is considering making an investment early in 2007 that annually will produce $45,000 of tax-exempt income. Balm is trying to decide between two alternatives. The first alternative is a tax-exempt bond that is a private activity bond. The second alternative is a tax-exempt bond that is not a private activity bond. Advise Balm on the preferable investment.

2. Cooper Partnership, a calendar year partnership, made qualifying rehabilitation expenditures to a building that it has used in its business for eight years. These improvements were placed in service on January 5, 2005. The amount of the rehabilitation expenditures credit was $40,000.

   Cooper is negotiating to sell the building in either December 2006 or January 2007. The sales price will be $600,000, and the recognized gain will be $100,000. Provide support for the CFO's position that Cooper should delay the sale until 2007.

3. For many years, Saul's sole proprietorship and his related Form 1040 have had a number of AMT tax preferences and AMT adjustments. He has made the AMT calculation each year, but the calculated amount always has been $0. Saul's regular taxable income and the AMT adjustments and preferences for 2006 are the same as for last year. Yet he must pay AMT this year. Explain how this could happen.

RESEARCH PROBLEMS

Note: Solutions to Research Problems can be prepared by using the **RIA Checkpoint®** **Student Edition** online research product, which is available to accompany this text. It is also possible to prepare solutions to the Research Problems by using tax research materials found in a standard tax library.

THOMSON RIA™

Research Problem 1. Miriam, an admirer of early twentieth-century architecture, discovers a 1920s-era house in the countryside outside Mobile, Alabama, during a recent Sunday excursion. She desires not only to purchase and renovate this particular house, but also to move the structure into Mobile so her community can enjoy its architectural features. Being aware of the availability of the tax credit for rehabilitation expenditures, she wishes to maximize her use of the provision, if it is available in this case, once the renovation work begins in Mobile. However, Miriam also informs you that she will pursue the purchase, relocation, and renovation of the house only if the tax credit is available. Comment on Miriam's decision and whether any renovation expenditures incurred will qualify for the tax credit for rehabilitation expenditures.

Partial list of research aids:
George S. Nalle, III, 99 T.C. 187 (1992).

Communications

Research Problem 2. Oriole Corporation is a large wholesaler of office products. To remain successful in a fiercely competitive industry, Oriole has automated and computerized many of its business operations. Specifically, the corporation has developed several new software programs to:

- Maintain files of customer histories.
- Create a paperless invoicing system.
- Develop a computer-to-computer order entry system.
- Monitor inventory levels more closely.

Oriole estimates that it spent more than $1 million to develop and test the new software programs that are used throughout the business. To date, Oriole has not sold the software programs to the public, but it is contemplating doing so. Oriole has claimed a research and experimentation deduction for the costs associated with developing the software programs. The corporation also wants to claim the research activities credit relating to the software development. Can Oriole do so? Write a memo to the tax research file summarizing your conclusions.

Communications

Research Problem 3. Your ophthalmologist, Dr. Hunter Francis (55 Wheatland Drive, Hampton, CT 06247), has been very pleased with the growth of his practice in the 15 years he has been in business. This growth has resulted, at least in part, because he has aggressively marketed his services and tried to accommodate clients with various needs. This year Dr. Francis purchased a sophisticated piece of equipment that enables him to diagnose persons with mental handicaps, hearing impairments, and physical disabilities without having to go through a series of questions. In addition, he can treat his patients who are not disabled much more accurately and efficiently by using this equipment.

Since purchasing the machine this year for $9,500, Dr. Francis has used it on many occasions. Unfortunately, he has not been able to attract any disabled patients, even though previously he referred such people to other ophthalmologists who owned the necessary equipment. Therefore, the primary purpose for acquiring the equipment (i.e., to attract disabled patients) has not been realized, but he has put it to good use in treating other patients. Write a letter to Dr. Francis explaining whether he may claim the disabled access credit for this acquisition.

Research Problem 4. Parrot, Inc., receives tax-exempt interest of $20,000 on bonds that are classified as private activity bonds. The corporation appropriately excludes the $20,000 from its gross income for regular income tax purposes under § 103(a) and § 103(b)(1). Parrot has asked you for advice on the treatment of the $20,000 for AMT purposes. Find the Code Section that addresses the AMT treatment for private activity bond interest. Provide Parrot with the advice it has requested.

Research Problem 5. Teal, Inc., owns two warehouses that were placed in service before 1987. Accelerated depreciation for 2006 on Warehouse A is $36,000 (straight-line depreciation would have been $30,000). On Warehouse B, accelerated depreciation was $16,000 (straight-line depreciation would have been $20,000). What is the amount of Teal's tax preference for excess depreciation in 2006?

Internet *Activity*

Use the tax resources of the Internet to address the following questions. Do not restrict your search to the World Wide Web, but include a review of newsgroups and general reference materials, practitioner sites and resources, primary sources of the tax law, chat rooms and discussion groups, and other opportunities.

Research Problem 6. The foreign tax credit is especially valuable when a U.S. business earns income in a country whose income tax rates exceed those of the United States. List five countries whose tax rates on business income exceed those of the United States, and five where the corresponding U.S. rates are higher.

Research Problem 7. Some parties believe that many corporations are paying little, if any, corporate income tax and blame the AMT for being ineffective. Examine both government and press sites on the Internet and summarize these complaints.

http://wft.swlearning.com

CHAPTER 15

Comparative Forms of Doing Business

LEARNING OBJECTIVES

After completing Chapter 15, you should be able to:

LO.1

Identify the principal legal and tax forms for conducting a business.

LO.2

Appreciate the relative importance of nontax factors in business decisions.

LO.3

Distinguish between the forms for conducting a business according to whether they are subject to single taxation or double taxation.

LO.4

Identify techniques for avoiding double taxation.

LO.5

Understand and apply the conduit and entity concepts as they affect operations, capital changes, and distributions.

LO.6

Analyze the effects of the disposition of a business on the owners and the entity for each of the forms for conducting a business.

OUTLINE

TAX *Talk*

[My law firm] had a rule—at least it seemed to be a rule—that everybody that came had to spend at least a year working on taxes. The general rationale for the rule as I could understand it was that taxes were so important to everything that you do, whatever the kind of case you are handling, you have to know something about the tax consequences of things.

—Charles A. Horsky

A variety of factors, both tax and nontax, can affect the choice of the form of business entity. The form that is appropriate at one point in the life of an entity and its owners may not be appropriate at a different time.

EXAMPLE 1

Eva is a tax practitioner in Kentwood, the Dairy Center of the South. Many of her clients are dairy farmers. She recently had tax planning discussions with two of her clients, Jesse, a Line Creek dairy farmer, and Larry, a Spring Creek dairy farmer.

Jesse recently purchased his dairy farm. He is 52 years old and just retired after 30 years of service as a chemical engineer at an oil refinery in Baton Rouge. Eva recommended that he incorporate his dairy farm and elect S corporation status for Federal income tax purposes.

Larry has owned his dairy farm since 2000. He inherited it from his father. At that time, Larry retired after 20 years of service in the U.S. Air Force. He has a master's degree in Agricultural Economics from LSU. His farm is incorporated, and shortly after the date of incorporation, Eva had advised him to elect S corporation status. She now advises him to revoke the S election. ■

Example 1 raises a number of interesting questions. Does Eva advise all of her dairy farmer clients to elect S corporation status initially? Why has she advised Larry to revoke his S election? Will she advise Jesse to revoke his S election at some time in the future? Will she advise Larry to make another S election at some time in the future? Why did she not advise Larry to dissolve his corporation outright? Could Larry and Jesse have achieved the same tax consequences for their dairy farms if they had operated the farms as limited liability entities or partnerships instead of

TAX in the News — **SHOULD YOU CHECK THAT BOX?**

The check-the-box rules have been evolving since their introduction into the Regulations in late 1996. They are designed to remove tax considerations from the owners' choice of the legal form in which to conduct business. These provisions act to reduce the owners' exposure to the double taxation of taxable business profits. But taxpayers considering the use of these rules have run into several complications.

- Changing tax entity classifications from year to year comes at a cost. Changing the business form from a corporation to a partnership might trigger taxes for both the entity and its owners, defeating the purpose of the entity change.
- State income tax laws do not always match those of the Code. Several states have been slow to adopt the check-the-box rules, and others have modified the rules in some way. For instance, in several states a one-member limited liability company does not receive the expected tax treatment as a partnership, but is reclassified as a corporation or sole proprietorship. Uncertainty as to the state income tax treatment of a check-the-box selection alone may keep the owners from exercising their supposed freedom of choice of tax entity.

incorporating? Does the way the farm is acquired (e.g., purchase versus inheritance) affect the choice of business entity for tax purposes?

This chapter provides the basis for comparing and analyzing the tax consequences of business decisions for various types of tax entities (sole proprietorship, partnership, corporation, limited liability entity, and S corporation). Understanding the comparative tax consequences for the different types of entities and being able to apply them effectively to specific fact patterns will result in effective tax planning, which is exactly what Eva was doing with her two clients. As the following discussion illustrates, a variety of potential answers may exist for each of the questions raised by Eva's advice.

Forms of Doing Business

Principal Forms

LO.1

Identify the principal legal and tax forms for conducting a business.

The principal *legal* forms for conducting a business entity are the sole proprietorship, partnership, limited liability entity, and corporation.[1] From a *Federal income tax* perspective, these same forms are available, but the corporate form can be taxed in either of two ways (S corporation and C or regular corporation). In most instances, the legal form and the tax form are the same.

The taxpayer generally is bound for tax purposes by the legal form that is selected. A major statutory exception to this is the ability of an S corporation to receive tax treatment similar to that of a partnership.[2] In addition, taxpayers sometimes can control which set of tax rules will apply to their business operations. The "check-the-box" Regulations provide an elective procedure that enables certain entities to be classified as partnerships for Federal income tax purposes even though they have corporate characteristics.[3] These Regulations have greatly simplified the determination of entity classification. See Chapter 9 for a more detailed discussion of the check-the-box provisions.

[1]A business entity can also be conducted in the form of a trust or estate.

[2]§§ 1361 and 1362. See Chapter 12.

[3]Reg. §§ 301.7701–1 through –4, and –6. Note that if the business has only one owner, the elective procedure enables the entity to be classified as a sole proprietorship.

TAX *in the News* **PROFESSIONAL SERVICE FIRMS AND ORGANIZATIONAL FORM**

Many professional service firms (e.g., accountants, architects, lawyers) have chosen to become limited liability partnerships. In the accounting profession, this includes all of the Big 4 (i.e., Deloitte, Ernst & Young, KPMG, and Pricewaterhouse-Coopers) and most regional and local accounting firms.

An LLP helps to provide protection for the purely personal assets of the partners. Under the LLP organizational structure, the only partners whose personal assets are at risk to pay a judgment are those actually involved in the negligence or wrongdoing at issue. Note, however, that the entity is still responsible for the full judgment. Thus, the capital of the entity is still at risk.

An individual conducting a sole proprietorship files Schedule C of Form 1040. If more than one trade or business is conducted, a separate Schedule C is filed for each trade or business. A partnership files Form 1065. A corporation files Form 1120, and an S corporation files Form 1120S. An LLC that has elected to be taxed as a partnership files Form 1065.

About 4.5 million corporations file U.S. income tax returns every year, and about 2 million of these use S corporation status. About 1.5 million partnership returns are filed every year, and more than 16 million individuals report sole proprietorship activities on Schedule C in a typical tax year.[4] The business entity forms that are growing in number the fastest are the sole proprietorship (twice as many as 15 years ago) and the partnership (perhaps due to the popularity of the new limited liability entities).

Limited Liability Companies

A **limited liability company (LLC)** is a hybrid business form that combines the corporate characteristic of limited liability for the owners with the tax characteristics of a partnership.[5] All of the states now permit this legal form for conducting a business.

The most frequently cited nontax benefit of an LLC is the limited liability of the owners. Compared to the other forms of ownership, LLCs offer additional benefits over other forms of business, including the following.

Advantages over S corporations

- Greater flexibility in terms of the number of owners, types of owners, special allocation opportunities, and capital structure.
- Inclusion of entity debt in the owner's basis for an ownership interest.
- More liberal deferral of gain recognition on contributions of appreciated property by an owner (determined under § 721 rather than § 351).
- For securities law purposes, an ownership interest in an LLC is not necessarily a security.

Advantages over C corporations

- Ability to pass tax attributes through to the owners.
- Absence of double taxation.

Advantages over limited partnerships

- Right of all owners to participate in the management of the business.
- Ability of all owners to have limited liability (no need for a general partner).
- For securities law purposes, an ownership interest in an LLC is not necessarily a security (the interest of a limited partner normally is classified as a security).

[4] *Statistics of Income Bulletin*, Summer 2003.

[5] Depending on state law, an LLC may be organized as a limited liability corporation or a limited liability partnership.

TAX FACT

Revenue Relevance of Corporate versus Individual Taxpayers

Federal income taxes (FIT) provide over half of the Federal budget receipts. As indicated below, the portion provided by individual taxpayers (which includes the effect of flow-through entities) far exceeds that provided by corporate taxpayers.

	2002	2003	2004	2005	2006
% of budget receipts from FIT	60%	57%	53%	54%	55%
% of FIT from individual taxpayers	83%	88%	83%	80%	80%
% of FIT from corporate taxpayers	17%	12%	17%	20%	20%

Source: *Federal Budget of the United States.*

Advantages over general partnerships

- Limited liability for owners.
- Greater continuity of life.
- Limitation on an owner's ability to withdraw from the business.

Among the disadvantages associated with LLCs are the following.

- Absence of a developed body of case law on LLCs.
- Requirement in most states that there be at least two owners.
- Inability to qualify for § 1244 ordinary loss treatment.

Nontax Factors

LO.2

Appreciate the relative importance of nontax factors in business decisions.

Taxes are only one of many factors to consider when making a business decision. Above all, any business decision should make economic sense.

EXAMPLE 2

Walter is considering investing $10,000 in a limited partnership. He projects that he will be able to deduct the $10,000 capital contribution within the next two years (as his share of partnership losses). Since Walter's marginal tax rate is 35%, the deductions will produce a positive cash-flow effect of $3,500 ($10,000 × 35%). However, there is a substantial risk that he will not recover any of his original investment. If this occurs, his negative cash flow from the investment in the limited partnership is $6,500 ($10,000 – $3,500). Walter must decide if the investment makes economic sense. ■

Capital Formation

The ability of an entity to raise capital is a factor that must be considered. A sole proprietorship has the narrowest capital base. Compared to the sole proprietorship, the partnership has a greater opportunity to raise funds through the pooling of owner resources.

EXAMPLE 3

Adam and Beth decide to form a partnership, AB. Adam contributes cash of $200,000, and Beth contributes land with an adjusted basis of $60,000 and a fair market value of $200,000. The partnership is going to construct an apartment building at a cost of $800,000. AB pledges the land and the building to secure a loan of $700,000. ■

The limited partnership offers even greater potential than the general partnership form because a limited partnership can secure funds from investors (i.e., future limited partners).

EXAMPLE 4

Carol and Dave form a limited partnership, CD. Carol contributes cash of $200,000, and Dave contributes land with an adjusted basis of $60,000 and a fair market value of $200,000. The partnership is going to construct a shopping center at a cost of $5 million. Included in this cost is the purchase price of $800,000 for land adjacent to that contributed by Dave. Thirty limited partnership interests are sold for $100,000 each to raise $3 million. CD then pledges the shopping center (including the land) and obtains nonrecourse creditor financing of another $2 million. ■

Both the at-risk limitations and the passive activity loss provisions reduce the tax attractiveness of investments in real estate, particularly in the limited partnership form. In effect, the tax rules themselves place a severe curb on the economic consequences. Chapter 6 presents these loss rules and their critical interaction.

Of the different business entities, the corporate form offers the greatest ease and potential for obtaining owner financing because it can issue additional shares of stock. The ultimate examples of this form are the large public companies that are listed on the stock exchanges.

Limited Liability

A corporation offers its owners limited liability under state law. This absence of personal liability on the part of the owners is the most frequently cited advantage of the corporate form.

EXAMPLE 5

Ed, Fran, and Gabriella each invest $25,000 for all the shares of stock of Brown Corporation. Brown obtains creditor financing of $100,000. Brown is the defendant in a personal injury suit resulting from an accident involving one of its delivery trucks. The court awards a judgment of $2.5 million to the plaintiff. The award exceeds Brown's insurance coverage by $1.5 million. Even though the judgment probably will result in Brown's bankruptcy, the shareholders will have no personal liability for the unpaid corporate debts. ■

Limited liability is not available to all corporations. For many years, state laws did not permit professional individuals (e.g., accountants, attorneys, architects, and physicians) to incorporate. Even though professionals now are allowed to incorporate, the statutes do not provide limited liability for the performance of professional services.

Even if state law provides for limited liability, the shareholders of small corporations may forgo this benefit. Quite often, a corporation may be unable to obtain external financing (e.g., a bank loan) at reasonable interest rates unless the shareholders guarantee the loan.

The limited partnership form provides limited liability to the limited partners. Their liability is limited to the amount invested. In contrast, a general partner has unlimited liability.

EXAMPLE 6

Hazel, the general partner, invests $250,000 in HIJ, a limited partnership. Iris and Jane, the limited partners, each invest $50,000. While the potential loss for Iris and Jane is limited to $50,000 each, Hazel's liability is unlimited. ■

Indirectly, it may be possible to provide the general partner with limited liability by establishing a corporation as the general partner (see Figure 15–1). When a venture is structured this way, the general partner (the corporation) has limited its liability under the corporate statutes. In the figure, individual A is protected from personal liability by being merely the shareholder of Corporation A.

FIGURE 15–1 **Limited Partnership with a Corporate General Partner**

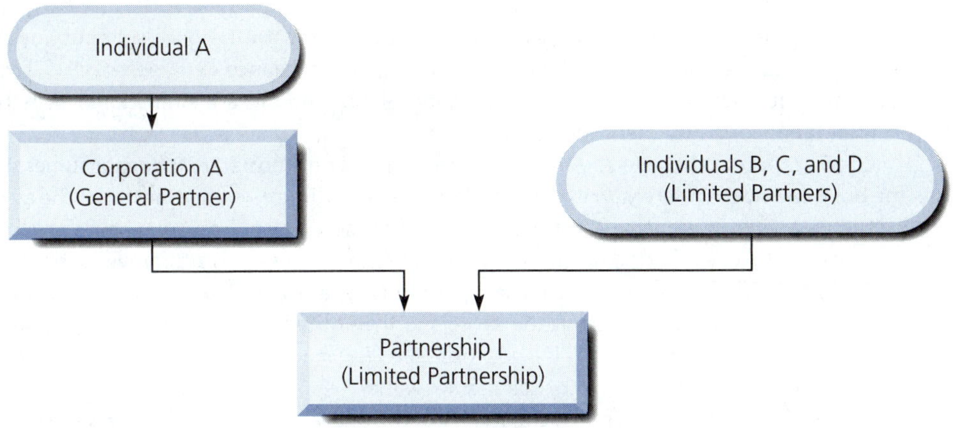

Other Factors

Other nontax factors may be significant in selecting an organization form, such as:

- Estimated life of the business.
- Number of owners and their roles in the management of the business.
- Freedom of choice in transferring ownership interests.
- Organizational formality, including the related cost and extent of government regulation.

Single versus Double Taxation

LO.3

Distinguish between the forms for conducting a business according to whether they are subject to single taxation or double taxation.

Overall Impact on Entity and Owners

The sole proprietorship, limited liability entity, and partnership are subject to *single* taxation. This result occurs because the owner(s) and the business generally are not considered separate entities for tax purposes. Therefore, the tax liability is levied at the owner level rather than at the entity level.

In contrast, a corporation and its owners can be subject to *double* taxation. This is frequently cited as the major tax disadvantage of the corporate form. The entity is taxed on the earnings of the corporation, and the owners are taxed on distributions to the extent they are made from corporate earnings.

The S corporation provides a way to avoid double taxation and possibly subject corporate earnings to a lower tax rate (the individual tax rate may be lower than the corporate tax rate). However, the ownership structure of an S corporation is restricted in both the number and type of shareholders. In addition, statutory exceptions subject the entity to taxation in certain circumstances.[6] To the extent these corporate-level taxes apply, double taxation results. Finally, the distribution policy of the S corporation may create difficulties under the *wherewithal to pay* concept.

EXAMPLE 7

Hawk Corporation has been operating as an S corporation since it began its business two years ago. For both of the prior years, Hawk incurred a tax loss. Hawk has taxable income of $75,000 this year and expects that its earnings will increase each year in the foreseeable

[6]Recall the Chapter 12 discussions of the taxes on an S corporation's built-in gains, LIFO recapture, and investment income.

BRIDGE *Discipline*

Bridge to Business Law and Financial Accounting

When a business entity is created and assets are transferred to the business entity by the owners, the tax balance sheet and the financial accounting balance sheet generally will contain different amounts for the assets. The balance sheet amounts are a function of whether conduit theory or entity theory is applied.

Conduit theory, also referred to as aggregate theory or proprietary theory, assumes that the business entity is merely an extension of the owners. Therefore, the transfer of the assets by the owners to the entity is not a taxable event. The owners' basis for their ownership interests is a carryover basis. The business entity's basis for its assets is a carryover basis.

Entity theory assumes that the business entity is separate and apart from the owners. Therefore, the transfer of assets by the owners to the entity is a taxable event. The owners' basis for their ownership interests is a new basis (i.e., fair market value). The business entity's basis for its assets is a new basis (i.e., fair market value).

Financial accounting uses entity theory. Thus, the critical value is the fair market value of each asset contributed by an owner to the business entity. Tax generally uses conduit theory. Thus, the critical value is the owner's adjusted basis for the contributed assets.

future. Part of this earnings increase results from Hawk's expansion into other communities in the state. Since most of this expansion will be financed internally, no dividend distributions will be made to Hawk's shareholders.

Assuming all of Hawk's shareholders are in the 33% tax bracket, their tax liability on corporate earnings will be $24,750 ($75,000 × 33%). Even though Hawk will not distribute any cash to the shareholders, they still will be required to pay the tax liability. This creates a wherewithal to pay problem. In addition, the corporate tax liability would have been less if Hawk had not been an S corporation [(15% × $50,000) + (25% × $25,000) = $13,750].

The shareholders' wherewithal to pay problem could be resolved by terminating the S corporation election. The tax liability would then be imposed at the corporate level. Since Hawk does not intend to make any dividend distributions, double taxation at the present time would be avoided. Terminating the election also reduces the overall tax liability by $11,000 ($24,750 – $13,750).[7]

In making the decision about the form of business entity, Hawk's shareholders should consider more than the current taxable year. If the S election is terminated, another election might not be available for five years. Thus, the decision to revoke the election should be made using at least a five-year planning horizon. Perhaps a better solution would be to retain the election and distribute enough dividends to the S corporation shareholders to enable them to pay the shareholder tax liability. ■

Two other variables that relate to the adverse effect of double taxation are the timing and form of corporate distributions. If no distributions are made, then only single taxation occurs in the short run.[8] To the extent that double taxation does occur in the future, the cash-flow effect should be discounted to its present value. Second, when the distribution is made, is it in the form of a dividend or a return of capital?[9] The owners likely would prefer to receive long-term capital gain (subject to lower tax rates) instead of ordinary income. Proper structuring of the distribution can accomplish this result. Note that for distributions made in 2003 and thereafter the availability of the 15%/5% rate for qualified dividends reduces the potential negative impact of double taxation (see Chapter 4).

[7] The absence of distributions to shareholders could create an accumulated earnings tax (AET) problem under § 531. However, as long as earnings are used to finance expansion, the "reasonable needs" provision will be satisfied, and the corporation will avoid any AET. Refer to the discussion of the AET in Chapter 10.

[8] This assumes there is no accumulated earnings tax problem. See especially Example 10 in the subsequent discussion of distributions in Minimizing Double Taxation.

[9] Redemptions of stock and corporate liquidations may be taxed as a sale of stock to shareholders (i.e., as capital gain or loss). See § 302 and Chapter 10.

TAX *in the News* **DO CORPORATIONS PAY TAXES?**

A disadvantage of being a C corporation is the potential for double taxation. This potential disappears, however, if the taxable income of the corporation is zero or negative.

A Government Accountability Office study indicates that for the period 1996–2000, more than 60 percent of U.S. corporations did not owe or pay any Federal income taxes. Neither did 70 percent of foreign-owned corporations doing business in the United States. By 2003, corporate tax receipts had fallen to 7.4 percent of overall Federal receipts, the lowest percentage since 1983.

Senator Carl Levin (who requested the GAO study) along with Senator Byron Dorgan, both Democrats, concluded that "too many corporations are finagling ways to dodge paying Uncle Sam, despite the benefits they receive from doing business in this country."

One motivation for this "finagling" has been temporarily reduced by a provision in the American Jobs Creation Act of 2004 (AJCA). Dividends earned by foreign subsidiaries of U.S. corporations are not taxed until repatriated back to the parent corporation. Since such dividends are not eligible for the dividends received deduction, they could be subject to a rate as high as 35 percent. Not only does the U.S. government not tax these unrepatriated foreign earnings, but earnings that are reinvested overseas are of no benefit to the U.S. economy.

To encourage corporations to bring these earnings back to the United States, the AJCA provided a temporary 85 percent dividends received deduction on any foreign subsidiary earnings that are repatriated to the U.S. parent.

Alternative Minimum Tax

All of the forms of business are directly or indirectly subject to the alternative minimum tax (AMT).[10] For the sole proprietorship and the C corporation, the effect is direct (the AMT liability calculation is attached to the tax form that reports the entity's taxable income—Form 1040 or Form 1120). For the partnership, limited liability entity, and S corporation, the effect is indirect; the tax preferences and adjustments pass through from the entity to the owners, and the AMT liability calculation is *not* assessed on the tax form that reports the entity's taxable income—Form 1065 or Form 1120S.

When compared to other entities, the C corporation appears to have a slight advantage. The corporate AMT rate of 20 percent is less than the individual AMT rates of 26 and 28 percent. An even better perspective is provided by comparing the maximum AMT rate with the maximum regular rate for both the individual and the corporation. For the individual, the AMT rate is 80 percent (28%/35%) of the maximum regular rate. The AMT rate for the corporation is 57 percent (20%/35%) of the maximum regular rate. Therefore, on the basis of comparative rates, the C corporation appears to offer lower AMT tax burdens. In addition, as presented below, under certain circumstances, a C corporation is exempt from the AMT.

The apparent corporate AMT rate advantage may be more than offset by the ACE adjustment, which applies only to C corporations.[11] If the ACE adjustment continually causes the C corporation to be subject to the AMT, the owners should consider electing S corporation status (if eligibility requirements can be satisfied). Since the S corporation does not compute an ACE adjustment, it may be possible to reduce the tax liability.

The AMT does not apply to modest-sized C corporations. To be exempt from the tax, the corporation must meet both of the following tests.

- Average annual gross receipts of not more than $5 million for the three tax years after 1993.
- Average annual gross receipts of not more than $7.5 million for every subsequent three-tax-year period.

[10] § 55.

[11] §§ 56(c)(1) and (f). Refer to the discussion of the corporate AMT in Chapter 14.

PLANNING *Strategies*

PLANNING FOR THE AMT

★ **Framework Focus: Tax Rate**

Strategy ★ Shift Net Income from High-Bracket Years to Low-Bracket Years.

If the AMT will apply in the current year, the entity should consider accelerating income and delaying deductions, so that current-year taxable income is taxed at the lower AMT rate. For a C corporation, the potential rate differential is 15 percentage points (20 percent AMT rate versus 35 percent regular tax rate). For an individual (i.e., as a sole proprietor, as a partner, or as an S corporation shareholder), the potential tax rate differential is 7 percentage points (28 percent highest AMT rate versus 35 percent regular tax rate). A present value analysis should be used to assure that the income acceleration and deduction deferral do not increase actual tax liabilities.

A corporation automatically is classified as a small corporation in the first year of existence. About 95 percent of all C corporations are likely to meet these tests and be exempt from the AMT in the future.

State Taxation

In selecting a form for doing business, the determination of the tax consequences should not be limited to Federal income taxes. Consideration also should be given to state income taxes and, if applicable, local income taxes.

The S corporation provides a good illustration of this point. Suppose that the forms of business being considered are a limited partnership or a corporation. An operating loss is projected for the next several years. The owners decide to operate the business in the corporate form. The principal nontax criterion for the decision is the limited liability attribute of the corporation. The owners consent to an S corporation election, so the corporate losses can be passed through to the shareholders to deduct on their individual tax returns. However, assume that state law does not permit the S corporation election. Thus, the owners will not receive the tax benefits of the loss deductions that would have been available on their state income tax returns if they had chosen the limited partnership form. As a result of providing limited liability to the owner who would have been the general partner for the limited partnership, the loss deduction at the state level is forgone.

LO.4

Identify techniques for avoiding double taxation.

Minimizing Double Taxation

Only the corporate form is potentially subject to double taxation. Several techniques are available for eliminating or at least reducing the second layer of taxation.

- Making distributions to the shareholders that are deductible to the corporation.
- Not making distributions to the shareholders.
- Making distributions that qualify for return of capital treatment at the shareholder level.
- Making the S corporation election.

Making Deductible Distributions

The following are typical distribution forms that will result in a deduction to the corporation.

TAX in the News — **WHO PAYS CORPORATE AMT?**

One of the issues often raised in debates over tax legislation is whether the corporate AMT should be repealed. Among the topics discussed are the revenue generated, the related compliance costs, and the number of corporations subject to the AMT.

According to the IRS, nearly 6 million corporate tax returns were filed in 2003. Of these returns, under 15,000 included any AMT.

Proponents of the corporate AMT argue that these statistics show that the AMT is being paid by corporations targeted by the law (i.e., large corporations). Opponents argue that the same statistics show that the compliance costs borne by the mass of corporations do not justify the continuation of this tax system.

The exemption from the AMT for small corporations may be providing the needed solution. Large corporations must make minimal Federal income tax payments when the AMT applies. Most C corporations no longer need to compute the tax.

Source: *IRS Tax Stats.*

- Salary payments to shareholder-employees.
- Lease or rental payments to shareholder-lessors.
- Interest payments to shareholder-creditors.

Recognizing the potential for abuse, the IRS scrutinizes these types of distributions carefully. All three forms are evaluated in terms of *reasonableness.*[12] In addition, interest payments to shareholders may lead to reclassification of some or all of the debt as equity.[13] IRS success with either approach raises the specter of double taxation.

EXAMPLE 8

Donna owns all the stock of Green Corporation and is also the chief executive officer. Green's taxable income before salary payments to Donna is as follows.

2004	2005	2006
$80,000	$50,000	$250,000

During the year, Donna receives a monthly salary of $3,000. In December of each year, Donna reviews the operations for the year and determines the year-end bonus she is to receive. Donna's yearly bonuses are as follows.

2004	2005	2006
$44,000	$14,000	$214,000

The apparent purpose of Green's bonus program is to reduce the corporate taxable income to zero and thereby avoid double taxation. An examination of Green's tax return by the IRS would likely result in a deduction disallowance for **unreasonable compensation**. ■

EXAMPLE 9

Tom and Vicki each contribute $20,000 to TV Corporation for all of its stock. In addition, they each lend $80,000 to TV. The loan is documented by formal notes, the interest rate is 8%, and the maturity date is 10 years from the date of the loan.

The notes provide the opportunity for the corporation to make payments of $6,400 each year to both Tom and Vicki and for the payments not to be subject to double taxation. This

[12] § 162(a)(1). *Mayson Manufacturing Co. v. Comm.*, 49–2 USTC ¶9467, 38 AFTR 1028, 178 F.2d 115 (CA–6, 1949); *Harolds Club v. Comm.*, 65–1 USTC ¶9198, 15 AFTR2d 241, 340 F.2d 861 (CA–9, 1965).

[13] § 385; Rev.Rul. 83–98, 1983–2 C.B. 40; *Bauer v. Comm.*, 84–2 USTC ¶9996, 55 AFTR2d 85–433, 748 F.2d 1365 (CA–9, 1984).

TAX *in the News* **WHO PAYS THE CORPORATE FEDERAL INCOME TAX AND WHY IT IS DECREASING**

C corporations and their shareholders potentially are subject to double taxation. Tax legislation enacted in 2003 substantially reduced the combined burden by making qualified dividends eligible for beneficial tax rates (i.e., 15%/5%). Another option considered at that time, but rejected by the administration and Congress, was to eliminate taxation at the C corporation level and have corporate profits taxed at the shareholder level.

A question that frequently arises in this continuing debate is just how heavy the corporate Federal income tax burden is. An analysis by the Government Accountability Office shows that larger companies (assets of more than $250 million or gross receipts over $50 million) are more likely to pay income taxes than smaller ones. In 2000, 55 percent of larger companies paid Federal income taxes whereas fewer than 50 percent did so in 2002. The authors of the report believe that many larger companies could bring their tax burden down to $0 if they chose to do so. To do so, however, would create "unwanted attention."

One of the reasons for the falling corporate tax burden is that larger portions of corporate earnings are being generated in countries that impose lower tax rates. General Electric is an example of this trend. GE paid income tax on earnings at a rate of 21.7 percent in 2003 compared with 28.3 percent in 2001. GE's annual report for 2003 attributed this decline in its tax burden to "the increasing share of earnings from lower taxed international operations."

happens because the interest payments are includible in the gross income of Tom and Vicki, but are deductible by TV in calculating its taxable income. At the time of repayment in 10 years, neither Tom nor Vicki recognizes gross income from the repayment; the $80,000 amount realized is equal to the basis for the note of $80,000.

If the IRS succeeded in reclassifying the notes as equity, Tom and Vicki still would have gross income of $6,400, but the interest would be reclassified as dividend income (which may be taxed at the 15% rate). Because dividend payments are not deductible by TV, the corporation's taxable income would increase by $12,800 ($6,400 × 2). To make matters worse, the repayment of the notes in 10 years would not qualify as a recovery of capital, resulting in additional dividend income for Tom and Vicki. ■

Note that for distributions made in 2003 and thereafter the availability of the 15%/5% rate for qualified dividends reduces the potential negative impact of double taxation (see Chapter 4).

Not Making Distributions

Double taxation will not occur unless the corporation makes (actual or deemed) distributions to the shareholders. A closely held corporation that does not make distributions may eventually encounter an accumulated earnings tax problem unless the reasonable needs requirement is satisfied. When making distribution decisions each year, the board of directors should be apprised of any potential accumulated earnings tax problem and take the appropriate steps to eliminate it. The accumulated earnings tax rate of 15 percent in 2006 is the same as the 15 percent rate for qualified dividends for individual taxpayers.[14]

EXAMPLE 10

According to an internal calculation made by Dolphin Corporation, its accumulated taxable income is $400,000. The board of directors would prefer not to declare any dividends, but is considering a dividend declaration of $400,000 to avoid the accumulated earnings tax. All of the shareholders are in the 35% bracket.

If a dividend of $400,000 is declared, the tax cost to the shareholders is $60,000 ($400,000 × 15%, assuming the dividends are qualified dividends). If a dividend is not declared and the IRS assesses the accumulated earnings tax, the tax cost to the corporation for the accumulated earnings tax also would be $60,000 ($400,000 × 15%).

To make matters worse, Dolphin will have incurred the accumulated earnings tax cost without getting any funds out of the corporation to the shareholders. If the unwise decision

[14]§ 531. Refer to the discussion of the accumulated earnings tax in Chapter 10.

were now made to distribute the remaining $340,000 ($400,000 − $60,000) to the shareholders, the additional tax cost at the shareholder level would be $51,000 ($340,000 × 15%). Therefore, the combined shareholder-corporation tax cost would be $111,000 ($60,000 + $51,000). This is 185% ($111,000/$60,000) of the tax cost that would have resulted from an initial dividend distribution of $400,000. ■

The legislation that created the special tax rate of 15 percent for qualified dividends also lowered the accumulated earnings tax rate from 35 percent to 15 percent. This tax rate reduction has substantially lowered the impact of the accumulated earnings tax. In Example 10, the penalty tax at the corporate level prior to the legislative change would have been $140,000 ($400,000 × 35%). Assuming the remaining $260,000 was distributed to the shareholders, the additional tax cost at the shareholder level would have been $91,000 ($260,000 × 35%). Therefore, the combined shareholder-corporation tax cost would have been $231,000 ($140,000 + $91,000) rather than the current $111,000. Thus, by reducing both the tax rate for the accumulated earnings tax and the tax rate on qualified dividends, this legislative change thereby reduced the taxpayer's net tax cost of the accumulated earnings tax.

Assuming that the accumulated earnings tax can be avoided (e.g., a growth company whose reasonable needs justify its failure to pay dividends), a policy of no distributions to shareholders can avoid the second layer of taxation on corporate earnings. The retained earnings will drive the value of the shares upward, equal to the accumulated after-tax cash. As a result of the step-up in basis rules for inherited property, the basis of the stock for the beneficiaries will be the fair market value at the date of the decedent's death rather than the decedent's basis.

Return of Capital Distributions

The exposure to double taxation can be reduced if the corporate distributions to the shareholders can qualify for return of capital rather than dividend treatment. This can occur when the corporation's earnings and profits (E & P) are low or negative in amount. Review Example 1 in Chapter 10. In some cases, the stock redemption provisions offer an opportunity to avoid dividend treatment altogether. Under these rules, the distribution may be treated as a sale of the shareholder's stock, resulting in a tax-free recovery of basis and then recognition of low-tax long-term capital gain.

Electing S Corporation Status

Electing S corporation status generally eliminates double taxation. Several factors, listed below, should be considered when making this election.

- Are all the shareholders willing to consent to the election?
- Can the qualification requirements under § 1361 be satisfied at the time of the election?
- Can the S corporation requirements continue to be satisfied?
- For what period will the conditions that make the election beneficial continue to prevail?
- Will the corporate distribution policy create wherewithal to pay problems at the shareholder level?

EXAMPLE 11

Emerald Corporation commenced business in January 2006. The two shareholders, Diego and Jaime, are both in the 28% tax bracket. The following operating results are projected for the first five years of operations.

2006	2007	2008	2009	2010
($50,000)	$400,000	$600,000	$800,000	$1,000,000

BRIDGE *Discipline*

Bridge to Economics

Corporations such as General Motors, IBM, Microsoft, Wal-Mart, and ExxonMobil are major players not only in their industries, but also in the world economy. However, people are also attracted to "mom and pop type stores," which cumulatively play a major role in the economy.

In recognition of the important role of small businesses and their size competitive disadvantage at times, Congress has provided small businesses with beneficial tax treatment that is not available to major business entities. Included among such beneficial treatments are the following.

- § 11 beneficial tax rates.
- § 44 disabled access credit.
- § 55(e) exemption from the AMT for small corporations.
- § 179 limited expensing for tangible personal property.
- § 1244 ordinary loss treatment.

Each of these provisions defines "small" in a different way. Sometimes, however, when beneficial tax treatment is provided for a business entity, the term "small" may be used inappropriately. The classic example is the small business corporation of Subchapter S. Some S corporations hold billions of dollars of assets. They are "small" only in the sense that the number of shareholders cannot exceed 100 unrelated shareholders.

The corporation plans to expand rapidly. Therefore, no distributions will be made to shareholders. In addition, beginning in 2007, preferred stock will be offered to a substantial number of investors to help finance the expansion.

If the S corporation election is made for 2006, the \$50,000 loss can be passed through to Diego and Jaime. The loss will generate a positive cash-flow effect of \$14,000 (\$50,000 × 28%). Assume that the election is either revoked or is involuntarily terminated at the beginning of 2007 as a result of the issuance of the preferred stock. The corporate tax liability for 2007 is \$136,000 (\$400,000 × 34%).

If the S corporation election is not made for 2006, the \$50,000 loss is a net operating loss. The amount can be carried forward to reduce the 2007 corporate taxable income to \$350,000 (\$400,000 – \$50,000). The resultant tax liability is \$119,000 (\$350,000 × 34%).

Should the S corporation election be made for just the one-year period? The answer is unclear. With an assumed after-tax rate of return to Diego and Jaime of 10%, the value of the \$14,000 one year hence is \$15,400 (\$14,000 × 110%). Even considering the time value of money, the combined corporation-shareholder negative cash-flow effect of \$120,600 (\$136,000 – \$15,400) in the case of an S election is not significantly different from the \$119,000 corporate tax liability that would result for a C corporation. ■

LO.5

Understand and apply the conduit and entity concepts as they affect operations, capital changes, and distributions.

Conduit versus Entity Treatment

Under the **conduit concept**, the entity is viewed as merely an extension of the owners. Under the **entity concept**, the entity is regarded as being separate and distinct from its owners. The effects of the conduit and entity concepts extend to a variety of tax rules, including the following.

- Recognition at time of contribution to the entity.
- Basis of ownership interest.
- Results of operations.
- Recognition at time of distribution.
- Passive activity losses.
- At-risk rules.
- Special allocations.

TAX FACT

Number of Income Tax Returns Filed by Different Types of Taxpayers (in Millions)

Type of Taxpayer	1980	1985	1990	1995	2000	2004
Individual	93.1	99.5	112.3	116.1	126.9	131.6
Partnership	1.4	1.8	1.8	1.6	2.1	2.5
C corporation	2.1	2.4	2.3	2.2	2.2	2.5
S corporation	.5	.7	1.5	2.2	2.8	3.5

The number of S corporation returns has increased dramatically since 1980. In addition, the number of S corporation returns now exceeds the number of C corporation returns. Since LLCs normally file as partnerships, it will be interesting to see what effect the popularity of this entity form will have on the number of partnership returns filed.

Source: *IRS Tax Stats.*

The sole proprietorship is not analyzed separately because the owner and the business are the same tax entity. In one circumstance, however, a tax difference can result. Income recognition does not occur when an owner contributes an asset to a sole proprietorship. Thus, the business generally takes a carryover basis. However, if the asset is a personal-use asset, the sole proprietorship's basis is the *lower of* the adjusted basis or the fair market value at the date of contribution. If a personal-use asset is contributed to a partnership or corporation, this same *lower-of* rule applies.

Effect on Recognition at Time of Contribution to the Entity

Since the conduit approach applies to partnerships, § 721 provides for no recognition on the contribution of property to a partnership in exchange for a partnership interest. Section 721 protects both a contribution associated with the formation of the partnership and later contributions. The partnership takes a carryover basis in the contributed property, and the partners have a carryover basis in their partnership interests.[15]

Since the entity approach applies to corporations, the transfer of property to a corporation in exchange for its stock is a taxable event. However, if the § 351 control requirement is satisfied, no gain or loss is recognized. In this case, both the corporate property and the shareholders' stock have a carryover basis.[16] This control requirement makes it possible for shareholders who contribute appreciated property to the corporation *after* its formation to recognize gain.

To the extent that the fair market value of property contributed to the entity at the time of formation is not equal to the property's adjusted basis, a special allocation may be desirable. With a special allocation, the owner contributing the property receives the tax benefit or detriment for any recognized gain or loss that subsequently results because of the initial difference between the adjusted basis and the fair market value. For the partnership, this special allocation treatment is mandatory. No such allocation is available for a C corporation because the gain or loss is recognized at the corporation level rather than at the shareholder level.

[15]Refer to the pertinent discussion in Chapter 11.

[16]Refer to the pertinent discussion in Chapter 9.

As with a C corporation, no such allocation is available for an S corporation. The recognized gain or loss is reported on the shareholders' tax returns according to their stock ownership.

EXAMPLE 12

Khalid contributes land with an adjusted basis of $10,000 and a fair market value of $50,000 for a 50% ownership interest. At the same time, Tracy contributes cash of $50,000 for the remaining 50% ownership interest. Because the entity is unable to obtain the desired zoning, it subsequently sells the land for $50,000.

If the entity is a C corporation, Khalid has a realized gain of $40,000 ($50,000 – $10,000) and a recognized gain of $0 resulting from the contribution. His basis in the stock is $10,000, and the corporation has a basis in the land of $10,000. The corporation realizes and recognizes a gain of $40,000 ($50,000 – $10,000) when it sells the land. Thus, what should have been Khalid's recognized gain is now the corporation's taxable gain. There is no way that the corporation can allocate the recognized gain directly to Khalid. The corporation could distribute the land to Khalid and let him sell it, but such a distribution is likely to be taxable to Khalid as a dividend, and gain on the distribution is also recognized at the corporate level.

If the entity is a partnership or limited liability entity, the tax consequences are the same as for the C corporation, except for the $40,000 recognized gain on the sale of the land. The partnership realizes and recognizes a gain of $40,000 ($50,000 – $10,000). However, even though Khalid's share of profits and losses is only 50%, all of the $40,000 recognized gain is allocated to him. If the entity is an S corporation, the tax consequences are the same as for the C corporation, except that Khalid reports $20,000 of the recognized gain on his tax return and Tracy reports $20,000. ■

Effect on Basis of Ownership Interest

In a partnership or limited liability entity, since the owner is the taxpayer, profits and losses of the partnership affect the owner's basis in the entity interest. Likewise, the owner's basis is increased by the share of entity liability increases and is decreased by the share of liability decreases. Accordingly, ownership basis changes frequently.[17]

Because a C corporation is a taxpaying entity, the shareholder's basis for the stock is not affected by corporate profits and losses or corporate liability changes.

The treatment of an S corporation shareholder falls between that of the partner and the C corporation shareholder. The S corporation shareholder's stock basis is increased by the share of profits and decreased by the share of losses, but it usually is not affected by corporate liability increases or decreases.[18]

EXAMPLE 13

Peggy contributes cash of $100,000 to an entity for a 30% ownership interest. The entity borrows $50,000 and repays $20,000 of this amount by the end of the taxable year. The profits for the year are $90,000.

If the entity is a partnership or limited liability entity, Peggy's basis at the end of the period is $136,000 ($100,000 investment + $9,000 share of net liability increase + $27,000 share of profits). If Peggy is a C corporation shareholder instead, her stock basis is $100,000 ($100,000 original investment). If the corporation is an S corporation, Peggy's stock basis is $127,000 ($100,000 + $27,000). ■

Effect on Results of Operations

The entity concept is responsible for producing potential double taxation for the C corporation if the corporation is taxed on its earnings, and the shareholders are taxed on the distribution of earnings. Thus, from the perspective of taxing the results of operations, the entity concept appears to provide a disadvantage to

[17]§§ 705 and 752.

[18]Recall from Chapter 12 that pass-through S losses can reduce a *shareholder's* basis in loans to the entity.

corporations. However, whether the entity concept actually produces disadvantageous results depends on the following.

- Whether the corporation generates positive taxable income.
- The tax rates that apply to the corporation and to the shareholders.
- The distribution policy of the corporation.

As discussed previously, techniques exist for getting cash out of the corporation to the shareholders without incurring double taxation (e.g., compensation payments to shareholder-employees, lease payments to shareholder-lessors, and interest payments to shareholder-creditors). Since these payments are deductible to the corporation, they reduce corporate taxable income. If the payments can be used to reduce corporate taxable income to zero, the corporation will have no tax liability.

The maximum individual tax rate currently is the same as the maximum corporate tax rate (35 percent). However, in a specific situation, the corporate tax rates that apply may be greater than or less than the applicable individual tax rates.

Double taxation occurs only if distributions (actual or constructive) are made to the shareholders. Thus, if no distributions (actual or constructive) are made and if the entity can avoid the accumulated earnings tax (e.g., based on the statutory credit or the reasonable needs adjustment) and the personal holding company tax (e.g., the corporation primarily generates active income), only one current level of taxation will occur. If the distribution can qualify for return of capital rather than dividend treatment, the shareholder tax liability is decreased. Finally, taxation of the earnings at the shareholder level can be avoided permanently if the stock passes through the decedent shareholder's estate.[19]

Application of the entity concept causes income and deductions to lose any unique tax characteristics when they are passed through to shareholders in the form of dividends. This may produce a negative result for capital gains. Since capital gains lose their identity when passed through in the form of dividends, they cannot be used to offset capital losses at the shareholder level. An even more negative result is produced when dividends are paid out of tax-exempt income. Tax-exempt income is excludible in calculating corporate taxable income, but is included in calculating current earnings and profits. Thus, exclusions from income may be taxed because of the entity concept.

Partnerships, limited liability entities, and S corporations use the conduit concept in reporting the results of operations. Any item that is subject to special treatment on the taxpayer-owner's tax return is reported separately to the owner. Other items are aggregated and reported as taxable income. Thus, taxable income merely represents the sum of income and deductions that are not subject to special treatment.[20]

Many of the problems that the entity concept may produce for the C corporation form are not present in pass-through entities. In particular, pass-through entities are not subjected to double taxation, problems with the reasonableness requirement, or loss of identity of the income or expense item at the owner level.

Only partnerships and limited liability entities completely apply the conduit concept when reporting the results of operations. In several circumstances, the S corporation is subject to taxation at the corporate level, including the tax on built-in gains. This limited application of the entity concept necessitates additional planning to attempt to avoid taxation at the corporate level.

Effect on Recognition at Time of Distribution

The application of the conduit concept results in distributions not being taxed to the owners. The application of the entity concept produces the opposite result.

[19]Recall Chapter 7's analysis of the basis step-up rules for property acquired from a decedent.

[20]§§ 701, 702, 1363, and 1366.

Therefore, tax-free distributions can be made to owners of flow-through entities, whereas distributions to C corporation shareholders may be taxable.

A combination entity/conduit concept applies to property distributions from S corporations. The conduit concept applies with respect to the shareholder. However, if the distributed property has appreciated in value, any realized gain is recognized at the corporate level.[21] This is the same treatment received by C corporations. Thus, corporate-level gain recognition is an application of the entity concept, whereas the pass-through of the gain to shareholders is an application of the conduit concept.

EXAMPLE 14

Tan, an S corporation, is equally owned by Leif and Matt. Tan distributes two parcels of land to Leif and Matt. Tan has a basis of $10,000 for each parcel. Each parcel has a fair market value of $15,000. The distribution results in a $10,000 ($30,000 – $20,000) recognized gain for Tan. Leif and Matt each report $5,000 of the gain on their individual income tax returns. ■

Stock redemptions and complete liquidations receive identical treatment whether a C or an S corporation is involved.[22]

Effect on Passive Activity Losses

The passive activity loss rules apply to flow-through entities, personal service corporations, and closely held C corporations. A *closely held C corporation* exists when more than 50 percent of the value of the outstanding stock at any time during the last half of the taxable year is owned by or for not more than five individuals. A corporation is classified as a *personal service corporation* if the following requirements are satisfied.[23]

- The principal activity of the corporation is the performance of personal services.
- The services are substantially performed by owner-employees.
- Owner-employees own more than 10 percent in value of the stock of the corporation.

The general passive activity loss rules apply to personal service corporations. Therefore, passive activity losses can be offset only against passive activity income. For closely held corporations, the application of the passive activity rules is less harsh. Passive activity losses can be offset against both active and passive income.

Since the conduit concept applies to partnerships, S corporations, and limited liability entities, the passive activity results are separately stated at the entity level and are passed through to the owners with their passive character maintained.

Effect of At-Risk Rules

The at-risk rules apply to all flow-through entities and to closely held C corporations. The rules produce a harsher result for partnerships and limited liability entities than for S corporations. This occurs because of the way liabilities affect partners' basis.

EXAMPLE 15

Walt is the general partner, and Ira and Vera are the limited partners in the WIV limited partnership. Walt contributes land with an adjusted basis of $40,000 and a fair market value of $50,000 for his partnership interest, and Ira and Vera each contribute cash of $100,000 for their partnership interests. They agree to share profits and losses equally. To finance

[21] § 311(b).
[22] §§ 302, 331, and 336.
[23] § 469, derived from the definition in § 269A.

TAX FACT

Partnership Income Tax Returns: Profits versus Losses

During the period from 1980 to 2000, the number of partnership income tax returns increased by 50 percent (i.e., from 1.4 million returns to 2.1 million returns). The beneficial tax treatment of LLCs is expected to cause this trend to continue. While the partnership provides a tax shelter opportunity by passing losses through to the partner, a majority of partnerships are profitable.

	1980	1985	1990	1995	2000
% of returns with profits	57%	53%	56%	63%	60%
% of returns with losses	43%	47%	44%	37%	40%

Source: *IRS Tax Stats.*

construction of an apartment building, the partnership obtains $600,000 of nonrecourse financing [not qualified nonrecourse financing under § 465(b)(6)] using the land and the building as the pledged assets. Each partner's basis for the partnership interest is as follows.

	Walt	Ira	Vera
Contribution	$ 40,000	$100,000	$100,000
Share of nonrecourse debt	200,000	200,000	200,000
Basis	$240,000	$300,000	$300,000

Without the at-risk rules, Ira and Vera could pass through losses up to $300,000 each even though they invested only $100,000 and have no personal liability for the nonrecourse debt. However, the at-risk rules limit the loss pass-through to the at-risk basis, which is $100,000 for Ira and $100,000 for Vera.

The at-risk rules also affect the general partner. Since Walt is not at risk for the nonrecourse debt, his at-risk basis is $40,000. If the mortgage were recourse debt, his at-risk basis would be $640,000 ($40,000 + $600,000).

If, instead, the entity were an S corporation and Walt received 20% of the stock and Ira and Vera each received 40%, the basis for their stock would be as follows.

Walt	Ira	Vera
$40,000	$100,000	$100,000

In S corporations, nonrecourse debt does not affect the calculation of stock basis. The stock basis for each shareholder would remain the same even if the debt were recourse debt. Only direct loans by the shareholders increase the ceiling on loss pass-through. ■

Effect of Special Allocations

An advantage of the conduit concept over the entity concept is the ability to make special allocations. Special allocations are not permitted in C corporations. Indirectly, however, the corporate form may be able to achieve results similar to those produced by special allocations through payments to owners (e.g., salary payments, lease rental payments, and interest payments) and through different classes of stock (e.g., preferred and common). However, even in these cases, the breadth of the treatment and the related flexibility are far less than that achievable under the conduit concept.

Although S corporations generally operate as conduits, they are treated more like C corporations than partnerships with respect to special allocations. This treatment results from the application of the per-share and per-day allocation rule in § 1377(a). Although S corporations are limited to one class of stock, they still can use salary, interest, and rental payments to owners to shift income to the desired recipient. However, the IRS has the authority to reallocate income among members of a family if fair returns are not provided for services rendered or capital invested.[24]

EXAMPLE 16

The stock of an S corporation is owned by Debra (50%), Helen (25%), and Joyce (25%). Helen and Joyce are Debra's adult children. Debra is subject to a 35% marginal tax rate, and Helen and Joyce have a 15% marginal tax rate. Only Debra is an employee of the corporation. She is paid an annual salary of $20,000, whereas employees with similar responsibilities in other corporations earn $100,000. The corporation generates earnings of approximately $200,000 each year.

It appears that the reason Debra is paid a low salary is to enable more of the earnings of the S corporation to be taxed to Helen and Joyce, who are in lower tax brackets. Thus, the IRS could use its statutory authority to allocate a larger salary to Debra. ■

Partnerships and limited liability entities have many opportunities to use special allocations, including the following (refer to Chapter 11).

- The ability to share profits and losses differently from the share in capital.
- The ability to share profits and losses differently.
- A required special allocation for the difference between the adjusted basis and the fair market value of contributed property.
- The special allocation of some items if a substantial economic effect rule is satisfied.

LO.6

Analyze the effects of the disposition of a business on the owners and the entity for each of the forms for conducting a business.

Disposition of a Business or an Ownership Interest

A key factor in evaluating the tax consequences of a business disposition is whether the disposition is viewed as the sale of an ownership interest or as a sale of assets. Generally, the tax consequences are more favorable to the seller if the transaction is treated as a sale of the ownership interest.

Sole Proprietorships

Regardless of the form of the transaction, the sale of a sole proprietorship is treated as the sale of individual assets. Thus, gains and losses must be calculated separately for each asset. Classification as capital gain or ordinary income depends on the nature and holding period of the individual assets. Ordinary income property such as inventory will result in ordinary gains and losses. Section 1231 property such as land, buildings, and machinery used in the business will produce § 1231 gains and losses (subject to depreciation recapture under §§ 1245 and 1250). Capital assets such as investment land and stocks qualify for capital gain or loss treatment.

[24] § 1366(e).

If the amount realized exceeds the fair market value of the identifiable assets, the excess is allocated to goodwill, which produces capital gain for the seller. If instead the excess payment is allocated to a covenant not to compete, the related gain is classified as ordinary income rather than capital gain. Both goodwill and covenants are amortized over a 15-year statutory period.[25]

EXAMPLE 17

Seth, who is in the 35% tax bracket, sells his sole proprietorship to Wilma for $600,000. The identifiable assets are as follows.

	Adjusted Basis	Fair Market Value
Inventory	$ 20,000	$ 25,000
Accounts receivable	40,000	40,000
Machinery and equipment*	125,000	150,000
Buildings**	175,000	250,000
Land	40,000	100,000
	$400,000	$565,000

*Potential § 1245 recapture of $50,000.

**Potential § 1250 recapture of $20,000.

The sale produces the following results for Seth.

	Gain (Loss)	Ordinary Income	§ 1231 Gain	Capital Gain
Inventory	$ 5,000	$ 5,000		
Accounts receivable	–0–			
Machinery and equipment	25,000	25,000		
Buildings	75,000	20,000	$ 55,000	
Land	60,000		60,000	
Goodwill	35,000			$35,000
	$200,000	$50,000	$115,000	$35,000

If the sale is structured this way, Wilma can deduct the $35,000 paid for goodwill over a 15-year period. If instead Wilma paid the $35,000 to Seth for a covenant not to compete for a period of seven years, she still would amortize the $35,000 over a 15-year period. However, Seth's $35,000 capital gain would now be taxed to him as ordinary income. If the covenant has no legal relevance to Wilma, in exchange for treating the payment as a goodwill payment, she should negotiate for a price reduction that reflects Seth's benefit from the lower capital gains tax. ■

Partnerships and Limited Liability Entities

The sale of a partnership or limited liability entity can be structured as the sale of assets or as the sale of an ownership interest. If the transaction takes the form of an asset sale, it is treated the same as for a sole proprietorship. The sale of an ownership interest is treated as the sale of a capital asset, although ordinary income potential exists for unrealized receivables and substantially appreciated inventory. Thus, if capital gain treatment can produce beneficial results for the taxpayer (e.g., he or she has capital losses to offset or has beneficially treated net capital gain), the sale of an ownership interest is preferable.

From a buyer's perspective, tax consequences are not affected by the form of the transaction. If the transaction is an asset purchase, the basis for the assets equals

[25] § 197.

TAX *in the News* **A NEW ONE-WAY STREET FOR PARTNERS**

Janel paid $800,000 for Waldo's partnership interest in the DWT Partnership. Waldo's outside basis was $600,000, which equaled his share of the partnership's inside basis for the partnership assets. Unless the partnership makes a § 754 election, Janel will eventually pay income taxes on the $200,000 difference between her outside basis of $800,000 and her share of the inside basis of $600,000. However, a § 754 election will activate § 743 and provide her with a special basis adjustment of $200,000. But does she recognize the need for making the § 754 election, and will the other partners cooperate?

Suppose the amounts are reversed (i.e., Janel paid $600,000 for an inside basis of $800,000). In this situation, Janel would prefer to avoid making the § 754 election. Congress in the American Jobs Creation Act of 2004 limited the ability to make this choice. The statutory language of § 743 was modified to require an automatic downward basis adjustment if the partnership has a "substantial built-in loss" at the time of the transfer.

Note that this new § 743 treatment applies only to losses. For built-in gains, an affirmative § 754 election still is necessary in order to receive a § 743 upward basis adjustment.

the amount paid. If a buyer intends to continue to operate as an LLC or a partnership, the assets can be contributed to the entity under § 721. Therefore, the owner's basis in the entity interest is equal to the purchase price for the assets. Likewise, if ownership interests are purchased, the owner's basis is the purchase price paid. The partnership's basis for the assets is the purchase price since the original partnership will have terminated.[26]

When the inside and outside basis of a partner's ownership interest differ (see Chapter 11), an election can be made to step up the partner's share of the entity's asset bases.[27] This tax-free basis step-up applies to all such exchanges by all of the partners as long as the election is in effect. The election allows asset basis to reflect increases in fair market value and the goodwill that a new partner has purchased.

EXAMPLE 18

Roz buys a one-third interest in the RST Partnership for $50,000 (outside basis). All of the entity's assets are depreciable, and their basis to the partnership (inside basis) is $90,000. If a § 754 election is in effect, the partnership can step up the basis of its depreciable assets by $20,000, the difference between Roz's outside and inside basis amounts [$50,000 − ($\frac{1}{3}$ × $90,000)]. All of the "new" asset basis is allocated to Roz. ■

C Corporations

The sale of a business held by a C corporation can be structured as either an asset sale or a stock sale. The stock sale has the dual advantage to the seller of being less complex both as a legal transaction and as a tax transaction. It also has the advantage of providing a way to avoid double taxation. Finally, any gain or loss on the sale of the stock is treated as a capital gain or loss to the shareholder.

EXAMPLE 19

Jane and Zina each own 50% of the stock of Purple Corporation. They have owned the business for 10 years. Jane's basis in her stock is $40,000, and Zina's basis in her stock is $60,000. They agree to sell the stock to Rex for $300,000. Jane recognizes a long-term capital gain of $110,000 ($150,000 − $40,000), and Zina recognizes a long-term capital gain of $90,000 ($150,000 − $60,000). Rex has a basis in his stock of $300,000. Purple's basis in its assets does not change as a result of the stock sale. ■

[26] § 708(b)(1)(B).

[27] § 754.

PLANNING *Strategies*

SELLING STOCK OR ASSETS

★ **Framework Focus: Tax Rate**

Strategy ★ Avoid Double Taxation.

Structuring the sale of the business as a stock sale may produce detrimental tax results for the purchaser. As Example 19 illustrates, the basis of the corporation's assets is not affected by the stock sale. If the fair market value of the stock exceeds the corporation's adjusted basis for its assets, the purchaser is denied the opportunity to step up the basis of the assets to reflect the amount in effect paid for them through the stock acquisition—no § 754 election is available to C corporations.

For an asset sale, the seller of the business can be either the corporation or its shareholders. If the seller is the corporation, the corporation sells the business (the assets), pays any debts not transferred, and makes a liquidating distribution to the shareholders. If the sellers are the shareholders, the corporation pays any debts that will not be transferred and makes a liquidating distribution to the shareholders; then the shareholders sell the business.

Regardless of the approach used for an asset sale, double taxation will occur. The corporation is taxed on the actual sale of the assets and is taxed as if it had sold the assets when it makes the liquidating distribution to the shareholders who then sell the distributed assets. The shareholders are taxed when they receive cash or assets distributed in-kind by the corporation.

The asset sale resolves the purchaser's problem of not being able to step up the basis of the assets to their fair market value. The basis for each asset is its purchase price. To operate in corporate form (assuming the purchaser is not a corporation), the purchaser needs to transfer the property to a corporation in a § 351 transaction.

From the perspective of the seller, the ideal form of the transaction is a stock sale. Conversely, from the purchaser's perspective, the ideal form is an asset purchase. Double taxation seldom can be avoided in either case. Therefore, the bargaining ability of the seller and the purchaser to structure the sale as a stock sale or an asset sale, respectively, is critical.

Rather than selling the entire business, an owner may sell only his or her ownership interest. Since the form of the transaction is a stock sale, the results for the selling shareholder will be the same as if all the shareholders had sold their stock (i.e., capital gain or capital loss).

S Corporations

Since the S corporation is a corporation, it is subject to the provisions for a C corporation discussed previously. Either an asset sale at the corporate level or a liquidating distribution of assets produces recognition at the corporate level. However, under the conduit concept applicable to the S corporation, the recognized amount is taxed at the shareholder level. Therefore, double taxation is avoided directly (only the shareholder is involved) for a stock sale and indirectly (the conduit concept ignores the involvement of the corporation) for an asset sale.

Double taxation might seem to be avoided by making an S corporation election prior to the liquidation of a C corporation, but the built-in gains tax closes this loophole; taxation occurs at the corporate level, and double taxation results.

Concept Summary 15–1 reviews the tax consequences of business dispositions.

Overall Comparison of Forms of Doing Business

Concept Summary 15–2 provides a detailed comparison of the tax consequences of the various forms of doing business.

CONCEPT SUMMARY 15–1

Tax Treatment of Disposition of a Business

Form of Entity	Form of Transaction	Tax Consequences: Seller	Tax Consequences: Buyer
Sole proprietorship	Sale of individual assets.	Gain or loss is calculated separately for the individual assets. Classification as capital or ordinary depends on the nature and holding period of the individual assets. If amount realized exceeds the fair market value of the identifiable assets, the excess is allocated to goodwill (except to the extent identified with a covenant not to compete), which is a capital asset.	Basis for individual assets is the allocated cost. Prefers that any excess of purchase price over the fair market value of identifiable assets be identified with a covenant not to compete if the covenant has legal utility. Otherwise, the buyer is neutral since both goodwill and covenants are amortized over a 15-year statutory period.
	Sale of the business.	Treated as a sale of the individual assets (as above).	Treated as a purchase of the individual assets (as above).
Partnership and limited liability entity	Sale of individual assets.	Treatment is the same as for the sole proprietorship.	Treatment is the same as for the sole proprietorship. If the intent is to operate in partnership form, the assets can be contributed to a partnership under § 721.
	Sale of ownership interest.	Entity interest is treated as the sale of a capital asset (subject to ordinary income potential for unrealized receivables and substantially appreciated inventory).	Basis for new owner's ownership interest is the cost. The new entity's basis for the assets is also the pertinent cost (i.e., contributed to the entity under § 721), since the original entity will have terminated.
C corporation	Sale of corporate assets by corporation (i.e., corporation sells assets, pays debts, and makes liquidating distribution to the shareholders).	Double taxation occurs. Corporation is taxed on the sale of the assets with the gain or loss determination and the classification as capital or ordinary treated the same as for the sole proprietorship. Shareholders calculate gain or loss as the difference between the stock basis and the amount received from the corporation in the liquidating distribution. Capital gain or loss usually results, since stock typically is a capital asset.	Basis for individual assets is the allocated cost. If the intent is to operate in corporate form, the assets can be contributed to a corporation under § 351.
	Sale of corporate assets by the shareholders (i.e., corporation pays debts and makes liquidating distribution to the shareholders).	Double taxation occurs. At the time of the liquidating distribution to the shareholders, the corporation is taxed as if it had sold the assets. Shareholders calculate gain or loss as the difference between the stock basis and the fair market value of the assets received from the corporation in the liquidating distribution. Capital gain or loss usually results, since stock typically is a capital asset.	Same as corporate asset sale.

Form of Entity	Form of Transaction	Tax Consequences: Seller	Tax Consequences: Buyer
	Sale of corporate stock.	Enables double taxation to be avoided. Since the corporation is not a party to the transaction, there are no tax consequences at the corporate level. Shareholders calculate gain or loss as the difference between the stock basis and the amount received for the stock. Capital gain or loss usually results, since stock typically is a capital asset.	Basis for the stock is its cost. The basis for the corporate assets is not affected by the stock purchase.
S corporation	Sale of corporate assets by corporation.	Recognition occurs at the corporate level on the sale of the assets, with the gain or loss determination and the classification as capital or ordinary treated the same as for the sole proprietorship. Conduit concept applicable to the S corporation results in the recognized amount being taxed at the shareholder level. Double taxation associated with the asset sale is avoided, because the shareholder's stock basis is increased by the amount of gain recognition and decreased by the amount of loss recognition. Shareholders calculate gain or loss as the difference between the stock basis and the amount received from the corporation in the liquidating distribution. Capital gain or loss usually results, since stock typically is a capital asset.	Basis for individual assets is the allocated cost. If the intent is to operate in corporate form (i.e., as an S corporation), the assets can be contributed to a corporation under § 351.
	Sale of corporate assets by the shareholders.	At the time of the liquidating distribution to the shareholders, recognition occurs at the corporation level as if the corporation had sold the assets. The resultant tax consequences for the shareholders and the corporation are the same as for the sale of corporate assets by the S corporation.	Same as corporate asset sale by the corporation.
	Sale of corporate stock.	Same as the treatment for the sale of stock of a C corporation.	Same as the treatment for the purchase of stock of a C corporation.

CONCEPT SUMMARY 15–2

Tax Attributes of Different Forms of Business (Assume Partners and Shareholders Are All Individuals)

	Sole Proprietorship	Partnership/Limited Liability Entity	S Corporation	C Corporation
Restrictions on type or number of owners	One owner. The owner must be an individual.	Must have at least 2 owners.	Only individuals, estates, certain trusts, and certain tax-exempt entities can be owners. Maximum number of shareholders limited to 100.*	None, except some states require a minimum of 2 shareholders.
Incidence of tax	Sole proprietorship's income and deductions are reported on Schedule C of the individual's Form 1040. A separate Schedule C is prepared for each business.	Entity not subject to tax. Owners in their separate capacity subject to tax on their distributive share of income. Entity files Form 1065.	Except for certain built-in gains and passive investment income when earnings and profits are present from C corporation tax years, entity not subject to Federal income tax. S corporation files Form 1120S. Shareholders are subject to tax on income attributable to their stock ownership.	Income subject to double taxation. Entity subject to tax, and shareholder subject to tax on any corporate dividends received. Corporation files Form 1120.
Highest tax rate	35% at individual level.	35% at owner level.	35% at shareholder level.	35% at corporate level plus 15%/5% on any corporate dividends at shareholder level (if qualified dividends; otherwise 35%).
Choice of tax year	Same tax year as owner.	Selection generally restricted to coincide with tax year of majority owners or principal owners, or to tax year determined under the least aggregate deferral method.	Restricted to a calendar year unless IRS approves a different year for business purposes or other exceptions apply.	Unrestricted selection allowed at time of filing first tax return.
Timing of taxation	Based on owner's tax year.	Owners report their share of income in their tax year within which the entity's tax year ends. Owners in their separate capacities are subject to payment of estimated taxes.	Shareholders report their shares of income in their tax year within which the corporation's tax year ends. Generally, the corporation uses a calendar year, but see "Choice of tax year." Shareholders may be subject to payment of estimated taxes. Corporation may be subject to payment of estimated taxes for the taxes imposed at the corporate level.	Corporation subject to tax at close of its tax year. May be subject to payment of estimated taxes. Dividends are subject to tax at the shareholder level in the tax year received.

*Spouses and family members can be treated as 1 shareholder.

	Sole Proprietorship	Partnership/Limited Liability Entity	S Corporation	C Corporation
Basis for allocating income to owners	Not applicable (only one owner).	Profit and loss sharing agreement. Cash basis items of cash basis entities are allocated on a daily basis. Other entity items are allocated after considering varying interests of owners.	Pro rata share based on stock ownership. Shareholder's pro rata share is determined on a daily basis, according to the number of shares of stock held on each day of the corporation's tax year.	Not applicable.
Contribution of property to the entity	Not a taxable transaction.	Generally not a taxable transaction.	Is a taxable transaction unless the § 351 requirements are satisfied.	Is a taxable transaction unless the § 351 requirements are satisfied.
Character of income taxed to owners	Retains source characteristics.	Conduit—retains source characteristics.	Conduit—retains source characteristics.	All source characteristics are lost when income is distributed to owners.
Basis for allocating a net operating loss to owners	Not applicable (only one owner).	Profit and loss sharing agreement. Cash basis items of cash basis entities are allocated on a daily basis. Other entity items are allocated after considering varying interests of owners.	Prorated among shareholders on a daily basis.	Not applicable.
Limitation on losses deductible by owners	Investment plus liabilities.	Owner's investment plus share of liabilities.	Shareholder's investment plus loans made by shareholder to corporation.	Not applicable.
Subject to at-risk rules?	Yes, at the owner level. Indefinite carryover of excess loss.	Yes, at the owner level. Indefinite carryover of excess loss.	Yes, at the shareholder level. Indefinite carryover of excess loss.	Yes, for closely held corporations. Indefinite carryover of excess loss.
Subject to passive activity loss rules?	Yes, at the owner level. Indefinite carryover of excess loss.	Yes, at the owner level. Indefinite carryover of excess loss.	Yes, at the shareholder level. Indefinite carryover of excess loss.	Yes, for closely held corporations and personal service corporations. Indefinite carryover of excess loss.
Tax consequences of earnings retained by entity	Taxed to owner when earned and increases his or her investment in the sole proprietorship.	Taxed to owners when earned and increases their respective interest bases in the entity.	Taxed to shareholders when earned and increases their respective interest bases in stock.	Taxed to corporation when earned and may be subject to penalty tax if accumulated unreasonably.
Nonliquidating distributions to owners	Not taxable.	Not taxable unless money received exceeds recipient owner's basis in entity interest. Existence of § 751 assets may cause recognition of ordinary income.	Generally not taxable unless the distribution exceeds the shareholder's AAA or stock basis. Existence of accumulated earnings and profits could cause some distributions to be dividends.	Taxable in year of receipt to extent of earnings and profits or if exceeds basis in stock.

	Sole Proprietorship	Partnership/Limited Liability Entity	S Corporation	C Corporation
Capital gains	Taxed at owner level using maximum rate of 5%, 15%, 25%, or 28%.	Conduit—owners must account for their respective shares. Taxed at owner level.	Conduit, with certain exceptions (a possible penalty tax)—shareholders must account for their respective shares. Tax treatment determined at shareholder level.	Taxed at corporate level with a maximum 35% rate. No other benefits.
Capital losses	Only $3,000 of capital losses can be offset each tax year against ordinary income. Indefinite carryover.	Conduit—owners must account for their respective shares. Tax treatment determined at owner level.	Conduit—shareholders must account for their respective shares. Tax treatment determined at shareholder level.	Carried back three years and carried forward five years. Deductible only to the extent of capital gains.
§ 1231 gains and losses	Taxable or deductible at owner level. Five-year lookback rule for § 1231 losses.	Conduit—owners must account for their respective shares. Tax treatment determined at owner level.	Conduit—shareholders must account for their respective shares. Tax treatment determined at shareholder level.	Taxable or deductible at corporate level only. Five-year lookback rule for § 1231 losses.
Foreign tax credits	Available at owner level.	Conduit—tax payments passed through to owners.	Generally conduit—tax payments passed through to shareholders.	Available at corporate level only.
§ 1244 treatment of loss on sale of interest	Not applicable.	Not applicable.	Available.	Available.
Basis treatment of entity liabilities	Not applicable.	Includible in interest basis.	Not includible in stock basis.	Not includible in stock basis.
Built-in gains	Not applicable.	Not applicable.	Possible corporate tax.	Not applicable.
Special allocations to owners	Not applicable (only one owner).	Available if supported by substantial economic effect.	Not available.	Not applicable.
Availability of fringe benefits to owners	None.	None.	None unless a 2% or less shareholder.	Available within antidiscrimination rules.
Effect of liquidation/redemption/reorganization on basis of entity assets	Not applicable.	Usually carried over from entity to owner.	Taxable step-up to fair market value.	Taxable step-up to fair market value.
Sale of ownership interest	Treated as the sale of individual assets. Classification of recognized gain or loss depends on the nature of the individual assets.	Treated as the sale of an entity interest. Recognized gain or loss is classified as capital, although appreciated inventory and receivables are subject to ordinary income treatment.	Treated as the sale of corporate stock. Recognized gain is classified as capital gain. Recognized loss is classified as capital loss, subject to ordinary loss treatment under § 1244.	Treated as the sale of corporate stock. Recognized gain is classified as capital gain. Recognized loss is classified as capital loss, subject to ordinary loss treatment under § 1244.

	Sole Proprietorship	Partnership/Limited Liability Entity	S Corporation	C Corporation
Distribution of appreciated property	Not taxable.	No recognition at the entity level.	Recognition at the corporate level to the extent of the appreciation. Conduit—amount of recognized gain is passed through to shareholders.	Taxable at the corporate level to the extent of the appreciation.
Splitting of income among family members	Not applicable (only one owner).	Difficult—IRS will not recognize a family member as an owner unless certain requirements are met.	Rather easy—gift of stock will transfer tax on a pro rata share of income to the donee. However, IRS can make adjustments to reflect adequate compensation for services.	Same as an S corporation, except that donees will be subject to tax only on earnings actually or constructively distributed to them. Other than unreasonable compensation, IRS generally cannot make adjustments to reflect adequate compensation for services and capital.
Organizational costs	Startup expenditures are eligible for $5,000 limited expensing (subject to phaseout) and amortizing balance over 180 months.	Organization costs are eligible for $5,000 limited expensing (subject to phaseout) and amortizing balance over 180 months.	Same as partnership.	Same as partnership.
Charitable contributions	Limitations apply at owner level.	Conduit—owners are subject to deduction limitations in their own capacities.	Conduit—shareholders are subject to deduction limitations in their own capacities.	Limited to 10% of taxable income before certain deductions.
Alternative minimum tax	Applies at owner level. AMT rates are 26% and 28%.	Applies at the owner level rather than at the entity level. AMT preferences and adjustments are passed through from the entity to the owners.	Applies at the shareholder level rather than at the corporate level. AMT preferences and adjustments are passed through from the S corporation to the shareholders.	Applies at the corporate level. AMT rate is 20%. Modest-sized C corporations are exempt.
ACE adjustment	Does not apply.	Does not apply.	Does not apply.	The adjustment is made in calculating AMTI. The adjustment is 75% of the excess of adjusted current earnings over unadjusted AMTI. If the unadjusted AMTI exceeds adjusted current earnings, the adjustment may be negative.

PLANNING *Strategies*

CHOOSING A BUSINESS FORM: CASE STUDY

★ **Framework Focus: Tax Rate**

Strategy ★ Avoid Double Taxation.
★ Shift Net Income from High-Bracket Taxpayers to Low-Bracket Taxpayers.

The chapter began with an example that illustrated the relationship between tax planning and the choice of business form; it also raised a variety of questions about the advice given by the tax practitioner. By this time, one should be able to develop various scenarios supporting the tax advice given. The actual fact situations that produced the tax adviser's recommendations were as follows.

- Jesse's experience in the dairy industry consists of raising a few heifers during the final five years of his employment. Eva anticipates that Jesse will generate tax losses for the indeterminate future. In addition, Jesse indicated that he and his wife must have limited liability associated with the dairy farm.
- Larry was born and raised on his father's dairy farm. Both his education and his Air Force managerial experience provide him with useful tools for managing his business. However, Larry inherited his farm when milk prices were at a low for the modern era. Since none of her dairy farm clients were profitable, Eva anticipated Larry would operate his dairy farm at a loss. Larry, like Jesse, felt that limited liability was imperative. Thus, he incorporated the dairy farm and made the S corporation election.
- For the first two years, Larry's dairy farm produced tax losses. Since then, the dairy farm has produced tax profits large enough to absorb the losses. Larry anticipates that his profits will remain relatively stable in the $50,000 to $75,000 range in the future. Since he is subject to a 28 percent marginal tax rate and anticipates that no dividend distributions will be made, his tax liability associated with the dairy farm will be reduced if he terminates the S corporation election.

As Jesse and Larry's example illustrates, selection of the proper business form can result in both nontax and tax advantages. Both of these factors should be considered in making the selection decision. Furthermore, this choice should be reviewed periodically, since a proper business form at one point in time may not be the proper form at a different time. Note that another business form Eva could have considered for Jesse is the limited liability entity.

In looking at the tax attributes, consideration should be given to the tax consequences of the following.

- Contribution of assets to the entity by the owners at the time the entity is created and at later dates.
- Taxation of the results of operations.
- Distributions to owners.
- Disposition of an ownership interest.
- Termination of the entity.

Suggested Further Readings

Sheldon I. Banoff, Paul Carman, and John Maxfield, "Prop. Regs. on Partnership Equity for Services: The Collision of Section 83 and Subchapter K," *Journal of Taxation*, August 2005.

Bruce D. Bernard, "Improve Tax Consequences of Business Purchase and Sale," *Practical Tax Strategies*, January 2002, pp. 4–7.

George Jackson III and David M. Maloney, "Buy-Sell Agreements—An Invaluable Tool," *The Tax Adviser*, April 2003, pp. 200–204 and May 2003, pp. 284–286.

Richard M. Lipton and Steven R. Dixon, "When Is a Partner Not a Partner? When Does a Partnership Exist?" *Journal of Taxation*, February 2004, pp. 73–84.

Mark A. Turner, "Excessive Involvement May Affect Benefits of Entity Choice," *Practical Tax Strategies*, March 2002, pp. 136–140.

Robert Willins, "When Will a Distribution Be a 'Dividend' and Who Bears the Tax Burden?" *Journal of Taxation*, June 2005, pp. 345–350.

KEY TERMS

Conduit concept, 15–14

Entity concept, 15–14

Limited liability company (LLC), 15–4

Unreasonable compensation, 15–11

PROBLEM MATERIALS

PROBLEMS

1. Using the legend provided, indicate which form of business entity each of the following characteristics describes. Some of the characteristics may apply to more than one form of business entity.

Legend
SP = Applies to sole proprietorship
P = Applies to partnership and LLC
S = Applies to S corporation
C = Applies to C corporation

a. Has limited liability.
b. Greatest ability to raise capital.
c. Subject to double taxation.
d. Subject to accumulated earnings tax.
e. Limit on types and number of shareholders.
f. Has unlimited liability.
g. Sale of the business can be subject to double taxation.
h. Contribution of property to the entity in exchange for an ownership interest can result in the nonrecognition of realized gain.
i. Profits and losses affect the basis for an ownership interest.
j. Entity liabilities affect the basis for an ownership interest.
k. Distributions of earnings are taxed as dividend income to the owners.

2. Using the legend provided, indicate which form of business entity each of the following characteristics describes. Some of the characteristics may apply to more than one form of business entity.

Legend
P = Applies to partnership and LLC
S = Applies to S corporation
C = Applies to C corporation

a. Basis for an ownership interest is increased by an investment by the owner.
b. Basis for an ownership interest is decreased by a distribution to the owner.
c. Basis for an ownership interest is increased by entity profits.
d. Basis for an ownership interest is decreased by entity losses.
e. Basis for an ownership interest is increased as the entity's liabilities increase.
f. Basis for an ownership interest is decreased as the entity's liabilities decrease.

3. A business entity has the following assets and liabilities on its balance sheet.

	Net Book Value	Fair Market Value
Assets	$675,000	$950,000
Liabilities	100,000	100,000

The business entity has just lost a product liability suit with damages of $5 million being awarded to the plaintiff. Although the business entity will appeal the judgment, legal counsel indicates the judgment is highly unlikely to be overturned by the appellate court. The product liability insurance carried by the business has a policy ceiling of $3 million. What is the amount of liability of the entity and its owners if the form of the business entity is:

a. A sole proprietorship?
b. A partnership or LLC?
c. A C corporation?
d. An S corporation?

Ethics

4. Bryan operates his business as a C corporation. He is the only shareholder. The accumulated E & P is $800,000. Starting next year, he plans on distributing $200,000. In future years, he intends to distribute all of the annual earnings. Recognizing that the distribution would be taxed as dividend income, he has developed the following tax strategy:

- Sell the corporate assets to himself for the fair market value.
- Have the corporation invest the sales proceeds in a mutual fund.
- Contribute the assets to an LLC and operate his business in this legal form.

Evaluate Bryan's proposal to avoid double taxation.

5. Red, White, Blue, and Orange generate taxable income as follows.

Corporation	Taxable Income
Red	$ 92,000
White	325,000
Blue	800,000
Orange	40,000,000

a. Calculate the marginal and effective tax rates for each of the C corporations.
b. Explain why the marginal tax rate for a C corporation can exceed 35%, but the effective tax rate cannot do so.

Decision Making
Communications

6. Amy and Jeff Barnes are going to operate their florist shop as a partnership or as an S corporation. Their mailing address is 5700 Richmond Highway, Alexandria, VA 22300. After paying salaries of $100,000 to each of the owners, the shop's earnings are projected to be about $150,000. The earnings are to be invested in the growth of the business. Write a letter to Amy and Jeff advising them of which of the two entity forms they should select.

Decision Making

7. Gerald is an entrepreneur who likes to be actively involved in his business ventures. He is going to invest $500,000 in a business that he projects will produce a tax loss of approximately $125,000 per year in the short run. However, once consumers become aware of the new product being sold by the business and the quality of the service it provides, he is confident the business will generate a profit of at least $200,000 per year. Gerald has substantial other income (from both business ventures and investment activities) each year. Advise Gerald on the business form he should select for the short run. He will be the sole owner.

Decision Making

8. Jack, an unmarried taxpayer, is going to establish a manufacturing business. He anticipates that the business will be profitable immediately due to a patent that he holds. He anticipates that profits for the first year will be about $200,000 and will increase at a rate of about 20% per year for the foreseeable future. He will be the sole

owner of the business. Advise Jack on the form of business entity he should select. Jack will be in the 35% tax bracket.

9. Clay Corporation will begin operations on January 1. Earnings for the next five years are projected to be relatively stable at about $90,000 per year. The shareholders of Clay are in the 33% tax bracket. *Decision Making*
   a. Clay will reinvest its after-tax earnings in the growth of the company. Should Clay operate as a C corporation or as an S corporation?
   b. Clay will distribute its after-tax earnings each year to its shareholders. Should Clay operate as a C corporation or as an S corporation?

10. Mabel and Alan, who are in the 35% tax bracket, recently acquired a fast-food franchise. Both of them will work in the business and receive a salary of $100,000. They anticipate that the annual profits of the business, after deducting salaries, will be approximately $300,000. The entity will distribute enough cash each year to Mabel and Alan to cover their Federal income taxes associated with the franchise.
    a. What amount will the entity distribute if the franchise operates as a C corporation?
    b. What amount will the entity distribute if the franchise operates as an S corporation?
    c. What will be the amount of the combined entity/owner tax liability in (a) and (b)?

11. Parrott is a closely held corporation owned by 10 shareholders (each has 10% of the stock). Selected financial information provided by Parrott follows.

Taxable income	$5,250,000
Positive AMT adjustments (excluding ACE adjustment)	425,000
Negative AMT adjustments	(30,000)
Tax preferences	6,000,000
Retained earnings	850,000
Accumulated E & P	775,000
ACE adjustment	720,000

    a. Calculate Parrott's tax liability as a C corporation.
    b. Calculate Parrott's tax liability as an S corporation.
    c. How would your answers in (a) and (b) change if Parrott is not closely held (e.g., 5,000 shareholders with no shareholder owning more than 2% of the stock)?

12. Offshore Fishing Corporation, a calendar year taxpayer, is going to sell real estate that it no longer needs. The real estate is located in Corpus Christi, Texas, and has an adjusted basis of $540,000 ($900,000 – $360,000 MACRS straight-line depreciation) and a fair market value of $840,000. (ADS straight-line depreciation would have been $312,000.) The buyer of the real estate would like to close the transaction prior to the end of the calendar year. Offshore Fishing, however, is uncertain whether the tax consequences would be better if it sold the real estate this year or next year. It is considering the following options. *Decision Making*

    - $840,000 in cash payable on December 31, 2006.
    - The sale will be closed on December 31, 2006, for consideration of an $840,000 note issued by the buyer. The maturity date of the note is January 2, 2007, with the real estate being pledged as security.

    Offshore projects its taxable income for 2006 and 2007 to be $900,000 (gross receipts of about $10 million) without the sale of the real estate. Determine the tax consequences to Offshore under each option and recommend the one that should be selected. Consider both the regular income tax and the AMT in making your recommendation.

13. Heron Corporation has been in operation for 10 years. Since Heron's creation, all of the stock has been owned by Andy, who initially invested $200,000 in the corporation. Heron has been successful far beyond Andy's expectations, and the current fair market value of the stock is $10 million. While he has been paid a salary of $200,000 per year by the corporation, all of Heron's earnings have been reinvested in the growth of the corporation. *Ethics*

    Heron is currently being audited by the IRS. One of the issues raised by the IRS agent is the possibility of the assessment of the accumulated earnings tax. Andy is not concerned about this issue because he believes Heron can easily justify the accumulations based on its past rapid expansion by opening new outlets. The expansion program is fully documented in the minutes of Heron's board of directors. Andy has provided this information to the IRS agent.

Two years ago, Andy decided that he would curtail any further expansion into new markets by Heron. In his opinion, further expansion would exceed his ability to manage the corporation effectively. Since the tax year under audit is three years ago, Andy sees no reason to provide the IRS agent with this information.

Heron will continue its policy of no dividend payments into the foreseeable future. Andy believes that if the accumulated earnings issue is satisfactorily resolved on this audit, it probably will not be raised again on any subsequent audits. Thus, double taxation in the form of the tax on dividends at the shareholder level or the accumulated earnings tax at the corporate level can be avoided.

What is Heron's responsibility to disclose to the IRS agent the expected change in its growth strategy? Are Andy's beliefs regarding future accumulated earnings tax issues realistic?

Extender

14. Two unmarried brothers own and operate a farm. The live on the farm and take their meals on the farm for the "convenience of the employer." The fair market value of their lodging is $20,000, and the fair market value of their meals is $12,000. The meals are prepared for them by the farm cook who prepares their meals along with those of the five other farm employees.
    a. Determine the tax consequences of the meals and lodging to the brothers if the farm is incorporated.
    b. Determine the tax consequences of the meals and lodging to the brothers if the farm is not incorporated.

Extender

15. A business entity's taxable income before the cost of certain fringe benefits paid to owners and other employees is $400,000. The amounts paid for these fringe benefits are as follows:

	Owners	Other Employees
Group term life insurance	$20,000	$40,000
Meals and lodging incurred for the convenience of the employer	50,000	75,000
Pension plan	30,000*	90,000

* H.R. 10 (Keogh) plan for partnership and S corporation.

The business entity is equally owned by four owners.
    a. Calculate the taxable income of the business entity if the entity is a partnership, a C corporation, or an S corporation.
    b. Determine the effect on the owners for each of the three business forms.

16. Turtle, a C corporation, has taxable income of $400,000 before paying salaries to the three equal shareholder-employees, Britney, Shania, and Alan. Turtle follows a policy of distributing all after-tax earnings to the shareholders.
    a. Determine the tax consequences for Turtle, Britney, Shania, and Alan if the corporation pays salaries to Britney, Shania, and Alan as follows.

Option 1		Option 2	
Britney	$180,000	Britney	$67,500
Shania	120,000	Shania	45,000
Alan	100,000	Alan	37,500

    b. Is Turtle likely to encounter any tax problems associated with either option?

17. Swallow, a C corporation, is owned by Sandra (50%) and Fran (50%). Sandra is the president, and Fran is the vice president for sales. Late in 2005, Swallow encounters working capital difficulties. Thus, Sandra and Fran each loan the corporation $300,000 on a 6% note that is due in five years with interest payable annually.

a. Determine the tax consequences to Swallow, Sandra, and Fran for 2006 if the notes are classified as debt.
b. Determine the tax consequences to Swallow, Sandra, and Fran for 2006 if the notes are classified as equity.

18. Laurie Gladin owns land and a building that she has been using in her sole proprietorship. She is going to incorporate her sole proprietorship as a C corporation. Laurie must decide whether to contribute the land and building to the corporation or to lease them to the corporation. The net income of the sole proprietorship for the past five years has averaged $250,000. Advise Laurie on the tax consequences. Summarize your analysis in a memo to the tax file.

Decision Making

Communications

19. Marci and Jennifer each own 50% of the stock of Lavender, a C corporation. After paying each of them a "reasonable" salary of $150,000, the taxable income of Lavender is normally around $800,000. The corporation is about to purchase a $2 million shopping mall ($1,500,000 allocated to the building and $500,000 allocated to the land). The mall will be rented to tenants at a net rental rate (including rental commissions, depreciation, etc.) of $600,000 annually. Marci and Jennifer will contribute $1 million each to the corporation to provide the cash required for the acquisition. Their CPA has suggested that Marci and Jennifer purchase the shopping mall as individuals and lease it to Lavender for a fair rental of $400,000. Both Marci and Jennifer are in the 35% tax bracket. The acquisition will occur on January 2, 2006. Determine whether the shopping mall should be acquired by Lavender or by Marci and Jennifer in accordance with their CPA's recommendation. Depreciation on the shopping mall in 2006 is $37,000.

Decision Making

20. Petal, Inc., has taxable income of $625,000 for 2006. Petal has been in business for many years and long ago used up the accumulated earnings credit. Petal has no additional "reasonable needs of the business" for the current tax year.
a. Determine the total potential tax liability for Petal if it declares no dividends.
b. Determine the total potential tax liability for Petal if it declares and pays dividends equal to the after-tax earnings.
c. Determine the total potential tax liability for Petal in (a) and (b) if Petal is an S corporation.

21. Frank owns 600 shares of the stock of Autumn, Inc., and Grace owns the remaining 400 shares. Frank's stock basis is $60,000, and Grace's is $40,000. As part of a stock redemption, Frank redeems 100 of his shares for $50,000, and Grace redeems 300 of her shares for $150,000.
a. Determine the tax consequences to Autumn, Inc., to Frank, and to Grace if Autumn, Inc., is a C corporation.
b. Determine the tax consequences to Autumn, Inc., to Frank, and to Grace if Autumn, Inc., is an S corporation.

22. Oscar created Lavender Corporation four years ago. The C corporation has paid Oscar as president a salary of $200,000 each year. Annual earnings after taxes approximate $700,000 each year. Lavender has not paid any dividends nor does it intend to do so in the future. Instead, Oscar wants his heirs to receive the stock with a step-up in stock basis when he dies. Identify the relevant tax issues.

Issue ID

23. Tammy and Arnold own 40% of the stock of Roadrunner, an S corporation. The other 60% is owned by 99 other shareholders, all of whom are single and unrelated. Tammy and Arnold have agreed to a divorce and are in the process of negotiating a property settlement. Identify the relevant tax issues for Tammy and Arnold.

Issue ID

24. Eagle Corporation has been an electing S corporation since its incorporation 10 years ago. During the first three years of operations, it incurred total losses of $250,000. Since then Eagle has generated earnings of approximately $150,000 each year. None of the earnings have been distributed to the three equal shareholders, Claire, Lynn, and Todd, because the corporation has been in an expansion mode. At the beginning of the year, Claire sells her stock to Nell for $400,000. Nell has reservations about the utility of the S election. Therefore, Lynn, Todd, and Nell are discussing whether the election should be continued. They expect the earnings to remain at approximately $150,000 each year. However, since they perceive that the company's expansion period is over and Eagle has adequate working capital, they

Decision Making

may start distributing the earnings to the shareholders. All of the shareholders are in the 33% tax bracket. Advise the three shareholders on whether the S election should be maintained.

Communications

25. Bob Bentz and Carl Pierce each own 50% of the stock of Deer, Inc., a C corporation. When the corporation was organized, Bob contributed cash of $200,000, and Carl contributed land with an adjusted basis of $125,000 and a fair market value of $240,000. Deer assumed Carl's $40,000 mortgage on the land. In addition to the capital contributions, Bob and Carl each loaned the corporation $75,000. The maturity date of the loan is in 10 years, and the interest rate is 8%, the same as the Federal rate.
    a. Determine the tax consequences to Bob, Carl, and Deer of the initial contribution of assets, the shareholder loans, and the annual interest payments if the loans are classified as debt.
    b. Determine the tax consequences if the loans are reclassified as equity.
    c. You met with Bob at lunch to discuss the tax consequences of the capital contributions and loans made by Carl and him to Deer, Inc. Prepare a memo for the files on your discussion.

26. Agnes, Becky, and Carol form a business entity with each contributing the following.

	Adjusted Basis	Fair Market Value
Agnes: Cash	$100,000	$100,000
Becky: Land	60,000	120,000
Carol: Services		50,000

Their ownership percentages will be as follows.

Agnes	40%
Becky	40%
Carol	20%

Becky's land has a $20,000 mortgage that is assumed by the entity. Carol is an attorney who receives her ownership interest in exchange for legal services. Determine the recognized gain to the owners, the basis for their ownership interests, and the entity's basis for its assets if the entity is:
    a. A partnership.
    b. A C corporation.
    c. An S corporation.

27. Eloise contributes $40,000 to a business entity in exchange for a 30% ownership interest. During the first year of operations, the entity earns a profit of $200,000. At the end of that year, the entity has liabilities of $75,000.
    a. Calculate Eloise's basis for her stock if the entity is a C corporation.
    b. Calculate Eloise's basis for her stock if the entity is an S corporation.
    c. Calculate Eloise's basis for her partnership interest if the entity is a partnership.

28. An entity has the following income for the current year:

Operations	$92,000
Tax-exempt interest income	19,000
Long-term capital gain	60,000

The entity has earnings and profits (AAA for an S corporation) of $900,000 at the beginning of the year. A distribution of $200,000 is made to the owners.
    a. Calculate the taxable income if the entity is (1) a C corporation and (2) an S corporation.
    b. Determine the effect of the distribution on the shareholders if the entity is (1) a C corporation and (2) an S corporation.

29. Amber holds a 20% interest in a business to which she contributed $100,000 as part of the initial ownership group. During the life of the business, the following have occurred.

- $200,000 cumulative losses, first three tax years.
- $150,000 operating profit in the fourth tax year.
- $75,000 distribution to owners at the end of the third tax year.
- $60,000 payment to redeem 25% of Amber's ownership interest at the end of the fourth year. No other ownership redemptions have occurred.

Determine the tax consequences to Amber if the entity is:

a. A partnership.
b. An S corporation.
c. A C corporation.

30. On January 1, 2006, John contributes assets with an adjusted basis of $80,000 and a fair market value of $212,000 for a 40% ownership interest in an interior design business. Maria contributes $300,000 cash for a 60% ownership interest. The entity assumes a $12,000 mortgage attributable to one of the assets contributed by John. During 2006, the business earns $130,000. In addition, the entity makes a $35,000 cash distribution to John and a $52,500 cash distribution to Maria during the year. John and Maria are each in the 33% tax bracket.

Decision Making

a. If the business entity is a C corporation, determine each of the following.
   - Recognized gain to the owners and the business entity on the creation of the business entity.
   - Original basis for John's and Maria's ownership interests.
   - Effect of the business entity earnings on the entity, John, and Maria.
   - Effect of the distributions on John and Maria.
   - Adjusted basis for John's and Maria's ownership interest at the end of the year.
b. Determine each of the above if the business entity is an S corporation.
c. If the objective is to minimize the income tax liability, should the business entity be a C corporation or an S corporation? Assume that 2006 is a representative year.

31. RK is a partnership that is owned by Rick and Kari. Rick's basis for his partnership interest is $85,000, and Kari's basis is $110,000. RK distributes $70,000 to Rick and $60,000 to Kari.

a. Determine the tax consequences of the distribution to Rick, Kari, and RK.
b. Assume that RK is a C corporation rather than a partnership. RK's earnings and profits are $220,000. Rick's basis for his stock is $85,000, and Kari's stock basis is $110,000. Determine the tax consequences of the distribution to Rick, Kari, and RK.

32. Beige, Inc., a personal service corporation, has the following types of income and losses.

Active income	$212,000
Portfolio income	20,000
Passive activity losses	216,000

a. Calculate Beige's taxable income.
b. Assume that instead of being a personal service corporation, Beige is a closely held corporation. Calculate Beige's taxable income.

33. Rosa contributes $50,000 to a business entity in exchange for a 10% ownership interest. Rosa materially participates in the business. The business entity incurs a loss of $900,000 for 2006. The entity liabilities at the end of 2006 are $700,000. Of this amount, $150,000 is for recourse debt, and $550,000 is for nonrecourse debt.

a. Assume the business entity is a partnership. How much of Rosa's share of the loss can be deducted on her 2006 individual tax return? What is Rosa's basis for her partnership interest at the end of 2006?
b. Assume the business entity is a C corporation. How much of Rosa's share of the loss can be deducted on her 2006 individual tax return? What is Rosa's basis for her stock at the end of 2006?

34. Sanford contributes land to a business entity in January 2006 for a 35% ownership interest. Sanford's basis for the land is $83,000, and the fair market value is $120,000. The business entity was formed three years ago by Pam and Rene, who have equal ownership. The entity is unsuccessful in getting the land rezoned from agricultural to residential use. In August 2006, the land is sold for $140,000. Determine the tax

consequences of the sale of the land for the business entity and the three owners if the organization is:

a. A C corporation.
b. An S corporation.
c. A partnership.

35. Abby and Velma are equal owners of the AV Partnership. Abby invests $75,000 cash in the partnership. Velma contributes land and a building (basis to her of $50,000, fair market value of $75,000). The entity then borrows $200,000 cash using recourse financing and $100,000 using nonrecourse financing.
    a. Compute the outside basis in the partnership interest for Abby and Velma.
    b. Compute the at-risk amount for Abby and Velma.

36. Indicate which of the following special allocations are available for a partnership (P), a C corporation (C), and an S corporation (S).
    a. Share profits and losses differently from the share in capital.
    b. Share profits in a different percentage than losses.
    c. Special allocation of precontribution gain.
    d. Special allocation supported by substantial economic effect.
    e. Allocation to eliminate difference between inside and outside basis.
    f. Special allocation of precontribution loss.

37. Sanjay contributes land to a business entity in January 2006 for a 30% ownership interest. Sanjay's basis for the land is $60,000, and the fair market value is $100,000. The business entity was formed three years ago by Polly and Rita, who have equal ownership. The entity is unsuccessful in getting the land rezoned from agricultural to residential. In October 2006, the land is sold for $110,000.

    Determine the tax consequences of the sale of the land for the entity and its owners if the entity is:
    a. A C corporation.
    b. An S corporation.
    c. A partnership.

38. Emily and Freda are negotiating with George to purchase the business that he operates in corporate form (Pelican, Inc.). The assets of Pelican, Inc., a C corporation, are as follows.

Asset	Basis	FMV
Cash	$ 20,000	$ 20,000
Accounts receivable	50,000	50,000
Inventory	100,000	110,000
Furniture and fixtures	150,000	170,000*
Building	200,000	250,000**
Land	40,000	150,000

* Potential depreciation recapture under § 1245 is $45,000.

**The straight-line method was used to depreciate the building. Accumulated depreciation is $340,000.

George's basis for the stock of Pelican, Inc., is $560,000. George is subject to a 35% marginal tax rate, and Pelican, Inc., faces a 34% marginal tax rate.

a. Emily and Freda purchase the *stock* of Pelican, Inc., from George for $908,000. Determine the tax consequences to Emily and Freda, Pelican, Inc., and George.
b. Emily and Freda purchase the *assets* from Pelican, Inc., for $908,000. Determine the tax consequences to Emily and Freda, Pelican, Inc., and George.
c. The purchase price is $550,000 because the fair market value of the building is $150,000, and the fair market value of the land is $50,000. No amount is assigned to goodwill. Emily and Freda purchase the *stock* of Pelican, Inc., from George. Determine the tax consequences to Emily and Freda, Pelican, Inc., and George.

39. Linda is the owner of a sole proprietorship. The entity has the following assets.

Decision Making

Asset	Basis	FMV
Cash	$10,000	$10,000
Accounts receivable	–0–	25,000
Office furniture and fixtures*	15,000	17,000
Building**	75,000	90,000
Land	60,000	80,000

* Potential depreciation recapture under § 1245 of $5,000.
**The straight-line method has been used to depreciate the building.

Linda sells the business for $260,000 to Juan.

a. Determine the tax consequences to Linda, including the classification of any recognized gain or loss.
b. Determine the tax consequences to Juan.
c. Advise Juan on how the purchase agreement could be modified to produce more beneficial tax consequences for him.

40. Gail and Harry own the GH Partnership. They have conducted the business as a partnership for 10 years. The bases for their partnership interests are as follows.

Decision Making

Gail	Harry
$100,000	$150,000

GH Partnership holds the following assets.

Asset	Basis	FMV
Cash	$ 10,000	$ 10,000
Accounts receivable	30,000	28,000
Inventory	25,000	26,000
Building*	100,000	150,000
Land	250,000	400,000

* The straight-line method has been used to depreciate the building.
Accumulated depreciation is $70,000.

Gail and Harry sell their partnership interests to Keith and Liz for $307,000 each.

a. Determine the tax consequences of the sale to Gail, Harry, and GH Partnership.
b. From a tax perspective, should it matter to Keith and Liz whether they purchase Gail and Harry's partnership interests or the partnership assets from GH Partnership?

41. Ted Jamison and Skip Arnold are going to purchase the Carp Partnership, as equal partners, from Jan and Gail for $900,000. Because of your negotiations on behalf of Ted and Skip, the transaction will be structured as a purchase of the partnership, not of its individual assets. Carp's inside basis in its assets is $720,000. Write a letter to Ted at 50 Lake Shore Drive, Erie, PA 16501, explaining the following.

Communications

a. What outside basis do Ted and Skip take in the partnership?
b. Can Carp change its inside asset basis as a result of the purchase of the entity?

42. Vladimir owns all the stock of Ruby Corporation. The fair market value of the stock (and Ruby's assets) is about four times his adjusted basis for the stock. Vladimir is negotiating with an investor group for the sale of the corporation. Identify the relevant tax issues for Vladimir.

Issue ID

43. Swallow, Inc., will purchase either the stock or the assets of Dane Corporation. All of the Dane stock is owned by Chuck. Bill Evans, Swallow's CFO, and Chuck agree that Dane is worth $625,000. The tax basis for Dane's assets is $400,000. Write a letter to Bill advising him on whether he should negotiate for Swallow to purchase the stock or the assets. Bill's address is 100 Village Green, Chattanooga, TN 37403.

Decision Making

Communications

BRIDGE *Discipline*

1. Parchment, Inc., is created with the following asset and liability contributions. Jake and Fran each receive 100 shares of Parchment common stock.

Shareholder	Assets	Basis	Fair Market Value
Jake	Cash	$100,000	$100,000
Fran	Land	40,000	120,000*

* The land has a mortgage of $20,000 that Parchment assumes.

   a. Prepare a financial accounting balance sheet. Discuss the relevance of conduit theory and entity theory.
   b. Prepare a tax balance sheet. Discuss the relevance of conduit theory and entity theory.
   c. Assume Parchment sells the land four months after the creation of the corporation for $150,000. Discuss the effect on the financial accounting balance sheet and the tax balance sheet.

2. Assume that Parchment in the preceding problem elects S corporation status at the time of its creation. Respond to (a), (b), and (c).

3. Assume that Parchment in (1) is a general partnership rather than a corporation. Respond to (a), (b), and (c). Would your answer change if Parchment were an LLC that "checked the box" to be taxed as a partnership?

4. Teal, Inc., has total assets of $100 million and annual revenues of $700 million. Lavender, Inc., has total assets of $12 million and annual revenues of $900,000. Both have been in existence for three years.
   a. Explain why neither Teal nor Lavender need make an AMT calculation for its first tax year.
   b. Explain why Teal must make an AMT calculation and why Lavender is not required to do so.
   c. Do you think that this different tax treatment for Teal and Lavender is equitable?

RESEARCH PROBLEMS

Note: Solutions to Research Problems can be prepared by using the **RIA Checkpoint® Student Edition** online research product, which is available to accompany this text. It is also possible to prepare solutions to the Research Problems by using tax research materials found in a standard tax library.

Research Problem 1. The stock of Ebony, Inc., is owned as follows:

	Percent Ownership	Basis	FMV
Alma	30%	$2,700	$270,000
Ben	30	2,700	270,000
Debbie	20	1,800	180,000
Clyde	20	1,800	180,000

Alma and Ben are the parents of Debbie and Clyde. Managerial positions in Ebony are as follows: Alma is the chief executive officer (CEO), Ben is the chief operating officer (COO), Debbie is the chief financial officer (CFO), and Clyde is the vice president for human resources. Alma and Ben have owned their stock for 30 years, and Debbie and Clyde have owned their stock for 10 years. Alma and Ben are considering disposing of their stock and would like to use the funds to acquire a more lucrative investment. Their initial plan was to have Ebony redeem their stock. However, their accountant has indicated that since they intend to retain their positions as officers, the redemption will not qualify under § 302(b)(3). The accountant suggests that they sell their stock to several outsiders who wish to acquire an interest in Ebony. As Debbie and Clyde expect to move into the CEO and COO positions in a few years, they oppose a sale to outsiders. They are concerned about the loss of family control that would result.

How can this family dilemma be resolved?

Internet *Activity*

Use the tax resources of the Internet to address the following questions. Do not restrict your search to the World Wide Web, but include a review of newsgroups and general reference materials, practitioner sites and resources, primary sources of the tax law, chat rooms and discussion groups, and other opportunities.

Research Problem 2. Find an anecdote about a professional consulting firm that recently converted to LLP status. Are the firm and its competition and clients agreeable to the conversion of operating status?

Research Problem 3. When did your state adopt LLC legislation? When did it receive IRS approval to apply partnership tax law to the entities?

Research Problem 4. Find an article describing how a specific business put together its employee fringe benefit package in light of the limitations presented by the tax law and its form of operation.

Research Problem 5. Determine whether your state income tax system permits an S corporation election.

Research Problem 6. Find a company that provides a service of identifying investment properties that are producing passive activity income.

http://wft.swlearning.com

PART 6

Taxation of Individuals

The primary orientation of this text is toward basic tax concepts as they apply to business entities. Although many of these concepts also apply to the individual taxpayer, numerous tax concepts have been designed to apply specifically to the individual taxpayer. The components of the basic tax model provide the framework for the presentation of these specifically designed tax concepts for the individual taxpayer.

http://wft.swlearning.com

CHAPTER 16

Introduction to the Taxation of Individuals

LEARNING OBJECTIVES

After completing Chapter 16, you should be able to:

LO.1

Understand and apply the components of the Federal income tax formula for individuals.

LO.2

Apply the rules for arriving at personal exemptions.

LO.3

Apply the rules for determining dependency exemptions.

LO.4

Use the proper method for determining the tax liability.

LO.5

Identify and work with kiddie tax situations.

LO.6

Recognize filing requirements and proper filing status.

LO.7

Identify specific inclusions and exclusions applicable to individuals.

LO.8

Determine an individual's allowable itemized deductions.

LO.9

Understand the adoption expenses credit, child tax credit, education tax credits, credit for child and dependent care expenses, and earned income credit.

OUTLINE

TAX *Talk*

I'm proud of paying taxes in the United States. The only thing is—I could be just as proud for half the money.

—Arthur Godfrey

The individual income tax accounts for approximately 35 percent of Federal budget receipts, compared to approximately 8 percent for the corporate income tax. The tax laws affecting individuals have become increasingly more complex in recent years as the government adds new laws to protect or increase this important source of revenue. Taxpayers respond to each new tax act with techniques to exploit loopholes, and the government responds with loophole-closing provisions, making the individual income tax law even more complex.[1]

LO.1

Understand and apply the components of the Federal income tax formula for individuals.

The Individual Tax Formula

Individuals are subject to Federal income tax based on taxable income. This chapter explains how taxable income and the income tax of an individual taxpayer are determined. To compute taxable income, it is necessary to understand the tax formula in Figure 16–1.

[1]Refer to the discussion of tax complexity in Chapter 1.

TAX FACT

The Government's Interest in Our Work

How much of the typical American's eight-hour work day goes to pay Federal, state, and local taxes? According to the Tax Foundation, the answer is 2 hours and 20 minutes. However, the required effort also depends on where the individual lives. In high-tax jurisdictions such as Connecticut and New York, people need to work on average nearly 3 hours, while in Alabama and Alaska, only about 2 hours are required.

Source: *Tax Foundation, 2005.*

FIGURE 16–1 **Individual Income Tax Formula**

Income (broadly conceived)	$xx,xxx
Less: Exclusions	(x,xxx)
Gross income	$xx,xxx
Less: Deductions *for* adjusted gross income	(x,xxx)
Adjusted gross income (AGI)	$xx,xxx
Less: The greater of—	
Total itemized deductions *or*	
Standard deduction	(x,xxx)
Less: Personal and dependency exemptions	(x,xxx)
Taxable income	$xx,xxx
Tax on taxable income (see Tax Tables or Tax Rate Schedules)	$ x,xxx
Less: Tax credits (including income taxes withheld and prepaid)	(xxx)
Tax due (or refund)	$ xxx

Although the tax formula is rather simple, determining an individual's taxable income can be quite complex because of the numerous provisions that govern the determination of gross income and allowable deductions.

After computing taxable income, the appropriate rates must be applied. This requires a determination of the individual's filing status, since different rates apply for single taxpayers, married taxpayers, and heads of household. The individual tax rate structure is progressive, with rates for 2006 ranging from 10 percent to 35 percent.[2] For comparison, the lowest rate structure, which was in effect from 1913 to 1915, ranged from 1 to 7 percent, and the highest, in effect during 1944–1945, ranged from 23 to 94 percent.

Once the individual's tax has been computed, prepayments and credits are subtracted to determine whether the taxpayer owes additional tax or is entitled to a refund.

Components of the Tax Formula

Before illustrating the application of the tax formula, a brief discussion of each of its components is helpful.

[2]Prior to the Tax Relief Reconciliation Act of 2001, the tax rates ranged from 15% to 39.6%. The Act established 10% as the new lowest bracket. Later legislation lowered the top tax rate to 35%.

EXHIBIT 16–1 **Partial List of Exclusions from Gross Income**

Accident and health insurance proceeds
Annuity payments (to the extent proceeds represent a recovery of the taxpayer's investment)
Child support payments
Damages for personal injury or sickness
Fringe benefits of employees:
- Educational assistance payments provided by employer
- Employer-provided accident and health insurance
- Group term life insurance (for coverage up to $50,000)
- Meals and lodging (if furnished for convenience of employer)
- Tuition reductions for employees of educational institutions
- Miscellaneous benefits

Gains from sale of principal residence (subject to statutory ceiling)
Gifts and inheritances received
Interest from state and local bonds
Life insurance paid on death of insured
Scholarship grants (to a limited extent)
Social Security benefits (to a limited extent)
Workers' compensation benefits

Income (Broadly Conceived). This includes all the taxpayer's income, both taxable and nontaxable. Although it is essentially equivalent to gross receipts, it does not include a return of capital or receipt of borrowed funds. Nor does gross income include unrealized appreciation in the value of a taxpayer's assets.

EXAMPLE 1

Dave needed money to purchase a house. He sold 5,000 shares of stock for $100,000. He had paid $40,000 for the stock. In addition, he borrowed $75,000 from a bank. Dave has income that is taxable of $60,000 from the sale of the stock ($100,000 selling price – $40,000 return of capital). He has no income from the $75,000 borrowed from the bank because he has an obligation to repay that amount. ■

Exclusions. For various reasons, Congress has chosen to exclude certain types of income from the income tax base. The principal income exclusions are listed in Exhibit 16–1. The exclusions most commonly encountered by individual taxpayers (employee fringe benefits) are discussed in detail in Chapter 17.

Gross Income. The Internal Revenue Code defines gross income broadly as "except as otherwise provided . . . all income from whatever source derived."[3] The "except as otherwise provided" refers to exclusions. Gross income includes, but is not limited to, the items in Exhibit 16–2.

EXAMPLE 2

Beth received the following amounts during the year:

Salary	$30,000
Interest on savings account	900
Gift from her aunt	10,000
Prize won in state lottery	1,000
Alimony from ex-husband	12,000

[3] § 61(a).

EXHIBIT 16–2 Partial List of Gross Income Items

Alimony	Interest
Bargain purchase from employer	Jury duty fees
Bonuses	Partnership income
Breach of contract damages	Pensions
Business income	Prizes (with some exceptions)
Commissions	Professional fees
Compensation for services	Punitive damages
Debts forgiven (with some exceptions)	Rents
Dividends	Rewards
Embezzled funds	Royalties
Farm income	Salaries
Fees	Severance pay
Gains from illegal activities	Strike and lockout benefits
Gains from sale of property	Tips and gratuities
Gambling winnings	Unemployment compensation
Hobby income	Wages

Child support from ex-husband	$ 6,000
Damages for injury in auto accident	25,000
Increase in the value of stock held for investment	5,000

Review Exhibits 16–1 and 16–2 to determine the amount Beth must include in the computation of taxable income and the amount she may exclude. Then check your answer in footnote 4.[4] ■

Deductions for Adjusted Gross Income. Individual taxpayers have two categories of deductions: (1) deductions *for* adjusted gross income (deductions to arrive at adjusted gross income) and (2) deductions *from* adjusted gross income. Deductions *for* adjusted gross income (AGI) include the following:[5]

- Ordinary and necessary expenses incurred in a trade or business.
- One-half of self-employment tax paid.
- Alimony paid.
- Certain payments to traditional Individual Retirement Accounts and Health Savings Accounts.
- Moving expenses.
- The capital loss deduction (limited to $3,000).

Adjusted Gross Income (AGI). AGI is an important subtotal that serves as the basis for computing percentage limitations on certain itemized deductions, such as medical expenses, charitable contributions, and certain casualty losses. For example, medical expenses are deductible only to the extent they exceed 7.5 percent of AGI, and charitable contribution deductions may not exceed 50 percent of AGI. These

[4]Beth must include $43,900 in computing taxable income ($30,000 salary + $900 interest + $1,000 lottery prize + $12,000 alimony). She can exclude $41,000 ($10,000 gift from aunt + $6,000 child support + $25,000 damages). The unrealized gain of $5,000 on the stock held for investment is not included in gross income. Such gain will be included in gross income only when it is realized upon disposition of the stock.

[5]See § 62 for a comprehensive list of items that are deductible *for* AGI. Deductions *for* AGI are sometimes known as *above-the-line* deductions because on the tax return they are taken before the "line" designating AGI.

CITIZENSHIP IS NOT TAX-FREE

Gross income from "whatever source derived" includes income from both U.S. and foreign sources. This approach to taxation, where the government taxes its citizens and residents on their worldwide income regardless of where earned, is referred to as a *global* system. Income earned by U.S. citizens outside the United States can be subject to additional taxes, however, because all countries maintain the right to tax income earned within their borders. Consequently, the U.S. tax law includes various mechanisms to alleviate the double taxation that arises when income is subject to tax in multiple jurisdictions. These mechanisms include the foreign tax deduction, the foreign tax credit, the foreign earned income exclusion for U.S. citizens and residents working abroad, and various tax treaty provisions.

Most industrialized countries use variants of the global system. An alternative approach is the *territorial* system, where a government taxes only the income earned within its borders. Hong Kong and Guatemala, for example, use a territorial approach.

limitations might be described as a 7.5 percent *floor* under the medical expense deduction and a 50 percent *ceiling* on the charitable contribution deduction.

EXAMPLE 3

Keith earned a salary of $65,000 in the current tax year. He contributed $4,000 to his traditional Individual Retirement Account (IRA) and sustained a $1,000 capital loss on the sale of Wren Corporation stock. His AGI is computed as follows:

Gross income		
Salary		$65,000
Less: Deductions *for* AGI		
IRA contribution	$4,000	
Capital loss	1,000	(5,000)
AGI		$60,000

■

EXAMPLE 4

Assume the same facts as in Example 3, and that Keith also had medical expenses of $5,800. Medical expenses may be included in his itemized deductions to the extent they exceed 7.5% of AGI. In computing his itemized deductions, Keith may include medical expenses of $1,300 [$5,800 medical expenses – $4,500 (7.5% × $60,000 AGI)]. ■

Itemized Deductions. As a general rule, personal expenditures are disallowed as deductions in arriving at taxable income. However, Congress has chosen to allow specific personal expenses as **itemized deductions**. Such expenditures include medical expenses, certain taxes and interest, and charitable contributions. Itemized deductions are discussed in detail later in this chapter.

EXAMPLE 5

Leo is the owner and operator of a video game arcade. All allowable expenses he incurs in connection with the arcade business are deductions *for* AGI. In addition, Leo paid medical expenses, mortgage interest, state income tax, and charitable contributions. These personal expenses are allowable as itemized deductions. ■

Standard Deduction. The **standard deduction** is used by taxpayers who do not have itemized deductions in excess of the allowable standard deduction amount. The standard deduction is a specified amount that depends on the filing status of the taxpayer (e.g., single, married filing jointly, married filing separately). In the past, Congress has attempted to set the amount of the standard deduction at a level

TABLE 16–1 Basic Standard Deduction Amounts

Filing Status	2005	2006
Single	$ 5,000	$ 5,150
Married, filing jointly	10,000	10,300
Surviving spouse	10,000	10,300
Head of household	7,300	7,550
Married, filing separately	5,000	5,150

that would exempt poverty-level taxpayers from the income tax,[6] but it has not always been consistent in doing so.

The standard deduction is the sum of two components: a *basic* standard deduction and an *additional* standard deduction.[7] Taxpayers who are allowed a *basic* standard deduction are entitled to the applicable amount listed in Table 16–1. The standard deduction amounts are subject to adjustment for inflation each year. Currently, about 70 percent of all individual taxpayers choose to use the standard deduction in lieu of itemizing deductions. However, certain taxpayers are not allowed to claim *any* standard deduction, and the standard deduction is *limited* for others.[8]

A taxpayer who is age 65 or over *or* blind qualifies for an *additional standard deduction* of $1,000 or $1,250, depending on filing status (see amount in Table 16–2). Two additional standard deductions are allowed for a taxpayer who is age 65 or over *and* blind. The additional standard deduction provisions also apply for a qualifying spouse who is age 65 or over or blind, but a taxpayer may not claim an additional standard deduction for a dependent.

To determine whether to itemize, the taxpayer compares the *total* standard deduction (the sum of the basic standard deduction and any additional standard deductions) to total itemized deductions. Taxpayers are allowed to deduct the *greater* of itemized deductions or the standard deduction. Taxpayers whose itemized deductions are less than the standard deduction compute their taxable income using the standard deduction rather than itemizing.

EXAMPLE 6

Sara, who is single, is 66 years old. She had total itemized deductions of $5,900 during 2006. Her total standard deduction is $6,400 ($5,150 basic standard deduction plus $1,250 additional standard deduction). Sara should compute her taxable income for 2006 using the standard deduction ($6,400), since it exceeds her itemized deductions ($5,900). ■

Personal and Dependency Exemptions. Exemptions are allowed for the taxpayer, for the taxpayer's spouse, and for each dependent of the taxpayer. The exemption amount is $3,200 in 2005 and $3,300 in 2006.

Application of the Tax Formula

The tax formula shown in Figure 16–1 is illustrated in Example 7.

EXAMPLE 7

Grace, age 25, is single and has no dependents. She is a high school teacher and earned a $40,000 salary in 2006. Her other income consisted of a $1,000 prize won in a sweepstakes

[6] S.Rep. No. 92–437, 92nd Cong., 1st Sess., 1971, p. 54. Another purpose of the standard deduction was discussed in Chapter 1 under Influence of the Internal Revenue Service—Administrative Feasibility. The size of the standard deduction has a direct bearing on the number of taxpayers who are in a position to itemize deductions. Reducing the number of taxpayers who itemize also reduces the audit effort required from the IRS.

[7] § 63(c)(1).

[8] § 63(c)(6).

TABLE 16–2 Amount of Each Additional Standard Deduction

Filing Status	2005	2006
Single	$1,250	$1,250
Married, filing jointly	1,000	1,000
Surviving spouse	1,000	1,000
Head of household	1,250	1,250
Married, filing separately	1,000	1,000

contest and $500 of interest on municipal bonds that she had received as a graduation gift in 2003. During 2006, she sustained a deductible capital loss of $1,000. Her itemized deductions are $5,400. Grace's taxable income for the year is computed as follows:

Income (broadly conceived)		
Salary		$40,000
Prize		1,000
Interest on municipal bonds		500
Total income		$41,500
Less: Exclusion—		
Interest on municipal bonds		(500)
Gross income		$41,000
Less: Deduction *for* adjusted gross income—		
Capital loss		(1,000)
Adjusted gross income (AGI)		$40,000
Less: The *greater* of—		
Total itemized deductions	$5,400	
or the standard deduction	5,150	(5,400)
Less: Personal and dependency exemptions (1 × $3,300)		(3,300)
Taxable income		$31,300

■

DIGGING DEEPER 1

Find more information on this topic at our Web site: ***http://wft-entities.swlearning.com.***

Special Limitations for Individuals Who can be Claimed as Dependents

Special rules apply to the standard deduction and personal exemption of an individual who can be claimed as a dependent on another person's tax return.

When filing his or her own tax return, a *dependent's* basic standard deduction in 2006 is limited to the greater of $850 or the sum of the individual's earned income for the year plus $300.[9] However, if the sum of the individual's earned income plus $300 exceeds the normal standard deduction, the standard deduction is limited to the appropriate amount shown in Table 16–1. These limitations apply only to the basic standard deduction. A dependent who is 65 or over or blind or both is also allowed the additional standard deduction amount on his or her own return (refer to Table 16–2). These provisions are illustrated in Examples 8 through 11.

[9] § 63(c)(5). Both the $850 amount and the $300 amount are subject to adjustment for inflation each year. The amounts were $800 and $250, respectively, for 2005.

EXAMPLE 8

Susan, who is 17 years old and single, is claimed as a dependent on her parents' tax return. During 2006, she received $1,200 of interest (unearned income) on a savings account. She also earned $400 from a part-time job. When Susan files her own tax return, her standard deduction is $850 (the greater of $850 or the sum of earned income of $400 plus $300). ■

EXAMPLE 9

Assume the same facts as in Example 8, except that Susan is 67 years old and is claimed as a dependent on her son's tax return. In this case, when Susan files her own tax return, her standard deduction is $2,100 [$850 (the greater of $850 or the sum of earned income of $400 plus $300) + $1,250 (the additional standard deduction allowed because Susan is age 65 or over)]. ■

EXAMPLE 10

Peggy, who is 16 years old and single, earned $600 from a summer job and had no unearned income during 2006. She is claimed as a dependent on her parents' tax return. Her standard deduction is $900 (the greater of $850 or the sum of earned income of $600 plus $300). ■

EXAMPLE 11

Jack, who is a 20-year-old, single, full-time college student, is claimed as a dependent on his parents' tax return. He worked as a musician during the summer of 2006, earning $5,900. Jack's standard deduction is $5,150 (the greater of $850 or the sum of earned income of $5,900 plus $300, but limited to the $5,150 standard deduction for a single taxpayer). ■

Personal Exemptions

LO.2

Apply the rules for arriving at personal exemptions.

The use of exemptions in the tax system is based in part on the idea that a taxpayer with a small amount of income should be exempt from income taxation. An exemption frees a specified amount of income from tax ($3,200 in 2005 and $3,300 in 2006). The exemption amount is indexed (adjusted) annually for inflation.

Exemptions that are allowed for the taxpayer and spouse are designated as **personal exemptions**. Those exemptions allowed for the care and maintenance of other persons are called dependency exemptions and are discussed in the next section.

An individual cannot claim a personal exemption if he or she is claimed as a dependent by another.

EXAMPLE 12

Assume the same facts as in Example 11. On his own income tax return,[10] Jack's taxable income is determined as follows:

Gross income	$ 5,900
Less: Standard deduction	(5,150)
Personal exemption	(–0–)
Taxable income	$ 750

Note that Jack is not allowed a personal exemption because he is claimed as a dependent by his parents. ■

When a husband and wife file a joint return, they may claim two personal exemptions. However, when separate returns are filed, a married taxpayer cannot claim an exemption for his or her spouse *unless* the spouse has no gross income and is not claimed as the dependent of another taxpayer.[11]

The determination of marital status generally is made at the end of the taxable year, except when a spouse dies during the year. Spouses who enter into a legal separation under a decree of divorce or separate maintenance before the end of the

[10]As noted on page 16–23 of the text, Jack's situation is such that he will be required to file an income tax return.

[11]§ 151(b).

TABLE 16–3 **Marital Status for Exemption Purposes**

Description	Marital Status and Personal Exemptions
• Walt is the widower of Helen who died on January 3, 2006.	Walt and Helen are considered to be married for purposes of filing the 2006 return. Walt may claim two exemptions on his 2006 return.
• Bill and Jane entered into a divorce decree that becomes effective on December 31, 2006.	Bill and Jane are considered to be unmarried for purposes of filing the 2006 return. Bill and Jane each may claim a personal exemption on their separate returns.

year are considered to be unmarried at the end of the taxable year. Table 16–3 illustrates the effect of death or divorce upon marital status.

For *Federal* tax purposes, the law does not recognize same-sex marriages. By virtue of the Defense of Marriage Act (Pub. L. No. 104–199), a marriage means a legal union only between a man and a woman as husband and wife.

The amount of the exemption is not reduced due to the taxpayer's death. For example, refer to the case of Helen in Table 16–3. Although she lived for only three days in 2006, the full personal exemption of $3,300 is allowed for the tax year. The same rule applies to dependency exemptions. As long as an individual qualified as a dependent at the time of death, the full amount of the exemption can be claimed.

LO.3

Apply the rules for determining dependency exemptions.

Dependency Exemptions

As is the case with personal exemptions, a taxpayer is permitted to claim an exemption of $3,300 in 2006 ($3,200 in 2005) for each person who qualifies as a dependent. A **dependency exemption** is available for either a qualifying child or a qualifying relative and must not run afoul of certain other rules (i.e., joint return, nonresident alien prohibitions).

Qualifying Child

One of the objectives of the Working Families Tax Relief Act of 2004 was to establish a uniform definition of qualifying child. Aside from minor modifications, the qualifying child definition applies to the following tax benefits:

- Dependency exemption.
- Head-of-household filing status.
- Earned income tax credit.
- Child tax credit.
- Credit for child and dependent care expenses.

A **qualifying child** must meet the relationship, abode, age, and support tests.[12]

Relationship Test. The relationship test includes a taxpayer's child (son, daughter), adopted child, stepchild, eligible foster child, brother, sister, half brother, half sister, stepbrother, stepsister, or a *descendant* of any of these parties (e.g., grandchild, nephew, niece). Note that *ancestors* of any of these parties (e.g., uncles and aunts) and in-laws (e.g., son-in-law, brother-in-law) *are not included.*

[12] § 152(c).

TABLE 16–4 Tiebreaker Rules for Claiming Qualified Child

Persons Eligible to Claim Exemption	Person Prevailing
One of the persons is the parent.	Parent
Both persons are the parents, and the child lives longer with one parent.	Parent with the longer period of residence
Both persons are the parents, and the child lives with each the same period of time.	Parent with the higher adjusted gross income (AGI)
None of the persons is the parent.	Person with highest AGI

An adopted child includes a child lawfully placed with the taxpayer for legal adoption even though the adoption is not final. An eligible foster child is one who is placed with the taxpayer by an authorized placement agency or by a judgment decree or other order of any court of competent jurisdiction.

EXAMPLE 13

Maureen's household includes her mother, grandson, stepbrother, stepbrother's daughter, uncle, and sister. All meet the relationship test for a qualifying child except the mother and uncle. ■

Abode Test. A qualifying child must live with the taxpayer for more than half of the year. For this purpose, temporary absences (e.g., school, vacation, medical care, military service, detention in a juvenile facility) are disregarded. Special rules apply in the case of certain kidnapped children.[13]

Age Test. A qualifying child must be under age 19 or under age 24 in the case of a student. A student is a child who, during any part of five months of the year, is enrolled full time at a school or government-sponsored on-farm training course.[14] The age test does not apply to a child who is disabled during any part of the year.[15]

Support Test. In order to be a qualifying child, the individual must not be self-supporting (i.e., provide more than one-half of his or her own support). In the case of a child who is a full-time student, scholarships are not considered to be support.[16]

EXAMPLE 14

Shawn, age 23, is a full-time student and lives with his parents and an older cousin. During 2006, Shawn receives his support from the following sources: 30% from a part-time job, 30% from a scholarship, 20% from his parents, and 20% from the cousin. Shawn is not self-supporting and can be claimed by his parents as a dependent. (Note: Shawn cannot be a qualifying child as to his cousin due to the relationship test.) ■

Tiebreaker Rules. In some situations, a child may be a qualifying child to more than one person. In this event, the tax law specifies which person has priority in claiming the dependency exemption.[17] Called "tiebreaker rules," these rules are summarized in Table 16–4.

DIGGING DEEPER 2

Find more information on this topic at our Web site: ***http://wft-entities.swlearning.com.***

[13] § 152(f)(6).

[14] § 152(f)(2).

[15] Within the meaning of § 22(e)(3) for purposes of the credit for elderly and disabled.

[16] § 152(f)(5).

[17] § 152(c)(4).

Qualifying Relative

Besides establishing the concept of a qualifying child, the Working Families Tax Relief Act of 2004 also provided for a second category of dependency exemption designated as the **qualifying relative**. The rules involved largely carried over then-existing law to post-2004 years.

A qualifying relative must meet the relationship, gross income, and support tests.[18] As in the case of the qualifying child category, qualifying relative status also requires that the joint return and nonresident alien restrictions be avoided (see Other Rules for Dependency Exemptions below).

Relationship Test. The relationship test for a qualifying relative is more expansive than for a qualifying child. Also included are the following relatives:

- Lineal ascendants (e.g., parents, grandparents).
- Collateral ascendants (e.g., uncles, aunts).
- Certain in-laws (e.g., son-, daughter-, father-, mother-, brother-, and sister-in- law).[19]

Children who do not satisfy the qualifying child definition may meet the qualifying relative criteria.

EXAMPLE 15

Inez provides more than half of the support of her son, age 20, who is neither disabled nor a full-time student. The son is not a qualifying child due to the age test, but is a qualifying relative if the gross income test is met. Consequently, Inez may claim a dependency exemption for her son. ■

The relationship test also includes unrelated parties who live with the taxpayer (i.e., are members of the household). Member-of-the-household status is not available for anyone whose relationship with the taxpayer violates local law or anyone who was a spouse during any part of the year.[20] However, an ex-spouse can qualify as a member of the household in a year following that of the divorce.

As the relationship test indicates, the category designation of "qualifying relative" is somewhat misleading. As just noted, persons other than relatives can qualify as dependents. Furthermore, not all relatives will qualify—notice the absence of the "cousin" grouping.

EXAMPLE 16

Charles provides more than half of the support of a family friend who lives with him and a cousin who lives in another city. Presuming the gross income test is met, the family friend is a qualifying relative, but the cousin is not. ■

Gross Income Test. A dependent's gross income must be *less* than the exemption amount—$3,200 in 2005 and $3,300 in 2006. Gross income is determined by the income that is taxable. In the case of scholarships, for example, include the taxable portion (e.g., amounts received for room and board) and exclude the nontaxable portion (e.g., amounts received for books and tuition).

EXAMPLE 17

Elsie provides more than half of the support of her son, Tom, who does not live with her. Tom, age 26, is a full-time student in medical school, earns $3,000 from a part-time job, and receives a $12,000 scholarship covering his tuition. Elsie may claim Tom as a dependent since he meets the gross income test and is a qualifying relative. (Note: Tom is not a qualifying child due to either the abode or the age test.) ■

[18] § 152(d).

[19] Once established by marriage, in-law status continues to exist and survives divorce.

[20] §§ 152(d)(2)(H) and (f)(3).

EXAMPLE 18

Aaron provides more than half of the support of his widowed aunt, Myrtle, who does not live with him. Myrtle's income for the year is as follows: dividend income of $1,100; earnings from pet sitting of $1,200; Social Security benefits of $6,000; and interest from City of Milwaukee bonds of $8,000. Since Myrtle's gross income is only $2,300 ($1,100 + $1,200), she meets the gross income test and can be claimed as Aaron's dependent. ■

In contrast, the qualifying child category of dependency exemptions does not contain a gross income test. Consequently, it is no longer necessary to have a special exception to the gross income test for a child of the taxpayer who is under age 19 or under age 24 and a full-time student.

Support Test. Over one-half of the support of the qualifying relative must be furnished by the taxpayer. Support includes food, shelter, clothing, toys, medical and dental care, education, and the like. However, a scholarship (both taxable and nontaxable portions) received by a student is not included for purposes of determining whether the taxpayer furnished more than half of the child's support.

EXAMPLE 19

Hal contributed $3,400 (consisting of food, clothing, and medical care) toward the support of his nephew, Sam, who lives with him. Sam earned $1,500 from a part-time job and received a $2,000 scholarship to attend a local university. Assuming that the other dependency tests are met, Hal can claim Sam as a dependent since he has contributed more than half of Sam's support. The $2,000 scholarship is not included as support for purposes of this test. ■

If an individual does not spend funds that have been received from any source, the unspent amounts are not counted for purposes of the support test.

EXAMPLE 20

Emily contributed $3,000 to her father's support during the year. In addition, her father received $2,400 in Social Security benefits, $200 of interest, and wages of $600. Her father deposited the Social Security benefits, interest, and wages in his own savings account and did not use any of the funds for his support. Thus, the Social Security benefits, interest, and wages are not considered to be support provided by Emily's father. Emily may claim her father as a dependent if the other tests are met. ■

Capital expenditures for items such as furniture, appliances, and automobiles are included for purposes of the support test if the item does, in fact, constitute support.

EXAMPLE 21

Norm purchased a television set costing $650 and gave it to his mother who lives with him. The television set was placed in the mother's bedroom and was used exclusively by her. Norm should include the cost of the television set in determining the support of his mother. ■

An exception to the support test involves a **multiple support agreement**. A multiple support agreement permits one of a group of taxpayers who furnish support for a qualifying relative to claim a dependency exemption for that individual even if no one person provides more than 50 percent of the support.[21] The group together must provide more than 50 percent of the support. Any person who contributed *more than 10 percent* of the support is entitled to claim the exemption if each person in the group who contributed more than 10 percent files a written consent. This provision frequently enables one of the children of aged dependent parents to claim an exemption when none of the children meets the 50 percent support test.

Each person who is a party to the multiple support agreement must meet all other requirements (except the support requirement) for claiming the exemption. A person who does not meet the relationship or member-of-the-household test, for instance,

[21] § 152(d)(3).

cannot claim the dependency exemption under a multiple support agreement. It does not matter if he or she contributes more than 10 percent of the individual's support.

EXAMPLE 22

Wanda, who resides with her son, Adam, received $12,000 from various sources during the year. This constituted her entire support for the year. She received support from the following individuals:

	Amount	Percentage of Total
Adam, a son	$ 5,760	48
Bob, a son	1,200	10
Carol, a daughter	3,600	30
Diane, a friend	1,440	12
	$12,000	100

If Adam and Carol file a multiple support agreement, either may claim the dependency exemption for Wanda. Bob may not claim Wanda because he did not contribute more than 10% of her support. Bob's consent is not required in order for Adam and Carol to file a multiple support agreement. Diane does not meet the relationship or member-of-the-household test and cannot be a party to the agreement. The decision as to who claims Wanda rests with Adam and Carol. It is possible for Carol to claim Wanda, even though Adam furnished more of Wanda's support. ■

DIGGING DEEPER 3

Find more information on this topic at our Web site: ***http://wft-entities.swlearning.com.***

PLANNING *Strategies* — MULTIPLE SUPPORT AGREEMENTS AND THE MEDICAL EXPENSE DEDUCTION

★ Framework Focus: Deductions

Strategy ★ Maximize Deductible Amounts.

Generally, medical expenses are deductible only if they are paid on behalf of the taxpayer, his or her spouse, and their dependents.[22] Since deductibility may rest on dependency status, planning is important in arranging multiple support agreements.

EXAMPLE 23

During the year, Zelda will be supported by her two sons (Vern and Vito) and her daughter (Maria). Each will furnish approximately one-third of the required support. If the parties decide that the dependency exemption should be claimed by Maria under a multiple support agreement, any medical expenses incurred by Zelda should be paid by Maria. ■

In planning a multiple support agreement, take into account which of the parties is most likely to exceed the 7.5 percent limitation. In Example 23, for instance, Maria might be a poor choice if she and her family do not expect to incur many medical expenses of their own.

Another exception to the support test applies when parents with children are divorced or separated under a decree of separate maintenance. For unmarried parents, living apart (for the last six months of the year) will suffice. A special rule applies if the parents meet the following conditions:

[22] See the discussion of medical expenses later in this chapter.

- Provide more than half of the support (either jointly or singly) of the child (or children).
- Have custody (either jointly or singly) of the child (or children) for more than half of the year.

The special rule grants the dependency exemption(s) to the noncustodial parent if the divorce (or separate maintenance) decree so specifies *or* the custodial parent issues a waiver.[23]

DIGGING DEEPER 4

Find more information on this topic at our Web site: ***http://wft-entities.swlearning.com.***

Other Rules for Dependency Exemptions

In addition to fitting into either the qualifying child or the qualifying relative category, a dependent must meet the joint return and the citizenship or residency tests.

Joint Return Test. If a dependent is married, the supporting taxpayer (e.g., the parent of a married child) generally is not permitted a dependency exemption if the married individual files a joint return with his or her spouse.[24] The joint return rule does not apply, however, if the following conditions are met:

- The reason for filing is to claim a refund for tax withheld.
- No tax liability would exist for either spouse on separate returns.
- Neither spouse is required to file a return.

EXAMPLE 24

Paul provides over half of the support of his son, Quinn. He also provides over half of the support of Vera, who is Quinn's wife. During the year, both Quinn and Vera had part-time jobs. To recover the taxes withheld, they file a joint return. If Quinn and Vera have income low enough that they are not *required* to file a return, Paul is allowed to claim both as dependents. ■

PLANNING *Strategies*

PROBLEMS WITH A JOINT RETURN

★ **Framework Focus: Deductions**

Strategy ★ Maximize Deductible Amounts.

A married person who files a joint return generally cannot be claimed as a dependent by another taxpayer. If a joint return has been filed, the damage may be undone if separate returns are substituted on a timely basis (on or before the due date of the return).

EXAMPLE 25

While preparing a client's 2005 income tax return on April 7, 2006, a tax practitioner discovered that the client's daughter had filed a joint return with her husband in late January of 2006. Presuming the daughter otherwise qualifies as the client's dependent, the exemption is not lost if she and her husband file separate returns on or before April 17, 2006. ■

Citizenship or Residency Test. To be a dependent, the individual must be either a U.S. citizen, a U.S. resident, or a resident of Canada or Mexico for some part of the calendar year in which the taxpayer's tax year begins.[25]

[23] § 152(e)

[24] § 152(b)(2).

[25] § 152(b)(3).

CONCEPT SUMMARY 16–1

Tests for Dependency Exemption after 2004

Category	
Qualifying Child	**Qualifying Relative**[1]
Relationship[2]	Support
Abode[3]	Relationship[4] or member of household[3]
Age	Gross income
Support	
Joint return[5]	Joint return[5]
Citizenship or residency[6]	Citizenship or residency[6]

[1] These rules are largely the same as those applicable to pre-2005 years.

[2] Children and their descendants, and siblings and stepsiblings and their descendants.

[3] The rules for abode are the same as for member of the household.

[4] Children and their descendants, siblings and their children, parents and their ascendants, uncles and aunts, stepparents and stepsiblings, and certain in-laws.

[5] The joint return rules are the same for each category.

[6] The citizenship or residency rules are the same for each category.

Comparison of Categories for Dependency Exemptions

Concept Summary 16–1 sets forth the tests for the two categories of dependency exemptions. In contrasting the two categories, the following observations are in order:

- As to the relationship tests, the qualifying relative category is considerably more expansive. Besides including those prescribed under the qualifying child grouping, other relatives are added. Nonrelated persons who are members of the household are also included.
- The support tests are entirely different. In the case of a qualifying child, support is not necessary. What is required is that the child not be self-supporting.
- The qualifying child category has no gross income limitation, whereas the qualifying relative category has no age restriction.

Phaseout of Exemptions

Several provisions of the tax law are intended to increase the tax liability of more affluent taxpayers who might otherwise enjoy some benefit from having some of their taxable income subject to the lower income tax brackets (e.g., 10 percent, 15 percent, 25 percent). One such provision phases out certain itemized deductions and is discussed later in this chapter. Another provision phases out personal and dependency exemptions and is considered below.[26] In 2001, however, Congress decided that both of these provisions imposed an unfair burden on high-income individual taxpayers and decided on their repeal. To avoid an immediate revenue loss, the repeal was postponed until 2006. Furthermore, to spread the impact of the revenue loss, the repeal is taking place in two stages and will not be complete until 2010. The personal and dependency exemption phaseout remains at two-thirds for 2006 and 2007 and at one-third for 2008 and 2009.

[26] § 151(d)(3).

TAX *in the News* — **HOW TO SUBTLY PLUCK THE CHICKEN**

No government likes to admit that it is enacting new taxes or even raising the rates on existing taxes. Needless to say, this is particularly true of the U.S. Congress. But there are more subtle ways to raise revenue (or to curtail revenue loss). The most popular way is to use a so-called *stealth tax*. A stealth tax is not really a tax at all. Instead, it is a means of depriving higher-income taxpayers of the benefits of certain tax provisions thought to be available to all.

The heart and soul of the stealth tax is the phaseout approach. Thus, as income increases, the tax benefit thought to be derived from a particular relief provision decreases. Since the phaseout is gradual and not drastic, many affected taxpayers are unaware of what has happened. Although the tax law is rampant with phaseouts, the two most flagrant limit the deductibility of personal and dependency exemptions and itemized deductions. (The itemized deduction phaseout is discussed later in this chapter.)

However, Congress has had some misgivings about the stealth tax imposed on personal and dependency exemptions and itemized deductions. These misgivings cannot be too severe since scheduled relief does not *start* until year 2006 and is not *completed* until year 2010!

The phaseout of exemptions occurs as AGI exceeds specified threshold amounts (indexed annually for inflation). For 2005 and 2006, the phaseout *begins* when AGI exceeds the following:

Filing Status	2005	2006
Joint return/surviving spouse	$218,950	$225,750
Head of household	182,450	188,150
Single	145,950	150,500
Married, filing separately	109,475	112,875

Exemptions are phased out by 2 percent for each $2,500 (or fraction thereof) by which the taxpayer's AGI exceeds the threshold amounts. For a married taxpayer filing separately, the phaseout is 2 percent for each $1,250 or fraction thereof. Then, the amount of the phased-out exemptions is multiplied by ⅔ (the reduction-of-phaseout fraction) for tax years 2006 and 2007.

The allowable exemption amount can be determined with the following steps:

1. AGI − threshold amount = excess amount.
2. Excess amount/$2,500 = reduction factor [rounded up to the next whole increment (e.g., 18.1 = 19)] × 2 = phaseout percentage.
3. Phaseout percentage (from step 2) × exemption amount = amount of exemptions phased out.
4. Amount of exemptions phased out × reduction-of-phaseout fraction = phaseout amount.
5. Exemption amount − phaseout amount = allowable exemption deduction.

EXAMPLE 26

Frederico is married but files a separate return. His 2006 AGI is $132,875. He is entitled to one personal exemption.

1. $132,875 − $112,875 = $20,000 excess amount.
2. [($20,000/$1,250) × 2] = 32% (phaseout percentage).
3. 32% × $3,300 = $1,056 amount of exemption phased out.
4. $1,056 × ⅔ = $704 phaseout amount.
5. $3,300 − $704 = $2,596 allowable exemption deduction. ■

The elimination of the phaseout of exemptions, as well as the phaseout of certain itemized deductions, will ultimately add much needed simplicity to the tax law. Unfortunately, reaching this objective by means of a gradual reduction of the phaseout (i.e., a phaseout of a phaseout) unduly adds further complexity to the existing rules.

LO.4

Use the proper method for determining the tax liability.

Tax Determination

Tax Table Method

The tax liability is computed using either the Tax Table method or the Tax Rate Schedule method. Most taxpayers compute their tax using the Tax Table. Eligible taxpayers compute taxable income (as shown in Figure 16–1) and *must* determine their tax by reference to the **Tax Table**.[27]

DIGGING DEEPER 5

Find more information on this topic at our Web site: ***http://wft-entities.swlearning.com.***

Although the Tax Table is derived by using the Tax Rate Schedules (discussed below), the tax calculated using the two methods may vary slightly. This variation occurs because the tax for a particular income range in the Tax Table is based on the midpoint amount.

EXAMPLE 27

Linda is single and has taxable income of $30,000 for calendar year 2005. To determine Linda's tax using the Tax Table, find the $30,000 to $30,050 income line. The tax of $4,171 is actually the tax the Tax Rate Schedules would yield on taxable income of $30,025 (i.e., the midpoint amount between $30,000 and $30,050). ■

Tax Rate Schedule Method

Prior to 2001 tax legislation, the **Tax Rate Schedules** contained rates of 15, 28, 31, 36, and 39.6 percent. These rates were scheduled to be reduced to 10, 15, 25, 28, 33, and 35 percent by year 2006. The Jobs and Growth Tax Relief Reconciliation Act of 2003 (JGTRRA of 2003), however, accelerated the phase-in and made the new rates effective as of January 1, 2003.[28] A sunset provision reinstates the original rates (pre-2001) after 2010.

The 2006 rate schedule for single taxpayers is reproduced in Table 16–5. This schedule is used to illustrate the tax computations in Example 28, 29, and 30.

EXAMPLE 28

Pat is single and had $5,870 of taxable income in 2006. His tax is $587 ($5,870 × 10%). ■

EXAMPLE 29

Chris is single and had taxable income of $50,000 in 2006. Her tax is $9,057.50 [$4,220 + 25%($50,000 – $30,650)]. ■

Note that $4,220, which is the starting point in the tax computation in Example 29, is 10 percent of the $7,550 taxable income in the first bracket + 15 percent of the $23,100 ($30,650 – $7,550) taxable income in the second bracket. Chris's income in excess of $30,650 is taxed at the 25 percent rate. This reflects the *progressive* (or graduated) rate structure on which the U.S. income tax system is based. A tax is progressive if a higher rate of tax applies as the tax base increases.

EXAMPLE 30

Carl is single and had taxable income of $80,000 in 2006. His tax is $16,731.50 [$15,107.50 + 28%($80,000 – $74,200)]. Note that the effect of this computation is to tax part of Carl's

[27] The 2005 Tax Table is located at **http://wft-entities.swlearning.com**. This table will be used to illustrate the tax computation. The 2006 Tax Table was not available at the date of publication of this text.

[28] § 1(i).

TABLE 16–5 **2006 Tax Rate Schedule for Single Taxpayers**

If Taxable Income Is			
Over	But Not Over	The Tax Is:	Of the Amount Over
$ –0–	$ 7,550	10%	$ –0–
7,550	30,650	$ 755.00 + 15%	7,550
30,650	74,200	4,220.00 + 25%	30,650
74,200	154,800	15,107.50 + 28%	74,200
154,800	336,550	37,675.50 + 33%	154,800
336,550		97,653.00 + 35%	336,550

income at 10%, part at 15%, part at 25%, and part at 28%. An alternative computational method provides a clearer illustration of the progressive rate structure of the individual income tax:

Tax on $7,550 at 10%	$ 755.00
Tax on $30,650 – $7,550 at 15%	3,465.00
Tax on $74,200 – $30,650 at 25%	10,887.50
Tax on $80,000 – $74,200 at 28%	1,624.00
Total	$16,731.50

Carl's marginal rate (refer to Chapter 1) is 28%, and his average rate is 20.9% ($16,731.50 tax/$80,000 taxable income). ■

A special computation limits the effective tax rate on qualified dividends (see Chapter 4) and net long-term capital gain (see Chapter 8).

PLANNING *Strategies*

SHIFTING INCOME AND DEDUCTIONS ACROSS TIME

★ **Framework Focus: Tax Rate**

Strategy ★ Shift Net Income from High-Bracket Years to Low-Bracket Years.

It is natural for taxpayers to be concerned about the tax rates they are paying. How does a tax practitioner communicate information about rates to clients? There are several possibilities. For example, a taxpayer who is in the 15 percent bracket this year and expects to be in the 28 percent bracket next year should, if possible, defer payment of deductible expenses until next year to maximize the tax benefit of the deduction.

A note of caution is in order with respect to shifting income and expenses between years. Congress has recognized the tax planning possibilities of such shifting and has enacted many provisions to limit a taxpayer's ability to do so. Some of these limitations on the shifting of income and deductions are discussed in Chapters 4 through 6.

Computation of Net Taxes Payable or Refund Due

The pay-as-you-go feature of the Federal income tax system requires payment of all or part of the taxpayer's income tax liability during the year. These payments take the form of Federal income tax withheld by employers or estimated tax paid by the taxpayer or both.[29] The payments are applied against the tax from the Tax Table or

[29]See § 3402 for withholding and § 6654 for estimated payments.

TAX FACT

The Tightening Tax Squeeze

How has the total tax burden changed over time? Many Americans would likely assert that more of their income than ever goes just to pay taxes. The Tax Foundation contends that such assertion is correct. It reports that the percentage of income claimed by Federal, state, and local taxes has increased from 5.9 percent in 1900 to 29.1 percent in 2005.

Source: *Tax Foundation, 2005.*

Tax Rate Schedules to determine whether the taxpayer will get a refund or pay additional tax.

Employers are required to withhold income tax on compensation paid to their employees and to pay this tax over to the government. The employer notifies the employee of the amount of income tax withheld on Form W–2 (Wage and Tax Statement). The employee should receive this form by January 31 after the year in which the income tax is withheld.

If taxpayers receive income that is not subject to withholding or income from which insufficient tax is withheld, they must pay estimated tax. These individuals must file Form 1040–ES (Estimated Tax for Individuals) and pay in quarterly installments the income tax and self-employment tax estimated to be due.

The income tax from the Tax Table or the Tax Rate Schedules also is reduced by the individual's tax credits. There is an important distinction between tax credits and tax deductions. Tax credits (including tax withheld) reduce the tax liability dollar-for-dollar. Tax deductions reduce taxable income on which the tax liability is based.

EXAMPLE 31

Gail is a taxpayer in the 25% tax bracket. As a result of incurring $1,000 in child care, she is entitled to a $200 credit for child and dependent care expenses ($1,000 child care expenses × 20% credit rate). She also contributed $1,000 to the American Cancer Society and included this amount in her itemized deductions. The credit for child and dependent care expenses results in a $200 reduction of Gail's tax liability for the year. The contribution to the American Cancer Society reduces taxable income by $1,000 and results in a $250 reduction in Gail's tax liability ($1,000 reduction in taxable income × 25% tax rate). ■

Selected tax credits for individuals are discussed later in this chapter. The following are some of the more common credits available to individuals:

- Child tax credit.
- Credit for child and dependent care expenses.
- Earned income credit.

EXAMPLE 32

Kelly, age 30, is a head of household whose 12-year-old daughter lives with him. During 2006, Kelly had the following: taxable income, $30,000; income tax withheld, $2,450; estimated tax payments, $600; and child tax credit, $1,000. Kelly's net tax payable (refund due) is computed as follows:

Income tax (from 2006 Tax Rate Schedule)		$ 3,963
Less: Tax credits and prepayments—		
Child tax credit	$1,000	
Income tax withheld	2,450	
Estimated tax payments	600	(4,050)
Net taxes payable (refund due if negative)		($ 87)

■

Unearned Income of Children under Age 14 Taxed at Parents' Rate

LO.5

Identify and work with kiddie tax situations.

Most individuals compute taxable income using the tax formula shown in Figure 16–1. Special provisions govern the computation of taxable income and the tax liability for children under age 14 who have **unearned income** in excess of specified amounts.

Recall that individuals who are claimed as dependents by other taxpayers cannot claim an exemption on their own return. This prevents parents from shifting the tax on investment income (such as interest and dividends) to a child by transferring ownership of the assets producing the income. Without this provision, the child would pay no tax on the income to the extent that it was sheltered by the child's exemption.

Current tax law also reduces or eliminates the possibility of saving taxes by shifting income from parents to children by taxing the net unearned income of children under age 14 as if it were the parents' income.[30] Unearned income includes such income as taxable interest, dividends, capital gains, rents, royalties, pension and annuity income, and income (other than earned income) received as the beneficiary of a trust.

This provision, commonly referred to as the **kiddie tax**, applies to any child for any taxable year if the child has not reached age 14 by the close of the taxable year, has at least one living parent, and has unearned income of more than $1,700. The kiddie tax provision does not apply to a child age 14 or older. However, the limitation on the use of the standard deduction and the unavailability of the personal exemption do apply to such a child as long as he or she is eligible to be claimed as a dependent by a parent.

Net Unearned Income.

Net unearned income of a dependent child is computed as follows:

Unearned income
Less: $850
Less: The *greater* of
  $850 of the standard deduction *or*
  The amount of allowable itemized deductions directly connected with the production of the unearned income
Equals: Net unearned income

If net unearned income is zero (or negative), the child's tax is computed without using the parents' rate. If the amount of net unearned income (regardless of source) is positive, the net unearned income will be taxed at the parents' rate. The $850 amounts in the preceding formula are subject to adjustment for inflation each year.

Find more information on this topic at our Web site: ***http://wft-entities.swlearning.com.***

DIGGING DEEPER
6

Election to Report Certain Unearned Income on Parent's Return.

If a child under age 14 is required to file a tax return and meets all of the following requirements, the parent may elect to report the child's unearned income that exceeds $1,700 on the parent's own tax return:

- Gross income is from interest and dividends only.
- Gross income is more than $850 but less than $8,500.
- No estimated tax has been paid in the name and Social Security number of the child, and the child is not subject to backup withholding.

[30] § 1(g).

If the parental election is made, the child is treated as having no gross income and then is not required to file a tax return.

The parent(s) must also pay an additional tax equal to the smaller of $85 or 10 percent of the child's gross income over $850. Parents who have substantial itemized deductions based on AGI may find that making the parental election increases total taxes for the family unit. Taxes should be calculated both with the parental election and without it to determine the appropriate choice.

PLANNING *Strategies*

INCOME OF MINOR CHILDREN

★ **Framework Focus: Tax Rate**

Strategy ★ Shift Net Income from High-Bracket Taxpayers to Low-Bracket Taxpayers.

Taxpayers can use several strategies to avoid or minimize the effect of the rules that tax the unearned income of certain minor children at the parents' rate. The kiddie tax rules do not apply once a child reaches age 14. Parents should consider giving a younger child assets that defer the inclusion in gross income until the child reaches age 14. For example, U.S. government Series EE savings bonds can be used to defer income until the bonds are cashed in.

Growth stocks typically pay little in the way of dividends. However, the unrealized appreciation on an astute investment may more than offset the lack of dividends. The child can hold the growth stock until he or she reaches age 14. If the stock is sold then at a profit, the profit is taxed at the child's low rates.

Taxpayers in a position to do so can employ their children in their business and pay them a reasonable wage for the work they actually perform (e.g., light office help, such as filing). The child's earned income is sheltered by the standard deduction, and the parents' business is allowed a deduction for the wages. The kiddie tax rules have no effect on earned income, even if it is earned from the parents' business.

LO.6

Recognize filing requirements and proper filing status.

Filing Considerations

Under the category of filing considerations, the following questions need to be resolved:

- Is the taxpayer required to file an income tax return?
- If so, which form should be used?
- When and how should the return be filed?
- In computing the tax liability, which column of the Tax Table or which Tax Rate Schedule should be used?

The first three questions are discussed under Filing Requirements, and the last is treated under Filing Status.

Filing Requirements

General Rules. An individual must file a tax return if certain minimum amounts of gross income have been received. The general rule is that a tax return is required for every individual who has gross income that equals or exceeds the sum of the exemption amount plus the applicable standard deduction.[31] For example, a single taxpayer under age 65 must file a tax return in 2006 if gross income equals or exceeds $8,450 ($3,300 exemption plus $5,150 standard deduction).[32]

DIGGING DEEPER 7

Find more information on this topic at our Web site: ***http://wft-entities.swlearning.com.***

[31]The exemption and standard deduction amounts for determining whether a tax return must be filed are adjusted for inflation each year.

[32]§ 6012(a)(1).

The additional standard deduction for being age 65 or older is considered in determining the gross income filing requirements. For example, the 2006 filing requirement for a single taxpayer age 65 or older is $9,700 ($5,150 basic standard deduction + $1,250 additional standard deduction + $3,300 exemption).

A self-employed individual with net earnings of $400 or more from a business or profession must file a tax return regardless of the amount of gross income.

Even though an individual has gross income below the filing level amounts and therefore does not owe any tax, he or she must file a return to obtain a tax refund of amounts withheld by employers. A return is also necessary to obtain the benefits of the earned income credit allowed to taxpayers with little or no tax liability.

Filing Requirements for Dependents. Computation of the gross income filing requirement for an individual who can be claimed as a dependent on another person's tax return is subject to more complex rules. For example, such an individual must file a return if he or she has earned income only and it is more than the total standard deduction (including any additional standard deduction) that the individual is allowed for the year.

DIGGING DEEPER 8

Find more information on this topic at our Web site: ***http://wft-entities.swlearning.com.***

Selecting the Proper Form. Although a variety of forms are available to individual taxpayers, the use of some of these forms is restricted. For example, Form 1040EZ cannot be used if the:

- Taxpayer claims any dependents;
- Taxpayer (or spouse) is 65 or older or blind; or
- Taxable income is $100,000 or more.

Taxpayers who desire to itemize deductions *from* AGI cannot use Form 1040A, but must file Form 1040 (the long form).

The E-File Approach. In addition to traditional paper returns, the **e-file** program is an increasingly popular alternative. Here, the required tax information is transmitted to the IRS electronically either directly from the taxpayer (i.e., an "e-file online return") or indirectly through an electronic return originator (ERO). EROs are tax professionals who have been accepted into the electronic filing program by the IRS. Such parties hold themselves out to the general public as "authorized IRS e-file providers." Providers often are also the preparers of the return.

The e-file approach has two major advantages. First, compliance with the format required by the IRS eliminates many errors that would otherwise occur. Second, the time required for processing a refund usually is reduced to three weeks or less.

When and Where to File. Tax returns of individuals are due on or before the fifteenth day of the fourth month following the close of the tax year. For the calendar year taxpayer, the usual filing date is on or before April 15 of the following year.[33] When the due date falls on a Saturday, Sunday, or legal holiday, the last day for filing falls on the next business day.

If a taxpayer is unable to file the return by the specified due date, an automatic six-month extension of time can be obtained.[34] Although obtaining an extension excuses a taxpayer from a penalty for failure to file, it does not insulate against the penalty for failure to pay. If more tax is owed, the extension request should be accompanied by an additional payment to cover the balance due. The return

[33]§ 6072(a).

[34]Reg. § 1.6081–4. File Form 4868 to receive the automatic extension.

TAX FACT

What Form of Tax Compliance Is Right for You?

Based on recent projections from the IRS, when preparing over 134 million individual income tax returns expected to be filed in 2006, taxpayers mostly will be using Forms 1040, 1040A, and 1040EZ. But importantly, the IRS expects the level of electronically filed returns to be at an all-time high.

	Percentage
Paper individual returns	44.68
Electronically filed individual returns	55.32
	100.00

Source: *Fiscal Year Return Projections for the United States: 2005–2012, Internal Revenue Service, Office of Research, October 2005.*

should be sent or delivered to the Regional Service Center listed in the instructions for each type of return or contained in software applications.[35]

Mode of Payment. Usually, payment is made by check. However, the IRS may now accept debit, credit, or charge cards for the payment of Federal income taxes. The entity providing the credit will charge the taxpayer a fee based on the size of the payment.

Filing Status

The amount of tax will vary considerably depending on which filing status is used. This is illustrated in the following example.

EXAMPLE 33

The following amounts of tax (rounded to the nearest dollar) are computed using the 2006 Tax Rate Schedules (inside the front cover of this text). The taxpayer (or taxpayers in the case of a joint return) is assumed to have $40,000 of taxable income.

Filing Status	Amount of Tax
Single	$6,558
Married, filing joint return	5,245
Married, filing separate return	6,558
Head of household	5,462

■

Rates for Single Taxpayers. A taxpayer who is unmarried or separated from his or her spouse by a decree of divorce or separate maintenance and does not qualify for another filing status must use the rates for single taxpayers. Marital status is determined as of the last day of the tax year, except when a spouse dies during the year. In that case, marital status is determined as of the date of death.

Rates for Married Individuals. The joint filing status was originally enacted to establish equity between married taxpayers in common law states and those in

[35]The Regional Service Centers and the geographic area each covers can also be found at **http://www.irs.gov/file** or in the tax forms packages.

GLOBAL *Tax Issues*

FILING A JOINT RETURN

John Garth is a U.S. citizen and resident, but spends a lot of time in London where his employer sends him on frequent assignments. John is married to Victoria, a citizen and resident of the United Kingdom.

Can John and Victoria file a joint return for U.S. Federal income tax purposes? Although § 6013(a)(1) specifically precludes the filing of a joint return if one spouse is a nonresident alien, another Code provision permits an exception. Under § 6013(g), the parties can elect to treat the nonqualifying spouse as a "resident" of the United States. This election would allow John and Victoria to file jointly.

But should John and Victoria make this election? If Victoria has considerable income of her own (from non-U.S. sources), the election could be ill-advised. As a nonresident alien, Victoria's non-U.S. source income *would not* be subject to the U.S. income tax. If she is treated as a U.S. resident, however, her non-U.S. source income *will be subject to U.S. tax*. Under the U.S. global approach to taxation, all income (regardless of where earned) of anyone who is a *resident* or *citizen* of the United States is subject to tax.

community property states. Before the joint return rates were enacted, taxpayers in community property states were in an advantageous position relative to taxpayers in common law states because they could split their income.

Taxpayers in common law states did not have this income-splitting option, so their taxable income was subject to higher marginal rates. This inconsistency in treatment was remedied by the joint return provisions. The progressive rates in the joint return Tax Rate Schedule are constructed based on the assumption that income is earned equally by the two spouses.

If married individuals elect to file separate returns, each reports only his or her own income, exemptions, deductions, and credits, and each must use the Tax Rate Schedule applicable to married taxpayers filing separately. It is generally advantageous for married individuals to file a joint return, since the combined amount of tax is lower. However, special circumstances (e.g., significant medical expenses incurred by one spouse subject to the 7.5 percent limitation) may warrant the election to file separate returns. It may be necessary to compute the tax under both assumptions to determine the most advantageous filing status.

When Congress enacted the joint return filing status, the result was to favor married taxpayers. In certain situations, however, the parties would incur less tax if they were not married and filed separate returns. The additional tax that a joint return caused, commonly called the **marriage penalty**, develop when *both* spouses had significant taxable incomes.

DIGGING DEEPER 9

Find more information on this topic at our Web site: ***http://wft-entities.swlearning.com.***

The joint return rates also apply for two years following the death of one's spouse, if the **surviving spouse** maintains a household for a dependent child.[36] The child must be a son, stepson, daughter, or stepdaughter who qualifies as a dependent of the taxpayer. This is referred to as surviving spouse status.

Rates for Heads of Household. Unmarried individuals who maintain a household for a dependent (or dependents) are entitled to use the **head-of-household** rates.[37] The tax liability resulting from the head-of-household rates falls between

[36] § 2(a). The IRS label for surviving spouse status is "Qualifying Widow(er) with Dependent Child."

[37] § 2(b).

BRIDGE *Discipline*

Bridge to Equity or Fairness

Much has been made in the press and in political circles in recent years concerning the so-called marriage penalty tax. This marriage penalty refers to the additional income tax that married couples pay over and above the aggregate amount two single individuals would pay with equal amounts of income. The marriage penalty arose because of the nature of the income tax rate structure that applies to individual taxpayers.

Relevant policy and ethical issues related to this dilemma are:

- Should the income tax system contain a bias against marriage?
- Should the income tax system require two people of economic means equal to that of two other people to pay a different amount of income taxes?
- Should the income tax system encourage two individuals to cohabit outside the commitment of marriage?

Long aware of the inequity of the marriage penalty, Congress reduced the effect of the problem in the JGTRRA of 2003. Beginning in 2003, the standard deduction available to married filers increased to 200 percent of that applicable to single persons. Furthermore and also beginning in 2003, the 15 percent bracket for joint filers increased to 200 percent of the size of that applicable to single filers.

the liability using the joint return Tax Rate Schedule and the liability using the Tax Rate Schedule for single taxpayers.

To qualify for head-of-household rates, a taxpayer must pay more than half the cost of maintaining a household as his or her home. The household must also be the principal home of a dependent. As a general rule, the dependent must live in the taxpayer's household for over half the year.

DIGGING DEEPER 10

Find more information on this topic at our Web site: ***http://wft-entities.swlearning.com.***

LO.7

Identify specific inclusions and exclusions applicable to individuals.

Overview of Income Provisions Applicable to Individuals

As indicated earlier in this chapter, the definition of gross income is broad enough to include almost all receipts of money, property, or services. However, the tax law provides for exclusion of many types of income. The following income provisions, which apply to all taxpayers (including individuals), were discussed in Chapter 4:

- Interest from state and local bonds.
- Life insurance paid on death of the insured.
- Imputed interest on below-market loans.
- Income from discharge of indebtedness.
- Income included under the tax benefit rule.

Most *exclusions* available only to individuals are for *fringe benefits* received by *employees* (refer to Exhibit 16–1). Fringe benefits are discussed in Chapter 17. Other specific inclusions and exclusions for individuals are discussed below.

Specific Inclusions Applicable to Individuals

The general principles of gross income determination as applied by the IRS and the courts have on occasion yielded results Congress found unacceptable.

BRIDGE *Discipline*

Bridge to Economics and Finance

As is the case for business entities, a primary financial goal for individual taxpayers should entail maximizing the *after-tax value* of their assets over time. This approach requires not only selecting the best investment alternatives, but also choosing those investments with the most favorable tax attributes. Fundamental to this notion is recognizing the key role that the government plays in all economic activity through its taxing authority. As a result, an investor should consider economically sound strategies that minimize the extent to which the government can stake a claim to his or her success. For example, taxpayers can reduce the government's share of their wealth accumulations by deferring the payment of taxes until future years and by taking advantage of investment strategies for which tax incentives are available. Taxpayers should choose the investment alternatives that provide the best after-tax return over time and not necessarily the ones that lead to the least amount of taxation.

These points can be illustrated by examining two classic strategies. One of the best ways for individuals to maximize their personal wealth is to invest to the extent possible in qualifying retirement savings programs [e.g., traditional Individual Retirement Accounts, § 401(k) accounts]. Not only do current additions to such accounts provide a current tax deduction, but earnings within the account are not subject to taxation until they are withdrawn, which, in most cases, is during the retirement years of the owner. Postponing the tax in these two ways reduces the present value of the tax cost, which increases the after-tax value of the investment. Another strategy involves investing in tax-free municipal bonds, which produce interest income that is free of Federal income tax. The returns from such investments, however, should be compared with the after-tax returns flowing from available taxable debt securities. For example, a relevant question is how the implicit tax (see Chapter 1) associated with a municipal bond compares with the explicit tax associated with a taxable bond.

Consequently, Congress has provided more specific rules for determining the amount of gross income from certain sources. Some of these special rules appear in §§ 71–90 of the Code. The following provisions applicable to individuals are covered in this chapter:

- Alimony and separate maintenance payments.
- Prizes and awards.
- Unemployment compensation.
- Social Security benefits.

Alimony and Separate Maintenance Payments

When a married couple divorce or become legally separated, state law generally requires a division of the property accumulated during the marriage. In addition, one spouse may have a legal obligation to support the other spouse. The Code distinguishes between the support payments (alimony or separate maintenance) and the property division in terms of the tax consequences.

Alimony and separate maintenance payments are deductible by the party making the payments and are includible in the gross income of the party receiving the payments.[38] Thus, taxation of the income is shifted from the income earner to the income beneficiary.

EXAMPLE 34

Pete and Tina are divorced, and Pete is required to pay Tina $15,000 of alimony each year. Pete earns $50,000 a year. Therefore, Tina must include the $15,000 in her gross income, and Pete is allowed to deduct $15,000 from his gross income. ■

[38]§§ 71 and 215.

A transfer of property other than cash to a former spouse under a divorce decree or agreement is not a taxable event. The transferor is not entitled to a deduction and does not recognize gain or loss on the transfer. The transferee does not recognize income and has a cost basis equal to the transferor's basis.[39]

EXAMPLE 35

Paul transfers stock to Rosa as part of a 2006 divorce settlement. The cost of the stock to Paul is $12,000, and the stock's fair market value at the time of the transfer is $15,000. Rosa later sells the stock for $16,000. Paul is not required to recognize gain from the transfer of the stock to Rosa, and Rosa has a realized *and* recognized gain of $4,000 ($16,000 – $12,000) when she sells the stock. ■

In the case of cash payments, however, it is often difficult to distinguish between support payments (alimony) and property settlements. In 1984, Congress developed objective rules to classify these payments.[40]

DIGGING DEEPER 11

Find more information on this topic at our Web site: ***http://wft-entities.swlearning.com.***

Child Support. While alimony is taxable, a taxpayer does *not* report income from the receipt of child support payments made by his or her former spouse. This result occurs because the money is received subject to the duty to use the money for the child's benefit. The payor is not allowed to deduct the child support payments because the payments are made to satisfy the payor's legal obligation to support the child.

In many cases, it is difficult to determine whether an amount received is alimony or child support. If the amount of the payments would be reduced upon the happening of a contingency related to a child (e.g., the child attains age 21 or dies), the amount of the future reduction in the payment is deemed child support.[41]

EXAMPLE 36

A divorce agreement provides that Matt is required to make periodic alimony payments of $500 per month to Grace. However, when Matt and Grace's child reaches age 21, marries, or dies (whichever occurs first), the payments will be reduced to $300 per month. Child support payments are $200 each month, and alimony is $300 each month. ■

Prizes and Awards

The fair market value of prizes and awards must be included in gross income.[42] Therefore, TV giveaway prizes, magazine publisher prizes, door prizes, and awards from an employer to an employee in recognition of performance are fully taxable to the recipient.

A narrow exception permits a prize or award to be excluded from gross income if *all* of the following requirements are satisfied:

- The prize or award is received in recognition of religious, charitable, scientific, educational, artistic, literary, or civic achievement (e.g., Nobel Prize, Pulitzer Prize).
- The recipient was selected without taking any action to enter the contest or proceeding.
- The recipient is not required to render substantial future services as a condition for receiving the prize or award.[43]

[39]Section 1041 was added to the Code in 1984 to repeal the rule of *U.S. v. Davis*, 62–2 USTC ¶9509, 9 AFTR2d 1625, 82 S.Ct. 1190 (USSC, 1962). Under the *Davis* rule, which applied to pre-1985 divorces, a property transfer incident to divorce was a taxable event.

[40]More complex rules existed for determining the nature of payments under pre-1985 agreements.

[41]§ 71(c)(2).

[42]§ 74.

[43]§ 74(b).

- The recipient arranges for the prize or award to be paid *directly* to a qualified governmental unit or nonprofit organization.

Another exception is provided to allow exclusion of certain employee achievement awards in the form of tangible personal property (e.g., a gold watch). The awards must be made in recognition of length of service or safety achievement. Generally, the ceiling on the excludible amount for an employee is $400 per taxable year. However, if the award is a *qualified plan award,* the ceiling on the exclusion is $1,600 per taxable year.[44]

Unemployment Compensation

The unemployment compensation program is sponsored and operated by the states and Federal government to provide a source of income for people who have been employed and are temporarily out of work. In a series of rulings over a period of 40 years, the IRS exempted unemployment benefits from tax. These payments were considered social benefit programs for the promotion of the general welfare. After experiencing dissatisfaction with the IRS's treatment of unemployment compensation, Congress amended the Code to provide that the benefits are taxable.[45]

Social Security Benefits

If a taxpayer's income exceeds a specified base amount, as much as 50 or 85 percent of Social Security retirement benefits must be included in gross income. The taxable amount of benefits is determined through the application of one of two complex formulas described in § 86.

Find more information on this topic at our Web site: ***http://wft-entities.swlearning.com.***

DIGGING DEEPER 12

Specific Exclusions Applicable to Individuals

Gifts and Inheritances

Beginning with the Income Tax Act of 1913 and continuing to the present, Congress has allowed the recipient of a **gift** to exclude the value of the property from gross income. The exclusion applies to gifts made during the life of the donor (*inter vivos* gifts) and transfers that take effect upon the death of the donor (bequests and inheritances).[46] However, the recipient of a gift of income-producing property is subject to tax on the income subsequently earned from the property. Also, as discussed in Chapter 1, the donor or the decedent's estate may be subject to gift or estate taxes on such transfers.

In numerous cases, gifts are made in a business setting. For example, a salesperson gives a purchasing agent free samples; an employee receives cash from his or her employer on retirement; a corporation makes payments to employees who were victims of a natural disaster; a corporation makes a cash payment to a deceased employee's spouse. In these and similar instances, it is frequently unclear whether the payment was a gift or whether it represents compensation for past, present, or future services.

The courts have defined a gift as "a voluntary transfer of property by one to another without adequate consideration or compensation therefrom."[47] If the payment is intended to be for services rendered, it is not a gift, even though the payment is made without legal or moral obligation and the payor receives no

[44] §§ 74(c) and 274(j).
[45] § 85.
[46] § 102.
[47] *Estate of D. R. Daly,* 3 B.T.A. 1042 (1926).

TAX *in the News* **BEGGING AS A TAX-DISFAVORED OCCUPATION**

In five recent decisions, the Tax Court ruled that amounts received from begging are nontaxable gifts. In a reversal of the normal roles, the beggars contended that the amounts received were earned income while the IRS argued that the taxpayers had merely received gifts. The beggars wanted the fruit of their efforts to be treated as earned income in order to qualify them for the earned income credit.

economic benefit from the transfer. To qualify as a gift, the payment must be made "out of affection, respect, admiration, charity or like impulses."[48] Thus, the cases on this issue have been decided on the basis of the donor's intent.[49]

In the case of cash or other property received by an employee from his or her employer, Congress has eliminated any ambiguity. Transfers from an employee to an employee cannot be excluded as a gift.[50]

DIGGING DEEPER 13

Find more information on this topic at our Web site: ***http://wft-entities.swlearning.com.***

Scholarships

General Information. Payments or benefits received by a student at an educational institution may be (1) compensation for services, (2) a gift, or (3) a scholarship. If the payments or benefits are received as compensation for services (past or present), the fact that the recipient is a student generally does not render the amounts received nontaxable.[51]

EXAMPLE 37

State University waives tuition for all graduate teaching assistants. The tuition waived is intended as compensation for services and is therefore included in the graduate assistant's gross income. ■

The **scholarship** rules are intended to provide exclusion treatment for education-related benefits that cannot qualify as gifts but are not compensation for services. According to the Regulations, "a scholarship is an amount paid or allowed to, or for the benefit of, an individual to aid such individual in the pursuit of study or research."[52] The recipient must be a candidate for a degree at an educational institution.[53]

EXAMPLE 38

Terry enters a contest sponsored by a local newspaper. Each contestant is required to submit an essay on local environmental issues. The prize is one year's tuition at State University. Terry wins the contest. The newspaper has a legal obligation to Terry (as the contest winner). Thus, the benefits are not a gift. However, since the tuition payment aids Terry in pursuing her studies and is not compensation for services, the payment is a scholarship. ■

A scholarship recipient may exclude from gross income the amount used for tuition and related expenses (fees, books, supplies, and equipment required for

[48] *Robertson v. U.S.*, 52–1 USTC ¶9343, 41 AFTR 1053, 72 S.Ct. 994 (USSC, 1952).

[49] See, for example, *Comm. v. Duberstein*, 60–2 USTC ¶9515, 5 AFTR2d 1626, 80 S.Ct. 1190 (USSC, 1960).

[50] § 102(c).

[51] Reg. § 1.117–2(a). See *C. P. Bhalla*, 35 T.C. 13 (1960), for a discussion of the distinction between a scholarship and compensation. See also *Bingler v. Johnson*, 69–1 USTC ¶9348, 23 AFTR2d 1212, 89 S.Ct. 1439 (USSC, 1969). For potential exclusion treatment, see the discussion of qualified tuition reductions in Chapter 17.

[52] Prop.Reg. § 1.117–6(c)(3)(i).

[53] § 117(a).

courses), provided the conditions of the grant do not require that the funds be used for other purposes.[54] Amounts received for room and board are taxable and are treated as earned income for purposes of calculating the standard deduction for a taxpayer who is another taxpayer's dependent.[55]

EXAMPLE 39

Kelly receives a scholarship of $9,500 from State University to be used to pursue a bachelor's degree. She spends $4,000 on tuition, $3,000 on books and supplies, and $2,500 for room and board. Kelly may exclude $7,000 ($4,000 + $3,000) from gross income. The $2,500 spent for room and board is includible in Kelly's gross income.

The scholarship is Kelly's only source of income. Her parents provide more than 50% of Kelly's support and claim her as a dependent. Kelly's standard deduction of $2,800 ($2,500 + $300) exceeds her $2,500 gross income. Thus, she has no taxable income. ■

Timing Issues. Frequently, the scholarship recipient is a cash basis taxpayer who receives the money in one tax year but pays the educational expenses in a subsequent year. The amount eligible for exclusion may not be known at the time the money is received. In that case, the transaction is held open until the educational expenses are paid.[56]

EXAMPLE 40

In August 2006, Sanjay received $10,000 as a scholarship for the academic year 2006–2007. Sanjay's expenditures for tuition, books, and supplies were as follows:

August–December 2006	$3,000
January–May 2007	4,500
	$7,500

Sanjay's gross income for 2007 includes $2,500 ($10,000 – $7,500) that is not excludible as a scholarship. None of the scholarship is included in his gross income in 2006. ■

Disguised Compensation. Some employers make scholarships available solely to the children of key employees. The tax objective of these plans is to provide a nontaxable fringe benefit to the executives by making the payment to the child in the form of an excludible scholarship. However, the IRS has ruled that the payments are generally includible by the parent-employee as compensation for services.[57]

Damages

A person who suffers harm caused by another is often entitled to **compensatory damages**. The tax consequences of the receipt of damages depend on the type of harm the taxpayer has experienced. The taxpayer may seek recovery for (1) a loss of income, (2) expenses incurred, (3) property destroyed, or (4) personal injury.

Generally, reimbursement for a loss of income is taxed in the same manner as the income replaced (see the exception under Personal Injury below). Damages that are a recovery of expenses previously deducted by the taxpayer are generally taxable under the tax benefit rule (refer to Chapter 4).

A payment for damaged or destroyed property is treated as an amount received in a sale or exchange of the property. Thus, the taxpayer has a realized gain if the damage payments received exceed the property's basis. Damages for personal injuries receive special treatment under the Code.

Personal Injury. The legal theory of personal injury damages is that the amount received is intended "to make the plaintiff [the injured party] whole as before the

[54]§ 117(b).
[55]Prop.Reg. § 1.117–6(h).
[56]Prop.Reg. § 1.117–6(b)(2).
[57]Rev.Rul. 75–448, 1975–2 C.B. 55 and *Richard T. Armantrout*, 67 T.C. 996 (1977).

CONCEPT SUMMARY 16–2

Taxation of Damages

Type of Claim	Taxation of Award or Settlement
Breach of contract (generally loss of income)	Taxable.
Property damages	Recovery of cost; gain to the extent of the excess over basis. A loss is deductible for business property and investment property to the extent of basis over the amount realized. A loss may be deductible for personal-use property (see discussion of casualty losses in Chapter 6).
Personal injury	
Physical	All compensatory amounts are excluded unless previously deducted (e.g., medical expenses). Amounts received as punitive damages are included in gross income.
Nonphysical	Compensatory damages and punitive damages are included in gross income.

injury."[58] It follows that if the damage payments received were subject to tax, the after-tax amount received would be less than the actual damages incurred and the injured party would not be "whole as before the injury."

With regard to personal injury damages, a distinction is made between compensatory damages and **punitive damages**. Under specified circumstances, compensatory damages may be excluded from gross income. Under no circumstances may punitive damages be excluded from gross income.

Compensatory damages are intended to compensate the taxpayer for the damages incurred. Only those compensatory damages received on account of *physical personal injury or sickness* can be excluded from gross income.[59] Such exclusion treatment includes amounts received for loss of income associated with the physical personal injury or physical sickness. Compensatory damages awarded on account of emotional distress are not received on account of physical injury or sickness and thus cannot be excluded from gross income (except to the extent of any amount received for medical care). Likewise, any amounts received for age discrimination or injury to one's reputation cannot be excluded.

Punitive damages are amounts the party that caused the harm must pay to the victim as punishment for outrageous conduct. Punitive damages are not intended to compensate the victim, but rather to punish the party that caused the harm. Thus, it follows that amounts received as punitive damages may actually place the victim in a better economic position than before the harm was experienced. Logically, punitive damages are thus included in gross income.

EXAMPLE 41

Tom, a television announcer, was dissatisfied with the manner in which Ron, an attorney, was defending the television station in a libel case. Tom stated on the air that Ron was botching the case. Ron sued Tom for slander, claiming damages for loss of income from clients and potential clients who heard Tom's statement. Ron's claim is for damages to his business reputation, and the amounts received are taxable.

Ron collected on the suit against Tom and was on his way to a party to celebrate his victory when a negligent driver, Norm, drove a truck into Ron's automobile, injuring Ron. Ron filed suit for the physical personal injuries and claimed as damages the loss of income for the

[58] *C. A. Hawkins*, 6 B.T.A. 1023 (1928).

[59] § 104(a)(2).

period he was unable to work as a result of the injuries. Ron also collected punitive damages that were awarded because of Norm's extremely negligent behavior. Ron's wife also collected damages for the emotional distress she experienced as a result of the accident. Ron may exclude the amounts he received for damages, except the punitive damages. Ron's wife must include the amounts she received for damages in gross income because the amounts were not received because of physical personal injuries or sickness. ■

Workers' Compensation

State workers' compensation laws require the employer to pay fixed amounts for specific job-related injuries. The state laws were enacted so that the employee will not have to go through the ordeal of a lawsuit (and possibly not collect damages because of some defense available to the employer) to recover the damages. Although the payments are intended, in part, to compensate for a loss of future income, Congress has specifically exempted workers' compensation benefits from inclusion in gross income.[60]

Accident and Health Insurance Benefits

The income tax treatment of **accident and health insurance benefits** depends on whether the policy providing the benefits was purchased by the taxpayer or the taxpayer's employer. Benefits collected under an accident and health insurance policy purchased by the taxpayer are excludible. In this case, benefits collected under the taxpayer's insurance policy are excluded even though the payments are a substitute for income.[61]

EXAMPLE 42

Bonnie purchases a medical and disability insurance policy. The insurance company pays Bonnie $1,000 per week to replace wages she loses while in the hospital. Although the payments serve as a substitute for income, the amounts received are tax-exempt benefits collected under Bonnie's insurance policy. ■

EXAMPLE 43

Joe's injury results in a partial paralysis of his left foot. He receives $20,000 for the injury from his accident insurance company under a policy he had purchased. The $20,000 accident insurance proceeds are tax-exempt. ■

A different set of rules applies if the accident and health insurance protection was purchased by the individual's employer, as discussed in Chapter 17.

Educational Savings Bonds

The cost of a college education has risen dramatically during the past 15 years. The U.S. Department of Education estimates that by the year 2007, the cost of attending a publicly supported university for four years will exceed $60,000. For a private university, the cost is expected to exceed $200,000. Consequently, Congress has attempted to assist low- to middle-income parents in saving for their children's college education.

The assistance is in the form of an interest income exclusion on **educational savings bonds**.[62] The interest on U.S. government Series EE savings bonds may be excluded from gross income if the bond proceeds are used to pay qualified higher education expenses. The exclusion applies only if both of the following requirements are satisfied:

[60] § 104(a)(1).

[61] § 104(a)(3).

[62] § 135.

- The savings bonds are issued after December 31, 1989.
- The savings bonds are issued to an individual who is at least 24 years old at the time of issuance.

The redemption proceeds must be used to pay qualified higher education expenses. Qualified higher education expenses consist of tuition and fees paid to an eligible educational institution for the taxpayer, spouse, or dependent. In calculating qualified higher education expenses, the tuition and fees paid are reduced by excludible scholarships and veterans' benefits received. If the redemption proceeds (both principal and interest) exceed the qualified higher education expenses, only a pro rata portion of the interest will qualify for exclusion treatment.

EXAMPLE 44

Tracy's redemption proceeds from qualified savings bonds during the taxable year are $6,000 (principal of $4,000 and interest of $2,000). Tracy's qualified higher education expenses are $5,000. Since the redemption proceeds exceed the qualified higher education expenses, only $1,667 [($5,000/$6,000) × $2,000] of the interest is excludible. ■

The exclusion is limited by the application of the wherewithal to pay concept. That is, once the *modified AGI (MAGI)* exceeds a threshold amount, the phaseout of the exclusion begins. The threshold amounts are adjusted for inflation each year. For 2006, the phaseout begins at $63,100 ($94,700 on a joint return).[63] The phaseout is completed when MAGI exceeds the threshold amount by more than $15,000 ($30,000 on a joint return). The otherwise excludible interest is reduced by the amount calculated as follows:

$$\frac{\text{MAGI} - \$63{,}100}{\$15{,}000} \times \begin{array}{c}\text{Excludible interest}\\ \text{before phaseout}\end{array} = \begin{array}{c}\text{Reduction in}\\ \text{excludible interest}\end{array}$$

On a joint return, $94,700 is substituted for $63,100 (in 2006), and $30,000 is substituted for $15,000.

EXAMPLE 45

Assume the same facts as in Example 44, except that Tracy's MAGI for 2006 is $70,000. The phaseout results in Tracy's interest exclusion being reduced by $767 {[($70,000 – $63,100)/$15,000] × $1,667}. Therefore, Tracy's exclusion is $900 ($1,667 – $767). ■

LO.8

Determine an individual's allowable itemized deductions.

Itemized Deductions

Taxpayers are allowed to deduct specified expenditures as itemized deductions. Itemized deductions, which are reported on Schedule A, can be classified as follows:

- Expenses that are purely *personal* in nature.
- Expenses incurred by *employees* in connection with their employment activities.
- Expenses related to (1) the *production or collection of income* and (2) the *management of property* held for the production of income.[64]

Expenses in the third category, sometimes referred to as *nonbusiness expenses*, differ from trade or business expenses (discussed previously). Trade or business expenses, which are deductions *for* AGI, must be incurred in connection with a trade or business. Nonbusiness expenses, on the other hand, are expenses incurred in connection with an income-producing activity that does not qualify as a trade or business. If the nonbusiness expense is incurred in connection with rent or royalty property, it is classified as a deduction *for* AGI. Otherwise, it is classified as a

[63] The indexed amounts for 2005 were $61,200 and $91,850.

[64] Section 212 allows itemized deductions for these types of activities. However, expenses related to the production of *rental or royalty income* are deductions *for* AGI, not itemized deductions, under § 62(a)(4).

EXHIBIT 16–3 **Partial List of Itemized Deductions**

Personal Expenditures
Medical expenses (in excess of 7.5% of AGI)
State and local income taxes or sales taxes
Real estate taxes
Personal property taxes
Interest on home mortgage
Charitable contributions (limited to a maximum of 50% of AGI)
Casualty and theft losses (in excess of 10% of AGI)
Tax return preparation fee (in excess of 2% of AGI)

Expenditures Related to Employment (in Excess of 2% of AGI)
Union dues
Professional dues and subscriptions
Certain educational expenses
Unreimbursed employee business expenses

Expenditures Related to Income-Producing Activities
Investment interest (to the extent of investment income)
Investment counsel fees (in excess of 2% of AGI)
Other investment expenses (in excess of 2% of AGI)

deduction *from* AGI. Itemized deductions include, but are not limited to, the expenses listed in Exhibit 16–3.

Allowable itemized deductions are deductible *from* AGI in arriving at taxable income if the taxpayer elects to itemize. The election to itemize is appropriate when total itemized deductions exceed the standard deduction based on the taxpayer's filing status. The more important itemized deductions are discussed below.

Medical Expenses

Medical Expenses Defined. **Medical expenses** paid for the care of the taxpayer, spouse, and dependents are allowed as an itemized deduction to the extent the expenses are not reimbursed. The medical expense deduction is limited to the amount by which such expenses exceed 7.5 percent of the taxpayer's AGI.

EXAMPLE 46

During the year, Iris had medical expenses of $4,800, of which $1,000 was reimbursed by her insurance company. If her AGI for the year is $40,000, the itemized deduction for medical expenses is limited to $800 [$4,800 – $1,000 = $3,800 – (7.5% × $40,000)]. ■

The term *medical care* includes expenditures incurred for the "diagnosis, cure, mitigation, treatment, or prevention of disease, or for the purpose of affecting any structure or function of the body."[65] Medical expense also includes premiums paid for health care insurance, prescribed drugs and insulin, and lodging while away from home for the purpose of obtaining medical care. Examples of deductible and nondeductible medical expenses appear in Exhibit 16–4.

Cosmetic Surgery. Amounts paid for unnecessary cosmetic surgery are not deductible medical expenses. However, if cosmetic surgery is deemed necessary, it is deductible as a medical expense. Cosmetic surgery is necessary when it ameliorates (1) a deformity arising from a congenital abnormality, (2) a personal injury, or (3) a disfiguring disease.

[65] § 213(d).

EXHIBIT 16–4 **Examples of Deductible and Nondeductible Medical Expenses**

Deductible	Nondeductible
Medical (including dental, mental, and hospital) care	Funeral, burial, or cremation expenses
Prescription drugs	Nonprescription drugs (except insulin)
Special equipment	Bottled water
Wheelchairs	Diaper service, maternity clothes
Crutches	Programs for the general improvement of health
Artificial limbs	Weight reduction
Eyeglasses (including contact lenses)	Health spas
Hearing aids	Social activities (e.g., dancing and swimming lessons)
Transportation for medical care	Unnecessary cosmetic surgery
Medical and hospital insurance premiums	
Long-term care insurance premiums (subject to limitations)	
Cost of alcohol and drug rehabilitation	
Certain costs to stop smoking	
Weight reduction programs related to obesity	

Nursing Home Care. The cost of care in a nursing home or home for the aged, including meals and lodging, can be included in deductible medical expenses if the primary reason for being in the home is to get medical care. If the primary reason for being there is personal, any costs for medical or nursing care can be included in deductible medical expenses, but the cost of meals and lodging must be excluded.

Capital Expenditures. The treatment of certain illnesses may require expenditures for equipment, special structures, or modification of the taxpayer's residence. Some examples of capital expenditures for medical purposes are swimming pools if the taxpayer does not have access to a neighborhood pool and air conditioners if they do not become permanent improvements (e.g., window units).[66] Other examples include dust elimination systems,[67] elevators,[68] and a room built to house an iron lung. These expenditures are medical in nature if they are incurred as a medical necessity upon the advice of a physician, the facility is used primarily by the patient alone, and the expense is reasonable.

Capital expenditures normally are adjustments to basis and are deductible only through depreciation. However, both a capital expenditure for a permanent improvement and expenditures made for the operation or maintenance of the improvement may qualify as medical expenses. If a capital expenditure qualifies as a medical expense, the allowable amount is deductible in the *year incurred.* The allowable amount is the excess of the cost of the capital expenditure over the increase in the value of the related property.

[66]Rev.Rul. 55–261, 1955–1 C.B. 307, modified by Rev.Rul. 68–212, 1968–1 C.B. 91.

[67]*F. S. Delp*, 30 T.C. 1230 (1958).

[68]*Riach v. Frank*, 62–1 USTC ¶9419, 9 AFTR2d 1263, 302 F.2d 374 (CA–9, 1962).

TAX *in the News* **THE PRESIDENT AND VICE PRESIDENT ITEMIZE**

Approximately two-thirds of all individual taxpayers take the standard deduction each year rather than itemize. President George W. Bush and Vice President Richard B. Cheney are among the one-third who itemize. The President, who files a joint return with his wife, released his 2004 tax return to the public. The itemized deductions, along with certain other information from the Bush tax return, are shown in the column to the right.

Vice President Cheney, who did not release Schedule A—Itemized Deductions, reported gross income of $1,747,794 and itemized deductions of $405,695.

Gross income	$784,219
Adjusted gross income	784,219
Itemized deductions:	
Medical expenses	–0–
Taxes	24,344
Interest	–0–
Charitable contributions	77,785
Job expenses and other miscellaneous deductions	28,544
Total itemized deductions	$130,673

Medical Expenses for Spouse and Dependents. In computing the medical expense deduction, a taxpayer may include medical expenses for a spouse and for a person who was a dependent at the time the expenses were paid or incurred. Of the requirements that normally apply in determining dependency status, neither the gross income nor the joint return test applies in determining dependency status for medical expense deduction purposes.

Transportation and Lodging. Payments for transportation to and from a hospital or other medical facility for medical care are deductible as medical expenses (subject to the 7.5 percent floor). Transportation expenses for medical care include bus, taxi, train, or plane fare, charges for ambulance service, and out-of-pocket expenses for the use of an automobile. A mileage allowance of 18 cents per mile[69] may be used instead of actual out-of-pocket automobile expenses. Whether the taxpayer chooses to claim out-of-pocket automobile expenses or the 18 cents per mile automatic mileage option, related parking fees and tolls can also be deducted. The cost of meals while en route to obtain medical care is not deductible.

Find more information on this topic at our Web site: ***http://wft-entities.swlearning.com.***

DIGGING DEEPER 14

Health Savings Accounts. Qualifying individuals may make deductible contributions to a **Health Savings Account (HSA)**. An HSA is a qualified trust or custodial account administered by a qualified HSA trustee, which can be a bank, insurance company, or other IRS-approved trustee. The HSA funds are used to pay for the individual's medical expenses in excess of the deductible amount under a high-deductible policy.[70]

A taxpayer can use an HSA in conjunction with a high-deductible medical insurance policy to help reduce the overall cost of medical coverage. The high-deductible policy provides coverage for extraordinary medical expenses (in excess

[69]This amount is adjusted periodically. The amount was 15 cents per mile from January 1 to August 31, 2005. The allowance was increased to 22 cents for the period September 1 through December 31, 2005.

[70]§ 223.

of the deductible), and expenses not covered by the policy can be paid with funds withdrawn from the HSA.

EXAMPLE 47

Sanchez, who is married and has three dependent children, carries a high-deductible medical insurance policy with a deductible of $4,400. He establishes an HSA and contributes the maximum allowable amount to the HSA in 2006. During 2006, the Sanchez family incurs medical expenses of $7,000. The high-deductible policy covers $2,600 of the expenses ($7,000 expenses – $4,400 deductible). Sanchez may withdraw $4,400 from the HSA to pay the medical expenses not covered by the high-deductible policy. ■

High-Deductible Plans. High-deductible policies are less expensive than low-deductible policies, so taxpayers with low medical costs can benefit from the lower premiums and use funds from the HSA to pay costs not covered by the high-deductible policy. A plan must meet two requirements to qualify as a high-deductible plan.[71]

1. The annual deductible is not less than $1,050 for self-only coverage ($2,100 for family coverage).
2. The sum of the annual deductible and other out-of-pocket costs (excluding the premiums) under the plan does not exceed $5,250 for self-only coverage ($10,500 for family coverage).

Tax Treatment of HSA Contributions and Distributions. To establish an HSA, a taxpayer contributes funds to a tax-exempt trust.[72] As illustrated in the preceding example, funds can be withdrawn from an HSA to pay medical expenses that are not covered by the high-deductible policy. The following general tax rules apply to HSAs:

1. Contributions made by the taxpayer to an HSA are deductible from gross income to arrive at AGI (deduction *for* AGI). Thus, the taxpayer does not need to itemize in order to take the deduction.
2. Earnings on HSAs are not subject to taxation unless distributed, in which case taxability depends on the way the funds are used.[73]
   - Distributions from HSAs are excluded from gross income if they are used to pay for medical expenses not covered by the high-deductible policy.
   - Distributions that are not used to pay for medical expenses are included in gross income and are subject to an additional 10 percent penalty if made before age 65, death, or disability. Such distributions made by reason of death or disability and distributions made after the HSA beneficiary becomes eligible for Medicare are taxed but not penalized.

HSAs have at least two other attractive features. First, an HSA is portable. Taxpayers who switch jobs can take their HSAs with them. Second, coverage is more widely available under the HSA rules than under the previous Archer Medical Savings Account rules. Generally, anyone under age 65 who has a high-deductible plan and is not covered by another policy that is not a high-deductible plan can establish an HSA.

Deductible Amount. The annual deduction for contributions to an HSA is limited to the sum of the monthly limitations. The monthly limitation is calculated for each month that the individual is an eligible individual. The monthly deduction is not allowed after the individual becomes eligible for Medicare coverage.

The amount of the monthly limitation for an individual who has self-only coverage in 2006 is the *lesser* of one-twelfth of the annual deductible under the high-deductible plan or $2,700. An individual who has family coverage in 2006 is limited

[71] § 223(c)(2).
[72] § 223(d).
[73] § 223(f).

to the *lesser* of one-twelfth of the annual deductible under the high-deductible plan or $5,450.[74] For an eligible taxpayer who in 2006 has attained the age of 55 by the end of the tax year, the limit on annual contributions is increased by $600. These amounts are subject to annual cost-of-living adjustments.

EXAMPLE 48

Liu, who is married and self-employed, carries a high-deductible medical insurance policy with an annual deductible of $4,000. In addition, he has established an HSA. Liu's maximum annual contribution to the HSA is $4,000 (the lesser of $5,450 or the annual deductible). ■

EXAMPLE 49

During 2006, Adam, who is self-employed, made 12 monthly payments of $700 for an HSA contract that provides medical insurance coverage with a $3,600 deductible. The plan covers Adam, his wife, and their two children. Of the $700 monthly fee, $400 was for the high-deductible policy, and $300 was deposited into an HSA. The deductible monthly contribution to the HSA is calculated as follows:

Amount of the annual deductible under the plan	$3,600
Maximum annual deduction for family coverage	5,450
Monthly limitation (1/12 of $3,600)	300

Because Adam is self-employed, he can deduct $4,800 of the amount paid for the high-deductible policy ($400 per month × 12 months) as a deduction *for* AGI (refer to Chapter 17). In addition, he can deduct the $3,600 ($300 × 12) paid to the HSA as a deduction *for* AGI. ■

Taxes

A deduction is allowed for certain state and local taxes paid or accrued by a taxpayer.[75] The deduction was created to relieve the burden of multiple taxes upon the same source of revenue.

Deductible taxes must be distinguished from nondeductible fees. Fees for special privileges or services are not deductible as itemized deductions if personal in nature. Examples include fees for dog licenses, automobile inspection, automobile titles and registration, hunting and fishing licenses, bridge and highway tolls, drivers' licenses, parking meter deposits, postage, etc. These items, however, could be deductible if incurred as a business expense or for the production of income (refer to Chapter 5). Deductible and nondeductible taxes for purposes of computing itemized deductions are summarized in Exhibit 16–5.

Personal Property Taxes. Deductible personal property taxes must be *ad valorem* (assessed in relation to the value of the property). Therefore, a motor vehicle tax based on weight, model, year, or horsepower is not an ad valorem tax. In contrast, a motor vehicle tax based on the value of the car is deductible.

EXAMPLE 50

A state imposes a motor vehicle registration tax on 4% of the value of the vehicle plus 40 cents per hundredweight. Belle, a resident of the state, owns a car having a value of $4,000 and weighing 3,000 pounds. Belle pays an annual registration fee of $172. Of this amount, $160 (4% of $4,000) is deductible as a personal property tax. The remaining $12, based on the weight of the car, is not deductible. ■

Real Estate Taxes. Real estate taxes of individuals are generally deductible. Taxes on personal-use property and investment property are deductible as itemized deductions. Taxes on business property are deductible as business expenses. Real

[74] § 223(b)(2). The limits were $2,650 and $5,250 in 2005.

[75] Most deductible taxes are listed in § 164, while the nondeductible items are included in § 275.

EXHIBIT 16-5 **Deductible and Nondeductible Taxes**

Deductible	Nondeductible
State, local, and foreign real property taxes	Federal income taxes
	FICA taxes imposed on employees
State and local personal property taxes	Employer FICA taxes paid on domestic household workers
State and local income taxes *or* sales/use taxes	Estate, inheritance, and gift taxes
	Federal, state, and local excise taxes (e.g., gasoline, tobacco, spirits)
Foreign income taxes	Taxes on real property to the extent such taxes are to be apportioned and treated as imposed on another taxpayer
The environmental tax	Special assessments for streets, sidewalks, curbing, and other similar improvements

property taxes on property that is sold during the year must be allocated between the buyer and the seller (refer to Chapter 5).

State and Local Income Taxes and Sales Taxes. The position of the IRS is that state and local *income* taxes imposed upon an individual are deductible only as itemized deductions, even if the taxpayer's sole source of income is from a business, rents, or royalties.

Cash basis taxpayers are entitled to deduct state income taxes withheld by the employer in the year the taxes are withheld. In addition, estimated state income tax payments are deductible in the year the payment is made by cash basis taxpayers even if the payments relate to a prior or subsequent year.[76] If the taxpayer overpays state income taxes because of excessive withholdings or estimated tax payments, the refund received is included in gross income of the following year to the extent that the deduction reduced the taxable income in the prior year.

EXAMPLE 51

Leona, a cash basis, unmarried taxpayer, had $800 of state income tax withheld during 2006. Additionally in 2006, Leona paid $100 that was due when she filed her 2005 state income tax return in 2006 and made estimated payments of $300 on her 2006 state income tax. When Leona files her 2006 Federal income tax return in April 2007, she elects to itemize deductions, which amount to $5,500, including the $1,200 of state income tax payments and withholdings. The itemized deductions reduce her taxable income.

As a result of overpaying her 2006 state income tax, Leona receives a refund of $200 early in 2007. She will include this amount in her 2007 gross income in computing her Federal income tax. It does not matter whether Leona received a check from the state for $200 or applied the $200 toward her 2007 state income tax. ■

Individuals can elect to deduct either their state and local income taxes *or* their sales/use taxes paid as an itemized deduction on Schedule A of Form 1040. This American Jobs Creation Act provision was effective beginning with 2004 returns. The annual election can reflect actual sales/use tax payments *or* an amount from an IRS table. The amount from the table may be increased by sales tax paid on the

[76]Rev.Rul. 71-190, 1971-1 C.B. 70. See also Rev.Rul. 82-208, 1982-2 C.B. 58, where a deduction is not allowed when the taxpayer cannot, in good faith, reasonably determine that there is additional state income tax liability.

GLOBAL *Tax Issues*

DEDUCTIBILITY OF FOREIGN TAXES

Josef, a citizen of the United States who works primarily in New York, also works several months each year in Austria. He owns a residence in Austria and pays income taxes to Austria on the income he earns there. Both the property tax he pays on his Austrian residence and the income tax he pays on his Austrian income are deductible in computing U.S. taxable income.

purchase of motor vehicles, boats, and other specified items. Most likely, the sales tax deduction will be elected by those living in states with no individual income tax (e.g., Texas and Washington).

PLANNING *Strategies*

TIMING THE PAYMENT OF DEDUCTIBLE TAXES

★ **Framework Focus: Deductions**

Strategy ★ Accelerate Recognition of Deductions to Achieve Tax Deferral.

It is sometimes possible to defer or accelerate the payment of certain deductible taxes, such as state income tax, real property tax, and personal property tax. For instance, the final installment of estimated state income tax is generally due after the end of a given tax year. However, accelerating the payment of the final installment could result in larger itemized deductions for the current year.

Interest

For Federal income tax purposes, interest must be divided into five categories: business interest, personal interest, interest on qualified education loans, qualified residence interest, and investment interest. Business interest is fully deductible as an ordinary and necessary expense. Personal (consumer) interest is not deductible. This includes credit card interest, interest on car loans, and any other interest that is not interest on qualified education loans, business interest, qualified residence interest, or investment interest. Interest on qualified education loans, investment interest, and qualified residence (home mortgage) interest are deductible, subject to limits discussed below.

Interest on Qualified Education Loans. Taxpayers who pay interest on a qualified education loan may deduct the interest as a deduction *for* AGI. A qualified education loan does not include indebtedness to certain related parties. For 2006, the maximum deduction is $2,500. The deduction is phased out for taxpayers with modified AGI (MAGI) between $50,000 and $65,000 ($105,000 and $135,000 on joint returns). The deduction is not available for taxpayers who are claimed as dependents or for married taxpayers filing separately.[77]

Investment Interest. Taxpayers frequently borrow funds that they use to acquire investment assets. When the interest expense is large relative to the income from the investments, substantial tax benefits could result. Congress has therefore

[77] § 221. See § 221(b)(2)(C) for the definition of MAGI. The phaseout amounts are subject to adjustments for inflation. The 2005 $2,500 limitation and the phaseout amounts were the same as for 2006.

limited the deductibility of interest on funds borrowed for the purpose of purchasing or continuing to hold investment property. **Investment interest** expense is limited to **net investment income** for the year.[78]

Investment income is gross income from interest, dividends (see below), annuities, and royalties not derived in the ordinary course of a trade or business. Income from a passive activity and income from a real estate activity in which the taxpayer actively participates are not included in investment income (see Chapter 6).

The following types of income are not included in investment income unless the taxpayer *elects* to do so.

- Net capital gain attributable to the disposition of (1) property producing the types of income just enumerated or (2) property held for investment purposes.
- Qualified dividends that are taxed at the same marginal rate that is applicable to a net capital gain.

A taxpayer may include net capital gains and qualified dividends as investment income by electing to do so. The election is available only if the taxpayer agrees to reduce amounts qualifying for the 15 percent (5 percent for low-income taxpayers) rates that otherwise apply to net capital gain (see Chapter 8) and qualified dividends (refer to Chapter 4) by an equivalent amount.

EXAMPLE 52

Terry incurred $13,000 of interest expense related to her investments during the year. Her investment income included $4,000 of interest, $2,000 of qualified dividends, and a $5,000 net capital gain on the sale of investment securities. If Terry does not make the election to include the net capital gain and qualified dividends in investment income, her investment income for purposes of computing the investment income limitation is $4,000 (interest income). If she does make the election, her investment income is $11,000 ($4,000 interest + $2,000 qualified dividends + $5,000 net capital gain). ■

Net investment income is the excess of investment income over investment expenses. Investment expenses are those deductible expenses directly connected with the production of investment income. Investment expenses do not include investment interest expense.

DIGGING DEEPER 15

Find more information on this topic at our Web site: ***http://wft-entities.swlearning.com.***

Qualified Residence Interest. **Qualified residence interest** is interest paid or accrued during the taxable year on indebtedness (subject to limitations) secured by any property that is a qualified residence of the taxpayer. Qualified residence interest falls into two categories: (1) interest on **acquisition indebtedness** and (2) interest on **home equity loans**. Before discussing each of these categories, however, the term *qualified residence* must be defined.

A qualified residence includes the taxpayer's principal residence and one other residence of the taxpayer or spouse. The principal residence is one that meets the requirement for nonrecognition of gain upon sale under § 121 (see Chapter 7). The one other residence, or second residence, refers to one that is used as a residence if not rented or, if rented, meets the requirements for a personal residence under the rental of vacation home rules. A taxpayer who has more than one second residence can make the selection each year of which one is the qualified second residence. A residence includes, in addition to a house in the ordinary sense, cooperative apartments, condominiums, and mobile homes and boats that have living quarters (sleeping accommodations and toilet and cooking facilities).

Although in most cases interest paid on a home mortgage is fully deductible, there are limitations.[79] Interest paid or accrued during the tax year on aggregate

[78] § 163(d).

[79] § 163(h)(3).

acquisition indebtedness of $1 million or less ($500,000 for married persons filing separate returns) is deductible as qualified residence interest. *Acquisition indebtedness* refers to amounts incurred in acquiring, constructing, or substantially improving a qualified residence of the taxpayer.

Qualified residence interest also includes interest on home equity loans. These loans utilize the personal residence of the taxpayer as security. Because the funds from home equity loans can be used for personal purposes (e.g., auto purchases, medical expenses), what would otherwise have been nondeductible consumer interest becomes deductible qualified residence interest. However, interest is deductible only on the portion of a home equity loan that does not exceed the lesser of:

- The fair market value of the residence, reduced by the acquisition indebtedness, or
- $100,000 ($50,000 for married persons filing separate returns).

EXAMPLE 53

Larry owns a personal residence with a fair market value of $150,000 and an outstanding first mortgage of $120,000. Therefore, his equity in his home is $30,000 ($150,000 − $120,000). Larry issues a lien on the residence and in return borrows $15,000 to purchase a new family automobile. All interest on the $135,000 of debt is treated as qualified residence interest. ■

EXAMPLE 54

Leon and Pearl, married taxpayers, took out a mortgage on their home for $200,000 in 1990. In March of the current year, when the home has a fair market value of $400,000 and they owe $195,000 on the mortgage, Leon and Pearl take out a home equity loan for $120,000. They use the funds to purchase an airplane to be used for recreational purposes. On a joint return, Leon and Pearl can deduct all of the interest on the first mortgage since it is acquisition indebtedness. Of the $120,000 home equity loan, only the interest on the first $100,000 is deductible. The interest on the remaining $20,000 is not deductible because it exceeds the statutory ceiling of $100,000. ■

Interest Paid for Services. Mortgage loan companies commonly charge a fee for finding, placing, or processing a mortgage loan. Such fees are often called **points** and are expressed as a percentage of the loan amount. Borrowers often have to pay points to obtain the necessary financing. To qualify as deductible interest, the points must be considered compensation to a lender solely for the use or forbearance of money. The points cannot be a form of service charge or payment for specific services if they are to qualify as deductible interest.[80]

Points must be capitalized and are amortized and deductible ratably over the life of the loan. A special exception permits the purchaser of a personal residence to deduct qualifying points in the year of payment.[81] The exception also covers points paid to obtain funds for home improvements.

EXAMPLE 55

During 2006, Thelma purchases a new residence for $130,000 and pays points of $2,600 to obtain mortgage financing. At Thelma's election, the $2,600 can be claimed as an interest deduction for 2006. ■

Points paid to refinance an existing home mortgage cannot be immediately expensed, but must be capitalized and amortized as interest expense over the life of the new loan.[82]

EXAMPLE 56

Sandra purchased her residence several years ago, obtaining a 30-year mortgage at an annual interest rate of 9%. In the current year, Sandra refinances the mortgage in order to reduce the interest rate to 6%. To obtain the refinancing, she has to pay points of $2,600. The

[80]Rev.Rul. 67–297, 1967–2 C.B. 87.

[81]§ 461(g)(2).

[82]Rev.Rul. 87–22, 1987–1 C.B. 146.

CONCEPT SUMMARY 16-3

Deductibility of Personal, Education, Investment, and Mortgage Interest

Type	Deductible	Comments
Personal (consumer) interest	No	Includes any interest that is not home mortgage interest, interest on qualified education loans, investment interest, or business interest. Examples include car loans, credit cards, etc.
Qualified education interest	Yes	Deduction *for* AGI; subject to limitations.
Investment interest (*not* related to rental or royalty property)	Yes	Itemized deduction; limited to net investment income for the year; disallowed interest can be carried over to future years.
Investment interest (related to rental or royalty property)	Yes	Deduction *for* AGI; limited to net investment income for the year; disallowed interest can be carried over to future years.
Qualified residence interest on acquisition indebtedness	Yes	Deductible as an itemized deduction; limited to indebtedness of $1 million.
Qualified residence interest on home equity indebtedness	Yes	Deductible as an itemized deduction; limited to indebtedness equal to lesser of $100,000 or FMV of residence minus acquisition indebtedness.

$2,600 paid comes under the usual rule applicable to points. That is, the $2,600 must be capitalized and amortized over the life of the mortgage. ■

Prepayment Penalty. When a mortgage or loan is paid off in full in a lump sum before its term, the lending institution may require an additional payment of a certain percentage applied to the unpaid amount at the time of prepayment. This is known as a prepayment penalty and is considered to be interest (e.g., personal, qualified residence, investment) in the year paid. The general rules for deductibility of interest also apply to prepayment penalties.

Interest Paid to Related Parties. Nothing prevents the deduction of interest paid to a related party as long as the payment actually took place and the interest meets the requirements for deductibility. However, a special rule applies for related taxpayers when the debtor uses the accrual basis and the related creditor is on the cash basis. If this rule is applicable, interest that has been accrued but not paid at the end of the debtor's tax year is not deductible until payment is made and the income is reportable by the cash basis recipient.

Tax-Exempt Securities. The tax law provides that no deduction is allowed for interest on debt incurred to purchase or carry tax-exempt securities.[83] A major problem for the courts has been to determine what is meant by the words "to purchase or carry." Refer to Chapter 5 for a detailed discussion of these issues.

Prepaid Interest. Accrual method reporting is imposed on cash basis taxpayers for interest prepayments that extend beyond the end of the taxable year.[84] Such payments must be allocated to the tax years to which the interest payments relate. These provisions are intended to prevent cash basis taxpayers from *manufacturing* tax deductions before the end of the year by prepaying interest.

Classification of Interest Expense. Whether interest is deductible *for* AGI or as an itemized deduction depends on whether the indebtedness has a business,

[83] § 265(a)(2).

[84] § 461(g)(1).

investment, or personal purpose. If the indebtedness is incurred in relation to a business (other than performing services as an employee) or for the production of rent or royalty income, the interest is deductible *for* AGI. If the indebtedness is incurred for personal use, such as qualified residence interest, any deduction allowed is reported on Schedule A of Form 1040 if the taxpayer elects to itemize. If the taxpayer is an employee who incurs debt in relation to his or her employment, the interest is considered to be personal, or consumer, interest. Business expenses appear on Schedule C of Form 1040, and expenses related to rents or royalties are reported on Schedule E.

Charitable Contributions

As noted in Chapter 5, individuals are allowed to deduct contributions made to qualified domestic organizations.[85] Contributions to qualified charitable organizations serve certain social welfare needs and thus relieve the government of the cost of providing these needed services to the community.

Criteria for a Gift. A **charitable contribution** is defined as a gift made to a qualified organization.[86] The major elements needed to qualify a contribution as a gift are a donative intent, the absence of consideration, and acceptance by the donee. Consequently, the taxpayer has the burden of establishing that the transfer was made from motives of disinterested generosity as established by the courts.[87] This test is quite subjective and has led to problems of interpretation (refer to the discussion of gifts in Chapter 4).

Benefit Received Rule. When a donor derives a tangible benefit from a contribution, he or she cannot deduct the value of the benefit.

EXAMPLE 57

Ralph purchases a ticket at $100 for a special performance of the local symphony (a qualified charity). If the price of a ticket to a symphony concert is normally $35, Ralph is allowed only $65 as a charitable contribution. ■

An exception to this benefit rule provides for the deduction of an automatic percentage of the amount paid for the right to purchase athletic tickets from colleges and universities.[88] Under this exception, 80 percent of the amount paid to or for the benefit of the institution qualifies as a charitable contribution deduction.

Contribution of Services. No deduction is allowed for the value of one's services contributed to a qualified charitable organization. However, unreimbursed expenses related to the services rendered may be deductible. For example, the cost of a uniform (without general utility) that is required to be worn while performing services may be deductible, as are certain out-of-pocket transportation costs incurred for the benefit of the charity. In lieu of these out-of-pocket costs for an automobile, a standard mileage rate of 14 cents per mile is allowed.[89] Deductions are permitted for transportation, reasonable expenses for lodging, and the cost of meals while away from home incurred in performing the donated services. The travel expenses are not deductible if the travel involves a significant element of personal pleasure, recreation, or vacation.[90]

[85] § 170.

[86] § 170(c).

[87] *Comm. v. Duberstein*, 60–2 USTC ¶9515, 5 AFTR2d 1626, 80 S.Ct. 1190 (USSC, 1960).

[88] § 170(l).

[89] § 170(i).

[90] § 170(j).

GLOBAL *Tax Issues*

CHOOSE THE CHARITY WISELY

Ibrahim, a U.S. citizen of Turkish descent, was distressed by the damage caused by a major earthquake in Turkey. He donated $100,000 to the Earthquake Victims' Relief Fund, a Turkish charitable organization that was set up to help victims of the earthquake. Ahmed, also a U.S. citizen of Turkish descent, donated $200,000 to help with the relief effort. However, Ahmed's contribution went to his mosque, which sent the proceeds of a fund drive to the Earthquake Victims' Relief Fund in Turkey. Ibrahim's contribution is not deductible, but Ahmed's is. Why? Contributions to charitable organizations are not deductible unless the organization is a U.S. charity.

Nondeductible Items. In addition to the benefit received rule and the restrictions placed on contribution of services, the following items may not be deducted as charitable contributions:

- Dues, fees, or bills paid to country clubs, lodges, fraternal orders, or similar groups.
- Cost of raffle, bingo, or lottery tickets.
- Cost of tuition.
- Value of blood given to a blood bank.
- Donations to homeowners associations.
- Gifts to individuals.
- Rental value of property used by a qualified charity.

Time of Deduction. A charitable contribution generally is deducted in the year the payment is made. This rule applies to both cash and accrual basis individuals. A contribution is ordinarily deemed to have been made on the date of delivery of the property to the donee. A contribution made by check is considered delivered on the date of mailing. Thus, a check mailed on December 31, 2006, is deductible on the taxpayer's 2006 tax return. If the contribution is charged on a bank credit card, the date the charge is made determines the year of deduction.

Record-Keeping Requirements. No deduction is allowed for contributions of $250 or more unless the taxpayer obtains written substantiation of the contribution from the charitable organization. Additional information is required if the value of the donated property is over $500 but not over $5,000. For noncash contributions with a claimed value in excess of $5,000 ($10,000 in the case of nonpublicly traded stock), the taxpayer must obtain a qualified appraisal. Failure to comply with these reporting rules may result in disallowance of the charitable contribution deduction.[91]

DIGGING DEEPER 16

Find more information on this topic at our Web site: ***http://wft-entities.swlearning.com.***

Valuation Requirements. Property donated to a charity is generally valued at fair market value at the time the gift is made. The Code and Regulations give very little guidance on the measurement of the fair market value except to say, "The fair market value is the price at which the property would change hands between a willing buyer and a willing seller, neither being under any compulsion to buy or sell and both having reasonable knowledge of relevant facts."

[91]The amounts discussed in this section ($250, $500, $5,000, and $10,000) apply to 2005 tax returns. Amounts for 2006 had not been announced at the time of this writing.

Generally, charitable organizations do not attest to the fair market value of the donated property. Nevertheless, the taxpayer must maintain reliable written evidence as to its value.

DIGGING DEEPER 17

Find more information on this topic at our Web site: ***http://wft-entities.swlearning.com.***

Limitations on Charitable Contribution Deduction. The potential charitable contribution deduction is the total of all donations, both money and property, that qualify for the deduction. After this determination is made, the actual amount of the charitable contribution deduction that is allowed for individuals for the tax year is limited as follows:

- If the qualifying contributions for the year total 20 percent or less of AGI, they are fully deductible.
- If the qualifying contributions are more than 20 percent of AGI, the deductible amount may be limited to either 20 percent, 30 percent, or 50 percent of AGI, depending on the type of property given and the type of organization to which the donation is made.
- In any case, the maximum charitable contribution deduction may not exceed 50 percent of AGI for the tax year.

To understand the complex rules for computing the amount of a charitable contribution, it is necessary to understand the distinction between **capital gain property** and **ordinary income property**. These rules, which were discussed in Chapter 5, are summarized in Concept Summary 16–4.

In addition, it is necessary to understand when the 50 percent, 30 percent, and 20 percent limitations apply. If a taxpayer's contributions for the year exceed the applicable percentage limitations, the excess contributions may be carried forward and deducted during a five-year carryover period. These topics are discussed in the sections that follow.

Fifty Percent Ceiling. Contributions made to public charities may not exceed 50 percent of an individual's AGI for the year. Excess contributions may be carried over to the next five years.[92] The 50 percent ceiling on contributions applies to the following types of public charities:

- A church or a convention or association of churches.
- An educational organization that maintains a regular faculty and curriculum.
- A hospital or medical school.
- An organization supported by the government that holds property or investments for the benefit of a college or university.
- A Federal, state, or local governmental unit.
- An organization normally receiving a substantial part of its support from the public or a governmental unit.

The 50 percent ceiling also applies to contributions to the following organizations:

- All private operating foundations.
- Certain private nonoperating foundations that distribute the contributions they receive to public charities and private operating foundations within two and one-half months following the year they receive the contributions.

[92] § 170(d); Reg. § 1.170A–10.

CONCEPT SUMMARY 16-4

Determining the Deduction for Contributions of Property by Individuals

If the Type of Property Contributed Is:	And the Property Is Contributed to:	The Contribution Is Measured by:	But the Deduction Is Limited to:
Capital gain property	A 50% organization	Fair market value of the property	30% of AGI
Ordinary income property	A 50% organization	The basis of the property*	50% of AGI
Capital gain property (and the property is tangible personal property put to an unrelated use by the donee)	A 50% organization	The basis of the property*	50% of AGI
Capital gain property (and the reduced deduction is elected)	A 50% organization	The basis of the property	50% of AGI
Capital gain property	A private nonoperating foundation that is not a 50% organization	The basis of the property*	The lesser of: 1. 20% of AGI 2. 50% of AGI minus other contributions to 50% organizations
Ordinary income property	A private nonoperating foundation that is not a 50% organization	The basis of the property*	30% of AGI

*If the FMV of the property is less than the adjusted basis (i.e., the property has declined in value instead of appreciating), the FMV is used.

- Certain private nonoperating foundations in which the contributions are pooled in a common fund and the income and principal sum are paid to public charities.

In the remaining discussion of charitable contributions, public charities and private foundations (both operating and nonoperating) that qualify for the 50 percent ceiling will be referred to as 50 percent organizations.

Thirty Percent Ceiling. A 30 percent ceiling applies to contributions of cash and ordinary income property to private nonoperating foundations that are not 50 percent organizations. The 30 percent ceiling also applies to contributions of appreciated capital gain property to 50 percent organizations unless the taxpayer makes a special election (see Example 59 below).

In the event the contributions for any one tax year involve both 50 percent and 30 percent property, the allowable deduction comes first from the 50 percent property.

EXAMPLE 58

During the year, Lisa makes the following donations to her church: cash of $2,000 and unimproved land worth $30,000. Lisa had purchased the land four years ago for $22,000 and held it as an investment. Therefore, it is long-term capital gain property. Lisa's AGI for the year is $60,000. Disregarding percentage limitations, Lisa's potential deduction is $32,000 [$2,000 (cash) + $30,000 (fair market value of land)].

In applying the percentage limitations, however, the current deduction for the land is limited to $18,000 [30% (limitation applicable to long-term capital gain property) × $60,000 (AGI)]. Thus, the total deduction is $20,000 ($2,000 cash + $18,000 land). Note that the total deduction does not exceed $30,000, which is 50% of Lisa's AGI. ■

Under a special election, a taxpayer may choose to forgo a deduction of the appreciation on capital gain property. Referred to as the reduced deduction election, this enables the taxpayer to move from the 30 percent limitation to the 50 percent limitation.

EXAMPLE 59

Assume the same facts as in Example 58, except that Lisa makes the reduced deduction election. Now the deduction becomes $24,000 [$2,000 (cash) + $22,000 (basis in land)] because both donations fall under the 50% limitation. Thus, by making the election, Lisa has increased her current charitable contribution deduction by $4,000 [$24,000 – $20,000 (Example 58)]. ■

Although the reduced deduction election appears attractive, it should be considered carefully. The election sacrifices a deduction for the appreciation on long-term capital gain property that might eventually be allowed. Note that in Example 58, the potential deduction was $32,000, yet in Example 59 only $24,000 is allowed. The reason the potential deduction is decreased by $8,000 ($32,000 – $24,000) is that no carryover is allowed for the amount sacrificed by the election.

Twenty Percent Ceiling. A 20 percent ceiling applies to contributions of appreciated long-term capital gain property to private nonoperating foundations that are not 50 percent organizations. Also, recall from Chapter 5 that only the basis of the contributed property is allowed as a deduction.

Contribution Carryovers. Contributions that exceed the percentage limitations for the current year can be carried over for five years. In the carryover process, such contributions do not lose their identity for limitation purposes. Thus, if the contribution originally involved 30 percent property, the carryover will continue to be classified as 30 percent property in the carryover year.

EXAMPLE 60

Assume the same facts as in Example 58. Because only $18,000 of the $30,000 value of the land is deducted in the current year, the balance of $12,000 may be carried over to the following year. But the carryover will still be treated as long-term capital gain property and will be subject to the 30%-of-AGI limitation. ■

In applying the percentage limitations, current charitable contributions must be claimed first before any carryovers can be considered. If carryovers involve more than one year, they are utilized in a first-in, first-out order.

Miscellaneous Itemized Deductions Subject to Two Percent Floor

No deduction is allowed for personal, living, or family expenses.[93] However, a taxpayer may incur a number of expenditures related to employment. If an employee or outside salesperson incurs unreimbursed business expenses or expenses that are reimbursed under a nonaccountable plan (see Chapter 17), including travel and transportation, the expenses are deductible as **miscellaneous itemized deductions**.[94] Certain other expenses also fall into the special category of miscellaneous itemized deductions. Some are deductible only to the extent they exceed 2 percent of the taxpayer's AGI. These miscellaneous itemized deductions include the following:

- Professional dues to membership organizations.
- Uniforms or other clothing that cannot be used for normal wear.

[93]§ 262.

[94]Actors and performing artists who meet certain requirements are not subject to this rule.

- Fees incurred for the preparation of one's tax return or fees incurred for tax litigation before the IRS or the courts.
- Job-hunting costs.
- Fee paid for a safe deposit box used to store papers and documents relating to taxable income-producing investments.
- Investment expenses that are deductible under § 212 as discussed previously in this chapter.
- Appraisal fees to determine the amount of a casualty loss or the fair market value of donated property.
- Hobby losses up to the amount of hobby income (see Chapter 17).
- Unreimbursed employee expenses (see Chapter 17).

Certain employee business expenses that are reimbursed are not itemized deductions, but are deducted *for* AGI. Employee business expenses are discussed in depth in Chapter 17.

Other Miscellaneous Deductions

Certain expenses and losses do not fall into any category of itemized deductions already discussed but are nonetheless deductible. The following expenses and losses are deductible on Schedule A as Other Miscellaneous Deductions:

- Gambling losses up to the amount of gambling winnings.
- Impairment-related work expenses of a handicapped person.
- Federal estate tax on income in respect of a decedent.
- Deduction for repayment of amounts under a claim of right if more than $3,000.

Unlike the expenses and losses discussed previously under Miscellaneous Itemized Deductions, the above expenses and losses are not subject to the 2 percent-of-AGI floor.

Overall Limitation on Certain Itemized Deductions

Congress has enacted several provisions limiting tax benefits for high-income taxpayers. These limitations include the exemption phaseout (discussed earlier in this chapter) and a phaseout of itemized deductions. For 2006, the phaseout of itemized deductions (also referred to as a *cutback adjustment*) applies to taxpayers whose AGI exceeds $150,500 ($75,250 for married taxpayers filing separately).[95] The limitation applies to the following frequently encountered itemized deductions:[96]

- Taxes.
- Home mortgage interest, including points.
- Charitable contributions.
- Unreimbursed employee expenses subject to the 2 percent-of-AGI floor.
- All other expenses subject to the 2 percent-of-AGI floor.

The following deductions are *not* subject to the limitation on itemized deductions:

- Medical and dental expenses.
- Investment interest expense.
- Nonbusiness casualty and theft losses.
- Gambling losses.

[95]For 2005, the limitation applied if AGI exceeded $145,950 ($72,975 for married taxpayers filing separately).

[96]Other deductions subject to the limitation include Federal estate tax on income in respect of a decedent, certain amortizable bond premiums, the deduction for repayment of certain amounts, certain unrecovered investments in an annuity, and impairment-related work expenses.

The overall limitation applicable to itemized deductions is being phased out over a four-year period, beginning in 2006. Therefore, taxpayers subject to the limitation must use a two-step computation to determine the reduction in itemized deductions required by the overall limitation.

Step 1

Calculate the lesser of:

- 3 percent of the amount by which AGI exceeds $150,500 ($75,250 if married filing separately).
- 80 percent of itemized deductions that are affected by the limit.

Step 2

Multiply the amount computed in Step 1 by the fraction that applies to the tax year involved. For 2006 and 2007, the phaseout is equal to two-thirds of the Step 1 amount. For 2008 and 2009, the phaseout is equal to one-third of the Step 1 amount. The overall limitation will no longer exist for taxable years beginning after 2009.

The overall limitation is applied after applying all other limitations to itemized deductions that are affected by the overall limitation. Other limitations apply to charitable contributions, certain meals and entertainment expenses, and certain miscellaneous itemized deductions.

EXAMPLE 61

Herman, who is single, had AGI of $200,000 for 2006. He incurred the following expenses and losses during the year:

Medical expenses before the 7.5%-of-AGI limitation	$16,000
State and local income taxes	3,200
Real estate taxes	2,800
Home mortgage interest	7,200
Charitable contributions	2,000
Casualty loss (after $100 floor, before 10%-of-AGI limitation)	21,500
Unreimbursed employee expenses subject to 2%-of-AGI limitation	4,300
Gambling losses (Herman had $3,000 gambling income)	7,000

Herman's itemized deductions before the overall limitation are computed as follows:

Medical expenses [$16,000 – (7.5% × $200,000)]	$ 1,000
State and local income taxes	3,200
Real estate taxes	2,800
Home mortgage interest	7,200
Charitable contributions	2,000
Casualty loss [$21,500 – (10% × $200,000)]	1,500
Unreimbursed employee expenses [$4,300 – (2% × $200,000)]	300
Gambling losses (limited to $3,000 of gambling income)	3,000
Total itemized deductions before overall limitation	$21,000

Herman's itemized deductions subject to the overall limitation are as follows:

State and local income taxes	$ 3,200
Real estate taxes	2,800
Home mortgage interest	7,200
Charitable contributions	2,000
Unreimbursed employee expenses	300
Total itemized deductions before overall limitation	$15,500

Step 1

Calculate the lesser of:

• 3% ($200,000 AGI – $150,500)	$ 1,485
• 80% of itemized deductions subject to limitation ($15,500 × .80)	12,400

Step 2

Multiply the Step 1 amount by two-thirds ($1,485 × ⅔)	$990

Therefore, the amount of the phaseout is $990, and Herman has $20,010 of deductible itemized deductions, computed as follows:

Deductible itemized deductions subject to overall limitation ($15,500 – $990)	$14,510
Itemized deductions not subject to overall limitation:	
Medical expenses	1,000
Casualty loss	1,500
Gambling losses	3,000
Deductible itemized deductions	$20,010

■

PLANNING *Strategies*

EFFECTIVE UTILIZATION OF ITEMIZED DEDUCTIONS

★ **Framework Focus: Deductions**

Strategy ★ Maximize Deductible Amounts.

An individual may use the standard deduction in one year and itemize deductions in another year. Therefore, it is frequently possible to obtain maximum benefit by shifting itemized deductions from one year to another. For example, if a taxpayer's itemized deductions and the standard deduction are approximately the same for each year of a two-year period, the taxpayer should use the standard deduction in one year and shift itemized deductions (to the extent permitted by law) to the other year. The individual could, for example, prepay a church pledge for a particular year or avoid paying end-of-the-year medical expenses to shift the deduction to the following year.

LO.9

Understand the adoption expenses credit, child tax credit, education tax credits, credit for child and dependent care expenses, and earned income credit.

Individual Tax Credits

Adoption Expenses Credit

Adoption expenses paid or incurred by a taxpayer may give rise to the **adoption expenses credit**.[97] The provision is intended to assist taxpayers who incur nonrecurring costs directly associated with the adoption process, such as adoption fees, attorney fees, court costs, social service review costs, and transportation costs.

In 2006, up to $10,960 of costs incurred to adopt an eligible child qualify for the credit. An eligible child is one who is:

- under 18 years of age at the time of the adoption, or
- physically or mentally incapable of taking care of himself or herself.

A taxpayer may claim the credit in the year qualifying expenses were paid or incurred if they were paid or incurred during or after the tax year in which the adoption was finalized. For qualifying expenses paid or incurred in a tax year prior to the year when the adoption was finalized, the credit must be claimed in the tax year following the tax year during which the expenses are paid or incurred. A married couple must file a joint return in order to claim the credit.

[97] § 23.

EXAMPLE 62

In late 2005, Sam and Martha pay $4,000 in legal fees, adoption fees, and other expenses directly related to the adoption of an infant daughter, Susan. In 2006, the year in which the adoption becomes final, they pay an additional $8,000. Sam and Martha are eligible for a $10,960 credit in 2006 (for expenses, limited by the $10,960 ceiling, paid in 2005 and 2006). ■

The amount of the credit that is otherwise available is subject to phaseout for taxpayers whose AGI (modified for this purpose) exceeds $164,410 in 2006, and is phased out completely when AGI reaches $204,410. The resulting credit is calculated by reducing the allowable credit (determined without this reduction) by the amount determined using the following formula:

$$\text{Allowable credit} \times \frac{\text{AGI} - \$164{,}410}{\$40{,}000}$$

EXAMPLE 63

Assume the same facts as in the previous example, except that Sam and Martha's AGI is $189,410 in 2006. As a result, their available credit in 2006 is reduced from $10,960 to $4,110 {$10,960 – [$10,960 × ($25,000/$40,000)]}. ■

The credit is nonrefundable and is available to taxpayers only in a year in which this credit and the other nonrefundable credits do not exceed the taxpayer's tax liability. However, any unused adoption expenses credit may be carried over for up to five years, being utilized on a first-in, first-out basis.

Child Tax Credit

The **child tax credit** provision allows individual taxpayers to take a tax credit based solely on the *number* of their qualifying children. This credit is one of several "family-friendly" provisions that currently are part of our tax law. To be eligible for the credit, the child must be under age 17, a U.S. citizen, and claimed as a dependent on the taxpayer's return.

Maximum Credit and Phaseouts. Under current law, the maximum credit available is $1,000 per child.[98] The available credit is phased out for higher-income taxpayers beginning when AGI reaches $110,000 for joint filers ($55,000 for married taxpayers filing separately) and $75,000 for single taxpayers. The credit is phased out by $50 for each $1,000 (or part thereof) of AGI above the threshold amounts.[99] Since the maximum credit available to taxpayers depends on the number of qualifying children, the income level at which the credit is phased out completely also depends on the number of children qualifying for the credit.

EXAMPLE 64

Juanita and Alberto are married and file a joint tax return claiming their two children, ages six and eight, as dependents. Their AGI is $122,400. Juanita and Alberto's available child tax credit is $1,350, computed as their maximum credit of $2,000 ($1,000 × 2 children) reduced by a $650 phaseout. Since Juanita and Alberto's AGI is in excess of the $110,000 threshold, the maximum credit must be reduced by $50 for every $1,000 (or part thereof) above the threshold amount {$50 × [($122,400 – $110,000)/$1,000]}. Thus, the credit reduction equals $650 [$50 × 13 (rounded up from 12.4)]. Therefore, Juanita and Alberto's child tax credit is $1,350. ■

[98] § 24. The maximum credit per child is scheduled to remain at $1,000 through 2010.

[99] AGI is modified for purposes of this calculation. The threshold amounts are *not* indexed for inflation. See §§ 24(a) and (b).

Credit for Child and Dependent Care Expenses

A credit is allowed to taxpayers who incur employment-related expenses for child or dependent care.[100] The **credit for child and dependent care expenses** is a specified percentage of expenses incurred to enable the taxpayer to work or to seek employment. Expenses on which the credit for child and dependent care expenses is based are subject to limitations.

Eligibility. To be eligible for the credit, an individual must have either of the following:

- A dependent under age 13.
- A dependent or spouse who is physically or mentally incapacitated and who lives with the taxpayer for more than one-half of the year.

Generally, married taxpayers must file a joint return to obtain the credit.

Eligible Employment-Related Expenses. Eligible expenses include amounts paid for household services and care of a qualifying individual that are incurred to enable the taxpayer to be employed. Child and dependent care expenses include expenses incurred in the home, such as payments for a housekeeper. Out-of-the-home expenses incurred for the care of a dependent under the age of 13 also qualify for the credit. In addition, out-of-the-home expenses incurred for an older dependent or spouse who is physically or mentally incapacitated qualify for the credit if that person regularly spends at least eight hours each day in the taxpayer's household. This makes the credit available to taxpayers who keep handicapped older children and elderly relatives in the home instead of institutionalizing them. Out-of-the-home expenses incurred for services provided by a dependent care center will qualify only if the center complies with all applicable laws and regulations of a state or unit of local government.

Child care payments to a relative are eligible for the credit unless the relative is a child (under age 19) of the taxpayer.

Earned Income Ceiling. The total for qualifying employment-related expenses is limited to an individual's earned income. For married taxpayers, this limitation applies to the spouse with the lesser amount of earned income. Special rules are provided for taxpayers with nonworking spouses who are disabled or are full-time students. If a nonworking spouse is physically or mentally disabled or is a full-time student, he or she is deemed to have earned income for purposes of this limitation. The deemed amount is $250 per month if there is one qualifying individual in the household or $500 per month if there are two or more qualifying individuals in the household. In the case of a student-spouse, the student's income is deemed to be earned only for the months that the student is enrolled on a full-time basis at an educational institution.[101]

Calculation of the Credit. In general, the credit is equal to a percentage of unreimbursed employment-related expenses up to $3,000 for one qualifying individual and $6,000 for two or more individuals. The credit rate varies between 20 percent and 35 percent, depending on the taxpayer's AGI. The following chart shows the applicable percentage for taxpayers as AGI increases:

[100] § 21.

[101] § 21(d).

Adjusted Gross Income		
Over	But Not Over	Applicable Rate of Credit
$ 0	$15,000	35%
15,000	17,000	34%
17,000	19,000	33%
19,000	21,000	32%
21,000	23,000	31%
23,000	25,000	30%
25,000	27,000	29%
27,000	29,000	28%
29,000	31,000	27%
31,000	33,000	26%
33,000	35,000	25%
35,000	37,000	24%
37,000	39,000	23%
39,000	41,000	22%
41,000	43,000	21%
43,000	No limit	20%

EXAMPLE 65

Nancy, who has two children under age 13, worked full-time while her spouse, Ron, attended college for 10 months during the year. Nancy earned $22,000 and incurred $6,200 of child care expenses. Ron is deemed to be fully employed and to have earned $500 for each of the 10 months (or a total of $5,000). Since Nancy and Ron have AGI of $22,000, they are allowed a credit rate of 31%. Nancy and Ron are limited to $5,000 in qualified child care expenses (the lesser of $6,000 or $5,000). Therefore, they are entitled to a tax credit of $1,550 (31% × $5,000) for the year. ■

Education Tax Credits

The **HOPE scholarship credit** and the **lifetime learning credit**[102] are available to help qualifying low- and middle-income individuals defray the cost of higher education. The credits, both of which are nonrefundable, are available for qualifying tuition and related expenses incurred by students pursuing undergraduate or graduate degrees or vocational training. Room, board, and book costs are ineligible for the credits.

Maximum Credit. The HOPE scholarship credit permits a maximum credit of $1,650 per year (100 percent of the first $1,100 of tuition expenses plus 50 percent of the next $1,100 of tuition expenses) for the *first two years* of postsecondary education.[103] The lifetime learning credit permits a credit of 20 percent of qualifying expenses (up to $10,000 per year) incurred in a year in which the HOPE scholarship credit is not claimed with respect to a given student. Generally, the lifetime learning credit is used for individuals who are beyond the first two years of postsecondary education.

[102] § 25A.

[103] The $1,100 qualifying expense base for the HOPE scholarship credit is subject to inflation adjustment. The base was $1,000 for years prior to 2006, and the maximum credit was $1,500.

Eligible Individuals. Both education credits are available for qualified expenses incurred by a taxpayer, taxpayer's spouse, or taxpayer's dependent. The HOPE scholarship credit is available per eligible student, while the lifetime learning credit is calculated per taxpayer. To be eligible for the HOPE scholarship credit, a student must take at least one-half the full-time course load for at least one academic term at a qualifying educational institution. No comparable requirement exists for the lifetime learning credit. Therefore, taxpayers who are seeking new job skills or maintaining existing skills through graduate training or continuing education are eligible for the lifetime learning credit. Taxpayers who are married must file joint returns in order to claim either education credit.

Income Limitations. Both education credits are subject to income limitations and are combined for purposes of the limitation calculation. The allowable credit amount is phased out, beginning when the taxpayer's AGI reaches $45,000 ($90,000 for married taxpayers filing jointly). The reduction in 2006 is equal to the extent to which AGI exceeds $45,000 ($90,000 for married filing jointly) as a percentage of the $10,000 ($20,000 for married filing jointly) phaseout range. The credits are completely eliminated when AGI reaches $55,000 ($110,000 for married filing jointly).

EXAMPLE 66

Dean and Audry are married, file a joint tax return, have modified AGI under $90,000 and have two children, Raymond and Kelsey. During fall 2006, Raymond is beginning his freshman year at State University, and Kelsey is beginning her senior year. During the prior semester, Kelsey completed her junior year. Both Raymond and Kelsey are full-time students and may be claimed as dependents on their parents' tax return. Raymond's qualifying expenses total $4,300 for the fall semester while Kelsey's qualifying expenses total $10,200 for the prior and current semesters. For 2006, Dean and Audry may claim a $1,650 HOPE scholarship credit [(100% × $1,100) + (50% × $1,100)] relating to Raymond's expenses and a $2,000 lifetime learning credit (20% × $10,000) relating to Kelsey's expenses. Kelsey's tuition expenses are ineligible for the HOPE scholarship credit because she is beyond her first two years of postsecondary education. ■

EXAMPLE 67

Assume the same facts as in Example 66, except that Dean and Audry's modified AGI for 2006 is $102,000. Dean and Audry are eligible to claim $1,460 in total education credits for 2006. Their available credits totaling $3,650 ($1,650 HOPE scholarship credit + $2,000 lifetime learning credit) must be reduced because their AGI exceeds the $90,000 limit for married taxpayers. The percentage reduction is computed as the amount by which modified AGI exceeds the limit, expressed as a percentage of the phaseout range, or [($102,000 − $90,000)/$20,000], resulting in a 60% reduction. Therefore, the maximum available credit for 2006 is $1,460 ($3,650 × 40% allowable portion). ■

Restrictions on Double Tax Benefit. Taxpayers are prohibited from receiving a double tax benefit associated with qualifying educational expenses. Therefore, taxpayers who claim an education credit may not deduct the expenses, nor may they claim the credit for amounts that are otherwise excluded from gross income (e.g., scholarships, employer-paid educational assistance). However, a taxpayer may claim an education tax credit and exclude from gross income amounts distributed from a Coverdell Education Savings Account (CESA) as long as the distribution is not used for the same expenses for which the credit is claimed.

Earned Income Credit

The **earned income credit**, which has been a part of the law for many years, has been justified as a means of providing tax equity to the working poor. In addition, the credit has been designed to help offset regressive taxes that are a part of our tax system, such as the gasoline and Social Security taxes. Further, the credit is intended to encourage economically disadvantaged individuals to become contributing members of the workforce.[104]

Eligibility Requirements. Eligibility for the credit may depend not only on the taxpayer meeting the earned income and AGI thresholds, but also on whether he or she has a qualifying child. The term *qualifying child* generally has the same meaning here as it does for purposes of determining who qualifies as a dependent.

In addition to being available for taxpayers with qualifying children, the earned income credit is also available to certain workers without children. However, this provision is available only to such taxpayers aged 25 through 64 who cannot be claimed as a dependent on another taxpayer's return.

Amount of the Credit. In 2006, the earned income credit is determined by multiplying a maximum amount of earned income by the appropriate credit percentage. Generally, earned income includes employee compensation and net earnings from self-employment but excludes items such as interest, dividends, pension benefits, nontaxable employee compensation, and alimony. If a taxpayer has children, the credit percentage used in the calculation depends on the number of qualifying children. Thus, in 2006, the maximum earned income credit for a taxpayer with one qualifying child is $2,747 ($8,080 × 34%) and $4,536 ($11,340 × 40%) for a taxpayer with two or more qualifying children. However, the maximum earned income credit is phased out completely if the taxpayer's earned income or AGI exceeds certain thresholds. To the extent that the greater of earned income or AGI exceeds $16,810 in 2006 for married taxpayers filing a joint return ($14,810 for other taxpayers), the difference, multiplied by the appropriate phaseout percentage, is subtracted from the maximum earned income credit.

It is not necessary for the taxpayer to actually compute the earned income credit. To simplify the compliance process, the IRS issues an Earned Income Credit Table for the determination of the appropriate amount of the credit. This table and a worksheet are included in the instructions available to individual taxpayers.

Advance Payment. The earned income credit is a form of negative income tax (a refundable credit for taxpayers who do not have a tax liability). An eligible individual may elect to receive advance payments of the earned income credit from his or her employer (rather than receiving the credit from the IRS upon filing the tax return). The amount that can be received in advance is limited to 60 percent of the credit that is available to a taxpayer with only one qualifying child. If this election is made, the taxpayer must file a certificate of eligibility (Form W–5) with his or her employer and must file a tax return for the year the income is earned.

Suggested Further Readings

"Easements Were Qualified Conservation Contributions," *Practical Tax Strategies*, July 2005, pp. 54–57.

Ellen D. Cook, "Innocent Spouse Provisions Evolve as IRS Clarifies Equitable Relief," *Practical Tax Strategies*, October 2004, pp. 196–209.

Karyn Bybee Friske and Darlene Pulliam, "The Marriage Penalty after the JGTRRA," *The Tax Adviser*, May 2004, pp. 284–288.

Michael E. Kitces, "Mortgage Interest Deductibility: More Than Meets the Eye," *Practical Tax Strategies*, September 2005, pp. 138–151.

David Lavin, Myron S. Lubell, and Angela F. Moree, "Tax Savings Ease the Task of Saving for College Tuition," *Practical Tax Strategies*, May 2004, pp. 283–297.

[104] § 32. This credit is subject to indexation.

KEY TERMS

Accident and health insurance benefits, 16–33
Acquisition indebtedness, 16–42
Adoption expenses credit, 16–52
Alimony and separate maintenance payments, 16–27
Capital gain property, 16–47
Charitable contribution, 16–45
Child tax credit, 16–53
Compensatory damages, 16–31
Credit for child and dependent care expenses, 16–54
Dependency exemption, 16–10
Earned income credit, 16–56
Educational savings bonds, 16–33
E-file, 16–23
Gift, 16–29
Head of household, 16–25
Health Savings Account (HSA), 16–37
Home equity loans, 16–42
HOPE scholarship credit, 16–55
Investment interest, 16–42
Itemized deductions, 16–6
Kiddie tax, 16–21
Lifetime learning credit, 16–55
Marriage penalty, 16–25
Medical expenses, 16–35
Miscellaneous itemized deductions, 16–49
Multiple support agreement, 16–13
Net investment income, 16–42
Ordinary income property, 16–47
Personal exemption, 16–9
Points, 16–43
Punitive damages, 16–32
Qualified residence interest, 16–42
Qualifying child, 16–10
Qualifying relative, 16–12
Scholarship, 16–30
Standard deduction, 16–6
Surviving spouse, 16–25
Tax Rate Schedules, 16–18
Tax Table, 16–18
Unearned income, 16–21

PROBLEM MATERIALS

PROBLEMS

1. Compute the taxable income for 2006 in each of the following independent situations:
   a. Sidney and Cora, ages 39 and 37, are married and file a joint return. In addition to two dependent children, they have AGI of $55,000 and itemized deductions of $8,300.
   b. Kay, age 66, is unmarried and supports her two dependent parents who live in their own home. She has AGI of $70,000 and itemized deductions of $8,100.
   c. Colin, age 60, is an abandoned spouse. The household he maintains includes two unmarried stepdaughters, ages 16 and 17, who qualify as his dependents. He has AGI of $81,000 and itemized deductions of $7,900.
   d. Angel, age 33, is a surviving spouse and maintains a household for her four dependent children. She has AGI of $48,000 and itemized deductions of $8,200.
   e. Dale, age 42, is divorced but maintains the home in which he and his daughter, Jill, live. Jill is single and qualifies as Dale's dependent. Dale has AGI of $54,000 and itemized deductions of $6,900.

2. Compute the taxable income for 2006 for Quincy on the basis of the following information. His filing status is head of household.

Salary	$40,000
Interest income from bonds issued by General Motors Corporation	1,200
Child support payments made	3,600
Alimony payments made	2,400
Contribution to traditional IRA	4,000
Gift from grandparents	30,000
Capital loss from stock investment	4,000
Amount won in football office pool (sports gambling is against the law where Quincy lives)	3,200
Number of dependents (parents, ages 66 and 68)	2
Age	40

3. Compute the taxable income for 2006 for Marjory on the basis of the following information. Marjory is married but has not seen or heard from her husband since 2004.

Salary	$ 60,000
Interest on bonds issued by the City of Independence (MO)	2,000
Interest on CD issued by Hibernia National Bank	1,800
Cash dividend received on GE common stock	2,300
Life insurance proceeds paid on death of aunt (Marjory was the designated beneficiary of the policy)	50,000
Inheritance received on death of aunt	110,000
Carlton (a cousin) repaid a loan Marjory made to him in 2003 (no interest was provided for)	5,000
Itemized deductions (state income tax, property taxes on residence, interest on home mortgage, charitable contributions)	7,200
Number of dependents (children, ages 13 and 15)	2
Age	40

4. Determine the amount of the standard deduction allowed for 2006 in the following independent situations. In each case, assume the taxpayer is claimed as another person's dependent.
   a. Hollis, age 17, has income as follows: $500 interest from a certificate of deposit and $4,900 from repairing cars.
   b. Sheila, age 18, has income as follows: $400 cash dividends from a stock investment and $3,400 from handling a paper route.
   c. Trent, age 15, has income as follows: $1,200 interest on a bank savings account and $400 for painting a neighbor's fence.
   d. Susan, age 15, has income as follows: $300 cash dividends from a stock investment and $600 from grooming pets.
   e. Molly, age 66 and a widow, has income as follows: $1,100 from a bank savings account and $1,900 from baby-sitting.

5. Using the legend provided below, classify each statement as to the taxpayer for dependency exemption purposes.

Legend		
QC	=	Could be a qualifying child
QR	=	Could be a qualifying relative
B	=	Could satisfy the definition of both a qualifying child and a qualifying relative
N	=	Could not satisfy the definition of *either* a qualifying child or a qualifying relative

   a. Taxpayer's son has gross income of $6,000.
   b. Taxpayer's niece has gross income of $6,000.
   c. Taxpayer's mother lives with him.
   d. Taxpayer's daughter is age 25 and not disabled.
   e. Taxpayer's daughter is age 18 but does not live with him.
   f. Taxpayer's cousin does not live with her.
   g. Taxpayer's brother lives with her.
   h. Taxpayer's sister does not live with him.
   i. Taxpayer's nephew is age 20 and a full-time student.
   j. Taxpayer's grandson does not live with her and has gross income of $7,000.

6. For tax year 2006, determine the number of personal and dependency exemptions in each of the following independent situations:
   a. Leo and Amanda (ages 48 and 46) are husband and wife and furnish more than 50% of the support of their two children, Elton (age 18) and Trista (age 24). During the year, Elton earns $4,500 providing transportation for elderly persons with disabilities, and Trista receives a $5,000 scholarship for tuition at the law school she attends.

b. Audry (age 65) is divorced and lives alone. She maintains a household in which her ex-husband, Clint, and his mother, Olive, live and furnishes more than 50% of their support. Olive is age 82 and blind.

c. Jacque (age 52) furnishes more than 50% of the support of his married daughter, Carin, and her husband, Pierce, who live with him. Both Carin and Pierce are age 18. During the year, Pierce earned $4,000 from a part-time job. All parties live in New York (a common law state).

d. Assume the same facts as in (c), except that all parties live in Nevada (a community property state).

Ethics

7. For the six years prior to his death in late 2006, Jesse lived with his daughter, Hannah. Because he had no source of income, Jesse was supported by equal contributions from Hannah and his two sons, Bill and Bob. At Jesse's funeral, his surviving children are amazed to discover that none of them has been claiming Jesse as a dependent. Upon the advice of the director of the funeral home, they decide to divide, among themselves, the dependency exemptions for the past six years. Multiple Forms 2120 are executed, and each of the three children files amended returns for different past years. As Jesse died before the end of the current year, no deduction is planned for 2006.

   Comment on the tax expectations of the parties involved.

8. Dudley and Lisa Berg are married and file a joint return. Their four children and Dudley's parents qualify as their dependents. If the Bergs have AGI of $250,000, what is their allowable deduction for personal and dependency exemptions for 2006?

9. Using the Tax Rate Schedules, compute the 2006 tax liability for each taxpayer:

   a. Hector (age 42) is a surviving spouse and provides all of the support of his three minor children who live with him. He also maintains the household in which his parents live and furnished 60% of their support. Besides interest on City of Flint bonds in the amount of $1,200, Hector's father received $2,400 from a part-time job. Hector has a salary of $70,000, a short-term capital loss of $4,000, a cash prize of $2,000 from a church raffle, and itemized deductions of $9,500.

   b. Penny (age 45) is single and provides more than 50% of the support of Rosalyn (a family friend), Flo (a niece, age 18), and Jerold (a nephew, age 18). Both Rosalyn and Flo live with Penny, but Jerold (a French citizen) lives in Canada. Penny earns a salary of $80,000, contributes $4,000 to a traditional IRA, and receives sales proceeds of $15,000 for an RV that cost $40,000 and was used for vacations. She has $8,000 in itemized deductions.

10. Which of the following taxpayers must file a Federal income tax return for 2006?

   a. Ben, age 19, is a full-time college student. He is claimed as a dependent by his parents. He earned $5,200 in wages during the year.

   b. Anita, age 12, is claimed as a dependent by her parents. She earned interest income of $1,200 during the year.

   c. Earl, age 16, is claimed as a dependent by his parents. He earned wages of $2,700 and interest of $1,100 during the year.

   d. Karen, age 16 and blind, is claimed as a dependent by her parents. She earned wages of $2,600 and interest of $1,200 during the year.

   e. Pat, age 17, is claimed as a dependent by her parents. She earned interest of $300 during the year. In addition, she earned $550 during the summer operating her own business at the beach, where she painted caricatures of her customers.

Decision Making

11. Each year, the Hundleys normally have itemized deductions of $9,500, including a $3,600 pledge payment to their church. Upon the advice of a friend, they do the following: in early January 2006, they pay their pledge for 2005; during 2006, they pay the pledge for 2006; and in late December 2006, they prepay their pledge for 2007.

   a. Explain what the Hundleys are trying to accomplish.

   b. What will be the tax saving if their marginal tax bracket is 25% for all three years? (Assume the standard deduction amounts for 2006 and 2007 are the same).

12. Under the terms of their divorce agreement, Barry is to transfer common stock (cost of $25,000, market value of $60,000) to Sandra. Barry and Sandra have a 14-year-old child. Sandra will have custody of the child, and Barry is to pay $300 per month as child support. In addition, Sandra is to receive $1,000 per month for 10 years. However, the payments will be reduced to $750 per month when their child reaches age 21. In the

first year under the agreement, Sandra receives the common stock and the correct cash payments for six months. How will the terms of the agreement affect Sandra's gross income?

13. For each of the following, determine the amount that should be included in gross income:
    a. Joe was selected as the most valuable player in the Super Bowl. In recognition of this, he was awarded a sports car worth $60,000 plus $150,000 in cash.
    b. Wanda won the Mrs. America beauty contest. She received various prizes valued at $100,000. None of the $100,000 was for a scholarship or travel expenses.
    c. George was awarded the Nobel Peace Prize. He directed the Nobel committee to pay the $900,000 prize to State University, his alma mater.

Extender

Decision Making

14. Linda and Don are married and file a joint return. In 2006, they received $9,000 in Social Security benefits and $35,000 in taxable pension benefits and interest.
    a. Compute the couple's adjusted gross income on a joint return.
    b. Don would like to know whether they should sell for $100,000 (at no gain or loss) a corporate bond that pays 8% in interest each year and use the proceeds to buy a $100,000 nontaxable State of Virginia bond that will pay $6,000 in interest each year.
    c. If Linda in (a) works part-time and earns $30,000, how much would Linda and Don's adjusted gross income increase?

15. Alejandro was awarded an academic scholarship to State University for the 2006–2007 academic year. He received $5,000 in August and $6,000 in December 2006. Alejandro had enough personal savings to pay all expenses as they came due. Alejandro's expenditures for the relevant period were as follows:

Tuition, August 2006	$ 3,300
Tuition, December 2006	3,400
Room and board	
August–December 2006	3,000
January–May 2007	2,400
Books and educational supplies	
August–December 2006	1,000
January–May 2007	1,200

Determine the effect on Alejandro's gross income for 2006 and 2007.

16. Liz sued an overzealous bill collector and received the following settlement:

Damage to her automobile the collector attempted to repossess	$ 1,000
Physical damage to her arm caused by the collector	8,000
Loss of income while her arm was healing	6,000
Punitive damages	30,000

    a. What effect does the settlement have on Liz's gross income?
    b. Assume Liz also collected $40,000 of damages for slander to her personal reputation caused by the bill collector misrepresenting the facts to Liz's employer and other creditors. Is this $40,000 included in Liz's gross income?

17. Doug and Karen are married and together have AGI of $80,000 in 2006. They have two dependents and file a joint return. They pay $3,000 for a high-deductible health insurance policy and contribute $2,400 to a qualified Health Savings Account. During the year, they paid the following amounts for medical care: $7,500 in doctor and dentist bills and hospital expenses, and $1,700 for prescribed medicine and drugs. In November 2006, they received an insurance reimbursement of $2,100 for hospitalization. They expect to receive an additional reimbursement of $1,000 in January 2007. Determine the maximum deduction allowable for medical expenses in 2006.

Ethics

18. Ron, who lives in Phoenix, has a chronic heart problem. He flies to Rochester, Minnesota several times each year for checkups and treatment at the Mayo Clinic, which has one of the most highly rated heart treatment programs in the United States. On each trip, he visits his two children, who live in Rochester with his ex-wife. Is Ron justified in deducting the cost of his airline tickets and his lodging in Rochester as a medical expense?

Issue ID

19. A local ophthalmologist's advertising campaign included a certificate for a free radial keratotomy for the lucky winner of a drawing. Ahmad held the winning ticket, which was drawn in December 2005. Ahmad had no vision problems and was uncertain what he should do with the prize. In February 2006, Ahmad's daughter, who lives with his former wife, was diagnosed with a vision problem that could be treated with either prescription glasses or a radial keratotomy. The divorce decree requires that Ahmad pay for all medical expenses incurred for his daughter. Identify the relevant tax issues for Ahmad.

20. Juan suffers from emphysema and severe allergies and, upon the recommendation of his physician, has a dust elimination system installed in his personal residence. In connection with the system, Juan incurs and pays the following amounts during the current year:

Dust elimination system	$7,500
Increase in utility bills due to the system	400
Cost of certified appraisal	300

The system has an estimated useful life of 10 years. The appraisal was to determine the value of Juan's residence with and without the system. The appraisal states that the system increased the value of Juan's residence by $1,500. How much of these expenditures qualifies for the medical expense deduction in the current year?

21. Dylan is a self-employed, calendar year taxpayer. He reports on the cash basis. Dylan made the following estimated state income tax payments:

Date	Amount
January 15, 2006	$1,800 (4th payment for 2005)
April 15, 2006	2,250 (1st payment for 2006)
June 15, 2006	2,250 (2nd payment for 2006)
September 15, 2006	2,250 (3rd payment for 2006)
January 15, 2007	2,250 (4th payment for 2006)

Dylan had a tax overpayment of $1,200 on his 2005 state income tax return and, rather than requesting a refund, had the overpayment applied to his 2006 state income taxes. What is the amount of Dylan's state income tax itemized deduction for his 2006 Federal income tax return?

Decision Making

Communications

22. Carol Sharp incurred $29,250 of interest expense related to her investments in 2006. Her investment income included $7,000 of interest, $5,500 of qualified dividends, and a $12,750 net capital gain on the sale of securities. Carol has asked you to compute the amount of her deduction for investment interest, taking into consideration any options she might have. In addition, she has asked for your suggestions as to any tax planning alternatives that might be available. Write a letter to her that contains your advice. Carol lives at 208 Lone Tree Circle, Napa, CA 94558.

Decision Making

23. Justine borrowed $100,000 to acquire a parcel of land to be held for investment purposes. During 2006, she paid interest of $11,000 on the loan. She had AGI of $75,000 for the year. Other items related to Justine's investments include the following:

Investment income	$10,000
Long-term capital gain on sale of stock	7,500
Investment counsel fees	2,000

Justine is unmarried and elects to itemize her deductions. She has no miscellaneous itemized deductions other than the investment counsel fees.

a. Determine Justine's investment interest deduction for 2006, assuming she does not make any special election regarding the computation of investment income.
b. Discuss the treatment of Justine's investment interest that is disallowed in 2006.
c. What election could Justine make to increase the amount of her investment interest deduction for 2006?

24. In 1997, Roland, who is single, purchased a personal residence for $340,000 and took out a mortgage of $200,000 on the property. In May of the current year, when the

residence had a fair market value of $440,000 and Roland owed $140,000 on the mortgage, he took out a home equity loan for $220,000. He used the funds to purchase a recreational vehicle, which he uses 100% for personal use. What is the maximum amount on which Roland can deduct home equity interest?

25. Pedro contributes a painting to an art museum in 2006. He has owned the painting for 12 years, and it is worth $130,000 at the time of the donation. Pedro's adjusted basis for the painting is $90,000, and his AGI for 2006 is $250,000. Pedro has asked you whether he should make the reduced deduction election for this contribution. Write a letter to Pedro Valdez at 1289 Greenway Avenue, Foster City, CA 94404 and advise him on this matter. *Decision Making* *Communications*

26. In December each year, Alice Young contributes 10% of her gross income to the United Way (a 50% organization). Alice, who is in the 35% marginal tax bracket, is considering the following alternatives as charitable contributions in December 2006: *Decision Making* *Communications*

	Fair Market Value
(1) Cash donation	$21,000
(2) Unimproved land held for six years ($3,000 basis)	21,000
(3) Blue Corporation stock held for eight months ($3,000 basis)	21,000
(4) Gold Corporation stock held for two years ($26,000 basis)	21,000

Alice has asked you to help her decide which of the potential contributions listed above will be most advantageous taxwise. Evaluate the four alternatives, and write a letter to Alice to communicate your advice to her. Her address is 2622 Bayshore Drive, Berkeley, CA 94709.

27. The Skins Game, which involves four of the top golfers on the PGA Tours, is held each year on the weekend after Thanksgiving. Total prize money amounts to $1 million, and the leading money winner also receives an automobile as a prize. Twenty percent of the money won by each player goes to charity. In addition, on the par three holes, the winner of the hole receives the keys to an automobile, which goes to the player's favorite charity. Identify the relevant tax issues for the players. Consider the following possibilities with respect to the car won by the leading money winner: (1) keep the car for personal use and sell his or her present car; (2) sell the new car; (3) give the car to a friend or relative; (4) donate the car to charity; or (5) give the car to his or her caddy. *Issue ID*

28. Eldrick, who is single, had an AGI of $350,000 during 2006. He incurred the following expenses and losses during the year:

Medical expenses before 7.5%-of-AGI limitation	$36,000
State and local income taxes	5,700
State sales tax	780
Real estate taxes	4,900
Home mortgage interest	5,900
Charitable contributions	5,200
Casualty loss before 10% limitation (after $100 floor)	44,000
Unreimbursed employee expenses subject to 2%-of-AGI limitation	8,200
Gambling losses (Eldrick had $6,800 of gambling income)	9,200

Compute Eldrick's itemized deductions before and after the overall limitation.

29. Ann and Bill were on the list of a local adoption agency for several years seeking to adopt a child. Finally, in 2005, good news comes their way and an adoption seems imminent. They pay qualified adoption expenses of $4,000 in 2005 and $11,000 in 2006. Assume the adoption becomes final in 2006. Ann and Bill always file a joint income tax return.
   a. Determine the amount of the adoption expenses credit available to Ann and Bill assuming their combined annual income is $90,000. In what year(s) will they benefit from the credit?
   b. Assuming Ann and Bill's modified AGI in 2005 and 2006 is $175,000, calculate the amount of the adoption expenses credit.

30. Kevin and Jane are husband and wife and have one dependent child, age 9. Kevin is a full-time student for all of the current year, while Jane earns $36,000 as a nurse's aide. To provide care for their child while Kevin attends classes and Jane works, they pay Sara (Jane's 17-year-old sister) $2,900. Sara is not a dependent of Kevin and Jane. Assuming Kevin and Jane file a joint return, what, if any, is their credit for child and dependent care expenses?

31. Ralph and Jill are husband and wife and have two dependent children under the age of 13. They both are gainfully employed and during the current year earn salaries as follows: $22,500 (Ralph) and $5,000 (Jill). To care for their children while they work, they pay Megan (Ralph's mother) $5,600. Assuming Ralph and Jill file a joint return, what, if any, is their credit for child and dependent care expenses?

Communications

32. Bernadette, a longtime client of yours, is an architect and president of the local Rotary chapter. To keep up to date with the latest developments in her profession, she attends continuing education seminars offered by the architecture school at State University. During 2006, Bernadette spends $2,000 on course tuition to attend such seminars. She also spends another $400 on architecture books during the year. Bernadette's son is a senior majoring in engineering at the University of the Midwest. During the 2006 calendar year, Bernadette's son incurs the following expenses: $8,200 for tuition ($4,100 per semester) and $750 for books and supplies. Bernadette's son, whom she claims as a dependent, lives at home while attending school full-time. Bernadette is married, files a joint return, and has a combined AGI with her husband of $95,000.
    a. Calculate Bernadette's education tax credit for 2006.
    b. In her capacity as president of the local Rotary chapter, Bernadette has asked you to make a 30–45 minute speech outlining the different ways the tax law helps defray (1) the cost of higher education and (2) the cost of continuing education once someone is in the workforce. Prepare an outline of possible topics for presentation. A tentative title for your presentation is "How Can the Tax Law Help Pay for College and Continuing Professional Education?"

33. Briefly discuss the requirements that must be satisfied for a taxpayer to qualify for the earned income tax credit.

Ethics

34. For many years, Loretta Johnson, a single mother of three children, has been struggling to make ends meet by working at two jobs that pay barely the minimum wage and together provide just over $15,000. Fortunately, her housing and food costs have been partially subsidized through various government programs. In addition, she has been able to take advantage of the earned income credit, which has provided around $3,000 annually to help her with living expenses. The credit has truly made a difference in the lives of Loretta and her family by helping them keep their creditors at bay. She is proud that she has worked hard and provided for her family for many years without having to accept welfare.

    Now, however, Loretta faces a problem as her children have grown up and moved out of her home. With no qualified children in her household, she no longer qualifies for the earned income credit. Although she will continue working at her two jobs, such a significant loss to her household budget cuts into her ability to be self-reliant. As a survival strategy and as a way of keeping the earned income credit, Loretta arranges to have one of her grandchildren live with her for just over six months every year. This enables a significant percentage of her household budget to be secure. How do you react to Loretta's strategy?

Extender

Decision Making

35. Joyce, a widow, lives in an apartment with her two minor children (ages 8 and 10) whom she supports. Joyce earns $32,000 during 2006. She uses the standard deduction.
    a. Calculate the amount, if any, of Joyce's earned income credit.
    b. During the year, Joyce is offered a new job that has greater future potential than her current job. If she accepts the job offer, her earnings for the year would be $36,500; however, she will not qualify for the earned income credit. Using after-tax cash-flow calculations, determine whether Joyce should accept the new job offer.

CUMULATIVE PROBLEMS

Tax Return Problem
Decision Making
Communications
TurboTax

36. Horace Fern, age 43, lives at 321 Grant Avenue, Cheyenne, WY 82002. Horace's mother, Kate (age 65), lived with him until her death in August 2005. Up to the time of her death, Kate qualified as Horace's dependent. Horace maintained the household where he and his mother lived.

Horace is a manager for Bison Lumber Company at a yearly salary of $72,000. Because his job duties will be expanded, Bison plans to increase Horace's salary by 10% starting in 2006.

During 2005, Horace paid $3,300 ($300 each month) in alimony to Janet, his ex-wife. As Janet was remarried in late November, Horace's alimony obligation has terminated.

Besides his salary, Horace received interest income of $6,700 from Western Bank and $7,300 from First Savings Bank on $400,000 in certificates of deposit (CDs) he owns. Horace received the CDs as a gift from his mother several years ago.

Except as otherwise noted, Horace's expenditures for 2005 are summarized below:

Interest on home mortgage	$3,300
Property taxes on home	1,200
Sales taxes (actual amount paid)	1,600
Charitable contributions	600

Relevant Social Security numbers are as follows:

Horace Fern	111–20–4444
Kate Fern	333–55–1111
Janet Fern	520–33–4432

Federal income taxes withheld from Horace's salary amounted to $13,000. FICA taxes withheld by his employer were $5,508 [($72,000 × 6.2% for Social Security) + ($72,000 × 1.45% for Medicare)].

Part 1—Tax Computation
Compute Horace's net tax payable or refund due for 2005. Horace does not wish to contribute to the Presidential Election Campaign Fund. If he has overpaid, he wants the amount refunded. If you use tax forms for your computations, you will need Form 1040 and Schedules A and B. Suggested software: TurboTax.

Part 2—Tax Planning
In addition to preparing the return for 2005, Horace has asked you to advise him regarding his tax situation for 2006. He is particularly concerned about the tax effects of the following:

- The death of Kate.
- The cessation of alimony payments due to Janet's remarriage.
- The salary increase.
- Interest income on the CDs.

Write a letter to Horace in which you summarize (in approximate amounts) how much more (or less) he will owe in income taxes for 2006. Also include recommendations on what can be done to mitigate the tax consequences resulting from the investment in CDs. Assume that Horace's itemized deductions will remain constant in 2006.

Tax Return Problem
Decision Making
TurboTax

37. Alice J. and Bruce M. Byrd are married taxpayers who file a joint return. Their Social Security numbers are 034–48–4382 and 016–50–9556, respectively. Alice's birthday is September 21, 1959, and Bruce's is June 27, 1958. They live at 473 Revere Avenue, Ames, MA 01850. Alice is the office manager for Ames Dental Clinic, 433 Broad Street, Ames, MA 01850 (employer identification number 37–4000456). Bruce is the manager of a Super Burgers fast-food outlet owned and operated by Plymouth Corporation, 1247 Central Avenue, Hauppauge, NY 11788 (employer identification number 37–6000987).

The following information is shown on their Wage and Tax Statements (Form W–2) for 2005.

Line	Description	Alice	Bruce
1	Wages, tips, other compensation	$52,600	$61,500
2	Federal income tax withheld	4,180	5,990
3	Social Security wages	52,600	61,500
4	Social Security tax withheld	3,261	3,813
5	Medicare wages and tips	52,600	61,500
6	Medicare tax withheld	763	892
15	State	Massachusetts	Massachusetts
16	State wages, tips, etc.	52,600	61,500
17	State income tax withheld	2,280	2,990

The Byrds provide over half of the support of their two children, Cynthia (born January 25, 1981, Social Security number 017–44–9126) and John (born February 7, 1983, Social Security number 017–27–4148), who live with them. Both children are full-time students and live with the Byrds except when they are away at college. Cynthia earned $3,700 from a summer internship in 2005, and John earned $3,400 from a part-time job.

During 2005, the Byrds furnished 60% of the total support of Bruce's widower father, Sam Byrd (born March 6, 1930, Social Security number 034–82–8583). Sam lived alone and covered the rest of his support with his Social Security benefits. Sam died in November, and Bruce, the beneficiary of a policy on Sam's life, received life insurance proceeds of $600,000 on December 28.

The Byrds had the following expenses relating to their personal residence during 2005:

Property taxes	$4,720
Interest on home mortgage	9,130
Repairs to roof	4,780
Utilities	3,810
Fire and theft insurance	2,290

The following facts relate to medical expenses for 2005:

Medical insurance premiums	$4,380
Doctor bill for Sam incurred in 2004 and not paid until 2005	7,760
Operation for Sam	7,310
Prescription medicines for Sam	860
Hospital expenses for Sam	2,850
Reimbursement from insurance company, received in 2005	3,000

The medical expenses for Sam represent most of the 60% Bruce contributed toward his father's support.

Other relevant information follows:

- When they filed their 2004 state return in 2005, the Byrds paid additional state income tax of $950.
- During 2005, Alice and Bruce attended a dinner dance sponsored by the Ames Police Disability Association (a qualified charitable organization). The Byrds paid $400 for the tickets. The cost of comparable entertainment would normally be $160.
- The Byrds contributed $4,800 to Ames Assembly Church and gave used clothing (cost of $1,100 and fair market value of $450) to the Salvation Army. All donations are supported by receipts.
- In 2005, the Byrds received interest income of $2,695, which was reported on a Form 1099–INT from Second National Bank.
- Alice's employer requires that all employees wear uniforms to work. During 2005, Alice spent $482 on new uniforms and $211 on laundry charges.
- Bruce paid $320 for an annual subscription to the *Journal of Franchise Management.*
- Neither Alice's nor Bruce's employer reimburses for employee expenses.
- The Byrds do not keep the receipts for the sales taxes they paid and had no major purchases subject to sales tax.

- Alice and Bruce paid no estimated Federal income tax. Neither Alice nor Bruce wishes to designate $3 to the Presidential Election Campaign Fund.

Part 1—Tax Computation
Compute net tax payable or refund due for Alice and Bruce Byrd for 2005. If they have overpaid, they want the amount to be refunded to them. If you use tax forms for your computations, you will need Form 1040 and Schedules A and B. Suggested software: TurboTax.

Part 2—Tax Planning
Alice and Bruce are planning some significant changes for 2006. They have provided you with the following information and asked you to project their taxable income and tax liability for 2006.

The Byrds will invest the $600,000 of life insurance proceeds in short-term certificates of deposit (CDs) and use the interest for living expenses during 2006. They expect to earn total interest of $21,000 on the CDs.

Bruce has been promoted to regional manager, and his salary for 2006 will be $85,000. He estimates that state income tax withheld will increase by $4,000.

Alice, who has been diagnosed with a serious illness, will take a leave of absence from work during 2006. The estimated cost for her medical treatment is $14,500, of which $5,500 will be reimbursed by their insurance company in 2006.

John will graduate from college in December 2005 and will take a job in New York City in January 2006. His starting salary will be $37,500.

Assume all the information reported in 2005 will be the same in 2006 unless other information has been presented above.

38. Paul and Donna Decker are married taxpayers, ages 44 and 42, who file a joint return for 2006. The Deckers live at 1121 College Avenue, Carmel, IN 46032. Paul is an assistant manager at Carmel Motor Inn, and Donna is a teacher at Carmel Elementary School. They present you with W–2 Forms that reflect the following information:

Tax Return Problem

	Paul	Donna
Salary	$58,000	$56,000
Federal tax withheld	10,300	9,700
State income tax withheld	900	800
FICA (Social Security and Medicare) withheld	4,437	4,284
Social Security numbers	222–11–4567	333–11–9872

Donna is the custodial parent of two children from a previous marriage who reside with the Deckers through the school year. The children, Larry and Jane Parker, reside with their father, Bob, during the summer. Relevant information for the children follows:

	Larry	Jane
Age	17	18
Social Security numbers	305–11–4567	303–11–9872
Months spent with Deckers	9	9

Under the divorce decree, Bob pays child support of $150 per month per child during the nine months the children live with the Deckers. Bob says he spends $200 per month per child during the three summer months they reside with him. Donna and Paul can document that they provide $2,000 of support per child per year. The divorce decree is silent as to which parent can claim the exemption for the children.

In August, Paul and Donna added a suite to their home to provide more comfortable accommodations for Hannah Snyder (Social Security number 263–33–4738), Donna's mother, who had moved in with them in February 2005 after the death of Donna's father. Not wanting to borrow money for this addition, Paul sold 300 shares of Acme Corporation stock for $50 per share on May 3, 2006, and used the proceeds of $15,000 to cover construction costs. The Deckers had purchased the stock on April 29, 2002, for $25 per share. They received dividends of $750 on the jointly owned stock a month before the sale.

Hannah, who is 66 years old, received $7,500 in Social Security benefits during the year, of which she gave the Deckers $2,000 to use toward household expenses and deposited the remainder in her personal savings account. The Deckers determine that they have spent $2,500 of their own money for food, clothing, medical expenses, and other items for Hannah. They do not know what the rental value of Hannah's suite would be, but they estimate it would be at least $300 per month.

Interest paid during the year included the following:

Home mortgage interest (paid to Carmel Federal Savings and Loan)	$7,890
Interest on an automobile loan (paid to Carmel National Bank)	1,490
Interest on Citibank Visa card	870

In July, Paul hit a submerged rock while boating. Fortunately, he was thrown from the boat, landed in deep water, and was uninjured. However, the boat, which was uninsured, was destroyed. Paul had paid $25,000 for the boat in June 2005, and its value was appraised at $18,000 on the date of the accident.

The Deckers paid doctor and hospital bills of $8,700 and were reimbursed $2,000 by their insurance company. They spent $640 for prescription drugs and medicines and $2,810 for premiums on their health insurance policy. They have filed additional claims of $1,200 with their insurance company and have been told they will receive payment for that amount in January 2007. Included in the amounts paid for doctor and hospital bills were payments of $380 for Hannah and $850 for the children.

Additional information of potential tax consequence follows:

Real estate taxes paid	$3,700
Sales taxes paid (per table)	1,379
Cash contributions to church	2,100
Appraised value of books donated to public library	740
Paul's unreimbursed employee expenses to attend hotel management convention:	
Airfare	340
Hotel	170
Meals	95
Registration fee	340
Refund of state income tax for 2005 (the Deckers itemized on their 2005 Federal tax return)	1,520

Compute net tax payable or refund due for the Deckers for 2006. Ignore the child tax credit in your computations. If they have overpaid, the amount is to be credited toward their taxes for 2007.

BRIDGE *Discipline*

1. George comes to you asking for your advice. He wishes to invest $10,000 either in a debt security or in an equity investment. His choices are as shown below:
   - Redbreast Corporation bond, annual coupon rate of 7.50%.
   - City of Philadelphia general obligation bond, coupon rate of 6.00%.
   - Blue Corporation 7.50% preferred stock (produces qualified dividend income).

   These alternatives are believed to carry comparable risk. Assuming George is in the 35% marginal tax bracket, which investment alternative could be expected to produce the superior annual after-tax rate of return?
2. Assume the same facts as in Problem 1, except that George is a C corporation rather than an individual and is in the 34% marginal tax bracket. Which investment strategy would maximize George, Inc.'s annual return?

RESEARCH PROBLEMS

Note: Solutions to Research Problems can be prepared by using the **RIA Checkpoint® Student Edition** online research product, which is available to accompany this text. It is also possible to prepare solutions to the Research Problems by using tax research materials found in a standard tax library.

THOMSON RIA

Communications

Research Problem 1. John and Marge Hudgens were married 26 years ago and have one child, Monica. Sometime in January 2005, after a particularly fierce argument, John packed his clothes and left for parts unknown. Marge has neither seen nor heard from him since.

Marge is employed and maintains the house where she and Monica live. Monica is a full-time student and will graduate from law school on May 9, 2006. During 2005 and 2006, Monica (age 22) earned over $9,000 each year from part-time jobs. She deposited part of her earnings in a savings account under her name and used the rest for her support. The remainder of Monica's support was provided by Marge.

Marge contacts you in March 2006 regarding tax advice. Specifically, she is interested in the answers to the following questions for tax year 2005 and 2006:

- What is her filing status?
- Can she claim Monica as a dependent?

a. Write a letter to Marge addressing her concerns. Marge lives at 1349 Center Street, Warrensburg, MO 64093.
b. Also prepare a memo for your firm's client files.

Research Problem 2. Bart and Arlene Keating are husband and wife and live in Mineola, Oregon. They have been married for 18 years and have four children, all of whom are teenagers. After the birth of her last child, Arlene took a job as a city clerk and, over the years, has become city treasurer. Since graduating from high school, Bart has worked as a dispatcher for the city fire and ambulance departments. As Arlene has some college training in finance and accounting, she handles the family's financial affairs, including reconciling the bank account, paying bills, and preparing all tax returns. She also takes care of major purchases (e.g., autos, furniture) and servicing of debt (e.g., home mortgage, auto loans, charge accounts).

The Keatings themselves maintain a modest lifestyle, but Arlene is quite generous with the children. All are well-dressed, attend summer camp, and have their own cars. Bart believes Arlene obtains any additional funds for the children's support through credit card financing and bank loans.

The Keatings filed joint returns for 2002 and 2003 that reflected their salary income. Arlene prepared the returns, and Bart signed them without reviewing them first. The returns did not show the $90,000 Arlene had embezzled from her employer over this two-year period.

The City of Mineola discovers the theft, and Arlene is tried and convicted of grand larceny. Due to the adverse publicity generated by these events, the Keatings are divorced, and Arlene moves to another state.

In 2006, the IRS assesses a deficiency against Bart for the income taxes that would have resulted if the embezzled amounts had been reported as income.

What are the rights of the parties?

Partial list of research aids:
§§ 6013(d)(3) and 6015.
Kathryn Cheshire, 115 T.C. 183 (2000).
Evelyn M. Martin, 80 TCM 665, T.C.Memo. 2000–346.

Research Problem 3. The taxpayer is an employee of a consulting firm and had over 50,000 miles of air travel in the current year. Her employer reimbursed all of the taxpayer's transportation expenses, but allows the taxpayer to retain the frequent-flyer miles. During the year, the taxpayer used the accumulated miles to purchase an airline ticket for her vacation. Without the frequent-flyer miles, the taxpayer would have been required to pay $1,200 for the ticket. Is the taxpayer required to recognize gross income from the receipt and use of the frequent-flyer miles?

Research Problem 4. Tom and Mary Smith, whose son was found murdered in a parking garage, offered a $100,000 reward for the city police to use to obtain information leading to the arrest and conviction of the murderer. As a result of the reward, a person who had overheard the murderer telling a friend about the crime reported the conversation to the police. The murderer was arrested and convicted, and the Smiths contributed the money to the police department, which gave the reward to the informant. Can the Smiths treat the payment as an itemized deduction?

Internet *Activity*

Use the tax resources of the Internet to address the following questions. Do not restrict your search to the World Wide Web, but include a review of newsgroups and general reference materials, practitioner sites and resources, primary sources of the tax law, chat rooms and discussion groups, and other opportunities.

Research Problem 5. A nonresident alien earns money in the United States that is subject to Federal income tax. What guidance does the IRS provide on what tax form needs to be used and on when it should be filed? In terms of the proper filing date, does it matter whether the earnings were subject to income tax withholding?

Research Problem 6. The IRS has unveiled a Web-based tool to help taxpayers determine whether they or their clients are eligible for the earned income credit. Locate this tool at the IRS Web site and then apply the facts related to a hypothetical taxpayer and determine if the earned income credit is available.

CHAPTER 17

Individuals as Employees and Proprietors

LEARNING OBJECTIVES

After completing Chapter 17, you should be able to:

LO.1

Distinguish between employee and self-employed status.

LO.2

Understand the exclusions from income available to employees who receive fringe benefits.

LO.3

Apply the rules for computing deductible expenses of employees including transportation, travel, moving, education, and entertainment expenses.

LO.4

Appreciate the difference between accountable and nonaccountable employee plans.

LO.5

Understand the tax provisions applicable to proprietors.

LO.6

Distinguish between business and hobby activities and apply the rules limiting the deduction of hobby losses.

OUTLINE

TAX *Talk*

The taxpayer—that's someone who works for the Federal government but doesn't have to take a civil service examination.

—Ronald Reagan

An individual may be an employee or may be self-employed. The terms *proprietor* and *independent contractor* are both used to describe self-employed individuals. These terms are used interchangeably throughout this chapter.

In many cases, it is difficult to distinguish between employees and self-employed individuals. This chapter begins with a discussion of the factors that must be considered in determining whether an individual is an employee or is self-employed. This is followed by a discussion of tax provisions applicable to employees and then by a discussion of tax provisions related to self-employed individuals.

LO.1

Distinguish between employee and self-employed status.

Employee versus Self-Employed

When one person performs services for another, the person performing the service is either an employee or self-employed (i.e., an **independent contractor**). Failure to recognize employee status can have serious consequences. Not only can interest and penalties result, but career opportunities, such as possible political opportunities or elected positions, can disappear in the wake of extensive negative media coverage.

The determination of employment status is already controversial and can be expected to become an even greater problem in the future. As a means for achieving greater flexibility and cost control, businesses are increasingly relying on self-employed persons (i.e., independent contractors) rather than employees for many services.

The IRS is very much aware that businesses have a tendency to wrongly classify workers as self-employed rather than as employees. In some cases, misclassification is unintentional and results from difficulty in applying the complex set of rules related to employee versus independent contractor status. In other cases, misclassification may be an intentional strategy to avoid certain costs that are associated with employees. Unlike employees, self-employed persons do not have to be included in

BRIDGE *Discipline*

Bridge to Equity or Fairness and Business Law

Max performs services for Calico, Inc. Amy performs services for Amber, Inc. They perform basically the same service. Yet Max is classified as an employee, and Amy is classified as an independent contractor. Does such a legal classification produce equitable results in terms of the effects it has on Max and Amy?

Employee status produces a number of potential perks. Included are coverage in the employer's fringe benefits programs such as medical insurance, group term life insurance, and § 132 fringe benefits. For an employee, the tax rate for Social Security is 6.2 percent and for Medicare, the rate is 1.45 percent (i.e., the employer is responsible for matching the employee amounts). For a self-employed person, the tax rates for Social Security and Medicare are 12.4 percent and 2.9 percent, respectively.

In distinguishing between an employee and an independent contractor, the overriding theme of common law is that the employee is subject to the will and control of the employer both as to what is to be done and as to how it is to be done. Put in more legal terminology, an employer has the right to control and direct the individual who performs the services, not only as to the result to be accomplished by the work but also as to the details and means by which the result is accomplished. Among the factors generally considered in determining whether this right exists are the following:

- Degree of control exercised over the details of the work.
- Provision of facilities used in the work.
- Opportunity for profit or loss.
- Right to discharge.
- Whether work is part of regular business.
- Permanency of the relationship.
- Relationship the parties believe they are creating.
- Manner of payment, by the job or by the hour.
- Skill required.
- Offering of the services to the general public rather than to one individual or entity.
- Distinct occupation or recognized trade or calling involved.
- Custom in the trade.

various fringe benefit programs and retirement plans. Furthermore, employers are not required to pay FICA and unemployment taxes (refer to Chapter 1) on compensation paid to independent contractors.

In terms of tax consequences, employment status also makes a great deal of difference to the worker. Allowable business expenses of self-employed taxpayers are classified as deductions *for* AGI and are reported on Schedule C (Profit or Loss from Business) of Form 1040.[1] On the other hand, unreimbursed business expenses incurred by employees are classified as itemized deductions and are deductible on Schedule A (as itemized deductions) only to the extent that the sum of certain miscellaneous itemized deductions exceeds 2 percent of the taxpayer's AGI. Unreimbursed employee expenses are reported on Form 2106 (Employee Business Expenses) and Schedule A (Itemized Deductions) of Form 1040.

Employee expenses that are reimbursed under an **accountable plan** (covered later in this chapter) are also reported as deductions *for* AGI. Employee expenses that are not reimbursed under an accountable plan are treated in the same way as unreimbursed expenses—deductible *from* AGI and limited to the excess over 2 percent of AGI.[2]

[1]§§ 62(a)(1) and 162(a).

[2]§ 67(a).

TAX *in the News* — **SELF-EMPLOYED OR EMPLOYED? MISCLASSIFICATION CAN BE COSTLY!**

Approximately a decade ago, the media sensation was the number of prominent persons who had run afoul of the so-called nanny tax. Simply stated, this meant not complying with payroll procedures applicable to domestics, baby sitters, and other household employees. This failure to comply with the tax law forced a President Clinton nominee for U.S. Attorney General, Zoe Baird, to withdraw from consideration. The publicity generated by this case, and others like it, had a sobering effect on the taxpaying public. By 1997, as many as 310,000 nanny tax forms (Schedule H, Form 1040) were being filed. Since then, however, the number of such returns has steadily declined. In 2001, for example, a new low of 263,000 was reached. This downward trend has continued with a new low of 239,810 nanny tax returns being filed in 2003.

What does this decline signify? Does it mean that a greater number of these household helpers are now self-employed (i.e., independent contractors) so as to be exempt from employee payroll procedures? Or does it mean that many taxpayers have forgotten about Zoe Baird and her costly lesson?

The Bernard Kerik incident in December 2004 must have been a touch of déjà vu. Nominated by President Bush to be head of Homeland Security, Kerik felt compelled to withdraw when it came to light that he had employed an illegal immigrant as a nanny. Ironically, as Secretary of Homeland Security, he would have overseen the enforcement of the nation's immigration laws. Furthermore, Kerik had compounded the wrongdoing by not paying any employment taxes on the wages earned by the nanny.

The moral of the story? If you aspire to a high-profile government appointment, avoid the nannygate trap!

Factors Considered in Classification

The pivotal issue in classifying an individual as an independent contractor or an employee is whether an employer-employee relationship exists. The IRS has created a complex *20-factor test* for determining whether a worker is an employee or an independent contractor. The courts, which have focused on a small number of these factors, generally hold that an individual is an employee if the individual or business acquiring the services:[3]

- has the right to specify the end result and the ways and means by which that result is to be attained,
- can exert will and control over the person providing the services with respect not only to *what* shall be done but also to *how* it shall be done,
- has the right to discharge, without legal liability, the person performing the service,
- furnishes tools or a place to work, and
- bases payment on time spent rather than the task performed.

Each case is tested on its own merits, and the right to control the means and methods of accomplishment is the definitive test. Generally, physicians, lawyers, dentists, contractors, subcontractors, and others who offer services to the public are not classified as employees.

DIGGING DEEPER 1

Find more information on this topic at our Web site: ***http://wft-entities.swlearning.com.***

EXAMPLE 1

Arnold is a lawyer whose major client accounts for 60% of his billings. He does the routine legal work and income tax returns at the client's request. He is paid a monthly retainer in addition to amounts charged for extra work. Arnold is a self-employed individual. Even though most of his income comes from one client, he still has the right to determine *how* the end result of his work is attained. ■

[3]Reg. § 31.3401(c)–(1)(b).

EXAMPLE 2

Ellen is a lawyer hired by Arnold to assist him in the performance of services for the client mentioned in Example 1. Ellen is under Arnold's supervision; he reviews her work and pays her an hourly fee. Ellen is Arnold's employee. ■

DIGGING DEEPER 2

*Find more information on this topic at our Web site: **http://wft-entities.swlearning.com.***

PLANNING *Strategies*

SELF-EMPLOYED INDIVIDUALS

★ **Framework Focus: Deductions**

Strategy ★ Maximize Deductible Amounts.

Some taxpayers have the flexibility to be classified as either employees or self-employed individuals. Examples include real estate agents and direct sellers. These taxpayers should carefully consider all factors and not automatically assume that self-employed status is preferable.

It is advantageous to deduct one's business expenses *for* AGI and avoid the 2 percent floor for miscellaneous itemized deductions. However, a self-employed individual may incur additional expenses, such as local gross receipts taxes, license fees, franchise fees, personal property taxes, and occupation taxes. Record-keeping and filing requirements can also be quite burdensome.

One of the most expensive considerations is the **self-employment tax** imposed on independent contractors and other self-employed individuals. For an employee in 2006, for example, the Social Security tax applies at a rate of 6.2 percent on a base amount of wages of $94,200, and the Medicare tax applies at a rate of 1.45 percent with no limit on the base amount. For self-employed persons, the rate, but not the base amount, for each tax doubles. Even though a deduction *for* AGI is allowed for one-half of the self-employment tax paid, an employee and a self-employed individual are not in the same tax position on equal amounts of earnings. For the applicability of these taxes to workers, see Chapter 1.

After analyzing all these factors, taxpayers in many cases may decide that employee status is preferable to self-employed status.

Exclusions Available to Employees

LO.2

Understand the exclusions from income available to employees who receive fringe benefits.

Several exclusions that are available to *all taxpayers* were discussed in Chapter 4; these include interest on obligations of state and local governments, life insurance proceeds, and income from discharge of indebtedness. Other exclusions, available only to *individuals*, were discussed in Chapter 16; these exclusions include gifts and inheritances, scholarships, and compensation for injuries and sickness. Exclusions available only to *employees* are discussed below.

Advantages of Qualified Fringe Benefits

Exclusions available only to *employees* are generally referred to as *qualified fringe benefits*. The popularity of fringe benefits is attributable to the fact that the cost of such benefits is deductible by employers and excludible by employees.

EXAMPLE 3

Cardinal Corporation, which has a marginal tax rate of 35%, provides health insurance coverage to employees at a cost of $1,000 per employee. Because Cardinal can deduct the health insurance premiums paid to provide this coverage, the net cost to the corporation is $650 per employee ($1,000 cost – $350 tax savings). The employee is allowed to exclude the value of this fringe benefit, so there is no tax cost to the employee.

The average employee of Cardinal Corporation is in the 28% bracket. If Cardinal did not provide the health insurance coverage and the employee paid a $1,000 premium, the employee would have to use after-tax dollars to acquire the coverage. The employee would have to earn $1,389 to pay for the coverage [$1,389 wages – ($1,389 × 28% tax)]. The after-tax cost to the corporation of $1,389 in wages is $903 ($1,389 wages – $486 corporate tax savings). Thus, the cost of health insurance coverage is $253 less per employee ($903 − $650) because it is both deductible by the corporation and excludible by the employee. ■

Employer-Sponsored Accident and Health Plans

Congress encourages employers to provide employees, retired former employees, and their dependents with accident and health benefits, disability insurance, and long-term care plans. The *premiums* are deductible by the employer and are excluded from the employee's gross income.[4] Although § 105(a) provides the general rule that the employee has includible income when he or she collects the insurance *benefits*, two exceptions are provided.

Section 105(b) generally excludes payments received for medical care of the employee, spouse, and dependents. However, if the payments are for expenses that do not meet the Code's definition of medical care,[5] the amount received must be included in gross income. In addition, the taxpayer must include in gross income any amounts received for medical expenses that were deducted by the taxpayer on a prior return.

EXAMPLE 4

In 2006, Tab's employer-sponsored health insurance plan paid $4,000 for hair transplants that did not meet the Code's definition of medical care. Tab must include the $4,000 in his gross income for 2006. ■

Section 105(c) excludes payments for the permanent loss or the loss of the use of a member or function of the body or the permanent disfigurement of the employee, spouse, or a dependent. However, payments that are a substitute for salary (e.g., related to the period of time absent) are included in income.

EXAMPLE 5

Jill lost an eye in an automobile accident unrelated to her work. As a result of the accident, Jill incurred $2,000 of medical expenses, which she deducted on her return. She collected $10,000 from an accident insurance policy carried by her employer. The benefits were paid according to a schedule of amounts that varied with the part of the body injured (e.g., $10,000 for loss of an eye, $20,000 for loss of a hand). Because the payment was for loss of a *member or function of the body*, the $10,000 is excluded from Jill's gross income. Jill was absent from work for a week as a result of the accident. Her employer also provided her with insurance that reimbursed her for the loss of income due to illness or injury. Jill collected $500, which is includible in her gross income. ■

Medical Reimbursement Plans

As noted above, the amounts received through the insurance coverage (insured plan benefits) are excluded from gross income under § 105. Unfortunately, because of cost considerations, the insurance companies that issue this type of policy usually require a broad coverage of employees. An alternative is to have a plan that is not funded with insurance (a self-insured arrangement). Under a self-insured plan, the employer reimburses employees directly for any medical expenses. The benefits received under a self-insured plan can be excluded from the employee's gross income, if the plan does not discriminate in favor of highly compensated employees.

Archer **Medical Savings Accounts (MSAs)** provided an alternative means of accomplishing a medical reimbursement plan. The MSA had two parts: catastrophic insurance coverage that kicked in after the deductible had been paid, and a savings account that could be tapped to pay the deductible and any uncovered medical expenses.

Legislation enacted in 2003 created the **Health Savings Account (HSA)**, which broadened the concept of MSAs and extended it to a larger set of taxpayers.[6] See additional discussion in Chapter 16.

[4] § 106, Reg. § 1.106–1, and Rev.Rul. 82–196, 1982–1 C.B. 106.

[5] See the discussion of medical care in Chapter 16.

[6] § 223.

BRIDGE *Discipline*

Bridge to Economic and Societal Needs

The media frequently report on the plight of our "senior citizens." Organizations such as the AARP effectively lobby for the rights of senior citizens through direct lobbying in Washington and through grassroots efforts throughout the country. With the graying of America, these concerns and lobbying efforts are likely to be magnified.

Congress, in the 1930s, enacted Social Security to partially provide for the retirement needs of our senior citizens. In the 1960s, Congress enacted Medicare to partially provide for the medical needs of our senior citizens.

The Internal Revenue Code contains a number of provisions that are "senior citizen friendly." Among these are the following:

- General exclusion, except for the "rich," of Social Security benefits from gross income (§ 86).
- Exclusion of life insurance proceeds from the gross income of the recipient (§ 101).
- Exclusion of medical insurance premiums and benefits from gross income (§ 105 and § 106).
- Limited exclusion from gross income of gain on the sale of a principal residence (§ 121).
- Limited exclusion from gross income of long-term care insurance premiums and benefits (§ 7702B).
- Beneficial treatment of retirement plans (Subchapter D).

Long-Term Care Benefits

Generally, long-term care insurance, which covers expenses such as the cost of care in a nursing home, is treated the same as accident and health insurance benefits. Thus, the employee does not recognize income when the employer pays the premiums. When benefits are received from the policy, whether the employer or the individual purchased the policy, the exclusion from gross income is limited to the *greater* of the following amounts:

- $250 (indexed amount for 2006) for each day the patient receives the long-term care.
- The actual cost of the care.

The excludible amount is reduced by any amounts received from other third parties (e.g., damages received).[7]

EXAMPLE 6

Hazel, who suffers from Alzheimer's disease, was a patient in a nursing home for the last 30 days of 2006. While in the nursing home, she incurred total costs of $7,800. Medicare paid $3,200 of the costs. Hazel received $5,100 from her long-term care insurance policy (which paid $170 per day while she was in the facility). The amount Hazel may exclude is calculated as follows:

Greater of:		
Daily statutory amount of $250 ($250 × 30 days)	$7,500	
Actual cost of the care	7,800	$ 7,800
Less: Amount received from Medicare		(3,200)
Amount of exclusion		$ 4,600

Therefore, Hazel must include $500 ($5,100 − $4,600) of the long-term care benefits received in her gross income. ■

[7] § 7702B.

The exclusion for long-term care insurance is not available if it is provided as part of a cafeteria plan or a flexible spending plan (discussed later in this chapter).

Meals and Lodging Furnished for the Convenience of the Employer

Income can take any form, including meals and lodging. However, § 119 excludes from gross income the value of meals and lodging provided to the employee and the employee's spouse and dependents under the following conditions:[8]

- The meals and/or lodging are *furnished by the employer*, on the employer's *business premises*, for the *convenience of the employer*.
- In the case of lodging, the *employee is required* to accept the lodging as a condition of employment.

The courts have construed these requirements strictly, as discussed below.

Furnished by the Employer. The following two questions have been raised with regard to the *furnished by the employer* requirement:

- Who is considered an *employee*?
- What is meant by *furnished*?

For the employee issue, the IRS and some courts have reasoned that because a partner is not an employee, the exclusion does not apply to a partner. However, the Tax Court and the Fifth Circuit Court of Appeals have ruled in favor of the taxpayer on this issue.[9]

On the issue of whether meals and lodging are *furnished* by the employer, the Supreme Court held that a *cash meal allowance* was ineligible for the exclusion because the employer did not actually furnish the meals.[10] Similarly, one court denied the exclusion where the employer paid for the food and supplied the cooking facilities but the employee prepared the meal.[11]

On the Employer's Business Premises. The *on the employer's business premises* requirement, applicable to both meals and lodging, has resulted in much litigation. The Regulations define business premises as simply "the place of employment of the employee."[12] Thus, the Sixth Circuit Court of Appeals held that a residence, owned by the employer and occupied by an employee, located two blocks from the motel that the employee managed was not part of the business premises.[13] However, the Tax Court considered an employer-owned house located across the street from the hotel that was managed by the taxpayer to be on the business premises of the employer.[14] Perhaps these two cases can be reconciled by comparing the distance from the lodging facilities to the place where the employer's business was conducted. The closer the lodging to the business operations, the more likely the convenience of the employer is served.

For the Convenience of the Employer. The *convenience of the employer* test is intended to focus on the employer's motivation for furnishing the meals and lodging rather than on the benefits received by the employee. If the employer furnishes

[8] § 119(a). The value of meals and lodging is also excluded from FICA and FUTA tax. *Rowan Companies, Inc. v. U.S.*, 81–1 USTC ¶9479, 48 AFTR2d 81–5115, 101 S.Ct. 2288 (USSC, 1981).

[9] Rev.Rul. 80, 1953–1 C.B. 62; *Comm. v. Doak*, 56–2 USTC ¶9708, 49 AFTR 1491, 234 F.2d 704 (CA–4, 1956); but see *G. A. Papineau*, 16 T.C. 130 (1951); *Armstrong v. Phinney*, 68–1 USTC ¶9355, 21 AFTR2d 1260, 394 F.2d 661 (CA–5, 1968).

[10] *Comm. v. Kowalski*, 77–2 USTC ¶9748, 40 AFTR2d 6128, 98 S.Ct. 315 (USSC, 1977).

[11] *Tougher v. Comm.*, 71–1 USTC ¶9398, 27 AFTR2d 1301, 441 F.2d 1148 (CA–9, 1971).

[12] Reg. § 1.119–1(c)(1).

[13] *Comm. v. Anderson*, 67–1 USTC ¶9136, 19 AFTR2d 318, 371 F.2d 59 (CA–6, 1966).

[14] *J. B. Lindeman*, 60 T.C. 609 (1973).

the meals and lodging primarily to enable the employee to perform his or her duties properly, it does not matter that the employee considers these benefits to be a part of his or her compensation.

The Regulations give the following examples in which the tests for excluding meals are satisfied:[15]

- A waitress is required to eat her meals on the premises during the busy lunch and breakfast hours.
- A bank furnishes a teller meals on the premises to limit the time the employee is away from his or her booth during the busy hours.
- A worker is employed at a construction site in a remote part of Alaska. The employer must furnish meals and lodging due to the inaccessibility of other facilities.

If more than half of the meals provided to employees are furnished for the convenience of the employer, then all such employee meals are treated as provided for the convenience of the employer. Thus, in this situation, all employees are treated the same (either all of the employees are allowed exclusion treatment, or none of the employees can exclude the meals from gross income).

EXAMPLE 7

Allison's Restaurant has a restaurant area and a bar. Nine employees work in the restaurant and three work in the bar. All of the employees are provided one meal per day. In the case of the restaurant workers, the meals are provided for the convenience of the employer. The meals provided to the bar employees do not satisfy the convenience of the employer requirement. Because more than half of the employees receive their meal for the convenience of the employer, all 12 employees qualify for exclusion treatment. ■

Required as a Condition of Employment.

The *required as a condition of employment* test applies only to lodging. If the employee's use of the housing would serve the convenience of the employer, but the employee is not required to use the housing, the exclusion is not available.

EXAMPLE 8

VEP, a utilities company, has all of its service personnel on 24-hour call for emergencies. The company encourages its employees to live near the plant so they can respond quickly to emergency calls. Company-owned housing is available rent-free. Only 10 of the employees live in the company housing because it is not suitable for families.

Although the company-provided housing serves the convenience of the employer, it is not required. Therefore, the employees who live in the company housing must include its value in gross income. ■

In addition, if the employee has the option of cash or lodging, the employer-required test is not satisfied.

EXAMPLE 9

Khalid is the manager of a large apartment complex. The employer gives Khalid the option of rent-free housing (value of $9,600 per year) or an additional $7,500 per year. Khalid selects the housing option. Therefore, he must include $9,600 in gross income. ■

Other housing exclusions are available for certain employees of educational institutions, ministers of the gospel, and military personnel.

Group Term Life Insurance

For many years, the IRS did not attempt to tax the value of life insurance protection provided to an employee by the employer. Some companies took undue advantage

[15] Reg. § 1.119–1(f).

TABLE 17–1 Uniform Premiums for $1,000 of Group Term Life Insurance Protection

5-Year Age Bracket	Cost of $1,000 of Protection for a One-Month Period*
Under 25	$ .05
25–29	.06
30–34	.08
35–39	.09
40–44	.10
45–49	.15
50–54	.23
55–59	.43
60–64	.66
65–69	1.27
70 and above	2.06

*Reg. § 1.79–3, effective for coverage after June 30, 1999.

of the exclusion by providing large amounts of insurance protection for key executives. In response, Congress enacted § 79, which created a limited exclusion for group term life insurance. Current law allows an exclusion of premiums on the first $50,000 of group term life insurance protection.

The benefits of this exclusion are available only to employees. Proprietors and partners are not considered employees. Moreover, the Regulations generally require broad-scale coverage of employees to satisfy the group requirement (e.g., shareholder-employees would not constitute a qualified group). The exclusion applies only to term insurance (protection for a period of time but with no cash surrender value) and not to ordinary life insurance (lifetime protection plus a cash surrender value that can be drawn upon before death).

As mentioned, the exclusion applies to the first $50,000 of group term life insurance protection. For each $1,000 of coverage in excess of $50,000, the employee must include the amounts indicated in Table 17–1 in gross income.[16]

DIGGING DEEPER 3

Find more information on this topic at our Web site: ***http://wft-entities.swlearning.com.***

EXAMPLE 10

Finch Corporation has a group term life insurance policy with coverage equal to the employee's annual salary. Keith, age 52, is president of the corporation and receives an annual salary of $75,000. Keith must include $69 in gross income from the insurance protection for the year.

$$[(\$75{,}000 - \$50{,}000)/\$1{,}000] \times \$0.23 \times 12 \text{ months} = \$69$$ ■

If the plan discriminates in favor of certain key employees (e.g., officers), the key employees are not eligible for the exclusion. In such a case, the key employees must include in gross income the *greater* of actual premiums paid by the employer or the amount calculated from the Uniform Premiums table in Table 17–1. The other employees are still eligible for the $50,000 exclusion and continue to use the Uniform Premiums table to compute the income from excess insurance protection.[17]

[16] Reg. § 1.79–3(d)(2).

[17] § 79(d).

Qualified Tuition Reduction Plans

Employees (including retired and disabled former employees) of nonprofit educational institutions are allowed to exclude a tuition waiver from gross income, if the waiver is pursuant to a qualified tuition reduction plan.[18] The plan may not discriminate in favor of highly compensated employees. The exclusion applies to the employee, the employee's spouse, and the employee's dependent children. The exclusion also extends to tuition reductions granted by any nonprofit educational institution to employees of any other nonprofit educational institution (reciprocal agreements).

EXAMPLE 11

ABC University allows the dependent children of XYZ University employees to attend ABC University with no tuition charge. XYZ University grants reciprocal benefits to the children of ABC University employees. The dependent children can also attend tuition-free the university where their parents are employed. Employees who take advantage of these benefits are not required to recognize gross income. ■

Generally, the exclusion is limited to undergraduate tuition waivers. However, in the case of teaching or research assistants, graduate tuition waivers may also qualify for exclusion treatment. According to the Proposed Regulations, the exclusion is limited to the value of the benefit in excess of the employee's reasonable compensation.[19] Thus, a tuition reduction that is a substitute for cash compensation cannot be excluded.

EXAMPLE 12

Susan is a graduate research assistant. She receives a $5,000 salary for 500 hours of service over a nine-month period. This pay, $10 per hour, is reasonable compensation for Susan's services. In addition, Susan receives a waiver of $6,000 for tuition. Susan may exclude the tuition waiver from gross income. ■

Other Specific Employee Fringe Benefits

Congress has enacted exclusions to encourage employers to (1) finance and make available child care facilities, (2) provide athletic facilities for employees, (3) finance certain education expenses of employees, and (4) assist employees who adopt children. These provisions are summarized as follows:

- The employee can exclude from gross income the value of child and dependent care services paid for by the employer and incurred to enable the employee to work. The exclusion cannot exceed $5,000 per year ($2,500 if married and filing separately). For a married couple, the annual exclusion cannot exceed the earned income of the spouse who has the lesser amount of earned income. For an unmarried taxpayer, the exclusion cannot exceed the taxpayer's earned income.[20]
- The value of the use of a gymnasium or other athletic facilities by employees, their spouses, and their dependent children may be excluded from an employee's gross income. The facilities must be on the employer's premises, and substantially all of the use of the facilities must be by employees and their family members.[21]
- Qualified employer-provided educational assistance (tuition, fees, books, and supplies) at the undergraduate and graduate levels is excludible from gross income. The exclusion is limited to a maximum of $5,250 annually.[22]
- The employee can exclude from gross income up to $10,960 of expenses incurred to adopt a child where the adoption expenses are paid or reimbursed

[18] § 117(d).

[19] Prop.Reg. § 1.117–6(d).

[20] § 129. The exclusion applies to the same types of expenses that, if paid by the employee (and not reimbursed by the employer), would be eligible for the credit for child and dependent care expenses, discussed in Chapter 16.

[21] § 132(j)(4).

[22] § 127.

TAX *in the News* **EMPLOYEES LOSE SOME UNDER "USE OR LOSE PLANS"**

Over 21 million Americans lose between $125 and $200 every year as a result of overfunding their flexible benefit accounts. If the employee overestimates the amount required to provide the flexible benefits, and thus the reduction in the employee's salary, the unused portion of the fund is forfeited to the employer. The total forfeited amounts exceed $2 billion annually. Thus, employees appear to be substantial losers under these "use-it-or-lose-it" plans. Even though employees can still be net beneficiaries from the portion of the accounts that is actually used, the employees simply are not maximizing the benefits.

Tax legislation has been proposed on several occasions recently to allow any unused amount in a flexible benefit account to be transferred to various types of employee retirement accounts or to otherwise carry over for the employee's benefit. To date, none of these proposals has been enacted.

However, in a recent Notice, the IRS announced that employers can now amend their plans to allow employees a grace period of two and one-half months. That is, the amount set aside in a calendar year plan can be used until March 15 of the following year. Employers will generally amend the plans to provide that payments made before March 15 of the current year be taken first from the beginning-of-the-year balance in the account.

by the employer under a qualified adoption assistance program.[23] The limit on the exclusion is the same even if the child has special needs (is not physically or mentally capable of caring for himself or herself). The exclusion is phased out over the AGI range from $164,410 to $204,410.

Cafeteria Plans

Generally, if an employee is offered a choice between cash and some other form of compensation, the employee is deemed to have constructively received the cash even when the noncash option is elected. Thus, the employee has gross income regardless of the option chosen.

An exception to this constructive receipt treatment is provided under the cafeteria plan rules. Under such a plan, the employee is permitted to choose between cash and nontaxable benefits (e.g., group term life insurance, health and accident protection, and child care). If the employee chooses the otherwise nontaxable benefits, the cafeteria plan rules allow the benefits to be excluded from the employee's gross income.[24] **Cafeteria plans** provide tremendous flexibility in tailoring the employee pay package to fit individual needs. Some employees (usually the younger group) prefer cash, while others (usually the older group) will opt for the fringe benefit program. However, long-term care insurance cannot be part of a cafeteria plan. Thus, an employer that wishes to provide long-term care benefits must provide such benefits separate from the cafeteria plan.[25]

EXAMPLE 13

Hawk Corporation offers its employees (on a nondiscriminatory basis) a choice of any one or all of the following benefits:

Benefit	Cost
Group term life insurance	$ 200
Hospitalization insurance for family members	2,400
Child care payments	1,800
	$4,400

[23] § 137.
[24] § 125.
[25] § 125(f).

If a benefit is not selected, the employee receives cash equal to the cost of the benefit.

Kay, an employee, has a spouse who works for another employer that provides hospitalization insurance but no child care payments. Kay elects to receive the group term life insurance, the child care payments, and $2,400 of cash. Only the $2,400 must be included in Kay's gross income. ■

Flexible Spending Plans

Flexible spending plans (often referred to as flexible benefit plans) operate much like cafeteria plans. Under these plans, the employee accepts lower cash compensation in return for the employer's agreement to pay certain costs that the employer can pay without the employee recognizing gross income. For example, assume the employer's health insurance policy does not cover dental expenses. The employee could estimate his or her dental expenses for the upcoming year and agree to a salary reduction equal to the estimated dental expenses. The employer then pays or reimburses the employee for the actual dental expenses incurred, up to the amount of the salary reduction. If the employee's actual dental expenses are less than the reduction in cash compensation, the employee cannot recover the difference. Hence, these plans are often referred to as *use or lose* plans. As is the case for cafeteria plans, flexible spending plans cannot be used to pay long-term care insurance premiums.

General Classes of Excluded Benefits

An employer can provide a variety of economic benefits to employees. Under the all-inclusive concept of income, the benefits are taxable unless one of the provisions previously discussed specifically excludes the item from gross income. The amount of the income is the fair market value of the benefit. This reasoning can lead to results that Congress considers unacceptable, as illustrated in the following example.

EXAMPLE 14

Vern is employed in New York as a ticket clerk for Trans National Airlines. Vern would like to visit his mother, who lives in Miami, Florida, but he has no money for plane tickets. Trans National has daily flights from New York to Miami that often leave with empty seats. The cost of a round-trip ticket is $500, and Vern is in the 25% tax bracket. If Trans National allows Vern to fly without charge to Miami, under the general gross income rules, Vern has income equal to the value of a ticket. Therefore, Vern must pay $125 tax (.25 × $500) on a trip to Miami. Because Vern does not have $125, he cannot visit his mother, and the airplane flies with another empty seat. ■

If Trans National in Example 14 will allow employees to use resources that would otherwise be wasted, why should the tax laws interfere with the employee's decision to take advantage of the available benefit? Thus, to avoid the economic inefficiency that occurs in Example 14 and in similar situations, as well as to create uniform rules for fringe benefits, Congress established seven broad classes of nontaxable employee benefits:[26]

- No-additional-cost services.
- Qualified employee discounts.
- Working condition fringes.
- *De minimis* fringes.
- Qualified transportation fringes.
- Qualified moving expense reimbursements.
- Qualified retirement planning services.

[26]See, generally, § 132.

No-Additional-Cost Services. Example 14 illustrates a no-additional-cost fringe benefit. **No-additional-cost services** are excluded from an employee's gross income if all of the following conditions are satisfied:

- The employee receives services, as opposed to property.
- The employer does not incur substantial additional costs, including forgone revenue, in providing the services to the employee.
- The services must be from the same line of business in which the employee works.
- The services are offered to customers in the ordinary course of the business in which the employee works.[27]

EXAMPLE 15

Assume that Vern in Example 14 can fly without charge only if the airline cannot fill the seats with paying customers. That is, Vern must fly on standby. Although the airplane may burn slightly more fuel because Vern is aboard and Vern may receive the same meal as paying customers, the additional costs would not be substantial. Thus, the trip could qualify as a no-additional-cost service.

On the other hand, assume that Vern is given a reserved seat on a flight that is frequently full. The employer would be forgoing revenue to allow Vern to fly. This forgone revenue would be a substantial additional cost, and thus the benefit would be taxable to Vern. ■

DIGGING DEEPER 4

Find more information on this topic at our Web site: ***http://wft-entities.swlearning.com.***

The no-additional-cost exclusion extends to the employee's spouse and dependent children and to retired and disabled former employees. In the Regulations, the IRS has conceded that partners who perform services for the partnership are employees for purposes of the exclusion.[28] However, the exclusion is not extended to highly compensated employees unless the benefit is available on a nondiscriminatory basis.

Qualified Employee Discounts. When the employer sells goods or services (other than no-additional-cost benefits just discussed) to the employee for a price that is less than the price charged regular customers, the employee ordinarily recognizes income equal to the discount. However, **qualified employee discounts** can be excluded from the gross income of the employee, subject to the following conditions and limitations:

- The exclusion is not available for discounted sales of real property (e.g., a house) or for personal property of the type commonly held for investment (e.g., common stocks).
- The property or services must be from the same line of business in which the employee works.
- In the case of property, the exclusion cannot exceed the gross profit component of the price to customers.
- In the case of services, the exclusion is limited to 20 percent of the customer price.[29]

EXAMPLE 16

Silver Corporation, which operates a department store, sells a television set to a store employee for $300. The regular customer price is $500, and the gross profit rate is 25%. The corporation also sells the employee a service contract for $100. The regular customer price for the contract is $150. The employee must recognize income of $95, computed as follows:

[27] Reg. § 1.132–2.

[28] Reg. § 1.132–1(b).

[29] § 132(c).

Customer price for property	$ 500	
Less: Qualifying discount (25% gross profit × $500 price)	(125)	
	$ 375	
Employee price	(300)	
Excess discount recognized as income		$75
Customer price for service	$ 150	
Less: Qualifying discount (20%)	(30)	
	$ 120	
Employee price	(100)	
Excess discount recognized as income		20
Total income recognized		$95 ■

EXAMPLE 17

Assume the same facts as in Example 16, except that the employee is a clerk in a hotel operated by Silver Corporation. Because the line of business requirement is not met, the employee must recognize $200 of income ($500 – $300) from the discount on the television and $50 of income ($150 – $100) from the service contract. ■

As in the case of no-additional-cost benefits, the exclusion applies to employees, their spouses and dependent children, and retired and disabled former employees. However, the exclusion does not extend to highly compensated individuals unless the discount is available on a nondiscriminatory basis.

Working Condition Fringes. Generally, an employee may exclude the cost of property or services provided by the employer if the employee could deduct the cost of those items if he or she had actually paid for them.[30] These benefits are called **working condition fringes**.

EXAMPLE 18

Mitch is a certified public accountant employed by an accounting firm. The employer pays Mitch's annual dues to professional organizations. Mitch is not required to include the payment of the dues in gross income because if he had paid the dues, he would have been allowed to deduct the amount as an employee business expense (as discussed later in this chapter). ■

In many cases, this exclusion merely avoids reporting income and an offsetting deduction. However, in two specific situations, the working condition fringe benefit rules allow an exclusion where the expense would not be deductible if paid by the employee:

- Some automobile salespeople are allowed to exclude the value of certain personal use of company demonstrators (e.g., commuting to and from work).[31]
- The employee business expense would be eliminated by the 2 percent floor on miscellaneous itemized deductions under § 67 (refer to Chapter 16).

Unlike the other fringe benefits discussed previously, working condition fringes can be made available on a discriminatory basis and still qualify for the exclusion.

***De Minimis* Fringes.** As the term suggests, ***de minimis* fringe benefits** are so small that accounting for them is impractical.[32] The House Report contains the following examples of *de minimis* fringes:

---

[30] § 132(d).

[31] § 132(j)(3).

[32] § 132(e).

- The typing of a personal letter by a company secretary, occasional personal use of a company copying machine, occasional company cocktail parties or picnics for employees, occasional supper money or taxi fare for employees because of overtime work, and certain holiday gifts of property with a low fair market value are excluded.
- The value of meals consumed in a subsidized eating facility (e.g., an employees' cafeteria) operated by the employer is excluded if the facility is located on or near the employer's business premises, if revenue equals or exceeds direct operating costs, and if nondiscrimination requirements are met.

When taxpayers venture beyond the specific examples contained in the House Report and the Regulations, there is obviously much room for disagreement as to what is *de minimis*. However, note that except in the case of subsidized eating facilities, *de minimis* fringe benefits can be granted in a manner that favors highly compensated employees.

Qualified Transportation Fringes. The intent of the exclusion for **qualified transportation fringes** is to encourage the use of mass transit for commuting to and from work. Qualified transportation fringes encompass the following transportation benefits provided by the employer to the employee:[33]

1. Transportation in a commuter highway vehicle between the employee's residence and the place of employment.
2. A transit pass.
3. Qualified parking.

Statutory dollar limits are placed on the amount of the exclusion. Categories (1) and (2) above are combined for purposes of applying the limit. In this case, the limit on the exclusion for 2006 is $105 per month. Category (3) has a separate limit. For qualified parking, the limit on the exclusion for 2006 is $205 per month. Both of these dollar limits are indexed annually for inflation.

A commuter highway vehicle is any highway vehicle with a seating capacity of at least six adults (excluding the driver). In addition, at least 80 percent of the vehicle's use must be for transporting employees between their residences and place of employment.

Qualified parking includes the following:

- Parking provided to an employee on or near the employer's business premises.
- Parking provided to an employee on or near a location from which the employee commutes to work via mass transit, in a commuter highway vehicle, or in a carpool.

Qualified transportation fringes may be provided directly by the employer or may be in the form of cash reimbursements.

EXAMPLE 19

Gray Corporation's offices are located in the center of a large city. The company pays for parking spaces to be used by the company officers. Steve, a vice president, receives $250 of such benefits each month. The parking space rental qualifies as a qualified transportation fringe. Of the $250 benefit received each month by Steve, $205 is excludible from gross income. The balance of $45 is included in his gross income. The same result would occur if Steve paid for the parking and was reimbursed by his employer. ■

Qualified Moving Expense Reimbursements. Qualified moving expenses that are reimbursed or paid by the employer are excludible from gross income. A qualified moving expense is one that would be deductible under § 217. See the discussion of moving expenses later in this chapter.

[33] § 132(f).

Qualified Retirement Planning Services. Qualified retirement planning services include any retirement planning advice or information provided by an employer who maintains a qualified retirement plan to an employee or the spouse.[34] Congress decided to exclude the value of such services from gross income because they are a key part of retirement income planning. Such an exclusion should motivate more employers to provide retirement planning services to their employees.

Nondiscrimination Provisions. For no-additional-cost services, qualified employee discounts, and qualified retirement planning services, if the plan is discriminatory in favor of *highly compensated employees,*[35] these key employees are denied exclusion treatment. However, any non-highly compensated employees who receive these benefits can still enjoy exclusion treatment.[36]

EXAMPLE 20

Dove Company's officers are allowed to purchase goods from the company at a 25% discount. Other employees are allowed only a 15% discount. The company's gross profit margin on these goods is 30%.

Peggy, an officer in the company, purchased goods from the company for $750 when the price charged to customers was $1,000. Peggy must include $250 in gross income because the plan is discriminatory.

Leo, an employee of the company who is not an officer, purchased goods for $850 when the customer price was $1,000. Leo is not required to recognize income because he received a qualified employee discount. ■

De minimis fringe benefits (except for subsidized eating facilities) and working condition fringe benefits can be provided on a discriminatory basis. Likewise, the qualified transportation fringe and the qualified moving expense reimbursement can be provided on a discriminatory basis.

DIGGING DEEPER 5

Find more information on this topic at our Web site: ***http://wft-entities.swlearning.com.***

Taxable Fringe Benefits

If fringe benefits cannot qualify for any of the specific exclusions or do not fit into any of the general classes of excluded benefits, the employee must recognize gross income equal to the fair market value of the benefits received. Obviously, problems are frequently encountered in determining values. To help taxpayers cope with these problems, the IRS has issued extensive Regulations addressing the valuation of personal use of an employer's automobiles and meals provided at an employer-operated eating facility.[37]

If a fringe benefit plan discriminates in favor of highly compensated employees, generally those employees are not allowed to exclude the benefits they receive that other employees do not enjoy. However, the highly compensated employees, as well as the other employees, are generally allowed to exclude the nondiscriminatory benefits.[38]

EXAMPLE 21

MED Company has a medical reimbursement plan that reimburses officers for 100% of their medical expenses, but reimburses all other employees for only 80% of their medical expenses. Cliff, the president of the company, was reimbursed $1,000 during the year for medical expenses. Cliff must include $200 in gross income [(1 − .80) × $1,000 = $200]. Mike, an

[34]§§ 132(a)(7) and (m).

[35]See § 414(q) for the definition of highly compensated employee.

[36]§§ 61, 132(j)(1), and 132(m)(2).

[37]Reg. § 1.61–2T(j). Generally, the income from the personal use of the employer's automobile is based on the lease value of the automobile (what it would have cost the employee to lease the automobile). Meals are valued at 150% of the employer's direct costs (e.g., food and labor) of preparing the meals.

[38]§§ 79(d), 105(h), 127(b)(2), and 132(j)(1).

employee who is not an officer, received $800 (80% of his actual medical expenses) under the medical reimbursement plan. None of the $800 is includible in his gross income. ■

Foreign Earned Income

A U.S. citizen is generally subject to U.S. tax on his or her income regardless of the income's geographic origin. The income may also be subject to tax in the foreign country, and thus the taxpayer must carry a double tax burden. Out of a sense of fairness and to encourage U.S. citizens to work abroad (so that exports might be increased), Congress has provided alternative forms of relief from taxes on foreign earned income. The taxpayer can elect *either* (1) to include the foreign income in his or her taxable income and then claim a credit for foreign taxes paid or (2) to exclude the foreign earnings from his or her U.S. gross income (the **foreign earned income exclusion**).[39] The foreign tax credit option is discussed in Chapter 14, but as is apparent from the following discussion, most taxpayers will choose the exclusion.

Foreign earned income consists of the earnings from the individual's personal services rendered in a foreign country (other than as an employee of the U.S. government). To qualify for the exclusion, the taxpayer must be either of the following:

- A bona fide resident of the foreign country (or countries).
- Present in a foreign country (or countries) for at least 330 days during any 12 consecutive months.

EXAMPLE 22

Sandra's trips to and from a foreign country in connection with her work were as follows:

Arrived in Foreign Country	Arrived in United States
March 10, 2005	February 1, 2006
March 7, 2006	June 1, 2006

During the 12 consecutive months ending on March 10, 2006, Sandra was present in the foreign country for at least 330 days (365 days less 28 days in February and 7 days in March 2006). Therefore, all income earned in the foreign country through March 10, 2006, is eligible for the exclusion. The income earned from March 11, 2006, through May 31, 2006, is also eligible for the exclusion because Sandra was present in the foreign country for 330 days during the 12 consecutive months ending on May 31, 2006. ■

The exclusion is *limited* to $80,000. For married persons, both of whom have foreign earned income, the exclusion is computed separately for each spouse. Community property rules do not apply (the community property spouse is not deemed to have earned one-half of the other spouse's foreign earned income). If all the days in the tax year are not qualifying days, then the taxpayer must compute the maximum exclusion on a daily basis ($80,000 divided by the number of days in the entire year and multiplied by the number of qualifying days).

EXAMPLE 23

Keith qualifies for the foreign earned income exclusion. He was present in France for all of 2006. Keith's salary for 2006 is $90,000. Since all of the days in 2006 are qualifying days, Keith can exclude $80,000 of his $90,000 salary.

Assume instead that only 335 days were qualifying days. Then, Keith's exclusion is limited to $73,425, computed as follows:

$$\$80{,}000 \times \frac{335 \text{ days in forign country}}{365 \text{ days in the year}} = \$73{,}425$$ ■

[39] § 911.

Employee Expenses

LO.3

Apply the rules for computing deductible expenses of employees including transportation, travel, moving, education, and entertainment expenses.

Once the employment relationship is established, employee expenses fall into one of the following categories:

- Transportation.
- Travel.
- Moving.
- Education.
- Entertainment.
- Other.

These expenses are discussed below in the order presented. Keep in mind, however, that these expenses are not necessarily limited to employees. A deduction for business transportation, for example, is equally available to taxpayers who are self-employed.

Transportation Expenses

Qualified Expenditures. An employee may deduct unreimbursed employment-related **transportation expenses** as an itemized deduction *from* AGI. Transportation expenses include only the cost of transporting the employee from one place to another when the employee is not away from home in travel status. Such costs include taxi fares, automobile expenses, tolls, and parking.

Commuting Expenses. Commuting between home and one's place of employment is a personal, nondeductible expense. The fact that one employee drives 30 miles to work and another employee walks six blocks is of no significance.[40]

EXAMPLE 24

Geraldo is employed by Sparrow Corporation. He drives 22 miles each way to work. The 44 miles he drives each workday are nondeductible commuting expenses. ■

The expenses of getting from one job to another job or from one work station to another work station are deductible transportation expenses rather than nondeductible commuting expenses.

DIGGING DEEPER 6

Find more information on this topic at our Web site: ***http://wft-entities.swlearning.com.***

EXAMPLE 25

In the current year, Cynthia holds two jobs, a full-time job with Blue Corporation and a part-time job with Wren Corporation. During the 250 days that she works (adjusted for weekends, vacation, and holidays), Cynthia customarily leaves home at 7:30 A.M. and drives 30 miles to the Blue Corporation plant, where she works until 5:00 P.M. After dinner at a nearby café, Cynthia drives 20 miles to Wren Corporation and works from 7:00 to 11:00 P.M. The distance from the second job to Cynthia's home is 40 miles. Her deduction is based on 20 miles (the distance between jobs). ■

Computation of Automobile Expenses. A taxpayer has two choices in computing deductible automobile expenses. The actual operating cost, which includes depreciation (refer to Chapter 5), gas, oil, repairs, licenses, and insurance, may be used. Records must be kept that detail the automobile's personal and business use. Only the percentage allocable to business transportation and travel is allowed as a deduction.

[40] *Tauferner v. U.S.*, 69–1 USTC ¶9241, 23 AFTR2d 69–1025, 407 F.2d 243 (CA–10, 1969).

CONCEPT SUMMARY 17–1

General Classes of Fringe Benefits

Benefit	Description and Examples	Coverage Allowed	Effect of Discrimination
1. No-additional-cost services	The employee takes advantage of the employer's excess capacity (e.g., free passes for airline employees).	Current, retired, and disabled employees; their spouses and dependent children; spouses of deceased employees. Partners are treated as employees.	No exclusion for highly compensated employees.
2. Qualified discounts on goods	The employee is allowed a discount no greater than the gross profit margin on goods sold to customers.	Same as (1) above.	Same as (1) above.
3. Qualified discounts on services	The employee is allowed a discount (maximum of 20%) on services the employer offers to customers.	Same as (1) above.	Same as (1) above.
4. Working condition fringes	Expenses paid by the employer that would be deductible if paid by the employee (e.g., a mechanic's tools). Also, includes auto salesperson's use of a car held for sale.	Current employees, partners, directors, and independent contractors.	No effect.
5. *De minimis* items	Expenses so immaterial that accounting for them is not warranted (e.g., occasional supper money, personal use of the copy machine).	*Any recipient* of a fringe benefit.	No effect.
6. Qualified transportation fringes	Transportation benefits provided by the employer to employees, including commuting in a commuter highway vehicle, a transit pass, and qualified parking.	Current employees.	No effect.
7. Qualified moving expense reimbursements	Qualified moving expenses that are paid or reimbursed by the employer. A qualified moving expense is one that would be deductible under § 217.	Current employees.	No effect.
8. Qualified retirement planning services	Qualified retirement planning services that are provided by the employer.	Current employees and spouses.	Same as (1) above.

Use of the **automatic mileage method** is the second alternative. For 2006, the deduction is based on 44.5 cents per mile for business miles.[41] Parking fees and tolls are allowed in addition to expenses computed using the automatic mileage method.

[41] Rev.Proc. 2005–78, I.R.B. No. 51, 1177. The mileage rate for 2005 was split as follows: 40.5 cents for January–August and 48.5 cents for September–December. The late-year increase of eight cents was due to the sudden rise in the cost of gasoline triggered by Hurricanes Katrina and Rita.

Generally, a taxpayer may elect either method for any particular year. However, the following restrictions apply:

- The vehicle must be owned or leased by the taxpayer.
- If five or more vehicles are in use (for business purposes) at the *same* time (not alternately), a taxpayer may not use the automatic mileage method.
- Use of the automatic mileage method in the first year the auto is placed in service is considered an election not to use the MACRS method of depreciation (refer to Chapter 5).
- A taxpayer may not switch to the automatic mileage method if the MACRS statutory percentage method or the election to expense under § 179 has been used.

DIGGING DEEPER 7

Find more information on this topic at our Web site: ***http://wft-entities.swlearning.com.***

Travel Expenses

Definition of Travel Expenses. An itemized deduction is allowed for *unreimbursed* **travel expenses** related to a taxpayer's employment. Travel expenses are more broadly defined in the Code than are transportation expenses. Travel expenses include transportation expenses and meals and lodging while away from home in the pursuit of a trade or business. Meals cannot be lavish or extravagant. A deduction for meals and lodging is available only if the taxpayer is away from his or her tax home. Deductible travel expenses also include reasonable laundry and incidental expenses.

DIGGING DEEPER 8

Find more information on this topic at our Web site: ***http://wft-entities.swlearning.com.***

Away-from-Home Requirement. The crucial test for the deductibility of travel expenses is whether the employee is away from home overnight. "Overnight" need not be a 24-hour period, but it must be a period substantially longer than an ordinary day's work and must require rest, sleep, or a relief-from-work period.[42] A one-day business trip is not travel status, and meals and lodging for such a trip are not deductible.

Temporary Assignments. The employee must be away from home for a temporary period. If the taxpayer-employee is reassigned to a new post for an indefinite period of time, that new post becomes his or her tax home. Temporary indicates that the assignment's termination is expected within a reasonably short period of time. The position of the IRS is that the tax home is the business location, post, or station of the taxpayer. Thus, travel expenses are not deductible if a taxpayer is reassigned for an indefinite period and does not move his or her place of residence to the new location.

EXAMPLE 26

Malcolm's employer opened a branch office in San Diego. Malcolm was assigned to the new office for three months to train a new manager and to assist in setting up the new office. He tried commuting from his home in Los Angeles for a week and decided that he could not continue driving several hours a day. He rented an apartment in San Diego, where he lived during the week. He spent weekends with his wife and children at their home in Los Angeles. Malcolm's rent, meals, laundry, incidentals, and automobile expenses in San Diego are deductible. To the extent that Malcolm's transportation expense related to his weekend trips

[42] *U.S. v. Correll*, 68–1 USTC ¶9101, 20 AFTR2d 5845, 88 S.Ct 445 (USSC, 1967); Rev.Rul. 75–168, 1975–1 C.B. 58.

TAX *in the News* **RELIEF FOR MEMBERS OF THE ARMED FORCES RESERVES**

In the Military Family Tax Relief Act of 2003, Congress provided various tax benefits for reservists, one of which deals with the classification of travel expenses. Members of the Reserves or National Guard who travel to drills and other service-related activities may claim the expenses as deductions *for* AGI. Previously, the expenses were not deductible unless the taxpayer itemized. (As miscellaneous itemized deductions, they were subject to the 2 percent-of-AGI floor.) To qualify for the deduction *for* AGI classification, the trip must be more than 100 miles from home and include an overnight stay. Any deduction is limited to the Federal per diem rates applicable to the area involved.

home exceeds what his cost of meals and lodging would have been, the excess is personal and nondeductible. ■

EXAMPLE 27

Assume that Malcolm in Example 26 was transferred to the new location to become the new manager permanently. His wife and children continued to live in Los Angeles until the end of the school year. Malcolm is no longer "away from home" because the assignment is not temporary. His travel expenses are not deductible. ■

To curtail controversy in this area, the Code specifies that a taxpayer "shall not be treated as temporarily away from home during any period of employment if such period exceeds 1 year."[43]

Determining the Tax Home. Under ordinary circumstances, determining the location of a taxpayer's tax home does not present a problem. The tax home is the area in which the taxpayer derives his or her principal source of income; when the taxpayer has more than one place of employment, the tax home is based on the amount of time spent in each area.

It is possible for a taxpayer never to be away from his or her tax home. In other words, the tax home follows the taxpayer.[44] Under such circumstances, all meals and lodging remain personal and are not deductible.

EXAMPLE 28

Bill is employed as a long-haul truck driver. He is single, stores his clothes and other belongings at his parents' home, and stops there for periodic visits. Most of the time, Bill is on the road, sleeping in his truck and in motels. It is likely that Bill is never in travel status, as he is not away from home. Consequently, none of his meals and lodging are deductible. ■

Combined Business and Pleasure Travel. To be deductible, travel expenses need not be incurred in the performance of specific job functions. Travel expenses incurred to attend a professional convention are deductible by an employee if attendance is connected with services as an employee. For example, an employee of a law firm can deduct travel expenses incurred to attend a meeting of the American Bar Association.

Travel deductions have been used in the past by persons who claimed a tax deduction for what was essentially a personal vacation. As a result, several provisions have been enacted to restrict deductions associated with combined business and pleasure trips. If the business/pleasure trip is from one point in the United States to another point in the United States (*domestic travel*), the transportation expenses are deductible only if the trip is primarily for business.[45] If the trip is primarily for

[43]§ 162(a).
[44]*Moses Mitnick*, 13 T.C. 1 (1949).
[45]Reg. § 1.162–2(b)(1).

pleasure, no transportation expenses qualify as a deduction. Meals, lodging, and other expenses are allocated between business and personal days.

Find more information on this topic at our Web site: ***http://wft-entities.swlearning.com.***

DIGGING DEEPER 9

EXAMPLE 29

In the current year, Hana travels from Seattle to New York primarily for business. She spends five days conducting business and three days sightseeing and attending shows. Her plane and taxi fare amounts to $560. Her meals amount to $100 per day, and lodging and incidental expenses are $150 per day. She can deduct the transportation expenses of $560, since the trip is primarily for business (five days of business versus three days of sightseeing). Deductible meals are limited to five days and are subject to the 50% cutback (discussed later in the chapter) for a total of $250 [5 days × ($100 × 50%)], and other deductions are limited to $750 (5 days × $150). If Hana is an employee, the unreimbursed travel expenses are miscellaneous itemized deductions subject to the 2%-of-AGI floor. ■

When the trip is outside the United States (*foreign travel*), special rules apply.[46] Transportation expenses must be allocated between business and personal days *unless* (1) the taxpayer is away from home for seven days or less or (2) less than 25 percent of the time was for personal purposes. No allocation is required if the taxpayer has no substantial control over arrangements for the trip or the desire for a vacation is not a major factor in taking the trip. If the trip is primarily for pleasure, no transportation charges are deductible. Days devoted to travel are considered business days. Weekends, legal holidays, and intervening days are considered business days, provided that both the preceding and succeeding days were business days.

Find more information on this topic at our Web site: ***http://wft-entities.swlearning.com.***

DIGGING DEEPER 10

EXAMPLE 30

In the current year, Robert takes a trip from New York to Japan primarily for business purposes. He is away from home from June 10 through June 19. He spends three days vacationing and seven days conducting business (including two travel days). His airfare is $2,500, his meals amount to $100 per day, and lodging and incidental expenses are $160 per day. Since Robert is away from home for more than seven days and more than 25% of his time is devoted to personal purposes, only 70% (7 days business/10 days total) of the transportation is deductible. His deductions are as follows:

Transportation (70% × $2,500)		$1,750
Lodging ($160 × 7)		1,120
Meals ($100 × 7)	$ 700	
Less: 50% cutback (discussed later in this chapter)	(350)	350
Total deductions		$3,220

If Robert is gone the same period of time but spends only two days (less than 25% of the total) vacationing, no allocation of transportation is required. Since the pleasure portion of the trip is less than 25% of the total, all of the airfare qualifies for the travel deduction. ■

The foreign convention rules do not operate to bar a deduction to an employer if the expense is *compensatory* in nature. For example, a trip to Rome won by a top salesperson is included in the gross income of the employee and is fully deductible by the employer.

[46] § 274(c) and Reg. § 1.274–4. For purposes of the seven-days-or-less exception, the departure travel day is not counted.

PLANNING *Strategies*

TRANSPORTATION AND TRAVEL EXPENSES

★ **Framework Focus: Deductions**

Strategy ★ Maximize Deductible Amounts.

Adequate detailed records of all transportation and travel expenses should be kept. Since the regular mileage allowance often is modest in amount, a new, expensive automobile used primarily for business may generate a higher expense based on actual cost. The election to expense part of the cost of the automobile under § 179, MACRS depreciation, insurance, repairs and maintenance, automobile club dues, and other related costs may result in automobile expenses greater than the automatic mileage allowance.

If a taxpayer wishes to sightsee or vacation on a business trip, it would be beneficial to schedule business on both a Friday and a Monday to turn the weekend into business days for allocation purposes. It is especially crucial to schedule appropriate business days when foreign travel is involved.

Moving Expenses

Moving expenses are deductible for moves in connection with the commencement of work at a new principal place of work.[47] Both employees and self-employed individuals can deduct these expenses. To be eligible for a moving expense deduction, a taxpayer must meet two basic tests: distance and time.

Distance Test. To meet the distance test, the taxpayer's new job location must be at least 50 miles farther from the taxpayer's old residence than the old residence was from the former place of employment. In this regard, the location of the new residence is not relevant. This eliminates a moving expense deduction for (1) taxpayers who purchase a new home in the same general area without changing their place of employment and (2) taxpayers who accept a new job in the same area as their old job.

EXAMPLE 31

Harry is permanently transferred to a new job location. The distance from Harry's former home to his new job (80 miles) exceeds the distance from his former home to his old job (30 miles) by at least 50 miles. Harry has met the distance test for a moving expense deduction.

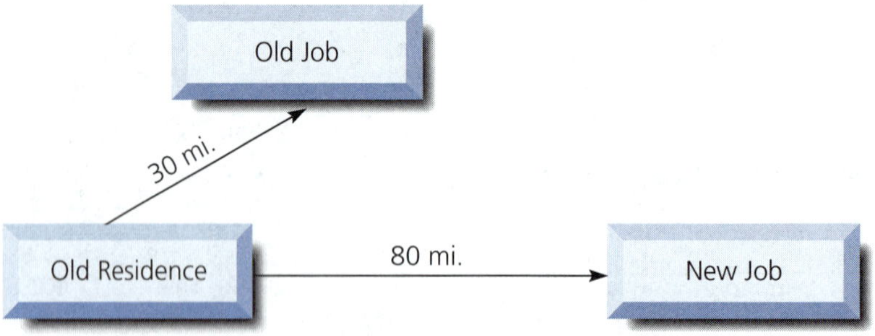

If Harry is not employed before the move, his new job must be at least 50 miles from his former residence. In this instance, Harry has also met the distance test if he was not previously employed. ■

Time Test. To meet the time test, an employee must be employed on a full-time basis at the new location for 39 weeks in the 12-month period following the move. If the taxpayer is a self-employed individual, he or she must work in the new location for 78 weeks during the two years following the move. The first 39 weeks must

47 § 217(a).

GLOBAL Tax Issues

EXPATRIATES AND THE MOVING EXPENSE DEDUCTION

Expatriates, U.S. persons who accept work assignments overseas, enjoy several favorable tax advantages regarding foreign moves. First, the cost of storing household goods qualifies as a moving expense. This could lead to a major tax saving since expatriates do not ship most of their household effects to the foreign location. Furthermore, the cost of storage, particularly in a climate-controlled facility, is not insignificant.

The second advantage expatriates may enjoy is an exemption from the time test. Those who return to the United States to retire are absolved from the 39-week or 78-week work requirement. Thus, the return home expenses are treated as qualified moving expenses.

be in the first 12 months. The time test is suspended if the taxpayer dies, becomes disabled, or is discharged or transferred by the new employer through no fault of the employee.

Find more information on this topic at our Web site: ***http://wft-entities.swlearning.com.***

DIGGING DEEPER 11

Treatment of Moving Expenses. *Qualified moving expenses* include reasonable expenses of:

- Moving household goods and personal effects.
- Traveling from the former residence to the new place of residence.

For this purpose, traveling includes lodging, but not meals, for the taxpayer and members of the household.[48] It does not include the cost of moving servants or others who are not members of the household. The taxpayer can elect to use actual auto expenses (no depreciation is allowed) or the automatic mileage method. In this case, moving expense mileage is limited in 2006 to 18 cents per mile for each car. The automatic mileage rate for 2005 depended on when the move was made—15 cents per mile for January through August and 22 cents per mile for September through December. These expenses are also limited by the reasonableness standard. For example, if one moves from Texas to Florida via Maine and takes six weeks to do so, the transportation and lodging must be allocated between personal and moving expenses.

EXAMPLE 32

Jill is transferred by her employer from the Atlanta office to the San Francisco office. In this connection, she spends the following amounts:

Cost of moving furniture	$6,800
Transportation	700
Meals	400
Lodging	900

Jill's total qualified moving expense is $8,400 ($6,800 + $700 + $900). ■

The moving expense deduction is allowed regardless of whether the employee is transferred by the existing employer or is employed by a new employer. It is allowed if the employee moves to a new area and obtains employment or switches from self-employed status to employee status (and vice versa). The moving expense deduction is also allowed if an individual is unemployed before obtaining employment in a new area.

[48] § 217(b).

What Is Not Included. In addition to meals while en route, the moving expense deduction does *not* include the following costs:

- New car tags and driver's licenses.
- Loss on the sale of a residence or penalty for breaking a lease.
- Forfeiture of security deposits and loss from disposing of club memberships.
- Pre-move house-hunting expenses.
- Temporary living expenses.

DIGGING DEEPER 12

Find more information on this topic at our Web site: ***http://wft-entities.swlearning.com.***

PLANNING *Strategies*

MOVING EXPENSES

★ **Framework Focus: Deductions**

Strategy ★ Maximize Deductible Amounts.

Persons who retire and move to a new location incur personal nondeductible moving expenses. If the retired person accepts a full-time job in the new location before moving and meets the time and distance requirements, the moving expenses are deductible.

EXAMPLE 33

At the time of his retirement from the national office of a major accounting firm, Gordon had an annual salary of $480,000. He moves from New York City to Seattle to retire, and accepts a full-time teaching position at a Seattle junior college at an annual salary of $22,000. If Gordon satisfies the 39-week test, his moving expenses are deductible. The disparity between the two salaries (previous and current) is of no consequence. ■

Education Expenses

General Requirements. Employees *and* self-employed individuals can deduct expenses incurred for education as ordinary and necessary business expenses, provided the expenses are incurred to maintain or improve existing skills required in the present job. An employee can also deduct expenses incurred to meet the express requirements of the employer or the requirements imposed by law to retain his or her employment status.

Education expenses are not deductible if the education is for either of the following purposes (except as discussed below under A Limited Deduction Approach):

- To meet the minimum educational standards for qualification in the taxpayer's existing job.
- To qualify the taxpayer for a new trade or business.[49]

Thus, fees incurred for professional exams (the bar exam, for example) and fees for review courses (such as a CPA review course) are not deductible.[50] If the education incidentally results in a promotion or raise, the deduction still can be taken as

[49]Reg. §§ 1.162–5(b)(2) and (3).

[50]Reg. § 1.212–1(f) and Rev.Rul. 69–292, 1969–1 C.B. 84.

TAX *in the News* **IS AN MBA DEGREE DEDUCTIBLE?**

Education that maintains or improves existing skills is deductible, but education that qualifies a taxpayer for a new field is not. But how do these basic rules apply to a conventional (i.e., nonspecialized) MBA degree? Does being a manager or a consultant require an MBA degree? Generally, the answer has always been that it does not. In this regard, therefore, the education does not create a new skill, so its cost should be deductible.

Several recent holdings, however, have found that an MBA degree can lead to qualifying for a new trade or business. But these holdings involved situations where the education resulted in a job change and satisfied different minimum requirements set by the employer. In one case, for example, the taxpayer moved from the position of investment analyst to become an investment banker, and the latter position required an MBA degree. Under these circumstances, the cost of the education was held to be nondeductible.

But barring a change to a job where the degree is required, the cost of an MBA degree should be deductible as merely improving existing managerial skills.

long as the education maintained and improved existing skills and did not qualify the person for a new trade or business. A change in duties is not always fatal to the deduction if the new duties involve the same general work. For example, the IRS has ruled that a practicing dentist's education expenses incurred to become an orthodontist are deductible.[51]

Requirements Imposed by Law or by the Employer for Retention of Employment. Taxpayers are permitted to deduct education expenses if additional courses are required by the employer or are imposed by law. Many states require a minimum of a bachelor's degree and a specified number of additional courses to retain a teaching job. In addition, some public school systems have imposed a master's degree requirement and require teachers to make satisfactory progress toward a master's degree in order to keep their positions. If the required education is the minimum degree required for the job, no deduction is allowed.

Professionals (such as physicians, attorneys, and CPAs) may deduct expenses incurred to meet continuing professional education requirements imposed by states as a condition for retaining a license to practice.

EXAMPLE 34

In order to meet continuing professional education requirements imposed by the State Board of Public Accountancy for maintaining her CPA license, Nancy takes an auditing course sponsored by a local college. The cost of the education is deductible. ■

DIGGING DEEPER 13

Find more information on this topic at our Web site: ***http://wft-entities.swlearning.com.***

Maintaining or Improving Existing Skills. The *maintaining or improving existing skills* requirement in the Code has been difficult for both taxpayers and the courts to interpret. For example, a business executive is permitted to deduct the costs of obtaining an MBA on the grounds that the advanced management education is undertaken to maintain and improve existing management skills. The executive is eligible to deduct the costs of specialized, nondegree management courses that are taken for continuing education or to maintain or improve existing skills. Expenses incurred by the executive to obtain a law degree are not deductible, however, because the education constitutes training for a new trade or business. The Regulations deny a self-employed accountant a deduction for expenses relating to law school.[52]

[51] Rev.Rul. 74–78, 1974–1 C.B. 44.

[52] Reg. § 1.162–5(b)(3)(ii) Example (1).

PLANNING *Strategies*

EDUCATION EXPENSES

★ **Framework Focus: Deductions**

Strategy ★ Maximize Deductible Amounts.

Education expenses are treated as nondeductible personal items unless the individual is employed or is engaged in a trade or business. A temporary leave of absence for further education is one way to assure that the taxpayer is still treated as being engaged in a trade or business. An individual was permitted to deduct education expenses even though he resigned from his job, returned to school full-time for two years, and accepted another job in the same field upon graduation. The court held that the student had merely suspended active participation in his field.[53]

If the time out of the field is too long, education expense deductions will be disallowed. For example, a teacher who left the field for four years to raise her child and curtailed her employment searches and writing activities was denied a deduction for education expenses. She was no longer actively engaged in the trade or business of being an educator.[54]

To secure the deduction, an individual should arrange his or her work situation to preserve employee or business status.

As discussed below under *A Limited Deduction Approach*, a limited exception is available for taxpayers who do not meet the above requirements.

Classification of Specific Items. Education expenses include books, tuition, typing, transportation (e.g., from the office to night school), and travel (e.g., meals and lodging while away from home at summer school).

EXAMPLE 35

Bill, who holds a bachelor of education degree, is a secondary education teacher in the Los Angeles school system. The school board recently raised its minimum education requirement for new teachers from four years of college training to five. A grandfather clause allows teachers with only four years of college to continue to qualify if they show satisfactory progress toward a graduate degree. Bill enrolls at the University of Washington during the summer and takes three graduate courses. His unreimbursed expenses for this purpose are as follows:

Books and tuition	$2,600
Lodging while in travel status (June–August)	1,150
Meals while in travel status	800
Laundry while in travel status	220
Transportation	600

Bill has an itemized deduction as follows:

Books and tuition	$2,600
Lodging	1,150
Meals less 50% cutback (discussed later in this chapter)	400
Laundry	220
Transportation	600
	$4,970

■

A Limited Deduction Approach

One of the major shortcomings of the education deduction, previously discussed, is that it is unavailable for taxpayers obtaining a basic skill. Thus, a taxpayer working

[53] *Stephen G. Sherman*, 36 TCM 1191, T.C.Memo. 1977–301.

[54] *Brian C. Mulherin*, 42 TCM 834, T.C.Memo. 1981–454; *George A. Baist*, 56 TCM 778, T.C.Memo. 1988–554.

TABLE 17–2 **Phase-in Rules for Qualified Tuition Deduction**

Filing Status	AGI Limit	Maximum Deduction Allowed
Single	$ 65,000	4,000
Married	130,000	
Single	65,001 to 80,000*	2,000
Married	130,001 to 160,000*	2,000

*No deduction at all is available if AGI exceeds this amount.

for an accounting firm cannot deduct the cost of earning a bachelor in accounting degree. Under 2001 tax legislation, this shortcoming has been partly resolved with the **deduction for qualified tuition and related expenses**.

A deduction *for* AGI is allowed for qualified tuition and related expenses involving higher education (i.e., postsecondary). The maximum amount of the deduction varies depending on the year involved. Further, the deduction is unavailable if the taxpayer's AGI exceeds a prescribed amount.[55] The current phase-ins and limitations are summarized in Table 17–2.

Various aspects of the new higher education tuition deduction are summarized below:

- Qualified tuition and related expenses include whatever is required for enrollment at the institution. Usually, student activity fees, books, and room and board are not included.[56]
- The expense need not be employment related, although it can be.
- The deduction is available for a taxpayer's spouse or anyone who can be claimed as a dependent and is an eligible student.
- The deduction is not available for married persons who file separate returns.[57]
- To avoid a "double benefit," the deduction must be coordinated with other education provisions (i.e., HOPE and lifetime learning credits). Along this same line, no deduction is allowed for a taxpayer who qualifies as another's dependent.[58]
- The deduction *for* AGI classification avoids the 2 percent-of-AGI floor on miscellaneous itemized deductions. See Chapter 16.[59]

EXAMPLE 36

Tina is single and a full-time employee of a CPA firm. During the current year, she attends law school at night and incurs the following expenses: $4,200 for tuition and $340 for books and supplies. Presuming she satisfies the AGI limitation (see Table 17–2), she can claim $4,000 as a deduction *for* AGI. If she itemizes her deductions for the year, can she claim the $540 not allowed under § 222 ($200 tuition in excess of $4,000 + $340 for books and supplies) as an education expense eligible for itemized deduction treatment? No, because obtaining a law degree leads to a new trade or business. ■

Another deduction item relating to education is the limited deduction of interest on education loans, which is covered in Chapter 16.[60]

[55] § 222(b)(2). Though this provision expired at the end of 2005, Congress is likely to extend it.
[56] § 222(d)(1).
[57] § 222(d)(4).
[58] § 222(c).
[59] §§ 61(a)(18) and 67.
[60] § 221.

Entertainment Expenses

Many taxpayers attempt to deduct personal **entertainment expenses** as business expenses. For this reason, the tax law restricts the deductibility of entertainment expenses. The Code contains strict record-keeping requirements and provides restrictive tests for the deduction of certain types of entertainment expenses.

The Fifty Percent Cutback. Only 50 percent of meal and entertainment expenses is deductible.[61] The limitation applies to employees, employers, and self-employed individuals. Although the 50 percent cutback can apply to either the employer or the employee, it will not apply twice. The cutback applies to the one who really pays (economically) for the meals or entertainment.

DIGGING DEEPER 14

Find more information on this topic at our Web site: ***http://wft-entities.swlearning.com.***

EXAMPLE 37

Jane, an employee of Pelican Corporation, entertains one of her clients. If Pelican Corporation does not reimburse Jane, she is subject to the cutback. If, however, Pelican Corporation reimburses Jane (or pays for the entertainment directly), Pelican suffers the cutback. ■

Transportation expenses are not affected by the cutback rule—only meals and entertainment expenses are reduced. The cutback also applies to taxes and tips relating to meals and entertainment. Cover charges, parking fees at an entertainment location, and room rental fees for a meal or cocktail party are also subject to the 50 percent cutback.

DIGGING DEEPER 15

Find more information on this topic at our Web site: ***http://wft-entities.swlearning.com.***

EXAMPLE 38

Joe pays a $30 cab fare to meet his client for dinner. The meal costs $120, and Joe leaves a $20 tip. His deduction is $100[($120 + $20) × 50% + $30 cab fare]. ■

Classification of Expenses. Entertainment expenses are classified either as *directly related* to business or *associated with* business.[62] Directly related expenses are related to an actual business meeting or discussion. These expenses are distinguished from entertainment expenses that are incurred to promote goodwill, such as maintaining existing customer relations. To obtain a deduction for directly related entertainment, it is not necessary to show that actual benefit resulted from the expenditure as long as there was a reasonable expectation of benefit. To qualify as directly related, the expense should be incurred in a business setting. If there is little possibility of engaging in the active conduct of a trade or business due to the nature of the social facility, it is difficult to qualify the expenditure as directly related to business.

Expenses associated with, rather than directly related to, business entertainment must serve a specific business purpose, such as obtaining new business or continuing existing business. These expenditures qualify only if the expenses directly precede or follow a bona fide business discussion. Entertainment occurring on the same day as the business discussion is considered associated with business.

EXAMPLE 39

Jerry, a manufacturers' representative, took his client to play a round of golf during the afternoon. They had dinner the same evening, during which time business was discussed. After dinner, they went to a nightclub to have drinks and listen to a jazz band. The business dinner

[61] § 274(n).

[62] § 274(a)(1)(A).

qualifies as directly related entertainment. The golf outing and the visit to the nightclub qualify as associated with entertainment. ■

PLANNING *Strategies*

ENTERTAINMENT EXPENSES

★ **Framework Focus: Deductions**

Strategy ★ Maximize Deductible Amounts.

Taxpayers should maintain detailed records of amounts, time, place, business purpose, and business relationships. A credit card receipt details the place, date, and amount of the expense. A notation made on the receipt of the names of the person(s) attending, the business relationship, and the topic of discussion should constitute sufficient documentation.[63] Failure to provide sufficient documentation could lead to disallowance of entertainment expense deductions.

Associated with or goodwill entertainment requires a business discussion to be conducted immediately before or after the entertainment. Furthermore, a business purpose must exist for the entertainment. Taxpayers should arrange for a business discussion before or after such entertainment. They also must document the business purpose, such as obtaining new business from a prospective customer.

Restrictions upon Deductibility of Business Meals. Business meals are deductible only if:[64]

- the meal is directly related to or associated with the active conduct of a trade or business,
- the expense is not lavish or extravagant under the circumstances, and
- the taxpayer (or an employee) is present at the meal.

A business meal with a business associate or customer is not deductible unless business is discussed before, during, or after the meal. This requirement does not apply to meals consumed while away from home in travel status.

EXAMPLE 40

Lacy travels to San Francisco for a business convention. She pays for dinner with three colleagues and is not reimbursed by her employer. They do not discuss business. She can deduct 50% of the cost of her meal. However, she cannot deduct the cost of her colleagues' meals. ■

EXAMPLE 41

Lance, a party to a contract negotiation, buys dinner for other parties to the negotiation but does not attend the dinner. No deduction is allowed because Lance was not present. ■

Restrictions upon Deductibility of Club Dues. The Code provides that "No deduction shall be allowed . . . for amounts paid or incurred for membership in any club organized for business, pleasure, recreation, or other social purpose."[65] Although this prohibition seems quite broad, it does not apply to clubs whose primary purpose is public service and community volunteerism (e.g., Kiwanis, Lions, Rotary). Although *dues* are not deductible, actual entertainment at a club may qualify.

EXAMPLE 42

During the current year, Vincent spent $1,400 on business lunches at the Lakeside Country Club. The annual membership fee was $6,000, and Vincent used the facility 60% of the time

[63] *Kenneth W. Guenther*, 54 TCM 382, T.C.Memo. 1987–440.

[64] § 274(k).

[65] § 274(a)(3).

for business. Presuming the lunches meet the business meal test, Vincent may claim $700 (50% cutback × $1,400) as a deduction. None of the club dues are deductible. ■

DIGGING DEEPER 16

Find more information on this topic at our Web site: ***http://wft-entities.swlearning.com.***

Business Gifts. Business gifts are deductible to the extent of $25 per donee per year.[66] An exception is made for gifts costing $4 or less (e.g., pens with the employee's or company's name on them) or promotional materials. Such items are not treated as business gifts subject to the $25 limitation. In addition, incidental costs such as engraving of jewelry and nominal charges for gift-wrapping, mailing, and delivery are not included in the cost of the gift in applying the limitation. Gifts to superiors and employers are not deductible. The $25 limitation on business gifts cannot be circumvented by having the donor's spouse join in the gift or by making multiple gifts that include the customer's family. Records must be maintained to substantiate business gifts.

Other Employee Expenses

Office in the Home. Employees and self-employed individuals are not allowed a deduction for **office in the home expenses** unless a portion of the residence is used *exclusively and on a regular basis* as either:

- The principal place of business for any trade or business of the taxpayer.
- A place of business used by clients, patients, or customers.

Employees must meet an additional test: The use must be for the convenience of the employer rather than merely being "appropriate and helpful."[67]

The precise meaning of "principal place of business" has been the subject of considerable controversy.[68] Congress ultimately resolved the controversy by amending the Code.[69]

The term "principal place of business" now includes a place of business that satisfies the following requirements:

- The office is used by the taxpayer to conduct administrative or management activities of a trade or business.
- There is no other fixed location of the trade or business where the taxpayer conducts these activities.

EXAMPLE 43

Dr. Smith is a self-employed anesthesiologist. During the year, he spends 30 to 35 hours per week administering anesthesia and postoperative care to patients in three hospitals, none of which provides him with an office. He also spends two or three hours per day in a room in his home that he uses exclusively as an office. He does not meet patients there, but he performs a variety of tasks related to his medical practice (e.g., contacting surgeons, bookkeeping, reading medical journals). A deduction will be allowed since he uses the office in the home to conduct administrative or management activities of his trade or business, and there is no other fixed location where these activities can be carried out. ■

The exclusive use requirement means that a specific part of the home must be used solely for business purposes. A deduction, if permitted, requires an allocation of total expenses of operating the home between business and personal use based on floor space or number of rooms.

[66] § 274(b)(1).

[67] § 280A(c)(1).

[68] See the restrictive interpretation arrived at in *Comm. v. Soliman*, 93–1 USTC ¶50,014, 71 AFTR2d 93–463, 113 S.Ct. 701 (USSC, 1993).

[69] § 280A(c)(1) as modified by TRA of 1997.

Even if the taxpayer meets the above requirements, the allowable home office expenses cannot exceed the gross income from the business less all other business expenses attributable to the activity. That is, the home office deduction cannot create a loss. Furthermore, the home office expenses that are allowed as itemized deductions anyway (e.g., mortgage interest and real estate taxes) must be deducted first. All home office expenses of an employee are miscellaneous itemized deductions, except those (such as interest and taxes) that qualify as other personal itemized deductions. Home office expenses of a self-employed individual are trade or business expenses and are deductible *for* AGI. Any disallowed home office expenses are carried forward and used in future years subject to the same limitations.

DIGGING DEEPER 17

Find more information on this topic at our Web site: ***http://wft-entities.swlearning.com.***

EXAMPLE 44

Rick is a certified public accountant employed by a regional CPA firm as a tax manager. He operates a separate business in which he refinishes furniture in his home. For this business, he uses two rooms in the basement of his home exclusively and regularly. The floor space of the two rooms constitutes 10% of the floor space of his residence. Gross income from the business totals $8,000. Expenses of the business (other than home office expenses) are $6,500. Rick incurs the following home office expenses:

Real property taxes on residence	$ 4,000
Interest expense on residence	7,500
Operating expenses of residence	2,000
Depreciation on residence (related to 10% business use)	250

Rick's deductions are determined as follows:

Business income		$ 8,000
Less: Other business expenses		(6,500)
		$ 1,500
Less: Allocable taxes ($4,000 × 10%)	$400	
Allocable interest ($7,500 × 10%)	750	(1,150)
		$ 350
Less: Allocable operating expenses of the residence ($2,000 × 10%)		(200)
		$ 150
Less: Allocable depreciation ($250, limited to remaining income)		(150)
		$ –0–

Rick has a carryover deduction of $100 (the unused excess depreciation). Because he is self-employed, the allocable taxes and interest ($1,150), the other deductible office expenses ($200 + $150), and $6,500 of other business expenses are deductible *for* AGI. ■

Certain Expenses for Teachers. The Job Creation and Worker Assistance Act of 2002 provided for a deduction *for* AGI for certain expenses of elementary and secondary school teachers.[70] Such teachers may deduct the costs they incur for books, supplies, computer equipment and related software and services, other equipment, and supplementary materials that they use in the classroom. The annual statutory ceiling on the deduction *for* AGI classification was $250 and applied for the 2002 and 2003 tax years. The Working Families Tax Relief Act of 2004 extended the provision through 2005.

[70] § 62(a)(2)(D).

TAX *in the News* ONE SIDE EFFECT OF 9/11

Telecommuting (or working at home) has always had its advantages. For the employee, it offers flexibility as to working hours and particularly in metropolitan areas, it avoids an often horrendous commute. For the employer, it offers the cost savings of not having to provide office space.

The tragedy of September 11 has added new variables to consider when evaluating the telecommuting approach. For the employee, there is the peace of mind that comes from the safety of the home. Although no place is entirely safe, the downtown high rise office building is clearly a more likely target of a terrorist attack. From an employer's standpoint, the "at home workplace" guarantees employee accessibility and precludes the complete destruction of job-related business data.

As working at home becomes more popular, an obvious result is the increased use of the office in the home deduction.

Although the educator expense provision expired at the end of 2005, there is good reason to believe that Congress will extend it. When such an extension occurs in 2006, it likely will be made retroactive in application to the beginning of 2006.

Miscellaneous Employee Expenses. Deductible miscellaneous employee expenses include special clothing and its upkeep, union dues, and professional expenses. Also deductible are professional dues, professional meetings, and employment agency fees for seeking new employment in the taxpayer's current trade or business, whether or not a new job is secured.

To be deductible, *special clothing* must be both specifically required as a condition of employment and not adaptable for regular wear. For example, a police officer's uniform is not suitable for off-duty activities. An exception is clothing used to the extent that it takes the place of regular clothing (e.g., some military uniforms).

EXAMPLE 45

Captain Roberts is on active duty in the U.S. Army. The cost of his regular uniforms is not deductible since such clothing is suitable for regular wear. Captain Roberts, however, spends over $1,100 to purchase "dress blues." Under military regulations, dress uniforms may be worn only during ceremonial functions (e.g., official events, parades). The $1,100 cost, to the extent it exceeds any clothing allowance, qualifies as a deduction. ■

The current position of the IRS is that expenses incurred in *seeking employment* are deductible if the taxpayer is seeking employment in the same trade or business. The deduction is allowed whether or not the attempts to secure employment are successful. An unemployed taxpayer can take a deduction providing there has been no substantial lack of continuity between the last job and the search for a new one. No deduction is allowed for persons seeking their first job or seeking employment in a new trade or business.

LO.4

Appreciate the difference between accountable and nonaccountable employee plans.

Classification of Employee Expenses

If employee expenses are reimbursed by the employer under an accountable plan, they are not reported by the employee at all. In effect, this result is equivalent to reporting the reimbursement as income and treating the expenses as deductions *for* AGI.[71] Alternatively, if the expenses are reimbursed under a nonaccountable plan or are not reimbursed at all, then they are classified as deductions *from* AGI and can be claimed only if the taxpayer itemizes (subject to the 2 percent-of-AGI floor). Exceptions are made for moving expenses and the employment-related expenses of a qualified performing artist, where a deduction *for* AGI is allowed. Thus, the tax treatment of reimbursements under accountable and nonaccountable plans differs significantly.

[71]§ 62(a)(2).

Accountable Plans. An accountable plan requires the employee to:

- Adequately account for (substantiate) the expenses. An employee renders an *adequate accounting* by submitting a record, with receipts and other substantiation, to the employer.[72]
- Return any excess reimbursement or allowance. An "excess reimbursement or allowance" is any amount that the employee does not adequately account for as an ordinary and necessary business expense.

The law provides that no deduction is allowed for any travel, entertainment, business gift, or listed property (automobiles, computers) expenditure unless properly substantiated by adequate records. The records should contain the following information:[73]

- The amount of the expense.
- The time and place of travel or entertainment (or date of gift).
- The business purpose of the expense.
- The business relationship of the taxpayer to the person entertained (or receiving the gift).

This means the taxpayer must maintain an account book or diary in which the above information is recorded at the time of the expenditure. Documentary evidence, such as itemized receipts, is required to support any expenditure for lodging while traveling away from home and for any other expenditure of $75 or more. If a taxpayer fails to keep adequate records, each expense must be established by a written or oral statement of the exact details of the expense and by other corroborating evidence.[74]

Find more information on this topic at our Web site: ***http://wft-entities.swlearning.com.***

DIGGING DEEPER 18

EXAMPLE 46

Bertha has travel expenses substantiated only by canceled checks. The checks establish the date, place, and amount of the expenditure. Because neither the business relationship nor the business purpose is established, the deduction is disallowed.[75] ■

EXAMPLE 47

Dwight has travel and entertainment expenses substantiated by a diary showing the time, place, and amount of the expenditure. His oral testimony provides the business relationship and business purpose; however, since he has no receipts, any expenditures of $75 or more are disallowed.[76] ■

Nonaccountable Plans. A **nonaccountable plan** is one in which an adequate accounting or return of excess amounts, or both, is not required. All reimbursements of expenses are reported in full as wages on the employee's Form W–2. Any allowable expenses are deductible in the same manner as are unreimbursed expenses.

An employer may have an accountable plan and require employees to return excess reimbursements or allowances, but an employee may fail to follow the rules of the plan. In that case, the expenses and reimbursements are subject to nonaccountable plan treatment.

Unreimbursed Expenses. Unreimbursed employee expenses are treated in a straightforward manner. Meals and entertainment expenses are subject to the 50 percent

[72] Reg. § 1.162–17(b)(4).

[73] § 274(d).

[74] Reg. § 1.274–5T(c)(3).

[75] *William T. Whitaker*, 56 TCM 47, T.C.Memo. 1988–418.

[76] *W. David Tyler*, 43 TCM 927, T.C.Memo. 1982–160.

limit. Total unreimbursed employee business expenses are usually reported as miscellaneous itemized deductions subject to the 2 percent-of-AGI floor (refer to Chapter 16). If the employee could have received, but did not seek, reimbursement for whatever reason, none of the employment-related expenses are deductible.

DIGGING DEEPER 19

Find more information on this topic at our Web site: ***http://wft-entities.swlearning.com.***

PLANNING *Strategies*

UNREIMBURSED EMPLOYEE BUSINESS EXPENSES

★ **Framework Focus: Deductions**

Strategy ★ Maximize Deductible Amounts.

The 2 percent floor for unreimbursed employee business expenses offers a tax planning opportunity for married couples. If one spouse has high miscellaneous expenses subject to the floor, it may be beneficial for the couple to file separate returns. If they file jointly, the 2 percent floor is based on the adjusted gross incomes of both. Filing separately lowers the reduction to 2 percent of only one spouse's adjusted gross income.

Other provisions of the law should be considered, however. For example, filing separately could cost a couple losses of up to $25,000 from self-managed rental units under the passive activity loss rules (discussed in Chapter 6).

Another possibility is to negotiate a salary reduction with one's employer in exchange for the 100 percent reimbursement of employee expenses. The employee is better off because the 2 percent floor does not apply. The employer is better off because certain expense reimbursements are not subject to Social Security and other payroll taxes.

Contributions to Individual Retirement Accounts

Traditional IRAs. Employees not covered by another qualified plan can establish their own tax-deductible **Individual Retirement Accounts (IRAs)**. The contribution ceiling is the smaller of $4,000 (or $8,000 for spousal IRAs) for years 2005–2007 or 100 percent of compensation.[77] If the taxpayer is an active participant in a qualified plan, the traditional IRA deduction limitation is phased out *proportionately* between certain AGI ranges, as shown in Table 17–3.[78]

An individual who attains the age of 50 by the end of the tax year can make additional catch-up IRA contributions. The maximum contribution limit is increased by $500 for 2005 and by $1,000 for years after 2005.

AGI is calculated taking into account any § 469 passive losses and § 86 taxable Social Security benefits and ignoring any § 911 foreign income exclusion, § 135 savings bonds interest exclusion, and the IRA deduction. There is a $200 floor on the IRA deduction limitation for individuals whose AGI is not above the phaseout range.

EXAMPLE 48

Dan, who is single, has compensation income of $56,000 in 2006. He is an active participant in his employer's qualified retirement plan. Dan contributes $4,000 to a traditional IRA. The deductible amount is reduced from $4,000 by $2,400 because of the phaseout mechanism:

$$\frac{\$6,000}{\$10,000} \times \$4,000 = \$2,400 \text{ reduction.}$$

Therefore, of the $4,000 contribution, Dan can deduct only $1,600 ($4,000 – $2,400). ■

[77] §§ 219(b)(1) and (c)(2). The ceiling was $3,000 for 2002–2004. It is increased to $5,000 for 2008. After 2008, the limit is adjusted annually for inflation in $500 increments.

[78] § 219(g).

TABLE 17–3 **Phaseout of Traditional IRA Deduction of an Active Participant in 2006**

AGI Filing Status	Phaseout Begins*	Phaseout Ends
Single and head of household	$50,000	$60,000
Married, filing joint return	75,000	85,000
Married, filing separate return	–0–	10,000

*The starting point for the phaseout is increased each year through 2007 for married filing jointly and through 2005 for other filing statuses.

EXAMPLE 49

Ben, an unmarried individual, is an active participant in his employer's qualified retirement plan. With AGI of $59,800, he would normally have an IRA deduction limit of $80 {$4,000 – [($59,800 – $50,000)/$10,000 × $4,000]}. However, because of the special floor provision, Ben is allowed a $200 IRA deduction. ■

An individual is not considered an active participant in a qualified plan merely because the individual's spouse is an active participant in such a plan for any part of a plan year. Thus, most homemakers may take a full $4,000 deduction regardless of the participation status of their spouse, unless the couple has AGI above $150,000. If their AGI is above $150,000, the phaseout of the deduction begins at $150,000 and ends at $160,000 (phaseout over the $10,000 range) rather than beginning and ending at the phaseout amounts in Table 17–3.[79]

EXAMPLE 50

Nell is covered by a qualified employer retirement plan at work. Her husband, Nick, is not an active participant in a qualified plan. If Nell and Nick's combined AGI is $135,000, Nell cannot make a deductible IRA contribution because she exceeds the income threshold for an active participant. However, since Nick is not an active participant, and their combined AGI does not exceed $150,000, he can make a deductible contribution of $4,000 to an IRA. ■

To the extent that an individual is ineligible to make a deductible contribution to an IRA, *nondeductible contributions* can be made to separate accounts. The nondeductible contributions are subject to the same dollar limits as deductible contributions ($4,000 of earned income, $8,000 for a spousal IRA). Income in the account accumulates tax-free until distributed. Only the account earnings are taxed upon distribution because the account basis equals the contributions made by the taxpayer. A taxpayer may elect to treat deductible IRA contributions as nondeductible. If an individual has no taxable income for the year after taking into account other deductions, the election would be beneficial. The election is made on the individual's tax return for the taxable year to which the designation relates.

Roth IRAs. A Roth IRA is a *nondeductible* alternative to the traditional deductible IRA. Introduced by Congress to encourage individual savings, earnings inside a Roth IRA are not taxable, and all qualified distributions from a Roth IRA are tax-free.[80] The maximum allowable annual contribution to a Roth IRA is the smaller of $4,000 ($8,000 for spousal IRAs) or 100 percent of the individual's compensation for the year. Contributions to a Roth IRA must be made by the due date (excluding extensions) of the taxpayer's tax return. Roth IRAs are not subject to the minimum distribution rules that apply to traditional IRAs.

[79] § 219(g)(7).

[80] § 408A.

TAX FACT

The Vacillating Popularity of IRAs

Individual Retirement Accounts (IRAs) became part of the tax law in 1974. The number of individual income tax returns indicating IRA contributions has varied over time, as the following table shows.

Year	Number of Returns (in Millions)
1975	1.2
1980	2.6
1985	16.2
1990	5.2
1995	4.3
2000	5.8
2002	3.3

What probably caused the substantial decline between 1985 and 1990? Tax legislation enacted in 1986 applied the *wherewithal to pay* concept in providing for the phaseout of the IRA deduction once an AGI threshold was reached. In addition, the legislation substantially reduced tax rates for the individual taxpayer.

Source: *IRS Tax Statistics.*

A taxpayer can make tax-free withdrawals from a Roth IRA after an initial five-year holding period if any of the following requirements is satisfied:

- The distribution is made on or after the date on which the participant attains age 59½.
- The distribution is made to a beneficiary (or the participant's estate) on or after the participant's death.
- The participant becomes disabled.
- The distribution is used to pay for qualified first-time homebuyer's expenses.

EXAMPLE 51

Edith establishes a Roth IRA at age 42 and contributes $3,000 per year for 20 years. The account is now worth $116,400, consisting of $60,000 of nondeductible contributions and $56,400 in accumulated earnings that have not been taxed. Edith may withdraw the $116,400 tax-free from the Roth IRA because she is over age 59½ and has met the five-year holding period requirement. ■

If the taxpayer receives a distribution from a Roth IRA and does not satisfy the aforementioned requirements, the distribution may be taxable. If the distribution represents a return of capital, it is not taxable. Conversely, if the distribution represents a payout of earnings, it is taxable. Under the ordering rules for Roth IRA distributions, distributions are treated as first made from contributions (return of capital).

EXAMPLE 52

Assume the same facts as in Example 51, except that Edith is only age 50 and receives a distribution of $55,000. Since her adjusted basis for the Roth IRA is $60,000 (contributions made), the distribution is tax-free, and her adjusted basis is reduced to $5,000 ($60,000 – $55,000). ■

Roth IRAs are subject to income limits. The maximum annual contribution of $4,000 is phased out beginning at AGI of $95,000 for single taxpayers and $150,000 for married couples who file a joint return. The phaseout range is $10,000 for married filing jointly and $15,000 for single taxpayers. For a married taxpayer filing separately, the contribution is phased out over a range beginning with AGI of $0 and ending with $10,000.

EXAMPLE 53

Bev, who is single, would like to contribute $4,000 to her Roth IRA. However, her AGI is $105,000, so her contribution is limited to $1,333 ($4,000 – $2,667) calculated as follows:

$$\frac{\$10,000}{\$15,000} \times \$4,000 = \$2,667 \text{ reduction.}$$ ■

Coverdell Education Savings Accounts (CESAs). Distributions from a **Coverdell Education Savings Account (CESA)** to pay for qualified education expenses receive favorable tax treatment.[81] Qualified education expenses include tuition, fees, books, supplies, and related equipment. Room and board qualify if the student's course load is at least one-half of the full-time course load. If the CESA is used to pay the qualified education expenses of the designated beneficiary, the withdrawals are tax-free. To the extent the distributions during a tax year exceed qualified education expenses, part of the excess is treated as a return of capital (the contributions), and part is treated as a distribution of earnings under the § 72 annuity rules. Thus, the distribution is presumed to be pro rata from each category. The exclusion for the distribution of earnings part is calculated as follows:

$$\frac{\text{Qualified education expenses}}{\text{Total distributions}} \times \text{Earnings} = \text{Exclusion.}$$

EXAMPLE 54

Meg receives a $2,500 distribution from her CESA. She uses $2,000 to pay for qualified education expenses. On the date of the distribution, Meg's CESA balance is $10,000, $6,000 of which represents her contributions. Since 60% ($6,000/$10,000) of her account balance represents her contributions, $1,500 ($2,500 × 60%) of the distribution is a return of capital, and $1,000 ($2,500 × 40%) is a distribution of earnings. The excludible amount of the earnings is calculated as follows:

$$\frac{\$2,000}{\$2,500} \times \$1,000 = \$800$$

Thus, Meg must include $200 ($1,000 – $800) in her gross income. ■

The maximum amount that can be contributed annually to a CESA for a beneficiary is $2,000. A beneficiary must be an individual and cannot be a group of children or an unborn child. The contributions are not deductible. A CESA is subject to income limits. The maximum annual contribution is phased out beginning at $95,000 for single taxpayers and $190,000 for married couples who file a joint return. The phaseout range is $30,000 for married filing jointly and $15,000 for single taxpayers. Contributions cannot be made to a CESA after the date on which the designated beneficiary attains age 18. Thus, a total of up to $36,000 can be contributed for each beneficiary—$2,000 in the year of birth and in each of the 17 following years.

A 6 percent excise tax is imposed on excess contributions to a CESA. A 10 percent excise tax is imposed on any distributions that are included in gross income.

The balance in a CESA must be distributed within 30 days after the death of a beneficiary or within 30 days after a beneficiary reaches age 30. Any balance at the close of either 30-day period is considered to be distributed at such time, and the earnings portion is included in the beneficiary's gross income. Before a beneficiary

[81] § 530.

reaches age 30, any balance can be rolled over tax-free into another CESA for a member of the beneficiary's family who is under age 30.

The CESA exclusion may be available in a tax year in which the beneficiary claims the HOPE credit or the lifetime learning credit (see Chapter 16). However, any excluded amount of the CESA distribution cannot be used for the same educational expenses for which the HOPE credit or the lifetime learning credit is claimed.

Contributions cannot be made to a beneficiary's CESA during any year in which contributions are made to a qualified tuition program on behalf of the same beneficiary.

LO.5

Understand the tax provisions applicable to proprietors.

Individuals as Proprietors

The Proprietorship as a Business Entity

A sole proprietorship is *not* a taxable entity separate from the individual who owns the proprietorship. A sole proprietor reports the results of business operations of the proprietorship on Schedule C of Form 1040. The net profit or loss from the proprietorship is then transferred from Schedule C to Form 1040, which is used by the taxpayer to determine tax liability. The proprietor reports all of the net profit or net loss from the business, regardless of the amount actually withdrawn from the proprietorship during the year.

Income and expenses of the proprietorship retain their character when reported by the proprietor. For example, ordinary income of the proprietorship is treated as ordinary income when reported by the proprietor, and capital gain of the proprietorship is treated as capital gain by the proprietor.

EXAMPLE 55

George is the sole proprietor of George's Record Shop. Gross income of the business in 2006 is $200,000, and operating expenses are $110,000. George also sells a capital asset held by the business for a $10,000 long-term capital gain. During 2006, he withdraws $60,000 from the business for living expenses. George reports the operating income and expenses of the business on Schedule C, resulting in net profit (ordinary income) of $90,000 ($200,000 – $110,000). Even though he withdrew only $60,000, George reports all of the $90,000 net profit from the business on Form 1040, where he computes taxable income and tax liability for the year. He also reports a $10,000 long-term capital gain on his personal tax return (Schedule D of Form 1040). ■

Income of a Proprietorship

The broad definition of gross income in § 61(a) applies equally to individuals and business entities, including proprietorships, corporations, and partnerships. Thus, it is assumed that asset inflows into a proprietorship are to be treated as income. Certain items may be excluded from gross income. Many of the exclusions available to an individual are related to the individual as an employee. Refer to Chapter 4 for a detailed discussion of gross income.

Deductions Related to a Proprietorship

Ordinary and Necessary Business Expenses. The provisions that govern business deductions also are general, and not entity specific. The § 162 requirement that trade or business expenses be *ordinary and necessary* (refer to Chapter 5) applies to proprietorships as well as corporations, partnerships, and other business entities. However, certain specific deductions are available only to self-employed taxpayers. These deductions are covered in detail below.

Health Insurance Premiums. A self-employed taxpayer may deduct 100 percent of insurance premiums paid for medical coverage as a deduction *for* AGI.[82] The deduction is allowed for premiums paid on behalf of the taxpayer, the taxpayer's spouse, and dependents of the taxpayer. The deduction is not allowed to any taxpayer who is eligible to participate in a subsidized health plan maintained by any employer of the taxpayer or of the taxpayer's spouse.

This deduction is reported in the Adjusted Gross Income section of Form 1040 rather than on Schedule C. Premiums paid for medical coverage of the *employees* of a self-employed taxpayer are deductible as business expenses on Schedule C, however.

EXAMPLE 56

Ellen, a sole proprietor of a restaurant, has two dependent children. During 2006, she paid health insurance premiums of $1,800 for her own coverage and $1,000 for coverage of her two children. Ellen can deduct $2,800 as a deduction *for* AGI. ■

Self-Employment Tax. The tax on self-employment income is levied to provide Social Security and Medicare benefits (old age, survivors, and disability insurance and hospital insurance) for self-employed individuals. Individuals with net earnings of $400 or more from self-employment are subject to the self-employment tax.[83] For 2006, the self-employment tax is 12.4 percent of self-employment earnings up to a $94,200 *ceiling amount* (for the Social Security portion) plus 2.9 percent of the *total* amount of self-employment earnings (for the Medicare portion). Thus, the combined self-employment tax rate on earnings up to $94,200 is 15.3 percent. The ceiling amount is adjusted periodically for inflation.

For purposes of computing the *self-employment tax,* self-employed taxpayers are allowed a deduction from net earnings equal to one-half of the self-employment tax rate.[84] This deduction of 7.65 percent (one-half of the 15.3 percent rate) is reflected by multiplying net earnings from self-employment by 92.35 percent (100% – 7.65%), as shown in Example 57. For purposes of computing *taxable income,* an income tax deduction is allowed for one-half the amount of self-employment tax paid.[85]

Example 57 illustrates the computation of the self-employment tax, as well as the income tax deduction for one-half of self-employment tax paid. For income tax purposes, the amount to be reported on Schedule C is net earnings from self-employment *before* the deduction for one-half of the self-employment tax. The deduction of one-half of the self-employment tax paid is reported separately on Form 1040 as a deduction *for* AGI.

EXAMPLE 57

Computation of the self-employment tax is determined using the steps below. The self-employment tax is determined for two taxpayers with net earnings from self-employment for 2006 as follows: Ned, $55,000 and Terry, $120,000.

Computation of Self-Employment Tax for Ned	
1. Net earnings	$55,000.00
2. Multiply line 1 by 92.35%.	$50,792.50
3. If the amount on line 2 is $94,200 or less, multiply the line 2 amount by 15.3%. This is the self-employment tax.	$ 7,771.25
4. If the amount on line 2 is more than $94,200, multiply the excess over $94,200 by 2.9% and add $14,412.60. This is the self-employment tax.	

[82] § 162(l).
[83] § 6017.
[84] § 1402(a)(12).
[85] § 164(f).

Computation of Self-Employment Tax for Terry	
1. Net earnings	$120,000.00
2. Multiply line 1 by 92.35%.	$110,820.00
3. If the amount on line 2 is $94,200 or less, multiply the line 2 amount by 15.3%. This is the self-employment tax.	
4. If the amount on line 2 is more than $94,200, multiply the excess over $94,200 by 2.9% and add $14,412.60. This is the self-employment tax.	$ 14,894.58

For income tax purposes, Ned has net earnings from self-employment of $55,000 and a deduction *for* AGI of $3,885.63 (one-half of $7,771.25). Terry has net earnings from self-employment of $120,000 and a deduction *for* AGI of $7447.29 (one-half of $14,894.58). Both taxpayers benefit from the deduction for one-half of the self-employment tax paid. ■

Wages of employees also are subject to Social Security and Medicare taxes. The total tax rate is also 15.3 percent, with 7.65 percent being withheld from the employee's wages and the employer paying at a 7.65 percent rate. If an individual who is self-employed also receives wages from working as an employee of another organization, the ceiling amount of the Social Security portion on which the self-employment tax is computed is reduced. Thus, the self-employment tax may be reduced if a self-employed individual also receives Social Security wages in excess of the ceiling amount.

Net earnings from self-employment include gross income from a trade or business less allowable trade or business deductions, the distributive share of any partnership income or loss derived from a trade or business activity, and net income from rendering personal services as an independent contractor. Gain or loss from the disposition of property (including involuntary conversions) is excluded from the computation of self-employment income unless the property involved is inventory.

Retirement Plans for Self-Employed Individuals

Self-employed individuals have several options for retirement funding. Individual Retirement Accounts (discussed earlier in this chapter) are available to both employees and self-employed individuals. Other options for self-employed individuals include, but are not limited to, H.R. 10 (Keogh) plans and SIMPLE plans, both of which are discussed below.

Keogh Plans. Self-employed individuals (e.g., partners and sole proprietors) are eligible to establish and receive qualified retirement benefits under **Keogh plans** (also known as H.R. 10 plans). Self-employed individuals who establish Keogh plans for themselves are also required to cover their *employees* under the plan.

Keogh investments can include a variety of funding vehicles, such as mutual funds, annuities, real estate shares, certificates of deposit, debt instruments, commodities, securities, and personal properties. When an individual decides to make all investment decisions, a *self-directed retirement plan* is established. Investment in most collectibles is not allowed in a self-directed plan.

A Keogh plan may be either a *defined contribution* plan or a *defined benefit* plan. In a defined contribution plan, the amount that can be contributed each year is subject to limitations. Retirement benefits depend on the amount contributed and the amount earned by the plan. In a defined benefit plan, the amount of retirement income is fixed and is determined on the basis of the employee's compensation while working, the number of years in the plan, and age on retirement.

TAX FACT

Increasing Popularity of Keogh Plans

Keogh plans are an increasingly popular retirement savings device for self-employed taxpayers. The number of individual income tax returns that included Keogh contributions is indicated below.

Year	Number of Returns (in Thousands)
1975	596
1980	569
1985	676
1990	824
1995	1,032
2000	1,228
2002	1,181

Source: *IRS Tax Statistics.*

A self-employed individual may annually contribute the smaller of $44,000 (in 2006) or 100 percent of earned income to a defined contribution Keogh plan.[86] If the defined contribution plan is a profit sharing plan or stock bonus plan, however, a 25 percent deduction limit applies. Under a defined benefit Keogh plan, the annual benefit is limited to the smaller of $175,000 (in 2006) or 100 percent of the average net earnings for the three highest years.[87]

Earned income refers to net earnings from self-employment.[88] Net earnings from self-employment means the gross income derived by an individual from any trade or business carried on by that individual, less appropriate deductions, plus the distributive share of income or loss from a partnership.[89] Earned income is reduced by contributions to a Keogh plan on the individual's behalf and by 50 percent of any self-employment tax.[90]

EXAMPLE 58

Pat, a partner, has earned income of $150,000 in 2006 (after the deduction for one-half of self-employment tax, but before any Keogh contribution). The maximum contribution Pat may make to a defined contribution Keogh plan is $44,000, the lesser of $150,000 or $44,000. ■

For discrimination purposes, the 25 percent limitation on the employee contribution to a profit sharing plan or stock bonus plan is computed on the first $220,000 (in 2006) of earned income. Thus, the maximum contribution in 2006 is $44,000 ($220,000 – .25X = X; X = $176,000). Therefore, $220,000 – $176,000 = $44,000. Alternatively, this can be calculated by multiplying $220,000 by 20 percent.

EXAMPLE 59

Terry, a self-employed accountant, has a profit sharing plan with a contribution rate of 15% of compensation. Terry's earned income after the deduction of one-half of self-employment tax, but before the Keogh contribution, is $250,000. Terry's contribution is limited to $28,696 ($220,000 – .15X = X), since X = $191,304 and .15 × $191,304 = $28,696. ■

[86] § 415(c)(1).

[87] § 415(b)(1). The amount is indexed annually.

[88] § 401(c)(2).

[89] § 1402(a).

[90] §§ 401(c)(2)(A)(v) and 164(f).

Although a Keogh plan must be established before the end of the year in question, contributions may be made up to the normal filing date for that year.

PLANNING *Strategies*

IMPORTANT DATES RELATED TO IRAs AND KEOGH PLANS

★ **Framework Focus: Deductions**

Strategy ★ Accelerate Recognition of Deductions to Achieve Tax Deferral.

A Keogh or IRA participant may make a deductible contribution for a tax year up to the time prescribed for filing the individual's tax return for that tax year. A Keogh plan must have been *established* by the end of the *prior* tax year (e.g., December 31, 2005) to obtain a deduction on the 2005 income tax return for the contribution made in the *current* year (2006). An individual can establish an IRA during the *current* tax year (up to the normal filing date) and still receive a deduction on the prior-year income tax return for the contribution made in the *current* year.

SIMPLE Plans. Employers with 100 or fewer employees who do not maintain another qualified retirement plan may establish a *savings incentive match plan for employees* (SIMPLE plan).[91] The plan can be in the form of a § 401(k) plan or an IRA. The SIMPLE plan is not subject to the nondiscrimination rules that are normally applicable to § 401(k) plans.

All employees who received at least $5,000 in compensation from the employer during any two preceding years and who reasonably expect to receive at least $5,000 in compensation during the current year must be eligible to participate in the plan. The decision to participate is up to the employee. A *self-employed individual* may also participate in the plan.

The contributions made by the employee (a salary reduction approach) must be expressed as a percentage of compensation rather than as a fixed dollar amount. The plan must not permit the elective employee contribution for the year to exceed $10,000 (in 2006).[92] The elective deferral limit is increased under the catch-up provision for employees age 50 and over. The amount is $2,000 for 2005 and $2,500 for 2006 and thereafter. The $2,500 amount is indexed for inflation in $500 increments beginning in 2007.

Generally, the employer must either match elective employee contributions up to 3 percent of the employee's compensation or provide nonmatching contributions of 2 percent of compensation for each eligible employee. Thus, the maximum amount that may be contributed to the plan for 2006 is $16,600 [$10,000 employee contributions + $6,600 ($220,000 compensation ceiling × 3%) employer match].

No other contributions may be made to the plan other than the employee elective contribution and the required employer matching contribution (or nonmatching contribution under the 2 percent rule). All contributions are fully vested. An employer is required to make contributions to a SIMPLE § 401(k) plan once it is established, whereas an employer's contributions to a traditional § 401(k) plan are optional.

An employer's deduction for contributions to a SIMPLE § 401(k) plan is limited to the greater of 25 percent of the compensation paid or accrued or the amount that the employer is required to contribute to the plan. Thus, an employer may deduct contributions to a SIMPLE § 401(k) plan in excess of 25 percent of the $220,000 salary cap. A traditional § 401(k) plan is limited to 25 percent of the total compensation of plan participants for the year.

[91] § 408(p).

[92] For 2005, the limit was $10,000. This amount is indexed for inflation in $500 increments in 2006 and thereafter. For 2006, the amount remains at $10,000.

An employer is allowed a deduction for matching contributions only if the contributions are made by the due date (including extensions) for the employer's tax return. Contributions to a SIMPLE plan are excludible from the employee's gross income, and the SIMPLE plan is tax-exempt.

EXAMPLE 60

The Mauve Company has a SIMPLE plan for its employees under which it provides nonmatching contributions of 2% of compensation for each eligible employee. The maximum amount that can be added to each participant's account in 2006 is $14,400, composed of the $10,000 employee salary reduction plus an employer contribution of $4,400 ($220,000 × 2%). ■

Distributions from a SIMPLE plan are taxed under the IRA rules. Tax-free rollovers can be made from one SIMPLE account to another. A SIMPLE account can be rolled over to an IRA tax-free after the expiration of a two-year period since the individual first participated in the plan. Withdrawals of contributions during the two-year period beginning on the date an employee first participates in the SIMPLE plan are subject to a 25 percent early withdrawal tax rather than the 10 percent early withdrawal tax that otherwise would apply.

PLANNING *Strategies*

FACTORS AFFECTING RETIREMENT PLAN CHOICES

★ **Framework Focus: Deductions**

Strategy ★ Maximize Deductible Amounts.

An IRA might not be the best retirement plan option for many self-employed taxpayers. The maximum amount that can be deducted is $4,000 per year ($8,000 for a spousal plan), which may be too low to provide funding for an adequate level of retirement income. Other options such as Keogh plans and SIMPLE plans allow larger contributions and larger deductions. However, a self-employed individual who establishes either a Keogh or a SIMPLE plan is required to cover employees under such plans. This can result in substantial expenditures, not only for the required contributions, but also for expenses of administering the plan. An advantage of an IRA is that coverage of employees is not required.

Accounting Periods and Methods

Proprietors may choose among accounting methods, just as other business entities do (refer to Chapter 4 and Chapter 5). The cash method is commonly used by proprietorships that provide services, while the accrual or hybrid method generally is required if inventory is a material income-producing factor.

The accounting period rules for proprietorships generally are much simpler than the rules for partnerships and S corporations. Because a proprietorship is not an entity separate from the proprietor, the proprietorship must use the same tax year-end as the proprietor. This does not preclude the use of a fiscal year for a proprietorship, but most proprietorships use the calendar year.

Estimated Tax Payments

Although the following discussion largely centers on self-employed taxpayers, some of the procedures may be applicable to employed persons. In many cases, for example, employed persons may be required to pay estimated tax if they have income that is not subject to withholding (e.g., income from rentals, dividends, or interest).

Estimated Tax for Individuals. **Estimated tax** is the amount of tax (including alternative minimum tax and self-employment tax) an individual expects to owe for the year after subtracting tax credits and income tax withheld. Any individual who has estimated tax for the year of $1,000 or more and whose withholding does not equal or exceed the required annual payment (discussed below) must make quarterly payments.[93] Otherwise, a penalty may be assessed. No quarterly payments are required, and no penalty will apply on an underpayment, if the taxpayer's estimated tax is under $1,000. No penalty will apply if the taxpayer had no tax liability for the preceding tax year, the preceding tax year was a taxable year of 12 months, and the taxpayer was a citizen or resident for the entire preceding tax year. In this regard, having no tax liability is not the same as having no additional tax to pay.

The required annual payment must first be computed. This is the smaller of the following amounts:

- Ninety percent of the tax shown on the current year's return.
- One hundred percent of the tax shown on the preceding year's return (the return must cover the full 12 months of the preceding year). If the AGI on the preceding year's return exceeds $150,000 ($75,000 if married filing separately), the 100 percent requirement is increased to 110 percent.

In general, one-fourth of this required annual payment is due on April 15, June 15, and September 15 of the tax year and January 15 of the following year. Thus, the quarterly installment of the required annual payment reduced by the applicable withholding is the estimated tax to be paid. An equal part of withholding is deemed paid on each due date, even if a taxpayer's earnings fluctuate widely during the year. Payments are to be accompanied by the payment voucher from Form 1040–ES for the appropriate date.

Penalty on Underpayments. A nondeductible penalty is imposed on the amount of underpayment of estimated tax. The rate for this penalty is the same as the rate for underpayments of tax and is adjusted quarterly to reflect changes in the average prime rate.

An *underpayment* occurs when any quarterly payment (the sum of estimated tax paid and income tax withheld) is less than 25 percent of the required annual payment. The penalty is applied to the amount of the underpayment for the period of the underpayment.[94]

EXAMPLE 61

Marta made the following payments of estimated tax for 2006 and had no income tax withheld:

April 17, 2006	$1,400
June 15, 2006	2,300
September 15, 2006	1,500
January 15, 2007	1,800

Marta's actual tax for 2006 is $8,000, and her tax in 2005 was $10,000. Therefore, each installment should have been at least $1,800 [($8,000 × 90%) × 25%]. Of the payment on June 15, $400 will be credited to the unpaid balance of the first quarterly installment due on April 17,[95] thereby effectively stopping the underpayment penalty for the first quarterly period. Of the remaining $1,900 payment on June 15, $100 is credited to the September 15 payment, resulting in this third quarterly payment being $200 short. Then $200 of the January 15, 2007 payment is credited to the September 15 shortfall, ending the period of underpayment for that portion due. The January 15, 2007 installment is now underpaid by $200, and a penalty will apply from January 15, 2007, to April 16, 2007 (unless paid sooner). Marta's underpayments for the periods of underpayment are as follows:

[93] § 6654(c)(1).
[94] § 6654(b)(2).
[95] Payments are credited to unpaid installments in the order in which the installments are required to be paid. § 6654(b)(3).

1st installment due:	$400 from April 17, 2006 to June 15, 2006
2nd installment due:	Paid in full
3rd installment due:	$200 from September 15, 2006 to January 15, 2007
4th installment due:	$200 from January 15, 2007 to April 16, 2007 ■

If a possible underpayment of estimated tax is indicated, Form 2210 should be filed to compute the penalty due or to justify that no penalty applies.

Hobby Losses

LO.6

Distinguish between business and hobby activities and apply the rules limiting the deduction of hobby losses.

Employee deductions and deductions related to a proprietorship were discussed in previous sections of this chapter. Employees are allowed to deduct certain expenditures incurred in connection with their work activities. Expenses incurred by a self-employed taxpayer are deductible only if the taxpayer can show that the activity was entered into for the purpose of making a profit.

Certain activities may have either profit-seeking or personal attributes, depending upon individual circumstances. Examples include raising horses and operating a farm that is also used as a weekend residence. While personal losses are not deductible, losses attributable to profit-seeking activities may be deducted and used to offset a taxpayer's other income. For this reason, losses generated by hobbies are not deductible.

General Rules

If an individual can show that an activity has been conducted with the intent to earn a profit, losses from the activity are fully deductible. The hobby loss rules apply only if the activity is not engaged in for profit. Hobby expenses are deductible only to the extent of hobby income.[96]

The Regulations stipulate that the following nine factors should be considered in determining whether an activity is profit seeking or a hobby:[97]

- Whether the activity is conducted in a businesslike manner.
- The expertise of the taxpayers or their advisers.
- The time and effort expended.
- The expectation that the assets of the activity will appreciate in value.
- The taxpayer's previous success in conducting similar activities.
- The history of income or losses from the activity.
- The relationship of profits earned to losses incurred.
- The financial status of the taxpayer (e.g., if the taxpayer does not have substantial amounts of other income, this may indicate that the activity is engaged in for profit).
- Elements of personal pleasure or recreation in the activity.

The presence or absence of a factor is not by itself determinative of whether the activity is profit seeking or a hobby. Rather, the decision is a subjective one that is based on an analysis of the facts and circumstances.

Presumptive Rule of § 183

The Code provides a rebuttable presumption that an activity is profit seeking if the activity shows a profit in at least three of any five prior consecutive years.[98] If the activity involves horses, a profit in at least two of seven consecutive years meets the presumptive rule. If these profitability tests are met, the activity is presumed to be a

[96] § 183(b)(2).

[97] Reg. §§ 1.183–2(b)(1) through (9).

[98] § 183(d).

trade or business rather than a personal hobby. In this situation, the burden of proof shifts from the taxpayer to the IRS. That is, the IRS bears the burden of proving that the activity is personal rather than trade or business related.

EXAMPLE 62

Camille, an executive for a large corporation, is paid a salary of $200,000. Her husband is a collector of antiques. Several years ago, he opened an antique shop in a local shopping center and spends most of his time buying and selling antiques. He occasionally earns a small profit from this activity but more frequently incurs substantial losses. If the losses are business related, they are fully deductible against Camille's salary income on a joint return. The following approach should be considered in resolving this issue:

- Initially determine whether the antique activity has met the three-out-of-five-years profit test.
- If the presumption is not met, the activity may nevertheless qualify as a business if the taxpayer can show that the intent is to engage in a profit-seeking activity. It is not necessary to show actual profits.
- Attempt to fit the operation within the nine criteria prescribed in the Regulations and listed above. These criteria are the factors considered in trying to rebut the § 183 presumption. ■

Determining the Amount of the Deduction

If an activity is deemed to be a hobby, the expenses are deductible only to the extent of the gross income from the hobby. These expenses must be deducted in the following order:

- Amounts deductible under other Code Sections without regard to the nature of the activity, such as property taxes and home mortgage interest.
- Amounts deductible under other Code Sections if the activity had been engaged in for profit, but only if those amounts do not affect adjusted basis. Examples include maintenance, utilities, and supplies.
- Amounts that affect adjusted basis and would be deductible under other Code Sections if the activity had been engaged in for profit.[99] Examples include depreciation, amortization, and depletion.

These deductions are deductible *from* AGI as itemized deductions to the extent they exceed 2 percent of AGI.[100] If the taxpayer uses the standard deduction rather than itemizing, all hobby loss deductions are wasted.

EXAMPLE 63

Jim, the vice president of an oil company, has AGI of $80,000. He decides to pursue painting in his spare time. He uses a home studio, comprising 10% of the home's square footage. During the current year, Jim incurs the following expenses:

Frames	$ 350
Art supplies	300
Fees paid to models	1,000
Expenses related to home:	
Total property taxes	900
Total home mortgage interest	10,000
Total home maintenance and utilities	3,600
Depreciation on 10% of home used as studio	500

During the year, Jim sold paintings for a total of $3,200. If the activity is held to be a hobby, Jim is allowed deductions as follows:

[99]Reg. § 1.183–1(b)(1).

[100]Reg. § 1.67–1T(a)(1)(iv) and Rev.Rul. 75–14, 1975–1 C.B. 90.

Gross income		$ 3,200
Deduct: Taxes and interest (10% of $10,900)		(1,090)
Remainder		$ 2,110
Deduct: Frames	$ 350	
Art supplies	300	
Models' fees	1,000	
Maintenance and utilities (10%)	360	(2,010)
Remainder		$ 100
Depreciation ($500, but limited to $100)		(100)
Net income		$ -0-

Jim includes the $3,200 of income in AGI, making his AGI $83,200. The taxes and interest are itemized deductions, deductible in full. Assuming Jim has no other miscellaneous itemized deductions, the remaining expenses of $2,110 are reduced by 2% of his AGI ($1,664); so the net deduction is $446. Since the property taxes and home mortgage interest are deductible anyway, the net effect is a $2,754 ($3,200 less $446) increase in taxable income. ■

EXAMPLE 64

If Jim's activity in Example 63 were held to be a business, he could deduct expenses totaling $3,600 *for* AGI, as shown below. All these expenses would be trade or business expenses. His reduction in AGI would be as follows:

Gross income		$ 3,200
Deduct: Taxes and interest	$1,090	
Other business expenses	2,010	
Depreciation	500	(3,600)
Reduction in AGI		($ 400)

As in Example 63, Jim can deduct the remaining property taxes and home mortgage interest of $9,810 ($10,900 – $1,090) as itemized deductions. ■

Suggested Further Readings

Shelton I. Banoff and Richard M. Lipton, Editors (Shop Talk), "Oprah's Audience Gets Another Lesson in Taxes," *Journal of Taxation*, January 2005, pp. 63–64.

Stanley D. Baum, "The Advantages of Health Savings Accounts—The Code's Newest Healthcare Arrangement," *Journal of Taxation*, February 2004, pp. 101–110.

Richard E. Coppage, Sidney J. Baxendale, and Lisa Blum, "Jobs Act Increases Prospect for ROTH IRA Conversions," *Practical Tax Strategies*, August 2005, pp. 99–108.

John B. Truskowski, "Tax Consequences of Renting Out a Second Home May Turn on How Often the Taxpayer Makes Use of It," *Journal of Taxation*, July 2004, pp. 26–40.

Donald T. Williamson, "Opportunities in Using the Office-in-Home Deduction for Code Sec. 280A," *Taxes—The Tax Magazine*, January 2002, pp. 19–32.

James L. Wittenbach and Ken Milani, "FICA Factors for S Corporation Payments to Owner/Employees," *Practical Tax Strategies*, December 2005, pp. 338–345.

KEY TERMS

Accountable plan, 17-3

Automatic mileage method, 17-20

Cafeteria plan, 17-12

Coverdell Education Savings Account (CESA), 17-39

De minimis fringe benefits, 17-15

Deduction for qualified tuition and related expenses, 17-29

Education expenses, 17-26

Entertainment expenses, 17-30

Estimated tax, 17-45

Flexible spending plan, 17-13

Foreign earned income exclusion, 17-18

Health Savings Account (HSA), 17-6

Independent contractor, 17-2

Individual Retirement Account (IRA), 17-36

Keogh plans, 17-42

Medical Savings Account (MSA), 17-6

Moving expenses, 17-24

No-additional-cost services, 17-14

Nonaccountable plan, 17-35

Office in the home expenses, 17-32

Qualified employee discounts, 17-14

Qualified transportation fringes, 17-16

Self-employment tax, 17-5

Transportation expenses, 17-19

Travel expenses, 17-21

Working condition fringes, 17-15

PROBLEM MATERIALS

PROBLEMS

1. In determining whether someone who performs services for another is an employee or is self-employed, a number of factors are considered. In each of the *independent* situations appearing below, which classification is indicated? In all cases, assume Heath performs services for Melvin.
   a. Melvin pays Heath based on units produced.
   b. Melvin sets Heath's working hours.
   c. Heath has his own tools.
   d. At any time he desires, Melvin has the right to terminate Heath's services.

2. Rex, age 45, is an officer of Blue Company, which provides him with the following nondiscriminatory fringe benefits in 2006:

   - Hospitalization insurance premiums for Rex and his dependents. The cost of the coverage for Rex is $2,700 per year, and the additional cost for his dependents is $3,600 per year. The plan has a $2,000 deductible, but his employer contributed $1,500 to Rex's Health Savings Account. Rex withdrew only $800 from the HSA, and the account earned $50 interest during the year.
   - Long-term care insurance premiums for Rex, at a cost of $3,600 per year.
   - Insurance premiums of $840 for salary continuation payments. Under the plan, Rex will receive his regular salary in the event he is unable to work due to illness. Rex collected $4,500 on the policy to replace lost wages while he was ill during the year.
   - Rex is a part-time student working on his bachelor's degree in engineering. His employer reimbursed his $5,200 tuition under a plan available to all full-time employees.

   Determine the amount Rex must include in gross income.

Decision Making

3. Paul is in the 15% marginal tax bracket, and Betty is in the 35% marginal tax bracket. They each pay $6,300 in health insurance premiums for themselves and their families. Their employer has offered to provide group health insurance, but each employee would have to forgo a $7,000 salary increase. How would the change in compensation affect Paul, Betty, and the employer?

4. Bertha spent the last 60 days of 2006 in a nursing home. The cost of the services provided to her was $12,000. Medicare paid $7,100 toward the cost of her stay. Bertha also received $8,000 of benefits under a long-term care insurance policy she purchased. What is the effect on Bertha's gross income?

5. Does the taxpayer recognize gross income in the following situations?
   a. Ann is a registered nurse working in a community hospital. She is not required to take her lunch on the hospital premises, but she can eat in the cafeteria at no charge. The hospital adopted this policy to encourage employees to stay on the premises and be available in case of emergencies. During the year, Ann ate most of her meals on the premises. The total value of those meals was $750.
   b. Ira is the manager of a hotel. His employer will allow him to live in one of the rooms rent-free or receive a $600 per month cash allowance for rent. Ira elected to live in the hotel.
   c. Seth is a forest ranger and lives in his employer's cabin in the forest. He is required to live there, and because there are no restaurants nearby, the employer supplies Seth with groceries that he cooks and eats on the premises.
   d. Rocky is a partner in the BAR Ranch (a partnership). He is the full-time manager of the ranch. BAR has a business purpose for Rocky's living on the ranch.

6. Sally and Bill are married and file joint returns. In 2006, Bill, an accountant, has a salary of $75,000, and Sally receives a salary of $25,000 as an apartment manager. What are the tax consequences of the following benefits that Bill and Sally's employers provide?
   a. Bill receives a reimbursement of $5,000 for child care expenses. Sally and Bill have three children who are not yet school age.
   b. Bill and Sally are provided a free membership at a local fitness and exercise club that allows them to attend three aerobic exercise sessions per week. The value of this type of membership is $1,600 per year.
   c. Bill is provided free parking at work. The value of the parking is $1,800 per year.
   d. Sally is provided with a free apartment. Living in this apartment is a condition of her employment. Similar apartments rent for $1,200 per month.

Communications

7. Finch Construction Company provides its employees who are carpenters with all of the required tools. However, the company believes that this has led to some employees not taking care of the tools and to the mysterious disappearance of some of the tools. The company is considering requiring all of its employees to provide their own tools. Employees' salaries would be increased by $1,500 to compensate for their additional costs. Write a letter to Finch's management explaining the tax consequences of this plan to the carpenters. Finch's address is 300 Harbor Drive, Vermillion, SD 57069.

Decision Making

8. Tara's employer provides a flexible benefits plan. Under the plan, medical and dental expenses incurred during the year that are not covered by the company's group health insurance plan will be paid by the flexible benefits plan. At the first of each year, the employee must set the amount to be covered by the plan. The employee's monthly salary is reduced by one-twelfth of the identified flexible benefit amount for the year. Tara thinks it is highly unlikely that she can accurately estimate her medical and dental expenses not covered by the company's group health insurance plan, but she feels these costs will probably be in the range of $1,500 to $2,500. She expects to be in the 25% marginal tax bracket. Tara would like your advice regarding how much she should reduce her salary in exchange for the expanded dental and medical benefits.

9. Canary Corporation would like you to review its employee fringe benefits program with regard to the tax consequences of the plan for the company's president (Polly), who is also the majority shareholder:
   a. All executives receive free tickets to State University football games. Polly is not a football fan and usually gives her tickets to another employee. The cost to the employer for Polly's tickets for the year was $600.
   b. The company owns a parking garage that is used by customers, employees, and the general public. Only the general public is required to pay for parking. The charge to the general public for Polly's parking for the year would have been $2,700 (a $225 monthly rate).
   c. All employees are allowed to use the company's fixed charge long-distance telephone services, as long as the privilege is not abused. Although no one has kept track of the actual calls, Polly's use of the telephone had a value (what she would have paid on her personal telephone) of approximately $600.
   d. The company owns a condominium at the beach, which it uses to entertain customers. Employees are allowed to use the facility without charge when the company has

no scheduled events. Polly used the facility 10 days during the year. Her use had a rental value of $1,000.

e. The company is in the household moving business. Employees are allowed to ship goods without charge whenever there is excess space on a truck. Polly purchased a dining room suite for her daughter. Company trucks delivered the furniture to the daughter. Normal freight charges would have been $750.

f. The company has a storage facility for household goods. Officers are allowed a 20% discount on charges for storing their goods. All other employees are allowed a 10% discount. Polly's discounts for the year totaled $900.

10. Ted works for Sage Motors, an automobile dealership. All employees can buy a car at the company's cost plus 2%. The company does not charge employees the $175 transfer service fee that nonemployees must pay. Ted purchased an automobile for $24,480 ($24,000 + $480). The company's cost was $24,000. The price for a nonemployee would have been $27,775 ($27,600 + $175 transfer service fee). What is Ted's gross income from the purchase of the automobile?

Ethics

11. Tom works for Roadrunner Motors, a company that manufactures automobiles. Tom purchased a new automobile from Roadrunner at the company's cost of $10,000. The retail selling price for the automobile is $15,000. Sue works for Coyote, Inc., an auto dealership, which sells the car manufactured by Roadrunner. Sue purchased an automobile identical to Tom's from Coyote. The price Sue pays is equal to Coyote's cost of the automobile ($13,500). Tom and Sue each receive a salary of $40,000 per year. Considering only the above information, do Tom and Sue have equal ability to pay income taxes for the year, and does equitable treatment occur? If not, how should the tax law be changed to produce equitable treatment?

Issue ID

12. Several of Egret Company's employees have asked the company to create a hiking trail that employees could use during their lunch hours. The company owns vacant land that is being held for future expansion, but would have to spend approximately $50,000 if it were to make a trail. Nonemployees would be allowed to use the facility as part of the company's effort to build strong community support. What are the relevant tax issues for the employees?

13. Redbird, Inc., does not provide its employees with any tax-exempt fringe benefits. The company is considering adopting a hospital and medical benefits insurance plan that will cost approximately $7,000 per employee. In order to adopt this plan, the company may have to reduce salaries and/or lower future salary increases. Redbird is in the 35% (combined Federal and state rates) income tax bracket. Redbird is also responsible for matching the Social Security and Medicare taxes withheld on employees' salaries. The benefits insurance plans will not be subject to the Social Security and Medicare taxes. The employees generally fall into three marginal tax rate groups:

Income Tax	Social Security and Medicare Tax	Total
.15	.0765	.2265
.25	.0765	.3265
.35	.0145	.3645

The company has asked you to assist in its financial planning for the benefits insurance plan by computing the following:

a. How much taxable compensation is the equivalent to $7,000 of exempt compensation for each of the three classes of employees?

b. What is the company's after-tax cost of the taxable compensation computed in (a) above?

c. What is the company's after-tax cost of the exempt compensation?

d. Briefly explain your conclusions from the above analysis.

14. George is a U.S. citizen who is employed by Hawk Enterprises, a global company. Beginning on July 1, 2006, George began working in London. He worked there until January 31, 2007, when he transferred to Paris. He worked in Paris the remainder of 2007.

His salary for the first six months of 2006 was $95,000, and it was earned in the United States. His salary for the remainder of 2006 was $135,000, and it was earned in London. George's 2007 salary from Hawk was $275,000, with part being earned in London and part being earned in Paris. What is George's gross income in 2006 and 2007?

15. Dena is the regional sales manager for the Burger Hut fast-food chain. Generally, she drives her personal automobile from her residence to the regional office, works for eight hours, and returns home. On many occasions, however, she leaves the office early and visits the four local outlets (starting with No. 1 through No. 4) as part of the workday. Relevant mileage is as follows:

	Miles
Residence to regional office	20
Regional office to Burger Hut No. 1	10
Burger Hut No. 1 to Burger Hut No. 2	15
Burger Hut No. 2 to Burger Hut No. 3	12
Burger Hut No. 3 to Burger Hut No. 4	16
Burger Hut No. 4 to residence	30

Dena works 230 days in 2006. Of these, 75 days involve visits to the outlets. If she uses the automatic mileage method, what is her deduction for the year?

16. Larry went from Cleveland to New York on business. His time was spent as follows:

Thursday	Travel
Friday	Business
Saturday and Sunday	Sightseeing
Monday and Tuesday	Business
Wednesday	Travel

During the trip, Larry incurred and paid expenses of $180 per day for lodging from Thursday night through Tuesday night and $110 per day for meals from Friday through Tuesday. Round-trip airfare was $400. Larry is a self-employed attorney who practices law in Cleveland.

a. How much can Larry deduct for the New York trip?
b. How will any deduction be classified?

17. In June of this year, Dr. and Mrs. Alvin Lord traveled to Memphis to attend a three-day conference sponsored by the American Society of Implant Dentistry. Alvin, a practicing oral surgeon, participated in scheduled technical sessions dealing with the latest developments in surgical procedures. On two days, Mrs. Lord attended group meetings where various aspects of family tax planning were discussed. On the other day, she went sightseeing. Mrs. Lord does not work for her husband, but she does their tax returns and handles the family investments. Expenses incurred in connection with the conference are summarized below:

Airfare (two tickets)	$1,040
Lodging (single and double occupancy are the same rate—$220 each day)	660
Meals ($200 × 3 days)*	600
Conference registration fee (includes $120 for Family Tax Planning sessions)	520
Car rental	240

*Split equally between Dr. and Mrs. Lord.

How much, if any, of these expenses can the Lords deduct?

18. On Thursday, Justin flies from Baltimore (his home office) to Cadiz (Spain). He conducts business on Friday and Tuesday; vacations on Saturday, Sunday, and Monday (a legal holiday in Spain); and returns to Baltimore on Thursday. Justin was scheduled to return home on Wednesday, but all flights were canceled due to bad weather. Therefore, he spent Wednesday watching floor shows at a local casino.

a. For tax purposes, what portion of Justin's trip is regarded as being for business?
b. Suppose Monday had not been a legal holiday. Would this change your answer to part (a)?
c. Under either (a) or (b), how much of Justin's airfare qualifies as a deductible business expense?

Ethics

19. Veronica is a key employee of Perdiz Corporation, an aerospace engineering concern located in Seattle. Perdiz would like to establish an office on the east coast of Florida and wants Veronica to be in charge of the branch. Veronica is hesitant about making the move because she fears she will have to sell her residence in Seattle at a loss. Perdiz buys the house from Veronica for $420,000, its cost to her. She has owned and occupied the house as her principal residence for eight years. One year later, Perdiz resells the property for $370,000. Nothing regarding the sale of the residence is ever reflected on Veronica's income tax returns. Needless to say, Perdiz absorbs all of Veronica's moving expenses. Do you have any qualms as to the way these matters have been handled for income tax purposes?

20. Doyle, a CPA, is a manager with a national accounting firm in Atlanta, Georgia. In 2006, he decides to quit his job and set up a private practice of public accounting in Santa Fe, New Mexico. In connection with the move, Doyle incurs the following expenses:

Penalty for breaking lease on Atlanta apartment	$3,200
Lodging during move	480
Meals during move	390
Packing and moving household goods	2,400
Mileage for personal autos	2,800 miles

How much, if any, of these expenses can Doyle deduct, and how are the deductible moving expenses classified (*for* or *from* AGI)?

Issue ID

21. Marvin is employed as a full-time high school teacher. The school district for which he works recently instituted a policy requiring all of its teachers to start working on a master's degree. Pursuant to this new rule, Marvin spent most of the summer of 2005 taking graduate courses at an out-of-town university. His expenses are as follows:

Tuition	$4,300
Books and course materials	650
Lodging	1,200
Meals	1,600
Laundry and dry cleaning	220
Campus parking	300

In addition, Marvin drove his personal automobile 1,500 miles in connection with the education. He uses the automatic mileage method.
a. How much, if any, of these expenses might qualify as a deduction *for* AGI?
b. How much, if any, of these expenses might qualify as a deduction *from* AGI?

Issue ID

22. In each of the following independent situations, determine how much, if any, qualifies as a deduction *for* AGI under § 222 (qualified tuition and related expenses):
a. Ruby is single and is employed as a nurse practitioner. During 2005, she spent $4,200 in tuition to attend law school at night. Her AGI is $64,000.
b. Jacque is single and is employed as a pharmacist. During 2005, he spent $2,100 ($1,900 for tuition and $200 for books) to take a course in herbal supplements at a local university. His AGI is $70,000.
c. How much, if any, of the above amounts *not allowed under § 222* might otherwise qualify as a deduction *from* AGI?

23. Elvis is a salesman who works for Crane Sales, Inc. Typically, Elvis spends several days out of town each week. Crane provides Elvis with a travel allowance of $1,100 per month, but requires no accountability. For the current year, Elvis had the following job-related travel expenses:

Meals	$ 5,040
Lodging	10,080
Transportation	1,400

a. What amount qualifies as a deductible travel expense?
b. What is the classification of any such deduction?

24. Felicia is employed full-time as an accountant for a national grocery chain. She also has a private consulting practice, which provides tax advice and financial planning to the general public. For this purpose, she maintains an office in her home. Expenses relating to the office are as follows:

Real property taxes	$4,800
Interest on home mortgage	4,200
Operating expenses of home	600
Depreciation allocated to 25% business use	1,800

Felicia's income from consulting is $18,000, and the related expenses are $6,000.
a. What is Felicia's office in the home deduction?
b. Suppose Felicia's income from the consulting is only $8,000 (not $18,000). How does this change the answer to part (a)?

25. Victor has AGI of $94,000 during the year and the following expenses related to his employment:

Lodging while in travel status	$3,400
Meals during travel	3,200
Business transportation	5,200
Entertainment of clients	2,200
Professional dues and subscriptions	900

Victor is reimbursed $10,000 under his employer's accountable plan. What are Victor's deductions *for* and *from* AGI?

26. Molly is unmarried and is an active participant in a qualified deductible (traditional) IRA plan. Her modified AGI is $55,000 in 2006.
a. Calculate the amount that Molly can contribute to the IRA and the amount she can deduct.
b. Assume instead that Molly is a participant in a SIMPLE IRA and that she elects to contribute 4% of her compensation to the account, while her employer contributes 3%. What amount will be contributed for 2006? What amount will be vested?

27. Karli and Jacob have been married for 12 years and are both active participants in employer qualified retirement plans. Their total AGI in 2006 is $156,000, and they earn salaries of $78,000 and $72,000, respectively.
a. What amount can Karli and Jacob contribute to traditional IRAs?
b. What amount can Karli and Jacob deduct for their contributions in (a)?
c. What amount can Karli and Jacob contribute to Roth IRAs?
d. What amount can Karli and Jacob deduct for their contributions in (c)?
e. What amount can they contribute to Coverdell Education Savings Accounts for their two children?

28. Monica, age 51, has a traditional deductible IRA with an account balance of $102,000. Of this amount, $72,000 represents contributions, and $30,000 represents earnings. In 2006, she converts her IRA into a Roth IRA. What amount must Monica include in her gross income in 2006?

29. In 2013, Joyce receives a $4,000 distribution from her Coverdell Education Savings Account (CESA) which has a fair market value of $10,000. Total contributions to her CESA have been $7,000. Joyce's AGI is $25,000.
a. Joyce uses the entire $4,000 to pay for qualified education expenses. What amount should she include in her gross income?
b. Assume instead that Joyce uses only $2,500 of the $4,000 distribution for qualified education expenses. What amount should she include in her gross income?

30. In 2006, Susan's sole proprietorship earns $210,000 of self-employment net income (after the deduction for one-half of self-employment tax).
a. Calculate the maximum amount that Susan can deduct for contributions to a defined contribution Keogh plan.

b. Suppose Susan contributes more than the allowable amount to the Keogh plan. What are the tax consequences to her?
c. Can Susan retire and begin receiving Keogh payments at age 55 without incurring a penalty?

31. Sammy is a self-employed accountant with earned income from the business of $130,000 (after the deduction for one-half of any self-employment tax). He has a profit sharing plan (i.e., defined contribution Keogh plan). What is the maximum amount Sammy can contribute to his retirement plan?

Extender

32. In each of the following *independent* situations, determine the amount of FICA (Social Security and Medicare) that should be withheld from the employee's 2006 salary by the employer.
a. Harry earns a $50,000 salary, files a joint return, and claims four withholding allowances.
b. Hazel earns a $100,000 salary, files a joint return, and claims four withholding allowances.
c. Tracey earns a $180,000 salary, files a joint return, and claims four withholding allowances.
d. Alicia's 17-year-old son, Carlos, earns $10,000 at the family business.

Extender

33. During 2006, Helen, the owner of a store, has the following income and expenses:

Gross profit on sales	$73,000
Income from part-time job (subject to FICA)	50,000
Business expenses (related to store)	15,000
Fire loss on store building	2,200
Dividend income	200
Long-term capital gain on the sale of a stock investment	2,000

Compute Helen's self-employment tax and allowable income tax deduction for the self-employment tax paid.

34. Samantha is an executive with an AGI of $100,000 before consideration of income or loss from her miniature horse business. Her other income comes from winning horse shows, stud fees, and sales of yearlings. Her home is on 20 acres, 10 of which she uses to pasture the horses and upon which she has erected stables, paddocks, fences, tack houses, and so forth.

Samantha uses an office in her home that is 10% of the square footage of the house. She uses the office exclusively for keeping records of breeding lines, histories, and show and veterinary records. Her records show the following income and expenses for the current year.

Income from fees, prizes, and sales	$22,000
Expenses	
Entry fees	1,000
Feed and veterinary bills	4,000
Supplies	900
Publications and dues	500
Travel to horse shows (no meals)	2,300
Salaries and wages of employees	8,000
Depreciation on horse equipment	3,000
Depreciation on horse farm improvements	7,000
Depreciation on 10% of home	1,000
Total home mortgage interest	24,000
Total property taxes on home	2,200
Total property taxes on horse farm improvements	800

The mortgage interest is only on her home. The horse farm improvements are not mortgaged.
a. How must Samantha treat the income and expenses of the operation if the miniature horse activity is held to be a hobby?
b. How would your answer in (a) differ if the horse operation was held to be a business?

COMPREHENSIVE TAX RETURN PROBLEM

TurboTax

35. Beth R. Jordan lives at 2322 Skyview Road, Mesa, AZ 85202. She is a tax accountant with Mesa Manufacturing Company, 1203 Western Avenue, Mesa, AZ 85201 (employer identification number 38–7788214). She also writes computer software programs for tax practitioners and has a part-time tax practice. Beth is single and has no dependents. Beth's birthday is July 4, 1971, and her Social Security number is 111–35–2222. She wants to contribute $3 to the Presidential Election Campaign Fund.

The following information is shown on Beth's Wage and Tax Statement (Form W–2) for 2005.

Line	Description	Amount
1	Wages, tips, other compensation	$63,000.00
2	Federal income tax withheld	11,000.00
3	Social Security wages	63,000.00
4	Social Security tax withheld	3,906.00
5	Medicare wages and tips	63,000.00
6	Medicare tax withheld	913.50
15	State	Arizona
16	State wages, tips, etc.	63,000.00
17	State income tax withheld	1,650.00

During 2005, Beth received interest of $1,300 from Home Federal Savings and Loan and $400 from Home State Bank. Each financial institution reported the interest income on a Form 1099–INT. She received qualified dividends of $500 from Gray Corporation, $400 from Blue Corporation, and $1,200 from Orange Corporation. Each corporation reported Beth's dividend payments on a Form 1099–DIV.

Beth received a $1,600 income tax refund from the state of Arizona on May 12, 2005. On her 2004 Federal income tax return, she reported total itemized deductions of $7,700, which included $2,400 of state income tax withheld by her employer.

Fees earned from her part-time tax practice in 2005 totaled $3,800. She paid $600 to have the tax returns processed by a computerized tax return service.

On February 1, 2005, Beth bought 500 shares of Gray Corporation common stock for $17.60 a share. On July 16, she sold the stock for $14 a share.

Beth bought a used sports utility vehicle for $3,000 on June 5, 2005. She purchased the vehicle from her brother-in-law, who was unemployed and was in need of cash. On November 2, 2005, she sold the vehicle to a friend for $3,400.

On January 2, 2005, Beth acquired 100 shares of Blue Corporation common stock for $30 a share. She sold the stock on December 19, 2005, for $55 a share.

During 2005, Beth received royalties of $16,000 on a software program she had written. Beth incurred the following expenditures in connection with her software-writing activities:

Cost of microcomputer (100% business use)	$7,000
Cost of printer (100% business use)	2,000
Office furniture	3,000
Supplies	650
Fee paid to computer consultant	3,500

Beth elected to expense the maximum portion of the cost of the microcomputer, printer, and furniture allowed under the provisions of § 179. This equipment and furniture were placed in service on January 15, 2005.

Although her employer suggested that Beth attend a convention on current developments in corporate taxation, Beth was not reimbursed for the travel expenses of $1,420 she incurred in attending the convention. The $1,420 included $200 for the cost of meals.

During 2005, Beth paid $300 for prescription medicines and $2,875 in doctor bills, hospital bills, and medical insurance premiums. Beth paid real property taxes of $1,766 on her home. Interest on her home mortgage was $3,845, and interest to credit card companies was $320. Beth contributed $30 each week to her church and $10 each week to the United Way. Professional dues and subscriptions totaled $350. Beth maintained her sales tax receipts. The total is $1,954. Beth paid estimated taxes of $1,000.

Part 1—Tax Computation
Compute the net tax payable or refund due for Beth R. Jordan for 2005. If you use tax forms for your solution, you will need Forms 1040, 2106-EZ, and 4562 and Schedules A, B, C, D, and SE. Suggested software: TurboTax.

Part 2—Tax Planning
Beth is anticipating significant changes in her life in 2006, and she has asked you to estimate her taxable income and tax liability for 2006. She just received word that she has been qualified to adopt a two-year-old daughter. Beth expects the adoption will be finalized in 2006 and that she will incur approximately $2,000 of adoption expenses. In addition, she expects to incur approximately $3,500 of child and dependent care expenses relating to the care of her new daughter, which will enable her to keep her job at Mesa Manufacturing Company. However, with the additional demands on her time because of her daughter, she has decided to discontinue her two part-time jobs (i.e., the part-time tax practice and her software business), and she will cease making estimated income tax payments. In your computations, assume all other income and expenditures will remain at approximately the same levels as in 2005.

Tax Return Problem

36. John R. Dorsey is single, age 36, and lives at 6240 Pinerock, Seattle, WA 98122. He is employed as a sales and claims agent for the commercial vehicle division of Hawk Corporation, a casualty insurance company. John's annual salary of $80,000 does not include a performance bonus. The bonus is announced in December of each year but is not paid until the following January. John received a bonus of $12,000 for 2005 (paid in 2006) and a bonus of $15,000 for 2006 (paid in 2007). Hawk withheld $15,000 for Federal income tax and $7,038 for FICA in 2006. Hawk *also* provides John with a modest expense account allowance of $4,000 but requires no accounting to be rendered as to how the amount is spent. John's Social Security number is 531–60–1890.

- John uses his personal automobile in his work and claims the automatic mileage method as to qualified business use. Typically, his work assignments follow one of three patterns. First, he may spend the entire day at the office where he meets with current and prospective policyholders and handles other business-related matters. Second, he goes to the office for a while and then visits various sites to assess the damage to clients' vehicles. Third, he goes directly from home to the claim sites. Mileage for 2006 is as follows: 3,200 for home to office; 4,000 for office to claim sites; and 3,300 for home to claim sites.
- John's other employment-related expenses are summarized below:

Business lunches for employees on special occasions (e.g., birthdays)	$ 610
Lunches, dinners, and other entertainment (e.g., nightclubs, sporting events) of clients	3,800
Christmas gifts for 24 key clients (e.g., managers of fleet car operations) consisting of a cheese tray ($25 cost + $4 shipping)	696
Dues to professional organizations and subscriptions to trade journals	520
Cost of attending three-day conference sponsored by an insurance trade group [$1,100 (airfare) + $390 (lodging) + $410 (meals) + $350 (registration) + $180 (car rental and parking)]	2,430
Job search expenses	1,200
Online continuing education program	800

- In connection with the job search expenses, John heard that a competing insurance company had a vacancy in a comparable position that paid a larger salary. Through a recruiting firm, he applied for the job but was turned down. The continuing education program dealt with procedures for maintaining and improving client relations.

- Besides the items already noted, John's receipts for 2006 are as follows:

Qualified dividends from GE common stock		$ 980
Interest income—		
City of Seattle bonds	$1,700	
Boeing Corporation bonds	1,100	
Wells Fargo Bank CD	1,300	4,100
Repayment of loan by Cindy Dorsey		4,200
City of Seattle medical reimbursement		7,800
Life insurance proceeds		50,000
Jury duty fees		180
Gambling winnings		900

Six months ago, John loaned his sister, Cindy, $4,000 to help her purchase a car. No note was signed, and no interest was provided for. When she repaid the loan in 2006, Cindy insisted on adding $200 in gratitude for the favor.

In 2005, John was hospitalized because of an injury caused by the operator of a public works vehicle. Since the city was at fault, it reimbursed John for the medical expenses caused by the accident [Note: John received no tax benefit from the $7,800 he paid in 2005.].

As a result of the death of their grandmother in early 2006, John and his brothers and sisters each received varying amounts as the beneficiaries of several life insurance policies she owned. John is paid his distribution of $50,000 in August of 2006.

- In addition to those already noted, John's expenditures for 2006 are as follows:

Medical—		
Insurance premiums	$3,600	
Medical and dental (including prescriptions) not covered by insurance	2,900	$ 6,500
Taxes—		
State and local sales taxes	$2,400	
Property taxes on residence	4,200	6,600
Interest on home mortgage		4,800
Charitable contributions		1,200
Purchase of SeaRay cabin cruiser		13,500
Jury duty expenses		210
Gambling losses		800

John keeps track of the sales taxes paid during the year and can substantiate the $2,400 listed. The state of Washington does not impose an income tax.

John acquired the cabin cruiser from a former classmate at a bargain price of $13,500—it had an appraised value of $18,000. Because the classmate was going through the financial throes of a divorce, he was in dire need of liquid assets. However, two days after the October purchase and before John could obtain any insurance coverage, the boat was stolen. The storage facility where the boat was kept limits its theft liability to $500 per item, and John was paid this amount in March 2007. As boats that are stolen are often taken to Canada and sold, John does not expect to recover his property.

Expenses related to the jury duty consisted of parking and meals and, as is frequently the case, exceeded what he was paid for serving on the jury.

As is true with all of his expenses, John can substantiate the gambling losses.

Based on the information given, determine John's income tax payable or refund due for 2006.

BRIDGE *Discipline*

1. Justin performs services for Partridge, Inc., and receives compensation of $85,000 for the year. Determine the tax consequences of Social Security and Medicare on Justin's take-home pay if:
   a. Justin is classified as an employee of Partridge.
   b. Justin is classified as an independent contractor.

2. Amanda has been an employee of Robin, Inc., for almost 5 years. She is a participant in Robin's defined contribution pension plan (money purchase plan). The total contributions made by Robin to the money purchase plan for Amanda are $60,000, and the balance in Amanda's account is $89,000. Amanda is considering accepting a job with a competitor of Robin's at an annual salary $7,000 higher than that received from Robin. Her boss, who is trying to convince her to stay, points out that she will not be vested in the money purchase plan until she has been employed by Robin for at least five years. In addition, she will have to start a new vesting schedule with the competitor.
   a. What is vesting, and how does it affect Amanda and her decision based on the information provided?
   b. What have been the tax consequences to Amanda of Robin's annual contribution of $14,000 to its money purchase plan for her?
   c. What effect would it have on Amanda's decision if the competitor does not provide retirement benefits?

3. The Code contains provisions that are "friendly" to specific groups of taxpayers. Among these are the following:

   - Seniors.
   - Married taxpayers.
   - Employed taxpayers.
   - Taxpayers with children.
   - Self-employed individuals.

   Provide justification for the special treatment for each of the above groups, and give an example of such special treatment for each group.

RESEARCH PROBLEMS

THOMSON RIA™

Note: Solutions to Research Problems can be prepared by using the **RIA Checkpoint® Student Edition** online research product, which is available to accompany this text. It is also possible to prepare solutions to the Research Problems by using tax research materials found in a standard tax library.

Communications

Research Problem 1. Tom Roberts, a chemical engineer, is a long-time employee of Teal Chemical Corporation. Tom's specialty is the design and construction of special-purpose chemical processing plants. Teal has decided to expand its presence in France and plans to transfer Tom to Paris on a three-year assignment. The planned foreign assignment will take Tom to age 65, Teal's normal retirement age.

Tom has been advised regarding the major income tax ramifications of working abroad. He has not, however, been told about the treatment of moving expenses. Since Teal Corporation pays its employees a substantial foreign service salary increment, it reimburses for moving expenses. In connection with the move, Tom plans to sell his residence and place most of his furniture in storage. Probabilities are good that the sale of the residence will result in a loss.

a. Write a letter to Tom regarding the income tax treatment of his moving expenses. Tom's address is 1389 Wilson Drive, Trent, NJ 08102. Be sure to include in the discussion the move from France back to the United States.
b. Prepare a memo for your firm's client files.

Communications

Research Problem 2. Rick Beam has been an independent sales representative for various textile manufacturers for many years. His products consist of soft goods, such as tablecloths, curtains, and drapes. Rick's customers are clothing store chains, department stores, and smaller specialty stores. The employees of these companies who are responsible for purchasing merchandise are known as buyers. These companies generally prohibit their buyers from accepting gifts from manufacturers' sales representatives.

Each year Rick gives cash gifts (never more than $25) to most of the buyers who are his customers. Generally, he cashes a large check in November and gives the money personally to the buyers around Christmas. Rick says, "This is one of the ways that I maintain my relationship with my buyers." He maintains adequate substantiation of all the gifts.

Rick's deductions for these gifts have been disallowed by the IRS, based on § 162(c)(2). Rick is confused and comes to you, a CPA, for advice.

a. Write a letter to Rick concerning his tax position on this issue. Rick's address is 948 Octavia Street, New Orleans, LA 70113.
b. Prepare a memo for your files supporting the advice you have given.

Research Problem 3. Al Hardee has been employed as a salesman by Robin Chevrolet at its Milwaukee dealership. In early May 2003, Al and the general manager of the office had a serious dispute over job procedures. When it became clear that the two could no longer work together amicably, Al contacted Robin's CEO regarding a possible solution. As the general manager planned to retire in five months, it was decided that Al would spend this period working at the Green Bay branch. After the manager's retirement, Al was to rejoin the Milwaukee office.

Al's residence is only a few blocks from the Milwaukee office, but it is 96 miles (one-way) from the Green Bay worksite. During the next five months (i.e., May to October), Al made 120 trips driving from his home in Milwaukee to the Green Bay job. His only records of his trips are a wall calendar with the workdays circled and the credit card receipts he received from gasoline purchases. The employee records of the Green Bay dealership can, however, support Al's on-the-job presence.

Upon termination of the five-month assignment and after the retirement of the general manager, Al requested a transfer back to the Milwaukee office. The CEO turned down the request on the grounds that Al was no longer needed in Milwaukee. During his absence and unknown to Al, his job position in Milwaukee had been eliminated. However, the CEO offered to make the Green Bay assignment permanent. Hurt and disgusted, Al quit and took a job with a competing Milwaukee car dealership.

On his Federal income tax return for 2003, Al claimed a deduction of $8,294 for employee transportation expenses, computed as follows: 120 (number of trips) × 192 (round-trip mileage) × $0.36 (automatic mileage rate for 2003) = $8,294 (rounded). The IRS disallowed the deduction on two grounds. First, Al's job status in Green Bay was *permanent*, not *temporary*. Thus, his tax home had changed from Milwaukee to Green Bay. This, in turn, made his transportation expenses nondeductible commuting expenses. Second, even if the transportation was warranted, the expenses were not properly substantiated. Consequently, the lack of substantiation precludes any deduction.

Should Al be allowed a deduction for his transportation expenses? Explain.

Partial list of research aids:
Reg. § 1.162–2(e).
Reg. § 1.274–5T(c)(3).
Rev.Rul. 99–7, 1999–1 C.B. 363.
Teresita T. Diaz, 84 TCM 148, T.C.Memo. 2002–192.
Richard M. Brockman, 85 TCM 733, T.C.Memo. 2003–3.

Research Problem 4. Herron, Inc., previously gave all of its employees a ham for Christmas. However, many of the employees do not eat ham. Therefore, Herron has decided to give each employee a coupon for $35 that can be redeemed (for food or cash) any time between December 1 and January 31 of the following year. Herron has asked you whether the coupons can be excluded from the employees' gross income as a *de minimis* fringe benefit.

Research Problem 5. You recently read an article in your school newspaper about Professor Rodney Taylor, one of your favorite professors in the religious studies department. According to the article, he and the university have been negotiating an early retirement package and have reached a stumbling block. Under the agreement, Professor Taylor is to receive a lump-sum payment equal to one year's salary in exchange for his retirement and the release of any and all rights associated with his tenure status. While recognizing that the payment would be subject to income tax, Taylor contends that the amount is not earned income and thus should not be subject to the FICA tax. The university negotiators say that they are not aware of any authority that supports Taylor's view. In fact, they have learned that other universities in the state system have been withholding amounts for FICA for years in situations involving early retirement buyout packages for high-level administrators. The university's position is that lacking the authority to not withhold for FICA and given the precedent of similar early retirement packages at other universities, they are obligated to withhold FICA from the payment. You want to come to the aid of Professor Taylor. Obviously, if the payments are considered wages subject to the FICA tax, the value of the offer to Professor Taylor will be significantly reduced. Can you find any authority for his position?

Internet *Activity*

Use the tax resources of the Internet to address the following questions. Do not restrict your search to the World Wide Web, but include a review of newsgroups and general reference materials, practitioner sites and resources, primary sources of the tax law, chat rooms and discussion groups, and other opportunities.

Research Problem 6. An employer allows its employees limited personal use of one of the corporate executive jets. Does the IRS provide any guidelines as to how much income the employee should recognize due to such use?

Research Problem 7. Check with a major CPA firm in your area. Does the firm provide office space for all of its field auditors? If so, what arrangements are made? If not, what workplace does the firm expect the staff to use?

APPENDIX A TAX RATE SCHEDULES AND TABLES

(The 2006 Tax Tables and 2006 Sales Tax Tables can be accessed at the IRS web site: [**http://www.irs.gov**] when released.)

2005 Tax Rate Schedules

Single—Schedule X

If taxable income is: Over—	But not over—	The tax is:	of the amount over—
$ 0	$ 7,300	........10%	$ 0
7,300	29,700	$ 730.00 + 15%	7,300
29,700	71,950	4,090.00 + 25%	29,700
71,950	150,150	14,652.50 + 28%	71,950
150,150	326,450	36,548.50 + 33%	150,150
326,450	....	94,727.50 + 35%	326,450

Head of household—Schedule Z

If taxable income is: Over—	But not over—	The tax is:	of the amount over—
$ 0	$ 10,450	........10%	$ 0
10,450	39,800	$ 1,045.00 + 15%	10,450
39,800	102,800	5,447.50 + 25%	39,800
102,800	166,450	21,197.50 + 28%	102,800
166,450	326,450	39,019.50 + 33%	166,450
326,450	....	91,819.50 + 35%	326,450

Married filing jointly or Qualifying widow(er)—Schedule Y–1

If taxable income is: Over—	But not over—	The tax is:	of the amount over—
$ 0	$ 14,600	........10%	$ 0
14,600	59,400	$ 1,460.00 + 15%	14,600
59,400	119,950	8,180.00 + 25%	59,400
119,950	182,800	23,317.50 + 28%	119,950
182,800	326,450	40,915.50 + 33%	182,800
326,450	....	88,320.00 + 35%	326,450

Married filing separately—Schedule Y–2

If taxable income is: Over—	But not over—	The tax is:	of the amount over—
$ 0	$ 7,300	........10%	$ 0
7,300	29,700	$ 730.00 + 15%	7,300
29,700	59,975	4,090.00 + 25%	29,700
59,975	91,400	11,658.75 + 28%	59,975
91,400	163,225	20,457.75 + 33%	91,400
163,225	....	44,160.00 + 35%	163,225

2006 Tax Rate Schedules

Single—Schedule X

If taxable income is: Over—	But not over—	The tax is:	of the amount over—
$ 0	$ 7,550	........10%	$ 0
7,550	30,650	$ 755.00 + 15%	7,550
30,650	74,200	4,220.00 + 25%	30,650
74,200	154,800	15,107.50 + 28%	74,200
154,800	336,550	37,675.50 + 33%	154,800
336,550	....	97,653.00 + 35%	336,550

Head of household—Schedule Z

If taxable income is: Over—	But not over—	The tax is:	of the amount over—
$ 0	$ 10,750	........10%	$ 0
10,750	41,050	$ 1,075.00 + 15%	10,750
41,050	106,000	5,620.00 + 25%	41,050
106,000	171,650	21,857.50 + 28%	106,000
171,650	336,550	40,239.50 + 33%	171,650
336,550	....	94,656.50 + 35%	336,550

Married filing jointly or Qualifying widow(er)—Schedule Y–1

If taxable income is: Over—	But not over—	The tax is:	of the amount over—
$ 0	$ 15,100	........10%	$ 0
15,100	61,300	$ 1,510.00 + 15%	15,100
61,300	123,700	8,440.00 + 25%	61,300
123,700	188,450	24,040.00 + 28%	123,700
188,450	336,550	42,170.00 + 33%	188,450
336,550	....	91,043.00 + 35%	336,550

Married filing separately—Schedule Y–2

If taxable income is: Over—	But not over—	The tax is:	of the amount over—
$ 0	$ 7,550	........10%	$ 0
7,550	30,650	$ 755.00 + 15%	7,550
30,650	61,850	4,220.00 + 25%	30,650
61,850	94,225	12,020.00 + 28%	61,850
94,225	168,275	21,085.00 + 33%	94,225
168,275	....	45,521.50 + 35%	168,275

2005 Tax Table

CAUTION *See the instructions for line 44 that begin on page 37 to see if you must use the Tax Table below to figure your tax.*

Example. Mr. and Mrs. Brown are filing a joint return. Their taxable income on Form 1040, line 43, is $25,300. First, they find the $25,300–25,350 taxable income line. Next, they find the column for married filing jointly and read down the column. The amount shown where the taxable income line and filing status column meet is $3,069. This is the tax amount they should enter on Form 1040, line 44.

Sample Table

At least	But less than	Single	Married filing jointly *	Married filing separately	Head of a household
			Your tax is—		
25,200	25,250	3,419	3,054	3,419	3,261
25,250	25,300	3,426	3,061	3,426	3,269
25,300	25,350	3,434	(3,069)	3,434	3,276
25,350	25,400	3,441	3,076	3,441	3,284

If line 43 (taxable income) is—		And you are—			
At least	But less than	Single	Married filing jointly *	Married filing separately	Head of a household
			Your tax is—		
0	5	0	0	0	0
5	15	1	1	1	1
15	25	2	2	2	2
25	50	4	4	4	4
50	75	6	6	6	6
75	100	9	9	9	9
100	125	11	11	11	11
125	150	14	14	14	14
150	175	16	16	16	16
175	200	19	19	19	19
200	225	21	21	21	21
225	250	24	24	24	24
250	275	26	26	26	26
275	300	29	29	29	29
300	325	31	31	31	31
325	350	34	34	34	34
350	375	36	36	36	36
375	400	39	39	39	39
400	425	41	41	41	41
425	450	44	44	44	44
450	475	46	46	46	46
475	500	49	49	49	49
500	525	51	51	51	51
525	550	54	54	54	54
550	575	56	56	56	56
575	600	59	59	59	59
600	625	61	61	61	61
625	650	64	64	64	64
650	675	66	66	66	66
675	700	69	69	69	69
700	725	71	71	71	71
725	750	74	74	74	74
750	775	76	76	76	76
775	800	79	79	79	79
800	825	81	81	81	81
825	850	84	84	84	84
850	875	86	86	86	86
875	900	89	89	89	89
900	925	91	91	91	91
925	950	94	94	94	94
950	975	96	96	96	96
975	1,000	99	99	99	99
1,000					
1,000	1,025	101	101	101	101
1,025	1,050	104	104	104	104
1,050	1,075	106	106	106	106
1,075	1,100	109	109	109	109
1,100	1,125	111	111	111	111
1,125	1,150	114	114	114	114
1,150	1,175	116	116	116	116
1,175	1,200	119	119	119	119
1,200	1,225	121	121	121	121
1,225	1,250	124	124	124	124
1,250	1,275	126	126	126	126
1,275	1,300	129	129	129	129

If line 43 (taxable income) is—		And you are—			
At least	But less than	Single	Married filing jointly *	Married filing separately	Head of a household
			Your tax is—		
1,300	1,325	131	131	131	131
1,325	1,350	134	134	134	134
1,350	1,375	136	136	136	136
1,375	1,400	139	139	139	139
1,400	1,425	141	141	141	141
1,425	1,450	144	144	144	144
1,450	1,475	146	146	146	146
1,475	1,500	149	149	149	149
1,500	1,525	151	151	151	151
1,525	1,550	154	154	154	154
1,550	1,575	156	156	156	156
1,575	1,600	159	159	159	159
1,600	1,625	161	161	161	161
1,625	1,650	164	164	164	164
1,650	1,675	166	166	166	166
1,675	1,700	169	169	169	169
1,700	1,725	171	171	171	171
1,725	1,750	174	174	174	174
1,750	1,775	176	176	176	176
1,775	1,800	179	179	179	179
1,800	1,825	181	181	181	181
1,825	1,850	184	184	184	184
1,850	1,875	186	186	186	186
1,875	1,900	189	189	189	189
1,900	1,925	191	191	191	191
1,925	1,950	194	194	194	194
1,950	1,975	196	196	196	196
1,975	2,000	199	199	199	199
2,000					
2,000	2,025	201	201	201	201
2,025	2,050	204	204	204	204
2,050	2,075	206	206	206	206
2,075	2,100	209	209	209	209
2,100	2,125	211	211	211	211
2,125	2,150	214	214	214	214
2,150	2,175	216	216	216	216
2,175	2,200	219	219	219	219
2,200	2,225	221	221	221	221
2,225	2,250	224	224	224	224
2,250	2,275	226	226	226	226
2,275	2,300	229	229	229	229
2,300	2,325	231	231	231	231
2,325	2,350	234	234	234	234
2,350	2,375	236	236	236	236
2,375	2,400	239	239	239	239
2,400	2,425	241	241	241	241
2,425	2,450	244	244	244	244
2,450	2,475	246	246	246	246
2,475	2,500	249	249	249	249
2,500	2,525	251	251	251	251
2,525	2,550	254	254	254	254
2,550	2,575	256	256	256	256
2,575	2,600	259	259	259	259
2,600	2,625	261	261	261	261
2,625	2,650	264	264	264	264
2,650	2,675	266	266	266	266
2,675	2,700	269	269	269	269

If line 43 (taxable income) is—		And you are—			
At least	But less than	Single	Married filing jointly *	Married filing separately	Head of a household
			Your tax is—		
2,700	2,725	271	271	271	271
2,725	2,750	274	274	274	274
2,750	2,775	276	276	276	276
2,775	2,800	279	279	279	279
2,800	2,825	281	281	281	281
2,825	2,850	284	284	284	284
2,850	2,875	286	286	286	286
2,875	2,900	289	289	289	289
2,900	2,925	291	291	291	291
2,925	2,950	294	294	294	294
2,950	2,975	296	296	296	296
2,975	3,000	299	299	299	299
3,000					
3,000	3,050	303	303	303	303
3,050	3,100	308	308	308	308
3,100	3,150	313	313	313	313
3,150	3,200	318	318	318	318
3,200	3,250	323	323	323	323
3,250	3,300	328	328	328	328
3,300	3,350	333	333	333	333
3,350	3,400	338	338	338	338
3,400	3,450	343	343	343	343
3,450	3,500	348	348	348	348
3,500	3,550	353	353	353	353
3,550	3,600	358	358	358	358
3,600	3,650	363	363	363	363
3,650	3,700	368	368	368	368
3,700	3,750	373	373	373	373
3,750	3,800	378	378	378	378
3,800	3,850	383	383	383	383
3,850	3,900	388	388	388	388
3,900	3,950	393	393	393	393
3,950	4,000	398	398	398	398
4,000					
4,000	4,050	403	403	403	403
4,050	4,100	408	408	408	408
4,100	4,150	413	413	413	413
4,150	4,200	418	418	418	418
4,200	4,250	423	423	423	423
4,250	4,300	428	428	428	428
4,300	4,350	433	433	433	433
4,350	4,400	438	438	438	438
4,400	4,450	443	443	443	443
4,450	4,500	448	448	448	448
4,500	4,550	453	453	453	453
4,550	4,600	458	458	458	458
4,600	4,650	463	463	463	463
4,650	4,700	468	468	468	468
4,700	4,750	473	473	473	473
4,750	4,800	478	478	478	478
4,800	4,850	483	483	483	483
4,850	4,900	488	488	488	488
4,900	4,950	493	493	493	493
4,950	5,000	498	498	498	498

(Continued on next page)

* This column must also be used by a qualifying widow(er).

2005 Tax Table—*Continued*

If line 43 (taxable income) is— At least	But less than	Single	Married filing jointly *	Married filing separately	Head of a household
		Your tax is—			
5,000					
5,000	5,050	503	503	503	503
5,050	5,100	508	508	508	508
5,100	5,150	513	513	513	513
5,150	5,200	518	518	518	518
5,200	5,250	523	523	523	523
5,250	5,300	528	528	528	528
5,300	5,350	533	533	533	533
5,350	5,400	538	538	538	538
5,400	5,450	543	543	543	543
5,450	5,500	548	548	548	548
5,500	5,550	553	553	553	553
5,550	5,600	558	558	558	558
5,600	5,650	563	563	563	563
5,650	5,700	568	568	568	568
5,700	5,750	573	573	573	573
5,750	5,800	578	578	578	578
5,800	5,850	583	583	583	583
5,850	5,900	588	588	588	588
5,900	5,950	593	593	593	593
5,950	6,000	598	598	598	598
6,000					
6,000	6,050	603	603	603	603
6,050	6,100	608	608	608	608
6,100	6,150	613	613	613	613
6,150	6,200	618	618	618	618
6,200	6,250	623	623	623	623
6,250	6,300	628	628	628	628
6,300	6,350	633	633	633	633
6,350	6,400	638	638	638	638
6,400	6,450	643	643	643	643
6,450	6,500	648	648	648	648
6,500	6,550	653	653	653	653
6,550	6,600	658	658	658	658
6,600	6,650	663	663	663	663
6,650	6,700	668	668	668	668
6,700	6,750	673	673	673	673
6,750	6,800	678	678	678	678
6,800	6,850	683	683	683	683
6,850	6,900	688	688	688	688
6,900	6,950	693	693	693	693
6,950	7,000	698	698	698	698
7,000					
7,000	7,050	703	703	703	703
7,050	7,100	708	708	708	708
7,100	7,150	713	713	713	713
7,150	7,200	718	718	718	718
7,200	7,250	723	723	723	723
7,250	7,300	728	728	728	728
7,300	7,350	734	733	734	733
7,350	7,400	741	738	741	738
7,400	7,450	749	743	749	743
7,450	7,500	756	748	756	748
7,500	7,550	764	753	764	753
7,550	7,600	771	758	771	758
7,600	7,650	779	763	779	763
7,650	7,700	786	768	786	768
7,700	7,750	794	773	794	773
7,750	7,800	801	778	801	778
7,800	7,850	809	783	809	783
7,850	7,900	816	788	816	788
7,900	7,950	824	793	824	793
7,950	8,000	831	798	831	798

If line 43 (taxable income) is— At least	But less than	Single	Married filing jointly *	Married filing separately	Head of a household
		Your tax is—			
8,000					
8,000	8,050	839	803	839	803
8,050	8,100	846	808	846	808
8,100	8,150	854	813	854	813
8,150	8,200	861	818	861	818
8,200	8,250	869	823	869	823
8,250	8,300	876	828	876	828
8,300	8,350	884	833	884	833
8,350	8,400	891	838	891	838
8,400	8,450	899	843	899	843
8,450	8,500	906	848	906	848
8,500	8,550	914	853	914	853
8,550	8,600	921	858	921	858
8,600	8,650	929	863	929	863
8,650	8,700	936	868	936	868
8,700	8,750	944	873	944	873
8,750	8,800	951	878	951	878
8,800	8,850	959	883	959	883
8,850	8,900	966	888	966	888
8,900	8,950	974	893	974	893
8,950	9,000	981	898	981	898
9,000					
9,000	9,050	989	903	989	903
9,050	9,100	996	908	996	908
9,100	9,150	1,004	913	1,004	913
9,150	9,200	1,011	918	1,011	918
9,200	9,250	1,019	923	1,019	923
9,250	9,300	1,026	928	1,026	928
9,300	9,350	1,034	933	1,034	933
9,350	9,400	1,041	938	1,041	938
9,400	9,450	1,049	943	1,049	943
9,450	9,500	1,056	948	1,056	948
9,500	9,550	1,064	953	1,064	953
9,550	9,600	1,071	958	1,071	958
9,600	9,650	1,079	963	1,079	963
9,650	9,700	1,086	968	1,086	968
9,700	9,750	1,094	973	1,094	973
9,750	9,800	1,101	978	1,101	978
9,800	9,850	1,109	983	1,109	983
9,850	9,900	1,116	988	1,116	988
9,900	9,950	1,124	993	1,124	993
9,950	10,000	1,131	998	1,131	998
10,000					
10,000	10,050	1,139	1,003	1,139	1,003
10,050	10,100	1,146	1,008	1,146	1,008
10,100	10,150	1,154	1,013	1,154	1,013
10,150	10,200	1,161	1,018	1,161	1,018
10,200	10,250	1,169	1,023	1,169	1,023
10,250	10,300	1,176	1,028	1,176	1,028
10,300	10,350	1,184	1,033	1,184	1,033
10,350	10,400	1,191	1,038	1,191	1,038
10,400	10,450	1,199	1,043	1,199	1,043
10,450	10,500	1,206	1,048	1,206	1,049
10,500	10,550	1,214	1,053	1,214	1,056
10,550	10,600	1,221	1,058	1,221	1,064
10,600	10,650	1,229	1,063	1,229	1,071
10,650	10,700	1,236	1,068	1,236	1,079
10,700	10,750	1,244	1,073	1,244	1,086
10,750	10,800	1,251	1,078	1,251	1,094
10,800	10,850	1,259	1,083	1,259	1,101
10,850	10,900	1,266	1,088	1,266	1,109
10,900	10,950	1,274	1,093	1,274	1,116
10,950	11,000	1,281	1,098	1,281	1,124

If line 43 (taxable income) is— At least	But less than	Single	Married filing jointly *	Married filing separately	Head of a household
		Your tax is—			
11,000					
11,000	11,050	1,289	1,103	1,289	1,131
11,050	11,100	1,296	1,108	1,296	1,139
11,100	11,150	1,304	1,113	1,304	1,146
11,150	11,200	1,311	1,118	1,311	1,154
11,200	11,250	1,319	1,123	1,319	1,161
11,250	11,300	1,326	1,128	1,326	1,169
11,300	11,350	1,334	1,133	1,334	1,176
11,350	11,400	1,341	1,138	1,341	1,184
11,400	11,450	1,349	1,143	1,349	1,191
11,450	11,500	1,356	1,148	1,356	1,199
11,500	11,550	1,364	1,153	1,364	1,206
11,550	11,600	1,371	1,158	1,371	1,214
11,600	11,650	1,379	1,163	1,379	1,221
11,650	11,700	1,386	1,168	1,386	1,229
11,700	11,750	1,394	1,173	1,394	1,236
11,750	11,800	1,401	1,178	1,401	1,244
11,800	11,850	1,409	1,183	1,409	1,251
11,850	11,900	1,416	1,188	1,416	1,259
11,900	11,950	1,424	1,193	1,424	1,266
11,950	12,000	1,431	1,198	1,431	1,274
12,000					
12,000	12,050	1,439	1,203	1,439	1,281
12,050	12,100	1,446	1,208	1,446	1,289
12,100	12,150	1,454	1,213	1,454	1,296
12,150	12,200	1,461	1,218	1,461	1,304
12,200	12,250	1,469	1,223	1,469	1,311
12,250	12,300	1,476	1,228	1,476	1,319
12,300	12,350	1,484	1,233	1,484	1,326
12,350	12,400	1,491	1,238	1,491	1,334
12,400	12,450	1,499	1,243	1,499	1,341
12,450	12,500	1,506	1,248	1,506	1,349
12,500	12,550	1,514	1,253	1,514	1,356
12,550	12,600	1,521	1,258	1,521	1,364
12,600	12,650	1,529	1,263	1,529	1,371
12,650	12,700	1,536	1,268	1,536	1,379
12,700	12,750	1,544	1,273	1,544	1,386
12,750	12,800	1,551	1,278	1,551	1,394
12,800	12,850	1,559	1,283	1,559	1,401
12,850	12,900	1,566	1,288	1,566	1,409
12,900	12,950	1,574	1,293	1,574	1,416
12,950	13,000	1,581	1,298	1,581	1,424
13,000					
13,000	13,050	1,589	1,303	1,589	1,431
13,050	13,100	1,596	1,308	1,596	1,439
13,100	13,150	1,604	1,313	1,604	1,446
13,150	13,200	1,611	1,318	1,611	1,454
13,200	13,250	1,619	1,323	1,619	1,461
13,250	13,300	1,626	1,328	1,626	1,469
13,300	13,350	1,634	1,333	1,634	1,476
13,350	13,400	1,641	1,338	1,641	1,484
13,400	13,450	1,649	1,343	1,649	1,491
13,450	13,500	1,656	1,348	1,656	1,499
13,500	13,550	1,664	1,353	1,664	1,506
13,550	13,600	1,671	1,358	1,671	1,514
13,600	13,650	1,679	1,363	1,679	1,521
13,650	13,700	1,686	1,368	1,686	1,529
13,700	13,750	1,694	1,373	1,694	1,536
13,750	13,800	1,701	1,378	1,701	1,544
13,800	13,850	1,709	1,383	1,709	1,551
13,850	13,900	1,716	1,388	1,716	1,559
13,900	13,950	1,724	1,393	1,724	1,566
13,950	14,000	1,731	1,398	1,731	1,574

* This column must also be used by a qualifying widow(er).

(Continued on next page)

2005 Tax Table—*Continued*

If line 43 (taxable income) is—		And you are—			
At least	But less than	Single	Married filing jointly *	Married filing separately	Head of a household
		Your tax is—			
14,000					
14,000	**14,050**	1,739	1,403	1,739	1,581
14,050	**14,100**	1,746	1,408	1,746	1,589
14,100	**14,150**	1,754	1,413	1,754	1,596
14,150	**14,200**	1,761	1,418	1,761	1,604
14,200	**14,250**	1,769	1,423	1,769	1,611
14,250	**14,300**	1,776	1,428	1,776	1,619
14,300	**14,350**	1,784	1,433	1,784	1,626
14,350	**14,400**	1,791	1,438	1,791	1,634
14,400	**14,450**	1,799	1,443	1,799	1,641
14,450	**14,500**	1,806	1,448	1,806	1,649
14,500	**14,550**	1,814	1,453	1,814	1,656
14,550	**14,600**	1,821	1,458	1,821	1,664
14,600	**14,650**	1,829	1,464	1,829	1,671
14,650	**14,700**	1,836	1,471	1,836	1,679
14,700	**14,750**	1,844	1,479	1,844	1,686
14,750	**14,800**	1,851	1,486	1,851	1,694
14,800	**14,850**	1,859	1,494	1,859	1,701
14,850	**14,900**	1,866	1,501	1,866	1,709
14,900	**14,950**	1,874	1,509	1,874	1,716
14,950	**15,000**	1,881	1,516	1,881	1,724
15,000					
15,000	**15,050**	1,889	1,524	1,889	1,731
15,050	**15,100**	1,896	1,531	1,896	1,739
15,100	**15,150**	1,904	1,539	1,904	1,746
15,150	**15,200**	1,911	1,546	1,911	1,754
15,200	**15,250**	1,919	1,554	1,919	1,761
15,250	**15,300**	1,926	1,561	1,926	1,769
15,300	**15,350**	1,934	1,569	1,934	1,776
15,350	**15,400**	1,941	1,576	1,941	1,784
15,400	**15,450**	1,949	1,584	1,949	1,791
15,450	**15,500**	1,956	1,591	1,956	1,799
15,500	**15,550**	1,964	1,599	1,964	1,806
15,550	**15,600**	1,971	1,606	1,971	1,814
15,600	**15,650**	1,979	1,614	1,979	1,821
15,650	**15,700**	1,986	1,621	1,986	1,829
15,700	**15,750**	1,994	1,629	1,994	1,836
15,750	**15,800**	2,001	1,636	2,001	1,844
15,800	**15,850**	2,009	1,644	2,009	1,851
15,850	**15,900**	2,016	1,651	2,016	1,859
15,900	**15,950**	2,024	1,659	2,024	1,866
15,950	**16,000**	2,031	1,666	2,031	1,874
16,000					
16,000	**16,050**	2,039	1,674	2,039	1,881
16,050	**16,100**	2,046	1,681	2,046	1,889
16,100	**16,150**	2,054	1,689	2,054	1,896
16,150	**16,200**	2,061	1,696	2,061	1,904
16,200	**16,250**	2,069	1,704	2,069	1,911
16,250	**16,300**	2,076	1,711	2,076	1,919
16,300	**16,350**	2,084	1,719	2,084	1,926
16,350	**16,400**	2,091	1,726	2,091	1,934
16,400	**16,450**	2,099	1,734	2,099	1,941
16,450	**16,500**	2,106	1,741	2,106	1,949
16,500	**16,550**	2,114	1,749	2,114	1,956
16,550	**16,600**	2,121	1,756	2,121	1,964
16,600	**16,650**	2,129	1,764	2,129	1,971
16,650	**16,700**	2,136	1,771	2,136	1,979
16,700	**16,750**	2,144	1,779	2,144	1,986
16,750	**16,800**	2,151	1,786	2,151	1,994
16,800	**16,850**	2,159	1,794	2,159	2,001
16,850	**16,900**	2,166	1,801	2,166	2,009
16,900	**16,950**	2,174	1,809	2,174	2,016
16,950	**17,000**	2,181	1,816	2,181	2,024

If line 43 (taxable income) is—		And you are—			
At least	But less than	Single	Married filing jointly *	Married filing separately	Head of a household
		Your tax is—			
17,000					
17,000	**17,050**	2,189	1,824	2,189	2,031
17,050	**17,100**	2,196	1,831	2,196	2,039
17,100	**17,150**	2,204	1,839	2,204	2,046
17,150	**17,200**	2,211	1,846	2,211	2,054
17,200	**17,250**	2,219	1,854	2,219	2,061
17,250	**17,300**	2,226	1,861	2,226	2,069
17,300	**17,350**	2,234	1,869	2,234	2,076
17,350	**17,400**	2,241	1,876	2,241	2,084
17,400	**17,450**	2,249	1,884	2,249	2,091
17,450	**17,500**	2,256	1,891	2,256	2,099
17,500	**17,550**	2,264	1,899	2,264	2,106
17,550	**17,600**	2,271	1,906	2,271	2,114
17,600	**17,650**	2,279	1,914	2,279	2,121
17,650	**17,700**	2,286	1,921	2,286	2,129
17,700	**17,750**	2,294	1,929	2,294	2,136
17,750	**17,800**	2,301	1,936	2,301	2,144
17,800	**17,850**	2,309	1,944	2,309	2,151
17,850	**17,900**	2,316	1,951	2,316	2,159
17,900	**17,950**	2,324	1,959	2,324	2,166
17,950	**18,000**	2,331	1,966	2,331	2,174
18,000					
18,000	**18,050**	2,339	1,974	2,339	2,181
18,050	**18,100**	2,346	1,981	2,346	2,189
18,100	**18,150**	2,354	1,989	2,354	2,196
18,150	**18,200**	2,361	1,996	2,361	2,204
18,200	**18,250**	2,369	2,004	2,369	2,211
18,250	**18,300**	2,376	2,011	2,376	2,219
18,300	**18,350**	2,384	2,019	2,384	2,226
18,350	**18,400**	2,391	2,026	2,391	2,234
18,400	**18,450**	2,399	2,034	2,399	2,241
18,450	**18,500**	2,406	2,041	2,406	2,249
18,500	**18,550**	2,414	2,049	2,414	2,256
18,550	**18,600**	2,421	2,056	2,421	2,264
18,600	**18,650**	2,429	2,064	2,429	2,271
18,650	**18,700**	2,436	2,071	2,436	2,279
18,700	**18,750**	2,444	2,079	2,444	2,286
18,750	**18,800**	2,451	2,086	2,451	2,294
18,800	**18,850**	2,459	2,094	2,459	2,301
18,850	**18,900**	2,466	2,101	2,466	2,309
18,900	**18,950**	2,474	2,109	2,474	2,316
18,950	**19,000**	2,481	2,116	2,481	2,324
19,000					
19,000	**19,050**	2,489	2,124	2,489	2,331
19,050	**19,100**	2,496	2,131	2,496	2,339
19,100	**19,150**	2,504	2,139	2,504	2,346
19,150	**19,200**	2,511	2,146	2,511	2,354
19,200	**19,250**	2,519	2,154	2,519	2,361
19,250	**19,300**	2,526	2,161	2,526	2,369
19,300	**19,350**	2,534	2,169	2,534	2,376
19,350	**19,400**	2,541	2,176	2,541	2,384
19,400	**19,450**	2,549	2,184	2,549	2,391
19,450	**19,500**	2,556	2,191	2,556	2,399
19,500	**19,550**	2,564	2,199	2,564	2,406
19,550	**19,600**	2,571	2,206	2,571	2,414
19,600	**19,650**	2,579	2,214	2,579	2,421
19,650	**19,700**	2,586	2,221	2,586	2,429
19,700	**19,750**	2,594	2,229	2,594	2,436
19,750	**19,800**	2,601	2,236	2,601	2,444
19,800	**19,850**	2,609	2,244	2,609	2,451
19,850	**19,900**	2,616	2,251	2,616	2,459
19,900	**19,950**	2,624	2,259	2,624	2,466
19,950	**20,000**	2,631	2,266	2,631	2,474

If line 43 (taxable income) is—		And you are—			
At least	But less than	Single	Married filing jointly *	Married filing separately	Head of a household
		Your tax is—			
20,000					
20,000	**20,050**	2,639	2,274	2,639	2,481
20,050	**20,100**	2,646	2,281	2,646	2,489
20,100	**20,150**	2,654	2,289	2,654	2,496
20,150	**20,200**	2,661	2,296	2,661	2,504
20,200	**20,250**	2,669	2,304	2,669	2,511
20,250	**20,300**	2,676	2,311	2,676	2,519
20,300	**20,350**	2,684	2,319	2,684	2,526
20,350	**20,400**	2,691	2,326	2,691	2,534
20,400	**20,450**	2,699	2,334	2,699	2,541
20,450	**20,500**	2,706	2,341	2,706	2,549
20,500	**20,550**	2,714	2,349	2,714	2,556
20,550	**20,600**	2,721	2,356	2,721	2,564
20,600	**20,650**	2,729	2,364	2,729	2,571
20,650	**20,700**	2,736	2,371	2,736	2,579
20,700	**20,750**	2,744	2,379	2,744	2,586
20,750	**20,800**	2,751	2,386	2,751	2,594
20,800	**20,850**	2,759	2,394	2,759	2,601
20,850	**20,900**	2,766	2,401	2,766	2,609
20,900	**20,950**	2,774	2,409	2,774	2,616
20,950	**21,000**	2,781	2,416	2,781	2,624
21,000					
21,000	**21,050**	2,789	2,424	2,789	2,631
21,050	**21,100**	2,796	2,431	2,796	2,639
21,100	**21,150**	2,804	2,439	2,804	2,646
21,150	**21,200**	2,811	2,446	2,811	2,654
21,200	**21,250**	2,819	2,454	2,819	2,661
21,250	**21,300**	2,826	2,461	2,826	2,669
21,300	**21,350**	2,834	2,469	2,834	2,676
21,350	**21,400**	2,841	2,476	2,841	2,684
21,400	**21,450**	2,849	2,484	2,849	2,691
21,450	**21,500**	2,856	2,491	2,856	2,699
21,500	**21,550**	2,864	2,499	2,864	2,706
21,550	**21,600**	2,871	2,506	2,871	2,714
21,600	**21,650**	2,879	2,514	2,879	2,721
21,650	**21,700**	2,886	2,521	2,886	2,729
21,700	**21,750**	2,894	2,529	2,894	2,736
21,750	**21,800**	2,901	2,536	2,901	2,744
21,800	**21,850**	2,909	2,544	2,909	2,751
21,850	**21,900**	2,916	2,551	2,916	2,759
21,900	**21,950**	2,924	2,559	2,924	2,766
21,950	**22,000**	2,931	2,566	2,931	2,774
22,000					
22,000	**22,050**	2,939	2,574	2,939	2,781
22,050	**22,100**	2,946	2,581	2,946	2,789
22,100	**22,150**	2,954	2,589	2,954	2,796
22,150	**22,200**	2,961	2,596	2,961	2,804
22,200	**22,250**	2,969	2,604	2,969	2,811
22,250	**22,300**	2,976	2,611	2,976	2,819
22,300	**22,350**	2,984	2,619	2,984	2,826
22,350	**22,400**	2,991	2,626	2,991	2,834
22,400	**22,450**	2,999	2,634	2,999	2,841
22,450	**22,500**	3,006	2,641	3,006	2,849
22,500	**22,550**	3,014	2,649	3,014	2,856
22,550	**22,600**	3,021	2,656	3,021	2,864
22,600	**22,650**	3,029	2,664	3,029	2,871
22,650	**22,700**	3,036	2,671	3,036	2,879
22,700	**22,750**	3,044	2,679	3,044	2,886
22,750	**22,800**	3,051	2,686	3,051	2,894
22,800	**22,850**	3,059	2,694	3,059	2,901
22,850	**22,900**	3,066	2,701	3,066	2,909
22,900	**22,950**	3,074	2,709	3,074	2,916
22,950	**23,000**	3,081	2,716	3,081	2,924

* This column must also be used by a qualifying widow(er).

(Continued on next page)

2005 Tax Table—*Continued*

If line 43 (taxable income) is— At least	But less than	And you are— Single	Married filing jointly *	Married filing separately	Head of a household
		Your tax is—			
23,000					
23,000	23,050	3,089	2,724	3,089	2,931
23,050	23,100	3,096	2,731	3,096	2,939
23,100	23,150	3,104	2,739	3,104	2,946
23,150	23,200	3,111	2,746	3,111	2,954
23,200	23,250	3,119	2,754	3,119	2,961
23,250	23,300	3,126	2,761	3,126	2,969
23,300	23,350	3,134	2,769	3,134	2,976
23,350	23,400	3,141	2,776	3,141	2,984
23,400	23,450	3,149	2,784	3,149	2,991
23,450	23,500	3,156	2,791	3,156	2,999
23,500	23,550	3,164	2,799	3,164	3,006
23,550	23,600	3,171	2,806	3,171	3,014
23,600	23,650	3,179	2,814	3,179	3,021
23,650	23,700	3,186	2,821	3,186	3,029
23,700	23,750	3,194	2,829	3,194	3,036
23,750	23,800	3,201	2,836	3,201	3,044
23,800	23,850	3,209	2,844	3,209	3,051
23,850	23,900	3,216	2,851	3,216	3,059
23,900	23,950	3,224	2,859	3,224	3,066
23,950	24,000	3,231	2,866	3,231	3,074
24,000					
24,000	24,050	3,239	2,874	3,239	3,081
24,050	24,100	3,246	2,881	3,246	3,089
24,100	24,150	3,254	2,889	3,254	3,096
24,150	24,200	3,261	2,896	3,261	3,104
24,200	24,250	3,269	2,904	3,269	3,111
24,250	24,300	3,276	2,911	3,276	3,119
24,300	24,350	3,284	2,919	3,284	3,126
24,350	24,400	3,291	2,926	3,291	3,134
24,400	24,450	3,299	2,934	3,299	3,141
24,450	24,500	3,306	2,941	3,306	3,149
24,500	24,550	3,314	2,949	3,314	3,156
24,550	24,600	3,321	2,956	3,321	3,164
24,600	24,650	3,329	2,964	3,329	3,171
24,650	24,700	3,336	2,971	3,336	3,179
24,700	24,750	3,344	2,979	3,344	3,186
24,750	24,800	3,351	2,986	3,351	3,194
24,800	24,850	3,359	2,994	3,359	3,201
24,850	24,900	3,366	3,001	3,366	3,209
24,900	24,950	3,374	3,009	3,374	3,216
24,950	25,000	3,381	3,016	3,381	3,224
25,000					
25,000	25,050	3,389	3,024	3,389	3,231
25,050	25,100	3,396	3,031	3,396	3,239
25,100	25,150	3,404	3,039	3,404	3,246
25,150	25,200	3,411	3,046	3,411	3,254
25,200	25,250	3,419	3,054	3,419	3,261
25,250	25,300	3,426	3,061	3,426	3,269
25,300	25,350	3,434	3,069	3,434	3,276
25,350	25,400	3,441	3,076	3,441	3,284
25,400	25,450	3,449	3,084	3,449	3,291
25,450	25,500	3,456	3,091	3,456	3,299
25,500	25,550	3,464	3,099	3,464	3,306
25,550	25,600	3,471	3,106	3,471	3,314
25,600	25,650	3,479	3,114	3,479	3,321
25,650	25,700	3,486	3,121	3,486	3,329
25,700	25,750	3,494	3,129	3,494	3,336
25,750	25,800	3,501	3,136	3,501	3,344
25,800	25,850	3,509	3,144	3,509	3,351
25,850	25,900	3,516	3,151	3,516	3,359
25,900	25,950	3,524	3,159	3,524	3,366
25,950	26,000	3,531	3,166	3,531	3,374

If line 43 (taxable income) is— At least	But less than	And you are— Single	Married filing jointly *	Married filing separately	Head of a household
		Your tax is—			
26,000					
26,000	26,050	3,539	3,174	3,539	3,381
26,050	26,100	3,546	3,181	3,546	3,389
26,100	26,150	3,554	3,189	3,554	3,396
26,150	26,200	3,561	3,196	3,561	3,404
26,200	26,250	3,569	3,204	3,569	3,411
26,250	26,300	3,576	3,211	3,576	3,419
26,300	26,350	3,584	3,219	3,584	3,426
26,350	26,400	3,591	3,226	3,591	3,434
26,400	26,450	3,599	3,234	3,599	3,441
26,450	26,500	3,606	3,241	3,606	3,449
26,500	26,550	3,614	3,249	3,614	3,456
26,550	26,600	3,621	3,256	3,621	3,464
26,600	26,650	3,629	3,264	3,629	3,471
26,650	26,700	3,636	3,271	3,636	3,479
26,700	26,750	3,644	3,279	3,644	3,486
26,750	26,800	3,651	3,286	3,651	3,494
26,800	26,850	3,659	3,294	3,659	3,501
26,850	26,900	3,666	3,301	3,666	3,509
26,900	26,950	3,674	3,309	3,674	3,516
26,950	27,000	3,681	3,316	3,681	3,524
27,000					
27,000	27,050	3,689	3,324	3,689	3,531
27,050	27,100	3,696	3,331	3,696	3,539
27,100	27,150	3,704	3,339	3,704	3,546
27,150	27,200	3,711	3,346	3,711	3,554
27,200	27,250	3,719	3,354	3,719	3,561
27,250	27,300	3,726	3,361	3,726	3,569
27,300	27,350	3,734	3,369	3,734	3,576
27,350	27,400	3,741	3,376	3,741	3,584
27,400	27,450	3,749	3,384	3,749	3,591
27,450	27,500	3,756	3,391	3,756	3,599
27,500	27,550	3,764	3,399	3,764	3,606
27,550	27,600	3,771	3,406	3,771	3,614
27,600	27,650	3,779	3,414	3,779	3,621
27,650	27,700	3,786	3,421	3,786	3,629
27,700	27,750	3,794	3,429	3,794	3,636
27,750	27,800	3,801	3,436	3,801	3,644
27,800	27,850	3,809	3,444	3,809	3,651
27,850	27,900	3,816	3,451	3,816	3,659
27,900	27,950	3,824	3,459	3,824	3,666
27,950	28,000	3,831	3,466	3,831	3,674
28,000					
28,000	28,050	3,839	3,474	3,839	3,681
28,050	28,100	3,846	3,481	3,846	3,689
28,100	28,150	3,854	3,489	3,854	3,696
28,150	28,200	3,861	3,496	3,861	3,704
28,200	28,250	3,869	3,504	3,869	3,711
28,250	28,300	3,876	3,511	3,876	3,719
28,300	28,350	3,884	3,519	3,884	3,726
28,350	28,400	3,891	3,526	3,891	3,734
28,400	28,450	3,899	3,534	3,899	3,741
28,450	28,500	3,906	3,541	3,906	3,749
28,500	28,550	3,914	3,549	3,914	3,756
28,550	28,600	3,921	3,556	3,921	3,764
28,600	28,650	3,929	3,564	3,929	3,771
28,650	28,700	3,936	3,571	3,936	3,779
28,700	28,750	3,944	3,579	3,944	3,786
28,750	28,800	3,951	3,586	3,951	3,794
28,800	28,850	3,959	3,594	3,959	3,801
28,850	28,900	3,966	3,601	3,966	3,809
28,900	28,950	3,974	3,609	3,974	3,816
28,950	29,000	3,981	3,616	3,981	3,824

If line 43 (taxable income) is— At least	But less than	And you are— Single	Married filing jointly *	Married filing separately	Head of a household
		Your tax is—			
29,000					
29,000	29,050	3,989	3,624	3,989	3,831
29,050	29,100	3,996	3,631	3,996	3,839
29,100	29,150	4,004	3,639	4,004	3,846
29,150	29,200	4,011	3,646	4,011	3,854
29,200	29,250	4,019	3,654	4,019	3,861
29,250	29,300	4,026	3,661	4,026	3,869
29,300	29,350	4,034	3,669	4,034	3,876
29,350	29,400	4,041	3,676	4,041	3,884
29,400	29,450	4,049	3,684	4,049	3,891
29,450	29,500	4,056	3,691	4,056	3,899
29,500	29,550	4,064	3,699	4,064	3,906
29,550	29,600	4,071	3,706	4,071	3,914
29,600	29,650	4,079	3,714	4,079	3,921
29,650	29,700	4,086	3,721	4,086	3,929
29,700	29,750	4,096	3,729	4,096	3,936
29,750	29,800	4,109	3,736	4,109	3,944
29,800	29,850	4,121	3,744	4,121	3,951
29,850	29,900	4,134	3,751	4,134	3,959
29,900	29,950	4,146	3,759	4,146	3,966
29,950	30,000	4,159	3,766	4,159	3,974
30,000					
30,000	30,050	4,171	3,774	4,171	3,981
30,050	30,100	4,184	3,781	4,184	3,989
30,100	30,150	4,196	3,789	4,196	3,996
30,150	30,200	4,209	3,796	4,209	4,004
30,200	30,250	4,221	3,804	4,221	4,011
30,250	30,300	4,234	3,811	4,234	4,019
30,300	30,350	4,246	3,819	4,246	4,026
30,350	30,400	4,259	3,826	4,259	4,034
30,400	30,450	4,271	3,834	4,271	4,041
30,450	30,500	4,284	3,841	4,284	4,049
30,500	30,550	4,296	3,849	4,296	4,056
30,550	30,600	4,309	3,856	4,309	4,064
30,600	30,650	4,321	3,864	4,321	4,071
30,650	30,700	4,334	3,871	4,334	4,079
30,700	30,750	4,346	3,879	4,346	4,086
30,750	30,800	4,359	3,886	4,359	4,094
30,800	30,850	4,371	3,894	4,371	4,101
30,850	30,900	4,384	3,901	4,384	4,109
30,900	30,950	4,396	3,909	4,396	4,116
30,950	31,000	4,409	3,916	4,409	4,124
31,000					
31,000	31,050	4,421	3,924	4,421	4,131
31,050	31,100	4,434	3,931	4,434	4,139
31,100	31,150	4,446	3,939	4,446	4,146
31,150	31,200	4,459	3,946	4,459	4,154
31,200	31,250	4,471	3,954	4,471	4,161
31,250	31,300	4,484	3,961	4,484	4,169
31,300	31,350	4,496	3,969	4,496	4,176
31,350	31,400	4,509	3,976	4,509	4,184
31,400	31,450	4,521	3,984	4,521	4,191
31,450	31,500	4,534	3,991	4,534	4,199
31,500	31,550	4,546	3,999	4,546	4,206
31,550	31,600	4,559	4,006	4,559	4,214
31,600	31,650	4,571	4,014	4,571	4,221
31,650	31,700	4,584	4,021	4,584	4,229
31,700	31,750	4,596	4,029	4,596	4,236
31,750	31,800	4,609	4,036	4,609	4,244
31,800	31,850	4,621	4,044	4,621	4,251
31,850	31,900	4,634	4,051	4,634	4,259
31,900	31,950	4,646	4,059	4,646	4,266
31,950	32,000	4,659	4,066	4,659	4,274

* This column must also be used by a qualifying widow(er).

(Continued on next page)

2005 Tax Table—*Continued*

If line 43 (taxable income) is—		And you are—			
At least	But less than	Single	Married filing jointly *	Married filing sepa-rately	Head of a house-hold
		Your tax is—			
32,000					
32,000	**32,050**	4,671	4,074	4,671	4,281
32,050	**32,100**	4,684	4,081	4,684	4,289
32,100	**32,150**	4,696	4,089	4,696	4,296
32,150	**32,200**	4,709	4,096	4,709	4,304
32,200	**32,250**	4,721	4,104	4,721	4,311
32,250	**32,300**	4,734	4,111	4,734	4,319
32,300	**32,350**	4,746	4,119	4,746	4,326
32,350	**32,400**	4,759	4,126	4,759	4,334
32,400	**32,450**	4,771	4,134	4,771	4,341
32,450	**32,500**	4,784	4,141	4,784	4,349
32,500	**32,550**	4,796	4,149	4,796	4,356
32,550	**32,600**	4,809	4,156	4,809	4,364
32,600	**32,650**	4,821	4,164	4,821	4,371
32,650	**32,700**	4,834	4,171	4,834	4,379
32,700	**32,750**	4,846	4,179	4,846	4,386
32,750	**32,800**	4,859	4,186	4,859	4,394
32,800	**32,850**	4,871	4,194	4,871	4,401
32,850	**32,900**	4,884	4,201	4,884	4,409
32,900	**32,950**	4,896	4,209	4,896	4,416
32,950	**33,000**	4,909	4,216	4,909	4,424
33,000					
33,000	**33,050**	4,921	4,224	4,921	4,431
33,050	**33,100**	4,934	4,231	4,934	4,439
33,100	**33,150**	4,946	4,239	4,946	4,446
33,150	**33,200**	4,959	4,246	4,959	4,454
33,200	**33,250**	4,971	4,254	4,971	4,461
33,250	**33,300**	4,984	4,261	4,984	4,469
33,300	**33,350**	4,996	4,269	4,996	4,476
33,350	**33,400**	5,009	4,276	5,009	4,484
33,400	**33,450**	5,021	4,284	5,021	4,491
33,450	**33,500**	5,034	4,291	5,034	4,499
33,500	**33,550**	5,046	4,299	5,046	4,506
33,550	**33,600**	5,059	4,306	5,059	4,514
33,600	**33,650**	5,071	4,314	5,071	4,521
33,650	**33,700**	5,084	4,321	5,084	4,529
33,700	**33,750**	5,096	4,329	5,096	4,536
33,750	**33,800**	5,109	4,336	5,109	4,544
33,800	**33,850**	5,121	4,344	5,121	4,551
33,850	**33,900**	5,134	4,351	5,134	4,559
33,900	**33,950**	5,146	4,359	5,146	4,566
33,950	**34,000**	5,159	4,366	5,159	4,574
34,000					
34,000	**34,050**	5,171	4,374	5,171	4,581
34,050	**34,100**	5,184	4,381	5,184	4,589
34,100	**34,150**	5,196	4,389	5,196	4,596
34,150	**34,200**	5,209	4,396	5,209	4,604
34,200	**34,250**	5,221	4,404	5,221	4,611
34,250	**34,300**	5,234	4,411	5,234	4,619
34,300	**34,350**	5,246	4,419	5,246	4,626
34,350	**34,400**	5,259	4,426	5,259	4,634
34,400	**34,450**	5,271	4,434	5,271	4,641
34,450	**34,500**	5,284	4,441	5,284	4,649
34,500	**34,550**	5,296	4,449	5,296	4,656
34,550	**34,600**	5,309	4,456	5,309	4,664
34,600	**34,650**	5,321	4,464	5,321	4,671
34,650	**34,700**	5,334	4,471	5,334	4,679
34,700	**34,750**	5,346	4,479	5,346	4,686
34,750	**34,800**	5,359	4,486	5,359	4,694
34,800	**34,850**	5,371	4,494	5,371	4,701
34,850	**34,900**	5,384	4,501	5,384	4,709
34,900	**34,950**	5,396	4,509	5,396	4,716
34,950	**35,000**	5,409	4,516	5,409	4,724

If line 43 (taxable income) is—		And you are—			
At least	But less than	Single	Married filing jointly *	Married filing sepa-rately	Head of a house-hold
		Your tax is—			
35,000					
35,000	**35,050**	5,421	4,524	5,421	4,731
35,050	**35,100**	5,434	4,531	5,434	4,739
35,100	**35,150**	5,446	4,539	5,446	4,746
35,150	**35,200**	5,459	4,546	5,459	4,754
35,200	**35,250**	5,471	4,554	5,471	4,761
35,250	**35,300**	5,484	4,561	5,484	4,769
35,300	**35,350**	5,496	4,569	5,496	4,776
35,350	**35,400**	5,509	4,576	5,509	4,784
35,400	**35,450**	5,521	4,584	5,521	4,791
35,450	**35,500**	5,534	4,591	5,534	4,799
35,500	**35,550**	5,546	4,599	5,546	4,806
35,550	**35,600**	5,559	4,606	5,559	4,814
35,600	**35,650**	5,571	4,614	5,571	4,821
35,650	**35,700**	5,584	4,621	5,584	4,829
35,700	**35,750**	5,596	4,629	5,596	4,836
35,750	**35,800**	5,609	4,636	5,609	4,844
35,800	**35,850**	5,621	4,644	5,621	4,851
35,850	**35,900**	5,634	4,651	5,634	4,859
35,900	**35,950**	5,646	4,659	5,646	4,866
35,950	**36,000**	5,659	4,666	5,659	4,874
36,000					
36,000	**36,050**	5,671	4,674	5,671	4,881
36,050	**36,100**	5,684	4,681	5,684	4,889
36,100	**36,150**	5,696	4,689	5,696	4,896
36,150	**36,200**	5,709	4,696	5,709	4,904
36,200	**36,250**	5,721	4,704	5,721	4,911
36,250	**36,300**	5,734	4,711	5,734	4,919
36,300	**36,350**	5,746	4,719	5,746	4,926
36,350	**36,400**	5,759	4,726	5,759	4,934
36,400	**36,450**	5,771	4,734	5,771	4,941
36,450	**36,500**	5,784	4,741	5,784	4,949
36,500	**36,550**	5,796	4,749	5,796	4,956
36,550	**36,600**	5,809	4,756	5,809	4,964
36,600	**36,650**	5,821	4,764	5,821	4,971
36,650	**36,700**	5,834	4,771	5,834	4,979
36,700	**36,750**	5,846	4,779	5,846	4,986
36,750	**36,800**	5,859	4,786	5,859	4,994
36,800	**36,850**	5,871	4,794	5,871	5,001
36,850	**36,900**	5,884	4,801	5,884	5,009
36,900	**36,950**	5,896	4,809	5,896	5,016
36,950	**37,000**	5,909	4,816	5,909	5,024
37,000					
37,000	**37,050**	5,921	4,824	5,921	5,031
37,050	**37,100**	5,934	4,831	5,934	5,039
37,100	**37,150**	5,946	4,839	5,946	5,046
37,150	**37,200**	5,959	4,846	5,959	5,054
37,200	**37,250**	5,971	4,854	5,971	5,061
37,250	**37,300**	5,984	4,861	5,984	5,069
37,300	**37,350**	5,996	4,869	5,996	5,076
37,350	**37,400**	6,009	4,876	6,009	5,084
37,400	**37,450**	6,021	4,884	6,021	5,091
37,450	**37,500**	6,034	4,891	6,034	5,099
37,500	**37,550**	6,046	4,899	6,046	5,106
37,550	**37,600**	6,059	4,906	6,059	5,114
37,600	**37,650**	6,071	4,914	6,071	5,121
37,650	**37,700**	6,084	4,921	6,084	5,129
37,700	**37,750**	6,096	4,929	6,096	5,136
37,750	**37,800**	6,109	4,936	6,109	5,144
37,800	**37,850**	6,121	4,944	6,121	5,151
37,850	**37,900**	6,134	4,951	6,134	5,159
37,900	**37,950**	6,146	4,959	6,146	5,166
37,950	**38,000**	6,159	4,966	6,159	5,174

If line 43 (taxable income) is—		And you are—			
At least	But less than	Single	Married filing jointly *	Married filing sepa-rately	Head of a house-hold
		Your tax is—			
38,000					
38,000	**38,050**	6,171	4,974	6,171	5,181
38,050	**38,100**	6,184	4,981	6,184	5,189
38,100	**38,150**	6,196	4,989	6,196	5,196
38,150	**38,200**	6,209	4,996	6,209	5,204
38,200	**38,250**	6,221	5,004	6,221	5,211
38,250	**38,300**	6,234	5,011	6,234	5,219
38,300	**38,350**	6,246	5,019	6,246	5,226
38,350	**38,400**	6,259	5,026	6,259	5,234
38,400	**38,450**	6,271	5,034	6,271	5,241
38,450	**38,500**	6,284	5,041	6,284	5,249
38,500	**38,550**	6,296	5,049	6,296	5,256
38,550	**38,600**	6,309	5,056	6,309	5,264
38,600	**38,650**	6,321	5,064	6,321	5,271
38,650	**38,700**	6,334	5,071	6,334	5,279
38,700	**38,750**	6,346	5,079	6,346	5,286
38,750	**38,800**	6,359	5,086	6,359	5,294
38,800	**38,850**	6,371	5,094	6,371	5,301
38,850	**38,900**	6,384	5,101	6,384	5,309
38,900	**38,950**	6,396	5,109	6,396	5,316
38,950	**39,000**	6,409	5,116	6,409	5,324
39,000					
39,000	**39,050**	6,421	5,124	6,421	5,331
39,050	**39,100**	6,434	5,131	6,434	5,339
39,100	**39,150**	6,446	5,139	6,446	5,346
39,150	**39,200**	6,459	5,146	6,459	5,354
39,200	**39,250**	6,471	5,154	6,471	5,361
39,250	**39,300**	6,484	5,161	6,484	5,369
39,300	**39,350**	6,496	5,169	6,496	5,376
39,350	**39,400**	6,509	5,176	6,509	5,384
39,400	**39,450**	6,521	5,184	6,521	5,391
39,450	**39,500**	6,534	5,191	6,534	5,399
39,500	**39,550**	6,546	5,199	6,546	5,406
39,550	**39,600**	6,559	5,206	6,559	5,414
39,600	**39,650**	6,571	5,214	6,571	5,421
39,650	**39,700**	6,584	5,221	6,584	5,429
39,700	**39,750**	6,596	5,229	6,596	5,436
39,750	**39,800**	6,609	5,236	6,609	5,444
39,800	**39,850**	6,621	5,244	6,621	5,454
39,850	**39,900**	6,634	5,251	6,634	5,466
39,900	**39,950**	6,646	5,259	6,646	5,479
39,950	**40,000**	6,659	5,266	6,659	5,491
40,000					
40,000	**40,050**	6,671	5,274	6,671	5,504
40,050	**40,100**	6,684	5,281	6,684	5,516
40,100	**40,150**	6,696	5,289	6,696	5,529
40,150	**40,200**	6,709	5,296	6,709	5,541
40,200	**40,250**	6,721	5,304	6,721	5,554
40,250	**40,300**	6,734	5,311	6,734	5,566
40,300	**40,350**	6,746	5,319	6,746	5,579
40,350	**40,400**	6,759	5,326	6,759	5,591
40,400	**40,450**	6,771	5,334	6,771	5,604
40,450	**40,500**	6,784	5,341	6,784	5,616
40,500	**40,550**	6,796	5,349	6,796	5,629
40,550	**40,600**	6,809	5,356	6,809	5,641
40,600	**40,650**	6,821	5,364	6,821	5,654
40,650	**40,700**	6,834	5,371	6,834	5,666
40,700	**40,750**	6,846	5,379	6,846	5,679
40,750	**40,800**	6,859	5,386	6,859	5,691
40,800	**40,850**	6,871	5,394	6,871	5,704
40,850	**40,900**	6,884	5,401	6,884	5,716
40,900	**40,950**	6,896	5,409	6,896	5,729
40,950	**41,000**	6,909	5,416	6,909	5,741

* This column must also be used by a qualifying widow(er).

(Continued on next page)

2005 Tax Table—*Continued*

If line 43 (taxable income) is—		And you are—			
At least	But less than	Single	Married filing jointly *	Married filing sepa-rately	Head of a house-hold
		Your tax is—			
41,000					
41,000	41,050	6,921	5,424	6,921	5,754
41,050	41,100	6,934	5,431	6,934	5,766
41,100	41,150	6,946	5,439	6,946	5,779
41,150	41,200	6,959	5,446	6,959	5,791
41,200	41,250	6,971	5,454	6,971	5,804
41,250	41,300	6,984	5,461	6,984	5,816
41,300	41,350	6,996	5,469	6,996	5,829
41,350	41,400	7,009	5,476	7,009	5,841
41,400	41,450	7,021	5,484	7,021	5,854
41,450	41,500	7,034	5,491	7,034	5,866
41,500	41,550	7,046	5,499	7,046	5,879
41,550	41,600	7,059	5,506	7,059	5,891
41,600	41,650	7,071	5,514	7,071	5,904
41,650	41,700	7,084	5,521	7,084	5,916
41,700	41,750	7,096	5,529	7,096	5,929
41,750	41,800	7,109	5,536	7,109	5,941
41,800	41,850	7,121	5,544	7,121	5,954
41,850	41,900	7,134	5,551	7,134	5,966
41,900	41,950	7,146	5,559	7,146	5,979
41,950	42,000	7,159	5,566	7,159	5,991
42,000					
42,000	42,050	7,171	5,574	7,171	6,004
42,050	42,100	7,184	5,581	7,184	6,016
42,100	42,150	7,196	5,589	7,196	6,029
42,150	42,200	7,209	5,596	7,209	6,041
42,200	42,250	7,221	5,604	7,221	6,054
42,250	42,300	7,234	5,611	7,234	6,066
42,300	42,350	7,246	5,619	7,246	6,079
42,350	42,400	7,259	5,626	7,259	6,091
42,400	42,450	7,271	5,634	7,271	6,104
42,450	42,500	7,284	5,641	7,284	6,116
42,500	42,550	7,296	5,649	7,296	6,129
42,550	42,600	7,309	5,656	7,309	6,141
42,600	42,650	7,321	5,664	7,321	6,154
42,650	42,700	7,334	5,671	7,334	6,166
42,700	42,750	7,346	5,679	7,346	6,179
42,750	42,800	7,359	5,686	7,359	6,191
42,800	42,850	7,371	5,694	7,371	6,204
42,850	42,900	7,384	5,701	7,384	6,216
42,900	42,950	7,396	5,709	7,396	6,229
42,950	43,000	7,409	5,716	7,409	6,241
43,000					
43,000	43,050	7,421	5,724	7,421	6,254
43,050	43,100	7,434	5,731	7,434	6,266
43,100	43,150	7,446	5,739	7,446	6,279
43,150	43,200	7,459	5,746	7,459	6,291
43,200	43,250	7,471	5,754	7,471	6,304
43,250	43,300	7,484	5,761	7,484	6,316
43,300	43,350	7,496	5,769	7,496	6,329
43,350	43,400	7,509	5,776	7,509	6,341
43,400	43,450	7,521	5,784	7,521	6,354
43,450	43,500	7,534	5,791	7,534	6,366
43,500	43,550	7,546	5,799	7,546	6,379
43,550	43,600	7,559	5,806	7,559	6,391
43,600	43,650	7,571	5,814	7,571	6,404
43,650	43,700	7,584	5,821	7,584	6,416
43,700	43,750	7,596	5,829	7,596	6,429
43,750	43,800	7,609	5,836	7,609	6,441
43,800	43,850	7,621	5,844	7,621	6,454
43,850	43,900	7,634	5,851	7,634	6,466
43,900	43,950	7,646	5,859	7,646	6,479
43,950	44,000	7,659	5,866	7,659	6,491
44,000					
44,000	44,050	7,671	5,874	7,671	6,504
44,050	44,100	7,684	5,881	7,684	6,516
44,100	44,150	7,696	5,889	7,696	6,529
44,150	44,200	7,709	5,896	7,709	6,541
44,200	44,250	7,721	5,904	7,721	6,554
44,250	44,300	7,734	5,911	7,734	6,566
44,300	44,350	7,746	5,919	7,746	6,579
44,350	44,400	7,759	5,926	7,759	6,591
44,400	44,450	7,771	5,934	7,771	6,604
44,450	44,500	7,784	5,941	7,784	6,616
44,500	44,550	7,796	5,949	7,796	6,629
44,550	44,600	7,809	5,956	7,809	6,641
44,600	44,650	7,821	5,964	7,821	6,654
44,650	44,700	7,834	5,971	7,834	6,666
44,700	44,750	7,846	5,979	7,846	6,679
44,750	44,800	7,859	5,986	7,859	6,691
44,800	44,850	7,871	5,994	7,871	6,704
44,850	44,900	7,884	6,001	7,884	6,716
44,900	44,950	7,896	6,009	7,896	6,729
44,950	45,000	7,909	6,016	7,909	6,741
45,000					
45,000	45,050	7,921	6,024	7,921	6,754
45,050	45,100	7,934	6,031	7,934	6,766
45,100	45,150	7,946	6,039	7,946	6,779
45,150	45,200	7,959	6,046	7,959	6,791
45,200	45,250	7,971	6,054	7,971	6,804
45,250	45,300	7,984	6,061	7,984	6,816
45,300	45,350	7,996	6,069	7,996	6,829
45,350	45,400	8,009	6,076	8,009	6,841
45,400	45,450	8,021	6,084	8,021	6,854
45,450	45,500	8,034	6,091	8,034	6,866
45,500	45,550	8,046	6,099	8,046	6,879
45,550	45,600	8,059	6,106	8,059	6,891
45,600	45,650	8,071	6,114	8,071	6,904
45,650	45,700	8,084	6,121	8,084	6,916
45,700	45,750	8,096	6,129	8,096	6,929
45,750	45,800	8,109	6,136	8,109	6,941
45,800	45,850	8,121	6,144	8,121	6,954
45,850	45,900	8,134	6,151	8,134	6,966
45,900	45,950	8,146	6,159	8,146	6,979
45,950	46,000	8,159	6,166	8,159	6,991
46,000					
46,000	46,050	8,171	6,174	8,171	7,004
46,050	46,100	8,184	6,181	8,184	7,016
46,100	46,150	8,196	6,189	8,196	7,029
46,150	46,200	8,209	6,196	8,209	7,041
46,200	46,250	8,221	6,204	8,221	7,054
46,250	46,300	8,234	6,211	8,234	7,066
46,300	46,350	8,246	6,219	8,246	7,079
46,350	46,400	8,259	6,226	8,259	7,091
46,400	46,450	8,271	6,234	8,271	7,104
46,450	46,500	8,284	6,241	8,284	7,116
46,500	46,550	8,296	6,249	8,296	7,129
46,550	46,600	8,309	6,256	8,309	7,141
46,600	46,650	8,321	6,264	8,321	7,154
46,650	46,700	8,334	6,271	8,334	7,166
46,700	46,750	8,346	6,279	8,346	7,179
46,750	46,800	8,359	6,286	8,359	7,191
46,800	46,850	8,371	6,294	8,371	7,204
46,850	46,900	8,384	6,301	8,384	7,216
46,900	46,950	8,396	6,309	8,396	7,229
46,950	47,000	8,409	6,316	8,409	7,241
47,000					
47,000	47,050	8,421	6,324	8,421	7,254
47,050	47,100	8,434	6,331	8,434	7,266
47,100	47,150	8,446	6,339	8,446	7,279
47,150	47,200	8,459	6,346	8,459	7,291
47,200	47,250	8,471	6,354	8,471	7,304
47,250	47,300	8,484	6,361	8,484	7,316
47,300	47,350	8,496	6,369	8,496	7,329
47,350	47,400	8,509	6,376	8,509	7,341
47,400	47,450	8,521	6,384	8,521	7,354
47,450	47,500	8,534	6,391	8,534	7,366
47,500	47,550	8,546	6,399	8,546	7,379
47,550	47,600	8,559	6,406	8,559	7,391
47,600	47,650	8,571	6,414	8,571	7,404
47,650	47,700	8,584	6,421	8,584	7,416
47,700	47,750	8,596	6,429	8,596	7,429
47,750	47,800	8,609	6,436	8,609	7,441
47,800	47,850	8,621	6,444	8,621	7,454
47,850	47,900	8,634	6,451	8,634	7,466
47,900	47,950	8,646	6,459	8,646	7,479
47,950	48,000	8,659	6,466	8,659	7,491
48,000					
48,000	48,050	8,671	6,474	8,671	7,504
48,050	48,100	8,684	6,481	8,684	7,516
48,100	48,150	8,696	6,489	8,696	7,529
48,150	48,200	8,709	6,496	8,709	7,541
48,200	48,250	8,721	6,504	8,721	7,554
48,250	48,300	8,734	6,511	8,734	7,566
48,300	48,350	8,746	6,519	8,746	7,579
48,350	48,400	8,759	6,526	8,759	7,591
48,400	48,450	8,771	6,534	8,771	7,604
48,450	48,500	8,784	6,541	8,784	7,616
48,500	48,550	8,796	6,549	8,796	7,629
48,550	48,600	8,809	6,556	8,809	7,641
48,600	48,650	8,821	6,564	8,821	7,654
48,650	48,700	8,834	6,571	8,834	7,666
48,700	48,750	8,846	6,579	8,846	7,679
48,750	48,800	8,859	6,586	8,859	7,691
48,800	48,850	8,871	6,594	8,871	7,704
48,850	48,900	8,884	6,601	8,884	7,716
48,900	48,950	8,896	6,609	8,896	7,729
48,950	49,000	8,909	6,616	8,909	7,741
49,000					
49,000	49,050	8,921	6,624	8,921	7,754
49,050	49,100	8,934	6,631	8,934	7,766
49,100	49,150	8,946	6,639	8,946	7,779
49,150	49,200	8,959	6,646	8,959	7,791
49,200	49,250	8,971	6,654	8,971	7,804
49,250	49,300	8,984	6,661	8,984	7,816
49,300	49,350	8,996	6,669	8,996	7,829
49,350	49,400	9,009	6,676	9,009	7,841
49,400	49,450	9,021	6,684	9,021	7,854
49,450	49,500	9,034	6,691	9,034	7,866
49,500	49,550	9,046	6,699	9,046	7,879
49,550	49,600	9,059	6,706	9,059	7,891
49,600	49,650	9,071	6,714	9,071	7,904
49,650	49,700	9,084	6,721	9,084	7,916
49,700	49,750	9,096	6,729	9,096	7,929
49,750	49,800	9,109	6,736	9,109	7,941
49,800	49,850	9,121	6,744	9,121	7,954
49,850	49,900	9,134	6,751	9,134	7,966
49,900	49,950	9,146	6,759	9,146	7,979
49,950	50,000	9,159	6,766	9,159	7,991

* This column must also be used by a qualifying widow(er).

(Continued on next page)

2005 Tax Table—*Continued*

If line 43 (taxable income) is—		And you are—			
At least	But less than	Single	Married filing jointly *	Married filing separately	Head of a household
		Your tax is—			
50,000					
50,000	50,050	9,171	6,774	9,171	8,004
50,050	50,100	9,184	6,781	9,184	8,016
50,100	50,150	9,196	6,789	9,196	8,029
50,150	50,200	9,209	6,796	9,209	8,041
50,200	50,250	9,221	6,804	9,221	8,054
50,250	50,300	9,234	6,811	9,234	8,066
50,300	50,350	9,246	6,819	9,246	8,079
50,350	50,400	9,259	6,826	9,259	8,091
50,400	50,450	9,271	6,834	9,271	8,104
50,450	50,500	9,284	6,841	9,284	8,116
50,500	50,550	9,296	6,849	9,296	8,129
50,550	50,600	9,309	6,856	9,309	8,141
50,600	50,650	9,321	6,864	9,321	8,154
50,650	50,700	9,334	6,871	9,334	8,166
50,700	50,750	9,346	6,879	9,346	8,179
50,750	50,800	9,359	6,886	9,359	8,191
50,800	50,850	9,371	6,894	9,371	8,204
50,850	50,900	9,384	6,901	9,384	8,216
50,900	50,950	9,396	6,909	9,396	8,229
50,950	51,000	9,409	6,916	9,409	8,241
51,000					
51,000	51,050	9,421	6,924	9,421	8,254
51,050	51,100	9,434	6,931	9,434	8,266
51,100	51,150	9,446	6,939	9,446	8,279
51,150	51,200	9,459	6,946	9,459	8,291
51,200	51,250	9,471	6,954	9,471	8,304
51,250	51,300	9,484	6,961	9,484	8,316
51,300	51,350	9,496	6,969	9,496	8,329
51,350	51,400	9,509	6,976	9,509	8,341
51,400	51,450	9,521	6,984	9,521	8,354
51,450	51,500	9,534	6,991	9,534	8,366
51,500	51,550	9,546	6,999	9,546	8,379
51,550	51,600	9,559	7,006	9,559	8,391
51,600	51,650	9,571	7,014	9,571	8,404
51,650	51,700	9,584	7,021	9,584	8,416
51,700	51,750	9,596	7,029	9,596	8,429
51,750	51,800	9,609	7,036	9,609	8,441
51,800	51,850	9,621	7,044	9,621	8,454
51,850	51,900	9,634	7,051	9,634	8,466
51,900	51,950	9,646	7,059	9,646	8,479
51,950	52,000	9,659	7,066	9,659	8,491
52,000					
52,000	52,050	9,671	7,074	9,671	8,504
52,050	52,100	9,684	7,081	9,684	8,516
52,100	52,150	9,696	7,089	9,696	8,529
52,150	52,200	9,709	7,096	9,709	8,541
52,200	52,250	9,721	7,104	9,721	8,554
52,250	52,300	9,734	7,111	9,734	8,566
52,300	52,350	9,746	7,119	9,746	8,579
52,350	52,400	9,759	7,126	9,759	8,591
52,400	52,450	9,771	7,134	9,771	8,604
52,450	52,500	9,784	7,141	9,784	8,616
52,500	52,550	9,796	7,149	9,796	8,629
52,550	52,600	9,809	7,156	9,809	8,641
52,600	52,650	9,821	7,164	9,821	8,654
52,650	52,700	9,834	7,171	9,834	8,666
52,700	52,750	9,846	7,179	9,846	8,679
52,750	52,800	9,859	7,186	9,859	8,691
52,800	52,850	9,871	7,194	9,871	8,704
52,850	52,900	9,884	7,201	9,884	8,716
52,900	52,950	9,896	7,209	9,896	8,729
52,950	53,000	9,909	7,216	9,909	8,741

If line 43 (taxable income) is—		And you are—			
At least	But less than	Single	Married filing jointly *	Married filing separately	Head of a household
		Your tax is—			
53,000					
53,000	53,050	9,921	7,224	9,921	8,754
53,050	53,100	9,934	7,231	9,934	8,766
53,100	53,150	9,946	7,239	9,946	8,779
53,150	53,200	9,959	7,246	9,959	8,791
53,200	53,250	9,971	7,254	9,971	8,804
53,250	53,300	9,984	7,261	9,984	8,816
53,300	53,350	9,996	7,269	9,996	8,829
53,350	53,400	10,009	7,276	10,009	8,841
53,400	53,450	10,021	7,284	10,021	8,854
53,450	53,500	10,034	7,291	10,034	8,866
53,500	53,550	10,046	7,299	10,046	8,879
53,550	53,600	10,059	7,306	10,059	8,891
53,600	53,650	10,071	7,314	10,071	8,904
53,650	53,700	10,084	7,321	10,084	8,916
53,700	53,750	10,096	7,329	10,096	8,929
53,750	53,800	10,109	7,336	10,109	8,941
53,800	53,850	10,121	7,344	10,121	8,954
53,850	53,900	10,134	7,351	10,134	8,966
53,900	53,950	10,146	7,359	10,146	8,979
53,950	54,000	10,159	7,366	10,159	8,991
54,000					
54,000	54,050	10,171	7,374	10,171	9,004
54,050	54,100	10,184	7,381	10,184	9,016
54,100	54,150	10,196	7,389	10,196	9,029
54,150	54,200	10,209	7,396	10,209	9,041
54,200	54,250	10,221	7,404	10,221	9,054
54,250	54,300	10,234	7,411	10,234	9,066
54,300	54,350	10,246	7,419	10,246	9,079
54,350	54,400	10,259	7,426	10,259	9,091
54,400	54,450	10,271	7,434	10,271	9,104
54,450	54,500	10,284	7,441	10,284	9,116
54,500	54,550	10,296	7,449	10,296	9,129
54,550	54,600	10,309	7,456	10,309	9,141
54,600	54,650	10,321	7,464	10,321	9,154
54,650	54,700	10,334	7,471	10,334	9,166
54,700	54,750	10,346	7,479	10,346	9,179
54,750	54,800	10,359	7,486	10,359	9,191
54,800	54,850	10,371	7,494	10,371	9,204
54,850	54,900	10,384	7,501	10,384	9,216
54,900	54,950	10,396	7,509	10,396	9,229
54,950	55,000	10,409	7,516	10,409	9,241
55,000					
55,000	55,050	10,421	7,524	10,421	9,254
55,050	55,100	10,434	7,531	10,434	9,266
55,100	55,150	10,446	7,539	10,446	9,279
55,150	55,200	10,459	7,546	10,459	9,291
55,200	55,250	10,471	7,554	10,471	9,304
55,250	55,300	10,484	7,561	10,484	9,316
55,300	55,350	10,496	7,569	10,496	9,329
55,350	55,400	10,509	7,576	10,509	9,341
55,400	55,450	10,521	7,584	10,521	9,354
55,450	55,500	10,534	7,591	10,534	9,366
55,500	55,550	10,546	7,599	10,546	9,379
55,550	55,600	10,559	7,606	10,559	9,391
55,600	55,650	10,571	7,614	10,571	9,404
55,650	55,700	10,584	7,621	10,584	9,416
55,700	55,750	10,596	7,629	10,596	9,429
55,750	55,800	10,609	7,636	10,609	9,441
55,800	55,850	10,621	7,644	10,621	9,454
55,850	55,900	10,634	7,651	10,634	9,466
55,900	55,950	10,646	7,659	10,646	9,479
55,950	56,000	10,659	7,666	10,659	9,491

If line 43 (taxable income) is—		And you are—			
At least	But less than	Single	Married filing jointly *	Married filing separately	Head of a household
		Your tax is—			
56,000					
56,000	56,050	10,671	7,674	10,671	9,504
56,050	56,100	10,684	7,681	10,684	9,516
56,100	56,150	10,696	7,689	10,696	9,529
56,150	56,200	10,709	7,696	10,709	9,541
56,200	56,250	10,721	7,704	10,721	9,554
56,250	56,300	10,734	7,711	10,734	9,566
56,300	56,350	10,746	7,719	10,746	9,579
56,350	56,400	10,759	7,726	10,759	9,591
56,400	56,450	10,771	7,734	10,771	9,604
56,450	56,500	10,784	7,741	10,784	9,616
56,500	56,550	10,796	7,749	10,796	9,629
56,550	56,600	10,809	7,756	10,809	9,641
56,600	56,650	10,821	7,764	10,821	9,654
56,650	56,700	10,834	7,771	10,834	9,666
56,700	56,750	10,846	7,779	10,846	9,679
56,750	56,800	10,859	7,786	10,859	9,691
56,800	56,850	10,871	7,794	10,871	9,704
56,850	56,900	10,884	7,801	10,884	9,716
56,900	56,950	10,896	7,809	10,896	9,729
56,950	57,000	10,909	7,816	10,909	9,741
57,000					
57,000	57,050	10,921	7,824	10,921	9,754
57,050	57,100	10,934	7,831	10,934	9,766
57,100	57,150	10,946	7,839	10,946	9,779
57,150	57,200	10,959	7,846	10,959	9,791
57,200	57,250	10,971	7,854	10,971	9,804
57,250	57,300	10,984	7,861	10,984	9,816
57,300	57,350	10,996	7,869	10,996	9,829
57,350	57,400	11,009	7,876	11,009	9,841
57,400	57,450	11,021	7,884	11,021	9,854
57,450	57,500	11,034	7,891	11,034	9,866
57,500	57,550	11,046	7,899	11,046	9,879
57,550	57,600	11,059	7,906	11,059	9,891
57,600	57,650	11,071	7,914	11,071	9,904
57,650	57,700	11,084	7,921	11,084	9,916
57,700	57,750	11,096	7,929	11,096	9,929
57,750	57,800	11,109	7,936	11,109	9,941
57,800	57,850	11,121	7,944	11,121	9,954
57,850	57,900	11,134	7,951	11,134	9,966
57,900	57,950	11,146	7,959	11,146	9,979
57,950	58,000	11,159	7,966	11,159	9,991
58,000					
58,000	58,050	11,171	7,974	11,171	10,004
58,050	58,100	11,184	7,981	11,184	10,016
58,100	58,150	11,196	7,989	11,196	10,029
58,150	58,200	11,209	7,996	11,209	10,041
58,200	58,250	11,221	8,004	11,221	10,054
58,250	58,300	11,234	8,011	11,234	10,066
58,300	58,350	11,246	8,019	11,246	10,079
58,350	58,400	11,259	8,026	11,259	10,091
58,400	58,450	11,271	8,034	11,271	10,104
58,450	58,500	11,284	8,041	11,284	10,116
58,500	58,550	11,296	8,049	11,296	10,129
58,550	58,600	11,309	8,056	11,309	10,141
58,600	58,650	11,321	8,064	11,321	10,154
58,650	58,700	11,334	8,071	11,334	10,166
58,700	58,750	11,346	8,079	11,346	10,179
58,750	58,800	11,359	8,086	11,359	10,191
58,800	58,850	11,371	8,094	11,371	10,204
58,850	58,900	11,384	8,101	11,384	10,216
58,900	58,950	11,396	8,109	11,396	10,229
58,950	59,000	11,409	8,116	11,409	10,241

* This column must also be used by a qualifying widow(er).

(Continued on next page)

2005 Tax Table—*Continued*

If line 43 (taxable income) is—		And you are—			
At least	But less than	Single	Married filing jointly *	Married filing sepa-rately	Head of a house-hold
		Your tax is—			
59,000					
59,000	**59,050**	11,421	8,124	11,421	10,254
59,050	**59,100**	11,434	8,131	11,434	10,266
59,100	**59,150**	11,446	8,139	11,446	10,279
59,150	**59,200**	11,459	8,146	11,459	10,291
59,200	**59,250**	11,471	8,154	11,471	10,304
59,250	**59,300**	11,484	8,161	11,484	10,316
59,300	**59,350**	11,496	8,169	11,496	10,329
59,350	**59,400**	11,509	8,176	11,509	10,341
59,400	**59,450**	11,521	8,186	11,521	10,354
59,450	**59,500**	11,534	8,199	11,534	10,366
59,500	**59,550**	11,546	8,211	11,546	10,379
59,550	**59,600**	11,559	8,224	11,559	10,391
59,600	**59,650**	11,571	8,236	11,571	10,404
59,650	**59,700**	11,584	8,249	11,584	10,416
59,700	**59,750**	11,596	8,261	11,596	10,429
59,750	**59,800**	11,609	8,274	11,609	10,441
59,800	**59,850**	11,621	8,286	11,621	10,454
59,850	**59,900**	11,634	8,299	11,634	10,466
59,900	**59,950**	11,646	8,311	11,646	10,479
59,950	**60,000**	11,659	8,324	11,659	10,491
60,000					
60,000	**60,050**	11,671	8,336	11,673	10,504
60,050	**60,100**	11,684	8,349	11,687	10,516
60,100	**60,150**	11,696	8,361	11,701	10,529
60,150	**60,200**	11,709	8,374	11,715	10,541
60,200	**60,250**	11,721	8,386	11,729	10,554
60,250	**60,300**	11,734	8,399	11,743	10,566
60,300	**60,350**	11,746	8,411	11,757	10,579
60,350	**60,400**	11,759	8,424	11,771	10,591
60,400	**60,450**	11,771	8,436	11,785	10,604
60,450	**60,500**	11,784	8,449	11,799	10,616
60,500	**60,550**	11,796	8,461	11,813	10,629
60,550	**60,600**	11,809	8,474	11,827	10,641
60,600	**60,650**	11,821	8,486	11,841	10,654
60,650	**60,700**	11,834	8,499	11,855	10,666
60,700	**60,750**	11,846	8,511	11,869	10,679
60,750	**60,800**	11,859	8,524	11,883	10,691
60,800	**60,850**	11,871	8,536	11,897	10,704
60,850	**60,900**	11,884	8,549	11,911	10,716
60,900	**60,950**	11,896	8,561	11,925	10,729
60,950	**61,000**	11,909	8,574	11,939	10,741
61,000					
61,000	**61,050**	11,921	8,586	11,953	10,754
61,050	**61,100**	11,934	8,599	11,967	10,766
61,100	**61,150**	11,946	8,611	11,981	10,779
61,150	**61,200**	11,959	8,624	11,995	10,791
61,200	**61,250**	11,971	8,636	12,009	10,804
61,250	**61,300**	11,984	8,649	12,023	10,816
61,300	**61,350**	11,996	8,661	12,037	10,829
61,350	**61,400**	12,009	8,674	12,051	10,841
61,400	**61,450**	12,021	8,686	12,065	10,854
61,450	**61,500**	12,034	8,699	12,079	10,866
61,500	**61,550**	12,046	8,711	12,093	10,879
61,550	**61,600**	12,059	8,724	12,107	10,891
61,600	**61,650**	12,071	8,736	12,121	10,904
61,650	**61,700**	12,084	8,749	12,135	10,916
61,700	**61,750**	12,096	8,761	12,149	10,929
61,750	**61,800**	12,109	8,774	12,163	10,941
61,800	**61,850**	12,121	8,786	12,177	10,954
61,850	**61,900**	12,134	8,799	12,191	10,966
61,900	**61,950**	12,146	8,811	12,205	10,979
61,950	**62,000**	12,159	8,824	12,219	10,991

If line 43 (taxable income) is—		And you are—			
At least	But less than	Single	Married filing jointly *	Married filing sepa-rately	Head of a house-hold
		Your tax is—			
62,000					
62,000	**62,050**	12,171	8,836	12,233	11,004
62,050	**62,100**	12,184	8,849	12,247	11,016
62,100	**62,150**	12,196	8,861	12,261	11,029
62,150	**62,200**	12,209	8,874	12,275	11,041
62,200	**62,250**	12,221	8,886	12,289	11,054
62,250	**62,300**	12,234	8,899	12,303	11,066
62,300	**62,350**	12,246	8,911	12,317	11,079
62,350	**62,400**	12,259	8,924	12,331	11,091
62,400	**62,450**	12,271	8,936	12,345	11,104
62,450	**62,500**	12,284	8,949	12,359	11,116
62,500	**62,550**	12,296	8,961	12,373	11,129
62,550	**62,600**	12,309	8,974	12,387	11,141
62,600	**62,650**	12,321	8,986	12,401	11,154
62,650	**62,700**	12,334	8,999	12,415	11,166
62,700	**62,750**	12,346	9,011	12,429	11,179
62,750	**62,800**	12,359	9,024	12,443	11,191
62,800	**62,850**	12,371	9,036	12,457	11,204
62,850	**62,900**	12,384	9,049	12,471	11,216
62,900	**62,950**	12,396	9,061	12,485	11,229
62,950	**63,000**	12,409	9,074	12,499	11,241
63,000					
63,000	**63,050**	12,421	9,086	12,513	11,254
63,050	**63,100**	12,434	9,099	12,527	11,266
63,100	**63,150**	12,446	9,111	12,541	11,279
63,150	**63,200**	12,459	9,124	12,555	11,291
63,200	**63,250**	12,471	9,136	12,569	11,304
63,250	**63,300**	12,484	9,149	12,583	11,316
63,300	**63,350**	12,496	9,161	12,597	11,329
63,350	**63,400**	12,509	9,174	12,611	11,341
63,400	**63,450**	12,521	9,186	12,625	11,354
63,450	**63,500**	12,534	9,199	12,639	11,366
63,500	**63,550**	12,546	9,211	12,653	11,379
63,550	**63,600**	12,559	9,224	12,667	11,391
63,600	**63,650**	12,571	9,236	12,681	11,404
63,650	**63,700**	12,584	9,249	12,695	11,416
63,700	**63,750**	12,596	9,261	12,709	11,429
63,750	**63,800**	12,609	9,274	12,723	11,441
63,800	**63,850**	12,621	9,286	12,737	11,454
63,850	**63,900**	12,634	9,299	12,751	11,466
63,900	**63,950**	12,646	9,311	12,765	11,479
63,950	**64,000**	12,659	9,324	12,779	11,491
64,000					
64,000	**64,050**	12,671	9,336	12,793	11,504
64,050	**64,100**	12,684	9,349	12,807	11,516
64,100	**64,150**	12,696	9,361	12,821	11,529
64,150	**64,200**	12,709	9,374	12,835	11,541
64,200	**64,250**	12,721	9,386	12,849	11,554
64,250	**64,300**	12,734	9,399	12,863	11,566
64,300	**64,350**	12,746	9,411	12,877	11,579
64,350	**64,400**	12,759	9,424	12,891	11,591
64,400	**64,450**	12,771	9,436	12,905	11,604
64,450	**64,500**	12,784	9,449	12,919	11,616
64,500	**64,550**	12,796	9,461	12,933	11,629
64,550	**64,600**	12,809	9,474	12,947	11,641
64,600	**64,650**	12,821	9,486	12,961	11,654
64,650	**64,700**	12,834	9,499	12,975	11,666
64,700	**64,750**	12,846	9,511	12,989	11,679
64,750	**64,800**	12,859	9,524	13,003	11,691
64,800	**64,850**	12,871	9,536	13,017	11,704
64,850	**64,900**	12,884	9,549	13,031	11,716
64,900	**64,950**	12,896	9,561	13,045	11,729
64,950	**65,000**	12,909	9,574	13,059	11,741

If line 43 (taxable income) is—		And you are—			
At least	But less than	Single	Married filing jointly *	Married filing sepa-rately	Head of a house-hold
		Your tax is—			
65,000					
65,000	**65,050**	12,921	9,586	13,073	11,754
65,050	**65,100**	12,934	9,599	13,087	11,766
65,100	**65,150**	12,946	9,611	13,101	11,779
65,150	**65,200**	12,959	9,624	13,115	11,791
65,200	**65,250**	12,971	9,636	13,129	11,804
65,250	**65,300**	12,984	9,649	13,143	11,816
65,300	**65,350**	12,996	9,661	13,157	11,829
65,350	**65,400**	13,009	9,674	13,171	11,841
65,400	**65,450**	13,021	9,686	13,185	11,854
65,450	**65,500**	13,034	9,699	13,199	11,866
65,500	**65,550**	13,046	9,711	13,213	11,879
65,550	**65,600**	13,059	9,724	13,227	11,891
65,600	**65,650**	13,071	9,736	13,241	11,904
65,650	**65,700**	13,084	9,749	13,255	11,916
65,700	**65,750**	13,096	9,761	13,269	11,929
65,750	**65,800**	13,109	9,774	13,283	11,941
65,800	**65,850**	13,121	9,786	13,297	11,954
65,850	**65,900**	13,134	9,799	13,311	11,966
65,900	**65,950**	13,146	9,811	13,325	11,979
65,950	**66,000**	13,159	9,824	13,339	11,991
66,000					
66,000	**66,050**	13,171	9,836	13,353	12,004
66,050	**66,100**	13,184	9,849	13,367	12,016
66,100	**66,150**	13,196	9,861	13,381	12,029
66,150	**66,200**	13,209	9,874	13,395	12,041
66,200	**66,250**	13,221	9,886	13,409	12,054
66,250	**66,300**	13,234	9,899	13,423	12,066
66,300	**66,350**	13,246	9,911	13,437	12,079
66,350	**66,400**	13,259	9,924	13,451	12,091
66,400	**66,450**	13,271	9,936	13,465	12,104
66,450	**66,500**	13,284	9,949	13,479	12,116
66,500	**66,550**	13,296	9,961	13,493	12,129
66,550	**66,600**	13,309	9,974	13,507	12,141
66,600	**66,650**	13,321	9,986	13,521	12,154
66,650	**66,700**	13,334	9,999	13,535	12,166
66,700	**66,750**	13,346	10,011	13,549	12,179
66,750	**66,800**	13,359	10,024	13,563	12,191
66,800	**66,850**	13,371	10,036	13,577	12,204
66,850	**66,900**	13,384	10,049	13,591	12,216
66,900	**66,950**	13,396	10,061	13,605	12,229
66,950	**67,000**	13,409	10,074	13,619	12,241
67,000					
67,000	**67,050**	13,421	10,086	13,633	12,254
67,050	**67,100**	13,434	10,099	13,647	12,266
67,100	**67,150**	13,446	10,111	13,661	12,279
67,150	**67,200**	13,459	10,124	13,675	12,291
67,200	**67,250**	13,471	10,136	13,689	12,304
67,250	**67,300**	13,484	10,149	13,703	12,316
67,300	**67,350**	13,496	10,161	13,717	12,329
67,350	**67,400**	13,509	10,174	13,731	12,341
67,400	**67,450**	13,521	10,186	13,745	12,354
67,450	**67,500**	13,534	10,199	13,759	12,366
67,500	**67,550**	13,546	10,211	13,773	12,379
67,550	**67,600**	13,559	10,224	13,787	12,391
67,600	**67,650**	13,571	10,236	13,801	12,404
67,650	**67,700**	13,584	10,249	13,815	12,416
67,700	**67,750**	13,596	10,261	13,829	12,429
67,750	**67,800**	13,609	10,274	13,843	12,441
67,800	**67,850**	13,621	10,286	13,857	12,454
67,850	**67,900**	13,634	10,299	13,871	12,466
67,900	**67,950**	13,646	10,311	13,885	12,479
67,950	**68,000**	13,659	10,324	13,899	12,491

* This column must also be used by a qualifying widow(er).

(Continued on next page)

2005 Tax Table—*Continued*

If line 43 (taxable income) is—		And you are—			
At least	But less than	Single	Married filing jointly *	Married filing separately	Head of a household
		Your tax is—			
68,000					
68,000	**68,050**	13,671	10,336	13,913	12,504
68,050	**68,100**	13,684	10,349	13,927	12,516
68,100	**68,150**	13,696	10,361	13,941	12,529
68,150	**68,200**	13,709	10,374	13,955	12,541
68,200	**68,250**	13,721	10,386	13,969	12,554
68,250	**68,300**	13,734	10,399	13,983	12,566
68,300	**68,350**	13,746	10,411	13,997	12,579
68,350	**68,400**	13,759	10,424	14,011	12,591
68,400	**68,450**	13,771	10,436	14,025	12,604
68,450	**68,500**	13,784	10,449	14,039	12,616
68,500	**68,550**	13,796	10,461	14,053	12,629
68,550	**68,600**	13,809	10,474	14,067	12,641
68,600	**68,650**	13,821	10,486	14,081	12,654
68,650	**68,700**	13,834	10,499	14,095	12,666
68,700	**68,750**	13,846	10,511	14,109	12,679
68,750	**68,800**	13,859	10,524	14,123	12,691
68,800	**68,850**	13,871	10,536	14,137	12,704
68,850	**68,900**	13,884	10,549	14,151	12,716
68,900	**68,950**	13,896	10,561	14,165	12,729
68,950	**69,000**	13,909	10,574	14,179	12,741
69,000					
69,000	**69,050**	13,921	10,586	14,193	12,754
69,050	**69,100**	13,934	10,599	14,207	12,766
69,100	**69,150**	13,946	10,611	14,221	12,779
69,150	**69,200**	13,959	10,624	14,235	12,791
69,200	**69,250**	13,971	10,636	14,249	12,804
69,250	**69,300**	13,984	10,649	14,263	12,816
69,300	**69,350**	13,996	10,661	14,277	12,829
69,350	**69,400**	14,009	10,674	14,291	12,841
69,400	**69,450**	14,021	10,686	14,305	12,854
69,450	**69,500**	14,034	10,699	14,319	12,866
69,500	**69,550**	14,046	10,711	14,333	12,879
69,550	**69,600**	14,059	10,724	14,347	12,891
69,600	**69,650**	14,071	10,736	14,361	12,904
69,650	**69,700**	14,084	10,749	14,375	12,916
69,700	**69,750**	14,096	10,761	14,389	12,929
69,750	**69,800**	14,109	10,774	14,403	12,941
69,800	**69,850**	14,121	10,786	14,417	12,954
69,850	**69,900**	14,134	10,799	14,431	12,966
69,900	**69,950**	14,146	10,811	14,445	12,979
69,950	**70,000**	14,159	10,824	14,459	12,991
70,000					
70,000	**70,050**	14,171	10,836	14,473	13,004
70,050	**70,100**	14,184	10,849	14,487	13,016
70,100	**70,150**	14,196	10,861	14,501	13,029
70,150	**70,200**	14,209	10,874	14,515	13,041
70,200	**70,250**	14,221	10,886	14,529	13,054
70,250	**70,300**	14,234	10,899	14,543	13,066
70,300	**70,350**	14,246	10,911	14,557	13,079
70,350	**70,400**	14,259	10,924	14,571	13,091
70,400	**70,450**	14,271	10,936	14,585	13,104
70,450	**70,500**	14,284	10,949	14,599	13,116
70,500	**70,550**	14,296	10,961	14,613	13,129
70,550	**70,600**	14,309	10,974	14,627	13,141
70,600	**70,650**	14,321	10,986	14,641	13,154
70,650	**70,700**	14,334	10,999	14,655	13,166
70,700	**70,750**	14,346	11,011	14,669	13,179
70,750	**70,800**	14,359	11,024	14,683	13,191
70,800	**70,850**	14,371	11,036	14,697	13,204
70,850	**70,900**	14,384	11,049	14,711	13,216
70,900	**70,950**	14,396	11,061	14,725	13,229
70,950	**71,000**	14,409	11,074	14,739	13,241

If line 43 (taxable income) is—		And you are—			
At least	But less than	Single	Married filing jointly *	Married filing separately	Head of a household
		Your tax is—			
71,000					
71,000	**71,050**	14,421	11,086	14,753	13,254
71,050	**71,100**	14,434	11,099	14,767	13,266
71,100	**71,150**	14,446	11,111	14,781	13,279
71,150	**71,200**	14,459	11,124	14,795	13,291
71,200	**71,250**	14,471	11,136	14,809	13,304
71,250	**71,300**	14,484	11,149	14,823	13,316
71,300	**71,350**	14,496	11,161	14,837	13,329
71,350	**71,400**	14,509	11,174	14,851	13,341
71,400	**71,450**	14,521	11,186	14,865	13,354
71,450	**71,500**	14,534	11,199	14,879	13,366
71,500	**71,550**	14,546	11,211	14,893	13,379
71,550	**71,600**	14,559	11,224	14,907	13,391
71,600	**71,650**	14,571	11,236	14,921	13,404
71,650	**71,700**	14,584	11,249	14,935	13,416
71,700	**71,750**	14,596	11,261	14,949	13,429
71,750	**71,800**	14,609	11,274	14,963	13,441
71,800	**71,850**	14,621	11,286	14,977	13,454
71,850	**71,900**	14,634	11,299	14,991	13,466
71,900	**71,950**	14,646	11,311	15,005	13,479
71,950	**72,000**	14,660	11,324	15,019	13,491
72,000					
72,000	**72,050**	14,674	11,336	15,033	13,504
72,050	**72,100**	14,688	11,349	15,047	13,516
72,100	**72,150**	14,702	11,361	15,061	13,529
72,150	**72,200**	14,716	11,374	15,075	13,541
72,200	**72,250**	14,730	11,386	15,089	13,554
72,250	**72,300**	14,744	11,399	15,103	13,566
72,300	**72,350**	14,758	11,411	15,117	13,579
72,350	**72,400**	14,772	11,424	15,131	13,591
72,400	**72,450**	14,786	11,436	15,145	13,604
72,450	**72,500**	14,800	11,449	15,159	13,616
72,500	**72,550**	14,814	11,461	15,173	13,629
72,550	**72,600**	14,828	11,474	15,187	13,641
72,600	**72,650**	14,842	11,486	15,201	13,654
72,650	**72,700**	14,856	11,499	15,215	13,666
72,700	**72,750**	14,870	11,511	15,229	13,679
72,750	**72,800**	14,884	11,524	15,243	13,691
72,800	**72,850**	14,898	11,536	15,257	13,704
72,850	**72,900**	14,912	11,549	15,271	13,716
72,900	**72,950**	14,926	11,561	15,285	13,729
72,950	**73,000**	14,940	11,574	15,299	13,741
73,000					
73,000	**73,050**	14,954	11,586	15,313	13,754
73,050	**73,100**	14,968	11,599	15,327	13,766
73,100	**73,150**	14,982	11,611	15,341	13,779
73,150	**73,200**	14,996	11,624	15,355	13,791
73,200	**73,250**	15,010	11,636	15,369	13,804
73,250	**73,300**	15,024	11,649	15,383	13,816
73,300	**73,350**	15,038	11,661	15,397	13,829
73,350	**73,400**	15,052	11,674	15,411	13,841
73,400	**73,450**	15,066	11,686	15,425	13,854
73,450	**73,500**	15,080	11,699	15,439	13,866
73,500	**73,550**	15,094	11,711	15,453	13,879
73,550	**73,600**	15,108	11,724	15,467	13,891
73,600	**73,650**	15,122	11,736	15,481	13,904
73,650	**73,700**	15,136	11,749	15,495	13,916
73,700	**73,750**	15,150	11,761	15,509	13,929
73,750	**73,800**	15,164	11,774	15,523	13,941
73,800	**73,850**	15,178	11,786	15,537	13,954
73,850	**73,900**	15,192	11,799	15,551	13,966
73,900	**73,950**	15,206	11,811	15,565	13,979
73,950	**74,000**	15,220	11,824	15,579	13,991

If line 43 (taxable income) is—		And you are—			
At least	But less than	Single	Married filing jointly *	Married filing separately	Head of a household
		Your tax is—			
74,000					
74,000	**74,050**	15,234	11,836	15,593	14,004
74,050	**74,100**	15,248	11,849	15,607	14,016
74,100	**74,150**	15,262	11,861	15,621	14,029
74,150	**74,200**	15,276	11,874	15,635	14,041
74,200	**74,250**	15,290	11,886	15,649	14,054
74,250	**74,300**	15,304	11,899	15,663	14,066
74,300	**74,350**	15,318	11,911	15,677	14,079
74,350	**74,400**	15,332	11,924	15,691	14,091
74,400	**74,450**	15,346	11,936	15,705	14,104
74,450	**74,500**	15,360	11,949	15,719	14,116
74,500	**74,550**	15,374	11,961	15,733	14,129
74,550	**74,600**	15,388	11,974	15,747	14,141
74,600	**74,650**	15,402	11,986	15,761	14,154
74,650	**74,700**	15,416	11,999	15,775	14,166
74,700	**74,750**	15,430	12,011	15,789	14,179
74,750	**74,800**	15,444	12,024	15,803	14,191
74,800	**74,850**	15,458	12,036	15,817	14,204
74,850	**74,900**	15,472	12,049	15,831	14,216
74,900	**74,950**	15,486	12,061	15,845	14,229
74,950	**75,000**	15,500	12,074	15,859	14,241
75,000					
75,000	**75,050**	15,514	12,086	15,873	14,254
75,050	**75,100**	15,528	12,099	15,887	14,266
75,100	**75,150**	15,542	12,111	15,901	14,279
75,150	**75,200**	15,556	12,124	15,915	14,291
75,200	**75,250**	15,570	12,136	15,929	14,304
75,250	**75,300**	15,584	12,149	15,943	14,316
75,300	**75,350**	15,598	12,161	15,957	14,329
75,350	**75,400**	15,612	12,174	15,971	14,341
75,400	**75,450**	15,626	12,186	15,985	14,354
75,450	**75,500**	15,640	12,199	15,999	14,366
75,500	**75,550**	15,654	12,211	16,013	14,379
75,550	**75,600**	15,668	12,224	16,027	14,391
75,600	**75,650**	15,682	12,236	16,041	14,404
75,650	**75,700**	15,696	12,249	16,055	14,416
75,700	**75,750**	15,710	12,261	16,069	14,429
75,750	**75,800**	15,724	12,274	16,083	14,441
75,800	**75,850**	15,738	12,286	16,097	14,454
75,850	**75,900**	15,752	12,299	16,111	14,466
75,900	**75,950**	15,766	12,311	16,125	14,479
75,950	**76,000**	15,780	12,324	16,139	14,491
76,000					
76,000	**76,050**	15,794	12,336	16,153	14,504
76,050	**76,100**	15,808	12,349	16,167	14,516
76,100	**76,150**	15,822	12,361	16,181	14,529
76,150	**76,200**	15,836	12,374	16,195	14,541
76,200	**76,250**	15,850	12,386	16,209	14,554
76,250	**76,300**	15,864	12,399	16,223	14,566
76,300	**76,350**	15,878	12,411	16,237	14,579
76,350	**76,400**	15,892	12,424	16,251	14,591
76,400	**76,450**	15,906	12,436	16,265	14,604
76,450	**76,500**	15,920	12,449	16,279	14,616
76,500	**76,550**	15,934	12,461	16,293	14,629
76,550	**76,600**	15,948	12,474	16,307	14,641
76,600	**76,650**	15,962	12,486	16,321	14,654
76,650	**76,700**	15,976	12,499	16,335	14,666
76,700	**76,750**	15,990	12,511	16,349	14,679
76,750	**76,800**	16,004	12,524	16,363	14,691
76,800	**76,850**	16,018	12,536	16,377	14,704
76,850	**76,900**	16,032	12,549	16,391	14,716
76,900	**76,950**	16,046	12,561	16,405	14,729
76,950	**77,000**	16,060	12,574	16,419	14,741

* This column must also be used by a qualifying widow(er).

(Continued on next page)

2005 Tax Table—*Continued*

If line 43 (taxable income) is— At least	But less than	Single	Married filing jointly *	Married filing separately	Head of a household
		Your tax is—			
77,000					
77,000	**77,050**	16,074	12,586	16,433	14,754
77,050	**77,100**	16,088	12,599	16,447	14,766
77,100	**77,150**	16,102	12,611	16,461	14,779
77,150	**77,200**	16,116	12,624	16,475	14,791
77,200	**77,250**	16,130	12,636	16,489	14,804
77,250	**77,300**	16,144	12,649	16,503	14,816
77,300	**77,350**	16,158	12,661	16,517	14,829
77,350	**77,400**	16,172	12,674	16,531	14,841
77,400	**77,450**	16,186	12,686	16,545	14,854
77,450	**77,500**	16,200	12,699	16,559	14,866
77,500	**77,550**	16,214	12,711	16,573	14,879
77,550	**77,600**	16,228	12,724	16,587	14,891
77,600	**77,650**	16,242	12,736	16,601	14,904
77,650	**77,700**	16,256	12,749	16,615	14,916
77,700	**77,750**	16,270	12,761	16,629	14,929
77,750	**77,800**	16,284	12,774	16,643	14,941
77,800	**77,850**	16,298	12,786	16,657	14,954
77,850	**77,900**	16,312	12,799	16,671	14,966
77,900	**77,950**	16,326	12,811	16,685	14,979
77,950	**78,000**	16,340	12,824	16,699	14,991
78,000					
78,000	**78,050**	16,354	12,836	16,713	15,004
78,050	**78,100**	16,368	12,849	16,727	15,016
78,100	**78,150**	16,382	12,861	16,741	15,029
78,150	**78,200**	16,396	12,874	16,755	15,041
78,200	**78,250**	16,410	12,886	16,769	15,054
78,250	**78,300**	16,424	12,899	16,783	15,066
78,300	**78,350**	16,438	12,911	16,797	15,079
78,350	**78,400**	16,452	12,924	16,811	15,091
78,400	**78,450**	16,466	12,936	16,825	15,104
78,450	**78,500**	16,480	12,949	16,839	15,116
78,500	**78,550**	16,494	12,961	16,853	15,129
78,550	**78,600**	16,508	12,974	16,867	15,141
78,600	**78,650**	16,522	12,986	16,881	15,154
78,650	**78,700**	16,536	12,999	16,895	15,166
78,700	**78,750**	16,550	13,011	16,909	15,179
78,750	**78,800**	16,564	13,024	16,923	15,191
78,800	**78,850**	16,578	13,036	16,937	15,204
78,850	**78,900**	16,592	13,049	16,951	15,216
78,900	**78,950**	16,606	13,061	16,965	15,229
78,950	**79,000**	16,620	13,074	16,979	15,241
79,000					
79,000	**79,050**	16,634	13,086	16,993	15,254
79,050	**79,100**	16,648	13,099	17,007	15,266
79,100	**79,150**	16,662	13,111	17,021	15,279
79,150	**79,200**	16,676	13,124	17,035	15,291
79,200	**79,250**	16,690	13,136	17,049	15,304
79,250	**79,300**	16,704	13,149	17,063	15,316
79,300	**79,350**	16,718	13,161	17,077	15,329
79,350	**79,400**	16,732	13,174	17,091	15,341
79,400	**79,450**	16,746	13,186	17,105	15,354
79,450	**79,500**	16,760	13,199	17,119	15,366
79,500	**79,550**	16,774	13,211	17,133	15,379
79,550	**79,600**	16,788	13,224	17,147	15,391
79,600	**79,650**	16,802	13,236	17,161	15,404
79,650	**79,700**	16,816	13,249	17,175	15,416
79,700	**79,750**	16,830	13,261	17,189	15,429
79,750	**79,800**	16,844	13,274	17,203	15,441
79,800	**79,850**	16,858	13,286	17,217	15,454
79,850	**79,900**	16,872	13,299	17,231	15,466
79,900	**79,950**	16,886	13,311	17,245	15,479
79,950	**80,000**	16,900	13,324	17,259	15,491

If line 43 (taxable income) is— At least	But less than	Single	Married filing jointly *	Married filing separately	Head of a household
		Your tax is—			
80,000					
80,000	**80,050**	16,914	13,336	17,273	15,504
80,050	**80,100**	16,928	13,349	17,287	15,516
80,100	**80,150**	16,942	13,361	17,301	15,529
80,150	**80,200**	16,956	13,374	17,315	15,541
80,200	**80,250**	16,970	13,386	17,329	15,554
80,250	**80,300**	16,984	13,399	17,343	15,566
80,300	**80,350**	16,998	13,411	17,357	15,579
80,350	**80,400**	17,012	13,424	17,371	15,591
80,400	**80,450**	17,026	13,436	17,385	15,604
80,450	**80,500**	17,040	13,449	17,399	15,616
80,500	**80,550**	17,054	13,461	17,413	15,629
80,550	**80,600**	17,068	13,474	17,427	15,641
80,600	**80,650**	17,082	13,486	17,441	15,654
80,650	**80,700**	17,096	13,499	17,455	15,666
80,700	**80,750**	17,110	13,511	17,469	15,679
80,750	**80,800**	17,124	13,524	17,483	15,691
80,800	**80,850**	17,138	13,536	17,497	15,704
80,850	**80,900**	17,152	13,549	17,511	15,716
80,900	**80,950**	17,166	13,561	17,525	15,729
80,950	**81,000**	17,180	13,574	17,539	15,741
81,000					
81,000	**81,050**	17,194	13,586	17,553	15,754
81,050	**81,100**	17,208	13,599	17,567	15,766
81,100	**81,150**	17,222	13,611	17,581	15,779
81,150	**81,200**	17,236	13,624	17,595	15,791
81,200	**81,250**	17,250	13,636	17,609	15,804
81,250	**81,300**	17,264	13,649	17,623	15,816
81,300	**81,350**	17,278	13,661	17,637	15,829
81,350	**81,400**	17,292	13,674	17,651	15,841
81,400	**81,450**	17,306	13,686	17,665	15,854
81,450	**81,500**	17,320	13,699	17,679	15,866
81,500	**81,550**	17,334	13,711	17,693	15,879
81,550	**81,600**	17,348	13,724	17,707	15,891
81,600	**81,650**	17,362	13,736	17,721	15,904
81,650	**81,700**	17,376	13,749	17,735	15,916
81,700	**81,750**	17,390	13,761	17,749	15,929
81,750	**81,800**	17,404	13,774	17,763	15,941
81,800	**81,850**	17,418	13,786	17,777	15,954
81,850	**81,900**	17,432	13,799	17,791	15,966
81,900	**81,950**	17,446	13,811	17,805	15,979
81,950	**82,000**	17,460	13,824	17,819	15,991
82,000					
82,000	**82,050**	17,474	13,836	17,833	16,004
82,050	**82,100**	17,488	13,849	17,847	16,016
82,100	**82,150**	17,502	13,861	17,861	16,029
82,150	**82,200**	17,516	13,874	17,875	16,041
82,200	**82,250**	17,530	13,886	17,889	16,054
82,250	**82,300**	17,544	13,899	17,903	16,066
82,300	**82,350**	17,558	13,911	17,917	16,079
82,350	**82,400**	17,572	13,924	17,931	16,091
82,400	**82,450**	17,586	13,936	17,945	16,104
82,450	**82,500**	17,600	13,949	17,959	16,116
82,500	**82,550**	17,614	13,961	17,973	16,129
82,550	**82,600**	17,628	13,974	17,987	16,141
82,600	**82,650**	17,642	13,986	18,001	16,154
82,650	**82,700**	17,656	13,999	18,015	16,166
82,700	**82,750**	17,670	14,011	18,029	16,179
82,750	**82,800**	17,684	14,024	18,043	16,191
82,800	**82,850**	17,698	14,036	18,057	16,204
82,850	**82,900**	17,712	14,049	18,071	16,216
82,900	**82,950**	17,726	14,061	18,085	16,229
82,950	**83,000**	17,740	14,074	18,099	16,241

If line 43 (taxable income) is— At least	But less than	Single	Married filing jointly *	Married filing separately	Head of a household
		Your tax is—			
83,000					
83,000	**83,050**	17,754	14,086	18,113	16,254
83,050	**83,100**	17,768	14,099	18,127	16,266
83,100	**83,150**	17,782	14,111	18,141	16,279
83,150	**83,200**	17,796	14,124	18,155	16,291
83,200	**83,250**	17,810	14,136	18,169	16,304
83,250	**83,300**	17,824	14,149	18,183	16,316
83,300	**83,350**	17,838	14,161	18,197	16,329
83,350	**83,400**	17,852	14,174	18,211	16,341
83,400	**83,450**	17,866	14,186	18,225	16,354
83,450	**83,500**	17,880	14,199	18,239	16,366
83,500	**83,550**	17,894	14,211	18,253	16,379
83,550	**83,600**	17,908	14,224	18,267	16,391
83,600	**83,650**	17,922	14,236	18,281	16,404
83,650	**83,700**	17,936	14,249	18,295	16,416
83,700	**83,750**	17,950	14,261	18,309	16,429
83,750	**83,800**	17,964	14,274	18,323	16,441
83,800	**83,850**	17,978	14,286	18,337	16,454
83,850	**83,900**	17,992	14,299	18,351	16,466
83,900	**83,950**	18,006	14,311	18,365	16,479
83,950	**84,000**	18,020	14,324	18,379	16,491
84,000					
84,000	**84,050**	18,034	14,336	18,393	16,504
84,050	**84,100**	18,048	14,349	18,407	16,516
84,100	**84,150**	18,062	14,361	18,421	16,529
84,150	**84,200**	18,076	14,374	18,435	16,541
84,200	**84,250**	18,090	14,386	18,449	16,554
84,250	**84,300**	18,104	14,399	18,463	16,566
84,300	**84,350**	18,118	14,411	18,477	16,579
84,350	**84,400**	18,132	14,424	18,491	16,591
84,400	**84,450**	18,146	14,436	18,505	16,604
84,450	**84,500**	18,160	14,449	18,519	16,616
84,500	**84,550**	18,174	14,461	18,533	16,629
84,550	**84,600**	18,188	14,474	18,547	16,641
84,600	**84,650**	18,202	14,486	18,561	16,654
84,650	**84,700**	18,216	14,499	18,575	16,666
84,700	**84,750**	18,230	14,511	18,589	16,679
84,750	**84,800**	18,244	14,524	18,603	16,691
84,800	**84,850**	18,258	14,536	18,617	16,704
84,850	**84,900**	18,272	14,549	18,631	16,716
84,900	**84,950**	18,286	14,561	18,645	16,729
84,950	**85,000**	18,300	14,574	18,659	16,741
85,000					
85,000	**85,050**	18,314	14,586	18,673	16,754
85,050	**85,100**	18,328	14,599	18,687	16,766
85,100	**85,150**	18,342	14,611	18,701	16,779
85,150	**85,200**	18,356	14,624	18,715	16,791
85,200	**85,250**	18,370	14,636	18,729	16,804
85,250	**85,300**	18,384	14,649	18,743	16,816
85,300	**85,350**	18,398	14,661	18,757	16,829
85,350	**85,400**	18,412	14,674	18,771	16,841
85,400	**85,450**	18,426	14,686	18,785	16,854
85,450	**85,500**	18,440	14,699	18,799	16,866
85,500	**85,550**	18,454	14,711	18,813	16,879
85,550	**85,600**	18,468	14,724	18,827	16,891
85,600	**85,650**	18,482	14,736	18,841	16,904
85,650	**85,700**	18,496	14,749	18,855	16,916
85,700	**85,750**	18,510	14,761	18,869	16,929
85,750	**85,800**	18,524	14,774	18,883	16,941
85,800	**85,850**	18,538	14,786	18,897	16,954
85,850	**85,900**	18,552	14,799	18,911	16,966
85,900	**85,950**	18,566	14,811	18,925	16,979
85,950	**86,000**	18,580	14,824	18,939	16,991

* This column must also be used by a qualifying widow(er).

(Continued on next page)

2005 Tax Table—*Continued*

If line 43 (taxable income) is—		And you are—			
At least	But less than	Single	Married filing jointly *	Married filing separately	Head of a household
		Your tax is—			
86,000					
86,000	**86,050**	18,594	14,836	18,953	17,004
86,050	**86,100**	18,608	14,849	18,967	17,016
86,100	**86,150**	18,622	14,861	18,981	17,029
86,150	**86,200**	18,636	14,874	18,995	17,041
86,200	**86,250**	18,650	14,886	19,009	17,054
86,250	**86,300**	18,664	14,899	19,023	17,066
86,300	**86,350**	18,678	14,911	19,037	17,079
86,350	**86,400**	18,692	14,924	19,051	17,091
86,400	**86,450**	18,706	14,936	19,065	17,104
86,450	**86,500**	18,720	14,949	19,079	17,116
86,500	**86,550**	18,734	14,961	19,093	17,129
86,550	**86,600**	18,748	14,974	19,107	17,141
86,600	**86,650**	18,762	14,986	19,121	17,154
86,650	**86,700**	18,776	14,999	19,135	17,166
86,700	**86,750**	18,790	15,011	19,149	17,179
86,750	**86,800**	18,804	15,024	19,163	17,191
86,800	**86,850**	18,818	15,036	19,177	17,204
86,850	**86,900**	18,832	15,049	19,191	17,216
86,900	**86,950**	18,846	15,061	19,205	17,229
86,950	**87,000**	18,860	15,074	19,219	17,241
87,000					
87,000	**87,050**	18,874	15,086	19,233	17,254
87,050	**87,100**	18,888	15,099	19,247	17,266
87,100	**87,150**	18,902	15,111	19,261	17,279
87,150	**87,200**	18,916	15,124	19,275	17,291
87,200	**87,250**	18,930	15,136	19,289	17,304
87,250	**87,300**	18,944	15,149	19,303	17,316
87,300	**87,350**	18,958	15,161	19,317	17,329
87,350	**87,400**	18,972	15,174	19,331	17,341
87,400	**87,450**	18,986	15,186	19,345	17,354
87,450	**87,500**	19,000	15,199	19,359	17,366
87,500	**87,550**	19,014	15,211	19,373	17,379
87,550	**87,600**	19,028	15,224	19,387	17,391
87,600	**87,650**	19,042	15,236	19,401	17,404
87,650	**87,700**	19,056	15,249	19,415	17,416
87,700	**87,750**	19,070	15,261	19,429	17,429
87,750	**87,800**	19,084	15,274	19,443	17,441
87,800	**87,850**	19,098	15,286	19,457	17,454
87,850	**87,900**	19,112	15,299	19,471	17,466
87,900	**87,950**	19,126	15,311	19,485	17,479
87,950	**88,000**	19,140	15,324	19,499	17,491
88,000					
88,000	**88,050**	19,154	15,336	19,513	17,504
88,050	**88,100**	19,168	15,349	19,527	17,516
88,100	**88,150**	19,182	15,361	19,541	17,529
88,150	**88,200**	19,196	15,374	19,555	17,541
88,200	**88,250**	19,210	15,386	19,569	17,554
88,250	**88,300**	19,224	15,399	19,583	17,566
88,300	**88,350**	19,238	15,411	19,597	17,579
88,350	**88,400**	19,252	15,424	19,611	17,591
88,400	**88,450**	19,266	15,436	19,625	17,604
88,450	**88,500**	19,280	15,449	19,639	17,616
88,500	**88,550**	19,294	15,461	19,653	17,629
88,550	**88,600**	19,308	15,474	19,667	17,641
88,600	**88,650**	19,322	15,486	19,681	17,654
88,650	**88,700**	19,336	15,499	19,695	17,666
88,700	**88,750**	19,350	15,511	19,709	17,679
88,750	**88,800**	19,364	15,524	19,723	17,691
88,800	**88,850**	19,378	15,536	19,737	17,704
88,850	**88,900**	19,392	15,549	19,751	17,716
88,900	**88,950**	19,406	15,561	19,765	17,729
88,950	**89,000**	19,420	15,574	19,779	17,741

If line 43 (taxable income) is—		And you are—			
At least	But less than	Single	Married filing jointly *	Married filing separately	Head of a household
		Your tax is—			
89,000					
89,000	**89,050**	19,434	15,586	19,793	17,754
89,050	**89,100**	19,448	15,599	19,807	17,766
89,100	**89,150**	19,462	15,611	19,821	17,779
89,150	**89,200**	19,476	15,624	19,835	17,791
89,200	**89,250**	19,490	15,636	19,849	17,804
89,250	**89,300**	19,504	15,649	19,863	17,816
89,300	**89,350**	19,518	15,661	19,877	17,829
89,350	**89,400**	19,532	15,674	19,891	17,841
89,400	**89,450**	19,546	15,686	19,905	17,854
89,450	**89,500**	19,560	15,699	19,919	17,866
89,500	**89,550**	19,574	15,711	19,933	17,879
89,550	**89,600**	19,588	15,724	19,947	17,891
89,600	**89,650**	19,602	15,736	19,961	17,904
89,650	**89,700**	19,616	15,749	19,975	17,916
89,700	**89,750**	19,630	15,761	19,989	17,929
89,750	**89,800**	19,644	15,774	20,003	17,941
89,800	**89,850**	19,658	15,786	20,017	17,954
89,850	**89,900**	19,672	15,799	20,031	17,966
89,900	**89,950**	19,686	15,811	20,045	17,979
89,950	**90,000**	19,700	15,824	20,059	17,991
90,000					
90,000	**90,050**	19,714	15,836	20,073	18,004
90,050	**90,100**	19,728	15,849	20,087	18,016
90,100	**90,150**	19,742	15,861	20,101	18,029
90,150	**90,200**	19,756	15,874	20,115	18,041
90,200	**90,250**	19,770	15,886	20,129	18,054
90,250	**90,300**	19,784	15,899	20,143	18,066
90,300	**90,350**	19,798	15,911	20,157	18,079
90,350	**90,400**	19,812	15,924	20,171	18,091
90,400	**90,450**	19,826	15,936	20,185	18,104
90,450	**90,500**	19,840	15,949	20,199	18,116
90,500	**90,550**	19,854	15,961	20,213	18,129
90,550	**90,600**	19,868	15,974	20,227	18,141
90,600	**90,650**	19,882	15,986	20,241	18,154
90,650	**90,700**	19,896	15,999	20,255	18,166
90,700	**90,750**	19,910	16,011	20,269	18,179
90,750	**90,800**	19,924	16,024	20,283	18,191
90,800	**90,850**	19,938	16,036	20,297	18,204
90,850	**90,900**	19,952	16,049	20,311	18,216
90,900	**90,950**	19,966	16,061	20,325	18,229
90,950	**91,000**	19,980	16,074	20,339	18,241
91,000					
91,000	**91,050**	19,994	16,086	20,353	18,254
91,050	**91,100**	20,008	16,099	20,367	18,266
91,100	**91,150**	20,022	16,111	20,381	18,279
91,150	**91,200**	20,036	16,124	20,395	18,291
91,200	**91,250**	20,050	16,136	20,409	18,304
91,250	**91,300**	20,064	16,149	20,423	18,316
91,300	**91,350**	20,078	16,161	20,437	18,329
91,350	**91,400**	20,092	16,174	20,451	18,341
91,400	**91,450**	20,106	16,186	20,466	18,354
91,450	**91,500**	20,120	16,199	20,483	18,366
91,500	**91,550**	20,134	16,211	20,499	18,379
91,550	**91,600**	20,148	16,224	20,516	18,391
91,600	**91,650**	20,162	16,236	20,532	18,404
91,650	**91,700**	20,176	16,249	20,549	18,416
91,700	**91,750**	20,190	16,261	20,565	18,429
91,750	**91,800**	20,204	16,274	20,582	18,441
91,800	**91,850**	20,218	16,286	20,598	18,454
91,850	**91,900**	20,232	16,299	20,615	18,466
91,900	**91,950**	20,246	16,311	20,631	18,479
91,950	**92,000**	20,260	16,324	20,648	18,491

If line 43 (taxable income) is—		And you are—			
At least	But less than	Single	Married filing jointly *	Married filing separately	Head of a household
		Your tax is—			
92,000					
92,000	**92,050**	20,274	16,336	20,664	18,504
92,050	**92,100**	20,288	16,349	20,681	18,516
92,100	**92,150**	20,302	16,361	20,697	18,529
92,150	**92,200**	20,316	16,374	20,714	18,541
92,200	**92,250**	20,330	16,386	20,730	18,554
92,250	**92,300**	20,344	16,399	20,747	18,566
92,300	**92,350**	20,358	16,411	20,763	18,579
92,350	**92,400**	20,372	16,424	20,780	18,591
92,400	**92,450**	20,386	16,436	20,796	18,604
92,450	**92,500**	20,400	16,449	20,813	18,616
92,500	**92,550**	20,414	16,461	20,829	18,629
92,550	**92,600**	20,428	16,474	20,846	18,641
92,600	**92,650**	20,442	16,486	20,862	18,654
92,650	**92,700**	20,456	16,499	20,879	18,666
92,700	**92,750**	20,470	16,511	20,895	18,679
92,750	**92,800**	20,484	16,524	20,912	18,691
92,800	**92,850**	20,498	16,536	20,928	18,704
92,850	**92,900**	20,512	16,549	20,945	18,716
92,900	**92,950**	20,526	16,561	20,961	18,729
92,950	**93,000**	20,540	16,574	20,978	18,741
93,000					
93,000	**93,050**	20,554	16,586	20,994	18,754
93,050	**93,100**	20,568	16,599	21,011	18,766
93,100	**93,150**	20,582	16,611	21,027	18,779
93,150	**93,200**	20,596	16,624	21,044	18,791
93,200	**93,250**	20,610	16,636	21,060	18,804
93,250	**93,300**	20,624	16,649	21,077	18,816
93,300	**93,350**	20,638	16,661	21,093	18,829
93,350	**93,400**	20,652	16,674	21,110	18,841
93,400	**93,450**	20,666	16,686	21,126	18,854
93,450	**93,500**	20,680	16,699	21,143	18,866
93,500	**93,550**	20,694	16,711	21,159	18,879
93,550	**93,600**	20,708	16,724	21,176	18,891
93,600	**93,650**	20,722	16,736	21,192	18,904
93,650	**93,700**	20,736	16,749	21,209	18,916
93,700	**93,750**	20,750	16,761	21,225	18,929
93,750	**93,800**	20,764	16,774	21,242	18,941
93,800	**93,850**	20,778	16,786	21,258	18,954
93,850	**93,900**	20,792	16,799	21,275	18,966
93,900	**93,950**	20,806	16,811	21,291	18,979
93,950	**94,000**	20,820	16,824	21,308	18,991
94,000					
94,000	**94,050**	20,834	16,836	21,324	19,004
94,050	**94,100**	20,848	16,849	21,341	19,016
94,100	**94,150**	20,862	16,861	21,357	19,029
94,150	**94,200**	20,876	16,874	21,374	19,041
94,200	**94,250**	20,890	16,886	21,390	19,054
94,250	**94,300**	20,904	16,899	21,407	19,066
94,300	**94,350**	20,918	16,911	21,423	19,079
94,350	**94,400**	20,932	16,924	21,440	19,091
94,400	**94,450**	20,946	16,936	21,456	19,104
94,450	**94,500**	20,960	16,949	21,473	19,116
94,500	**94,550**	20,974	16,961	21,489	19,129
94,550	**94,600**	20,988	16,974	21,506	19,141
94,600	**94,650**	21,002	16,986	21,522	19,154
94,650	**94,700**	21,016	16,999	21,539	19,166
94,700	**94,750**	21,030	17,011	21,555	19,179
94,750	**94,800**	21,044	17,024	21,572	19,191
94,800	**94,850**	21,058	17,036	21,588	19,204
94,850	**94,900**	21,072	17,049	21,605	19,216
94,900	**94,950**	21,086	17,061	21,621	19,229
94,950	**95,000**	21,100	17,074	21,638	19,241

* This column must also be used by a qualifying widow(er).

(Continued on next page)

2005 Tax Table—*Continued*

If line 43 (taxable income) is—		And you are—			
At least	But less than	Single	Married filing jointly *	Married filing separately	Head of a household
		Your tax is—			
95,000					
95,000	95,050	21,114	17,086	21,654	19,254
95,050	95,100	21,128	17,099	21,671	19,266
95,100	95,150	21,142	17,111	21,687	19,279
95,150	95,200	21,156	17,124	21,704	19,291
95,200	95,250	21,170	17,136	21,720	19,304
95,250	95,300	21,184	17,149	21,737	19,316
95,300	95,350	21,198	17,161	21,753	19,329
95,350	95,400	21,212	17,174	21,770	19,341
95,400	95,450	21,226	17,186	21,786	19,354
95,450	95,500	21,240	17,199	21,803	19,366
95,500	95,550	21,254	17,211	21,819	19,379
95,550	95,600	21,268	17,224	21,836	19,391
95,600	95,650	21,282	17,236	21,852	19,404
95,650	95,700	21,296	17,249	21,869	19,416
95,700	95,750	21,310	17,261	21,885	19,429
95,750	95,800	21,324	17,274	21,902	19,441
95,800	95,850	21,338	17,286	21,918	19,454
95,850	95,900	21,352	17,299	21,935	19,466
95,900	95,950	21,366	17,311	21,951	19,479
95,950	96,000	21,380	17,324	21,968	19,491
96,000					
96,000	96,050	21,394	17,336	21,984	19,504
96,050	96,100	21,408	17,349	22,001	19,516
96,100	96,150	21,422	17,361	22,017	19,529
96,150	96,200	21,436	17,374	22,034	19,541
96,200	96,250	21,450	17,386	22,050	19,554
96,250	96,300	21,464	17,399	22,067	19,566
96,300	96,350	21,478	17,411	22,083	19,579
96,350	96,400	21,492	17,424	22,100	19,591
96,400	96,450	21,506	17,436	22,116	19,604
96,450	96,500	21,520	17,449	22,133	19,616
96,500	96,550	21,534	17,461	22,149	19,629
96,550	96,600	21,548	17,474	22,166	19,641
96,600	96,650	21,562	17,486	22,182	19,654
96,650	96,700	21,576	17,499	22,199	19,666
96,700	96,750	21,590	17,511	22,215	19,679
96,750	96,800	21,604	17,524	22,232	19,691
96,800	96,850	21,618	17,536	22,248	19,704
96,850	96,900	21,632	17,549	22,265	19,716
96,900	96,950	21,646	17,561	22,281	19,729
96,950	97,000	21,660	17,574	22,298	19,741
97,000					
97,000	97,050	21,674	17,586	22,314	19,754
97,050	97,100	21,688	17,599	22,331	19,766
97,100	97,150	21,702	17,611	22,347	19,779
97,150	97,200	21,716	17,624	22,364	19,791
97,200	97,250	21,730	17,636	22,380	19,804
97,250	97,300	21,744	17,649	22,397	19,816
97,300	97,350	21,758	17,661	22,413	19,829
97,350	97,400	21,772	17,674	22,430	19,841
97,400	97,450	21,786	17,686	22,446	19,854
97,450	97,500	21,800	17,699	22,463	19,866
97,500	97,550	21,814	17,711	22,479	19,879
97,550	97,600	21,828	17,724	22,496	19,891
97,600	97,650	21,842	17,736	22,512	19,904
97,650	97,700	21,856	17,749	22,529	19,916
97,700	97,750	21,870	17,761	22,545	19,929
97,750	97,800	21,884	17,774	22,562	19,941
97,800	97,850	21,898	17,786	22,578	19,954
97,850	97,900	21,912	17,799	22,595	19,966
97,900	97,950	21,926	17,811	22,611	19,979
97,950	98,000	21,940	17,824	22,628	19,991

If line 43 (taxable income) is—		And you are—			
At least	But less than	Single	Married filing jointly *	Married filing separately	Head of a household
		Your tax is—			
98,000					
98,000	98,050	21,954	17,836	22,644	20,004
98,050	98,100	21,968	17,849	22,661	20,016
98,100	98,150	21,982	17,861	22,677	20,029
98,150	98,200	21,996	17,874	22,694	20,041
98,200	98,250	22,010	17,886	22,710	20,054
98,250	98,300	22,024	17,899	22,727	20,066
98,300	98,350	22,038	17,911	22,743	20,079
98,350	98,400	22,052	17,924	22,760	20,091
98,400	98,450	22,066	17,936	22,776	20,104
98,450	98,500	22,080	17,949	22,793	20,116
98,500	98,550	22,094	17,961	22,809	20,129
98,550	98,600	22,108	17,974	22,826	20,141
98,600	98,650	22,122	17,986	22,842	20,154
98,650	98,700	22,136	17,999	22,859	20,166
98,700	98,750	22,150	18,011	22,875	20,179
98,750	98,800	22,164	18,024	22,892	20,191
98,800	98,850	22,178	18,036	22,908	20,204
98,850	98,900	22,192	18,049	22,925	20,216
98,900	98,950	22,206	18,061	22,941	20,229
98,950	99,000	22,220	18,074	22,958	20,241
99,000					
99,000	99,050	22,234	18,086	22,974	20,254
99,050	99,100	22,248	18,099	22,991	20,266
99,100	99,150	22,262	18,111	23,007	20,279
99,150	99,200	22,276	18,124	23,024	20,291
99,200	99,250	22,290	18,136	23,040	20,304
99,250	99,300	22,304	18,149	23,057	20,316
99,300	99,350	22,318	18,161	23,073	20,329
99,350	99,400	22,332	18,174	23,090	20,341
99,400	99,450	22,346	18,186	23,106	20,354
99,450	99,500	22,360	18,199	23,123	20,366
99,500	99,550	22,374	18,211	23,139	20,379
99,550	99,600	22,388	18,224	23,156	20,391
99,600	99,650	22,402	18,236	23,172	20,404
99,650	99,700	22,416	18,249	23,189	20,416
99,700	99,750	22,430	18,261	23,205	20,429
99,750	99,800	22,444	18,274	23,222	20,441
99,800	99,850	22,458	18,286	23,238	20,454
99,850	99,900	22,472	18,299	23,255	20,466
99,900	99,950	22,486	18,311	23,271	20,479
99,950	100,000	22,500	18,324	23,288	20,491

$100,000 or over — use the Tax Rate Schedules on page A–2

* This column must also be used by a qualifying widow(er).

Income Tax Rates—Estates and Trusts

Tax Year 2005

Taxable Income		The Tax Is:	
Over—	But not Over—		Of the Amount Over—
$ 0	$2,000	15%	$ 0
2,000	4,700	$ 300 + 25%	2,000
4,700	7,150	975 + 28%	4,700
7,150	9,750	1,661 + 33%	7,150
9,750	....	2,519 + 35%	9,750

Tax Year 2006

Taxable Income		The Tax Is:	
Over—	But not Over—		Of the Amount Over—
$ 0	$ 2,050	15%	$ 0
2,050	4,850	$ 307.50 + 25%	2,050
4,850	7,400	1,007.50 + 28%	4,850
7,400	10,050	1,721.50 + 33%	7,400
10,050	....	2,596.00 + 35%	10,050

Income Tax Rates—Corporations

Taxable Income		The Tax Is:	
Over—	But not Over—		Of the Amount Over—
$ 0	$ 50,000	15%	$ 0
50,000	75,000	$ 7,500 + 25%	50,000
75,000	100,000	13,750 + 34%	75,000
100,000	335,000	22,250 + 39%	100,000
335,000	10,000,000	113,900 + 34%	335,000
10,000,000	15,000,000	3,400,000 + 35%	10,000,000
15,000,000	18,333,333	5,150,000 + 38%	15,000,000
18,333,333	....	35%	0

Unified Transfer Tax Rates

For Gifts Made and for Deaths After 1983 and Before 2002

If the Amount with Respect to Which the Tentative Tax to Be Computed Is:	The Tentative Tax Is:
Not over $10,000	18 percent of such amount.
Over $10,000 but not over $20,000	$1,800, plus 20 percent of the excess of such amount over $10,000.
Over $20,000 but not over $40,000	$3,800, plus 22 percent of the excess of such amount over $20,000.
Over $40,000 but not over $60,000	$8,200, plus 24 percent of the excess of such amount over $40,000.
Over $60,000 but not over $80,000	$13,000, plus 26 percent of the excess of such amount over $60,000.
Over $80,000 but not over $100,000	$18,200, plus 28 percent of the excess of such amount over $80,000.
Over $100,000 but not over $150,000	$23,800, plus 30 percent of the excess of such amount over $100,000.
Over $150,000 but not over $250,000	$38,800, plus 32 percent of the excess of such amount over $150,000.
Over $250,000 but not over $500,000	$70,800, plus 34 percent of the excess of such amount over $250,000.
Over $500,000 but not over $750,000	$155,800, plus 37 percent of the excess of such amount over $500,000.
Over $750,000 but not over $1,000,000	$248,300, plus 39 percent of the excess of such amount over $750,000.
Over $1,000,000 but not over $1,250,000	$345,800, plus 41 percent of the excess of such amount over $1,000,000.
Over $1,250,000 but not over $1,500,000	$448,300, plus 43 percent of the excess of such amount over $1,250,000.
Over $1,500,000 but not over $2,000,000	$555,800, plus 45 percent of the excess of such amount over $1,500,000.
Over $2,000,000 but not over $2,500,000	$780,800, plus 49 percent of the excess of such amount over $2,000,000.
Over $2,500,000 but not over $3,000,000	$1,025,800, plus 53 percent of the excess of such amount over $2,500,000.
Over $3,000,000	$1,290,800, plus 55 percent of the excess of such amount over $3,000,000.

Unified Transfer Tax Rates

For Gifts Made and for Deaths in 2002

If the Amount with Respect to Which the Tentative Tax to Be Computed Is:	The Tentative Tax Is:
Not over $10,000	18 percent of such amount.
Over $10,000 but not over $20,000	$1,800, plus 20 percent of the excess of such amount over $10,000.
Over $20,000 but not over $40,000	$3,800, plus 22 percent of the excess of such amount over $20,000.
Over $40,000 but not over $60,000	$8,200, plus 24 percent of the excess of such amount over $40,000.
Over $60,000 but not over $80,000	$13,000, plus 26 percent of the excess of such amount over $60,000.
Over $80,000 but not over $100,000	$18,200, plus 28 percent of the excess of such amount over $80,000.
Over $100,000 but not over $150,000	$23,800, plus 30 percent of the excess of such amount over $100,000.
Over $150,000 but not over $250,000	$38,800, plus 32 percent of the excess of such amount over $150,000.
Over $250,000 but not over $500,000	$70,800, plus 34 percent of the excess of such amount over $250,000.
Over $500,000 but not over $750,000	$155,800, plus 37 percent of the excess of such amount over $500,000.
Over $750,000 but not over $1,000,000	$248,300, plus 39 percent of the excess of such amount over $750,000.
Over $1,000,000 but not over $1,250,000	$345,800, plus 41 percent of the excess of such amount over $1,000,000.
Over $1,250,000 but not over $1,500,000	$448,300, plus 43 percent of the excess of such amount over $1,250,000.
Over $1,500,000 but not over $2,000,000	$555,800, plus 45 percent of the excess of such amount over $1,500,000.
Over $2,000,000 but not over $2,500,000	$780,800, plus 49 percent of the excess of such amount over $2,000,000.
Over $2,500,000	$1,025,800, plus 50 percent of the excess of such amount over $2,500,000.

Unified Transfer Tax Rates

For Gifts Made and for Deaths in 2003

If the Amount with Respect to Which the Tentative Tax to Be Computed Is:	The Tentative Tax Is:
Not over $10,000	18 percent of such amount.
Over $10,000 but not over $20,000	$1,800, plus 20 percent of the excess of such amount over $10,000.
Over $20,000 but not over $40,000	$3,800, plus 22 percent of the excess of such amount over $20,000.
Over $40,000 but not over $60,000	$8,200, plus 24 percent of the excess of such amount over $40,000.
Over $60,000 but not over $80,000	$13,000, plus 26 percent of the excess of such amount over $60,000.
Over $80,000 but not over $100,000	$18,200, plus 28 percent of the excess of such amount over $80,000.
Over $100,000 but not over $150,000	$23,800, plus 30 percent of the excess of such amount over $100,000.
Over $150,000 but not over $250,000	$38,800, plus 32 percent of the excess of such amount over $150,000.
Over $250,000 but not over $500,000	$70,800, plus 34 percent of the excess of such amount over $250,000.
Over $500,000 but not over $750,000	$155,800, plus 37 percent of the excess of such amount over $500,000.
Over $750,000 but not over $1,000,000	$248,300, plus 39 percent of the excess of such amount over $750,000.
Over $1,000,000 but not over $1,250,000	$345,800, plus 41 percent of the excess of such amount over $1,000,000.
Over $1,250,000 but not over $1,500,000	$448,300, plus 43 percent of the excess of such amount over $1,250,000.
Over $1,500,000 but not over $2,000,000	$555,800, plus 45 percent of the excess of such amount over $1,500,000.
Over $2,000,000	$780,800, plus 49 percent of the excess of such amount over $2,000,000.

Unified Transfer Tax Rates

For Gifts Made and for Deaths in 2004

If the Amount with Respect to Which the Tentative Tax to Be Computed Is:	The Tentative Tax Is:
Not over $10,000	18 percent of such amount.
Over $10,000 but not over $20,000	$1,800, plus 20 percent of the excess of such amount over $10,000.
Over $20,000 but not over $40,000	$3,800, plus 22 percent of the excess of such amount over $20,000.
Over $40,000 but not over $60,000	$8,200, plus 24 percent of the excess of such amount over $40,000.
Over $60,000 but not over $80,000	$13,000, plus 26 percent of the excess of such amount over $60,000.
Over $80,000 but not over $100,000	$18,200, plus 28 percent of the excess of such amount over $80,000.
Over $100,000 but not over $150,000	$23,800, plus 30 percent of the excess of such amount over $100,000.
Over $150,000 but not over $250,000	$38,800, plus 32 percent of the excess of such amount over $150,000.
Over $250,000 but not over $500,000	$70,800, plus 34 percent of the excess of such amount over $250,000.
Over $500,000 but not over $750,000	$155,800, plus 37 percent of the excess of such amount over $500,000.
Over $750,000 but not over $1,000,000	$248,300, plus 39 percent of the excess of such amount over $750,000.
Over $1,000,000 but not over $1,250,000	$345,800, plus 41 percent of the excess of such amount over $1,000,000.
Over $1,250,000 but not over $1,500,000	$448,300, plus 43 percent of the excess of such amount over $1,250,000.
Over $1,500,000 but not over $2,000,000	$555,800, plus 45 percent of the excess of such amount over $1,500,000.
Over $2,000,000	$780,800, plus 48 percent of the excess of such amount over $2,000,000.

Unified Transfer Tax Rates

For Gifts Made and for Deaths in 2005

If the Amount with Respect to Which the Tentative Tax to Be Computed Is:	The Tentative Tax Is:
Not over $10,000	18 percent of such amount.
Over $10,000 but not over $20,000	$1,800, plus 20 percent of the excess of such amount over $10,000.
Over $20,000 but not over $40,000	$3,800, plus 22 percent of the excess of such amount over $20,000.
Over $40,000 but not over $60,000	$8,200, plus 24 percent of the excess of such amount over $40,000.
Over $60,000 but not over $80,000	$13,000, plus 26 percent of the excess of such amount over $60,000.
Over $80,000 but not over $100,000	$18,200, plus 28 percent of the excess of such amount over $80,000.
Over $100,000 but not over $150,000	$23,800, plus 30 percent of the excess of such amount over $100,000.
Over $150,000 but not over $250,000	$38,800, plus 32 percent of the excess of such amount over $150,000.
Over $250,000 but not over $500,000	$70,800, plus 34 percent of the excess of such amount over $250,000.
Over $500,000 but not over $750,000	$155,800, plus 37 percent of the excess of such amount over $500,000.
Over $750,000 but not over $1,000,000	$248,300, plus 39 percent of the excess of such amount over $750,000.
Over $1,000,000 but not over $1,250,000	$345,800, plus 41 percent of the excess of such amount over $1,000,000.
Over $1,250,000 but not over $1,500,000	$448,300, plus 43 percent of the excess of such amount over $1,250,000.
Over $1,500,000 but not over $2,000,000	$555,800, plus 45 percent of the excess of such amount over $1,500,000.
Over $2,000,000	$780,800, plus 47 percent of the excess of such amount over $2,000,000.

Unified Transfer Tax Rates

For Gifts Made and for Deaths in 2006

If the Amount with Respect to Which the Tentative Tax to Be Computed Is:	The Tentative Tax Is:
Not over $10,000	18 percent of such amount.
Over $10,000 but not over $20,000	$1,800, plus 20 percent of the excess of such amount over $10,000.
Over $20,000 but not over $40,000	$3,800, plus 22 percent of the excess of such amount over $20,000.
Over $40,000 but not over $60,000	$8,200, plus 24 percent of the excess of such amount over $40,000.
Over $60,000 but not over $80,000	$13,000, plus 26 percent of the excess of such amount over $60,000.
Over $80,000 but not over $100,000	$18,200, plus 28 percent of the excess of such amount over $80,000.
Over $100,000 but not over $150,000	$23,800, plus 30 percent of the excess of such amount over $100,000.
Over $150,000 but not over $250,000	$38,800, plus 32 percent of the excess of such amount over $150,000.
Over $250,000 but not over $500,000	$70,800, plus 34 percent of the excess of such amount over $250,000.
Over $500,000 but not over $750,000	$155,800, plus 37 percent of the excess of such amount over $500,000.
Over $750,000 but not over $1,000,000	$248,300, plus 39 percent of the excess of such amount over $750,000.
Over $1,000,000 but not over $1,250,000	$345,800, plus 41 percent of the excess of such amount over $1,000,000.
Over $1,250,000 but not over $1,500,000	$448,300, plus 43 percent of the excess of such amount over $1,250,000.
Over $1,500,000 but not over $2,000,000	$555,800, plus 45 percent of the excess of such amount over $1,500,000.
Over $2,000,000	$780,800, plus 46 percent of the excess of such amount over $2,000,000.

Table for Computation of Maximum Credit for State Death Taxes**

(A) Adjusted Taxable Estate* Equal to or More Than	(B) Adjusted Taxable Estate Less Than	(C) Credit on Amount in Column (A)	(D) Rate of Credit on Excess Over Amount in Column (A) (Percentage)
0	$ 40,000	0	None
$ 40,000	90,000	0	0.8
90,000	140,000	$ 400	1.6
140,000	240,000	1,200	2.4
240,000	440,000	3,600	3.2
440,000	640,000	10,000	4.0
640,000	840,000	18,000	4.8
840,000	1,040,000	27,600	5.6
1,040,000	1,540,000	38,800	6.4
1,540,000	2,040,000	70,800	7.2
2,040,000	2,540,000	106,800	8.0
2,540,000	3,040,000	146,800	8.8
3,040,000	3,540,000	190,800	9.6
3,540,000	4,040,000	238,800	10.4
4,040,000	5,040,000	290,800	11.2
5,040,000	6,040,000	402,800	12.0
6,040,000	7,040,000	522,800	12.8
7,040,000	8,040,000	650,800	13.6
8,040,000	9,040,000	786,800	14.4
9,040,000	10,040,000	930,800	15.2
10,040,000		1,082,800	16.0

*Adjusted Taxable Estate = Taxable Estate – $60,000.

**Although the § 2011 credit has been completely phased out for Federal estate tax purposes, the schedule continues to be used by some states as the measure of state death tax imposed.

Scheduled phaseout:

Year	Percentage Allowed
2002	75
2003	50
2004	25
2005	0

2005 Optional Sales Tax Tables

When Used. The election to deduct state and local general sales taxes requires that the taxpayer forgo any deduction for state and local income taxes. Whether this is advisable or not depends on a comparison of the amounts involved. In making the choice, however, the outcome could be influenced by the additional sales tax incurred due to any "big ticket" purchases that were made. For example, a taxpayer who chose to deduct state and local income taxes for 2004 might well prefer the sales tax deduction in 2005 if a new family SUV was purchased during the year. To make the sales tax election, the taxpayer must check **box b** on **line 5** of Schedule A to Form 1040.

If the sales tax election is made, the amount of the deduction can be determined by use of the *actual expense method* or the *optional sales tax tables* issued by the IRS. The actual expense method can be used only when the taxpayer has actual receipts to support the deduction claimed. In the absence of receipts, the usual case with most taxpayers, resort to the optional sales tax tables is necessary. Under neither method, however, is the purchase of items used in a taxpayer's trade or business to be considered.

Adjustments Necessary. The optional sales tax tables are based on a number of assumptions that require adjustments to be made. As the starting point for the use of the tables is AGI, nontaxable receipts have not been included. Examples of receipts that should be added include: tax-exempt interest, veterans' benefits, workers' compensation, nontaxable Social Security and other retirement benefits. But do not include any large nontaxable items that are not likely to be spent. For example, a $100,000 inheritance should not be added if it was invested in a certificate of deposit.

The tables represent the sales tax on the average (and recurring) expenditures based on level of income by family size and do not include exceptional purchases. Therefore, add to the table amount any sales taxes on major purchases (such as motor vehicles, aircraft, boats, and home building materials, etc.).

When the optional sales tax tables are utilized, special adjustments may be needed when a taxpayer has lived in more than one taxing jurisdiction (e.g., state, county, city) during the year. The adjustments involve apportionment of taxes based on days involved and are illustrated in the 2005 Instructions for Schedules A & B (Form 1040), pages A–3 to A–5.

Local Sales Taxes. Local sales taxes (i.e., those imposed by counties, cities, transit authorities) may or may not require a separate determination. In those states where they are not imposed (such as Connecticut, Hawaii, Indiana, and others), no further computations are necessary. This is also the case where the local taxes are uniform and are incorporated into the state sales tax table (Virginia). In other situations, another step is necessary to arrive at the optional sales tax table deduction. Depending on where the taxpayer lives, one of two procedures need be used. In one procedure, the local sales tax is arrived at by using the **state table** amount—see the Example 1 worksheet. In the other procedure, special **local tables** issued by the IRS for enumerated state and local jurisdictions are modified (if necessary) and used—see the Example 2 worksheet.

Use Illustrated.

EXAMPLE 1 The Archers file a joint return for 2005 reflecting AGI of $88,000 and claiming three exemptions. They have tax-exempt interest of $3,000, and during the year they incurred sales tax of $1,650 on the purchase of an automobile for their dependent teenage son. They live in Bellaire, Texas, where the general sales tax rates are 6.25% for state and 2% for local. Since the IRS *has not issued* optional local sales tax tables for Texas, use the Worksheet below to arrive at the Archers' general sales tax deduction of $3,057.

Sales Tax Deduction Worksheet
(To be used when *no* IRS Optional Local Sales Tax Table Available)

Adjusted Gross Income (AGI) as listed on line 37 of Form 1040		$88,000
Add nontaxable items		3,000
Table income to be used for purposes of line 1 below		$91,000
1. Use table income to determine table amount—go to state of residence and find applicable range of table income and exemption column* for *state* sales tax		$ 1,066
2a. Enter local general sales tax rate	2.0	
2b. Enter state general sales tax rate	6.25	
2c. Divide 2a by 2b	0.32	
2d. Multiply line 1 by line 2c for the local sales tax		341
3. Enter general sales tax on large purchases		1,650
4. Deduction for general sales tax (add lines 1 + 2d + 3) and report on line 5 of Schedule A of Form 1040		$ 3,057

* Use total of personal and dependency exemptions as reported in item 6d of Form 1040.

EXAMPLE 2 The Hardys file a joint return for 2005, reporting AGI of $40,000 and claiming four exemptions (two personal and two dependency). They received $30,000 in nontaxable pension benefits. Although the Hardys do not keep sales tax receipts, they can prove that they paid $4,800 in sales tax on the purchase of a new RV in 2005. The Hardys are residents of Georgia and live in a jurisdiction that imposes a 2% local sales tax. Since the IRS *has issued* optional local sales tax tables for Georgia, use the Worksheet below to arrive at the Hardys' general sales tax deduction of $5,686.

Sales Tax Deduction Worksheet
[To be used for Alaska, Arizona, Arkansas (Texarkana), California (Los Angeles County), Colorado, Georgia, Illinois, Louisiana, New York (New York City) and North Carolina]

Adjusted Gross Income (AGI) as listed on line 37 of Form 1040		$40,000
Add nontaxable income		30,000
Table income to be used for purpose of line 1 below		$70,000
1. Use the table income to determine *state* sales tax amount—go to table for state of residence and find applicable income range and exemption column*		$ 552
2a. Enter local general sales tax rate	2.0	
2b. Enter IRS *local* sales tax table amount (based on 1%)	$167	
2c. Multiply line 2b by 2a for the local sales tax		334
3. Enter general sales tax on large purchases		4,800
4. Deduction for general sales tax (add lines 1 + 2c + 3) and report on line 5 of Schedule A of Form 1040		$ 5,686

* Use total of personal and dependency exemptions as reported in item 6d of Form 1040

2005 Optional State Sales Tax Tables

Alabama 4.0000%

Income At least	But less than	Exemptions 1	2	3	4	5	Over 5
$0	$20,000	195	236	265	288	307	333
20,000	30,000	299	361	404	437	466	506
30,000	40,000	351	423	473	512	545	591
40,000	50,000	396	476	532	575	612	663
50,000	60,000	436	524	584	632	671	728
60,000	70,000	472	567	632	683	725	786
70,000	80,000	507	607	676	731	776	841
80,000	90,000	538	645	718	775	823	891
90,000	100,000	568	680	757	817	867	939
100,000	120,000	608	726	808	872	925	1001
120,000	140,000	662	790	878	947	1005	1086
140,000	160,000	709	845	939	1012	1074	1161
160,000	180,000	756	901	1000	1077	1142	1234
180,000	200,000	799	950	1054	1136	1204	1300
200,000 or more		1010	1198	1326	1426	1510	1628

Arizona 5.6000%

Income At least	But less than	Exemptions 1	2	3	4	5	Over 5
$0	$20,000	183	212	231	245	257	274
20,000	30,000	324	374	407	432	453	482
30,000	40,000	400	462	502	533	559	595
40,000	50,000	468	539	587	623	653	694
50,000	60,000	530	610	664	705	738	785
60,000	70,000	587	676	735	781	818	869
70,000	80,000	643	740	804	853	894	950
80,000	90,000	694	799	868	922	965	1026
90,000	100,000	744	856	930	987	1034	1099
100,000	120,000	810	932	1013	1074	1125	1196
120,000	140,000	903	1038	1127	1196	1252	1330
140,000	160,000	984	1132	1229	1303	1365	1450
160,000	180,000	1067	1226	1331	1412	1478	1571
180,000	200,000	1142	1313	1425	1511	1582	1680
200,000 or more		1530	1755	1905	2019	2113	2244

Arkansas 6.0000%

Income At least	But less than	Exemptions 1	2	3	4	5	Over 5
$0	$20,000	297	358	399	432	459	498
20,000	30,000	478	573	638	690	732	793
30,000	40,000	570	683	760	821	871	943
40,000	50,000	650	777	865	933	991	1072
50,000	60,000	721	862	959	1034	1098	1187
60,000	70,000	787	940	1044	1126	1195	1292
70,000	80,000	848	1013	1125	1213	1287	1391
80,000	90,000	906	1080	1200	1294	1372	1483
90,000	100,000	960	1145	1271	1370	1453	1569
100,000	120,000	1032	1229	1364	1470	1559	1684
120,000	140,000	1130	1346	1493	1608	1705	1841
140,000	160,000	1216	1447	1605	1729	1832	1978
160,000	180,000	1302	1548	1717	1849	1958	2114
180,000	200,000	1380	1640	1818	1957	2073	2237
200,000 or more		1769	2097	2321	2496	2643	2849

California[1] 7.2500%

Income At least	But less than	Exemptions 1	2	3	4	5	Over 5
$0	$20,000	195	227	249	265	279	298
20,000	30,000	346	401	438	467	491	524
30,000	40,000	427	495	541	576	605	646
40,000	50,000	499	578	631	672	706	753
50,000	60,000	565	655	715	761	799	852
60,000	70,000	627	726	792	843	885	943
70,000	80,000	686	794	866	921	967	1031
80,000	90,000	741	858	935	995	1044	1113
90,000	100,000	794	919	1002	1066	1119	1192
100,000	120,000	865	1000	1090	1160	1217	1297
120,000	140,000	964	1114	1214	1291	1355	1444
140,000	160,000	1052	1215	1324	1407	1477	1573
160,000	180,000	1140	1317	1434	1525	1600	1704
180,000	200,000	1221	1410	1535	1632	1712	1823
200,000 or more		1637	1887	2053	2181	2287	2435

Colorado 2.9000%

Income At least	But less than	Exemptions 1	2	3	4	5	Over 5
$0	$20,000	93	107	117	124	130	138
20,000	30,000	155	179	194	206	216	229
30,000	40,000	188	216	235	249	261	277
40,000	50,000	217	249	270	287	300	318
50,000	60,000	243	279	303	321	335	356
60,000	70,000	267	306	332	352	368	391
70,000	80,000	290	332	360	382	399	423
80,000	90,000	312	357	387	409	428	454
90,000	100,000	332	380	412	436	456	483
100,000	120,000	359	411	445	471	492	522
120,000	140,000	397	453	491	519	543	575
140,000	160,000	430	491	531	562	587	622
160,000	180,000	463	529	572	605	632	670
180,000	200,000	493	563	609	644	673	712
200,000 or more		646	736	795	841	878	929

Connecticut[2] 6.0000%

Income At least	But less than	Exemptions 1	2	3	4	5	Over 5
$0	$20,000	179	202	217	228	238	250
20,000	30,000	317	358	384	404	421	443
30,000	40,000	392	442	475	499	520	548
40,000	50,000	458	516	555	584	607	640
50,000	60,000	519	585	628	661	687	724
60,000	70,000	575	648	696	732	762	803
70,000	80,000	629	709	761	801	833	878
80,000	90,000	680	766	823	865	900	949
90,000	100,000	729	821	881	927	965	1016
100,000	120,000	793	894	960	1009	1050	1106
120,000	140,000	884	996	1069	1124	1169	1232
140,000	160,000	964	1086	1165	1226	1275	1343
160,000	180,000	1044	1176	1263	1328	1381	1455
180,000	200,000	1118	1259	1351	1421	1478	1557
200,000 or more		1495	1684	1807	1900	1976	2081

District of Columbia[2] 5.7500%

Income At least	But less than	Exemptions 1	2	3	4	5	Over 5
$0	$20,000	153	175	190	201	210	223
20,000	30,000	273	312	337	357	373	396
30,000	40,000	338	386	417	442	462	489
40,000	50,000	395	451	488	517	540	572
50,000	60,000	448	511	553	585	612	648
60,000	70,000	497	567	614	649	678	719
70,000	80,000	544	621	672	710	742	787
80,000	90,000	588	671	726	768	802	850
90,000	100,000	631	720	778	823	860	911
100,000	120,000	687	784	848	897	937	992
120,000	140,000	766	874	945	999	1044	1105
140,000	160,000	836	953	1031	1090	1138	1206
160,000	180,000	907	1034	1117	1181	1234	1307
180,000	200,000	971	1107	1197	1265	1321	1399
200,000 or more		1302	1484	1603	1694	1769	1873

Florida 6.0000%

Income At least	But less than	Exemptions 1	2	3	4	5	Over 5
$0	$20,000	192	226	249	266	281	301
20,000	30,000	335	393	431	462	486	521
30,000	40,000	411	482	529	566	596	639
40,000	50,000	479	561	615	658	693	743
50,000	60,000	541	632	694	742	782	837
60,000	70,000	598	699	767	820	863	924
70,000	80,000	653	763	837	894	941	1008
80,000	90,000	704	822	902	964	1015	1086
90,000	100,000	753	880	964	1030	1085	1161
100,000	120,000	819	956	1047	1119	1178	1260
120,000	140,000	910	1061	1163	1242	1307	1398
140,000	160,000	990	1155	1265	1351	1421	1520
160,000	180,000	1072	1249	1368	1460	1536	1643
180,000	200,000	1146	1335	1462	1560	1641	1755
200,000 or more		1524	1773	1940	2069	2176	2326

Georgia 4.0000%

Income At least	But less than	Exemptions 1	2	3	4	5	Over 5
$0	$20,000	137	156	169	179	187	197
20,000	30,000	230	261	282	298	311	328
30,000	40,000	278	316	341	360	376	397
40,000	50,000	321	364	393	414	432	457
50,000	60,000	359	408	439	464	483	511
60,000	70,000	394	448	482	509	530	560
70,000	80,000	428	486	523	552	575	607
80,000	90,000	460	521	562	592	617	651
90,000	100,000	490	555	598	630	657	693
100,000	120,000	530	600	646	681	710	749
120,000	140,000	585	662	713	751	783	826
140,000	160,000	634	717	772	813	847	893
160,000	180,000	682	772	831	875	911	961
180,000	200,000	727	822	884	931	970	1023
200,000 or more		952	1075	1155	1216	1265	1334

Hawaii[2] 4.0000%

Income At least	But less than	Exemptions 1	2	3	4	5	Over 5
$0	$20,000	207	250	279	302	321	349
20,000	30,000	333	401	447	483	513	556
30,000	40,000	398	477	532	575	611	661
40,000	50,000	453	544	605	654	694	752
50,000	60,000	503	603	671	725	769	833
60,000	70,000	549	657	731	789	838	906
70,000	80,000	592	708	788	850	902	976
80,000	90,000	632	756	840	907	962	1040
90,000	100,000	670	801	890	960	1019	1101
100,000	120,000	720	860	956	1031	1093	1182
120,000	140,000	789	941	1045	1127	1195	1292
140,000	160,000	849	1012	1124	1212	1285	1388
160,000	180,000	909	1083	1202	1296	1374	1484
180,000	200,000	963	1147	1273	1372	1454	1570
200,000 or more		1235	1467	1626	1750	1854	2001

Idaho 5.5000%

Income At least	But less than	Exemptions 1	2	3	4	5	Over 5
$0	$20,000	266	323	363	394	420	458
20,000	30,000	408	494	553	599	638	693
30,000	40,000	479	579	647	701	746	810
40,000	50,000	540	651	727	787	838	909
50,000	60,000	595	716	799	865	919	997
60,000	70,000	644	774	864	934	993	1077
70,000	80,000	691	830	925	1000	1063	1152
80,000	90,000	734	881	981	1061	1127	1221
90,000	100,000	775	929	1035	1118	1187	1286
100,000	120,000	829	992	1105	1193	1267	1372
120,000	140,000	903	1079	1200	1295	1375	1488
140,000	160,000	967	1155	1284	1385	1470	1590
160,000	180,000	1031	1230	1366	1474	1563	1690
180,000	200,000	1089	1298	1441	1554	1648	1781
200,000 or more		1378	1635	1812	1950	2066	2230

Illinois 6.2500%

Income At least	But less than	Exemptions 1	2	3	4	5	Over 5
$0	$20,000	199	233	256	273	288	308
20,000	30,000	346	403	442	472	497	531
30,000	40,000	424	494	542	578	608	650
40,000	50,000	493	574	629	671	706	755
50,000	60,000	556	648	709	756	795	850
60,000	70,000	615	715	783	835	878	938
70,000	80,000	671	780	853	910	957	1022
80,000	90,000	723	841	920	980	1031	1101
90,000	100,000	773	899	983	1048	1101	1176
100,000	120,000	840	976	1067	1137	1195	1276
120,000	140,000	933	1083	1184	1261	1326	1415
140,000	160,000	1015	1178	1287	1371	1441	1538
160,000	180,000	1098	1274	1391	1482	1557	1662
180,000	200,000	1173	1360	1486	1583	1662	1774
200,000 or more		1558	1805	1969	2096	2201	2347

Indiana[2] 6.0000%

Income At least	But less than	Exemptions 1	2	3	4	5	Over 5
$0	$20,000	208	243	266	283	298	318
20,000	30,000	343	398	435	463	487	519
30,000	40,000	413	479	523	556	584	623
40,000	50,000	474	549	599	637	669	713
50,000	60,000	529	612	668	710	745	794
60,000	70,000	580	671	731	777	815	869
70,000	80,000	628	726	791	841	882	939
80,000	90,000	673	777	846	900	944	1005
90,000	100,000	716	826	900	956	1002	1067
100,000	120,000	773	891	970	1030	1080	1150
120,000	140,000	851	981	1067	1133	1188	1264
140,000	160,000	920	1059	1152	1223	1282	1364
160,000	180,000	989	1138	1237	1313	1376	1464
180,000	200,000	1052	1210	1315	1395	1462	1554
200,000 or more		1369	1571	1705	1808	1892	2010

Iowa 5.0000%

Income At least	But less than	Exemptions 1	2	3	4	5	Over 5
$0	$20,000	177	204	223	237	248	264
20,000	30,000	308	355	387	411	431	458
30,000	40,000	378	436	474	504	528	562
40,000	50,000	440	507	551	585	614	653
50,000	60,000	496	572	622	660	692	736
60,000	70,000	548	631	687	729	764	813
70,000	80,000	598	689	749	795	833	886
80,000	90,000	645	742	807	857	898	955
90,000	100,000	689	794	863	916	959	1020
100,000	120,000	749	862	937	994	1042	1107
120,000	140,000	831	956	1039	1103	1155	1228
140,000	160,000	904	1040	1130	1199	1256	1335
160,000	180,000	978	1124	1222	1296	1358	1443
180,000	200,000	1044	1201	1305	1384	1450	1541
200,000 or more		1386	1592	1729	1833	1920	2040

Kansas 5.3000%

Income At least	But less than	Exemptions 1	2	3	4	5	Over 5
$0	$20,000	256	313	352	383	409	446
20,000	30,000	408	495	556	604	644	702
30,000	40,000	485	588	659	716	763	831
40,000	50,000	551	667	748	811	865	941
50,000	60,000	611	738	827	897	956	1040
60,000	70,000	665	803	899	975	1039	1129
70,000	80,000	716	864	967	1048	1117	1214
80,000	90,000	763	921	1030	1116	1189	1292
90,000	100,000	808	975	1090	1181	1257	1366
100,000	120,000	868	1045	1168	1265	1347	1463
120,000	140,000	949	1142	1276	1381	1470	1596
140,000	160,000	1020	1227	1370	1482	1577	1712
160,000	180,000	1091	1311	1463	1583	1684	1827
180,000	200,000	1155	1387	1547	1674	1780	1931
200,000 or more		1475	1766	1967	2125	2258	2447

Kentucky[2] 6.0000%

Income At least	But less than	Exemptions 1	2	3	4	5	Over 5
$0	$20,000	202	234	255	271	285	303
20,000	30,000	335	387	421	447	469	499
30,000	40,000	405	466	507	539	564	600
40,000	50,000	465	536	582	618	647	688
50,000	60,000	520	599	650	690	723	768
60,000	70,000	571	656	713	756	792	841
70,000	80,000	619	711	772	819	857	910
80,000	90,000	664	762	827	877	918	975
90,000	100,000	707	811	880	933	976	1037
100,000	120,000	763	876	950	1007	1053	1118
120,000	140,000	842	965	1046	1108	1159	1230
140,000	160,000	911	1043	1131	1198	1253	1329
160,000	180,000	980	1122	1216	1287	1346	1428
180,000	200,000	1043	1193	1293	1369	1431	1518
200,000 or more		1361	1555	1682	1779	1859	1970

Louisiana 4.0000%

Income At least	But less than	Exemptions 1	2	3	4	5	Over 5
$0	$20,000	141	161	175	185	194	205
20,000	30,000	245	281	304	322	336	356
30,000	40,000	302	345	373	395	413	437
40,000	50,000	351	401	434	459	480	508
50,000	60,000	396	452	490	518	541	573
60,000	70,000	438	500	541	572	598	633
70,000	80,000	478	545	590	624	652	691
80,000	90,000	515	588	636	673	703	744
90,000	100,000	551	629	680	719	751	796
100,000	120,000	598	683	739	781	816	864
120,000	140,000	664	758	820	867	905	959
140,000	160,000	723	825	892	943	984	1042
160,000	180,000	782	892	964	1019	1064	1127
180,000	200,000	835	953	1030	1088	1137	1203
200,000 or more		1109	1264	1365	1443	1506	1594

Maine[2] 5.0000%

Income At least	But less than	Exemptions 1	2	3	4	5	Over 5
$0	$20,000	129	151	165	177	186	199
20,000	30,000	228	266	291	311	327	350
30,000	40,000	282	328	359	383	403	431
40,000	50,000	329	383	419	447	470	503
50,000	60,000	373	433	474	506	532	568
60,000	70,000	413	480	525	560	589	629
70,000	80,000	452	525	574	612	643	687
80,000	90,000	489	567	620	661	695	742
90,000	100,000	524	608	664	708	744	794
100,000	120,000	570	662	723	770	809	864
120,000	140,000	635	737	805	857	901	961
140,000	160,000	693	803	877	934	981	1048
160,000	180,000	751	870	950	1012	1063	1134
180,000	200,000	805	932	1017	1083	1137	1214
200,000 or more		1078	1247	1359	1447	1519	1619

Maryland[2] 5.0000%

Income At least	But less than	Exemptions 1	2	3	4	5	Over 5
$0	$20,000	158	184	202	215	227	242
20,000	30,000	275	319	349	372	391	418
30,000	40,000	338	392	428	456	479	512
40,000	50,000	394	456	498	530	557	594
50,000	60,000	445	514	561	597	627	670
60,000	70,000	492	568	620	660	693	739
70,000	80,000	537	620	676	719	755	806
80,000	90,000	580	669	729	775	814	868
90,000	100,000	620	715	779	829	870	927
100,000	120,000	674	777	846	900	944	1006
120,000	140,000	749	863	939	999	1048	1116
140,000	160,000	816	939	1022	1086	1139	1214
160,000	180,000	883	1016	1105	1174	1231	1311
180,000	200,000	945	1086	1181	1254	1315	1400
200,000 or more		1259	1444	1568	1664	1743	1855

Massachusetts[2] 5.0000%

Income At least	But less than	Exemptions 1	2	3	4	5	Over 5
$0	$20,000	145	164	177	187	196	207
20,000	30,000	250	284	306	323	337	356
30,000	40,000	307	348	375	395	412	436
40,000	50,000	357	404	435	459	478	505
50,000	60,000	402	456	490	517	539	569
60,000	70,000	444	503	541	571	595	628
70,000	80,000	485	548	590	622	648	684
80,000	90,000	522	591	636	670	698	737
90,000	100,000	558	631	679	716	746	787
100,000	120,000	606	685	737	777	809	854
120,000	140,000	673	760	818	861	897	946
140,000	160,000	732	827	889	936	975	1028
160,000	180,000	791	893	960	1011	1053	1110
180,000	200,000	845	954	1025	1080	1124	1185
200,000 or more		1121	1264	1357	1428	1486	1567

Michigan[2] 6.0000%

Income At least	But less than	Exemptions 1	2	3	4	5	Over 5
$0	$20,000	196	228	250	266	280	299
20,000	30,000	340	395	431	460	483	515
30,000	40,000	417	484	528	563	591	631
40,000	50,000	485	562	614	653	686	732
50,000	60,000	546	633	691	736	773	824
60,000	70,000	604	700	763	812	853	909
70,000	80,000	659	763	832	885	929	991
80,000	90,000	710	822	896	954	1001	1067
90,000	100,000	759	879	958	1019	1070	1140
100,000	120,000	825	954	1040	1106	1161	1237
120,000	140,000	915	1058	1154	1227	1287	1371
140,000	160,000	996	1151	1254	1333	1399	1490
160,000	180,000	1077	1244	1355	1441	1511	1610
180,000	200,000	1151	1329	1447	1539	1614	1718
200,000 or more		1528	1762	1917	2037	2135	2273

Minnesota 6.5000%

Income At least	But less than	Exemptions 1	2	3	4	5	Over 5
$0	$20,000	184	210	228	242	253	269
20,000	30,000	323	369	400	424	443	470
30,000	40,000	398	455	493	522	546	579
40,000	50,000	465	531	575	608	636	674
50,000	60,000	526	600	650	688	719	762
60,000	70,000	582	665	719	761	795	843
70,000	80,000	636	726	786	831	869	921
80,000	90,000	687	784	848	897	937	993
90,000	100,000	736	839	908	960	1003	1063
100,000	120,000	801	913	987	1044	1091	1156
120,000	140,000	891	1016	1098	1161	1213	1285
140,000	160,000	971	1107	1196	1264	1321	1399
160,000	180,000	1052	1198	1295	1369	1429	1514
180,000	200,000	1126	1282	1385	1464	1529	1619
200,000 or more		1504	1710	1846	1950	2036	2155

Mississippi[2] 7.0000%

Income At least	But less than	Exemptions 1	2	3	4	5	Over 5
$0	$20,000	347	418	466	505	536	581
20,000	30,000	558	669	745	805	855	926
30,000	40,000	666	797	887	958	1017	1101
40,000	50,000	759	908	1010	1090	1156	1251
50,000	60,000	842	1007	1119	1207	1281	1385
60,000	70,000	918	1097	1219	1315	1395	1508
70,000	80,000	990	1182	1313	1416	1502	1623
80,000	90,000	1057	1261	1401	1510	1601	1730
90,000	100,000	1121	1336	1483	1599	1695	1831
100,000	120,000	1204	1435	1592	1716	1819	1965
120,000	140,000	1319	1570	1742	1877	1989	2148
140,000	160,000	1420	1689	1873	2017	2137	2307
160,000	180,000	1520	1807	2003	2157	2285	2466
180,000	200,000	1611	1914	2121	2283	2418	2610
200,000 or more		2065	2447	2708	2913	3083	3324

Missouri 4.2250%

Income At least	But less than	Exemptions 1	2	3	4	5	Over 5
$0	$20,000	153	179	196	209	220	236
20,000	30,000	252	293	321	343	360	385
30,000	40,000	303	353	386	411	433	462
40,000	50,000	348	405	442	471	495	529
50,000	60,000	389	451	493	525	552	589
60,000	70,000	426	494	540	575	604	644
70,000	80,000	461	535	584	622	653	696
80,000	90,000	494	573	625	665	699	745
90,000	100,000	526	609	664	707	742	791
100,000	120,000	567	657	716	762	800	853
120,000	140,000	625	723	788	838	879	937
140,000	160,000	676	781	851	905	949	1011
160,000	180,000	726	839	914	971	1019	1085
180,000	200,000	772	891	971	1032	1082	1152
200,000 or more		1005	1157	1258	1336	1400	1490

Nebraska 5.5000%

Income At least	But less than	Exemptions 1	2	3	4	5	Over 5
$0	$20,000	194	223	242	256	268	285
20,000	30,000	337	387	420	445	466	494
30,000	40,000	414	475	515	546	571	606
40,000	50,000	482	553	599	635	664	705
50,000	60,000	544	623	676	716	749	794
60,000	70,000	601	689	747	791	827	877
70,000	80,000	656	751	814	862	902	957
80,000	90,000	707	810	878	929	972	1031
90,000	100,000	756	866	938	994	1039	1102
100,000	120,000	821	940	1019	1079	1128	1196
120,000	140,000	912	1044	1131	1197	1252	1327
140,000	160,000	992	1135	1230	1302	1361	1443
160,000	180,000	1073	1227	1329	1407	1471	1560
180,000	200,000	1146	1311	1420	1503	1571	1666
200,000 or more		1521	1739	1882	1991	2081	2206

(Continued)

2005 Optional State Sales Tax Tables *(Continued)*

Nevada[3] 6.5000%

Income At least	Income But less than	Exemptions 1	2	3	4	5	Over 5
$0	$20,000	213	246	269	286	300	320
20,000	30,000	368	426	464	493	517	550
30,000	40,000	451	521	568	603	633	673
40,000	50,000	525	605	659	700	734	781
50,000	60,000	592	682	742	789	827	880
60,000	70,000	654	753	820	871	912	971
70,000	80,000	713	821	893	949	994	1057
80,000	90,000	768	885	962	1022	1071	1139
90,000	100,000	821	946	1028	1092	1144	1216
100,000	120,000	892	1027	1116	1185	1241	1320
120,000	140,000	990	1139	1238	1314	1376	1463
140,000	160,000	1077	1239	1346	1428	1496	1590
160,000	180,000	1164	1339	1454	1543	1616	1717
180,000	200,000	1244	1430	1553	1647	1725	1833
200,000 or more		1651	1895	2056	2180	2282	2423

New Jersey[2,4] 6.0000%

Income At least	Income But less than	Exemptions 1	2	3	4	5	Over 5
$0	$20,000	178	202	217	229	239	253
20,000	30,000	314	356	384	405	422	446
30,000	40,000	388	440	474	500	521	551
40,000	50,000	453	514	554	584	609	643
50,000	60,000	513	582	627	661	689	728
60,000	70,000	569	645	694	732	763	806
70,000	80,000	622	705	759	800	834	881
80,000	90,000	672	761	820	865	901	952
90,000	100,000	720	815	878	926	965	1019
100,000	120,000	784	888	956	1008	1050	1109
120,000	140,000	872	988	1064	1122	1169	1234
140,000	160,000	951	1077	1160	1222	1274	1345
160,000	180,000	1030	1167	1256	1324	1380	1457
180,000	200,000	1103	1249	1344	1417	1476	1559
200,000 or more		1473	1668	1795	1892	1971	2081

New Mexico 5.0000%

Income At least	Income But less than	Exemptions 1	2	3	4	5	Over 5
$0	$20,000	184	213	231	246	257	274
20,000	30,000	321	369	401	426	446	475
30,000	40,000	393	453	492	522	547	582
40,000	50,000	458	527	572	607	636	676
50,000	60,000	516	594	645	685	717	762
60,000	70,000	571	656	713	756	792	841
70,000	80,000	622	716	777	824	863	917
80,000	90,000	671	771	838	888	930	988
90,000	100,000	717	824	895	950	994	1056
100,000	120,000	779	895	972	1031	1079	1146
120,000	140,000	865	994	1079	1144	1197	1272
140,000	160,000	941	1080	1173	1243	1302	1382
160,000	180,000	1017	1168	1267	1344	1406	1494
180,000	200,000	1087	1247	1354	1435	1502	1595
200,000 or more		1441	1653	1793	1900	1988	2111

New York 4.1034%

Income At least	Income But less than	Exemptions 1	2	3	4	5	Over 5
$0	$20,000	140	163	177	189	198	211
20,000	30,000	246	284	309	329	345	367
30,000	40,000	302	349	380	404	423	451
40,000	50,000	352	406	442	470	493	525
50,000	60,000	397	459	499	530	556	592
60,000	70,000	439	507	552	586	615	654
70,000	80,000	480	553	602	640	671	714
80,000	90,000	518	597	650	690	723	770
90,000	100,000	554	638	695	738	774	823
100,000	120,000	602	694	755	802	840	894
120,000	140,000	669	771	838	890	933	993
140,000	160,000	728	839	912	969	1015	1080
160,000	180,000	788	907	987	1048	1098	1168
180,000	200,000	842	970	1054	1119	1173	1248
200,000 or more		1119	1288	1400	1486	1557	1655

North Carolina 4.5000%

Income At least	Income But less than	Exemptions 1	2	3	4	5	Over 5
$0	$20,000	152	179	197	211	222	239
20,000	30,000	262	307	337	361	380	408
30,000	40,000	321	375	412	441	464	497
40,000	50,000	372	435	478	511	538	576
50,000	60,000	419	490	537	574	605	648
60,000	70,000	463	540	593	633	667	714
70,000	80,000	504	589	645	689	726	777
80,000	90,000	543	634	695	742	781	835
90,000	100,000	580	677	742	792	834	892
100,000	120,000	629	734	804	859	904	966
120,000	140,000	698	813	891	951	1001	1070
140,000	160,000	758	884	968	1033	1086	1161
160,000	180,000	819	954	1045	1115	1172	1253
180,000	200,000	875	1018	1115	1189	1251	1337
200,000 or more		1158	1346	1472	1569	1649	1762

North Dakota 5.0000%

Income At least	Income But less than	Exemptions 1	2	3	4	5	Over 5
$0	$20,000	163	191	210	225	237	254
20,000	30,000	281	328	360	385	406	435
30,000	40,000	345	402	441	471	496	531
40,000	50,000	401	467	511	546	575	616
50,000	60,000	452	526	576	615	647	693
60,000	70,000	499	581	635	678	714	764
70,000	80,000	545	633	692	739	777	831
80,000	90,000	587	682	746	795	837	895
90,000	100,000	628	729	797	850	894	955
100,000	120,000	682	791	864	922	969	1036
120,000	140,000	757	877	958	1022	1074	1148
140,000	160,000	824	954	1042	1110	1167	1246
160,000	180,000	891	1031	1125	1199	1260	1346
180,000	200,000	952	1101	1202	1280	1345	1436
200,000 or more		1266	1460	1590	1692	1777	1896

Ohio 5.7500%

Income At least	Income But less than	Exemptions 1	2	3	4	5	Over 5
$0	$20,000	204	236	258	274	288	306
20,000	30,000	351	405	441	469	492	524
30,000	40,000	429	495	539	573	600	639
40,000	50,000	497	574	624	663	695	740
50,000	60,000	559	645	702	746	782	832
60,000	70,000	617	711	774	822	862	917
70,000	80,000	672	774	842	895	938	997
80,000	90,000	723	833	906	962	1009	1073
90,000	100,000	772	890	967	1027	1076	1145
100,000	120,000	838	964	1049	1113	1166	1240
120,000	140,000	928	1068	1161	1232	1291	1373
140,000	160,000	1008	1159	1260	1337	1401	1490
160,000	180,000	1088	1251	1360	1443	1512	1607
180,000	200,000	1161	1335	1450	1539	1612	1713
200,000 or more		1531	1759	1910	2026	2122	2254

Oklahoma 4.5000%

Income At least	Income But less than	Exemptions 1	2	3	4	5	Over 5
$0	$20,000	205	246	274	297	315	342
20,000	30,000	333	398	443	478	508	549
30,000	40,000	399	477	530	571	606	655
40,000	50,000	457	544	604	651	691	747
50,000	60,000	509	605	672	724	767	829
60,000	70,000	556	661	733	790	837	904
70,000	80,000	601	714	791	852	903	975
80,000	90,000	643	763	846	910	964	1041
90,000	100,000	683	810	897	965	1022	1103
100,000	120,000	736	872	965	1038	1099	1186
120,000	140,000	809	957	1058	1138	1205	1299
140,000	160,000	873	1031	1140	1226	1297	1398
160,000	180,000	937	1106	1222	1313	1389	1497
180,000	200,000	995	1174	1296	1392	1473	1586
200,000 or more		1288	1513	1668	1789	1891	2034

Pennsylvania 6.0000%

Income At least	Income But less than	Exemptions 1	2	3	4	5	Over 5
$0	$20,000	176	201	219	232	242	257
20,000	30,000	307	352	381	404	423	449
30,000	40,000	378	432	468	496	519	551
40,000	50,000	440	503	545	578	604	641
50,000	60,000	497	568	616	652	682	723
60,000	70,000	549	628	681	721	754	800
70,000	80,000	600	686	743	786	822	872
80,000	90,000	647	740	801	848	887	941
90,000	100,000	692	791	857	907	948	1006
100,000	120,000	752	860	931	985	1030	1093
120,000	140,000	836	955	1033	1094	1144	1213
140,000	160,000	909	1039	1124	1190	1244	1319
160,000	180,000	984	1124	1216	1287	1345	1427
180,000	200,000	1052	1201	1299	1375	1437	1524
200,000 or more		1397	1594	1725	1825	1907	2022

Rhode Island[2] 7.0000%

Income At least	Income But less than	Exemptions 1	2	3	4	5	Over 5
$0	$20,000	201	230	249	264	276	293
20,000	30,000	352	402	435	460	481	510
30,000	40,000	433	494	534	565	591	626
40,000	50,000	504	575	622	658	687	728
50,000	60,000	570	650	702	743	776	822
60,000	70,000	631	719	777	821	858	909
70,000	80,000	689	785	848	896	936	991
80,000	90,000	744	847	915	967	1010	1069
90,000	100,000	796	906	979	1034	1080	1143
100,000	120,000	865	985	1064	1124	1174	1242
120,000	140,000	962	1095	1182	1249	1304	1380
140,000	160,000	1048	1192	1287	1359	1419	1501
160,000	180,000	1135	1290	1392	1470	1535	1624
180,000	200,000	1213	1379	1488	1572	1640	1735
200,000 or more		1617	1835	1979	2089	2180	2305

South Carolina 5.0000%

Income At least	Income But less than	Exemptions 1	2	3	4	5	Over 5
$0	$20,000	235	288	324	353	378	412
20,000	30,000	374	456	512	557	595	648
30,000	40,000	445	541	608	660	705	768
40,000	50,000	506	614	689	749	799	870
50,000	60,000	561	680	763	828	883	961
60,000	70,000	611	740	829	900	959	1044
70,000	80,000	658	796	892	968	1032	1122
80,000	90,000	702	849	951	1031	1099	1195
90,000	100,000	744	899	1006	1091	1162	1263
100,000	120,000	798	964	1079	1169	1245	1353
120,000	140,000	874	1054	1179	1277	1360	1477
140,000	160,000	940	1133	1266	1371	1459	1585
160,000	180,000	1006	1211	1353	1465	1559	1692
180,000	200,000	1066	1282	1432	1550	1649	1789
200,000 or more		1366	1637	1824	1972	2096	2272

South Dakota 4.0000%

Income At least	Income But less than	Exemptions 1	2	3	4	5	Over 5
$0	$20,000	199	240	269	291	310	337
20,000	30,000	320	385	430	466	495	537
30,000	40,000	382	460	513	554	589	639
40,000	50,000	436	523	583	631	670	726
50,000	60,000	484	581	647	699	743	804
60,000	70,000	528	633	705	761	809	876
70,000	80,000	570	682	760	820	871	943
80,000	90,000	608	728	810	875	929	1006
90,000	100,000	645	771	858	927	984	1065
100,000	120,000	693	829	922	995	1056	1142
120,000	140,000	759	907	1009	1088	1155	1249
140,000	160,000	817	976	1085	1170	1241	1342
160,000	180,000	875	1044	1160	1251	1327	1435
180,000	200,000	928	1106	1229	1325	1405	1519
200,000 or more		1190	1415	1570	1691	1792	1935

Tennessee 7.0000%

Income At least	Income But less than	Exemptions 1	2	3	4	5	Over 5
$0	$20,000	322	386	430	465	494	534
20,000	30,000	525	627	697	752	798	863
30,000	40,000	629	751	835	900	954	1032
40,000	50,000	719	858	953	1027	1089	1177
50,000	60,000	801	955	1059	1142	1210	1307
60,000	70,000	876	1043	1157	1246	1321	1426
70,000	80,000	946	1126	1249	1345	1425	1539
80,000	90,000	1012	1203	1334	1437	1522	1643
90,000	100,000	1074	1277	1416	1524	1614	1742
100,000	120,000	1156	1374	1523	1639	1736	1873
120,000	140,000	1270	1508	1670	1797	1903	2052
140,000	160,000	1369	1625	1799	1935	2049	2209
160,000	180,000	1469	1741	1927	2073	2194	2366
180,000	200,000	1558	1847	2044	2198	2326	2507
200,000 or more		2009	2376	2626	2822	2985	3214

Texas 6.2500%

Income At least	Income But less than	Exemptions 1	2	3	4	5	Over 5
$0	$20,000	216	250	273	291	305	325
20,000	30,000	377	436	475	505	530	565
30,000	40,000	464	536	584	621	651	693
40,000	50,000	540	624	679	722	757	806
50,000	60,000	610	704	767	815	854	909
60,000	70,000	674	778	847	900	944	1005
70,000	80,000	736	849	924	982	1030	1096
80,000	90,000	794	916	997	1059	1110	1181
90,000	100,000	849	979	1066	1132	1187	1263
100,000	120,000	923	1064	1158	1230	1289	1372
120,000	140,000	1025	1181	1285	1365	1431	1523
140,000	160,000	1115	1285	1398	1485	1556	1656
160,000	180,000	1206	1390	1512	1606	1683	1790
180,000	200,000	1289	1485	1615	1715	1798	1912
200,000 or more		1713	1972	2143	2275	2384	2535

Utah 4.7500%

Income At least	Income But less than	Exemptions 1	2	3	4	5	Over 5
$0	$20,000	232	282	315	342	365	397
20,000	30,000	371	448	501	543	578	627
30,000	40,000	442	533	595	645	686	744
40,000	50,000	503	606	676	732	778	844
50,000	60,000	558	671	749	810	861	934
60,000	70,000	608	730	815	881	937	1015
70,000	80,000	655	787	877	948	1008	1092
80,000	90,000	699	839	935	1010	1073	1163
90,000	100,000	741	888	989	1069	1136	1230
100,000	120,000	795	953	1061	1146	1218	1319
120,000	140,000	871	1042	1160	1253	1330	1440
140,000	160,000	936	1120	1246	1345	1428	1546
160,000	180,000	1002	1197	1332	1437	1526	1651
180,000	200,000	1061	1268	1409	1521	1614	1746
200,000 or more		1358	1617	1795	1935	2052	2218

Vermont 6.0000%

Income At least	Income But less than	Exemptions 1	2	3	4	5	Over 5
$0	$20,000	116	130	139	146	152	160
20,000	30,000	216	243	260	273	284	298
30,000	40,000	273	306	327	344	357	376
40,000	50,000	323	363	388	408	424	446
50,000	60,000	370	415	445	467	485	511
60,000	70,000	414	465	498	523	543	571
70,000	80,000	457	513	549	576	599	630
80,000	90,000	497	558	597	627	652	686
90,000	100,000	536	601	644	676	703	739
100,000	120,000	589	660	707	742	771	811
120,000	140,000	662	742	795	835	867	912
140,000	160,000	728	816	874	917	953	1003
160,000	180,000	794	891	954	1001	1040	1094
180,000	200,000	856	959	1027	1079	1121	1179
200,000 or more		1175	1318	1410	1481	1539	1618

Virginia[5] 5.0000%

Income At least	Income But less than	Exemptions 1	2	3	4	5	Over 5
$0	$20,000	168	196	214	228	240	256
20,000	30,000	278	323	352	375	394	420
30,000	40,000	336	389	424	451	474	505
40,000	50,000	386	446	487	518	543	579
50,000	60,000	431	498	543	578	606	646
60,000	70,000	473	546	595	633	664	707
70,000	80,000	512	592	644	685	718	765
80,000	90,000	549	634	690	733	769	819
90,000	100,000	585	674	734	780	817	870
100,000	120,000	631	728	792	841	882	938
120,000	140,000	696	802	872	926	970	1032
140,000	160,000	753	867	942	1000	1048	1114
160,000	180,000	810	932	1012	1074	1126	1197
180,000	200,000	862	991	1076	1142	1196	1271
200,000 or more		1124	1290	1399	1483	1552	1649

Washington 6.5000%

Income At least	Income But less than	Exemptions 1	2	3	4	5	Over 5
$0	$20,000	229	266	291	310	325	347
20,000	30,000	395	458	500	532	559	596
30,000	40,000	484	560	611	650	683	728
40,000	50,000	562	650	709	754	792	844
50,000	60,000	633	732	798	849	891	949
60,000	70,000	698	808	880	936	982	1046
70,000	80,000	761	880	959	1019	1069	1139
80,000	90,000	820	947	1032	1097	1151	1226
90,000	100,000	876	1012	1102	1172	1229	1309
100,000	120,000	950	1097	1195	1270	1333	1419
120,000	140,000	1053	1216	1324	1407	1476	1572
140,000	160,000	1144	1321	1438	1528	1603	1706
160,000	180,000	1236	1426	1552	1650	1730	1842
180,000	200,000	1319	1522	1657	1760	1846	1965
200,000 or more		1744	2009	2186	2322	2434	2590

West Virginia[2] 6.0000%

Income At least	Income But less than	Exemptions 1	2	3	4	5	Over 5
$0	$20,000	299	358	399	432	458	496
20,000	30,000	480	574	639	689	731	791
30,000	40,000	573	684	760	820	870	940
40,000	50,000	653	779	865	933	989	1068
50,000	60,000	724	864	959	1034	1096	1183
60,000	70,000	790	941	1045	1126	1193	1288
70,000	80,000	852	1015	1126	1212	1285	1387
80,000	90,000	910	1083	1201	1293	1370	1479
90,000	100,000	964	1147	1272	1369	1450	1565
100,000	120,000	1036	1232	1365	1470	1557	1679
120,000	140,000	1135	1348	1494	1607	1702	1836
140,000	160,000	1222	1450	1606	1728	1829	1973
160,000	180,000	1308	1552	1718	1848	1956	2109
180,000	200,000	1386	1644	1819	1956	2070	2231
200,000 or more		1777	2102	2323	2496	2640	2843

Wisconsin 5.0000%

Income At least	Income But less than	Exemptions 1	2	3	4	5	Over 5
$0	$20,000	177	203	220	233	244	259
20,000	30,000	308	353	383	406	424	450
30,000	40,000	379	434	470	498	521	552
40,000	50,000	441	505	547	579	606	642
50,000	60,000	498	570	617	653	683	724
60,000	70,000	550	630	682	722	755	800
70,000	80,000	600	687	744	787	823	873
80,000	90,000	647	741	802	849	887	941
90,000	100,000	692	792	857	907	949	1005
100,000	120,000	752	860	931	986	1030	1092
120,000	140,000	835	955	1034	1094	1143	1212
140,000	160,000	909	1039	1124	1190	1243	1318
160,000	180,000	983	1123	1216	1286	1344	1424
180,000	200,000	1051	1200	1299	1374	1436	1521
200,000 or more		1395	1592	1722	1822	1903	2016

Wyoming 4.0000%

Income At least	Income But less than	Exemptions 1	2	3	4	5	Over 5
$0	$20,000	195	236	264	287	305	332
20,000	30,000	312	377	421	456	485	527
30,000	40,000	372	448	501	542	577	626
40,000	50,000	424	510	569	616	655	711
50,000	60,000	470	565	631	682	725	786
60,000	70,000	513	616	687	742	789	855
70,000	80,000	553	663	739	799	849	920
80,000	90,000	590	707	788	852	905	981
90,000	100,000	625	749	835	902	958	1038
100,000	120,000	671	804	896	967	1028	1113
120,000	140,000	735	880	979	1058	1123	1216
140,000	160,000	791	946	1052	1136	1206	1306
160,000	180,000	847	1012	1125	1215	1289	1395
180,000	200,000	897	1071	1191	1285	1364	1476
200,000 or more		1149	1368	1519	1637	1736	1877

[1] The California table includes the 1% uniform local sales tax rate in addition to the 6.25% state sales tax rate.
[2] This state does not have a local general sales tax.
[3] The Nevada table includes the 2.25% uniform local sales tax rate in addition to the 4.25% state sales tax rate.
[4] Residents of Salem County, NJ should deduct only half of the amount in the state table.
[5] The state and local general sales taxes are combined in the Virginia table.

2005 Optional Local Sales Tax Tables

Which Optional Local Sales Tax Table Should I Use?

IF you live in the state of...	AND you live in...	THEN use Local Table...
Alaska	Any locality	C
Arizona	Any locality	B
Arkansas	Texarkana	B
California	Los Angeles County	B
Colorado	Aurora, Greeley, Longmont, or City of Pueblo	B
	Arvada, City of Boulder, Fort Collins, Lakewood, Thornton, or Westminster	C
	Boulder County, Pueblo County, or any other locality	A
Georgia	Any locality	B
Illinois	Arlington Heights, Aurora, Bloomington, Champaign, Chicago, Cicero, Decatur, Elgin, Evanston, Joliet, Palatine, Peoria, Schaumburg, Skokie, Springfield, or Waukegan	B
	Any other locality	A
Louisiana	Any locality	C
New York	New York City	B
North Carolina	Any locality	C

2005 Optional Local Sales Tax Tables A, B, and C

(Based on a local sales tax rate of 1 percent)

Income		Local Table A						Local Table B						Local Table C					
		Exemptions						Exemptions						Exemptions					
At least	But less than	1	2	3	4	5	Over 5	1	2	3	4	5	Over 5	1	2	3	4	5	Over 5
$0	$20,000	32	37	40	43	45	48	41	48	53	57	60	65	50	60	67	72	77	83
20,000	30,000	54	62	67	71	75	79	66	78	87	93	98	105	80	96	107	115	122	132
30,000	40,000	65	75	81	86	90	96	80	94	104	111	118	126	96	114	127	137	145	157
40,000	50,000	75	86	93	99	103	110	92	108	119	127	134	144	109	130	144	155	165	178
50,000	60,000	84	96	104	111	116	123	102	120	132	142	149	161	121	144	160	172	182	197
60,000	70,000	92	106	115	121	127	135	112	131	145	155	163	175	132	157	174	187	198	214
70,000	80,000	100	115	124	132	138	146	121	142	156	167	176	189	142	169	187	202	214	230
80,000	90,000	107	123	133	141	148	157	129	152	167	179	189	202	151	180	200	215	228	245
90,000	100,000	114	131	142	150	157	167	137	161	177	190	200	215	160	191	211	227	241	260
100,000	120,000	124	141	153	162	170	180	148	174	191	204	216	231	172	205	227	244	258	279
120,000	140,000	137	156	169	179	187	198	163	191	210	225	237	254	189	224	248	267	282	304
140,000	160,000	148	169	183	194	202	214	176	206	226	242	255	273	203	241	266	286	303	327
160,000	180,000	159	182	197	208	218	231	189	221	243	260	274	293	217	257	285	306	324	349
180,000	200,000	170	194	210	222	232	245	201	235	258	276	290	311	230	273	301	324	343	369
200,000 or more		222	253	274	289	302	320	260	304	333	356	374	401	295	348	384	413	436	470

APPENDIX B

TAX FORMS

(Tax forms can be obtained from the IRS web site: **http://www.irs.gov**)

Form **1040** Department of the Treasury—Internal Revenue Service
U.S. Individual Income Tax Return **2005** (99) IRS Use Only—Do not write or staple in this space.

For the year Jan. 1–Dec. 31, 2005, or other tax year beginning , 2005, ending , 20 — OMB No. 1545-0074

Label (See instructions on page 16.) **Use the IRS label.** Otherwise, please print or type.

LABEL HERE

Your first name and initial	Last name	**Your social security number**
If a joint return, spouse's first name and initial	Last name	**Spouse's social security number**
Home address (number and street). If you have a P.O. box, see page 16.	Apt. no.	▲ You **must** enter your SSN(s) above. ▲
City, town or post office, state, and ZIP code. If you have a foreign address, see page 16.		Checking a box below will not change your tax or refund.

Presidential Election Campaign ▶ Check here if you, or your spouse if filing jointly, want $3 to go to this fund (see page 16) ▶ ☐ **You** ☐ **Spouse**

Filing Status

Check only one box.

1 ☐ Single
2 ☐ Married filing jointly (even if only one had income)
3 ☐ Married filing separately. Enter spouse's SSN above and full name here. ▶
4 ☐ Head of household (with qualifying person). (See page 17.) If the qualifying person is a child but not your dependent, enter this child's name here. ▶
5 ☐ Qualifying widow(er) with dependent child (see page 17)

Exemptions

6a ☐ **Yourself.** If someone can claim you as a dependent, **do not** check box 6a
b ☐ **Spouse**
c **Dependents:**

(1) First name Last name	(2) Dependent's social security number	(3) Dependent's relationship to you	(4)✓ if qualifying child for child tax credit (see page 19)
			☐
			☐
			☐
			☐

If more than four dependents, see page 19.

d Total number of exemptions claimed

Boxes checked on 6a and 6b ______
No. of children on 6c who:
• **lived with you** ______
• **did not live with you due to divorce or separation (see page 20)** ______
Dependents on 6c not entered above ______
Add numbers on lines above ▶ ☐

Income

Attach Form(s) W-2 here. Also attach Forms W-2G and 1099-R if tax was withheld.

If you did not get a W-2, see page 22.

Enclose, but do not attach, any payment. Also, please use **Form 1040-V.**

7	Wages, salaries, tips, etc. Attach Form(s) W-2		7	
8a	**Taxable** interest. Attach Schedule B if required		8a	
b	**Tax-exempt** interest. **Do not** include on line 8a	8b		
9a	Ordinary dividends. Attach Schedule B if required		9a	
b	Qualified dividends (see page 23)	9b		
10	Taxable refunds, credits, or offsets of state and local income taxes (see page 23)		10	
11	Alimony received		11	
12	Business income or (loss). Attach Schedule C or C-EZ		12	
13	Capital gain or (loss). Attach Schedule D if required. If not required, check here ▶ ☐		13	
14	Other gains or (losses). Attach Form 4797		14	
15a	IRA distributions 15a	**b** Taxable amount (see page 25)	15b	
16a	Pensions and annuities 16a	**b** Taxable amount (see page 25)	16b	
17	Rental real estate, royalties, partnerships, S corporations, trusts, etc. Attach Schedule E		17	
18	Farm income or (loss). Attach Schedule F		18	
19	Unemployment compensation		19	
20a	Social security benefits 20a	**b** Taxable amount (see page 27)	20b	
21	Other income. List type and amount (see page 29)		21	
22	Add the amounts in the far right column for lines 7 through 21. This is your **total income** ▶		22	

Adjusted Gross Income

23	Educator expenses (see page 29)	23		
24	Certain business expenses of reservists, performing artists, and fee-basis government officials. Attach Form 2106 or 2106-EZ	24		
25	Health savings account deduction. Attach Form 8889	25		
26	Moving expenses. Attach Form 3903	26		
27	One-half of self-employment tax. Attach Schedule SE	27		
28	Self-employed SEP, SIMPLE, and qualified plans	28		
29	Self-employed health insurance deduction (see page 30)	29		
30	Penalty on early withdrawal of savings	30		
31a	Alimony paid **b** Recipient's SSN ▶	31a		
32	IRA deduction (see page 31)	32		
33	Student loan interest deduction (see page 33)	33		
34	Tuition and fees deduction (see page 34)	34		
35	Domestic production activities deduction. Attach Form 8903	35		
36	Add lines 23 through 31a and 32 through 35		36	
37	Subtract line 36 from line 22. This is your **adjusted gross income** ▶		37	

For Disclosure, Privacy Act, and Paperwork Reduction Act Notice, see page 78. Cat. No. 11320B Form **1040** (2005)

Form 1040 (2005) Page 2

Tax and Credits

Standard Deduction for—

- People who checked any box on line 39a or 39b **or** who can be claimed as a dependent, see page 36.
- All others:

Single or Married filing separately, $5,000

Married filing jointly or Qualifying widow(er), $10,000

Head of household, $7,300

Line	Description		
38	Amount from line 37 (adjusted gross income)		38
39a	Check if: ☐ **You** were born before January 2, 1941, ☐ Blind. ☐ **Spouse** was born before January 2, 1941, ☐ Blind. **Total boxes checked** ▶ 39a		
b	If your spouse itemizes on a separate return or you were a dual-status alien, see page 35 and check here ▶39b ☐		
40	**Itemized deductions** (from Schedule A) **or** your **standard deduction** (see left margin)		40
41	Subtract line 40 from line 38		41
42	If line 38 is over $109,475, or you provided housing to a person displaced by Hurricane Katrina, see page 37. Otherwise, multiply $3,200 by the total number of exemptions claimed on line 6d		42
43	**Taxable income.** Subtract line 42 from line 41. If line 42 is more than line 41, enter -0-		43
44	**Tax** (see page 37). Check if any tax is from: **a** ☐ Form(s) 8814 **b** ☐ Form 4972		44
45	**Alternative minimum tax** (see page 39). Attach Form 6251		45
46	Add lines 44 and 45 ▶		46
47	Foreign tax credit. Attach Form 1116 if required	47	
48	Credit for child and dependent care expenses. Attach Form 2441	48	
49	Credit for the elderly or the disabled. Attach Schedule R	49	
50	Education credits. Attach Form 8863	50	
51	Retirement savings contributions credit. Attach Form 8880	51	
52	Child tax credit (see page 41). Attach Form 8901 if required	52	
53	Adoption credit. Attach Form 8839	53	
54	Credits from: **a** ☐ Form 8396 **b** ☐ Form 8859	54	
55	Other credits. Check applicable box(es): **a** ☐ Form 3800 **b** ☐ Form 8801 **c** ☐ Form ______	55	
56	Add lines 47 through 55. These are your **total credits**		56
57	Subtract line 56 from line 46. If line 56 is more than line 46, enter -0- ▶		57

Other Taxes

Line	Description		
58	Self-employment tax. Attach Schedule SE		58
59	Social security and Medicare tax on tip income not reported to employer. Attach Form 4137		59
60	Additional tax on IRAs, other qualified retirement plans, etc. Attach Form 5329 if required		60
61	Advance earned income credit payments from Form(s) W-2		61
62	Household employment taxes. Attach Schedule H		62
63	Add lines 57 through 62. This is your **total tax** ▶		63

Payments

If you have a qualifying child, attach Schedule EIC.

Line	Description		
64	Federal income tax withheld from Forms W-2 and 1099	64	
65	2005 estimated tax payments and amount applied from 2004 return	65	
66a	**Earned income credit (EIC)**	66a	
b	Nontaxable combat pay election ▶ 66b		
67	Excess social security and tier 1 RRTA tax withheld (see page 59)	67	
68	Additional child tax credit. Attach Form 8812	68	
69	Amount paid with request for extension to file (see page 59)	69	
70	Payments from: **a** ☐ Form 2439 **b** ☐ Form 4136 **c** ☐ Form 8885	70	
71	Add lines 64, 65, 66a, and 67 through 70. These are your **total payments** ▶		71

Refund

Direct deposit? See page 59 and fill in 73b, 73c, and 73d.

Line	Description		
72	If line 71 is more than line 63, subtract line 63 from line 71. This is the amount you **overpaid**		72
73a	Amount of line 72 you want **refunded to you** ▶		73a
▶ b	Routing number ▶ **c** Type: ☐ Checking ☐ Savings		
▶ d	Account number		
74	Amount of line 72 you want **applied to your 2006 estimated tax** ▶	74	

Amount You Owe

Line	Description		
75	**Amount you owe.** Subtract line 71 from line 63. For details on how to pay, see page 60 ▶		75
76	Estimated tax penalty (see page 60)	76	

Third Party Designee

Do you want to allow another person to discuss this return with the IRS (see page 61)? ☐ **Yes.** Complete the following. ☐ **No**

Designee's name ▶ Phone no. ▶ ( ) Personal identification number (PIN) ▶

Sign Here

Joint return? See page 17. Keep a copy for your records.

Under penalties of perjury, I declare that I have examined this return and accompanying schedules and statements, and to the best of my knowledge and belief, they are true, correct, and complete. Declaration of preparer (other than taxpayer) is based on all information of which preparer has any knowledge.

Your signature	Date	Your occupation	Daytime phone number ( )
Spouse's signature. If a joint return, **both** must sign.	Date	Spouse's occupation	

Paid Preparer's Use Only

Preparer's signature	Date	Check if self-employed ☐	Preparer's SSN or PTIN
Firm's name (or yours if self-employed), address, and ZIP code		EIN	
		Phone no.	( )

Form **1040** (2005)

SCHEDULE C (Form 1040)

Department of the Treasury Internal Revenue Service (99)

Profit or Loss From Business

(Sole Proprietorship)

▶ **Partnerships, joint ventures, etc., must file Form 1065 or 1065-B.**

▶ **Attach to Form 1040 or 1041.** ▶ **See Instructions for Schedule C (Form 1040).**

OMB No. 1545-0074

2005

Attachment Sequence No. **09**

Name of proprietor | **Social security number (SSN)**

A Principal business or profession, including product or service (see page C-2 of the instructions) | **B Enter code from pages C-8, 9, & 10** ▶

C Business name. If no separate business name, leave blank. | **D Employer ID number (EIN), if any**

E Business address (including suite or room no.) ▶
City, town or post office, state, and ZIP code

F Accounting method: **(1)** ☐ Cash **(2)** ☐ Accrual **(3)** ☐ Other (specify) ▶

G Did you "materially participate" in the operation of this business during 2005? If "No," see page C-3 for limit on losses ☐ **Yes** ☐ **No**

H If you started or acquired this business during 2005, check here . . . ▶ ☐

Part I Income

1	Gross receipts or sales. **Caution.** If this income was reported to you on Form W-2 and the "Statutory employee" box on that form was checked, see page C-3 and check here . . . ▶ ☐	1	
2	Returns and allowances	2	
3	Subtract line 2 from line 1	3	
4	Cost of goods sold (from line 42 on page 2)	4	
5	**Gross profit.** Subtract line 4 from line 3	5	
6	Other income, including Federal and state gasoline or fuel tax credit or refund (see page C-3)	6	
7	**Gross income.** Add lines 5 and 6 ▶	7	

Part II Expenses. Enter expenses for business use of your home **only** on line 30.

8	Advertising	8		**18**	Office expense	18	
9	Car and truck expenses (see page C-3)	9		**19**	Pension and profit-sharing plans	19	
10	Commissions and fees	10		**20**	Rent or lease (see page C-5):		
11	Contract labor (see page C-4)	11		**a**	Vehicles, machinery, and equipment	20a	
12	Depletion	12		**b**	Other business property	20b	
13	Depreciation and section 179 expense deduction (not included in Part III) (see page C-4)	13		**21**	Repairs and maintenance	21	
14	Employee benefit programs (other than on line 19)	14		**22**	Supplies (not included in Part III)	22	
15	Insurance (other than health)	15		**23**	Taxes and licenses	23	
16	Interest:			**24**	Travel, meals, and entertainment:		
a	Mortgage (paid to banks, etc.)	16a		**a**	Travel	24a	
b	Other	16b		**b**	Deductible meals and entertainment (see page C-5)	24b	
17	Legal and professional services	17		**25**	Utilities	25	
				26	Wages (less employment credits)	26	
				27	Other expenses (from line 48 on page 2)	27	

28	**Total expenses** before expenses for business use of home. Add lines 8 through 27 in columns ▶	28	
29	Tentative profit (loss). Subtract line 28 from line 7	29	
30	Expenses for business use of your home. Attach **Form 8829**	30	
31	**Net profit or (loss).** Subtract line 30 from line 29. • If a profit, enter on **Form 1040, line 12,** and **also** on **Schedule SE, line 2** (statutory employees, see page C-6). Estates and trusts, enter on Form 1041, line 3. • If a loss, you **must** go to line 32.	31	

32 If you have a loss, check the box that describes your investment in this activity (see page C-6).
- If you checked 32a, enter the loss on **Form 1040, line 12,** and **also** on **Schedule SE, line 2** (statutory employees, see page C-6). Estates and trusts, enter on Form 1041, line 3.
- If you checked 32b, you **must** attach **Form 6198.** Your loss may be limited.

32a ☐ All investment is at risk.
32b ☐ Some investment is not at risk.

Schedule C (Form 1040) 2005 Page 2

Part III Cost of Goods Sold (see page C-6)

33 Method(s) used to value closing inventory: a ☐ Cost b ☐ Lower of cost or market c ☐ Other (attach explanation)

34 Was there any change in determining quantities, costs, or valuations between opening and closing inventory? If "Yes," attach explanation . . . ☐ Yes ☐ No

35	Inventory at beginning of year. If different from last year's closing inventory, attach explanation	35	
36	Purchases less cost of items withdrawn for personal use	36	
37	Cost of labor. Do not include any amounts paid to yourself	37	
38	Materials and supplies	38	
39	Other costs	39	
40	Add lines 35 through 39	40	
41	Inventory at end of year	41	
42	**Cost of goods sold.** Subtract line 41 from line 40. Enter the result here and on page 1, line 4	42	

Part IV Information on Your Vehicle.

Complete this part **only** if you are claiming car or truck expenses on line 9 and are not required to file Form 4562 for this business. See the instructions for line 13 on page C-4 to find out if you must file Form 4562.

43 When did you place your vehicle in service for business purposes? (month, day, year) ► ____/____/____ .

44 Of the total number of miles you drove your vehicle during 2005, enter the number of miles you used your vehicle for:

a Business ________ b Commuting (see instructions) ________ c Other ________

45 Do you (or your spouse) have another vehicle available for personal use? . . . ☐ Yes ☐ No

46 Was your vehicle available for personal use during off-duty hours? . . . ☐ Yes ☐ No

47a Do you have evidence to support your deduction? . . . ☐ Yes ☐ No

b If "Yes," is the evidence written? . . . ☐ Yes ☐ No

Part V Other Expenses.

List below business expenses not included on lines 8–26 or line 30.

48 **Total other expenses.** Enter here and on page 1, line 27	48	

Schedule C (Form 1040) 2005

Form **1065**
Department of the Treasury
Internal Revenue Service

U.S. Return of Partnership Income

For calendar year 2005, or tax year beginning ...., 2005, ending ...., 20.....
▶ See separate instructions.

OMB No. 1545-0099

2005

A Principal business activity	Use the IRS label. Otherwise, print or type.	Name of partnership	D Employer identification number
B Principal product or service		Number, street, and room or suite no. If a P.O. box, see the instructions.	E Date business started
C Business code number		City or town, state, and ZIP code	F Total assets (see the instructions) $

G Check applicable boxes: (1) ☐ Initial return (2) ☐ Final return (3) ☐ Name change (4) ☐ Address change (5) ☐ Amended return

H Check accounting method: (1) ☐ Cash (2) ☐ Accrual (3) ☐ Other (specify) ▶ ....

I Number of Schedules K-1. Attach one for each person who was a partner at any time during the tax year ▶ ....

Caution. *Include **only** trade or business income and expenses on lines 1a through 22 below. See the instructions for more information.*

Income	1a	Gross receipts or sales	1a			
	b	Less returns and allowances	1b		1c	
	2	Cost of goods sold (Schedule A, line 8)			2	
	3	Gross profit. Subtract line 2 from line 1c			3	
	4	Ordinary income (loss) from other partnerships, estates, and trusts *(attach statement)*			4	
	5	Net farm profit (loss) *(attach Schedule F (Form 1040))*			5	
	6	Net gain (loss) from Form 4797, Part II, line 17 (attach Form 4797)			6	
	7	Other income (loss) *(attach statement)*			7	
	8	**Total income (loss).** Combine lines 3 through 7			8	
Deductions (see the instructions for limitations)	9	Salaries and wages (other than to partners) (less employment credits)			9	
	10	Guaranteed payments to partners			10	
	11	Repairs and maintenance			11	
	12	Bad debts			12	
	13	Rent			13	
	14	Taxes and licenses			14	
	15	Interest			15	
	16a	Depreciation *(if required, attach Form 4562)*	16a			
	b	Less depreciation reported on Schedule A and elsewhere on return	16b		16c	
	17	Depletion **(Do not deduct oil and gas depletion.)**			17	
	18	Retirement plans, etc.			18	
	19	Employee benefit programs			19	
	20	Other deductions *(attach statement)*			20	
	21	**Total deductions.** Add the amounts shown in the far right column for lines 9 through 20			21	
	22	**Ordinary business income (loss).** Subtract line 21 from line 8			22	

Sign Here

Under penalties of perjury, I declare that I have examined this return, including accompanying schedules and statements, and to the best of my knowledge and belief, it is true, correct, and complete. Declaration of preparer (other than general partner or limited liability company member) is based on all information of which preparer has any knowledge.

▶ Signature of general partner or limited liability company member manager ▶ Date

May the IRS discuss this return with the preparer shown below (see instructions)? ☐ Yes ☐ No

Paid Preparer's Use Only

Preparer's signature	Date	Check if self-employed ▶ ☐	Preparer's SSN or PTIN
Firm's name (or yours if self-employed), address, and ZIP code ▶		EIN ▶	
		Phone no. ( )	

Form 1065 (2005) Page **2**

Schedule A Cost of Goods Sold (see the instructions)

1	Inventory at beginning of year	1	
2	Purchases less cost of items withdrawn for personal use	2	
3	Cost of labor	3	
4	Additional section 263A costs *(attach statement)*	4	
5	Other costs *(attach statement)*	5	
6	**Total.** Add lines 1 through 5	6	
7	Inventory at end of year	7	
8	**Cost of goods sold.** Subtract line 7 from line 6. Enter here and on page 1, line 2	8	

9a Check all methods used for valuing closing inventory:

(i) ☐ Cost as described in Regulations section 1.471-3

(ii) ☐ Lower of cost or market as described in Regulations section 1.471-4

(iii) ☐ Other (specify method used and attach explanation) ▶

b Check this box if there was a writedown of "subnormal" goods as described in Regulations section 1.471-2(c) ▶ ☐

c Check this box if the LIFO inventory method was adopted this tax year for any goods *(if checked, attach Form 970)*. ▶ ☐

d Do the rules of section 263A (for property produced or acquired for resale) apply to the partnership? ☐ **Yes** ☐ **No**

e Was there any change in determining quantities, cost, or valuations between opening and closing inventory? ☐ **Yes** ☐ **No**
If "Yes," attach explanation.

Schedule B Other Information

		Yes	No
1	What type of entity is filing this return? Check the applicable box: **a** ☐ Domestic general partnership **b** ☐ Domestic limited partnership **c** ☐ Domestic limited liability company **d** ☐ Domestic limited liability partnership **e** ☐ Foreign partnership **f** ☐ Other ▶		
2	Are any partners in this partnership also partnerships?		
3	During the partnership's tax year, did the partnership own any interest in another partnership or in any foreign entity that was disregarded as an entity separate from its owner under Regulations sections 301.7701-2 and 301.7701-3? If yes, see instructions for required attachment		
4	Did the partnership file Form 8893, Election of Partnership Level Tax Treatment, or an election statement under section 6231(a)(1)(B)(ii) for partnership-level tax treatment, that is in effect for this tax year? See Form 8893 for more details		
5	Does this partnership meet all three of the following requirements? **a** The partnership's total receipts for the tax year were less than $250,000; **b** The partnership's total assets at the end of the tax year were less than $600,000; and **c** Schedules K-1 are filed with the return and furnished to the partners on or before the due date (including extensions) for the partnership return. If "Yes," the partnership is not required to complete Schedules L, M-1, and M-2; Item F on page 1 of Form 1065; or Item N on Schedule K-1.		
6	Does this partnership have any foreign partners? If "Yes," the partnership may have to file Forms 8804, 8805 and 8813. See the instructions		
7	Is this partnership a publicly traded partnership as defined in section 469(k)(2)?		
8	Has this partnership filed, or is it required to file, a return under section 6111 to provide information on any reportable transaction?		
9	At any time during calendar year 2005, did the partnership have an interest in or a signature or other authority over a financial account in a foreign country (such as a bank account, securities account, or other financial account)? See the instructions for exceptions and filing requirements for Form TD F 90-22.1. If "Yes," enter the name of the foreign country. ▶		
10	During the tax year, did the partnership receive a distribution from, or was it the grantor of, or transferor to, a foreign trust? If "Yes," the partnership may have to file Form 3520. See the instructions		
11	Was there a distribution of property or a transfer (for example, by sale or death) of a partnership interest during the tax year? If "Yes," you may elect to adjust the basis of the partnership's assets under section 754 by attaching the statement described under *Elections Made By the Partnership* in the instructions		
12	Enter the number of Forms 8865, Return of U.S. Persons With Respect to Certain Foreign Partnerships, attached to this return ▶		

Designation of Tax Matters Partner (see the instructions)

Enter below the general partner designated as the tax matters partner (TMP) for the tax year of this return:

Name of designated TMP ▶ Identifying number of TMP ▶

Address of designated TMP ▶

Form 1065 (2005) Page 3

Schedule K Partners' Distributive Share Items

				Total amount
Income (Loss)	1 Ordinary business income (loss) (page 1, line 22)		1	
	2 Net rental real estate income (loss) *(attach Form 8825)*		2	
	3a Other gross rental income (loss)	3a		
	b Expenses from other rental activities *(attach statement)*	3b		
	c Other net rental income (loss). Subtract line 3b from line 3a		3c	
	4 Guaranteed payments		4	
	5 Interest income		5	
	6 Dividends: a Ordinary dividends		6a	
	b Qualified dividends	6b		
	7 Royalties		7	
	8 Net short-term capital gain (loss) *(attach Schedule D (Form 1065))*		8	
	9a Net long-term capital gain (loss) *(attach Schedule D (Form 1065))*		9a	
	b Collectibles (28%) gain (loss)	9b		
	c Unrecaptured section 1250 gain *(attach statement)*	9c		
	10 Net section 1231 gain (loss) *(attach Form 4797)*		10	
	11 Other income (loss) *(see instructions)* Type ▶		11	
Deductions	12 Section 179 deduction *(attach Form 4562)*		12	
	13a Contributions		13a	
	b Investment interest expense		13b	
	c Section 59(e)(2) expenditures: **(1)** Type ▶ **(2)** Amount ▶		13c(2)	
	d Other deductions *(see instructions)* Type ▶		13d	
Self-Employment	14a Net earnings (loss) from self-employment		14a	
	b Gross farming or fishing income		14b	
	c Gross nonfarm income		14c	
Credits & Credit Recapture	15a Low-income housing credit (section 42(j)(5))		15a	
	b Low-income housing credit (other)		15b	
	c Qualified rehabilitation expenditures (rental real estate) *(attach Form 3468)*		15c	
	d Other rental real estate credits *(see instructions)* Type ▶		15d	
	e Other rental credits *(see instructions)* Type ▶		15e	
	f Other credits and credit recapture *(see instructions)* Type ▶		15f	
Foreign Transactions	16a Name of country or U.S. possession ▶			
	b Gross income from all sources		16b	
	c Gross income sourced at partner level		16c	
	Foreign gross income sourced at partnership level			
	d Passive ▶ e Listed categories *(attach statement)* ▶ f General limitation ▶		16f	
	Deductions allocated and apportioned at partner level			
	g Interest expense ▶ h Other ▶		16h	
	Deductions allocated and apportioned at partnership level to foreign source income			
	i Passive ▶ j Listed categories *(attach statement)* ▶ k General limitation ▶		16k	
	l Total foreign taxes (check one): ▶ Paid ☐ Accrued ☐		16l	
	m Reduction in taxes available for credit *(attach statement)*		16m	
	n Other foreign tax information *(attach statement)*			
Alternative Minimum Tax (AMT) Items	17a Post-1986 depreciation adjustment		17a	
	b Adjusted gain or loss		17b	
	c Depletion (other than oil and gas)		17c	
	d Oil, gas, and geothermal properties—gross income		17d	
	e Oil, gas, and geothermal properties—deductions		17e	
	f Other AMT items *(attach statement)*		17f	
Other Information	18a Tax-exempt interest income		18a	
	b Other tax-exempt income		18b	
	c Nondeductible expenses		18c	
	19a Distributions of cash and marketable securities		19a	
	b Distributions of other property		19b	
	20a Investment income		20a	
	b Investment expenses		20b	
	c Other items and amounts *(attach statement)*			

Form **1065** (2005)

Analysis of Net Income (Loss)

1	Net income (loss). Combine Schedule K, lines 1 through 11. From the result, subtract the sum of Schedule K, lines 12 through 13d, and 16l	1	

2 Analysis by partner type:	(i) Corporate	(ii) Individual (active)	(iii) Individual (passive)	(iv) Partnership	(v) Exempt organization	(vi) Nominee/Other
a General partners						
b Limited partners						

Note: Schedules L, M-1, and M-2 are not required if Question 5 of Schedule B is answered "Yes."

Schedule L Balance Sheets per Books

Assets	Beginning of tax year (a)	(b)	End of tax year (c)	(d)
1 Cash				
2a Trade notes and accounts receivable				
b Less allowance for bad debts				
3 Inventories				
4 U.S. government obligations				
5 Tax-exempt securities				
6 Other current assets *(attach statement)*				
7 Mortgage and real estate loans				
8 Other investments *(attach statement)*				
9a Buildings and other depreciable assets				
b Less accumulated depreciation				
10a Depletable assets				
b Less accumulated depletion				
11 Land (net of any amortization)				
12a Intangible assets (amortizable only)				
b Less accumulated amortization				
13 Other assets *(attach statement)*				
14 Total assets				
Liabilities and Capital				
15 Accounts payable				
16 Mortgages, notes, bonds payable in less than 1 year				
17 Other current liabilities *(attach statement)*				
18 All nonrecourse loans				
19 Mortgages, notes, bonds payable in 1 year or more				
20 Other liabilities *(attach statement)*				
21 Partners' capital accounts				
22 Total liabilities and capital				

Schedule M-1 Reconciliation of Income (Loss) per Books With Income (Loss) per Return

1 Net income (loss) per books		6 Income recorded on books this year not included on Schedule K, lines 1 through 11 (itemize):	
2 Income included on Schedule K, lines 1, 2, 3c, 5, 6a, 7, 8, 9a, 10, and 11, not recorded on books this year (itemize):		a Tax-exempt interest $	
3 Guaranteed payments (other than health insurance)		7 Deductions included on Schedule K, lines 1 through 13d, and 16l, not charged against book income this year (itemize):	
4 Expenses recorded on books this year not included on Schedule K, lines 1 through 13d, and 16l (itemize):		a Depreciation $	
a Depreciation $			
b Travel and entertainment $		8 Add lines 6 and 7	
5 Add lines 1 through 4		9 Income (loss) (Analysis of Net Income (Loss), line 1). Subtract line 8 from line 5	

Schedule M-2 Analysis of Partners' Capital Accounts

1 Balance at beginning of year		6 Distributions: a Cash	
2 Capital contributed: a Cash		b Property	
b Property		7 Other decreases (itemize):	
3 Net income (loss) per books			
4 Other increases (itemize):			
		8 Add lines 6 and 7	
5 Add lines 1 through 4		9 Balance at end of year. Subtract line 8 from line 5	

651105

☐ Final K-1 ☐ Amended K-1 OMB No. 1545-0099

Schedule K-1 (Form 1065) **2005**

Department of the Treasury
Internal Revenue Service

For calendar year 2005, or tax year beginning ____________, 2005 ending ____________, 20____

Partner's Share of Income, Deductions, Credits, etc.

► See back of form and separate instructions.

Part I Information About the Partnership

A Partnership's employer identification number

B Partnership's name, address, city, state, and ZIP code

C IRS Center where partnership filed return

D ☐ Check if this is a publicly traded partnership (PTP)

E ☐ Tax shelter registration number, if any ____________

F ☐ Check if Form 8271 is attached

Part II Information About the Partner

G Partner's identifying number

H Partner's name, address, city, state, and ZIP code

I ☐ General partner or LLC member-manager ☐ Limited partner or other LLC member

J ☐ Domestic partner ☐ Foreign partner

K What type of entity is this partner? ____________

L Partner's share of profit, loss, and capital:

	Beginning	Ending
Profit	%	%
Loss	%	%
Capital	%	%

M Partner's share of liabilities at year end:

Nonrecourse . . . . $____________

Qualified nonrecourse financing . .$____________

Recourse . . . . $____________

N Partner's capital account analysis:

Beginning capital account . . . . $____________

Capital contributed during the year . $____________

Current year increase (decrease) . . $____________

Withdrawals & distributions . . . $(____________)

Ending capital account . . . . $____________

☐ Tax basis ☐ GAAP ☐ Section 704(b) book

☐ Other (explain)

Part III Partner's Share of Current Year Income, Deductions, Credits, and Other Items

1	Ordinary business income (loss)	15	Credits & credit recapture
2	Net rental real estate income (loss)		
3	Other net rental income (loss)	16	Foreign transactions
4	Guaranteed payments		
5	Interest income		
6a	Ordinary dividends		
6b	Qualified dividends		
7	Royalties		
8	Net short-term capital gain (loss)		
9a	Net long-term capital gain (loss)	17	Alternative minimum tax (AMT) items
9b	Collectibles (28%) gain (loss)		
9c	Unrecaptured section 1250 gain		
10	Net section 1231 gain (loss)	18	Tax-exempt income and nondeductible expenses
11	Other income (loss)		
		19	Distributions
12	Section 179 deduction		
13	Other deductions	20	Other information
14	Self-employment earnings (loss)		

*See attached statement for additional information.

For IRS Use Only

For Privacy Act and Paperwork Reduction Act Notice, see Instructions for Form 1065. Cat. No. 11394R **Schedule K-1 (Form 1065) 2005**

Form **1120** Department of the Treasury Internal Revenue Service

U.S. Corporation Income Tax Return

For calendar year 2005 or tax year beginning ...., 2005, ending ...., 20....
▶ See separate instructions.

OMB No. 1545-0123

2005

A Check if:
1 Consolidated return (attach Form 851) ☐
2 Personal holding co. (attach Sch. PH) ☐
3 Personal service corp. (see instructions) ☐
4 Schedule M-3 required (attach Sch. M-3) ☐

Use IRS label. Otherwise, print or type.

Name

Number, street, and room or suite no. If a P.O. box, see instructions.

City or town, state, and ZIP code

B Employer identification number

C Date incorporated

D Total assets (see instructions) $

E Check if: **(1)** ☐ Initial return **(2)** ☐ Final return **(3)** ☐ Name change **(4)** ☐ Address change

Income

1a	Gross receipts or sales ____ **b** Less returns and allowances ____ **c** Bal ▶	1c	
2	Cost of goods sold (Schedule A, line 8)	2	
3	Gross profit. Subtract line 2 from line 1c	3	
4	Dividends (Schedule C, line 19)	4	
5	Interest	5	
6	Gross rents	6	
7	Gross royalties	7	
8	Capital gain net income (attach Schedule D (Form 1120))	8	
9	Net gain or (loss) from Form 4797, Part II, line 17 (attach Form 4797)	9	
10	Other income (see instructions—attach schedule)	10	
11	**Total income.** Add lines 3 through 10 ▶	11	

Deductions (See instructions for limitations on deductions.)

12	Compensation of officers (Schedule E, line 4)	12	
13	Salaries and wages (less employment credits)	13	
14	Repairs and maintenance	14	
15	Bad debts	15	
16	Rents	16	
17	Taxes and licenses	17	
18	Interest	18	
19	Charitable contributions (see instructions for 10% limitation)	19	
20a	Depreciation (attach Form 4562) 20a		
b	Less depreciation claimed on Schedule A and elsewhere on return 20b	20c	
21	Depletion	21	
22	Advertising	22	
23	Pension, profit-sharing, etc., plans	23	
24	Employee benefit programs	24	
25	Domestic production activities deduction (attach Form 8903)	25	
26	Other deductions (attach schedule)	26	
27	**Total deductions.** Add lines 12 through 26 ▶	27	
28	Taxable income before net operating loss deduction and special deductions. Subtract line 27 from line 11	28	
29	**Less:** **a** Net operating loss deduction (see instructions) 29a		
	b Special deductions (Schedule C, line 20) 29b	29c	

Tax and Payments

30	**Taxable income.** Subtract line 29c from line 28 (see instructions if Schedule C, line 12, was completed)	30	
31	**Total tax** (Schedule J, line 11)	31	
32	**Payments: a** 2004 overpayment credited to 2005 32a		
b	2005 estimated tax payments 32b		
c	Less 2005 refund applied for on Form 4466 32c ( ) **d Bal** ▶ 32d		
e	Tax deposited with Form 7004 32e		
f	Credits: **(1)** Form 2439 ____ **(2)** Form 4136 ____ 32f	32g	
33	Estimated tax penalty (see instructions). Check if Form 2220 is attached ▶ ☐	33	
34	**Tax due.** If line 32g is smaller than the total of lines 31 and 33, enter amount owed	34	
35	**Overpayment.** If line 32g is larger than the total of lines 31 and 33, enter amount overpaid	35	
36	Enter amount of line 35 you want: **Credited to 2006 estimated tax** ▶ **Refunded** ▶	36	

Sign Here

Under penalties of perjury, I declare that I have examined this return, including accompanying schedules and statements, and to the best of my knowledge and belief, it is true, correct, and complete. Declaration of preparer (other than taxpayer) is based on all information of which preparer has any knowledge.

Signature of officer ▶ Date ▶ Title

May the IRS discuss this return with the preparer shown below (see instructions)? ☐ **Yes** ☐ **No**

Paid Preparer's Use Only

Preparer's signature ▶ Date Check if self-employed ☐ Preparer's SSN or PTIN

Firm's name (or yours if self-employed), address, and ZIP code ▶ EIN Phone no. ( )

For Privacy Act and Paperwork Reduction Act Notice, see separate instructions. Cat. No. 11450Q Form **1120** (2005)

Form 1120 (2005) Page **2**

Schedule A Cost of Goods Sold (see instructions)

1	Inventory at beginning of year	1	
2	Purchases	2	
3	Cost of labor	3	
4	Additional section 263A costs (attach schedule)	4	
5	Other costs (attach schedule)	5	
6	**Total.** Add lines 1 through 5	6	
7	Inventory at end of year	7	
8	**Cost of goods sold.** Subtract line 7 from line 6. Enter here and on page 1, line 2	8	

9a Check all methods used for valuing closing inventory:
- *(i)* ☐ Cost
- *(ii)* ☐ Lower of cost or market
- *(iii)* ☐ Other (Specify method used and attach explanation.) ▶

b Check if there was a writedown of subnormal goods ▶ ☐

c Check if the LIFO inventory method was adopted this tax year for any goods (if checked, attach Form 970) ▶ ☐

d If the LIFO inventory method was used for this tax year, enter percentage (or amounts) of closing inventory computed under LIFO | **9d** |

e If property is produced or acquired for resale, do the rules of section 263A apply to the corporation? ☐ Yes ☐ No

f Was there any change in determining quantities, cost, or valuations between opening and closing inventory? If "Yes," attach explanation ☐ Yes ☐ No

Schedule C Dividends and Special Deductions (see instructions)

		(a) Dividends received	(b) %	(c) Special deductions (a) × (b)
1	Dividends from less-than-20%-owned domestic corporations (other than debt-financed stock)		70	
2	Dividends from 20%-or-more-owned domestic corporations (other than debt-financed stock)		80	
3	Dividends on debt-financed stock of domestic and foreign corporations		see instructions	
4	Dividends on certain preferred stock of less-than-20%-owned public utilities		42	
5	Dividends on certain preferred stock of 20%-or-more-owned public utilities		48	
6	Dividends from less-than-20%-owned foreign corporations and certain FSCs		70	
7	Dividends from 20%-or-more-owned foreign corporations and certain FSCs		80	
8	Dividends from wholly owned foreign subsidiaries		100	
9	**Total.** Add lines 1 through 8. See instructions for limitation			
10	Dividends from domestic corporations received by a small business investment company operating under the Small Business Investment Act of 1958		100	
11	Dividends from affiliated group members and certain FSCs		100	
12	Dividends from controlled foreign corporations (attach Form 8895)		85	
13	Dividends from foreign corporations not included on lines 3, 6, 7, 8, 11, or 12			
14	Income from controlled foreign corporations under subpart F (attach Form(s) 5471)			
15	Foreign dividend gross-up			
16	IC-DISC and former DISC dividends not included on lines 1, 2, or 3			
17	Other dividends			
18	Deduction for dividends paid on certain preferred stock of public utilities			
19	**Total dividends.** Add lines 1 through 17. Enter here and on page 1, line 4 ▶			
20	**Total special deductions.** Add lines 9, 10, 11, 12, and 18. Enter here and on page 1, line 29b ▶			

Schedule E Compensation of Officers (see instructions for page 1, line 12)

Note: *Complete Schedule E only if total receipts (line 1a plus lines 4 through 10 on page 1) are $500,000 or more.*

	(a) Name of officer	(b) Social security number	(c) Percent of time devoted to business	Percent of corporation stock owned (d) Common	(e) Preferred	(f) Amount of compensation
1			%	%	%	
			%	%	%	
			%	%	%	
			%	%	%	
			%	%	%	

2	Total compensation of officers	
3	Compensation of officers claimed on Schedule A and elsewhere on return	
4	Subtract line 3 from line 2. Enter the result here and on page 1, line 12	

Form 1120 (2005) Page 3

Schedule J Tax Computation (see instructions)

1 Check if the corporation is a member of a controlled group ▶ ☐

Important: Members of a controlled group, see instructions.

2a If the box on line 1 is checked, enter the corporation's share of the $50,000, $25,000, and $9,925,000 taxable income brackets (in that order):

(1) $ ______ (2) $ ______ (3) $ ______

b Enter the corporation's share of: (1) Additional 5% tax (not more than $11,750) $ ______

(2) Additional 3% tax (not more than $100,000) $ ______

3 Income tax. Check if a qualified personal service corporation (see instructions) ▶ ☐ 3

4 Alternative minimum tax (attach Form 4626) 4

5 Add lines 3 and 4 5

6a Foreign tax credit (attach Form 1118) 6a

b Possessions tax credit (attach Form 5735) 6b

c Credits from: ☐ Form 8834 ☐ Form 8907, line 23 6c

d General business credit. Check box(es) and indicate which forms are attached:

☐ Form 3800 ☐ Form(s) (specify) ▶ ______ 6d

e Credit for prior year minimum tax (attach Form 8827) 6e

f Bond credits from: ☐ Form 8860 ☐ Form 8912 6f

7 **Total credits.** Add lines 6a through 6f 7

8 Subtract line 7 from line 5 8

9 Personal holding company tax (attach Schedule PH (Form 1120)) 9

10 Other taxes. Check if from: ☐ Form 4255 ☐ Form 8611 ☐ Form 8697 ☐ Form 8866 ☐ Form 8902 ☐ Other (attach schedule) 10

11 **Total tax.** Add lines 8 through 10. Enter here and on page 1, line 31 11

Schedule K Other Information (see instructions)

	Yes	No
1 Check accounting method: a ☐ Cash b ☐ Accrual c ☐ Other (specify) ▶ ______		
2 See the instructions and enter the: a Business activity code no. ▶ ______ b Business activity ▶ ______ c Product or service ▶ ______		
3 At the end of the tax year, did the corporation own, directly or indirectly, 50% or more of the voting stock of a domestic corporation? (For rules of attribution, see section 267(c).)		
If "Yes," attach a schedule showing: (a) name and employer identification number (EIN), (b) percentage owned, and (c) taxable income or (loss) before NOL and special deductions of such corporation for the tax year ending with or within your tax year.		
4 Is the corporation a subsidiary in an affiliated group or a parent-subsidiary controlled group?		
If "Yes," enter name and EIN of the parent corporation ▶ ______		
5 At the end of the tax year, did any individual, partnership, corporation, estate, or trust own, directly or indirectly, 50% or more of the corporation's voting stock? (For rules of attribution, see section 267(c).) If "Yes," attach a schedule showing name and identifying number. (Do not include any information already entered in **4** above.) Enter percentage owned ▶ ______		
6 During this tax year, did the corporation pay dividends (other than stock dividends and distributions in exchange for stock) in excess of the corporation's current and accumulated earnings and profits? (See sections 301 and 316.)		
If "Yes," file **Form 5452,** Corporate Report of Nondividend Distributions.		
If this is a consolidated return, answer here for the parent corporation and on **Form 851,** Affiliations Schedule, for each subsidiary.		

	Yes	No
7 At any time during the tax year, did one foreign person own, directly or indirectly, at least 25% of **(a)** the total voting power of all classes of stock of the corporation entitled to vote or **(b)** the total value of all classes of stock of the corporation?		
If "Yes," enter: **(a)** Percentage owned ▶ ______ and **(b)** Owner's country ▶ ______		
c The corporation may have to file **Form 5472,** Information Return of a 25% Foreign-Owned U.S. Corporation or a Foreign Corporation Engaged in a U.S. Trade or Business. Enter number of Forms 5472 attached ▶ ______		
8 Check this box if the corporation issued publicly offered debt instruments with original issue discount ▶ ☐		
If checked, the corporation may have to file **Form 8281,** Information Return for Publicly Offered Original Issue Discount Instruments.		
9 Enter the amount of tax-exempt interest received or accrued during the tax year ▶ $ ______		
10 Enter the number of shareholders at the end of the tax year (if 100 or fewer) ▶ ______		
11 If the corporation has an NOL for the tax year and is electing to forego the carryback period, check here ▶ ☐		
If the corporation is filing a consolidated return, the statement required by Temporary Regulations section 1.1502-21T(b)(3) must be attached or the election will not be valid.		
12 Enter the available NOL carryover from prior tax years (Do not reduce it by any deduction on line 29a.) ▶ $ ______		
13 Are the corporation's total receipts (line 1a plus lines 4 through 10 on page 1) for the tax year **and** its total assets at the end of the tax year less than $250,000?		
If "Yes," the corporation is not required to complete Schedules L, M-1, and M-2 on page 4. Instead, enter the total amount of cash distributions and the book value of property distributions (other than cash) made during the tax year. ▶ $ ______		

Note: *If the corporation, at any time during the tax year, had assets or operated a business in a foreign country or U.S. possession, it may be required to attach* ***Schedule N (Form 1120),*** *Foreign Operations of U.S. Corporations, to this return. See Schedule N for details.*

Form **1120** (2005)

Note: *The corporation is not required to complete Schedules L, M-1, and M-2 if Question 13 on Schedule K is answered "Yes."*

Schedule L Balance Sheets per Books

	Beginning of tax year		End of tax year	
Assets	**(a)**	**(b)**	**(c)**	**(d)**
1 Cash				
2a Trade notes and accounts receivable				
b Less allowance for bad debts	( )		( )	
3 Inventories				
4 U.S. government obligations				
5 Tax-exempt securities (see instructions)				
6 Other current assets (attach schedule)				
7 Loans to shareholders				
8 Mortgage and real estate loans				
9 Other investments (attach schedule)				
10a Buildings and other depreciable assets				
b Less accumulated depreciation	( )		( )	
11a Depletable assets				
b Less accumulated depletion	( )		( )	
12 Land (net of any amortization)				
13a Intangible assets (amortizable only)				
b Less accumulated amortization	( )		( )	
14 Other assets (attach schedule)				
15 Total assets				
Liabilities and Shareholders' Equity				
16 Accounts payable				
17 Mortgages, notes, bonds payable in less than 1 year				
18 Other current liabilities (attach schedule)				
19 Loans from shareholders				
20 Mortgages, notes, bonds payable in 1 year or more				
21 Other liabilities (attach schedule)				
22 Capital stock: a Preferred stock				
b Common stock				
23 Additional paid-in capital				
24 Retained earnings—Appropriated (attach schedule)				
25 Retained earnings—Unappropriated				
26 Adjustments to shareholders' equity (attach schedule)				
27 Less cost of treasury stock		( )		( )
28 Total liabilities and shareholders' equity				

Schedule M-1 Reconciliation of Income (Loss) per Books With Income per Return (see instructions)

1 Net income (loss) per books		7 Income recorded on books this year not included on this return (itemize): Tax-exempt interest $	
2 Federal income tax per books			
3 Excess of capital losses over capital gains			
4 Income subject to tax not recorded on books this year (itemize):			
5 Expenses recorded on books this year not deducted on this return (itemize):		8 Deductions on this return not charged against book income this year (itemize):	
a Depreciation $		a Depreciation $	
b Charitable contributions $		b Charitable contributions $	
c Travel and entertainment $			
		9 Add lines 7 and 8	
6 Add lines 1 through 5		10 Income (page 1, line 28)—line 6 less line 9	

Schedule M-2 Analysis of Unappropriated Retained Earnings per Books (Line 25, Schedule L)

1 Balance at beginning of year		5 Distributions: a Cash	
2 Net income (loss) per books		b Stock	
3 Other increases (itemize):		c Property	
		6 Other decreases (itemize):	
		7 Add lines 5 and 6	
4 Add lines 1, 2, and 3		8 Balance at end of year (line 4 less line 7)	

Form **1120S**

Department of the Treasury
Internal Revenue Service

U.S. Income Tax Return for an S Corporation

▶ **Do not file this form unless the corporation has filed Form 2553 to elect to be an S corporation.**

▶ **See separate instructions.**

OMB No. 1545-0130

2005

For calendar year 2005, or tax year beginning , 2005, ending , 20

A Effective date of S election	**Use the IRS label. Otherwise, print or type.**	Name	**C Employer identification number**
		Number, street, and room or suite no. If a P.O. box, see instructions.	**D** Date incorporated
B Business code number (see instructions)		City or town, state, and ZIP code	**E** Total assets (see instructions) $

F Check applicable boxes: **(1)** ☐ Initial return **(2)** ☐ Final return **(3)** ☐ Name change **(4)** ☐ Address change **(5)** ☐ Amended return

G Enter number of shareholders in the corporation at end of the tax year . . . . . ▶

Caution. *Include **only** trade or business income and expenses on lines 1a through 21. See the instructions for more information.*

Income

1a	Gross receipts or sales ____ **b** Less returns and allowances ____ **c** Bal ▶	**1c**	
2	Cost of goods sold (Schedule A, line 8)	**2**	
3	Gross profit. Subtract line 2 from line 1c	**3**	
4	Net gain (loss) from Form 4797, Part II, line 17 *(attach Form 4797)*	**4**	
5	Other income (loss) *(attach statement)*	**5**	
6	**Total income (loss).** Add lines 3 through 5 ▶	**6**	

Deductions (see the instructions for limitations)

7	Compensation of officers			**7**	
8	Salaries and wages (less employment credits)			**8**	
9	Repairs and maintenance			**9**	
10	Bad debts			**10**	
11	Rents			**11**	
12	Taxes and licenses			**12**	
13	Interest			**13**	
14a	Depreciation *(attach Form 4562)*	**14a**			
b	Depreciation claimed on Schedule A and elsewhere on return	**14b**			
c	Subtract line 14b from line 14a			**14c**	
15	Depletion **(Do not deduct oil and gas depletion.)**			**15**	
16	Advertising			**16**	
17	Pension, profit-sharing, etc., plans			**17**	
18	Employee benefit programs			**18**	
19	Other deductions *(attach statement)*			**19**	
20	**Total deductions.** Add the amounts shown in the far right column for lines 7 through 19 ▶			**20**	
21	**Ordinary business income (loss).** Subtract line 20 from line 6			**21**	

Tax and Payments

22	**Tax: a** Excess net passive income tax *(attach statement)*	**22a**			
b	Tax from Schedule D (Form 1120S)	**22b**			
c	Add lines 22a and 22b (see the instructions for additional taxes)			**22c**	
23	**Payments: a** 2005 estimated tax payments and amount applied from 2004 return	**23a**			
b	Tax deposited with Form 7004	**23b**			
c	Credit for Federal tax paid on fuels *(attach Form 4136)*	**23c**			
d	Add lines 23a through 23c			**23d**	
24	Estimated tax penalty (see instructions). Check if Form 2220 is attached ▶ ☐			**24**	
25	**Tax due.** If line 23d is smaller than the total of lines 22c and 24, enter amount owed			**25**	
26	**Overpayment.** If line 23d is larger than the total of lines 22c and 24, enter amount overpaid			**26**	
27	Enter amount of line 26 you want: **Credited to 2006 estimated tax** ▶ **Refunded** ▶			**27**	

Sign Here

Under penalties of perjury, I declare that I have examined this return, including accompanying schedules and statements, and to the best of my knowledge and belief, it is true, correct, and complete. Declaration of preparer (other than taxpayer) is based on all information of which preparer has any knowledge.

▶ Signature of officer | Date | ▶ Title

May the IRS discuss this return with the preparer shown below (see instructions)? ☐ **Yes** ☐ **No**

Paid Preparer's Use Only

Preparer's signature ▶	Date	Check if self-employed ☐	Preparer's SSN or PTIN
Firm's name (or yours if self-employed), address, and ZIP code ▶		EIN	
		Phone no. ( )	

For Privacy Act and Paperwork Reduction Act Notice, see the separate instructions. Cat. No. 11510H Form **1120S** (2005)

Form 1120S (2005) Page **2**

Schedule A Cost of Goods Sold (see instructions)

1	Inventory at beginning of year	1	
2	Purchases	2	
3	Cost of labor	3	
4	Additional section 263A costs *(attach statement)*	4	
5	Other costs *(attach statement)*	5	
6	**Total.** Add lines 1 through 5	6	
7	Inventory at end of year	7	
8	**Cost of goods sold.** Subtract line 7 from line 6. Enter here and on page 1, line 2	8	

9a Check all methods used for valuing closing inventory: *(i)* ☐ Cost as described in Regulations section 1.471-3
(ii) ☐ Lower of cost or market as described in Regulations section 1.471-4
(iii) ☐ Other (specify method used and attach explanation) ▶

b Check if there was a writedown of subnormal goods as described in Regulations section 1.471-2(c) ▶ ☐

c Check if the LIFO inventory method was adopted this tax year for any goods (if checked, attach Form 970) ▶ ☐

d If the LIFO inventory method was used for this tax year, enter percentage (or amounts) of closing inventory computed under LIFO **9d**

e If property is produced or acquired for resale, do the rules of Section 263A apply to the corporation? ☐ Yes ☐ No

f Was there any change in determining quantities, cost, or valuations between opening and closing inventory? ☐ Yes ☐ No
If "Yes," attach explanation.

Schedule B Other Information (see instructions)

		Yes	No
1	Check method of accounting: **(a)** ☐ Cash **(b)** ☐ Accrual **(c)** ☐ Other (specify) ▶		
2	See the instructions and enter the: **(a)** Business activity ▶ **(b)** Product or service ▶		
3	At the end of the tax year, did the corporation own, directly or indirectly, 50% or more of the voting stock of a domestic corporation? (For rules of attribution, see section 267(c).) If "Yes," attach a statement showing: **(a)** name, address, and employer identification number and **(b)** percentage owned.		
4	Was the corporation a member of a controlled group subject to the provisions of section 1561?		
5	Has this corporation filed, or is it required to file, a return under section 6111 to provide information on any reportable transaction?		
6	Check this box if the corporation issued publicly offered debt instruments with original issue discount ▶ ☐ If checked, the corporation may have to file **Form 8281,** Information Return for Publicly Offered Original Issue Discount Instruments.		
7	If the corporation: **(a)** was a C corporation before it elected to be an S corporation **or** the corporation acquired an asset with a basis determined by reference to its basis (or the basis of any other property) in the hands of a C corporation **and (b)** has net unrealized built-in gain (defined in section 1374(d)(1)) in excess of the net recognized built-in gain from prior years, enter the net unrealized built-in gain reduced by net recognized built-in gain from prior years ▶ $		
8	Check this box if the corporation had accumulated earnings and profits at the close of the tax year ▶ ☐		
9	Are the corporation's total receipts (see instructions) for the tax year **and** its total assets at the end of the tax year less than $250,000? If "Yes," the corporation is not required to complete Schedules L and M-1.		

Note: *If the corporation had assets or operated a business in a foreign country or U.S. possession, it may be required to attach* ***Schedule N (Form 1120),*** *Foreign Operations of U.S. Corporations, to this return. See Schedule N for details.*

Schedule K Shareholders' Shares of Income, Deductions, Credits, etc.

	Shareholders' Pro Rata Share Items				Total amount
Income (Loss)	1 Ordinary business income (loss) (page 1, line 21)			1	
	2 Net rental real estate income (loss) *(attach Form 8825)*			2	
	3a Other gross rental income (loss)	3a			
	b Expenses from other rental activities *(attach statement)*	3b			
	c Other net rental income (loss). Subtract line 3b from line 3a			3c	
	4 Interest income			4	
	5 Dividends: **a** Ordinary dividends			5a	
	b Qualified dividends	5b			
	6 Royalties			6	
	7 Net short-term capital gain (loss) *(attach Schedule D (Form 1120S))*			7	
	8a Net long-term capital gain (loss) *(attach Schedule D (Form 1120S))*			8a	
	b Collectibles (28%) gain (loss)	8b			
	c Unrecaptured section 1250 gain *(attach statement)*	8c			
	9 Net section 1231 gain (loss) (attach Form 4797)			9	
	10 Other income (loss) *(see instructions)* Type ▶			10	

Form **1120S** (2005)

Form 1120S (2005) Page 3

	Shareholders' Pro Rata Share Items (continued)		Total amount
Deductions	**11** Section 179 deduction *(attach Form 4562)*	11	
	12a Contributions	12a	
	b Investment interest expense	12b	
	c Section 59(e)(2) expenditures **(1)** Type ▶ ______ **(2)** Amount ▶	12c(2)	
	d Other deductions *(see instructions)* Type ▶ ______	12d	
Credits & Credit Recapture	**13a** Low-income housing credit (section 42(j)(5))	13a	
	b Low-income housing credit (other)	13b	
	c Qualified rehabilitation expenditures (rental real estate) *(attach Form 3468)*	13c	
	d Other rental real estate credits (see instructions) Type ▶ ______	13d	
	e Other rental credits (see instructions) Type ▶ ______	13e	
	f Credit for alcohol used as fuel *(attach Form 6478)*	13f	
	g Other credits and credit recapture *(see instructions)* Type ▶ ______	13g	
Foreign Transactions	**14a** Name of country or U.S. possession ▶ ______		
	b Gross income from all sources	14b	
	c Gross income sourced at shareholder level	14c	
	Foreign gross income sourced at corporate level:		
	d Passive	14d	
	e Listed categories *(attach statement)*	14e	
	f General limitation	14f	
	Deductions allocated and apportioned at shareholder level:		
	g Interest expense	14g	
	h Other	14h	
	Deductions allocated and apportioned at corporate level to foreign source income:		
	i Passive	14i	
	j Listed categories *(attach statement)*	14j	
	k General limitation	14k	
	Other information:		
	l Total foreign taxes (check one): ▶ ☐ Paid ☐ Accrued	14l	
	m Reduction in taxes available for credit *(attach statement)*	14m	
	n Other foreign tax information *(attach statement)*		
Alternative Minimum Tax (AMT) Items	**15a** Post-1986 depreciation adjustment	15a	
	b Adjusted gain or loss	15b	
	c Depletion (other than oil and gas)	15c	
	d Oil, gas, and geothermal properties—gross income	15d	
	e Oil, gas, and geothermal properties—deductions	15e	
	f Other AMT items *(attach statement)*	15f	
Items Affecting Shareholder Basis	**16a** Tax-exempt interest income	16a	
	b Other tax-exempt income	16b	
	c Nondeductible expenses	16c	
	d Property distributions	16d	
	e Repayment of loans from shareholders	16e	
Other Information	**17a** Investment income	17a	
	b Investment expenses	17b	
	c Dividend distributions paid from accumulated earnings and profits	17c	
	d Other items and amounts *(attach statement)*		
	e Income/loss reconciliation. (Required only if Schedule M-1 must be completed.) Combine the amounts on lines 1 through 10 in the far right column. From the result, subtract the sum of the amounts on lines 11 through 12d and 14l	17e	

Form **1120S** (2005)

Form 1120S (2005) Page **4**

Note: The corporation is not required to complete Schedules L and M-1 if question 9 of Schedule B is answered "Yes."

Schedule L **Balance Sheets per Books**

Assets	Beginning of tax year (a)	(b)	End of tax year (c)	(d)
1 Cash				
2a Trade notes and accounts receivable				
b Less allowance for bad debts				
3 Inventories				
4 U.S. government obligations				
5 Tax-exempt securities				
6 Other current assets *(attach statement)*				
7 Loans to shareholders				
8 Mortgage and real estate loans				
9 Other investments *(attach statement)*				
10a Buildings and other depreciable assets				
b Less accumulated depreciation				
11a Depletable assets				
b Less accumulated depletion				
12 Land (net of any amortization)				
13a Intangible assets (amortizable only)				
b Less accumulated amortization				
14 Other assets *(attach statement)*				
15 Total assets				
Liabilities and Shareholders' Equity				
16 Accounts payable				
17 Mortgages, notes, bonds payable in less than 1 year				
18 Other current liabilities *(attach statement)*				
19 Loans from shareholders				
20 Mortgages, notes, bonds payable in 1 year or more				
21 Other liabilities *(attach statement)*				
22 Capital stock				
23 Additional paid-in capital				
24 Retained earnings				
25 Adjustments to shareholders' equity *(attach statement)*				
26 Less cost of treasury stock		( )		( )
27 Total liabilities and shareholders' equity				

Schedule M-1 **Reconciliation of Income (Loss) per Books With Income (Loss) per Return**

1 Net income (loss) per books		5 Income recorded on books this year not included on Schedule K, lines 1 through 10 (itemize):	
2 Income included on Schedule K, lines 1, 2, 3c, 4, 5a, 6, 7, 8a, 9, and 10, not recorded on books this year (itemize):		a Tax-exempt interest $	
3 Expenses recorded on books this year not included on Schedule K, lines 1 through 12 and 14l (itemize):		6 Deductions included on Schedule K, lines 1 through 12 and 14l, not charged against book income this year (itemize):	
a Depreciation $		a Depreciation $	
b Travel and entertainment $		7 Add lines 5 and 6	
4 Add lines 1 through 3		8 Income (loss) (Schedule K, line 17e). Line 4 less line 7	

Schedule M-2 **Analysis of Accumulated Adjustments Account, Other Adjustments Account, and Shareholders' Undistributed Taxable Income Previously Taxed** (see instructions)

	(a) Accumulated adjustments account	**(b)** Other adjustments account	**(c)** Shareholders' undistributed taxable income previously taxed
1 Balance at beginning of tax year			
2 Ordinary income from page 1, line 21			
3 Other additions			
4 Loss from page 1, line 21	( )		
5 Other reductions	( )	( )	
6 Combine lines 1 through 5			
7 Distributions other than dividend distributions			
8 Balance at end of tax year. Subtract line 7 from line 6			

Form **1120S** (2005)

671105

☐ Final K-1 ☐ Amended K-1 OMB No. 1545-0130

Schedule K-1 (Form 1120S) **2005**

Department of the Treasury
Internal Revenue Service

For calendar year 2005, or tax year beginning ________, 2005
ending ________, 20__

Shareholder's Share of Income, Deductions, Credits, etc.

► See back of form and separate instructions.

Part I Information About the Corporation

A Corporation's employer identification number

B Corporation's name, address, city, state, and ZIP code

C IRS Center where corporation filed return

D ☐ Tax shelter registration number, if any ________

E ☐ Check if Form 8271 is attached

Part II Information About the Shareholder

F Shareholder's identifying number

G Shareholder's name, address, city, state and ZIP code

H Shareholder's percentage of stock ownership for tax year . . . . . . ________ %

For IRS Use Only

Part III Shareholder's Share of Current Year Income, Deductions, Credits, and Other Items

1	Ordinary business income (loss)	13	Credits & credit recapture
2	Net rental real estate income (loss)		
3	Other net rental income (loss)		
4	Interest income		
5a	Ordinary dividends		
5b	Qualified dividends	14	Foreign transactions
6	Royalties		
7	Net short-term capital gain (loss)		
8a	Net long-term capital gain (loss)		
8b	Collectibles (28%) gain (loss)		
8c	Unrecaptured section 1250 gain		
9	Net section 1231 gain (loss)		
10	Other income (loss)	15	Alternative minimum tax (AMT) items
11	Section 179 deduction	16	Items affecting shareholder basis
12	Other deductions		
		17	Other information

* See attached statement for additional information.

Form **2553** (Rev. March 2005) Department of the Treasury Internal Revenue Service

Election by a Small Business Corporation

(Under section 1362 of the Internal Revenue Code)

▶ See Parts II and III on back and the separate instructions.

▶ The corporation may either send or fax this form to the IRS. See page 2 of the instructions.

OMB No. 1545-0146

Notes: 1. ***Do not*** *file* ***Form 1120S,*** *U.S. Income Tax Return for an S Corporation, for any tax year before the year the election takes effect.*

2. *This election to be an S corporation can be accepted only if all the tests are met under* ***Who May Elect*** *on page 1 of the instructions; all shareholders have signed the consent statement; an officer has signed this form; and the exact name and address of the corporation and other required form information are provided.*

Part I Election Information

Please Type or Print		
	Name (see instructions)	**A Employer identification number**
	Number, street, and room or suite no. (If a P.O. box, see instructions.)	**B** Date incorporated
	City or town, state, and ZIP code	**C** State of incorporation

D Check the applicable box(es) if the corporation, after applying for the EIN shown in **A** above, changed its name ☐ or address ☐

E Election is to be effective for tax year beginning (month, day, year) . . . . ▶ / /

F Name and title of officer or legal representative who the IRS may call for more information

G Telephone number of officer or legal representative ( )

H If this election takes effect for the first tax year the corporation exists, enter month, day, and year of the **earliest** of the following: (1) date the corporation first had shareholders, (2) date the corporation first had assets, or (3) date the corporation began doing business . . . . ▶ / /

I Selected tax year: Annual return will be filed for tax year ending (month and day) ▶

If the tax year ends on any date other than December 31, except for a 52-53-week tax year ending with reference to the month of December, complete Part II on the back. If the date you enter is the ending date of a 52-53-week tax year, write "52-53-week year" to the right of the date.

J Name and address of each shareholder or former shareholder required to consent to the election. (See the instructions for column K)	**K** Shareholders' Consent Statement. Under penalties of perjury, we declare that we consent to the election of the above-named corporation to be an S corporation under section 1362(a) and that we have examined this consent statement, including accompanying schedules and statements, and to the best of our knowledge and belief, it is true, correct, and complete. We understand our consent is binding and may not be withdrawn after the corporation has made a valid election. (Sign and date below.)		**L** Stock owned or percentage of ownership (see instructions)		**M** Social security number or employer identification number (see instructions)	**N** Share-holder's tax year ends (month and day)
	Signature	Date	Number of shares or percentage of ownership	Date(s) acquired		

Under penalties of perjury, I declare that I have examined this election, including accompanying schedules and statements, and to the best of my knowledge and belief, it is true, correct, and complete.

Signature of officer ▶ **Title ▶** **Date ▶**

Form 2553 (Rev. 3-2005) Page 2

Part II **Selection of Fiscal Tax Year** (All corporations using this part must complete item O and item P, Q, or R.)

O Check the applicable box to indicate whether the corporation is:

1. ☐ A new corporation **adopting** the tax year entered in item I, Part I.
2. ☐ An existing corporation **retaining** the tax year entered in item I, Part I.
3. ☐ An existing corporation **changing** to the tax year entered in item I, Part I.

P Complete item P if the corporation is using the automatic approval provisions of Rev. Proc. 2002-38, 2002-22 I.R.B. 1037, to request **(1)** a natural business year (as defined in section 5.05 of Rev. Proc. 2002-38) or **(2)** a year that satisfies the ownership tax year test (as defined in section 5.06 of Rev. Proc. 2002-38). Check the applicable box below to indicate the representation statement the corporation is making.

1. Natural Business Year ▶ ☐ I represent that the corporation is adopting, retaining, or changing to a tax year that qualifies as its natural business year as defined in section 5.05 of Rev. Proc. 2002-38 and has attached a statement verifying that it satisfies the 25% gross receipts test (see instructions for content of statement). I also represent that the corporation is not precluded by section 4.02 of Rev. Proc. 2002-38 from obtaining automatic approval of such adoption, retention, or change in tax year.

2. Ownership Tax Year ▶ ☐ I represent that shareholders (as described in section 5.06 of Rev. Proc. 2002-38) holding more than half of the shares of the stock (as of the first day of the tax year to which the request relates) of the corporation have the same tax year or are concurrently changing to the tax year that the corporation adopts, retains, or changes to per item I, Part I, and that such tax year satisfies the requirement of section 4.01(3) of Rev. Proc. 2002-38. I also represent that the corporation is not precluded by section 4.02 of Rev. Proc. 2002-38 from obtaining automatic approval of such adoption, retention, or change in tax year.

Note: *If you do not use item P and the corporation wants a fiscal tax year, complete either item Q or R below. Item Q is used to request a fiscal tax year based on a business purpose and to make a back-up section 444 election. Item R is used to make a regular section 444 election.*

Q Business Purpose—To request a fiscal tax year based on a business purpose, check box Q1. See instructions for details including payment of a user fee. You may also check box Q2 and/or box Q3.

1. Check here ▶ ☐ if the fiscal year entered in item I, Part I, is requested under the prior approval provisions of Rev. Proc. 2002-39, 2002-22 I.R.B. 1046. Attach to Form 2553 a statement describing the relevant facts and circumstances and, if applicable, the gross receipts from sales and services necessary to establish a business purpose. See the instructions for details regarding the gross receipts from sales and services. If the IRS proposes to disapprove the requested fiscal year, do you want a conference with the IRS National Office?
☐ Yes ☐ No

2. Check here ▶ ☐ to show that the corporation intends to make a back-up section 444 election in the event the corporation's business purpose request is not approved by the IRS. (See instructions for more information.)

3. Check here ▶ ☐ to show that the corporation agrees to adopt or change to a tax year ending December 31 if necessary for the IRS to accept this election for S corporation status in the event (1) the corporation's business purpose request is not approved and the corporation makes a back-up section 444 election, but is ultimately not qualified to make a section 444 election, or (2) the corporation's business purpose request is not approved and the corporation did not make a back-up section 444 election.

R Section 444 Election—To make a section 444 election, check box R1. You may also check box R2.

1. Check here ▶ ☐ to show the corporation will make, if qualified, a section 444 election to have the fiscal tax year shown in item I, Part I. To make the election, you must complete **Form 8716,** Election To Have a Tax Year Other Than a Required Tax Year, and either attach it to Form 2553 or file it separately.

2. Check here ▶ ☐ to show that the corporation agrees to adopt or change to a tax year ending December 31 if necessary for the IRS to accept this election for S corporation status in the event the corporation is ultimately not qualified to make a section 444 election.

Part III **Qualified Subchapter S Trust (QSST) Election Under Section 1361(d)(2)***

Income beneficiary's name and address	Social security number
	: :
Trust's name and address	Employer identification number
	:

Date on which stock of the corporation was transferred to the trust (month, day, year) . . . . ▶ / /

In order for the trust named above to be a QSST and thus a qualifying shareholder of the S corporation for which this Form 2553 is filed, I hereby make the election under section 1361(d)(2). Under penalties of perjury, I certify that the trust meets the definitional requirements of section 1361(d)(3) and that all other information provided in Part III is true, correct, and complete.

Signature of income beneficiary or signature and title of legal representative or other qualified person making the election — Date

*Use Part III to make the QSST election only if stock of the corporation has been transferred to the trust on or before the date on which the corporation makes its election to be an S corporation. The QSST election must be made and filed separately if stock of the corporation is transferred to the trust **after** the date on which the corporation makes the S election.

Form **4562** (Rev. January 2006) Department of the Treasury Internal Revenue Service

Depreciation and Amortization
(Including Information on Listed Property)

▶ See separate instructions. ▶ Attach to your tax return.

OMB No. 1545-0172
2005
Attachment Sequence No. **67**

Name(s) shown on return	Business or activity to which this form relates	Identifying number

Part I **Election To Expense Certain Property Under Section 179**
Note: *If you have any listed property, complete Part V before you complete Part I.*

1	Maximum amount. See the instructions for a higher limit for certain businesses	1	$105,000
2	Total cost of section 179 property placed in service (see instructions)	2	
3	Threshold cost of section 179 property before reduction in limitation	3	$420,000
4	Reduction in limitation. Subtract line 3 from line 2. If zero or less, enter -0-	4	
5	Dollar limitation for tax year. Subtract line 4 from line 1. If zero or less, enter -0-. If married filing separately, see instructions	5	

	(a) Description of property	(b) Cost (business use only)	(c) Elected cost
6			

7	Listed property. Enter the amount from line 29	7	
8	Total elected cost of section 179 property. Add amounts in column (c), lines 6 and 7	8	
9	Tentative deduction. Enter the **smaller** of line 5 or line 8	9	
10	Carryover of disallowed deduction from line 13 of your 2004 Form 4562	10	
11	Business income limitation. Enter the smaller of business income (not less than zero) or line 5 (see instructions)	11	
12	Section 179 expense deduction. Add lines 9 and 10, but do not enter more than line 11	12	
13	Carryover of disallowed deduction to 2006. Add lines 9 and 10, less line 12 ▶	13	

Note: *Do not use Part II or Part III below for listed property. Instead, use Part V.*

Part II **Special Depreciation Allowance and Other Depreciation (Do not** include listed property.) (See instructions.)

14	Special allowance for certain aircraft, certain property with a long production period, and qualified NYL or GO Zone property (other than listed property) placed in service during the tax year (see instructions)	14	
15	Property subject to section 168(f)(1) election	15	
16	Other depreciation (including ACRS)	16	

Part III **MACRS Depreciation (Do not** include listed property.) (See instructions.)

Section A

17	MACRS deductions for assets placed in service in tax years beginning before 2005	17	
18	If you are electing to group any assets placed in service during the tax year into one or more general asset accounts, check here ▶ ☐		

Section B—Assets Placed in Service During 2005 Tax Year Using the General Depreciation System

(a) Classification of property	(b) Month and year placed in service	(c) Basis for depreciation (business/investment use only—see instructions)	(d) Recovery period	(e) Convention	(f) Method	(g) Depreciation deduction
19a 3-year property						
b 5-year property						
c 7-year property						
d 10-year property						
e 15-year property						
f 20-year property						
g 25-year property			25 yrs.		S/L	
h Residential rental property			27.5 yrs.	MM	S/L	
			27.5 yrs.	MM	S/L	
i Nonresidential real property			39 yrs.	MM	S/L	
				MM	S/L	

Section C—Assets Placed in Service During 2005 Tax Year Using the Alternative Depreciation System

20a Class life					S/L	
b 12-year			12 yrs.		S/L	
c 40-year			40 yrs.	MM	S/L	

Part IV **Summary** (see instructions)

21	Listed property. Enter amount from line 28	21	
22	**Total.** Add amounts from line 12, lines 14 through 17, lines 19 and 20 in column (g), and line 21. Enter here and on the appropriate lines of your return. Partnerships and S corporations—see instr.	22	
23	For assets shown above and placed in service during the current year, enter the portion of the basis attributable to section 263A costs	23	

For Paperwork Reduction Act Notice, see separate instructions. Cat. No. 12906N Form **4562** (2005) (Rev. 1-2006)

Form 4562 (2005) (Rev. 1-2006) Page **2**

Part V **Listed Property** (Include automobiles, certain other vehicles, cellular telephones, certain computers, and property used for entertainment, recreation, or amusement.)

Note: *For any vehicle for which you are using the standard mileage rate or deducting lease expense, complete* ***only*** *24a, 24b, columns (a) through (c) of Section A, all of Section B, and Section C if applicable.*

Section A—Depreciation and Other Information (Caution: *See the instructions for limits for passenger automobiles.***)**

24a Do you have evidence to support the business/investment use claimed? ☐ **Yes** ☐ **No** | **24b** If "Yes," is the evidence written? ☐ **Yes** ☐ **No**

(a) Type of property (list vehicles first)	**(b)** Date placed in service	**(c)** Business/ investment use percentage	**(d)** Cost or other basis	**(e)** Basis for depreciation (business/investment use only)	**(f)** Recovery period	**(g)** Method/ Convention	**(h)** Depreciation deduction	**(i)** Elected section 179 cost
25 Special allowance for certain aircraft, certain property with a long production period, and qualified NYL or GO Zone property placed in service during the tax year and used more than 50% in a qualified business use (see instructions)						**25**		
26 Property used more than 50% in a qualified business use:								
		%						
		%						
		%						
27 Property used 50% or less in a qualified business use:								
		%				S/L –		
		%				S/L –		
		%				S/L –		
28 Add amounts in column (h), lines 25 through 27. Enter here and on line 21, page 1.						**28**		
29 Add amounts in column (i), line 26. Enter here and on line 7, page 1.							**29**	

Section B—Information on Use of Vehicles

Complete this section for vehicles used by a sole proprietor, partner, or other "more than 5% owner," or related person.
If you provided vehicles to your employees, first answer the questions in Section C to see if you meet an exception to completing this section for those vehicles.

	(a) Vehicle 1		**(b)** Vehicle 2		**(c)** Vehicle 3		**(d)** Vehicle 4		**(e)** Vehicle 5		**(f)** Vehicle 6	
30 Total business/investment miles driven during the year (**do not** include commuting miles)												
31 Total commuting miles driven during the year												
32 Total other personal (noncommuting) miles driven												
33 Total miles driven during the year. Add lines 30 through 32												
	Yes	**No**	**Yes**	**No**	**Yes**	**No**	**Yes**	**No**	**Yes**	**No**	**Yes**	**No**
34 Was the vehicle available for personal use during off-duty hours?												
35 Was the vehicle used primarily by a more than 5% owner or related person?												
36 Is another vehicle available for personal use?												

Section C—Questions for Employers Who Provide Vehicles for Use by Their Employees

Answer these questions to determine if you meet an exception to completing Section B for vehicles used by employees who **are not** more than 5% owners or related persons (see instructions).

	Yes	**No**
37 Do you maintain a written policy statement that prohibits all personal use of vehicles, including commuting, by your employees?		
38 Do you maintain a written policy statement that prohibits personal use of vehicles, except commuting, by your employees? See the instructions for vehicles used by corporate officers, directors, or 1% or more owners		
39 Do you treat all use of vehicles by employees as personal use?		
40 Do you provide more than five vehicles to your employees, obtain information from your employees about the use of the vehicles, and retain the information received?		
41 Do you meet the requirements concerning qualified automobile demonstration use? (See instructions.)		

Note: *If your answer to 37, 38, 39, 40, or 41 is "Yes," do not complete Section B for the covered vehicles.*

Part VI **Amortization**

(a) Description of costs	**(b)** Date amortization begins	**(c)** Amortizable amount	**(d)** Code section	**(e)** Amortization period or percentage	**(f)** Amortization for this year
42 Amortization of costs that begins during your 2005 tax year (see instructions):					
43 Amortization of costs that began before your 2005 tax year.				**43**	
44 **Total.** Add amounts in column (f). See the instructions for where to report.				**44**	

Form **4562** (2005) (Rev. 1-2006)

Form **4626**

Department of the Treasury
Internal Revenue Service

Alternative Minimum Tax—Corporations

▶ See separate instructions.
▶ Attach to the corporation's tax return.

OMB No. 1545-0175

2005

Name | Employer identification number

Note: *See the instructions to find out if the corporation is a small corporation exempt from the alternative minimum tax (AMT) under section 55(e).*

1	Taxable income or (loss) before net operating loss deduction	1	
2	**Adjustments and preferences:**		
a	Depreciation of post-1986 property	2a	
b	Amortization of certified pollution control facilities	2b	
c	Amortization of mining exploration and development costs	2c	
d	Amortization of circulation expenditures (personal holding companies only)	2d	
e	Adjusted gain or loss	2e	
f	Long-term contracts	2f	
g	Merchant marine capital construction funds	2g	
h	Section 833(b) deduction (Blue Cross, Blue Shield, and similar type organizations only)	2h	
i	Tax shelter farm activities (personal service corporations only)	2i	
j	Passive activities (closely held corporations and personal service corporations only)	2j	
k	Loss limitations	2k	
l	Depletion	2l	
m	Tax-exempt interest income from specified private activity bonds	2m	
n	Intangible drilling costs	2n	
o	Other adjustments and preferences	2o	
3	Pre-adjustment alternative minimum taxable income (AMTI). Combine lines 1 through 2o	3	
4	**Adjusted current earnings (ACE) adjustment:**		
a	ACE from line 10 of the ACE worksheet in the instructions — 4a		
b	Subtract line 3 from line 4a. If line 3 exceeds line 4a, enter the difference as a negative amount (see instructions) — 4b		
c	Multiply line 4b by 75% (.75). Enter the result as a positive amount — 4c		
d	Enter the excess, if any, of the corporation's total increases in AMTI from prior year ACE adjustments over its total reductions in AMTI from prior year ACE adjustments (see instructions). **Note:** *You **must** enter an amount on line 4d (even if line 4b is positive)* — 4d		
e	ACE adjustment. • If line 4b is zero or more, enter the amount from line 4c • If line 4b is less than zero, enter the **smaller** of line 4c or line 4d as a negative amount	4e	
5	Combine lines 3 and 4e. If zero or less, stop here; the corporation does not owe any AMT	5	
6	Alternative tax net operating loss deduction (see instructions)	6	
7	**Alternative minimum taxable income.** Subtract line 6 from line 5. If the corporation held a residual interest in a REMIC, see instructions	7	
8	**Exemption phase-out** (if line 7 is $310,000 or more, skip lines 8a and 8b and enter -0- on line 8c):		
a	Subtract $150,000 from line 7 (if completing this line for a member of a controlled group, see instructions). If zero or less, enter -0- — 8a		
b	Multiply line 8a by 25% (.25) — 8b		
c	Exemption. Subtract line 8b from $40,000 (if completing this line for a member of a controlled group, see instructions). If zero or less, enter -0-	8c	
9	Subtract line 8c from line 7. If zero or less, enter -0-	9	
10	Multiply line 9 by 20% (.20)	10	
11	Alternative minimum tax foreign tax credit (AMTFTC) (see instructions)	11	
12	Tentative minimum tax. Subtract line 11 from line 10	12	
13	Regular tax liability before applying all credits except the foreign tax credit and possessions tax credit	13	
14	**Alternative minimum tax.** Subtract line 13 from line 12. If zero or less, enter -0-. Enter here and on Form 1120, Schedule J, line 4, or the appropriate line of the corporation's income tax return	14	

For Paperwork Reduction Act Notice, see the instructions. Cat. No. 12955I Form **4626** (2005)

Form **4797**

Department of the Treasury
Internal Revenue Service (99)

Sales of Business Property

(Also Involuntary Conversions and Recapture Amounts Under Sections 179 and 280F(b)(2))

▶Attach to your tax return. ▶See separate instructions.

OMB No. 1545-0184

2005

Attachment Sequence No. **27**

Name(s) shown on return | **Identifying number**

1 Enter the gross proceeds from sales or exchanges reported to you for 2005 on Form(s) 1099-B or 1099-S (or substitute statement) that you are including on line 2, 10, or 20 (see instructions) 1

Part I Sales or Exchanges of Property Used in a Trade or Business and Involuntary Conversions From Other Than Casualty or Theft—Most Property Held More Than 1 Year (see instructions)

(a) Description of property	(b) Date acquired (mo., day, yr.)	(c) Date sold (mo., day, yr.)	(d) Gross sales price	(e) Depreciation allowed or allowable since acquisition	(f) Cost or other basis, plus improvements and expense of sale	(g) Gain or (loss) Subtract (f) from the sum of (d) and (e)
2						

3 Gain, if any, from Form 4684, line 42 3

4 Section 1231 gain from installment sales from Form 6252, line 26 or 37 4

5 Section 1231 gain or (loss) from like-kind exchanges from Form 8824 5

6 Gain, if any, from line 32, from other than casualty or theft 6

7 Combine lines 2 through 6. Enter the gain or (loss) here and on the appropriate line as follows: 7

Partnerships (except electing large partnerships) and S corporations. Report the gain or (loss) following the instructions for Form 1065, Schedule K, line 10, or Form 1120S, Schedule K, line 9. Skip lines 8, 9, 11, and 12 below.

Individuals, partners, S corporation shareholders, and all others. If line 7 is zero or a loss, enter the amount from line 7 on line 11 below and skip lines 8 and 9. If line 7 is a gain and you did not have any prior year section 1231 losses, or they were recaptured in an earlier year, enter the gain from line 7 as a long-term capital gain on the Schedule D filed with your return and skip lines 8, 9, 11, and 12 below.

8 Nonrecaptured net section 1231 losses from prior years (see instructions) 8

9 Subtract line 8 from line 7. If zero or less, enter -0-. If line 9 is zero, enter the gain from line 7 on line 12 below. If line 9 is more than zero, enter the amount from line 8 on line 12 below and enter the gain from line 9 as a long-term capital gain on the Schedule D filed with your return (see instructions). 9

Part II Ordinary Gains and Losses (see instructions)

10 Ordinary gains and losses not included on lines 11 through 16 (include property held 1 year or less):

11 Loss, if any, from line 7. . . . . 11 ( )

12 Gain, if any, from line 7 or amount from line 8, if applicable 12

13 Gain, if any, from line 31 13

14 Net gain or (loss) from Form 4684, lines 34 and 41a 14

15 Ordinary gain from installment sales from Form 6252, line 25 or 36 15

16 Ordinary gain or (loss) from like-kind exchanges from Form 8824 16

17 Combine lines 10 through 16 17

18 For all except individual returns, enter the amount from line 17 on the appropriate line of your return and skip lines a and b below. For individual returns, complete lines a and b below:

a If the loss on line 11 includes a loss from Form 4684, line 38, column (b)(ii), enter that part of the loss here. Enter the part of the loss from income-producing property on Schedule A (Form 1040), line 27, and the part of the loss from property used as an employee on Schedule A (Form 1040), line 22. Identify as from "Form 4797, line 18a." See instructions 18a

b Redetermine the gain or (loss) on line 17 excluding the loss, if any, on line 18a. Enter here and on Form 1040, line 14 . . . . 18b

For Paperwork Reduction Act Notice, see separate instructions. Cat. No. 13086I Form **4797** (2005)

Part III Gain From Disposition of Property Under Sections 1245, 1250, 1252, 1254, and 1255 (see instructions)

19 (a) Description of section 1245, 1250, 1252, 1254, or 1255 property:	(b) Date acquired (mo., day, yr.)	(c) Date sold (mo., day, yr.)
A		
B		
C		
D		

These columns relate to the properties on lines 19A through 19D. ▶		Property A	Property B	Property C	Property D
20 Gross sales price (**Note:** *See line 1 before completing.*)	20				
21 Cost or other basis plus expense of sale	21				
22 Depreciation (or depletion) allowed or allowable	22				
23 Adjusted basis. Subtract line 22 from line 21	23				
24 Total gain. Subtract line 23 from line 20	24				
25 **If section 1245 property:**					
a Depreciation allowed or allowable from line 22	25a				
b Enter the **smaller** of line 24 or 25a	25b				
26 **If section 1250 property:** If straight line depreciation was used, enter -0- on line 26g, except for a corporation subject to section 291.					
a Additional depreciation after 1975 (see instructions)	26a				
b Applicable percentage multiplied by the **smaller** of line 24 or line 26a (see instructions)	26b				
c Subtract line 26a from line 24. If residential rental property **or** line 24 is not more than line 26a, skip lines 26d and 26e	26c				
d Additional depreciation after 1969 and before 1976	26d				
e Enter the **smaller** of line 26c or 26d	26e				
f Section 291 amount (corporations only)	26f				
g Add lines 26b, 26e, and 26f	26g				
27 **If section 1252 property:** Skip this section if you did not dispose of farmland or if this form is being completed for a partnership (other than an electing large partnership).					
a Soil, water, and land clearing expenses	27a				
b Line 27a multiplied by applicable percentage (see instructions)	27b				
c Enter the **smaller** of line 24 or 27b	27c				
28 **If section 1254 property:**					
a Intangible drilling and development costs, expenditures for development of mines and other natural deposits, and mining exploration costs (see instructions)	28a				
b Enter the **smaller** of line 24 or 28a	28b				
29 **If section 1255 property:**					
a Applicable percentage of payments excluded from income under section 126 (see instructions)	29a				
b Enter the **smaller** of line 24 or 29a (see instructions)	29b				

Summary of Part III Gains. Complete property columns A through D through line 29b before going to line 30.

30 Total gains for all properties. Add property columns A through D, line 24	30	
31 Add property columns A through D, lines 25b, 26g, 27c, 28b, and 29b. Enter here and on line 13	31	
32 Subtract line 31 from line 30. Enter the portion from casualty or theft on Form 4684, line 36. Enter the portion from other than casualty or theft on Form 4797, line 6	32	

Part IV Recapture Amounts Under Sections 179 and 280F(b)(2) When Business Use Drops to 50% or Less (see instructions)

		(a) Section 179	(b) Section 280F(b)(2)
33 Section 179 expense deduction or depreciation allowable in prior years	33		
34 Recomputed depreciation (see instructions)	34		
35 Recapture amount. Subtract line 34 from line 33. See the instructions for where to report	35		

Form **6251**

(Rev. January 2006)
Department of the Treasury
Internal Revenue Service (99)

Alternative Minimum Tax—Individuals

▶ See separate instructions.

▶ Attach to Form 1040 or Form 1040NR.

OMB No. 1545-0074

2005

Attachment Sequence No. **32**

Name(s) shown on Form 1040 | **Your social security number**

Part I Alternative Minimum Taxable Income (See instructions for how to complete each line.)

1	If filing Schedule A (Form 1040), enter the amount from Form 1040, line 41 (minus any amount on Form 8914, line 2), and go to line 2. Otherwise, enter the amount from Form 1040, line 38 (minus any amount on Form 8914, line 2), and go to line 7. (If less than zero, enter as a negative amount.)	1	
2	Medical and dental. Enter the **smaller** of Schedule A (Form 1040), line 4, **or** 2½ % of Form 1040, line 38	2	
3	Taxes from Schedule A (Form 1040), line 9	3	
4	Enter the home mortgage interest adjustment, if any, from line 6 of the worksheet on page 2 of the instructions	4	
5	Miscellaneous deductions from Schedule A (Form 1040), line 26	5	
6	If Form 1040, line 38, is over $145,950 (over $72,975 if married filing separately), enter the amount from line 9 of the **Itemized Deductions Worksheet** on page A-9 of the Instructions for Schedules A & B (Form 1040)	6	( )
7	Tax refund from Form 1040, line 10 or line 21	7	( )
8	Investment interest expense (difference between regular tax and AMT)	8	
9	Depletion (difference between regular tax and AMT)	9	
10	Net operating loss deduction from Form 1040, line 21. Enter as a positive amount	10	
11	Interest from specified private activity bonds exempt from the regular tax	11	
12	Qualified small business stock (7% of gain excluded under section 1202)	12	
13	Exercise of incentive stock options (excess of AMT income over regular tax income)	13	
14	Estates and trusts (amount from Schedule K-1 (Form 1041), box 12, code A)	14	
15	Electing large partnerships (amount from Schedule K-1 (Form 1065-B), box 6)	15	
16	Disposition of property (difference between AMT and regular tax gain or loss)	16	
17	Depreciation on assets placed in service after 1986 (difference between regular tax and AMT)	17	
18	Passive activities (difference between AMT and regular tax income or loss)	18	
19	Loss limitations (difference between AMT and regular tax income or loss)	19	
20	Circulation costs (difference between regular tax and AMT)	20	
21	Long-term contracts (difference between AMT and regular tax income)	21	
22	Mining costs (difference between regular tax and AMT)	22	
23	Research and experimental costs (difference between regular tax and AMT)	23	
24	Income from certain installment sales before January 1, 1987	24	( )
25	Intangible drilling costs preference	25	
26	Other adjustments, including income-based related adjustments	26	
27	Alternative tax net operating loss deduction	27	( )
28	**Alternative minimum taxable income.** Combine lines 1 through 27. (If married filing separately and line 28 is more than $191,000, see page 7 of the instructions.)	28	

Part II Alternative Minimum Tax

29 Exemption. (If this form is for a child under age 14, see page 7 of the instructions.)

IF your filing status is . . .	**AND line 28 is not over . . .**	**THEN enter on line 29 . . .**
Single or head of household	$112,500	$40,250
Married filing jointly or qualifying widow(er)	150,000	58,000
Married filing separately	75,000	29,000

If line 28 is **over** the amount shown above for your filing status, see page 7 of the instructions. → 29

30	Subtract line 29 from line 28. If zero or less, enter -0- here and on lines 33 and 35 and stop here	30	
31	• If you reported capital gain distributions directly on Form 1040, line 13; you reported qualified dividends on Form 1040, line 9b; **or** you had a gain on both lines 15 and 16 of Schedule D (Form 1040) (as refigured for the AMT, if necessary), complete Part III on the back and enter the amount from line 55 here. • **All others:** If line 30 is $175,000 or less ($87,500 or less if married filing separately), multiply line 30 by 26% (.26). Otherwise, multiply line 30 by 28% (.28) and subtract $3,500 ($1,750 if married filing separately) from the result.	31	
32	Alternative minimum tax foreign tax credit (see page 7 of the instructions)	32	
33	Tentative minimum tax. Subtract line 32 from line 31	33	
34	Tax from Form 1040, line 44 (minus any tax from Form 4972 and any foreign tax credit from Form 1040, line 47). If you used Schedule J to figure your tax, the amount for line 44 of Form 1040 must be refigured without using Schedule J (see page 9 of the instructions)	34	
35	**Alternative minimum tax.** Subtract line 34 from line 33. If zero or less, enter -0-. Enter here and on Form 1040, line 45	35	

For Paperwork Reduction Act Notice, see page 9 of the instructions. Cat. No. 13600G Form **6251** (2005) (Rev. 1-2006)

Part III Tax Computation Using Maximum Capital Gains Rates

36 Enter the amount from Form 6251, line 30		36	
37 Enter the amount from line 6 of the Qualified Dividends and Capital Gain Tax Worksheet in the instructions for Form 1040, line 44, or the amount from line 13 of the Schedule D Tax Worksheet on page D-9 of the instructions for Schedule D (Form 1040), whichever applies (as refigured for the AMT, if necessary) (see page 9 of the instructions)	37		
38 Enter the amount from Schedule D (Form 1040), line 19 (as refigured for the AMT, if necessary) (see page 9 of the instructions)	38		
39 If you did not complete a Schedule D Tax Worksheet for the regular tax or the AMT, enter the amount from line 37. Otherwise, add lines 37 and 38, and enter the **smaller** of that result or the amount from line 10 of the Schedule D Tax Worksheet (as refigured for the AMT, if necessary)	39		
40 Enter the **smaller** of line 36 or line 39		40	
41 Subtract line 40 from line 36		41	
42 If line 41 is $175,000 or less ($87,500 or less if married filing separately), multiply line 41 by 26% (.26). Otherwise, multiply line 41 by 28% (.28) and subtract $3,500 ($1,750 if married filing separately) from the result ▶		42	
43 Enter: • $59,400 if married filing jointly or qualifying widow(er), • $29,700 if single or married filing separately, or • $39,800 if head of household.	43		
44 Enter the amount from line 7 of the Qualified Dividends and Capital Gain Tax Worksheet in the instructions for Form 1040, line 44, or the amount from line 14 of the Schedule D Tax Worksheet on page D-9 of the instructions for Schedule D (Form 1040), whichever applies (as figured for the regular tax). If you did not complete either worksheet for the regular tax, enter -0-	44		
45 Subtract line 44 from line 43. If zero or less, enter -0-	45		
46 Enter the **smaller** of line 36 or line 37	46		
47 Enter the **smaller** of line 45 or line 46	47		
48 Multiply line 47 by 5% (.05) ▶		48	
49 Subtract line 47 from line 46	49		
50 Multiply line 49 by 15% (.15) ▶		50	
If line 38 is zero or blank, skip lines 51 and 52 and go to line 53. Otherwise, go to line 51.			
51 Subtract line 46 from line 40	51		
52 Multiply line 51 by 25% (.25) ▶		52	
53 Add lines 42, 48, 50, and 52		53	
54 If line 36 is $175,000 or less ($87,500 or less if married filing separately), multiply line 36 by 26% (.26). Otherwise, multiply line 36 by 28% (.28) and subtract $3,500 ($1,750 if married filing separately) from the result		54	
55 Enter the **smaller** of line 53 or line 54 here and on line 31		55	

Form **8582**

Department of the Treasury
Internal Revenue Service (99)

Passive Activity Loss Limitations

▶ See separate instructions.
▶ Attach to Form 1040 or Form 1041.

OMB No. 1545-1008
2005
Attachment Sequence No. 88

Name(s) shown on return | Identifying number

Part I 2005 Passive Activity Loss

Caution: *Complete Worksheets 1, 2, and 3 on page 2 before completing Part I.*

Rental Real Estate Activities With Active Participation (For the definition of active participation see **Special Allowance for Rental Real Estate Activities** on page 3 of the instructions.)

1a Activities with net income (enter the amount from Worksheet 1, column (a))	1a		
b Activities with net loss (enter the amount from Worksheet 1, column (b))	1b	( )	
c Prior years unallowed losses (enter the amount from Worksheet 1, column (c))	1c	( )	
d Combine lines 1a, 1b, and 1c			1d

Commercial Revitalization Deductions From Rental Real Estate Activities

2a Commercial revitalization deductions from Worksheet 2, column (a)	2a	( )	
b Prior year unallowed commercial revitalization deductions from Worksheet 2, column (b)	2b	( )	
c Add lines 2a and 2b			2c ( )

All Other Passive Activities

3a Activities with net income (enter the amount from Worksheet 3, column (a))	3a		
b Activities with net loss (enter the amount from Worksheet 3, column (b))	3b	( )	
c Prior years unallowed losses (enter the amount from Worksheet 3, column (c))	3c	( )	
d Combine lines 3a, 3b, and 3c			3d

4 Combine lines 1d, 2c, and 3d. If the result is net income or zero, all losses are allowed, including any prior year unallowed losses entered on line 1c, 2b, or 3c. **Do not** complete Form 8582. Report the losses on the forms and schedules normally used . . . **4**

If line 4 is a loss and:
- Line 1d is a loss, go to Part II.
- Line 2c is a loss (and line 1d is zero or more), skip Part II and go to Part III.
- Line 3d is a loss (and lines 1d and 2c are zero or more), skip Parts II and III and go to line 15.

Caution: *If your filing status is married filing separately and you lived with your spouse at any time during the year,* ***do not*** *complete Part II or Part III. Instead, go to line 15.*

Part II Special Allowance for Rental Real Estate With Active Participation

Note: *Enter all numbers in Part II as positive amounts. See page 8 of the instructions for an example.*

5 Enter the **smaller** of the loss on line 1d or the loss on line 4			5
6 Enter $150,000. If married filing separately, see page 8	6		
7 Enter modified adjusted gross income, but not less than zero (see page 8)	7		
Note: *If line 7 is greater than or equal to line 6, skip lines 8 and 9, enter -0- on line 10. Otherwise, go to line 8.*			
8 Subtract line 7 from line 6	8		
9 Multiply line 8 by 50% (.5). **Do not** enter more than $25,000. If married filing separately, see page 8			9
10 Enter the **smaller** of line 5 or line 9			10

If line 2c is a loss, go to Part III. Otherwise, go to line 15.

Part III Special Allowance for Commercial Revitalization Deductions From Rental Real Estate Activities

Note: *Enter all numbers in Part III as positive amounts. See the example for Part II on page 8 of the instructions.*

11 Enter $25,000 reduced by the amount, if any, on line 10. If married filing separately, see instructions	11
12 Enter the loss from line 4	12
13 Reduce line 12 by the amount on line 10	13
14 Enter the **smallest** of line 2c (treated as a positive amount), line 11, or line 13	14

Part IV Total Losses Allowed

15 Add the income, if any, on lines 1a and 3a and enter the total	15
16 **Total losses allowed from all passive activities for 2005.** Add lines 10, 14, and 15. See pages 10 and 11 of the instructions to find out how to report the losses on your tax return	16

For Paperwork Reduction Act Notice, see page 12 of the instructions. Cat. No. 63704F Form **8582** (2005)

Form 8582 (2005) Page 2

Caution: *The worksheets must be filed with your tax return. Keep a copy for your records.*

Worksheet 1—For Form 8582, Lines 1a, 1b, and 1c (See page 7 of the instructions.)

Name of activity	Current year		Prior years	Overall gain or loss	
	(a) Net income (line 1a)	(b) Net loss (line 1b)	(c) Unallowed loss (line 1c)	(d) Gain	(e) Loss
Total. Enter on Form 8582, lines 1a, 1b, and 1c . . . . ▶					

Worksheet 2—For Form 8582, Lines 2a and 2b (See pages 7 and 8 of the instructions.)

Name of activity	(a) Current year deductions (line 2a)	(b) Prior year unallowed deductions (line 2b)	(c) Overall loss
Total. Enter on Form 8582, lines 2a and 2b . . . . ▶			

Worksheet 3—For Form 8582, Lines 3a, 3b, and 3c (See page 8 of the instructions.)

Name of activity	Current year		Prior years	Overall gain or loss	
	(a) Net income (line 3a)	(b) Net loss (line 3b)	(c) Unallowed loss (line 3c)	(d) Gain	(e) Loss
Total. Enter on Form 8582, lines 3a, 3b, and 3c . . . . ▶					

Worksheet 4—Use this worksheet if an amount is shown on Form 8582, line 10 or 14 (See page 9 of the instructions.)

Name of activity	Form or schedule and line number to be reported on (see instructions)	(a) Loss	(b) Ratio	(c) Special allowance	(d) Subtract column (c) from column (a)
Total . . . . ▶			1.00		

Worksheet 5—Allocation of Unallowed Losses (See page 9 of the instructions.)

Name of activity	Form or schedule and line number to be reported on (see instructions)	(a) Loss	(b) Ratio	(c) Unallowed loss
Total . . . . ▶			1.00	

Form **8582** (2005)

Form 8582 (2005) Page **3**

Worksheet 6—Allowed Losses (See pages 9 and 10 of the instructions.)

Name of activity	Form or schedule and line number to be reported on (see instructions)	(a) Loss	(b) Unallowed loss	(c) Allowed loss
Total . . . . ▶				

Worksheet 7—Activities With Losses Reported on Two or More Forms or Schedules (See page 10 of the instructions.)

Name of Activity:	(a)	(b)	(c) Ratio	(d) Unallowed loss	(e) Allowed loss
Form or schedule and line number to be reported on (see instructions): ----------					
1a Net loss plus prior year unallowed loss from form or schedule. ▶					
b Net income from form or schedule . . . . . . ▶					
c Subtract line 1b from line 1a. If zero or less, enter -0- ▶					
Form or schedule and line number to be reported on (see instructions): ----------					
1a Net loss plus prior year unallowed loss from form or schedule. ▶					
b Net income from form or schedule . . . . . . ▶					
c Subtract line 1b from line 1a. If zero or less, enter -0- ▶					
Form or schedule and line number to be reported on (see instructions): ----------					
1a Net loss plus prior year unallowed loss from form or schedule. ▶					
b Net income from form or schedule . . . . . . ▶					
c Subtract line 1b from line 1a. If zero or less, enter -0- ▶					
Total . . . . ▶			1.00		

Form **8832**
(Rev. January 2006)
Department of the Treasury
Internal Revenue Service

Entity Classification Election

OMB No. 1545-1516

Type or Print

Name of entity	EIN ▶
Number, street, and room or suite no. If a P.O. box, see instructions.	
City or town, state, and ZIP code. If a foreign address, enter city, province or state, postal code and country.	

1 **Type of election** (see instructions):

a ☐ Initial classification by a newly-formed entity.

b ☐ Change in current classification.

2 **Form of entity** (see instructions):

a ☐ A domestic eligible entity electing to be classified as an association taxable as a corporation.

b ☐ A domestic eligible entity electing to be classified as a partnership.

c ☐ A domestic eligible entity with a single owner electing to be disregarded as a separate entity.

d ☐ A foreign eligible entity electing to be classified as an association taxable as a corporation.

e ☐ A foreign eligible entity electing to be classified as a partnership.

f ☐ A foreign eligible entity with a single owner electing to be disregarded as a separate entity.

3 **Disregarded entity information** (see instructions):

a Name of owner ▶ ....

b Identifying number of owner ▶ ....

c Country of organization of entity electing to be disregarded (if foreign) ▶ ....

4 Election is to be effective beginning (month, day, year) (see instructions) . . . . ▶ ___/___/___

5 Name and title of person whom the IRS may call for more information

6 That person's telephone number ( )

Consent Statement and Signature(s) (see instructions)

Under penalties of perjury, I (we) declare that I (we) consent to the election of the above-named entity to be classified as indicated above, and that I (we) have examined this consent statement, and to the best of my (our) knowledge and belief, it is true, correct, and complete. If I am an officer, manager, or member signing for all members of the entity, I further declare that I am authorized to execute this consent statement on their behalf.

Signature(s)	Date	Title

APPENDIX C

GLOSSARY OF TAX TERMS

The key terms in this glossary have been defined to reflect their conventional use in the field of taxation. The definitions may therefore be incomplete for other purposes.

A

Accelerated cost recovery system (ACRS). A method in which the cost of tangible property is recovered over a prescribed period of time. The approach disregards salvage value, imposes a period of cost recovery that depends upon the classification of the asset into one of various recovery periods, and prescribes the applicable percentage of cost that can be deducted each year. § 168.

Accident and health insurance benefits. Employee fringe benefits provided by employers through the payment of health and accident insurance premiums or the establishment of employer-funded medical reimbursement plans. Employers generally are entitled to a deduction for such payments, whereas employees generally exclude such fringe benefits from gross income. §§ 105 and 106.

Accountable plan. An accountable plan is a type of expense reimbursement plan that requires an employee to render an adequate accounting to the employer and return any excess reimbursement or allowance. If the expense qualifies, it will be treated as a deduction *for* AGI.

Accounting income. The accountant's concept of income is generally based upon the realization principle. Financial accounting income may differ from taxable income (e.g., accelerated depreciation might be used for Federal income tax and straight-line depreciation for financial accounting purposes). Differences are included in a reconciliation of taxable and accounting income on Schedule M–1 or Schedule M–3 of Form 1120 for corporations.

Accounting method. The method under which income and expenses are determined for tax purposes. Important accounting methods include the cash basis and the accrual basis. Special methods are available for the reporting of gain on installment sales, recognition of income on construction projects (the completed contract and percentage of completion methods), and the valuation of inventories (last-in, first-out and first-in, first-out). §§ 446–474.

Accounting period. The period of time, usually a year, used by a taxpayer for the determination of tax liability. Unless a fiscal year is chosen, taxpayers must determine and pay their income tax liability by using the calendar year (January 1 through December 31) as the period of measurement. An example of a fiscal year is July 1 through June 30. A change in accounting period (e.g., from a calendar year to a fiscal year) generally requires the consent of the IRS. Some new taxpayers, such as a newly formed corporation, are free to select either an initial calendar or a fiscal year without the consent of the IRS. §§ 441–444.

Accrual method. A method of accounting that reflects expenses incurred and income earned for any one tax year. In contrast to the cash basis of accounting, expenses need not be paid to be deductible, nor need income be received to be taxable. Unearned income (e.g., prepaid interest and rent) generally is taxed in the year of receipt regardless of the method of accounting used by the taxpayer. § 446(c)(2).

Accumulated adjustments account (AAA). An account that aggregates an S corporation's post-1982 income, loss, and deductions for the tax year (including nontaxable income and nondeductible losses and expenses). After the year-end income and expense adjustments are made, the account is reduced by distributions made during the tax year. § 1368(e)(1).

Accumulated earnings and profits. Net undistributed tax-basis earnings of a corporation aggregated from March 1, 1913, to the end of the prior tax year. Used to determine the amount of dividend income associated with a distribution to shareholders. § 316 and Reg. § 1.316–2.

Acquiescence. Agreement by the IRS on the results reached in certain judicial decisions; sometimes abbreviated *Acq.* or *A*.

Acquisition indebtedness. Debt incurred in acquiring, constructing, or substantially improving a qualified residence of the taxpayer. The interest on such loans is deductible as qualified residence interest. However, interest on such debt is deductible only on the portion of the indebtedness that does not exceed $1,000,000 ($500,000 for married persons filing separate returns). § 163(h)(3).

Active income. Active income includes wages, salary, commissions, bonuses, profits from a trade or business in which the taxpayer is a material participant, gain on the sale or other disposition of assets used in an active trade or business, and income from intangible property if the taxpayer's personal efforts significantly contributed to the creation of the property. The passive activity loss rules require classification of income and losses into three categories with active income being one of them. § 465.

Ad valorem tax. A tax imposed on the value of property. The most common ad valorem tax is that imposed by states, counties, and cities on real estate. Ad valorem taxes can be imposed on personal property as well.

Additional depreciation. The excess of the amount of depreciation actually deducted over the amount that would have been deducted had the straight-line method been used. § 1250(b).

Adjusted basis. The cost or other basis of property reduced by depreciation allowed or allowable and increased by capital improvements. Other special adjustments are provided in § 1016 and the related Regulations.

Adjusted current earnings (ACE). An adjustment in computing corporate alternative minimum taxable income (AMTI), computed at 75 percent of the excess of adjusted current earnings (ACE) over unadjusted AMTI. ACE computations reflect longer and slower cost recovery deductions and other restrictions on the timing of certain recognition events. Exempt interest, life insurance proceeds, and other receipts that are included in earnings and profits but not in taxable income also increase the ACE adjustment. If unadjusted AMTI exceeds ACE, the ACE adjustment is negative. The negative adjustment is limited to the aggregate of the positive adjustments under ACE for prior years, reduced by any previously claimed negative adjustments. § 56(g).

Adoption expenses credit. A provision intended to assist taxpayers who incur nonrecurring costs directly associated with the adoption process such as legal costs, social service review costs, and transportation costs. Up to $10,960 ($10,960 for a child with special needs regardless of the actual adoption expenses) of costs incurred to adopt an eligible child qualify for the credit. A taxpayer may claim the credit in the year qualifying expenses are paid or incurred if the expenses are paid during or after the year in which the adoption is finalized. For qualifying expenses paid or incurred in a tax year prior to the year the adoption is finalized, the credit must be claimed in the tax year following the tax year during which the expenses are paid or incurred. § 23.

Alimony and separate maintenance payments. Alimony deductions result from the payment of a legal obligation arising from the termination of a marital relationship. Payments designated as alimony generally are included in the gross income of the recipient and are deductible *for* AGI by the payer. §§ 62(a)(10), 71, and 215.

Allocate. The assignment of income for various tax purposes. A multistate corporation's nonbusiness income usually is allocated to the state where the nonbusiness assets are located; it is not apportioned with the rest of the entity's income. International taxpayers allocate certain expenses in computing the taxable income from specific activities. Partnerships can allocate specific items of income, deduction, and credit if certain requirements are met.

Alternative depreciation system (ADS). A cost recovery system that produces a smaller deduction than would be calculated under ACRS or MACRS. The alternative system must be used in certain instances and can be elected in other instances. § 168(g).

Alternative minimum tax (AMT). The AMT is a fixed percentage of alternative minimum taxable income (AMTI). AMTI generally starts with the taxpayer's adjusted gross income (for individuals) or taxable income (for other taxpayers). To this amount, the taxpayer (1) adds designated preference items (e.g., tax-exempt interest income on private activity bonds), (2) makes other specified adjustments (e.g., to reflect a longer, straight-line cost recovery deduction), (3) subtracts certain AMT itemized deductions for individuals (e.g., interest incurred on housing but not taxes paid), and (4) subtracts an exemption amount (e.g., $40,000 on a C corporation's return). The taxpayer must pay the greater of the resulting AMT (reduced by only the foreign tax credit) or the regular income tax (reduced by all allowable tax credits). The AMT does not apply to certain small C corporations. AMT preferences and adjustments are assigned to partners and S corporation shareholders. § 55–59.

Alternative minimum taxable income (AMTI). The base (prior to deducting the exemption amount) for computing a taxpayer's alternative minimum tax. This consists of the taxable income for the year modified for AMT adjustments and AMT preferences. § 55(b)(2).

Amortization. The tax deduction for the cost or other basis of an intangible asset over the asset's estimated useful life. Examples of amortizable intangibles include patents, copyrights, and leasehold interests. The intangible goodwill can be amortized for income tax purposes over a 15-year period. § 197.

Amount realized. The amount received by a taxpayer upon the sale or exchange of property. Amount realized is the sum of the cash and the fair market value of any property or services received by the taxpayer, plus any related debt assumed by the buyer. Determining the amount realized is the starting point for arriving at realized gain or loss. § 1001(b).

Apportion. The assignment of the business income of a multistate corporation to specific states for income taxation. Usually, the apportionment procedure accounts for the property, payroll, and sales activity levels of the various states, and a proportionate assignment of the entity's total income is made, using a three-factor apportionment formula. Some states exclude nonbusiness income from the apportionment procedure; they allocate nonbusiness income to the states where the nonbusiness assets are located.

Arm's length concept. The standard under which unrelated parties would carry out a transaction. Suppose Bint Corporation sells property to its sole shareholder for $10,000. In determining whether $10,000 is an arm's length price, one would ascertain the amount for which the corporation could have sold the property to a disinterested third party.

Arm's length price. See *arm's length concept.*

Assignment of income. A procedure whereby a taxpayer attempts to avoid the recognition of income by assigning to another the property that generates the income. Such a procedure will not avoid the recognition of income by the taxpayer making the assignment if it can be said that the income was earned at the point of the transfer. In this case, usually referred to as an anticipatory assignment of income, the income will be taxed to the person who earns it.

Assumption of liabilities. In a corporate formation, corporate takeover, or asset purchase, the new owner often takes assets and agrees to assume preexisting debt. Such actions do not create boot received on the transaction for the new shareholder, unless there is no *bona fide* business purpose for the exchange, or the principal purpose of the debt assumption is the avoidance of tax liabilities. Gain is recognized to the extent that liabilities assumed exceed the aggregated bases of the transferred assets. § 357.

At-risk limitation. Generally, a taxpayer can deduct losses related to a trade or business, S corporation, partnership, or investment asset only to the extent of the at-risk amount.

Automatic mileage method. Automobile expenses are generally deductible only to the extent the automobile is used in business or for the production of income. Personal commuting expenses are not deductible. The taxpayer may deduct actual expenses (including depreciation and insurance), or the standard (automatic) mileage rate may be used (37.5 cents per mile for 2004, 40.5 cents per mile for 2005 for January–August and 48.5 cents per mile for September–December, and 44.5 cents per mile for 2006) during any one year. Automobile expenses incurred for medical purposes or in connection with job-related moving expenses are deductible to the extent of actual out-of-pocket expenses or at the rate of 18 cents per mile in 2006 (15 cents per mile in 2005 for January through August and 22 cents per mile for September through December). For charitable activities, the rate is 14 cents per mile.

B

Bad debts. A deduction is permitted if a business account receivable subsequently becomes partially or completely worthless, providing the income arising from the debt previously was included in income. Available methods are the specific charge-off method and the reserve method. However, except for certain financial institutions, TRA of 1986 repealed the use of the reserve method for 1987 and thereafter. If the reserve method is used, partially or totally worthless accounts are charged to the reserve. A nonbusiness bad debt deduction is allowed as a short-term capital loss if the loan did not arise in connection with the creditor's trade or business activities. Loans between related parties (family members) generally are classified as nonbusiness. § 166.

Basis in partnership interest. The acquisition cost of the partner's ownership interest in the partnership. Includes purchase price and associated debt acquired from other partners and in the course of the entity's trade or business. § 705.

Boot. Cash or property of a type not included in the definition of a nontaxable exchange. The receipt of boot causes an otherwise nontaxable transfer to become taxable to the extent of the lesser of the fair market value of the boot or the realized gain on the transfer. For example, see transfers to controlled corporations under § 351(b) and like-kind exchanges under § 1031(b).

Brother-sister controlled group. More than one corporation owned by the same shareholders. If, for example, Chris and Pat each own one-half of the stock in Wren Corporation and Redbird Corporation, Wren and Redbird form a brother-sister controlled group. § 1563(a)(2).

Built-in gains tax. A penalty tax designed to discourage a shift of the incidence of taxation on unrealized gains from a C corporation to its shareholders, via an S election. Under this provision, any recognized gain during the first 10 years of S status generates a corporate-level tax on a base not to exceed the aggregate untaxed built-in gains brought into the S corporation upon its election from C corporation taxable years. § 1374.

Business bad debt. A tax deduction allowed for obligations obtained in connection with a trade or business that have become either partially or completely worthless. In contrast to nonbusiness bad debts, business bad debts are deductible as business expenses. § 166.

Buy-sell agreement. An arrangement, particularly appropriate in the case of a closely held corporation or a partnership, whereby the surviving owners (shareholders or partners) or the entity agrees to purchase the interest of a withdrawing owner. The buy-sell agreement provides for an orderly disposition of an interest in a business and may aid in setting the value of the interest for death tax purposes.

C

C corporation. A separate taxable entity, subject to the rules of Subchapter C of the Code. This business form may create a double taxation effect relative to its shareholders. The entity is subject to the regular corporate tax and a number of penalty taxes at the Federal level.

Cafeteria plan. An employee benefit plan under which an employee is allowed to select from among a variety of employer-provided fringe benefits. Some of the benefits may be taxable, and some may be statutory nontaxable benefits (e.g., health and accident insurance and group term life insurance). The employee is taxed only on the taxable benefits selected. A cafeteria benefit plan is also referred to as a flexible benefit plan. § 125.

Capital account. The financial accounting analog of a partner's tax basis in the entity.

Capital asset. Broadly speaking, all assets are capital except those specifically excluded by the Code. Major categories of noncapital assets include property held for resale in the normal course of business (inventory), trade accounts and notes receivable, and depreciable property and real estate used in a trade or business (§ 1231 assets). § 1221.

Capital contribution. Various means by which a shareholder makes additional funds available to the corporation (placed at the risk of the business), sometimes without the receipt of additional stock. If no stock is received, the contributions are added to the basis of the shareholder's existing stock investment and do not generate gross income to the corporation. § 118.

Capital gain. The gain from the sale or exchange of a capital asset.

Capital gain property. Property contributed to a charitable organization that, if sold rather than contributed, would have resulted in long-term capital gain to the donor.

Capital interest. Usually, the percentage of the entity's net assets that a partner would receive on liquidation. Typically determined by the partner's capital sharing ratio.

Capital loss. The loss from the sale or exchange of a capital asset.

Capital sharing ratio. A partner's percentage ownership of the entity's capital.

Cash receipts method. A method of accounting that reflects deductions as paid and income as received in any one tax year. However, deductions for prepaid expenses that benefit more than one tax year (e.g., prepaid rent and prepaid interest) usually must be spread over the period benefited rather than deducted in the year paid. For fixed assets, the cash basis taxpayer claims deductions through depreciation or amortization in the same manner as an accrual basis taxpayer. § 446(c)(1).

Casualty loss. A casualty is defined as "the complete or partial destruction of property resulting from an identifiable event of a sudden, unexpected or unusual nature" (e.g., floods, storms, fires, auto accidents). Individuals may deduct a casualty loss only if the loss is incurred in a trade or business or in a transaction entered into for profit or arises from fire, storm, shipwreck, or other casualty or from theft. Individuals usually deduct personal casualty losses as itemized deductions subject to a $100 nondeductible amount and to an annual floor equal to 10 percent of adjusted gross income that applies after the $100 per casualty floor has been applied. Special rules are provided for the netting of certain casualty gains and losses. § 165(c)(3).

Charitable contributions. Contributions are deductible (subject to various restrictions and ceiling limitations) if made to qualified nonprofit charitable organizations. A cash basis taxpayer is entitled to a deduction solely in the year of payment. Accrual basis corporations may accrue contributions at year-end if payment is properly authorized before the end of the year and payment is made within two and one-half months after the end of the year. § 170.

Check-the-box Regulation. A business entity can elect to be taxed as a partnership, S corporation, or C corporation by indicating its preference on the tax return. Legal structure and operations are irrelevant in this regard. Thus, by using the check-the-box rules prudently, an entity can select the most attractive tax results offered by the Code, without being bound by legal forms. Not available if the entity is incorporated under state law.

Child tax credit. A tax credit based solely on the number of qualifying children under age 17. The maximum credit available is $1,000 per child through 2010. A qualifying child must be claimed as a dependent on a parent's tax return in order to qualify for the credit. Taxpayers who qualify for the child tax credit may also qualify for a supplemental credit. The supplemental credit is treated as a component of the earned income credit and is therefore refundable. The credit is phased out for higher-income taxpayers. § 24.

Circuit Court of Appeals. Any of 13 Federal courts that consider tax matters appealed from the U.S. Tax Court, a U.S. District Court, or the U.S. Court of Federal Claims. Appeal from a U.S. Court of Appeals is to the U.S. Supreme Court by *Certiorari.*

Citator. A tax research resource that presents the judicial history of a court case and traces the subsequent references to the case. When these references include the citing cases' evaluations of the cited case's precedents, the research can obtain some measure of the efficacy and reliability of the original holding.

Claim of right doctrine. A judicially imposed doctrine applicable to both cash and accrual basis taxpayers that holds that an amount is includible in income upon actual or constructive receipt if the taxpayer has an unrestricted claim to the payment. For the tax treatment of amounts repaid when previously included in income under the claim of right doctrine, see § 1341.

Closely held C corporation. A regular corporation (i.e., the S election is not in effect) for which more than 50 percent of the value of its outstanding stock is owned, directly or indirectly, by five or fewer individuals at any time during the tax year. The term is relevant in identifying C corporations that are subject to the passive activity loss provisions. § 469.

Collectibles. A special type of capital asset, the gain from which is taxed at a maximum rate of 28 percent if the holding period is more than one year. Examples include art, rugs, antiques, gems, metals, stamps, some coins and bullion, and alcoholic beverages held for investment. § 1(h).

Compensatory damages. Damages received or paid by the taxpayer can be classified as compensatory damages or as punitive damages. Compensatory damages are those paid to compensate one for harm caused by another. Compensatory damages are excludible from the recipient's gross income. § 104(a)(2).

Conduit concept. An approach assumed by the tax law in the treatment of certain entities and their owners. Specific tax characteristics pass through the entity without losing their identity. For example, items of income and expense, capital gains and losses, tax credits, etc., realized by a partnership pass through the partnership (a conduit) and are subject to taxation at the partner level. Also, in an S corporation, certain items pass through and are reported on the returns of the shareholders.

Constructive dividend. A taxable benefit derived by a shareholder from his or her corporation that is not actually called a dividend. Examples include unreasonable compensation, excessive rent payments, bargain purchases of corporate property, and shareholder use of corporate property. Constructive dividends generally are found in closely held corporations.

Constructive receipt. If income is unqualifiedly available although not physically in the taxpayer's possession, it is subject to the income tax. An example is accrued interest on a savings account. Under the constructive receipt of income concept, the interest is taxed to a depositor in the year available, rather than the year actually withdrawn. The fact that the depositor uses the cash basis of accounting for tax purposes is irrelevant. See Reg. § 1.451–2.

Control. Holding a specified level of stock ownership in a corporation. For § 351, the new shareholder(s) must hold at least 80 percent of the total combined voting power of all voting classes of stock and at least 80 percent of the shares of all nonvoting classes. Other tax provisions require different levels of control to bring about desired effects, such as 50 or 100 percent.

Controlled foreign corporation (CFC). A non-U.S. corporation in which more than 50 percent of the total combined voting power of all classes of stock entitled to vote or the total value of the stock of the corporation is owned by "U.S. shareholders" on any day during the taxable year of the foreign corporation. For purposes of this definition, a U.S. shareholder is any U.S. person who owns, or is considered to own, 10 percent or more of the total combined voting power of all classes of voting stock of the foreign corporation. Stock owned directly, indirectly, and constructively is used in this measure. Certain Subpart F income of the CFC is taxed to the U.S. shareholders when it is earned, not when it is later repatriated.

Controlled group. A controlled group of corporations is required to share the lower-level corporate tax rates and various other tax benefits among the members of the group. A controlled group may be either a brother-sister or a parent-subsidiary group. §§ 1561 and 1563.

Cost depletion. Depletion that is calculated based on the adjusted basis of the asset. The adjusted basis is divided by the expected recoverable units to determine the depletion per unit. The depletion per unit is multiplied by the units sold during the tax year to calculate cost depletion. § 612.

Cost recovery system. The system which provides for the write-off of the cost of an asset under ACRS or MACRS. The cost recovery system replaced the depreciation system as the method of writing off the cost of an asset for most capitalized assets placed in service after 1980 (after 1986 for MACRS). § 168.

Court of Federal Claims. A trial court (court of original jurisdiction) that decides litigation involving Federal tax matters. Appeal from this court is to the Court of Appeals for the Federal Circuit.

Court of original jurisdiction. The Federal courts are divided into courts of original jurisdiction and appellate courts. A dispute between a taxpayer and the IRS is first considered by a court of original jurisdiction (i.e., a trial court). The four Federal courts of original jurisdiction are the U.S. Tax Court, U.S. District Court, the Court of Federal Claims, and the Small Cases Division of the U.S. Tax Court.

Coverdell Education Savings Account (CESA). A savings account established to pay for qualified education expenses (i.e., tuition, fees, books, supplies, related equipment, room and board if the student's course load is at least one-half of the full-time course load). The maximum annual contribution to the savings account of a beneficiary is $2,000. The maximum annual contribution is subject to phaseout beginning at $95,000 for single taxpayers and $150,000 for married couples who file a joint return. Contributions are not deductible and cannot be made to a savings account once the beneficiary attains age 18. Distributions used to pay for qualified education expenses for a designated beneficiary are tax-free. § 530.

Credit for child and dependent care expenses. A tax credit ranging from 20 percent to 35 percent of employment-related expenses (child and dependent care expenses) for amounts of up to $6,000 is available to individuals who are employed (or deemed to be employed) and maintain a household for a dependent child under age 13, disabled spouse, or disabled dependent. § 21.

Credit for employer-provided child care. A nonrefundable credit is available to employers who provided child care facilities to their employees during normal working hours. The credit, limited to $150,000, is comprised of two components. The portion of the credit for qualified child care expenses is equal to 25 percent of these expenses while the portion of the credit for qualified child care resources and referral services is equal to 10 percent of these expenses. Any qualifying expenses otherwise deductible by taxpayer must be reduced by the amount of the credit. In addition, the taxpayer's basis for any property used for qualifying purposes is reduced by the amount of the credit. § 45F.

Credit for small employer pension plan startup costs. A nonrefundable credit available to small businesses based on administrative costs associated with establishing and maintaining certain qualified plans. While such qualifying costs generally are deductible as ordinary and necessary business expense, the availability of the credit is intended to lower the costs of starting a qualified retirement program, and therefore encourage qualifying businesses to establish retirement plans for their employees. The credit is available for eligible employers at the rate of 50 percent of qualified startup costs. The maximum credit is $500 (based on a maximum of $1,000 of qualifying expenses). § 45E.

Current earnings and profits. Net tax-basis earnings of a corporation aggregated during the current tax year. A corporate distribution is deemed to be first from the entity's current earnings and profits and then from accumulated earnings and profits. Shareholders recognize dividend income to the extent of the earnings and profits of the corporation. A dividend results to the extent of current earnings and profits, even if there is a larger negative balance in accumulated earnings and profits.

D

***De minimis* fringe benefits.** Benefits provided to employees that are too insignificant to warrant the time and effort required to account for the benefits received by each employee and the value of those benefits. Such amounts are excludible from the employee's gross income. § 132.

Death tax. A tax imposed on property transferred by the death of the owner.

Deduction for qualified tuition and related expenses. Taxpayers are allowed a deduction of up to $4,000 for higher education expenses. Certain taxpayers are not eligible for the deduction: those whose AGI exceeds a specified amount and those who can be claimed as a dependent by another taxpayer. These expenses are classified as a deduction *for* AGI and they need not be employment related. § 222.

Deemed-paid credit. A foreign tax credit allowed to a U.S. taxpayer that has received an actual or constructive dividend from a non-U.S. corporation that has paid foreign income taxes. The credit is computed using the proportion of foreign income taxes paid by the payor corporation to its post-1986 undistributed earnings. Under § 78, the U.S. taxpayer claiming a deemed-paid credit includes the same amount in gross income for the tax year.

Dependency exemption. The tax law provides an exemption for each individual taxpayer and an additional exemption for the taxpayer's spouse if a joint return is filed. An individual may also claim a dependency exemption for each dependent, provided certain tests are met. The amount of the personal and dependency exemptions is $3,300 in 2006 ($3,200 in 2005). The exemption is subject to phase-out once adjusted gross income exceeds certain statutory threshold amounts. This phaseout provision is subject to partial phaseout beginning in 2006. §§ 151 and 152.

Depletion. The process by which the cost or other basis of a natural resource (e.g., an oil or gas interest) is recovered upon extraction and sale of the resource. The two ways to determine the depletion allowance are the cost and percentage (or statutory) methods. Under cost depletion, each unit of production sold is assigned a portion of the cost or other basis of the interest. This is determined by dividing the cost or other basis by the total units expected to be recovered. Under percentage (or statutory) depletion, the tax law provides a special percentage factor for different types of minerals and other natural resources. This percentage is multiplied by the gross income from the interest to arrive at the depletion allowance. §§ 611–613 and 613A.

Depreciation rules. The depreciation system that existed prior to the enactment of the Accelerated Cost Recovery System (ACRS). This system applies to depreciable assets placed in service prior to January 1, 1981, and to certain post-1980 assets that do not qualify for ACRS. § 167.

Determination letter. Upon the request of a taxpayer, an IRS Area Director will comment on the tax status of a completed transaction. Determination letters frequently are used to clarify employee status, determine whether a retirement or profit sharing plan qualifies under the Code, and determine the tax-exempt status of certain nonprofit organizations.

Disabled access credit. A tax credit designed to encourage small businesses to make their facilities more accessible to disabled individuals. The credit is equal to 50 percent of the eligible expenditures that exceed $250 but do not exceed $10,250. Thus, the maximum amount for the credit is $5,000. The adjusted basis for depreciation is reduced by the amount of the credit. To qualify, the facility must have been placed in service before November 6, 1990. § 44.

Disaster area loss. A casualty sustained in an area designated as a disaster area by the President of the United States. In such an event, the disaster loss may be treated as having occurred in the taxable year immediately preceding the year in which the disaster actually occurred. Thus, immediate tax benefits are provided to victims of a disaster. § 165(i).

Disguised sale. When a partner contributes property to the entity and soon thereafter receives a distribution from the partnership, the transactions are collapsed, and the distribution is seen as a purchase of the asset by the partnership. § 707(a)(2)(B).

District Court. A Federal District Court is a trial court for purposes of litigating (among others) Federal tax matters. It is the only trial court where a jury trial can be obtained.

Dividend. A nondeductible distribution by a corporation to a shareholder. A dividend constitutes gross income to the recipient if it is from the current or accumulated earnings and profits of the corporation.

Dividends received deduction. A deduction allowed a shareholder that is a corporation for dividends received from a domestic corporation. The deduction usually is 70 percent of the dividends received, but it could be 80 or 100 percent depending upon the ownership percentage held by the recipient corporation. §§ 243–246.

Domestic production gross receipts (DPGR). A key component in computing the production activities deduction (PAD). Includes receipts from the sale and other disposition of qualified production property produced in significant part within the United States. DPGR is defined in § 199(c)(4). See also *production activities deduction (PAD).*

E

Earned income credit. A tax credit designed to provide assistance to certain low-income individuals who generally have a qualifying child. This is a refundable credit. To receive the most beneficial treatment, the taxpayer must have qualifying children. However, it is possible to qualify for the credit without having a child. To calculate the credit for a taxpayer with one or more children for 2006, a statutory rate of 34 percent for one child (40 percent for two or more children) is multiplied by the earned income (subject to a statutory maximum of $8,080 with one qualifying child or $11,340 with two or more qualifying children). Once the earned income exceeds certain thresholds, the credit is phased out using a 15.98 percent rate for one qualifying child and a 21.06 percent rate for two qualifying children. For the qualifying taxpayer without children, the credit is calculated on a maximum earned income of $5,380 applying a 7.65 percent rate with the phaseout beginning later applying the same rate. § 32.

Earnings and profits (E & P). Measures the economic capacity of a corporation to make a distribution to shareholders that is not a return of capital. Such a distribution results in dividend income to the shareholders to the extent of the corporation's current and accumulated earnings and profits. §§ 312 and 316.

Economic effect test. Requirements that must be met before a special allocation may be used by a partnership. The premise behind the test is that each partner who receives an allocation of income or loss from a partnership bears the economic benefit or burden of the allocation.

Economic income. The change in the taxpayer's net worth, as measured in terms of market values, plus the value of the assets the taxpayer consumed during the year. Because of the impracticality of this income model, it is not used for tax purposes.

Education expenses. Employees may deduct education expenses that are incurred either (1) to maintain or improve existing job-related skills or (2) to meet the express requirements of the employer or the requirements imposed by law to retain employment status. The expenses are not deductible if the education is required to meet the minimum educational standards for the taxpayer's job or if the education qualifies the individual for a new trade or business. Reg. § 1.162–5.

Educational savings bonds. U.S. Series EE bonds whose proceeds are used for qualified higher educational expenses for the taxpayer, the taxpayer's spouse, or a dependent.

The interest may be excluded from gross income, provided the taxpayer's adjusted gross income does not exceed certain amounts. § 135.

Effectively connected income. Income of a nonresident alien or non-U.S. corporation that is attributable to a trade or business operating in the United States. Income effectively connected to a U.S. trade or business usually is subject to U.S. income taxation, after deductions and allowing other credits, using the appropriate progressive tax rate schedule.

e-file. The electronic filing of a tax return. The filing is either direct or indirect. As to direct, the taxpayer goes online using a computer and tax return preparation software. Indirect filing occurs when a taxpayer utilizes an authorized IRS e-file provider. The provider often is the tax return preparer.

Employment taxes. Employment taxes are those taxes that an employer must pay on account of its employees. Employment taxes include FICA (Federal Insurance Contributions Act) and FUTA (Federal Unemployment Tax Act) taxes. Employment taxes are paid to the IRS in addition to income tax withholdings at specified intervals. Such taxes can be levied on the employees, the employer, or both. §§ 1401 and 1402.

Entertainment expenses. These expenses are deductible only if they are directly related to or associated with a trade or business. Various restrictions and documentation requirements have been imposed upon the deductibility of entertainment expenses to prevent abuses by taxpayers. See, for example, the provision contained in § 274(n) that disallows 50 percent of entertainment expenses. § 274.

Entity concept. The theory of partnership taxation under which a partnership is treated as a separate and distinct entity from the partners and has its own tax attributes.

Estate tax. A tax imposed on the right to transfer property by death. Thus, an estate tax is levied on the decedent's estate and not on the heir receiving the property. §§ 2001–2058.

Estimated tax. The amount of tax (including alternative minimum tax and self-employment tax) a taxpayer expects to owe for the year after subtracting tax credits and income tax withheld. The estimated tax must be paid in installments at designated intervals (e.g., for the individual taxpayer, by April 15, June 15, September 15, and January 15 of the following year). § 6654.

Excise tax. A tax on the manufacture, sale, or use of goods; on the carrying on of an occupation or activity; or on the transfer of property. Thus, the Federal estate and gift taxes are, theoretically, excise taxes.

F

Fair market value. The amount at which property would change hands between a willing buyer and a willing seller, neither being under any compulsion to buy or to sell, and both having reasonable knowledge of the relevant facts. Reg. §§ 1.1001–1(a) and 20.2031–1(b).

FDAP. Income of a nonresident alien or non-U.S. corporation that is received in the form of dividends, interest, rents, royalties, certain compensation, premiums, annuities, and other "fixed, determinable, annual, or periodic" forms. FDAP income usually is subject to U.S. income taxation at a flat 30 percent tax rate.

FICA tax. An abbreviation that stands for Federal Insurance Contributions Act, commonly referred to as the Social Security tax. The FICA tax is comprised of the Social Security tax (old age, survivors, and disability insurance) and the Medicare tax (hospital insurance) and is imposed on both employers and employees. The employer is responsible for withholding from the employee's wages the Social Security tax at a rate of 6.2 percent on a maximum wage base of $94,200 (for 2006) and the Medicare tax at a rate of 1.45 percent (no maximum wage base). The employer is required to match the employee's contribution. § 3101.

Fifty percent additional first-year depreciation. This provision, which was effective for property acquired after May 5, 2003, and placed in service before January 1, 2005, provided for an additional cost recovery deduction of 50 percent in the tax year the qualified property was placed in service. Qualified property included most types of new property other than buildings. The taxpayer could elect to forgo this bonus depreciation. The taxpayer also could elect to use 30 percent bonus depreciation rather than the 50 percent bonus depreciation. See also *cost recovery system* and *thirty percent additional first-year depreciation.*

Final Regulation. The U.S. Treasury Department Regulations (abbreviated Reg.) represent the position of the IRS as to how the Internal Revenue Code is to be interpreted. Their purpose is to provide taxpayers and IRS personnel with rules of general and specific application to the various provisions of the tax law. Regulations are published in the *Federal Register* and in all tax services.

Flexible spending plan. An employee benefit plan that allows the employee to take a reduction in salary in exchange for the employer paying benefits that can be provided by the employer without the employee being required to recognize income (e.g., medical and child care benefits).

Foreign earned income exclusion. The foreign earned income exclusion is a relief provision that applies to U.S. citizens working in a foreign country. To qualify for the exclusion, the taxpayer must be either a bona fide resident of the foreign country or present in the foreign country for 330 days during any 12 consecutive months. The exclusion is limited to $80,000 per year. § 911.

Foreign tax credit. A U.S. citizen or resident who incurs or pays income taxes to a foreign country on income subject to U.S. tax may be able to claim some or all of these taxes as a credit against the U.S. income tax. §§ 27 and 901–905.

Franchise. An agreement that gives the transferee the right to distribute, sell, or provide goods, services, or facilities within a specified area. The cost of obtaining a franchise may be amortized over a statutory period of 15 years. In general, the franchisor's gain on the sale of franchise rights is an ordinary gain because the franchisor retains a significant power, right, or continuing interest in the subject of the franchise. §§ 197 and 1253.

Franchise tax. A tax levied on the right to do business in a state as a corporation. Although income considerations may come into play, the tax usually is based on the capitalization of the corporation.

Fruit and tree metaphor. The courts have held that an individual who earns income from property or services cannot assign that income to another. For example, a father cannot assign his earnings from commissions to his child and escape income tax on those amounts.

FUTA tax. An employment tax levied on employers. Jointly administered by the Federal and state governments, the tax provides funding for unemployment benefits. FUTA applies at a rate of 6.2 percent on the first $7,000 of covered wages paid during the year for each employee. The Federal government allows a credit for FUTA paid (or allowed under a merit rating system) to the state. The credit cannot exceed 5.4 percent of the covered wages. § 3301.

G

General business credit. The summation of various nonrefundable business credits, including the tax credit for rehabilitation expenditures, business energy credit, welfare-to-work credit, work opportunity credit, research activities credit, low-income housing credit, disabled access credit, credit for small employer pension plan startup costs, and credit for employer-provided child care. The amount of general business credit that can be used to reduce the tax liability is limited to the taxpayer's net income tax reduced by the greater of (1) the tentative minimum tax or (2) 25 percent of the net regular tax liability that exceeds $25,000. Unused general business credits can be carried back 1 year and forward 20 years. § 38.

General partnership. A partnership that is owned by one or more general partners. Creditors of a general partnership can collect amounts owed them from both the partnership assets and the assets of the partners individually.

Gift. A transfer of property for less than adequate consideration. Gifts usually occur in a personal setting (such as between members of the same family). They are excluded from the income tax base but may be subject to a transfer tax.

Gift tax. A tax imposed on the transfer of property by gift. The tax is imposed upon the donor of a gift and is based on the fair market value of the property on the date of the gift. §§ 2501–2524.

Goodwill. The reputation and built-up business of a company. For accounting purposes, goodwill has no basis unless it is purchased. In the purchase of a business, goodwill generally is the difference between the purchase price and the fair market value of the assets acquired. Since acquired goodwill is a § 197 intangible asset, it is amortized for tax purposes over a 15-year period. Reg. § 1.167(a)–3.

Gross income. Income subject to the Federal income tax. Gross income does not include all economic income. That is, certain exclusions are allowed (e.g., interest on municipal bonds). For a manufacturing or merchandising business, gross income usually means gross profit (gross sales or gross receipts less cost of goods sold). § 61 and Reg. § 1.61–3(a).

Guaranteed payments. Payments made by a partnership to a partner for services rendered or for the use of capital to the extent that the payments are determined without regard to the income of the partnership. The payments are treated as though they were made to a nonpartner and thus are usually deductible by the entity. § 707(c).

H

Half-year convention. The half-year convention is a cost recovery convention that assumes all property is placed in service at mid-year and thus provides for a half-year's cost recovery for that year.

Head of household. An unmarried individual who maintains a household for another and satisfies certain conditions set forth in § 2(b). This status enables the taxpayer to use a set of income tax rates that are lower than those applicable to other unmarried individuals but higher than those applicable to surviving spouses and married persons filing a joint return.

Health Savings Account (HSA). A medical savings account created in legislation enacted in December 2003 that is designed to replace and expand Archer Medical Savings Accounts. See also *medical savings account.*

Holding period. The period of time during which property has been held for income tax purposes. The holding period is significant in determining whether gain or loss from the sale or exchange of a capital asset is long term or short term. § 1223.

Home equity loans. Loans that utilize the personal residence of the taxpayer as security. The interest on such loans is deductible as qualified residence interest. However, interest is deductible only on the portion of the loan that does not exceed the lesser of (1) the fair market value of the residence, reduced by the acquisition indebtedness, or (2) $100,000 ($50,000 for married persons filing separate returns). A major benefit of a home equity loan is that there are no tracing rules regarding the use of the loan proceeds. § 163(h)(3).

HOPE scholarship credit. A tax credit for qualifying expenses paid for the first two years of postsecondary education. Room, board, and book costs are ineligible for the credit. The maximum credit available is $1,650 per year per student, computed as 100 percent of the first $1,100 of qualifying expenses, plus 50 percent of the second $1,100 of qualifying expenses. Eligible students include the taxpayer, taxpayer's spouse, and taxpayer's dependents. To qualify for the credit, a student must take at least one-half the full-time course load for at least one academic term at a qualifying educational institution. The credit is phased out for higher-income taxpayers. § 25A.

Hybrid method. A combination of the accrual and cash methods of accounting. That is, the taxpayer may account for some items of income on the accrual method (e.g., sales and cost of goods sold) and other items (e.g., interest income) on the cash method.

I

Implicit tax. A tax that is paid through higher prices or lower returns on tax-favored investments rather than being paid directly to the government (i.e., an explicit tax). The value added tax is an example of an implicit tax.

Inbound taxation. U.S. tax effects when a non-U.S. person undertakes an investment or business activity in the United States.

Income. For tax purposes, an increase in wealth that has been realized.

Income tax treaties. An agreement between the U.S. State Department and another country designed to alleviate potential double taxation and to share administrative information useful to tax agencies in both countries, relative to taxpayers with investment or business activities in both countries.

Independent contractor. A self-employed person as distinguished from one who is employed as an employee.

Individual Retirement Account (IRA). A type of retirement plan to which an individual with earned income can contribute a maximum of $3,000 ($3,000 each in the case of a married couple with a spousal IRA) per tax year for 2002–2004. The maximum amount increases to $4,000 in 2005 and to $5,000 in 2008. IRAs can be classified as traditional IRAs or Roth IRAs. With a traditional IRA, an individual can contribute and deduct a maximum of $4,000 per tax year in 2006. The deduction is a deduction *for* AGI. However, if the individual is an active participant in another qualified retirement plan, the deduction is phased out proportionally between certain AGI ranges (note that the phaseout limits the amount of the deduction and not the amount of the contribution). With a Roth IRA, an individual can contribute a maximum of $4,000 per tax year in 2006. No deduction is permitted. However, if a five-year holding period requirement is satisfied and if the distribution is a qualified distribution, the taxpayer can make tax-free withdrawals from a Roth IRA. The maximum annual contribution is phased out proportionally between certain AGI ranges. §§ 219 and 408A.

Inheritance tax. A tax imposed on the right to receive property from a decedent. Thus, theoretically, an inheritance tax is imposed on the heir. The Federal estate tax is imposed on the estate.

Inside basis. A partnership's basis in the assets it owns.

Intangible drilling and development costs (IDC). Taxpayers may elect to expense or capitalize (subject to amortization) intangible drilling and development costs. However, ordinary income recapture provisions apply to oil and gas properties on a sale or other disposition if the expense method is elected. §§ 263(c) and 1254(a).

Interpretive Regulation. A Regulation issued by the Treasury Department that purports to explain the meaning of a particular Code Section. An interpretive Regulation is given less deference than a legislative Regulation.

Investment interest. Payment for the use of funds used to acquire assets that produce investment income. The deduction for investment interest is limited to net investment income for the tax year.

Involuntary conversion. The loss or destruction of property through theft, casualty, or condemnation. Any gain realized on an involuntary conversion can, at the taxpayer's election, be deferred for Federal income tax purposes if the owner reinvests the proceeds within a prescribed period of time in property that is similar or related in service or use. § 1033.

Itemized deductions. Personal and employee expenditures allowed by the Code as deductions from adjusted gross income. Examples include certain medical expenses, interest on home mortgages, state income taxes, and charitable contributions. Itemized deductions are reported on Schedule A of Form 1040. Certain miscellaneous itemized deductions are reduced by 2 percent of the taxpayer's adjusted gross income. In addition, a taxpayer whose adjusted gross income exceeds a certain level (indexed annually) must reduce the itemized deductions by 3 percent of the excess of adjusted gross income over that level. Medical, casualty and theft, and investment interest deductions are not subject to the 3 percent reduction. The 3 percent reduction may not reduce itemized deductions that are subject to the reduction to below 20 percent of their initial amount. Beginning in 2006, this reduction is subject to partial phaseout. §§ 63(d), 67, and 68.

K

Keogh plan. A retirement plan that is available to self-employed taxpayers; also referred to as an H.R. 10 plan. Under such plans, in 2006, a taxpayer may deduct each year up to either 100 percent of net earnings from self-employment or $44,000, whichever is less. If the plan is a profit sharing plan, the percentage is 25 percent.

Kiddie tax. Passive income, such as interest and dividends, that is recognized by a child under age 14 is taxed to him or her at the rates that would have applied had the income been incurred by the child's parents, generally to the extent that the income exceeds $1,700. The additional tax is assessed regardless of the source of the income or the income's underlying property. If the child's parents are divorced, the custodial parent's rates are used. The parents' rates reflect any applicable alternative minimum tax and the phaseouts of lower tax brackets and other deductions. § 1(g).

L

Legislative Regulation. Some Code Sections give the Secretary of the Treasury or his delegate the authority to prescribe Regulations to carry out the details of administration or to otherwise complete the operating rules. Regulations issued pursuant to this type of authority truly possess the force and effect of law. In effect, Congress is almost delegating its legislative powers to the Treasury Department.

Lessee. One who rents property from another. In the case of real estate, the lessee is also known as the tenant.

Lessor. One who rents property to another. In the case of real estate, the lessor is also known as the landlord.

Letter ruling. The written response of the IRS to a taxpayer's request for interpretation of the revenue laws, with respect to a proposed transaction (e.g., concerning the tax-free status of a reorganization). Not to be relied on as precedent by other than the party who requested the ruling.

Life insurance proceeds. A specified sum (the face value or maturity value of the policy) paid to the designated beneficiary of the policy by the life insurance company upon the death of the insured.

Lifetime learning credit. A tax credit for qualifying expenses for taxpayers pursuing education beyond the first two years of postsecondary education. Individuals who are completing their last two years of undergraduate studies, pursuing graduate or professional degrees, or otherwise seeking new job skills or maintaining existing job skills are all eligible for the credit. Eligible individuals include the taxpayer, taxpayer's spouse, and taxpayer's dependents. The maximum credit is 20 percent of the first $10,000 of qualifying expenses and is computed per taxpayer. The credit is phased out for higher-income taxpayers. § 25A.

Like-kind exchange. An exchange of property held for productive use in a trade or business or for investment (except inventory and stocks and bonds) for other investment or trade or business property. Unless non-like-kind property (boot) is received, the exchange is fully nontaxable. § 1031.

Limited liability company (LLC). A form of entity allowed by all of the states. The entity is taxed as a partnership in which all members or owners of the LLC are treated much like limited partners. There are no restrictions on ownership, all members may participate in management, and none has personal liability for the entity's debts.

Limited liability partnership (LLP). A form of entity allowed by many of the states, where a general partnership registers with the state as an LLP. Owners are general partners, but a partner is not liable for any malpractice committed by other partners. The personal assets of the partners are at risk for the entity's contractual liabilities, such as accounts payable. The personal assets of a specific partner are at risk for his or her own professional malpractice and tort liability, and for malpractice and torts committed by those whom he or she supervises.

Limited partnership. A partnership in which some of the partners are limited partners. At least one of the partners in a limited partnership must be a general partner.

Listed property. The term listed property includes (1) any passenger automobile, (2) any other property used as a means of transportation, (3) any property of a type generally used for purposes of entertainment, recreation, or amusement, (4) any computer or peripheral equipment (with an exception for exclusive business use), (5) any cellular telephone (or other similar telecommunications equipment), and (6) any other property of a type specified in the Regulations. If listed property is predominantly used for business, the taxpayer is allowed to use the statutory percentage method of cost recovery. Otherwise, the straight-line cost recovery method must be used. § 280F.

Long-term nonpersonal-use capital assets. Includes investment property with a long-term holding period. Such property disposed of by casualty or theft may receive § 1231 treatment.

M

Marriage penalty. The additional tax liability that results for a married couple when compared with what their tax liability would be if they were not married and filed separate returns.

Material participation. If an individual taxpayer materially participates in a nonrental trade or business activity, any loss from that activity is treated as an active loss that can be offset against active income. Material participation is achieved by meeting any one of seven tests provided in the Regulations. § 469(h).

Medical expenses. Medical expenses of an individual, spouse, and dependents are allowed as an itemized deduction to the extent that such amounts (less insurance reimbursements) exceed 7.5 percent of adjusted gross income. § 213.

Medical savings account (MSA). A plan available to employees of small firms (50 or fewer employees) with high-deductible health insurance. The employee can place money in the fund and then deduct the contributions (within limits) from gross income. If the employer contributes to the fund, the employee can exclude the contribution from gross income. Income earned from the fund and withdrawals for medical care are not subject to tax. See also *Health Savings Account (HSA)*. §§ 106(b) and 220.

Mid-month convention. A cost recovery convention that assumes property is placed in service in the middle of the month that it is actually placed in service.

Mid-quarter convention. A cost recovery convention that assumes property placed in service during the year is placed in service at the middle of the quarter in which it is actually placed in service. The mid-quarter convention applies if more than 40 percent of the value of property (other than eligible real estate) is placed in service during the last quarter of the year.

Minimum tax credit (AMT). When a corporation pays an alternative minimum tax (AMT), a minimum tax credit is created on a dollar-for-dollar basis, to be applied against regular tax liabilities incurred in future years. The credit is carried forward indefinitely, but it is not carried back. The effect of the credit for corporate taxpayers alternating between the AMT and regular tax models is to make the AMT liabilities a prepayment of regular taxes. Noncorporate AMT taxpayers are allowed the credit only with respect to the elements of the AMT that reflect timing differences between the two tax models. § 53.

Miscellaneous itemized deductions. A special category of itemized deductions that includes such expenses as professional dues, tax return preparation fees, job-hunting costs, unreimbursed employee business expenses, and certain investment expenses. Such expenses are deductible only to the extent they exceed 2 percent of adjusted gross income. § 67.

Modified accelerated cost recovery system (MACRS). A method in which the cost of tangible property is recovered over a prescribed period of time. Enacted by the Economic Recovery Tax Act (ERTA) of 1981 and substantially modified by the Tax Reform Act (TRA) of 1986 (the modified system is referred to as MACRS), the approach disregards salvage value, imposes a period of cost recovery that depends upon the classification of the asset into one of various recovery periods, and prescribes the applicable percentage of cost that can be deducted each year. § 168.

Modified adjusted gross income. A key determinant in computing the production activities deduction (PAD). The deduction is limited to a percentage of the *lesser of* qualified production activities income (QPAI) or modified adjusted gross income. Aside from limited changes required by § 199(d)(2)(A), modified adjusted gross income is AGI as usually determined but without any production activities deduction (PAD). See also *production activities deduction (PAD)*.

Moving expenses. A deduction *for* AGI is permitted to employees and self-employed individuals provided certain tests are met. The taxpayer's new job must be at least 50 miles farther from the old residence than the old residence was from the former place of work. In addition, an employee must be employed on a full-time basis at the new location for 39 weeks in the 12-month period following the move. Deductible moving expenses include the cost of moving the household and personal effects, transportation, and lodging expenses during the move. The cost of meals during the move is not deductible. Qualified moving expenses that are paid (or reimbursed) by the employer can be excluded from the employee's gross income. In this case, the related deduction by the employee is not permitted. §§ 62(a)(15), 132(a)(6), and 217.

Multiple support agreement. To qualify for a dependency exemption, the support test must be satisfied. This requires that over 50 percent of the support of the potential dependent be provided by the taxpayer. Where no one person provides more than 50 percent of the support, a multiple support agreement enables a taxpayer to still qualify for the dependency exemption. Any person who contributed more than 10 percent of the support is entitled to claim the exemption if each person in the group who contributed more than 10 percent files a written consent (Form 2120). Each person who is a party to the multiple support agreement must meet all the other requirements for claiming the dependency exemption. § 152(c).

Multistate corporation. A corporation that has operations in more than one of the states of the United States. Issues arise relative to the assignment of appropriate amounts of the entity's taxable income to the states in which it has a presence. See also *allocate, apportion,* and *nexus.*

Multistate Tax Commission (MTC). A regulatory body of which about half of the U.S. states are members. The MTC develops operating rules and regulations to compute and assign the total taxable income of a multistate taxpayer to specific states.

N

Net capital gain. The excess of the net long-term capital gain for the tax year over the net short-term capital loss. The net capital gain of an individual taxpayer is eligible for the alternative tax. § 1222(11).

Net capital loss. The excess of the losses from sales or exchanges of capital assets over the gains from sales or exchanges of such assets. Up to $3,000 per year of the net capital loss may be deductible by noncorporate taxpayers against ordinary income. The excess net capital loss carries over to future tax years. For corporate taxpayers, the net capital loss cannot be offset against ordinary income, but it can be carried back three years and forward five years to offset net capital gains. §§ 1211, 1212, and 1221(10).

Net investment income. The excess of investment income over investment expenses. Investment expenses are those deductible expenses directly connected with the production of investment income. Investment expenses do not include investment interest. The deduction for investment interest for the tax year is limited to net investment income. § 163(d).

Net operating loss. To mitigate the effect of the annual accounting period concept, § 172 allows taxpayers to use an excess loss of one year as a deduction for certain past or future years. In this regard, a carryback period of 2 years and a carryforward period of 20 years currently are allowed.

Nexus. A multistate taxpayer's taxable income can be apportioned to a specific state only if the taxpayer has established a sufficient presence, or nexus with that state. State law, which often follows the UDITPA, specifies various activities that lead to nexus in various states.

No-additional-cost services. Services that the employer may provide the employee at no additional cost to the employer. Generally, the benefit is the ability to utilize the employer's excess capacity (e.g., vacant seats on an airliner). Such amounts are excludible from the recipient's gross income. § 132(b).

Nonaccountable plan. An expense reimbursement plan that does not have an accountability feature. The result is that employee expenses must be claimed as deductions *from* AGI. An exception is moving expenses that are deductions *for* AGI.

Nonacquiescence. Disagreement by the IRS on the result reached in certain judicial decisions. *Nonacq.* or *NA.*

Nonbusiness bad debt. A bad debt loss that is not incurred in connection with a creditor's trade or business. The loss is classified as a short-term capital loss and is allowed only in the year the debt becomes entirely worthless. In addition to family loans, many investor losses are nonbusiness bad debts. § 166(d).

Nonrecourse debt. Debt secured by the property that it is used to purchase. The purchaser of the property is not personally liable for the debt upon default. Rather, the creditor's recourse is to repossess the related property. Nonrecourse debt generally does not increase the purchaser's at-risk amount.

Nonresident alien. An individual who is neither a citizen nor a resident of the United States. Citizenship is determined under the immigration and naturalization laws of the United States. Residency is determined under § 7701(b) of the Internal Revenue Code. Certain activities of the nonresident alien are subject to U.S. taxation.

Nontaxable exchange. A transaction in which realized gains or losses are not recognized. The recognition of gain or loss is postponed (deferred) until the property received in the nontaxable exchange is subsequently disposed of in a taxable transaction. Examples are § 1031 like-kind exchanges and § 1033 involuntary conversions.

O

Occupational tax. A tax imposed on various trades or businesses. A license fee that enables a taxpayer to engage in a particular occupation.

Office in the home expenses. Employment and business-related expenses attributable to the use of a residence (e.g., den or office) are allowed only if the portion of the residence is exclusively used on a regular basis as a principal place of business of the taxpayer or as a place of business that is used by patients, clients, or customers. If the expenses are incurred by an employee, the use must be for the convenience of the employer as opposed to being merely appropriate and helpful. § 280A.

Options. The sale or exchange of an option to buy or sell property results in capital gain or loss if the property is a capital asset. Generally, the closing of an option transaction results in short-term capital gain or loss to the writer of the call and the purchaser of the call option. § 1234.

Ordinary and necessary. An ordinary expense is one that is common and accepted in the general industry or type of activity in which the taxpayer is engaged. It comprises one of the tests for the deductibility of expenses incurred or paid in connection with a trade or business; for the production or collection of income; for the management, conservation, or maintenance of property held for the production of income; or in connection with the determination, collection, or refund of any tax. §§ 162(a) and 212. A necessary expense is one that is appropriate and helpful in furthering the taxpayer's business or income-producing activity. §§ 162(a) and 212.

Ordinary income property. Property contributed to a charitable organization that, if sold rather than contributed, would have resulted in other than long-term capital gain to the donor (i.e., ordinary income property and short-term capital gain property). Examples are inventory and capital assets held for less than the long-term holding period.

Organizational expenditures. Items incurred early in the life of a corporate entity, qualifying for a special treatment under Federal tax law. A corporation can elect to immediately expense the first $5,000 (subject to phaseout) of organizational expenditures and generally amortize the balance over a period of 180 months or more. Amortizable expenditures exclude those incurred to obtain capital (underwriting fees) or assets (subject to cost recovery). Typically, amortizable expenditures include legal and accounting fees and state incorporation payments. Such items must be incurred by the end of the entity's first tax year. § 248.

Original issue discount. The difference between the issue price of a debt obligation (e.g., a corporate bond) and the maturity value of the obligation when the issue price is *less than* the maturity value. OID represents interest and must be amortized over the life of the debt obligation using the effective interest method. The difference is not considered to be original issue discount for tax purposes when it is less than one-fourth of 1 percent of the redemption price at maturity multiplied by the number of years to maturity. §§ 1272 and 1273(a)(3).

Outbound taxation. U.S. tax effects when a U.S. person undertakes an investment or business activity outside the United States.

Outside basis. A partner's basis in his or her partnership interest.

P

Parent-subsidiary controlled group. A controlled or affiliated group of corporations, where at least one corporation is at least 80 percent owned by one or more of the others. The affiliated group definition is more difficult to meet.

Passive investment holding company. A means by which a multistate taxpayer can reduce its overall effective tax rate by isolating investment income in a no- or low-tax state.

Passive investment income (PII). Gross receipts from royalties, certain rents, dividends, interest, annuities, and gains from the sale or exchange of stock and securities. With certain exceptions, if the passive investment income of an S corporation exceeds 25 percent of the corporation's gross receipts for three consecutive years, S status is lost. In another circumstance, if the S corporation has excessive passive income, a penalty tax is imposed on the S corporation. §§ 1362(d)(3) and 1375.

Passive loss. Any loss from (1) activities in which the taxpayer does not materially participate or (2) rental activities (subject to certain exceptions). Net passive losses cannot be used to offset income from nonpassive sources. Rather, they are suspended until the taxpayer either generates net passive income (and a deduction of such losses is allowed) or disposes of the underlying property (at which time the loss deductions are allowed in full). One relief provision allows landlords who actively participate in the rental activities to deduct up to $25,000 of passive losses annually. However, a phaseout of the $25,000 amount commences when the landlord's AGI exceeds $100,000. Another relief provision applies for material participation in a real estate trade or business. § 469.

Patent. A patent is an intangible asset that may be amortized over a statutory 15-year period as a § 197 intangible. The sale of a patent usually results in favorable long-term capital gain treatment. §§ 197 and 1235.

Payroll factor. The proportion of a multistate corporation's total payroll that is traceable to a specific state. Used in determining the taxable income that is to be apportioned to that state.

Percentage depletion. Percentage depletion is depletion based on a statutory percentage applied to the gross income from the property. The taxpayer deducts the greater of cost depletion or percentage depletion. § 613.

Permanent establishment (PE). A level of business activity, as defined under an income tax treaty, that subjects the taxpayer to taxation in a country other than that in which the taxpayer is based. Often evidenced by the presence of a plant, office, or other fixed place of business. Inventory storage and temporary activities do not rise to the level of a PE. PE is the treaty's equivalent to nexus.

Personal and dependency exemptions. The tax law provides an exemption for each individual taxpayer and an additional exemption for the taxpayer's spouse if a joint return is filed. An individual may also claim a dependency exemption for each dependent, provided certain tests are met. The amount of the personal and dependency exemptions is $3,200 in 2005 and $3,300 in 2006. The amount is indexed for inflation. The exemption is subject to phaseout once adjusted gross income exceeds certain statutory threshold amounts. This phaseout provision is subject to partial phaseout beginning in 2006. §§ 151 and 152.

Personal service corporation (PSC). A corporation whose principal activity is the performance of personal services (e.g., health, law, engineering, architecture, accounting, actuarial science, performing arts, or consulting) and where such services are substantially performed by the employee-owners. The 35 percent statutory income tax rate applies to PSCs.

Personalty. All property that is not attached to real estate (realty) and is movable. Examples of personalty are machinery, automobiles, clothing, household furnishings, inventory, and personal effects.

Points. Loan origination fees that may be deductible as interest by a buyer of property. A seller of property who pays points reduces the selling price by the amount of the points paid for the buyer. While the seller is not permitted to deduct this amount as interest, the buyer may do so. § 461(g).

Portfolio income. Income from interest, dividends, certain rentals, royalties, capital gains, or other investment sources. Net passive losses cannot be used to offset net portfolio income. § 469.

Precedent. A previously decided court decision that is recognized as authority for the disposition of future decisions.

Precontribution gain or loss. Partnerships allow for a variety of special allocations of gain or loss among the partners, but gain or loss that is "built in" on an asset contributed to the partnership is assigned specifically to the contributing partner. § 704(c)(1)(A).

Private activity bond. Interest on state and local bonds is excludible from gross income. § 103. Certain such bonds are labeled private activity bonds. Although the interest on such bonds is excludible for regular income tax purposes, it is treated as a tax preference in calculating the AMT.

Procedural Regulation. A Regulation issued by the Treasury Department that is a housekeeping-type instruction indicating information that taxpayers should provide the IRS as well as information about the internal management and conduct of the IRS itself.

Production activities deduction (PAD). A deduction based on 3 percent of the lesser of qualified production activities income (QPAI) or modified adjusted gross income but not to exceed 50 percent of the W–2 wages paid. In the case of a corporate taxpayer, taxable income is substituted for modified AGI. The deduction rate increases to 6 percent for 2007 to 2009 and to 9 percent for 2010 and thereafter. § 199. See also *qualified production activities income (QPAI)*.

Profit and loss sharing ratios. Specified in the partnership agreement and used to determine each partner's allocation of ordinary taxable income and separately stated items. Profits and losses can be shared in different ratios. The ratios can be changed by amending the partnership agreement. § 704(a).

Profits (loss) interest. A partner's percentage allocation of partnership operating results, determined by the profit and loss sharing ratios.

Property. Assets defined in the broadest legal sense. Property includes the unrealized receivables of a cash basis taxpayer, but not services rendered. § 351.

Property dividend. Generally treated in the same manner as a cash distribution, measured by the fair market value of the property on the date of distribution. The portion of the distribution representing E & P is a dividend; any excess is treated as a return of capital. Distribution of appreciated property causes the distributing corporation to recognize gain. The distributing corporation does not recognize loss on property that has depreciated in value. §§ 301 and 311.

Property factor. The proportion of a multistate corporation's total property that is traceable to a specific state. Used in determining the taxable income that is to be apportioned to that state.

Proposed Regulation. A Regulation issued by the Treasury Department in proposed, rather than final, form. The interval between the proposal of a Regulation and its finalization permits taxpayers and other interested parties to comment on the propriety of the proposal.

Proprietorship. A business entity for which there is a single owner. The net profit of the entity is reported on the owner's Federal income tax return (Schedule C of Form 1040).

Public Law 86–272. A congressional limit on the ability of the state to force a multistate taxpayer to assign income to that state. Under P.L. 86–272, where orders for tangible personal property are both filled and delivered outside the state, the entity must establish more than the mere solicitation of such orders took place in-state before any income can be apportioned to the state.

Punitive damages. Damages received or paid by the taxpayer can be classified as compensatory damages or as punitive damages. Punitive damages are those awarded to punish the defendant for gross negligence or the intentional infliction of harm. Such damages are includible in gross income. § 104(a)(2).

Q

Qualified dividend income. Dividends that are eligible for the beneficial 5 percent or 15 percent tax rate. Excluded are certain dividends from foreign corporations, dividends from tax-exempt entities, and dividends that do not satisfy the holding period requirement. A dividend from a foreign corporation is eligible for qualified dividend status only if one of the following requirements is met: (1) the foreign corporation's stock is traded on an established U.S. securities market, or (2) the foreign corporation is eligible for the benefits of a comprehensive income tax treaty between its country of incorporation and the United States. To satisfy the holding period requirement, the stock on which the dividend is paid must have been held for more than 60 days during the 120-day period beginning 60 days before the ex-dividend date.

Qualified employee discounts. Discounts offered employees on merchandise or services that the employer ordinarily sells or provides to customers. The discounts must be generally available to all employees. In the case of property, the discount cannot exceed the employer's gross profit (the sales price cannot be less than the employer's cost). In the case of services, the discounts cannot exceed 20 percent of the normal sales price. § 132.

Qualified nonrecourse debt. Debt issued on realty by a bank, retirement plan, or governmental agency. Included in the at-risk amount by the investor. § 465(b)(6).

Qualified production activities income (QPAI). A key determinant in computing the production activities deduction (PAD). It consists of domestic production gross receipts (DPGR) reduced by cost of goods sold and other assignable expenses. Thus, QPAI represents the profit derived from production activities. § 199. See also *domestic production gross receipts (DPGR)* and *production activities deduction (PAD)*.

Qualified real property business indebtedness. Indebtedness that was incurred or assumed by the taxpayer in connection with real property used in a trade or business and is secured by such real property. The taxpayer must not be a C corporation. For qualified real property business indebtedness, the taxpayer may elect to exclude some or all of the income realized from cancellation of debt on qualified real property. If the election is made, the basis of the property must be reduced by the amount excluded. The amount excluded cannot be greater than the excess of the principal amount of the outstanding debt over the fair market value (net of any other debt outstanding on the property) of the property securing the debt. § 108(c).

Qualified residence interest. A term relevant in determining the amount of interest expense the individual taxpayer may deduct as an itemized deduction for what otherwise would be disallowed as a component of personal interest (consumer interest). Qualified residence interest consists of interest paid on qualified residences (principal residence and one other residence) of the taxpayer. Debt that qualifies as qualified residence interest is limited to $1 million of debt to acquire, construct, or substantially improve qualified residences (acquisition indebtedness) plus $100,000 of other debt secured by qualified residences (home equity indebtedness). The home equity indebtedness may not exceed the fair market value of a qualified residence reduced by the acquisition indebtedness for that residence. § 163(h)(3).

Qualified small business stock. Stock in a qualified small business corporation, purchased as part of an original issue after August 10, 1993. The shareholder may exclude from gross income 50 percent of the realized gain on the sale of the stock, if he or she held the stock for more than five years. § 1202.

Qualified transportation fringes. Transportation benefits provided by the employer to the employee. Such benefits include (1) transportation in a commuter highway vehicle between the employee's residence and the place of employment, (2) a transit pass, and (3) qualified parking. Qualified transportation fringes are excludible from the employee's gross income to the extent categories (1) and (2) above do not exceed $105 per month in 2006 and category (3) does not exceed $205 per month in 2006. These amounts are indexed annually for inflation. § 132(f).

Qualifying child. An individual who, as to the taxpayer, satisfies the relationship, abode, and age tests. To be claimed as a dependent, such individual must also meet the citizenship and joint return tests and not be self-supporting. §§ 152(a)(1) and (c). See also *personal and dependency exemptions.*

Qualifying relative. An individual who, as to the taxpayer, satisfies the relationship, gross income, support, citizenship, and joint return tests. Such an individual can be claimed as a dependent of the taxpayer. §§ 152(a)(2) and (d). See also *personal and dependency exemptions.*

R

Realized gain or loss. The difference between the amount realized upon the sale or other disposition of property and the adjusted basis of the property. § 1001.

Realty. Real estate.

Reasonableness requirement. The Code includes a reasonableness requirement with respect to the deduction of salaries and other compensation for services. What constitutes reasonableness is a question of fact. If an expense is unreasonable, the amount that is classified as unreasonable is not allowed as a deduction. The question of reasonableness generally arises with respect to closely held corporations where there is no separation of ownership and management. § 162(a)(1).

Recognized gain or loss. The portion of realized gain or loss subject to income taxation.

Recourse debt. Debt for which the lender may both foreclose on the property and assess a guarantor for any payments due under the loan. A lender may also make a claim against the assets of any general partner in a partnership to which debt is issued, without regard to whether the partner has guaranteed the debt.

Recovery of capital doctrine. When a taxable sale or exchange occurs, the seller may be permitted to recover his or her investment (or other adjusted basis) in the property before gain or loss is recognized.

Regular corporation. See *C corporation.*

Rehabilitation expenditures credit. A credit that is based on expenditures incurred to rehabilitate industrial and commercial buildings and certified historic structures. The credit is intended to discourage businesses from moving from older, economically distressed areas to newer locations and to encourage the preservation of historic structures. § 47.

Rehabilitation expenditures credit recapture. When property that qualifies for the rehabilitation expenditures credit is disposed of or ceases to be used in the trade or business of the taxpayer, some or all of the tax credit claimed on the property may be recaptured as additional tax liability. The amount of the recapture is the difference between the amount of the credit claimed originally and what should have been claimed in light of the length of time the property was actually held or used for qualifying purposes. § 50.

Related corporation. See *controlled group.*

Related-party transactions. Various Code Sections define related parties and often include a variety of persons within this (usually detrimental) category. Generally, related parties are accorded different tax treatment from that applicable to other taxpayers who enter into similar transactions. For instance, realized losses that are generated between related parties are not recognized in the year of the loss (§ 267). However, these deferred losses can be used to offset recognized gains that occur upon the subsequent sale of the asset to a nonrelated party. Other uses of a related-party definition include the conversion of gain upon the sale of a depreciable asset into all ordinary income (§ 1239) and the identification of constructive ownership of stock relative to corporate distributions, redemptions, liquidations, reorganizations, and compensation.

Rental activity. Any activity where payments are received principally for the use of tangible property is a rental activity. Temporary Regulations provide that in certain circumstances activities involving rentals of real and personal property are not to be *treated* as rental activities. The Temporary Regulations list six exceptions.

Research activities credit. A tax credit whose purpose is to encourage research and development. It consists of two components: the incremental research activities credit and the basic research credit. The incremental research activities credit is equal to 20 percent of the excess qualified research expenditures over the base amount. The basic research credit is equal to 20 percent of the excess of basic research payments over the base amount. § 41.

Research and experimental expenditures. The Code provides three alternatives for the tax treatment of research and experimental expenditures. They may be expensed in the year paid or incurred, deferred subject to amortization, or capitalized. If the taxpayer does not elect to expense such costs or to defer them subject to amortization (over 60 months), the expenditures must be capitalized. § 174. Two types of research activities credits are available: the basic research credit and the incremental research activities credit. The rate for each type is 20 percent. § 41.

Reserve method. A method of accounting whereby an allowance is permitted for estimated uncollectible accounts. Actual write-offs are charged to the reserve, and recoveries of amounts previously written off are credited to the reserve. The Code permits only certain financial institutions to use the reserve method. § 166.

Residential rental real estate. Buildings for which at least 80 percent of the gross rents are from dwelling units (e.g., an apartment building). This type of building is distinguished from nonresidential (commercial or industrial) buildings in applying the recapture of depreciation provisions. The term also is relevant in distinguishing between buildings that are eligible for a 27.5-year life versus a 39-year life for MACRS purposes. Generally, residential buildings receive preferential treatment. § 168(e)(2)(A).

Revenue Procedure. A matter of procedural importance to both taxpayers and the IRS concerning the administration of the tax laws is issued as a Revenue Procedure (abbreviated Rev.Proc.). A Revenue Procedure is first published in an *Internal Revenue Bulletin* (I.R.B.) and later transferred to the appropriate *Cumulative Bulletin* (C.B.). Both the *Internal Revenue Bulletins* and the *Cumulative Bulletins* are published by the U.S. Government Printing Office.

Revenue Ruling. A Revenue Ruling (abbreviated Rev.Rul.) is issued by the National Office of the IRS to express an official interpretation of the tax law as applied to specific transactions. It is more limited in application than a Regulation. A Revenue Ruling is first published in an *Internal Revenue Bulletin* (I.R.B.) and later transferred to the appropriate *Cumulative Bulletin* (C.B.). Both the *Internal Revenue Bulletins* and the *Cumulative Bulletins* are published by the U.S. Government Printing Office.

S

S corporation. The designation for a small business corporation. See also *Subchapter S.*

Sale or exchange. A requirement for the recognition of capital gain or loss. Generally, the seller of property must receive money or relief from debt in order to have sold the property. An exchange involves the transfer of property for other property. Thus, collection of a debt is neither a sale nor an exchange. The term *sale or exchange* is not defined by the Code.

Sales factor. The proportion of a multistate corporation's total sales that is traceable to a specific state. Used in determining the taxable income that is to be apportioned to that state.

Sales tax. A state- or local-level tax on the retail sale of specified property. Generally, the purchaser pays the tax, but the seller collects it, as an agent for the government. Various taxing jurisdictions allow exemptions for purchases of specific items, including certain food, services, and manufacturing equipment. If the purchaser and seller are in different states, a use tax usually applies.

Schedule M–1. On the Form 1120, a reconciliation of book net income with Federal taxable income. Accounts for timing and permanent differences in the two computations, such as depreciation differences, exempt income, and nondeductible items. On Forms 1120S and 1065, the Schedule M–1 reconciles book income with owners' aggregate ordinary taxable income.

Schedule M–3. An *expanded* reconciliation of book net income with Federal taxable income (see *Schedule M–1*). Applies to corporations with total assets of $10 million or more.

Scholarships. Scholarships are generally excluded from the gross income of the recipient unless the payments are a disguised form of compensation for services rendered. However, the Code imposes restrictions on the exclusion. The recipient must be a degree candidate. The excluded amount is limited to amounts used for tuition, fees, books, supplies, and equipment required for courses of instruction. Amounts received for room and board are not eligible for the exclusion. § 117.

Section 179 expensing election. The ability to deduct a capital expenditure in the year an asset is placed in service rather than over the asset's useful life or cost recovery period. The annual ceiling on the deduction is $108,000 for 2006 ($105,000 for 2005). However, the deduction is reduced dollar for dollar when § 179 property placed in service during the taxable year exceeds $430,000 in 2006 ($420,000 in 2005). In addition, the amount expensed under § 179 cannot exceed the aggregate amount of taxable income derived from the conduct of any trade or business by the taxpayer.

Section 1231 gains and losses. If the combined gains and losses from the taxable dispositions of § 1231 assets plus the net gain from business involuntary conversions (of both § 1231 assets and long-term capital assets) is a gain, the gains and losses are treated as long-term capital gains and losses. In arriving at § 1231 gains, however, the depreciation recapture provisions (e.g., §§ 1245 and 1250) are first applied to produce ordinary income. If the net result of the combination is a loss, the gains and losses from § 1231 assets are treated as ordinary gains and losses. § 1231(a).

Section 1231 lookback. In order for gain to be classified as § 1231 gain, the gain must survive the § 1231 lookback. To the extent of nonrecaptured § 1231 losses for the five prior tax years, the gain is classified as ordinary income. § 1231(c).

Section 1231 property. Depreciable assets and real estate used in trade or business and held for the required long-term holding period. Under certain circumstances, the classification also includes timber, coal, domestic iron ore, livestock (held for draft, breeding, dairy, or sporting purposes), and unharvested crops. § 1231(b).

Section 1245 property. Property that is subject to the recapture of depreciation under § 1245. For a definition of § 1245 property, see § 1245(a)(3).

Section 1245 recapture. Upon a taxable disposition of § 1245 property, all depreciation claimed on the property is recaptured as ordinary income (but not to exceed recognized gain from the disposition).

Section 1250 property. Real estate that is subject to the recapture of depreciation under § 1250. For a definition of § 1250 property, see § 1250(c).

Section 1250 recapture. Upon a taxable disposition of § 1250 property, some of the depreciation or cost recovery claimed on the property may be recaptured as ordinary income.

Securities. Generally, stock, debt, and other financial assets. To the extent securities other than the stock of the transferee corporation are received in a § 351 exchange, the new shareholder realizes a gain.

Self-employment tax. In 2006, a tax of 12.4 percent is levied on individuals with net earnings from self-employment (up to $94,200) to provide Social Security benefits (i.e., the old age, survivors, and disability insurance portion) for such individuals. In addition, in 2006, a tax of 2.9 percent is levied on individuals with net earnings from self-employment (with no statutory ceiling) to provide Medicare benefits (i.e., the hospital insurance portion) for such individuals. If a self-employed individual also receives wages from an employer that are subject to FICA, the self-employment tax will be reduced if total income subject to Social Security is more than $94,200 in 2006. A partial deduction is allowed in calculating the self-employment tax. Individuals with net earnings of $400 or more from self-employment are subject to this tax. §§ 1401 and 1402.

Separate foreign tax credit limitation category. The foreign tax credit of a taxpayer is computed for each of several types of income sources, as specified by the Code to limit the results of tax planning. FTC income "baskets" include passive, ordinary, and shipping income. The FTC for the year is the sum of the credits as computed within all of the taxpayer's separate FTC baskets used for the tax year.

Separately stated item. Any item of a partnership or S corporation that might be taxed differently to any two owners of the entity. These amounts are not included in ordinary income of the entity, but are instead reported separately to the owners; tax consequences are determined at the owner level. §§ 702(a) and 1366(a)(1).

Short sale. A short sale occurs when a taxpayer sells borrowed property (usually stock) and repays the lender with substantially identical property either held on the date of the short sale or purchased after the sale. No gain or loss is recognized until the short sale is closed, and such gain or loss is generally short term. § 1233.

Significant participation activity. There are seven tests to determine whether an individual has achieved material participation in an activity, one of which is based on more than 500 hours of participation in significant participation activities. A significant participation activity is one in which the individual's participation exceeds 100 hours during the year. Reg. § 1.469–5T.

Small business corporation. A corporation that satisfies the definition of § 1361(b), § 1244(c), or both. Satisfaction of § 1361(b) permits an S election, and satisfaction of § 1244 enables the shareholders of the corporation to claim an ordinary loss on the worthlessness of stock.

Small business stock. See *small business corporation.*

Small Cases Division of the U.S. Tax Court. Jurisdiction is limited to claims of $50,000 or less. There is no appeal from this court.

Solicitation. A level of activity brought about by the taxpayer within a specific state. Under Public Law 86-272, certain types of solicitation activities do not create nexus with the state. Exceeding mere solicitation, though, creates nexus.

Special allocation. Any amount for which an agreement exists among the partners of a partnership outlining the method used for spreading the item among the partners.

Specific charge-off method. A method of accounting for bad debts in which a deduction is permitted only when an account becomes partially or completely worthless.

Standard deduction. The individual taxpayer can either itemize deductions or take the standard deduction. The amount of the standard deduction depends on the taxpayer's filing status (single, head of household, married filing jointly, surviving spouse, or married filing separately). For 2006, the amount of the standard deduction ranges from $5,150 (for married, filing separately or unmarried) to $10,300 (for married, filing jointly). Additional standard deductions of either $1,000 (for married taxpayers) or $1,250 (for single taxpayers) are available if the taxpayer is either blind or age 65 or over. Limitations exist on the amount of the standard deduction of a taxpayer who is another taxpayer's dependent. The standard deduction amounts are adjusted for inflation each year. § 63(c).

Stock dividend. Not taxable if pro rata distributions of stock or stock rights on common stock. Section 305 governs the taxability of stock dividends and sets out five exceptions to the general rule that stock dividends are nontaxable.

Stock redemption. A corporation buys back its own stock from a specified shareholder. Typically, the corporation recognizes any realized gain on the noncash assets that it uses to effect a redemption, and the shareholder obtains a capital gain or loss upon receipt of the purchase price. §§ 301 and 302.

Subchapter S. Sections 1361–1379 of the Internal Revenue Code. An elective provision permitting certain small business corporations (§ 1361) and their shareholders (§ 1362) to elect to be treated for income tax purposes in accordance with the operating rules of §§ 1363–1379. S corporations usually avoid the corporate income tax, and corporate losses can be claimed by the shareholders.

Subpart F income. Certain income earned by a controlled foreign corporation. Usually, Subpart F income is included in the gross income of a U.S. shareholder of the CFC when the income is earned, not when it is later repatriated.

Supreme Court. The highest appellate court or the court of last resort in the Federal court system and in most states. Only a small number of tax decisions of the U.S. Courts of Appeal are reviewed by the U.S. Supreme Court under its certiorari procedure. The Supreme Court usually grants certiorari to resolve a conflict among the Courts of Appeal (e.g., two or more appellate courts have assumed opposing positions on a particular issue) or when the tax issue is extremely important (e.g., size of the revenue loss to the Federal government).

Surviving spouse. When a husband or wife predeceases the other spouse, the survivor is known as a surviving spouse. Under certain conditions, a surviving spouse may be entitled to use the income tax rates in § 1(a) (those applicable to married persons filing a joint return) for the two years after the year of death of his or her spouse. § 2.

Syndication costs. Incurred in promoting and marketing partnership interests for sale to investors. Examples include legal and accounting fees, printing costs for prospectus and placement documents, and state registration fees. These items are capitalized by the partnership as incurred, with no amortization thereof allowed.

T

Tax avoidance. The minimization of one's tax liability by taking advantage of legally available tax planning opportunities. Tax avoidance can be contrasted with tax evasion, which entails the reduction of tax liability by illegal means.

Tax benefit rule. A provision that limits the recognition of income from the recovery of an expense or loss properly deducted in a prior tax year to the amount of the deduction that generated a tax saving. Assume that last year Gary had medical expenses of $3,000 and adjusted gross income of $30,000. Because of the 7.5 percent limitation, Gary could deduct only $750 of these expenses [$3,000 – (7.5% × $30,000)]. If, this year, Gary is reimbursed by his insurance company for $900 of these expenses, the tax benefit rule limits the amount of income from the reimbursement to $750 (the amount previously deducted with a tax saving). § 111.

Tax Court. The U.S. Tax Court is one of four trial courts of original jurisdiction that decides litigation involving Federal income, death, or gift taxes. It is the only trial court where the taxpayer must not first pay the deficiency assessed by the IRS. The Tax Court will not have jurisdiction over a case unless a statutory notice of deficiency (90-day letter) has been issued by the IRS and the taxpayer files the petition for hearing within the time prescribed.

Tax credits. Tax credits are amounts that directly reduce a taxpayer's tax liability. The tax benefit received from a tax credit is not dependent on the taxpayer's marginal tax rate, whereas the benefit of a tax deduction or exclusion is dependent on the taxpayer's tax bracket.

Tax evasion. The reduction of the taxpayer's tax liability through the use of illegal means. Tax evasion can be contrasted with tax avoidance, which entails the reduction of tax liability through the use of legal means.

Tax preference items. Various items that may result in the imposition of the alternative minimum tax. §§ 55–58.

Tax rate schedules. Rate schedules that are used by upper-income taxpayers and those not permitted to use the tax table. Separate rate schedules are provided for married individuals filing jointly, head of household, single taxpayers, estates and trusts, and married individuals filing separate returns. § 1.

Tax shelters. The typical tax shelter generated large losses in the early years of the activity. Investors would offset these losses against other types of income and, therefore, avoid paying income taxes on this income. These tax shelter investments could then be sold after a few years and produce capital gain income, which is taxed at a lower rate than ordinary income. The passive activity loss rules and the at-risk rules now limit tax shelter deductions.

Tax table. A tax table that is provided for taxpayers with less than $100,000 of taxable income. Separate columns are provided for single taxpayers, married taxpayers filing jointly, head of household, and married taxpayers filing separately. § 3.

Taxable year. The annual period over which income is measured for income tax purposes. Most individuals use a calendar year, but many businesses use a fiscal year based on the natural business year.

Technical advice memoranda (TAMs). TAMs are issued by the National Office of the IRS in response to questions raised by IRS field personnel during audits. They deal with completed rather than proposed transactions and are often requested for questions related to exempt organizations and employee plans.

Temporary Regulation. A Regulation issued by the Treasury Department in temporary form. When speed is critical, the Treasury Department issues Temporary Regulations that take effect immediately. These Regulations have the same authoritative value as Final Regulations and may be cited as precedent for three years. Temporary Regulations are also issued as proposed Regulations.

Theft loss. A loss from larceny, embezzlement, or robbery. It does not include misplacement of items.

Thin capitalization. When debt owed by a corporation to the shareholders becomes too large in relation to the corporation's capital structure (i.e., stock and shareholder equity), the IRS may contend that the corporation is thinly capitalized. In effect, this means that some or all of the debt is reclassified as equity. The immediate result is to disallow any interest deduction to the corporation on the reclassified debt. To the extent of the corporation's earnings and profits, interest payments and loan repayments on the reclassified debt are treated as dividends to the shareholders. § 385.

Thirty percent additional first-year depreciation. This provision, which was effective for property acquired after September 10, 2001, and before September 11, 2004, provided for an additional cost recovery deduction of 30 percent in the tax year that qualified property was placed in service. Qualified property included most types of new property other than buildings. The property had to be placed in service before January 1, 2005. § 168(k). See also *cost recovery system* and *fifty percent additional first-year depreciation.*

Throwback rule. If there is no income tax in the state to which a sale otherwise would be apportioned, the sale essentially is exempt from state income tax, even though the seller is domiciled in a state that levies an income tax. Nonetheless, if the seller's state has adopted a throwback rule, the sale is attributed to the seller's state, and the transaction is subjected to a state-level tax.

Transportation expenses. Transportation expenses for an employee include only the cost of transportation (taxi fares, automobile expenses, etc.) in the course of employment when the employee is not away from home in travel status. Commuting expenses are not deductible.

Travel expenses. Travel expenses include meals (generally subject to a 50 percent disallowance) and lodging and transportation expenses while away from home in the pursuit of a trade or business (including that of an employee).

U

Unearned income. Income received but not yet earned. Normally, such income is taxed when received, even for accrual basis taxpayers. In certain cases involving advance payments for goods and services, income may be deferred. See Revenue Procedure 2004–34 (I.R.B. No. 22,991) and Reg. § 1.451–5.

Unitary approach. Sales, property, and payroll of related corporations are combined for nexus and apportionment purposes, and the worldwide income of the unitary entity is apportioned to the state. Subsidiaries and other affiliated corporations found to be part of the corporation's unitary business (because they are subject to overlapping ownership, operations, or management) are included in the apportionment procedure. This approach can be limited if a waters'-edge election is in effect.

Unreasonable compensation. A deduction is allowed for "reasonable" salaries or other compensation for personal services actually rendered. To the extent compensation is "excessive" ("unreasonable"), no deduction is allowed. The problem of unreasonable compensation usually is limited to closely held corporations, where the motivation is to pay out profits in some form that is deductible to the corporation. Deductible compensation therefore becomes an attractive substitute for nondeductible dividends when the shareholders also are employed by the corporation. § 162(a)(1).

Unrecaptured § 1250 gain (25 percent gain). Gain from the sale of depreciable real estate held more than one year. The gain is equal to or less than the depreciation taken on such property and is reduced by § 1245 and § 1250 gain.

U.S. shareholder. For purposes of classification of an entity as a controlled foreign corporation, a U.S. person who owns, or is considered to own, 10 percent or more of the total combined voting power of all classes of voting stock of a foreign corporation. Stock owned directly, indirectly, and constructively is counted for this purpose. The U.S. shareholder may be currently taxed on a proportionate share of Subpart F income.

U.S. trade or business. A set of activities that is carried on in a regular, continuous, and substantial manner. A non-U.S. taxpayer is subject to U.S. tax on the taxable income that is effectively connected with a U.S. trade or business.

Use tax. A sales tax that is collectible by the seller where the purchaser is domiciled in a different state.

V

Value added tax (VAT). A national sales tax that taxes the increment in value as goods move through the production process. A VAT is much used in other countries but has not yet been incorporated as part of the U.S. Federal tax structure.

Voluntary revocation. The owners of a majority of shares in an S corporation elect to terminate the S status of the entity, as of a specified date. The day on which the revocation is effective is the first day of the corporation's C tax year.

W

W–2 wages. The production activities deduction (PAD) cannot exceed 50 percent of the W–2 wages paid for any particular year. Prop.Reg. § 199–2(f)(2) provides several methods for calculating the W–2 wages, but the payments must involve common law employees. To qualify, however, they need not be involved in the production process. § 199. See also *production activities deduction (PAD).*

Wash sale. A loss from the sale of stock or securities that is disallowed because the taxpayer, within 30 days before or after the sale, has acquired stock or securities substantially identical to those sold. § 1091.

Waters'-edge election. A limitation on the worldwide scope of the unitary approach to computing state taxable income. If a waters'-edge election is in effect, the state can consider only the activities that occur within the boundaries of the United States in the apportionment procedure.

Welfare-to-work credit. A tax credit available to employers hiring individuals who have been long-term recipients of family assistance welfare benefits. In general, long-term recipients are those individuals who are certified by a designated local agency as being members of a family receiving assistance under a public aid program for at least an 18-month period ending on the hiring date. The welfare-to-work credit is available for qualified wages paid in the first two years of employment. The maximum credit is equal to $8,500 per qualified employee, computed as 35 percent of the first $10,000 of qualified wages paid in the first year of employment, plus 50 percent of the first $10,000 of qualified wages paid in the second year of employment. § 51A.

Wherewithal to pay. This concept recognizes the inequity of taxing a transaction when the taxpayer lacks the means with which to pay the tax. Under it, there is a correlation between the imposition of the tax and the ability to pay the tax. It is particularly suited to situations in which the taxpayer's economic position has not changed significantly as a result of the transaction.

Work opportunity tax credit. Employers are allowed a tax credit equal to 40 percent of the first $6,000 of wages (per eligible employee) for the first year of employment. Eligible employees include certain hard-to-employ individuals (e.g., qualified ex-felons, high-risk youth, food stamp recipients, and veterans). The employer's deduction for wages is reduced by the amount of the credit taken. For qualified summer youth employees, the 40 percent rate is applied to the first $3,000 of qualified wages. §§ 51 and 52.

Working condition fringe. A type of fringe benefit received by the employee that is excludible from the employee's gross income. It consists of property or services provided (paid or reimbursed) by the employer for which the employee could take a tax deduction if the employee had paid for them. § 132(d).

Worthless securities. A loss (usually capital) is allowed for a security that becomes worthless during the year. The loss is deemed to have occurred on the last day of the year. Special rules apply to securities of affiliated companies and small business stock. § 165.

Writ of Certiorari. Appeal from a U.S. Court of Appeals to the U.S. Supreme Court is by Writ of Certiorari. The Supreme Court need not accept the appeal, and it usually does not (*cert. den.*) unless a conflict exists among the lower courts that must be resolved or a constitutional issue is involved.

APPENDIX D–1

TABLE OF CODE SECTIONS CITED

[See Title 26 U.S.C.A.]

APPENDIX D–2

TABLE OF REGULATIONS CITED

Temporary Treasury Regulations

Treasury Regulations

APPENDIX D–3

TABLE OF REVENUE PROCEDURES AND REVENUE RULINGS CITED

Revenue Procedures

Revenue Rulings

Revenue Rulings

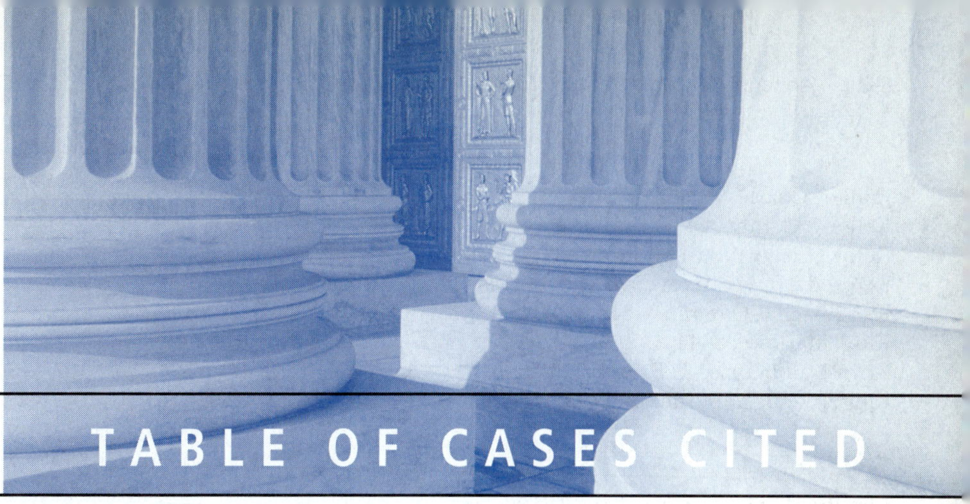

APPENDIX E

TABLE OF CASES CITED

APPENDIX F

PRESENT VALUE AND FUTURE VALUE TABLES

Present Value of $1

N/R	4%	5%	6%	7%	8%	9%	10%	11%	12%	13%	14%
1	0.9615	0.9524	0.9434	0.9346	0.9259	0.9174	0.9091	0.9009	0.8929	0.8850	0.8772
2	0.9246	0.9070	0.8900	0.8734	0.8573	0.8417	0.8264	0.8116	0.7972	0.7831	0.7695
3	0.8890	0.8638	0.8396	0.8163	0.7938	0.7722	0.7513	0.7312	0.7118	0.6931	0.6750
4	0.8548	0.8227	0.7921	0.7629	0.7350	0.7084	0.6830	0.6587	0.6355	0.6133	0.5921
5	0.8219	0.7835	0.7473	0.7130	0.6806	0.6499	0.6209	0.5935	0.5674	0.5428	0.5194
6	0.7903	0.7462	0.7050	0.6663	0.6302	0.5963	0.5645	0.5346	0.5066	0.4803	0.4556
7	0.7599	0.7107	0.6651	0.6227	0.5835	0.5470	0.5132	0.4817	0.4523	0.4251	0.3996
8	0.7307	0.6768	0.6274	0.5820	0.5403	0.5019	0.4665	0.4339	0.4039	0.3762	0.3506
9	0.7026	0.6446	0.5919	0.5439	0.5002	0.4604	0.4241	0.3909	0.3606	0.3329	0.3075
10	0.6756	0.6139	0.5584	0.5083	0.4632	0.4224	0.3855	0.3522	0.3220	0.2946	0.2697
11	0.6496	0.5847	0.5268	0.4751	0.4289	0.3875	0.3505	0.3173	0.2875	0.2607	0.2366
12	0.6246	0.5568	0.4970	0.4440	0.3971	0.3555	0.3186	0.2858	0.2567	0.2307	0.2076
13	0.6006	0.5303	0.4688	0.4150	0.3677	0.3262	0.2897	0.2575	0.2292	0.2042	0.1821
14	0.5775	0.5051	0.4423	0.3878	0.3405	0.2992	0.2633	0.2320	0.2046	0.1807	0.1597
15	0.5553	0.4810	0.4173	0.3624	0.3152	0.2745	0.2394	0.2090	0.1827	0.1599	0.1401
16	0.5339	0.4581	0.3936	0.3387	0.2919	0.2519	0.2176	0.1883	0.1631	0.1415	0.1229
17	0.5134	0.4363	0.3714	0.3166	0.2703	0.2311	0.1978	0.1696	0.1456	0.1252	0.1078
18	0.4936	0.4155	0.3503	0.2959	0.2502	0.2120	0.1799	0.1528	0.1300	0.1108	0.0946
19	0.4746	0.3957	0.3305	0.2765	0.2317	0.1945	0.1635	0.1377	0.1161	0.0981	0.0829
20	0.4564	0.3769	0.3118	0.2584	0.2145	0.1784	0.1486	0.1240	0.1037	0.0868	0.0728

Present Value of an Ordinary Annuity of $1

N/R	4%	5%	6%	7%	8%	9%	10%	11%	12%	13%	14%
1	0.9615	0.9524	0.9434	0.9346	0.9259	0.9174	0.9091	0.9009	0.8929	0.8850	0.8772
2	1.8861	1.8594	1.8334	1.8080	1.7833	1.7591	1.7355	1.7125	1.6901	1.6681	1.6467
3	2.7751	2.7232	2.6730	2.6243	2.5771	2.5313	2.4869	2.4437	2.4018	2.3612	2.3216
4	3.6299	3.5460	3.4651	3.3872	3.3121	3.2397	3.1699	3.1024	3.0373	2.9745	2.9137
5	4.4518	4.3295	4.2124	4.1002	3.9927	3.8897	3.7908	3.6959	3.6048	3.5172	3.4331
6	5.2421	5.0757	4.9173	4.7665	4.6229	4.4859	4.3553	4.2305	4.1114	3.9975	3.8887
7	6.0021	5.7864	5.5824	5.3893	5.2064	5.0330	4.8684	4.7122	4.5638	4.4226	4.2883
8	6.7327	6.4632	6.2098	5.9713	5.7466	5.5348	5.3349	5.1461	4.9676	4.7988	4.6389
9	7.4353	7.1078	6.8017	6.5152	6.2469	5.9952	5.7590	5.5370	5.3282	5.1317	4.9464
10	8.1109	7.7217	7.3601	7.0236	6.7101	6.4177	6.1446	5.8892	5.6502	5.4262	5.2161
11	8.7605	8.3064	7.8869	7.4987	7.1390	6.8052	6.4951	6.2065	5.9377	5.6869	5.4527
12	9.3851	8.8633	8.3838	7.9427	7.5361	7.1607	6.8137	6.4924	6.1944	5.9176	5.6603
13	9.9856	9.3936	8.8527	8.3577	7.9038	7.4869	7.1034	6.7499	6.4235	6.1218	5.8424
14	10.5631	9.8986	9.2950	8.7455	8.2442	7.7862	7.3667	6.9819	6.6282	6.3025	6.0021
15	11.1184	10.3797	9.7122	9.1079	8.5595	8.0607	7.6061	7.1909	6.8109	6.4624	6.1422
16	11.6523	10.8378	10.1059	9.4466	8.8514	8.3126	7.8237	7.3792	6.9740	6.6039	6.2651
17	12.1657	11.2741	10.4773	9.7632	9.1216	8.5436	8.0216	7.5488	7.1196	6.7291	6.3729
18	12.6593	11.6896	10.8276	10.0591	9.3719	8.7556	8.2014	7.7016	7.2497	6.8399	6.4674
19	13.1339	12.0853	11.1581	10.3356	9.6036	8.9501	8.3649	7.8393	7.3658	6.9380	6.5504
20	13.5903	12.4622	11.4699	10.5940	9.8181	9.1285	8.5136	7.9633	7.4694	7.0248	6.6231

Future Value of $1

N/R	4%	5%	6%	7%	8%	9%	10%	11%	12%	13%	14%
1	1.0400	1.0500	1.0600	1.0700	1.0800	1.0900	1.1000	1.1100	1.1200	1.1300	1.1400
2	1.0816	1.1025	1.1236	1.1449	1.1664	1.1881	1.2100	1.2321	1.2544	1.2769	1.2996
3	1.1249	1.1576	1.1910	1.2250	1.2597	1.2950	1.3310	1.3676	1.4049	1.4429	1.4815
4	1.1699	1.2155	1.2625	1.3108	1.3605	1.4116	1.4641	1.5181	1.5735	1.6305	1.6890
5	1.2167	1.2763	1.3382	1.4026	1.4693	1.5386	1.6105	1.6851	1.7623	1.8424	1.9254
6	1.2653	1.3401	1.4185	1.5007	1.5869	1.6771	1.7716	1.8704	1.9738	2.0820	2.1950
7	1.3159	1.4071	1.5036	1.6058	1.7138	1.8280	1.9487	2.0762	2.2107	2.3526	2.5023
8	1.3686	1.4775	1.5938	1.7182	1.8509	1.9926	2.1436	2.3045	2.4760	2.6584	2.8526
9	1.4233	1.5513	1.6895	1.8385	1.9990	2.1719	2.3579	2.5580	2.7731	3.0040	3.2519
10	1.4802	1.6289	1.7908	1.9672	2.1589	2.3674	2.5937	2.8394	3.1058	3.3946	3.7072
11	1.5395	1.7103	1.8983	2.1049	2.3316	2.5804	2.8531	3.1518	3.4785	3.8359	4.2262
12	1.6010	1.7959	2.0122	2.2522	2.5182	2.8127	3.1384	3.4985	3.8960	4.3345	4.8179
13	1.6651	1.8856	2.1329	2.4098	2.7196	3.0658	3.4523	3.8833	4.3635	4.8980	5.4924
14	1.7317	1.9799	2.2609	2.5785	2.9372	3.3417	3.7975	4.3104	4.8871	5.5348	6.2613
15	1.8009	2.0789	2.3966	2.7590	3.1722	3.6425	4.1772	4.7846	5.4736	6.2543	7.1379
16	1.8730	2.1829	2.5404	2.9522	3.4259	3.9703	4.5950	5.3109	6.1304	7.0673	8.1372
17	1.9479	2.2920	2.6928	3.1588	3.7000	4.3276	5.0545	5.8951	6.8660	7.9861	9.2765
18	2.0258	2.4066	2.8543	3.3799	3.9960	4.7171	5.5599	6.5436	7.6900	9.0243	10.5752
19	2.1068	2.5270	3.0256	3.6165	4.3157	5.1417	6.1159	7.2633	8.6128	10.1974	12.0557
20	2.1911	2.6533	3.2071	3.8697	4.6610	5.6044	6.7275	8.0623	9.6463	11.5231	13.7435

Future Value of an Ordinary Annuity of $1

N/R	4%	5%	6%	7%	8%	9%	10%	11%	12%	13%	14%
1	1.0000	1.0000	1.0000	1.0000	1.0000	1.0000	1.0000	1.0000	1.0000	1.0000	1.0000
2	2.0400	2.0500	2.0600	2.0700	2.0800	2.0900	2.1000	2.1100	2.1200	2.1300	2.1400
3	3.1216	3.1525	3.1836	3.2149	3.2464	3.2781	3.3100	3.3421	3.3744	3.4069	3.4396
4	4.2465	4.3101	4.3746	4.4399	4.5061	4.5731	4.6410	4.7097	4.7793	4.8498	4.9211
5	5.4163	5.5256	5.6371	5.7507	5.8666	5.9847	6.1051	6.2278	6.3528	6.4803	6.6101
6	6.6330	6.8019	6.9753	7.1533	7.3359	7.5233	7.7156	7.9129	8.1152	8.3227	8.5355
7	7.8983	8.1420	8.3938	8.6540	8.9228	9.2004	9.4872	9.7833	10.0890	10.4047	10.7305
8	9.2142	9.5491	9.8975	10.2598	10.6366	11.0285	11.4359	11.8594	12.2997	12.7573	13.2328
9	10.5828	11.0266	11.4913	11.9780	12.4876	13.0210	13.5795	14.1640	14.7757	15.4157	16.0853
10	12.0061	12.5779	13.1808	13.8164	14.4866	15.1929	15.9374	16.7220	17.5487	18.4197	19.3373
11	13.4864	14.2068	14.9716	15.7836	16.6455	17.5603	18.5312	19.5614	20.6546	21.8143	23.0445
12	15.0258	15.9171	16.8699	17.8885	18.9771	20.1407	21.3843	22.7132	24.1331	25.6502	27.2707
13	16.6268	17.7130	18.8821	20.1406	21.4953	22.9534	24.5227	26.2116	28.0291	29.9847	32.0887
14	18.2919	19.5986	21.0151	22.5505	24.2149	26.0192	27.9750	30.0949	32.3926	34.8827	35.5811
15	20.0236	21.5786	23.2760	25.1290	27.1521	29.3609	31.7725	34.4054	37.2797	40.4175	43.8424
16	21.8245	23.6575	25.6725	27.8881	30.3243	33.0034	35.9497	39.1899	42.7533	46.6717	50.9804
17	23.6975	25.8404	28.2129	30.8402	33.7502	36.9737	40.5447	44.5008	48.8837	53.7391	59.1176
18	25.6454	28.1324	30.9057	33.9990	37.4502	41.3013	45.5992	50.3959	55.7497	61.7251	68.3941
19	27.6712	30.5390	33.7600	37.3790	41.4463	46.0185	51.1591	56.9395	63.4397	70.7494	78.9692
20	29.7781	33.0660	36.7856	40.9955	45.7620	51.1601	57.2750	64.2028	72.0524	80.9468	91.0249

INDEX

A

B

C

D

E

F

G

H

I

J

K

L

M

Q

R

T

U

AMT Formula for Individuals

Regular Taxable Income	
Plus or minus:	Adjustments
Plus:	Tax preferences
Equals:	Alternative minimum taxable income
Minus:	Exemption
Equals:	Alternative minimum tax base
Times:	26% and 28% graduated rates
Equals:	Tentative minimum tax before foreign tax credit
Minus:	Alternative minimum tax foreign tax credit
Equals:	Tentative minimum tax
Minus:	Regular income tax liability
Equals:	Alternative minimum tax (if amount is positive)

AMT Formula for Corporations

Regular Taxable Income before NOL Deduction	
Plus or minus:	Adjustments (except ACE adjustment)
Plus:	Tax preferences
Equals:	AMTI before ATNOL deduction and ACE adjustment
Plus or minus:	ACE adjustment
Equals:	Alternative minimum taxable income (AMTI) before ATNOL deduction
Minus:	ATNOL deduction (limited to 90% of AMTI before ATNOL deduction)
Equals:	Alternative minimum taxable income (AMTI)
Minus:	Exemption
Equals:	Alternative minimum tax base
Times:	20% rate
Equals:	AMT before AMT foreign tax credit
Minus:	AMT foreign tax credit
Equals:	Tentative minimum tax
Minus:	Regular income tax liability before credits minus regular foreign tax credit
Equals:	Alternative minimum tax (AMT) if positive

Tax Formula for Corporate Taxpayers

Income (broadly conceived)	$xxx,xxx
Less: Exclusions (income that is not subject to tax).	(xx,xxx)
Gross income	$xxx,xxx
Less: Certain business deductions	(xx,xxx)
Taxable income	$xxx,xxx
Federal income tax (see Tax Rate Schedule inside front cover of text).	$ xx,xxx
Less: Tax credits (including Federal income tax withheld and other prepayments of Federal income taxes)	(x,xxx)
Tax owed (or refund due)	$ xx,xxx

AMT Formula for Individuals

Regular Taxable Income	
Plus or minus:	Adjustments
Plus:	Tax preferences
Equals:	Alternative minimum taxable income
Minus:	Exemption
Equals:	Alternative minimum tax base
Times:	26% and 28% graduated rates
Equals:	Tentative minimum tax before foreign tax credit
Minus:	Alternative minimum tax foreign tax credit
Equals:	Tentative minimum tax
Minus:	Regular income tax liability
Equals:	Alternative minimum tax (if amount is positive)

AMT Formula for Corporations

Regular Taxable Income before NOL Deduction	
Plus or minus:	Adjustments (except ACE adjustment)
Plus:	Tax preferences
Equals:	AMTI before ATNOL deduction and ACE adjustment
Plus or minus:	ACE adjustment
Equals:	Alternative minimum taxable income (AMTI) before ATNOL deduction
Minus:	ATNOL deduction (limited to 90% of AMTI before ATNOL deduction)
Equals:	Alternative minimum taxable income (AMTI)
Minus:	Exemption
Equals:	Alternative minimum tax base
Times:	20% rate
Equals:	AMT before AMT foreign tax credit
Minus:	AMT foreign tax credit
Equals:	Tentative minimum tax
Minus:	Regular income tax liability before credits minus regular foreign tax credit
Equals:	Alternative minimum tax (AMT) if positive

Tax Formula for Corporate Taxpayers

Income (broadly conceived)	$xxx,xxx
Less: Exclusions (income that is not subject to tax).	(xx,xxx)
Gross income	$xxx,xxx
Less: Certain business deductions	(xx,xxx)
Taxable income	$xxx,xxx
Federal income tax (see Tax Rate Schedule inside front cover of text).	$ xx,xxx
Less: Tax credits (including Federal income tax withheld and other prepayments of Federal income taxes)	(x,xxx)
Tax owed (or refund due)	$ xx,xxx